THE NORTON/GROVE
HANDBOOKS IN MUSIC

ETHNOMUSICOLOGY
HISTORICAL AND REGIONAL STUDIES

To the Memory of Klaus P. Wachsmann
(1907–1984)

Ethnomusicologist, Humanist

IN THE SAME SERIES

ETHNOMUSICOLOGY
An Introduction
Edited by Helen Myers
A companion to the present volume

PERFORMANCE PRACTICE
Edited by Howard Mayer Brown and Stanley Sadie
in two volumes

HISTORY OF OPERA
Edited by Stanley Sadie

MUSIC PRINTING AND PUBLISHING
Edited by D. W. Krummel and Stanley Sadie

ANALYSIS
Ian Bent with William Drabkin

THE NORTON/GROVE
HANDBOOKS IN MUSIC

ETHNOMUSICOLOGY

HISTORICAL AND REGIONAL
STUDIES

Edited by HELEN MYERS

W. W. NORTON & COMPANY
New York   London

The New Grove and *The New Grove Dictionary of Music and Musicians*
are registered trademarks of Macmillan Publishers Limited, London.

First published in the UK 1993 by
THE MACMILLAN PRESS LTD
London and Houndmills, Basingstoke, Hampshire RG21 2XS
Companies and representatives throughout the world

British Library Cataloguing in Publication Data
Ethnomusicology: Vol. 2
Historical and regional studies – (The New Grove handbooks in musicology).
I. Myers, Helen   II. Series 780'.89
ISBN 0–333–57632–2 (Vol. 2)
ISBN 0–333–44444–2 (2-volume set)

First American edition 1993

All rights reserved.

W. W. Norton & Company, Inc.,
500 Fifth Avenue, New York, NY 10110

W. W. Norton & Company, Ltd,
10 Coptic Street, London WC1A 1PU

ISBN 0–393–03378–3

Typeset at The Spartan Press Ltd,
Lymington, Hants, Great Britain
Printed in the United States of America

1 2 3 4 5 6 7 8 9 0

Contents

Contents

General Abbreviations

AD	anno Domini
add, addl	additional
add(s), addn(s)	addition(s)
ad lib	ad libitum
AK	Alaska (USA)
AL	Alabama (USA)
Alta.	Alberta (Canada)
anon.	anonymous(ly)
appx	appendix
AR	Arkansas (USA)
attrib.	attribution, attributed to
AZ	Arizona
BBC	British Broadcasting Corporation
BC	British Columbia (Canada)
BC	before Christ
bk	book
BL	British Library
BM	British Museum
Bros.	Brothers
c	circa (about)
CA	California (USA)
CBC	Canadian Broadcasting Corporation
cf	confer (compare)
chap.	chapter
Chin.	Chinese
Cie	Compagnie
cm	centimetre(s)
CO	Colorado (USA)
Co.	Company; County
col.	column
coll.	collection, collected by
collab.	collaborator, in collaboration with
comp(s).	compiler(s), compiled by
contribs.	contributors, contributions
CT	Connecticut (USA)

DC	District of Columbia (USA)
DE	Delaware (USA)
Dept	Department
dir.	director, directed by
diss.	dissertation
ed., eds.	editor(s), edited by
edn(s)	edition(s)
e.g.	exempli gratia [for example]
Eng.	English
enl.	enlarged
esp.	especially
etc	et cetera [and so on]
ex., exx.	example, examples
f., ff.	folio, folios
facs.	facsimile
fasc.	fascicle
ff	following pages
fig.	figure [illustration]
FL	Florida (USA)
Fr.	French
frag., frags.	fragment(s)
GA	Georgia (USA)
Ger.	German
Gk.	Greek
Heb.	Hebrew
HI	Hawaii (USA)
Hon.	Honorary; Honourable
HRH	His/Her Royal Highness
Hung.	Hungarian
Hz	Hertz (cycles per second)
IA	Iowa (USA)
ibid	ibidem [in the same place]
ID	Idaho (USA)
i.e.	id est [that is]
IL	Illinois (USA)
IN	Indiana (USA)
inc.	incomplete

incl.	includes, including		PA	Pennsylvania (USA)
It.	Italian		p.a.	per annum
			Pol.	Polish
Jap.	Japanese		pseud.	pseudonym
Jb	*Jahrbuch* [yearbook]		pt(s)	part(s)
Jg.	*Jahrgang* [year of publication, volume]		pubd	published
			pubn	publication
jr	junior			
			R	photographic reprint
kHz	kilohertz [1000 cycles per second]		repr.	reprinted
			rev.	revision, revised (by/for)
km	kilometre(s)		RI	Rhode Island (USA)
KS	Kansas (USA)		Rom.	Romanian
KY	Kentucky (USA)		rpm	revolutions per minute
			Russ.	Russian
LA	Louisiana (USA)			
LP	long-playing record		S	San, Santa, Santo, Sao [saint]
Ltd	Limited		Sask.	Saskatchewan (Canada)
			SC	South Carolina (USA)
m	metre(s)		SD	South Dakota (USA)
MA	Massachusetts (USA)		ser.	series
MD	Maryland (USA)		St	Saint, Sint, Szent
ME	Maine (USA)		suppl.	supplement, supplementary
MI	Michigan (USA)			
mm	millimetre(s)		TN	Tennessee (USA)
MN	Minnesota (USA)		trans.	translation, translated by
MO	Missouri (USA)		transcr.	transcription
MS(S)	manuscript(s)		TV	television
MS	Mississippi (USA)		TX	Texas (USA)
MT	Montana (USA)			
			U.	University
NC	North Carolina (USA)		UCLA	University of California at Los Angeles (USA)
ND	North Dakota (USA)			
n.d.	no date of publication		UK	United Kingdom of Great Britain and Northern Ireland
NE	Nebraska (USA)			
NH	New Hampshire (USA)		unattrib.	unattributed
NJ	New Jersey (USA)		unpubd	unpublished
NM	New Mexico (USA)		US	United States [adjective]
no., nos.	number(s)		USA	United States of America
n.p.	no place of publication		USSR	Union of Soviet Socialist Republics
nr	near			
NV	Nevada (USA)		UT	Utah (USA)
NY	New York State (USA)			
			VA	Virginia (USA)
OH	Ohio (USA)		VHF	very high frequency
OK	Oklahoma (USA)		viz	videlicet [namely]
Ont.	Ontario (Canada)		vol.,vols.	volume(s)
op., opp.	opus, opera			
opt.	optional		WA	Washington State (USA)
op. cit.	opere citato [in the work cited]		WI	Wisconsin (USA)
OR	Oregon (USA)		WV	West Virginia (USA)
orig.	original(ly)		WY	Wyoming (USA)
p., pp.	page, pages			

Bibliographical Abbreviations

AcM	Acta musicologica
AmF	Archiv für Musikforschung
AMw	Archiv für Musikwissenschaft
AMZ	Allgemeine musikalische Zeitung
AMz	Allgemeine Musik-Zeitung
AnM	Anuario musical
AnMc	Analecta musicologica
BAMS	Bulletin of the American Musicological Society
BMw	Beiträge zur Musikwissenschaft
CMc	Current Musicology
DJbM	Deutsches Jahrbuch der Musikwissenschaft
EM	Ethnomusicology
EMDC	Encylopédie de la musique et dictionnaire du Conservatoire
FAM	Fontes artis musicae
Grove1 (–5)	G. Grove, ed.: A Dictionary of Music and Musicians, 2nd–5th edns. as Grove's Dictionary of Music and Musicians
Grove6	The New Grove Dictionary of Music and Musicians
GSJ	The Galpin Society Journal
IIM	Izvestiya na Instituta za muzika
IMSCR	International Musicological Society Congress Report
IRASM	International Review of the Aesthetics and Sociology of Music
JAMIS	Journal of the American Musical Instrument Society
JAMS	Journal of the American Musicological Society

JbMP	Jahrbuch der Musikbibliothek Peters
JEFDSS	Journal of the English Folk Dance and Song Society
JFSS	Journal of the Folk-song Society
JIFMC	Journal of the International Folk Music Council
JMT	Journal of Music Theory
Mf	Die Musikforschung
MGG	Die Musik in Geschichte und Gegenwart
ML	Music and Letters
MM	Modern Music
MQ	Musical Quarterly
MT	The Musical Times
NOHM	The New Oxford History of Music, ed. E. Wellesz, J. Westrup and G. Abraham (London, 1954–)
PAMS	Papers of the American Musicological Society
PMA	Proceedings of the Musical Association
PRMA	Proceedings of the Royal Musical Association
RdM	Revue de musicologie
ReM	La revue musicale
RISM	Répertoire international des sources musicales
RMI	Rivista musicale italiana
SIMG	Sammelbände der Internationalen Musik-Gesellschaft
SM	Studia musicologica Academiae scientarum hungaricae

SMz	*Schweizerische Musikzeitung/Revue*		*Music Council*
	musicale suisse	*YTM*	*Yearbook for Traditional Music*
STMf	*Svensk tidskrift for musikforskning*		
		ZIMG	*Zeitschrift der Internationalen*
VMw	*Vierteljahrschrift für Musikwissen-*		*Musik-Gesellschaft*
	schaft	*ZL*	*Zenei lexikon*
YIFMC	*Yearbook of the International Folk*	*ZMw*	*Zeitschrit für Musikwissenschaft*

Contributors

HELEN MYERS, editor and contributor, is Professor of Music at Trinity College in Hartford, Conn., where she teaches a wide range of courses from ethnomusicology to historical musicology. She holds degrees in performance, music education, music theory, and historical musicology from Ithaca College, Syracuse University, the Ohio State University and the University of Edinburgh. She has done extensive fieldwork in the Bhojpuri villages of Uttar Pradesh and Bihar, India, and with the Bhojpuri Indian immigrant community in Trinidad, West Indies. The author of innumerable articles, in *The New Oxford Companion to Music, The New Grove Dictionaries of Music, of Musical Instruments, and of American Music,* and of *Felicity Trinidad: the Musical Portrait of a Hindu Village* (1984), she is co-author of an introduction to folk music in the United States and editorial consultant in ethnomusicology for all the New Grove titles.

DOROTHY SARA LEE is a curator at the Archives of Traditional Music, Indiana University. She has conducted field research in Fiji as well as amongst Native Americans. She has been a main collaborator on the Federal Cylinder Project, Library of Congress, and has produced the Omaha recordings of Alice Cunningham Fletcher and her Omaha collaborator Francis La Flesche. Her writings include *The Federal Cylinder Project. A Guide to Field Cylinder Collections in Federal Agencies* (1984–1985), and *Music Performance and the Negotiation of Identity in Viti Levu, Fiji* (1984).

WILLIAM W. WESTCOTT is a freelance musician and educator living in Toronto, Ontario. He taught music history and general musicianship at York University throughout the 1980s. His research interest centres on African-American music. He is active as a performer, composer, arranger and general writer on music.

JAMES ROBBINS has taught ethnomusicology at York University and Reed College and is a Caribbean specialist. His fieldwork has been in Cuba with a focus on popular forms. His writings include *Practical and Abstract Taxonomy in Cuban Music.*

ALBRECHT SCHNEIDER is Professor of Systematic Musicology at the University of Hamburg. His speciality is the history of comparative musicology and ethnomusicology, especially the German school. He is author of *Musikwissenschaft und Kulturkreislehre* (1976) and *Analogie und Rekonstruktion: Studien zur Methodologie der Musikgeschichtsschreibung und zur Frühgeschichte der Musik* (1984).

MAX PETER BAUMANN conducts research at the Institut für Vergleichende Musikstudien und Dokumentation, Berlin. His diverse field-work includes study in Switzerland, France, Ethiopia, and Bolivia. His writings include *Bibliographie zur ethnomusikologischen Literatur der Schweiz* (1981) and *Volkmusik in der Schweiz* (1985).

ERNST HEINS is on the faculty of the Ethnomusicology Centre 'Jaap Kunst', The Netherlands. His research has been in Java, following in the traditions of his eminent teacher Jaap Kunst. An expert on gamelan traditions, he is author of *Cueing the Gamelan in Javanese Wayang Performance* (1970) and *Goong Renteng: Aspects of Orchestral Music in a Sundanese Village* (1977).

MIRIAM ROVSING OLSEN, daughter of the late Poul Rovsing Olsen, is assistant lecturer at the University of Paris. Her fieldwork in North Africa includes research in Morocco, especially with Berber women.

MARTIN CUNNINGHAM is a lecturer in the Department of Spanish at University College, Dublin. He is a specialist in medieval literature and historical linguistics, with a particular interest in Hispanic vocal music. His recent publications include a musical transcription and study of the first New World Opera (Lima, 1701), Torrejón's setting of Calderón's libretto *La púrpura de la rosa* (1990).

ROBERTO LEYDI is Professor of Music at the University of Milan. His research interests include musical iconography and traditional Italian music. His writings include *La zampogne in Italia* (1985) and *Strumenti musicali e tradizioni popolari in Italia* (1985).

The late BREANDÁN BREATNACH of County Dublin, a foremost authority on Irish music, was editor and publisher of *Ceol*, a magazine devoted to traditional Irish music. An accomplished performer on the Union pipes, he was the chairman of Na Piobairi (Association of Union Pipes). He was the author of *Ceol Rince na hEireann* ['Dance Music of Ireland'] (1963) and *Folk Music and Dances of Ireland* (1971).

NICHOLAS CAROLAN, who updated the Breathnach article for this volume, is Administrator of Taisce Cheol Duchais Eireann (Irish Traditional Music Archive), Dublin. He is author of 'Two Irish harps in Co. Dublin' (1984).

JAN LING is Professor of Music at the University of Göteborg, Sweden. His research investigates European folk music, the ideology and sociology of music and contemporary Nordic music. His writings include *Vi äro musikanter alltifrån Skaraborg: Studier i västgötsk musikhistoria* (We are the musicians that come from Skaraborg: Studies in the history of music in the province of Västergötland, Sweden) (1983) and *Folkmusiken 1730–1980 (Europas Musikhistoria)* (1989).

BARBARA KRADER, former President of the Society for Ethnomusicology, has conducted exhaustive research in eastern Europe, particularly Albania, Romania, Bosnia-Herzegovina, Greece, Russia and other peoples in the former USSR. Fluent in the languages of these regions, for over 30 years she has promoted collaborations amongst local scholars in this area. Her publications include the seminal article 'Ethnomusicology' in *The New Grove Dictionary of Music and Musicians* (1980).

BÁLINT SAROSI teaches and conducts research at the Institute of Musicology, Budapest. An expert on gypsy music, from 1958 onwards he has conducted fieldwork in Hungary, Transylvania/Romania, Slovakia, Ethiopia and Armenia. His principal publications include *Népi hangszereink* (Our folk instruments) (1976) and *Folk music: Hungarian musical idiom* (1986).

MARGARITA MAZO teaches musicology at the Ohio State University. A native of St Petersburg (formerly Leningrad), she is expert on the historical and modern traditions of peoples of the former USSR. She is author of 'Dynamics of a local song cycle' (1977).

JAMES PORTER is Professor of Ethnomusicology and Folklore at the University of California, Los Angeles, and teaches courses in the musics of Europe, Britain and Ireland, as well as seminars on ethnomusicological topics. His field research has been conducted in Scotland (with travelling people), Brittany and Spain. He has published widely in scholarly journals and is currently co-editing an encyclopedia of world music. His books include *The ballad image: Essays presented to Bertrand Harris Bronson* (coed., 1983) and *The Traditional Music of Britain and Ireland: A Research and Reference Guide* (1989).

CHRISTOPHER A. WATERMAN, son of the pioneering ethnomusicologist the late Richard A. Waterman, teaches music at the University of Washington, Seattle. His fieldwork in Nigeria resulted in the publication of *Jùjú: a Social History and Ethnography on an African Popular Music* (1990).

AMNON SHILOAH is Professor of Musicology at the Hebrew University of Jerusalem. Trained in France as a flautist and musicologist, he has been Head of the Folklore Department of the Israel Radio, Director of the Jewish Music Research Center and Provost of the School for Overseas Students, Jerusalem. His research interests involve Near Eastern music history and theory combined with the exploration of living musical practice of both Arabic and Jewish music. His publications include *Ha-Moreshet ha-musikalit shel kehitol yistra el* (The musical heritage of Jewish communities) (ed., 1985–87) and *The Theory of Music in Arabic Writings* (RISM B/10).

NAZIR ALI JAIRAZBHOY, former President of the Society for Ethnomusicology, is Professor of Ethnomusicology at the University of California, Los Angeles. He was born in India and trained in London; his research in South Asia has included the folk, classical, popular and regional traditions, as well as historical and theoretical work with the Hindustani theoretical canon. He is founder of the Archives and Research Centre for Ethnomusicology, New Delhi. He is author of *The Rāgā of North Indian Music* (1971), chapters on Indian Music in *A Cultural History of India* (1975), *Ethnomusicology in the Indian Context* (1984), *Bake Restudy* (1990) and *High-Tech Shiva* (1991).

CYRIL DE SILVA KULATILLAKE is Music Research Officer at the Aesthetic Studies Institute of Kelaniya University, Sri Lanka. For many years he worked for the Broadcasting Corporation Service of Sri Lanka. His research is on the traditional music of Sri Lanka. His publications include *Metre, Melody and Rhythm in Sinhala Music* (1966), 'Buddhist chant in Sri Lanka and its musical elements' (1982), and '*Kiri-amma* Worship and its relevant songs' (1984).

THEODORE LEVIN teaches ethnomusicology at Dartmouth College. His field research has been in Uzbekistan, Siberia, Russia, Georgia and Bosnia-Herzegovina. His PhD dissertation, written under the supervision of Harold Powers, Princeton University, is 'The Music and Tradition of the Bukharan Shashmaqam in Soviet Uzbekistan', 1984. He has also written 'Music in Modern Uzbekistan' (1980).

MIREILLE HELFFER is Directeur de recherche au C.N.R.S. Département d'Ethnomusicologie, Musée de l'Homme, Paris. She has conducted research in North India and the Himalayan Regions, including Nepal, Ladakh and Bhutan. Her publications include *Les chants dans l'épopée tibétaine de Ge-sar, d'après le livre de la course de cheval* (1977), and she has also written numerous record notes on Tibetan and Nepalese music.

ALAN R. THRASHER teaches at the University of British Columbia, Vancouver, Canada. He has done fieldwork in South China and Taiwan. His publications include articles in the Journals *Ethnomusicolgy* and *Asian Music*, entries in *The New Grove Dictionary of Musical Instruments* and *La-li-lio Dance-songs of the Chuxiong Yi, Yunnan Province, China*.

DAVID HUGHES teaches ethnomusicology at the School of Oriental and African Studies, University of London. His research in Japan has focused on folk traditions. His writings include numerous entries on Japanese instruments in *The New Grove Dictionary of Musical Instruments* (1984) as well as his doctoral dissertation, *The heart's home town: Traditional Folk Song in Modern Japan* (diss., 1985), and *The Archaeology of Early Music Cultures* (1988, ed).

ROBERT PROVINE teaches historical musicology and ethnomusicology at the University of Durham, England. He was trained at Harvard; his interest in East Asian music first developed during military service with the US Armed

Forces in Korea. His research embraces historical and contemporary forms. He is author of 'Chinese ritual music in Korea: The origins, codification, and cultural role of aak' (1980) and *Essays on Sino-Korean Musicology* (1988).

JUDITH BECKER teaches ethnomusicology at the University of Michigan. Her research in Southeast Asia covers the mainland (Burma) and the islands (Java). Drawing on linguistic theory she has contributed to the critical literature on theory and practice of Indonesian gamelan music. Writings include *Traditional Music in Modern Java* (1980) and *Karawitan: Source readings in Javanese gamelan and vocal music* (ed.: 3v., 1984, 1987, 1988).

MERVYN McLEAN, pioneer in the study of Oceanic music, teaches at the University of Auckland, New Zealand. He has directed the project 'Territorial Survey of Oceanic Music', resulting in the documentation of hitherto unknown traditions. He is author of *An Annotated Bibliography of Oceanic Music and Dance* (1977) and *Tikopia Songs* (1990).

GERARD BÉHAGUE is Professor of Music at the University of Texas at Austin, USA. He has conducted field research in South America, especially Brazil and the Andean countries, and in West Africa. His publications include *Music in Latin America: an Introduction* (1979), *The Beginning of Musical Nationalism in Brazil* (1971) and *Performance Practice: Ethnomusicological Perspectives* (ed.) (1984), among others. He is the founder/editor of *Latin American Music Review*.

List of Illustrations

Picture Credits

We are grateful to the following for permission to reproduce illustrative material (every effort has been made to contact copyright holders: we apologize to anyone who may have been omitted):
Bartók Archives, Budapest: pp.5 and 189; Eva Wachsmann: p.9; National Anthropological Archive, Smithsonian Institution, Washington, D.C.: pp.22 and 28; Nebraska State Historical Society/photo Melvin Gilmore: p.26; Barker Texas History Center, The University of Texas at Austin (John A. Lomax Family Papers): p.40; American Folklife Center, Library of Congress, Washington, D.C. (Archive of Folk Culture)/photo Robert Hemming: p.43; Paul Oliver, Woodstock: p.50; Ethnomusicology Centre 'Jaap Kunst', University of Amsterdam: pp.86, 104–5, 108 and 109; Schweizerische Landesbibliothek, Berne: p.98 (fig.2); Bibliothèque Nationale, Paris: p.112; Musée de l'Homme, Paris: p.115; English Folk Dance and Song Society, London: p.135; Great Grimsby Borough Council Museum & Heritage Service (W. E. R. Hallgarth Collection): p.137; Irish Traditional Music Archive, Dublin: p.150; Svenska Litteratursällskapet i Finland/photo Gösta Widbom: p.154; Suomalaisen Kirjallisuuden Seura, Helsinki/photo Dr. A. O. Väisänen: p.155; Institute of Musicology, Belgrade: p.165 (fig.2).

Acknowledgements

Many individuals have helped in the preparation of this volume. In particular I would like to thank my editorial assistant and Malaysian music specialist, Margaret Sarkissian, who generously checked hundreds of bibliographic entries to source, and was untiring in her efforts to ensure factual accuracy. The publishers of this work owe much to my mother, Elsie Myers Stainton, who has used her professional editing skills in full measure on this project.

For the section on the USA by Lee, thanks go to the staff of the National Anthropological Archives, Washington, D.C., particularly Vyrtis Thomas and Kathy Creek; to the Archives of Traditional Music, Indiana University, particularly Marilyn Graf for help with the George Herzog collection; and to Erika Brady for comments and suggestions on early drafts. The chapter on the history of ethnomusicology in Canada and Greenland benefited enormously from the advice and assistance of Robert Witmer and Beverley Diamond Cavanagh (both of York University). Thanks are also due to Mary Hayes of the Ethnology Department of the Royal Ontario Museum and Gordon Smith (Queen's University), who provided useful information on the ROM and publishing history of Ernest Gagnon's *Chansons populaires du Canada*, respectively.

For my section on the early history of ethnomusicology in Great Britain, I wish to thank Ian Russell of The Centre for English Cultural Tradition and Language, University of Sheffield, Malcolm Taylor, Librarian of the English Folk Dance and Song Society, Cecil Sharp House, Edward O. Henry of San Diego State University and Gordon Thompson of Skidmore College for their helpful comments. For the chapter on Scandinavia, Jan Ling has asked me to remind the reader of his debt to his mentor, pioneer in Nordic musicology, the late Ernst Emsheimer.

For the sections on eastern European folk music research our gratitude goes to Dr. Jerko Bezic of the Institute for Folklore Research in Zagreb, for reading the Yugoslav section and making corrections and suggestions; to Dr. Oskar Elschek of the Institute of Arts of the Slovak Academy of Sciences for valuable suggestions on Czechoslovakia; for the Polish section, to Professor Anna Czeckanowska, Director of the Institute of Musicology of the University of Warsaw, for suggestions and bibliographical assistance, and to Professor Jan Steszewski for providing his recent unpublished article and further information about Oskar Kolberg. For assistance with the chapter on Southeast Asia by Becker we thank Deborah Wong and Mohd. Anis Md. Nor, at the

University of Michigan, and R. Anderson Sutton at the University of Wisconsin, Madison. Appreciation is also extended to Huang Jinpei, Xinghai Conservatory of Music, Guangzhou, Han Kuo-huang, Northern Illinois University, and Kenneth DeWoskin, University of Michigan, who read drafts of the chapter on Chinese ethnomusicology by Thrasher.

For the chapter on ethnomusicology in North America after World War II, I would like to thank Wayne State University Press for their gracious permission to publish revised and updated paragraphs of *Folk Music in the United States* (Bruno Nettl and Helen Myers, 1976). For the material on Italian-American music, I am indebted to my colleague Anthony Rauche of the University of Hartford.

Several editors deserve special thanks for their painstaking work, including Mara M. Vilcinskas of Macmillan, London, and Susan Pohl and Joanne Hinman of Cornell University. For translation work from the French and German thanks are due to Anthea Bell of Cambridge. Helen Ottaway, illustrations editor for this Handbook series, pursued a picture search around the world to bring this lively subject – ethnomusicology – to life on the printed page. Particular thanks are due to Elisabeth Ingles and Suzanne La Plante, who coordinated the editorial and production schedules in London and New York respectively. I am particularly grateful of Marilyn Bliss of *RILM*, New York City, for checking the page proofs and for the thoughtful preparation of the index.

I owe special gratitude to Christopher Paterson, Director of Macmillan Press, who patiently sponsored this book and its companion volume, *Ethnomusicology: an Introduction*, from conception to publication.

I would like to thank my colleagues at Trinity College, particularly Professor Gerald Moshell and Dean Jan Cohn, for their encouragement, and also the College administration for financial support during the final stages of this work.

This project could never have come to fruition without the unfailing sponsorship of Claire Brook, Vice President and Music Editor of W. W. Norton and Company; her vision of ethnomusicology as part of a musical education at any level, her professional wisdom and her lively innovative thinking have enlightened our work. This volume on the history of ethnomusicology appears as she moves on in life from her career at Norton to other ventures (she has asked her friends not to mention retirement). I and my generation of musicologists thank her for the books that taught us and for the opportunity to write anew for our students.

Finally, my warmest thanks go to Stanley Sadie, editor of *The New Grove Dictionary of Music and Musicians*, 6th ed., and series editor for these Handbooks, who has supported this volume since its inception and guided it steadily to publication. Stanley Sadie early honoured ethnomusicology and has contributed immeasurably to its flourishing around the world. Through the years, I have observed his zeal for perfection, his dedication to detail, and his scholarly daring in contemplating the whole musical world – all the places, all the peoples, and all the things of that musical universe. It takes greatness of spirit, strong intellectual capacities, organizational skills, and even physical stamina to present the music of the world to the world. This he has done.

H.M.

Klaus Wachsmann recording during his Uganda years (1948–57)

Preface

A famous classic was the first to claim the title 'Ethno-musicology'; Jaap Kunst's compendium of 1958 introduced the nature, problems, methods, representative personalities and bibliography of a fledgling discipline. Now we use this title a second time for two volumes, *Ethnomusicology: an Introduction* and *Ethnomusicology: Historical and Regional Studies*, appearing in the series of New Grove Handbooks in Music. The growing discipline deserves and has needed this new effort to show the various directions that scholarship in this field has taken and to present the tremendously detailed information that has been discovered in the last half-century. Today, when Eurocentricity is being challenged throughout the world, both philosophically and politically, these glimpses into a discipline that focusses on ethnic diversity will inform everyone confronting the issue.

Although these companion volumes do not remotely resemble a 'World Music Survey', they do make available the tools by which one may look at the music of other cultures systematically and scientifically, historically and geographically. A second timely factor relates to the teaching of ethnomusicology; there has been up till now no adequate introduction to the subject to serve as a textbook for music majors, be they historians, theorists, composers, performers or educators.

The two volumes consist completely of contributions written especially for this project. They are intended to serve as a general and wide-ranging guide to the entire field of ethnomusicology. Each volume is self-sustaining and separate but complementary; the first, systematic, discusses theories and methods, and the second, regional, outlines the early history of ethnomusicology and explores the later manifestations of this study in the continents of the world. The search for contributors reached beyond Britain and the Continent to the USA, Russia, the Near East, India and the Antipodes.

The Introduction presents a brief survey of ethnomusicological research. Part Two, 'History to World War II', treats the broad historical and intellectual trends that contributed to the birth of comparative musicology in the 1880s, including developments in linguistics, philology, folklore and anthropology as well as nationalism and Orientalism in late 19th-century Europe. It describes the role of comparative musicology in Guido Adler's scheme for musicology (1885) and the influence of 19th-century anthropological theories, particularly evolutionism and diffusionism, on the new field of *vergleichende Musikwissenschaft*. The discussion is organized not by the music under study but by national schools of scholarship: hence the research of Cecil Sharp and Maud Karpeles in the Southern Appalachians of the USA, for example, is treated in the section on Great Britain (not under 'British-American').

The divisions are as follows: For 'North America', Native Americans by Dorothy Sara Lee (Bloomington, Indiana), African-Americans by William Westcott (Toronto), British-Americans by myself, and Canada (including Greenland) by James Robbins (Toronto). For 'Northern and Western Europe', Germany and Austria by Albrecht Schneider (Hamburg), Switzerland by Max Peter Baumann (Berlin), the Netherlands by Ernst Heins (Amsterdam), France and Belgium by Miriam Rovsing Olsen (Paris), Iberia by Martin Cunningham (Dublin), Italy by Roberto Leydi (Milan), Great Britain by myself, Ireland by the late Breandán Breatnach and Scandinavia by Jan Ling (Göteborg). For 'Southern and Eastern Europe', Bulgaria, Slovenia, Croatia, Serbia, Poland, Czechoslovakia and Greece by Barbara Krader (Berlin); Hungary and Romania by Bálint Sarosi (Budapest); and 'Russia and the Former USSR' by Margarita Mazo (Columbus, Ohio; formerly of Leningrad, now St Petersburg, Russia).

Part Three presents regional studies, up-to-date reports by world area on the state of ethnomusicological research since World War II: topics that have been studied; topics awaiting research; bibliographic resources relating to the area; relationship of the musical culture of the area to ethnomusicological research that has been conducted there; special problems the ethnomusicologist may encounter in the area. This discussion is organized by the music under study. Accordingly, the research conducted by Bruno Nettl in Teheran, for example, is included in Chapter VIII, 'West Asia', whereas his research amongst the Montana Blackfeet is treated in Chapter XV, 'North America'.

'Europe' by James Porter (Los Angeles) includes ethnic Russia, Ukraine, Belorussia, Moldavia and the Baltic States; 'Africa' by Christopher Waterman (Seattle) discusses the sub-Saharan cultures including Madagascar; 'West Asia' by Amnon Shiloah (Jerusalem) discusses lands of the Middle East including the Maghrib, the Arab states of Egypt, Syria, Lebanon, Jordan, Iraq, nations of the Arabian Peninsula, the Gulf states, and Israel, Turkey and Iran; 'South Asia' includes India and Pakistan by Nazir Ali Jairazbhoy (Los Angeles) and Sri Lanka by Cyril de Silva Kulatillake (Ambalangoda); 'Western Central Asia' by Theodore Levin (Andover, Vermont) includes Afghanistan, Kazakhstan, Kyrgyzstan, Turkmenistan, Uzbekistan, Tajikistan, Azerbaijan and the Caucasus; 'Eastern Central Asia' by Mireille Helffer (Paris) includes Nepal, Bhutan, Sikkim, Ladakh, Tibet, Mongolia and adjacent areas; 'East Asia' includes China by Alan Thrasher (Vancouver), Japan by David Hughes (Cambridge, UK), and Korea by Robert Provine (Durham, UK); 'Southeast Asia' by Judith Becker (Ann Arbor) includes the mainland countries, Indonesia and the Philippines; 'Oceania' by Mervyn McLean (Auckland) includes Polynesia, Melanesia, Micronesia and Australia; 'North America' by myself includes Native Americans, African-, Asian-, European- and Hispanic-Americans; 'The West Indies', also by me, includes the British, French and Dutch islands; 'Latin America' by Gerard Béhague (Austin, Texas) includes South and Central America and the Hispanic Caribbean.

Hartford, Connecticut, 1992   Helen Myers

PART ONE

Ethnomusicology

CHAPTER I

Introduction

Helen Myers

The history of comparative musicology, later ethnomusicology, has traditionally been portrayed as the development of German and American research, beginning in the 1880s, and culminating in the synthesis of the two schools as reflected in the work of the German-Jewish émigré George Herzog, assistant to the Berliner Erich M. von Hornbostel, and later in New York City of Franz Boas. The contributors to this volume offer a richer and more thoroughly researched perspective – inclusive rather than exclusive – not only of the development of *vergleichende Musikwissenschaft* but of the modern international effort to understand the music of the world's peoples.

Characteristics

Ethnomusicology includes the study of folk and traditional music, Eastern art music, contemporary music in oral tradition as well as conceptual issues such as the origins of music, musical change, composition and improvisation, music as symbol, universals in music, the function of music in society, the comparison of musical systems and the biological basis of music and dance. Western art traditions are not ruled out, although few studies in this area have been conducted by ethnomusicologists. In general, music in oral tradition and living musical systems are the realms that have most appealed to scholars in this field. Nevertheless most ethnomusicological research also involves history, and for many studies history is the focus. Often ethnomusicologists study cultures other than their own, a situation that distinguishes this field from most historical musicology. As a consequence of its broad scope, definitions of ethnomusicology abound, ranging from 'the study of music as culture' and the 'comparative study of musical cultures' to 'the hermeneutic science of human musical behaviour'. Charles Seeger (1970) suggested that the term 'musicology' is more suitable for ethnomusicology, whose purview includes the music of all peoples of all times, than it is for historical musicology, which is limited generally to Western art music.

Early developments

What we now call ethnomusicology began long before that term was invented. Amateur interest in non-Western music dates back to the voyages of discovery, and the philosophical rationale for study of foreign cultures derives from the Age of Enlightenment. The *Dictionnaire de musique* of Jean-Jacques Rousseau (1768) reflects the spirit of the age by including samples of European folk, North American Indian and Chinese music. During the 18th and 19th centuries, missionaries, civil servants and world travellers took an interest in 'exotic music', resulting in studies of Chinese music by Jean-Baptiste du Halde (1735) and Joseph Amiot (1779), of Arab music by Guillaume André Villoteau (1809–22) and Raphael Kiesewetter (1842), of Indian music by William Jones (1784) and Charles Russell Day (1891) and of Japanese music by Francis Taylor Piggott (1893).

Although scholars of music have long been aware that China, Korea, India, and Japan had distinguished traditions of music theory, some dating back 5000 years, the study of these historical documents was not originally considered by European comparative musicologists to be part of what they regarded as their essentially scientific, psychological research. In the struggle to achieve recognition in the Western academy, scholars have particularly cited the late 19th-century experiments conducted in Berlin by Carl Stumpf (1848–1936) and Erich M. von Hornbostel (1877–1935), and in London those on pitch and scale measurements made by the phonetician and acoustician Alexander J. Ellis (1814–90) as proof of scientific respectability of their work.

The late 19th century

As an academic pursuit, comparative musicology, like historical musicology, is reckoned to have a history of just over one hundred years, dating from the publication of the Viennese scholar Guido Adler, 'Umfang, Methode und Ziel der Musikwissenschaft' (1885). Adler lists the comparative study of non-Western music as a division of systematic musicology together with music theory, aesthetics and the psychology of music.

Adler's schemata notwithstanding, scientific investigation of non-Western music was in fact made possible by two technical innovations of the late 19th century: the invention of the phonograph in 1877 by the American scientist Thomas Edison, and the development of the cents system of pitch measurement in 1885 by Ellis. The phonograph facilitated fieldwork, offering the possibility of playback from which to transcribe and analyse. The cents system, by which the octave is divided into 1200 equal units, made possible a more objective measurement of non-Western scales; in 'On the Musical Scales of Various Nations' (1885), Ellis concludes that 'the Musical Scale is not one, not "natural", nor even founded necessarily on the laws of the constitution of musical sound so beautifully worked out by Helmholtz, but very diverse, very artificial, and very capricious' (p.526). This finding brought into question the assumed superiority of Western tempered tuning and led the way to open-minded cross-cultural comparison of tonal systems.

Musicologists of the 19th century quickly took advantage of these technological advances, recording small samples on wax cylinders, which they added to their collection of musical artefacts – instruments, song notations and photographs. Many early cylinders were collected during general ethnological fieldwork. Psychologists and acousticians of the Berlin Phonogrammarchiv, including Carl Stumpf and Erich M. von Hornbostel, studied hundreds of cylinders recorded by ethnologists in the German colonies. From analysis of this limited and diverse material they proposed theories about the distribution of musical styles, instruments, and tunings – including evolutionary schemes and later historical reconstructions of music history based on the *Kulturkreislehre* ('school of culture circles'). Scholars of the Berlin school worked in the laboratory, rarely conducted fieldwork and gave little note in their work to music as a cultural manifestation.

This account of the history of ethnomusicology, which continues with the unification of the German and American schools, has been taught to generations of students. Inasmuch as it displays the essential elements of an academic discipline (theory, method) it promotes academic legitimacy. Less often mentioned is the role of nationalism elsewhere in Europe during the 19th century – a fervour that motivated a revival of interest in local folk song. In Hungary, Béla Vikár began recording in the field in 1896. Béla Bartók notated his first Hungarian folk song in 1904 and in 1905 began collaboration with Zoltán Kodály; from 1906, Bartók used the Edison phonograph in Hungary, Romania and Transylvania. In England, Cecil Sharp began the study of traditional English folk song during the same decade. In his search for old

1. Béla Bartók transcribing from a phonograph

5

authentic material, he visited the USA (1916–18), where he and his assistant Maud Karpeles discovered some 1600 English tunes and variants. Harmonizing the material they had collected, Sharp fought for the introduction of folk song in English public schools. The Australian composer Percy Grainger emigrated to England, where he began recording Lincolnshire folk song on wax cylinders in 1906, and issued in 1908 the first commercial recording of folk song with the Gramophone Company, London. Nationalist composers throughout Europe turned to peasant song to enrich the classical musical idiom of their countries. Composers and amateur collectors made arrangements of folk songs for piano or orchestra; from their love of indigenous folk music, composers also drew inspiration for new compositions based on folk idioms.

American studies during the late 19th and early 20th centuries were practical, descriptive, and based on fieldwork, particularly amongst the indigenous peoples at their doorstep, the American Indians. Early writings on Native American musical life were rich in data and independent of the speculations of contemporary German thinkers. Fearful that native cultures were vanishing, American scholars used the phonograph to preserve samples of Indian music. The ethnologist Jesse Walter Fewkes (1850–1930) was the first to use the Edison cylinder machine in the field, during his research with the Passamaquoddy Indians of the northeastern USA (March 1890), and later with the Zuni and Hopi Pueblos of Arizona (1890–91).

Especially sensitive American fieldworkers of this generation were women: Alice Cunningham Fletcher (1838–1923), noteworthy for her lifelong collaboration with the Omaha Indian Francis La Flesche (1857–1932), who is now recognized as the first native American ethnomusicologist (Mark, 1982); and Frances Densmore (1867–1957), the most prolific collector of the period, for 50 years collaborator in the Bureau of American Ethnology at the Smithsonian Institution, and author of over a dozen monographs on individual Indian groups. The anthropologist Franz Boas (1858–1942) taught the holistic study of musical cultures through contemporary anthropological fieldwork methods to a new generation of students at Columbia University, including Helen Heffron Roberts (1888–1985) and George Herzog (1901–84). Herzog was the first to combine in his fieldwork the Boasian anthropological approach with the theories of the Berlin school, a synthesis exemplified in 'The Yuman Musical Style' (1928), an early application of the culture area concept in ethnomusicology. He saw comparative musicology as a field analogous to comparative linguistics.

Development of the modern discipline

Historical musicologists acknowledged the contributions of these early studies, finding in them some evidence for the superiority of Western classical music. On the other hand, for historical musicologists in European and American universities it became helpful to have an adjunct sub-topic to which they could assign issues – often obscure and challenging – beyond the normal scope of their own work. Thus, while comparative musicologists struggled to give their field a sharp theoretical focus, historical musicologists offered to ethnomusicology topics that their subject could not accommodate, such as the psychology of music, organology, dance, and the study of non-Western music, folk music and popular music. These scraps from the table of historical musicology were as the ethnomusicologist perceived them indeed the feast. But, as with any pot-luck supper, the variety and amount proved to be somewhat indigestible.

After World War II, two professional societies were founded, the International Folk Music Council in 1947 (after 1982, the International Council for Traditional Music) and the Society for Ethnomusicology in 1955. The term 'ethnomusicology' gained currency in the mid-1950s (the hyphen was officially dropped by the Society in 1957), replacing 'comparative musicology'. Over and again the view was expressed, by George Herzog, Jaap Kunst, Willard Rhodes, George List and Curt Sachs, that this study was no more comparative than all other fields of knowledge.

By the late 1950s, American ethnomusicologists had divided into two camps: those with anthropological training, led by Alan Merriam (1923–80), and those with musicological backgrounds, led by Mantle Hood (b1918) (Merriam, 1969, 'Ethnomusicology Revisited'). In 1960, Merriam spoke as anthropologist when he defined ethnomusicology not in terms of subject matter but approach as 'the study of music in culture' (p.109). In 1973 he modified his definition to 'the study of music as culture', and in 1975 gave even greater emphasis to the cultural and social factors, stating 'music *is* culture and what musicians do *is* society' (1977, p.204; 1975, p. 57; also see Herndon and McLeod, 1979). He criticized the laboratory-based comparative research of the Berlin school, in which 'cultural facts were applied more or less indiscriminately to "prove" the already deduced theory' (1964, p.52). Merriam regarded personal fieldwork as an essential part of any ethnomusicological study and proposed a model for the study of musical cultures: the investigation of concepts about music, musical behaviour, and musical sound (pp. 32–3). In his dissatisfaction with deductive research, Merriam spoke for most American ethnomusicologists, who considered their current grasp of world music too sketchy to warrant theoretical generalization. Merriam's positivist and particularist approach was nurtured by an increase in fieldwork, made possible by the advances in commercial aviation following World War II. Studies written during the 1950s and 1960s reflect caution; most are self-contained ethnographic reports based on fieldwork in a particular tradition, an individual ethnic group, or a geographic region, aimed at filling the gaps on a map of world musical styles.

The American musicological approach stressed mastery of a foreign musical language, 'bi-musicality' (an analogue to bi-linguality), through extended stays in the field (a year or more; Hood, 1960, 1971). This method had its rationale in the teachings of Charles Seeger, the Connecticut Yankee philosopher of musicology, who held that speech and music are incompatible modes of communication. This dilemma, which Seeger called 'the musicological juncture', left the scholar, who must use words to describe music, in a curious position (Seeger, 1977).

One solution Seeger proposed was the study of non-Western performance at home and in the field. Hood gathered at the UCLA Institute of Ethno-

7

musicology a distinguished circle of foreign musician-teachers including José Maceda (Philippines), Kwabena Nketia (Ghana) and Hardja Susilo (Java); beginning in 1960, Hood's programme offered instruction in Javanese, Persian, Japanese, Mexican, Indian, Balinese, Greek and African musics. The critical mission of ethnomusicology was explicit in his pronouncement of 1961, that 'in the latter half of the twentieth century it may well be that the very existence of man depends on the accuracy of his communications'. These words fired the imagination of American music students and university administrators alike, and ethnomusicology graduates from UCLA found jobs in major American universities. In the series of short articles in the inaugural issue of the *SEM Newsletter*, Hood was one of the first to proclaim ethnomusicology to be the study of any and all musics, paraphrasing the 'Report of the Committee on Graduate Studies', *JAMS*, 1955.

The 1970s to 1990s

The nature of ethnomusicological studies has been transformed during the last hundred years, although the field has not yet 'come of age' (as was claimed at the 25th meeting of the Society for Ethnomusicology, 1980). The armchair has been abandoned; scholars now conduct their own fieldwork, and experience first-hand the cultures whose music they analyse. Inevitably this development has improved the standard of work and led to new understanding of the role of music in human life. But have the fundamental issues really changed?

The 1970s and 1980s saw unification in ethnomusicological theory and method despite a diversification of topics. Anthropological and musicological concerns fused; interest shifted from pieces of music to processes of musical creation and performance – composition and improvisation – and the focus shifted from collection of repertory to examination of these processes. New approaches to the analysis of music and of its cultural setting were used; these include aspects of cybernetics (the study of control systems), information theory (how information is generated, transmitted and stored), semiotics (the interpretation of phenomena in terms of signs and symbols), and structuralism (the identification of the structural rules governing cultural phenomena). Increased emphasis was placed on decoding the meaning of the musical message. New methods have also stimulated more rigorous musical ethnography, for example, the ethnography of musical performance (Herndon and McLeod, 1980) and the microethnographic analysis of the musical event (Stone, 1982).

The distinction between diachronic and synchronic studies lost importance. Historical studies returned, making new demands on fieldworkers, for example, studies of modernization and Westernization (Nettl, 1985). Many traditional historians of South and East Asian musics began to amplify their research with field studies of contemporary music. New subjects came under investigation: ethnopoetics and aesthetic anthropology (Feld, 1982), gender and music (Keeling, 1989), urban music (Nettl, 1978), the music of refugee populations, film music of India and Japan (Skillman, 1986), the impact of tourism on music in rural and urban settings, street music and busking, and the new traditional musics – popular Westernized forms in burgeoning non-Western cities, including Latin salsa, African 'high life', Congolese, *juju, kwela* and *tarabu* (Blum, 1978; Waterman, 1985, 1990). Local cassette industries sprang up overnight in Africa and Asia (Wallis and Malm, 1984). The international music industry brought a mixing and matching of musical styles that would have astonished early fieldworkers of the 20th century who searched in their travels only for idealized authentic folk music. Fieldwork took on new dimensions, as the field came to the scholar through media broadcasts and locally produced records; artists from Africa and Asia began to visit Western capitals on concert tours. As a consequence of international exchange and renewed ethical awareness, indigenous performers and informants were given recognition for their contribution to music scholarship (Nettl, 1984). Ethics in fieldwork and research received more attention, and attempts were made to deposit copies of recordings and scholarly publications in archives and libraries of the countries under study.

New methods of field investigation were born of new technology, for example Ruth Stone's video recording and playback in analysis of musical events amongst the Kpelle of Liberia (Stone, 1982). To facilitate transcription of complex polyphonic, polyrhythmic compositions from the Central African Republic, Simha Arom used stereo recording and audio playback techniques in the field, a method involving the musicians as 'true scientific collaborators' who 'assume totally the determination of the successive stages of the experimental work' (1976, p.495).

2. Klaus Wachsmann recording in Uganda

9

With innovative studies of modern musical life, the 1970s and 1980s also saw fieldwork resumed in societies largely untouched by Western life, for example Anthony Seeger's research among the Suyá, a remote community of the Amazon (1987), and Marina Roseman's study of the Temiar of the Malaysian rain forest (1984). Steven Feld had to master the local ornithology of the Kaluli people of highland Papua New Guinea, and Monique Brandily that of the Teda of Chad, before either could understand these complex musical systems (Feld, 1982, 1988; Brandily, 1982). In isolated settings scholars adapted field techniques to suit the situation. Hugo Zemp elicited the rich detailed musical vocabulary of the 'Are'are people of the Solomon Islands during informal music and language lessons, rather than formal interviews (1978, 1979, 1981).

Beginning in the late 1970s, renewed enthusiasm was voiced for ethno-musicological studies of Western classical music, but little work was actually published in this area (however, see Wachsmann, 1981 and 1982; Herndon, 1988). Conversely, musicologists (perhaps with a glance over their shoulders at ethnomusicological methods) began taking greater cognizance of extra-musical factors, particularly the social milieu, in their analyses of standard repertories.

Beginning in the 1980s, the biology of music-making united ethno-musicologists with musicologists, performers and music educators, as well as psychologists and neurologists (Wilson, 1983, 1985). Through teamwork, fresh approaches were tested to understand the music-specific aspects of brain and motor functions. Ethnomusicologists contributed by comparing findings from different cultures, hearkening back, in spirit if not in method, to the cross-cultural psycho-acoustic studies of the Berlin school in the late 19th century. Are the basic biological functions of human musicality universal, or are they determined by culture? The old nature/nurture question was raised once again.

Abiding central issues

After a century of work, certain fundamental issues still occupy centre stage in ethnomusicology. Ethnomusicologists generally study non-Western and folk music, and are particularly interested in the match of cultural context to musical style. With the whole world as their oyster, and the essential links between music and the rest of life their abiding concern, ethnomusicologists have resorted to methods and theories from various allied disciplines. Many a recent article describes Mongolian or Bolivian or Samoan music in the terminology of linguistics, interactionism, phenomenological sociology, in-formation theory, structuralism, and so on; this makes life hard for experts and amateurs alike, to say nothing of the musicians whose music is under discussion. Delving into the pages of the music periodicals of the field, *Ethnomusicology* and *Yearbook For Traditional Music*, is not light reading. After wading through pages devoted to definitions of familiar terms like 'perform-ance', 'event' and 'assumption', you may unexpectedly find yourself drowning in a sea of undefined matrices and paradigms, pondering the nature of 'sonic ideation', 'cantometric profiles', 'thick description' or 'semiotico-cybernetic theory'.

Conflicts continue: between scholars searching for universally applicable systems of analysis and those attempting to use the cognitive framework of a particular culture as the basis for analysis of its music; between those who believe that detailed analysis of music leads to understanding and those who believe that music can be understood only on its own terms through performance. Although approaches vary and orientations differ, some tenets of ethnomusicology are held in common. Fieldwork remains the focal point of research, and each scholar is expected to collect his own material for analysis. Ethnomusicologists continue to acknowledge the value of written notation; some use mechanical music writers, including computers and the melograph, but a surprising number, armed with various special symbols, still rely on conventional Western notation.

At the very heart of ethnomusicology, the astute reader may discern the fundamental irony of the subject. On the one hand, each scholar is eager to defend the music of his or her own people as special and unique; on the other, no ethnomusicologist will rank the music of his culture over that of his colleague. Value judgements are not the fashion in today's ethnomusicology – perhaps a small price to pay for an even-handed treatment of the world's music. So ethnomusicologists, with their bewildering array of new topics, their barrage of jargon and their pedantic definitions, find their place of pride as the great egalitarians of musicology.

Towards the year 2000

No particular logic can be imposed on the materials that have come to ethnomusicology other than the examination of all the music of all the peoples of all times and all places. Scholars have shied away from trying to organize a comprehensive text on this subject because of the diversity and incompatibility of material. The study of ancient Indian manuscripts has little to do with the study of contemporary Indian film music. The texts so far published suggest a limited range of activities for ethnomusicologists. Hence there are books on the history of ethnomusicology, its methods, its theories, performance, fieldwork, and many representative studies of particular cultures. Any attempt to provide the full picture is bound to reflect the anomaly of the subject.

This book cheerfully presents a full account beginning with the tales of explorers, missionaries, travellers, as well as the ancient theories of the Orient, leading to the high-tech world of the 1980s and the new humanism of the 1990s. Ethnomusicologists are travelling everywhere with pad and pencil, recorders and cameras (still, video and movie), endeavouring to document the music of the world. Such a task happily is never-ending, as music is ever-changing and the world is vast.

This book, *Ethnomusicology: Historical and Regional Studies*, and its companion volume, *Ethnomusicology: an Introduction*, provide a comprehensive survey of the field. *Ethnomusicology: Historical and Regional Studies* has two parts, one giving the early history of the field (to World War II), the other up-to-date reports on post-war research. These volumes boldly carry the title *Ethnomusicology*. Critics may argue, indeed have argued, that before the 1950s there was no ethnomusicology and before the 1880s no comparative musicology. These arguments to limit the subject for want of a term run contrary to common usage, which allows change and lets words mean what users wish. (The venerable *Oxford English Dictionary*, with its continuing supplements, keeps the English-speaking populace abreast of these changes.) Ethnomusicologists have long needed a broad-minded label and a comprehensive survey, as presented here.

The reader will find that continents of the world have inspired different styles of research. What is available is what is studied. For China, Korea, Japan, India and West Asia there is a body of historical material analogous to the Western canon of music theory. For Africa a sophisticated technique for the study of oral history has developed, whereas cultures with long-standing written traditions have inspired methods for the study of ancient texts – analysis of ink, paper, folding, etc. This unevenness characterizes the field of ethnomusicology. What initially fascinated Westerners in Tibet was the Buddhist monastic tradition; in the West Indies, topical songs (calypso, reggae), and festival music; in Southeast Asia the court traditions of various gong-chime ensembles. In India, scholars initially were interested in the high musical traditions (the 'great' tradition). Only recently has interest turned to peasant music of the countryside (the 'little' tradition) and modern devotional music. The real music of India for Indians – film music – has been investigated only in the late 1980s.

We know much about peasant music of Eastern Europe but little about peasant music of India, even less about peasant music of China. We know much about urban theatrical forms in China but little about the village theatrical forms of India.

The musical traditions that have attracted the attention of Western scholars appear to be random, but in fact the studies reflect either what crossed the eyes and ears of the researchers and engaged their imaginations or what local people valued and presented as significant. This mélange is part of the charm of the subject and part of the difficulty in presenting to the world neat categories or an evenly balanced scholarly analysis. It also marks the richness of ethnomusicology. And as our continuing research has prospered, some unanticipated and surprising developments have been reported. Merriam found when visiting the Basongye village of Lupupa Ngye that music there had changed in ways he had never anticipated. More disturbing, he learned that the single most important event in the musical life of the village was thought to be his previous visit 14 years previously (1977, 'Music Change'). That gave the ethnomusicologists pause!

The hope of being a fly on the wall was dashed and a new issue, 'reflexivity', arose. What would they be doing if I weren't here? How is my presence affecting what they are doing? How can I modify my behaviour so that they would more nearly do what they would have done if I weren't here? Should I tell my life story so the reader of my study can answer these questions?

If these are mischievous questions, perhaps they will lead us to abandon hope of a false objectivity, and to become resigned to our wholesome subjectivity. Let us come to savour the personal insights of our many scholars.

Eventually what Westerners think of non-Western music may be overshadowed by what the people we have studied think of their own music. Finding ways of helping native observers, literate or illiterate, to describe their own music – their likes and dislikes, their sense of the beautiful and the ugly – is a present task for ethnomusicologists, perhaps an ethical responsibility.

This volume includes accounts of both local and foreign observers.

Bibliography

J. B. de Halde: *Description de l'Empire de la Chine* (Paris, 1735)

J.-J. Rousseau: *Dictionnaire de musique* (Paris, 1768/*R*1969; many edns. to 1825; Eng. trans. by W. Waring, London, 1771, 2/1779/*R*1975)

J. M. Amiot: *Mémoire sur la musique des chinois* (Paris, 1779)

W. Jones: 'On the Musical Modes of the Hindoos', *Asiatick Researches*, iii (1792), 55–87; repr. in S. M. Tagore: *Hindu Music from Various Authors* (Calcutta, 1875, 2/1882 in 2 pts., 3/1965)

G.-A. Villoteau: 'De l'état actuel de l'art musical en Egypte' and 'Description historique, technique et littéraire des instrumens de musique des orientaux', *Description de l'Egypte: état moderne*, i, ed. E. P. Jomard (Paris, 1809), 607–845, 846–1016

R. G. Kisewetter: *Die Musik der Araber* (Leipzig, 1842)

G. Adler: 'Umfang, Methode und Ziel der Musikwissenschaft', *VMw*, i (1885), 5; Eng. trans. in Mugglestone, (1981)

A. J. Ellis: 'On the Musical Scales of Various Nations', *Journal of the Society of Arts*, xxxiii (1885), 485–527

J. W. Fewkes: 'A Contribution to Passamaquoddy Folk-Lore', *Journal of American Folklore*, iii (1890), 257

C. R. Day: *The Music and Musical Instruments of Southern India and the Deccan* (London and New York, 1891/*R*1974)

A. C. Fletcher with F. La Flesche and J. C. Fillmore: *A Study of Omaha Indian Music* (Cambridge, MA, 1893) [pp.35ff repr. as 'The Wa-wan, or Pipe Dance of the Omahas', *Music*, iv (1893), 468]

F. T. Piggott: *The Music and Musical Instruments of Japan* (London, 1893)

G. Herzog: 'The Yuman Musical Style', *Journal of American Folklore*, xli (1928), 183–231

C. Seeger: 'Music and Musicology', *Encyclopedia of the Social Sciences*, ed. E. R. A. Seligman, xi (New York, 1933), 143

H. H. Roberts: 'The Viewpoint of Comparative Musicology', *Volume of Proceedings of the Music Teachers National Association, Thirty-First Series. Annual Meeting of the Sixtieth Year. Chicago, Illinois. December 28–31, 1936*, ed. K. W. Gehrkens (Oberlin, OH, 1936), 233

G. Haydon: *Introduction to Musicology: a Survey of the Fields, Systematic and Historical, of Musical Knowledge and Research* (Chapel Hill, NC, 1941)

C. Sachs: *The Rise of Music in the Ancient World, East and West* (New York, 1943)

W. Apel: 'Comparative Musicology', 'Exotic Music', *Harvard Dictionary of Music*, ed. W. Apel, (Cambridge, MA, 1944), 167, 250

G. Herzog: 'Comparative Musicology', *Music Journal*, iv/6 (1946), 11

J. Kunst: *Musicologica* (Amsterdam, 1950, enl. 3/1959/*R*1975 as *Ethnomusicology*)

C. Seeger: 'Systematic Musicology: Viewpoints, Orientations, and Methods', *JAMS*, iv (1951), 240

M. F. Bukofzer: 'Observations on the Study of Non-Western Music', *Les Colloques de Wégimont*, ed. P. Collaer (Brussels, 1956), 33

D. P. McAllester: 'The Organizational Meeting in Boston', *EM*, i/6 (1956), 3

B. Nettl: *Music in Primitive Culture* (Cambridge, MA, 1956)

W. Rhodes: 'Toward a Definition of Ethnomusicology', *American Anthropologist*, lviii (1956), 457

M. Hood: 'Training and Research Methods in Ethnomusicology', *EM*, i/11 (1957), 2

M. Kolinski: 'Ethnomusicology, its Problems and Methods', *EM*, i/10 (1957) 1

M. Schneider: 'Primitive Music', *New Oxford History of Music*, i, *Ancient and Oriental Music*, ed. E. Wellesz (London, 1957), 1–82

G. Chase: 'A Dialectical Approach to Music History', *EM*, ii (1958), 1

'Whither Ethnomusicology?' *EM*, iii (1959), 99 [essays by Hood, Kolinski, Nettl, Chilkovsky, List, Seeger, Miller, McAllester, Meyer]

13

M. Hood: 'The Challenge of "Bi-musicality"', *EM*, iv (1960), 55

A. P. Merriam: 'Ethnomusicology – Discussion and Definition of the Field', *EM*, iv (1960), 107

M. Hood: *Institute of Ethnomusicology* (Los Angeles, 1961)

N. Schiørring: 'The Contribution of Ethnomusicology to Historical Musicology', *Report of the Eighth Congress of the International Musicological Society, New York, 1961, Papers*, ed. J. La Rue, (Kassel, 1961), 380

C. Seeger: 'Semantic, Logical and Political Considerations Bearing Upon Research in Ethnomusicology', *EM*, v (1961), 77

G. List: 'Ethnomusicology in Higher Education', *Music Journal*, xx/8 (1962), 20

C. Sachs: *The Wellsprings of Music* (The Hague, 1962)

M. Hood: 'Music, the Unknown', *Musicology*, ed. F. Ll. Harrison, M. Hood and C. V. Palisca (Englewood Cliffs, NJ, 1963), 217–326

O. Kinkeldey: 'Musicology', *The International Cyclopedia of Music and Musicians*, ed. O. Thompson, (New York, 9/1964), 1428

A. P. Merriam: *The Anthropology of Music* (Evanston, IL, 1964)

B. Nettl: *Theory and Method in Ethnomusicology* (Glencoe, IL, 1964)

C. Marcel-Dubois: 'L'ethnomusicologie, sa vocation et sa situation', *Revue de l'enseignement supérieur*, iii (1965), 38

J. Blacking: 'Review of *The Anthropology of Music*', *Current Anthropology*, vii (1966), 217

M. Kolinski: 'Recent Trends in Ethnomusicology', *EM*, xi (1967), 1

A. Merriam: 'The Use of Music as a Technique of Reconstructing Culture History in Africa', *Reconstructing African Culture History*, ed. C. Gabel and N. R. Bennett (Boston, 1967), 83–114

C. Seeger: 'Factorial Analysis of the Song as an Approach to the Formation of a Unitary Field Theory', *JIFMC*, xx (1968), 33

M. Hood: 'Ethnomusicology', *Harvard Dictionary of Music*, ed. W. Apel (Cambridge, MA, 2/1969), 298

A. P. Merriam: 'Ethnomusicology Revisited', *EM*, xiii (1969), 213

K. P. Wachsmann: 'Music', *Journal of the Folklore Institute*, vi (1969), 164

C. Seeger: 'Toward a Unitary Field Theory for Musicology', *Selected Reports in Ethnomusicology*, i/3 (1970), 171–210

A. Czekanowska: *Etnografia muzyczna: metodologia i metodyka* (Warsaw, 1971)

M. Hood: *The Ethnomusicologist* (New York, 1971/R1982)

C. Seeger: 'Reflections Upon a Given Topic: Music in Universal Perspective', *EM*, xv (1971), 385

G. Chase: 'American Musicology and the Social Sciences', *Perspectives in Musicology*, ed. B. S. Brook, E. O. D. Downes and S. Van Solkema (New York, 1972), 202

V. Duckles: 'Musicology at the Mirror: a Prospectus for the History of Musical Scholarship', *Perspectives in Musicology*, ed. B. S. Brook, E. O. D. Downes, and S. Van Solkema (New York, 1972), 32

F. Ll. Harrison: 'Music and Cult: The Functions of Music in Social and Religious Systems', *Perspectives in Musicology*, ed. B. S. Brook, E. O. D. Downes and S. Van Solkema (New York, 1972), 307

J. Blacking: *How Musical Is Man?* (Seattle, 1973)

——: 'Ethnomusicology as a Key Subject in the Social Sciences', *In Memoriam António Jorge Dias*, iii (Lisbon, 1974), 71

S. Blum: 'Towards a Social History of Musicological Technique', *EM*, xix (1975), 207

A. P. Merriam: 'Ethnomusicology Today', *CMc*, xx (1975), 50

B. Nettl: 'Ethnomusicology Today', *World of Music*, xvii/4 (1975), 11

——: 'The State of Research in Ethnomusicology, and Recent Developments', *CMc*, xx (1975), 67

S. Arom: 'The Use of Play-Back Techniques in the Study of Oral Polyphonies', *EM*, xx (1976), 483–519

A. Lomax: *Cantometrics: an Approach to the Anthropology of Music* (Berkeley, 1976)

A. P. Merriam: 'Definitions of "Comparative Musicology" and "Ethnomusicology": an Historical-Theoretical Perspective', *EM*, xxi (1977), 189

——: 'Music Change in a Basengye Village (Zaire),' *Anthropos*, lxxii (1977), 806–46

C. Seeger: 'The Musicological Juncture: 1976', *EM*, xxi (1977), 179

J. Blum: 'Problems of *Salsa* Research', *EM*, xxii (1978), 137

C. J. Frisbie and D. P. McAllester, eds.: *Navajo Blessingway Singer: the Autobiography of Frank Mitchell 1881–1967* (Tucson, 1978)

K. A. Gourlay: 'Towards a Reassessment of the Ethnomusicologist's Role in Research', *EM*, xxii (1978), 1–35

B. Nettl, ed.: *Eight Urban Musical Cultures: Tradition and Change* (Urbana, 1978)

H. Zemp: ''Are'are Classification of Musical Types and Instruments', *EM*, xxii (1978), 37–67

M. Herndon and N. McLeod: *Music as Culture* (Norwood, PA, 1979 *R*/1982)

G. List: 'Ethnomusicology: a Discipline Defined', *EM*, xxiii (1979), 1

D. P. McAllester: 'The Astonished Ethno-Muse', *EM*, xxiii (1979), 179

B. Whyte: *The Yellow on the Broom: the Early Days of a Traveller Woman* (Edinburgh, 1979)

H. Zemp: 'Aspects of 'Are'are Musical Theory', *EM*, xxiii (1979), 6–48

N. McLeod and M. Herndon: *The Ethnography of Musical Performance* (Norwood, PA, 1980)

K. K. Shelemay: '"Historical Ethnomusicology": Reconstructing Falasha Liturgical History', *EM*, xxiv (1980), 233

E. Mugglestone: 'Guido Adler's "The Scope, Method, and Aim of Musicology" (1885): an English Translation with an Historico-Analytical Commentary', *YTM*, xiii (1981), 1

H. P. Myers: '"Normal" Ethnomusicology and "Extraordinary" Ethnomusicology', *Journal of the Indian Musicological Society*, xii/3–4 (1981), 38

K. P. Wachsmann: 'Applying Ethnomusicological Methods to Western Art Music', *World of Music*, xxiii/2 (1981), 74

H. Zemp: 'Melanesian Solo Polyphonic Panpipe Music', *EM*, xxv (1981), 383–418

M. Brandily: 'Songs to Birds among the Teda of Chad', *EM*, xxvi (1982), 371

S. Feld: *Sound and Sentiment: Birds, Weeping, Poetics, and Song in Kaluli Expression* (Philadelphia, 1982)

J. Mark: 'Francis La Flesche: the American Indian as Anthropologist', *Isis*, lxxii (1982), 497

R. M. Stone: *Let the Inside Be Sweet: the Interpretation of Music Event Among the Kpelle of Liberia* (Bloomington, IN, 1982)

K. P. Wachsmann: 'The Changeability of Musical Experience', *EM*, xxvi (1982), 197

H. P. Myers: 'Ethnomusicology', *The New Oxford Companion to Music*, ed. D. Arnold, (Oxford, 11/1983), 645

B. Nettl: *The Study of Ethnomusicology: Twenty-nine Issues and Concepts* (Urbana, 1983)

H. P. Myers: 'Ethnomusicology', *The New Grove Dictionary of American Music*, ed. H. W. Hitchcock and S. Sadie, (London, 1984)

B. Nettl: 'In Honor of Our Principal Teachers', *EM*, xxviii (1984), 173

M. Roseman: 'The Social Structuring of Sound: the Temiar of Peninsular Malaysia, *EM*, xxviii (1984), 411–45

R. Wallis and K. Malm: *Big Sounds from Small Peoples: the Music Industry in Small Countries* (New York, 1984)

C. A. Waterman: 'Juju', in B. Nettl: *The Western Impact on World Music: Change, Adaptation, and Survival* (New York, 1985), 87

T. Skillman: 'The Bombay Hindi Film Song Genre: a Historical Survey', *YTM*, xviii (1986), 133

A. Seeger: *Why Suyá Sing: a Musical Anthropology of an Amazonian People* (Cambridge, MA, 1987)

S. Feld: 'Aesthetics as Iconicity of Style, or "Lift-up-over Sounding": Getting into the Kaluli Groove'. *YTM*, xx (1988), 74–113

M. Herndon: 'Cultural Engagement: the Case of the Oakland Symphony Orchestra', *YTM*, xx (1988), 134

F. R. Wilson and R. L. Roehmann, eds.: *The Biology of Music Making: Proceedings of the 1984 Denver Conference* (St Louis, 1988)

R. Keeling, ed.: *Women in North American Indian Music: Six Essays.* (Bloomington, IN, 1989)

F. R. Wilson and R. L. Roehmann, eds.: *Music and Child Development: Proceedings of the 1987 Denver Conference* (St Louis, 1990)

C. A. Waterman: *Jùjú: a Social History and Ethnography of an African Popular Music* (Chicago, 1990)

B. Nettl and P. V. Bohlman, eds.: *Comparative Musicology and Anthropology of Music: Essays on the History of Ethnomusicology* (Chicago, 1991)

15

PART TWO

History to World War II

CHAPTER II

North America

DOROTHY SARA LEE, HELEN MYERS,
WILLIAM WESTCOTT, JAMES ROBBINS

1: NATIVE AMERICAN

DOROTHY SARA LEE

Ethnomusicology, like other disciplines developing in the USA during the late 19th century, resulted from conflicting social, scientific and governmental pressures. Scientific interest in the American Indian had escalated since the late 1700s; rapid westward expansion during the 19th century brought increased awareness of the diversity of Native American culture as well as corresponding increase in brutal hostilities between the still fragile US government and native peoples determined to halt encroachment on their lands. By the late 1860s, the USA was at war with many tribes west of the Mississippi, yet within three decades most of the tribes had been defeated and consigned to reservations.

Ethnological field research had persisted – government sponsorship of scientific activity began long before creation of the Bureau of American Ethnology (BAE) in 1879. In addition to geographical and geological surveys, Congress appropriated funds in the early 1830s for an extensive exploration of the Pacific Ocean under the command of Lieutenant Charles Wilkes. The United States South Seas Exploring Expedition (1838–42) included a full complement of botanists, geologists and artist-illustrators, as well as philologist Horatio Hale (1817–96), who made the first objective study of Fijian prosody.

The need to know more about the peoples with whom it was at war gave impetus to further ethnological research by soldiers in the Army. Washington Matthews (1843–1905), an army surgeon during campaigns in the Southwest, began an intensive field relationship with the Navajo, and Captain John Gregory Bourke's (1846–96) anthropological career resulted from his experiences fighting tribes in the Plains.

Others, such as James Mooney (1861–1921) and Frank Hamilton Cushing (1857–1900), came to ethnology as talented amateurs and found employment with the BAE at the Smithsonian Institution. Mandated by Congress to study

19

the American Indian, the Bureau, under the command of Major John Wesley Powell, himself a veteran of Indian wars and geological surveys, crystallized prevailing Victorian theories of social and cultural evolution into government dogma and shaped this direction of cultural studies in the USA for over two decades.

Most important for ethnomusicology, the Bureau confirmed the primacy of Washington over Boston as the national centre for anthropology. During the 1880s and 1890s it was a thriving intellectual community with nearly two dozen scientific and literary societies drawing most of their membership from squadrons of federal workers engaged in scholarly research. At society-sponsored meetings, members offered papers and worked towards building credibility for emerging cultural sciences.

This Washington intellectual community embodied an accumulation of cultural paradoxes characteristic of North America in the so-called Gilded Age. In a tumultuous century, evolutionary teachings assured white Americans of their so-called place as the dominant race, and rapid strides in technology guaranteed the centrality of science and progress in the post-revolutionary search for a national identity. While 19th-century romanticism fostered an idealization of Indian culture and lamented its passing, 19th-century reformers hastened its end through policies that deliberately broke down cultural institutions. The same ethnologists who rushed to record Native American culture before it disappeared helped to formulate policies accelerating acculturation.

Before 1890

Although French and Spanish missionaries and explorers had documented American Indian music and dance performances since the discovery of the New World (Crawford, 1967; Harrison, 1973; Stevenson, 1973), the subject excited little scientific interest in the USA until well after the turn of the 19th century, perhaps because of public hostility towards Indian subjects. As explorers and settlers pushed westward across the continent, descriptions of music were imbedded in narratives recounting social and ceremonial events. However, for early 19th-century American society music was merely a diversion or amusement and most chroniclers failed to grasp its fundamental role in Native American culture.

Theodore Baker's (1854–1928) doctoral dissertation, *Über die musik der Nordamerikanischen Wilden* (1882), is recognized as the first significant examination of American Indian music. Baker transcribed songs directly from Seneca performers during a visit to their New York reservation in the summer of 1880, supplementing these with songs notated at the Carlisle Indian School, Pennsylvania. His study combined direct, although limited, field observation with a broad summary of current sources.

During the 1880s, increased awareness of the importance of music in Native American ceremonialism led ethnologists to include song transcriptions in their monographs and articles. Linguist and Episcopal missionary James Owen Dorsey (1848–95) published a selection of Ponca and Omaha songs in the *Journal of American Folklore*; one of his field assistants was a young Francis La Flesche (1857–1932). Franz Boas (1858–1943) wrote about Kwakiutl and

Chinook songs for the same journal and included Central Eskimo songs in his 1884 BAE annual report. Many fieldworkers transcribed Indian melodies in standard Western notation but were frustrated by the potential for inaccuracy and the growing perception that a more scientific method for preservation – matching the methods in archaeology and material culture – was needed. The invention of the phonograph in 1879 and its use for anthropological fieldwork in 1890 provided a welcome resolution to the problem.

The 1890s

The first major studies of American Indian music came in the 1890s, along with the first major theoretical controversies, which went to the heart of the emerging discipline. Field research intensified throughout the Plains and the Southwest as the last of the hostile tribes were consigned to reservations and the scare of the Ghost Dance, an inter-tribal movement against whites, 1870–90, ended. Government-sponsored and privately funded expeditions gathered artefacts for major museums in Chicago, New York and Washington, and the disciplines of anthropology and folklore tested their theoretical wings in the public arena of the 1893 Chicago World's Fair.

By far, the major impetus for the developing study of 'exotic' music was the adoption of the cylinder phonograph by field researchers. The phonograph liberated the ethnologist from the tedium of linguistic and musical field transcriptions, and enabled the scholar to bring songs and texts back to laboratories for scientific study. Jesse Walter Fewkes was the earliest to use the phonograph in the field, recording Passamaquoddy Indian songs and narratives in February and March 1890, during a trial field trip to the Passamaquoddy reservation at Calais, Maine ('A Contribution to Passamaquoddy Folklore'). This initial effort was sponsored by Mary Thaw Hemenway, a major stockholder in the Edison company who wished to test the phonograph's usefulness for ethnographic work, and who probably furnished the machine. At the time, the phonograph was only available through lease from the company (Brady, 1985). Hemenway funded Fewkes's summer researches at the Zuni (1889–90) and Hopi (1891–4). Fewkes used his treadle-operated phonograph to record Zuni and Hopi sacred and secular music, and handed the cylinders over to Benjamin Ives Gilman (1852–1933) for transcription and analysis (Gilman, 1891, 1908).

Gilman, a psychologist with no prior experience in non-Western music, was acutely aware of the pioneering nature of his study and with Fewkes conducted experiments to establish the accuracy of the machines used in transcription. Accepting the cylinder as the primary document, he used a harmonium tuned to concert pitch as referent, and found deviations from the Western tempered scale that could not be explained by the eccentricities of the phonograph. His decision to publish the Zuni melodies without key or time signatures sparked a bitter debate with John Comfort Fillmore (1843–98) who used the universality of diatonic harmony.

Other ethnologists were quick to adapt the phonograph for field use, and by the 1890s music was regularly included in ethnographies. James Mooney recorded Caddoan songs during the last stages of his Ghost Dance field research in 1893; Franz Boas recorded Kwakiutl music in British Columbia and at the 1893 Chicago World's Fair; and George Bird Grinnell (1849–1938) and Walter McClintock (1870–1949) collected social and ceremonial songs in Montana.

Most credit for the development of ethnomusicology in the USA must go to Alice Cunningham Fletcher (1838–1923; see fig.1). With no professional training in anthropology yet available, Fletcher began her studies in the mid-1870s with Frederick Ward Putnam (1839–1915), curator at Harvard's Peabody Museum of Archaeology and Ethnology, and, like many of her contemporaries, launched a lecture career in anthropology based primarily upon library research. Direct field experience came in 1881 with her first Nebraska trip to study Omaha Indian people, and this background inspired her second vocation as an activist for Native American reform and education (March, 1980, p.67). Through her work administering land allotments for the Pawnee, Arapaho, Dakota, Winnebago, Nez Perce, Omaha, Cheyenne and other tribes in the central and western areas of the country, Fletcher became acquainted with the distressing problems facing contemporary Indian cultures.

Although Fletcher was affiliated with the BAE, writing articles on music and Plains Indian culture for the Bureau's *Handbook of North American Indians* and later producing two monographs for its Annual Reports, she was never actually employed by the Bureau. Rather, she lived an independent scholarly life in Washington, supported through Harvard University by a lifetime

1. *Alice Cunningham Fletcher at her writing desk*

personal fellowship from Mary Copley Thaw. Washington supplied a surprisingly active arena for secondary field research since members of various Indian delegations visiting government offices would stop at Fletcher's Capitol Hill home, where much of her recording was conducted.

Early in her ethnological studies Fletcher recognized the importance of music in Indian ritual and began collecting melodies. While she was able to notate these melodies by ear, she preferred to work with professional musicians to realize her transcriptions. Her earliest and most celebrated collaborator was John Comfort Fillmore, an Oberlin- and Leipzig-trained teacher at the Milwaukee School of Music (DeVale, 1986), who prepared the harmonizations for her monograph, *A Study of Omaha Indian Music* (1893).

Fletcher's early lectures on Indian music reveal a belief in the uniqueness of native musical systems. In 'Indian Music', an unpublished manuscript dated 1888, she writes: 'The Indian Scale is different from our own; but there are songs that come very near to our scales and yield very readily to our keyboard . . . I am sorry that it is impossible for me to exemplify to you the Indian scale. It could only be done by the violin. There is no notation in common use that would make it feasible to describe it' (p.6, National Anthropological Archives, MS 4558, box 15). Fillmore, on the other hand, embraced the evolutionary perspective of his day, developing a theory of musical analysis that assumed a common harmonic foundation for all music, European and exotic (McNutt, 1984, 1985; Pantaleoni, 1985). He attributed Indian deviations from the diatonic scale to an underdeveloped sense of pitch discrimination. For the 1893 monograph, Fillmore developed his harmonizations of Omaha melodies almost exclusively from Fletcher's field transcriptions, although he did make several trips during 1891–2 to the Omaha reservation to refine his work. Fillmore distrusted the phonograph, and he accused Gilman of failing to use the machine properly (letter to Alice Cunningham Fletcher, 27 December 1891, National Anthropological Archives, MS 4558).

Fillmore worked with other ethnologists as well. He began transcribing Kwakiutl cylinders for Franz Boas in 1893 ('Dr Boas has been here and has brought me 72 cylinders. A sweet job I shall have with them. The rhythm is so abominably complicated': letter to Alice Cunningham Fletcher, 12 November 1893, National Anthropological Archives, MS 4558). He notated Navajo melodies for Washington Matthews and, after his move to Pomona College in California, worked briefly with the collections of Charles Lummis (1859–1928) (McNutt, 1984). Fillmore clearly wanted to devote his full attention to studying American music and hoped for a Smithsonian appointment, but Bureau support for his work was not forthcoming. Towards the end of his life, his letters to Fletcher were increasingly bitter about perceived opposition from Bureau ethnologists who leaned towards Gilman's approach. In one such letter, dated 26 February 1894, he wrote, 'what bothers me is, that men like Mason should not know without being told, that such questions as we are at work on have to be solved by *musicians* [italics Fillmore's], not by physicists' (National Anthropological Archives, Alice Fletcher collection, MS 4558).

Fletcher's life-long interest in Indian reform gave her music studies a sense of vocation and imparted an almost missionary tone to the emerging discipline. She maintained a wide correspondence with other researchers, encouraging younger ethnologists like Walter McClintock (1870–1949) to study Indian music. Fletcher wrote passionately about her participation in Native American life – her descriptions of music performances in magazines such as *Century* were a revelation to late-Romantic American composers searching for a foundation for a national musical identity. Granted, the richness of American native material had already been cited by such European musicians as Dvořák, who urged American composers to explore the ethnic diversity in their own land, rather than continuing to look towards Europe for inspiration. Some of Dvořák's students at the National Conservatory of Music, among them Harvey Worthington Loomis (1865–1930), heeded his warnings and published compositions based on Indian themes. But Fletcher's published studies of Omaha Indian music galvanized a direct involvement with Native American culture; *A Study of Omaha Indian Music* and *Indian Story and Song* (1900) were primers for many subsequent Americanist compositions and guided several composers into the field for firsthand experience.

The 1893 World's Fair Columbian Exposition in Chicago was, like fairs before it, a showplace for American technology and a visible symbol of the achievements reached in the progress of American civilization. Anthropology also found an arena in Chicago; in a departure from earlier fairs which displayed American Indians and occasionally such exotics as Fijians at sideshows on the peripheries of fairgrounds, the Smithsonian Institution orchestrated a major exhibit demonstrating current evolutionary theories. The ethnology building housed collections of tribal artefacts arranged as a visual illustration of the accepted evolutionary scale.

The highlight of the fair was the Midway Plaisance, which featured living ethnological displays of people from Dahomey, Samoa, Java, Syria, China and several Native American tribes. Such a fertile research laboratory attracted ethnologists and students of exotic music who measured, analysed and recorded the colonials. Boas and Fillmore made cylinders of Kwakiutl performers, while Benjamin Gilman recorded full performances from the Javanese, Samoan and Kwakiutl villages (Lee, 1984). It is reported that Frances Densmore was frightened by the Indian music at the fair.

1900–1920

The end of the 19th century marked a widening of hegemony to embrace Pacific and Caribbean territories acquired after the Spanish–American War, and a corresponding expansion of research outside the North American continent. In 1906, Congress augmented the mandate of the BAE to include Hawaii. At the same time, Washington's tight rein on anthropology began to loosen, with the focus of activity shifting to museums and anthropological centres in New York, Chicago, Philadelphia and California. The turn of the century also marked the coming of age of academic anthropology; opportunities for training opened up at Columbia University, under Boas, and the University of California at Berkeley, under Alfred Kroeber (a Boas student). These new centres attracted funding for ethnological research and organized field trips to Africa, South America and the Pacific.

Ethnomusicology was coming of age as well, shifting its focus from American Indian to other North American cultures. Scholars turned to African-American music in the Caribbean as well as in the American South;

John Lomax started recording American cowboy music in 1910; Charles Lummis and Eleanor Hague amassed collections of Latin American folk songs; and Albert Gale analysed 15 cylinders of Philippine music brought back by Fay-Cooper Cole in 1906.

Work on American Indian music continued. European ethnomusicologists – Erich Mortiz von Hornbostel (1877–1935), Carl Stumpf (1848–1936) and Christian Leden – journeyed to the USA to record American Indian music *in situ.* The cylinder phonograph had become standard field equipment, with major cylinder collections accumulating at the Smithsonian Institution, the American Museum of Natural History in New York and the Chicago Field Museum. Alice Fletcher turned to Pawnee ceremonialism, joining with Pawnee ethnologist James Murie (1862–1921) to produce a monograph on the Pawnee Hako ceremony (1904). Murie also worked with George A. Dorsey and Melvin Gilmore (1868–1940), researched Pawnee tradition on his own as a collaborator for the BAE, and amassed a large cylinder collection of his own. In 1911, Alice Fletcher and Francis La Flesche published *The Omaha Tribe,* which went beyond Fletcher's 1893 monograph to integrate Omaha culture and Omaha music in what may be termed the first truly ethnomusicological work.

The 1904 St Louis Louisiana Purchase Exposition provided ethnologists with further opportunities for observation of tribal peoples. By this time, the USA had acquired a small colonial empire and was anxious to demonstrate to the American people that its newly dependent peoples were unable to govern themselves. Thus, Philippine ethnic groups replaced Native Americans as primary evidence of anthropological theories of the evolution of mankind, and hundreds of native people were invited to take up residence at the Philippine village.

Natalie Curtis (1875–1921) and Frances Densmore (1867–1957) attended the 1904 fair. Curtis, a composer and pianist who had studied at the National Conservatory, was reportedly converted to the study of American Indian music by experiences at the fair (Haywood, 1986), although she actually began collecting songs in the Southwest as early as 1901. (Her cylinder collection dates from 1903; Frisbie, 1977.) Like Alice Fletcher, Curtis combined music study with advocacy and her work had wide popular appeal. She considered herself simply an interpreter for American Indian, and later African and African-American, culture – her articles frequently ended with appeals for an end to racial bias. She is best known for *The Indian's Book* (1907), a blend of narrative, verse, art and melody which featured transcriptions abandoning the harmonizing convention of her day. Instead, she presented melodic lines tied to prosodic structure. Except for the Hopi and Navajo songs, her transcriptions were mostly taken directly from performers in the field. Her 1903 field collection of Hopi and Navajo songs contains nearly 150 cylinders.

In response to a request to employ her methods on the study of African-American music, Curtis worked with students at the Hampton Institute in Virginia, publishing a series of folk songs and spirituals harmonized directly from the singing of the Hampton Quartet and a collection of East and South African music and narrative based on the recollections of two African students at the Institute (some 30 cylinders ; Curtis-Burlin, 1918). She also wrote more

2. Lone Buffalo, an Omaha Indian elder and historian, singing into a phonograph, August 1905

general articles for *Southern Workman, The Outlook* and *Musical Quarterly.*

Frances Densmore's career closely follows the growth of ethnomusicology in the 20th century. She began her pursuit of Indian music in 1895, giving lectures based on Alice Fletcher's Omaha monograph. At the St Louis fair she tackled both Philippine Sultans (1906) and Geronimo, whom she virtually stalked until she had the chance to notate his song. Hers was the first and only Smithsonian appointment dedicated specifically to the study of music but her title was collaborator; she was never a permanent employee of the BAE.

Densmore was commissioned in 1907 to study the Medicine Ceremony at the White Earth Chippewa Reservation. Over the next 50 years she recorded more than 3000 cylinders among dozens of tribal groups from British Columbia to Florida, publishing close to 20 monographs and scores of articles on American Indian music. By her own admission, Densmore was less concerned with current ethnological theory than with collecting and transcribing melody. In a letter of 6 May 1953 to Willard Rhodes, she wrote: 'My present attitude toward the study of Indian, or primitive, music is definite and is opposed to its becoming highly technical. As you may be aware, I have always used the term "study of Indian music" instead of the term "musicology"' (Hoffman, 1968, p.62).

But Densmore was not adverse to exploiting current technology for transcription and analysis. She experimented with graphic representations or plots to show melodic contour, used phonophotography to analyse the relationship between voice and drum (1922, pp.206–10), and had her aptitude for pitch discrimination tested by Carl E. Seashore. She shared a romantic devotion to 'the work' with other students of American Indian music but not their activism, preferring to remain aloof from both advocacy and intense involvement with professional organizations.

The new century was also a time for reflection on the accomplishments of the emerging discipline of exotic music. Benjamin Gilman, having completed his final analysis of Hopi song from the Hemenway Expedition in 1905, produced a summary of research in the area of exotic music to date. This paper, 'The Science of Exotic Music' (1909), placed American studies within the wider context of a European scholarship which attributed its methodological framework to psychology and physics as well as musicology. Five years later, W. V. Bingham of Dartmouth College noted a doubling of publications in the field (1914). However, while European scholars, paralleling in part the spread of European colonial empires to Africa and Asia, built extensive phonographic archives and concentrated on the comparative analysis of diverse musical systems, most American scholars remained committed to the empirical grounding of American ethnology and continued to generate what were essentially ethnographies of music.

On the other hand, in the early part of the 20th century the rise of the Americanist movement in American composition influenced public images of American folk, African-American and American-Indian music. It is easy to dismiss Americanist composers as popularizers, but in fact, as many of the battles for the legitimization of the new disciplines of folklore, anthropology and the study of 'exotic music' were fought in public lecture halls and on the pages of newspapers and popular magazines as were waged in professional journals.

For years, American composers shared the scientific enterprise with their colleagues in ethnology. After Fillmore's death in 1898, Alice Fletcher worked with Charles Wakefield Cadman (1881–1946) and Edwin S. Tracey, music director at Morris High School in New York. Both Cadman and Fletcher provided transcriptions for Francis La Flesche's monographs on Osage ritual, and Cadman accompanied La Flesche to the Omaha reservation in 1909, where he recorded cylinders of Omaha and Winnebago music (Perison, 1982). R. Carlos Troyer (1837–1920) joined Frank Cushing in the field to notate Zuni melodies; Arthur Nevin (1871–1943), who collaborated with Walter McClintock in the writing of *Poia*, an opera based on Blackfoot Indian themes, travelled to Montana to experience Blackfoot music firsthand (Nevin, 1916); and Thurlow Lieurance (1878–1963) recorded Crow, Gros Ventre and Cheyenne music in Montana. Frederick Burton researched Ojibwa music for his book, *American Primitive Music* (1909), which, he says, was written from a composer's perspective.

Arthur Farwell (1872–1952), who adapted both Omaha melodies and the spirit of the Omaha pipes of fellowship (*wa-wa^n*) ceremony for his American music publishing enterprise, the Wa-Wan Press 1904, not only advocated the use of Indian material by American composers but also wrote and lectured extensively on Indian music in general.

1920–1939

The entry of the USA into World War I curtailed research and publication in American ethnology, but work resumed in force after the war. The Bernice

P. Bishop Museum (Honolulu) expeditions yielded large cylinder collections from the Pacific – the Bayard Dominick Expedition conducted research in the Marquesas in 1920–21, and the Museum sent researchers to the Tuamotus in 1929–31, and Uvea and Futuna in 1932; Chicago's Field Museum sent researchers to Madagascar in 1923 and Wilfrid D. Hambly to Angola and Nigeria in 1929–30. In addition, increasing anti-Semitism in Europe and the threat of a second world war forced the emigration of European scholars to the USA, including Erich M. von Hornbostel.

Ethnological research was again disrupted in the 1930s, this time by the Depression, and while the Smithsonian continued to fund small field projects, little money outside private philanthropy was available. The Works Project Administration (1935–43), established by the federal government to support writers, artists and musicians displaced by the depression, sponsored the Federal Writer's Project and the Federal Theater Project, which sent researchers into the field collecting folk tales and songs.

3. *Francis La Flesche*

Research in American Indian music continued, particularly in the Southwest: Francis La Flesche published the last volume of his massive study of the Osage tribe for the Bureau; Densmore ranged through Texas and the Southwest; and George Herzog recorded southwestern Indian music for the American Museum of Natural History in the late 1920s and for Mary Cabot Wheelwright during the early 1930s. The Laboratory of Anthropology at Santa Fe also sponsored field trips.

Helen Heffron Roberts (1888–1985) and George Herzog (1901–84), both students of Franz Boas, began their ethnomusicological careers around this time. Roberts, who supplemented her conservatory education with training in anthropology under Boas (1916–19), found her talents as a transcriber in demand by ethnologists. She worked with Boas students H. K. Haeberlin on Salish music (1918), Martha Beckwith on Jamaican folklore (early 1920s) and Diamond Jenness on Copper Eskimo music (1925), then collaborated with Smithsonian ethnologist John Peabody Harrington (1884–1961) on California Indian music and transcribed James Murie's collection of cylinders for a monograph (unpublished) on Pawnee ceremonialism. In 1923–4, the Hawaiian Folklore Commission sponsored a survey of Hawaiian music with Roberts as principal investigator. She returned to the subject of California Indian music, publishing *Form in Primitive Music* (1933), based on her own 1926 field research.

George Herzog's position in 20th-century ethnomusicology paralleled Alice Fletcher's 19th-century role as mediator between ethnology and musicology. He worked with Erich M. von Hornbostel in Berlin before emigrating to the USA in 1925, where he sought to combine European and American theoretical and methodological perspectives. His talents and interests as linguist, ethnologist, musicologist and folklorist led him to culture areas as diffuse as Liberia and the southwestern USA, making him the ideal candidate to found an academic discipline of comparative musicology in the USA during the 1920s and 1930s. He began teaching courses in folk and primitive music at Columbia University while working on a doctorate under Franz Boas, and in 1932 instituted general courses in comparative musicology for the anthropology department at Yale University.

During the 1930s, Herzog surveyed resources of folk and primitive music and summarized American research in comparative musicology for the American Council of Learned Societies (1936). He and Roberts collaborated on a Yale-sponsored project to collect recorded examples of non-Western music for comparative purposes. The venture included the re-recording of cylinders onto disk for preservation. Both Roberts and Herzog were also concerned with questions of distribution of cultural traits, and each attempted to delineate stylistic areas for North American Indian music (Herzog, 1923; Roberts, 1936).

The decade also saw an attempt to organize interest in comparative musicology. Herzog, Roberts and Charles Seeger, who were among the founders of the American Musicological Society, launched the American Society for Comparative Musicology in 1933. This organization, which was affiliated with the German *Gesellschaft zur Erforschung der Musik Des Orients*, set out to encourage and sponsor research in the field, support publication of works in comparative musicology and establish the New York equivalent of Berlin's Phonogrammarchiv. The Society also published a recording of Navajo music, before the war curtailed its efforts.

On the eve of World War II, ethnomusicology in the USA had come to an important juncture in its development. During the late 19th and early 20th centuries American ethnomusicology had closely paralleled the development of American anthropology, sharing an emphasis on American ethnography and drawing many adherents from anthropology's closely knit intellectual community. Increased European influence broadened US concerns to include comparative approaches to the study of non-Western music, thus opening new horizons for a new generation of scholars.

Bibliography

MANUSCRIPT COLLECTIONS

Alice Cunningham Fletcher and Francis La Flesche papers. Smithsonian Institution, National Anthropological Archives, MS 4558

George Herzog papers. Indiana University, Archives of Traditional Music

Walter McClintock papers. Yale University, Beinecke Library, Western Americana Collection, Manuscript Group Number S1175

GENERAL

J. W. Fewkes: 'A Contribution to Passamaquoddy Folklore', *Journal of American Folklore*, iii (1890), 257

——: 'On the Use of the Phonograph Among the Zuni Indians', *American Naturalist*, xxiv (1890), 687

J. C. Eastman: 'Village Life at the World's Fair', *Chautauquan*, xvii (1893), 602

E. F. Bauer: 'The Development of an Empire', *Music Trade Review, Special Edition: Lewis and Clark Exposition Number 41* (30 September 1905)

H. Adams: *The Education of Henry Adams* (Boston, MA, 1907)

B. I. Gilman: 'The Science of Exotic Music', *Science*, xxx (1909), 532

W. V. Bingham: 'Five Years of Progress in Comparative Music Science', *Psychological Bulletin*, xi (1914), 421

N. Curtis-Burlin: *Hampton Series, Negro Folk-Songs* (New York, 1918)

E. Sapir: 'Representative Music', *MQ*, iv (1918), 161

G. Herzog: 'Musical Styles in North America', *Proceedings, 23rd International Congress of Americanists* (1923), 455

L. H. Sullivan: *The Autobiography of an Idea* (New York, 1926)

F. Boas: 'Primitive Literature, Music, and Dance', *Primitive Art* (New York, 1927, R/1955), 299–348

F. Densmore: 'The Study of American Indian Music in the Nineteenth Century', *American Anthropologist*, xxix (1927), 77

F. Boas: 'History and Science in Anthropology: a Reply', *American Anthropologist*, xxxviii (1936), 137

G. Herzog: 'Research in Primitive and Folk Music in the United States', *American Council of Learned Societies*, Bulletin xxiv (Washington, DC, 1936)

A. L. Kroeber: 'An Outline of the History of American Indian Linguistics', *American Council of Learned Societies*, Bulletin xxix (Washington, DC, 1939), 116

C. Seeger: 'Music and Government – Field for an Applied Musicology', *Papers Read at the International Congress of Musicology*, ed. A. Mendel, G. Reese, and G. Chase (New York, 1939), 11

H. S. Mekeel: 'Report in Retrospect on Laboratory of Anthropology Training Parties', *American Anthropologist*, xliii (1941), 315

F. Densmore: 'The Study of Indian Music', *Annual Report of the Smithsonian Institution for the Year Ended June 30, 1941* (Washington, DC, 1942), 527

C. Wissler: 'The American Indian and the American Philosophical Society', *Proceedings of the American Philosophical Society*, lxxxvi (1943), 189

D. Collier and H. Tschopik Jr: 'The Role of Museums in American Anthropology', *American Anthropologist*, lvi (1954), 768

R. Welter: 'The Idea of Progress in America', *Journal of the History of Ideas*, xiv (1955), 401

A. Ellegard: 'The Darwinian Theory and Nineteenth-Century Philosophies of Science', *Journal of the History of Ideas*, xviii (1957), 362–93

P. Winch: *The Idea of a Social Science and its Relation to Philosophy* (London, 1958)

A. I. Hallowell: 'The Backwash of the Frontier: the Impact of the Indian on American Culture', *Annual Report of the Smithsonian Institution for 1958* (Washington, DC, 1959), 447

F. de Laguna, ed.: *Selected Papers from the American Anthropologists: 1888–1920* (Washington, DC, 1960, 2/1976)

W. Stanton: *The Leopard's Spots: Scientific Attitudes Toward Race in America, 1815–59* (Chicago, IL, 1960)

G. W. Stocking: 'Franz Boas and the Founding of the American Anthropological Association', *American Anthropologist*, lxii (1960) 1

W. D. Allen: *Philosophies of Music History: a Study of General Histories of Music, 1600–1960* (New York, 1962)

H. Pedersen: *The Discovery of Language* (Bloomington, IN, 1962)

J. W. Burrow: 'Evolution and Anthropology in the 1860s: the Anthropological Society of London, 1863–71', *Victorian Studies*, vii (1963), 137

W. Cannon: 'History in Depth: the Early Victorian Period', *History of Science*, iii (1964), 20

A. W. Coates: 'American Scholarship Comes of Age: the Louisiana Purchase Exposition of 1904', *Journal of the History of Ideas*, xxii (1964), 404

M. T. Hogden: *Early Anthropology in the Sixteenth and Seventeenth Centuries* (Philadelphia, PA, 1964)

H. Baudet: *Paradise on Earth: Some Thoughts on European Images of Non-European Man*, trans. E. Wenthold (New Haven, CT, 1965)

J. F. Freeman: 'University Anthropology: Early Departments in the United States', *Kroeber Anthropological Society Papers*, xxxii (1965), 78

A. I. Hallowell: 'The History of Anthropology as an Anthropological Problem', *Journal of the History of the Behavioral Sciences*, i (1965), 24

G. W. Stocking: 'On the Limits of "Presentism" and "Historicism" in the Historiography of the Behavioral Sciences', *Journal of the History of the Behavioral Sciences*, i (1965), 211

J. W. Burrow: *Evolution and Society, a Study in Victorian Social Theory* (Cambridge, 1966)

R. W. Dexter: 'Putnam's Problems Popularizing Anthropology', *American Scientist*, liv (1966), 315

W. H. Goetzmann: *Exploration and Empire: the Explorer and the Scientist in the Winning of the American West* (New York, 1966)

J. Gruber: 'In Search of Experience: Biography as an Instrument for the History of Anthropology', *Pioneers of American Anthropology*, ed. J. Helm (Seattle, WA, 1966)

J. Helm, ed.: *Pioneers in American Anthropology: the Uses of Biography* (Seattle, WA, 1966)

W. E. Washburn: 'The Influence of the Smithsonian Institution on Intellectual Life in Mid-Nineteenth Century Washington', *Records of the Columbia Historical Society of Washington, D.C. 1963–1965* (Washington, DC, 1966), 96

L. Ziff: *The American 1890s: the Life and Times of a Lost Generation* (New York, 1966)

J. F. Freeman: 'The American Philosophical Society in American Anthropology', *The Philadelphia Anthropological Society*, ed. J. W. Gruber (Philadelphia, PA, 1967), 32

J. W. Gruber, ed.: *The Philadelphia Anthropological Society* (New York, 1967)

A. I. Hallowell: 'Anthropology in Philadelphia', *The Philadelphia Anthropological Society*, ed. J. W. Gruber (Philadelphia, PA, 1967), 1–31

F. W. Voget: 'Process Science, History and Evolution in Eighteenth and Nineteenth-Century Anthropology', *Journal of the History of the Behavioral Sciences*, iii (1967), 132

R. J. Wilson, ed.: *Darwin and the American Intellectuals* (Homewood, IL, 1967)

D. B. Tyler: 'The Wilkes Expedition: the First United States Exploring Expedition, 1838–1942', *American Philosophical Society Memoir*, lxxiii (1968)

P. F. Boller Jr: *American Thought in Transition: the Impact of Evolutionary Naturalism, 1865–1900* (Chicago, IL, 1969)

D. H. Fischer: *Historians' Fallacies: Toward a Logic of Historical Thought* (New York, 1970)

I. Lakatos and A. Musgrave, eds.: *Criticism and the Growth of Knowledge* (Cambridge, 1970)

G. W. Stocking: *Anthropology at Chicago: Tradition, Discipline, Department* (Chicago, IL, 1970)

A. Symondson, ed.: *The Victorian Crisis of Faith* (London, 1970)

R. M. Young: *Mind, Brain, and Adaptation in the Nineteenth Century* (Oxford, 1970)

R. Darnell: 'The Professionalization of American Anthropology: a Case Study in the Sociology of Knowledge', *Social Science Information*, x (1971), 83

M. Mandelbaum: *History, Man & Reason: a Study in Nineteenth-Century Thought* (Baltimore, MD, 1971)

R. C. Tobey: *The American Ideology of Science, 1919–1930* (Pittsburgh, PA, 1971)

R. Bannister: *Social Darwinism: Science and Myth in Anglo-American Social Thought* (Philadelphia, PA, 1972)

G. H. Daniels: *Nineteenth-Century American Science: a Reappraisal* (Evanston, IL, 1972)

J. A. Rogers: 'Darwinism and Social Darwinism', *Journal of the History of Ideas*, xxxiii (1972), 265

31

F. Harrison, ed.: *Time, Place and Music* (Amsterdam, 1973)

R. Darnell: *Readings in the History of Anthropology* (New York, 1974)

T. Glick, ed.: *The Comparative Reception of Darwinism* (Austin, TX, 1974)

M. Horkheimer: *Eclipse of Reason* (New York, 1974)

E. Lurie: *Nature and the American Mind: Louis Agassiz and the Culture of Science* (New York, 1974)

A. de W. Malefijt: *Images of Man: a History of Anthropological Thought* (New York, 1974)

G. W. Stocking: *The Shaping of American Anthropology 1883–1911: a Franz Boas Reader* (New York, 1974)

J. L. Allen: *Passage Through the Garden: Lewis and Clark and the Image of the American Northwest* (Urbana, IL, 1975)

L. K. Barnett: *Ignoble Savage: American Literary Racism, 1790–1890* (Westport, CT, 1975)

J. K. Flack: *Desideratum in Washington: the Intellectual Community in the Capital City, 1870–1900* (Cambridge, MA, 1975)

M. O. Furner: *Advocacy & Objectivity: a Crisis in the Professionalization of American Social Science, 1865–1905* (Lexington, KY, 1975)

L. Hanke: *Aristotle and the American Indians: a Study of Race Prejudice in the Modern World* (Bloomington, IN, 1975)

T. Bender: 'Science and the Culture of American Communities: the Nineteenth Century', *History of Education Quarterly*, xvi (1976), 63

R. W. Dexter: 'The Role of F. W. Putnam in Developing Anthropology at the American Museum of Natural History', *Curator*, xix (1976), 303

B. Hindle, ed.: *Early American Science* (New York, 1976)

C. M. Hinsley Jr: 'Amateurs and Professionals in Washington Anthropology. 1879–1903', *American Anthropology: the Early Years*, ed. J. V. Murra (St Paul, MN, 1976), 36–68

S. Kohlstedt: 'A Step Toward Scientific Self-Identity in the United States: the Failure of the National Institute, 1844', *Science in America Since 1820*, ed. N. Reingold (New York, 1976), 79

R. L. Meek: *Social Science and the Ignoble Savage* (Cambridge, 1976)

J. V. Murra, ed.: *American Anthropology: the Early Years* (St Paul, MN, 1976)

F. P. Prucha: *American Indian Policy in Crisis: Christian Reformers and the Indian, 1865–1900* (Norman, OK, 1976)

N. Reingold, ed.: *Science in America Since 1820* (New York, 1976)

D. N. Robinson: *An Intellectual History of Psychology* (New York, 1976)

D. D. Zochert: 'Science and the Common Man in Ante-Bellum America', *Science in America Since 1820*, ed. N. Reingold (New York, 1976), 7

R. Darnell: 'History of Anthropology in Historical Perspective', *Annual Review of Anthropology*, vi (1977), 399

R. Godoy: 'Franz Boas and his Plans for an International School of American Archaeology and Ethnology in Mexico', *Journal of the History of the Behavioral Sciences*, xiii (1977), 228

S. J. Gould: *Ever Since Darwin: Reflections in Natural History* (New York, 1977)

M. N. Penkower: *The Federal Writer's Project: a Study in Government Patronage of the Arts* (Urbana, IL, 1977)

H. H. Thorenson: 'Art, Evolution, and History: a Case Study of Paradigm Change in Anthropology', *Journal of the History of the Behavioral Sciences*, xiii (1977), 107

R. F. Berkofer Jr: *The White Man's Indian: Images of the American Indian from Columbus to the Present* (New York, 1978)

S. F. Cannon: *Science in Culture: the Early Victorian Period* (New York, 1978)

J. O'Connor and L. Brown, eds.: *Free, Adult, Uncensored: the Living History of the Federal Theatre Project* (Washington, DC, 1978)

F. M. Turner: 'The Victorian Conflict between Science and Religion: a Professional Dimension', *ISIS*, lxix (1978), 356

G. Barraclough: *Main Trends in History* (New York, 1979)

J. R. Moore: *The Post-Darwinian Controversies: a Study of the Protestant Struggle to Come to Terms with Darwin in Great Britain and American 1870–1900* (Cambridge, 1979)

R. Drinnon: *Facing West: the Metaphysics of Indian-Hating and Empire Building* (New York, 1980)

S. J. Gould: 'Flaws in a Victorian Veil', *The Panda's Thumb: More Reflections in Natural History* (New York, 1980), 169

C. M. Hinsley Jr: 'The Problem with Mr Hewett: Academics and Popularizers in American Anthropology, c. 1910', *History of Anthropology Newsletter*, vii/3 (1980), 7

J. Paradis and T. Postlewait, eds.: *Victorian Science and Victorian Values: Literary Perspectives* (New York, 1980)

B. Sheehan: *Savagism and Civility: Indians and Englishmen in Colonial Virginia* (Cambridge, 1980)

B. Chauvenet: *Hewett and Friends: the Biography of a Vibrant Era* (Albuquerque, NM, 1981)

S. W. Gould: *The Mismeasure of Man* (New York, 1981)

D. W. Krummel and others, eds.: *Resources of American Music History* (Urbana, IL, 1981)

S. Silverman, ed.: *Totems and Teachers: Perspectives on the History of Anthropology* (New York, 1981)

A. Spoehr: 'Lewis Henry Morgan and His Pacific Collaborators', *Proceedings of the American Philosophical Society*, cxxv/6 (1981), 449

A. Pagden: *The Fall of Natural Man: the American Indian and the Origins of Comparative Ethnology* (Cambridge, 1982)

G. W. Stocking: 'The Santa Fe Style in American Anthropology: Regional Interest, Academic Initiative, and Philanthropic Policy in the First Two Decades of The Laboratory of Anthropology, Inc.', *Journal of the History of the Behavioral Sciences*, xviii (1982), 3

S. A. Freed and R. S. Freed: 'Clark Wissler and the Development of Anthropology in the United States', *American Anthropologist*, lxxxv (1983), 800

L. Graham, W. Lepenies and P. Weingart, eds.: *Functions and Uses of Disciplinary Histories* (Boston, MA, 1983)

D. Hymes: *Essays in the History of Linguistic Anthropology* (Amsterdam, 1983)

B. Scholte: 'Cultural Anthropology and the Paradigm-Concept: a Brief History of Their Recent Convergence', *Functions and Uses of Disciplinary Histories*, ed. L. Graham, W. Lepenies and P. Weingart (Boston, MA, 1983), 229–78

J. Helm, ed.: *Social Contexts of American Ethnology, 1840–1984* (Washington, DC, 1985)

A. Kuper: 'The Historian's Revenge: Review of G. W. Stocking Jr., ed. *Functionalism Historicized: Essays on British Social Anthropology*', *American Ethnologist*, xii/3 (1985), 523

——: 'The Development of Lewis Henry Morgan's Evolutionism', *Journal of the History of the Behavioral Sciences*, xxi (1985), 3

R. E. Beider: *Science Encounters the Indian, 1820–1880: the Early Years of American Ethnology* (Norman, OK, 1986)

INDIVIDUALS

C. Hoffman: *Frances Densmore and American Indian Music* (New York, 1968)

M. Liberty, ed.: *American Indian Intellectuals* (St Paul, MN, 1978)

J. Marks: *Four Anthropologists: an American Science in its Early Years* (New York, 1980)

J. C. McNutt: 'John Comfort Fillmore: a Student of Indian Music Reconsidered', *American Music*, ii (1984), 61

L. G. Moses: *The Indian Man: a Biography of James Mooney* (Urbana, IL, 1984)

J. McNutt: 'Reply to Pantaleoni', *American Music*, iii (1985), 229

H. Pantaleoni: 'A Reconsideration of Fillmore Reconsidered', *American Music*, iii (1985), 217

S. C. DeVale: 'Fillmore, John Comfort', *The New Grove Dictionary of American Music* (London, 1986)

C. Haywood: 'Natalie Curtis (Burlin)', *The New Grove Dictionary of American Music* (London, 1986)

J. C. Porter: *Paper Medicine Man: John Gregory Bourke and His American West* (Norman, OK, 1986)

AMERICAN ROMANTIC MOVEMENT

C. W. Cadman: 'The "Idealization" of Indian Music', *MQ*, i (1916), 386

A. Nevin: 'Two Summers with the Blackfeet Indians of Montana', *MQ*, ii (1916), 257

E. N. Waters: 'The Wa-Wan Press: an Adventure in Musical Idealism', *A Birthday Offering to Carl Engel* (New York, 1943)

G. Chase: 'The Wa-Wan Press: a Chapter in American Enterprise', *The Wa-Wan Press, 1901–1911*, ed. V. B. Lawrence (New York, 1970), ix

V. B. Lawrence, ed.: *The Wa-Wan Press, 1901–1911* (New York, 1970) [reprint of entire press run]

H. D. Perison: 'The "Indian" Operas of Charles Wakefield Cadman', *College Music Symposium*, xxii (1982), 20

A. H. Levy: *Musical Nationalism: American Composer's Search for Identity* (Westport, CT, 1983)

——: 'The Search for Identity in American Music, 1890–1920', *American Music*, ii (1984), 70

AREA STUDIES

T. Baker: *On the Music of the North American Indians* (New York, 1882, R/1977)

J. W. Fewkes: 'Additional Studies of Zuñi Songs and Rituals with the Phonograph', *American Naturalist*, xxiv (1890), 1094

33

——: 'On the Use of the Phonograph Among the Zuñi Indians', *American Naturalist*, xxiv (1890), 687

B. I. Gilman, 'Zuñi Melodies', *Journal of American Archaeology and Ethnology*, i (1891), 63

H. E. Krehbiel: 'Chinese Music', *Century Magazine*, xl (1891), 449

B. I. Gilman: 'Some Psychological Aspects of the Chinese Musical System', *Philosophical Review*, i (1892), 54, 154

A. C. Fletcher: *A Study of Omaha Indian Music* (Boston, MA, 1893)

——: 'Personal Studies of Indian Life: Politics and "Pipe-Dancing"', *Century Magazine*, new ser., xlv (1893), 441

W. Matthews: 'Indian Music and its Investigators', *Music*, iv (1893), 452

F. Boas: 'Review, *A Study of Omaha Indian Music*, A. C. Fletcher', *Journal of American Folklore*, vii (1894), 169

L. W. Colby: 'Wanagi Olowan Kin: the Ghost Songs of the Dakotas', *Proceedings and Collections*, Nebraska State Historical Society, i (1894–95), 131

J. C. Fillmore: 'Review, *Primitive Music*, R. Wallaschek', *Journal of American Folklore*, vii (1894), 165

——: 'A Study of Indian Music', *Century Magazine*, xlvii (1894), 616

W. Matthews: 'Songs of Sequence of the Navajos', *Journal of American Folklore*, vii (1894), 185

J. C. Fillmore: 'What Do the Indians Mean to Do When They Sing and How Far Do They Succeed?', *Journal of American Folklore*, ix (1895), 138

F. Boas: 'Songs of the Kwakiutl Indians', *Internationales Archiv für Ethnographie*, ix (1896), 1

A. C. Fletcher: 'Tribal Life Among the Omahas', *Century Magazine*, li (1896), 450

J. Mooney: 'The Ghost Dance Religion and the Sioux Outbreak of 1890', *Fourteenth Annual Report of the Bureau of American Ethnology, 1892–1893* (Washington, DC, 1896), 641–1110

F. Boas: *The Social Organization and Secret Societies of the Kwakiutl* (Washington, DC, 1897), 311–738

J. C. Fillmore: 'The Harmonic Structure of Indian Music', *American Anthropologist*, ii (1899), 297

A. C. Fletcher: 'The Hako: a Pawnee Ceremony', *Twenty-second Annual Report of the Bureau of American Ethnology, 1900–1901* (Washington, DC, 1904)

F. Densmore: 'The Music of the Filipinos', *American Anthropologist*, viii (1906), 611

C. G. DuBois: 'Two Types or Styles of Diegueño Religious Dancing: the Old and the New in Southern California', *Proceedings of the 15th International Congress of Americanists*, ii (Quebec, 1906–7), 135

N. Curtis: *The Indian's Book* (New York, 1907/R1968)

C. G. DuBois: 'The Religion of the Luiseno and Diegueño Indians of Southern California', *University of California Publications in American Archaeology and Ethnology*, viii (1908), 69–186

——: 'Ceremonies and Traditions of the Diegueño Indians', *Journal of American Folklore*, xxi (1908), 228

B. I. Gilman: 'Hopi Songs', *Journal of American Archaeology and Ethnology*, v (1908/R1977), 1–226

C. Mindeleff: 'Preserving the Last Relics of Indian Music Through Aid of the Phonograph', *Metronome*, xxiii (1908), 6, 17

F. Densmore: 'Scale Formation in Primitive Music', *American Anthropologist*, xi (1909), 1

——: *Chippewa Music* (Washington, DC, 1910–13)

E. Sapir: 'Song Recitative in Paiute Mythology', *Journal of American Folklore*, xxiii (1910), 455

A. C. Fletcher and F. La Flesche: 'The Omaha Tribe', *Twenty-seventh Annual Report of the Bureau of American Ethnology, 1905–1906* (Washington, DC, 1911)

F. G. Speck: *Ceremonial Songs of the Creek and Yuchi Indians* (Philadelphia, PA, 1911)

A. Nevin: 'Two Summers with the Blackfeet Indians of Montana', *MQ*, ii (1916), 257

S. A. Barrett: 'Ceremonies of the Pomo Indians', *University of California Publications in American Archaeology and Ethnology*, xii (1917), 397–441

F. Densmore: *Teton Sioux Music* (Washington, DC, 1918)

N. Curtis: *Songs and Tales from the Dark Continent* (New York, 1920)

F. La Flesche: 'The Osage Tribe: Rite of the Chiefs, Sayings of the Ancient Men', *Thirty-sixth Annual Report of the Bureau of American Ethnology, 1914–1915* (Washington, DC, 1921/R1970)

F.-C. Cole: *The Tinguian: Social, Religious and Economic Life of a Philippine Tribe. Field Museum of Natural History Anthropological Series*, xiv/2 (1922)

F. Densmore: *Northern Ute Music* (Washington, DC, 1922), 206

H. H. Roberts: 'New Phases in the Study of Primitive Music', *American Anthropologist*, xxiv (1922), 144

——: 'Chakwena Songs of Zuñi and Laguna', *Journal of American Folklore*, xxxvi (1923), 177

—— and D. Jenness: 'Songs of the Copper Eskimo', *Report of the Canadian Arctic Expedition, 1913–1918*, xiv (Ottawa, 1923)

E. S. Handy and C. and J. L. Winne: 'Music in the Marquesas Islands', *Bernice P. Bishop Museum Bulletin*, cix (Honolulu, HI, 1925)

F. La Flesche and H. H. Roberts: 'The Osage Tribe: the Rite of Vigil', *Thirty-ninth Annual Report of the Bureau of American Ethnology, 1917–1918* (Washington, DC, 1925)

H. H. Roberts: 'Indian Music from the Southwest', *Natural History*, xxvii (1927), 257

G. Herzog: 'The Yuman Musical Style', *Journal of American Folklore*, xli (1928), 181–231

——: 'Musical Styles in North America', *Proceedings of the 23rd International Congress of Americanists* (1928), 455

F. La Flesche and H. H. Roberts: 'The Osage Tribe: Two Versions of the Child Naming Rite' (Washington, DC, 1928)

—— and H. H. Roberts: 'The Osage Tribe, Rite of the Wa-xo'-be', *Forty-fifth Annual Report of the Bureau of American Ethnology, 1927–1928* (Washington, DC, 1930)

J. de Angulo and M. B. d'Harcourt: 'La Musique des Indiennes de la Californie du Nord', *Journal de la Société des Américanistes de Paris*, xxiii (1931), 189–228

F. Densmore: *Menominee Music* (Washington, DC, 1932)

E. G. Burrows: 'Native Music of the Tuamotus', *Bernice P. Bishop Museum Bulletin*, cix (Honolulu, HI, 1933)

H. H. Roberts: *Form in Primitive Music* (New York, 1933)

G. Herzog: 'Plains Ghost Dance and Great Basin Music', *American Anthropologist*, xxxvii (1935), 403

——: 'Special Song Types in North American Indian Music', *Zeitschrift für Vergleichende Musikwissenschaft*, iii (1935), 23

H. H. Roberts: 'Musical Areas in Aboriginal North America', *Yale University Publications in Anthropology*, xii (1936)

W. D. Hambly: *Source Book for African Anthropology, Field Museum of Natural History, Fieldiana: Anthropology*, xxvi (1937), 454

F. La Flesche: *War Ceremony and Peace Ceremony of the Osage Indians* (Washington, DC, 1939)

G. Herzog: 'African Influences in North American Indian Music', *PAMS* (1939), 130

W. Rhodes: 'North American Indian Music: a Bibliographic Survey of Anthropological Theory', *Music Library Association Notes*, x (1952), 33

D. K. Wilgus: *Anglo-American Folksong Scholarship Since 1898* (New Brunswick, NJ, 1959)

F. Boas: *Kwakiutl Ethnography*, ed. H. Codere (Chicago, IL, 1966)

D. E. Crawford: 'The Jesuit Relations and Allied Documents: Early Sources for an Ethnography of Music Among American Indians', *EM*, xi (1967), 199

H. H. Roberts: *Ancient Hawaiian Music* (New York, 2/1967)

H. Hale: *Ethnography and Philology: United States Exploring Expedition During the Years 1838, 1839, 1840, 1841, 1842, 1846* (Ridgewood, NJ, 1968)

R. Stevenson: 'Written Sources for Indian Music Until 1882', *EM*, xvii (1973), 1–40, 399–442

G. Catlin: *Letters and Notes on the North American Indians*, ed. M. M. Mooney (New York, 1975)

C. J. Frisbie: *Music and Dance Research of Southwestern United States Indians* (Detroit, MI, 1977)

J. P. Murie: *Ceremonies of the Pawnee*, i: *The Skiri*, ed. D. R. Parks (Washington, DC, 1981)

——: *Ceremonies of the Pawnee*, ii: *The South Bands*, ed. D. R. Parks (Washington, DC, 1981)

D. S. Lee, ed.: *The Federal Cylinder Project*, viii: *Early Anthologies* (Washington, DC, 1984)

J. C. McNutt: 'John Comfort Fillmore: a Student of Indian Music Reconsidered', *American Music*, ii (1984), 61

F. Boas: 'The Central Eskimo', *Sixth Annual Report of the Bureau of American Ethnology, 1884–1885* (Washington, DC, 1988), 399–669

WORLD'S FAIRS

J. C. Eastman: 'Village Life at the World's Fair', *Chautauquan*, xvii (1893), 602

J. Mooney: 'The Indian Congress at Omaha', *American Anthropologist* (1899), 126

J. Hawthorne: 'Foreign Folk at the Fair', *Cosmopolitan Magazine*, xxxi (1901), 483

E. F. Bauer: 'The Development of an Empire', *Music Trade Review, Special Edition: Lewis and Clark Exposition*, xli (1905)

'Indian Chants and Indian Footfalls', *World's Fair Weekly* (30 July 1933), 3

A. W. Coates: 'American Scholarship Comes of Age: the Louisiana Purchase Exposition of 1904', *Journal of the History of Ideas*, xxii (1964), 404

E. McCullough: *World's Fair Midways: an Affectionate Account of American Amusement Areas from the Crystal Palace to the Crystal Ball* (New York, 1966)

D. F. Burg: *Chicago's White City of 1893* (Lexington, KY, 1976)

J. Allwood: *The Great Exhibitions* (London, 1977)

W. D. Andrews: 'Women and the Fairs of 1876 and 1893', *Hayes Historical Journal*, i (1977), 173

R. R. Badger: *The Great American Fair: the World's Columbian Exposition and American Culture* (Chicago, IL, 1979)

J. Mark: *Four Anthropologists: an American Science in its Early Years* (New York, 1980)

H. Harrison, ed.: *Dawn of a New Day: the New York World's Fair 1939/40* (New York, 1980)

R. W. Rydell: 'The Trans-Mississippi and International Exposition: "To Work Out the Problem of Universal Civilization"', *American Quarterly*, xxxiii (1981), 587–607

B. Benedict and others: *The Anthropology of World's Fairs: San Francisco Panama-Pacific International Exposition, 1915* (Berkeley, CA, 1983)

E. Brady: 'The Box That Got The Flourishes: the Cylinder Phonograph in Folklore Fieldwork, 1890–1937' (diss., U. of Indiana, 1985)

R. W. Rydell: *All the World's a Fair: Visions of Empire at American International Expositions, 1876–1916* (Chicago, IL, 1985)

——: 'The Fan Dance of Science: American World's Fairs in the Great Depression', *ISIS*, lxxvi (1986), 525

2: BRITISH-AMERICANS

HELEN MYERS

Theories: communalism and individualism

Ballad study in the USA, as in the British Isles, began as an aspect of antiquarian literary scholarship. During the 19th century scholars were preoccupied with the historical dimension of folk song, particularly its origin, with opinion divided between 'communalists' and 'individualists' ('the ballad war'; Wilgus, 1959, pp.3–52). Communalists took their lead from two Germans, folklorist-philologist Jacob Grimm (1785–1863) and mythologist-philosopher Johann Gottfried von Herder (1744–1803), who popularized the notion of folk music as a natural, instinctive, and spontaneous expression of the peasant soul. Folk song, they maintained, was composed collectively; it preceded and is antithetical to art song. The ballad was seen as an antique literary text surviving in oral tradition, in which was captured the essence of a people. Led by American literary academicians Francis Barton Gummere (1855–1919) and George Lyman Kittredge (1860–1941), communalists claimed that ballads were derived from group-composed dance songs of antiquity (Gummere, 1896, 1903–4, 1907).

Related to communalism was the theory of *gesunkenes Kulturgut* ('debased or lowered cultural element'), of German scholars of the 19th and early 20th centuries including Rochus von Liliencron, Hans Naumann and John Meier. They held that folk songs are degenerated art songs, filtered down from city and court to countryside where in the hands of the common man they become debased (Pulikowski, 1933, pp.167–8; Naumann, 1921, pp.4–6). Attempts to apply this theory to the unified corpus of Anglo-American ballads were unsuccessful.

The opponents of communalism, including British literati William John Courthope (1842–1917) and Scottish folklorist Andrew Lang (1844–1912), argued that folk ballads were inventions of individual composers, not themselves necessarily of the folk. Lang, originally a communalist (1878), modified his position, accepting individual creation and re-creation (1903). The most vigorous challenge was mounted by American linguist Louise Pound (1872–1958) in *Poetic Origins and the Ballad* (1921). Attacking communalism from all sides, she cited evidence from groups then called primitive who have dance without song, song without dance, and groups altogether without narrative song. Examining the characteristically lyric dance songs from the European Middle Ages, she found no correspondence to narratives of the Child canon. She noted that many Child texts derive from written sources, probably aristocratic, and cited 14th- and 15th-century poetic language and literary devices in the ballad texts (Wilgus, 1959, pp.89–98).

The American collector Phillips Barry (1880–1937) and scholar Gordon Hall Gerould (1877–1953) put forward the widely accepted theory of communal re-creation, whereby ballads are individually composed by singers who voice in their composition sentiments of the community; then as the song enters oral tradition and is enhanced by variants, it achieves the status of genuine ballad.

Child canon and regional collecting

Preoccupied with theoretical concerns, scholars conducted little empirical research on Anglo-American folk song prior to the publication (1883–98) of *The English and Scottish Popular Ballads* by Francis James Child (1825–96). Educator and scholar, renowned for his systematic study and collection of British folk song, Child studied at Harvard, where he became Professor of English in 1851. His monumental five-volume work contains some of the oldest ballads of the English tradition, including multiple versions, and a variety of topics: apocryphal legends, Christian miracles, outlaw tales, history and lore, feuds and raids and domestic quarrels. The 'Child ballads' mentioned in practically every subsequent study refer to the 305 songs in his collection. Over 100 Child texts and around 80 tunes have been collected in the USA (Child himself made no special search for New World variants, discovering only 18). Child's sources are held at the Harvard library, which became a centre for folk-song research. His collection stimulated literary controversy and focussed research on a limited corpus of material, an orientation that has persisted well into the 20th century.

During the late 19th and early 20th centuries, folk-song study developed from an antiquarian pastime into an academic pursuit. American collecting methods differed from those of the British, due in part to the size of the continent (the Appalachians alone are larger than the UK). Americans, natives of a new land, were more inclined to accept newly composed popular folk songs, and although they did not come from folk backgrounds, were generally more in sympathy with folkways than were their middle-class English colleagues. Some collections were based on fieldwork, but many were assembled through correspondence with friends, relatives, students, and state folklore societies.

The earliest systematic collection was *Games and Songs of American Children* (1883) by poet and literary scholar, William Wells Newell (1839–1907), a Harvard student of Child's. This collection of tunes, texts, formulas, rules and movements was gathered during fieldwork with children (some on the streets of

New York) and interviews with adults, and is a product of the late 19th-century romanticized vision of the freedom and adventure of childhood. Literary annotations and comparisons with Continental sources testify to the antiquity and distribution of many items. In later collections, Newell included diverse material, mainly from the northeastern USA – broadsides as well as songs in oral tradition, older songs and recently composed pieces. Newell challenged the communalist theory of Gummere at its ethnological roots, and proposed a ballad history for the Old and New Worlds, based on literary evidence (biography and bibliography for Newell in Chamberlain, 1907).

By the last decades of the 19th century, the notion of an American folklore had evolved. In 1888, the American Folklore Society was founded by literary scholars Newell and Child, and anthropologist Franz Boas (1858–1942), with the intention of gathering and publishing relics of old English song and story, southern Negro lore, American Indian culture, and folk traditions of Mexico and French Canada. Modelled on the Folklore Society of Britain, the American counterpart reflected the intellectual links between Old World and New World literati. The centennial of American independence, a celebration of American achievement, stimulated a review of national culture incorporating folklore of the frontier experience, the social experiment of democracy and American social pluralism. Newell, executive secretary of the Society up to the time of his death, served as editor of the *Journal of American Folklore* (1888–1900) and the first nine issues of *Memoirs* on various topics (African, Cajun, Bahamian, Mexican, and Native American). These publications served as a forum for early collectors, the issues reflecting changing approaches and attitudes in American folk-song research.

Music found its place in folk-song study, first in the UK with the work of the Folk-Song Society (founded 1898), and in the USA with the work of Phillips Barry, who investigated all aspects of folk art: text, tune, performance and transmission. Unlike his English counterpart Cecil Sharp (1859–1924), Barry collected broadsides and music-hall ballads, refusing to make a distinction not recognized by the folk. Folk song for Barry, and most American collectors, was song sung from memory:

> It refers, not to an event, but to a process, . . . The process is one by which a simple event in human experience, of subjective interest, narrated in simple language, set to a simple melody is progressively objectivated (1913, pp.4–5).

Barry demonstrated the history of communal re-creation by comparing ancient ballads with their modern variants including those he had collected in New England, beginning in 1903. He argued for the vitality of the ballad tradition, self-renewing, flourishing in cities as well as countryside, embracing vulgar and popular forms, and at times perpetuated via the printed page ('no ballad . . . ever died of printers' ink'), a progressive approach contrary to the conservative thinking of English Folk-Song Society members studying similar traditions on the other side of the Atlantic.

Henry Marvin Belden (1865–1954), a contemporary of Barry, began collecting in Missouri in 1904. In 'The Study of Folk-Song in America' (1905) he proposed a programme to recover American versions of Child ballads and to answer questions regarding origins of the American repertory. Belden emphasized documentation of collections, including circumstances of recording, biographical information on the singer, family and racial background, and local concepts of song origin. He argued for comprehensive collection (including printed versions), contrary to the selective methods of English contemporaries, who rejected popular and broadside material. While acknowledging Gummere to have made 'by far the most important contribution to ballad study . . . in our time' (1911, p.4), he mounted a vigorous attack on his communalist theories in a review of *The Popular Ballad* (1909).

In the early years of the 20th century, state folklore societies were founded, dedicated to collecting and preserving Old World folk song, especially the Child canon: Missouri (1906), Texas (1909), North Carolina (1912), Kentucky (1912), Virginia (1913), Nebraska (1913), West Virginia (1915) and Oklahoma (1915). In 1914, the US Department of Education instigated a 'rescue' mission for ballads and folk songs, stimulating an era of collecting by local enthusiasts and academics that lasted through the Depression until World War II. The extensive regional collections between the two world wars reflect the amount of unstudied material, reaction against the theoretical preoccupations of the earlier generation, and the search for a sense of national tradition in the face of striking regional diversity. Collections included those of Henry Marvin Belden (Missouri, 1907, 1940), Henry W. Shoemaker (Pennsylvania, 1919, 1931), Roland Palmer Gray (Maine, 1924), Josiah H. Combs (Kentucky and environs, 1925, 1939), John Harrington Cox (West Virginia, 1925, 1939, 'Folk-Songs'; 1939, 'Traditional Ballads'), W. Roy MacKenzie (Nova Scotia, 1928), Arthur Kyle Davis Jr (Virginia, 1929, 1949), Helen Creighton (Nova Scotia, 1932), Elizabeth Bristol Greenleaf and Grace Yarrow Mansfield (Newfoundland, 1933), Earl J. Stout (Iowa, 1936), Emelyn Elizabeth Gardner (Schoharie Hills, New York, 1937), Charles Neely (southern Illinois, 1938), Louis W. Chappell (North Carolina, 1939), Gardner and Geraldine Jencks Chickering (southern Michigan, 1939), Mary O. Eddy (Ohio, 1939), Paul G. Brewster (Indiana, 1940), Vance Randolph (Ozark, 1946–50), Creighton and Doreen H. Senior (Nova Scotia, 1950) and Alton C. Morris (Florida, 1950).

These eclectic collections are nondiscriminatory, literary and true to recovered texts; they tend to include all material sung from memory and to cite all known variants, in contrast to contemporary English collections, which are discriminatory, freely edited and tune-oriented. The American collections include imported and native narratives, lyric songs, 'parlor' songs (popular music-hall songs), game songs, instrumental music and Negro songs (mostly collected from white informants). Topics are diverse, from outlaws, domestic tragedy, lovers, catastrophes and war, to hobo songs and occupational songs of the cowboy, shantyboy, sailor and railroadsman. Some organizations specialized in the collection of Child ballads (C. Alphonso Smith, Virginia Folklore Society), and several early publications are specialist studies of the Child canon (Reed Smith, 1928; Barry and others, 1929; Davis, 1929; Scarborough, 1937). Most collections include texts to the total neglect of tunes, though publications vary in presentation: those prepared by academics follow the Child canon, with comparative and bibliographical notes; some collections include essays; others present unordered and unannotated samples, or offer folk songs arranged for performance.

Three typical essays of the early 20th century illustrate cross-cultural historical studies of ballad themes: G. H. Gerould, 'The Ballad of the Bitter Withy' (1908), Walter R. Nelles, 'The Ballad of Hind Horn' (1909) and Paull Franklin Baum, 'The English Ballad of Judas Iscariot' (1916). Characterized by broad comparisons, they are summations of the sparse evidence then available.

The first major collection of southern folk song, Negro and white, was Tennessee native E. C. Perrow's 'Songs and Rhymes from the South' (*Journal of American Folklore*, 1912), including 270 items from Tennessee, Kentucky, Mississippi, Missouri, West Virginia and Alabama. The introduction describes the social milieu of the mountains, and cites Negro repetition and improvisation in dance, revival, and work songs as a living illustration of the formation of a ballad tradition.

By the 1930s and 1940s, with much of the American Child repertory notated, collectors turned to new genres and detailed studies of individual ballads (Barry, 'The Two Sisters', 1931; Archer Taylor, '*Edward*' and '*Sven i Rosengård*', 1931). Occupational songs were collected by Roland Palmer Gray (Maine lumberjacks, 1924), Franz Rickaby (Minnesota lumberjacks, 1926), Earl Clifton Beck (Michigan lumberjacks, 1941, 1948) and George G. Korson (anthracite and bituminous coal miners in Pennsylvania and 19 other states,

1. *John Avery Lomax: portrait by J. Anthony Wills*

1927, 1938, 1943, 1949). Songs of drifters and down-and-outs were documented by Charles J. Finger (1927), George Milburn (1930) and the poet-performer Carl Sandburg in his famous anthology, *The American Songbag* (1927). The most prolific fieldworker of the period was Robert Winslow Gordon, who, sponsored by Harvard University, recorded some 1000 cylinders on a grand tour in 1927 of the southern Appalachians, the southeastern coast, Georgia, north along the Mississippi River to Minnesota, the Dakotas, to the Great Lakes region of Canada, ending in Nova Scotia and Newfoundland (Wilgus, 1959, p.180).

John Avery Lomax (1867–1948; see fig.1), pioneer in the study of southwestern lore, grew up on a farm in Bosque county, Texas, beside a branch of the Chisholm Trail. As a teenager he notated local cowboy songs, but later burnt these manuscripts when scorned by an instructor at the University of Texas, Austin. At Harvard in 1907, he encountered folklorists Kittredge and Barrett Wendell, who encouraged him on a venture to collect songs of cowboys, miners, stage drivers, freighters and hunters, through correspondence with western newspaper editors as well as summer field trips, on which he was the first scholar to collect Anglo-American folk songs with the Edison phonograph (reminiscences in Lomax and others, 1947). Despite the written endorsement of Theodore Roosevelt, Lomax's *Cowboy Songs and Other Frontier Ballads* (1910), with 112 song texts and 18 tunes, was rejected by two publishers before its appearance in 1910 under the imprint of Sturgis & Waltor. Lomax presented his collection as 'indigenous popular songs that have sprung up as has the grass on the plains' (1911, pp.1–2), a romantic interpretation that supported the communalist views of Kittredge (also of Wendell, who wrote an introduction to the Lomax collection). Any song 'the most gifted man could produce must bear the criticism of the entire camp, and agree with the ideas of a group of men . . . Any song that came from such a group would be the joint product of a number of them' (Lomax, 1911, p.16). His documentation is suspect, with many texts lacking dates and sources, and difficult to verify because only 47 of the 250 cylinders recorded in Texas and Oklahoma, 1908–10, are extant at the Library of Congress. Lomax was unmoved by later discoveries that 'communally composed' songs in his collection had named composers (e.g. 'The Railroad Corral' by J. M. Hanson). Lomax cleaned up tough cowpuncher language and combined lines from different versions to produce a 'complete' song, violating 'the ethics of ballad-gatherers, in a few instances, by selecting and putting together what seemed to be the best lines from different versions, all telling the same story. Frankly, the volume is meant to be popular' (1910, p.xxiii). A second anthology included works of western poets E. A. Brinistool, Henry Herbert Knibbs, Badger Clark and James Barton Adams (1919).

A different style of cowboy collection was prepared by Nathan Howard (Jack) Thorp (1867–1940), an easterner who drifted West in search of folklore, beginning in 1889. He collected songs first hand and through correspondence, combining verses freely from different sources. *Songs of Cowboys* (1908), a slim red booklet that included five of his own compositions, sold all over the West at roundups, cow camps, and fairs for 50 cents, and was used as a songbook by a generation of ranch hands.

Other collections presenting folk songs for performance include *Lonesome*

Tunes (1916) by Loraine Wyman and Howard Brockway and *Folk Songs of the Kentucky Mountains* (1917) by Josephine McGill; material for these was collected in the same districts and at the same time as Cecil Sharp's and Maud Karpeles's fieldwork for *English Folk Songs from the Southern Appalachians* (1932). McGill's volume has 13 Child versions; Wyman and Brockway include broadsides, lyrics, and religious, nursery and nonsense songs in addition to Child material. Both collections present the melodies harmonized for domestic performance.

Archives and commercialism

In 1928, the Archive of American Folk Song of the Library of Congress was established through the support of Carl Engel of the Division of Music. The private collection of Robert W. Gordon, the first archivist, formed the heart of the new institution. In 1934, John Lomax joined as honorary consultant and curator; it is largely through his personal charisma and showmanship, and that of his son Alan (*b* 1915), who became his assistant in 1937, that the Archive became renowned. The recording laboratory was built in 1940 with duplicating equipment and field equipment available for loan; beginning in 1943, commercial albums of folk song were issued.

In 1931, beset by illness and financial problems, John Lomax resumed his collecting career, setting out with Alan on a four-month, 16,000-mile trip to record Negro songs (1934). In southern prison camps, they discovered prisoners who still sang old work songs. In 1933, Lomax discovered Leadbelly [Huddie Ledbetter] (1885–1949), African-American songster, blues singer and guitarist, in jail for murder. Lomax arranged his parole and engaged him to record many of his repertory of some 500 songs for the Library of Congress Archive (1935–40). *Negro Folk Songs as Sung by Lead Belly* (1936) is one of the first extensive presentations of an individual repertory.

Ruth Crawford Seeger transcribed, arranged and edited hundreds of recordings from the Archive, many of which were published by John and Alan Lomax in *Our Singing Country* (1941). In the collection, *Folk Song U.S.A.: the 111 Best American Ballads*, John and Alan Lomax and Charles and Ruth Seeger presented a popular anthology with piano arrangements and annotations (1947).

A market for commercial folk music steadily developed through the 1920s to the 1940s as recording technology improved. With the popularization of folk radio broadcasts prior to World War I, record sales plummeted (Alan Lomax was featured as a radio personality for many years – 'Well-springs of America', 'Transatlantic Call', 'Your Ballad Man'). During the 1920s, in a search for new material, record producers turned to folk song, African and Anglo (especially race and hillbilly – pejorative terms later replaced by blues, soul, country, and western). In 1939, Moses Asch (1905–86) founded Asch Records (later Folkways), releasing recordings of Leadbelly and Woody Guthrie. Other labels featured Josh White, Burl Ives and Carl Sandburg. On the Folkways label, Asch amassed the largest collection of commercial folk music, with help from colleagues Henry Cowell and Pete Seeger. By the 1920s, scholars were transcribing from commercial records and citing them in their studies (e.g. Guy B. Johnson and Howard W. Odum in 'John Henry' studies;

Green, 1983, pp.434–5). Academic reviews of commercial recording began in the late 1940s and 1950s (Herbert Halpert, Claude M. Simpson, Charles Seeger and D. K. Wilgus).

2. Fiddler Will Neal playing for collectors Robert Sonkin (centre) and Charles Todd (right), Summer 1940. The recording machine is a Presto Model K.

Bibliography

A. Lang: 'Ballads', *Encyclopaedia Britannica*, iii (New York, 1878), 283
F. J. Child: *The English and Scottish Popular Ballads* (Boston, MA, and New York, 1883–98/R1956, 1965)
W. W. Newell: *Games and Songs of American Children* (New York, 1883, rev. and enl. 2/1903/R1963)
F. B. Gummere: 'The Ballad and Communal Poetry', *Harvard Studies and Notes in Philology and Literature*, v (1896), 41
A. Lang, ed.: *A Collection of Ballads* (London, 1897/R1910)
——: 'Notes on Ballad Origins', *Folk-Lore* (1903)
F. B. Gummere: 'Primitive Poetry and the Ballad', *Modern Philology*, i (1903–4), 193, 217, 373
P. Barry: 'Some Traditional Songs', *Journal of American Folklore*, xviii/68 (1905), 49
H. M. Belden: 'The Study of Folk-Song in America', *Modern Philology*, ii (1905), 573
——: *A Partial List of Song-Ballads and Other Popular Poetry Known in Missouri* (Columbia, MO, 1907, rev. and enl. 2/1910)
A. F. Chamberlain: '[Newell]', *American Anthropologist*, ix (1907), 366
F. B. Gummere: 'Ballad Origins', *The Nation*, lxxxv (1907), 184
——: *The Popular Ballad* (Boston, MA, and New York, 1907)

43

G. H. Gerould: 'The Ballad of the Bitter Withy', *Publications of the Modern Language Association*, xxiii (1908), 141

N. H. Thorp: *Songs of the Cowboys* (Estancia, NM, 1908, rev. and enl. 2/1921)

P. Barry: 'Folk Music in America', *Journal of American Folklore*, xxii/83 (1909), 72

H. M. Belden: 'Review, *The Popular Ballad*, F. B. Gummere', *Journal of English and Germanic Philology*, viii (1909), 114

W. R. Nelles: 'The Ballad of Hind Horn', *Journal of American Folklore*, xxii/83 (1909), 42

P. Barry: 'The Origin of Folk-Melodies', *Journal of American Folklore*, xxiii/87 (1910), 440

J. A. Lomax: *Cowboy Songs and Other Frontier Ballads* (New York, 1910, enl. 2/1916, rev. and enl. 3/1938)

H. M. Belden: 'The Relation of Balladry to Folk-lore', *Journal of American Folklore*, xxiv/91 (1911), 1

J. A. Lomax: 'Cowboy Songs of the Mexican Border', *Sewanee Review*, xix (1911), 1

P. Barry: 'Some Aspects of Folk-Song', *Journal of American Folklore*, xxv/97 (1912), 274

E. C. Perrow: 'Songs and Rhymes from the South', *Journal of American Folklore*, xxv/97 (1912), 137

P. Barry: 'An American Homiletic Ballad', *Modern Language Notes*, xxviii (1913), 1

——: 'The Transmission of Folk-Song', *Journal of American Folklore*, xxvii/103 (1914), 67

P. F. Baum: 'The English Ballad of Judas Iscariot', *Publications of the Modern Language Association*, xxxi (1916), 181

L. Wyman and H. Brockway, comps.: *Lonesome Tunes: Folk Songs from the Kentucky Mountains* (New York, 1916)

J. McGill, comp. and arr.: *Folk Songs of the Kentucky Mountains* (New York, 1917)

J. A. Lomax, comp.: *Songs of the Cattle Trail and Cow Camp* (New York, 1919)

H. W. Shoemaker, comp.: *North Pennsylvania Minstrelsy: as Sung in the Backwood Settlements, Hunting Cabins and Lumber Camps in Northern Pennsylvania 1840–1910* (Altoona, PA, 1919, 2/1923)

L. Wyman and H. Brockway, comps.: *Twenty Kentucky Mountain Songs* (Boston, MA, 1920)

H. Naumann: *Primitive Gemeinschaftskultur, Beiträge zur Volkskunde und Mythologie* (Jena, 1921)

L. Pound: *Poetic Origins and the Ballad* (New York, 1921)

R. P. Gray, ed.: *Songs and Ballads of the Maine Lumberjacks, with Other Songs from Maine* (Cambridge, MA, 1924)

L. Pound: 'The Term "Communal"', *Publications of the Modern Language Association of America*, xxxix (1924), 440

J. H. Combs: *Folk-Songs du Midi des États-Unis* (Paris, 1925)

J. H. Cox, ed.: *Folk-Songs of the South* (Cambridge, MA, 1925)

F. L. Rickaby: *Ballads and Songs of the Shanty-Boy* (Cambridge, MA, 1926)

C. J. Finger: *Frontier Ballads* (Garden City, NJ, 1927)

G. G. Korson, comp. and ed.: *The Miner Sings: a Collection of Folk Songs and Ballads of the Anthracite Miner* (New York, 1927)

C. Sandburg, ed.: *The American Songbag* (New York, 1927)

W. R. MacKenzie: *Ballads and Sea Songs from Nova Scotia* (Cambridge, MA, 1928)

R. Smith, ed.: *South Carolina Ballads, with a Study of the Traditional Ballad To-day* (Cambridge, MA, 1928)

P. Barry, F. H. Eckstorm and M. W. Smyth: *British Ballads from Maine: the Development of Popular Songs with Texts and Airs* (New Haven, CT, 1929)

A. K. Davis Jr, ed.: *Traditional Ballads of Virginia* (Cambridge, MA, 1929)

G. Milburn, comp.: *The Hobo's Hornbook: a Repertory for a Gutter Jongleur* (New York, 1930)

P. Barry: 'The Two Sisters', *Bulletin of the Folk-Song Society of the Northeast*, iii (1931), 11

H. W. Shoemaker, comp.: *Mountain Minstrelsy of Pennsylvania* (Philadelphia, PA, 1931) [3rd rev. and enl. edition of *North Pennsylvania Minstrelsy* (Altoona, PA, 1919)]

A. Taylor: *'Edward' and 'Sven i Rosengård', a Study in the Dissemination of a Ballad* (Chicago, IL, 1931)

H. Creighton: *Songs and Ballads from Nova Scotia* (Toronto, 1932/R1966)

G. H. Gerould: *The Ballad of Tradition* (Oxford, 1932/R1960)

C. J. Sharp and M. Karpeles, comps.: *English Folk Songs from the Southern Appalachians* (London, 1932, 2/1952)

E. B. Greenleaf and G. Y. Mansfield, eds.: *Ballads and Sea Songs of Newfoundland* (Cambridge, MA, 1933)

G. P. Jackson: *White Spirituals in the Southern Uplands* (Chapel Hill, NC, 1933/R1965)

J. von Pulikowski: *Geschichte des Begriffes Volkslied im musikalischen Schrifttum, ein Stück deutscher Geistesgeschichte* (Heidelberg, 1933)

J. A. Lomax and A. Lomax, comps.: *American Ballads and Folksongs* (New York, 1934)

——: *Negro Folk Songs as Sung by Lead Belly* (New York, 1936)

E. J. Stout, ed.: *Folklore from Iowa* (New York, 1936)

E. E. Gardner: *Folklore from the Schoharie Hills, New York* (Ann Arbor, MI, 1937)

D. Scarborough: *A Song Catcher in Southern Mountains: American Folk Songs of British Ancestry* (New York, 1937)

G. G. Korson, ed.: *Minstrels of the Mine Patch: Songs and Stories of the Anthracite Industry* (Philadelphia, PA, 1938)

G. Herzog: 'Phillips Barry', *Journal of American Folklore*, li/202 (1938), 439

C. Neely: *Tales and Songs of Southern Illinois* (Menasha, WI, 1938)

P. Barry: *Folk Music in America* (New York, 1939)

S. P. Bayard: 'Aspects of Melodic Kinship and Variation in British-American Folk-tunes', *PAMS* (1939), 122

L. W. Chappell: *Folk-songs of Roanoke and the Albermarle* (Morgantown, WV, 1939)

J. H. Combs, ed.: *Folk-Songs from the Kentucky Highlands* (New York, 1939)

J. H. Cox: *Folk-Songs Mainly from West Virginia* (New York, 1939)

———: *Traditional Ballads Mainly from West Virginia* (New York, 1939)

M. O. Eddy, comp.: *Ballads and Songs from Ohio* (New York, 1939)

E. E. Gardner and G. J. Chickering: *Ballads and Songs of Southern Michigan* (Ann Arbor, MI, 1939)

H. M. Belden, ed.: *Ballads and Songs Collected by the Missouri Folk-Lore Society* (Columbia, MO, 1940, 2/1955)

P. G. Brewster, ed.: *Ballads and Songs of Indiana* (Bloomington, IN, 1940)

E. C. Beck: *Songs of the Michigan Lumberjacks* (Ann Arbor, MI, 1941)

J. A. Lomax and A. Lomax, comps.: *Our Singing Country: a Second Volume of American Ballads and Folk Songs* (New York, 1941, 2/1948) [R. C. Seeger, music ed.]

A. Lomax and S. R. Cowell: *American Folk Song and Folk Lore: a Regional Bibliography* (New York, 1942/R1972)

G. G. Korson, ed.: *Coal Dust on the Fiddle: Songs and Stories of the Bituminous Industry* (Philadelphia, PA, 1943)

G. P. Jackson: *White and Negro Spirituals* (New York, 1943)

N. H. Thorp and N. M. Clark: *Pardner of the Wind* (Cadwell, ID, 1945)

V. Randolph, ed.: *Ozark Folksongs* (Columbia, MO, 1946–50)

J. A. Lomax: *Adventures of a Ballad Hunter* (New York, 1947)

J. A. Lomax, A. Lomax, C. Seeger, and R. C. Seeger: *Folk Song U.S.A.: the 111 Best American Ballads* (New York, 1947, rev. 2/1975)

E. C. Beck: *Lore of the Lumber Camps* (Ann Arbor, MI, 1948) [rev. and enl. edition of *Songs of the Michigan Lumberjacks* (Ann Arbor, MI, 1941)]

A. K. Davis Jr: *Folk-songs of Virginia, a Descriptive Index and Classification of Material Collected under the Auspices of the Virginia Folklore Society* (Durham, NC, 1949)

G. G. Korson, ed.: *Pennsylvania Songs and Legends* (Philadelphia, PA, 1949)

T. P. Coffin: *The British Traditional Ballad in North America* (Philadelphia, PA, 1950, rev. 2/1963/R1977 with suppl.)

H. Creighton and D. H. Senior, comps.: *Traditional Songs from Nova Scotia* (Toronto, 1950)

G. M. Laws Jr: *Native American Balladry: a Descriptive Study and a Bibliographical Syllabus* (Philadelphia, PA, 1950, rev. 2/1964)

A. Lomax: *Mister Jelly Roll: the Fortunes of Jelly Roll Morton, New Orleans Creole and 'Inventor of Jazz'* (New York, 1950, 2/1973)

A. C. Morris, ed.: *Folksongs of Florida* (Gainesville, FL, 1950)

C. Haywood: *A Bibliography of North American Folklore and Folksong* (New York, 1951, rev. 2/1961)

A. Taylor: 'Trends in the Study of Folksong, 1937–1950', *Southern Folklore Quarterly*, xvii (1953), 97

J. A. Lomax and A. Lomax: *Leadbelly: a Collection of World-Famous Songs* (New York, 1959, enl. 2/1965 as *The Leadbelly Legend*)

D. K. Wilgus: *Anglo-American Folksong Scholarship Since 1898* (New Brunswick, NJ, 1959/R1982)

R. M. Lawless: *Folksingers and Folksongs in America: a Handbook of Biography, Bibliography, and Discography* (New York, 1960, rev. 2/1965/R1968)

M. C. Boatright, W. M. Hudson and A. Maxwell, eds.: *A Good Tale and a Bonnie Tune* (Dallas, TX, 1964)

A. Green: 'Sound Recordings, Use and Challenge', *Handbook of American Folklore*, ed. R. M. Dorson (Bloomington, IN, 1983), 434

3: AFRICAN-AMERICAN

WILLIAM WESTCOTT

The Colonial period through the Civil War

Written documentation of African-American music in North America dates from the early 17th century. African explorers, slave-ship captains, European and American travellers, Christian missionaries and ministers, slave owners, free blacks, freed and escaped slaves and general observers have left numerous accounts of music making among blacks in Africa, in the 'middle passage' and in the New World. Some of these accounts were published at the time while others were made available for study only in the 19th and 20th centuries. Many early accounts give vivid descriptions (and in some cases, transcriptions) of a musical style of clear, West African character; others attest to various degrees of musical acculturation.

Captain and explorer Richard Jobson, travelling in West Africa for the Company of Adventurers in 1620–21, described singers of a *griot* type and several instruments in use, including long-necked gourd lutes, drums and a 'Ballards' (Balofo) (Jobson, 1623). Thomas Edward Bowdich, on a commercial mission in 1817, gave a remarkable account of music, including transcriptions of texts and melodies found among the Fanti and Ashanti peoples, in his *Mission from Cape Coast to Ashantee* (1819). George Pinckard (*Notes on the West Indies*, 1806) and Bryan Edwards (*The History, Civil and Commercial, of the British Colonies in the West Indies*, 1793–1801) are only two among many who noted the widespread practice of forcing slaves to dance aboard ship as well as the occasional employment of African instruments (Epstein, 1977, p.7). Until the early 19th century, commercial and cultural ties between the West Indies and the North American mainland were strong, and information on the slave trade from the West Indies shed light on mainland conditions, which were less well-documented (Epstein, 1977, p.xvi; Abrahams and Szwed, eds., 1983).

Documents before the Civil War attesting to the persistence of West African styles in singing and improvisation in the daily life of mainland slaves and freedmen are numerous and occasionally lengthy (Epstein, 1977, p.128). Outstanding descriptions of slave festivities and celebrations preserving and perpetuating West African practices in the colonial and post-colonial periods include Benjamin Latrobe's account of dancing in Place Congo (*Impressions of New Orleans . . .*, 1819), where he described drums, a stringed instrument, singing and dancing of evident West African types. He saw this regular Sunday event as 'brutally savage, and at the same time dull and stupid'. An account at once friendlier and more objective in tone than Latrobe's is that of James Eights, writing around the time of the Revolutionary War, who describes the Pinkster celebrations of blacks in New York, detailing a week of festivities including singing, dancing, drumming and a ceremonial surrounding a 'King' (1867).

A more acculturated music-making in the daily life of slaves in the colonial and pre-Civil War periods is documented by advertisements of slaves for sale and descriptions of runaway slaves characterized frequently as being good fiddlers (Southern, 1971, *Readings . . .*, p.31). Thomas Jefferson (*Notes on the State of Virginia . . .*, 1782) not only noted the use among slaves of the 'banjar' but commented that 'in music they [the slaves] are more generally gifted than the whites . . . and they have been found capable of imagining a small catch' (Chase, 2/1966, p.66). Simeon Gilliat, a slave fiddler, was according to his own statement a 'court fiddler' attached to the Governor's Palace at Williamsburg. His obituary of 16 October 1820 described him as 'a man of color, very celebrated as a Fiddler, and much caressed by polished society who will long deplore the loss' (Epstein, 1977, p.116).

The first systematic efforts to christianize the Africans were undertaken by the Anglican-based Society for the Preservation of the Gospel in Foreign Parts in the 1720s. Letters from missionary ministers, requesting hymnals and commenting on the usefulness of sacred song in the missionary work, survive. The Great Awakening of the mid-18th century sparked similar efforts by Methodists, Baptists and Presbyterians. Ministers and missionaries of these groups all left accounts of black religious singing, commenting on the differences in style and approach from their white brethren and on their general enthusiasm for the exercise (Epstein, 1977, p.100).

In the post-revolutionary years black students attended singing schools and in some cases became music teachers (Southern, 1971, *The Music*, p.69). In 1801, Richard Allen, the first Bishop of the A(frican) M(ethodist) E(piscopal) church compiled a tune book for the use of his black congregation in Philadelphia containing hymns with 'wandering strains', this being arguably the first collection of 'Negro Spirituals' (Southern, 1971, *The Music*, p.73).

Accounts beginning in the early 19th century reflect the ever-increasing importance of Christian worship among black slaves, as resistance by their owners to their religious observances gradually receded. The end of the legal importation of slaves in 1808 also reduced the direct influence of African culture on the American black population, while the industrial revolution made chattel slavery increasingly profitable in the South. The abolitionist movement developing in the 30 years prior to the Civil War sparked an interest by Northern idealists in the music of the slaves, especially in the sacred music, which in contrast to the apparent trifles of the black-face minstrels could be adduced as evidence of the moral development of the slaves and the justice of their claims to freedom and citizenship. Southern proponents of slavery were correspondingly given to publishing examples of black song and folklore as evidence of the uncivilized and childlike character of the slaves.

The first camp meetings of the Second Great Awakening were attended by both races, a pattern that persisted until the middle of the century (Epstein, 1977, p.197). Observers of these meetings noted the presence of blacks as well as their unique behaviour and enthusiasm. Typical of disapproving earlier accounts is John F. Watson's *Methodist Error* (1819), where blacks are criticized for dancing while at worship and for singing 'merry airs' (Epstein, 1977, p.218). Friendlier accounts typical of many European travellers are given by Fanny Kemble (1863, *Journal of a Residence*) and Fredrika Bremer, who attended a camp meeting near Charleston in 1850. In her *Homes of the New World* (1853), Bremer described the voices of the numerous black worshippers as 'naturally beautiful and pure', and accepted the 'Holy Dance' without opprobrium (Epstein, 1977, p.218).

The rise of black-face Negro minstrelsy, beginning in the late 1820s with the successes of 'Daddy Rice' and others, brought a general public interest, however superficial, in the music of the slaves. Some of the more perceptive observers raised questions regarding the 'authenticity' of this popular idiom. J. Kinnard, writing in the *Knickerbocker Magazine* (1845), argued confusingly that the slaves were 'national poets' who lacked sufficient subsidy to become 'spoiled' or correctly recognized. On the other hand, a person like 'Thomas Rice . . . learned their poetry, music and dancing, blacked his face, and made his fortune by giving to the world his counterfeit presentment of the American national opera' (B. Jackson, 1967, p.23).

Accounts in the years before the Civil War show a general increase in the attention paid to sacred music. This reflects progress in missionary conversions as well as the biases of abolitionists. Also many Christian fundamentalists prohibited dancing as a profane activity and the frequent notices of 'shouts' suggest a redirection of African-derived dancing into this form of worship. Secular forms such as corn songs and rowing songs are nevertheless commonly noted, and communal singing while at work was generally encouraged. In these genres the boundary between 'sacred' and 'secular' was frequently obscure. William J. Grayson, a pro-slavery advocate recalling his boyhood in South Carolina, remembered being ferried in canoes by slaves:

> The singers were the negro oarsmen. One served as chief performer, the rest as chorus. The songs were partly traditionary [sic], partly improvised. They were simple . . . consisting of one line only and the chorus. The singer worked into his rude strain any incident that came in his way relating to the place of destination, the passengers on board, the wife or sweetheart at home, his work or amusement . . . The voices were generally good, the tunes pleasing and various, sometimes gay, sometimes plaintive. They were sung *con amore* (Epstein, 1977, p.166–7).

Many such accounts portraying the slaves as happy in their condition were advanced in defence of institutional slavery, while abolitionists were quick to interpret the same data otherwise. In an oft-quoted letter to *Dwight's Journal of Music* (1862) accompanying her 'Songs of the Port Royal "Contrabands"', Lucy McKim asserted that the songs she had transcribed are

> valuable as an expression of the character and life of the race which is playing such a conspicuous part in our history. The wild sad strains tell, as the sufferers themselves never could, of crushed hopes, keen sorrow, and a dull daily misery which covered them as hopelessly as the fog from the rice swamps . . . [One of McKim's informants is quoted:] . . . 'Pshaw! dont har to dese yer chil'en, misse. Dey just rattles it off, – dey dont know how for sing it. I likes "Poor Rosy" better dan all de songs, but it cant be sung widout a *full heart and a troubled sperrit!*' (Katz, 1969, p.10, and B. Jackson, 1967, p.61).

The first printed spirituals with music came out of the early Civil War years, when Northerners first came into daily contact with Southern blacks. In September 1861, the Rev. Lewis Lockwood, representing the American Missionary Association and the New York YMCA, visited Fortress Monroe in Virginia, where he heard the singing of 'contrabands'. By the end of the year a commercial sheet-music version of the spiritual known today as 'Go Down Moses' was published as 'The Song of the Contrabands: "O let My People go"' with 'words and music obtained through the rev. L. C. Lockwood, Chaplain of the "Contrabands" at Fortress Monroe'. The arrangement had been made by Thomas Baker, who cast the tune into an unlikely and awkward 6/8 *andante* (facsimile in Epstein, 1977, p.365). Other notable examples from the war years include the two commercial efforts of Lucy McKim, gathered on her rather brief visit to Port Royal, SC, in 1861 ('Poor Rosy, Poor Gal' and 'Roll, Jordan Roll'; see Epstein, 1977, p.365) and the five tunes with texts in Henry George Spaulding's article, 'Under the Palmetto', which appeared in the *Continental Monthly* (1863). Other articles from the war years appeared in *Dwight's Journal* (without music), including 'Contraband Singing' by C.W.D. (1861) and 'Negro Songs' by James Miller McKim, Lucy's father (1862). Outstanding among wartime accounts (though published afterward and lacking musical transcriptions) is Thomas Wentworth Higginson's *Atlantic Monthly* article (1967), 'Negro Spirituals', giving texts and commentary for 37 songs. This article was incorporated later into his book *Army Life in a Black Regiment* (1870), an account of Higginson's war experiences as commanding officer of the First South Carolina Volunteers, the first Union Army regiment composed entirely of freed slaves.

Reconstruction era through 1900

The collecting and publishing activities of William Francis Allen, Charles Pickard Ware and Lucy McKim Garrison (all dedicated abolitionists working together in the Georgia Sea Islands for the Freedman's Bureau at Port Royal during the War) mark the beginning of the systematic collection, transcription and study of African-American music in North America. Their efforts resulted in the publication of *Slave Songs of the United States* (1867). This collection of 136 songs, with texts and an introductory essay by W. F. Allen, reflects the usual preoccupation of the abolitionists with sacred music but is nevertheless a landmark in scope, method and objectivity. Songs were solicited from a number of collectors other than themselves and grouped on the basis of geography into three regions: Southeastern slave states, including South Carolina, Georgia and the Sea Islands (102 songs), inland slave states, including Tennessee, Arkansas and Mississippi River (9 songs), Gulf states, including Florida, Louisiana and miscellaneous (25 songs). Recognizing the difficulty of providing a 'correct text', the editors supplied multiple variants of some of the melodies and at least one complete text for each song. Allen's introductory essay was the first effort to deal seriously with issues of repertory structure and performance practice. He regretted the lack of secular song in the collection, which if included would have demonstrated more 'barbaric' qualities, and noted that since the abolition of slavery the repertory had already begun to change. He also recognized that given versions of songs have a local provenance but travel as well; and that the local repertory varied according to denominational preferences. Regarding performance practice, he described the shout in considerable detail noting regional variations. He noted the variability of tempo depending on performance context, the roles of the leader and 'basers', a characteristic use of harmony, variable intonation and irregularities of rhythm. His essay also presented an extended analysis, the first, of the Sea Island (Gullah) dialect.

It has been fashionable to undervalue the musical transcriptions in this collection on the basis that the collectors were not qualified musicians and could not be relied upon to record the music with sufficient detail and correctness to be useful. Dena J. Epstein has pointed out that these people were as qualified as anyone reasonably could have been – especially Lucy McKim Garrison, a trained pianist with some experience on the violin, who was primarily responsible for reading the proofs (1977, p.303).

The lucrative concert tours of the Fisk University Jubilee Singers in the 1870s (see illustration), quickly followed by tours of other student vocal groups from newly established Negro colleges (notably, Hampton Institute), resulted in the publication of narratives of their successful activities and four-part arrangements of their songs. The intent of these collections was clearly to capitalize on the sudden popularity of the spirituals. Other collections (some with a more folkloric intent containing commentaries on the origins or significance of each song) began to appear in the 1890s and continued steadily through the middle of the 20th century (Horn, 1977, p.273). Some of these provided the melody only (Mary Allen Grissom's *The Negro Sings a New Heaven*, 1930) but the majority presented the songs either in four-part format (John Wesley Work's *American Negro Songs and Spirituals*, 1940) or as vocal solos with piano accompaniment (James Weldon Johnson and J. Rosamond Johnson's *Book(s) of American Negro Spirituals* of 1925 and 1926).

The Fisk Jubilee Singers in 1875

The late 19th century saw the elaboration on a tradition of romantic journalism already begun before the Civil War, centring on black culture (and music), best remembered today through the works of Joel Chandler Harris. This literature frequently shows a condescending nostalgia for the lost forever days of slavery and an increasing contempt for minstrelsy, coon songs and ragtime, the black-influenced products of the popular music industry. This extensive literature is nevertheless valuable as a whole. The accounts of Lafcadio Hearn and George W. Cable document songs and dances of New Orleans Creoles and other black urban groups of the 19th century in stylish prose. Cable's article 'The Dance in Place Congo' (1886) romantically recreates the scene from his probable memories of it at around the middle of the 19th century and gives descriptions and transcriptions of 'Bamboula,' 'Counjaille' and 'Calinda' dancing and music – a welcome sequel to Latrobe's earlier account. Cable's 'Creole Slave Songs' (1886) gives several songs of interest, including songs and rituals of voodoo as practised in New Orleans in (presumably) the mid-19th century. The same era saw the gradual rise of formal folklore studies in the USA, and considerable attention was paid to the Negro, especially after the success in the early 1880s of Harris's 'Uncle Remus' stories. Early articles in the 'scientific' spirit appeared first in mainstream periodicals but eventually found a permanent home in the *Journal of American Folklore*, beginning in 1888 (see B. Jackson, 1967, p.356, for an index to pertinent articles in the journal 1888 to 1900). Thus, by the end of the 19th century, black sacred music was established in the mainstream culture in the form of the spiritual and a 'Negroid' strain in popular music was also generally, if grudgingly, acknowledged by some.

Antonin Dvořák's ill-informed, but influential remarks, beginning in 1893, on the singular appropriateness of black folk music and American Indian music, but especially the tunes of the spirituals, as the most hopeful basis for a genuinely American style in serious music, brought the character and pedigree of the Negro spiritual under close examination (1895). In fairness to Dvořák, it should be noted that he denied any real knowledge of American folk music and that in singling out Negroes and Indians he was merely applying to music a position taken more than ten years before by T. F. Crane regarding American folk tales. In his review of Harris's *Uncle Remus: His Songs and His Sayings*, appearing in *Popular Science Monthly*, 1881, Crane stated that there were no native American legends save those of the Indians and the Negroes. Until this time, those who were interested in Negro music assumed logically that the salient features of this music distinguishing it from other musics must be African in essence. Richard Wallaschek's dismissive remarks in his study *Primitive Music* (1893), that the transcriptions of Negro spirituals he had examined showed little explicit African character, but rather that they were 'overvalued . . . imitations' of European models, opened up the possibility that this music was not the product of an African genius, but merely a debased form of European musical type (p.60). The debate that ensued from these two contrasting positions lasted for nearly 70 years and was carried out often in an atmosphere of racial and national pridefulness, wilful disregard by opposing parties of the research and findings of their opponents and by an only gradually reducing ignorance of both African music and white American folk music. Moreover, political, economic and moral crises facing the USA at this time attached themselves to the origins debate, which came to dominate discussion of African–American music in the first half of the 20th century.

1900 to 1950

THE SPIRITUALS CONTROVERSY AND MODELS OF ETHNIC ASSIMILATION   The study and interpretation of Negro spirituals and black folk music generally in the first third of the 20th century was informed by two contrasting models of ethnic assimilation: the 'melting-pot' hypothesis advanced by Frederic Jackson Turner (a pupil of W. F. Allen), first presented in his article 'The Significance of the Frontier in American History' (1893) and the ideal of 'Anglo conformity'. (For an elaborate exposition and historiographic discussion of these two models as well as that of 'cultural pluralism', see Milton M. Gordon's *Assimilation in American Life*, 1964.) Although these models were advanced as general notions of how American culture operates (or should operate), at least two social conditions facing the black population at that time lent a particular urgency to the discussion: (i) of all ethnic or racial groups ever to attempt political assimilation into American society (except possibly North American Indians), blacks remained the most identifiable and, over all, the least successful; (ii) of behaviours unique to American blacks, their music received by far the widest general acceptance and approval from the core society. The success of black music as such (whether spirituals, ragtime or jazz) offered moderate thinkers grounds for a belief in the melting pot and tended to validate psychological urges towards cultural assimilation; but the obvious disenfranchisement of the black population could be seen either as validating the ideal of Anglo-conformity as a necessary precondition to assimilation or (beginning in the 1930s), as grounds for a pluralist, even black-nationalist stance in history, politics and music criticism.

The implications of the melting-pot hypothesis for the future of Negro assimilation were not lost on black intellectuals. W. E. B. DuBois formed the Niagara Movement in 1903 opposing the 'separate but equal' policies of Booker T. Washington and calling for, among other things, manhood suffrage, the abolition of all caste distinctions based simply on colour and race, the recognition of the principle of human brotherhood as a practical and present need, and the recognition of a highest and best human training as the monopoly of no class or race (Ottley and Weatherby, 1967, p.127). The NAACP and the National Urban League soon emerged as advocates of Negro integration into the American melting pot. DuBois, in his book *The Souls of Black Folk* (1903), included a chapter, 'Of the Sorrow Songs', in which he proposed a four-stage historical model of the development of black song supported by 13 texted melodies consonant with the melting-pot ideology, and an implicit rebuttal of Wallaschek:

> . . . The first [stage] is African music, the second Afro-American, while the third is a *blending* of Negro music with the music heard in the foster land. The result is still distinctively Negro and the *method of blending original, but the elements are both Negro and Caucasian.* One might go further and find a fourth step . . . where the songs of White America have been distinctively influenced by the slave songs.' (Katz, 1969, pp.xxii–xxiv – italics, mine)

This line of thought was ably advanced by Henry Edward Krehbiel in 1914 (then musical reviewer for the New York *Tribune* for more than 30 years) in his *Afro-American Folksongs: a Study in Racial and National Music.* Consistent with Dvořák's position, Krehbiel intended to show that Negro song could be used as the basis for an American school of composition and that the songs he studied were crucial to that school because they were the final product of folk-song history in the USA (see his 'conclusions', pp.153–5). Krehbiel analysed 527 songs found in six collections, including the Allen–Ware–McKim *Slave Songs*, the Hampton and Fisk collections, the unusually careful *Calhoun Plantation Songs* by Emily Hallowell (1902–07) and Charles L. Edwards's *Bahama Songs and Stories: a Contribution to Folklore* (1895). Krehbiel gives a lengthy discussion of scalar characteristics and the relationship of mode to ethos in the spirituals. He notes that the major mode predominates in this repertory with a distinct tendency toward pentatonicism. Both of these traits he holds to be characteristic of African practice. He also notes the pronounced use of the flatted 7th and the variable intonation given to this scale degree and to the 3rd. Deeply influenced by the performances of Dahoman musicians at the World's Columbian Exposition in Chicago in 1893, his study is also a good résumé of information then available on African, West Indian and Latin American musics, giving considerable emphasis to complex rhythmic practices previously undiscussed and printing some of his private correspondence with Lafcadio Hearn. However informative, the book fails (as nearly all contributions to this field did and do) to address the problem of comparison with appropriately selected samples of white musics (or black musics, as the case may be). It is a landmark, however, in establishing the feasibility of gathering data from across the Atlantic and presenting it as germane to a question that had been to that time largely conceived in terms of the continental USA only.

A belief in the existence of an 'Africanness' in black music was a logical necessity for anyone interested in forming an argument that asserted the originality (*contra* Wallaschek) of black American culture. Otherwise, any 'characteristic' behaviour of blacks could too easily be interpreted as a dilution or debasement of what had been originally an Anglo-Saxon trait. The premise of black originality was necessary in order to show how blacks could make their contribution to the American alloy. John Wesley Work, using Krehbiel's research to bolster DuBois's historical proposition, makes the emotional urgency of this line of reasoning quite plain in his treatise of the following year, *Folk Songs of the American Negro*:

> The evolution of African to American song correctly indicates the evolution of the African himself. The process was thorough and both singer and song became American . . . His song is new in thought and spirit . . . [but] The vehicle is as old as the African himself. This vehicle, the framework of his musical creation, has remained ever the same, and even the new life, though powerful, has not been able to change it. Africa fashioned the body, but America breathed into it the breath of life (1915, pp.17–18).

The collection and study of Negro folk song continued through the next 40 years with an ever-broadening focus to include various genres of secular song including blues, a wider understanding of performance practices and contexts, and an exploration of Caribbean and Creole phenomena. N. G. J. Ballanta, a native of Sierra Leone, was able to notice connections previously overlooked between West African practices and those of the Sea Islands (1925). G. B. Johnson studied the Sea Islands and advanced an argument against African origins based on melodic and textual comparisons between white revival music of the 19th century and the music he heard there (1930). Lydia Parrish (1942) and Lorenzo Turner (1949) contributed more information from the Sea Islands on the African side of the argument. Lengthy studies of the 'John Henry' ballad were written by Guy B. Johnson (1929) and L. W. Chappell (1933). Helen Roberts, Maude Cuney-Hare and others contributed studies of Caribbean musics (Cunard, 1933). Zora Neale Hurston (1935) gathered folk tales and songs from across the South and recorded music and rites of 'Hoodoo' as a participant observer. Milton Metfessel, using the technique of phonophotography developed by Carl Seashore and others, demonstrated a methodology for describing fine nuances of vocal behaviour which he applied inconclusively to a small sample of Negro singing (1928). Abbe Niles in his foreword and notes to W. C. Handy's *Blues: an Anthology* (1926), presented a thorough stylistic and historical analysis of the genre and considerable background on Handy. Hughes Panassie (1942) and Winthrop Sargent (1938) contributed early interpretations of jazz. Other notable contributors include H. W. Odum (1911), Dorothy Scarborough (1925), Odum and G. B. Johnson in collaboration (1925, 1926) and Newman Ivey White (1928).

This period, however, saw a dramatic change in the demographic structure of the USA. Unrestricted immigration from Europe continued until 1921, but unlike before, it brought a preponderance of people from the South and East. Italians, Slavs and Jews arrived in the cities of the northern and eastern USA in unprecedented numbers. They were joined in the industrial metropolis by rural Southern blacks and by rural and small-town whites from all sectors. By 1921, North America had transformed itself into a predominantly urban society. Industrial expansion was tapering off, joblessness was rising and consequent interracial and interethnic tensions were increasing. The melting pot was cooling down. These developments placed greater strain on the credibility of Turner's hypothesis both in the eyes of nativists, who were attracted to notions of the integrity of Anglo-Saxon traditions, and in the eyes of emergent cultural pluralists, who were coming to see a viable solution in the ideal of cultural autonomy for ethnic groups within national civic unity.

During the 1920s radical cultural pluralism had great appeal only in the lower economic strata of the black community, where it took the form of Marcus Garvey's 'Back to Africa' movement. Black intellectuals and community leaders, recognizing the connection between the Anglo-conformity of American nativism and the ethos of white supremacy as expressed by the re-emergent Ku Klux Klan, nevertheless continued in their attachment to the melting-pot model. James Weldon Johnson, in his preface to the (first) *Book of American Negro Spirituals* (1925), paraphrases Krehbiel, adding many original observations, and echoes DuBois and Work in his emphasis on the 'dignity' and 'originality' of the music. The melting-pot interpretation was shared by liberal whites such as Isaac Goldberg, who becomes explicit about the significance of the melting-pot for blacks, and Jews as well, in his general discussion of the impact of jazz on the popular song industry (1930, p.268).

Although jazz and ragtime seemed to lend themselves well to the melting-pot argument, a staid, upper-crust, white resistance to these musics as allegedly emblematic of modern moral degeneracy threatened to tear a rent in the ark of Afro-American culture (Leonard, 1962). Already in 1915, Work had recourse to the following line of defence: 'Against the words and ideas of ragtime songs, all moral people . . . have just complaint; but let the spirit of ragtime be changed, and let the writers of it express high ideals . . . and the public, all, would welcome it, and hail it as a new development of the musical art' (p.38).

Under such pressures the Africanisms controversy came to a head. Those who opposed the notion of African origins for Negro music did so on the grounds that the 'Africanness' of the music, especially of the spirituals, was an illusion. Guy B. Johnson (1930), Newman I. White (1928), and George Pullen Jackson (1933) cogently argued (using textual and melodic comparisons) that the alleged African traits were really borrowings from antebellum white practice. In a review of Jackson's *White Spirituals in the Southern Uplands*, Carter G. Woodson took the author to task for the racist implications of his work:

> The best he has done is merely to identify himself with those who from time immemorial have tried to prove that the Negro is not and has never been capable of originating anything worthwhile and must therefore be branded as an inferior and treated accordingly. The author does not say so, but by innuendo he will not have it appear any longer that the Negro has risen to any high level of his own volition and power (1934, p.93).

Jackson, White and Johnson had hastened to assure their readers that they had every respect for the Negro spiritual, that only its 'Africanness' was at question; but respect for the songs themselves was not enough. Stripped from their African 'framework', they could no longer stand as symbols of a unique African character, and the melting-pot could consequently hold no promise for the Negro.

Illogically enough, during the 1920s the argument seemed to be working in any case. Jazz had given its name to the decade in the minds of the liberal people who were important. Black music, African or not, was attracting as much praise as censure in the popular imagination, and even though blacks held few positions of real power in the music industry, their impact as performers in classical and popular fields was undeniable. Furthermore, ever since Dvořák had made his much-heeded remarks on the suitability of Negro and Indian folk songs as a basis for the formation of an American nationalist school of art music, black and white composers of popular and concert music had been using American Negro, or even African scenarios, titles and programmes to enhance their efforts.

The brief story of Harry Pace's ill-fated *Black Swan* phonograph company, however, offered a compelling demonstration of the economic significance of Afro-American music for Afro-American assimilation (DuBois, 1921). White society at that time generally preferred to hear its Africanisms from Milhaud, Beiderbecke and Sophie Tucker than from Fletcher Henderson, Louis Armstrong or Bessie Smith. The nocturnal glow of the Harlem renaissance and the restricted middle-class prosperity of the jazz age tended to blur the fundamental disparity between white acceptance of black culture and white acceptance of black people. Many social workers and some social scientists saw the realities of ghetto life behind the veil of the entertainment industry, but a reformulation of the problem of African-American music awaited the sobriety of the Great Depression.

CULTURAL PLURALISM AND A THEORY OF AFRO-AMERICAN MUSICAL ACCULTUR-ATION   For many students of African–American music the social upheavals of the Depression provoked a change in belief away from the melting-pot ideology towards a pluralist view. The efforts of Americanizers to force cultural assimilation on European immigrants (especially Germans during the war years) impressed many people with the virulent and damaging potential of ideological Anglo-conformity. The anti-Semitism traditional in American culture, which was encountered by older as well as more recent Jewish immigrants, also lent ample evidence to the cause of those who felt that democratic principles had to be interpreted as protecting the rights of individuals to be different – to associate with others of like background and persuasion in primary relationships through generations, to preserve residential communities, and to retain the language and literature of their traditional culture – without encountering discrimination from the core society in social status and economic opportunity. Though the idea of cultural pluralism did not originate in the black community, and though it was not necessarily tailored to meet their political needs, black intellectuals of the Harlem renaissance and afterwards showed increasing concern for the values of Negro culture for its own sake. Alain Locke, in *The Negro and His Music* (1936), expressed this change in attitude by asserting that black musical culture *per se* should be held on a par with, or even on a level above that of American musical culture in general. Further, its significance should be primarily for blacks themselves. No longer need black music be offered as a rich ore for the melting-pot, but rather as the source for a (black) nationalist school of composition (Locke, 1936, p.4). In this climate it was necessary as never before to demonstrate the reality of an African basis for the music of black Americans, but a new theory of ethnic culture and its role in American history and society was required to advance the discussion beyond the impasse it had reached by the 1930s.

In 1963, Richard Waterman confidently maintained that the conceptual conflicts implicit in the controversial literature of Afro-American music in the first part of the century had been largely resolved through the efforts of subsequent anthropological and ethnomusicological research. According to Waterman, the question 'Did the American Negro create his own folk song or did he borrow it?' was effectively transformed into the formulation 'How did the musical heritage of West Africans change over generations of contact with alien musical forms?' (1963). He cites five factors that made this new formulation possible: (i) the development of anthropological theory concerning acculturation; (ii) an increasing knowledge of the characteristics of West African music; (iii) increased awareness of a greater Afro-American culture; (iv) abandonment of the concept of racially inherited musical talent; (v) increased awareness of music as an aspect of culture (1963, pp.83–7).

In 1928, Erich M. von Hornbostel had stated that 'African and (modern) European music are constructed on entirely different principles, and therefore . . . cannot be fused into one, and only one or the other can be used without compromise' (p.30). Although Hornbostel had already stated in 1926 that 'had the Negro slaves been taken to China instead of America, they would have developed folk songs in Chinese style' (p.751), his 1928 article certainly was not taking Afro-American acculturation for its subject. Here, he was addressing Christian missionaries in Africa, whose intention it was to adapt African forms to Christian worship. Hornbostel's view of the matter rested upon his discussion of the potential among Africans for the development of genuine polyphonic forms from the current manner of antiphony and 'organum in parallel motion' (1928, p.42).

As to the situation in the USA, Hornbostel might well have felt himself in a delicate position. It must not have been easy to reconcile his and Wallaschek's perception of the European character of the melodic and harmonic materials of North American Negro music as found in the printed spiritual collections with the humanitarian need to render these folk songs culturally respectable. For Hornbostel, the best way to do this was to separate the issue of authenticity from that of origins. Krehbiel had been somewhat overzealous in his attempt to transfer the sense of high regard traditionally associated with English folk song to American Negro folk song. He had tried to do this by defining the Anglo-American variety out of existence. Hornbostel understood more clearly than Krehbiel that authentic human culture requires no 'proof' and that attempting to prove it at the expense of the dominant tradition could too easily be interpreted as a *de facto* admission to the lack of same.

Rhythm was a different matter. Here Hornbostel gave the 'Negro race' its due: 'Not what he sings is so characteristic of his race, but the way he sings. This way of the Negro is identical in Africa and America, and it is totally different than the way of any other race, but it is difficult, if not impossible to describe or analyse it' (1926, p.752). By pointing to characteristics of rhythmic behaviour (including overlapping call-and-response patterns as well as an ambivalence about upbeat and downbeat) resulting, in his view, from the disparity between the moment of muscular tension at the lifting of a drum stick, and its audible consequence at the moment of relaxation, Hornbostel articulated a musical insight important for subsequent literature with a cultural relativist viewpoint. These observations went unheeded in certain quarters, especially by George Pullen Jackson, who had an incomparable grasp of 19th-century revivalist folk music and used it very effectively to bolster the case for the priority of poor Southern whites in the creation of 'spirituals' (1943).

Cultural relativism was an intellectual mood developing in American anthropology at this time. It tended to stress the importance of subjectively held cultural values in the analysis of any society. The most immediate corollary to this position was the realization by the analyst that his own perceptions were conceived in cultural biases which he must seek to objectify and compensate for. Hence, the literature of cultural relativism tended to eliminate the language of absolute value judgment from its analysis.

Melville J. Herskovits (1895–1963) was the person most responsible for the substantial increase since 1942 in our anthropological and ethnomusicological knowledge of Afro-American cultures. Born in Ohio, Herskovits lectured on

African history and art in the liberating atmosphere of the Harlem renaissance. His earliest fieldwork (1928–9) was done in the Surinam bush and the city of Paramaribo, where he was forcibly struck by the degree of African cultural retention there among the blacks whom he studied. Subsequent fieldwork in West Africa and other parts of the New World provided the basis for a tentative historical reconstruction of the African experience in the Americas. His broadly conceived work, *The Myth of the Negro Past* (1942), relies upon a wealth of ethnographic and historical documentation plainly demonstrating the capacity of the Afro-American to retain and transmit his African heritage in whatever degree local circumstances made it possible or desirable. He was sensitive to music as an important element of culture, and enlisted the aid of Mieczyslaw Kolinski in transcribing and interpreting field recordings. It was largely as a consequence of his work that the five factors contributing to Waterman's 'reformation' came about. As an anthropologist he attempted to erect a theory of the history of Afro-American culture as 'a special instance of culture contact', which would illustrate the workings of cultural dynamics (Herskovits, 1942). African America was of compelling interest to him since he felt that instances of contact between dramatically differing cultures provide the best laboratories for observing social processes.

Fundamental to Herskovits's method of 'ethno-history' in the serious study of culture contact were the following: to establish the cultural baseline from which the process of change began (this would be the province of ethnology); to know facts concerning the culture or cultures emerging from the contact (and ethnological and historical activity); and to comprehend how, and under what circumstances the phenomena as observed in the culture that has resulted from the contact actually developed, thus being susceptible of primarily historical treatment (Herskovits, 1966, p.52). Using this compound method, Herskovits was able to develop a scale of intensity of New World Africanisms in various cultural categories for black populations across the entire Western hemisphere (1945). It is important to realize that his table is an idealization: that is, the particular entries in each category represent the maximum degree of retention noted in that population regardless of the social stratum or geographical location at which it may have been encountered. In general, the USA shows the slightest degree of retention, but both music and magic show a 'quite African' rating in all three American regions: Gullah Islands, rural South and urban North. The only 'very African' rating is given to folklore in the Gullah islands while this category in the urban North receives a rating of only 'a little African' (1966, p.53). The categories of social organization and religion in all three areas show ratings of 'somewhat African' while the categories of technology, nonkinship institutions, economic organization, art and language all show ratings of 'a little African', or '. . . absent'. An exception is found in the Gullah Islands, which tend to show higher ratings in these categories, especially in language.

Herskovits does not here say upon exactly what analytic basis these values for musical retention were derived, or what examples were used as representative of the areas. In all likelihood, however, Kolinski's comparative method (developed from Hornbostel's ideas) as he applied it in *Suriname Folklore* (Herskovits and Herskovits, 1936, pp.525ff) had been brought into play. In this publication Kolinski stresses the importance of both an 'aesthetic' and an 'analytical' method of comparison. The aesthetic method involved the noting of traits that Hornbostel had already mentioned, such as (overlapping) of call-and-response phrases, percussive emphasis and use of falsetto, while the analytic method is largely devoted to the comparison of melodies on the basis of such categories as selection and arrangement of pitches in a scale or mode, relation of subjective tonic to duration tone, overall contour of song, frequency of any and all intervals used, total range measured in semitones, and characteristic movement (pendular swings, ascending or descending interlocking 3rds).

Whatever the weaknesses of this 'analytical' (tonal) method may be, the aesthetic (one might add 'rhythmic') approach to analysis proved fruitful. The universally cited discussions are Waterman's two articles, 'Hot Rhythm in Negro Music' (1948) and 'African Influence on the Music of the Americas' (1952), in which he lays greatest stress on rhythm – 'the outstanding feature' that sets African music apart from that of Europe. This characteristic rhythmic behaviour is predicated, according to Waterman, on a powerful subconsciously held value, a 'cultural imponderable' in Herskovits's language, which he dubs the 'metronome sense': 'It entails habits of conceiving any music as structured along a theoretical framework of beats regularly spaced in time, and co-operating in terms of overt or inhibited motor behavior with the pulse of the metric pattern' (1952, p.211).

Corollaries of the metronome sense include polymeter, overlapping of call-and-response phrases, offbeat phrasing of melodic accents, the dominance of percussion and a concern for music as inextricable from dance. Specific musical behaviours of West Africans retained by New World populations include the tendency towards variable intonation of the 3rd and 7th of the scale which Waterman allows 'has occasionally been noted in West African musics' (he dubs it 'the blues scale'); 'contrapuntal duet, with or without a recurrent chorus phrase; use of song as a device for social control, venting of aggressions and contests of virtuosity; counter-clockwise circle dancing; use of falsetto; and ambiguity of sacred and secular music' (1952, p.212).

The particular processes of social dynamics by which this acculturation has taken place were developed by Herskovits and taken over by Waterman. They are 'syncretism' and 'reinterpretation'. Of syncretism Herskovits says: 'Under contact elements of a culture are more effectively retained in the degree that they bear resemblance to newly experienced patterns of behavior or institutions. Syncretism [is] the tendency to identify those patterns in a new culture with similar elements in the old one, enabling persons experiencing the contact to move from one to the other with psychological ease' (1966, p.57). Waterman points out that there is no lack of elements common to African and European music capable of being syncretized. He cites basic scale characteristics and the deliberate use of vertical harmony. 'Greatly increased understanding of the distribution of musical characteristics over the world made it possible to recognize that in contrast to the "never the twain shall meet" hypothesis of Hornbostel, basic scale characteristics, and particularly the frequent deliberate use of harmony were shared by West African and European musical traditions' (1963, p.84). Waterman believed furthermore that there was a prehistorical reason for these fortuitous similarities in the existence of a harmony – and diatonic scale – using the belt of cultures that originally occupied the western third of the Old World land mass (1952, p.207). He felt that 'a broad intrusive belt of Arabic and Arabic-influenced music' has 'masked the previous existence of a harmony-using belt of cultures established earlier in the area.' He cites no studies by students of neolithic culture that may or may not have brought corroborating evidence to bear on such a hypothesis, and we are left with an innuendo concerning ultimate origins, subsequent divergence and re-assimilation.

Collecting and study of Afro-American music from around the Atlantic continued through the 1930s and 1940s. Although some opponents of the African origins notion remained stalwart (Guy B. Johnson and George Pullen Jackson) the impact of Herskovits's thought was felt in ever-widening circles, especially in the emerging field of jazz research. Ernest Borneman (1946) and Rudi Blesh (1946) wrote histories of black music and jazz from an unabashed ethno-historical perspective inconceivable before the 1940s. It is safe to say that Herskovits's contribution, as applied to Afro-American music by Waterman, Alan Merriam and others, laid a theoretical foundation on which the majority of serious writing would subsequently be based.

Bibliography

R. Jobson: *The Golden Trade* (London, 1623/*R*1968); excerpts repr. in E. Southern, ed.: *Readings* (1971, 2/1983), 1

T. Jefferson: *Notes on the State of Virginia, Written in the Year 1781* (Paris, 1782)

B. Edwards: *The History, Civil and Commercial, of the British Colonies in the West Indies* (London, 1793–1801); excerpts repr. in J. D. Abrahams and J. F. Szwed, eds. (1983), 291

R. Allen: *A Collection of Hymns and Spiritual Songs by Various Authors: by Richard Allen, Minister of the African Methodist Episcopal Church* (Philadelphia, PA, 1801); excerpts repr. in E. Southern, ed.: *Readings* (1971, 2/1983), 52

G. Pinckard: *Notes on the West Indies* (London, 1806); excerpts repr. in J. D. Abrahams and J. F. Szwed, eds. (1983), 293

T. E. Bowdich: *Mission from Cape Coast Castle to Ashantee* (London, 1819); excerpts repr. in E. Southern, ed.: *Readings* (1971, 2/1983), 8

J. F. Watson: *Methodist Error, or, Friendly Christian Advice to those Methodists who indulge in Extravagant Religious Emotions* (Trenton, NJ, 1819); excerpts repr. in E. Southern, ed.: *Readings* (1971, 2/1983), 62

J. K.[innard]: 'Who are our National Poets?', *Knickerbocker Magazine*, xxvi (1845), 331; repr. in B. Jackson, ed. (1967), 23

F. Bremer: *Hemmen i den nya veriden* (Stockholm, 1853–4); Eng. trans. as *Homes of the New World: Impressions of America* (New York, 1853–); excerpts repr. in E. Southern, ed.: *Readings* (1971, 2/1983), 103

Y. S. Nathanson: 'Negro Minstrelsy – ancient and modern', *Putnam's Monthly*, v (1855); repr. in B. Jackson, ed. (1967), 36

C.W.D.: 'Contraband Singing', *Dwight's Journal of Music*, xix (1861), 182; repr. in B. Jackson, ed. (1967), 55

J. M. McKim: 'Negro Songs', *Dwight's Journal of Music*, xix (1862), 148

L. McKim Garrison: 'Songs of the Port Royal "Contraband"', *Dwight's Journal of Music*, xxi (1862), 254; repr. in B. Jackson, ed. (1967), 57

F. A. Kemble: *Journal of a Residence on a Georgian Plantation in 1838–1839* (London, 1863/*R*1961); excerpts repr. in G. Chase (2/1966), 232

H. G. Spaulding: 'Under the Palmetto', *Continental Monthly*, iv (1863), 188; excerpts repr. in B. Jackson, ed. (1967), 64, and in B. Katz (1969), 3

W. F. Allen, C. P. Ware and L. McKim Garrison: *Slave Songs of the United States* (New York, 1867/*R*1929, 1971)

J. Eights: 'Pinkster Festivities in Albany', *Collections on the History of Albany*, ed. J. Munsell (Albany, NY, 1867), 323; repr. in E. Southern, ed.: *Readings* (1971, 2/1983), 41

T. W. Higginson: 'Negro Spirituals', *Atlantic Monthly*, xix (1867), 685; repr. in B. Jackson, ed. (1967), 82

———: *Army Life in a Black Regiment* (Boston, MA, 1870); excerpts repr. in E. Southern, ed.: *Readings* (1971, 2/1983), 175

J. M. Trotter: *Music and Some Highly Musical People* (Boston, MA, 1878/R1968); excerpts repr. in E. Southern, ed.: *Readings* (1971, 2/1983), 142

J. B. T. M[arsh]: *The Story of the Jubilee Singers, with their Songs* (Boston, MA, 1875)

F. T. Crane: 'Plantation Folk-Lore', *Popular Science Monthly*, xviii (1881), 824; repr. in B. Jackson, ed. (1967), 157

G. W. Cable: 'The Dance in Place Congo', *Century Magazine*, xxxi (1886), 517

———: 'Creole Slave Songs', *Century Magazine*, xxxi (1886), 807

F. J. Turner: 'The Significance of the Frontier in American History', *Annual Report for 1893 of the American Historical Association* (1893/R1961), 199

R. Wallaschek: *Primitive Music: an Inquiry into the Origin and Development of Music: Songs, Instruments, Dances and Pantomimes of Savage Races* (London, 1893/R1970, enl. 2/1903 as *Anfänge der Tonkunst*)

A. Dvořák: 'Music in America', *Harper's New Monthly Magazine*, xc (1895), 428; repr. in B. Jackson, ed. (1969), 263

C. L. Edwards: *Bahama Songs and Stories: a Contribution to Folklore* (Boston, MA, 1895)

E. Hallowell: *Calhoun Plantation Songs* (Boston, MA, 1901–07)

W. E. B. DuBois: *The Souls of Black Folk* (Chicago, IL, 1903); excerpts repr. in E. Southern, ed.: *Readings* (1971, 2/1983), 203

C. Peabody: 'Notes on Negro Music', *Journal of American Folk-Lore*, xvi (1903), 148

T. Fenner, ed.: *Religious Folk Songs of the Negro as Sung on the Plantations* (Hampton, VA, 1909, enl. 5/1918)

H. W. Odum: 'Folk-song and Folk-poetry as found in the Secular Songs of the Southern Negroes', *Journal of American Folk-Lore*, xxiv (1911), 255–94, 351–96

H. E. Krehbiel: *Afro-American Folksongs: a Study in Racial and National Music* (New York, 1914/R1962)

J. W. Work: *Folk Song of the American Negro* (Nashville, TN, 1915/R1969)

W. E. B. DuBois: 'Phonograph Records', *The Crisis*, xxi/4 (1921), 152

N. G. J. Ballanta: *Saint Helena Island Spirituals* (New York, 1925)

J. W. Johnson and J. R. Johnson, eds.: *The Book of American Negro Spirituals* (New York, 1925/R1940, 1969)

H. W. Odum and G. B. Johnson: *The Negro and his Songs: a Study in Typical Negro Songs of the South* (Chapel Hill, NC, 1925)

D. Scarborough: *On the Trail of Negro Folk-songs* (Cambridge, MA, 1925)

W. C. Handy: *Blues: an Anthology* (New York, 1926/R1949, 1972)

J. W. Johnson and J. R. Johnson, eds.: *The Second Book of Negro Spirituals* (New York, 1926/R1940, 1969)

H. W. Odum and G. B. Johnson: *Negro Workaday Songs* (Chapel Hill, NC, 1926)

E. M. von Hornbostel: 'African Negro Music', *Africa*, i/1 (1928), 30–62; repr. in *International Institute of African Languages and Cultures: Memorandum*, iv (London, 1928), 1–35

M. Metfessel: *Phonophotography in Folk Music: American Negro Songs in New Notation* (Chapel Hill, NC, 1928)

N. I. White: *American Negro Folksongs* (Cambridge, MA, 1928)

G. B. Johnson: *John Henry: Tracking down a Negro Legend* (Chapel Hill, NC, 1929)

I. Goldberg: *Tin Pan Alley* (New York, 1930/R1961)

M. A. Grissom: *The Negro Sings a New Heaven* (Chapel Hill, NC, 1930/R1969)

G. B. Johnson: *Folk Culture on St Helena Island, South Carolina* (Chapel Hill, NC, 1930/R1968)

L. W. Chapell: *John Henry: a Folk-lore Study* (Jena, 1933)

N. Cunard, ed.: *Negro: Anthology Made by Nancy Cunard, 1931–1933* (New York, 1933)

M. Cuney-Hare: 'Negro Music in Puerto Rico', *Negro: Anthology Made by Nancy Cunard, 1931–1933*, ed. N. Cunard (New York, 1933)

G. P. Jackson: *White Spirituals in the Southern Uplands* (New York, 1933/R1964)

H. H. Roberts: 'Jamaica Negro "Digging Sings"', *Negro: Anthology Made by Nancy Cunard, 1931–1933*, ed. N. Cunard (New York, 1933)

J. Lomax and A. Lomax: *American Ballads and Folksongs* (New York, 1934)

Z. N. Hurston: *Mules and Men* (Philadelphia, PA, 1935/R1963)

M. Cuney-Hare: *Negro Musicians and their Music* (Washington, DC, 1936/R1974)

L. Gellert: *Negro Songs of Protest* (New York, 1936)

M. J. Herskovits and F. Herskovits: *Suriname Folklore* (New York, 1936) [with musicological transcriptions and analysis by M. Kolinski]

A. Locke: *The Negro and his Music* (New York, 1936/R1969)

W. Sargent: *Jazz Hot and Hybrid* (New York, 1938/R1959)

F. Ramsey Jr and C. E. Smith, eds.: *Jazzmen* (New York, 1939/R1967)

J. W. Work: *American Negro Songs and Spirituals: a Comprehensive Collection of 230 Folk Songs, Religious and Secular; with a Foreword* (New York, 1940/Rn.d.)

M. J. Herskovits: *The Myth of the Negro Past* (Boston, MA, 1942/R1958)

H. Panassié: *The Real Jazz*, trans. by A. S. Williams (New York, 1942/R1960, 1967)

L. Parrish: *Slave Songs of the Georgia Sea Islands* (New York, 1942/R1965)

G. P. Jackson: *White and Negro Spirituals: their Life Span and Kinship* (New York, 1943/R1975)

M. J. Herskovits: 'Drums and Drummers in Afro-Brazilian Cult Life', *MQ*, xxx/4 (1944), 47; repr. in M. J. Herskovits, ed.: *The New World Negro* (1966/R1969), 183

——: 'Problem, Method and Theory in Afro-American Studies', *Afroamerica*, i (1945), 5; repr. in M. J. Herskovits, ed.: *The New World Negro* (1966/R1969), 43

R. Blesh: *Shining Trumpets* (New York, 1946, 4/1958)

E. Bornemann: *A Critic Looks at Jazz* (London, 1946)

W. J. Grayson: 'The Autobiography of William John Grayson', *South Carolina Historical and Genealogical Magazine*, xlviii (1947), 125

R. Waterman: 'Hot Rhythm in Negro Music', *JAMS*, i/1 (1948), 24

J. Lomax and A. Lomax: *Our Singing Country: a Second Volume of American Ballads and Folk Songs* (New York, 1949)

L. D. Turner: *Africanisms in the Gullah Dialect* (Chicago, IL, 1949)

J. W. Work: 'Changing Patterns in Negro Folk Songs', *Journal of American Folk-Lore*, lxii (1949), 136

B. H. B. Latrobe: *Impressions Respecting New Orleans: Diary & Sketches, 1818–1820*, ed. S. Wilson Jr (New York, 1952)

R. A. Waterman: 'African Influence on the Music of the Americas', *Acculturation in the Americas*, ed. S. Tax (Chicago, IL, 1952), 207

G. Chase: *America's Music: From the Pilgrims to the Present* (New York, 1955, rev. 2/1966)

D. K. Wilgus: *Anglo-American Folk Song Scholarship since 1898* (New Brunswick, NJ, 1959) [see Appx I, 'The Negro-White Spiritual']

N. Leonard: *Jazz and the White Americans: the Acceptance of a New Art Form* (Chicago, IL, 1962)

R. A. Waterman: 'On Flogging a Dead Horse: Lessons learned from the Africanisms Controversy', *EM*, vii/2 (1963), 83

M. J. Herskovits, ed.: *The New World Negro: Selected Papers in Afroamerican Studies* (1966/R1969)

B. Jackson, ed.: *The Negro and His Folklore in Nineteenth-century Periodicals* (Austin, TX, 1967)

R. Ottley and W. Weatherby, eds.: *The Negro in New York: an Informal Social History* (New York, 1967)

E. Southern: *The Music of Black Americans: a History* (New York, 1971, 2/1983)

——, ed.: *Readings in Black American Music* (New York, 1971, 2/1983)

J. Lovell Jr: *Black Song: the Forge and the Flame* (New York, 1972)

P. Maultsby: 'Selective Bibliography: U.S. Black Music', *EM*, xix (1975), 421

L. Malson: *Histoire du jazz et de la musique afro-américaine* (Paris, 1976)

D. Epstein: *Sinful Tunes and Spirituals: Black Folk Music to the Civil War* (Urbana, IL, 1977)

D. Horn: *The Literature of American Books and Folk Music Collections: a Fully Annotated Bibliography* (Metuchen, NJ, 1977)

L. W. Levine: *Black Culture and Black Consciousness* (New York, 1977)

I. V. Jackson-Brown: *Afro-American Gospel Music: a Bibliography* (Westport, CT, 1979)

D. R. DeLerma: *Bibliography of Black Music* (Westport, CT, 1981–)

J. D. Abrahams and J. F. Szwed, eds.: *After Africa: Extracts from British Travel Accounts* (New Haven, CT, 1983) [see especially entries 'Drums', 'Dance', 'Music', 'Songs']

S. A. Floyd Jr: *Black Music in the United States: an Annotated Bibliography of Selected Reference and Research Materials* (New York, 1983)

4. CANADA

James Robbins

The products of inquiry into the music of Canada's and Greenland's ethnic groups yielded results of several kinds: incidental descriptions in explorers' or travellers' reports and in novels; collections of songs; ethnographic, analytical and comparative studies; and institutions for the study, preservation and promotion of traditional musics. In Canada, the division between scholarly and other types of activity, such as missionary, commercial and political pursuits, has not always been clear.

Early reports of explorers, travellers and novelists

Jacques Cartier observed Indian singing and dancing on his first (1534) and second (1535–6) voyages to Canada; those events recorded in his travel accounts took place after exchanges of gifts between his crew and natives (Biggar, 1924, pp.62, 134). After one such exchange with the Iroquois of Hochelaga, Cartier's crew themselves provided music with 'trompettes et aultres instrumens de musicque'; this exposure to European music was well received (Biggar, 1924, p.167).

The first known transcriptions of Indian songs were made by Marc Lescarbot (*c*1570–*c*1630) during his stay at Port Royal (near Annapolis, Royal Nova Scotia) in 1606–7; three Micmac Indian melodies sung by a medicine man were published along with a description of typical performance in his *Histoire de la Nouvelle-France* (1617, vi, p.729). While the notation is in solfège syllables, without rhythmic indication, the same songs were republished, harmonized, with rhythmic notation in Father Gabriel Sagard Théodat's *Histoire du Canada* (1636). Sagard had previously recorded part of the text of a Wyandot (Huron) dance song collected during his stay among the Wyandot during the winter of 1623–4 and first published in his earlier version of the *Histoire, Le Grand Voyage du Pays des Hvrons* (1632). Sagard's detailed description emphasizes the importance of dreams in curative singing and dancing. For purposes of comparison, both Lescarbot and Sagard provided transcriptions of two Tupinambá songs collected in Brazil by Jean de Léry, which have since been confused with the Canadian songs by numerous writers (e.g. Rousseau).

Notable among the many references to Indian music by later missionaries are the descriptions of Iroquois singing, drumming and dancing in the diary of Paul Le Jeune (1591–1664) made during his tenure as superior of the Canadian missions from 1632–9 (Thwaites, 1959, v, p.27, vi, p.183ff). In the manuscript 'Recit des voyages et des découvertes du Père Jacques Marquette de la Compagnie du Jésus en l'année 1673,' held in Chantilly, there is a description of a Calumet ceremony performed by the Illinois Indians and notation of 'quelqu'une des Chansons qu'ils ont coûtume de chanter' (Thwaites, 1959, lix, p.136 – the description of the dance is found on pp.130– 36, an inaccurately copied version of the transcription in Thwaites's notes, p.311, a facsimile of the recit version in R. Stevenson, 1973, 'Written Sources', p.20). The transcriber and source of the melody are uncertain; it indeed might be a Calumet song transcribed by Marquette, but Delanglez speculated that it is a song inserted by the editor of the manuscript, Claude Dablon (1619–97), who could have collected it on his 1670 trip to present-day Wisconsin (Delanglez, 1946, p.240). Dablon had commented on 'quelques airs très mélodieux qu'ils [the Oumami, one of the Illinois Nations, in present-day Wisconsin] chantoient de très bon accord' (Thwaites, 1959, lv, p.204). The transcriber remarked on the inadequacy of Western notation to transcribe those very features that gave the melody 'tout la grace'. This, in addition to confronting one of the central problems of transcription, makes unlikely a third possibility, namely that Dablon, a musician, recorded the song as sung by Louis Jolliet, Marquette's companion, who had lost his journal when his boat capsized in the St Lawrence River and consequently dictated an account of the journey to Dablon.

Travel accounts such as those by Louis-Armand de Lahontan (1703), Pehr Kalm (1770–71) and Isaac Weld (1799) describe music, dance and instruments of Indians in areas around the lower Great Lakes and St Lawrence River. Early references to music of Indians in the Queen Charlotte Islands (as well as a transcription from Baranof Island, Alaska) are found in William Beresford's *A Voyage Round the World* (1789).

The Danish missionary Hans Egede described several types of songs, including drum-singing in Greenland (1741, p.85), and provides the text with translation of a song by a West Greenland Inuit, Frederick Christian, which clearly shows the missionary's influence. David Cranz provided some description of Greenland melody (although without transcription) in *Historie von Grönland*, i (1765, p.229). The journal of explorer W. E. Parry contains transcriptions (probably the first of Eskimo music) and descriptions of East Greenland Eskimo singing (1824, p.541). The earliest European observation of music of the Smith Sound (Polar) Eskimo appears to have been made by John Ross during his 1818 expedition; notation of Smith Sound songs made by Kane at Cape York during the period 1853–5 (both are cited in Stein, 1902, pp.338–39). An early regional comparison was made when Ross noted differences between the singing and dance of Inuit in the vicinity of Repulse Bay and that of Greenlanders (Ross, 1835, p.287). Scattered reports of Inuit drum-dancing in Ungava appear in the late 19th century (e.g. Lucien M. Turner, 1894).

Both Kalm and Weld were among early travellers to comment on the singing of French colonists and their descendants, as was François-Alexandre-Frédéric, duc de La Rochefoucauld-Liancourt (*Voyage dans les Etats-Unis d'Amérique*, 1799). Weld and La Rochefoucauld were among the first to mention the songs of voyageurs, which were to spark the interest of European visitors for the next 50 years.

According to L. F. R. Masson (1889–90), the Norwegian Ferdinand Wentzel collected voyageur songs in the early 19th century. Perhaps the first international hit song associated with Canada was Thomas Moore's 'Canadian Boat Song' (1805). Although Moore was inspired by hearing the voyageur song 'Dans mon chemin j'ai rencontré' on a boat trip on the St Lawrence in 1804, and said that he wrote new words 'to an air, which our boatmen sung to us very frequently' (Moore, 1806, p.305), he later claimed to have totally reworked the 'glee' (i.e. tune), preserving only the 'time' (Moore, 1840, p.xxiii). John Bradbury mentioned hearing 'Trois beaux canards' in *Travels in the Interior of America* (1817), and John M. Duncan described voyageur singing, comparing the songs to 'our Scotish [sic] airs' (1823, ii, p.121). Texts of voyageur songs were transcribed by John MacTaggart, who described the composition of 'extemporaneous songs, somewhat smutty, but never intolerant' (1829, i, pp.254–5), and Anna Jameson (1839). By 1848, R. M. Ballantyne lamented the passing of voyageur singing as steamboats came into use on the Ottawa river, but in the late 1850s, Johann Georg Kohl (1808–78) observed the practice on the Great Lakes, and noted three types of songs, 'classified according to the nature of the work' (1859; Eng. trans., 1985, p.255). Throughout the 19th century numerous novelists and playwrights included descriptions and texts of French Canadian singing, ranging from passing remarks to virtual collections of song texts (Phillipe Aubert de Gaspé's *Les Anciens Canadiens*, 1863; see Laforte, 1973).

Indications of a parallel literature for English Canada exist, in which the most distinctive musical feature is Protestant hymn singing. C.H.C.'s travel account *It Blows, It Snows* (1846) describes ubiquitous hymn and psalm singing among English Canadians and in the household of a 'Pensylvania [sic] Dutchman', by former 'inhabitants of the Netherlands' (C.H.C., 1846, p.135). A remarkable description of lining out, with a transcription of 'St Paul's' showing 'the extraordinary slides and slurs [which] almost obliterated the notes of the original tune' lent local colour to Ralph Connor's historical novel *The Man from Glengarry: a Tale of the Ottawa* (1901, pp.127–41).

Early observations of secular social dancing are found among the writings of missionaries (e.g. Le Jeune, in Thwaites, 1959, ix, p.269). Numerous travellers' reports from the late 18th and early 19th centuries comment on the popularity of social dance in Canada, including Pierre de Sales Laterrière (père), who in the late 1760s saw 'contre-danses françoises et les menuets, qu'ils [the Canadians] entre-mêlent de danses angloises' (Garneau, ed., 1873, p.61). Pre-Confederation 'apple-bees' were described by W. L. Smith (1923), where settlers danced to fiddle music, or in the absence of a fiddle, to the same tunes whistled or sung through a paper-covered comb.

Folk music collections

FRENCH Throughout the 19th century, there was much collecting in Lower (French) Canada. Several early manuscript collections were made presumably for use by the collectors. These include an untitled notebook of French Canadian songs made in 1817 by Cécile Lagueux (possibly the earliest such manuscript) and a collection made by Edward Ermatinger, an employee of the Hudson's Bay Company from 1818–26; this latter was published in 1954 by Marius Barbeau as 'The Ermatinger Collection of Voyageur Songs (*c*1830)'.

A second type of song collection comprised publications for commercial sale. The first of these was *Canadian Airs* (1823), based on melodies collected by Lieut. George Back. The compilers supplied new texts for the melodies. During the period from the 1837 rebellion to the early years of Confederation, a number of song collections were published aimed at a Canadian market. Possibly the first was made by a law student, Jos. Laurin, *Le chansonnier canadien: ou, Nouveau recueil de chansons* (1838). Later similar collections included

Marius Barbeau

literary items as well as folk-song texts and some music. Two titles that went through several editions were *La lyre canadienne* 'par un amateur' (1847), and *Le chansonnier des collèges* (1850). The third edition of the latter was subsequently republished as *Le chansonnier des collèges mis en musique* (1860). A late example of this type of publication, aimed at expatriates, was *Le chansonnier canadien du Michigan* (1886).

In 1863, a collection of song texts appeared which, for the first time, included a study of the songs: F. A. Hubert LaRue's 'Les chansons populaires et historiques du Canada' (1863). This was followed two years later by the serial publication in *Le foyer canadien* of Ernest Gagnon's *Chansons populaires du Canada*, whose bound versions constituted this work's first edition (1865). Gagnon's work, which has gone through numerous editions and was for a time considered a comprehensive collection of Québecois folk songs, included studies of each song and a final analytical chapter. In the latter, he drew upon the racist scale theories of F.-J. Fétis (1784–1871) and d'Ortigue to explain a relationship of similar modality which he saw between plainchant and folk song. Gagnon does not postulate a historical connection via tradition but rather via virtuous stock. Musical material is not a matter of choice, as Rousseau would have it (Gagnon, 1880, p.322), but rather determined by character, and given that 'le peuple de nos campagnes canadiennes est un peuple à moeurs simples, honnête et religieux' (p.324), it necessarily follows that they would eschew chromaticism and leading tones. In some respects, Gagnon anticipated the work of 20th-century ethnomusicologists. For example, the notation of the melodies in the first edition included grace notes that were dropped from later editions in order to make them easier to sing. While the alterations were slight, they nevertheless show an awareness of different purposes and levels of detail in transcription; what Charles Seeger later called 'prescriptive' and 'descriptive' transcription. Gagnon made a Bartók-like distinction between two types of rhythm used in folk song:

> l'un appelé *poétique*, qui se combine avec la mesure; l'autre appellé *prosaïque* ou *oratoire*, qui n'est entravé par aucune mesure et qui est le rhythme propre du plain-chant (1880, p.195).

Several collections of French-Canadian folk song followed that of Gagnon, including Ernest Myrand's *Noëls anciens de la Nouvelle-France* (1899) and Julien Tiersot's *Forty-Four French Folk-songs and Variants from Canada, Normandy and Brittany* (1910). The important manuscript collection 'Annales musicales du Petit-Cap' was made by Monsigneur Thomas-Etienne Hamel between 1866 and 1908, now in the archives of the Séminaire de Québec.

In 1919, E.-Z. Massicotte (1867–1947) and Marius Barbeau (1883–1969; see illustration) collaborated on a collection published as 'Chants Populaires du Canada'. Massicotte had kept a notebook of folk songs in Quebec and Ontario between 1883 and 1911, but most of the songs in the 1919 article had been collected on cylinder recordings between 1917 and 1918. Barbeau transcribed the recordings, devising special symbols to provide accurate notation. Barbeau himself had been collecting songs in Quebec since 1916, ultimately assembling some 10,000 songs in manuscript or wax cylinder for the National Museum. In the proceedings of the 1919 *Veillées du bon vieux temps*, he included transcriptions of several instrumental pieces for violin or *guimbarde* (jew's harp) as well as a number of songs from Massicotte's collection (La Société historique de Montréal et la Société de Folklore d'Amérique [Section de Québec]; 1920; see pp.86–93ff). Throughout his life Barbeau continued to publish an enormous amount of French Canadian folk song under the auspices of the National Museum (e.g. *Romancero du Canada*, 1937). His motivations were as much nationalistic as scholarly; he felt Canadians should use their own folk music as a basis for artistic creation rather than regard Canadian music as epitomized by some set of 'variations banales pour piano, composées il y a un demi-siècle par un Allemand en voyage' (1920, p.4).

Barbeau's nationalism was shared by other promoters of folk song who did not necessarily share his concern for authentic presentation. The Abbé F.-X. Burque, in the preface to his *Chansonnier canadien-français* (1921), expressed the feeling that folk songs needed 'les retouches' so that they would remain popular; in particular problems such as poor grammar in the texts needed correction (pp.vii–viii).

In the 1920s, there was a return to the commercial presentation of traditional music collections, this time in the form of commercial recordings of *violoneux*, such as J. B. Roy for Victor. A new area for French Canadian folk-song collecting was entered in the 1940s when Father Anselme Chiasson and Brother Daniel Boudreau began publishing a series of collections of Acadian music from New Brunswick (1942, 1945, 1948, 1972, 1979).

BRITISH There are no extant manuscript collections of folk songs from Upper (English) Canada to parallel those of Ermatinger and Lagueux. However, there are several manuscript collections of instrumental music, for example, a 28-page manuscript book that belonged to the Ontario farmer Alan Ash (1800–89), containing waltzes, reels, galops, hornpipes and other dances, written on one staff by a professional hand. While broadsides are mentioned in modern ballad scholarship, they have not received the bibliographic attention of Lower Canadian chansonniers. The 19th-century commercial collections such as *Canadian National and Patriotic Songs* (1890) may have contained folk songs. Commercial publication of folk songs flourished in the early 20th century, particularly in the Maritimes. The first of a number of text collections by James Murphy appeared in 1902 (*Songs and Ballads of Newfoundland, Ancient and Modern*); he produced several subsequent collections of 'old songs' and 'sealers' songs' (1903, 1904, 1905, 1912, 1923, 1925). A collection made by the St John's merchant Gerald S. Doyle in 1927, *The Old-Time Songs and Poetry of Newfoundland*, went through four editions; in the 1940 edition, music was added. Later editions at least (e.g. 1955) were distributed free of cost; expenses were evidently covered by the inclusion (following a precedent set by Murphy) of advertisements for constipation remedies and other useful domestic items. J. M. Gibbon's popular collection *Canadian Folksongs, Old and New* (1927) contained songs from Gagnon's collection with English translations of the texts. Text-only collections known as 'come-all-ye's' appear from the late 1920s, for example, Stuart McCawley's *Cape Breton Come all ye* (1929). In 1925 the first recordings of traditional Anglo fiddling were made for commercial release by Apex.

A somewhat narrower range of material was collected by a number of folklorists beginning with a student of George Lyman Kittredge, W. Roy Mackenzie ('Ballad-Singing in Nova Scotia' (1909)) and *Ballads and Sea Songs from Nova Scotia* (1928). In his account of his collecting activities, *Quest of the Ballad*, which he wished to be 'free from taint of theory' (1919, p.xi), he explains that 'it is axiomatic that he who reads the newspaper shall cease to be a perpetuator of folk-lore' (1919, p.1). Two Vassar students, Elisabeth Greenleaf and Grace Mansfield, began collecting in Newfoundland in the early 1920s; and published the results in *Ballads and Sea Songs of Newfoundland* (1933). They were followed by Maud Karpeles, who, during two trips to Newfoundland in 1929 and 1930, collected 200 songs, some of which were published in *Folk Songs from Newfoundland* (1934). Cecil Sharp had planned visits to Newfoundland in 1918 and 1925 which were never made; Karpeles commented regretfully that 'the original settlement of Newfoundland is very much older than that of the Appalachian Mountains, but the island has not had the same immunity from modern civilization, for the sea does not isolate to the same extent as does a mountain range' (1934, p.iii). She typically excluded 'composed' songs from her collection (1934, p.iii). Around the same time, Helen Creighton, inspired by the work of Mackenzie, began collecting songs in Nova Scotia, at first transcribing them on the spot aided by a portable hand organ, and later using mechanical recording devices. The first of her many published collections was *Songs and Ballads from Nova Scotia* (1932/*R*1966), wherein she abided by the dictates of the English Folk-Song Society in classifying the songs as 'Good and worthy of publication' and 'Genuine, but better variants known elsewhere' (1966, p.xv); to her credit she published both categories. Phillips Barry included 39 songs from New Brunswick in 'Songs and Traditions of the Miramichi' (1935–7) as well as some texts collected in the southern part of the province in *British Ballads from Maine* (1929).

OTHER NON-NATIVE GROUPS Very few collections exist of music of other non-native groups in Canada or Greenland. 19th-century African-American music is represented by a late collection (Famous Canadian Jubilee Singers, *Plantation Lullabies. Songs Sung by the famous Canadian Jubilee Singers, The Royal Paragon Male Quartette and Imperial Orchestra, c* 1900). In 1903, Alexander Fraser published a collection 'The Gaelic Folk Songs of Canada'. Huff Fauset's *Folklore of Nova Scotia* (1931) contains 20 song texts mostly collected from blacks. Laura Boulton made recordings of Gaelic music in Nova Scotia in 1941 and of Ukrainian and Polish music in Winnipeg and Winnipeg Beach in 1942; the collections are in the Center for Studies in Ethnomusicology at Columbia University (Rahn, 1977). Oleksander Koshetz (or Koshyts') (1875–1944) preserved a number of Ukrainian folk songs in choral settings (e.g. Koshyts', 1949) and wrote on Ukrainian ritual songs (1945).

NATIVE-INDIAN Collection of native music has been primarily scholarly in intent. Almost all of the material cited here contains a substantial amount of ethnographic or analytic material in addition to the music collected. Among the early collectors of Indian songs were Gagnon (*Les Sauvages de l'Amérique et l'art musical*, 1907), Father Lionel de Saint-Georges Lindsay ('Notre-Dame de Lorette en la Nouvelle France' (1902)), and John Reade ('Some Wabanaki Songs . . .', 1887). The German-American anthropologist Franz Boas began collecting songs of West Coast Indians in the 1880s; his early publications (e.g. 'Chinook Songs', 1888; 'On Certain Songs and Dances of the Kwakiutl', 1888) inspired a generation of collecting activity in British Columbia by persons such as Henri Tate, Marius Barbeau, Edward Sapir, Thomas McIlwraith and James A. Teit. (Unpublished field material collected by the latter is used extensively in Wickwire, 1978.) 'Chinook Songs' remains a remarkable study in that it anticipates many later developments in ethnomusicology: it focusses on music in urban settings; acknowledges the impact of Christian missionaries on secular music; deals with acculturation; and deliberately presents data in the form of song texts – that is, shows sensitivity to what has become known as 'writing culture'. Teit, in British Columbia in the 1890s under the auspices of the Geological Survey of Canada, made some of the first phonograph recordings of Indian songs to be made in Canada; these were submitted by Boas to Otto Abraham and Erich M. von Hornbostel, who then transcribed and analysed them in 'Phonographierte Indianermelodien aus Britisch-Columbia' (1906). While most collections were made of individual tribes, Frances Densmore collected from a variety of 'tribes and locations' who had gathered at a BC hop-picking camp (1943).

Music of Eastern Woodlands Indians received considerable attention as well during this period. A. T. Cringan made cylinder recordings of Iroquois songs from c1898–1902; his transcriptions were published in 'Iroquois music' (1898) and later reports. In 1911, W. H. Mechling transcribed Malecite and Micmac songs in New Brunswick; the same year, Barbeau began recording songs of various native groups including Hurons, Algonquins and Iroquois. Both Mechling and Barbeau were collecting for the new Anthropology Division of the Museum Branch of the Geological Survey of Canada. In 1925, Gertrude Kurath began recording at the Six Nations Reserve (for her publications see Kealiinohomoku and Gillis, 1970).

Plains Indians in Canada were not subject to collecting activity before the recordings made of Blackfoot music in Alberta by Jane Richardson Hanks in 1939. Recorded collections, however, dating from the turn of the century, made in Montana by Grinnell (1897), McClintock (1898), Wissler (1903–4) and others, are important sources for Canadian music history; the native musicians in the prairie provinces at the time were not concerned with the national boundary (see Nettl, 1989, pp.18–21, 174–5). Descriptions of musical life in Canada among Plains natives from around the same time and earlier are found in the Annual Reports of the Department of Indian Affairs (see Witmer, 1982, pp.91–7).

Collections made in other areas include those by Pliny E. Goddard of Sarcee songs over the period 1905–44, and by Alden J. Mason of Sikani songs at Fort Rae in 1913 (Mason, 1946).

NATIVE-INUIT The first published collection of Inuit music, *Otte grønlanske Smaasange* (Godthaab, 1859), contains West Greenland melodies 'which are intermediate forms between European and Greenland songs' (Thuren, 1911, p.42); three of these, with eight other melodies recorded by Mrs Janssen appeared in A. P. Berggreen's *Folkesange og Melodier*, x (1870). These are remarkable among early collections of native music in that the music was apparently recorded by residents of the area, rather than visiting investigators.

The beginning of outside interest in Inuit music is marked by Boas's *The Central Eskimo* (1888), which contains 19 melodies, 15 newly collected. Other songs from the same expedition were published in three reports titled 'Eskimo Tales and Songs' in the *Journal of American Folklore* (Rink and Boas, 1889, 1894, 1897). The first of these contains an example of staffless notation for transcription. Most of the songs were collected on Baffin Island, with some comparative material from Greenland. Boas later worked with material collected by Capt. George Comer in 1897–9, who recorded four and a half hours of Inuit songs (and some hymns) on cylinders (Boas, 1901; see Lee, 1979, p.54). Robert Stein's chapter 'Eskimo music' (in Rudolf Kersting, ed., *The White World*, 1902; pp.337–56) contains 38 songs from the Smith Sound

(Polar) Eskimos, collected during the winter of 1899–1900. A collection was made in the following year from Northwest Greenland by William Thalbitzer, published in 'North-Greenlandic Contributions to Eskimo Folklore' (1904). When, in 1911, Hjalmar Thuren published 129 melodies from East Greenland, he felt able, on reviewing his and previous accomplishments, to state:

> We are thus in possession now of such an extensive material that we can lay claim to complete knowledge of the whole musical system of the Eskimo (1911).

Even so, collectors continued activities among Greenland and Canadian Inuit. The Norwegian composer and traveller Christian Leden made recordings in 1914 of Inuit music from the Keewatin (now housed at the Musée de Neuchâtel, Switzerland, with copies at the Canadian Museum of Civilization); he also collected music from Smith Sound and Angmagssalik in Greenland. Diamond Jenness recorded 137 songs while with the Canadian Arctic Expedition of 1913–18 which formed the basis for his and Helen H. Roberts's *Eskimo Songs: Songs of the Copper Eskimos* (1925). Other expeditions produced notable collections: five hours of music were recorded on Donald Baxter MacMillan's 1917 Croker Land expedition (see Lee, 1979, p.55); Rasmussen collected a large number of texts on the Fifth Thule Expedition (1921–4). In 1938, Jean Gabus recorded three hours of Caribou music from the area west of Hudson Bay; the collection of 78 rpm discs is housed in Neuchâtel and provided the basis for analytical work by Zygmunt Estreicher (e.g., 'La musique des Esquimaux-Caribous', 1948). During 1935–7 and 1946–7, Eric Holtved gathered song texts in the Thule district of Greenland (later published in 'The Polar Eskimos: Language and Folklore, i: Texts', 1951). Laura Boulton began recording music on the west coast of Hudson Bay in 1941, and later in 1942; her collections are housed at the Center for Studies in Ethnomusicology at Columbia University (see Rahn, 1977).

Synthesis and comparative work

Canadian examples have been used in many of the early efforts at comparison of world musics, including those by Marin Mersenne (*Harmonie universelle*, 1637) and Jean-Jacques Rousseau (*Dictionnaire de la musique*, 1768). Some of the pioneer works of ethnomusicology as a distinct discipline (*vergleichende Musikwissenschaft*) were based to a large extent on Canadian material, including those by Theodore Baker (*Über die Musik der nordamerikanischen Wilden*, 1882), and Carl Stumpf ('Lieder der Bellakula Indianer', 1886) as well as the aforementioned article by Abraham and Hornbostel, 'Phonographierte Indianermelodien aus Britisch Columbia' (1906). Studies by Julien Tiersot ('Notes d'ethnographie musicale: La musique chez les peuples indigènes de l'Amérique du Nord [États Unis et Canada]', 1910), Frances Densmore (*Chippewa Music*, 1910–13) and Frederick R. Burton (*American Primitive Music*, 1909), while dealing to a large extent with Indian music in the USA, included material from Canada.

Several attempts were made at broad area studies drawing on existing field reports from Canada or Greenland. Perhaps the first was Thuren's 'On the Eskimo music in Greenland' (1911), described in 1914 as 'one of the finest studies issued during the recent period' (Bingham, 1914, p.422). Bingham, in his survey of 'comparative musical science' to date, used melodies collected by Thuren as examples of 'melodies unfettered by the restrictions of scale', demonstrating that '[t]he interval is not the mental unit with which he [the primitive musician] works. His unit is the motif' (Bingham, 1914, p.427). The Greenland examples provided ammunition for a feisty relativistic effort to 'shatter one's provincial conviction that the only true God-given music must be cast in our own diatonic modern-European mould', with a consequent reappraisal of European music history (Bingham, 1914, p.429). George Herzog ('Musical Styles in North America', 1930) studied geographical trait distribution of North American Indian music; Roberts pursued the same end of determining musical style areas, basing her study on trait clustering in areas accepted as standard in language-distribution studies (Roberts, 1936). A strictly Canadian example was Margaret Sargent's 'The Native and Primitive Music of Canada' (1942).

While all of the aforementioned works in this section deal with native music of North America, Cyrus MacMillan's PhD dissertation, *The Folk Songs of Canada* (1909), treated French Canadian music. And Barbeau wrote comparative studies that went beyond the confines of the continent, including 'Asiatic Survivals in Indian Songs' (1934) and 'Slavonic Cultural Influences on the North Pacific Coast' (unpublished).

Institutions

In 1910, the German-born anthropologist and linguist Edward Sapir was hired to head the newly established Anthropology Division of the Museum Branch of the National Geographical Survey, in Ottawa. Barbeau was appointed as ethnologist and anthropologist in 1911 and began extensive collecting of Canadian music. Diamond Jenness succeeded Sapir in 1926. The museum (restructured and renamed the National Museum of Canada in 1927; then the National Museum of Man; and as of summer 1989 the Canadian Museum of Civilization) continued, and continues, to be the stimulus and repository for much of the ethnomusicological work done in Canada. The Ontario Provincial Museum (Norman School) was the repository for some 50 cylinders of Iroquois, Seneca and Cayuga songs recorded by A. T. Cringan as well as a collection of instruments started in the 19th century; by the 1920s they were donated to the Ethnology Department of the Royal Ontario Museum.

The Mary Mellish Archibald collection, in the R. P. Bell Library of Mt Allison University, was established in 1905 and contains some folk music. Of considerable importance was the founding in 1944 of the Archives de folklore at Laval University (Quebec City) by Luc Lacourcière, one of Barbeau's students. The Archives initiated a publication series in 1946. Summer courses in folklore and folk music were offered at Laval in 1939; a chair in folklore, occupied until 1977 by Lacourcière, was established in 1944.

Festivals have been and continue to be important focusses of ethnomusicological activity in Canada. In 1919, the Société historique de Montréal and the Quebec Section of the American Folklore Society put on the first 'Veillées [or soirées] du bon vieux temps' at the Bibliothèque Saint-Sulpice (later the Bibliotèque National du Québec). The programme, which covered two evenings and was prepared by Massicotte and Barbeau, included performances of traditional music, story telling, lectures and slide shows on folk art and architecture. The Veillées brought together traditional musicians from Quebec, scholars and professional performers in front of the Montreal audience from 1921 to 1941. One of the main motivations for these festivals was described by Victor Morin, head of the Montreal Historical Society, who noted that while efforts had long been made to preserve French language and laws in Quebec, 'nos traditions seules paraissent avoir été négligées' (La Société historique de Montréal and la Société de Folklore d'Amérique (Section de Québec), *Veillées du bon vieux temps*, Montréal: G. Ducharme, 1920, p.12).

A somewhat less idealistic motive lay behind the CPR Festivals, organized for the Canadian Pacific Railway by John Murray Gibbon. A total of 17 festivals were held at CPR hotels in various cities from 1927 to 1931. Their purpose as far as their sponsor was concerned was to promote tourism. The first, the Canadian Folk Song and Handicraft Festival, was held in Quebec City; the same year a Highland/Scottish Gathering and Music Festival was held in Banff. The 1928 New Canadian Folksong and Handicraft Festival in Winnipeg featured songs of settlers of 'European Continental extraction'; that same year, Indian Week took place in Banff. In the 1929 Regina Great West Canadian Folksong, Folkdance and Handicraft Festival, almost 30 ethnic groups were featured – far more than had received scholarly attention in the literature at that time.

Bibliography

M. Lescarbot: *Histoire de la Nouvelle-France* (Paris, 1609, 3/1617)

G. Sagard Théodat: *Le Grand Voyage du Pays des Hvrons* (Paris, 1632)

——: *Histoire du Canada* (Paris, 1636)

M. Mersenne: *Harmonie universelle* (Paris, 1637)

L.-A. de Lahontan: *Nouveaux voyages dans l'Amérique septentironale* (The Hague, 1703)

H. Egede: *Det gamle Grønlands nye Perlustration eller Naturel-Historie* (Copenhagen, 1741; Eng. trans., 2/1818 as *A Description of Greenland*)

D. Cranz: *Histoire von Grönland* (Leipzig, 1765)

J.-J. Rousseau: *Dictionnaire de la musique* (Paris, 1768/*R*1969)

P. Kalm: *Travels into North America* (London, 1770–71/*R*1966; Eng. trans. of *En resa til Norra America*)

W. Beresford: *A Voyage Round the World: but More Particularly to the North-West Coast of America: Performed in 1785, 1786, 1787 and 1788 . . . by Capt. George Dixon* (London, 1789)

F.-A.-F. de La Rochefoucauld-Liancourt: *Voyage dans les Etats-Unis d'Amérique fait en 1795, 1796 et 1797, par La Rochefoucauld-Liancourt*, ii: *Excursion dans le Haut-Canada* (Paris, 1799)

I. Weld: *Travels through the States of North America and the Provinces of Upper and Lower Canada, during the Years 1795, 1796, and 1797* (London, 1799)

T. Moore: *Canadian Boat Song* (London, 1805)

——: *Epistles, Odes and Other Poems* (London, 1806)

J. Bradbury: *Travels in the Interior of America, in the Year 1809, 1810, and 1811* (London, 1817, 2/1819)

Canadian Airs (London, 1823)

J. M. Duncan: *Travels through Part of the United States and Canada in 1818 and 1819* (Glasgow, 1823)

W. E. Parry: *Journal of a Second Voyage for the Discovery of a North-West Passage from the Atlantic to the Pacific* (London, 1824)

J. MacTaggart: *Three Years in Canada: an Account of the Actual State of 1826–7–8*, i (London, 1829)

J. Ross: *Narrative of a Second Voyage in Search of Northwest Passage and of a Residence in the Arctic Regions During the Years 1829, 1830, 1831, 1832, 1833* (London, 1835)

J. Laurin: *Le chansonnier canadien: ou, Nouveau recueil de chansons* (Quebec, 1838)

A. Jameson: *Winter Studies and Summer Rambles in Canada, 1836–37* (New York, 1839/*R*1923)

T. Moore: *The Poetical Works of Thomas Moore, Collected by Himself*, ii: *Juvenile Poems, Poems Relating to America* (London, 1840)

C.H.C.: *It Blows, It Snows* (Dublin, 1846)

La lyre canadienne (Quebec, 1847)

R. M. Ballantyne: *Hudson's Bay* (Edinburgh, 1848)

Le Chansonnier des collèges (Quebec, 1850, rev. 3/1860)

Otte grønlanske smaasanges (Godthaab, 1859)

J. G. Kohl: *Kitchi-Gami: oder Erzählungen vom Obern See. Ein Beitrag zur Characteristik der amerikanischen Indianer* (Bremen, 1859; Eng. trans., 1860/*R*1985)

P. A. de Gaspé: *Les anciens Canadiens* (Quebec, 1863)

F. A. Hubert LaRue: 'Les chansons populaires et historiques du Canada', *Le foyer canadien*, i (1863), 321–84

E. Gagnon: *Chansons populaires du Canada* (Quebec, 1865, 7/1880)

T.-E. Hamel: 'Annales musicales du Petit-Cap' (Quebec, 1866–1908) [unpubd MS collection]

A. P. Berggreen: *Folke-Sange og Melodie*, x (Copenhagen, 3/1870)

M. A. Garneau, ed.: *Mémoires de P. de Sales Laterrière et de ses traverses* (Quebec, 1873)

T. Baker: *Über die Musik der nordamerikanischen Wilden* (Leipzig, 1882)

Le chansonnier canadien du Michigan (Michigan, 1886)

C. Stumpf: 'Lieder der Bellakula Indianer', *VMW*, ii (1886), 405

J. Reade: 'Some Wabanaki Songs', *Transactions of the Royal Society of Canada*, ser. 1, v/2 (1887), 1

F. Boas: *The Central Eskimo* (Washington, DC, 1888)

——: 'Chinook Songs', *Journal of American Folklore*, i (1888), 220

——: 'On Certain Songs and Dances of the Kwakiutl of British Columbia', *Journal of American Folklore*, i (1888), 49

L. F. R. Masson: *Les bourgeois de la compagnie du Nord-Ouest*, i (Quebec, 1889–90)

H. Rink and F. Boas: 'Eskimo Tales and Songs', *Journal of American Folklore*, ii (1889), 123; vii (1894), 45; x (1897), 109

Canadian National and Patriotic Songs (Toronto, 1890)

L. M. Turner: 'Ethnology of the Ungava District', *Eleventh Annual Report of the Bureau of Ethnology to the Secretary of the Smithsonian Institution 1889–90* (Washington, DC, 1894), 167–350; repr. as L. M. Turner: *Indians and Eskimos in the Quebec-Labrador Peninsula: Ethnology of the Ungava District* (Quebec, 1979)

A. T. Cringan: 'Iroquois Music', *Report of the Minister of Education of Ontario* (Toronto, 1898), appx

E. Myrand: *Noëls anciens de la Nouvelle-France* (Quebec, 1899)

Famous Canadian Jubilee Singers: *Plantation Lullabies. Songs Sung by the Famous Canadian Jubilee Singers, The Royal Paragon Male Quartette and Imperial Orchestra* (Hamilton)

F. Boas: *The Eskimo of Baffin Land and Hudson Bay* (New York, 1901)

R. Connor: *The Man from Glengarry: a Tale of the Ottawa* (Chicago, IL, New York and Toronto, 1901)

L. de St.-G. Lindsay: 'Notre-Dame de Lorette en la Nouvelle France, étude historique', xii: 'La langue et les chants des Hurons', *La revue canadienne*, xl (1901), 266

J. Murphy: *Songs and Ballads of Newfoundland, Ancient and Modern* (St John's, 1902)

R. Stein: 'Eskimo Music', *The White World*, ed. R. Kersting (New York, 1902), 337

A. Fraser: 'The Gaelic Folk Songs of Canada', *Transactions of the Royal Society of Canada*, ser. 3, ix/2 (1903), 49

J. Murphy: *Songs and Ballads of Terra Nova* (St John's, 1903)

——: *Songs of Our Land* (St John's, 1904)

W. Thalbitzer: 'North-Greenlandic Contributions to Eskimo Folk-lore', *Meddelelser om Grønland*, xxxi (1904), 375

J. Murphy: *Murphy's Sealers' Song Book* (St John's, 1905)

O. Abraham and E. M. von Hornbostel: 'Phonographierte Indianermelodien aus Britisch-Columbia', *Boas Anniversary Volume* (New York, 1906), 447

E. Gagnon: *Les sauvages de l'Amérique et l'art musical* (Quebec, 1907)

F. R. Burton: *American Primitive Music* (New York, 1909)

W. R. Mackenzie: 'Ballad-Singing in Nova Scotia', *Journal of American Folklore*, xxii (1909), 327

C. MacMillan: 'The Folk Songs of Canada' (diss., Harvard U., 1909)

F. Densmore: *Chippewa Music* (Washington, DC, 1910–13)

J. Tiersot: 'Notes d'ethnographie musicale: La musique chez les peuples indigènes de l'Amérique du Nord (Etats Unis et Canada)', *SIMG*, xi (1909–10), 141–231; repr. as *Notes d'ethnographie musicale (Deuxième Série): La musique chez les peuples indigènes de l'Amérique du Nord (Etats-Unis et Canada)* (Paris, 1910)

——: *Forty-Four French Folk-songs and Variants from Canada, Normandy and Brittany* (New York, 1910)

H. Thuren: 'On the Eskimo Music in Greenland', *Meddelelser om Grønland*, xl (1911)

J. Murphy: *Old Songs of Newfoundland* (St John's, 1912)

W. V. Bingham: 'Five Years of Progress in Comparative Musical Science', *Psychological Bulletin*, ix/11 (1914), 421

W. R. Mackenzie: *Quest of the Ballad* (Princeton, NJ, 1919)

E.-Z. Massicotte and C.-M. Barbeau: 'Chants Populaires du Canada', *Journal of American Folklore*, xxxii (1919), 1–89

C.-M. Barbeau: 'Preface', in 'La Société historique de Montréal et la Société de Folklore d'Amérique (Section de Québec)': *Veillées du bon vieux temps* (Montréal, 1920), 1

'La Société historique de Montréal et la Société de Folklore d'Amérique (Section de Québec)': *Veillées du bon vieux temps* (Montréal, 1920)

F.-X. Burque: *Chansonnier canadien-français* (Québec City, 1921)

J. Murphy: *Songs their Fathers Sung, for Fishermen. Old Time Ditties* (St John's, 1923)

W. L. Smith: *The Pioneers of Old Ontario* (Toronto, 1923)

H. P. Biggar: *The Voyages of Jacques Cartier Published from the Originals with Translations. Notes and Appendices* (Ottawa, 1924)

D. Jenness and H. H. Roberts: *Eskimo Songs: Songs of the Copper Eskimos* (Ottawa, 1925)

J. Murphy: *Songs Sung by Old-Time Sealers of Many Years Ago* (St John's, 1925)

G. S. Doyle: *The Old-Time Songs and Poetry of Newfoundland* (St John's, 1927, 4/1966)

J. M. Gibbon: *Canadian Folksongs. Old and New* (London and Toronto, 1927)

W. R. Mackenzie: *Ballads and Sea Songs from Nova Scotia* (Cambridge, MA, 1928)

P. Barry, F. H. Eckstorm, and M. W. Smyth: *British Ballads from Maine* (New Haven, CT, 1929)

S. McCawley: *Cape Breton Come All Ye* (Glace Bay, Nova Scotia, 1929)

G. Herzog: 'Musical Styles in North America', *Proceedings of the 23rd International Congress of Americanists* (New York, 1930), 455

H. Fauset: *Folklore of Nova Scotia* (New York, 1931)

H. Creighton: *Songs and Ballads from Nova Scotia* (Toronto, 1932/R1966)

E. Greenleaf and G. Mansfield: *Ballads and Sea Songs of Newfoundland* (Cambridge, MA, 1933)

C.-M. Barbeau: 'Asiatic Survivals in Indian Songs', *MQ*, xx (1934), 106

M. Karpeles: *Folk Songs from Newfoundland* (London, 1934)

P. Barry: 'Songs and Traditions of the Miramichi', *Bulletin of the Folksong Society of the Northeast*, x (1935), 15; xi (1936), 21; xii (1937), 23

H. H. Roberts: *Musical Areas in Aboriginal North America* (New Haven, CT, 1936/R1970)

M. Barbeau: *Romancero du Canada* (Montreal, 1937)

A. Chiasson and D. Boudreau: *Chansons d'Acadie*, i–iii (Montreal, 1942–48)

M. Sargent: 'The Native and Primitive Music of Canada' (diss., U. of Toronto, 1942)

F. Densmore: *Music of the Indians of British Columbia* (Washington, DC, 1943)

O. A. Koshyts' [Koshetz]: *Prohenetychnyï zviazok ta hrupuvannïa ukraïns'kykh obrïadovykh pisen'* [Genetic Relationship and Classification of Ukrainian Ritual Songs] (Winnipeg, 1945)

J. Delanglez: 'The "Récit des voyages et des découvertes du Père Jacques Marquette"', *Mid-America*, xxviii/3 (1946), 173; xxviii/4 (1946), 211

A. J. Mason: *Notes on the Indians of the Great Slave Lake Area* (New Haven, 1946)

Z. Estreicher: 'La Musique des Esquimaux-Caribous', *Bulletin de la Société Neuchâteloise de Géographie*, v/1 (1948), 1–54

O. A. Koshyts' [Koshetz]: *Muzychni trory* (Winnipeg, 1949)

E. Holtved: *The Polar Eskimos: Language and Folklore*, i (Copenhagen, 1951)

M. Barbeau: 'The Ermatinger Collection of Voyageur Songs (ca. 1830)', *Journal of American Folklore*, lxvii (1954), 147

R. G. Thwaites, ed.: *The Jesuit Relations and Allied Documents: Travels and Explorations of the Jesuit Missionaries in New France, 1610–1791*; v: *Quebec: 1632–1633*; vi: *Quebec: 1633–1634*; ix: *Quebec: 1636* [P. Le Jeune]; lv: *Lower Canada, Iroquois, Ottawas: 1670–1672* [C. Dablon]; lix: *Lower Canada, Illinois, Ottawas: 1673–1677* [J. Marquette] (New York, 1959) [orig. pubd 1896]

H. Kallmann: *A History of Music in Canada, 1534–1919* (Toronto, 1960)

J. W. Kealiinohomoku and F. J. Gillis: 'Special Bibliography: Gertrude Prokosch Kurath', *EM*, xiv (1970), 114

A. Chiasson and D. Boudreau: *Chansons d'Acadie* (Moncton, 1972–9) iv–v

I. J. Katz, ed.: *EM*, xvi/3 (1972) [special Canadian issue]

C. Laforte: *La Chanson folklorique et les écrivains du XIX siècle (en France et au Québec)* (Montreal, 1973)

R. Stevenson: 'Written Sources for Indian Music until 1882', *EM*, xvii (1973), 1–40

——: 'English Sources for Indian Music until 1882', *EM*, xvii (1973), 399–442

P. Mercer: 'A Supplementary Bibliography on Newfoundland Music', *Canadian Folk Music Journal*, ii (1974), 52–6

G. A. Proctor: *Sources in Canadian Music: a Bibliography of Bibliographies* (Sackville, New Brunswick, 1975)

J. Rahn: 'Canadian Folk Music Holdings at Columbia University', *Canadian Folk Music Journal*, v (1977), 46

Canadian Folk Music Society and The Canadian Music Centre: *A Reference List on Canadian Folk Music* (Calgary and Toronto, 1978)

W. Wickwire: *Songs of the Canadian Interior Salish Tribes: an Anthology and Ethnography* (diss., York U., Toronto, 1978)

D. S. Lee: *Native North American Music and Oral Data: a Catalogue of Sound Recordings (1893–1976)* (Bloomington, IN, 1979)

P. Mercer: *Newfoundland Songs and Ballads in Print 1842–1974: a Title and First-line Index* (St John's, 1979)

E. Fowke and C. H. Carpenter: *A Bibliography of Canadian Folklore in English* (Toronto, 1981)

H. Kallman, G. Potvin, and K. Winters, eds.: *Encyclopedia of Music in Canada* (Toronto, 1981)

G. P. Kurath: *Tutelo Rituals on Six Nations Reserve, Ontario* (Ann Arbor, MI, 1981)

R. Witmer: *The Musical Life of the Blood Indians* (Ottawa, 1982)

B. Nettl: *Blackfoot Musical Thought: Comparative Perspectives* (Kent, OH, 1989)

G. E. Smith: *Ernest Gagnon (1834–1915): Musician and Pioneer Folksong Scholar* (diss., U. of Toronto, 1989)

CHAPTER III

Northern and Western Europe

Albrecht Schneider, Max Peter Baumann,
Ernst Heins, Miriam Rovsing Olsen,
Martin Cunningham, Roberto Leydi,
Helen Myers, Breandán Breatnach,
Nicholas Carolan, Jan Ling

1: GERMANY AND AUSTRIA

Albrecht Schneider

The beginnings of ethnomusicology in Germany and Austria can be dated to the second half of the 19th century with a number of forerunners and earlier achievements well before that time. However, as musicology was re-established in many universities as an academic discipline only between 1861 and 1900, it follows that comparative musicology hardly existed before 1885, the year of Alexander J. Ellis's well-known article generally acknowledged as the take-off of ethnomusicology as an independent scientific endeavour. In this context already in the 19th century there were different concepts of comparative musicology and ethnomusicology with respect to research strategies, methodology, and goals, and it is necessary to distinguish between two approaches, one of which is more systematic and uses scientific methods (for instance, acoustical measurements), while the other is more descriptive, based on fieldwork, and thus cultural (Graf, 1980; Födermayr, 1983). However, this distinction is one of two related fields rather than a dichotomy and it should be clear that comparative musicology as developed and outlined between about 1885 and 1930 differs considerably from ethnomusicology as it was practised after World War II.

Early writings and research

Non-Western musics were mentioned quite frequently in accounts of travels published in many European countries from the 16th century onwards (see, for example, Harrison, 1973). Such accounts, among many other topics, provide information about non-Western instruments, their use and function

77

(Schüller, 1972), while in some of the literature devoted to cultural history we find a comparative examination of musical systems of several nations, for instance of China, Japan, Persia, India etc (Francisci, 1670). Unfortunately, music very often was only one subject among many treated in such accounts so that information is meagre, or of limited value for lack of details. Music often seems to be mentioned because of obvious differences compared to European experiences, while sometimes writers point to certain 'similarities' or 'analogies'. For example, several writers notice that Chinese music employs pentatonic scales, and thus is similar to Celtic music.

Since the Enlightenment, studies of world history have grown in Europe both in content and number, and historiography now includes music on a large scale (Allen, 1939; Schneider, 1984, pp.326–77). Major works such as written by Charles Burney (1776), Sir John Hawkins (1776), and Johann Forkel (1788–1801) include chapters on the music in antiquity as well as in ancient civilizations such as Egypt and China (see also Forkel, 1784). The aspects most prominently featured are instruments, scales and tone systems, and sometimes so in a comparative perspective, to illustrate convergence, similarities and differences in order to ascertain which system was probably established earliest, and if there are historical relationships between musical cultures in the East and in the West. Such comparisons after 1800 were further kindled by translations into German of the works of Sir William Jones (*The Music of the Indians*, translated by Friedrich Dalberg as *Die Musik der Inder*, Erfurt, 1802) and of Guillaume André Villoteau ('Mémoire sur la musique de l'antique Egypte', translated as 'Abhandlung über die Musik des alten Ägypten', Leipzig, 1821). The theologian and well-known music critic Gottfried Wilhelm Fink (1783–1846) published studies of Chinese music (1827), and of the early history of music among the Hindustanis and the Chinese (1831, 'Einiges über die Begründungsweise'). Fink also attempted to give a coherent account of the spread and early history of music in Europe, in a book partly historical in its approach and partly mere speculation (1831, *Erste Wanderung der ältesten Tonkunst*). The interesting point about this book is that it extensively employs the diffusionist theory of the dissemination of 'culture elements', an approach originally taken in the history and philosophy of religion, and advanced by, among others, Johann Gottfried Herder (1744–1803) and Friedrich Wilhelm Schelling (1775–1854). The diffusionist theory stems from the view that mankind was created at one time, and at a certain place (probably Central Asia), to spread from there to all quarters of the world later by 'waves' of migrations (see fig.1; from Schneider, 1976, p.29). According to this view, not only mankind but also most human inventions (e.g. the cart-wheel, bronze casting, the outrigger, also musical instruments such as the xylophone with tuned resonators etc) are believed to be 'monogenetic', that is, created at one place, and to be disseminated from there as part of 'diffusion' in the course of time. Thus 'early history' would be largely a reconstruction of ancient migrations of both people and 'culture elements', a concept that was well to the fore in German ethnology and anthropology up to the 1950s, and figured most prominently in the so-called *Kulturkreislehre* which also was influential on comparative musicology (see Schneider, 1976).

As diffusionism for the lack of archaeological records or written sources remains speculative or, at best, conjectural (see Mühlmann, 1968; Harris,

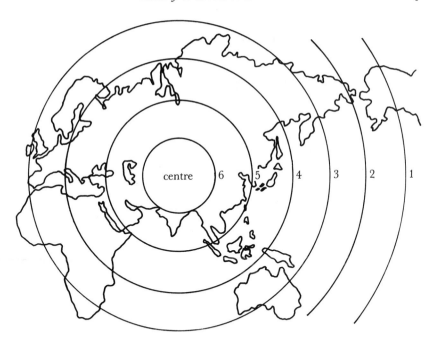

1. Waves of cultural spread (diffusion)

1969), this approach met criticism from the very beginning. With respect to music, especially Raphael Georg Kiesewetter (1773–1850) pointed out the importance of written sources and their philological evaluation. In his famous book, *Die Musik der Araber* (1842), he expressly warns against attempts to deduce the nature of early art music from relics and from ethnographical 'parallels'. In that respect, Kiesewetter rejected the notion of possible continuity, and he denied any connection between ancient Greek music and the music of the Greeks of Byzantium (1838). His view, that of a historicist, seems to be rather restrictive in the light of modern approaches such as ethnohistory yet underlines the fact that research into musical systems of several non-European civilizations calls for philological method.

Musicology and comparative musicology

Most of the ethnographical, anthropological, and also musicological literature of the 19th century was based on a Eurocentric perspective which is obvious in the prevailing classification of 'civilized' peoples, and 'primitive' peoples believed to live in a natural state. The dichotomy of *Naturvölker* and *Kulturvölker* (Vierkandt, 1896) reflects not only that of nature and culture but also includes ethnocentric value judgements. In Eduard Hanslick's (1825–1904) best-known treatise on musical aesthetics, *Vom Musikalisch-Schönen* (1854), he contrasts European art music (*Tonkunst*) with the 'incomprehensible howl' of so-called savages. Without comparative research, and from a strictly Euro-

79

pean point of view, such musics had to be incomprehensible as there was no methodology available to properly analyse and understand them.

The need to enlarge the scope of musicology was felt as early as 1863 when Friedrich Chrysander founded the *Jahrbücher für musikalische Wissenschaft*, one of the earliest periodicals in musicology. In his introduction he underscores the necessity to compare the melodies of various nations in order to ascertain the relative age of a corpus of melodies according to musical criteria, and to find the origins of particular melodies (see Chrysander, 1863, p.14). His ideas eventually led to the concept of comparative folk-song research pursued by Oskar Fleischer (1901–02), Hans Mersmann (1922–4), Walter Wiora (1957) and others. Musicology was established primarily as a subject to investigate European art music, and within the context of the other historic-philological disciplines such as art history, classical philology etc. The core of musicology according to Guido Adler's (1855–1941) well-known article is music history, the edition and analysis of the work of art, along with the 'systematic' subjects of music theory, aesthetics of music, and music pedagogy (1885; see also Heinz, 1968; Kalisch, 1988). Within the systematic section, we find comparative musicology (simply labelled '*Musikologie*') which is allotted the task to compare the music, and songs in particular, of various nations, countries, and territories in order to classify the source material with respect to similarities and differences. Thus Adler's concept of comparative musicology seems to have been the kind of musical ethnography that should contribute to our knowledge of musical styles (the notion of 'style' is central to Adler's thought; cf. Kalisch, 1988).

Although there have been a number of contributions to musical ethnography (a term later to be discussed by Robert Lach [1874–1958], successor to Adler as professor of musicology at Vienna, and eminent scholar in comparative musicology; see Lach, 1930), these hardly were restricted to the description, and formal analysis, of non-European musics. One of the early contributions, Karl Hagen's dissertation, *Über die Musik einiger Naturvölker* (1892), leaves no doubt that a comparative ethnography of music simultaneously should address the question of the ultimate origins of music in terms of 'evolution' and continuous development. Moreover, comparative musicology should investigate such aspects relevant also to the psychology of music, a view that was stressed also by Carl Stumpf (1848–1936), founder of the 'Berlin School' of comparative musicology, as well as by Erich Moritz von Hornbostel (1877–1935), first his co-worker and then the most prominent representative of this discipline until his untimely death in 1935.

The concept of comparative musicology thus contained several ingredients to be outlined here (for a detailed discussion, see Schneider, 1976, 1978, 1980, 1988, 1990; Graf, 1974, 1980; Simon, 1979; Nettl, 1983). To begin with, the comparative approach was taken over from linguistics where especially in Indo-European studies comparison has been employed to detect and trace genetic relationships (Katičić, 1970, pp.9–10) which were always interpreted also as historic relationships. In this, linguistic methodology is equivalent to that of genetic classification in biology, and there are obvious interdependencies between biological and linguistic approaches (Maher, 1966; Koerner, 1981). Both served as a model for other disciplines devoted to comparative research, and thus it is clear that comparative musicology was expected to establish historic and/or genetic relationships between the music of various countries and peoples (Lach, 1924, 1930; Sachs, 1930). With genetic classification in biology, the goal was to disclose the course of evolution, and to reconstruct its natural history. This approach again was taken over by various disciplines (for instance, prehistory, archaeology, ethnology and anthropology; see Mühlmann, 1968; Harris, 1969), and generally is known as 'evolutionism' with respect to the prevailing idea of a linear and continuous development from the simple form to a complex and sophisticated one, the aspect of genetic relationships between various forms compared morphologically, and the idea that 'evolution' notwithstanding continuous development leads to certain 'stages' (Ger.: *Entwicklungsstadien*). In a simple graph, basic aspects of evolutionism may be modelled (see fig.2).

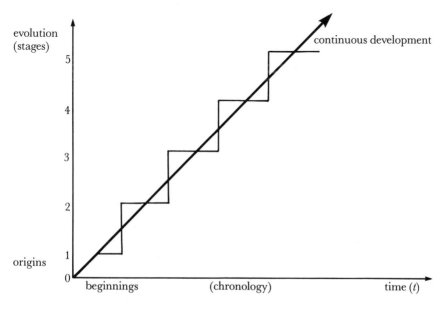

2. *Graph showing the basic aspects of evolutionism*

The attraction of 'evolutionism' in general, and of concepts of ethnography and historiography devised as *Entwicklungsgeschichte* ('developmental history'; see Schneider, 1976, 1984, for further explanations) cannot be overemphasized. The influence of this line of thought (see Goll, 1972) is felt in many studies vigorously disputing the origins of music, its 'early stages', and subsequent 'evolution' (Simmel, 1881–2; Stumpf, 1885; Wallaschek, 1891, 1893, 1897, 1903). Still, in 1928, Hornbostel presented a paper, *Geburt und erste Kindheit der Musik* (1973), that by its very title reflects the approach sketched above, which combined historic and systematic elements in that simple and elementary forms of music are judged to be the most ancient ones. Thus music recorded from the Vedda (Wertheimer, 1909), the Andaman islanders (Portman, 1888), or the Selk'nam and Yamana of Tierra del Fuego (Hornbostel, 1936) for its simplicity was believed to constitute the core of all music as well as to illustrate its possible origins. It is this aspect that was treated quite systematically in Stumpf's *Anfänge der Musik* (1911). Unfortunately, the temporal or chronological aspect in several contributions is confused with that of classification and typology as the 'origins' of music (the most basic phenomena even within 'primitive' music; see Wallaschek, 1893; Stumpf, 1911; Sachs, 1930, 1962) are taken to represent also the very 'beginnings' of music. As we have little if any factual evidence of the beginnings of music in time (besides a few artefacts collected by archaeologists, some rock engravings and similar iconographic sources), it was hoped that comparative musicology might supply 'ethnographic parallels' to music history as its 'first chapter'. In fact, many books on the history of music open with 'origins' to employ findings of comparative musicology (i.e. musical ethnography), to be followed by 'antiquity' (history of music in ancient Egypt, Greece, and the Roman Empire). It was the scientific construct of *Entwicklungsgeschichte*, and the concept of evolutionism which allowed for such a strategy; as can be gathered from fig.2, there is a linear correlation of 'development' and chronology ('evolution' and time), so that the most 'primitive' music rightly can be considered to make up the 'first stage' of music history, and to be the 'oldest' stratum even if recorded in the 19th and 20th centuries.

In a programmatic lecture of 1905, Hornbostel said that the problems investigated by comparative musicology point to 'the most common questions: those of the origin and development of music as well as its nature' (1905–06, p.85). He placed comparative musicology at the point of intersection of three disciplines – ethnology, musicology and psychology. It was his conviction that systematic musicology, in particular studies in the field of music psychology and psycho-acoustics, can only be valid if combined with comparative research (1910, 'Über vergleichende akustische und musikpsychologische Untersuchungen'). This basic view which was and still is up-to-date, was shared by Carl Stumpf, who in particular contributed to music psychology (see his *Tonpsychologie*, 1883–90). He was mainly interested in comparative musicology as he hoped this field of study would make available a broad sample of empirical data suited to enhance the discussion concerning musical scale formation, consonance and harmony, foundations of rhythmic pattern recognition etc. It should be remembered that according to Adler's system of musicology (1885), the subjects classified as 'systematic' (music theory, aesthetics, pedagogics, and comparative musicology as well as a number of auxiliary sciences such as acoustics, physiology, psychology) were allotted the task to establish and eventually prove the 'ultimate laws' of musical art. Thus systematic and comparative musicology were expected to settle questions at issue such as whether musical harmony is a 'natural gift' or a cultural achievement of the sophisticated peoples. Musical ethnography therefore could provide data from outside Europe, and could even make available subjects unbiased as they had not been exposed to 'Western' tonality, and Western music in general.

This perspective was considered important by both Stumpf and Hornbostel (see Stumpf, 1901; Stumpf and Hornbostel, 1911; Hornbostel, 1905–06, 1910, 'Über vergleichende akustische und musikpsychologische Untersuchungen') who rightly stressed that observations of musical behaviour restricted to European countries and modern art music only, could rarely yield generalized, representative results valid in an anthropological perspective.

Comparative and systematic musicology according to the concept outlined by Stumpf and Hornbostel at Berlin, and similarly by Richard Wallaschek (1860–1917) and Robert Lach (1874–1958) at Vienna (see Wallaschek, 1893, 1905; Lach, 1913, 1924; Graf, 1974), had to be combined to allow for an integrated approach comprising 'scientific' as well as cultural aspects and methods. Thus, comparative musicology from its very beginnings was shaped as an interdisciplinary research strategy (Graf, 1973, 1980), especially the systematic component which is marked in many writings devoted to the analysis of specific problems in non-Western musical cultures (see, for example, Hornbostel, 1906–07, 1912, 1928, 'African Negro Music'). This distinguishes the concept of comparative musicology from ethnomusicology which after 1945 took a more descriptive stand close to ethnographic particularism and cultural relativism (Harris, 1969; Nettl, 1983).

The schools of Vienna and Berlin

A look at both the works and the members of the two schools of Vienna and Berlin perhaps may suffice to underline the fact that comparative musicology can be defined as a combination of systematic and ethnological studies. At Vienna, Wallaschek published several works on aesthetics and psychology as well as his musicological studies (Graf, 1974); Lach not only contributed to our knowledge of general principles in music (1913, 1924, 1925) but also transcribed and analysed a large number of recordings made from prisoners of World War I, representing various ethnic groups of the USSR (1926–52). Other members of the Vienna school such as Siegfried Nadel (1903–56), Walter Graf (1903–82) and Albert Wellek (1904–72), contributed to a wide variety of problems and issues in comparative musicology, stretching from the intricate polyphony of the Caucasian peoples, the analysis of xylophone music (Nadel, 1931, 1933) to foundations of music psychology treated in numerous publications of Wellek. After World War II Walter Graf (*b* 1903) re-established the Vienna school, and has published on central topics of comparative musicology such as transcription and analysis, documentation, acoustics and tonometrics, biological factors in music production and perception etc (see Graf, 1980, for full bibliography). Another of Lach's pupils, Ida Halpern (1910–87), emigrated to Canada and made a name as a specialist in Indian music of the Northwest coast. Lach's interest in Oriental music (1916) at Vienna was shared by his colleague Egon J. Wellesz (1885–1974) who became an expert in the music of Byzantium, co-founder of Monumenta musicae byzantinae (1931), and published on the relations of music of the Near East and Europe (see Wellesz, 1914, 1947).

The Berlin school, at the time it was founded around 1900, consisted of a few but very gifted people. Besides Hornbostel who had joined Stumpf in 1900 (or early 1901), there was Otto Abraham (1872–1926), a physician who worked as Stumpf's assistant and was particularly interested in absolute pitch as well as other questions of music psychology (1901–02, 1923). He co-authored many articles with Hornbostel, among them 'Studien über das Tonsystem und die Musik der Japaner' (1902–03), 'Über die Bedeutung des

Phonographen für vergleichende Musikwissenschaft' (1904), and the important 'Vorschläge für die Transkription exotischer Melodien' (1909–10), a proposal of rules for transcription which for a large part are still in use to this day. Other members of Stumpf's Institute of Psychology (which contained a laboratory as well as the rapidly growing sound archive; at Vienna, the Phonogrammarchiv was established in 1899, see Hajek, 1928) were Erich Fischer who published on the music of Patagonia and China (1910), and Max Wertheimer (1880–1943), who soon became a leading figure in *Gestaltpsychologie* ('Gestalt psychology'); he investigated the music of the Vedda (1909–10), and joined Hornbostel in some of the acoustical projects.

Probably in 1912 or 1913 Curt Sachs (1881–1959) joined forces with Hornbostel to produce a landmark in organology, the *Systematik der Musikinstrumente* (1914). Sachs had first graduated in art history, then in musicology with a major in music history, a subject he frequently took up in publications dealing with music of ancient civilizations (1920, 1921, 1924, 1943). His view was to enhance music history by results of ethnographic and comparative research, so that historiography of music should rest on foundations established by comparative musicology (1930, 1962). With Sachs and other musicologists working at Berlin, above all, Georg Schünemann (1884–1945), comparative musicology gained a historic orientation (see Schünemann, 1920) to be felt also in several of Hornbostel's papers as well as in publications by his own students (e.g. Bose, 1934, 'Neue Aufgaben'). Marius Schneider (1903–82), assistant to Hornbostel at the Berlin Phonogrammarchiv, in his *Geschichte der Mehrstimmigkeit* (1934–5) tried to combine ethnographical and historical sources, and to outline principles of multi-part singing and polyphony on a comparative basis.

Many of the publications launched by members of the Berlin school may be viewed as contributions to musical ethnography, a field that Stumpf had entered already in 1886 with his article 'Lieder der Bellakula-Indianer' that was based on his own notations of songs obtained from Indians brought to Germany in 1885. Stumpf had especially one of the Indians repeatedly sing a number of melodies which he noted on paper to analyse melodic contour, ambitus, rhythmic organization, and intonation in particular. The phonograph, invented by Thomas Edison in 1877, and soon available to the ethnographer and musicologist, offered the opportunity to record music all over the world, and to analyse it thereafter in the laboratory as was done at Vienna and Berlin. With the steady flow of recordings made by travellers, missionaries, anthropologists etc, not only was music documented as it actually sounds (it is this aspect in which comparative musicology differed from more conventional views according to which 'music' in the strict sense of the word is a work of art put down in a score), but also the archives soon expanded to provide a basis of comparative studies. After Stumpf's initial discussion in 'Phonographierte Indianermelodien' (1892), Otto Abraham and Hornbostel published a series of articles all bearing the title of 'Phonographierte . . . Melodien' (e.g. 'Phonographierte türkische Melodien' [1904]; 'Phonographierte indische Melodien' [1904–05]; 'Phonographierte tunesische Melodien' [Hornbostel, 1906–07]). These papers, often containing remarks relevant to method, scales, tone systems etc, were mainly aiming for the publication of material already collected, and analysed so that the musical public might gain a better understanding of non-Western music. To the same end, a series of recordings entitled *Musik des Orients* was issued in 1931 making use of the Berlin Phonogrammarchiv. The collection provided a survey of 'Oriental music from Japan to Tunis', edited by Hornbostel; it was also published in London (1934) and in the USA (1951; the so-called *Demonstration Collection* was re-issued in 1963 on Ethnic Folkways FE 4175, ed. G. List and K. Reinhard).

In 1930, in Berlin the Gesellschaft zur Erforschung der Musik des Orients was founded, shortly after renamed the Gesellschaft für vergleichende Musikwissenschaft (GVM) in 1933. With the Nazi regime in power (January 1933), some of the most prominent members of the Berlin group had to emigrate or lose their jobs. Hornbostel first went to New York where he was offered a professorship at the New School for Social Research, and then to England where he died at Cambridge in November 1935. Curt Sachs left in 1933 to work at the Musée de l'Homme in Paris, but settled in the USA in 1937 to teach at New York University (and later at Columbia). Robert Lachmann (1892–1939), who had been editor-in-chief of the *Zeitschrift für vergleichende Musikwissenschaft* (founded in 1933), emigrated to Israel in 1935 to die prematurely in 1939. Georg Schünemann and Johannes Wolf, both founder members of the GVM, and musicologists of international repute, lost their jobs in 1933 and 1934. Pupils of Hornbostel and Sachs such as Mieczyslaw Kolinski (1901–81), Walter Kaufmann (1907–84), and Hans Hickmann (1908–68) left Germany, as did other young musicologists outside the Berlin school such as Ernst Emsheimer (1904–89; see Emsheimer, 1943), and Edith Gerson-Kiwi (*b* 1908).

By the end of 1935, the *Zeitschrift für vergleichende Musikwissenschaft* was discontinued after only three volumes (1933–5), though there had been plans to publish the journal in the USA where in February 1933 the American Society for Comparative Musicology was founded and whose members automatically were enrolled in the GVM (see *The New York Musicological Society Bulletin*, ii and iii, 1933). Notwithstanding the exodus as well as many impediments, Marius Schneider, who in 1934 was appointed head of the Phonogrammarchiv (moved from the University to the Museum für Völkerkunde of Berlin), tried to keep up with collecting material as well as its publication (Schneider, 1937, 1938, 1940) until World War II. Some of the former students like Heinrich Husmann (1908–83) and Walter Wiora (*b* 1906) produced articles in the tradition of the Berlin school (Husmann, 1936, 1939; Wiora, 1941). So did eventually Werner Danckert (1900–70) who after having held a professorship in the University of Jena came to Berlin in 1939 and set out to continue in particular the culture-historical investigations with respect to music Hornbostel had begun in the first decade of the century.

Concepts, methods, results

As comparative musicology was interdisciplinary, and a combination of systematic and ethnological approaches, investigations such as Stumpf's famous 'Tonsystem und Musik der Siamesen' (1901) covered aspects of perception and cognition as well as tonometrical measurements, music transcription and analysis. Tonometrical studies in particular became a centre of research and resulted in many interesting findings, and finally in the ill-fated *Blasquintentheorie* ('blown 5ths theory') elaborated by Hornbostel (1927).

The point of departure however for all these efforts was the assumption propagated by Alexander J. Ellis (1885) that several if not many non-European scales exhibit equal temperament, among them *laras slendro* and *pelog* of Java as well as some scales of Thailand (Siam). Stumpf, who at first had doubts about this hypothesis, carried out measurements on Siamese instruments and interviewed musicians of a Siamese *pi phāt* ensemble visiting Berlin in 1900. In fact recordings and measurements undertaken with the help of Abraham formed the very core of the Berlin archive, and were published subsequently (Stumpf, 1901; Stumpf and Hornbostel, 1911; Hornbostel, 1919–20). Notwithstanding considerable deviations from equal temperament, the data obtained according to Stumpf's interpretation point to a scale that is intended as an equidistant sectioning of the octave (1200 cents) into five (*slendro*) or seven (*pelog* as well as Siamese) parts. The problem involved is one of the most subtle in psychophysics, namely how stimulus and sensation relate to each other with respect to such scales (Schneider, 1986, 1988, 'Musikwissenschaftliche Theorienbildung', 1990) based on pitches which make up no simple intervals but incorporate steps of the size $^{7}\sqrt{2} = 1{,}1040895$ in the heptatonic, and $^{5}\sqrt{2} = 1{,}148984$ in equipentatonic tuning. Due to Stumpf's essay, any such scales and in particular the equiheptatonic Siamese

3. Erich Moritz von Hornbostel, c1930

one as found on the *ranats* (xylophones, metallophones of Thailand) are likely to support the theory of G. T. Fechner according to which the relation of a sensation (E) and the stimulus (R) can be formulated as $E = k \cdot \log R$ (see also Beurmann and Schneider, 1989; Schneider and Beurmann, 1990). It is quite obvious that Stumpf's curiosity was stimulated for the consequences comparative research might yield for psychological theory in Europe beyond the musical and ethnographic outcome.

Hornbostel and Abraham, both trained in natural sciences as well as in psychology, took up Stumpf's position to conclude that in non-Western music the principle of 'tone distance' that gives rise to equipentatonic and equiheptatonic scales is as important as is the overtone series (frequencies $f_n = n \cdot f_1$), or simple ratio intervals in general (see Abraham and Hornbostel, 1926; Hornbostel, 1910, 'Über vergleichende akustische und musikpsychologische Untersuchungen', 1926). It is this basic hypothesis which governed much of Hornbostel's research as well as that of his co-workers and pupils (see, for example, Hornbostel, 1906–07, 1909, 1910, 1912, 1923; Husmann, 1936, 1939, 1961), and provided for an interpretation of data which aimed at finding tone systems independent of the experience of elementary intervals such as the 4th and 5th. A closer look, however, reveals that mere speculation set in quite early (see Hornbostel, 1909, p.148 and the 'deduction' of *slendro* and *pelog* offered there) to end up with the circle of blown 5ths, a highly sophisticated construct yet without empirical foundations. This hypothesis claims that a number of non-Western tone systems are based on a cycle of 5ths which are all somewhat reduced in pitch so that the average size of the basic interval is 678 instead of 702 cents (pure 5ths $3/2 = 702$ cents). Hornbostel allegedly had found the 'blown 5th' when measuring panpipes of Brazil which did not exhibit a clear pattern of intervals to be assigned to the common major or minor scale. The only interval that came close to those known from Western practice was a 4th, however, much too wide compared to the pure interval ($4/3 = 498$ cents). Hornbostel hypothesized that such an interval could be obtained if the maker of the instrument had established the scale of the panpipe by means of overblowing one of the pipes. As these are stopped, only the odd partials above the fundamental will be produced so that their respective frequency ratios will equal $1:3:5:7: \ldots :n$. Hornbostel now surmised that the 12th above the fundamental generated by overblowing would not correspond to the frequency ratio of 3:1 but would be flattened a little as well as all the other partials should be. According to this assumption, the 12th would have the 'tone distance' of 1878 cents in relation to the fundamental instead of 1902 ($2/1 + 3/2 = 1902$ cents; see Hornbostel, 1910, 'Über vergleichende akustische musikpsychologische Untersuchungen', 1927). If we now allow for subtraction of an octave ($2/1 = 1200$ cents), the so-called *Blasquinte* ('blown 5th') of 678 cents is left. Hornbostel was of the persuasion that with the blown 5th a cycle could be formed analogous to the well-known *Quintenzirkel* ('circle of 5ths') we know from elementary music theory: as this one generally consists of 12 steps ($702 \times 12 = 8424$ cents) which exceed the 7th octave by 24 cents (the 'Pythagorean comma'), so Hornbostel's cycle of blown 5ths consists of 23 steps ($678 \times 23 = 15,594$ cents) almost equal to the 13th octave ($1200 \times 13 = 15,600$ cents).

It should be clear, however, that Hornbostel had only assumed that the deviation in pitch caused by overblowing constantly would be 24 cents; thus, his theory, ironically to be published in a handbook of physics, was by no means based on empirical facts. Manfred Bukofzer (1910–55), testing the hypothesis in the laboratory, found that the size of intervals generated by overblowing stopped pipes is dependent on several parameters so that there is no constant deviation, and in fact no such 'blown 5th' as Hornbostel had postulated (Bukofzer, 1936, 1937). With the *Blasquintentheorie* refuted and eventually abandoned, comparative musicology lost a good deal of its scientific reputation; the discipline, once in high esteem for the 'exactness' gained in tonometrical measurements (Schneider, 1976), in reality was prone to speculation (Schneider, 1986, pp.158ff).

This becomes particularly clear when considering the involvement of comparative musicology in what was termed 'culture-historical ethnology', a movement not restricted to, yet especially active in, Germany and Austria, and scientifically condensed in the concept of *Kulturkreislehre* ('theory of culture circles'; see Mühlmann, 1968; Harris, 1969; Schneider, 1976). This approach, advanced by the historian Fritz Graebner (1877–1954), and the ecclesiastics Father Wilhelm Schmidt (1868–1954) and Father Wilhelm Koppers (1886–1961), initially was planned to allow (ethno-)historical research to cover the entire globe, and all peoples that cannot boast of historiography based on written records (so-called *schriftlose Kulturen* which by conservatory historiographers were believed to have 'no history' for the lack of written sources; see Graebner, 1911). Positive as this new orientation appeared to be, it was hindered by ideological constraints as especially Father Schmidt, being as passionate a scholar as he was a missionary, wanted to fight 'evolutionism' in anthropology, and to prove certain tenets of Catholic doctrine by means of ethnology.

Basically, *Kulturkreislehre* held that cultural parallels (obvious similarities in material goods, social institutions etc) are the result of migrations that took place in the remote past or more recent times. According to their belief in monogenesis of mankind as well as of culture traits (see fig.1), Schmidt and his followers claimed that most of human achievements had been invented only once, and then spread over the globe in the course of migrations of ethnic groups as well as by trade relations over sometimes very long distances, thus connecting Africa to Indonesia, and American Indian culture to those of East Asia. Even though some of the findings of this ethnologic school were stimulating in that allegedly 'primitive' cultures ('peoples without history', so-called *Naturvölker*, in the view of ethnography in the colonial era) were put into a historic and intercultural perspective, the approach as a whole was a failure, as *Kulturkreislehre* avoided neither dogmatism nor the model of linear development 'evolutionism' was criticized for. Thereby the heuristic tool of 'culture circles' was turned into a rigid scheme as cultures were classified with respect to certain culture traits, among them being musical instruments. Cultures due to *Kulturkreislehre* thus were defined as an inventory of so-called *Kulturmerkmale* ('culture traits'), an approach which is not unlike that of archaeology.

With respect to method, the approach sketched here worked on the principle of 'age-to-area': according to the basic belief in migrations and a single centre of all culture somewhere in Asia, one may hypothesize that similar 'elements' found in locations far away from the point of departure (Inner Asia), belong to one of the first 'waves' (fig.1) of culture spread, and thus are very old. In general, a rule could be formulated saying that the more distant culture traits are found in relation to the centre supposed, the older they are. Hornbostel, who was interested in ethnological theory (1911, 1933), contacted Father Schmidt most likely around 1906. From that year on he published articles in which 'culture-historical relations' were discussed (e.g. 1909, 1910, 'Über einige Panpfeifen', 1911, 1912, 1923, 1928, 'Die Massnorm'; see Schneider, 1976, 1988, 'Erich Moritz von Hornbostel') whereby Hornbostel himself tried to establish and render likely some of such relations by means of tonometrical data obtained from instruments belonging to different cultures. If, for example, xylophones in Southeast Asia and Africa, or panpipes of Brazil and the Solomon Islands yield similar sets of pitches (measured with tuning forks or similar devices whereby frequencies were tabulated and the intervals ['tone distances'] expressed in cents), such findings might indicate historic and/or genetic relationships, especially if there are more such 'culture parallels'. Unfortunately, seeking for 'culture-historical relationships' in practice sometimes lacked source criticism and was based only on apparent 'similarities'. A good case in point is an article by Hornbostel and Lachmann, 'Asiatische Parallelen zur Berbermusik' (1933), in which comparison of melodies and singing styles accounts for the establishment of 'parallels' which in turn are interpreted in a historic-genetic sense to tenets of *Kulturkreislehre* (see also Schneider, 1988, 'Erich Moritz von Hornbostel').

Other scholars adhering to this approach were Marius Schneider (see especially 1938) who also addressed the problem of 'parallels', namely with respect to Caucasian and medieval polyphony (1940), and Werner Danckert who set out to develop a scheme of musical areas analogous to that of culture circles (1937). His pupil Herbert Hübner in his dissertation (1938) also made use of *Kulturkreislehre* when analysing the music of the Bismarck Archipelago (1935, 1938).

As comparison of *Kulturelemente* mostly was done on a strictly morphological level (the method of comparison is one genuine to biological classification; cf. Picken, 1975, Appendix), it follows that musical instruments as material objects are suited best to be compared with respect to 'similarities'. Ethno-organological studies such as produced by Bernhard Ankermann (1902) on African musical instruments introduced typological ordering which employs the criterion of similarity in shape, elements, material etc, and also discussed questions of mutual relationships, culture contacts and the like. Curt Sachs, who had written on non-Western musical instruments (e.g. 1915, 'Die Musikinstrumente', 1923), and also employed typology as a means to establish genetic relationships (1917, 'Die Maultrommel') with respect to jew's harps, in his book *Geist und Werden der Musikinstrumente* (1929) made use of an approach that combined a strictly 'evolutionist' view with that of 'migrations' and culture-historical relationships as proposed by *Kulturkreislehre*. In this way Sachs for example connects clapping of hands (a most rudimentary 'concussion idiophone' according to the Hornbostel–Sachs system) with highly sophisticated musical instruments, and presents a sample that covers most of the world. Sachs employed the 'age-to-area' principle to arrive at a presentation which was impressive yet much too schematic in terms of chronology. Hornbostel, who basically agreed to Sachs's classification and findings, gave a lucid discussion of issues of the 'culture-historical' methodology, and himself outlined yet another 'tentative grouping of African sound-producing instruments with reference to their extra-African distribution' (1933).

Though speculative thought evident in the *Blasquintentheorie* as well as in ethnomusicological contributions to *Kulturkreislehre* cannot be denied (Schneider, 1976, 1988 'Erich Moritz von Hornbostel'), and strains of evolutionism are clearly present in works of Wallaschek, Lach, Sachs and others, it would be presumptuous and unjust to reduce comparative musicology to an approach close to 'armchair anthropology'. First, a discipline had to be established that differed considerably from conventional (historic-philological) musicology, and needed a methodology of its own to meet the requirements of interdisciplinary research (see Stumpf and Hornbostel, 1911; Hornbostel, 1905–06, 1910, 'Über vergleichende akustische und musikpsychologische Untersuchungen', Abraham and Hornbostel, 1904 'Über die Bedeutung', 1909–10; Hornbostel and Sachs, 1914; Lach, 1924, 1930; see also Graf, 1980; Nettl, 1983, pp.52ff). Second, fieldwork which is considered in modern ethnomusicology as *conditio sine qua non*, was much less easy to organize in 1900 than it was by 1950, to the effect that even leading figures in comparative musicology had relatively little experience in the field. For the most part they had to rely on information provided by anthropologists, missionaries, colonial officers etc who supplied many of the recordings stored in the archives of Vienna and Berlin. However, there was awareness that music needs to be studied with regard to its cultural and historical background (see Hornbostel, 1905–06; Lachmann, 1922–23, 1929), and it was Hornbostel who in his paper 'Fuegian Songs' (1936) explicitly discussed music in culture ('Stellung der Musik innerhalb der Kultur'). Thus, comparative musicology did not consist only of laboratory investigations (though these were considered necessary, and rightly so), nor did comparison dominate the many publications which on the one hand aim at a description and the analysis of recorded material (cf. Abraham and Hornbostel, 1902–03; 1904, 'Phonographierte türkische Melodien', 1904–05; Hornbostel, 1906–07, 1908, 1909, 1912, 1917, 1919–20, 1923, 1936; Lachmann, 1922–3; Lach, 1926–52; Bose, 1934, 'Neue Aufgaben'; Kolinski, 1930; Heinitz, 1931; Herzog, 1932, 1936; Hübner, 1935, 1938; Reinhard, 1939; Emsheimer, 1943; Graf, 1950), and on the other hand contain chapters on 'parallels' as well as on more systematic issues such as tone systems, singing styles, or musical development (see Nettl, 1983).

To be sure, comparison was by no means the only method used within a scientific concept which covers many aspects of music and musical behaviour (see Wiora, 1975; Graf, 1980). The comparative approach moreover was not restricted to non-Western music and figures prominently also in European folk-song research (see Fleischer, 1899–1900, 1901–02; Mersmann, 1922; Schünemann, 1923; Danckert, 1939; Sichardt, 1939; Heinitz, 1921, 1929–30; Wiora, 1941). As here sources in general are more homogeneous, comparison sometimes can be based on a statistically significant body of songs, and 'parallels' are often very obvious. However, due to the morphological nature of methods such as synoptic ordering of melodies (see Mersmann, 1922; Wiora, 1941, 1957), similarities in melodic contour, stanza form etc first indicate a typological relationship which may also point to historic and/or genetic relationship especially if continuity can be assumed with respect to certain traditions (a case study worth reading is Hornbostel's 'Phonographierte isländische Zwiegesänge' [1930], an investigation of Iceland's *tvisöngvar* in relation to medieval organa).

Conclusion

Comparative musicology in Germany and Austria was initiated around 1885 on a professional level, and soon was established as a discipline in its own right. As the concept from the very beginning was inter-disciplinary, and the perspective global, relatively few scholars in practice had to cope with a multitude of tasks, a rich variety of musical cultures, as well as methodological and technical problems. Given these circumstances, what was achieved in a few decades deserves admiration. At the same time one must admit that certain shortcomings in methodology, perhaps lack of field experience, and not least of all a fair amount of speculative thought did affect validity of results presented, especially in works devoted to 'culture-historical' issues. Yet already in the 1920s and 1930s a process of specialization and revision of concepts set in (see, for example, Lachmann, 1922–3, 1935; Hornbostel, 1928, 'African Negro Music', 1933) which was stopped for political reasons outlined above. Comparative musicology thus fell victim to totalitarian power, and in Germany and Austria little by little had to be restored in the 1950s, with objectives and methods considerably changed. The orientation in Germany mainly became that of ethnomusicology with majors in music description and analysis, while at Vienna Walter Graf succeeded in working out a new concept of comparative research, still including the systematic aspects (see Graf, 1980; Födermayr, 1971, 1983). It should be noted, finally, that of Hornbostel's colleagues and students forced to leave Germany, some were able to maintain and further develop ideas of comparative musicology, namely Curt Sachs (1961) and Mieczyslaw Kolinski (see Falck and Rice, 1982; Nettl, 1983).

Bibliography

E. Francisci: 'Die Music', *Neu polirter Geschict-, Kunst- und Sittenspiegel* (Nuremberg, 1670), 1314–24

J. N. Forkel: 'Von der Musik der Chinesen', *Musikalischer Almanach auf 1784* (Leipzig, 1784), 233–74

——: *Allgemeine Geschicte der Musik* (Leipzig, 1788–1801/R1967)

G. W. Fink: 'Einiges über die Begrundungsweise des älltesten Zustandes der Tonkunst, insonderheit über den Werth geschichtlier Überreste der frühesten gebildeten Völker, namentlich der Hindostaner und Chinesen', *AMZ*, xxxiii (1831), 785

——: *Erste Wanderung der ältesten Tonkunst, als Vorgeschichte der Musik oder als erste Periode derselben* (Essen, 1831)

R. G. Kiesewetter: Über die Musik der neueren Griechen nebst freien Gedanken über alt-ägyptische und alt-griechische Musik (Leipzig, 1838)

——: *Die Musik der Araber, nach Originalquellen dargestellt* (Leipzig, 1842/R1968)

E. Hanslick: *Von Musikalisch-Schönen: ein Beitrag zur Revision der Ästhetik der Tonkunst* (Leipzig, 1854/R1965, 16/1966; Eng. trans., 1891/R1974)

G. Simmel: 'Psychologische und ethnologische Studien über Musik', *Zeitschrift für Völkerpsychologie*, xiii (1882), 261–305

C. Stumpf: *Tonpsychologie* (Leipzig, 1883–90/R1965)

G. Adler: 'Umfang, Methode und Ziel der Musikwissenschaft', *VMw*, i (1885), 5

A. J. Ellis: 'On the Musical Scales of Various Nations', *Journal of the Society of Arts*, xxxiii (1885), 485–527

C. Stumpf: 'Musikpsychologie in England. Betrachtungen über Herleitung der Musik aus der Sprache und aus dem thierischen Entwicklungsprozess, über Empirismus und Nativismus in der Musiktheorie', *VMw*, i (1885), 261–349

——: 'Lieder der Bellakula-Indianer', *VMw*, ii (1886), 405

M. V. Portman: 'Andamanese Music', *Journal of the Royal Asiatic Society*, xx (1888), 181–218

R. Wallaschek: 'On the Origin of Music', *Mind*, xvi (1891), 375

K. Hagen: *Über die Musik einiger Naturvölker* (diss., U. of Hamburg, 1892)

C. Stumpf: 'Phonographierte Indianermelodien', *VMw*, viii (1892), 127

R. Wallaschek: *Primitive Music: Inquiry into the Origin and Development of Music of Savage Tribes* (London, 1893/*R*1970; Ger. trans., enl. 2/1903 as *Anfänge der Tonkunst*)

A. Vierkandt: *Naturvölker und Kulturvölker: ein Beitrag zur Sozialpsychologie* (Leipzig, 1896)

R. Wallaschek: 'Anfänge unseres Musiksystems in der Urzeit', *Mittheilungen der Anthropologische Gesellschaft in Wien, Sitzungsberichte*, xxvii (1897), 10

O. Fleischer: 'Ein Kapitel vergleichender Musikwissenschaft', *SIMG*, i (1899–1900), 1–53

R. Wallaschek: 'Die Entstehung der Scala', *Sitzungsberichte der Kaiserliche Akademie der Wissenschaften, Wien, Mathematisch–naturwissenschaftliche Klasse*, cviii/2 (1899), 905–49

O. Abraham: 'Das absolute Tonbewusstsein: psychologisch-musikalische Studie', *SIMG*, iii (1901–02), 1–86

O. Fleischer: 'Zur vergleichenden Liedforschung', *SIMG*, iii (1901–02), 185

C. Stumpf: 'Tonsystem und Musik der Siamesen', *Beiträge zur Akustik und Musikwissenschaft*, iii (1901), 69–152

O. Abraham and E. M. von Hornbostel: 'Studien über das Tonsystem und die Musik der Japaner', *SIMG*, iv (1902–03), 302–60; repr. in *Sammelbände für vergleichende Musikwissenschaft*, i (1922), 179–231 as 'Tonsystem und Musik der Japaner'

B. Ankermann: *Die afrikanischen Musikinstrumente* (diss., U. of Leipzig, 1902)

O. Abraham and E. M. von Hornbostel: 'Über die Bedeutung des Phonographen für die vergleichende Musikwissenschaft', *Zeitschrift für Ethnologie*, xxxvi (1904), 222

——: 'Phonographierte türkische Melodien', *Zeitschrift für Ethnologie*, xxxvi (1904), 203; repr. in *Sammelbände für vergleichende Musikwissenschaft*, i (1922), 233

——: 'Phonographierte indische Melodien', *SIMG*, v (1903–4), 348–401; repr. in *Sammelbände für vergleichende Musikwissenschaft*, i (1922), 251–90

E. M. von Hornbostel: 'Die Probleme der vergleichenden Musikwissenschaft', *ZIMG*, viii (1905–06), 85

R. Wallaschek: *Psychologie und Pathologie der Vorstellung: Beiträge zur Grundlegung der Ästhetik* (Leipzig, 1905)

E. M. von Hornbostel: 'Phonographierte tunesische Melodien', *SIMG*, viii (1906–07), 1–43; repr. in *Sammelbände für vergleichende Musikwissenschaft*, i (1922), 311–48

——: 'Über die Musik der Kubu', *Die Orang-Kubu auf Sumatra*, D. Hagen (Frankfurt am Main, 1908), 245; repr. in *Sammelbände für vergleichende Musikwissenschaft*, i (1922), 359

O. Abraham and E. M. von Hornbostel: 'Vorschläge für die Transkription exotischer Melodien', *SIMG*, xi (1909–10), 1

E. M. von Hornbostel: 'Phonographierte Melodien aus Madagaskar und Indonesien', *Anthropologie und Ethnographie*, v: *Forschungsreise S.M.S. 'Planet' 1906–7*, A. Kramer (Berlin, 1909), 139

C. Stumpf: 'Die Anfänge der Musik', *Internationale Wochenschrift*, iii (1909); pubd separately (Leipzig, 1911)

M. Wertheimer: 'Musik der Wedda', *SIMG*, xi (1909–10), 300

E. M. von Hornbostel: 'Über einige Panpfeifen zus Nordwestbrasilien', *Zwei Jahre unter den Indianern*, ii, T. Koch-Grunberg (Berlin, 1910), 378

——: 'Über vergleichende akustische und musikpsychologische Untersuchungen', *Zeitschrift für angewandte Psychologie und psychologische Sammelforschung*, iii (1910), 465; repr. in *Beiträge zur Akustik und Musikwissenschaft*, v (1910), 143

F. Graebner: *Methode der Ethnologie* (Heidelberg, 1911)

E. M. von Hornbostel: 'Über ein akustisches Kriterium für Kulturzusammenhänge', *Zeitschrift für Ethnologie*, xliii (1911), 601

C. Stumpf and E. M. von Hornbostel: 'Über die Bedeutung ethnologisher Untersuchungen für die Psychologie und Ästhetik der Tonkunst', *4. Kongress für experimentelle Psychologie: Innsbruck 1910* (Innsbruck, 1911)

E. M. von Hornbostel: 'Die Musik auf den nordwestlichen Salomo-Inseln', *Forschungen auf den Salomo-Inseln und dem Bismarck-Archipel*, i, R. Thurnwald (Berlin, 1912), 461–504

——: 'Melodie und Skala', *JbMP12*, 11

R. Lach: *Zur Entwicklungsgeschichte der ornamentalen Melopöie: Beiträge zur Geschichte der Melodie* (Leipzig, 1913)

E. M. von Hornbostel and C. Sachs: 'Systematik der Musikinstrumente', *Zeitschrift für Ethnologie*, xlvi (1914), 553–90 [Eng. trans. in *GSJ*, xiv (1961), 3]

E. Wellesz: 'Fragen und Aufgaben musikalischer Orientforschung', *Österreichische Monatsschrift für den Orient*, xl (1914), 332

C. Sachs: *Die Musikinstrumente Indiens und Indonesiens. Zugleich eine Einführung in die Instrumentenkunde* (Berlin and Leipzig, 1915, 2/1923)

R. Lach: 'Orientalistik und vergleichende Musikwissenschaft', *Wiener Zeitschrift für die Kunde des Morgenlandes*, xxix (1916), 463–501

E. M. von Hornbostel: 'Gesänge aus Ruanda', *Forschungen im Nil-Kongo- Zwischengebiet*, i, J. Czekanowski (Leipzig, 1917), 379–412

C. Sachs: *Die Musikinstrumente Birmas und Assams im K. Ethnographischen Museum zu München*, *Sitzungsberichte der Königliche Bayerischen Akademie der Wissenschaften, Philosophisch-historische Klasse*, ii (Munich, 1917)

——: 'Die Maultrommel: eine typologische Vorstudie', *Zeitschrift für Ethnologie*, xlix (1917), 185

E. M. von Hornbostel: 'Formanalysen an siamesischen Orchesterstücken', *AMw*, ii (1919–20), 306

C. Sachs: 'Die Tonkunst der alten Ägypter', *AMw*, ii (1920), 9

G. Schünemann: 'Über die Beziehungen der vergleichenden Musikwissenschaft zur Musikge- schichte, *AMw*, ii (1920), 175

W. Heinitz: 'Eine lexikalische Ordnung für die vergleichende Beitrachtung von Melodien', *AMw*, iii (1921), 247

C. Sachs: *Die Musikinstrumente des alten Ägyptens* (Berlin, 1921)

R. Lachmann: *Die Musik in den tunesischen Städten* (diss., U. of Berlin, 1922); *AMw*, v (1923), 136–71

H. Mersmann: 'Grundlagen einer musikalischen Volksliedforschung', *AMw*, iv (1922), 141, 289– 321; v (1923), 81–135; vi (1924), 127–64

O. Abraham: 'Tonometrische Untersuchungen an einem deutschen Volkslied', *Psychologische Forschung*, iv (1923), 1

E. M. von Hornbostel: 'Musik der Makuschi, Taulipang und Yekunda', *Von Roroima zum Orinoco*, iii, T. Koch-Grunberg (Stuttgart, 1923), 397–442; Eng. trans., M. Herndon, *Inter-American Music Bulletin* (1969), no.71, pp.1–42

G. Schünemann: *Das Lied der deutschen Kolonisten in Russland* (Munich, 1923)

R. Lach: *Die vergleichende Musikwissenchaft: ihre Methoden und Probleme* (Vienna and Leipzig, 1924)

C. Sachs: *Musik des Altertums* (Breslau, 1924)

R. Lach: *Das Konstruktionsprinzip der Wiederholung in Musik, Sprache und Literatur*, Sitzungsberichte der Akademie der Wissenschaften Wien, Philosophisch-historische Klasse, cci/2 (Vienna, 1925)

O. Abraham and E. M. von Hornbostel: 'Zur Psychologie der Tondistanz', *Zeitschrift für Psychologie und Physiologie der Sinnersorgane* (1926), no.98, p.233

E. M. von Hornbostel: 'Psychologie der Gehörserscheinungen', *Handbuch der normalen und pathologischen Physiologie*, xi, A. Bethe and others (Berlin, 1926), 701

R. Lach: *Gesänge russischer Kriegsgefangener/Volksgesänge von Völkern Russlands* (Vienna, 1926–52)

E. M. von Hornbostel: 'Musikalische Tonsysteme', *Handbuch der Physik*, viii, ed. H. Geiger and K. Scheel (Berlin, 1927)

L. Hajek: *Das Phonogrammarchiv der Akademie der Wissenschaften in Wien von seiner Gründung bis zur Neueinrichtung im Jahre 1927* (Vienna and Leipzig, 1928)

E. M. von Hornbostel: 'Die Massnorm als kulturgeschichtliches Forschungsmittel', *Festschrift: Publication d'hommage offerte au P. W. Schmidt* (Vienna, 1928), 303

——: 'African Negro Music', *Africa*, i (1928), 30–62; repr. in *International Institute of African Languages and Cultures: Memorandum*, iv (London, 1928), 1–35

C. Sachs: 'Der Ursprung der Saiteninstrumente', *Festschrift: Publication d'hommage offerte au P. W. Schmidt* (Vienna, 1928), 629

W. Heinitz: 'Vergleichende Betrachtung zweier neugriechischer Choralvarianten', *ZMw*, xii (1929–30), 330

R. Lachmann: *Musik des Orients* (Breslau, 1929/R1965)

C. Sachs: *Geist und Werden der Musikinstrumente* (Berlin, 1929/R1975)

E. M. von Hornbostel: 'Phonographierte isländische Zwiegesänge', *Deustsche Islandforschung*, i, ed. W. H. Vogt (Breslau, 1930), 300

M. Kolinski: 'Die Musik der Primitivstämme auf Malaka und ihre Beziehungen zur samoanischen Musik', *Anthropos*, xxv (1930), 585–648

R. Lach: 'Musikalische Ethnographie', *Mitteilung der Anthropologischen Gesellschaft zu Wien*, lx (1930), 356

C. Sachs: *Vergleichende Musikwissenschaft in ihren Grundzügen* (Leipzig, 1930)

W. Heinitz: *Strukturprobleme in primitiver Musik* (Habilitationsschrift, U. of Hamburg, 1931; Hamburg, 1931)

S. F. Nadel: Marimba-Musik (Vienna, 1931)

G. Herzog: 'Die Musik auf Truk', *Truk, Ergebnisse der Südsee-Expedition 1908–1910*, ii/5, A. Kramer (1932), 385–404

E. M. von Hornbostel: 'The Ethnology of African Sound-instruments', *Africa*, vi (1933), 129, 257– 311 [comments on C. Sachs: *Geist und Werden der Musikinstrumente*]

—— and R. Lachmann: 'Asiatische Parallelen zur Berbermusik', *Zeitschrift für vergleichende Musikwissenschaft*, i (1933), 4

S. Nadel: *Georgische Gesänge* (Berlin and Leipzig, 1933)

C. Sachs: *Eine Weltgeschichte des Tanzes* (Berlin, 1933; Eng. trans. 1937/R1963)

F. Bose: 'Neue Aufgaben der vergleichenden Musikwissenschaft', *ZMw*, xvi (1934), 229

——: *Die Musik der Uitoto* (diss., Humboldt U., Berlin, 1934; Berlin, 1934)

M. Schneider: *Geschichte der Mehrstimmigkeit: historische und phaenomenologische Studien*, i: *Die Naturvölker*; ii: *Die Anfänge in Europa* (Berlin, 1934–5, 2/1968 with iii: *Die Kompositionsprinzipen und ihre Verbreitung*)

H. Hübner: 'Studien zur Musik im Bismarck-Archipel', *Anthropos*, xxx (1935), 669

R. Lachmann: 'Musiksysteme und Musikauffassung', *Zeitschrift fur vergleichende Musikwissenschaft*, iii (1935), 1

M. Bukofzer: 'Präzisionsmessungen an primitiven Musikinstrumenten', *Zeitschrift für Physik*, xcix (1936), 643

G. Herzog: 'Die Musik der Karolinen-Inseln aus dem Phonogramm-Archiv', in A. Eilers: *Westkarolinen, Ergebnisse der Sudsee-Expedition*, iib/9 (Hamburg, 1936)

E. M. von Hornbostel: 'Fuegian Songs', *American Anthropologist*, new ser. xxxviii (1936), 357; enl. as 'The Music of the Fuegians', *Ethnos*, xiii (1948), 62–102; repr. in *Tonart und Ethos: Aufsätze zur Musikethnologie und Musikpsychologie*, ed. E. Stockmann and C. Kaden (Leipzig, 1968)

H. Husmann: 'Marimba und Sansa der Sambesikultur', *Zeitschrift für Ethnologie*, lxviii (1936), 197

M. Bukofzer: 'Kann die "Blasquintentheorie" zur Erklärung exotischer Tonsysteme beitragen?', *Anthropos*, xxxii (1937), 402

W. Danckert: 'Musikwissenschaft und Kulturkreislehre', *Anthropos*, xxxii (1937), 1

H. Husmann: 'Sieben afrikansischer Tonleitern', *JbMP46*, 1937, 44

M. Schneider: 'Über die Verbreitung afrikanscher Chorformen', *Zeitschrift für Ethnologie*, lxix (1937), 78

H. Hübner: 'Die Musik im Bismarck-Archipel', *Musikethnologische Studien zur Kulturgeschichte und Rassenforschung* (Jena, 1938)

M. Schneider: 'Die musikalischen Beziehungen zwischen Urkulturen, Altpflanzern und Hirtenvölkern', *Zeitschrift für Ethnologie*, lxx (1938), 287

W. D. Allen: *Philosophies of Music History: a Study of General Histories of Music* (New York, 1939/R1962)

W. Danckert: *Grundriss der Volksliedkunde* (Berlin, 1939)

——: *Das europäische Volkslied* (Berlin, 1939, 2/1970)

K. Reinhard: *Die Musik Birmas* (Würzburg, 1939)

W. Sichardt: *Der alpenländische Jodler und Ursprung des Jodelns* (Berlin, 1939)

H. Simbriger: *Gong und Gongspiele* (diss., U. of Vienna, 1939; *Internationales Archiv für Ethnographie*, xxxvi [1939])

M. Schneider: 'Kaukasische Parallelen zur mitteralterlichen Mehrstimmigkeit', *AcM*, xii (1940), 12, 52

W. Wiora: 'Systematik der musikalischen Erscheinungen der Umsingens', *Jb für Volksliedforschung*, vii (1941), 128–95

E. Emsheimer: 'Preliminary Remarks on Mongolian Music and Instruments', 'Music of Eastern Mongolia', *The Music of the Mongols*, i (Stockholm, 1943), 69–100, 1–97

C. Sachs: *The Rise of Music in the Ancient World: East and West* (New York, 1943)

E. J. Wellesz: *Eastern Elements in Western Chant: Studies in the Early History of Ecclesiastical Music* (Boston, MA, 1947, 2/1967)

W. Graff: *Die musikwissenschaftlichen Phonogrammer Rudolf Pöchs von der Nordküste Neuguineas* (Habilitationsscrift, U. of Vienna, 1952; Vienna, 1950)

W. Wiora: 'On the Method of Comparative Melodic Research', *JIFMC*, ix (1957), 55

K. Husmann: *Grundlagen der antiken und orientalischen Musikkultur* (Berlin, 1961)

C. Sachs: *The Wellsprings of Music: an Introduction to Ethnomusicology* (Leiden and The Hague, 1962/R1977)

J. Maher: 'More on the History of the Comparative Method: the Tradition of Darwinism in August Schleicher's Work', *Anthropological Linguistics*, viii (1966), 1

R. Heinz: *Geschichtsbegriff und Wissenschaftscharakter der Musikwissenschaft in der zweiten Hälfte des 19. Jahrhunderts* (Regensburg, 1968)

W. Mühlmann: *Geschichte der Anthropologie* (Frankfurt am Main, 2/1968)

M. Harris: *The Rise of Anthropological Theory: a History of Theories of Culture* (London, 1969)

R. Katičić: *A Contribution to the General Theory of Comparative Linguistics* (The Hague, 1970)

F. Födermayr: *Zur gesanglichen Stimmgebung in der aussereuropäischen Musik* (Vienna, 1971)

R. Goll: *Der Evolutionismus: Analyse eines Grundbegriffs neuzeitlichen Denkens* (Munich, 1972)

D. Schüller: *Beziehungen zwischen west- und westzentralafrikanischen Staaten von 1482 bis 1700* (Vienna, 1972)

W. Graf: 'Zum interdisziplinären Charakter der vergleichenden Musikwissenschaft', *Mitteilungen der Anthropologischen Gesellschaft zu Wien*, cii (1973), 91

F. Ll. Harrison: *Time, Place and Music: an Anthology of Ethnomusicological Observation c1550 to c1800* (Amsterdam, 1973)

E. M. von Hornbostel: 'Geburt und erste Kindheit der Musik', *Jb für musikalische Volks- und Völkerkunde*, vii (1973), 9 [post. publ. of lecture delivered in 1928]

W. Graf: 'Die vergleichende Musikwissenschaft in Österreich seit 1896', *YIFMC*, vi (1974), 15–43

L. E. R. Picken: *Folk Music Instruments of Turkey* (London, 1975)

W. Wiora: *Ergebnisse und Aufgaben vergleichender Musikforschung* (Darmstadt, 1975)

A. Schneider: *Musikwissenschaft und Kulturkreislehre, Zur Methodik und Geschichte der vergleichende Musikwissenschaft* (Bonn, 1976)

——: 'Stil, Schicht, Stratigraphie und Geschichte der Volksmusik: zur historischen Erforschung oral tradierter Music', *Studia musicologica Academia Scientica Hungaricae*, xx (1978), 339

——: 'Vergleichende Musikwissenschaft als Morphologie und Stilkritik: Werner Danckerts Stellung in der Volksliedforschung und Musikethnologie', *Jb für Volksliedforschung*, xxiv (1979), 11

A. Simon: 'Probleme, Aufgaben und Ziele der Ethnomusikologie', *Jb für musikalische Volks- und Völkerkunde*, ix (1979), 8–52

W. Graff: *Vergleichende Musikwissenschaft: ausgewählte Aufsätze* (Vienna, 1980)

E. F. K. Koerner: 'Schleichers Einfluss auf Haeckel: Schlaglichter auf die wechselseitige Abhängigkeit zwischen linguistischen und biologischen Theorien im 19. Jahrhundert', *Zeitschrift für vergleichende Sprachforschung*, xcv (1981), 1

R. Falck and T. Rice, eds.: *Cross-cultural Perspectives on Music* (Toronto, 1982)

F. Födermayr: 'Zum Konzept einer vergleichend-systematischen Musikwissenschaft', *Musikethnologische Sammelbände*, vi (1983), 25

B. Nettl: *The Study of Ethnomusicology: Twenty-nine Issues and Concepts* (Urbana, Chicago and London, 1983)

A. Schneider: *Analogie und Rekonstruktion: Studien zur Methodologie der Musikgeschichtsschreibung und zur Frühgeschichte der Musik*, i (Bonn, 1984)

——: 'Tonsystem und Intonation', *Hamburger Jb der Musikwissenschaft*, ix (1986), 153–99

V. Kalisch: *Entwurf einer Wissenschaft von der Musik: Guido Adler* (Baden Baden, 1988)

A. Schneider: 'Musikwissenschaftliche Theorienbildung, aussereuropäische Musik und (psycho-)akustische Forschung', *Colloquium: Festschrift Martin Vogel zum 65, Geburtstag* (Bonn, 1988), 145

——: 'Erich Mortiz von Hornbostel: Tonart und Ethos', *Jb für Volkslied forschung*, xxxiii (1988), 156

A. Beurmann and A. Schneider: 'Probleme und Aufgaben akustisch-tonometrischen Forschung in der vergleichenden Musikwissenschaft', *Acustica*, lxix (1989), 156

H. Schneider and A. Beurmann: 'Tonsysteme, Frequenzdistanz, Klangformen und die Bedeutung experimenteller Forschung für die vergleichende Musikwissenschaft', *Hamburger Jb der Musikwissenschaft*, xi (1990), 179

A. Schneider: 'Psychological Theory and Comparative Musicology', *Comparative Musicology and Anthropology of Music: Essays on the History of Ethnomusicology*, ed. B. Nettl and P. Bohlman (Chicago, IL, and London, 1991), 293

2: SWITZERLAND

MAX PETER BAUMANN

Although there was sporadic interest in Swiss folk customs during the Renaissance, it was not focussed specifically on songs or instrumental music. Publications of the period give specific pointers on the nature and distribution of folk music at that time: the *Kühreihen* or *ranz des vaches* (herdsman's song) from the Appenzell in Georg Rhaw's *Bicinia* (1545); the Swiss dance *Der Sibentaler genandt* (1556) by Urban Weiss, in Wolff Heckel's *Lautten-Buch* (1562); and references to *Alpsegen*, dancing, singing at Easter and New Year, *Sternsingen* (Epiphany songs) and nightwatchmen's songs in Cyssat's *Colletanea chronica und denkwürdige Sachen* (1565; ed. J. Schmid, 1969–72). Other brief references to folk music occur in such contemporary sources, *Ein Lebensbild aus dem Jahrhundert der Reformation* by Thomas Platter the Elder (ed. H. Kohl, 1921) and *Tagebuchblätter . . . des 16. Jahrhunderts* by Felix Platter (ed. H. Kohl, 1913). The first detailed account of the alphorn and its use appeared in *De raris et admirandis herbis* by Conrad Gesner (1555). General interest in historical battle songs was shown by 15th- and 16th-century chroniclers following the rise of the Confederation. However, these and other lesser sources tell little about the music itself. Johannes Hofer's medical dissertation, printed in 1688, refers to the homesickness experienced by exiled shepherds when they heard the *Cantilena Helvetica*. This was the first of a long series of references to the effect of alphorn music, or of the *ranz des vaches*, on Swiss expatriates, particularly those engaged in foreign military service.

During the 18th century, with the growth of Helvetian patriotism and Jean-Jacques Rousseau's 'return to nature', the ranz des vaches, whether sung or played (on alphorn or bagpipe), was increasingly regarded as the essence of Swiss *Nationalmelodie*. From the 17th century onwards, secular songs had been shunned by the upper classes and censured by the authorities as 'frivolous', to be replaced by compulsory psalm-singing. The authorities aimed, in the words of M. P. Planta, 'to suppress vexatious and corrupting songs and introduce beneficial ones in their place'. These aims were partly supported by men like Johan Jakob Bodmer (1698–1783), Johan Kaspar Lavater (1741–1801) and their followers, who were often offended by the real folk songs of the period; such genres as the *Kiltlieder* (courting songs), cowherds' sayings and teasing verses were considered unworthy of attention. Later, in the 2nd edition of the *Sammlung von Schweizer-Kühreihen . . . Volkliedern* (1805, rev. and enl. 2/1812), there appears the regretful, ironic and self-accusing statement: 'Our old national songs are in part lost or extinct, in part spoiled and misrepresented'.

The ideas of the Enlightenment as proposed by Bodmer and Albrecht von Haller (1707–1737) gained influence when applied to the 'return to nature' movement. Already in 1724 Bodmer and Laurenz Zellweger had searched for the famous *Küh-Reyhen* and *Senenspruch* to prove that 'human nature is alike in all reasonable people' (Bodmer to Zellweger, 14 September 1724). Mountain life and customs were extolled in the poem *Die Alpen* (1729) by Haller, which was a far-reaching influence toward idealization of the herdsmen's life from the view of the urban dweller. With Rousseau's musical notation of the *ranz des vaches* in the *Dictionnaire de musique* (1768), this interest found a scientific basis (see fig.1).

Before 1788 and before the numerous and (mostly) German travel accounts about Switzerland were published towards the end of the 18th century (Karl Gottlob Küttner, Karl Spazier, Christoph Meiners, Count Friedrich Leopold zu Stolberg, Heinrich Zschokke and Johan Gottfried Ebel), the scholar and official scribe from Langnau, Gottlieb Sigmund Studer (1761–1808), started with the *Berner Bergfreunde* (groups of Bernese mountain-lovers) to collect and document folk songs, *ranz de vaches* and songs of herdsmen of the Bernese Oberland, Alpenzell, Uri, Schwyz and Unterwalden. This early collecting activity, inspired by Ossian and Haller (but hardly under the influence of Johann Gottfried von Herder), resulted in the first edition of a genuine folk-song collection – The *Acht Schweizer-Kühreihen, mit Musik und Text* by Sigmund von Wagner. It appeared in 1805 on the occasion of the pastoral festival at Unspunnen near Interlaken on 17 August. This was the beginning of Swiss folk-song research, and by the 4th edition in 1826 included 76 songs with guitar or piano accompaniment. A few art songs by Gottlieb Jakob Kuhn and Ferdinand Huber were also inserted, for the aim was to offer the people new and better folk songs as well as old ones. It was hoped to satisfy the 'townsman's longing for the idyllic' by reviving extinct customs and songs, and to inspire visiting tourists with an interest in Swiss folk life. There was also a political aspect to the Unspunnen festival, for it marked the reinstatement of Berne as the 'directing canton' for that year, following Napoleon's Act of Mediation in 1803. By means of public exercises in alphorn playing, by singing and by Alpine contests, country folk were prepared for later self-glorification in the *ranz des vaches* and cowherd songs (*Küher-* and *Sennenlieder*) composed in popular style during the 19th and 20th centuries. Thus *Musikfolklorismus*, the use of traditional folklore to create and rationalize history, was established in the early 19th century.

Folk-song collection and study first began in educated circles among the followers of Johann Rudolf Wyss, Sigmund Wagner, Gottlieb Jakob Kuhn and Ferdinand Huber in Berne, and of Martin Usteri, D. H. Hess and J. U. Hegner in Zurich. Isolated songs and *airs* soon appeared in calendars, weekly journals and almanacs, and individual collections also appeared, such as the *Allgemeines Schweizer-Liederbuch* (1825) and the *Schweizerisches Taschen-Liederbuch 'Alpenröschen'* (1849). The attention of the German romantic literary movement introduced a philological approach. In addition to the object lessons provided by Herder, L. Achim von Arnim, Clemens Brentano, Rochus von Liliencron, Ludwig Erk and Franz M. Böhme, the work of a long succession of immigrants and scholars from Germany (Stolberg, Meisner,

1. *Musical notation of the 'ranz des vaches' in Rousseau's 'Dictionnaire de musique' (1768)*

2. *The Alpsegen: woodcut by Joseph Balmer from 'Schweizerisches Kunst-Album' (1862)*

Manfred Szadrowsky, Ernst Ludwig Rochholz and John Meier) first stimulated and later paved the way for systematic collecting. Interests were still
predominantly philological under the foundation of the Schweizerisches
Archiv für Volkskunde, but conditions improved from 1906 with the founding,
under the inspiration of J. Meier, of the Volksliedarchiv (Basle), first for
collections of German-Swiss folk tunes, then (from 1907) of French, and soon
afterwards of Rhaeto-Romanic and Italian. Since then the research findings of
A. Tobler, H. In der Gand, O. von Greyerz, A. Rossat, G. Züricher,
S. Grolimund, A. L. Gassmann, M. Maisen and many others have been
published regularly in the *Schriften der Schweizerischen Gesellschaft für Volkskunde*.
But research was mostly geared towards local interest which centred around
the *Heimatschutz* by fostering regional values and identities and was oriented by
the 'undeniable and sacred duty' to save from oblivion the inherited folk
treasures with one great national piece of work. Until World War II,
therefore, the goal was collecting and preserving through registering rather
than promoting scientifically based debates and the exchange of views on the
Swiss folk music tradition and the oral practice of transmission.

Bibliography

GENERAL

P. Geiger: *Volksliedinteresse und Volksliedforschung in der Schweiz vom Anfang des 18. Jahrhunderts bis zum Jahre 1830* (Berne, 1912)
W. Merian: 'Das schweizerische Volkslied in musikalischer Beziehung', *Die Garbe*, ii (1918), no.4, p.116; no.5, p.149; no.6, p.176
O. von Greyerz: *Das Volkslied der deutschen Schweiz* (Frauenfeld and Leipzig, 1927)
P. Budry, ed.: *Die Schweiz, die singt: illustrierte Geschichte des Volksliedes, des Chorgesanges und der Festspiele in der Schweiz* (Erlenbach and Zurich, 1932)
R. Weiss: 'Musik und Gesang', *Volkskunde der Schweiz* (Erlenbach, 1946), 223
W. Wiora: *Zur Frühgeschichte der Musik in den Alpenländern* (Basle, 1949)
A. Geering: 'Schweiz', §E, *MGG*
M. Zulauf: *Das Volkslied in der Schweiz im 19. Jahrhundert* (Berne, 1972)
M. P. Baumann: *Bibliographie zur ethnomusikologischen Literatur der Schweiz. Mit einem Beitrag zu Geschichte, Gegenstand und Problemen der Volksliedforschung* (Winterthur, 1981)
P. Budry, ed.: *La Suisse qui chante: Histoire illustrée de la chanson populaire, du chant choral et du Festspiel en Suisse* (Geneva, 1981)

COLLECTIONS

Acht Schweizer-Kühreihen (Berne, 1805, rev. and enl., 2/1812 as *Sammlung von Schweizer-Kühreihen und alten Volksliedern*, 4/1826)
S. Wagner: *Sammlung aller Lieder, Gedichte und andern Schriften auf das schweizerische Alphirten-Fest zu Unspunnen im Kanton Bern* (Berne, 1805)
E. L. Rocholz, ed.: *Eidgenössische Lieder-Chronik: Sammlung der ältesten und werthvollsten Schlacht-, Bundes- und Parteilieder* (Berne, 1835, 2/1842)
——: *Alemannisches Kinderlied und Kinderspiel aus der Schweiz* (Leipzig, 1857)
F. J. Schild: *Der Grossätti aus dem Leberberg* (Solothurn, 1863–73)
A. von Flugi: *Die Volkslieder des Engadin* (Strasbourg, 1873)
L. Tobler: *Schweizerische Volkslieder* (Frauenfeld, 1882–4/R1975)
A. Tobler: *Kühreihen oder Kühreigen, Jodel und Jodellied in Appenzell* (Leipzig, 1890)
P. J. Derin: 'Chanzuns popularas engiadinaisas', *Annalas della Societad Rhaeto-Romanscha* vi (1891), 34–75; vii (1892), 45
A. Rossat: 'Chants patois jurassiens', *Schweizerisches Archiv für Volkskunde*, iii (1899), 257–90; iv (1900), 133–66; v (1901), 81–112, 201; vi (1902), 161, 257; vii (1903), 81, 241

C. Decurtins, ed.: *Rätoromanische Chrestomathie*, ii (Erlangen, 1901), 180–625, 680ff; iii (1902); iv (1911), 264–337, 416ff, 1014ff; ix (1908); x (1916), 1104ff

M. E. Marriage and J. Meier: 'Volkslieder aus dem Kanton Bern', *Schweizerisches Archiv für Volkskunde*, v (1901), 1–47

A. L. Gassmann: *Das Volkslied im Luzerner Wiggertal und Hinterland* (Basle, 1906)

V. Pellandini: 'Canti popolari ticinesi', *Schweizerisches Archiv für Volkskunde*, xii (1908), 36, 268

O. von Greyerz: *Im Röseligarte: schweizerische Volkslieder* (Berne, 1908–25)

S. Grolimund: *Volkslieder aus dem Kanton Solothurn* (Basle, 1910)

——: *Volkslieder aus dem Kanton Aargau* (Basle, 1911)

A. L. Gassmann: *'s Alphorn: 100 echte Volkslieder, Jodel und G'sätzli* (Zurich and Leipzig, 1913)

——: *Juhui! Volksliedbüchlein für die Schweizer Jugend: 60 echte Volkslieder, Jodel und Gsätzli für eine Vor- und Nachstimme (Naturbegleitung)* (Zurich, 1914)

K. Aeschbacher: *50 Appenzeller Volkstänze* (Trogen, 1915, 6/1944)

H. In der Gand: *Das Schwyzerfähnli: ernste und heitere Kriegs-, Soldaten- und Volkslieder der Schweiz aus dem 16., 17., 18. und 19. Jahrhundert* (Biel, 1915–17)

A. Rossat: *Les chansons populaires recueillies dans la Suisse romande* (Basle, 1917–31)

A. L. Gassmann: *D'Ländlermusik: 100 Ländler und Buuretänz aus dem Hügelland und den Schweizer Bergen* (Zurich, 1920)

A. Stoecklin: *Weihnachts- und Neujahrslieder aus der Schweiz* (Basle, 1921)

G. Züricher: *Kinderlieder der deutschen Schweiz* (Basle, 1926)

E. Fisch: *22 canti popolari ticinesi* (Zurich, 1927–31)

F. R. Berger: *Das Basler Trommeln: nebst vollständigem Lehrgang und einer Sammlung aller Basler Trommelmärsche* (Basle, 1928)

T. Dolf: 'Las melodias dellas canzuns popularas de Schons', *Annalas de la Società retoromantscha*, xlii (1929), 131

A. Maissen, A. Schorta and W. Wehrli, eds.: *Die Lieder der Consolaziun dell'olma devoziusa*, Rätoromanische Volkslieder, i (Basle, 1945)

G. G. Cloetta: *Chanzunettas populeras rumauntschas* (Basle, 1958)

A. L. Gassmann: *Was unsere Väter sangen: Volkslieder und Volksmusik vom Vierwaldstättersee, aus der Urschweiz und dem Entlebuch* (Basle, 1961)

M. Vernet: *Les carillons du Valais* (Basle, 1965)

Schweizer Liedermacher, i: *Ernst Born, Martin Hauzenberger, Jürg Jegge, Walter Lietha, Fritz Widmer: Portraits und Materialen* (Berne, 1976)

M. P. Baumann: *Hausbuch der Schweizer Volkslieder. Mit einem geschichtlichen Überblick zu Volkslied und Volksmusik* (Berne, 1980)

B. Bachmann-Geiser and others: *Volksmusik in der Schweiz* (Zofingen, 1985)

C. Brăiloiu: *Musique populaire Suisse* (Geneva, 2/1986) [established on the basis of recordings made between 1927–51; 2 discs]

STUDIES

G. Tarenne: *Recherches sur les ranz des vaches, ou sur les chansons pastorales des bergers de la Suisse* (Paris, 1813)

H. Szadrowsky: 'Nationaler Gesang bei den Alpenbewohnern', *Jb des Schweizer Alpenclub*, i (1864), 504

——: 'Die Musik und die tonerzeugenden Instrumente der Alpenbewohner', *Jb des Schweizer Alpenclub*, iv (1867–8), 275–352

L. Gauchat: *Etude sur le ranz des vaches fribourgeois* (Zurich, 1899)

A. Tobler: *Das Volkslied im Appenzellerlande* (Zurich, 1903)

——: 'Der Volkstanz im Apenzellerlande', *Schweizerisches Archiv für Volkskunde*, viii (1905), 1, 100, 178

A. Rossat: *La chanson populaire dans la Suisse romande* (Basle, 1917)

M. Bukofzer: 'Magie und Technik in der Alpenmusik', *Schweizer Annalen* (1936), 205

H. In der Gand: 'Volkstümliche Musikinstrumente der Schweiz', *Schweizerisches Archiv für Volkskunde*, xxxvi (1937), 73–120

W. Sichardt: *Der alpenländische Jodler und der Ursprung des Jodelns* (Berlin, 1939)

V. Alford: 'Music and Dance of the Swiss Folk', *MQ*, xxxvii (1941), 500

H. Spreng: *Die Alphirtenfeste zu Unspunnen 1805 und 1808* (Interlaken, 1946)

L. Witzig: *Dances of Switzerland* (London, 1949)

A. Geering: 'Von der Tessiner Volksmesse', *Schweizerisches Archiv für Volkskunde*, xlvii (1951), 55

J. Burdet: *La danse populaire dans le pays de Vaud sous le régime bernois* (Basle, 1958)

W. Senn: 'Jodeln: ein Beitrag zur Entstehung und Verbreitung des Wortes', *Jb des Österreichischen Volksliedwerkes*, xi (1962), 150

K. Klenk: 'Der Volkstanz in der Schweiz', *Jb herausgegeben von den Sekundarlehrerkonferenzen der Ostschweiz* (1963), 54

M. Vernet: *Cloches et musique* (Neuchâtel, 1963)

G. Duthaler: 'Die Melodien der alten Schweizermärsche', *Schweizerisches Archiv für Volkskunde*, lx (1964), 18

J. Burdet: 'Chansons populaires', *La musique dans le canton de Vaud au XIXe siècle* (Lausanne, 1971), 330–406 [with disc]

M. P. Baumann: *Aus Tradition und Gegenwart der Volksmusik im Oberwallis* (Brig, 1972)

W. Meyer and H. Oesch: 'Maultrommelfunde in der Schweiz', *Festschrift Arnold Geering* (Berne, 1972), 211

A. Schmid and B. Geiser: *Chlefeli: Instrumente zur Fastenzeit* (Schwyz, 1973)

M. P. Baumann: 'Zur Lage der Volksmusikforschung in der Schweiz', *SMz*, xv (1975), 249

H. van der Meer, B. Geiser and K. H. Schickhaus: *Das Hackbrett, ein alpenländisches Musikinstrument* (Herisau and Trogen, 1975)

M. P. Baumann: *Musikfolklore und Musikfolklorismus: eine ethnomusikologische Untersuchung zum Funktionswandel des Jodels* (Winterthur, 1976)

B. Geiser: *Das Alphorn in der Schweiz* (Berne, 1976) [with Fr. and Eng. summary]

M. -J. Glanzmann: *My nächste Lied: 20 Jahre Schweizer Chanson* (Zurich and Cologne, 1976)

B. Bachmann-Geiser: *Die Volksmusikinstrumente der Schweiz* (Leipzig, 1981)

R. Wolfram: 'Die Volkstänze der Schweiz', *Beiträge zur Musik in Vorarlberg und im Bodenseeraum*, ed. W. Deutsch and E. Schneider (Vienna, 1983), 185

B. Bremberger and S. Döll: 'Der Betruf auf dem Urnerboden im Umfeld von Geschichte, Inhalt und Funktion', *Jahrbuch für Volksliedforschung* (1984), 65–96

C. Collenberg: *Wandel im Volkslied. Langfristige Veränderungen in der Zusammensetzung eines Volkslied-bestandes, dargestellt am räto-romanischen Volksliedkorpus* (Freiburg, 1986)

3: THE NETHERLANDS

ERNST HEINS

The forerunners of contemporary ethnomusicology in the Netherlands must be placed in the 19th-century colonial context. By 1800 the Dutch government had possessions both in the East Indies (chiefly Java) and the West Indies (a few islands in the Caribbean called the Dutch Antilles, and along the South American northern coast, Dutch Guyana or Surinam). Until the end of the century the Dutch ruled additionally over only the Moluccas and a few scattered regions in Sumatra and Sulawesi.

From the beginning, the Dutch focussed their ethnographic attention mainly on Java, the most densely populated island of the Indonesian archipelago. The first diffuse ethnomusicological studies 'avant la lettre' were written by philologists and historians, whose linguistic, ethnographic and socio-historical knowledge was found to be of value for the effectiveness of colonial administration. Thus the government's need to know about the inhabitants of the colonies and their habitat singularly coincided with geological, zoological, botanical, historical, linguistical and ethnological curiosity.

Among those who foreshadowed modern Dutch ethnomusicology was the philologist J. A. Wilkens, who wrote a lengthy description of the gamelan – including an inventory of its instruments – in a linguistic study on Javanese poetry (1850). In his classic study on Java (1875), the historian J. P. Veth summarized the current knowledge about Javanese music, which had been observed haphazardly by travelling scholars, missionaries and civil servants.

In the 1870s, with the development of industrial capitalism, Dutch colonial policy underwent a radical change. Traditional indifference to the so-called Outer Regions (i.e. all islands other than Java) turned into avid interest. By 1914 the whole of Indonesia as it is known today was firmly under Dutch administrative control. In the colonies the industrial revolution brought about sudden recognition of European technical supremacy. The development of empirical and observational sciences marked the next stage of early ethnomusicology in the Netherlands.

Jan P. N. Land (1834–97) was its most outspoken forerunner. He taught philosophy and Oriental languages at the universities of Amsterdam and Leyden, but, as a scholar of universal interest, he also examined the scale structures and intervals of non-European musics. This concern, shared with his friend A. J. Ellis, was a by-product of his studies of ancient Dutch music theory (e.g. Christian Huygens's tone-systems and Thysius's lute-book), musicological writings that precede his 'Recherches sur l'histoire de la gamme arabe' (1883). This work on classical Arabic tone material is one of the first European books to approach the subject analytically. In the same year the Dutchman J. A. van Aalst published his famous monograph, *Chinese Music*.

Land and Ellis worked together on tone measurements of (randomly encountered) Javanese gamelan instruments. Although Land had never been to Indonesia, he had been exposed several times to Javanese gamelan music. As early as 1857 he witnessed what was probably the very first gamelan performance by Europeans. Students of the Royal Academy of Delft, most of whom were to become colonial civil servants, carried a museum gamelan through the town in a festive reconstruction of a *garebeg* procession to celebrate the anniversary of the school. The anonymous author of the programme notes, dating from 1857, puts a 19th-century ethnomusicological dilemma into words. Bearing in mind that no two gamelan have the same tuning, he states:

> A difference of a quarter tone does not mean 'off pitch' for a Javanese; for instance, in this gamelan the tone *manis* equals in *f*, and in another gamelan it equals a tone between *f* and *f♯*, while in both, the preceding note is equal to *e*. One may attribute this difference to particular taste; one person would prefer this tone-relation, another would prefer other nuances in the tone scale.

Instead of leaving the argument at this point, he cannot help but go on:

> However, it may well be a deficiency of the instruments themselves, because the gongs and keys have to have the same thickness throughout. And because a Javanese has no knowledge of the mechanics necessary to make them all the same, his work simply has to be deficient . . . The hearing gets accustomed to this imperfection, however, and this explains the said difference in taste.

The writer states that there are two kinds of gamelan, the five-tone *slendro* and the seven-tone *pelog*. Little did he know that the scales, interval structures and tunings of non-European music would dominate the writings of successive generations of ethnomusicologists. That gamelan musicians can play as many as 300 pieces by heart he also attributes to a 'default':

> The variety of sounds and the simplicity of style cause all pieces to sound almost alike.

This strange reconstruction was followed 22 years later in 1879 by the performances of Javanese gamelan musicians playing

> a chamber-gamelan which the ruler of Solo, H.H. Prince Mangkunegoro, had sent to the Netherlands to perform at the Colonial Exhibition in Arnhem. I went there several times and enjoyed these performances. I also suggested to my friend, the musician Daniel de Lange, who studied this gamelan, that he should make a comparison with the Delft instruments, that in the meantime had moved to the Ethnographical Museum in Leyden . . .

The dismal gamelan performances during the Colonial Exhibition at Amsterdam in 1883, probably badly organized due to lack of funds, merely resulted in strengthening the visitors' natural dislike of the musical art of other races (Land, 1890, pp.1, 3; see also Mellema, 1960).

The extensive essay 'On Our Knowledge of Javanese Music', published as an introduction to J. Groneman (1890), prompted Land to become the first Western musical scientist to occupy himself with Javanese music. To establish the acoustical properties of the instruments, he consulted Ellis. As for the musical aspects, his own limited experience was supplemented by that of Groneman. Groneman lived in Jogja Karta, the centre of Javanese culture, where he was the sultan's personal physician. A sharp observer, he co-operated locally with a professional photographer. He wrote to Land and sent him his manuscript which contained inventories and descriptions of various uses of most Jogjanese palace gamelan. Land had it published as *De gamelan te Jogjakarta* to which he added his 'Voorrede' (Foreword). Groneman and Land's book (1890) soon became a landmark in 19th-century Javanology. As late as 1934 Jaap Kunst and others still leaned heavily on Groneman.

New information from a variety of sources was the basis of a new landmark, characterized by conscientious scholarship – Johan F. Snelleman's articles in the leading reference work on the Dutch colony, the *Encyclopaedie van Nederlandsch Indië* (1899–1905; enl. 2/1917–21). In collaboration with the Dutch composer-conductor Daniël de Lange, Snelleman reworked his encyclopedia for inclusion in Lavignac's French music encyclopedia (1922).

Meanwhile, in parallel with other magnificent monographs on Indonesian arts and crafts and amid an increasing number of smaller musicological publications, the monumental, bi-lingual *De gongfabricatie te Semarang* by E. Jacobsen and J. H. van Hassalt (1907) was devoted with painstaking ethnographic precision to a description of the manufacture of gongs at the Javanese centre of the gong industry.

Outside Indonesia, but equally remote from his own country, van Aalst published one of the first European monographs on Chinese music while working in Shanghai (1884). He was a close observer and published his studies in English, making them accessible to international scholars. Van Aalst states

---

1. *Is the only difference between Ladrang and Ketawang that in a Ketawang there are twice as many gong strokes as in Ladrang?*

2. *Are there other differences between various types of compositions apart from the number of ketuk-, kenong-, kempool-[sic] and gong strokes? If so, which?*

3. *Why is there no pathet jangga or pathet tengah?*

4. *Are the following musical terms known in the Mangkunegaran?*
   lumampah – nesek – ngracak – nyendal – pancer – ngrangkep – imbal – dhawahi – minjal – ngepinjal – ngencot – wela – soewook [sic] – majeng – rep – kendhu – dhedheg – antal – napas.

5, 6 *[deleted]*

7. *Is the difference between gambang nem and gambang barang known in the Mangkunegaran?*

8. *What is pangkon?*

9. *Is Groneman's statement correct saying that there is a low kenong nem called japan? Does this apply to the Mangkunegaran? In any case this does not apply to gamelan Kanyut Mesem, but is this the case with other gamelan?*

10. *Further, Groneman states, 'Pelog places in pl.lima and pl.barang need a kenong tuned to lima or barang instead of a kenong nem [. . .].' Is this correct?*

11. *Are kemanak known?*

12. *I have noticed that in every pathet certain melody tones seem to stand out.*
    In pathet nem slendro these seemed to me to be jangga, tengah and nem; in pathet nem pelog: penunggul, jangga, nem. Is this correct?

13. *Tumbuk nem is used to change easily from slendro into pelog vice versa. Tumbuk gulu or tumbuk lima also?*

14. *In which (type of) compositions does such a transition occur?*

15. *Could the mantri langenpraja add to the list of compositions played or known in the Mangkunegaran: a. pathet; b. type of buka; c. category of compositions to which the piece belongs (ageng, ketawang, ladrang, etc.); d. with gending ageng also the number of kethuk strokes; e. at which occasion in particular a composition is usually played.*

---

1. *Questionnaire (a), used by Jaap Kunst in the early stages of his research into Javanese gamelan and (b) autograph in Javanese script of the reply letter from Prince Suryokusumo of Solo, a gamelan connoisseur at the Mangkunegaran Court in Surakarta:*

This letter is graciously presented to my brother Mr J. Kunst and his wife.

I have received my Brother's letter, dated 27 October 1921. Its contents are clear to me. With much pleasure I would like to reply to your request for information on the foundations ('babagan' in Javanese) of Javanese gamelan-theory. In order to keep this information together and neatly arranged I will gather it in book form, if you have no objections. The information cannot be abbreviated since there appears to be a substantial amount. In the first place the answers to your questions are extensive, and secondly they are related to many other issues.

I plan to explain everything as clearly as possible, for example, the transition of one scale to the other, with or without defining the distance ('godhagan' in Javanese) between the tones. If that transition contains intervals, how many tone-distances make up each interval? In European music they are perhaps called whole tone and semitone, but in Javanese gamelan we could speak of one and a half tone. In fact, the Javanese do not yet know this, or rather they do not want to take this into account. I plan to demonstrate all basics to the smallest detail in the hope to meet your demands as fully as possible. I agree with your point that the explanations in the existing literature are unsatisfactory. That is why for a long time I have cherished the wish to write about the theory of Javanese gamelan. I have delighted in gamelan ever since I was a child, but until now I have neglected to collect this information.

Since His Highness has requested me to answer all your questions and you addressed yourself directly to me, I will certainly hasten to realize my plans as soon as possible.

Besides I also possess a collection of Javanese compositions ('gendhing-gendhing') notated in cipher script and provided with 'pathet'. This collection is a sequel to the work of my late father-in-law, R. M. T. Wreksodiningrat. At a later date I shall give you this collection, too.

Because it will take some time to finish this work, I humbly ask your forgiveness for having to be patient until then.

Surakarta, 7 November 1921.   *Soerjokoesoemo.*

The original and the collection of compositions mentioned in the letter are kept in the Ethnomusicology Centre 'Jaap Kunst', University of Amsterdam. (Translations by Ernst Heins)

in his foreword that he hoped to obliterate general misunderstandings about Chinese music. Yet, a certain Eurocentric bias is not easily suppressed. Commenting on heterophony, he writes:

> All these instruments play, or at least try to play, in unison; still it seems to a foreigner not acquainted with their music that each performer has a part of his own, and that each aims to distinguish himself above his colleagues by making as much noise as he can (1884, p.36).

All these books have become classics. Significantly, the pioneering Dutchmen were quoted over and over in the many early works by others; Erich M. von Hornbostel, Curt Sachs, Robert Lachmann and later Manfred Bukofzer all read Dutch fluently.

The Dutch colonies in the West did not attract nearly as much ethnomusicological attention as those in the East. However, some work was done on music in Surinam by L. van Panhuys, the predecessor of Melville Herskovitz and T. A. C. Comvalius.

Early ethnomusicologists in Europe either worked in their own countries or else turned their backs on their own society and chose a remote region. Jaap Kunst (1891–1960) was one of the few scholars who did both.

A musically gifted law student in Groningen (he played the violin from the age of six and later became the only licensed music critic in the Netherlands), he spent much time in the island of Terschelling, where he systematically collected songs and dance melodies through observation, interviews and participation and also re-introduced the fiddle to the island. His *Terschellinger Volksleven* was published in 1915, and in 1916–18 the three-volume collection *Noord-Nederlandse Volksliederen en -dansen* appeared, both titles being reprinted one year after publication. *Terschellinger Volksleven* especially set the style of Kunst's future work in which 'he was to give the scales back to the Javanese'. It contains songs and dances, related to their uses and functions, of the only region in the Netherlands that can claim an unbroken folk song and dance tradition to the present day. With a third edition in 1951, it is still used by the Terschelling islanders as a local reference tool. They refer to it as the 'Konsteboek', a good example of feedback from local culture that Kunst intended.

In 1917 Kunst graduated as a doctor of law, worked for a few months as a lawyer in a bank and then became a clerk in the Department of Education at the Amsterdam City Hall. But after one year he joined a *diseuse lyrique* and a young pianist in a varied programme of 'vieilles chansons de France en costume de l'époque', chamber music, fairy tales with slide projections, music and animal imitations and living folk songs from the Netherlands. Kunst's role in the trio was as a violinist and animal imitator. With borrowed money this unorthodox freelance group set off for Indonesia in 1919 and undertook an extensive, eight-month tour throughout the archipelago, performing no fewer than 95 times and earning enough money to pay back their loan.

His two companions returned to the Netherlands, but Kunst, having heard 'the best' Javanese gamelan music in the palace of Prince Paku Alam in Jogjakarta, decided to stay behind to learn more about it. To earn a living he acquired a position in the section of Social and Legal Affairs of the Department of State Colonial Enterprises, which kept him occupied daily from 7 am till 2 pm. The afternoons, evenings, early morning hours and all his free days were spent entirely on musicological research, either behind his desk or in his musical instruments collection (the Museum), if not in the field. Kunst was one of the first ethnomusicologists to do systematic fieldwork; it was a *sine qua non* for him. In 1921 he married Katy van Wely; their honeymoon in Bali resulted in a detailed study of Balinese instrumental and vocal genres, the first in its kind. Other firsts included his articles on Sundanese (West-Javanese) music.

Kunst's immense correspondence with leading ethnomusicologists all over the world dates from this time. To Hornbostel alone, Kunst wrote an estimated 160 letters (see fig.2). Quotations from Kunst's letters illustrate some of his ideas and working methods. Unhappy with the articles by Snelleman (1918, 1927) on Indonesian music and inspired by Fox Strangways (1914), he wrote to Hornbostel, whom he always regarded and approached as his guru:

> I am writing an article that has to replace the outdated and faulty present encyclopedia-article. Progress is slow and the work threatens to become cannily exhaustive (23 October 1930) . . . The last months I have put more energy than ever in completing that study about Javanese music (which has become much too large for an Encyclopedia article and is now being prepared as a book) (14 December 1931).

He was referring here to his *De toonkunst van Java* (*Music in Java*), which was published in 1934.

Hornbostel knew and appreciated the earlier studies by Land and Groneman. He had planned a German translation in the series *Sammelbände für Vergleichende Musikwissenschaft*. But, he writes to Kunst:

> Through your work it has been completely overtaken and it does not pay the trouble any longer to republish it again. Now I would like to ask you if you would be willing in principle to take a volume on Indonesian music upon you or to co-operate in it (8 October 1923).

What fascinated Kunst were, in his own words, tone systems and interval measurements. The first thing he confides to Hornbostel after his return from the island of Nias, where he filmed as well as photographed, recorded (wax cylinders) and collected a wealth of instruments, is that: 'Almost all their songs contain a pure tritonus!' In his second letter to Hornbostel (2 August 1923) he writes:

> The last year Katy and I have been concerned with the question of origin and age of *slendro* and *pelog*. I am therefore strongly convinced that at least in Java *pelog* is the older, although the Javanese themselves think that *slendro* came first, basing themselves on the strangest arguments.

Hornbostel sent Kunst, in exchange for the offprints of Sundanese and Balinese music, which Kunst had sent him because of the photographs, his *Blasquintenzirkel* theory. To Hornbostel, the Sundanese and Balinese scales that Kunst had outlined in these early studies were no less than a godsend:

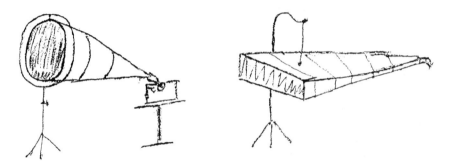

2. *Two types of an extendable device to be attached to a phonograph, as drawn by E. M. von Hornbostel in a letter to Jaap Kunst in Java. He writes, '. . . To record polyphonic choirs, "gamelan" etc., I advise you to have a large funnel made from aluminium and resting on a tripod. In conical form and with a circular opening, one can have it constructed in such a way with separate rings, that the funnel can be folded up like a camper's drinking cup (see enclosed sketch).' (Hornbostel to Kunst, 8 October 1923.) To which Kunst replied, '. . . For the recordings with the Amberola cylinder recorder we have extended our apparatus with a large wooden funnel, 1 metre long. Further we had quite some trouble in finding a recording position for the instruments that would make the phonogram as natural as possible. Prince Alam was very satisfied with the results.' (Kunst to Hornbostel, 22 November 1923.)*

> I like to believe that the *Blasquintensystem* is the origin of all instrumental scales in the entire world, and in any case heuristically valuable in bringing order in chaos. In addition, I very much hope ever to reach a relative chronology, which until now I still have been unable to do. The theory dates from 1919. I am very happy that I have not yet made in public extensively, because the theory has first to be put to the proof by means of your large amount of measurement material. I have already started to work your scales through (8 October 1923).

Thus he concludes his private, two-page explanation of the *Blasquintenzirkel* theory to Kunst. Here we can witness the genesis of the formation of ethnomusicological theory going beyond mere description.

To this letter Kunst replied:

> We have appreciated very much that you have been so kind as to explain your theory of the blown fifth cycle to us. Of course, we have never looked at our scales from this angle.

The theory of the cycle of blown fifths occupied them until Manfred Bukofzer disproved it in 1936. After Bukofzer wrote to Kunst, Kunst replied:

> Naturally I was quite taken aback when I learned from you that von Hornbostel's theory on the cycle of blown fifths has proven to be untenable at closer examination. If ever I had had any confidence in a theory, it was this one (15 May 1936).

Kunst remained in the field, establishing instrumental tunings by means of his self-devised monochord, collecting hundreds of instruments, taking photographs and making recordings and films. He sent most of his valuable phonograms to Hornbostel in Berlin, who then had them galvanized and stored in the Phonogrammarchiv (they remained Kunst's property), and had copies made for the archive and for Kunst. He also advised Kunst to record, not only complete gamelan ensembles, but in such a way that with each repetition of the piece the recording equipment was moved to highlight a different instrument. If this were not possible he suggested that the punctuating instruments, *kenong* and gong, should be recorded with each of the successive solo parts. 'Only this way is it possible to write a score afterwards' (8 October 1923). Kunst's first set of phonograms sent to Berlin were recorded

3. Jaap Kunst during fieldwork in Irian Jaya, West New Guinea, 1932

in Paku Alam's palace and consisted of the following *gending bonang* (*ladrang*): *Igo-Igo Sl.*9; *Eling-Eling Sl.*9; *Dirodo Meto Pel.*6 and *Bima Kurda Pel.*bar.; *Tedak Saking* (*Pel. bar.*). He was also permitted to make gamelan recordings in the palaces of other Javanese rulers.

By 1930 the Musicological Archives, founded and run by the Kunsts, contained 500 instruments, 450 × 2" × 2" slides, 600 negatives and 250 wax cylinders, each with one copy.

Kunst's scholarly productivity seemed to be unlimited, especially when he was officially appointed government musicologist from 1930–32. Apart from all his other work Kunst has a place in the history of ethnomusicology as the author of a series of monographs that opened up the rich musical traditions of

Indonesia (Bali, 1925; Java, 1934; Flores, 1942; Nias, 1939; Hindu Java, 1929
– all standard works and still unsurpassed).

Yet, in spite of his apparent love for and involvement with Javanese music
Kunst, the fervent string-quartet player, never touched a gamelan instrument
except for measuring purposes. We can only guess how different *Music in Java*
(and perhaps even the field of ethnomusicology itself) might have been if he
had. The reason for his attitude, which we find hard to understand nowadays,
was the tremendous social barrier that divided colonizer and colonized before
Indonesian Independence (1949). In the colonial situation it was unthinkable
for a European to play in a Javanese or Balinese gamelan, or even take private
lessons.

In 1950, Kunst launched the term 'Ethno-musicologica' to his colleagues
Wiora and Brăiloiu, which marks the end of early ethnomusicology. In the
same year that Kunst first landed in Indonesia, the controversial Dutch music
critic Johan Sebastiaan Brandts Buys (1879–1939) arrived there. Brandts
Buys saw himself as a trained critic of music and culture and a creative artist.
While Kunst worked closely with the Javanese and Sundanese nobility over
the years, Brandts Buys's true interest lay in the understanding of folk music.
The two had very close scholarly contact, exchanging each other's notes and
articles, and were interested in each other's opinion of their work. (For a
revealing account of Brandts Buys as a scholar and fieldworker in East Java
and Madura, see Burman-Hall, 1985.)

Bibliography

J. A. Wilkens: 'Sewaka, een Javaansch gedicht', *Tijdschrift voor Nederlandsch-Indië*, xii/2 (1850),
  383–461; xiii/1 (1851), 464

J. P. Veth: *Java, geographisch, ethnologisch, historisch* (Haarlem, 1875, 2/1896–1907)

J. P. N. Land: 'Recherches sur l'histoire de la gamme arabe', *VIe congrès international des orientalistes,
  Leiden, 1883*, 35–168

J. A. van Aalst: *Chinese Music* (Shanghai, 1884)

J. Groneman: *De gamelan te Jogjakarta: Uitgegeven met eene voorrede: over onze kennis der Javaansche
  Muziek, door J. P. N. Land* (Amsterdam, 1890)

J. P. N. Land: 'Over onze kennis der Javaansche Muziek', *De gamelan te Jogjakarta*, ed. J.
  Groneman (Amsterdam, 1890)

J. F. Snelleman: 'Muziek en Muziekinstrumenten', *Encyclopaedie van Nederlandsch-Indië* (The
  Hague and Leiden, 1899–1905; enl. 2/1917–21), 812

E. Jacobson and J. H. van Hasselt: *De gongfabricatie te Semarang* (Leiden, 1907; Eng. trans., as 'The
  Manufacture of Gongs in Semarang' in *Indonesia*, no.19 [1975], 127–72)

L. C. van Panhuys: 'Mitteilungen über surinamische Ethnographie und Kolonisations-
  geschichte', *Verhandlung der XVI Internationalen Amerikanisten Kongresses* (Vienna, 1909), 521

——: 'Les chansons et la musique de la Guyane Neerlandaise', *Journal de la Société des Américanistes
  de Paris*, new ser., ix (1912), 27

A. H. Fox Strangways: *The Music of Hindostan* (Oxford, 1914/*R*1965, 1967)

J. Kunst: *Terschellinger Volksleven* (Uithuizen, 1915, 3/1951)

——: *Noord-Nederlandsche Volksliederen en -dansen* (Groningen, 1916–18, 2/1918–19)

D. de Lange and J. F. Snelleman: 'La musique et les instruments de musique dans les Indes
  Orientales néerlandaises', *EMDC*, v (1922)

J. Kunst and C. J. A. Kunst-van Wely: 'Over Balische muziek', *Djåwå*, ii (1922), 117, 194

——: 'Over toonschalen instrumenten van West-Java', *Djåwå*, iii (1923), 26

——: *De toonkunst van Bali* (Weltevreden, 1925); pt.2 in *Tijdschrift voor Indische taal-, land- en
  volkenkunde*, lxv (1925), 369–508

J. Kunst and R. Goris: *Hindoe-Javaansche muziekinstrumenten, speciaal die van Oost Java* (Batavia, 1927; rev. 2/1968 as *Hindu-Javanese Musical Instruments*)

J. S. Brandts Buys and A. Brandts Buys-van Zijp: 'De toonkunst bij de Madoereezen', *Djâwâ*, viii (1928), 1–290

J. Kunst: *De toonkunst van Java* (The Hague, 1934; Eng. trans., 1949 as *Music in Java*, enl. 3/1973)

T. A. C. Comvalius: 'Het Surinam'sche negerlied: de banja en de doe', *De West-Indische Gids*, xvii (1935–6), 211

L. C. van Panhuys: 'Surinaamsche Folklore', *De West-Indische Gids*, xvii (1935–6), 282

T. A. C. Comvalius: 'Een der vormen van het Surinaamse lied na 1863', *De West-Indische Gids*, xxi (1939), 335

J. Kunst: *Music in Nias* (Leiden, 1939)

——: *Music in Flores* (Leiden, 1942)

——: *Music in New Guinea* (The Hague, 1967)

L. Burman-Hall: 'The Life and Times of J. S. Brandts Buys (1879–1939)' (1985) [typescript]

4: FRANCE

MIRIAM ROVSING OLSEN

The first documentary records of French music pertinent to ethnomusicological research are to be found in the travel writings of explorers and missionaries. Intent upon omitting no detail of the manners and customs of the distant peoples they visited, these travellers provided first-hand observations of musical performance, sometimes with quasi-photographic illustrations of musical instruments and musical notation written down in the field. Among many works now considered classics are *Histoire d'un voyage faict en la terre du Brésil* (1585) by Jean de Léry, *Voyages en Perse, et d'autres lieux de l'Orient* (1711) by Jean Chardin and *Nouvelle relation de l'Afrique occidentale* (1728) by Jean-Baptiste Labat. The musical notation found in these accounts, unique evidence of music as a living phenomenon, began to attract the attention of scholars as early as the 17th century, and made a fundamental contribution to the development of this field of study. Thus, in his *Harmonie Universelle* (1636–7) Marin Mersenne (1588–1648) published a 'Chanson canadoise' and 'Trois chansons des Amériquains' (taken from the work of Jean de Léry). These specimens were reprinted a century later by Jean-Jacques Rousseau (1712–78) in the appendix to his *Dictionnaire de musique* (1768), under the titles of 'Danse Canadienne' and 'Chanson des sauvages du Canada' along with 'Air chinois', an 'Air suisse appelé le rans des vaches' and 'Chanson persane' (taken from Chardin's work).

At that period, too, the first serious studies of non-European music appeared, and these are still of great interest to ethnomusicologists. They include *Essai sur la musique orientale comparée à la musique européenne* (1751) by Charles Fonton, a study of Turco-Persian music first published in 1985; *Mémoire sur la musique des Chinois tant anciens que modernes* (1779) by Jean-Joseph Marie Amiot (1718–93), a missionary in Peking; and *Essai sur la musique ancienne et moderne* (1780) by Jean-Benjamin de La Borde (1734–94), which

111

included Oriental music for the first time in a general history of music. Early in the 19th century were published the works undertaken by Guillaume André Villoteau (1759–1839; see fig.1) at the request of General Bonaparte at the time of his Egyptian campaign: *De l'état actual de l'art musical en Égypte* (1812), *Description historique, technique et littéraire des instruments de musique des Orientaux* (1813) and *Mémoire sur la musique de l'antique Égypte* (1816). Villoteau's studies covered both Arab art music and folk music, recording many details on how and when this music was performed in Egypt; his doctrine of a scale in 3rds of tones was to influence research into Arab music over a long period. Villoteau also studied the music of minority ethnic groups who had settled in Egypt, originally from black Africa, Asia and Europe, his most important chapters being devoted to Ethiopian, Armenian and Greek music.

1. *Guillaume André Villoteau: portrait*

Although non-European music was a subject of ethnomusicological study in the modern sense of the term as early as the end of the 18th century, a different approach was taken to the folk music of France itself, being limited to making song collections; it was to gather strength in the middle of the 19th century and to last until the middle of the 20th. Interest in this oral traditional music was initially linked to the Romantic movement in literature (in the work of such authors as Gérard de Nerval and George Sand), and priority was given to textual study until the 1860s, while the melodies were printed in a separate section at the end of the volume. In 1852 an official project for collecting French country songs was launched, a survey, by order of Prince Louis Napoleon. Since vocal music is the natural vehicle of poetry in the oral tradition, the musical as well as the poetic side of folk song was soon recognized. More and more collections covering different regions of France came out, and from then on the tunes of songs, noted down from oral performance, were presented systematically and included in the body of the text.

At the end of the 19th century, exotic as well as French folk music was largely the province of composers who did research of their own in the field (for example, Camille Saint-Saëns, who went to Algeria and Egypt). Colonial exhibitions and visits to France by troupes of musicians from the colonies gave the general public an opportunity of hearing music from the whole world. Such music encouraged composers to broaden the musical language of Western art music, particularly modality. Greek music, a central interest, was compared with Oriental music and European folk music. Characteristic of this tendency were the efforts of the composer Francisco Salvador-Daniel, who lived in Algeria between 1853 and 1865, to unite East and West in his scholarly works and in his own compositions. In his essay *La musique arabe, ses rapports avec la musique grecque et le chant grégorien* (1863), he showed that Arab musical modes were the same as Greek modes, contradicting Villoteau's theory. The same ideas were subsequently upheld in France by the composer Louis-Albert Bourgault-Ducoudray. In 1877 he published *Trente mélodies de Grèce et d'Orient*, and the next year at the World Exhibition gave a lecture which became famous on modality in Greek music. In 1885, after an expedition to Brittany, he published a French equivalent of his 1877 collection, *Trente mélodies populaires de Basse-Bretagne*. In Breton songs, as in the folk music of many other European countries, Bourgault-Ducoudray observed musical modes similar to those of ancient Greece.

At a period when interest in foreign music was centred on Greek music and on musical modes, Jules Combarieu's book *La musique et la magie* (1909) was innovative in both subject and method. Combarieu saw magical song as a universal phenomenon and considered examples from all over the world, including American Indian, Chinese, Hindu and Scandinavian. He observed its functions and its various uses, such as in relation to rain, fine weather, birth and medicine, and established the principal features of its musical language, including rhythm, scales, modes, the musical ethos and the symbolism of numbers.

The first French phonograph recordings were concerned not with music but with linguistics and phonetics in the whole world. However, since song is particularly efficacious in getting people from societies with an oral tradition to pronounce words in front of a recording machine, music naturally began to make its mark. At the World Exhibition of 1900, Dr L. Azoulay, who aimed to record as many languages as possible, made recordings on over 400 wax cylinders, mainly of sung music, which represented a remarkable variety of ethnic groups (corresponding to 74 standard languages and dialects), chiefly from Asia, Europe and Africa. They were the basis of the first phonographic archives, set up on this occasion – the archives of the Musée Phonographique de la Société d'Anthropologie de Paris. In 1911 the Archives de la Parole opened at the University of Paris (the Sorbonne), later to become Le Musée de la Parole et du Geste. These archives, for which musical recordings were made in France before World War I and farther afield after the war, are now in the Phonothèque Nationale, established in 1938.

A monumental *Encyclopédie de la Musique et Dictionnaire du Conservatoire* (1920–3), by Albert Lavignac and Lionel de La Laurencie, contained the sum of contemporary knowledge of world music in its ethnological, historical and archaeological aspects – profusely illustrated. Some of the articles have remained standard works, particularly those on Japan, China and Korea by Maurice Courant, on India by Joanny Grosset and on Arab music and the music of the Maghreb by Jules Rouanet. Regarding Asiatic music in the wider sense, the encyclopedia shows that up to the end of the 19th century scholars had paid most attention to art music, theories of scales and intervals and musical instruments. These facets continued to be central to research on music in the French North African colonies during the 1920s and 1930s, by French musicologists living there.

At the time, the general opinion was that Arab art music was in decline, and one object of the Congress of Cairo (1932) was to find means of safeguarding it. Baron Rodolphe d'Erlanger, the translator of some important treatises on medieval Arab music, organized the congress. The principal musicologists of Europe and the Arab countries had been invited, and recordings were made of the Arab orchestras also invited for the occasion. Baron d'Erlanger's own contribution to the congress was a codification of the rules underlying the modal and rhythmic systems of Arab art music of his time, which he published in the last two of the six volumes of his major work *La musique arabe* (1930–59). Conventional symbols for the notation of Arab music were laid down, although the problems linked with fixing that music by notation were not solved. Alexis Chottin published substantial work on the music of Morocco: *Corpus de la musique marocaine* i and ii (1931, 1933) and *Tableau de la musique marocaine* (1939), which concentrate on art music, although they also contain the first major studies of Berber music.

Encompassing a different part of the world, Raoul and Marguerite d'Harcourt's work, *La musique des Incas et ses survivances* (1925), was one of the first studies to introduce what later became a general method, research into ethnic music based on fieldwork – in the high Andes valleys of the Equator, Peru and part of Bolivia. It contains a section devoted to festivals and dances, an analysis of 204 pieces of transcribed music (texts and melodies, three-quarters of them taken down from live performance) and descriptions of musical instruments with photographs in a separate volume.

Institutes were set up in museums of ethnography where the scattered sound recordings and the collections of primitive musical instruments could be brought together, with qualified staff to look after this material and use it. This contact with ethnologists led ethnomusicologists to concentrate on ethnic rather than on art music, basing their research on fieldwork and integrating the social context of the music they were studying into their research and their thinking. In 1929 André Schaeffner set up in Paris a Department of Musical Organology in the Musée d'Ethnographie du Trocadéro (renamed the Musée de l'Homme in 1937). Initially intended to contain musical instruments from all over the world, the department acquired a record library in 1932, and was rechristened the Department of Musical Ethnology. (Its present title of Department of Ethnomusicology dates from 1954.) Many ethnomusicologists from all over the world have passed through this department. Curt Sachs, for instance, worked there while in exile (1933–37), and his study 'Les instruments de musique de Madagascar' (1938) was based on the Museum's collections.

2. André Schaeffner notating the music of a Dogon drummer, Mali, 1931

Field recordings became more and more numerous in the 1930s. Schaeffner's favourite field was West Africa, to which he made several expeditions from 1931 onwards. He collaborated with ethnologists and made recordings, particularly among the Dogon people of Mali (formerly the French Sudan; see fig.2), who were the subject of major studies both before and after World War II. Schaeffner's experience in the field, as well as his reading of Curt Sachs's *Geist und Werden der Musikinstrumente* (1929), resulted in the publication of his *Origine des instruments de musique. Introduction ethnologique à l'histoire de la musique instrumentale* (1936) – a true work of comparative musicology, including Western art music. As Schaeffner searched for the origins of musical instruments and instrumental music, he observed their use throughout the world, combining both fieldwork and research in the abundant literature on the subject, including accounts by travellers, and was led to consider music in relation to dance, drama, work, play, religion and magic. Moreover, he considered at length concepts relating to polyphony and throughout his book based his analyses on ethnological or sociological observations. In the appendix to his work, Schaeffner presented his own system of classification, dividing musical instruments into two great categories; first, 'instruments with a solid vibrating body' and second, 'instruments using vibrating air'. Those in the first category are further divided into (i) 'solid bodies incapable of tension'; (ii) 'flexible solid bodies; and (iii) 'solid bodies capable of tension'.

The different approach to non-European music on the one hand and to the folk music of France on the other, as established in the 19th century, led to the creation of separate research institutes. In 1937 Claudie Marcel-Dubois set up a Department of Musical Ethnology devoted to traditional French music, first in the Palais de Chaillot and then at the Musée des Arts et Traditions Populaires. The basis of the collections there consisted of recordings brought back from an expedition to Lower Brittany in 1939. The approach adopted to the music of Lower Brittany was similar to that taken to music outside France, with field investigations involving sociological, psychological and linguistic observations, and it inaugurated a type of research which was to become general in France after World War II.

A special Asian musical section was set up by Philippe Stern at the Musée Guimet in 1932. The basis of these archives consisted of recordings made at the Colonial Exhibition of 1931 in Paris and the Congress of Arab Music in Cairo in 1932.

Bibliography

J. de Léry: *Histoire d'un voyage faict en la terre du Brésil* (3rd edn, with musical notations, La Rochelle, 1585; reissued Geneva, 1975)

M. Mersenne: *Harmonie universelle* (Paris, 1636–7/*R*1963)

J. Chardin: *Voyages en Perse, et d'autres lieux de l'Orient* (Amsterdam, 1711)

J.-B. Labat: *Nouvelle relation de l'Afrique occidentale* (Paris, 1728)

J.-J. Rousseau: *Dictionnaire de musique* (Paris, 1768/*R*1969; many edns. to 1825; Eng. trans. by W. Waring, London, 1771, 2/1779/*R*1975)

J.-M. Amiot: *Mémoire sur la musique des Chinois tant anciens que modernes* (Paris, 1779/*R*1973)

J.-B. de La Borde: *Essai sur la musique ancienne et moderne* (Paris, 1780)

G. A. Villoteau: *De l'état actuel de l'art musical en Egypte* (Paris, 1812)

——: *Description historique, technique et littéraire des instruments de musique des Orientaux* (Paris, 1813)

——: *Mémoire sur la musique de l'antique Egypte* (Paris, 1816)

F. Salvador-Daniel: *La musique arabe, ses rapports avec la musique grecque et le chant grégorien* (Algiers, 1863, repr. in *Musique et instruments de musique du Maghreb*, 1986; Eng. trans. by H. G. Farmer in *The Music and Musical Instruments of the Arab*, 1915/*R*1975)

J. Tiersot: *Histoire de la chanson populaire en France* (Paris, 1889)

L. Azoulay: 'Liste des phonogrammes composant le Musée phonographique de la Société d'Anthropologie', *Revue de la Société d'Anthropologie de Paris*, iii (1902), 652

J. Combarieu: *La musique et la magie: Etude sur les origines populaires de l'art musical, son influence et sa fonction dans les sociétés* (Paris, 1909/*R*1978)

L. Azoulay: 'Les musées et archives phonographiques avant et depuis la fondation du musée phonographique de la société d'Anthropologie en 1900' (paper delivered at the meeting of 2 November 1911), *Revue de la Société d'Anthropologie de Paris*, ii (1911), 450

A. Lavignac and L. de La Laurencie, eds.: *Encyclopédie de la Musique et Dictionnaire du Conservatoire*, i, v (Paris 1920–3)

R. and M. d'Harcourt: *La musique des Incas et ses survivances* (Paris, 1925)

C. Sachs: *Geist und Werden der Musikinstrumente* (Berlin, 1926)

Baron R. d'Erlanger: *La musique arabe* (Paris, 1930–59)

J. Tiersot: *La chanson populaire et les écrivans romantiques* (Paris, 1931)

A. Chottin: *Corpus de musique marocaine*, i: *Nouba de Ochchâk*; ii: *Musique et danses berbères du pays Chleuh* (Paris, 1931, 1933)

Egyptian Ministry of Education: *Recueil des Travaux du Congrès de Musique Arabe qui s'est tenu au Caire en 1932 (Hég. 1350) sous le Haut Patronage de S. M. Fouad 1er, Roi d'Egypte* (Cairo, 1934)

A. Schaeffner: *Origine des instruments de musique: Introduction ethnologique à l'histoire de la musique instrumentale* (Paris, 1936; rev. 2/1968)

C. Sachs: 'Les instruments de musique de Madagascar', *Travaux et mémoires de l'Institut d'Ethnologie*, xxviii (1938), 70

A. Chottin: *Tableau de la musique marocaine* (Paris, 1939)

G. Rouget: 'L'ethnomusicologie', *Ethnologie générale* (*Encyclopédie de la Pléiade*) (Paris, 1968), 1339–90

F. H. Harrison: *Time, Place and Music: an Anthology of Ethnomusicological Observation c. 1550 to c. 1800* (Amsterdam, 1973)

M. Helffer and others: 'L'enseignement de l'ethnomusicologie en France', *RdM*, lix (1973), 18

C. Boilès and J.-J. Nattiez: 'Petite histoire critique de l'ethnomusicologie', *Musique en jeu*, xxviii (1977), 26

Les fantaisies du voyageur, XXXIII Variations Schaeffner (Paris, 1982)

C. Fonton: *Essai sur la musique orientale comparée à la musique européenne*, ed. E. Neubauer (1751), *Zeitschrift für Geschichte der arabisch-islamischen Wissenschaften*, ii (1985), 277–324

E. Neubauer: 'Der *Essai sur la musique orientale* von Charles Fonton mit Zeichnungen von Adanson', *Zeitschrift für Geschichte der arabisch-islamischen Wissenschaften*, iii (1986), 335, 376

J. Cheyronnaud: *Mémoires en recueils: jalons pour une histoire des collectes musicales en terrain français* (Paris, 1986)

P. V. Bohlman: 'Missionaries, Magical Muses and Magnificent Menageries: Images and Imagination in the Early History of Ethnomusicology', *World of Music*, iii (1988), 5

M. Brandily: 'Ethnomusicologie: musiques et civilisations', *Clartes: L'encyclopédie du présent*, ix: *L'homme et les sciences de la vie* (Paris, 1989), 4895

5: BELGIUM

Miriam Rovsing Olsen

One of the great ancestors of comparative musicology, François-Joseph Fétis (1784–1871), was a Belgian. His *Histoire générale de la musique, depuis les temps les plus anciens jusqu'à nos jours*, published in five volumes between 1869 and 1876, covers not only Western art music but also European folk music and non-European music. Refusing to regard music as a phenomenon in itself, separate from the people who made it, Fétis took account of the way people thought, their history, surroundings and the outside influences to which they had been exposed in explaining their various musical systems. He thus advocated the use by the music historian of all related disciplines that could cast light on the musical cultures of the world: ethnology, anthropology and linguistics.

Fétis had a large collection of musical instruments from all over the world. This collection, together with another, an Indian collection given to King Leopold II by Sir Sourindro Mohun Tagore (1840–1914), constitutes the basis of the Musée Instrumental du Conservatoire Royal de Musique of Brussels, set up in 1877. Taking as his starting point these music collections, constantly augmented over the years by acquisitions from many different sources (among others, some Arab instruments collected by Guillaume André Villoteau (1759–1839) and acquired in 1878), Victor-Charles Mahillon (1841–1924), the museum's curator, published a *Catalogue descriptif et analytique du Musée Instrumental du Conservatoire royal de musique de Bruxelles*, in five volumes, which came out between 1880 and 1892. The first volume was prefaced by an *Essai de classification méthodique de tous les instruments anciens et modernes*. This system of classification into four main categories – autophones, membranophones, chordophones and aerophones – according to the material set in vibration, was to be the basis of the classification system established by Curt Sachs and Erich M. von Hornbostel in 'Systematik der Musikinstrumente'

(1914), since adopted by most organologists. Ernest Closson (1870'-1950), a former assistant of Victor-Charles Mahillon who succeeded him in 1924, published several studies on musical instruments, in particular *La facture des instruments de musique en Belgique* (1935). His interest also extended to Belgian folk song.

Foundations also were laid for a long tradition of research concentrating on Central Africa, particularly Zaire (formerly the Belgian Congo), with which Belgium had historical links. Although these researches were mainly ethnographical, music had an important place in them. Systematic surveys were carried out at the end of the 20th century in the form of detailed questionnaires, addressed to all local administrators, on various aspects of social and religious life including music and dance. Such was the accumulation of documents that it soon became necessary to collect and classify all the information. In 1907 the Bureau international d'ethnographie undertook to publish a *Collection de monographies ethnographiques*, with a section on music in each. Publication of these monographs ceased at the beginning of World War I.

Research on Central Africa was undertaken for the Musée du Congo Belge at Tervuren, set up in 1897 (now the Musée Royal d'Afrique Centrale). These researches began early in the 20th century with the publication by E. Coart and A. de Haulleville in the *Annales du Musée du Congo Belge* of a work on the music and musical instruments of Zaire, deriving from research done at the Museum. The first ethnographers were sent to the field in 1910, and some of them took an interest in music. Between 1910 and 1912, A. Hutereau recorded 210 wax cylinders in northeast Zaire, particularly among the Zande people. However, it was organology above all that attracted field ethnographers. Joseph Maes published a series of studies on musical instruments from 1912 until after World War II. A survey in the form of a questionnaire organized by Gaston Knosp in Zaire between 1934 and 1935 gives much information about musical instruments; these findings were deposited in the Musée du Congo (although they were not published until 1968 by P. Collaer). The collections of instruments preserved in the Musée du Congo have been the subject of some major systematic works. With her now classic work 'Les xylophones du Congo Belge' (1936), Olga Boone inaugurated a type of study which continued after World War II.

Bibliography

Fr.-J. Fétis: *Résumé philosophique de l'histoire de la musique* (Paris, 1835)
——: *Biographie universelle des musiciens et bibliographie générale de la musique* (Paris, 1860–65)
——: *Histoire générale de la musique, depuis les temps les plus anciens jusqu'à nos jours* (Paris, 1869–76)
V.-Ch. Mahillon: *Catalogue descriptif et analytique du Musée instrumental du Conservatoire royal de musique de Bruxelles* (Ghent, 1880–1922; i, 2/1893; ii, 2/1909)
E. Coart and A. de Haulleville: 'La Musique', *Annales du Musée du Congo Belge*, III, i/1 (1902), 145–315
E. Closson: *Chansons populaires des provinces belges* (Brussels, 1905)
E. M. von Hornbostel and C. Sachs: 'Systematik der Musikinstrumente', *Zeitschrift für Ethnologie*, xlvi (1914), 553–90; Eng. trans. in *GSJ*, xiv (1961), 3
J. Maes: 'La sanza du Congo Belge', *Congo*, i (1921), 542

E. Closson: *La facture des instruments de musique en Belgique* (Brussels, 1935)

O. Boone: 'Les xylophones du Congo Belge', *Annales du Musée du Congo Belge*, iii/2 (1936), 69–144

J. Maes: 'Sculpture decorative ou symbolique des instruments de musique du Congo Belge', *Artes Africanae*, x/7 (Brussels, 1937), 1

J. Maes: 'Les Lukombe ou instruments de musique à cordes des populations du Kasai – Lac Léopold II – Lukenie', *Zeitschrift für Ethnologie*, 70 (1938), 240

P. Collaer: *Enquête sur la vie musicale au Congo Belge 1934–1935 (Questionnaire Knosp)* (Tervuren, 1968)

N. Meeus: *Le musée instrumental de Bruxelles* (Brussels, 1976)

Etudes africaines en Europe, bilan et inventaire (Paris, 1981)

J. Gansemans and B. Schmidt-Wrenger: *Zentralafrika, Musikgeschichte in Bildern*, i/9 (Leipzig, 1986)

6: IBERIA

MARTIN CUNNINGHAM

Scientific collection of folk songs began in Spain as early as the 16th century, when Francisco de Salinas (1513–90) used folk songs collected in the Salamanca region to illustrate theoretical points about rhythm and metre (1577). He has generally been regarded as a reliable source, and some of the melodies he includes are undoubtedly old: one of them resembles 'Polorum regina' from the 14th-century Catalan *Llibre Vermell*; another is the purportedly Arab tune 'Qalbi bi qalbi', mentioned by the 14th-century author, the Arcipreste de Hita. The survival of Salinas's material in the modern tradition has been studied by M. García Matos (1963).

During the 18th century, interest in folk music and dance was shown (albeit within the context of general aesthetic discussions about music) by the essayist Benoit Feijoo (1676–1734), the musical theorist Antonio Eximeno (1729–1808) and the jurist and scholar Gaspar Melchor de Jovellanos (1744–1811); the remark attributed to Eximeno that 'a nation's music should be based on its folk song', although taken up as a rallying cry by later musical nationalists, is undoubtedly an oversimplification of his views. In 1799 José González Torres de Nava suggested, in a memorandum to the government, that folk music should be collected systematically and notated from live performance; his enterprise, considerably ahead of its time, bore no fruit. The same year, however, saw the publication of a selection of texts by Zamácola, whose intention was to demonstrate the superiority of Spanish forms over foreign genres then in vogue.

The principal contribution of the Romantic era was a new interest in folk-song texts; this centred initially on *romances* (ballads), as an object both of aesthetic appreciation (thus responding to the declassicizing thrust of the period) and of antiquarian interest (arising from the persistence of the genre over many centuries in both folk and art traditions). The first modern stimulus to further collection of folk songs was thus given in Spain by A. Durán's series of ballad collections, begun in 1828, and in Portugal, by that of J. B. Almeida Garrett, begun in 1843. To the *costumbrismo* movement (an offshoot of Spanish Romanticism which sought to define the essence of Spanish life by recording

119

contemporary customs) are owed the description of Andalusian dance by Estébanez Calderón (1850) and the collection of Andalusian texts by Fernán Caballero (1859). Other important early text collections are those of E. Lafuente y Alcántara (2/1865), J. Pérez Ballersteros (1886) in Spain, and T. Braga (1867, 1867–9, 1869), S. P. M. Estácio da Veiga (1870), A. Rodrígues de Azevedo (1880) and J. Leite de Vasconcellos (1882, 1886) in Portugal. The separate publication of folk-song texts has continued (for a bibliography of important text collections, see *Enciclopedia de la cultura española*, 'Canción popular').

Collection of music lagged behind the text collections. Apart from a remarkable early Basque contribution by J. I. de Iztueta (1824), the earliest publications containing music date from the 1870s. Some were primarily text anthologies with music included only in appendices or notes, as in the works of F. Rodríguez Marín (1881–3), M. Milá y Fontanals (1882) and P. Bertrán y Bros (1885). Others contain more music (e.g. F. Pelay Briz), but the first proper music collections were those of A. A. das Neves e Melo (1872) in Portugal, and E. Ocón (1874) and J. Inzenga (1888) in Spain. A tendency towards regional specialization was apparent from the beginning in both countries, particularly in regions such as Galicia, Catalonia and the Basque country, where there was a greater awareness of separate cultural identity. In the same period, consideration was given to the methodology of folk-song collection by A. Machado y Álvarez (1890). A less scientific strand is represented by the provision of accompaniments, suitable for drawing-room use, in collections such as those of J. A. Santesteban (1862–70) and F. Alió (1891).

More exhaustive musical collection began in the early 20th century; although the most productive period in Portugal was not to come until the second quarter of the century, fieldwork carried out in Spain before the Civil War (1936) bore impressive results in published volumes, even though several areas remained uninvestigated. (The date of publication of some later volumes is deceptive: they really belong to this earlier period.) By the 1920s, sufficient material had been amassed to permit useful surveys such as those of R. Laparra (1920) and E. López-Chavarri (1927); E. M. Torner, in his 1920 Asturian anthology, was the first to give detailed and sensitive treatment of the problems of melodic shape, while in the following decade the debate began, not yet concluded, over modal classification of songs, and in particular over the distinction between various types of E-mode and their possible origins. The 1931 studies of song, by Torner, and dance, by A. Capmany, remain indispensable. Other features of studies at this date were the search for regional differences and the search for folk elements in the music of earlier centuries (hence the inclusion of melodies from the medieval and later periods in the anthologies of F. Pedrell [1918–22] and others). Underlying both collections and studies in this period was increased respect for the intricacies of folk material, making artificially regularized barring and phrase-lengths, and other such editorial 'improvements' unacceptable. The great Catalan *Obra* (F. Pujol, 1926–9) is a milestone in the increasingly scientific attitude.

An important occasion in the history of Spanish ethnic music was the festival of *cante jondo* held in June 1922 in Granada, directed among others by the composer M. de Falla and the poet and dramatist (also accomplished musician) García Lorca. The significance of the event lay principally in the heightening of awareness of *cante jondo*, and the stimulation of a desire to perpetuate genres in danger of extinction. A number of descriptive studies of *cante jondo* date from the 1920s and 1930s, some arising directly from the 1922 festival. Transcriptions, however, both of *cante jondo* and of *flamenco* in general, are broadly of rather later date, perhaps reflecting the problems of transcribing intricate, even microtonal ornamentation which varies spontaneously from one performance to another.

The scientific approach to folk-song collection was greatly helped by the introduction of field recording, pioneered by such researchers as J. Bal y Gay in the 1930s. K. Schindler's anthology claims to be the first to be transcribed entirely from mechanically recorded material and may be taken as signalling a transition to the modern period of ethnomusicological research.

In the decades following the Civil War, the work of individual collectors was supplemented by two organizations. First was the Sección Femenina (the women's section of the Falange party, now disbanded), which aimed to preserve folk material from extinction by encouraging performance, particularly of dances, by non-professional groups. The Sección issued publications giving surveys of the songs and dances that the organization brought to a wide audience through festivals, competitions and television. Its archives contained a wealth of recorded and transcribed material. The second group is the Instituto de Musicología (part of the Consejo Superior de Investigaciones Científicas), under whose auspices much collection has been carried out, especially in missions to areas hitherto neglected or where the survival of traditional genres seemed threatened. A key figure in both organizations was M. García Matos (1912–74), for his indefatigable recording missions, his perceptive studies and his devising of a choreographic notation for traditional dance. Much material collected in this period remains unpublished; important collections are housed in the archives of the Instituto de Musicología in Madrid and Barcelona, in the Centro de Historia del Folklore y de la Danza (part of the Real Escuela Superior de Arte Dramático y Danza, Madrid) and in the archives of the recording company Hispavox, under whose label the recorded anthologies of García Matos were issued. Material collected for the Catalan *Obra* (Pujol), whose publication was interrupted, is housed in the Biblioteca del Orfeó Català (Barcelona).

In the decade or more since democratization, a new generation of scholars has come to the fore, who, although not neglecting continued collection of material, seem set to focus their efforts on systematic, analytical studies (as opposed to merely descriptive ones), based in part on statistical methods. A willingness is also seen to treat music as but one ingredient in a wider ethnological and anthropological approach. Even so, and in spite of the wealth of published data, it is possible to lament that collection began too late, and that the abundance of folk music, Iberia's heritage until relatively recently, led to its being undervalued, just as surely as dearth leads to appreciation (J. Crivillé i Bargalló, 1983).

Bibliography

Salinas

F. de Salinas: *De musica libri septem* (Salamanca, 1577; repr. (facsimile) Kassel, 1958); Spanish trans. I. Fernández de la Cuesta (Madrid, 1983)

J. B. Trend: 'Salinas: a Sixteenth-century Collector of Folk-songs', *ML* viii (1927), 13

M. García Matos: 'Pervivencia en la tradición actual de canciones populares recogidas en el siglo XVI por Salinas en su tratado *De musica libri septem*', *AnM*, xviii (1963), 67

Eighteenth century

Don Preciso [pseud. of J. A. (Iza) de Zamácola]: *Colección de las mejores coplas de seguidillas, tiranas y polos* (Madrid, 1799, 2/1816/*R* Córdoba, 1982)

D. Hergueta Martín: 'Don Preciso, su vida y sus obras', *Revista de Archivos, Bibliotecas y Museos*, xxxiii (1929), 19, 23, 159, 328; xxxiv (1930), 56, 61, 63

A. M. Pollin: 'Towards an understanding of Antonio Eximeno', *JAMS*, x (1957), 89

A. Martín Moreno: *El padre Feijoo y las ideologías musicales del siglo XVIII* (Orense, 1976)

Spain

Anon.: *Coplas de seguidillas y tiranas jocosas, malagueñas y polos* (Seville, 1807)

J. I. de Iztueta: *Gipuzkoa'ko dantzak/Danzas de Guipúzcoa* (San Sebastián, 1824, 3/1968) [texts]; (San Sebastián, 1826, 3/1973) [melodies]

A. Durán: *Colección de romances castellanos anteriores al siglo xvii* (Madrid, 1828–32)

S. Estébanez Calderón: *Un baile en Triana* (Seville, 1850)

F. Caballero [pseud. of Cecilia Böhl de Faber]: *Cuentos y poesías populares andaluces* (Seville, 1859)

J. A. Santesteban: *Colección de aires vascongados para canto y piano* (San Sebastián, 1862–70, 2/1889)

E. Lafuente y Alcántara: *Cancionero popular: coplas y seguidillas* (Madrid, 2/1865)

F. Pelay Briz: *Cançons de la terra*, i–v (Barcelona, 1866–77)

J. D. J. Sallaberry: *Chants populaires du pays basque* (Bayonne, 1870, 2/1930)

E. Ocón: *Cantos españoles con notas explicativas y biográficas* (Málaga, 1874, 2/1906)

J. Calvo: *Colección de cantares populares murcianos* (Murcia, 1877)

J. Manterola: *Cancionero vasco* (San Sebastián, 1877–80)

Demófilo [pseud. of A. Machado y Álvarez]: *Colección de cantos flamencos* (Seville, 1881/*R*1975)

F. Rodríguez Marín: *Cantos populares españoles* (Seville, 1881–3)

M. Milá y Fontanals: *Romancerillo catalán: canciones tradicionales* (Barcelona, 1882)

M. Díaz Marín: *Colección de cantares andaluces* (Seville, 1884)

P. Bertrán y Bros: *Cançons i folies recullides al peu de Montserrat* (Barcelona, 1885)

J. Pérez Ballesteros: *Cancionero popular gallego*, i–iii (Madrid, 1886)

J. Inzenga: *Cantos y bailes populares de España* (Madrid, 1888)

J. Hurtado: *Cien cantos populares asturianos* (Madrid, c1890)

A. Machado y Álvarez: *Cantos flamencos* (Madrid, 1890)

F. Alió: *Cançons populars catalanas* (Barcelona, 1891)

A. Noguera: *Memoria sobre los cantos, bailes y tocatas populares de la isla de Mallorca* (Barcelona, 1893)

C. Bordes: *Cent chansons populaires basques* (Paris, 1894)

——: *12 noëls basques anciens* (Paris, 1897)

——: *La tradition au pays basque* (Paris, 1899)

F. Pedrell: 'Folk-lore musical castillian du XVIe siècle', *SIMG* (1899–1900), 372

R. Calleja: *Colección de canciones populares de la provincia de Santander* (Madrid, 1901)

A. Capmany: *Cançoner popular* (Barcelona, 1901–13/*R*1980)

F. Olmeda: *Folk-lore de Castilla o Cancionero popular de Burgos* (Seville, 1903, 2/1975)

V. Llinione y Boule: *Colección de cantos populares de Murcia* (Barcelona, 1906)

J. Verdú: *Colección de cantos populares de Murcia* (Barcelona, 1906)

D. Ledesma: *Folklore o cancionero salamantino* (Madrid, 1907/*R*1972)

M. Fernández Núñez: *Cantos populares leonesas* (Madrid, 1909)

V. Blanco: *Las mil y una canciones populares de la región leonesa*, 3 vols (Astorga, 1910, 1932, 1934)

A. Carrera: *Cançons populars catalanes*, i–iv (Barcelona, 1910–16)

C. Bordes: *12 chansons amoureuses du pays basque français* (Paris, 1910)
F. Echevarría: *Cantos y bailes populares de Valencia* (Valencia, 1912)
M. Machado: *Cante jondo* (Madrid, 1912)
L. Millet: *El cante popular religiós* (Barcelona, 1912)
F. Gaskué: *Origen de la música popular vascongada* (Paris, 1913)
———: *Materiales para el estudio del folklore músico vasco* (San Sebastián, 1917)
L. Millet: *De la cançó popular catalana* (Barcelona, 1917)
A. Pol: *Un conrador: folklore musical mallorquín* (Barcelona, 1917)
F. Camps i Mercadal: *Folklore menorquí* (Mahón, 1918)
N. Otaño: *Canciones montañesas* (Valencia, 1918)
F. Pedrell: *Cancionero musical popular español* (Vals, 1918–22, 3/1958)
K. Schindler: *Spanish Sacred and Secular Songs* (Boston, MA, 1918)
J. A. de Donostia: *Euskel eres-sorta (cancionero vasco)* (Madrid, 1919)
F. Gaskué: *El aurresku en Guipúzcoa* (San Sebastián, 1919)
R. Laparra: 'La musique et la danse populaires en Espagne', *EMDC*, I/iv (1920), 2353–400
E. M. Torner: *Cancionero musical de la lírica popular asturiana* (Madrid, 1920)
A. Sevilla: *Cancionero popular murciano* (Murcia, 1921)
J. B. Trend: *Picture of Modern Spain* (London, 1921)
M. de Falla: *El 'cante jondo' (canto primitivo andaluz)* (Granada, 1922)
G. M. Vergara: *El cante jondo* (Madrid, 1922)
K. Schindler: *Songs of the Spanish Provinces* (Boston, MA, 1922–3)
R. M. de Azkue: *Cancionero popular vasco* (Barcelona, 1923–4/R1968)
J. A. de Donostia: 'Apuntes de folklore vasco; toberas', *Revista internacional de los estudios vascos*, xv (1924), 1
G. de [W. von] Humboldt: 'Bocetos de un viaje a través del país vasco', *Revista internacional de los estudios vascos*, xv (1924), 448
H. Möller: *Spanische, katalanische, portugiesische und baskische Volkslieder* (Mainz, 1924)
J. B. Trend: 'Music in Spanish Galicia', *MQ*, v (1924), 15
G. Castrillo Hernández: *Estudio sobre el canto popular castellano* (Valencia, 1925)
H. Olazarán de Estella: *Mutil dantza del Baztán* (Pamplona, 1925)
A. Pol: *Colecció de cançons populars mallorquines* (Barcelona, 1925)
J. Ribera: 'De música y métrica gallegas', *Homenaje ofrecido a Ramón Menéndez Pidal*, iii (Madrid, 1925), 7
E. M. Torner: 'Ensayo de clasificación de las melodías de romance', *Homenaje ofrecido a Ramón Menéndez Pidal*, ii (Madrid, 1925), 391
F. de P. Bové: *El Penedés: Folklore dels balls, danses i comparses populars* (Vendrell, 1926)
J. C. de Luna: *De cante grande y cante chico* (Madrid, 1926, 3/1942)
F. Pujol and others, eds.: *Obra del cançoner popular de Catalunya: materials*, i–iii (Barcelona, 1926–9)
M. Arnaudas Larrodé: *Colección de cantos populares de la provincia de Teruel* (Zaragoza, 1927)
P. Díaz Carbonell: *Cancionero de Madrid* (Madrid, 1927)
E. López-Chavarri: *Música popular española* (Barcelona, 1927)
M. van Eys: 'Second voyage au pays basque, 1868', *Revista internacional de estudios vascos*, xviii (1927), 527
J. A. de Donostia: *Gure herria* [Our People] (Paris, 1928)
R. A. Gallop: *Vingt-cinq chansons populaires d'Eskual-herria* (Bayonne, 1928)
J. Llongueres: *Els cants de la Passió* (Barcelona, 1928)
J. Ribera: *La música de la jota aragonesa* (Madrid, 1928)
I. Brown: *Deep Song* (New York, 1929)
P. E. González Pastrana: *La Montaña de León: cien canciones leonesas* (Madrid, 1929)
E. M. del Portillo: *Cante jondo* (Madrid, 1929)
F. Rodríguez Marín: *El alma de Andalucía en sus mejores coplas amorosas* (Madrid, 1929)
A. Capmany: *La dansa a Catalunya* (Barcelona, 1930)
B. Estornés Lasa: 'De arte popular', *Revista internacional de estudios vascos*, xxi (1930), 206
A. Martínez Hernández: *Antología de cantos populares españoles* (Barcelona, 1930)
A. Capmany: 'El baile y la danza', *Folklore y costumbres de España*, ed. F. Carreras y Candi, ii (Barcelona, 1931), 169–418
M. Fernández Núñez: *Folk-lore leonés: canciones, romances y leyendas* (Madrid, 1931/R1980)
B. Gil García: *Cancionero popular de Extremadura*, i (Valls, 1931); ii (Badajoz, 1956)
J. Llongueras: *Cançoner popular de Nadal* (Barcelona, 1931)
S. Llorens de Serra: *El cançoner de Pineda* (Barcelona, 1931)

F. de Onís: *Canciones españolas* (New York, 1931)
E. M. Torner: 'La canción tradicional española', *Folklore y costumbres de España*, ed. F. Carreras y Candi, ii (Barcelona, 1931), 7–166
F. Baldelló: *Cançoner popular religiós de Catalunya* (Barcelona, 1932)
A. José: *Colección de cantos populares burgaleses: nuevo cancionero burgalés* (Madrid, 1980 [material collected in 1932])
C. Caba and P. Caba: *Andalucía, su comunismo y su cante jondo* (Madrid, 1933)
G. M. Vergara Martín: *Seguidillas populares recogidas en diferentes regiones de España* (Madrid, 1933)
J. Moreira: *Del folklore tortosí* (Tortosa, 1934)
A. Araux: *Vox y cuerda (soleares, saetas, polos, seguiriyas, malagueñas)* (Madrid, 1935)
G. Arenal: *Salerosas canciones del Bajo Aragón* (Madrid, 1935)
W. F. Starkie: *Don Gypsy* (London, 1936)
H. Anglès: 'Das spanische Volkslied', *AMf*, iii (1938), 331–62
J. Bal y Gay: *Folklore musical: Espagne* (Paris, 1939)
A. Chottin: *Chants arabes d'Andalousie* (Paris, 1939)
M. J. Kahn: 'Chant populaire andalou et musique synagogale', *Cahiers d'art*, xiv (1939), 155; Eng. trans. (1956)
L. M. Fernández Espinosa: *Canto popular gallego* (Madrid, 1940)
K. Schindler: *Folk Music and Poetry of Spain and Portugal* (New York, 1941)
J. A. de Donostia and F. de Madina: *De música vasca* (Buenos Aires, 1943)

Portugal
J. B. Almeida Garrett: *Romanceiro e cancioneiro geral* (Lisbon, 1843–51, 3/1900–01)
C. F. Bellerman: *Portugiesische Volkslieder und Romanzen* (Leipzig, 1864)
T. Braga: *História da poesia popular portugueza* (Oporto, 1867, 3/1902)
——: *Cancioneiro e romanceiro geral português* (Coimbra, 1867–9; rev. and enl. 2/1906–09)
——: *Cantos populares do archipélago açoriano* (Oporto, 1869)
S. P. M. Estácio da Veiga: *Romanceiro do Algarve* (Lisbon, 1870)
A. A. das Neves e Melo: *Músicas e canções populares coligidas da tradição* (Lisbon, 1872)
A. Rodrígues de Azevedo: *Romanceiro do archipélago da Madeira* (Funchal, 1880)
J. Leite de Vasconcellos: *Tradições populares de Portugal* (Oporto, 1882)
——: *Romanceiro português* (Lisbon, 1886; rev. 2/1958–60)
T. Braga: 'Ampliações ao romanceiro das ilhas dos Açores', *Revista lusitana*, i (1887–9), 99
C. Michaelis de Vasconcellos: 'Estudos sobre o romanceiro peninsular', *Revista lusitana*, ii (1890–92), 156–240; pubd separately (Coimbra, 1907–9, 2/1934)
A. Pimentel: *A dança em Portugal* (Esposende, 1892)
F. M. Sousa Viterbo: *Artes e artistas em Portugal* (Lisbon, 1892, rev. 2/1920)
P. F. Tomás: *Canções populares da Beira* (Figueira da Foz, 1896, 2/1923)
A. J. de Morais Ferreira: *Dialecto mirandês* (Lisbon, 1898)
J. Leite de Vasconcellos: *Estudos de filologia mirandesa*, i (Lisbon, 1900), 43ff
P. de Carvalho: *História do fado* (Lisbon, 1903)
F. M. de Sousa Viterbo: 'Musica e poesia popular portugueza: cantos maritimos', *Arte musical*, v (1903), 169
M. Lambertini: *Chansons et instruments: renseignements pour l'étude du folklore portugais* (Lisbon, 1904)
A. Pimentel: *A triste cançao do sul* (Lisbon, 1904)
F. X. d'Athaide Oliveira: *Romanceiro e cancioneiro de Algarve (Lição de Loulé)* (Oporto, 1905)
J. do Rio [pseud. of P. Barreto]: *Fados, canções e dansas de Portugal* (Rio de Janeiro and Paris, 1909)
P. F. Tomás: *Velhas canções e romances populares portugueses* (Coimbra, 1913)
C. Basto: 'Falas e tradições do distrito de Viana-do-Castelo', *Revista lusitana*, xvii (1914), 55
A. C. Pires de Lima: 'Tradições populares de Santo Tirso', *Revista lusitana*, xvii (1914), 282–337; xx (1917), 1–39
S. Costa: 'Auto do Natal', *Terra portuguesa*, ii (1916), 97
M. A. Lambertini: *Bibliophilie musicale* (Lisbon, 1918)
F. A. Coelho: *Jogos e rimas infantais* (Oporto, 2/1919)
P. F. Tomás: *Cantares do povo* (Coimbra, 1919)
J. L. Dias: *Etnografia da Beira*, ii (Lisbon, 1927)
F. A. Martins: *Folclore do concelho de Vinhais* (Coimbra, 1928)
M. Lopes: 'Da minha terra', *Revista lusitana*, xxxi (1933), 138
P. F. Tomás: *Canções portuguesas* (Coimbra, 1934)
J. Lopes Dias: *A Beira Baixa da mocrofone da Emissora nacional de radiodifusão* (Lisbon, 1936)

L. Moita: *O fado: canção de vencidos* (Lisbon, 1936)

L. Claves: 'Pantomimas, danças e bailados populares', *Revista lusitana*, xxxv (1937), 140; xxxvi (1938), 218

J. L. Dias: *Etnografia da Beira*, iv: *O que a nossa gente canta* (Lisbon, 1937)

R. Gallop: *Cantares do povo português: estudo crítico* (Lisbon, 1937)

C. M. Santos: *Tocares e cantares da ilha: estudo do folklore da Madeira* (Funchal, 1937)

J. Diogo Correia: *Cantares da Malpica (Beira Baixa)* (Lisbon, 1938)

A. Leça: 'Danças e cantigas', *Vida e arte do povo português* (1940), 185

M. Maria de Melo: 'Musica regional açoreana', *Portucale*, xi (1938), 142

A. Avelino Joyce: 'Acerca das canções populares de Monsanto e Paul', *Revista ocidente*, iv (1939), 276, 445

A. Leça: 'Músico caminheiro', *Revista ocidente*, iv (1939), 25, 86, 241; v (1939), 86, 370; xiii (1941), 418; xii (1941), 97, 320; xiv (1941), 109, 249

Further bibliography

The entries listed below will provide supplementary bibliographies both for the period before 1941 and for more recent works.

J. A. de Donastia: *Essai d'une bibliographie musicale basque* (Bayonne, 1932)

E. M. Torner: *Temas folklóricos: música y poesía* (Madrid, 1935)

G. Chase: *The Music of Spain* (New York, 1941, rev. 2/1959)

L. de Hoyos Sáinz and N. de Hoyos Sancho: *Manual de folklore* (Madrid, 1947)

F. Pérez Embid, ed.: *Enciclopedia de la cultura española* (Madrid, 1962–8); see entries. 'Canción popular', 'Cancioneros populares', 'Cante flamenco', 'Copla', 'Coros', 'Danzas', 'Flamenco, baile', 'Instrumentos musicales populares', 'Música popular', etc.

A. González Climent: *Bibliografía flamenco* (Madrid, 1965)

B. E. Pereira: *Bibliografia analítica de etnografia portuguesa* (Lisbon, 1965)

A. González Climent and J. Blas Vega: *Segunda bibliografía flamenco* (Málaga, 1966)

S. G. Armistead and J. H. Silverman: *Folk Literature of the Sephardic Jews*, i: *The Judeo-Spanish Chapbooks of Yacob Abraham Yoná* (Berkeley, CA, 1971)

I. J. Katz: 'The Traditional Folk Music of Spain: Explorations and Perspectives', *YIFMC*, vi (1974), 64

Bibliografía de romancero oral (Madrid, 1980)

Grove 6; see entries. 'Basque music', 'Cante hondo', 'Flamenco', 'Portugal, §II. Folk music', 'Spain, §II. Folk music'; see also articles on individual collectors, *viz*: 'Alió', 'Azkue', 'Bordes', 'Capmany', 'Donostia', 'Eximeno', 'Gallop', 'García Matos', 'Gil García', 'inzenga', 'Katz', 'Laparra', 'Ledesma', 'López-Chavarri', 'Olmeda', 'Otaño', 'Pedrell', '[Franciso] Pujol', 'Ribera', 'Salinas', '[Kurt] Schindler', '[Marius] Schneider', 'Starkie', 'Trend', 'Torner', 'Zamácola'.

P. Lopez de Osaba, ed.: *Historia de la música española*, vii (Madrid, 1983)

7: ITALY

ROBERTO LEYDI

Interest in the musical aspects of Italian folk tradition started late and developed only after World War II. Folklorists of the 19th century and the early 20th had, with few exceptions, been interested only in song texts, following the trend of folklore studies and strong Italian literary and humanistic traditions.

Although there are few documented 19th-century contributions, a few names deserve mention: Giovan Battista Bolza in 1867 published in Vienna a number of popular tunes from his Lake Como collections in 1867; Constantino Nigra included in his very important collection of song texts *I Canti popolari del Piemonte* [Folk songs of Piedmont] (1888) only about ten tunes; Giuseppe Ungarelli provided a considerable contribution on the folk dances of the Bolognian Apennines; and Ella von Schultz Adaiewski, although she was not Italian, lived and worked in the Venice area and left excellent transcriptions of songs and dance music.

Straddling the 19th and 20th centuries is Alberto Favara (1863–1923), who created a large and systematic collection of Sicilian songs and instrumental music. Favara collected 1090 musical themes, covering much of the Sicilian musical repertory, and applied to his transcriptions (by ear) a method that was advanced for his time. Favara's collection remained unrecognized until 1957 when it was published under the direction of Ottavio Tiby.

Also of note is the work on Sardinia by Giulio Fara (1880–1949). With a solid set of examples, Fara provided the first contribution to knowledge of Sardinian folk music, in particular instrumental music, and subsequently with the book *L'anima della Sardegna* [The Soul of Sardinia] (1940) attempted a general synthesis of the island's traditional music.

Francesco Balilla Pratella (1880–1955), who took part in the futurist movement, documented and elucidated the music of oral tradition in the Romagna region. He also started to create a general 'body' of Italian folk music. In 1933 under his influence the Italian National Committee of Folk Art circulated a questionnaire among the provincial committees which asked them to transcribe and send to Rome as many folk songs and instrumental passages as possible. Since this quest was entrusted more to private individuals than to professionals, the resulting publication (*Primo Documentario per la storia dell'Etnofonia in Italia* [First Document of the History of Folk Music in Italy], 1941) was inadequate quantitatively, unequally distributed over the regions and hardly reliable.

Cesare Caravaglios is remembered for his research into the calls and cries of Neapolitan pedlars (pub. 1931), an interesting and neglected area of study. His attempt in 1936 at synthesis of Italian research and ethnomusicological studies (*Il Folklore musicale in Italia* [Musical Folklore in Italy]) came decidedly late in the panorama of international study.

Alfredo Bonaccorsi (*b* 1887), mainly a student of 19th-century Italian music, devoted attention to the music of the Tuscan folk theatre (1934, 1935). Colacicchi turned his attention to the peasants of Ciociaria (Latium) and to the sacred representation of the 'Mourning of the Virgins' of Vallepietra (Latium).

Giorgio Nataletti (*b* 1907) began his intensive investigation of the Italian folk music of the 1930s with research and study on Latium.

Vito Fedeli, composer and music teacher, merits particular acknowledgment among the pioneers of Italian ethnomusicology. Although he was only occasionally concerned with folk music, to him belongs the most serious study of folk organology published in Italy before World War II, a work devoted to the Calabrian *zampogna a poro* (bagpipes) and to the double flute of the same region (1911).

While the systematic recording of folk music began in Italy only in 1948, some important documents were preserved before World War II on discs, although very little was recorded by scientific means: records of Sardinian music (*tenores* of the Barbagia and *tasgia* of Aggius, in Gallura), carried out in 1929 (Barbagia) and 1933 (Gallura) on the initiative of Gavino Gabriel, a founder of the Discoteca di Stato (State Record Library); improvised songs of Latin peasants (Nataletti, on l'EIAR, the state radio, in 1936); and, perhaps, some cries of Neapolitan pedlars, collected by Cesare Caravaglios. Authentic urban music was recorded by Zonophone (Vienna) in 1910 in an area not yet Italian, to wit Trieste.

On the other hand, much more material was published (on 78 rpm records) for commercial purposes designed for local and regional markets. Practically ignored until recently, the exploration and cataloguing of this collection was begun in 1987, including the most important and complete collection of the music of the bagpipe (first cut 1907), the music of Sardinia (1922), the Ligurian *trallalero* (1928) and other aspects of Italian folk music. Records produced (since 1917) in the USA for the Italian-American market also provide relevant documents. This material is ordered and classified in Richard Spottswood's record list.

In 1948 stimulus towards the collection and transcription of Italian folk music was provided by the incorporation of the Centro nazionale studi di musica popolare (National Centre of Folk Music) in Rome (on the initiative of Giorgio Nataletti) and the start of more continuous activity by the Discoteca di Stato (State Record Library). Much material has been collected by private individuals and institutions and by local governments. Calculated approximately, in the absence of any complete catalogues, Italy has just under 100,000 recordings available.

In the first years after World War II there were few researchers and their view was that the primary urgency was to record a musical tradition which was disappearing. In the 1980s publication and study increased notably.

A characteristic of research since the 1960s has been development of work in the northern regions, an area that was initially neglected since it was regarded as being by then completely corrupted by industrial development. This research has demonstrated that, on the contrary, there is a remarkable and important permanence of the traditional musical culture even in the north. One can say that almost all of Italy, with a gap or two such as the Veneto region, has been well documented by recorded material.

Bibliography

G. B. Bolza: 'Canzoni popolari comasche', *Sitzungsberichte der K. Adakemie der Musikwissenschaft*, liii (Vienna, 1867)

C. Nigra: *Canti popolari del Piemonte* (Turin, 1888/R1957)

A. Parisotti: 'Le melodie popolari romane', *Il volgo di Roma*, ed. F. Sabatini (Rome, 1890)

L. Mastrigli: *La Sicilia musicale* (Bologna, 1891)

E. von Schultz Adaiewsky: '*Chansons et airs de danses populaires, précédés de textes, reveillis dans la vallée de Résia*' (St Petersburg, 1891)

——: 'La berceuse populaire. Analyse comparée', *RMI*, i (1894), 240; ii (1895), 420; iv (1897), 484

——: 'Tableau synoptique des chansons résiens', *Materialen zur südslavischen Dialektologie und*

Ethnologie, ed. J. Baudouin de Courtenay (St Petersburg, 1895), 430–75

B. Pergoli: *Saggio di canti popolari romagnoli* (Forli, 1894/*R*1967)

U. Ungarelli: *Le vecchie danze italiane ancora in uso nella provincia bolognese* (Rome, 1894)

C. Ferrara: *La musica dei vanniaturi di piazza notigiana* (Noto, 1896)

E. Schultz Adaiewsky: 'Vecchia canzone di Natale', *Rivista della tradizioni popolari*, ii (1904), 116

A. Favara: 'Le melodie tradizionali di Val Mazzara', *Atti del congresso internazionale di scienze storiche*, viii (Rome, 1905)

E. Ferrero: 'La musica dei negri americani', *RMI*, xiii (1906), 391

A. Parisotti: 'Le melodie popolari romane', *Canti popolari romani*, ed. G. Zanazzo (Rome, 1907–10)

G. F. Checcacci: 'La musica dell'Hindustan', *RMI*, xv (1908), 1, 295, 519, 655

E. Schultz Adaiewsky: 'Anciennes mélodies et chansons populaires d'Italie', *RMI*, xvi (1909), 143, 311; xviii (1911), 137

G. Fara: 'Musica popolare sarda', *RMI*, xvi (1909), 713

G. Gabriel: 'Canti e cantadori della Gallura', *RMI*, xvii (1910), 926

S. Baglioni: 'Contributo alla conoscenta della musica naturale: i scopo e metodo delle ricerche', *Rivista di antropologia*, xv (1909–10), 313–60

——: 'Strumenti musicali sardi'; 'Strumente musicali dei popoli asiatici'; 'Ulteri ricerche sulle launeddas', *Rivista di antropologia*, xvi (1911), 75, 365, 391

V. Fedeli: 'Zampogne calabresi', *Sammelbände der Intern. Musikwissenschaft, Wien*, xiii (1911–1912)

G. Fara: 'Su uno strumento musicale sardo', *RMI*, xx (1913), 763; xxi (1914), 13, 51

L. Sinigaglia: *Vecchie canzoni popolari del Piemonte* (Leipzig, 1914)

G. Fara: 'Dello zufolo pastorale in Sardegna', *RMI*, xxiii (1916), 509

——: 'Giocattoli di musica rudimentale in Sardegna', *Archivo storico sardo* (Cagliari), xi (1916)

——: 'Il pifaro y tamborillo in Sardegna', *Archivio storico sardo*, xii (1917)

——: 'Di alcuni costumi musicali in Sardegna', *RMI*, xxv (1918), 63

——: 'Sull'etimologia di *launeddas*', *RMI*, xxv (1918), 259

F. B. Pratella: *Saggio di gridi, canzoni, cori e danze del popolo italiano* (Bologna, 1919/*R*1976)

V. Gui and P. Jahier: *Canti di soldati* (Trento, 1919, 2/1919)

G. Fara: *L'anima musicale d'Italia* (Rome, 1920)

C. Caravaglios: *Le origini della canzone napoletana* (Naples, 1921)

G. Fara: 'Studi comparati d'etnofonia religiosa', *Musica d'oggi*, iii (1921), 333

——: 'Studi comparati di etnofonia', *La cultura musicale*, i (1922), 22, 81

——: 'Appunti di etnografia comparata', *RMI*, xxix (1922), 277

A. Favara: 'Il ritmo nella vita e nell'arte popolare in Sardegna', *Rivista d'Italia*, xxvi (1923), 78

——: 'Canti e leggende della Conca d'oro', *Rivista d'Italia*, xxvi (1923), 287

G. Fara: 'Bricciche di etnofonia sarda', *Musica d'oggi*, v (1923), 209; x (1928), 45

G. Gabriel: *Canti di Sardegna* (Milan, 1923)

G. Fara: 'I canti del popolo d'Italia. Montagnana', *Musica d'oggi*, vi (1924), 193

A. Bonaccorsi: 'Canti di Lucchesia', *Musica d'oggi*, vii (1925), 243

C. Caravaglios: 'Gridi di venditori napoletani trascritti musicalmente', *Il folklore musicale*, i (1925), 87

G. Fara: 'Bricciche di etnofonia marchigiana. Saggio sul Piceno', *Musica d'oggi*, vii (1925), 143, 175

A. Bonaccorsi: 'Le strade di Firenze (Gridi d'ogni genere)', *Musica d'oggi*, ix (1927), 40

G. Fara: 'Bricciche di etnofonia marchigiana. Saggio sul Maceratese', *Musica d'oggi*, xi (1929), 345; xiv (1932), 13

M. Barbi: *Scibilia Nobili e la raccolta dei canti popolari (nota musicale di Vito Frazzi)* (Turin, 1929)

A. Bonaccorsi: 'Il teatro delle campagne toscane. Il Maggio', *RMI*, xxxvii (1930), 108

C. Caravaglios: *I canti delle trincee* (Rome, 1930, 2/1935)

G. Fara: 'Saggio di geografia etnofonica', *Il folklore italiano*, v (1930), 25

G. Nataletti: 'Voci della vecchia Roma', *Il folklore italiano*, v (1930), 78

—— and G. Petrassi: *Canti popolari della campagna romana* (Milan, 1930)

C. Caravaglios: *Voci e gridi di venditori in Napoli* (Catania, 1931)

G. Fara: 'I canti del popolo d'Italia. Montagnana Ferrarese', *Musica d'oggi*, xiii (1931), 161

G. Nataletti: 'Alcuni canti della campagna romana', *Rassegna Dorica*, ii (1931), 84

L. Cocchi: 'I canti della Sardegna', *Musica d'oggi*, xiii (1931), 397

C. Caravaglios: 'Il contenuto poetico e il contenuto musicale dei gridi dei venditori ambulanti napoletani', *Atti dell'Accademia pontiniana*, xii (1932)

G. Fara: 'Scorcio di etnofonia marcigiana', *Musica d'oggi*, xxi (1933), 305

S. Di Massa: 'Cori campestri del popolo di Solopaca', *Lares*, iv (1933), 55

A. Bonaccorsi: 'Il teatro nelle campagne toscane. Il Bruscello', *Musica d'oggi*, xvi (1934), 52

F. B. Pratella, G. Nataletti and A. Anzellotti: 'Per la storia critica della musica del popolo', *Lares*, v (1934), 93

G. Nataletti: 'Su una orazione in dialetto siciliano e su alcuni canti della campagna romana', *Rassegna Dorica*, v (1934), 148

——: 'Otto canti popolari della campagna romana', *Lares*, v (1934), 35

A. Bonaccorsi: 'L'ultimo giorno di carnevale a Bibbiena e la canzone della Brunetta', *Lares*, vi (1935), 173

——: 'Il teatro nelle campagne toscane. La Zinganetta', *Lares*, vi (1935), 40

F. B. Pratella: 'Primo riassunto intorno alla canzone della Donna lombarda', *Lares*, vi (1935), 9

G. Fara: 'Etnofonia pugliese', *Lapigia*, vi (1935), 67

G. Nataletti: 'Improvvisatoni di popolo', *Musica d'oggi*, xvii (1935), 301

S. Di Massa: 'Canti del popolo di Solopaca', *Lares*, vi (1935), 50

A. Bonaccorsi: 'Divertimenti fanciulleschi. Il mercato fiorentino', *Lares*, vii (1936), 303

——: 'La Befana nella valle del Serchio', *Lares*, vii (1936), 61

C. Caravaglios: *Il folklore musicale in Italia* (Naples, 1936)

F. B. Pratella: 'Erosimo italiano e poesia e musica popolare. Da Dogali ad Adua e a Domokos', *Lares*, vii (1936), 13, 83

G. Nataletti: 'I poeti a braccio della campagna romana', *Atti del 3° Congresso nazionale delle arti e tradizioni popolari, Trento 1934* (Rome, 1936), 383

L. Colacicchi: 'Il pianto delle zitelle', *Lares*, vii (1936), 98

——: 'Canti popolari di Ciociaria', *Atti del 3° Congresso nazionale delle arti e tradizioni popolari, Trento 1934* (Rome, 1936), 289

A. Bonaccorsi: 'Canti dell'emigrazione. La rondinella', *Lares*, viii (1937), 143

L. De Angelis: 'Canti etnofonici piceni', *Lares*, viii (1937), 145

A. Bonaccorsi: 'La storia dell'Asinaro', *Lares*, ix (1938), 473

C. Caravaglios: 'Per lo studio della musica indigena delle nostre Colonie', *Saggi di folklore* (Naples, 1938), 157

F. B. Pratella: *Etnofonia di Romagna* (Udine, 1938)

——: 'La Girometta', *Lares*, ix (1938), 5, 97

L. De Angelis: 'Natale e Pasqua nelle tradizioni popolari di Macerata', *Lares*, ix (1938), 253

S. Zanon, G. Mazzotti and S. Cancian: *Cento canzoni popolari della Marca trevigiana* (Treviso, 1938)

A. Capurro: 'Appunti sul Maggio nel territori di Chiavari', *Lares*, x (1939), 131

A. Frescura and G. Re: *Canzoni popolari milanesi* (Milan, 1939)

G. Fara: 'Scorcio di etnofonia marchigiana (Treia)', *Musica d'oggi*, xxi (1939), 305

L. De Angelis: 'Saggio sul folklore della terra picena', *ARSTPI*, xiv (1939), 69

M. Barbi: *Poesia popolare italiana* (Florence, 1939/R1974)

F. B. Pratella: 'Nota sulla musica della canzone della Finta monacella', *Lares*, xi (1940), 14

G. Bollini and A. Frescura: *I canti della filana* (Milan, 1940)

G. Fara: *L'anima della Sardegna* (Udine, 1940)

F. B. Pratella: *Primo documentario per la storia dell'etnofonia in Italia* (Udine, 1940)

L. De Angelis: 'Canti della terra picena', *Lares*, xii (1941), 130

——: 'Canti della terra picena', *ARSTPI*, xvi (1941), 150

A. Bonaccorsi: *La musica popolare* (Florence, 1943)

F. B. Pratella: *Saggio di comparazione etnofonica* (Rome, 1943)

8: GREAT BRITAIN

Helen Myers

The roots of ethnomusicology in Great Britain can be traced to three distinct developments: the first, inward-looking and nationalistic, was the collection and study of indigenous folk song, which has a history in Britain nearly as long as that of printing; the second, exploratory and wide-ranging, was the investigation of non-Western music (particularly of colonial holdings), dating from the writings of 18th- and 19th-century civil servants and travellers such as Francis Taylor Piggott on Japan (1893), William Jones on Hindustan (1792) and Charles Russell Day on southern India and the Deccan (1891); and the third, scientific and systematic, was the acoustical analysis of folk and non-Western music, dating from the 1880s and the seminal work of Alexander J. Ellis on musical pitch, tunings and scales. Scholars often date the birth of ethnomusicology from the investigations of Ellis, and tend to dismiss the more descriptive work of folk-song collectors in Britain and amateur colonial writers abroad. But it is the growth and interaction of these three movements that have determined the orientation of modern ethnomusicology in the British Isles. Of these, the first, the long-standing tradition of folk-song collection, has proved the most important, although in recent decades this activity falls between two stools: on the one hand it has been rejected by anthropologically trained British ethnomusicologists as dilettantism; on the other it has been scorned by folk music enthusiasts as elitist, patronizing and overly academic.

Indigenous folk music: 16th–18th centuries

The history of folk-song study in Great Britain properly begins in the 16th century with the collection of popular broadside ballads, often composed by professional song writers, and so named because they were printed on folio-size unfolded sheets. The first collection, a sequence of Robin Hood ballads, was printed by Wynkyn de Worde (*c*1495), only two decades after the introduction of printing to England. During the 17th and 18th centuries, broadsides were the primary medium for sensational news among the urban working classes. Hyder Rollins cites over 3000 broadsides listed for the period 1557 to 1709, not including numerous items not registered with the Company of Stationers (1924). During the early 19th century, heyday of the broadside, London boasted some 50 broadside publishers, including the prolific Pitts family of Seven Dials, their rival James Catnach, and Bachelor of Moorfields, Henry Such of the Borough and others. The popularity of this form dwindled only during the early 20th century.

From the 16th century onwards, broadside texts were preserved by antiquarian collectors interested primarily in their literary value. (The systematic collection of tunes from living singers only began in the mid-19th century, with the work of John Broadwood and Cecil Sharp.) Samuel Pepys (1633–1703), the famous English diarist, composer and performer, acquired the extensive broadside collection of John Selden (1584–1654), to which he added broadsides purchased on the streets of London; Pepys amassed some 1800 items, now housed at Magdalene College, Cambridge (Rollins, 1929–32).

During the 18th century, the anthologies of Thomas D'Urfey [Durfey] (*c*1653–1723) and Thomas Percy (1729–1811) influenced English literary circles. D'Urfey's *Wit and Mirth; or, Pills to Purge Melancholy* (1719–20) contained some 1000 texts including broadsides, songs by composers of the day, older traditional items, and texts by D'Urfey and set to traditional ballad tunes. Percy's *Reliques of Ancient English Poetry* (1765) roused unprecedented interest among Romantic poets in the traditional songs of England and Scotland and stimulated the 'ballad revival' (Wordsworth claimed: 'I do not think that there is an able writer in verse at the present time who would not be proud to acknowledge his obligation to the *Reliques*' [Hutchinson, 1895, p.949]). Around 40 songs in the collection were drawn from a 15th-century manuscript found by Percy in the Shropshire home of Humphrey Pitt, where it was systematically being demolished – so the oft-repeated story goes – by the chamber maid, who was using its leaves to kindle the daily fire. *Reliques* also includes manuscripts of ballads, romances and other songs provided by Percy's friends, including items from the Bodleian and Ashmolean Libraries at Oxford, the Pepys collection at Cambridge, the Library of the London Society of Antiquaries and the British Museum. In editing these materials, Percy freely altered texts, literary licence which was only revealed a century later with the publication of the complete Pitt Folio manuscript by J. W. Hales and F. J. Furnivall, who claimed that Percy had 'powdered everything' (Hales and Furnivall, 1867–8, i, pp.22–3).

Percy's editorial policies were much attacked by the 18th-century English collector, Joseph Ritson (1752–1803), who brought out several anthologies of songs and ballads from the border district of England and Scotland (1783, 1790, 1794, 1795). In *The Bishopric Garland* (1784), Ritson supplied a few early examples of songs collected from living singers, including items by Stockton shoemakers James McLean and George Knight, and 'Rookhope Ryde' collected from George Collingwood the elder of Boltsburn. But he was wary of folk performance, 'a species of alchemy which converts gold to lead', and folk performers, 'persons, in short, altogether uncultivated'.

Scottish collections from the late 18th century include David Herd's *The Ancient and Modern Scottish Songs* (1769). Robert Burns (1759–96) pioneered the study of Scottish lyrical song, travelling throughout the lowlands and highlands to collect a representative anthology of tunes and English-language texts from native singers. He freely revised folk texts, exercising his poetic genius in filling out incomplete lines and verses, composing new texts for existing airs and setting English lowland Scots texts to Gaelic tunes; as Burns's popularity ascended, these revised and newly composed songs passed back into oral tradition, and by the time of his death, broadsides of his compositions were being sold in the streets of Edinburgh. Burns collaborated in the publication of this repertory, first with James Johnson (*The Scots Musical Museum*, 1787–1803) and later with George Thomson (*A Select Collection of Original Scottish Airs*, 1793–1841, with accompaniments by Pleyel, Haydn, and Beethoven). Burns considered this work a service to his native land, refused payment for either project, and addressed a defence of folklore to the sophisticated urbanite critic (from the preface to *The Scots Musical Museum*):

> Ignorance and Prejudice may perhaps affect to sneer at the simplicity of the poetry or music of some of these pieces, but their having been for ages the favourites of Nature's Judges – the Common People – was to the Editor a sufficient test of their merit.

The most famous collector of lowland Scots ballads was Sir Walter Scott, who presented in *Minstrelsy of the Scottish Border* (1802) material collected from printed sources and from oral tradition, particularly in Liddesdale, Ettrick Forest and the Vale of Yarrow, as well as manuscripts from collaborators John Leyden, Skene of Rubislaw, C. K. Sharpe, William Laidlaw and James Hogg. Scott edited the texts, sometimes collating variants and adding original lines. The first published collection of Gaelic tunes was Patrick MacDonald's *A Collection of Highland Vocal Airs* (1784), which includes instrumental and vocal melodies and four pibroch compositions. In 1816, Simon Fraser published his *Airs and Melodies Peculiar to the Highlands of Scotland and the Isles*, a fine collection (despite Fraser's conversions of modal cadences to minor). Later Gaelic collections include those of Francis Tolmie (1911), Margaret Fay Shaw (1955) and J. L. Campbell and F. Colinson (1969–81).

The appetite in Britain and on the continent for lowland ballads continued unabated during the decades after the publication of Scott's *Minstrelsy*, giving rise to an abundance of anthologies, including those of R. Jamieson (1806), R. H. Cromek (1810), Sharpe (1823), A. Cunningham (1825), P. Buchan (1825), G. R. Kinloch (1827) and W. Motherwell (1827).

From the mid-19th century, publications reflect the growing interest in collecting from living singers. The Sussex parson John Broadwood published an anthology under an exceptional title which describes the contents of the volume and the orientation of the collector:

> *Old English Songs, as now sung by the Peasantry of the Weald of Surrey and Sussex, and collected by one who has learnt them by hearing them Sung every Christmas from early Childhood, by The Country People, who go about to the Neighbouring Houses, Singing, or 'wassailing', as it is called, at that season. The Airs are set to Music exactly as they are now Sung, to rescue them from oblivion, and to afford a specimen of genuine Old English Melody. The words are given in their original rough state, with an occasional slight alteration to render the sense intelligible. Harmonized for the Collector, in 1843, by G. A. Dusart, organist to the Chapel of Ease at Worthing.*

Broadwood's anthology was the first attempt to present the performing practices of living informants:

> He was before his time in sympathising with the dialect, music and customs of country-folk . . . When Mr Dusart, the Worthing organist, was asked to harmonize Mr Broadwood's collection he made great outcries over intervals which shocked his musical standards. A flat seventh never *was*, and never *could* be! . . . Mr Broadwood, confirming his intervals by vehement blasts on his flute, replied '*Musically* it may be wrong, but I *will* have it exactly as my singers sang it' (niece Lucy Broadwood, *JFSS*, vii, p.81, London, 1923).

The Rev. Sabine Baring-Gould (1834–1924) was last in the great line of 19th-century country parsons with wide-ranging amateur interests, a man of intense and varied intellectual and creative talents extending from mythology and religion to travel and topography and from the writing of fiction to folklore and folk song. He turned to folk-song study in his later years (from 1887), concentrating on the music of his native West country. Working largely in isolation, before the study of folk song had acquired any methodological canons, Baring-Gould nevertheless influenced later collectors, particularly Cecil Sharp, through his interest in fieldwork, his close personal relationships with informants and his care, singular at the time, in notating tunes as well as texts. His first published folk-song collection, *Songs and Ballads of the West: a Collection Made from the Mouths of the People* (1889–92), contains 110 items from singers throughout Devon and Cornwall, together with notes about local customs and history and related printed sources for textual variants. He collaborated with the Rev. H. Fleetwood Sheppard, who transcribed the tunes, harmonized and arranged them for piano, in this and later collections (1895, 1895–9). Baring-Gould altered the texts as he saw fit, substituting printed versions for verses he considered unsuitable for popular publication. So began the process by which the songs of harvest suppers and Whitsun ales, of village fields and village greens, found their way, harmonized and simplified after the fashion of the day, into the parlours of middle-class Victorian homes, where the piano, the hallmark of learning and respectability, was a more common fixture then than now.

Indigenous folk music: 19th–20th centuries

During the Victorian era, the focus in folk-song study shifted from the collection of texts alone to the notation of both texts and tunes, from emphasis on the literary value of the songs to their musical features and their role in daily life, from antiquarian curiosity to interest in folk song as a living and ever-changing source of national culture, a native musical idiom that should be learned by all British children (much as they learn their mother tongue) and from which composers could draw in the creation of a new national art music. A parallel interest in native folklore, led by the anthropologically orientated scholars Andrew Lang (1844–1912), George Laurence Gomme (1853–1916), Alfred Trübner Nutt (1856–1910), Edwin Sidney Hartland (1848–1927), Edward Clodd (1840–1930) and William Alexander Clouston (1843–96), resulted in the formation of the Folk-Lore Society in 1878 (Dorson, 1968).

The developing interest in folk song took place within the overall renaissance of English music (usually dated from 1880 to 1900), a movement that restored English music to a position of international prominence and, for the first time since the age of Purcell, ended the domination of foreign composers and performers, the centuries of continental hegemony during which England had hosted a parade of foreign musicians including Handel, Clementi, J. C. Bach, Haydn, the infant Mozart, Mendelssohn, Spohr, Chopin and Berlioz. Developments in 19th-century English musical life included many innovations: the establishment of provincial festivals, the formation of choral societies and provincial orchestras including the Hallé (Manchester, 1857) and the Bournemouth (1893); the inauguration in London of the Henry Wood Queen's Hall summer Promenade concerts (1895); a fresh concern for musical scholarship and criticism as demonstrated in the writings of J. A. Fuller Maitland, chief music critic for *The Times*, and George Bernard Shaw of *The Star* and *The World*; the foundation of musical associations, including the Purcell Society (1876) and the Musical Association (1874, now the Royal Music Association); a renewed concern for musical scholarship (Hubert Parry held the professorship at Cambridge, Charles Stanford the Chair of Music at Oxford); the foundation of new music schools including the Royal Academy of Music (1822), Trinity College (1872) and the Guildhall School of Music (1880); and new musical publications including the

Oxford History (1901–5) and George Grove's *Dictionary of Music and Musicians* (1st fascicle, 1877; 1st edn., 1890).

The folk-song revival drew together individuals with divergent interests, all of whom were inspired to contribute to this growing English musical nationalism, all of whom were animated by the fear that traditional English folk song was dying before receiving the recognition that Scots and Irish traditional material had gained in earlier decades. The leading figures were English collector-educators such as Cecil Sharp (1859–1924) and his assistant Maud Karpeles (1885–1976), Lucy E. Broadwood (1858–1929), niece of John Broadwood and daughter of Henry Fowler Broadwood of the piano firm; musical antiquaries Anne Gilchrist (1863–1954) and Frank Kidson (1855–1926); and composer-collectors Ralph Vaughan Williams (1872–1958), George Butterworth (1885–1916), Edward Elgar (1857–1934), Gustav Holst (1874–1934) and the Australian eccentric, Percy Grainger (1882–1961). The formation of the Folk-Song Society in 1898 (after 1932, the English Folk Dance and Song Society) by these enthusiasts, as well as such leading figures from the mainstream of English musical life as Hubert Parry (1848–1918), John Stainer (1840–1901), Charles Stanford (1852–1924) and Alexander Campbell Mackenzie (1847–1935), provided a forum for their activities – to discover, collect, publish and disseminate folk song – and the eight volumes (35 numbers) of the *Journal of the Folk Song Society* (1899–1931), chronicle the history of their work throughout England, Ireland, Scotland and the Isle of Man. Similar organizations were founded in Ireland (1904) and in Wales (1906, with the first journal appearing in 1909).

Early numbers of the *Journal* and other contemporary publications reflect the diversity of their work within their unity of purpose: Kidson's collections in Yorkshire (1891) and his pioneering publication in the English folk dance revival (1890); Lucy Broadwood's material from Surrey, Sussex, southern Ireland and the highlands of Scotland, and (with J. A. Fuller Maitland) her classic *English Country Songs* (1893); Vaughan Williams's tunes and variants from Norfolk, Essex and Sussex (1908); and Butterworth's collections of Morris dances, made with Sharp. Most of these collections are presented with piano accompaniment in the belief that 'many of the tunes have harmonic implications and it is possible for a perceptive and sensitive musician to harmonize them without doing violence to their nature, provided always that he keeps the tune in the forefront of his mind' (Karpeles, 1973, p.90).

The oft-praised and oft-criticized champion of the English folk-song revival was Cecil Sharp, educated at Clare College, Cambridge, as a musician and teacher, later to become folk music collector, arranger and editor. The anecdotes relating his discovery of English folk song are told in every account on the subject, how he first became interested in folk music in the summer of 1899 when he saw the Headington Morris side dance at Oxford, and later in 1903 during a stay at Hambridge, Somerset, when he heard a gardener sing 'The Seeds of Love'. From the age of 40 he devoted his life to the collection, preservation and dissemination of English folk song and folk dance and published numerous collections beginning with *Folk Songs from Somerset* (1904–9, 1905, 1906, 1908–25, 1909–12, 1912, 1914, 1917, 1920, 1961; Karpeles, 1973). Sharp and his contemporaries believed that authentic traditions were dying, that scholarly interest in traditional culture had come only after the Industrial Revolution, general education and urbanization had wrought their inevitable changes on folkways; they hoped to save English vocal music from German influence and, in the interests of urgent preservation, sought most of their material from singers over the age of 60. For Sharp, folk song was not an antiquarian curiosity, nor its study an armchair activity, but a vital part of the living cultural heritage of the English people. Sharp was an active fieldworker, collecting widely but with emphasis on Somerset. He was an early exponent of 'applied ethnomusicology', advocating the use of folk song at many levels in national life, returning folk culture to the people through many methods from primary education to the invention of an authentic English repertory of classical music based on folk idioms. He gained notoriety with his campaign in the daily press pressuring the Board of Education to recommend authentic folk songs (those passed on in oral transmission) to be taught in English schools. In 1911 he founded the English Folk Dance Society, which, unlike the Folk-Song Society, was more concerned with the propagation of surviving dance traditions than with publication. Maud Karpeles and her sister Helen (later Mrs Douglas Kennedy) were leading figures with Sharp in this folk-dance movement. The two organizations amalgamated in 1932 to form the English Folk Dance and Song Society. In *English Folk Songs: Some Conclusions* (1907), the first comprehensive study of the subject, Sharp set out his three principles of folk-song evolution: continuity (the unfailing accuracy of the oral record), variation (spontaneous invention, the product of the individual) and selection (based on the taste of the folk community). He stressed the distinction between art and folk music:

1. Cecil Sharp transcribing a song with his assistant, Maud Karpeles, in the Appalachian Mountains

> *Art music*, then is the work of the individual, and expresses his own personal ideals and aspirations; it is composed in, comparatively speaking, a short period of time, and, by being committed to paper, it is for ever fixed in one unalterable form.
>
> *Folk music*, on the other hand, is the product of a race, and reflects feelings and tastes that are communal rather than personal; it is always in solution; its creation is never completed; while, at every moment of its history, it exists not in one form but in many (1907, pp.19–20).

Sharp collected 4977 tunes during his relatively short career, published 1118 of these, composed accompaniments for 501, and stimulated a generation of composers including Vaughan Williams, Holst and Butterworth to draw on folk-song material. During 1916–18, Sharp and Karpeles extended their research on English folk song to the USA, where they collected 1612 tunes and variants from scattered and remote communities of English, Lowland-Scots, and Scots-Irish descent living in the Southern Appalachian mountains of North Carolina, Virginia, Tennessee and Kentucky (1919–21, 1921–3; see fig.1). This monumental work ensured their place in the history of folk-song research and remains the most impressive illustration of the theory of 'marginal survival', whereby old traditions long lost in their native environment have been preserved by isolated immigrant groups.

A maverick figure in the English folk-song movement was the Australian-American composer and collector, Percy Grainger. Grainger immigrated to England in 1901 as a concert pianist, joined the Folk-Song Society in 1905 and in 1906 began to study folk song. He collected some 500 songs in four years, mainly from Lincolnshire (see fig.2), Gloucestershire and Worcestershire, as well as sea shanties from Dartmouth and a few vendor's cries from the streets of London. In 1914 he moved to the USA but later returned to folk-song study, collaborating with the Danish scholar, Evald Tang Kristensen, in Jutland in 1922, 1925 and 1927.

Grainger was keen to use scientific methods in the study of folk song. Against protests of Society members he advocated use of the Edison phonograph in fieldwork, presenting his case in the seminal article 'Collecting with the Phonograph' (1908–9), which also includes transcriptions of 27 songs (mainly from Lincolnshire), texts, variants, and a discussion of alternative forms of transcription giving a complete 'voice picture', displaying minute variations in rhythm or pitch. Upon reading Grainger's article Sharp argued, 'In transcribing a song, our aim should be to record its artistic effect, not necessarily the exact means by which that effect was produced . . . It is not an exact, scientifically accurate memorandum that is wanted, so much as a faithful artistic record of what is actually heard by the ordinary auditor' (Sharp to Grainger, 23 May 1908; quoted in Bird, 1976, p.114). Through use of the phonograph, however, Grainger was able to demonstrate that apparent irregularities in folk song were systematic; variations between verses significant; accents, dynamics and ornamentation essential to style; and that folk song rarely could be analysed in terms of conventional modes as advocated by Sharp. Sharp rejected the Edison cylinder because he thought it unreliable and felt it made the singer nervous. (Lincolnshire singer Joseph Taylor confessed to Grainger, 'Irt's lahk singin' with a muzzle on'.) Nevertheless, in 1908 and under the persuasion of Grainger, Taylor issued nine songs with the Gramophone Company – these the first commercial recordings of folk song. Grainger's painstaking transcriptions (mostly unpublished) demonstrate the importance of recorded sound in the aid of accuracy and detail. But Sharp's arguments prevailed within the conservative circles of the Folk-Song Society and only in recent years are Grainger's pioneering efforts – viewed by contemporaries as threatening and eccentric – being applauded (Bird, 1976; Dreyfus, 1985; Blacking, 1987).

2. Percy Grainger with Lincolnshire singers at Brigg Manor House in 1906: (from left to right, back) George Gouldthorpe, Grainger, Joseph Leaning, (front) Joseph Taylor and George Wray

After Sharp's death, Karpeles devoted herself to completing his work, editing two volumes, *English Folk Songs from the Southern Appalachians* (1917, 3/1960), revising the Fox Strangways biography (1967) and publishing the definitive edition of Sharp's English folk-song collection (1973). She carried on his New World research, returning to the southern Appalachians in 1950 and 1955 to discover that, with increasing modernization, many of the traditional songs they had earlier collected had vanished from living tradition. She fulfilled Sharp's desire to study the vestiges of British song in Newfoundland, where she collected 191 songs, 30 of which were published with piano accompaniment by Vaughan Williams, Hubert Foss and others (1934). In 1935, she was instrumental in the organization of the International Folk Dance Conference at Cecil Sharp House, hosting 800 dancers from 18

137

countries. After the conference a body of correspondents was established as the International Folk Dance Council.

The momentum to create an international scholarly body was halted by World War II; in September 1947, under the advice of UNESCO, Karpeles convened a meeting in London to re-establish such an organization. This gathering, which included delegates from 28 countries, resolved to form the International Folk Music Council (1947, first president Vaughan Williams), still the premier international society for ethnomusicology. Karpeles served as secretary and later as lifetime honorary president. To the end of her days she at once entertained and challenged the transformation of Sharp's values within the forum of the IFMC, especially his fundamental belief in an authentic folk culture, a notion opposed by the new generation of American and Western European ethnomusicologists in the 1960s and 1970s, who favoured a dynamic model for music with change at its very heart. With the renaming of this organization as The International Council for Traditional Music at the 1981 meeting in Seoul, Korea, Sharp's theories of an ideal 'folk' were silently ushered from scholarly practice to the history of ethnomusicology.

Acoustics and organology

The English phonetician, Alexander John Ellis (1814–90), expert in spelling reform, the psychology of hearing, and acoustics, is often said to be the father of modern ethnomusicology, and his publication 'On the Musical Scales of Various Nations' (1885), the first scientific and fair-minded appraisal of non-Western tuning systems, to mark the birth of the new study. Musical scales, Ellis maintained, were the product of cultural invention and not based on natural acoustical laws. Although he was considered tone deaf (or perhaps for this very reason), he devised the 'cents' system of pitch measurement, still used in the 1990s, whereby the Western tempered semitone is divided into 100 cents, the octave into 1200 cents. The precision this system offered made possible for the first time the objective measurement of non-Western scales. Such objectivity dealt a lethal blow to the pernicious theory of the 'contemporary ancestor' as applied to music, whereby so-called primitive music was understood to represent an early phase in the evolution of European art music. Ellis was assisted in his investigations by Alfred James Hipkins (1826–1903), specialist on temperament and pitch, of the Broadwood piano firm. They measured the tunings of non-Western instruments, breaking precedent by basing research on performance rather than on theoretical principles – studying Japanese music (1885), Central Javanese music at the Aquarium (1882), and Chinese court musicians at the International Health Exhibition (1884; Ellis found they had difficulty playing a Scots air and the English National Anthem). Ellis argued that 'there is no practical way of arriving at the real pitch of a musical scale, when it cannot be heard as played by a native musician; and even in the latter case, we only obtain that particular musician's tuning of the scale, not the theory on which it was founded' (1885, pp.490–91). He dismissed the prevalent notion that pentatonic scales had developed in Asian cultures because oriental peoples were insensitive to the subtleties of the semitone. 'It is found that intervals of three-quarters and five-quarters of a

Tone, and even more, occur. Hence the real division of the Octave in a pentatonic scale is very varied' (p.508).

The Ellis system of cents supplied the mathematical foundations necessary for scientific comparison of scales and, together with the newly available Edison cylinder recordings, made possible the objective study of non-Western musical systems. Within the intellectual climate of the late 19th century and, moreover, with cylinder collections from colonial holdings steadily mounting in the archives of Berlin, Vienna and other European capitals, these innovations contributed directly to the development of *vergleichende Musikwissenschaft* ('comparative musicology'). The issue of absolute pitch measurement – a topic that has receded in recent years in favour of anthropological preoccupations – was one of the earliest concerns of this young science, especially evident in the works of Erich M. von Hornbostel, Jaap Kunst and Curt Sachs, all of whom used these measurements to support their various theories of the history and diffusion of musical systems. Ellis's work was enthusiastically received on the continent and his treatise on scales was translated into the German by Hornbostel (1922).

Contributions in organology were made by Henry Balfour (1863–1939), who published findings about various non-Western instruments including the musical bow (1899), Aboriginal trumpets (1901) and the African *goura* (1902). He argued from an evolutionary perspective, identifying, for example, stages in the development of the African friction drum, postulating its evolution from the stick-and-membrane bellows; this hypothesis was based on the similar distribution patterns of the two forms (1907).

Francis William Galpin (1858–1945), clergyman, archaeologist and authority on instruments also contributed to non-Western organology. He studied a wide range of topics from Babylonian and Assyrian practices (1937/ *R*) to the 'music of electricity' (1937–8), from old English instruments (1910) to American Indian instruments (1902–3). The Galpin Society was founded in 1946 to commemorate and continue his work, particularly in the realm of old instruments.

The Empire and other territories

As early as the 17th century, British musical amateurs including travellers, explorers, mariners, civil servants, military personnel, businessmen, land owners, educators and missionaries made substantial contributions to music research in the British colonies and other territories, through both casual references in diaries and journals and monographs dedicated to musical topics: for the Pacific, Captain James Cook (1784; see fig.3 overleaf); for Africa, Mungo Park (1799); for China, John Barrow (1806) and the Earl of MacCartney (1793–4; published, 1962); for Japan, Francis Taylor Piggott (1893) and A. C. Moule (1908); and for the Arab world, Henry George Farmer (many writings, 1915–).

Particularly distinguished is the roster of British colonial writings on Indian music beginning with the eminent jurist and orientalist, Sir William Jones (1746–94), author of 'On the Musical Modes of the Hindoos' (1792). Harrow and Oxford trained, Jones was expert in Greek, Latin, Hebrew, Arabic, Persian, Chinese and later Sanskrit; his pioneering work in linguistics, leading

3. *Tall drums played at a Marae sacrificial ceremony on Tahiti: engraving from the atlas of Captain Cook's 'Voyage to the Pacific Ocean' (1784)*

to recognition of a Proto-Indo-European language now dead, encouraged oriental studies in the West and led to later achievements in comparative philology. In 1783 Jones was appointed judge of the Supreme Court at Calcutta (then Fort William), during the tenure of which he founded the Asiatic Society of Bengal (1784), serving as its president until his death. His music treatise, the first in English, was based in part on his reading (in a poor Persian translation) of the *Saṅgīta-darpaṇa* of Dāmodara-paṇḍita (*c*1625), the *Saṅgīta-pārijāta* of Ahobala-paṇḍita (17th century, also in Persian translation) and his most valued source, the *Rāga-vibodha* ('Doctrine of Musical Modes', 1609) of Somanātha. The value of Jones's treatise lies not in its essential accuracy or strength of argument but in the role it had in bringing to the attention of Western scholars the sophisticated musical traditions of North India (Powers, 1965).

More sound in its factual and theoretical foundations is Captain N. Augustus Willard's *A Treatise on the Music of Hindoostan* (1834), that includes descriptions of forms and glossary definitions still considered accurate. Willard is an obscure figure about whom few biographical facts have emerged. He was appointed by the Nawab of the small princely state of Banda, Uttar Pradesh, but his name does not appear in the India Office Records, possibly indicating that he was of Anglo-Indian birth. His essay was reprinted, together with that of Jones and a score of others, by the Bengali musicologist and patron Sir Sourindro Mohun Tagore [Ṣaurīndramohana Ṭhākura]

(1840–1914) in *Hindu Music from Various Authors* (1875); this early anthology served to preserve scarce items on Indian music.

The success of Tagore's anthology reflects the interest 19th-century Indian scholars took in British writings. By 1835, English had been established as the official language of British India; through English the exchange of ideas between Indian and British experts was achieved, with Indian scholars often drawing heavily on British thought – a development one might not expect in a culture with its own scholastic models and long-standing traditions of musicological discourse. Collaboration between Indian and English writers was not uncommon as with Herbert A. Popley (of the National Council of YMCA), author of *The Music of India* (1921), who consulted over his manuscript with the eminent Indian theorist, composer (and lawyer) Vishnu Narayan Bhātkhaṇḍe (1860–1936). The Indian scholar K. B. Deval drew heavily on Western acoustical research in his *The Hindu Musical Scale and the Twenty-Two Shrutees* (1910) in which he parallels Western findings with excerpts from the Sanskrit literature, especially the 13th-century *Saṅgīta Ratnākara*. Ernest Clements, an Indian Civil Service officer and musical amateur, used Deval's interpretation of scales as a basis for his *Introduction to the Study of Indian Music* (1913/R1981), in which he attempts to correlate modern Hindustani scales with historical scales as described in the early theoretical Sanskrit treatises. In *The Ragas of Hindustan* (1918), Clements illustrated his findings with examples from compositions in various North Indian ragas. In *The Ragas of Tanjore: Songs and Hymns from the Répertoire of the Karnatic Singer, Natrajan* (1920) he applied the same principles to the South Indian repertory. The new and seemingly scientific methods of Deval and Clements – review of ancient theoretical scales in light of 19th-century acoustics and the measurement of modern scales as performed – came immediately into vogue both with local and foreign experts, as for example the works of Alain Daniélou, C. S. Ayyar, and more recently, Nazir Ali Jairazbhoy (see also Powers, 1965).

The music of the Karnatak tradition, south of Hyderabad and dominated by Dravidian culture, was less studied during the British period. Exceptions are *The Music and Musical Instruments of Southern India and the Deccan* (1891) by Charles Russell Day, Captain of the Oxfordshire Light Infantry. He offers a full description of the classical Karnatak system, its theoretical treatises, raga and tala, instruments, and includes pitch measurements made by Ellis and Hipkins. The earliest survey of the vernacular folk song of South India is *The Folk-Songs of South India* (1871) by Charles E. Gover, Member of the Royal Asiatic Society, the Society of Arts, and Fellow of the Anthropological Society. He gives contextual information and generous samples of English translations from the Canarese, Bagada, Coorg, Tamil, Malayalam and Telugu poetic repertories, but offers little indication of the musical content of the songs. The earliest works on the vernacular traditions of northeast India are 'Some Bihārī Folk-Songs' (1884) and 'Some Bhoj'pūrī Folk-Songs' (1886) by the linguist Sir George Grierson of the Bengal Civil Service and member of the Royal Asiatic Society. These collections are complete with Devanagari transcriptions, English translations and meticulous linguistic annotations; however, musical commentary is lacking. Early work in Gujarat was done by the Scotsman Alexander Kinlock Forbes [Farbas], a civil servant and judge who collected an historical account of the area from regional bards. Some of the earliest sources for popular devotional tunes and texts are found in Christian hymnals compiled by missionaries (Parsons, 1861; Ullmann, 1878; Bate, 1886).

From the early 20th century, studies were made by professional musicians. A. H. Fox Strangways (1859–1948), the Oxford-trained musicologist, critic and editor visited India in 1904 and again during 1910–11. Fascinated by the music, he wrote *The Music of Hindostan* (1914), which includes, in addition to his detailed analysis of raga, tala, and form in the North Indian classical repertory, a 57-page 'Musical Diary' of his travels through various districts including the Central Provinces, Madras, Bangalore, Mysore, Travancore, Tanjore, Calcutta and Lahore. This survey, one of the earliest accounts of Indian music outside the classical tradition, includes devotional songs, street cries, beggars' songs, songs of the boy acrobats of Bombay, grinding songs and dance tunes from railway stations. Fox Strangways's interpretation of ancient Indian music should be read with caution but his discussion of contemporary practice is masterful and his analytic comparisons of Indian and Western music enlightening, even in view of more recent and detailed research.

One of the last scholar-administrators under the Raj was William G. Archer (1907–79), appointed to the Indian Civil Service, Bihar, in 1931. His interest in folk music, poetry and art persisted throughout his 16-year stay in India; in each of several appointments he mastered the local dialect, rituals and customs, and published major anthologies of song texts and poetry in the vernacular language in collaboration with local colleagues. He first studied Indian tribal song from 1934 to 1937 during his post as Joint Magistrate and Deputy Collector of Gumla subdivision of Chota Nagpur, where he investigated the culture of the Uraon tribes (1940, 1941, 1948). From 1939 he was posted to Hazaribhag as Provincial Census Superintendent, where he studied Kharia, Ho, and Munda poetry (1942, *Ho Durang*; 1942, *Kharia Along*; 1942, *Munda Durang*; 1943, *Hor Seren*). From 1942 to 1946 he served as Deputy Commissioner of the Santal Parganas, Dumka, Bihar, working and living with these tribal peoples, collecting their folk art (1944, 'More Santal'; 1945; 1974) alongside his appointed task of recording and codification of Santal civil law.

These civil servants in India and throughout the Empire worked largely within the forum of the Royal Asiatic Society. Their contemporaries in other camps, for example the 'great team' of folklorists (especially Lang, Gomme and Nutt), were tirelessly searching out the roots of traditional British folkways within the work of the Folk-Lore Society; the new imperial view in folklore was set out in C. S. Burne's *The Handbook of Folklore* (1914). During the same decades, the roots of British social anthropology were established with the evolutionary theories of Edward B. Tylor (1832–1917) and Lewis Henry Morgan (1818–81). Contemporary organologists and acousticians including Ellis and Hipkins were actively pursuing their independent aims within the Society of Arts and the [Royal] Musical Association. This period also marked the most intensive work of Folk-Song Society collectors Broadwood, Butterworth, Grainger, Karpeles and Sharp. Only in retrospect can we synthesize these separate developments in England and in the Empire to posit an intellectual history of British ethnomusicology. Indeed, the lack of actual contact and interaction between these movements may account for the relatively underdeveloped state of ethnomusicological studies in modern Britain.

Bibliography

England: COLLECTIONS

T. D'Urfey: *Wit and Mirth; or, Pills to Purge Melancholy* (London, 1719–20/*R*1959)

T. Percy, ed.: *Reliques of Ancient English Poetry* (London, 1765)

J. Ritson, comp.: *A Select Collection of English Songs, with Their Original Airs and a Historical Essay on the Origin and Progress of National Song* (London, 1783, 2/1813)

——comp.: *The Bishopric Garland: or, Durham Minstrel* (Stockton, 1784, 2/1792/*R*1809)

——comp.: *Ancient Songs and Ballads from the Reign of King Henry the Second to the Revolution* (London, 1790, 3/1877/*R*1968)

——: *Robin Hood: a Collection of all the Ancient Poems, Songs, and Ballads, now extant, relating to that Celebrated English Outlaw* (London, 1795, 2/1832)

J. Broadwood, comp.: *Old English Songs* (London, 1843) [pubd with additional songs by L. E. Broadwood as *Sussex Songs* (Popular Songs of Sussex), arr. H. F. B. Reynardson (London, 1889)]

W. Chappell: *Popular Music of the Olden Time* (London, 1855–9)

J. W. Hales and F. J. Furnivall, eds.: *Bishop Percy's Folio Manuscript: Ballads and Romances* (London, 1867–8)

J. C. Bruce and J. Stokoe, eds.: *Northumbrian Minstrelsy: a Collection of the Ballads, Melodies, and Small-pipe Tunes of Northumbria* (Newcastle upon Tyne, 1882/*R*1965)

F. J. Child: *The English and Scottish Popular Ballads* (Boston, MA, and New York, 1882–98/*R*1956, 1965)

Journal of the Folk-Song Society (London, 1889–1931) [index, 1951]

S. Baring-Gould and H. F. Sheppard, comps.: *Songs and Ballads of the West: a Collection Made from the Mouths of the People* (London, 1889–92, 2/1891–5, rev. 7/1928)

W. A. Barrett: *English Folk Songs* (London, 1891)

F. Kidson: *Traditional Tunes: a Collection of Ballad Airs, chiefly obtained in Yorkshire and the South of Scotland* (Oxford, 1891/*R*1970)

L. E. Broadwood and J. A. Fuller Maitland, eds.: *English County Songs, Words and Music* (London, 1893)

S. Baring-Gould and H. F. Sheppard, comps. *A Garland of Country Song: English Folk Songs with Their Traditional Melodies* (London, 1895)

——eds.: *English Minstrelsie: a National Monument of English Song* (1895–6)

C. J. Sharp and C. L. Marson, eds.: *Folk Songs from Somerset* (London, 1904–9)

C. J. Sharp, S. Baring-Gould and others, eds.: *Songs of the West* (London, 1905, 5/1913) [rev. of S. Baring-Gould and H. Sheppard, comps. (1889–92)]

C. J. Sharp and S. Baring-Gould, eds.: *English Folk-Songs for Schools* (London, 1905)

C. J. Sharp: Folk Songs Without Accompaniment, *JFSS*, ii/6 (1905); v/18 (1914); v/20 (1916); viii/31 (1927)

——ed.: *English Folk-Carols* (London, 1906/*R*1911)

L. E. Broadwood, comp.: *English Traditional Songs and Carols* (London, 1908)

H. E. D. Hammond, comp.: *Folk Songs from Dorset* (London 1908, repr. in Sharp, 1961)

C. J. Sharp, ed.: *Novello's School Series* (London, 1908–25) [songs collected by C. Sharp, R. Vaughan Williams and H. E. D. Hammond]

R. Vaughan Williams, comp.: *Folk-Songs from the Eastern Counties* (London, 1908, repr. in Sharp, 1961)

A. B. Gomme and C. J. Sharp, eds.: *Children's Singing Games* (London, 1909–12)

G. B. Gardiner, comp.: *Folk-Songs from Hampshire* (London, 1909, repr. in Sharp, 1961)

W. P. Merrick, comp.: *Folk Songs from Sussex* (London, 1911, repr. in Sharp, 1961)

C. J. Sharp, ed.: *Folk-Songs from Various Counties* (London, 1912, repr. in Sharp, 1961)

R. Vaughan Williams: *Folk-Songs for Schools* (London, 1912)

G. Butterworth: *Folk Songs from Sussex* (London, 1913)

C. J. Sharp, ed.: *English Folk-chanteys* (London, 1914)

C. J. Sharp and O. D. Campbell, comps.: *English Folk Songs from the Southern Appalachians* (London, 1917, 2/1932, ed. M. Karpeles, 3/1960) [without acc.]

C. J. Sharp: *Folk-Songs of English Origin collected in the Appalachian Mountains* (London, 1919–21/*R*1927)

R. Vaughan Williams, ed.: *Eight Traditional English Carols* (London, 1919)

C. J. Sharp, ed.: *English Folk Songs* (London, 1920, 2/1959)

R. Vaughan Williams and E. M. Leather, eds.: *Twelve Traditional Carols from Herefordshire* (London, 1920)

C. J. Sharp: *Nursery Songs from the Appalachian Mountains* (London, 1921–3)

A. Williams, ed.: *Folk-songs of the Upper Thames* (London, 1923)

Journal of the English Folk Dance and Song Society (London, 1932–64)

M. Karpeles: *Folk Songs from Newfoundland* (London, 1934, enl. 2/1971) [with pianof acc. by R. Vaughan Williams, C. Carey, H. J. Foss and M. Mullinar]

B. H. Bronson: *The Traditional Tunes of the Child Ballads with their Texts according to the Extant Records of Great Britain and America* (Princeton, NJ, 1959–72)

R. Vaughan Williams and A. L. Lloyd, eds.: *The Penguin Book of English Folk Songs* (London, 1959)

C. J. Sharp, ed.: *English County Folk Songs* (London, 1961)

R. Vaughan Williams: *A Yacre of Land: 16 Folk-songs from the Manuscript Collection of Ralph Vaughan Williams*, ed. I. Holst and U. Vaughan Williams (London, 1961)

Folk Music Journal (1965–)

P. Grainger: *Seven Lincolnshire Folk Songs*, ed. P. O'Shaughnessy (London, 1966)

——: *Twenty-one Lincolnshire Folk Songs*, ed. P. O'Shaughnessy (London, 1968)

——: *More Folk Songs from Lincolnshire*, ed. P. O'Shaughnessy (London, 1971)

M. Karpeles, ed.: *Cecil Sharp's Collection of English Folk Songs* (London, 1973)

——: *The Crystal Spring* (London, 1975)

B. H. Bronson, ed.: *The Singing Tradition of Child's Popular Ballads* (Princeton, NJ, 1976)

For further bibliography see M. Dean-Smith: *A Guide to English Folk Song Collections, 1822–1952, with an Index to their Contents, Historical Annotations, and an Introduction* (Liverpool, 1954)

ON FOLK MUSIC AND COLLECTORS

T. Hutchinson, ed.: *The Poetical Works of William Wordsworth* (Oxford, 1895)

L. E. Broadwood: 'On the Collecting of English Folk-Song', *PRMA* (1904–5), 89

C. J. Sharp: *English Folk Song: Some Conclusions* (London, 1907, 3/1954/R1972, ed. M. Karpeles)

P. Grainger: 'Collecting with the Phonograph', *JFSS*, iii/12 (1908–9), 147

C. J. Sharp: *Folk Singing in Schools* (London, 1912)

C. S. Burne: *The Handbook of Folklore* (London, 1914)

H. E. Rollins, comp.: *An Analytical Index to the Ballad Entries (1557–1709) in the Registers of the Company of Stationers of London* (Chapel Hill, NC, 1924/R1967)

J. Fuller-Maitland: 'The Beginning of the Folk-Song Society', *JFSS*, viii/1 (1927), 46

W. Ford: 'Lucy Etheldred Broadwood', *JFSS*, viii/3 (1929), 168

H. E. Rollins, ed.: *The Pepys Ballads (1535–1702)* (Cambridge, MA, 1929–32)

G. H. Gerould: *The Ballad of Tradition* (Oxford, 1932/R1960)

A. H. Fox Strangways and M. Karpeles: *Cecil Sharp: His Life and Work* (London, 1933, rev. 2/1955, rev. 3/1967)

R. Vaughan Williams: *National Music* (London, 1934; repr. in *National Music and Other Essays*, 1963)

E. K. Wells: *The Ballad Tree: a Study of British and American Ballads* (London and New York, 1950)

M. Karpeles, ed.: *The Collecting of Folk Music and Other Ethnomusicological Material: a Manual for Field Workers* (London, 1958)

M. Dean-Smith: 'The Work of Anne Geddes Gilchrist O.B.E., F.S.A., 1863–1954', *PRMA* (1957–8), 43

J. Reeves, ed.: *The Idiom of the People: English Traditional Verse* (London, 1958)

——: 'Letters to Lucy Broadwood', *JEFDSS*, ix (1964), 233–68

C. M. Simpson: *The British Broadside Ballad and its Music* (New Brunswick, 1966)

A. L. Lloyd: *Folk Song in England* (London, 1967)

R. M. Dorson: *The British Folklorists: a History* (Chicago, IL, 1968)

B. H. Bronson: *The Ballad as Song* (Berkeley and Los Angeles, CA, 1969)

I. Clissold: 'Alfred Williams, Song Collector', *Folk Music Journal*, i (1969), 293

F. S. Howes: *Folk Music of Britain – and Beyond* (London, 1969)

M. Karpeles: *An Introduction to English Folk Song* (London, 1973)

J. Bird: *Percy Grainger* (London, 1976)

M. Dawney: 'George Butterworth's Folk Music Manuscripts', *Folk Music Journal*, iii (1976), 99

Grainger Journal [Percy Grainger Society] (1978–)

K. Dreyfus, ed.: *The Farthest North of Humanness: Letters of Percy Grainger 1901–1914* (St Louis, MO, 1985)

D. Harker: *Fakesong: the Manufacture of British 'Folksong' 1700 to the Present Day* (Milton Keynes, 1985)

J. O'Brien: *The Grainger English Folksong Collection* (Nedlands, Western Australia, 1985)

J. Blacking: *'A Commonsense View of All Music': Reflections on Percy Grainger's Contribution to Ethnomusicology and Music Education* (Cambridge, 1987)

FOLK DANCE COLLECTIONS AND BOOKS ON FOLK DANCE

F. Kidson, ed.: *Old English Country Dances, Gathered from Scarce Printed Collections, and from Manuscripts* (London, 1890)

C. J. Sharp and H. C. Macilwaine: *The Morris Book* (London, 1907, rev. 2/1912–24)

C. J. Sharp: *The Country Dance Book* (London, 1909–16)

—— and H. C. Macilwaine: *Morris Dance Tunes* (London, 1909–19, 2/1923)

C. J. Sharp: *The Sword Dances of Northern England: Songs and Dance Airs* (London, 1911–13)

Journal of the English Folk Dance Society (London, 1914–15; 1927–31)

D. N. Kennedy: *England's Dances: Folk-dancing To-day and Yesterday* (London, 1949)

Scotland: VOCAL COLLECTIONS

J. Forbes: *Cantus, Songs and Fancies to Three, Foure, or Five Partes, Both Apt for Voices and Viols* (Aberdeen, 1662, 2/1666)

D. Herd: *The Ancient and Modern Scottish Songs, Heroic Ballads, &c.* (Edinburgh, 1769, 2/1776/R1870)

J. Johnson, comp.: *The Scots Musical Museum* (Edinburgh, 1787–1803, rev. 3/1853) [with notes]

G. Thomson, ed.: *A Select Collection of Original Scottish Airs for the Voice* (Edinburgh, 1793–1841)

J. Ritson, comp.: *Scottish Song* (London, 1794, 2/1869) [with historical essay]

W. Scott: *Minstrelsy of the Scottish Border* (Edinburgh, 1802, many edns/R1932)

R. Jamieson: *Popular Ballads and Songs, from Tradition, Manuscripts, and Scarce Editions* (Edinburgh, 1806)

R. H. Cromek: *Remains of Nithsdale and Galloway Song* (London, 1810/R1880)

C. K. Sharpe, comp.: *A Ballad Book* (Edinburgh, 1823/R1883)

P. Buchan: *Gleanings of Scotch, English and Irish Scarce Old Ballads* (Peterhead, 1825)

A. Cunningham, ed.: *The Songs of Scotland, Ancient and Modern* (London, 1825)

G. R. Kinloch, ed.: *Ancient Scottish Ballads, Recovered from Tradition, and Never Before Published* (London, 1827)

W. Motherwell: *Minstrelsy: Ancient and Modern, with an Historical Introduction and Notes* (Glasgow, 1827, 2/1873)

F. J. Child: *The English and Scottish Popular Ballads* (Boston, MA, and New York, 1882–98/R1956, 1965)

H. Hecht, ed.: *Songs from David Herd's Manuscripts* (London, 1904)

G. Grieg: *Last Leaves of Traditional Ballads and Ballad Airs*, ed. A. Keith (Aberdeen, 1925)

B. H. Bronson: *The Traditional Tunes of the Child Ballads with their Texts, According to the Extant Records of Great Britain and America* (Princeton, NJ, 1959–72)

GAELIC COLLECTIONS

P. MacDonald, comp.: *A Collection of Highland Vocal Airs, Never Hitherto Published* (Edinburgh, 1784, 2/1788)

S. Fraser, ed.: *The Airs and Melodies Peculiar to the Highlands of Scotland and the Isles* (Edinburgh, 1816, 2/1874/R1918)

F. Tolmie: 'A Collection of Gaelic Songs', *JFSS*, iv (1911)

M. F. Shaw: *Folksongs and Folklore of South Uist* (London, 1955)

J. L. Campbell and F. Collinson: *Hebridean Folksongs* (Oxford, 1969–81)

BOOKS ON FOLK MUSIC

J. C. Dick, ed.: *The Songs of Robert Burns* (London, 1903/R1962)

——: *Notes on Scottish Song by Robert Burns* (London, 1908/R1962)

H. G. Farmer: *A History of Music in Scotland* (London, 1947/R1970)

F. M. Collinson: *The Traditional and National Music of Scotland* (London, 1966/R1970)

International Folk Music Council

Journal of the International Folk Music Council (Cambridge, 1949–68) 20 vols., yearly, cumulative index 1949–63, 1954–8, 1959–63; continued as *Yearbook of the International Folk Music Council* (Urbana, IL, 1969–70; UNESCO, 1971–80); continued as *Yearbook for Traditional Music* (UNESCO, 1981–), yearly

N. Fraser, ed.: *International Catalogue of Recorded Folk Music* (London, 1954)

International Folk Music Council: *Bulletin*, from 1957 (no.11), *Bulletin of the International Folk Music Council* (London, 1948–67; Copenhagen, 1967–9; Kingston, Ont., 1969–80), from 1981, *Bulletin of the International Council for Traditional Music* (New York, approx. yearly; from 1957 semiannually)

K. P. Wachsmann, ed.: *International Catalogue of Published Records of Folk Music* (London, 1961) [sequel to Fraser, 1954]

R. W. I. Band, ed.: *Directory of Institutions and Organizations Concerned Wholly or in Part with Folk Music* (London, 1964)

K. Vetterl, ed.: *A Select Bibliography of European Folk Music* (Prague, 1966)

The International Folk Directory of Ethnic Music and Related Traditions (Dartington, 1973)

D. and N. Christensen, eds.: *ICTM Directory of Interests and Projects* (New York, 1985), rev. and enl. as *ICTM Directory of Traditional Music* (1987)

Acoustics and organology

A. J. Ellis, trans.: *On the Sensations of Tone as a Physiological Basis for the Theory of Music* (London, 1875, 2/1885, 6/1948) [trans. of H. L. F. von Helmholtz, *Die Lehre von den Tonempfindungen als physiologische Grundlage für die Theorie der Musik* (Brunswick, 1863), with addns]

A. J. Hipkins: 'Pitch', *Encyclopaedia Britannica* (London, 9/1875–89)

A. J. Ellis: 'Tonometrical Observations on Some Existing Non-harmonic Scales', *Proceedings of the Royal Society*, xxvii (1884), 368

——: 'On the Musical Scales of Various Nations', *Journal of the Society of Arts*, xxxiii (1885), 485–527 [rev., enl. version of preceding essay Ger. trans. by E. M. von Hornbostel as 'Über die Tonleitern verschiedener Völker', *Sammelbände für vergleichende Musikwissenschaft*, i (1922), 1–75]

A. J. Hipkins: *Musical Instruments, Historic, Rare and Unique* (Edinburgh, 1888, 3/1945) [examples from India, China, Japan and South Africa]

——: 'Preface', C. R. Day; *The Music and Musical Instruments of Southern India and the Deccan* (London and New York, 1891/*R*1974)

H. Balfour: *The Natural History of the Musical Bow* (Oxford, 1899)

——: 'Three Bambu Trumpets from Northern Territory, South Australia', *Man*, i/28 (1901), 33

——: 'The Goura: a Stringed Wind Musical Instrument of the Bushmen Hottentots', *Journal of the Royal Anthropological Institute*, xxxii (1902), 156

F. W. Galpin: 'The Whistles and Reed Instruments of the American Indians of the North-west Coast', *PMA*, xxix (1902–3), 115

H. Balfour: 'The Friction Drum', *Journal of the Royal Anthropological Institute of Great Britain and Ireland*, xxxvii (1907), 67

F. W. Galpin: *Old English Instruments of Music, their History and Character* (London, 1911, rev. 4/1965 by T. Dart)

A. H. Fox Strangways: 'Interval', *Grove 3*

J. A. Fuller Maitland: 'Hipkins, Alfred James', *Grove 3*

A. J. Hipkins: 'Ellis, Alexander John', *Grove 3*

F. W. Galpin: *The Music of the Sumerians and Their Immediate Successors, the Babylonians and Assyrians* (Cambridge, 1937/*R*)

——: 'The Music of Electricity', *PMA*, lxiv (1937–8), 71

J. Kunst: *Musicologica: a Study of the Nature of Ethno-musicology, its Problems, Methods and Representative Personalities* (Amsterdam, 1950, enl. 3/1959/*R*1975 as *Ethnomusicology*)

H. Balfour: 'Ritual and Secular Uses of Vibrating Membranes as Voice Disguisers', *Journal of the Royal Anthropological Institute of Great Britain and Ireland*, xxxviii (1951), 86

C. Sachs: *The Wellsprings of Music* (The Hague, 1962)

M. Hood: *The Ethnomusicologist* (New York, 1971, rev. 2/1982)

K. Wachsmann: 'Spencer to Hood: a Changing View of Non-European Music', *Proceedings of the Royal Anthropological Institute for 1973* (1974), 5

The Empire and other territories

Africa

M. Park: *Travels in the Interior Districts of Africa Performed in the Years 1795, 1796, and 1797* (London, 1799)

A. M. Jones: 'African Drumming', *Bantu Studies*, viii (1934), 1

——: 'The Study of African Rhythm', *Bantu Studies*, xi (1937), 295

——: *Studies in African Music* (Oxford, 1959)

———: 'Indonesia and Africa: the Xylophone as Culture-Indicator', *African Music*, ii (1960), 36

Arab

H. G. Farmer, ed.: *The Music and Musical Instruments of the Arab* (London, 1915/*R*1975) [trans. and rev. of F. Salvador-Daniel: *La musique arabe* (Algiers, 1863)]

———: *Clues for the Arabian Influence on Musical Theory* (London, 1925)

———: 'A North African Folk Instrument', *Journal of the Royal Asiatic Society* (1928), 25

———: 'Ibn Khurdadhbih on Musical Instruments', *Journal of the Royal Asiatic Society* (1928), 509

———: *A History of Arabian Music to the XIIIth Century* (London, 1929/*R*1973)

———: 'Meccan Musical Instruments', *Journal of the Royal Asiatic Society* (1929), 489

———: 'The Congress of Arabian Music, Cairo, 1932', *Transactions of the Glasgow University Oriental Society*, vi (1929–33), 61

———: *Historical Facts for the Arabian Musical Influence* (London, 1930/*R*1970)

———: *Studies in Oriental Musical Instruments* (London, 1931–9)

———: *Al-Fārābī's Arabic-Latin Writings on Music* (London, 1934/*R*1965)

———, ed. and trans.: *Turkish Instruments of Music in the Seventeenth Century* (Glasgow, 1937)

———: *The Sources of Arabian Music* (Glasgow, 1939, rev. 2/1965)

———: *Instruments of Music: History and Development* (Glasgow, 1941)

———: *Oriental Studies, Mainly Musical* (London, 1953)

———: Many articles in *Grove 5, MGG, The Encyclopedia of Islam* (Leiden, 1928–38, rev. 2/1960) and the *Journal of the Royal Asiatic Society*

India

W. Jones: 'On the Musical Modes of the Hindoos', *Asiatick Researches*, iii (1792), 55–87; repr. in S. M. Tagore, ed. (1875)

N. A. Willard: *A Treatise on the Music of Hindoostan, Comprising a Detail of the Ancient Theory and Modern Practice* (Calcutta, 1834; repr. in S. M. Tagore, ed., 1875)

J. Parsons: *The Hindustani Choral Book, or Swar Sangrah* (Benares, 1861)

C. E. Gover: *The Folk-songs of Southern India* (Madras, 1871)

S. M. Tagore, ed.: *Hindu Music from Various Authors* (Calcutta, 1875, 2/1882 in 2 pts., 3/1965)

J. F. Ullmann: *Gītāwalī: Containing Hymns and Songs, for Children, in Hindustani, with Their Music* (London, 1878)

G. A. Grierson: 'Some Bihārī Folk-Songs', *Journal of the Royal Asiatic Society of Great Britain and Ireland*, xvi (1884), 196–246

J. D. Bate: *The North India Tune-Book, Containing Bhajans and Ghazals with Native Tunes as Usually Sung* (London, 1886)

G. A. Grierson: 'Some Bhoj'pūrī Folk-Songs', *Journal of the Royal Asiatic Society of Great Britain and Ireland*, xviii (1886), 207–67

C. R. Day: *The Music and Musical Instruments of Southern India and the Deccan* (London and New York, 1891/*R*1974)

A. C. Wilson: *A Short Account of the Hindu System of Music* (Lahore, 1904)

A. H. Fox Strangways: 'The Hindu Scale', *SIMG*, ix (1907–8), 449–511

K. B. Deval: *The Hindu Musical Scale and the Twenty-Two Shrutees* (Poona, 1910)

E. Clements: *Introduction to the Study of Indian Music* (London, 1913/*R*1981)

A. H. Fox Strangways: *The Music of Hindostan* (Oxford, 1914/*R*1975)

E. Clements: *The Ragas of Hindustan* (Poona, 1918)

———: *The Rāgas of Tanjore, Songs and Hymns from the Répertoire of the Karnatic Singer, Natrajan, Arranged in Staff Notation, With an Introduction* (London, 1920)

H. A. Popley: *The Music of India* (London, 1921, 3/1966)

A. H. Fox Strangways: 'Exotic Music', *ML*, vi (1925), 119

———: 'Music', *The Legacy of India*, ed. G. T. Garratt (Oxford, 1937), 305

W. G. Archer, ed. and trans.: *The Blue Grove: the Poetry of the Uraons* (London, 1940/*R*1972)

A. H. Fox Strangways: 'Indian Music', *Grove 4*

W. G. Archer, F. Hahn and D. Lakra: *Lil Khora Khekhel: a Collection of 2600 Uraon Songs and 40 Riddles in Uraon and Gaonwari* (Laheriasarai, 1941)

W. G. Archer: 'Seasonal Songs of Patna District', *Man in India* (Ranchi), xxii (1942), 233

W. G. Archer, B. K. Dutt and Ram Chandra Birua: *Ho Durang: a Collection of 935 Ho Songs and 400 Riddles in Ho* (Patna, 1942)

W. G. Archer, D. Hans and S. Hans: *Munda Durang: a Collection of 1641 Munda Songs and 380 Riddles in Mundari* (Patna, 1942)

W. G. Archer, J. Kharia, D. Dungdung and M. Totetohran: *Kharia Along: a Collection of 1528 Kharia Songs and 446 Riddles in Kharia* (Ranchi, 1942)

W. G. Archer and S. Prasad: 'Bhojpurī Village Songs', *The Journal of Bihar and Orissa Research Society* (1942), 1–48

W. G. Archer and G. G. Soren: *Don Soren: a Collection of 1954 Santal Cultivation and Marriage Songs in Santali* (Dumka, 1943)

——: *Santal Songbook, paḥil ḥaṭiń* (Chapa Akana, 1942)

——: *Hoṛ Sereń, a Collection of 1676 Santal Songs in Santali* (Dumka, 1943)

W. G. Archer: 'Festival Songs', *Man in India* (Ranchi), xxiv (1944), 70

——: 'More Santal Songs', *Man in India* (Ranchi), xxiv (1944), 141

——: 'Santal Rebellion Songs', *Man in India* (Ranchi), xxv (1945), 207

——ed. and trans.: *The Dove and the Leopard: More Uraon Poetry* (Bombay, 1948)

H. S. Powers: 'Indian Music and the English Language', *EM*, ix (1965), 1

W. G. Archer: *The Hill of Flutes: Life, Love and Poetry in Tribal India: a Portrait of the Santals* (London, 1974)

M. D. Rosse: 'Tagore, Sir Sourindro Mohun', *Grove 6*

W. G. Archer: *Songs for the Bride: Wedding Rites of Rural India* (New York, 1985)

J. Bor: 'The Rise of Ethnomusicology: Sources on Indian Music c. 1780–c. 1890', *YTM*, xx (1988), 51

East and Southeast Asia

J. Barrow: *A Voyage to Cochinchina in the Years 1792 and 1793* (London, 1806)

F. T. Piggott: *The Music and Musical Instruments of Japan* (London, 1893)

The Earl of Macartney: *An Embassy to China, Being the Journal Kept by Lord Macartney During his Embassy to the Emperor Ch'ien-lung 1793–1794*, ed. J. L. Crabmer-Byng (London, 1962)

A. C. Moule: 'A List of the Musical Instruments of the Chinese', *Journal of the North-China Branch of the Royal Asiatic Society*, xxxiii (1908), 37

Pacific

J. Cook: *A Voyage to the Pacific Ocean . . . in the Years 1776, 1777, 1778, 1779, and 1780* (London, 1784)

9: IRELAND

BREANDÁN BREATNACH, NICHOLAS CAROLAN

Although some Irish airs are found in 17th-century English publications, and a few pieces of an even earlier date in English manuscript collections, the first collection consisting of Irish music was not published until 1724 (J. and W. Neal). As the century progressed, Irish airs appeared in increasing numbers in English and Scots collections, in the ballad operas of the period and in local collections published by such Dublin printers as J. and E. Lee. But it was 1796 before Bunting published the results of first-hand collecting in the field.

Edward Bunting (1773–1843; see illustration, p. 148) first became acquainted with Irish music when he was engaged as musical scribe to the Belfast Harp Festival in 1792. He continued his collecting after the festival, visiting some of the harpers he had met there as well as venturing further into the field. His 1796 volume, the first of three, contained 66 airs, many of which had not been published before; Thomas Moore took 12 of the 24 airs printed in his *Irish*

Melodies from it. When collecting the music for his second volume (1809) Bunting engaged the service of an Irish scholar to note the words of the Irish songs but unfortunately he did not use the texts collected. His final volume (1840) consisted mostly of material already collected by 1809, but he also included a description of the methods of playing employed by the harpers, along with notes on their lives and habits, and a list of technical terms in Irish relating to harping and music in general. Bunting was the first of the great collectors of Irish folk music and his collections contain beautiful airs, many of which are known throughout the English-speaking world because of their adoption by Thomas Moore. Bunting's theories about this music have long since been outmoded; his printed versions of tunes do not always correspond with his manuscript settings. The airs of the three volumes have been re-edited by D. O'Sullivan (1927–39, 1983), together with the related Irish verses which Bunting had not used.

George Petrie (1790–1866), a distinguished antiquary and artist, was the next important collector of Irish folk music. He was largely responsible for the founding of the Society for the Preservation and Publication of the Melodies of Ireland, the first organization to concern itself with native music. This society planned to issue five annual publications, each containing 200 airs, suitably arranged and copiously annotated, but in fact the society's only publication was Petrie's *The Ancient Music of Ireland* (1853–5). This volume contains only 147 airs, introduced in many cases by extensive historical and descriptive notes. A further selection similarly annotated was published posthumously in 1882; many of the airs in these two volumes were altered to fit the harmonic idiom of the day. Petrie's manuscript collections containing 2148 pieces were finally entrusted to Charles Stanford for editing and publication. His edition (1902–5) contains 1582 tunes. He eliminated some 500 duplicates and variants but failed to detect many others and made no attempt to arrange the material systematically.

Patrick Weston Joyce (1827–1914) made the greatest single contribution to the Petrie collection. His own first volume (1873) contains 100 airs with piano accompaniment and notes on the sources of the airs. His major work (1909) contains 842 airs drawn principally from the Forde and Pigot manuscript collections but also from his own collecting, from transcriptions received from friends and from broadsheets. This collection has been criticized for containing airs of English and Scots origin although these were current in Ireland. A more serious fault is that the notation cannot be trusted, as evidence from his work on other manuscripts shows that he habitually altered source melodies (Hegarty, 1966).

Three other major 19th-century collections remain unpublished. They are those of W. Forde (*c*1795–1850), who was the first collector to adopt a systematic approach to the collecting of variants and whose manuscripts include the results of fieldwork in Munster, Leitrim and adjacent areas; J. E. Pigot (1822–71), whose manuscript (mostly compiled from second-hand sources) is housed in the Royal Irish Academy along with that of Forde; and J. Goodman (1828–96), whose manuscript (in the library of Trinity College, Dublin) contains much dance music noted down from the playing of Munster pipers.

Francis O'Neill (1849–1936), born in West Cork, spent most of his life in

Edward Bunting: etching (1811) by James Sidebotham

Chicago. His *Music of Ireland* (1903) is the largest published collection of Irish music and contains 1850 pieces garnered from all sources; borrowings from printed material are sometimes disguised under altered titles, but over half the items in the collection were noted down from the singing and playing of Chicago residents. O'Neill's second collection, *The Dance Music of Ireland* (1907), contains 1001 tunes (based mostly on his first volume with additional material); it won immediate acceptance among traditional players. His *Waifs and Strays of Gaelic Melody* (1922) is compiled from manuscript and early Irish and Scots printed sources. In *Irish Folk Music* (1910) and *Irish Minstrels and Musicians* (1913) O'Neill has left a fund of information about Irish music and musicians.

Only desultory efforts were made in the fields of collection and publication in the years between the wars. Of considerable interest however are the commercially produced 78 rpm recordings of traditional instrumentalists made in the 1920s and 1930s, chiefly in the USA. Sam Henry (1878–1954), a collector from Coleraine, Co. Derry, published about 850 songs in the Coleraine newspaper *The Northern Constitution* between 1923 and 1939. Coimisiún Béaloideasa Éireann (The Folklore Commission of Ireland), founded in Dublin in 1935, collected songs on phonograph which now survive mostly in transcriptions.

Bibliography

VOCAL AND INSTRUMENTAL MUSIC

J. and W. Neal: *A Collection of the Most Celebrated Irish Tunes proper for the Violin, German Flute or Hautboy* (Dublin, 1724/*R*1986)

W. Jackson: *Jackson's Celebrated Irish Tunes* (Dublin, *c*1780)

J. Lee: *A Favourite Collection of . . . Irish Tunes* (Dublin, 1780)

J. Aird: *A Selection of Scotch, English, Irish and Foreign Airs* (Glasgow, 1782–1803)

S., A. and P. Thompson: *The Hibernian Muse* (London, *c*1786)

E. Bunting: *A General Collection of the Ancient Irish Music* (Dublin and London, 1796/*R*1969)

O'Farrell: *O'Farrell's Collection of National Irish Music for the Union Pipes* (London, *c*1804)

S. Holden: *Collection of Old-established Irish Slow and Quick Tunes* (Dublin, 1806–7)

E. Bunting: *A General Collection of the Ancient Music of Ireland* (London, 1809/*R*1969)

J. Murphy: *A Collection of Irish Airs and Jiggs* (Paisley, 1809)

J. Mulholland: *A Collection of Irish Airs* (Belfast, 1810)

O'Farrell: *O'Farrell's Pocket Companion for the Irish or Union Pipes* (London, *c*1811)

E. Bunting: *The Ancient Music of Ireland* (Dublin, 1840/*R*1969)

J. Clinton: *Gems of Ireland* (London, *c*1840)

G. Petrie: *The Ancient Music of Ireland* (Dublin, 1853–5)

P. M. Haverty: *One Hundred Irish Airs*, i–iii (New York, 1858–9)

R. M. Levey: *The Dance Music of Ireland*, i–ii (London, 1858–73)

P. W. Joyce: *Ancient Irish Music* (Dublin, 1873)

F. Hoffman: *Ancient Music of Ireland from the Petrie Collection* (Dublin, 1877)

G. Petrie: *Music of Ireland* (Dublin, 1882)

P. W. Joyce: *Irish Music and Song* (Dublin, 1888)

A Moffat: *The Minstrelsy of Ireland* (London, 1898)

C. V. Stanford, ed.: *The Complete Collection of Irish Music as Noted by George Petrie* (London, 1902–5)

F. O'Neill: *The Music of Ireland* (Chicago, IL, 1903)

P. W. Joyce: *Irish Peasant Songs in the English Language* (Dublin, 1906)

F. O'Neill: *The Dance Music of Ireland* (Chicago, IL, 1907, rev. and enl 2/1976 by M. Krassen)

C. G. Hardebeck: *Gems of Melody, Seoda Ceóil 1–3* (Belfast, 1908–?1916)

P. W. Joyce: *Old Irish Folk Music and Songs* (London and Dublin, 1909)

F. Roche: *Irish Airs, Marches and Dance Tunes*, i–iii (Dublin, 1911–27)

A. Darley and P. J. McCall: *Feis Ceoil Collection of Irish Airs Hitherto Unpublished 1* (Dublin, 1914/ *R*1984)

F. O'Neill: *Waifs and Strays of Gaelic Melody* (Chicago, IL, 1922)

D. O'Sullivan: 'The Bunting Collection of Irish Folk Music', *Journal of the Irish Folk Song Society*, xxii–xxix (1927–39/*R*1969)

C. Hegarty: *Thematic Index and Analytical Investigation of the Joyce Manuscripts* (diss., National U. of Ireland, 1966)

M. Deasy: *New Edition of Airs and Dance Tunes from the Music Manuscripts of George Petrie . . .* (diss., National U. of Ireland, 1982)

D. O'Sullivan with M. ÓSúilleabháin: *Bunting's Ancient Music of Ireland* (Cork, 1983)

SONG COLLECTIONS

C. Brooke: *Reliques of Irish Poetry consisting of Heroic Poems, Odes, Elegies and Songs* (Dublin, 1789)

T. Connellan: *An Duanaire . . .* [The Poem-book], *A Selection of Irish Poems and Moral Epigrams Collected from Ancient Manuscripts and Oral Tradition* (Dublin, 1829)

J. Hardiman: *Irish Minstrelsy or Bardic Remains of Ireland* (London, 1831/*R*1971)

E. Walsh: *Irish Popular Songs* (Dublin, 1847)

J. O'Daly: *The Poets and Poetry of Munster* (Dublin, 1849, rev. 5/1884)

F. J. Child: *English and Scottish Popular Ballads* (Boston, MA, 1882–98/*R*1965)

D. Hyde: *Abhráin grádha Chúige Chonnacht* [Love-songs of Connacht] (Dublin, 1893/*R*1968, enl. 2/1931)

M. and T. Ó Máille: *Abhráin Chlainne Gaedheal* [Songs of the Children of the Gael] (Dublin, 1905, 2/1925)

M. Ó Tiománaidhe: *Abhráin Ghaedhilge an Iarthair* [Gaelic Songs of the West] (Dublin, 1906)

H. Hughes: *Irish Country Songs*, i–iv (London, 1909–36)

P. Breathnach: *Fuinn na smól* [Tunes of the Thrushes] (Dublin, 1913, enl. 2/1923 as *Ceól ár Sinsear* [The Music of our Ancestors])

E. Ó Muirgheasa: *Céad de Cheoltaibh Uladh* [100 Ulster Songs] (Dublin, 1915)

E. Costelloe: *Amhráin mhuighe seóla* [Traditional Songs from Galway and Mayo] (London, 1919, 2/1923)

P. Breathnach: *Ár gceól féinig* [Our own Music] (Dublin, 1920)

A. M. Freeman: 'Irish Folk Songs from Ballyvourney', *JFSS*, vi (1920–21), 95–342

P. Breathnach: *Ceól ár sinsear* [The Music of our Ancestors] (Dublin, 1923)

S. Henry: 'Songs of the People' [series in *The Northern Constitution* newspaper] (Coleraine, 1923–39/*R* 1990)

F. Mac Coluim: *Cosa buidhe árda* [Long Yellow Legs] (Dublin, 1924)

P. Breathnach: *Sidh-cheól* [Fairy Music] (Dublin, 1924–6)

M. Ní Annagáin and S. de Chlanndiolúin: *Londubh an chairn* [Blackbird of the Cairn] (Oxford, 1927)

T. Ó Ceallaigh: *Ceól na n-oileán* [Music of the Islands] (Dublin, 1931)

E. Ó Muirgheasa: *Dhá Céad de Cheoltaibh Uladh* [200 Ulster Songs] (Dublin, 1934/*R*1969)

C. Ó Lochlainn: *Irish Street Ballads* (Dublin, 1939)

F. Mac Coluim: *Amhráin na nGleann 1* [Songs of the Glens] (Dublin, *c*1940)

J. Moulden: *Songs of the People 1* [selection from S. Henry series] (Belfast, 1979)

GENERAL

J. C. Walker: *Historical Memoirs of the Irish Bards* (Dublin, 1786, enl. 2/1818)

T. Croker: *Researches in the South of Ireland* (London, 1824)

E. O'Curry: *Of the Manners and Customs of the Ancient Irish* (Dublin, 1873)

J. C. Culwick: *The Distinctive Characteristics of Ancient Irish Melody* (Dublin, 1897)

R. B. Armstrong: *Musical Instruments*, i: *The Irish and the Highland Harps* (Edinburgh, 1904/*R*1969)

W. H. G. Flood: *A History of Irish Music* (Dublin, 1904, rev. 3 1913/*R*1970)

Journal of the Irish Folk Song Society (London and Dublin, 1905–39)

F. O'Neill: *Irish Folk Music: a Fascinating Study* (Chicago, IL, 1910/*R*1973)

——: *Irish Minstrels and Musicians* (Chicago, IL, 1913/*R*1973)

R. Henebry: *A Handbook of Irish Music* (Dublin, 1928)

10: SCANDINAVIA

JAN LING

Ethnomusicology in the Scandinavian countries (Denmark, the Faroe Islands, Finland, Norway, Iceland and Sweden) up to World War II has been concerned primarily with folk music on a national level and music of peoples in the northern and northeastern hemisphere such as the Lapps (Sames), Eskimos (Inuit) and Ostjaks. Research on folk music can be divided into the study and collecting of folk songs and of instrumental music and musical instruments; properly scientific research on local traditions; and ethnomusicological studies outside the Nordic area. The last mentioned have been few and have not resulted in comparable research traditions to the first and second.

By the end of the 18th century a nationalistic antiquarian interest in old popular poetry gave rise to the collecting of folk songs. The collectors also had ambitions to give the songs back to the people. Three approaches to the tunes were made: preparing them for a drawing-room performance by 'correcting' them in a major or minor tonality and harmonizing them; trying to trace their medieval roots and 'reconstruct' their 'degenerate, destroyed' origin; and providing an unadorned notated version. Most early collections belong to the first category. The first edition of Swedish ballads collected by Erik Gustav Geijer and Arvid August Afzelius from 1814–18 stimulated a lively debate about how the melodies should be harmonized, resulting in an extensive correspondence between collectors and scholars. Composers, organists and teachers were involved, indicating the importance of folk song at this time. Andreas Peter Berggreen (1801–80) emphasizes in his Danish edition of folk songs (1860–71) that melodies should be edited and performed with accompaniment, and the Norwegian collector Ludvig Mathias Lindemann (1812–87) presented his collection of Norwegian melodies from 1841 as already 'harmonized'.

In the debate concerning the origin of the melodies, scholars tried to trace them to classical antiquity or to classify them as a specific Nordic type (Haeffner, 1818). Thomas Laub (1852–1927) first classified the melodies according to church modes and later 'restored' them using Gregorian plainsong as a model (1892–3). The Swedish scholar and composer Karl Valentin (1853–1918), also tried to find connections between Gregorian chant and folk melodies in his dissertation (1885) and Erik Abrahamsen strongly emphasizes the same idea in his dissertation (1923). Even among the very first collectors and scholars, however, are representatives of a rather modern approach to folk song: The Swedish vicar Levin Christian Wiede (1804–82), the Danish teacher Evald Tang Kristensen (1843–1929) and the Norwegian composer and organist Martin Ludvig Lindeman (1812–87) made efforts to capture peculiarities of performance such as neutral intervals and the subtlety of rhythmic agogics. But these efforts can only be seen in the manuscripts; the published melodies were submitted to conventional notation.

Of great importance in the study of folk song was the founding of the Dansk folkemindesamling (Danish Folklore Collection) in 1905, based on Tang Kristensen's huge collection. In Norway, Ole Mørk Sandvik (1875–1976) was the initiator of the Norsk musiksamling (Norwegian Music Collection) in 1927. In Finland the Svenska litteratursällskapet (Swedish Society of Literature), founded in 1885, was responsible for collecting and publishing Swedish folk songs in Finland and later of instrumental music.

The founder of Finnish musicology, Ilmari Krohn (1867–1960), wrote his dissertation on Finnish sacred folk melodies (1899). He did extensive fieldwork not only in Finland and Sweden but also in other parts of Europe. Besides studies of folk music (1933, 1935) and ethnomusicology he devised a system of arranging tunes as in a dictionary according to melodic characteristics (1906).

In Sweden interest in folk music was focussed more on instrumental than on vocal genres. After World War II the Svenskt visarkiv (Swedish Centre for Folk Song and Folk Music Research, founded 1951) took responsibility for the scientific recording of folk song and the copying of manuscript material from archives and private collections.

In the early 1800s chain-dancing with sung ballads in the medieval manner on the Faroe Islands was observed and reported by Hjalmar Thuren, in his important study published in 1908. Two years before, Bjarni Thorsteinsson had begun the first comprehensive collection of Icelandic folktunes old and new.

The pioneer in the scientific study of herding music was the Swedish antiquarian Richard Dybeck (1811–77). In 1846 he published a collection of herding calls, vocal and instrumental, and continued to give examples of this genre in his journal *Runa* during the following decades. Dybeck considered herding calls and songs the essence of the folk and the nation, an ideology that has lived on. The founder of musicology in Sweden, Tobias Norlind, characterized herding calls and the *joik* of the Sames as the first primitive step in a process of musical evolution (1930).

The study of instrumental folk music was most significant in Finland, Sweden and Norway, where collectors were driven not by scholarly interest but by their desire to preserve traditions for future generations of fiddlers. Working towards this practical goal, they discovered peculiarities of tunes and performance, observations that were the first steps toward scientific research of instrumental folk music. Most of the early collectors and scholars were amateurs.

In Sweden collections of instrumental folk music were published at the beginning of the 19th century, such as *Svenska folkdansar* (Swedish Folk-dances) in 1814, but only by the end of the century were more comprehensive and

1. Otto Andersson notating music played by Erik Lönnbergin, 1912

2. *A Samu woman recorded on a phonograph by A. O. Väisänen*

reliable editions prepared (Andersson, 1895–1916). Some of the collectors were fiddlers themselves and part of a local tradition (Fredin, 1909–33). The Swedish lawyer Nils Andersson (1864–1921), an enthusiastic propagandist of folk music, compiled a collection of instrumental music covering most parts of the country; the collection comprises some 15,000 tunes, of which half are published in *Svenska låtar* (Swedish Tunes) (1922–40/*R*1974).

Collecting in Norway was more or less the same as in Sweden, but the closest equivalent to *Svenska låtar*, *Hardingfeleslåttar* (Hardanger Fiddle Music) was not published until 1958–67, with modern transcriptions. Studies of tunes to find out their origin and age started in the 1920s with the work of E. Eggen (1923) and E. Groven (1927). These studies though have been criticized as to method as well as theory.

In Finland 'Dansmelodies' were published in the famous series *Suomen kansan sävälmiä* (Tunes of the Finnish People) in 1893, a forerunner of the Swedish *Svenska låtar*. Finnish musicologist and folklorist Otto Andersson (1879–1969) also played an important role in the Scandinavian folk music movement as collector, scholar, administrator and as the initiator of the folk music revival (see fig.1). In his research he synthesized theories and methods from different branches of musicology and other disciplines. Some of his articles are reprinted in *Studier i musik och folklore* (1964, 2/1969). His monograph on the bowed harp (1923) was for its time a revolutionary study in which Andersson combined ethnomusicological, historical and linguistic research in an attempt to give the bowed harp a convenient place in his evolutionary scheme for the development of string instruments. Mats Rehnberg's study of the Swedish bagpipe (1943) also deals with one instrument in history and modern times.

Early in the 20th century the first scientific research of Lappish *joik* was made in Finland and Sweden. In 1908 the Finnish musicologist Armas Launis (1884–1959) published more than 850 *joiks*. In Sweden a station-master, Karl Tirén (1869–1955) spent his summers with Swedish Sames, recording and learning the art of joiking (1942). The studies of E. Manker (1938) and E. Emsheimer (1944, 1947) were the first analytical and reflective studies on the subject.

Material for ethnomusicological studies in Scandinavia, collections of recorded melodies, instruments and notes about music were brought by expeditions of linguists and ethnographers. K. F. Karjalainen and A. Kannisto, two prominent Finnish linguists, collected music from the Ostjaks and Woguls and the Danish ethnographer H. Hasslund-Christensen recorded music on the Swedish explorer S. Hedin's expedition to Mongolia. Later this material was the object of a scientific interpretation by A. O. Väisänen (1930, 1937, 1939) and E. Emsheimer (1943), who was musicological adviser to the scientific expeditions led by Hedin.

In 1903, W. Thalbitzer recorded a large collection of melodies from Northwest Greenland, and in 1905–6 he did the same for the Ammassalik Inuit. He passed the material to Thuren, who transcribed the songs, with very interesting analyses and remarks partly in collaboration with Thalbitzer (1910–11, 1911, 1923).

In 1935, Karl Gustav Izikowitz published his study of the instruments of the South American Indians, and three years later the first part of Ernst Manker's monograph on the Lappish *trum* appeared. Together with Emsheimer's studies (1941, 1943, 1946) these publications restored the international reputation that ethnomusicology in Scandinavia had at the beginning of the century.

Bibliography

COLLECTIONS

A. A. Afzelius and O. Åhlström: *Traditioner of svenska folkdansar* [Swedish Folk Dances in Tradition] (Stockholm, 1814–15/R1972)

E. G. Geijer and A. A. Afzelius: *Svenska folk-visor från forntiden* [Ancient Swedish Folk Songs, Ballads] (1814–18, 2/1880, 3/1957–60)

A. I. Arwidsson: *Svenska fornsånger* [Ancient Swedish Folk Songs] (Stockholm, 1834–42)

L. M. Lindemann: *Norske fjeldemelodier harmoniskt bearbeidede* [Norwegian Melodies harmonized] (Christiania, 1841)

R. Dybeck: *Svenska vallvisor och hornlåtar, med norska artförändringar* (Stockholm, 1846/R1974)

E. T. Kristensen: *Jydske folkeminder* (Copenhagen, 1842–55, 2/1871, 1874)

A. P. Berggreen: *Folke-sange og melodier, faedrelandske og fremmede* [Folk Songs and Melodies, Native and Foreign], i–xi (1860–71)

A. G. Rosenberg: *420 svenska danspolskor* [420 Swedish *polskas*] (Stockholm, 1876–82/*R*1969)

J. Nordlander: *Svenska barnvisor och barnrim* [Swedish Children's Songs and Rhymes] (Stockholm, 1886/*R*1971)

N. Andersson: *Skånska melodier* [Melodies from Schoene] (Stockholm, 1895–1916)

I. Krohn: *Soumen kansan sävelmiä* [Tunes of the Finnish People] (Helsinki, 1898–1933)

K. P. Leffler: *Folkmusik från norra Södermanland* [Folk music from north Södermanland] (Stockholm, 1899–1900)

I. Krohn: 'Melodien der Berg-Tscheremissen und Wotjaken', *SIMG*, iii (1901–2), 430, 741

A. Bondeson: *Visbok* [Songbook] (Stockholm, 1902–3/*R*1940)

B. Thorsteinsson: *Islenzk thjodlög* (Copenhagen, 1906–09)

A. Launis: *Soumen kansan savelmia: Runosävelmiä* [Tunes of the Finnish People: Runotunes] (Helsinki, 1908)

H. Thuren: *Folkesangen paa Faeröerna* [The Folk Song of the Faroes] (Copenhagen, 1908)

A. Fredin: *Gotlandstoner* [Melodies from Gotland] (Stockholm, 1909–33)

W. Thalbitzer and H. Thuren: 'Musik aus Ostgrønland: Eskimoische Phonogramme', *ZIMG*, xii (1910–11), and

——: 'The Eskimo Music', 'On the Eskimo Music', *Meddelelser om Grønland* [Melodies from East Greenland], xl (Copenhagen, 1911)

O. M. Sandvik: *Folkemusikk i Gundbrandsdalen* (Oslo, 1919/*R*1948)

K. P. Leffler: *Folkmusiken i Norrland* [Folk Music in Norrland] (Härnösand, 1921–4)

N. Andersson: *Svenska låtar* [Swedish Tunes] (Stockholm, 1922–40/*R*1974)

W. Thalbitzer: 'Melodies from the Cape Farewell District', *Meddelelser om Grønland* (Copenhagen, 1923), 49

H. Thuren and others: *Danmarks gamle Folkeviser*, xi (Copenhagen, 1933–6/*R*1976)

O. Andersson: *Folkvisor: den äldre folkvisan* [Folksongs: the Old Folksongs], *Finlands svenska folkdiktning*, v/l (Helsinki, 1934)

A. O. Väisänen: 'Mordwinische Melodien phonographisch aufgenommen von A. Kannisto und K. F. Karjalainen', *Mémoirs de la Société Finno-ougrienne*, ed. A. O. Väisänen, xcii (Helsinki, 1937)

——: 'Wogulische und ostjakische Melodien, phonographisch aufgenommen von A. Kannisto und K. F. Karjalainen', *Mémoires de la Société Finno-ougrienne*, ed. A. O. Väisänen, lxxiii (Helsinki, 1937)

Y. Heykel: *Folkdans, dansbeskrivningar Finland svenska folkdiktning*, vi B (Helsinki, 1938)

P. A. Säve: *Gotländska visor* [Folksongs from Gotland] (Uppsala, 1949–55)

O. Gurvin, ed.: *Hardingfeleåtar* [Hardanger Fiddle Music], *Norsk folkemusikk*, I/i–v (Oslo, 1958–67)

O. Andersson: *Folkdans: instrumentalmusik: menuetter, polskor, polonäser, Finlands svenska folkdiktning*, vi/A1 (Turku, 1963)

O. Andersson and others: *Sånglekar* [Game Songs], *Finlands svenska folkdiktning*, vi/A3 (Turku, 1967)

E. Ala-Könni: 'Kansanmusiikin keruun ja tutkikuksen vaiheta' [History of Folk Music Collection and Research], *Kalevalaseuran vousikirja*, xlix (1969)

S. Nyhus: *Pols i Rörostrakten* [The Poles in the Rörs Region] (Oslo, 1973)

O. Andersson and G. Dahlström, eds.: *Folkdans: Yngre dansmelodier Finlands svenska folkdiktning*, vi/A2 (Turku, 1975)

J. Dicander: *Folkliga koraler från Dalarna* [Folk Hymns from Dalarna] (Falun, 1975)

M. Ramsten: *Einar Övergaards folkmusiksamling* (Uppsala, 1982)

S. Ahlbäck: *Jernbergs låtar* [The Tunes of a Fiddler, with an Analysis] (Gävle, 1986)

M. Jersild: *K. P. Lefflers folkmusiksamling* (Örsköldsvik, 1987)

J. H. Koudal: *Rasmus Storms nodebog* [The Notebook of R.S.] (Copenhagen, 1987)

STUDIES

J. C. Fr Haeffner with E. G. Geijer: 'Anmärkningar öfver gamla nordiska sången' [Comments concerning the old Nordic Scale], *Svea* (Uppsala, 1818), 78

K. Valentin: *Studien über die schwedischen Volksmelodien* (diss., U. of Leipzig, 1885)

T. Laub: 'Studier över vore folkevisemelodiers oprindelse og musikaliske bygning', *Dania*, ii (1892–3), 1, 149–179

A. Hammerich, 'Studien über isländische Musik', *SIMG*, i (1899–1900), 341–71

I. Krohn: *Über die Art und Enstehung der geistlichen Volksmelodien in Finnland* (diss., U. of Helsinki,

1900; Helsinki, 1899)

H. Thuren: 'Dichtung und Gesang auf der Färöern', *SIMG*, iii (1901–2), 222–69

I. Krohn: 'Welche ist die beste Methode um Folks-und volksmässige Melodien nach ihrer melodischen (nicht textlichen Beschaffenheit lexikalisch zu ordnen?', *SIMG*, iv (1902–3), 634–70

T. Laub: 'Vore folkevisemelodier og deres fornyelse', *Danske studier*, i (1904), 177–209

I. Krohn: 'Über das lexikalische Orden von Volksmelodien', *Bericht über den II. Kongress der internationalen Musikgesellschaft zu Basel* (1906), 66

A. Launis: 'Lappische Juoigos-Melodien', *Mémoires de la Société Finno-ougrienne*, i (1908), 26

T. Norlind: 'Melodier till svenska folkvisor och folkdanser, upptecknade före år 1800' [Swedish Folk Tunes and Folk Dances, Collected Before 1800], *Svenska landsmålen* (1906), 67

O. Andersson: 'Über schwedische Volkslieder und Volkstänze in Finnland', *Brage*, iii (1909), 145–76

H. Thuren: 'On the Eskimo Music in Greenland', *Meddelelser om Grønland*, xl/1 (1914), 1–45

C. Elling: Vore Kjaempeviser belyst fra musikalisk Synspunkt [Musical Aspects of our Giant Songs, Ballads], *Videnskapsselskapets Sunifter. II Hist.-filos Klasse 1913* (1914)

H. Grüner-Nielsen: *Vore aeldste folkdanse, langdans og polskdans* (Copenhagen, 1917)

E. O. Abrahamsen: *Eléments romans et allemands dans le chant grégorien et la chanson popoulaire en Danemark* (diss., U. of Fribourg, 1923; Copenhagen, 1923)

O. Andersson: *Stråkharpan: En studie i nordisk instrumenthistoria* [The Bowed Harp] (Helsingfors, 1923)

E. Eggen: *Skalastudier: studier over skalaens genesis på norrönt område* [Study of the Langeleik and Intervals in Norwegian Folk Music] (Oslo, 1923)

E. Groven: 'Natureskalaen' [The Natural Scale], *Norsk folkekultur* (1927), 1–46

A. O. Väisänen: 'Das Zupfinstrument gusli bei den Wolgavölkern', *Mémoires de la Société Finno-ougrienne*, lviii (1928), 303

O. Andersson: *The Bowed Harp* (London, 1930) [rev. Eng. version of *Stråkharpan*, 1923]

T. Norlind: *Svensk folkmusik och folkdans* [Swedish Folk Music and Folk Dance] (Stockholm, 1930)

A. O. Väisänen: 'Die Leier der ob-ugrischen Völker: Ihr Bau, Gebrauch und Ursprung', *Eurasia Septentrionalis Antiqua*, vi (1930), 15

I. Krohn: *Die Sammlung und Erforschung der Volksmusik in Finland* (Helsinki, 1933)

K. G. Izikowitz: *Musical and Other Sound Instruments of the South American Indians* (diss., U. of Göteborg, 1934; Göteborg, 1935)

I. Krohn: *Die finnische Volksmusik* (Greifswald, 1935)

A. O. Väisänen: 'Die obugrische Harfe', *Finnisch-ugrischen Forschungen*, xxiv (1937), 127

E. Manker: *Die lappische Zaubertrommel: Die Trommel als Denkmal materieller Kultur* (Stockholm, 1938)

A. O. Väisänen: 'Wirklichkeitsgrund der Finnische-Estnischen Kanteleruner', *Acta ethnologica*, i (1938), 31

C. A. Moberg, 'De folkliga koralvarianterna på Runö' [Choral Singing on Runö], *STMf*, xix (1939), 9–47

A. O. Väisänen: *Untersuchungen über die ob-ugrischen Melodien. Eine vergleichende Studie nebst methodischer Einleitung* (diss., U. of Helsinki, 1939)

K. Tirén: *Die Lappische Volksmusik* (Uppsala, 1942)

E. Emsheimer: *Preliminary Remarks on Mongolian Music and Instruments. Music of Eastern Mongolia, The Music of the Mongols*, i (Stockholm, 1943)

M. Rehnberg: *Den svenska säckpipan* [The Swedish Bagpipe] (Stockholm, 1943)

E. Emsheimer: 'Schamanentrommel und Trommelbaum', *Ethnos*, xi (1946), 166

C.-A. Moberg: 'Två kapitel om svensk folkmusik' [The Problem of Tonality in Swedish Folk Music and Study of a Tune], *STMf*, xxxiii (1950), 5–49

N. Schiörring: *Det 16. og 17. århundredes verdslige danske visesang* [16th- and 17th-century Danish Secular Folk Songs], i-ii (Copenhagen, 1950)

C.-A. Moberg: 'Från kämpevisa till locklåt' [A Survey of the Swedish Folk Music Collectors and Collections], *STMf*, xxxix (1951), 5–52

S. Walin: *Die schwedische Hummel* (Stockholm, 1952)

C.-A. Moberg: 'Om vallåtar: en studie i de svenska fäbodarnas musikaliska organisation' [Of Herdsmen's Songs: a Study of the Musical Organization of the Swedish *fäbodar*], *STMf*, xxxvii (1955), 7–95

E. Ala-Könni: *Die Polska-Tänze in Finnland: eine ethnomusikologische Untersuchung* (Helsinki, 1956)

E. Dal: *Nordisk folkeviseforskning siden 1800* [Scandinavian Ballad Research] (Copenhagen, 1956)

C.-A. Moberg: 'Om vallåter II: musikaliska strukturproblem', *STMf*, xli (1959), 10–57

M. Arnberg: *Den medeltida balladen: en orientering och kommentar till Sveriges radios inspelningar* [The Medieval Ballad: Introduction and Commentary on Swedish Radio Recordings] (Stockholm, 1962)

O. Andersson: *Studier i musik och folklore* [Studies in Music and Folklore], ed. A. Forslin (Åbo, 1964) [collected essays as 85th birthday tribute with list of writings]

J. Ling: *Svensk folkmusik: bondens musik i helg och söcken* [Swedish Folk Music: Peasant Music for Holy Days and Week Days] (Stockholm, 1964)

H. Huldt-Nyström: *Det najonale tonefall* [The National Accent] (Oslo, 1966)

O. K. Ledang: *Song, syngemåte og stemmekarakter* [Singing, Vocal Technique and Style] (Oslo, 1967)

B. R. Jonsson: *Svensk balladtradition* [The Medieval Popular Ballad in Swedish Tradition] (Stockholm, 1967) [with an English summary]

J. Ling: *Levin Christian Wiedes vissamling: en studie i 1800-talets folkiga vissång* [Levin Christian Wiedes Song Collection: a Study of 19th-Century Folk Song] (Uppsala, 1965) [with English summary]

J. Ling: *Nyckelharpan: studier i ett folklight musikinstrument* [The Keyed Fiddle: Studies of a Folk Instrument] (diss., U. of Uppsala, 1967; Stockholm, 1967) [with abbrev. version in Eng.]

C. -A. Moberg: *Studien zur schwedischen Volksmusik* [Translation of Studies in Swedish] (Uppsala, 1971)

P. Helistö: *Finnish Folk Music* (Helsinki, 1973)

R. Sevåg: *Det gjallar og det laet* [The Ring and the Soft Sound: On Norwegian folk instruments] (Oslo, 1973)

M. Jersild: *Skillingtryck: studie i svensk folklig vissång före 1800* [Broadsheets: Studies on the Swedish Popular Ballads before 1800] (Stockholm, 1975) [with Eng. summary]

B. Kjellström: *Dragspel* [The accordion] (Stockholm, 1976)

M. Ramsten: *Hurven: En polska och dess miljö'* [A Dance Tune and its Environment], *Årsbok för vis-och folkmusikforskning* (1976), 67–155

K.-O. Edström: *Den samiska musikkulturen: en källkritisk översikt* [The Music Culture of the Laplanders: a Critical Survey of the Sources] (diss., U. of Göteborg, 1978)

H. Larsen: 'Vallhornstillverkning i Sverige', *SUMLEN* (1980), 9–46

J. Ling and others: *Folkmusikboken* [A Survey of Swedish Folk Music] (Stockholm, 1980)

S. Nielsen: *Stability in Musical Improvisation. A Repertoire of Icelandic Epic Songs* (Rimur) (Copenhagen, 1982)

T. Leisiö: *Soumen ja Karjalan vanhakantaiset torvi-ja pillisoittimet I. Nimisto: rakenteet ja historia* [Finnish and Karelian Wind Instruments as Historical Indicators] (diss., U. of Tampere, 1983; Kaustinen, 1983)

P. Suojanen: *Finnish Folk Hymn Singing* (diss., U. of Tampere, 1984)

B. Kjellström: and others: *Folkmusikvågen* [The Folk Music Vogue] (Stockholm, 1985) [abbrev. version in Eng.]

CHAPTER IV

Southern and Eastern Europe

Barbara Krader, Bálint Sarosi

Introduction

This chapter discusses seven very different countries from the 19th century up to 1939. Poland was entirely under foreign rule for over a century. Bohemia and Moravia, of the Austrian Empire, were industrializing, and, especially in Bohemia, rapidly losing village traditions. Slovakia, an integral part of Hungary from the 11th century until 1918, was poor, isolated, traditional. Hungary proper, ruler of an empire, was relatively poor, industrialization was beginning, often led by foreigners. She, and her non-Hungarian population as well, became ever more nationalistic. The Romanian state dates from 1861, uniting Moldavia and Walachia, which had been ruled by the Turkish and Russian Empires. It gained Transylvania from Hungary in 1919. Bulgaria was under Turkish rule for 500 years until 1878. Greece was freed from Turkish rule, piece by piece, by 1914. Yugoslavia and Czechoslovakia were founded only in 1918, both from diverse ethnic groups with different histories. Throughout the area, nationalism was strong, affecting interest in and study of traditional music.

1: BULGARIA

Barbara Krader

The year 1878 marks the liberation of Bulgaria from the Turks. By 1939 this small country with its limited resources had reached a remarkably high level in folk music research.

One of the leading figures in pre-war Bulgarian ethnomusicology was Dobri Christov (1875–1941), a composer and professor at the Music Academy (Kamburov, 1942?; Kŭrstev, 1954; Kaufman, 1975). He was the first to systematize the remarkable Bulgarian asymmetric metres in his classic treatise on the rhythmic bases of Bulgarian folk music (1913), including a famous table of asymmetric patterns known to him, followed by song and dance examples of each and discussion. He defined the asymmetric metres as

160

composed of shorter and longer units of measure, in a ratio of 2:3. A revised version of this work, completed about 1925–8, was published posthumously in his collected writings (Christov, 1967–70). Bartók knew this study and cited it in his own brief article on the subject (1938). Bartók called such rhythms Bulgarian (although he refers to their presence in other countries), and also used them in his compositions – in the Fifth String Quartet and *Mikrokosmos*. Christov also notated the music of 215 songs from a single traditional singer (IAnkov, 1913), which was a sequel to a much admired collection of 333 song texts made by IAnkov from his mother Elena IAnkova (1825–1901), published in 1908. Christov's singer, the daughter, Kira IAneva, had learned her repertory from her remarkable mother (Dzhudzhev, 1952). Christov later published a broader analytic work on the technical structure of Bulgarian folk music (1928) and a collection of Macedonian folksongs (1939). The latter contains an analytic study in Bulgarian and French (pp.1–35) and also notes the place of origin of each song and provides piano accompaniments with song texts in Bulgarian and French. His writings also include valuable information on 19th-century Greek, Turkish and Czech influences on urban songs (1928, introduction). Venelin Kŭrstev later compiled and edited Christov's works in two volumes (Christov, 1967, 1970). Both volumes include articles on Macedonian folk music, intended to prove its intrinsic Bulgarian nature.

The second important Bulgarian figure is Vasil Stoin (1880–1938), a professor of music who devoted his last years, from 1927, to collecting, systematizing and publishing Bulgarian folk songs. With a few assistants, he organized the collection of some 24,000 folk songs from all parts of Bulgaria (Dinekov, 1980; Katsarova, 1980; Krader, 1980). The four volumes published by 1939 contain 9730 songs and instrumental tunes, all but the last provided with his systematic indices, classifying the rhythms, metres and scales (Stoin, 1928, 1931, 1934, 1939). He also published a solid theoretical study on the metrics and rhythm of Bulgarian folk music (Stoin, 1927), which was consulted by E. M. von Hornbostel, Béla Bartók and Klyment Kvitka, among others. Boris Kremenliev presents the analyses of Christov and Stoin in his *Bulgarian–Macedonian Folk Music* (1952). Stoin's extraordinary collection – remarkably reliable even though recording equipment was not available – documents an archaic tradition and affords rich material for Slavic comparative analysis and for the more refined Bulgarian analyses made after 1945.

Stoian Dzhudzhev (*b*1902) and Raina Katsarova (1901–1984) belong to the next generation of Bulgarian music scholars. Although they were most active after 1945, both made significant contributions before the war. Dzhudzhev's Sorbonne doctoral dissertation, *Rythme et mesure dans la musique folklorique populaire bulgare* (1931), already emphasized his lifelong interest in theory and his international comparative perspective. It discusses poetic versification and rhythm, the musical metres, poetry, music and dance (the first treatment of Bulgarian folk dances); the introduction states: 'In confronting the folk melodies of the *Near Eastern countries* (Greece, Turkey, Persia, Romania, Bulgaria etc) we discover striking analogies in their rhythmic structure' (p.5). This international viewpoint set him apart from other Bulgarian ethnomusicologists. (For a survey of his work and bibliography, see B. Nikolova-Tomova, 1977.)

Katsarova's pre-war articles, including scholarly studies of bagpipe-making

(1936, 1937), of a town's musical life before 1878 (1938), and an analysis of the Bulgarian epic recitative (1939), all reflect her emphasis on fieldwork and examine subjects never previously investigated in her country (Krader, 1981).

Although the folk music specialists in Sofia acquired recording equipment only in 1938 (Katsarova-Kukudsva, 1961), Bartók recorded Bulgarian music in a Banat region (now within Yugoslavia) as early as 1912. (Transcriptions of his Serbian and Bulgarian Banat recordings are published in Dille, ed., 1970, vol.4, pp.222–4.)

A Russian scholar, Nikolai S. Derzhavin, recorded songs of Bulgarian colonies in the Russian empire in 1910 and 1911 (1914). He did fieldwork from 1900 to 1915 in the Taurian, Kherson and Bessarabian provinces. His work has been transcribed and studied recently by Nikolai Kaufman (1982, pp.21–7), who included some Derzhavin melodies with his own large field collection made in the Ukraine and in Soviet Moldavia.

Bibliography

D. Christov: 'Ritmichnite osnovi na narodnata ni muzika' [The Rhythmic Bases of our Folk Music], *Sbornik za narodni umotvoreniia i narodopis*, xxvii (1913), 1–51; (rev. 2/1967), 33–98

Colonel IAnkov: 'Bulgarski narodni pesni ot Besarabiia subral Polkovnik Iankov, notiral Dobri Khristov' [Bulgarian Folk Songs from Besarabiia, Collected by Colonel IAnkov, Notated by Dobri Christov], *Sbornik za narodni umotvoreniia i narodopis*, xxvii (1913), 1–75

N. S. Derzhavin: 'Bolgarskie kolonii v Rossii' [Bulgarian Colonies in Russia]: *Sbornik za narodni umetvareniia i narodopis*, xxiv (Sofia, 1914)

V. Stoin: *Bulgarska narodna muzika: metrika i ritmika* [Bulgarian Folk Music: Metrics and Rhythm] (Sofia, 1927); repr. in Stoin (1956), 11–60

D. Christov: *Tekhnicheskiiat stroezn na bulgarskata narodna muzika* [The Technical Structure of Bulgarian Folk Music] (Sofia, 1928); repr. in Christov (1967–70), 63–124

V. Stoin: *Narodni pesni ot Timok do Vita. Chants populaires bulgares du Timok à la Vita* (Sofia, 1928)

S. Djoudjeff [Dzhudzhev]: *Rythme et mesure dans la musique folklorique populaire bulgare* (Paris, 1931)

V. Stoin: *Narodni pesni ot Sredna Severna Bulgariia. Chants populaires bulgares de la partie centrale de la Bulgarie du Norde* (Sofia, 1931)

V. Stoin: 'Rodopski narodni pesni' [Rhodope Folk Songs], *Sbornik za narodni umotvoreniia*, xxxix (1934), 1–324

R. D. Katsarova: 'Gaidite na edin shumenski maistor' [The Bagpipes Made by a Craftsman in Shumen], *Izvestiia na Narodniia Etnografski Muzei v Sofiia*, xii (1936), 89

R. D. Katsarova: 'Koprishki gaidi i gaidari' [Koprivshtitsa Bagpipes and Bagpipe Players], *Vjesnik Etnografskog Muzeja u Zagrebu*, iii (1937), 14

B. Bartók: 'Az úgynevezett bolgár ritmus', *Énekszó*, v (1938), 537; Eng. trans., as 'The so-called Bulgarian Rhythm', in B. Bartók (1976), 40; Ger. trans., as 'Die sogenannte bulgarische Rhythmus', in Bartók (1972), 94

R. D. Katsarova: 'Churtitsi ot muzikalniia zhivot na Koprishtitsa [sic] predi Osvobozhdenieto' [Sketches from the musical life of Koprivshtitsa before the Liberation], *Iubileen Sbornik-Koprivshtitsa*, ii (1938), 378–423

D. Christov: *66 narodni pesni na makedonskite bulgari. 66 Chansons populaires des Bulgares Macédoniens* (Sofia, 1939)

R. D. Katsarova: 'Dneshnoto sustoianie na epichniia retsitativ v Bulgariia' [The present state of the epic recitatif in Bulgaria], *Izvestiia na Narodniia Etnografski Muzei v Sofiia*, xiii (1939), 182

V. Stoin: *Narodni pesni ot Iztochna i Zapadna Trakiia. Chansons populaires bulgares de Thrace Orientale et Occidentale* (Sofia, 1939)

I. Kamburov: *Dobri Christov* (Sofia, c1942)

S. Dzhudzhev: 'Elena IAnkova i pesnite na besarabskite bulgari' [Elena IAnkov and the Songs of the Bessarabian Bulgarians], *Izvestiia na Instituta za Muzika*, i (1952), 149

B. Kremenliev: *Bulgarian–Macedonian Folk Music* (Berkeley and Los Angeles, CA, 1952)

V. Kŭrstev: *Dobri Christov* (Sofia, 1954; Russ. trans., 1960)

V. Stoin: *Bulgarska narodna muzika* [Bulgarian folk music], ed. S. Dzhudzhev (Sofia, 1956)

R. D. Katsarova-Kukudova: 'Spomeni na Bela Bartok' [Recollections of Béla Bartók], *Bulgarska muzika*, xii/3 (1961), 15

D. Christov: *Muzikalno-teoretichesko i publistichesko nasledstvo* [Musical theoretical and journalistic writings], ed. V. Kŭrstev (Sofia, 1967–70)

D. Dille, ed.: *Documenta Bartókiana*, iv (Mainz, 1970), 222

B. Bartók: *Musiksprachen: Aufsätze und Vorträge* (Leipzig, 1972)

N. Kaufman: 'Krupen teoretik na bulgarskata narodna muzika' [(Christov) A Powerful Theoretician of Bulgarian Folk Music], *Bulgarska muzika*, xxvi/10 (1975), 31

B. Bartók: *Béla Bartók Essays*, ed. B. Suchoff (New York, 1976)

B. Nikolova-Tomova: 'Stoian Dzhudzhev', in *S. Dzudzhev, Muzikografski eseta i studii* [Musicological Essays and Studies] (Sofia, 1977), 5, 203

P. Dinekov: 'Deloto na Vasil Stoin' [The Work of Vasil Stoin], *Bulgarski folkor*, vi/4 (1980), 3

R. D. Katsarova: 'Ot Timok do Vita' [From the Timok to the Vita rivers], *Bulgarska muzika*, xxxi/10 (1980), 23

B. Krader: 'Vasil Stoin, Bulgarian Folk Song Collector', *YIFMC*, xii (1980), 27

——: 'Raina D. Katsarova: A Birthday Appreciation and List of Publications', *EM*, xxv (1981), 287

N. Kaufman: *Narodni pesni na bulgarite ot Ukrainska i Moldavska SSR* [Folksongs of Bulgarians from the Ukrainian and Moldavian Soviet Socialist Republics] (Sofia, 1982)

2: SOUTH SLAVS

Barbara Krader

Yugoslavia was formed in 1918 from lands previously under Austrian, Hungarian, Italian and Turkish rule, thus with very different historical experiences; they are now breaking apart again. Great poverty in the south, and in some northern areas, has persisted almost to the 1990s. Here the discussion will focus on folk music research in the three northern-most lands, now republics (R. Petrović, 1970) (*see* also 'Czechoslovakia', 'L. Kuba').

Slovenia

The Slovenes, for centuries under Austrian rule, collected their folk songs beginning in the late 18th and all through the 19th centuries, focussing almost exclusively on song texts. The culmination was a great four-volume text collection, published from 1895 to 1923, compiled and edited by Karol Štrekelj (1862–1912). It included over 8000 song texts and some 200 melodies, and was praised at once by leading Slavic scholars as the finest scholarly classified folk-song collection of any Slavic nation (Štrekelj, 1895–1923).

In 1904 a drive to collect melodies began at the instigation of the Viennese project *Das Volkslied in Oesterreich*. The Slovenian language section was headed at first by Štrekelj and from 1912 by Matija Murko. Some 12,000 Slovenian songs with melodies were systematically collected between 1906 and 1914

(Murko, 1929). For the same project a German collection was gathered, mainly by Hans Tschinkel, from a German colony, Gottschee (Kočevje in Slovenian), part of Slovenian territory from the 14th century. This collection contains some of the most archaic ballads known in the German language and is rich in religious ballads (as is the Slovenian tradition; see Brednich, 1966). The Slovenian and Gottschee collections had to wait until after 1945 for publication (Kumer and others, 1970–; Brednich, Suppan and Kumer, 1969–).

A pioneering achievement in Slovenia was Yugoslavia's Folklorni Institut, founded in 1934 in Ljubljana, under the leadership of France Marolt, with sections devoted to music, song texts and dance.

Croatia

The earliest preserved notations of folk songs in Croatia are considered to be those by Petar Hektorović (1487–1572). His book *Ribanje i ribarsko prigovaranje* (Fishing and Fishermen's Conversations) contains four folk-song texts with two melodies in Renaissance mensural notation (Hektorović, 1568; see R. Petrović, 1965; Bezić, 1969, 1970; Županović, 1969).

The most important 19th-century South Slavic folk-song collection was made by the Croat Franjo Ksaver Kuhač (1834–1911; see fig.1). The four volumes contain 1600 songs, melodies and texts, with piano accompaniment, almost all of which he collected in the field from 1861 to 1869, in Slavonia, central Croatia. Slovenia, Vojvodina, Istria, Serbia, Dalmatia, Bosnia and Hercegovina, and what are now Bulgaria and Macedonia. Although some are urban songs and the non-Western rhythms are not always correctly notated, it continues to be a standard work (Kuhač, 1878–81). Kuhač was nearly bankrupt after publishing the first four volumes at his own expense. Volume 5, containing 400 songs without accompaniment, was published from his remaining material by the Yugoslav Academy of Sciences in Zagreb (Širola and Dukat, eds., 1941). About 300 secular and 400 religious songs are still unpublished (see Marošević, 1984).

Kuhač was the father of Croatian folk music research as well, for he also published a detailed descriptive and historical account of South Slavic folk instruments (1877–82) and an analytic work, after long study, which included a comparative analysis of Croatian, German, Italian and Hungarian folk songs (1905–9; see Širola, 1942, pp.76–86 for a critique of Kuhač's analysis). Kuhač's 1899 study of the Turkish element in Croatian, Serbian and Bulgarian folk music is still of interest. Kuhač became known abroad for articles on the Croatian folk-song tunes used by Haydn and Beethoven (see Žganec, 1962; Andreis, 1974, pp.214–23).

Between the wars Božidar Širola (1889–1956), a composer and ethnomusicologist, was the leading figure in the field. He developed a musical instrument collection at the Ethnographic Museum in Zagreb and did much field collection of instruments and songs, some recorded. His thorough study of wind instruments that use free beating reeds is a standard work (1937), and his small book on Croatian folk music is useful and remains unsurpassed (1940; see also Širola, 1932, 1956 and the critique and overall study by Bezić, 1985).

Vinko Žganec (1890–1976), trained in theology, law and music, published two song collections and a few articles on folk music before 1945, after which he became the leading Croatian ethnomusicologist. His collections of songs from his native Medjimurje, a region long under Hungarian rule, are very fine (1924–5) and Bartók was much interested in the archaic pentatonic tunes Žganec found there (letter to Žganec, 27 Oct. 1934, in Bartók, 1971, pp.229–33).

1. *Franjo Ksaver Kuhač*   2. *Vladimir R. Djordjević*

Serbia

Stevan St Mokranjac (1856–1914) was the first great Serbian nationalist composer, among whose finest works are the set of 14 choral compositions called *Rukoveti* ('Sheaves'), based on folk songs of Serbia, Macedonia, Kosovo, Montenegro and Bosnia. He also laid the foundation for serious study of Serbian folk music: in a local collection of folk songs from one Serbian region, for which he notated the tunes from the song collector, he wrote the first general analysis of Serbian folk music (Bušetić and Mokranjac, 1902). In 1896, he made a systematic collection of Serbian folk music from the Kosovo region, published with the other folk songs he collected only in 1966 (Mokranjac, 1966). From 1897 to 1912 he notated a great body of oral musical tradition, almost the entire repertory of Serbian Church chant, a record of inestimable value to the Church itself and to research in Byzantine and Eastern Orthodox Church music (Mokranjac, 1908, 1935; also D. Petrović, 1973, pp.275–92; Bingulac, 1971, pp.13–38).

The first Serb to devote his life primarily to ethnomusicology was Vladimir

R. Djordjević (1869–1938; see fig.2), whose folk-song collecting began in the 1890s. His two collections of melodies and texts, of 428 Macedonian (1928) and 528 Serbian folk songs (1931), notated by ear (he had no access to a phonograph), with place and function indicated, are still highly regarded, and were praised by Bartók. Djordjević also prepared, with Božidar Joksimović, a remarkable questionnaire for collecting musical customs, with much attention to context (1899; also L. Janković, 1969). His brother Tihomir R. Djordjević (1868–1941), the leading Serbian folklorist of his time and a prolific scholar, wrote an article on gypsy music in Serbia and three articles with material for the questionnaire (Janković, 1975). But most important is his early study of Serbian folk dances (1907), for on its basis Danica and Ljubica C. Janković began their pioneering work on folk dances in the 1930s (1934; 1937; also L. C. Janković, 1975).

Kosta P. Manojlović (1890–1949) was an ethnomusicologist, a scholar and a composer active in Belgrade's musical life. As early as 1923 he started a folk music section in the Ethnographic Museum for systematic collection and classification of folk melodies. He notated by ear 1074 songs from southern Serbia, Macedonia and Kosovo between 1923 and 1933 (unpublished). Manojlović was also among the first Serbs to record folk songs mechanically. The song archive was transferred to the Musicological Institute of the Serbian Academy after World War II (see Dević, 1960, pp.105–8; Milojković-Djurić, 1967, pp.8–11; Matović, 1973, p.318; R. Petrović, 1973).

In the southern part of Yugoslavia – Montenegro, Macedonia, and what are today Bosnia and Hercegovina – almost all research in folk music before 1939 was carried out by outsiders: the Croat, Kuhač; the Czech, Kuba; the Serbs Mokranjac, Djordjević and Manojlović; and some foreign recording expeditions. The Macedonian Marko K. Cepenkov (1829–1920), a tailor from Prilep, whose vast collection of folklore texts was gathered basically from 1856 to 1900, left material also on folk music instruments, with drawings, which were published in 1972 (see Sazdov, 1970; Dinekov, 1980).

Two important works by German scholars are the solid study by Peter Brömse on wind instruments of the South Slavs (1937), and the pioneer work by Walter Wünsch on *gusle* playing techniques (1934).

Recording

In 1940, Béla Bartók, in a lecture at Harvard University, said, 'The Serbo-Croatian scholars never used recording instruments, for reasons unknown to me' (Bartók, 1976, p.186). In fact, Yugoslavs did record before 1940. Above all, the Slovenian Slavicist Matija Murko (1861–1952), not a musician but an outstanding investigator of Yugoslav heroic songs, made three expeditions to Bosnia and Hercegovina in 1912 and 1913 with a phonograph lent by the Phonogram Archive in Vienna. Copies of these survived World War II, and several were analysed in 1975 by Walter Graf. Unfortunately Murko's many field recordings of 1930–32 were made on poor equipment; many have now been lost, although some of those preserved at the Yugoslav Academy of Sciences in Zagreb are barely usable. Nevertheless his writings, based on eight field expeditions (see fig.3), present a rich account of the singers, their musical instruments, their repertory, terms, attitudes and methods of learning, laying

3. Matija Murko (centre, smiling) photographed with a large group of people including the performers Stevo Mršula and Savo Cetković (seated) in Gornji Grbalj, near the Bay of Kotor (Boka Kotorska), 1932

the groundwork for Milman Parry and Albert B. Lord (M. Murko, 1933, 1951; V. Murko, 1963). In *Serbocroatian Heroic Songs*, Parry tells how important Murko's writings were to him as he prepared his expedition (Lord, ed., 1954, p.3).

In Slovenia the earliest recordings of folk music appear to have been those made in 1913 by the Slovene Juro Adlešič in Bela Krajina for the Vienna project begun in Slovenia in 1906 (Kumer, 1977, p.59), and also by the Russian ethnomusicologist Evgeniia Lineva. The cylinders recorded by Adlešič have not survived, although the music was transcribed. Lineva visited Gorenjsko and Bela Krajina in September 1913. About 100 Slovenian folk songs have been preserved on her cylinders, which are housed in the Phonogram Archive in Leningrad, with their texts ([Report] *Leptopis*, 1958, pp.140–41).

In Croatia in the 1920s, recordings were made by the new section for folk music in the Ethnographic Division of the Croatian National Museum in Zagreb. The Phonogram Archive in Vienna provided recording apparatus, and the recording was made by Božidar Širola and the ethnographer Milovan Gavazzi, on the islands of Krk, Korčula, Rab, in Medjimurje (with collaboration from Žganec) and elsewhere. They provided details of time, place and songs recorded and a list of contents of 120 discs (Širola and Gavazzi, 1931). The section eventually sent some 120 wax discs to Vienna, copies of which are preserved on magnetic tape at the Phonogrammarchiv (Bezić, 1974, p.174).

The Serbian scholar Kosta P. Manojlović made recordings on wax discs from 1932 to 1940 in Serbia, Kosovo and Macedonia, many of which are now preserved in the Musicological Institute of the Serbian Academy, but, like nearly all of the others, are not yet transcribed (Dević, 1960, p.109).

There was considerable interest among German scholars in South Slavic heroic songs before 1939. Especially active was Gerhard Gesemann (1888–1948), professor at the German University in Prague from 1922. He apparently arranged the recording of the heroic-song singer Tanasije Vučić in Berlin in 1929 (20 discs), subsequently analysed by eminent scholars (Becking, 1933; Jakobson, 1933; Gesemann, 1933).

An expedition for heroic songs in Macedonia in May 1931, with the participation of Becking, Gesemann and outstanding Yugoslav ethnographers, used faulty recording equipment, apparently with no lasting results (Gesemann, 1932; Medenica, 1937; Dević, 1960, p.109).

One more expedition, in 1937, was successful. Sponsored by German institutions and led by Gesemann, recordings were made in Sarajevo from mid-September to mid-October, among them recordings of heroic-song singers, village singing, playing of the *tamburica* and *dvojnice* instruments, singing with rolling of a tray (*uz tepsiju*) and, especially, of the characteristic Bosnian urban song, the *sevdalinka*. These were copied on magnetic tape in 1969 (Gesemann, 1937; Medenica, 1937; Milošević, 1973).

Intent upon heroic songs, like so many other collectors in Yugoslavia, the young American classics scholar from Harvard, Milman Parry (1902–35), first explored in 1933, and then, with Albert B. Lord, worked in Hercegovina, Bosnia, Montenegro and Macedonia from June 1934 to September 1935 making records and writing from dictation. Parry was investigating the oral composition of South Slavic heroic-song texts in order to analyse Homer's art as an oral one. To this end, his field recordings included 350 very long heroic songs, in full, on about 2200 double-faced discs (along with some 800 heroic-song texts taken from dictation). Also recorded were about 250 much shorter women's songs, as well as some 55 songs in Macedonian, Turkish and Albanian, and 16 instrumental pieces. The Parry Collection comprises over 12,500 texts, most of which were written from dictation (Bartók and Lord, 1951, pp.xv, 247).

In addition to the collection's great importance for Homeric studies and research, and theory in world epic, Parry and Lord documented on aluminium discs, with recording quality better than any other field records in Yugoslavia before World War II, the music of an ancient South Slavic tradition of narrative singing, mostly with instrumental accompaniment, performed by expertly selected traditional singers, an art which has now almost disappeared. These records of the music were supplemented by long interviews with the singers, providing rich contextual information; 75 of the recorded lyric songs, mostly from Gacko, a small town in Hercegovina, were transcribed and analysed by Bartók (Bartók and Lord, 1951, 1978). Bartók transcribed from a Parry recording one entire heroic song, voice and *gusle* accompaniment, which was later published with his comments (Lord, ed., 1954, pp.437–67; Bartók's study and analysis of Serbo-Croatian folk melodies is discussed in 'Hungary and Romania').

Bibliography

P. Hektorović: *Ribanje i ribarsko prigovaranje* [Fishing and Fishermen's Conversations] (Venice, 1568)

F. K. Kuhač: 'Prilog za povjest glazbe južnoslovjenske' [A Contribution to the History of South Slavic Music], *Rad Jugoslavenske Akademije Znanosti i Umjetnosti*, xxxviii, xxxix, xli, xlv, l, lxii, lxiii (1877–82)

——: *Južno-slovjenske narodne popievke* [South Slavic Folk Songs] (Zagreb, 1878–81), 4 vols.

K. Štrekelj: *Slovenske narodne pesmi* [Slovenian Folk Songs] (Ljubljana, 1895–1923), 4 vols.

V. R. Djordjević and B. Joksimović: 'Pitanja za prikupljanje muzičkih običaja u Srba' [Questions for Collecting Musical Customs among Serbs], *Karadžić*, i/6, supp. (1899)

F. K. Kuhač: *Das türkische Element in der Volksmusik der Croaten, Serben und Bulgaren* (Vienna, 1899)

T. M. Bušetić and S. S. Mokranjac: 'Srpske narodne pesme i igre s melodijama iz Levča' [Serbian Folk Songs and Dances with Melodies from Levač], *Srpski etnografski zbornik*, iii (1902)

S. S. Mokranjac: *Srpsko narodno crkveno pojanje* [Serbian Traditional Church Chant], i: *Osmoglasnik u note stavio St. St. Mokranjac* [The Octoechos, notated by S. S. Mokranjac] (Belgrade, 1902, 2/1922/R1964)

F. K. Kuhač: *Osobine narodne glazbe naročito hrvatske* [Characteristics of Folk Music, especially Croatian] (Zagreb, 1905–9)

T. R. Djordjević: 'Srpske narodne igre' [Serbian Folk Dances], *Srpski etnografski zbornik*, ix (1907)

V. Žganec: *Hrvatske pučke popijevke iz Medjumurja* [Croatian Folk Songs from Medjimurje]: i. *Svjetovne* [Secular] (Zagreb, 1924), ii: *Crkvene* [Religious] (Zagreb, 1925)

V. R. Djordjević: *Srpske narodne melodije (Južna Srbija)* [Serbian Folk Melodies of 'South Serbia' (Macedonia)] (Skopje, 1928)

M. Murko: 'Velika zbirka slovenskih narodnih pesmi s melodijami' [The Great Collection of Slovenian Folk Songs with Tunes], *Etnolog*, iii (1929), 5–54

V. R. Djordjević: *Srpske narodne melodije (predratna Srbija)* [Serbian Folk Melodies of Prewar Serbia] (Beograd, 1931)

B. Širola and M. Gavazzi: *Muzikološki rad Etnografskog muzeja u Zagrebu* [Musicological Work of the Ethnographic Museum in Zagreb] (Zagreb, 1931)

G. Gesemann: 'Izveštaji o proučavanju Južne Srbije na terenu' [Report on a Field Study of South Serbia (Macedonia)], *Glasnik Skopskog naučnog društva*, xi (1932), 191

B. Širola: *Sopile i zurle* [Sopilas and Zurlas] (Zagreb, 1932)

G. Becking: 'Der musikalische Bau des montenegrinischen Volksepos', *Archives Néérlandaises de phonétique expérimentale*, viii–ix (1933), xxx

G. Gesemann: 'Die Vortragsweise der südslavischen Volksepik', *Archives Néérlandaises de phonétique expérimentale*, viii–ix (1933), xxx

R. Jakobson: 'Über den Versbau der serbokroatischen Volksepen', *Archives Néérlandaises de phonétique expérimentale*, viii–ix (1933), 135

M. Murko: 'Nouvelles observations sur l'état actuel de la poésie épique en Yougoslavie', *Revue des études Slaves*, xiii (1933), 16

D. and L. C. Janković: *Narodne igre* [Folk Dances], i [Belgrade, 1934)

W. Wünsch: *Die Geigentechnik der südslawischen Guslaren* (Brünn, 1934)

S. S. Mokranjac: *Srpsko narodno crkveno pojanje* [Serbian Traditional Church Music]: ii. *Opšte pojanje* [General Chant], ed. K. P. Manojlović (Belgrade, 1935)

P. Brömse: *Flöten, Schalmeien und Sackpfeifen Südslawiens* (Brünn, 1937)

G. Gesemann: 'Prolegomena povodom gramofonskog snimanja bosanske narodne pesme' [Thoughts on the Occasion of Phonograph Recording of the Bosnian Folk Song], *Prilozi proučavanju narodne poezije*, iv (1937), 222

D. and L. C. Janković: *Narodne igre* [Folk Dances], ii (Belgrade, 1937)

R. Medenica: 'Fonografsko snimanje naših narodnih pesama u Sarajevu' [Phonograph Recordings of our Folk Songs in Sarajevo], *Prilozi proučavanju narodne poezije*, iv (1937), 272

B. Širola: *Sviraljke s udarnim jezičkom* [Wind Instruments with a Beating Reed] (Zagreb, 1937)

——: *Hrvatska narodna glazba* [Croatian Folk Music] (Zagreb, 1940, 2/1942)

—— and V. Dukat, eds.: *Kuhač, F. K.: Južno-slovjenske narodne popievke*, v (Zagreb, 1941)

B. Bartók and A. B. Lord: *Serbo-Croatian Folk Songs* (New York, 1951)

M. Murko: *Tragom srpsko-hrvatske narodne epike: putovania u godinama 1930–1932* [On the Track of the Serbo-Croatian Folk Epic: Journeys in 1930–1932] (Zagreb, 1951)

A. B. Lord, ed.: *Serbocroatian Heroic Songs, Collected by Milman Parry*, i (Cambridge, MA, and Belgrade, 1954)

B. Širola: 'Die Volksmusik der Kroaten', *Studia memoriae Belae Bartók sacra* (Budapest, 1956), 89 [Report]: *Letopis Slovenske Akademije Znanosti in Umetnosti, 8, 1956–7* (Ljubljana, 1958), 140

D. Dević: 'Sakupljači naših narodnih pesama' [Collectors of our Folk Songs], *Glasnik etnografskog muzeja u Beogradu*, xxii–xxiii (1960), 99

V. Žganec: 'Kuhačev rad, život i značenje za našu muzičku kulturu' [Kuhač's Work, Life and Importance for our Musical Culture], *Zvuk*, liv (1962), 435

V. Murko: 'Sudbine literarne ostavštine i fonografskih snimaka srpskohrvatskih pjesama Matije Murka' [The Fate of the Literary Papers, Letters and Phonograph Recordings of Serbo-Croatian Epic Songs of Matija Murko], *Narodna umjetnost*, ii (1963), 107–37

R. Petrović: 'The Oldest Notation of Folk Tunes in Yugoslavia', *JIFMC*, xvi (1965), pt.2, 109 = *Studia Musicologica*, vii (1965), 109

R. W. Brednich: 'Gottscheer Volkslieder: ein Vorbericht zu ihrer Gesamtausgabe', *Jb für Volksliedforschung*, xi (1966), 123

S. S. Mokranjac: *Zapisi narodnih melodija* [Notations of Folk Melodies] (Belgrade, 1966)

J. Milojković-Djurić: 'Zapisi narodnih pesama kompozitora Koste P. Manojlovića' [Notations of Folk Songs by K. P. Manojlović], *Zvuk*, lxxix (1967), 8

J. Bezić: 'Kakve je napjeve Hektorović priložio svom "Ribanju i ribarskom prigovaranju"?' [What Sorts of Melodies did Hektorović add to his 'Fishing and Fishermen's Conversations'?], *Arti musices*, i (1969), 75

R. W. Brednich, W. Suppan and Z. Kumer, eds.: *Gottscheer Volkslieder* (Mainz, 1969–)

L. S. Janković: 'Vladimir R. Djordjević – pionir etnomuzikologije u Srbiji', in V. R. Djordjević: *Ogled srpske musičke bibliografije do 1914 g.* (Beograd, 1969), 9

L. Županović: 'Napjevi iz Hektorovićeva "Ribanja" u svjetlu suvremene muzikološke interpretacije' [The Melodies from Hektorović's 'Ribanje' in the Light of Current Musicological Interpretation], *Zvuk*, c (1969), 477

J. Bezić: 'Etnomuzikološki osvrt na napjeve u Hektorovićeovom Ribanju' [An Ethnomusicological Examination of the Melodies in Hektorović's 'Ribanje'], *Zvuk*, civ–cv (1970), 218

Z. Kumer and others, eds.: *Slovenske ljudske pesmi* [Slovenian Folk Songs] (Ljubljana, 1970–)

R. Petrović: 'The Place of Ethnomusicology in Yugoslav Music Study', *Papers of the Yugoslav-American Seminar on Music*, ed. M. H. Brown (Bloomington, IN, 1970), 164

T. Sazdov: 'Marko K. Cepenkov (1829–1920)', *Makedonski folklor*, iii/5–6 (1970), 113

B. Bartók: *Letters*, ed. J. Demény (London, 1971)

P. Bingulac: 'Stevan Mokranjac i crkvena muzika' [Stevan Mokranjac and Church Music], *Zbornik radova o Stevanu Mokranjcu* [Collection of Studies on Stevan Mokranjac], ed. M. Vukdragović (Belgrade, 1971), 13

M. K. Cepenkov: 'Muzički narodni instrumenti' [Folk Music Instruments], in M. Cepenkov: *Makedonski narodni umotvorbi* [Macedonian Folklore], x (Skopje, 1972), 147

A. Matović: 'Recueils manuscrits de mélodies populaires à l'Institut de musicologie', *Srpska muzika kroz vekove – La musique serbe à travers les siècles* (Belgrade, 1973), 314

V. Milošević: 'Rad ekipe dra Gerharda Gezemana na fonografisanju narodnih pjesama u Sarajevu 1937. godine' [The Work of Gerhard Gesemann's Team in Recording Folk Songs in Sarajevo in 1937], *Radovi Akademija nauka i umjetnosti Bosne i Hercegovine*, xlvii (1973), 185

D. Petrović: 'Le chant populaire sacré et ses investigateurs', *Srpska muzika kroz vekove – La musique serbe à travers les siècles* (Belgrade, 1973), 275

R. Petrović: 'Les recherches ethnomusicologiques', *Srpska musika kroz vekove – La musique serbe à travers les siècles* (Belgrade, 1973), 239–50

J. Andreis: *Music in Croatia* (Zagreb, 1974)

J. Bezić: 'Hrvatska muzika, narodna' [Croatian Music, Folk], *Muzička enciklopedija*, ii (Zagreb, 2/1974)

W. Graf: 'Murko's Phonogramme bosnischer Epenlieder aus dem Jahre 1912', *Grazer musikwissenschaftliche Arbeiten*, i (1975), 41–76

L. S. Janković: 'The Brothers Tihomir and Vladimir Djordjević: Pioneers of Ethnomusicology in Serbia', *YIFMC*, vii (1975), 67

———: 'The System of the Sisters Ljubica and Danica Janković for the Recording, Description and Analysis of Folk Dances', *EM*, xix (1975), 31

B. Bartók: *Béla Bartók Essays*, ed. B. Suchoff (New York, 1976)

Z. Kumer: *Etnomuzikologija: razgled po znanosti o ljudski glasbi* [Ethnomusicology: a Survey of Scholarship in Folk Music] (Ljubljana, 1977)

B. Bartók and A. B. Lord: *Yugoslav Folk Music*, i: *Serbo-Croatian Folk Songs and Instrumental Pieces from the Milman Parry Collection*, ed. B. Suchoff (Albany, NY, 1978)

P. Dinekov: 'Edin ot golemite maîstori: Marko K. TSepenkov (1829–1920)' [One of the Great Masters: M. K. TS.], *Bulgarski folklor*, vi/1 (1980), 5

G. Marošević: 'Kuhačev etnomuzikološki rad u svjetlu sbirke "Južno-slovjenske narodne popievke"' [Kuhač's Ethnomusicological Work in the Light of the Collection 'South Slavic Folk Songs'], *Zbornik radova sa znanstvenog skupa održanog u povodu 150. obljetnice rodjenja Franje Ksavera Kuhača (1834–1911)* [Collected Papers of the Scholarly Session on the Occasion of the 150th Anniversary of the Birth of Franjo Ksaver Kuhač], ed. J. Bezić (Zagreb, 1984), 77–110

J. Bezić: 'Etnomuzikološka djelatnost Božidara Širole' [The Ethnomusicological Activity of Božidar Širola], *Arti musices*, xvi (1985), 5–39

3: POLAND

BARBARA KRADER

Collections

Publication of Polish folk-song collections began in the early 19th century. At first the volumes contained only texts, but even when melodies were included, piano accompaniments were felt to be necessary. An early example is the collection of Polish and Ukrainian songs compiled by Wacław z Oleska, which contains 1450 song texts and 160 tunes with piano accompaniment (Oleska, 1833). (For more detail on this early period of collecting, see the surveys of Polish folk music by Ludwik Bielawski, 1965; Jan Stęszewski, 1980; and Anna Czekanowska, 1990.)

Yet one man dominated both folk-song collecting and the broader field of folk culture in 19th-century Poland. The earliest ambition of Oskar Kolberg (1814–90) was to be a composer. He had excellent musical training in Warsaw and Berlin, but after only moderate success as a composer he turned decisively to collecting folk songs and tunes, which he began to take down as early as 1839 (Górski, 1974, p.41). He soon developed a new focus, starting from his recognition that folk song 'is closely related to rites, customs and the entire life of the people' (Kolberg, 1885, p.2; see also Burszta, 1968, p.28). He then embarked, with amazing energy and singlemindedness, on his life's work, collecting and compiling both folklore and songs from every possible region of Poland within its borders before the partitions, and even from areas beyond. He also amassed data on the history and economy of each region – occupations, food, costume (with documentary drawings) and more (see illustration). All this he organized into regional monographs, 33 published in his lifetime with the general title *Lud: Jego zwyczaje, sposób życia, mowa, podania, przysłowia, obrzędy, gusła, zabawy, pieśni, muzyka i tańce* (The Folk: their Customs, Ways of Life, Language, Legends, Proverbs, Rituals, Spells, Entertainments,

Songs, Instrumental Music and Dances) and 11 with the general title *Obrazy etnograficzne* (Ethnographic Pictures). The Polish Ethnographic Society has undertaken to publish a new edition of this monument of Polish ethnography and folklore, including the large body of materials in manuscript, with critical commentaries and scholarly apparatus (*Dzieła wszystkie*, 1961–) (Complete Works). (See also the shorter survey of his complete works in Burszta, 1968; the longer study by Krzyżanowski, in the introduction to *Dzieła wszystkie*, 1961–; and Millerowa and Skrukwa, 1982. The fullest critical discussion appeared in the journal *Lud*, xlii, 1956.)

1. *Illustration from Oskar Kolberg's 'Mazowske' (1885) showing a fiddle player from Warsaw*

Kolberg's first published folk-song collection (1842) was in an old tradition, with melodies prettified, a few non-folk songs included, and with piano accompaniment. But his next collection (1857) was on a totally different level, with no piano accompaniment and melodies as close to the original as possible. Here Kolberg's aim was to represent all regions of former united Poland, reflecting his interim goal to work only on songs. This landmark collection was the first in Poland to have music as its main object. It contains 910 melodies, of which 444 are texts and melodies of 41 ballads and songs with their variants. The rest are dances, not always with texts. About a quarter of the songs were taken from the already published collections of Oleska (Załeski), Wójcicki and Pauli, and one unpublished collection, but all the sources are acknowledged. His inclusion of variants is remarkable, in advance of many contemporary collectors abroad.

The first of Kolberg's regional monographs was published in 1865 (*Sandomierskie*), and from that time the songs he collected appeared in these volumes; the total number of songs in the 38 regional volumes published by 1910 was over 12,000. The new edition, with its 80 planned volumes, including some 12 regional volumes to his manuscripts, has already added hundreds more songs with tunes.

On the critical side, perhaps the most serious shortcoming is that, as his work expanded, Kolberg depended more and more on correspondents who sent him materials, including song notations. Much of their material was incorporated into his own work without identification of the source. Even the current editors, dealing with manuscripts, cannot always be sure what is his and what is not. In the case of individual songs Kolberg noted the place of origin but not the date of collection or the informant's name. And his notation, reflecting his musical training, normalized the scales, metres and rhythms to a great extent (see Sobieski, 1961; Stęszewski, 1986). Nevertheless his work has great documentary value and is an astonishing achievement for a man who was relatively poor, with little regular financial support for his magnificent undertaking. The new edition is an appropriate act of national recognition.

Władisław Skierkowski (1886–1941) collected over 2000 songs from 1913 to 1923 in the Kurpie district, about 70 miles northeast of Warsaw. Some of these were published in a collection of songs from the Kurpie forest (Skierkowski, 1928–34). This unique Polish musical style, with its narrow-range songs, recurring pentatonic or modal scales, complex rhythmic systems and frequent five-beat measures had not been noticed before (see also Stęszewski, 1955, pp.3–6; Wozaczyńska, 1956). The composer Karol Szymanowski arranged songs from this published collection for voice and piano, and for chorus, thus making the style more widely known.

The vocal and instrumental style of Podhale, a mountain region 40 to 60 miles south of Kraków, has long attracted interest in Poland because it is different from the folk music elsewhere in the country. Part-singing occurs only in the mountains; the lydian scale is typical; and the rhythm is free and difficult to notate. Stanisław Mierczyński (1894–1952) was the first to issue a collection of instrumental music from this area, having begun to notate it by ear from 1914 (Mierczyński, 1930). A trained violinist, he learned to play in Podhale ensembles, with their special fiddle, and he notated much music performed by the legendary fiddler Bartolomiej (Bartek, Bartko) Obrochta, who died in 1926. Mierczyński neglected the songs, but his instrumental notations have documentary value to this day.

Ignac Jan Paderewski (in 1884) and Kolberg also notated songs of Podhale during the 19th century. Volumes xliv and xlv of the *Dzieła wszystkie* 1961–), entitled *Góry i podgórze* (Mountains and Foothills), comprise previously unpublished Kolberg materials, with 992 melodies, mostly collected by him from Podhale and other areas. After some hesitation, Kolberg notated all the melodies in regular metres with bar lines. The melodies collected by Paderewski, originally published in his *Album tatrzanski* op. 12 for piano (1883), are also included in the volumes of *Dzieła wszystkie*, as copied by Kolberg but are not identified as Paderewski's.

Mierczyński also notated music, mostly instrumental, from the Ukrainian Hutsuls between 1934 and 1938 (Mierczyński, 1965). This area, then Polish, became part of the Soviet Ukraine. A detailed study of Podhale music and an evaluation of Mierczyński is given by Kotoński (1953–4) and Chybiński (1961). Chybiński includes a collection of 281 Podhale folk songs assembled by himself, a few notated by him and many drawn from other manuscript collections.

The small published collection of 102 songs, with variants, from Orawa, collected by Emil Mika from 1924 to 1934, also deserves attention (1934). It was the first collection from that mountainous region west of Podhale and provided a basis for analysis of the style. The second edition contains an important study of Polish folk music of Orawa by Adolf Chybiński (Mika, 2/1957, pp.77–168). Part of Orawa lies in Slovakia.

Research

Helena Windakiewiczowa (1868–1956) was the earliest Polish scholar to work primarily on folk-music analysis. One of her first studies was on rhythm (1897), another on the pentatonic scale (1933) and a third on a particular circular structural form – $a\,a^l\,b\,a$ – (1930). Most important, relating to musical rhythm, is her long study of the verse line and strophe in Polish folk poetry (1913). Her useful catalogue of parallels between Polish and Moravian folk songs (1908), followed by a long commentary, lists 145 Polish songs alphabetically by their first lines, cites one Polish source and gives the numbers of related songs in the basic Moravian song collections of Sušil and Bartoš, and in a Čelakovský collection. She also analysed folk-song elements in Chopin's mazurkas (1926).

Adolf Chybiński (1880–1952) was Poland's leading music historian, specializing in early music. No fieldworker, he nevertheless wrote on the methodology of folk-music collection and classification, in addition to his basic study of folk instruments of the Podhale region and his pioneering work on the ties of Podhale melodies across the border to those of Slovaks, Hungarians, Romanians and others (Chybiński, 1961).

Kazimierz Moszyński (1887–1959) was an ethnographer and Slavicist, a great organizer of team research and a dedicated fieldworker. In our field he contributed reports on Belorussia and Polesie (1932). In his 1932 expedition to Polesie, Moszyński was accompanied by the outstanding Ukrainian ethnomusicologist, Filaret Kolessa. Moszyński's magnificent work, *Kultura ludowa Słowian* (The Folk Culture of the Slavs) in vol. ii (*Kultura duchowa*) contains a systematic comparative analysis of Slavic folk music which is unmatched to this day, although in part outdated because so much more data are now available.

Recording

Two Poles – one an anthropologist who became one of his country's leading scholars, the other exiled to Sakhalin, the author of several studies of the Ainu – made cylinder recordings outside Poland before World War I and these recordings have survived. The first, Jan Czekanowski (1882–1965), took part in the German Central Africa Expedition of 1907–9, led by Grand Duke Friedrich of Mecklenburg, with specialists from the Royal Ethnographic

Museum in Berlin. Czekanowski gathered copious materials at this time, which constitute invaluable scholarly data on the Congo (Czekanowski, 1911–27). The Museum provided him with a phonograph, 75 cylinders and other equipment; he took 100 additional cylinders of his own. He recorded 83 of these cylinders in Africa. In August 1986, the Ethnomusicological Section of the Ethnographical Museum in West Berlin possessed copies of 13 songs recorded by Czekanowski in Rwanda in 1907–8. Artur Simon, director of the Ethnomusicological Section, reports that the original cylinders are now in East Berlin. E. M. von Hornbostel subsequently published two articles with musical transcriptions based on these cylinder recordings: a short study of a melody of the Wasukuma (1911) and a transcription and analysis of 44 songs from Rwanda (1917).

The second Pole to make early cylinder recordings was Bronisław Piłsudski (1866–1918), an ethnographer, linguist and the elder brother of Józef Piłsudski, the famous Marshal of Poland. In 1886, Bronisław was involved in a plot to assassinate Tsar Alexander III, and was sentenced to 15 years of hard labour in eastern Siberia. He soon reached the island of Sakhalin where he studied the Ainu (1912), Gilyaks and Orochi, among others, from about 1896 to 1905. He was the first Pole to make systematic phonograph recordings (from 1902 to 1905). In 1906 he brought 100 cylinders of Ainu songs to Kraków. In June 1953, 83 of these cylinders were preserved in the Phonographic Institute (Zakład Fonograficzny) of the University of Poznań, and efforts were under way to copy them on tape (Kaczmarek, 1952, pp.23–4).

Piłsudski also played a role in the first phonograph recording of Polish folk music, for he urged Julian Zborowski to record in the Tatra region.

Zborowski (*b*1888) proceeded to record during late 1913 and 1914 in Podhale. Then a teacher in Nowy Targ (later a director of the Tatra Museum in Zakopane), he became an authority on the folklore of this distinctive area. His recordings were transcribed in 1920 by Adolf Chybiński, though the cylinders were ruined in the process. The most valuable recordings were some 50 tunes from the great fiddler, Bartek Obrochta, brought to Nowy Targ in 1914. Zborowski also recorded his Podhale school children and mountaineers passing through Nowy Targ (see Bielawski in Chybiński, 1961, p.428ff)

Institutional systematic recording, archiving and research began on a high level in 1930 in Poznań, western Poland (Wielkopolska). The Regionalne Archiwum Fonograficzne was established in that year under the direction of Łucjan Kamieński (1885–1964) as part of the Institute of Musicology of the University of Poznań. They recorded at first on wax cylinders but changed to electro-acoustic recordings on gelatine discs in 1934. About 4000 phonogrammes were recorded in the field, mostly in western Poland, but also in Pomerania, the Pieniny mountains and Mazovia, all with documentation (Kamieński, 1936, *Z badań nad śpiewem*; Kazmarek, 1953, pp.28–30). Several studies were subsequently based on this fieldwork (Kamieński, 1933, 1936 *Pieśni ludu pomorskiego*; Pietruszyńska, 1936).

In 1935, after the example of Poznań, Julian Pulikowski (1908–44) organized the Centralne Archiwum Fonograficzne in Warsaw. About 20,000 melodies were collected for this archive, some by amateurs less well-trained than the staff in Poznań.

All the Poznań recordings were destroyed deliberately by the army of occupation during World War II. Near the end of the war, during the Warsaw uprising, Pulikowski perished and the Warsaw Archive was destroyed by fire. Since 1945, with government support, the work in ethnomusicology, recording, research and publication has developed rapidly, and its achievements have won wide respect.

Bibliography

W. z Oleska [pseud. of W. Zaleski]: *Pieśni polskie i ruskie ludu galicyjskiego* [Polish and Ukrainian Songs of the Galician Folk] (Lwów, 1833)

K. Wójcicki: *Pieśni ludu Biatochropatów, Mazurów i Rusi znad Buga* [Folk Songs of Bialochrobata, Mazury and Ukraine beyond the Bug] (n.p., 1836)

Ż. Pauli: *Pieśni ludu polskiego w Galicji* (Lwów, 1838) [Polish Folk Songs in Galicia]
——: *Pieśni ludu ruskiego w Galicji* (Lwów, 1839) [Ukrainian Folk Songs in Galicia]

O. Kolberg: *Pieśni ludu polskiego* [Songs of the Polish Folk] (Poznań, 1842)
——: *Pieśni ludu polskiego* [Songs of the Polish Folk] (Warsaw, 1857); repr. as vol. i of *Dzieła wszystkie* [Complete Works] (Wrocław and Poznań, 1961)
——: *Lud: Jego zwyczaje, sposób życia, mowa, podania, przysłowia, obrzędy, gusta, zabawy, pieśni, muzika i tańce.* [The Folk: their Customs, Ways of Life, Language, Legends, Proverbs, Rituals, Spells, Entertainments, Songs, Music and Dance] (Warsaw, 1865); repr. as vol. ii of *Dzieła wszystkie* (Kraków, 1962)
——: *Mazowsze* [Mazurkas], i (Kraków, 1885); repr. as vol xxiv of *Dieła wszystkie* (Wrocław and Poznań, 1961–)

H. Windakiewiczowa: 'Rytmika ludowej muzyki polskiej' [Rhythmics of Polish Folk Music] *Wisła*, xi (1897), 716
——: 'Katalog pieśni polsko-morawskich' [Catalogue of Polish–Moravian Songs] i: *Materiały antropologiczno-archeologiczne i etnograficzne, wydawne staraniem Komisyi Antropologicznej Akademii Umiejętności w Krakowie* [Anthropological, Archaeological and Ethnographic Materials, Published under the Auspices of the Anthropological Commission of the Academy of Learning in Kraków], x (1908), ii: *Dział etnograficzny* [Ethnographic section] (1908), 3–43

J. Czekanowski: *Forschungen in Nil-Kongo Zwischengebiet* (Leipzig, 1911–27)

E. M. von Hornbostel: 'Melodya Wasukumska, podług zapisek Dra. J. Czekanowskiego. Wasukuma-Melodie, nach der Aufnahme von Dr J. Czekanowski', *Bulletin international de l'Académie des Sciences de Cracovie*, Series B, Sciences naturelles, Année 1910 (1911), 711

B. Piłsudski: 'Ainu Folk-Lore', *Journal of American Folklore*, xxv/95 (1912)
——: *Materials for the Study of the Ainu Language and Folklore* (Kraków, 1912)

H. Windakiewiczowa: 'Studia nad wierszem i zwrotką poezji polskiej ludowej' [Study of Polish Folk Poetry and Poetic Verse], *Rozprawy Akademii Umiejętności* [Treatises of the Academy of Learning], lii (1913), 175–269

E. M. von Hornbostel: 'Gesänge aus Ruanda', *Forschungen in Nil-Kongo Zwischengebeit*, i, J. Czekanowski (Leipzig, 1917), 379–412

H. Windakiewiczowa: *Wzory ludowej muzyki w mazurkach Fryderyka Chopina* [Examples of Folk Music in Chopin's Mazurkas] (Kraków, 1926)

W. Skierkowski: *Puszcza Kurpiowska w pieśni* [The Kurpie Forest in Song] (Płock, 1928–34)

K. Moszyński: *Kultura ludowa Słowian* [The Folk Culture of the Slavs], i: *Kultura materialna* (1929)

S. Mierczyński: *Muzyka Podhala* (Lwów and Warsaw, 1930, 2/1973)

H. Windakiewiczowa: 'Ze studjów nad formą muzyczną pieśni ludowych: okres kolisty' [From Studies on the Musical Form of Folk Songs: the Era of the Round], *Księga pamiątkowa ku czci Profesora Dr. Adolfa Chybińskiego* [Festschrift for Adolf Chybiński] (Kraków, 1930), 115

K. Moszyński: 'Stan obecny melografji rdzennej Bia orusi i Polesia' [The Situation Till Now of Folk Music Collection in Soviet Belorussia and Polesie], *Lud Słowiański*, iii/1 (1932), B61

H. Windakiewiczowa: 'O badaniach muzyczno-etnograficznych na Polesiu w r. 1932' [On Ethnomusicological Research in Polesie in 1932], *Lud Słowiański*, iii/1 (1932), B69

L. Kamieński: 'Diafonja ludowa w Pieninach' [Folk Diaphony in the Pieniny], *Sprawozdania*

Poznańskiego Towarzystwo Przyjaciół Nauk [Report of the Poznań Society of Friends of Learning], vii (1933), 5

H. Windakiewiczowa: 'Pentatonika w muzyce polskiej ludowej' [Pentatonic Scales in Polish Folk Music], *Kwartalnik muzyczny* [Musical Quarterly], v/17–18 (1933), 1

E. Mika: *Pieśni orawski* [Songs from Orawa] (Lipnica Wielka, 1934, 2/1957)

K. Moszyński: *Kultura ludowa Słowian* [The Folk Culture of the Slavs], ii: *Kultura duchowa* [Spiritual Culture] (Kraków, 1939)

L. Kamieński: *Pieśni ludu pomorskiego* [Songs of the Pomeranian Folk], i: *Pieśni z Kaszub południowych* [Songs from Southern Cassubia] (Torun, 1936)

———: 'Z badań nad śpiewem i muzyka ludu polskiego: problemy i prace Zakładu Muzykologicznego Uniwersytetu Poznańskiego' [Research on Polish Folk Song and Instrumental Music: the Problems and Work of the Musicological Institute of the University of Poznań], *Balticoslavica*, ii (1936), 129

J. Pietruszyńska [Sobieska]: *Dudy wielkopolskie* [The Bagpipes of Wielkopolska] (Poznań, 1936); repr. in J. and M. Sobiescy (1973), 75–136

L. Kaczmarek: 'Fonograf na usługach dialektologii i etnografii muzyczne w Polsce' [The Phonograph in the Service of Dialectology and Ethnomusicology in Poland], *Biuletyn fonograficzny* [Phonographic Bulletin], i (1953), 19–54

W. Kotoński: 'Uwagi o muzyce ludowej Podhala' [Remarks on the Music of Podhale], *Muzyka*, v–vi (1953), 4; vii–viii (1953), 43; xi–xii (1953), 26; i–ii (1954), 14

J. Stęszewski, comp.: *Piosenki kurpiów* [Kurpie Songs] (Kraków, 1955)

A. Wozaczyńska: 'Pieśni kurpiowskie: Ich struktura i charakterystyka w świetle zbiorów W. Skierkowskiego' [Kurpie Songs: Their Style and Characteristics in the Light of the Collections of W. Skierkowski], *Materiały etnograficzne* [Ethnographic Materials], xii (1956)

A. Chybiński: *O polskiej muzyce ludowej: wybór prac etnograficznych* [On Polish Folk Music: a Selection of Ethnographic Works], ed. L. Bielawski (Warsaw, 1961)

Dzieła wszystkie Oskara Kolberga [The Complete Works of Oskar Kolberg], ed. J. Burszta (Warsaw, 1961–) with introductory survey by J. Krzyżanowski, i, xix–xlii

M. Sobieski: 'Wartość zbiorów Oskara Kolberga dla polskiej kultury muzycznej' [The Value of Kolberg's Collections for Polish Musical Culture], *Muzyka*, i (1961), 105; rev. and repr. in J. and M. Sobiescy (1973), 512

L. Bielawski: 'Muzyka ludowa Polska' [Polish Folk Music], *Słownik folkloru polskiego* [Dictionary of Polish Folklore], ed. J. Krzyżanowski (Warsaw, 1965), 240

S. Mierczyński: *Muzyka Huculszczyzny* [Music of Huculszczyna], ed. J. Stęszewski (Krakow, 1965)

J. Burszta: 'The Documentary Value of Oskar Kolberg's Complete Works', *Zaszyty Panstwowego Muzeum Etnograficznego w Warszawie* [Papers of the National Ethnographic Museum in Warsaw], vi–vii, 1965/66 (1968), 27

O. Kolberg: *Góry i podgórze* [Hills and Foothills] (Wrocław and Poznań, 1968)

J. and M. Sobiescy: *Polska muzyka ludowa i jej problemy* [Polish Folk Music and its Problems], ed. L. Bielawski (Kraków, 1973)

R. Górski: *Oskar Kolberg: zarys życia i działalności* [Oskar Kolberg: an Outline of his Life and Works] (Warsaw, 2/1974)

J. Stęszewski: 'Poland, §II. Folk music', *Grove 6*

E. Millerowa and A. Skrukwa: 'Oskar Kolberg'? *Dzieje folklorystyki polskiej 1864–1918* [History of Polish Folklore Research 1864–1918], ed. H. Kapeluś and J. Krzyżanowski (Warsaw, 1982), 25–103

J. Stęszewski: 'O zawartości informacyjnej i wiarogodności zbioru etnomuzycznego Oskara Kolberga' [On the Information, Content and Reliability of Oskar Kolberg's Ethnomusicological Collection] (unpublished manuscript, 1986)

A. Czekanowska: *Polish Folk Music* (London, 1990)

4: BOHEMIA, MORAVIA AND SLOVAKIA

BARBARA KRADER

Serious collection and analysis of folk songs and melodies began in the early 19th century in Bohemia and Moravia, and somewhat later in Slovakia. Although notated by ear, the major collections still stand as documents for modern research.

Bohemia and Moravia

The classic Czech folk-song collection, by Karel Jaromír Erben (1811–70; see fig.1), gathered by him and his friends in almost every locality in Bohemia, contains in the definitive edition 811 melodies and over 2200 texts of songs, rhymes, riddles and children's games (Erben, 1862–4; earliest edition 1842–3). The time of collection, essentially the 1840s, was crucial, for after 1848

1. Karel Jaromír Erben

village isolation in Bohemia (less true for Moravia) all but ended and urban influences spread rapidly. Erben, a distinguished poet and prose stylist, made his selection with taste and a deep feeling for the language and the traditional musical style. His work is notable for the quality of his selection as well as for skilled classification and the indication of place of collection and reference to variants in other Slavic collections. Erben's collection is still the basic source for Czech folk poetry and folk-song melodies (Horák, 1912; Grund, 1935;

Markl, 1959, 'Nápěvy českých'). The songs soon spread widely, through the 500 arrangements for voice and piano by Jan Pavel Martinovský (1845–70).

The earliest published Czech folk-song collection with tunes, that of Jan Rittersberk in 1825, has recently attracted new attention for its inclusion of a few texts with coarse humour and some urban songs, thus offering a fuller picture of the contemporary repertory. Most of the items in the collection, which contains 300 Czech secular songs, 50 German songs and a supplement of 50 Czech and German instrumental folk-dance tunes, were taken from a collection made in 1819 in Bohemia and Moravia by Austrian decree, initiated by the Vienna Gesellschaft für Musikfreunde. The rest were taken from a late 18th-century manuscript collection of folk, urban and erotic songs collected by Jan Nepomuk Jeník z Bratřic (1756–1845), which was published by J. Markl in 1959 ('Deutsche Volkslieder'; 1967, Vetterl, 1973). The romantic principles of Erben, Sušil and Bartoš forbade the inclusion of songs like these. Markl's important song anthology, published posthumously in 1987, reprints the entire Rittersberk collection of 1825 and three others, also pre-1830, never previously published. These are preceded by a long study (pp.15–193).

Moravia is the Czech-speaking province between Bohemia and Slovakia, long attached to Bohemia, but with a firm sense of identity. Western Moravia has folk-song melodies like the Czech, relatively regular and easy to notate by schooled musicians. In the East, however, as in Slovakia, the melodies are freer in rhythm, there are more melodies than texts, the scales are not limited to major and minor, and quarter tones occur. The composer Alois Hába came from Valašsko, where this style dominates, and Leoš Janáček from Lašsko, just to the north.

František Sušil (1809–68) was a Catholic priest and a respected professor of theology in Brno, now remembered for his folk-song collection published in 1860. Sušil gathered approximately 1890 melodies and the 2361 song texts singlehandedly during his summer vacations in the 1840s and 1850s from villages in all parts of Moravia. Following the general practice of the time, he made an aesthetic selection (like Erben), and some 'corrections' of texts, seeking the best from several variants, but otherwise was painstakingly accurate. The collecting was so thorough that only a few songs in later Moravian collections are not found in Sušil's. His volume is rich in religious legendary songs, spiritual lyric songs (some stemming from broadside ballads), ballads and love songs. Places of collection are indicated and reference made to variants in a dozen other song collections, Czech, Slovak, Polish, Sorbian and South Slavic. No coarse language appears and there are few group songs, dance songs or drinking songs (Hýsek, 1911, pp.59–71; Václavek and Smetana, 1941 and 1951).

The second great Moravian song collection (Bartoš, 1899–1901) was made by František Bartoš (1837–1906), a schoolmaster and philologist trained in Vienna. His goal was to collect and publish Moravia's folklore heritage before it disappeared, and his writings include many books and articles on Moravian folklore, folk poetry and a basic work on Moravian dialects. The Bartoš song collection is marred by editorial faults – he changed words, omitted stanzas without indication and did not always copy precisely – but the work is still important for the number of songs, the wealth of folk dances and instrumental music from Slovácko and Valašsko (of the eastern musical style), and the

179

many traditional religious songs (Bartoš, 1882 and later expanded editions). From 1886 he enlisted Janáček's help to review the music. Unlike Sušil, Bartoš relied on other collectors and expert musicians, although he collected song texts extensively himself. He possessed a deep sense of folklore and its context, a feeling Sušil lacked (Sirovátka, 1966; Vysloužil, 1956; Hýsek, 1911, pp.189–98; Gregor, 1968).

The composer Leoš Janáček (1854–1928) worked actively with Moravian folk music, chiefly from the 1880s until 1914. He edited the music in the 1889 and 1899–1901 editions of the Bartoš collection and wrote an important treatise on Moravian folk music, published in the later edition (reprinted in Janáček, 1955). He also collected some 300 folk songs in the field, primarily for his own use as a composer (Janáček, 1955, pp.29–78; Novák, 1962). His greatest contribution to folk-song scholarship was related to the multinational project for song collection initiated in Vienna in 1904, *Das Volkslied in Oesterreich*. As director of the Czech language Moravian and Silesian section (Hostinský directed the Bohemian Czech area), he issued instructions on how to collect, contacted teachers throughout Moravia, refined methods of notation and organized the first recordings on cylinders. Eventually in 1917 Janáček refused to send the collection of over 10,000 songs and melodies to Vienna and it remains in Brno (Hrabalová, 1983, pp.7–52). He also prepared the first fully scholarly folk-song anthology of Moravian love songs, published posthumously (Janáček and Váša, 1930–36). The collection contains 150 Moravian songs, with many variants selected mainly from the 1906–14 collecting project, and an index of melodic types by Vladimír Helfert. (Janáček's introduction, written in 1913, was not published with the anthology but appears in Janáček, 1955; see also Černík, 1969.)

Otakar Hostinský (1847–1910), professor of music history and aesthetics at the university in Prague, laid the foundation for scholarly study of Czech folk music in two studies of 1892 and 1906. He established in the first, from early written sources, over 30 secular folk-song melodies known in the 16th century and in the second, partly by the statistical analysis of more than 1000 Czech folk melodies, the essential features of the so-called Czech instrumental song type (Horák and Zich, 1910; Markl, 1960; Sychra, 1961, pp.5–22).

Otakar Zich (1879–1934), composer, ethnomusicologist and pupil of Hostinský, contributed a fine study of Czech folk dances with changing metre (1916) and another of songs and dances of the *do kolečka* type (1906–10; see also Markl, 1981).

In the 1930s, the research on broadside ballads by Bedřich Václavek and Robert Smetana was especially valuable (Smetana and Václavek, 1937), as was Václavek's theoretical work on folk song (1938) which stimulated further study of urban social singing of broadside ballads (bourgeois and proletarian) and of the interweaving of folklore with literature. Their postscript to the 1941 edition of Sušil's collection is one of the best studies of Moravian folk song since Janáček (Václavek and Smetana, 1941, 1951).

The fullest survey of Czech and Slovak folklore scholarship until 1930 is by Horák (1933). On folk-song collecting in Moravia see Hrabalová (1983).

The first mechanical recording of folk music in Bohemia, 14 wax cylinders of more than 18 pieces, was made by Otakar Zich in May 1909 in the Chodsko region of southwest Bohemia, which retains a characteristic regional instrumental style (an ensemble of clarinet, violin and bagpipes). Although these recordings were imperfect, after 1945 they were copied on tape and the bagpipe part painstakingly transcribed by Zdeněk Blaha. Ten of these pieces are published in Markl, 1962, *Dudy a dudáci*. The first recordings by Janáček's Moravian collecting team were made in November 1909 of Slovak agricultural workers. From 1909–12 they recorded 90 cylinders, several of which were of Slovak folk music, including 25 Terchov songs, sung in parts. The early Moravian recordings were partly damaged by frequent playing, some being completely ruined, but the remainder were copied in 1955 and again in 1978 on to magnetic tape (Hrabalová, 1983, pp.27–9, 49).

The best recordings in Czechoslovakia before 1945 were made in 1929 by the French company Pathé, in co-operation with the Paris Institut Phonétique, for the Czech Academy's Phonograph Commission (Chlumský, 1930; Devigne, 1939, pp.300–301). Singers and bands came to Prague for recording on discs. Zich and Jindřich Jindřich supervised the instrumental music from Chodsko, which is especially well-chosen and documented (Chlumský, 1930 p.191; see also Markl's 1962 *Antologie autentických* brochure notes – the third 7-inch disc in this collection, issued for the 1962 International Folk Music Council meeting in Czechoslovakia, reproduces ten of the Pathé recordings of 1929 from Chodsko).

Slovakia

Although collections of Slovak folk-song texts were published as early as the 1820s and 1830s, the classic collection with tunes is *Slovenské spevy*, published from 1880–1926 (Galko, 1966, 1971). In 1875 the government had closed the new Slovak cultural centre, Matica Slovenská, and the new Slovak-language secondary schools. When a call was issued by Slovak cultural leaders four years later to collect folk songs with tunes, the appeal was understood and response came from all parts of modern Slovakia. Though notated by amateurs and not organized systematically, it remains an important folk-song source and a national monument.

The greatest scholarly pre-1939 Slovak folk-song collection was made, mostly by recordings, by Béla Bartók from 1906 to 1918. Although it was prepared during 1924–8 and presented to Matica Slovenská in 1928, its publication is still not completed (Bartók, 1959, 1970; volume iii has been in preparation since the early 1960s).

The first phonograph recordings (30 songs) were made by Karol Medvecký in 1902 in the Detva region of central Slovakia and transcribed roughly by Milan Lichard (Medvecký, 1905; see also Elscheková and Elschek, 1962, i, pp.31–5). This distinctive regional musical style is central to Slovak folk music study. It is significant that the first recording took place there and that Bartók recorded the long *fujara* flute there four years later. The Hungarian Béla Vikár recorded in northwest Slovakia (Trenčiansko) during 1903–7. His cylinders, containing 115 songs, were transcribed by Bartók and included in his Slovak collection, with Kodály's early Slovak collections by ear, beginning in 1900. Other phonograph recordings made in 1913 by the Russian ethnomusicologist Evgeniia Lineva in Slovakia (Kysúcke villages) and eastern Moravia are preserved with the song texts in the Leningrad Phonogram

Archive. The best pre-war stationary recording of folk music was made on discs in 1929 in Prague by the French company Pathé. Among these studio recordings made in Prague of singers and instrumentalists brought from all over the country, including Subcarpathian Russia (a Ukrainian region, then part of Czechoslovakia), the largest number of discs (over 130) were devoted to Slovak folk music, the performers chosen by Karel Plicka. Plicka (1894–1987), a musician, creative artist, photographer and film-maker, was engaged by Matica Slovenská from 1924 to 1939 to collect folk songs. In the field, he notated by ear almost 8500 melodies and texts and 10,000 song texts without tunes (Elscheková and Elschek, 1962, i, p.41). Only about 500 songs from his collection have been published (Plicka, 1961); the manuscript collection remains at Matica Slovenská in Martin (Markl, 1965; Elscheková and Elschek, 1962, i, pp.40–43). One of Potúček's many bibliographies of Slovak folk music is Potúček, 1966, pp.201–27. A detailed critical survey of Slovak folk music study up to 1957 is found in Elscheková and Elschek, 1962, i, pp.18–61.

Ludvík Kuba

The Czech Ludvík Kuba (1863–1956) needs special consideration. He was a professional musician, later in his career an eminent painter, and always an evocative and witty writer. In his early twenties he began to publish a series of albums of folk songs of the Slavic peoples (1884–1929). The enterprise prospered at first, but gradually the sales dropped and in 1894–5 he turned to painting, studying in Paris, Munich and Vienna, then returning to Prague as a prominent and successful artist. The final song albums were published in the 1920s with the support of President Masaryk. This series was the impetus for his folk-song collecting but is today, with its piano accompaniments and generally popular appeal, of minor interest to ethnomusicology.

Of greater importance now are two separately published collections, one of Lusatian Serbian folk songs and instrumental tunes (Kuba, 1887, 1922; see also Raupp, 1963), and the other of 1127 songs gathered in 1893, mainly in small towns in Bosnia and Hercegovina (Kuba, 2/1984). His notations by ear from 1893 of Czech instrumental ensembles in the Chodsko region are also outstanding (published in Markl, 1962, *Dudy a dudáci*; pp.82–231). Kuba was the first to document Lusatian Serbian instruments, songs and instrumental melodies, and among the first to notate Ukrainian folk choruses (in 1886–7). In his extensive and early collecting among the south Slavs (although after Kuhač), he spent more time, gathered more material and gained deeper insights in Istria, Dalmatia (coastal and inland), Croatia, Bosnia and Hercegovina. In Serbia, Macedonia and Bulgaria he collected less, and his notations of metres and rhythms in these less-Western styles are criticized.

Everywhere he travelled he made sketches, drawings and even paintings. Those of musical instruments and costumes are ethnographic documents (see fig.2). He mastered all the languages of the lands and regions he visited. The song texts he collected are a solid source for native folklorists.

Kuba wrote a great number of magazine and newspaper articles, often of ethnographic value, about his travels, accompanied by his own illustrations and by song melodies and texts. (A selection of these, revised, appears in Kuba, 1933–5.) There are also major scholarly articles, including a small book on

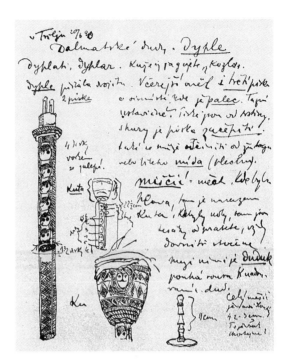

2. Drawing by Ludvík Kuba from his 'Cesty za slovanskou písní' (Journeys after the Slavic song) showing the construction of a simple bagpipe (diple)

Yugoslav folk music (1923), which contains valuable comparative observations. A lengthy book on his travels in Montenegro was published in 1892, and later five book collections of his articles on particular areas: on Lusatia, Old Serbia, Macedonia, Dalmatia, and Bosnia and Hercegovina. Each is illustrated and includes music. Kuba never used a phonograph, but he had perfect pitch and enormous practice in notation by ear. Most of his musical notations in the field and many of his writings, especially the lengthy studies of Dalmatian song, with the other accounts of performance practices and the views of the performers, are of permanent scholarly value.

Bibliography

J. R. z Rittersberk and B. D. Weber, comps. and eds.: *České narodnj pjsně/Böhmische Volkslieder* (Prague, 1825); repr. in Markl (1987), 221–445

K. J. Erben: *Prostonárodní české písně a říkadla* [Czech Folk Songs and Riddles] (Prague, 1842–3, 3/1862–4/*R*1886)

J. P. Martinovský: *Nàpěvy písní národních v Čechách* [Melodies of Folk Songs in Bohemia] (Prague, 1845–70/*R*1951)

F. Sušil: *Moravské národní písně s nápěvy do textu vřaděnými* [Moravian Folk Songs with Melodies Placed with the Text] (Brno, 1860/*R*1941/*R*1951, ed. B. Václavek and R. Smetana, with commentary)

Slovenské spevy [Slovak Songs] (Turčiansky Sv Martin, 1880–1926); new critical edn., ed. L. Galko (Bratislava, 1972–89)

F. Bartoš: *Národní písné moravské v nové nasbírané* [Moravian Folk Songs Newly Collected] (Brno, 1882, enl. 2/1889, enl. with studies by Bartoš and Janáček, 3/1899–1901 with study by Janáček, pp.i–cxxxvi)

L. Kuba: *Slovanstvo ve svých zpěvech* [The Slavic World in its Songs], i: *Písně české* [Czech Songs] (1884–8); ii: *Písně moravské* [Moravian Songs] (1888); iii: *Písně slovenské* [Slovak Songs] (1888); iv: *Písně polské* [Polish Songs] (1887); v: *Písně lužické* [Lusation Serb, Wend, or Sorb Songs] (1885–7); vi: *Písně ruské* [Russian – Including Great Russian, Ukrainian, and Belorussian – Songs] (1885–8); vii: *Písně jihoslovanské* [South Slavic – Slovenian, Montenegrin, Croatian, Dalmatian, Serbian Kingdom, Bosnian and Hercegovinian, Macedonian, Old Serbian and Bulgarian – songs] (1890–1929)

———: *Nowa zběrka melodiji k hornjołužiskim pesnjam (223 čisła) zhromadził Ludwík Kuba* [A New Collection of Melodies to Upper Lusatian Songs (223 numbers) Gathered by Ludvík Kuba] (Budyšin, 1887)

O. Hostinský: *36 nápěvů světských písní českéno lidu z XVI. století* [36 Secular Song Melodies of the Czech Folk from the 16th Century] (Prague, 1892/*R*1956), with postword by J. Markl

K. Medvecký: *Detva* (Detva, 1905)

O. Hostinský: *Česká světská píseň lidová* [The Czech Secular Folk Song] (Prague, 1906); repr. in Hostinský (1961)

O. Zich: 'Písně a tance "do kolečka" na Chodsku' [*Do kolečka* Songs and Dances in the Chodsko Region], *Český lid*, xv–xix (1906–10)

J. Horák and O. Zich: 'Význam Otakara Hostinského pro theorii lidové písné české' [The Significance of Otakar Hostinský for the Theory of the Czech Folk Song], *Národopisný věstník českoslovanský*, v (1910), 97

M. Hýsek: *Literární Morava v letech 1849–1885* [Literary Moravia in the Years 1849–1885] (Prague, 1911)

J. Horák: 'Erbenova sbírka českých písní lidových' [Erben's collection of Czech Folk Songs], *Národopisný věstník českoslovanský*, vii (1912), 1

O. Zich: 'České lidové tance s proměnlivým taktem' [Czech Folk Dances with Changing Metre], *Národopisný věstník českoslovanský*, xi (1916)

L. Kuba: *Píseň srbů lužických* [The Song of the Lusatian Serbs] (Prague, 1922)

———: *Píseň jihoslovanská: Přehled celkový* [The Yugoslav Song: a Survey of the Whole] (Prague, 1923)

J. Chlumský: 'Fonografický a gramofonický archiv České akademie věd a umění v Praze' [The Phonographic and Gramophone Archive of the Czech Academy of Sciences and Arts in Prague], *Časopis pro moderní filologii*, xvi/2 (1930), 189

L. Janáček and P. Váša: *Moravské písně milostné* [Moravian Love Songs] (Prague, 1930–36)

J. Horák: 'Národopis československý', in *Československá Vlastivěda*, ii: *Člověk* (Prague, 1933), 305–472

L. Kuba: *Cesty za slovanskou písní 1885–1929* (Journeys after the Slavic Song) (Prague, 1933–5, 2/1953)

A. Grund: *Karel Jaromír Erben* (Prague, 1935)

R. Smetana and B. Václavek, eds.: *České písně kramářské* [Czech Broadside Ballads] (Prague, 1937, 2/1947)

B. Václavek: *Písemnictví a lidová tradice: obraz jejich vztahů v české písní lidové a zlidovělé* [Literature and Folk Tradition: a Picture of Their Relations in the Czech Folk and Folkicized Song] (Prague, 1938, 2/1947)

R. Devigne: 'France: La Phonothèque du Musée de la parole et du geste de l'Université de Paris', *Folklore musical* (Paris, 1939), 293

B. Václavek and R. Smetana: 'Doslov' [Afterword], in F. Sušil, *Moravské národní písně s nápěvy vřaděnými* [Moravian Folk Songs with Melodies Placed with the Text] (Prague, 4/1951), 747

L. Janáček: *O lidové písní a lidové hudbě: dokumenty a studie* [On Folk Song and Instrumental Folk Music], ed. J. Vysloužil (Prague, 1955)

J. Vysloužil: 'Nad folkloristickým dílem Františka Bartoše' [On the Scholarly Folklore Works of František Bartoš], *Český lid*, xliii (1956), 110

B. Bartók: *Slovenské l'udové piesne* [Slovak Folk Songs], ed. A. Elscheková, O. Elschek, and J. Kresánek, i (Bratislava, 1959)

J. Markl: 'Deutsche Volkslieder gesammelt im Jahre 1819', *BMw*, i (1959), 23

———: 'Nápěvy českých lidových písní podle sbírky K. J. Erbena' [The Melodies of Czech Folk Songs According to K. J. Erben's Collection], *Český lid*, xlvi (1959), 248

———, ed.: *Rozmarné písničky Jana Jeníka z Bratřic* [Humorous Little Songs of Jan Jeník z Bratřic] (Prague, 1959)

J. Markl: 'Živý odkaz Otakara Hostinského 2. I. 1847–19. I. 1910' [The Living Legacy of Otakar Hostinský], *Český lid*, xlvii (1960), 49

O. Hostinský: *O hudbě* [Writings on Music] (Prague, 1961)

K. Plicka: *Slovenský spevník* (Bratislava, 1961)

A. Sychra: 'Badatelský odkaz Otakara Hostinského a dnešek' [The Scholarly Legacy of Otakar Hostinský Today], in O. Hostinský, *O hudbě* (Prague, 1961), 5

A. Elscheková and O. Elschek: *Úvod do štúdia slovenskej ľudovej hudby* [Introduction to the Study of Slovak Folk Music] (Bratislava, 1962)

J. Markl: *Antologie autentických forem československého hudebního folkloru* [An Anthology of Authentic Forms of Czechoslovak Folk Music] (Prague, 1962), 16 7-inch discs and brochure

——: *Česká dudácká hudba* [Czech Bagpipe Music] (Prague, 1962)

——: *Dudy a dudáci: o jihočeských písních a lidové hudbě* [Bagpipes and Pipers: On South Bohemian Songs and Instrumental Folk Music] (České Budějovice, 1962)

P. Novák: 'Hudebně folkloristická historiografie ve Slezsku a na severovýchodní Moravě' [Historiography of Scholarly Folk Music Study in Czech Silesia and Northeastern Moravia], *Slezský sborník*, lx (1962), 187

J. Raupp: *Sorbische Volksmusikanten und Musikinstrumente* (Budyšin [Bautzen], 1963)

J. Markl: 'Karel Plicka siebzig Jahre', *Demos*, vi/1 (1965), cols. 19–20

L. Galko: 'Vydávanie a ohlas "Slovenských spevov"' [The Publication and Resonance of *Slovenské spevy*], *Hudobnovedné štúdie*, vii (1966), 109

J. Potúček: 'Slovenská hudobnofolkloristická literatúra: výberová bibliografia za roky 1823–1961' [Slovak Folk Music Research Literature: a Selective Bibliography, 1823–1961], *Hudobnovedné štúdia*, vii (1966), 201

O. Sirovátka: 'Bartoš národopisec' [Bartoš as Ethnographer], *Zprávy Oblastního muzea jihovýchodní Moravy v Gottwaldově*, iii (1966), 97

J. Markl: 'Guberniální sběr písní z roku 1819' [The State Collection of Songs from 1819], *Český lid*, liv (1967), 133

A. Gregor: *O životě a díle Františka Bartoše* [On the Life and Works of František Bartoš] (Brno, 1968)

J. Černík: 'Vztah Leoše Janáčka k lidové písní' [Janáček's Relation to the Folk Song], *Časopis slezského muzea*, ser. B/18 (1969), 46

B. Bartók: *Slovenské ľudové piesne* [Slovak Folk Songs], ii, ed. A. Elscheková, O. Elschek, and J. Kresánek (Bratislava, 1970)

L. Galko: 'O redigovaní Slovenských spevov' [On the Editing of *Slovenské spevy*], *Musicologica Slovaca*, iii (1971), 141

K. Vetterl: 'Volkslied-Sammelergebnisse in Mähren und Schlesien aus dem Jahre 1819', *Sborník prací Filosofické fakulty Brněnské university*, ser. H/B (1973), 95

J. Markl: 'Otakar Zich a hudební folklor Čech' [Otakar Zich and the Folk Music of Bohemia], *Vědecký odkaz Otakara Zicha. Sborník* [The Scholarly Heritage of Otakar Zich. A Collection] (Prague, 1981), 231

O. Hrabalová, comp.: *Průvodce písňovými rukopisnými sbírkami Ústavu pro etnografii a folkloristiku ČSAV, pracoviště v Brně* [Guide to the Manuscript Song Collections in the Institute for Ethnography and Folklore of the Czechoslovak Academy, Brno Branch], i (Brno, 1983), 7–52

L. Kuba: *Pjesme i napjevi iz Bosne i Hercegovine* [Songs and Melodies from Bosnia and Hercegovina], ed. C. Rihtman with L. Simić, M. Fulanović-Šošić, and D. Rihtman-Šotrić (Sarajevo, 2/1984) [see review in *YTM*, xviii (1986), 177, for background information]

J. Markl: *Nejstarší sbírky českých lidových písní* [The Oldest Collections of Czech Folk Songs] (Prague, 1987)

5: GREECE

Barbara Krader

The earliest known notations of Greek folk melodies are found in the books of Fr. J. Sulzer (1781–2), Daniel H. Sanders (1844, pp.351–8) and in the Haxthausen collection, evidently assembled by 1814. The collection was admired in manuscript form by Goethe and the Grimm brothers, although it was not published until 1935 (*Neugriechische Lieder*; see also Spyridakis, 1968). The first larger collection of songs with music, by Louis A. Bourgault-Ducoudray (1876), contained songs found in Smyrna and Athens (town songs, according to Samuel Baud-Bovy, 1959, p.342; 1982).

Of folk songs with melodies gathered by Greeks themselves, Georgios Pachtikos (1869–1916) in 1905 published a classic collection, which he gathered from 1888 to 1904 in Asia Minor, Thrace, Macedonia, Epirus, Albania, central Greece, Crete, the Aegean Islands and Cyprus. Also important are the early collections of songs from Skyros (1910–11) and Gortynia (1923) by Konstantin Psachos (1869–1949) and of songs from Roumelia (1931) by Melpo Merlier (1890–1979).

The first field recordings of Greek folk music were made on cylinders by the French scholar Hubert Pernot on the island of Chios in 1898–9. A collection of 114 of these melodies, which were published in 1903 with faulty transcriptions by Paul Le Flem, were subsequently harmonized by Ravel (Baud-Bovy, 1975). The first mechanical field recordings in mainland Greece were undertaken in the Peloponnesus by the Conservatory of Athens in 1910. The transcriptions, by Konstantin Psachos, were not published until 1930, together with his 1911 collection (made by ear) from western Crete (Syllogi Odeiou Athinon, 1930; Dragoumis, 1974).

In 1930 the Archives of Folk Music were founded in Athens, soon to be led by Melpo Merlier. They were later incorporated into the Study Centre on Asia Minor, founded by Merlier in 1931 for research into the traditions of Greek refugees from Asia Minor (Merlier, 1960, p.71). Between 1930 and 1933 a programme of finest-quality stationary recording on discs, initiated by Pernot and financed by the Greek government, was carried out for the archive by the French company Pathé. Merlier and an assistant chose as informants refugees from Asia Minor and Thrace, and folk musicians from the least studied Greek regions (Merlier, 1935; Formozis, 1939; Devigne, 1939, pp.300–02). Copies of these discs are at the Athens Archives; the original matrices and copies are preserved in Paris. From these recordings – about 220 discs containing over 600 songs – 70 songs and dances from the Dodecanese islands were transcribed and published by the Swiss scholar Samuel Baud-Bovy (1906–86) in his outstanding collection *Chansons du Dodécanèse* (Baud-Bovy, 1935–8). This collection, which includes some 350 tunes with variants, 281 notated by ear, the rest transcribed from discs, documents almost the entire repertory of the Dodecanese islands, permitting scholarly analysis of a Greek tradition of Asia minor and comparison with that of continental Greece and Crete. His separate study of the folk-song texts (Baud-Bovy, 1936) remains a classic work; it contains an analysis of the relations of the poetic and musical rhythms, the distich and its form, and traces the origin, date and diffusion of the narrative songs (especially the akritic), and the areas of their creation and diffusion. A further volume on the music was apparently never completed. After 1945, Baud-Bovy continued to study Greek folk music, especially the *clephtic* song and the music of Crete (see the preface by Merlier in Baud-Bovy, 1958, pp.v–xv and 'Hommage', 1987).

The important Folklore Archive of the Academy of Athens, founded in 1918, has long collected folklore materials but its music section only began in 1950 (Spyridakis, 1968, pp.183–4).

Bibliography

Fr. J. Sulzer: *Geschichte des transalpinischen Daciens* (Vienna, 1781–2)

D. H. Sanders: *Das Volksleben der Neugriechen* (Mannheim, 1844)

L. A. Bourgault-Ducoudray: *Trente mélodies populaires de Grèce et d'Orient: Recueillies et harmonisées* (Paris, 1876)

Mélodies populaires grecques de l'île de Chio: Recueillies en phonograph par Hubert Pernot et mises en musiques par Paul Le Flem (Paris, 1903)

G. Pachtikos: *260 dimodi ellinika asmata. . .* [260 Greek Folk Songs] (Athens, 1905)

K. Psachos: *Dimodi asmata Skyrou* [Folk Songs of Skyros] (Athens, 1910–11)

——: *Dimodi asmata Gortynias* [Folk Songs of Gortynia] (Athens, 1923)

Syllogi Odeiou Athinon [Collection of the Athens Conservatory]: *50 dimodi asmata Peloponnisou kai Kritis* [50 Folk Songs of the Peloponnesus and Crete] (Athens, 1930)

M. Merlier: *Tragoudia tis Roumelis* [Songs of Roumelia] (Athens, 1931)

S. Baud-Bovy: *Chansons du Dodécanèse* (Athens and Paris, 1935–8), 2 vols.

M. Merlier: *Essai d'un tableau du folklore musical grec* (Athens, 1935)

Neugriechische Lieder, gesammelt von Werner von Haxthausen: Urtext und übersetzung (Münster, 1935)

S. Baud-Bovy: *La chanson populaire grecque du Dodécanèse, i: Les textes* (Paris, 1936)

R. Devigne: 'France: La Phonothèque du Musée de la parole et du geste de l'Université de Paris', *Folklore musical*, ii (Paris, 1939), 293

P. Formozis: 'Grèce', *Folklore musical*, ii (Paris, 1939), 130

S. Baud-Bovy: *Études sur la chanson cleftique* (Athens, 1958)

——: 'Musique grecque. §II Grèce moderne. 1. Musique populaire', *Fasquelle E*, ii (Paris, 1959), 342

M. Merlier: 'La chanson populaire grecque', *AcM*, xxxii (1960), 68

G. Spyridakis: 'Volksliedforschung in Griechenland', *Jb für Volksliedforschung*, xiii (1968), 181

M. F. Dragoumis: 'Konstantin A. Psachos', *Laografia*, xxix (1974), 311

S. Baud-Bovy: 'Les chansons populaires grecques harmonisées par Maurice Ravel', *Maurice Ravel au XXe siècle* (Paris, 1975), 24

——: 'Bourgault-Ducoudray et la musique grecque écclésiastique et profane', *RdM*, lxviii (1982), 153

'Hommage à Samuel Baud-Bovy', *Revue musicale de Suisse romande*, xl (1987), 13

6: HUNGARY and ROMANIA

BÁLINT SAROSI

Interest in folk music in Hungary and Romania developed in roughly the same way as it did in Western Europe. Since Johann Herder's example, a high value has been set on oral poetic tradition, a tradition especially precious to peoples striving for independence and wanting to prove their ground for national identity by means of their individual culture – and within it, not to a small extent, by songs.

The well-known convention of 19th-century studies, that the term folk song can be used for the words only, also applies to Hungary and Romania. Indeed until the middle of the 20th century folk song was central in ethnomusicology even if we speak mostly about folk music research.

Furthermore, Hungarian and Romanian folk music has meant exclusively peasant music.

Before the 19th century Hungarian folk music was noted down infrequently and haphazardly, although there are a few printed collections of religious songs including folk hymns from the 16th and 17th centuries – some of them Hungarian in origin, some of foreign origin but adapted to Hungarian taste. A number of representative Hungarian bagpipe melodies were noted down and published at the end of the 16th century by foreigners, following the West European fashion for Hungarian dances under such titles as *Ungarescha*, *Heiducken dantz* or *Ungarischer tantz*. There are also miscellaneous Hungarian manuscript collections from the 17th and 18th centuries with notations or tablatures. In terms of vocal folk music the student songbooks that have survived from the end of the 18th century are important; these were compiled in simple notation by students for their own use. In its melodic scope and its method of notation Ádám Pálóczi Horváth's great manuscript collection of 450 songs, completed in 1813 (ed. Bartha, 1953), can also be classified among these student manuals. Besides the fashionable Hungarian songs of the period and Pálóczi Horváth's own compositions, it contains many songs from previous centuries and can thus be considered the first great achievement in Hungarian folk music collection. A Romanian collection of similar import-ance, although of different conception, is that of the versatile Anton Pann (1797?–1854), teacher, singer and man of letters, who published more than 200 secular songs of his era in Bucharest between 1830 and 1854 (Ciobanu, 1955). Information about the wealth of songs current in Hungary in the first half of the 19th century, known also in middle-class circles, is still found only in manuscript collections, for instance those of István Tóth, Sámuel Almási, Dániel Mindszenty, Dénes Kiss and János Udvardy Cserna.

Since 1832 the Hungarian Academy of Sciences has undertaken the collection and publication of folk songs. The Academy sponsored a project including two kinds of folk-song collections. One type intended for use in scientific research consequently had to preserve folk songs in their original unchanged form. The other was to serve directly in forming national taste; accordingly it contained songs in somewhat embellished variants.

This academic decision, however, did not change the practice already existing all over Europe, so in Hungary as elsewhere, the so-called folk-song collections contained original folk songs, in a more or less unchanged form, together with other kinds of national songs and new songs by writers inspired by the spirit of the people. These songs were usually provided with piano accompaniment. Such collections, of heterogeneous content and with piano accompaniment, in Romania were those compiled by Dimitri Vulpian (1848–1922) between 1885 and 1891. Among his several collections, the first one entitled *Muzica populară, ballade, colinde, doine, idyle* [Folk Music, Ballads, Christmas Carols, Doina Songs, Idylls] contains 381 pieces. A Hungarian collection of similar character, compiled by István Bartalus (1821–99), is the impressive seven-volume *Magyar népdalok: egyetemes gyűjtemény* [Hungarian Folk songs: a Universal Collection, 1873–96]. This extensive collection contains some 730 melodies with piano accompaniment, acquired largely through correspondence and not always competently noted down; most of them are 19th-century tunes, including recent popular Hungarian ones by known composers. Earlier, in 1865, Károly Szini's collection *A magyar nép dalai és dallamai* [Songs and Tunes of the Hungarian Folk], containing 200 melodies, had appeared. Although its content is as heterogeneous as that of the other 19th-century collections, it has the advantage of presenting the songs in their original form, without piano accompaniment, and in reliable notation. Only one branch of folk music – the collection of children's games – produced a pioneering work that is still highly regarded: Áron Kiss's *Magyar gyermekjáték gyűjtemény* ('Collection of Hungarian Children's Games', 1891).

The collecting of Hungarian peasant music with the help of the Edison phonograph was started in 1895 by Béla Vikár (1859–1945), a philologist and literary man. The young Zoltan Kodály (1882–1967) in 1904 started to transcribe Vikár's cylinders (still preserved), together with further recordings of Kodály, Béla Bartók (1881–1945), László Lajtha (1892–1963), Antal Molnár (1890–1983) and others in the Ethnographic Department of the National Museum, which grew into the present Museum of Ethnography.

The first to undertake folk music collection methodically in Hungary was János Seprődi (1874–1923), who began noting down folk songs from peasants in 1897.

1. *Béla Bartók (left) and Zoltan Kodály in 1908*

Modern Hungarian folk music research, however, can be said to have commenced when Kodály and Bartók set out on their first collecting trips in 1905 and 1906 respectively. From the outset they worked concertedly and systematically. They made a geographical division between them of the territories to be covered; the scholarly work that followed, however, was largely shared. World War I, then World War II, prevented them for a long time from carrying out this plan. Kodály, by reason of his higher philological education and his collecting activity, studied the musical historical background of Hungarian folk music, listing also the songs taken down in preceding centuries (mainly the 19th). Bartók extended his collecting to neighbouring peoples dealing with the issues of international comparative study. He started on Slovak folk music almost at the same time as his Hungarian, collecting 3223 Slovak melodies between 1906 and 1918. His Slovak collection was published in the 1920s (see also Bartók, 1959–70). His complete Hungarian collection runs to 2721 items (1924). The number of Romanian melodies he collected between 1908 and 1917 is even larger – 3500 (Bartók, 1913, 1923, 1935; see also Suchoff, ed., 1967–75; Alexandru, 1958). In 1913 Bartók collected Arab peasant music in Biskra, North Africa and environs. In 1936 he managed to travel to Turkey on his first and last collecting trip after 1918 (Bartók, 1976; see also L. Vikár, 1976).

According to the definition of Kodály and Bartók, folk music is the unwritten music surviving in the peasant tradition. It is generally distinguished from the stratum of melody created in the 19th century (mainly in the second half of the century) by amateur composers which also spread largely in unwritten form: in contemporary collections these songs were also called folk songs. The modern specialist term for them in Hungarian is *népies dal* (popular art song), though they are also known as *nóta* (popular melody) or *magyarñota* (Hungarian melody). As gypsy bands led the way in popularizing them, they are also referred to as *cigányzene* (gypsy music).

In his paper 'Why and How Do We Collect Folk Music?' (1936), Bartók emphasized that it was not enough to collect songs as 'isolated items', because

'it would be like the entomologist or lepidopterist who would be satisfied with the assembly and preparation of the different species of insects or butterflies. If his satisfaction rests there, then his collection is an inanimate material. The genuine, scientific naturalist, therefore, not only collects and prepares but also studies and describes, as far as possible, the most hidden moments of animal life . . . Similar reasons direct the folk-music collector to investigate in detail the conditions surrounding the real life of the melodies' (Bartók, 1976, pp.19–20).

Bartók first summarized his joint collecting with Kodály in 1921 when he wrote *A magyar népdal* ('Hungarian Folk Song'), published in Hungarian in 1924. This fundamental handbook was based on over 8000 collected and systematized Hungarian melodies. Ten years later, after a thorough observation of the music of neighbouring countries, he wrote a detailed analytical account of the relationship between Hungarian folk music and that of neighbouring peoples, chiefly Slovak and Romanian *Népzenénk és azomszéd népek népzenéje* [Our Folk Music and that of Neighbouring Peoples] (1934; also B. Szabolcsi, ed., 1966, pp.403–61). In the atmosphere of Central and Eastern Europe of the 1930s which was not free from national bias, Bartók's scientific clear-sightedness and immovable objectivity enabled him to write a delicate work of great importance.

Kodály wrote his synthesis, *A magyar népzene* ('Hungarian Folk Music'), in

1937. This comprehensive work, issued in several editions and in foreign languages (English, German and Russian), covers the entire oral Hungarian musical tradition including music of folk customs and of instrumental performances. Besides presenting the various branches and strata of Hungarian folk music and their interrelationship, it also illuminates the most important links that connect Hungarian folk music organically with Hungarian and international culture: it remains the basic textbook of Hungarian folk music. According to a plan outlined in 1913, between 1934 and 1940 Bartók completed the editing of Hungarian folk melodies (about 14,000) collected up to that time on behalf of the Hungarian Academy of Sciences prepared for publication.

Characterizing ethnomusicology in Hungary early in the 20th century, Bartók stated in 1932:

> The present renaissance of ethno-musicology in Hungary differs from its parallels abroad in two basic points: (1) its participants are creative musicians who are doing their laborious task not with the attitude of a fastidious esthetician but with strict scientific methods and (2) their field of interest does not only cover Hungarian folk songs but folk songs of the neighbouring peoples as well (Szőllősy, ed., 1966, p.366).

In 1953 the Folk Music Research Group of the Hungarian Academy of Sciences was formed under Kodály's leadership. Since January 1974 this institution has continued its activities as the Folk Music Research Department of the Institute for Musicology, publishing among other things the *Corpus musicae popularis hungaricae*. The first volume of this collection, containing children's songs, appeared in 1951; the melodies are grouped according to pairs of bars (motifs), and the games that belong to the songs are also systematically arranged. About 25 volumes were projected, and seven had been completed by 1990. The first five contain songs connected with folk customs. From the sixth onwards, publication is in musical sequence: the editors have classified the melodies according to type, and the types follow each other according to their relationship and stylistic stratum. The publishing of a new general work on Hungarian folk songs (*A magyar népdaltípusok kalalógusa* [Catalogue of Hungarian folk-song types]), arranged according to styles and edited by László Dobszary and Janka Szendrei, was started in 1988.

The entire corpus of Hungarian folk music, with a few insignificant exceptions, is now in the archives of the Folk Music Research Department of the Institute for Musicology; the collection expanded rapidly, especially with the increased availability of recording facilities in the 1950s, and it now consists of between 100,000 and 150,000 melodies. In certain Hungarian-speaking areas (particularly Transylvania and Moldavia in Romania) it was still possible to record large quantities of archaic vocal and instrumental peasant music in the second half of the 20th century. Valuable material is also being gathered throughout Hungary, and in many cases this can substantially supplement and modify the picture of Hungarian folk music sketched by Kodály and Bartók.

The scholarly studies that have been carried out since 1950 have produced particularly significant results in the clarification of questions concerning the history of Hungarian folk music (by Rajeczky, Dobszary, Vargyas, Szendrei);

the systemization of folk music (Járdányi, Dobszary, Szendrei); and research into instrumental folk music (by Lajtha and Sárosi). Apart from the Institute for Musicology, the Ethnographical Museum in Budapest also conducts systematic research into folk music, chiefly by collecting. It holds most of the original phonograph recordings made before World War II (most of the recordings by Vikár, Bartók and Kodály etc), as well as the original transcriptions made from them. It also holds the only collection of Hungarian folk instruments that can be considered complete. Outside Hungary intensive research into folk music has been carried out notably by the Romanian Hungarians, especially in the 1950s, at the Cluj department of the Bucharest Folklore Institute under János Jagamas.

The first series of Hungarian folk music discs, the Patria series, began to be produced in Budapest in 1936. Under the original direction of Bartók and Kodály, and later of Lajtha, 250 discs in the series had been completed by the end of the 1950s. The first disc to be made with modern microgroove techniques for widespread distribution was issued in 1964 in honour of the conference of the International Folk Music Council held in Budapest; this disc was followed by three series, each consisting of four discs, edited by Rajeczky.

Modern Romanian ethnomusicology did not start with the explosiveness of the Hungarian. Its great personality, Constantin Brăiloiu (1893–1958), emerged more than 20 years after Bartók and Kodály. However, we cannot omit a significant observation: Bartók's first Transylvanian-Romanian collection was published in 1913 in Bucharest, prior to any Hungarian collections of similar gravity (Bartók, 1913).

The immediate predecessors of Brăiloiu were the composer Dimitrie Georgescu Kiriac, Brăiloiu's professor in Bucharest, and Tiberiu Brediceanu, a productive amateur folk-music collector in Transylvania. Their, for the most part, phonographic collections remained unpublished until the last half of the 20th century (see Brediceanu, 1957; Kinac, 1960).

Brăiloiu received a comprehensive musical education at home and abroad (Austria, Switzerland and Paris), thus starting ethnomusicological research with a thorough grounding. In 1928 he founded the Folklore Archives of the Society of Romanian Composers. This archive soon became one of the world's most modern workshops in ethnomusicology (see fig.2). In collaboration with the outstanding sociologists D. Gusti and H. Stahl, he adopted a method of collecting which is unsurpassed in thoroughness. He outlined his method in an essay published in 1931 in Bucharest and Paris, 'Esquisse d'une méthode de folklore musical' (Brăiloiu in Rouget, ed., 1973, pp.3–39). With his questionnaires fully worked out, with Edison phonograph, photo camera and even cinematograph, he was seeking to give answers to the questions: 'Que chante-t-on? Quand et où chante-t-on? Comment chante-t-on? Pourquoi chante-t-on comme on chante? D'où viennent les chansons? Comment naissent les chansons?' 'What is being sung? When and where is it sung? How is it sung? Why do they sing as they do? Where do the songs come from? How do the songs come into being?' (Brăiloiu, 1973, p.36). Around the 1930s Brăiloiu's main interest was in musical folklore customs: *colinda* (carol singing), wedding songs, and especially laments (e.g. Brăiloiu, 1967–81, i).

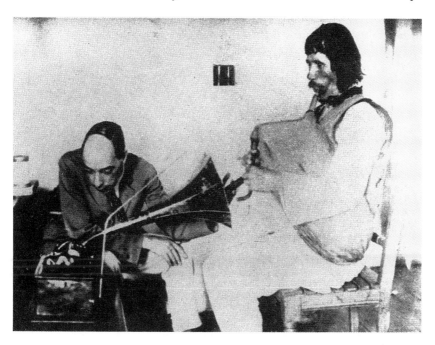

2. Constantin Brăiloiu recording a bagpiper during his first monographic collection for the Folklore Archives of the Society of Romanian Composers, Fundu-Moldovei, Suceava, 1928

In both Romania and Hungary the first half of the 20th century was the period of collecting according to scientific norms. The proliferation of the material and its preparation for publishing inevitably raised the question of classification, the more so since musically unsettled melodies cannot be compared. In their classification, Kodály and Bartók transposed the melodies to a common final tone and adopted with some modification the method of the Finn Ilmari Krohn, who regarded the final tone of the sections in a strophic structure as the distinguishing mark of the melody (cf. Bartók, 1924). Further methods of classification, among them that according to genres, were outlined by Bartók (in B. Suchoff, ed., 1967, i, 7; ii, 7).

Instrumental music, in particular that played by professional musicians, was rarely collected and studied except in the first volume of Bartók's *Romanian Folk Music* (Suchoff, ed., 1967).

As in the 19th century, folk music in the 20th century has been regarded as a focus and inspiring source of modern national music. Ethnomusicology, however, does not gain when the national mission of its subject is stressed.

Since 1949 the collection and study of Romanian folk music has been entrusted to a scientific institute – until 1963 the Institutul de folclor (Institute of Folklore), later the Institutul de etnografi și folclor (Institute of Ethnography and Folklore), then in the last two decades Institutul de cercetări etnologice și dialectologice (Institute of Ethnological and Dialectological Researches) – in Bucharest, where by the end of 1973 the collections

193

comprised approximately 100,000 items of musical folklore, recorded on cylinder, disc or magnetic tape.

Bibliography

Hungary: COLLECTIONS

K. Szini: *A magyar nép dalai és dallamai* [Songs and Tunes of the Hungarian Folk] (Pest, 1865)
I. Bartalus: *Magyar népdalok: egyetemes gyűjtemény* [Hungarian Folk Songs: a Universal Collection] (Budapest, 1873–96)
E. Limbay: *Magyar daltár* [Hungarian Song Collection] (Győr, 1879–88)
Á. Kiss: *Magyar gyermekjáték gyűjtemény* [Collection of Hungarian Children's Games] (Budapest, 1891)
B. Bartók: 'A hangszeres zene folkloreja Magyarországon' [Instrumental Musical Folklore in Hungary], *Zeneközlöny*, ix (1911), 141, 207, 309; x (1912), 601
——: 'A magyarnép hangszerei' [Hungarian Folk Instruments], *Ethnographia*, xxii (1911), 305; xxiii (1912), 110
——: 'Primitiv népi hangszerek *Magyarországon'* [Primitive Folk Instruments in Hungary], *Zenei szemle*, i (1917), 273, 311
—— and Z. Kodály: *Erdélyi magyarság: népdalok* [The Hungarians of Transylvania: Folk Songs] (Budapest, 1923; Fr. trans., 1925)
B. Bartók: *A magyar népdal* [Hungarian Folk Song] (Budapest, 1924/*R*1965; Eng. trans., 1931); repr. in Hung. and Ger. in Dille (1965–8)
P. P. Domokos: *Moldvai magyarság* [Hungarians of Moldavia] (Csiksomlyó, 1931)
G. Kerényi, ed.: *Gyermekjátékok* [Children's Games], *Corpus musicae popularis hungaricae*, i, ed. B. Bartók and Z. Kodály (Budapest, 1951)
D. Bartha and J. Kiss, eds.: *Ötödfélszáz énekek: Pálóczi Horváth Ádám dalgyűjteménye az 1813: évből* [450 Songs from Adam Páloczi Horvath's Collection of 1813] (Budapest, 1953)
G. Kerényi, ed.: *Jeles napok* [Tunes of the Calendar Customs], *Corpus musicae popularis hungaricae*, ii, ed. B. Bartók and Z. Kodály (Budapest, 1953)
Z. Kodály and Á. Gyulai, eds.: *Arany János népdalgyűjteménye* [The Folk Song Collection of János Arany] (Budapest, 1953)
L. Kiss, ed.: *Lakodalom* [Wedding Songs], *Corpus musicae popularis hungaricae*, iii, ed. B. Bartók and Z. Kodály (Budapest, 1955–6)
G. Kerényi, ed.: *Párosítók* [Matchmaking Songs], *Corpus musicae popularis hungaricae*, iv, ed. B. Bartók and Z. Kodály (Budapest, 1959)
D. Dille, ed.: *Bartók, Béla: Ethnomusikologische Schriften: Faksimile Nachdrucke* (Budapest, 1965–8)
B. Rajeczky and L. Kiss, eds.: *Siratók* [Laments], *Corpus musicae popularis hungaricae*, v, ed. B. Bartók and Z. Kodály (Budapest, 1966)
B. Rajeczky, ed.: 'Magyar népzene' [Hungarian Folk Music], Qualiton LPX 10095–8, 18001–4 [disc notes]
A. Szőllősy, ed.: *Bartók Béla összegyűjtött irásai* [The Collected Essays of B. Bartók], i [Budapest, 1966)
P. Járdányi and I. Olsvai, eds.: *Népdaltipusok* [Folk Song Types], *Corpus musicae popularis hungaricae*, vi and vii, ed. B. Bartók and Z. Kodály (Budapest, 1973–87)

STUDIES

B. Bartók: 'Az összehasonlító zenefolklore' [Comparative Musical Folklore], *Új élet népművelés*, i (1912), 109
——: 'The Relation of Folk-song to the Development of the Art Music of our Time', *The Sackbut*, ii (1921), 5
——: 'La musique populaire hongroise', *ReM*, ii/1 (1921), 8
——: 'The Folksongs of Hungary', *Pro musica* (1928), 28
——: 'Zenefolklore-kutatások Magyarországon' [Research on Hungarian Musical Folklore], *Zenei szemle*, xiii (1929), 13; rev. Fr. trans in *1er Congrès international des arts populaires: Prague 1928*, ii, 127

E. Major: *A népies magyar műzene és a népzene kapcsolatai* [The Relation of Popular Hungarian Composed Music to Folk Music] (Budapest, 1930); repr. in *Fejezetek a magyar zene történetéből* (Budapest, 1967)

B. Bartók: 'Cigányzene? Magyarzene? (Magyar népdalok a német zeneműpiacon)' [Gypsy Music? Hungarian Music? (On the Edition of Hungarian Folk Songs)], *Ethnographia*, xlii (1931), 49; Ger. trans., *Ungarische Jb*, xi (1931), 191

——: 'Mi a népzene? A parasztzene hatása az újabb műzenére: a népzene jelentőséről' [What is Folk Music? The Influence of Peasant Music on Contemporary Composition], *Új idők*, xxxvii (1931), 626, 718, 818; Ger. trans., abridged, *Mitteilungen der Österreichischen Musiklehrerschaft* (1932), no.2, p.6; no.3, p.5

——: 'Hungarian Peasant Music', *MQ*, xix (1933), 267

——: *Népzenénk és a szomszéd népek népzenéje* [The Folk Music of the Magyars and Neighbouring Peoples] (Budapest, 1934); Ger. trans., *Ungarische Jb*, xv (1935), 194–258; Fr. trans., *Archivum europae centro-orientalis*, ii (1936), 197–232 and i–xxxii

——: *Miért és hogyan gyüjtsünk népzenét? A zenei folklore trvénykönyve* [Why and How Do We Collect Folk Music?] (Budapest, 1936)

——: 'Nachwort zu dem "Volksmusik der Magyaren und der benachbarten Völker" – Antwort auf einen rumänischen Angriff', *Ungarische Jb*, xvi (1936), 276; Fr. trans., *Archivum europae centro-orientalis*, ii (1936), 233; Hung. orig., *Szép szó*, ii (1937), 263

——: 'Népdalkutatás és nacionalizmus' [Folksong Research and Nationalism], *Tükör*, v (1937), 166; Fr. and Ger. trans., *Revue internationale de musique*, i (1938), 608

——: 'Az úgynevezett bolgár ritmus' [The so-called Bulgarian Rhythm], *Énekszó*, v (1937–8), 537

Z. Kodály: *A magyar népzene* [Hungarian Folk Music] (Budapest, 1937, enl. 3/1952 by L. Vargyas, 6/1973; Eng. trans. 1960, rev., enl. 2/1971, 3/1982)

B. Bartók: 'Race Purity in Music', *MM*, xix/3–4 (1941–2), 153

L. Vargyas: *Áj falu zenei élete* [The Music of the Village of Aj] (Budapest, 1941)

P. Járdányi: *A Kidei magyarság világi zenéje* [The Secular Music of the Hungarians of Kide] (Kolozsvár, 1943)

Z. Kodály: 'A folklorista Bartók', *Uj zenei szemle*, i (1950), 33; Ger. trans., *Musik der Zeit* (1954), no. 9, p.33

C. Mason: 'Béla Bartók and Folksong', *MR*, xi (1950), 292

B. Suchoff, ed.: *Béla Bartók Essays* (London, 1976)

Romania: COLLECTIONS

P. Pirvescu: *Hora din Cartal: cu arii notate de C. M. Cordoneanu* (Bucharest, 1908)

B. Bartók: *Cîntece poporale românești din Comitatul Bihor (Ungaria)* [Romanian Folk Songs from the Bihor District] (Bucharest, 1913) [incl. Fr. summary]; repr. in *Béla Bartók: Ethnomusikologische Schriften: Faksimile Nachdrucke*, iii, ed. D. Dille (Budapest, 1967)

G. Fira: *Cîntece și hore* (Bucharest, 1916)

B. Bartók: 'A hunyadi román nép zenedialektusa' [The Folk Music Dialect of the Hunedoara Romanians], *Ethnographia*, xxv (1914), 108; Ger. trans., *ZMw*, ii (1919–20), 352

——: *Volkmusik der Rumänen von Maramureş* (Munich, 1923); repr. in *Béla Bartók: Ethnomusikologische Schriften: Faksimile Nachdrucke*, ii, ed. D. Dille (Budapest, 1966), and in *Béla Bartók: Rumanian Folk Music*, v, ed. B. Suchoff (The Hague, 1975)

S. V. Drăgoi: *303 colinde* (Craiova, 1930)

C. Brăiloiu: *Colinde și cîntece de stea* [*Colinde* and Star Songs] (Bucharest, 1931)

——: *Cîntece bătrînești din Oltenia, Muntenia, Moldova și Bucovina* [Ballads from Oltenia, Wallachia, Moldavia and Bukovina] (Bucharest, 1932)

B. Bartók: *Melodien der rumänischen Colinde (Weihnachtslieder)* (Vienna, 1935); repr. in *Béla Bartók: Ethnomusikologische Schriften: Faksimile Nachdrucke*, iv, ed. D. Dille (Budapest, 1968) [incl. texts] and in *Béla Bartók: Rumanian Folk Music*, iv, ed. B. Suchoff (The Hague, 1975)

C. Brăiloiu: *Ale mortului' din Gorj* ['The Songs of the Dead' from Gorj District] (Bucharest, 1936); also in *Mesures*, v/4 (1939), 85; repr. in *Constantin Brăiloiu: Opere*, v, ed. E. Comișel (Bucharest, 1981), 107

——, ed.: *G. Gucu: 200 colinde populare* (Bucharest, 1936)

I. Caranica: *130 de melodii populare aromânești* [130 Aromanian Folk Melodies] (Bucharest, 1937)

S. V. Drăgoi: *122 melodii populare din județul Caraş* [122 Folk Tunes from the Caraş District] (Bucharest, 1937)

C. Brăiloiu: *Bocete din Oaş* [Laments from Oaş] (Bucharest, 1938); repr. in *Constantin Brăiloiu: Opere*, v, ed. E. Comișel (Bucharest, 1981), 195

M. Friedwagner: *Rumänische Volkslieder aus der Bukowina*, i (Würzburg, 1940)

G. Ciobanu and V. D. Nicolescu: *200 cîntece şi doine* [200 Songs and Doine] (Bucharest, 1955, 2/1962)

G. Ciobanu, ed.: *Anton Pann: cîntece de lume* [Secular Songs] (Bucharest, 1955)

T. Brediceanu: *170 melodii populare româneşti din Maramure* (Bucharest, 1957)

D. G. Kiriac: *Cîntece populare româneşti* (Bucharest, 1960)

B. Suchoff, ed.: *Béla Bartók: Rumanian Folk Music* (The Hague, 1967–75)

BOOKS AND ARTICLES

G. Fira: *Nunta în judeţul Vilcea* [The Wedding in the Vilcea District] (Bucharest, 1928)

C. Brăiloiu: *Despre bocetul de la Drăguş (Jud. Făgăraş)* [On the Lament in the Village of Drăguş District)] (Bucharest, 1932) [incl. Fr. summary]; repr. in *Constantin Brăiloiu: Opere*, v, ed. E. Comişel (Bucharest, 1981), 115

C. Brăiloiu and H. H. Stahl: 'Vicleiul din Tîrgu-Jiu' [The Nativity Play from the Town of Tîrgu Jiu], *Sociologie românească* (1936), no.12, p.15

C. Brăiloiu: 'La musique populaire roumaine', *ReM* (1940), no.196, p.146

E. Riegler-Dinu: *Das rumänische Volkslied: eine musikwissenschaftliche Studie mit 162 Liederbeispielen und 2 Tabellen* (Berlin, 1940)

G. Breazul: *Patrium Carmen: contribuţii la studiul muzicii româneşti* (Craiova, 1941)

I. Cocişiu: 'Folclor muzical din judeţul Tîrnava Mare (Sighişoara, 1944), 393–492

C. Brăiloiu: 'Béla Bartók folkloriste', *SMz*, lxxxviii (1948), 92

T. Alexandru: *Béla Bartók despre folclorul românesc* [Bartók on Romanian Folklore] (Bucharest, 1958)

C. Brăiloiu: *Vie musicale d'un village: recherches sur le répertoire de Drăguş (Roumaine) 1929–1932* (Paris, 1960)

E. Comişel, ed.: *Constantin Brăiloiu: Opere* (Bucharest, 1967–81) [in Rom. and Fr.]

G. Rouget, ed.: *Constantin Brăiloiu: problèmes d'ethnomusicologie* (Geneva, 1973)

Bartók research outside Hungary and Romania

B. Bartók: 'A Biskra-vidéki arabok népzenéje' [The Folk Music of the Arabs of the Biskra Region], *Szimfónia*, i (1917), 308; Ger. trans., *ZMw*, ii (1919–20), 489–522

——: 'Népdalgyűjtes Tőrőkországban' [Collecting Folk Songs in Anatolia], *Nyugat*, iii (1937); Eng. trans., *Hungarian Quarterly*, iii (1937), 337

—— with A. B. Lord: *Serbo-Croatian Folk Songs* (New York, 1951)

B. Bartók: *Serbocroatian Heroic Songs*, i, ed. A. B. Lord (Cambridge, MA, and Belgrade, 1954)

——: *Slovenské l'udové piesne/Slowakische Volkslieder*, i–ii [Slovak Folk Songs], ed. O. and A. Elschek (Bratislava, 1959–70) [vol. iii unpubd]

B. Bartók: *Turkish Folk Music from Asia Minor*, ed. B. Suchoff (Princeton and London, 1976)

L. Vikár, ed.: *A. A. Saygun: Béla Bartók's Folk Music Research in Turkey* (Budapest, 1976)

CHAPTER V

Russia, the USSR and the Baltic States

MARGARITA MAZO

The study of traditional music in Russia and the USSR developed differently in various ethnic-cultural areas. Its early history can best be seen through short studies and published collections, and through examining what was collected and where, how it was presented, and which concerns were expressed by authors, compilers, observers and transcribers.

For logistical reasons, the Baltic republics have been included in this chapter, although they were not of course incorporated into the USSR until 1940.

RUSSIA, BELORUSSIA, UKRAINE   Early printed songbooks, starting in 1776 with a collection by Vasily Trutovsky, were addressed to the musically literate general public and did not pursue scientific goals. They included harmonizations of Russian and some Ukrainian (Malorossiikie) folk songs collected in St Petersburg and Moscow.

In 1790 the landmark collection by Nikolay Lvov and Ivan Prach appeared. Lvov's preface contained the first discussion in print of folk-song specifics; his classification of Russian songs by genre is still used. The publication of Kirsha Danilov's manuscript collection, the only record of mid-18th-century rural tradition, was historically important, although not representative of mainstream publications. A collection by Mikhail Maksimovich, dedicated solely to Ukrainian songs, appeared in 1834.

A new trend began in the early 1850s, when Mikhail Stakhovich, influenced by ideas of the young Russian nationalists, intentionally collected songs in villages and identified the regions of his work in the Central-Russian Orel, Tambov, Voronezh and Riazan' gubernii. Stakhovich realized that arrangements render village songs unrecognizable. As all earlier collectors, he presented songs traditionally sung *a cappella* with accompaniment for piano or guitar.

In St Petersburg during the mid-19th century, Prince V. Odoevsky and A. Serov sought to establish Russian folk song as a subject of scientific study, which they viewed as closely connected with ethnography, culture history, philology, and physiology. They considered only folk songs dating before Peter the Great as distinctly 'Russian'. Advocating the study of folk song according to its own parameters, and not by the standards of European music, they strove to 'translate' the modal and rhythmic properties of folk song into technical concepts which they related to ancient Greek theory. Odoevsky studied folk song concurrently with his research on Russian Orthodox chants (1867, 1871). Serov was more concerned with problems of harmonization and use of folk song by composers (1870–71).

In the 1860s and 1870s leading composers pioneered the collecting of folk music. Mily Balakirev, Nikolay Rimsky-Korsakov, Modest Musorgsky and Mykola Lysenko acknowledged folk songs decades before scholars considered them – Russian seasonal songs transcribed by Rimsky-Korsakov and Ukrainian *dumy* (traditional epic songs) collected by Lysenko. (Lysenko later published over 1000 Ukrainian songs and several studies.) The others were essentially interested in exploring folk songs as a source of new musical means. After the publication of Balakirev's collection (1866) the tasks of artistic arrangement and scholarly investigation of folk music became separated. Russian ethnographic publications focussed on choral polyphony, or part-singing, 'discovered' in peasant tradition. Yuly Melgunov and Nikolay Palchikov presented evidence of this phenomenon and published the first experiments in transcribing choral songs 'as they are sung by peasants'. Working independently in different regions, they reached similar conclusions: a folk chorus sings *a cappella*; each participant improvises his or her own variant of the melody; and only the aggregate of these melodic variants, which Melgunov called *podgoloski*, should be recognized as the song. Without experience in transcribing part-singing, they noted down the melodies from individual performers, a method that produced a distorted picture of the choral song. Melgunov attempted to combine the individual variants into a piano score; in search of scientific grounds for a satisfactory harmonization, he undertook a theoretical study of folk-song scale and rhythm. Palchikov organized his solo transcriptions in a table, noted in parallel, without harmonization. Palchikov's collection, gathered from one village, also represented new aims such as the growing interest in local musical dialects.

The 1889 collection by Nikolay Lopatin and Vasily Prokunin was the first effective collaboration of a philologist and a musician. It was also the first systematic study of one song category – lyric *protiazhnaia* long-drawn-out songs. Lopatin emphasized the coherence of song text and melody and analysed all known text variants of presented songs from different regions. Prokunin's piano arrangements endeavoured to imitate choral *podgoloski* as he had heard them in the field; he distinguished solo from choral variants.

A theoretical study of Russian and Ukrainian folk song, P. Sokalsky's monograph of 1888 was an attempt to understand the development of musical folklore as a coherent logical concept. He addressed a wide scope of problems: structural inseparability of song melody and text, notation that 'imprisons' the folk-song rhythm and intonation and common roots of Russian and Ukrainian folk song. Sokalsky viewed the development of song melodies in terms of three subsequent periods which he defined as epochs of the intervals of the 4th, the 5th and the 3rd. Historical studies on *skomorokhi* and folk instruments were published by Alexander Famintsyn.

Belorussian folk songs were published by Z. Radchenko (1881–1911) and P. Shein (1887–1902) and collections of Ukrainian songs by O. Hulak-Artemovsky (1868), A. Rubets (1872) and A. Konoshchenko (1900–2; southern Ukraine). Songs of Belorussia and Western Ukraine were collected mostly by Polish scholars M. Federowsky, Oskar Kolberg (1882–8, 1890, 1891) and Ludvík Kuba, the Czech (1933). (*See* Chapter III, 'Czechoslovakia', 'Poland'.)

Since the 1880s, the activities of collecting, studying and propagandizing folk music in concerts were organized under the aegis of scholarly institutions: the Song Commission (PK) of the Russian Geographic Society (RGO) in St Petersburg (1884; members: Terty I. Filippov, Mily Balakirev, Anatoly Lyadov, Sergey Lyapunov and others), Naukove tovarystvo im. Shevchenko and Polish Towarzystwo Iudoznaweze in Lvov (1895; members: Ivan Franko, Filaret Kolessa, V. Hnatyuk and others), and the larger interdisciplinary Music-Ethnographic Commission (MEK) of the Society of Supporters of Natural Sciences, Physical Anthropology and Ethnography (OLEAE) in Moscow (1901; almost 60 members, including N. Yanchuk, N. Melgunov, V. Paskhalov, A. Maslov, S. Taneev, E. Lineva, D. Arakchiev, M. Pyatnitsky, B. Yavorsky, M. Ippolitov-Ivanov and others). The periodicals *Zhivaya starina*, *Kievskaya starina*, *Lud*, *Zhite i slovo*, *Etnograficheskoe obozrenie*, as well as regular *Transactions* of the academic institutions, published materials on rituals, customs, beliefs, proverbs, legends as well as song texts, melodies and instrumental music. RGO expeditions of Fedor Istomin with Georgy Dyutsh (1886) and Lyapunov (1893) resulted in two well-documented collections of Russian traditional repertory, including funeral and wedding laments, in field transcriptions without any harmonization. Songs originating in urban tradition were excluded, even though, according to Istomin's report to the RGO, they occupied a considerable place in the local repertory.

The quest for a scientific approach in study and for precision in music notation was intensified with the invention of the phonograph. The first stationary recordings were made in Moscow by Blok around 1894 of the *byliny* (Russian epic songs) chanter Ivan Ryabinin, and in 1896 of the songs of and by Fedosova. In 1897 Irina Evgeniya Lineva was the first to make sound recordings in the field. MEK supported early phonographic field recordings of *byliny* in 1901 by A. Grigoriev (Arkhangel'sk district), A. Maslov, A. Markov, and V. Bogoslovsky (White Sea region), Don Cossacks part-singing by Alexander Listopadov in 1904, choral songs in the Voronezh district by Mitrofan Pyatnitsky, and also recordings in Georgia, Siberia, Belorussia and Ukraine. MEK issued five significant volumes on current research, collections, pedagogy, methodology of collecting, notation and analysis of folk music. These publications advanced knowledge on traditional culture: they included material on non-Russian peoples living in Imperial Russia; they also published transcriptions of street pedlars' cries. MEK publications had important scholarly and artistic consequences during the following decades.

Lineva recorded songs in the Central-Russian and Novgorod provinces (1897–1901) and Ukraine (1903), the Caucasus from the Russian Sectarians (1910), and in Austria-Hungary (1913); she also recorded an ensemble of wooden horn (*rozhok*) players from Vladimir. Her major publications were transcriptions of phonographically recorded Russian part- singing, where the *podgoloski*, for the first time, were reliably presented. Invaluable today are her reports on performers' behaviour and verbal expressions. Her notion of the 'variant type', understood as the basic melodic, modal and rhythmic structures common for all variants of a particular song, was picked up in later Soviet studies.

In Belorussia during the 1900s and 1910s, E. Romanov (1910), A. Hrinevič (1910) and Čurkin gathered valuable collections transcribed by ear. In Ukraine the phonograph was used in 1900 by O. Rozdolsky in Galitsiya and later in Bukovina, Lemkovshchina, Kholmshchina and Pridneprovie; Lyudkevich systematized part of Rozdolsky material according to rhythmic structures. In 1908 Filaret Kolessa, an influential Ukrainian musicologist, recorded *dumy* in Poltavshchina. Kolessa's most important research, carried on over the next decades, was on rhythm in Ukrainian song, Ukrainian musical dialects and their affinity with music of other Slavs, also on *dumy*, their folk origins and relations to laments.

After the 1917 Revolution numerous politically oriented editions of songs of the Revolution and the Civil War, and satirical *chastushki* (short topical songs) came out. The Association of Proletarian Musicians (RAPM, 1923–32) declared that traditional village music must be destroyed as harmful to proletarian ideology (see discussions on the role of folklore in *Literatura i Marksizm* [Literature and Marxism], May and June, 1931). Fortunately, opinions were not unanimous; the folk choruses of Pyatnitsky and Yarkov continued their concerts; instructions for local collectors were issued; recordings made in Moscow included traditional Russian repertory and also songs of Far Eastern peoples, participants of the All-Union Exhibition in 1923. Some archival material (F. Lagovsky) and documents unearthed by N. Findeizen were also published. Discussions in many articles and brochures by N. Briusova, L. Lebedinsky, A. Kastalsky, Nikolsky, Kulakovsky, A. Finagin and others centred on the connections of folk music with the 'culture of masses', folk music and composers, contemporary songs, also the social, administrative, educational and propaganda aspects of the study of traditional music.

The number of expeditions and publications during the 1930s is impressive though not all are reliable, as some 'folk songs' were concocted by collectors bent hard on the 'reflection of Soviet reality' in folk art.

Government scholarly institutions financed all research and fieldwork, including interdisciplinary expeditions in 1926 to Northern Russia, in 1932 to Belorussian Polesie and in 1937 to the Vologda region; collected material included not only traditional repertory but also songs of urban origin and *chastushki*. Scholars in Moscow and Leningrad became involved in recording and studying music of the non-Russian peoples of the USSR: Victor Paskhalov made recordings in Crimea, Zinaida Evald, Evgeny Gippius and Feodosy Rubtsov in Belorussia, Gippius in Armenia, Boris Galaev in Osetia, Danilin in the Altay and Lidiya Kershner in Buryatia. Sofiya Magid and particularly Moisei Beregovsky, of Ukraine, worked on Jewish music.

The fieldwork and research of Filaret Kolessov, Klyment Kvitka and Gippius established the standards of modern ethnomusicology in the USSR. Kvitka started collecting Ukrainian folksongs in 1896 and made more than 6000 recordings of folk music in Ukraine, South-Russia, Belorussia, Moldavia and Crimea. His research advanced comparative studies on the music of Slavic and neighbouring peoples. Kvitka advocated the examination of the geographical distribution of song types and structural and morphologic characteristics, particularly of songs related to rituals, regardless of administrative borders. Kvitka also initiated the investigation of instrumental music. In 1922 he organized the Bureau of Musical Ethnography of the Ukrainian Academy of Science, and in 1937 the Bureau on Study Musical Creation of Peoples of USSR at Moscow Conservatory.

Gippius's most important fieldwork was done during the 1926–30 expeditions along the North-Russian rivers, in collaboration with Evald (528 cylinders). Some of the Pinezhie material was published in transcriptions attempting to render the intonation and phonetics of the local dialect (1937). Gippius's research on musical dialects suggested a description of all local forms and genres prior to stylistic generalizations. The idea of the dependence of newly formed songs on distinctive 'tune-formulas' of local ritual songs was further developed by Evald on Belorussian material. Gippius's 1933 article addressed subject and methodology in the study of folk music, but with political overtones; he criticized Western ethnomusicological thought and considered a 'production-consumption' function of music in a society as a key problem. In 1926–7 Gippius organized the Music-Ethnographic Bureau at Leningrad Conservatory and the Phonogram-Archive (now the Phonogram-Archive of the Pushkin House, Institute of Russian Literature), where he assembled all available pre-revolutionary phonographic recordings.

Systematic collection of the folk music of other peoples living in pre-Revolutionary Russia, often initiated by major local composers, began around the 1870s; scholarly study did not start until the 1920s.

VOLGA-URAL PEOPLES   In the 1890s studies on the music of the Volga-Ural peoples were published notably by V. Moshkov (1893) and S. Rybakov (1894; 1897). In the 1880s and 1890s songs of the Tatars and Bashkirs were recorded on metal discs by Enikeev, Ovodov and later by S. Saifullin. The first significant publication of Mari songs by V. Vasiliev came out in 1919. In the 1920s S. Maksimov (1932), F. Pavlov (1927), Ilin and Vorobiev collected music of the Chuvashs; Tatar and Bashkir songs were collected (some phonographically) and studied by S. Gabyashi; also collections of Robert Lach, Alexander Zataevich (1933) and K. Gubaydulin's ('Pesni Kasimov-skikh tatar', 1935) unpublished manuscript (now in the Phonogram-Archiv of the Pushkin House in Leningrad) were important. Shortly before 1939 A. Eihenvald, A. Klyucharyov and V. Vinogradov began working on Tatar music.

ARMENIA   In Armenia, Erznik Ersnkyan, Xr. Kara-Murza and M. Ekmalyan started collecting in the 1880s; the most productive was Sogomon Komitas, who transcribed several thousands of specimens (mostly in Armenian neume notation, *khaz*) which represented all dialects and forms of traditional music, including ancient agricultural songs and improvisations of *gusan* (traditional professional musician, simultaneously singer, narrator and instrumentalist). Komitas also made the first transcriptions of Kurdish songs. From 1913–30 S. Melikyan recorded phonographically more than 1000 songs, solely in villages. Scholarly expeditions (Kushnaryov, Gippius, Evald, Ter-Ovanesyan) were organized from 1927–9.

GEORGIA   In Georgia A. Benashvili (1886), Z. Chkhikvadze (1896), and I. Kargareteli (1899–1909) published first collections of vocal and instrumental music in arrangements. The use of the phonograph by D. Arakishvili (Arakchiev) since 1901 and in some field trips by Z. Paliashvili allowed an accurate presentation ofcomplex part-singing in distinct local forms. Arakishvili also initiated study of the history and specifics of Georgian music (1906, 1911, 1913, 1916). Starting in 1907, the British *Gramophone* opened its office in Tiflis and issued several commercial recordings of traditional music of various peoples from the Transcaucasus.

AZERBAIJAN   The first published collection in Azerbaijan (1927) included mostly arrangements by U. Hajibeyov and M. Magomaev, who started transcriptions by ear at the end of the 1890s. In 1910–1912, the London firms *Gramophone* and *Sport Record* recorded the famous musicians D. Kariyagdy, Primov and others. Expeditions of the Azerbaijan Conservatory (1932–1939) recorded folk and classic repertory in Shusha, Nukha, Kirovabad and some regions of Armenia and Georgia. Many *ashugs* (folk poets and singers) were also recorded during olympiads and conventions of folk musicians in Baku.

CENTRAL ASIA   In Central Asia during the 1870s and 1880s the Russian military musicians Leisek, Pfennig and particularly Alexander Eichhorn initiated the collection and harmonizations of traditional melodies (Eichhorn, 1885). S. Rybakov published a description of Kazakh songs in 1897, and Zarubin gathered an outstanding collection of Pamir musical instruments in 1914. More thorough collecting began in the 1920s by Nikolay Mironov (1931, 1932; Uzbek and Tajik music), Alexander Zataevich (1931, Kazakh; 1934, Kirghiz; and 1933 Kazakhstan Tatar), and Victor Uspensky (Turkmen, Uzbek and Kirghiz). Elena Romanovskaya joined the field in the 1930s. All notated by ear. They gathered thousands of folk and classic specimens, including the entire cycle of Bukhara *shashmaqom* (six *magoms*) transcribed by Uspensky. The research on the music cultures of Central Asia was originated by Victor Belyaev; most influential was his *Turkmenskaya muzyka* (1928) based on Uspensky's transcriptions.

BALTIC STATES   Research was most active in the Baltic areas. During the 1870s, national Song Festivals in Estonia and Latvia stimulated folk-song collecting and publication in choral arrangements (K. Hermann, Jānis Cimze). In Latvia, Andrejs Jurjāns gathered a sizeable folk-song collection, starting in the late 1880s; a major collector from the 1920s to the 1940s was Emīlis Melngailis. Significant collections and studies on Lithuanian music were published by A. Juškevičius (1883), C. Bartsch (1886–9), O. Kolberg (1879) and A. Sabaliauskas (1916). The initial scholarly studies by K. Launis and Bartsch were picked up in the 1920s and 1930s, and were particularly fruitful for continuing research (Launis, A. Väisänen, T. Brazys, J. Graubiņš, Z. Slaviūnas and others) and were carried further by a new generation of ethnomusicologists (H. Tampere, J. Vītoliņš and J. Čiurlionytė).

Bibliography

Armenia

S. Komitas: *Shar Akna zhoghovrdakan ergeri* [Folk Songs from Akn Region] (Vagharshapat, 1895) [In Armenian notation]

V. Korganov: *Kavkazskaya muzyka* [Caucasian Music] (Tbilisi, 1900)

S. Komitas: 'La musique rustique arménienne', *BSIM*, iii (1907)

S. Demuryan: *K'nar* (St Petersburg, 1908) [A Collection of Armenian Songs in European Notation]

S. Melikyan: *Shiraki erger* [Songs from Shirak] (Tbilisi, 1917) [collected in collaboration with A. Ter-Ghevondyan]

S. Komitas: *Hay zhoghovrdakan erazhshut'yun/Musique populaire arménienne*, new ser., i-vii (Paris, 1925–37)

S. Melikyan and G. Gardashyan: *Vana zhoghovrdakan erger* [Folk Songs from Van] (Tbilisi, 1927–8)

S. Komitas: 'Zhoghovrdakan erger' [Folk Songs], *Etnografichesky sbornik*, i (Erevan, 1931) [special issue]

S. Melikyan: *Urvagids hay erazhshtut'yan patmut'yan* [An Outline History of Armenian Music] (Erevan, 1935)

S. Komitas: *Hay geghdjuk erazhshtut'yan* [Armenian Peasant Music] (Paris, 1938)

A. Koch'aryan: *Armyanskaya narodnaya muzyka* [Armenian Folk Music] (Moscow, 1938)

S. Melikyan: *Hay zhoghovrdakan erger ev parerger* [Armenian Folk Songs and Dances] (Erevan, 1949–52)

S. Komitas: 'Hay zhoghovrdakan erger ev parerger' [Armenian Folk Songs and Dances], *Etnografichesky sbornik*, ii (Erevan, 1950) [special issue]

——: *Sobranie sochineniy* [Collected Works], ed. R. Atayan (Erevan, 1960–69)

Azerbaijan

P. Vostrikov: 'Muzyka i pesnya u azerbaydjanskikh tatar' [Music and Song of Azerbaijani Tatars], *Sbornik materialov dlya opisaniya mestnostey i plemyon Kavkaza*, xlii (1912)

U. Hajibeyov and M. Magomaev: *Azerbayjanskie tyurkskie narodnye pesni* [Azerbaijani Turkic Folk Songs] (Baku, 1927)

T. Kuliev and Z. Bagirov: *Rast dastgakhy zabit dastgakhy, dugiakh dastgakhy*, 3 parts (Baku, 1936) [Three Complete *mugams* Sung by Mansur Mansurov, Transcribed by T. Kuliev (1, 2) and Z. Basgirov (3), and Arranged for Piano by L. Rudolf]

V. Krivonosov: 'Ashugi Azerbaydjana' [The *Ashugs* of Azerbaijan], *SovM* (April, 1938)

S. Rustamov, ed.: *50 azerbaidjanskikh narodnykh pesen* [50 Azerbaijani Folk Songs] (Baku, 1938) [Songs of D. Kariyagdy Transcribed from Phonograph Cylinders, no Harmonization]

——: *Azerbaidjanskie ashugskie pesni* [Songs of Azerbaijani *Ashug*] (Baku, 1938) [transcriptions from voice and *saz*, no harmonization]

V. Vinogradov: *Useir Gadzhibekov i azerbaidzhanskaya muzyka* [Uzeir Gajibekov and Azerbaijani Music] (Moscow, 1938)

V. Krivonosov: 'Pesni Dzhabbara Kariyagdy' [Songs of D. Kariyagdy), *SovM*, ii (1940)

I. Sviridova: 'Iz istorii zapisey i publikatsiy Azebaydzhanskogo muzykal'nogo folklora' [From a History of Collection and Publications of Azerbaijani Musical Folklore], *Muzykal'naya folkloristika*, i, ed. A. Banin (Moscow, 1973), 189

Belorussia

Z. Radchenko: *Sbornik malorusskikh i belorussikikh narodnykh pesen (Gomel'skogo uezda). Zapisannye dlya golosa s akkompanementom fortep'yano Zinaidoy Radchenko* [A Collection of Ukrainian and Belorussian Folk Songs (Gomel' district). Transcribed for Voice and Piano by Z. Radchenko] (St Petersburg, 1881–1911)

P. Shein: *Materialy dlya izycheniya byta i yazyka russkogo naseleniya Severo-Zapadnogo kraya* [Material for Study on Everyday Life and Language of the Russian Population of the Northwest], *Sbornik Otdeleniya russkogo yazyka i slovesnisti Akademii nauk*, xli (1887), no.3; li (1890), no.3; lvii (1893), lxxii; (1902), no.4 (St Petersburg) [melodies only in i, ii]

O. Kolberg, 'Zwyczaje i obrze.dy weselne z Polesia. Podal Oskar Kolberg' [Wedding Customs and Rituals in Polesie], in *Zbior wiadomosci do antropologii krajowej*, xiii (Kraków, 1889)

A. Černy: *Pieśni białoruskie z powiatu Dzisnienskiego, gubernii Wileńskij* [Belorussian Songs from the Vilna Province] (Kraków, 1894)

E. Romanov: 'Belorusskie narodnye melodii' [Belorussian Folk Melodies], *Belorusskiy sbornik E. P. Romanova*, vii (Vilna, 1910)

A. Hrinevič: *Bielarusskije pieśni z notami. Sabrau i wydau A. Hryniewič* [Belorussian Songs with Music, Collected and Published by A. Hrinevič], i (St Petersburg, 1910); ii, *Bielarusskije pieśni z notami. Sabrali A. Hryniewič i A. Zyazyula* [Belorussian Songs with Music. Collected by A. Hrinevič and A. Zyazyula] (St Petersburg, 1912)

A. Egoray: 'Narodnyya pesni z melyodyyami' [Folk Songs with Melodies], *Bielaruskaya etnagrafiya u dosledakh i materyyalakh*, iv (Minsk, 1928)

I. Zdanovich: *Narodnye pesni Zapadnoy Belorussii* [Folk Songs of West Belorussia] (Moscow, 1931)

L. Kuba: *Cesty za slovanskou pisni. Svazek prvy. Slovansky zapad a vychod* [Journeys after the Slavic Song] (Prague, 1933–5, 2/1953)

Z. Evald: 'Sotsial'noe pereosmyslenie zhnivnykh pesen Belorusskogo Polesiya', *Sovetskaya etnografiya*, v (1934), 17; Ger. trans. by Z. V. Evald as 'Die soziale Umdeutung von Ernteliedern im belorussischen Polesie', *Sowjetische Volkslied- und Volksmusikforschung* (Berlin, 1967)

B. Gawronska: *Pieśni ludowe ziemi Wilensiej i Nowogródzkiej* [Folk Songs of the Vilno and Nowogrud Regions] (Vilnius, 1935)

Z. Evald, ed.: *Belorusskie narodnye pesni* [Belorussian Folk Songs], series *Pesni narodov SSSR*, ed. E. Gippius (Moscow, 1941) [in addition to folk songs, included articles by E. Gippius and Z. Evald, 'Zamechaniya o belorusskoi narodnoy pesne' [Observations on the Belorussian Folk Song]; K. Kvitka, 'Ob oblastyakh rasprostraneniya nekotorykh tipov Belorusskikh kalendarnykh i svadebnykh pesen' [On the Regions of Distribution of Certain Types of Belorussian Calendar and Wedding Songs]; V. Belyaev, 'Spravka o belorusskikh narodnykh muzykalnykh instrumentakh' [Information on Belorussian Folk Musical Instruments]]

V. Belyaev: *Belorusskaya narodnaya muzyka* [Belorussian Folk Music] (Leningrad, 1941)

M. Federowski: *Materialy do etnografij slowianskiej zgromadzone w latach 1877–1905* [Slavic Ethnographical Materials Collected 1877–1905] (Warsaw, 1958–69)

Central Asia

A. Eichhorn: *Polnaya kollektsiya muzykal'nykh instrumentov narodov Tsentral'noy Azii* [A Complete Collection of Musical Instruments of the Peoples of Central Asia] (St Petersburg, 1885) [A Catalogue of the Instruments Sent by Eichhorn to the 1885 International Exhibition; present whereabouts of the collection unknown]

S. Rybakov: *Muzyka i pesni ural'skikh musul'man s ocherkom ikh byta* [Music and Songs of the Ural Muslims with an Essay on Their Everyday Life] (St Petersburg, 1897)

V. Uspensky: *Shest' muzykalnykh poem (maqom)* [Six Musical Poems (*maqom*)] (Bukhara, 1924)

A. Zataevich: *1000 pesen kirgizskogo naroda* [1000 songs of Kirghiz People] (Orenburg, 1925, 2/1963)

V. Belyaev and V. Uspensky: *Turkmenskaya muzyka* [Turkmenian Music], i (Moscow, 1928) [ii not pubd]

N. Mironov: *Muzyka uzbekov* [The Music of the Uzbeks] (Moscow, 1929)

——: *Pesni Fergany, Bukhary i Khivy* [Songs of the Fergana, Bukhara and Khivy] (Moscow, 1931)

A. Zataevich: *500 kazakhskikh pesen i kyuyev* [500 Kazakh Songs and Instrumental Compositions] (Alma-Ata, 1931)

N. Mironov: *Obzor muzykalnykh kul'tur uzbekov i drugikh narodov Vostoka* [A Survey of Music Cultures of the Uzbeks and Other Eastern Peoples] (Samarkand, 1931)

——: *Musyka tadjikov* [The Music of the Tadzhiks] [musical-ethnographic material collected and written down at the first All-Tajik convention of singers, musicians and dancers in Stalinabad] (Stalinabad, 1932)

A. Zataevich: *Pesni kazakhstanskikh tatar* [Songs of the Kazakhstan Tatars] (Moscow, 1933)

V. Belyaev: *Musykal'nye instrumenty Uzbekistana* [Musical Instruments of Uzbekistan] (Moscow, 1933)

A. Zataevich: *250 kirgizskikh instrumental'nykh p'es i napevov* [250 Kirgiz Instrumental Pieces and Melodies] (Moscow, 1934; rev. 2/1971)

V. Belyaev: 'Formy uzbekskoy muzyki' [Form in Uzbek Music], *SovM*, vii–viii (1935)

E. Romanovskaya: *Khoresmskaya klassicheskaya muzyka* [Khoresmian Classic Music] (Tashkent, 1939)

E. Romanovskaya and I. Akbarov, eds.: *Uzbekskie narodnye pesni* [Uzbek Folk Songs] (Tashkent, 1939) [in Uzbek]

E. Alekseev: 'O dvukh tomakh "Turkmenskoy muzyki" i eye avtorakh' [About Two Volumes of

204

Turkmenskaya muzyka and its Authors], *SovM*, x (1973), 29–37
M. Slobin: *Music of Central Asia and the Volga-Ural Peoples: Teaching Aids for the Study of Inner Asia*, v (Bloomington, IN)
T. Solomonova: 'Muzykalnaya folkloristika i muzykovedenie (obozrenie)' [Ethnomusicology and Musicology (an Overview)], *Muzykalnaya kul'tura Uzbekskoy SSR* (Moscow, 1981), 310

Estonia

K. Hermann: *Über estnische Volksweisen* (Dorpat, 1891)
O. Kallas: *Lutsi maarahvas* [Country Folk from Lutsi] (Helsinki, 1894)
A. Launis: *Über Art, Entstehung und Verbreitung der estnischfinnischen Runenmelodien* (Helsinki, 1910)
A. Väisänen: 'Eesti rahva vana laulumuusika' [Old Estonian Folk Songs], *Odamees* (Tartu, 1923)
——: 'Seto lauluaale' ja manguriista' [Songs and Instruments of the Setos], *Kodotulo'* (Tartu, 1924)
K. Launis: *Eesti runoviisid* [Runic Estonian Melodies] (Tartu, 1930)
H. Tampere: 'Tahelepanekuid rahvaviisidest ja rahvalaulude ettekandmisest lounapoolses Laane- Eestis' [Observations on Folk Melodies and Performance of Folk Songs in the South Part of Eastern Estonia], *Kultuuri ja teaduse teilt* (Tartu, 1932); Russ. trans., H. Tampere, *Estonskaya narodnaya pesnya*, ed. I. Rüütel (Leningrad, 1983)
E. Arro: *Geschichte der estonischen Musik*, i (Tartu, 1933)
J. Zeiger: *Eesti rahvaviisid* [Estonian Folk Melodies] (Tallin, 1934)
H. Tampere: 'Moningaid motteid eesti rahvaviisist ja selle uurimismeetodist' [Observations on Estonian Folk Melody and Methods of its Analysis], *Eesti Muusika Almanak*, i (Tallin, 1934); Russ. trans., H. Tampere, *Estonskaya narodnaya pesnya*, ed. I. Rüütel (Leningrad, 1983)
——: *Eesti rahvaviiside antologia* [Anthology of Estonian Folk Songs] (Tallin, 1935); [the major part of the preface in Russ. trans., H. Tampere, *Estonskaya narodnaya pesnya*, ed. I. Rüütel (Leningrad, 1983)]
——: 'Tekstimuutusi eesti rahvalaulude ettekandmisel' [Text Changes in Performance of Estonian songs], *Opetatud Eesti seltsi kirjad*, iii (Tartu, 1935); Russ. trans., H. Tampere, *Estonskaya narodnaya pesnya*, ed. I. Rüütel (Leningrad, 1983)
O. Loorits: *Volkslieder der Liven* (Tartu, 1936)
H. Tampere: 'Über das Problem des Rhythmus im alten estnischen Volkslied', *Acta Ethnologica* (1937), in Estonian, 'Eesti rahvalaulu rutmiprobleemist', *Looming* (1937); Russ. trans., H. Tampere, *Estonskaya narodnaya pesnya*, ed. I. Rüütel (Leningrad, 1983)
R. Põldmäe: H. Tampere, *Valimik eesti rahvatantse* [Collection of Estonian Folk Dances] (Tartu, 1938) [Ger. summary]
H. Tampere: 'Kuusalu vanad rahvalaulud' [Old Folk Songs from Kuusalu], *Vana kannel*, iii (Tallin, 1938)

Georgia

A. Benashvili: *Kartuli khmebi* [Georgian Songs] (Tbilisi, 1886) [in Georgian]
K. Grozdov: *Mingrel'skie narodnye pesni* [Folk Songs from Mengrelia] (Tbilisi, 1894)
M. Ippolitov-Ivanov: 'Gruzinskaya narodnaya pesnya i eye sovremennoe sostoyanie' [Georgian Folk Song and its Modern Stage], *Artist*, i/5 (1894)
Z. Chkhikvadze: *Salamuri* [Georgian Flute] (Tbilisi, 1896) [in Georgian]
I. Kargareteli: *Kartuli sakhlkho simgerebi* [Georgian Folk Songs] (Tbilisi, 1899–1909) [in Georgian]
F. Koridze: *Mitsvalebulis sagalobelni* [The Melodies of Laments] (Tbilisi, 1899)
D. Arakchiev [Arakishvili]: 'Kratkiy ocherk razvitiya gruzinskoy, kartalino-kakhetinskoi, narodnoy pesni' [A Brief Essay on the Development of Georgian Kartalin-Kakhetin Folk Song], *Trudy MEK*, i (Moscow, 1906), 269–344
Z. Paliashvili [Paliev]: *Kartuli khalkhuri simgerebi* [Georgian Folk Songs] (Tbilisi, 1910) [in Georgian] [Contained 40 songs, other transcriptions of Paliashvili are most probably lost]
D. Arakcheev [Arakishvili]: 'Sravnitel'nyi obzor narodnoi pesni i myzykal'nykh instrumentov Zapadnoi Gruzii (Imeretii)' [A Comparative Survey of Folk Song and Music Instruments of West Georgia (Imeretia)], *Trudy MEK*, ii (Moscow, 1911), 119–203
——: 'Gruzinskoe narodnoe muzykal'noe tvorchestvo', *Trudy MEK*, v (Moscow, 1916)
V. Belyaev: 'The Folk-Music of Georgia', *MQ*, xix (1933), 417
S. Nadel: *Georgische Gesänge* (Berlin, 1933)
A. Partskhaladze: *Acharis khalkhuri tsekva da simgera* [Adjarian Folk Dance and Song] (Batumi, 1936)
I. Djavakhishvili: *Kartuli musikis istoriis dziritadi sakithkhebi* [Basic Questions of the History of Georgian Music] (Tbilisi, 1938) [in Georgian]

Latvia

J. Cimze: *Dziesmu rota* [Garland of Songs] (Riga, 1872–1884) [arrangements for four-voice chorus]

E. Vinger: *Latvia* (Riga, 1873–74) [arrangements for male chorus]

A. Jurjāns: *Latviešu tautas mūzikas materiāli* [Materials on Latvian Folk Music] (Riga, 1894–1926)

A. Bielenstein: *Die Holzbanten und Holzgeräte det Letten*, ii (Petrograd, 1918)

J. Vītoliņš: *200 Latviu tautas dziesmas klavieru pavadijumā* [200 Latvian Folk Songs with Piano Accompaniment] (Riga, 1919)

E. Melngailis: *Birzes un noras* [Forests and Fields] (Riga, 1902–57) [arrangements of Latvian folk songs for vocal and instrumental ensembles, voice and piano]

J. Rinka and J. Ošs: *Latvju tautas dejas* [Latvian Folk Dances] (Riga, 1934–6)

J. Graubiņš: 'Latviešu tautas dziesmu mūzika' [The Music of Latvian Folk Song], *Latviesu literatūras vēsture*, i (Riga, 1935)

——: *Talsu novada tautas melodijas* [Folk Melodies from Talsi] (Riga, 1935)

E. Siliņa: *Latviešu deja* [The Latvian Dance] (Riga, 1939)

A. Jurjāns: *Kopotas driesmas* [A Collection of Songs] (Riga, 1939)

E. Melngailis: *Latviešu mūzikas folkloras materiāli* [Latvian Folk Music Material] (Riga, 1951–3) [4345 melodies, 1000 collected in 1940–41]

E. Vitolin [J. Vītoliņš]: 'Latyshskoe narodnoe muzykal'noe tvorchestvo (sobiranie, publikatsii, issledovaniya)' [Latvian Folk Music (the Collection, Publication, and Research)], *Muzykalnaya kul'tura Latviiskoy SSR* (Moscow, 1976), 90

Lithuania

O. Kolberg: *Piesni ludu litewskiego* [Folk Songs of the Lithuanian People] (Kraków, 1879)

C. Bartsch: 'Über das litauische Volklieed oder die Daina', *Mitteilingen der litauischen literischen Gesellschaft*, i/4 (Köningsberg, 1881)

A. Juškevičius [Juška]: *Lietuviškos švotbines dajnos uzrašytos par Antano Juškeviče ir isspaudintos par Jona Juškevič* [Lithuanian Wedding Songs Transcribed by A. Juškevičius and Printed by J. Juškevičius] (Moscow, 1883)

C. Bartsch: *Dainŭ Balsai. Melodien litauischer Volkslieder* (Heidelberg, 1886–9)

A. Juškevičius [Juška]: *Melodie ludowe litewskie, zebrane przez s. p. Antoniego Juszkiewicza* [Lithuanian Folk Melodies Collected by A. Juškevičius] (Kraków, 1900)

A. Niemiy and A. Sabaliauskas: *Lietuvių dainos ir giesmēs šiaurytineje Lietuvoje* [Lithuanian Songs and sutartines of Southeastern Lithuania] (Helsinki, 1912)

A. Sabaliauskas: *Lietuvių dainų ir giesmių gaidos* [Melodies of Lithuanian Songs and Choral *Gaidos*] (Helsinki, 1916)

C. Sachs: 'Die litauischen Musikihstrumente in der Königl', *Sammlung für deutsche Volkskunde zu Berlin. Internationales Archiv für Ethnographie*, xxiii (1916), 1

T. Brazys: *Apie tatutinēs lietuvių dainų gaidas* [About Collections of Lithuanian Folk Songs] (Tilže, 1920)

——: 'Lietuvių liaudies daina vestuvēse' [Lithuanian Wedding Folk Songs], *Tauta ir žodis*, ii (Kaunas, 1924)

——: 'Die Singweisen der litauischen Dainos', *Tauta ir žodis*, iv (1926)

——: *Lietuvių tautinių dainų melodijos* [Melodies of Lithuanian Folk Songs] (Kaunas, 1927)

B. Scruoga: 'Lithuanian Folk Songs', *Folklore*, xliii (1932), 301–37

J. Balys: 'Lithuanian Folk Dance', *JEFDSS*, ii (1935)

J. Zilevičius: 'Native Lithuanian Musical Instruments', *MQ*, xxi (1935), 99

Z. Slaviūnas: 'Lietuvių kankles' [Lithuanian *kankles*], *Tautosakos darbai*, iii (1937), 244–318 [Summary in Eng.]

J. Čiurlionytė: 'Lietuvių liaudies melodijos' [Lithuanian Folk Melodies], *Tautosakos darbai*, v (1938) [350 melodies]

Z. Slaviūnas: 'Lietuvių etnografines muzikos bibliografija' [Lithuanian Ethnography-Musical Bibliography], *Tautosakos darbai*, v (1938)

A. Paterson: *Old Lithuanian Songs* (Kaunas, 1939)

J. Čiurlionytė: *Litovskoe narodnoe pesennoe tvorchestvo* [Lithuanian Folk Song] (Moscow, 1966)

Russia

V. Trutovsky: *Sobranie russkikh prostykh pesen s notami* [Collection of Russian Simple Songs with Music] (St Petersburg, 1776–95, 2/1953)

N. Lvov and I. Prach: *Sobranie Russkikh narodnykh pesen s ikh golosami. Na muzyku polozhil Ivan Prach* [Collection of Russian Folk Songs with Their Tunes. Set to Music by I. Prach] (St Petersburg,

1790; enl. 2/1806; 5/1955) [facsimile of 2nd edn. with English introduction and appx. by M. Mazo (Ann Arbor, MI, 1987)]

K. Danilov: *Drevnie Rossiiskie stikhotvoreniya sobrannye Kirsheyu Danilovym* [Old Russian Poems Collected by Kirsha Danilov] (Moscow, 1804) [texts only]; 2/*Drevnie Rossiiskie stikhotvoreniya sobrannye Kirsheyu Danilovym i vtorichno izdannye s pribavleniem 35 pesen i skazok, dosele neizvestnykh* (2/1818) [with melodies ed. D. Sprevits]

I. Rupin: *Narodnye russkie pesni arranzhirovannye dlya golosa i khorov s akkompanementom fortepiano . . . Ivan Rupini* [Russian Folk Songs Arranged for Voice and Chorus with Piano Accompaniment], 2 parts (St Petersburg, 1831–3, rev. 3/1955)

M. Stakhovich: *Sobranie russkikh narodnyke pesen. Tekst i melodii sobral i muzyku aranzhiroval dlya fortepiano i semistrunnoy gitary Mikhail Stakhovich* [Collection of Russian Folk Songs. Texts and Melodies Collected and Arranged for the Piano, and for Seven-String Guitar by M. Stakhovich] (St Petersburg, 1851–4, 2/1964)

M. Balakirev: *Sbornik Russkikh narodnykh pesen sostavlennyi M. Balakirevym* [A Collection of Russian Folk Songs Compiled by Balakirev] (St Petersburg, 1866) [for voice and piano]; rev. M. Balakirev, *Russkie narodnye pesni dlya odnogo golosa s soprovozhdeniem fortepiano* [Russian Folk Songs for Voice and Piano], ed. with the preface, research and comments by E. V. Gippius (Moscow, 1957)

V. Odoevsky: 'Russkaya i tak nazyvaemaya obshchaya muzyka' [Russian and So-called General Music], *Russkiy* (1867); repr. in *Muzykal'no-literaturnoe nasledie* (Moscow, 1956), 318

A. Serov: 'Russkaya narodnaya pesnya kak predmet nauki' [Russian Folk Song as a subject of Science], *Muzykal'nyi sezon* (1870–71), vi, xiii; repr. in *Izbrannye stat'i*, i (Moscow, 1950), 81

V. Odoevsky: 'Voprosy predlozhennye k obsuzhdeniyu na s'ezde' [Problems Suggested for a Discussion on the (first archaeological) Convention], *Trudy Pervogo arkheologischeskogo s'ezda v Moskve, 1869 g.*, i (Moscow, 1871)

———: 'Mirskaya pesnya napisannaya na vosem' glasov kryukami s kinovarnymi pometami' [A Folk Song written in Eight *Glasy* by *Kryuki* with Cinnabar], *Trudy Pervogo arkheologicheskogo s'ezda v Moskve, 1869 g.*, ii (Moscow, 1871), 484; repr. in *Muzykal'no-literaturnoe nasledie* (Moscow, 1956), 371

V. Prokunin, *Pesni dlya odnogo golosa s soprovozhdeniem fortepiano, sobrannye i perelozhennye Prokuninym, pod redaktsiey professora, P. Tchaikovskogo* [Songs for One Voice and Piano, collected by Prokunin, edited by Prof. Tchaikovsky] (Moscow, 1872)

N. Rimsky-Korsakov: *Sbornik russkikh narodnykh pesen, Op. 24* [A Collection of Russian Folk Songs] (St Petersburg, 1876–7) [for voice and piano]

F. Lagovsky: *Narodnye pesni Kostromskoy, Vologodskoy, Novgorodskoy, Nizhegorodskoy i Yaroslavskoy guberniy sobrannye i polozhennye na noty uchitelem peniya pri Cherepovetskom tehhnicheskom uchilishchaa Lagovskim* [Folk Songs of the Kostroma, Vologda, Novgorod, Nizhniy Novgorod, and Yaroslavl' *Gubernii*, Collected and Transcribed by a Voice Teacher at Cherepovets Technical Vocational School Lagovsky], i (Cherepovets, 1877) [first publication of Russian folk songs without harmonization]; ii in *Trudy Kostromskogo nauchnogo obshchestva po izucheniyu mestnogo kraya* (Kostroma, 1923)

N. Rimsky-Korsakov: *40 russkikh narodnykh pesen sobrannykh T. I. Filippovym i garmonizovannykh N. A. Rimskim-Korsakovym* [40 Russian Folk Songs Collected by Filippov and Harmonized by Rimsky-Korsakov] (Moscow, 1882) [songs transcribed from Filippov's singing and arranged for voice and piano by Rimsky-Korsakov]

Y. Melgunov: *Russkie narodnye pesni neprosredstvenno s golosov naroda zapisannye i s ob'yasneniyami izdannye Yu. N. Melgunovym* [Russian Folk Songs Written Down Directly from People's Voices and with Explanations Published by Y. Melgunov] (Moscow, 1879–85) [arranged for piano by N. Klenovsky and P. Blaramberg]

N. Palchikov: *Krest'yanskie pesni zapisannye v sele Nilolaevka Menzelinskogo yez'da Ufimskoy gubernii N. Palchikovym* [Peasant Songs Written Down by N. Pal'chikov in the Village Nikolaevka, Menzelinsk District of the Ufa *Guberniya*] (St Petersburg, 1888) [songs collected in one village over the period of 30 years]

N. Lopatin and V. Prokunin: *Russkie narodnye liricheskie pesni; Opyt systematicheskogo svoda liricheskikh pesen s ob'yasneniyami variantov so storony bytovogo i khudozhestvennogo ikh soderzhaniya N. M. Lopatina, s polozhenniem pesen dlya golosa i fortepiano V. P. Prokunina i s prilozheniem polnoy rasstanovki slov nekotorykh variantov po ikh napevu* [Russian Folk Lyric Song; an Attempt of Systematic Assembly of Russian Lyric Songs with Explanations of the Variants, Their Everyday Life and Artistic Contents by Lopatin; Songs Set for Voice and Piano by Prokunin; Also Included a Complete Text Underlay for Some of the Variants] (Moscow, 1889, 3/1956)

A. Famintsyn: *Skomorokhi na Rusi* [The *Skomorokh* in Russia] (St Petersburg, 1889)

——: *Gusli-russkiy narodnyi myzykal'nyi instrument* [Russian Folk Instrument *Gusli*] (St Petersburg, 1890)

——: *Domra i srodnye ey myzykal'nye instrumenty russkogo naroda* [*Domra* and Related Instruments of the Russian People] (St Petersburg, 1891)

E. Lyatsky: 'Skazitel' I. T. Ryabinin i ego byliny' [Chanter I. Ryabinin and His *byliny*], *Etnograficheskoe obozreniie*, iv/23 (1894), 105–53

F. Istomin and G. Dyutsh [Deutsch]: *Pesni Russkogo naroda. Sobrany v guberniyakh Arkhangelskoy i Olonetskoy v 1886 g. Zapisali: slova F. M. Istomin, napevy G. O. Dyutsh* [Songs of the Russian People. Collected in the Arkhangelsk and Olonets *Gubernii* in 1886. Texts Transcribed by Istomin, Melodies by Dyutsh] (St Petersburg, 1894)

S. Lyapunov and F. Istomin: *Pesni Russkogo naroda. Sobrany v guberniyakh Vologodskoy, Vyatskoy i Kostromskoy v 1893 g. Zapisali: slova F. M. Istomin, napevy S. M. Lyapunov* [Songs of the Russian People. Collected in the Vologda, Vyatka, and Kostroma *Gubernii* in 1893. Texts transcribed by Istomin, Melodies by Lyapunov] (St Petersburg, 1899)

E. Lineva: *Velikorusskie pesni v narodnoy garmonizatsii. Zapisany E. Linyevoi* (St Petersburg, 1904, 1909); Eng. trans. as *The Peasant Songs of Great Russia as they are in the Folk's Harmonization: Collected and Transcribed from Phonograms by Eugenie Lineff* (Moscow, 1905–12)

A. Grigoriev: *Arkhangelskie byliny i istoricheskie pesni* [*Byliny* and Historical Songs of the Arkhangelsk District] (Moscow, 1902–10) [transcriptions by I. Tezarovsky from Grigoriev's recordings; these were the first attempt to notate peculiarities of intonation in folk singing]

Trudy muzykalno-etnograhicheskoy komissii [Transactions of the Music-Ethnographic Commission], 5 vols (Moscow, 1906, 1907, 1911, 1913, 1916) [Simultaneously *Izvestiya Obshchestva Lyubiteley Estestvoznaniya, Antropologii i Etnografii*, cxiii, cxiv, cxv, cxviii, cxx]

A. Maslov: '*Byliny*, ikh proiskhozhdenie, ritmicheskiy i melodicheskiy sklad' [*Byliny*, Their Origin, Rhythmic and Melodic Structures], *Transactions of the Music-Ethnographic Commission*, ii (Moscow, 1911), 301

N. Yanchuk: 'O muzyke bylin v svyazi s istoriiey ikh izucheniya' [On the Music of *Byliny* in Relation to the History of Their Study], *Russkaya slovesnost'*, ii: *Byliny*, ed. M. Speransky (Moscow, 1919)

A. Kastalsky: *Osobennosti narodno-russkoy muzykal'noy sistemy* [Peculiarities of Folk Musical Systems] (Moscow, 1923)

V. Paskhalov, 'Deyatel'nost' moskovskikh muzykantov-etnografov za poslednie vosem' let' [The Activity of Moscow Musicians-Ethnographers During the Past Eight Years], *Etnografiya*, i–ii (1926), 193

N. Findeizen: 'Kratkaya programma dlya sobiraniya materialov po muzykal'noy etnografii' [A Short Guide for Collection Materials on Musical Ethnography], *Muzykal'naya etnografiya* (Leningrad, 1926)

Krest'yanskoe iskusstvo Severa [Peasant Arts of the North] (Leningrad, 1926)

Iskusstvo Severa [Arts of the North], 2 vols. (Leningrad, 1927–8) [includes articles by Evald and Gippius on North-Russian songs]

N. Findeizen: *Ocherki po istorii muzyki v Rossii s drevneyshikh vremen do kontsa XVIII veka, vyp. 1–2* [Essays on the History of Music in Russia from Ancient Time to the End of the 18th c.] (Moscow and Leningrad, 1928–9)

Pesni katorgi i ssylki [Songs of Convict Colonies and Exile] (Moscow, 1930)

B. Asafiev [I. Glebov]: *Russkaya muzyka ot nachala XIX stoletiya* [Russian Music from the Beginning of the 19th c.] (Moscow, 1930; Eng. trans. by A. Swann, 1953) [analysis of folk song publications with instrumental accompaniment]

E. Gippius: 'Problema muzykalnogo fol'klora' [A Problem of Musical Folklore], *SovM*, vi (1933)

B. Steinpress: *K istorii 'tsyganskogo peniya' v Rossii* [On the History of the 'Gypsy Song' in Russia] (Moscow, 1934) [review, M. Druskin, *SovM*, xii (1934)]

L. Lebedinsky: *8 let borby za proletarskuyu muzyku* [Eight Years of a Struggle for Proletarian Music] (Moscow, 1931)

E. Gippius: 'Intonatsionnye elementy russkoi chastushki' [*Intonasiya* Elements of Russian *chastushka*], *Sovetskiy fol'klor*, iv/v (Moscow, 1936), 97

A. Novikov: *Russkie narodnye pesni* [Russian Folk Songs] (Moscow, 1936–7)

E. Gippius and Z. Evald: *Pesni Pinezh'ya; materialy fonogramm-arkhiva sobrannye i razrabotannye E. V. Gippius i Z. V. Evald* [Songs from the Pinega River Area; Material of the Phonogram-Archiv Collected and Processed by Gippius and Evald], ii (Moscow, 1937) [i, with song

texts, was not pubd.]
M. Druskin: *50 russkikh revolyutsionnykh pesen* [50 Revolution Songs] (Leningrad, 1938)
E. Gippius and Z. Evald, eds.: *Narodnye pesni Vologodskoy oblasti. Sbornik fonograficheskikh zapisey pod redaktsiey E. V. Gippius i Z. V. Evald. Zapisi tekstov A. M. Astakhovoy i N. P. Kolpakovoy. Muzykal'nye zapisi E. V. Velikanova i F. A. Rubtsova.* [Folk Songs of the Vologda District. Collection of Phonograph Recordings edited by E. Gippius and Z. Evald. Texts Transcribed by A. Astakhova and N. Kolpakova, Melodies by E. Velikanov and F. Rubtsov] (Leningrad, 1938)
E. Gippius and V. Chicherov: 'Sovetskaya fol'kloristika za 30 let' [Soviet Studies on Folklore and Musical Folklore during the Past 30 Years], *Sovetskaya etnografiya*, iv (1947), 29
M. Azadovsky: *Istoriya russkoi fol'kloristiki* [A History of Studies on Russian Folklore] (Moscow, 1958–63)
T. Popova: *Russkoe narodnoe muzykal'noe tvorchestvo* [Russian Folk Music], ii (Moscow, 1964)
M. Meltts: *Russkiy fol'klor. Bibliograficheskiy ukazatel'* [Russian Folklore. Bibliography], 1917–1944 (Leningrad, 1966); 1901–1916 (Leningrad, 1981)
I. Zemtsovsky: 'Russkaya sovetskaya muzykal'naya fol'kloristika' [Soviet Russian Studies on Musical Folklore], *Voprosy teorii i estetiki muzyki*, vi/vii (Leningrad, 1967)
B. Krader: 'Folk Music Archive of the Moscow Conservatory, with a Brief History of Russian Field Recording', *Folklore and Folk Music Archivist*, x/2 (1967–8), 13
I. Zemtovsky: 'Fol'kloristika kak nauka' [Studies on Folklore as a Science], *Slavyanskiy muzykal'nyi fol'klor. Stat'i i materialy* [Slavic Musical Folklore. Articles and Materials], ed. I. Zemtsovsky (Moscow, 1972)
P. Vulfius: *Russkaya mysl' o muzykal'nom folklore* [Russian Thought on Musical Folklore] (Moscow, 1979)

Ukraine

M. Maksimovich: *Golosa ukrainskikh pesen* [Melodies of Ukrainian Songs] (Moscow, 1834, rev. 2/1961) [Songs collected by Maksimovich, arranged for voice and piano by Alyabiev]
A. Serov: 'Muzyka yuzhno-russkikh pesen' [Music of South Russian (Ukrainian) Songs], *Osnova* (1861); repr. in *Izbrannye stat'i*, i (Moscow, 1950), 109
M. Lysenko: *Ukrains'ki narodni pisni* [Ukrainian Folk Songs] (Leipzig and Kiev, 1868–1906); rev. in *Zibranny tvoriv* [Collected Works] (Kiev, 1950–59)
O. Hulak-Artemovsky: *Narodni ukrains'ki pisni z holosom* [Ukrainian Folk Songs with the Melodies] (Kiev, 1868, rev. 2/1883)
A. Rubets: *216 narodnykh ukrainskikh napevov* [216 Ukrainian Folk Melodies] (Moscow, 1872, 2/1882)
M. Lysenko: 'Kharacteristika muzichnikh osoblivostey ukraïns'kikh dum i pisen, u vikonanni kobzaria Veresa' [Musical Characteristics of Ukrainian *Dumy* and Songs performed by *kobzar'* Veresay], *Zapiski Yugo-Zapadnogo otdela Russkogo Geograficheskogo Obshchestva*, i (Kiev, 1874, 2/1978)
O. Kolberg: *Pokucie: obraz etnograficzny* [Ethnographic Sketch on Pokuchie] (Kraków, 1882–8/*R*1962–3)
P. Sokalsky: *Russkaya narodnaya muzyka velilorusskaya i malorusskaya v ee stroenii melodicheskom i ritmicheskom i otlichiya eye ot osnov sovremennoy garmonicheskoy muzyki* [Russian Music of Great- and Malo-Russia, its Melodic and Rhythmic Structures and its Dissimilarity with the Bases of Contemporary Harmonic Music] (Kharkov, 1888)
O. Kolberg: *Chelmskie: obraz ethnograficzny* (Kraków, 1890/*R*1964)
——: *Przemyskie: zarys etnograficzny* (Kraków, 1891/*R*1964)
M. Lysenko: 'Narodni myzichni instrumenty na Ukraini' [Folk Musical Instruments in Ukraine], *Zorya*, i–x (1894, 2/1907, 3/1955)
——: *Ukrains'ki obryadovi pisni* [Ukrainian Ritual Songs] (Kiev, 1896); rev. in *Zibrannya tvoriv*, xx (1956)
A. Konoshchenko: *Ukrains'ki pisni z notami* [Ukrainian Songs with Melodies] (Odessa, 1900–02, 2/1909)
I. Kolessa: 'Halyts'ko-rus'ki narodni pisni z melodiyami. Zibrav y s. Khodovychakh Ivan Kolessa' [Galicia-Russian Folk Songs with Melodies. Collected in the Village Khodovichi by I. Kolessa], *Etnografichny zbirnik*, xi (Lemberg, 1902) [special issue]
——: 'Rytmika ukrains'kykh narodnykh pisen' [Rhythmics of Ukrainian Folk Songs], *Zapiski naukovoho tovarystva im. Shevchenka* (Lemberg, 1906–07); repr. in *Muzykoznavchi pratsi* (Kiev, 1970)
O. Rozdolsky and S. Lyudkevich: *Halyts'ko-rus'ki narodni melodii* [Galicia-Russian Folk Melodies]

(Lemberg, 1906–08) [recorded by Rozdolsky, transcribed and classified by Lyudkevich]
V. Hnatyuk, O. Rozdol'sky and F. Kolessa: *Hayivky* (Lemberg, 1909) [Ger. summary]
F. Kolessa: 'Über den melodischen und rhythmischen Aufbau der ukrainischen (Kleinrussischen) rezitierenden Gesange, der sogenannten 'Kosakenlieder'', *IMusSCR*, iii (Vienna, 1909)
——: *Melodii ukrains'kykh narodnykh dum* [Melodies of Ukrainian *dumy*], i/ii (Lemberg, 1910, 1913 [intro. in Ger.], rev. 2/1969)
——: 'Das ukrainische Volkslied, sein melodischer und rhythmischer Aufbau', *Osterreichische Monatschrift für den Orient*, xlii (1916); enl. version in Ukrainian in *Muzykoznavchi pratsi* (Kiev, 1970)
K. Kvitka: *Narodni melodiyi z holosu Lesi Ukrayinky* [Folk Melodies From the Voice of Lesya Ukrainka] (Kiev, 1917–18, enl. 2/1971)
F. Kolessa: *Pro genezu ukrains'kykh narodnykh dum (ukrains'ki narodny dumy u vidnoshenni do pisen', virshiv i pokhoronnykh holosin')* [On the Origin of Ukrainian Folk *Duma* (Ukrainian Folk *dumy* and Their Relations to Songs, Religious Songs, and Funeral Laments)] (Lvov, 1920–2)
K. Kvitka: *Ukrains'ki narodni melodii* [Ukrainian Folk Melodies] (Kiev, 1922)
——: 'Ritmichni paraleli v pisnyakh slov'yans'kikh narodiv. Rytmichna forma ABBA v budovi strofy' [Rhythmic Parallels in Folk Songs of Slavic Peoples. A Rhythmic Form ABBA in a Song Stanza], *Muzyka* (January 1923); trans. in Russian in K. Kvitka, *Izbrannye trudy v dvukh tomakh*, i (Moscow, 1971), 37
——: 'Professional'ni narodni spivtsy y muzykanty na Ukraini: prohrama dlya doslidu yikh diyal'nosti ta pobutu' [Professional Folk Singers and Instrumentalists in the Ukraine: a Programme for Study of Their Activity and Everyday Life] (Kiev, 1924); trans. in Russian in K. Kvitka, *Izbrannye trudy v dvukh tomakh*, ii (Moscow, 1973), 279–325
——: 'Vstupni uvagi do muzichno-etnografichnikh studiy' [Introductory Notes to Ethnomusicological Research], *Zapiski Etnografochnogo tovarystva*, i (1925); trans. in Russian in K. Kvitka, *Izbrannye trudy v dvukh tomakh*, ii (Moscow, 1973), 3
——: 'Pervisni tonoryady' [Earliest Tone Rows], *Pervicne gromadyanstvo i yogo perezhytky na Ykraini*, iii (Kiev, 1926); trans. in Russian in K. Kvitka, *Izbrannye trudy v dvukh tomakh*, i (Moscow, 1971), 215–74
D. Revuts'ky: *Zoloti klyuchi* (Kiev, 1926–9, rev. 2/1964)
K. Kvitka: 'Muzykal'naya etnografiya na Ukraine v poslerevolyutsionnye gody' [Musical Ethnography in Ukraine in the Post-Revolution Years], *Etnografiya*, i/ii (1926)
——: 'La système anhémitonique pentatonique chez les peuples slaves', *II Zjazd Slowianskich geografow i etnografow* (Kraków, 1927)
——: 'Do pytannya pro tyurks'kyi vplyv na ukrains'ku narodnu melodiku' [The Question of Turkish Influence on Ukrainian Folk Melody], *Yubileyny zbirnik na poshanu akad. M. Hrushevs'kogo*, ii (Kiev, 1928); trans. in Russian in K. Kvitka, *Izbrannye trudy v dvukh tomakh*, i (Moscow, 1971), 336
M. Hayday: *Zrazky narodnoy polifoniyi* [Examples of Folk Polyphony] (Kiev, 1928–9)
F. Kolessa: *Narodni pisni z halyts'koi Lemkivshchiny: teksty i melodiyi* [Folk Songs from the Lemkovshchina of Galicia] (Lvov, 1929)
——: 'Poryadkovannya i kharakterisichny pryznaki lemkivs'kykh piesennykh melodii' [Systematization and Characteristic Features of Song Melodies from Lemkovshchina], *Etnografichnyi zbirnik*, xxxix–xl (L'vov, 1929) [Ger. summary]
——: ''Karpats'ky tsykl narodnikh piesen' (spil'nykh ukraintsyam, slovakam, chekhami i polyakam)' [The 'Karpathian Cycle' (Folk Songs Common to Ukrainians, Slovaks, Moravian Czechs, and Poles)], *Sbornik praci, i Sjezdu slovanskych filologu v Praze 1929*, ii (Prague, 1932) [Fr. summary]
M. Beregovsky: *Evreysky muzykal'nyi fol'klor* [Jewish Musical Folklore] (Moscow, 1934), Eng. trans. by M. Slobin as *Old Jewish Folksongs and Fiddle Tunes: the Writings and Collections of Moshe Beregovski* (Philadelphia, PA, 1982)
F. Kolessa: 'Formuly zaklyuchennya v ukrains'kykh narodnykh dumakh u zv'yazku z pitannyam pro naverstvuvannya dum' [Cadence Formulas in Ukrainian *Duma* and the Problems of Their Classification], *Zapiski naukovogo tovarystva im. Shevchenka*, cliv (L'vov, 1935)
M. Beregovsky: *Evreyskaya narodnaya instrumental'naya muzyka* [Jewish Folk Instrumental Music], i (Kiev, 1937) [in Yiddish]; iii (Moscow, 1987) [in Russian]
F. Kolessa: 'Narodni pisni z pidkarpats'koy Rusi' [Folk Songs from the Sub-Karpatian Russia], *Naukovyi zbirnik tovarystva 'Prosvita' v Uzhhorodi*, xiii–xiv (1938), 40
R. Harasymchuk: *Tan'tsy hutsuls'kie* [Hutsuls' Dances] (L'vov, 1939)

F. Kolessa: *Muzykoznavchi pratsi* [Works on Musicology] (Kiev, 1970)

——: *Fol'kloristichi pratsi* [Works on Folklore] (Kiev, 1970)

K. Kvitka: *Izbrannye trudy v dvukh tomakh* [Selected Works in Two Volumes] (Moscow, 1971–3)

O. Pravdyuk: *Ukrains'ka muzichna fol'kloristika* [Ukrainian Studies on Musical Folklore] (Kiev, 1978)

Volga-Ural peoples

A. Rittikh: *Materialy dlya etnografii Rossii. Kazanskaya guberniya* [Material on Ethnography of Russia. Kazan' *Guberniya*] (Kazan', 1870)

V. Moshkov: *Muzyka chuvashskikh pesen* [Music of Chuvash Songs] (Kazan, 1893)

——: 'Materialy dlya kharakteristiki muzykal'nogo tvorchestva inorodtsev Volzhsko-Kamsogo kraya' [Material on Music of non-Russian Peoples of Volka-Kama Region], *Izvestiya Obshchestva arkheologii, etnografii i istorii pri Kazanskom universitete*, xi–xvii (Kazan', 1893–1901)

S. Rybakov: 'O narodnykh pesnyakh tatar, bashkir i teptyarey' [On Folk Songs of the Tatars, Bashkirs, and Teptyars], *Zhivaya starina*, iii–iv (1894), 323–64

G. Schünemann: 'Kasantatarische Lieder', *AMw*, i (Leipzig, 1918–1919), 499

V. Vasiliev: *Mari muro* [Mari Folk Songs] (Kazan, 1919, rev. 2/1937)

R. Lach: *Gesänge russischer Kriegsgefangener* (Vienna and Leipzig, 1926–52)

F. Pavlov: *Chuvashi i ikh pesennoe i muzykal'noe tvorchestvo* [The Chuvash and their Music and Songs] (Cheboksary, 1927)

S. Maksimov: *Turi chavashsen yurrisem* [Folk Songs of the Northern Chuvash] (Cheboksary, 1932)

A. Zataevich: *Pesni kazakhstanskikh tatar* [Songs of the Kazakhstan Tatars] (Moscow, 1933)

G. Fedarav: *146 yura* [146 Songs] (Cheboksary and Moscow, 1934) [Chuvash Songs Sung by Fedarav]

A. Zataevich: *Pesni raznykh narodov* [Songs of Various Peoples], ed. V. Dernova (Alma-Ata, 1958)

PART THREE

Regional Studies

CHAPTER VI

Europe

JAMES PORTER

The idea of an 'ethnomusicology of Europe' in the contemporary sense of the term is fairly recent, although the goal of a comparative synthesis of popular musical and poetic forms in Europe goes back to Johann Herder and the 19th-century search for a common Indo-European cultural heritage. Stimulated in the 1930s by the *Kulturkreis* ('culture circle') anthropological theory with its emphasis on historical cultures, the concept was anticipated in publications by Werner Danckert (1939/*R*1970, 1966) and later, shed of the *Kulturkreis* influence, in those of Walter Wiora (1952, 1957) (*see* Chapter III, 'Northern and Western Europe', 'Germany and Austria'). An outgrowth of this post-war development was the formation of study groups within the International Folk Music Council to examine more closely problems of melodic classification, historical sources and organology, the compass of these investigations being almost entirely confined to Europe. The study of Europe's traditional music has been closely allied to folklore methods and institutions, and scholars have generally conceived of such music in folk communities ('folk music') as the chief object of their research.

With the increasing influence of cultural anthropology in the tradition of Malinowski (cf. Merriam, 1964) and European ethnology as conceived by Sigurd Erixon (1967) and others, the need for greater ethnographic depth was recognized as an essential component in an ethnomusicology of Europe (Suppan, 1970; Porter, 1977). Important dimensions to this more complex picture of music-making and its contexts have been studies of musical life in European emigrant communities in North America and elsewhere (Erdely, 1979; Porter, 1978; *see also* Chapter II, 'North America'), as well as field studies in Europe, sometimes among uprooted minorities, by a younger generation of scholars from Australia (Holst, 1975), New Zealand (Dunn, 1980) 'and especially North America (e.g. Bohmann, 1984; Chianis, 1965; Garfias, 1984; Hopkins, 1986; Katz, 1972–5; Kuter, 1981; Markoff, 1976; Rice, 1980). Useful additions to the view of musical activity at the popular or folk level in Europe, especially in industrialized countries, have come from sociological perspectives (e.g. Karbusicky, 1975; Ling, 1970; Shepherd and others, 1977; and Wallis and Malm, 1984).

General developments since World War II

The urge to continue work from before 1939, yet to promote new frameworks and methodologies for the study of traditional music in Europe, led quickly to two events of major importance for the field in general: the founding of the International Folk Music Council (IFMC) in London in 1947, and the introduction of the term *ethno-musicology* by the Dutch scholar Jaap Kunst in his book *Musicologica* (1950).

Dominated at its inception and ever since by Europeans, the IFMC originally aimed at 'furthering the study of folk music and dance, and of assisting in their practice, preservation and dissemination', as Maud Karpeles, the first honorary secretary of the body, wrote in 1954 (1980). This description needs considerable updating in the light of changing concepts of folk music and the growth of ethnomusicology since the 1950s. Nevertheless, the IFMC has continued its work under a new name (International Council for Traditional Music) since 1980 and, with its study groups, has met annually or biennially since 1948, most often in European centres but also in Africa, Asia and the Americas (*see* Chapter III, 'Northern and Western Europe', 'Great Britain').

Kunst's term, which was explicitly intended to replace 'comparative musicology', has had a lasting effect because of its adoption in the English-speaking world, leading to the founding of the Society for Ethnomusicology in the USA (1955), and through the use of equivalent terms in other languages (e.g. Fr. *ethnomusicologie*, It. *etnomusicologia*). In German-speaking usage the parallel term *Musikethnologie*, with the emphasis on the ethnological rather than the musicological component, had already appeared before 1950 (Bose, 1949), though as European scholars came increasingly under American influence this term has coexisted with the adapted form *Ethnomusikologie* (Stęszewski, 1972; Baumann, 1976; Simon, 1978). More significantly, the concept of comparative musicology as developed between the world wars in Berlin and Vienna has persevered in Germany and Austria, if with diminished impact, in the systematic work of Walter Graf and the historical and comparative studies of Wiora (e.g. 1952, 1961, 1975).

Usage in Eastern Europe and the Soviet Union has varied according to whether the subject matter was conceived as *Musikfolklore*, a term used by Béla Bartók and others to signify the method as well as the material (Bartók, 1919), or *ethnographie musicale*, a name for the field popularized by Julien Tiersot in 1900 after the Italian scholar Amintore Galli (1898). In Russia the most common term, even after 1950, has been *muzikal'naya fol'kloristika* (see Banin, 1973, 1978; Gusev, 1977; Zemtsovsky, 1973), while in Poland, for instance, the nomenclature of *etnografia muzyczna* has also reflected the influence of West European terminology (Bielawski, 1970; Czekanowska, 1971). In recent times neologisms derived from *ethnomusicology* have begun to appear in East European writings. Just as strikingly, the subject matter has been redefined as the perception of changing functions for traditional music has come about.

The initial impetus to establish the IFMC came from Great Britain, where enthusiastic associates of Cecil Sharp in the English Folk Dance and Song Society, including Vaughan Williams the IFMC's first president, introduced Sharp's ideas into discussions on the nature and role of 'folk music'. This culminated in an attempt to formulate a definition based on Sharp's linking of continuity, variation and selection as the key features of origin and transmission in folk music (Sharp, 1907). Sharp had viewed folk music as the product of a highly stable, conservative, and rural society unaffected by industrialization, literacy or urban tastes and had consequently idealized 'the folk' and their musical life. In contrast Bartók, who had similarly been preoccupied with the collection and classification of rural music, though in Eastern Europe, included urban popular forms as worthy of scholarly consideration under the rubric of folk music (e.g. Bartók, 1931). As the modern world began to impinge even more palpably after World War II, mainly through radio, records and later, television, the position of the purists within the IFMC became untenable since technological advance in Europe, as everywhere else, was accompanied by changing cultural and political attitudes.

In Western Europe the influential developments in traditional music took place under the aegis of a 'folk revival' that had its roots in the USA, where notable figures such as Charles Seeger and Alan Lomax promoted engagement by college students and intellectuals in the ideals of populist folk song. During prolonged trips to Europe in the 1950s, Lomax collaborated with local scholars in publishing the results of extensive field collecting on the Columbia World Library series of commercial recordings. In some instances (England and Wales, Ireland, Scotland, Spain) these recordings were largely from tapes made by Lomax and his local associates: in others (Bulgaria, France, Romania, Yugoslavia) the contents were assembled by specialists who would occasionally draw on archival sources. Lomax subsequently made available supplementary field material from Italy (Folkways), Scotland (Tradition) and Spain (Westminster).

By 1960 several countries in Western Europe had begun to issue examples of their indigenous traditional music through institutions such as university research units, sometimes using major record companies as distributors (e.g. RCA Victor). Denmark, Norway, Scotland and later Germany, Italy, Spain and Sweden all produced notable albums or multiple sets of discs, the larger purpose being to assert national identity and cultural continuity in the face of American-inspired 'pop' music emanating from urban centres and backed by powerful commercial interests (see Wallis and Malm, 1984). Yet the radio in particular was also manipulated effectively to create awareness of traditional music: active broadcasters affiliated with the IFMC at this time included Matts Arnberg (Sweden), Hendrik Daems (Belgium), Rolf Myklebust and Liv Greni (Norway), Giorgio Nataletti (Italy) and Marie Slocombe (UK). From the mid-1960s, films on traditional music began to proliferate (see selected list in Rahkonen, 1983).

In socialist Central and Eastern Europe, by contrast, scholars were enjoined after World War II to stress the concept of traditional music as a collective phenomenon originating in the village, a trend that Brăiloiu and others had continued from the 1920s (Brăiloiu, 1960; Vargyas, 1957). Ideology, however, sometimes dictated that the emphasis should rather fall on the revolutionary songs of urban workers, lauding these as 'optimistic' as against the 'depressing' cast of traditional rural idioms (Tokaji, 1983). Researchers in Bulgaria tried, with some success, to follow the pattern of 19th-century Russian folklorists in exploring the life and repertory of individual performers:

especially notable are publications by Katsarova (1952), Keremidchiev (1954) and Vranska (1953; Rihtman's 1951 study of a singer in Bosnia could also be considered part of this perspective). Issues arising therefrom included consideration of popular aesthetics in the performance of traditional music (Vakarelski, 1957). But a de-emphasis of the individual creative personality was a striking feature of analysis between the mid-1950s and the 1970s, when increased contact with Western scholars and a relaxation of official sanctions on such work was effected (Elschek, 1981). This largely explains the conventional adherence to Bartók's methods during the interwar period, which concentrate almost exclusively on analysis and classification (Bartók, 1951, 1959–, 1967–75, 1978, 1981).

State record labels were primarily concerned with issuing recordings of folk ensembles for a popular market, while discs of authentic traditional music would appear only intermittently (see Krader, 1971). When the 78 rpm record was discontinued by the Soviet company Melodiya in 1969, for example, the number of ethnic and folk recordings decreased markedly, but then began to rise again slowly (Gronow, 1975). Other state record concerns have produced outstanding sets of traditional music on disc, notably Bulgaria, Hungary, Romania and Yugoslavia, and the English scholar A. L. Lloyd brought out a useful record of Albanian music after a visit there in 1965 (Topic 12T154). In the 1970s, the Society for the Dissemination of National Music (founded 1929) in Greece produced a handsome series of albums underwritten by the Rockefeller Foundation, a significant venture that has provided the most detailed sound documentation of regional Greek styles to date.

The intensive recording of traditional music in Europe during the post-war years was considered by some to represent the last great phase of an exercise that had begun with the antiquarians of the 18th century and received its final incentive from Edison's invention of the phonograph in 1877. Field collections published in the first few decades after 1945 generally assumed a 'devolution-ary' hypothesis of folk music's decline though many, following in the footsteps of such as Bartók, were models of their kind (annotated in Vetterl, 1966, listed in Elschek and others, 1967–).

This concept of traditional music as a phenomenon that had to be captured before vanishing continued to dominate thinking within the IFMC until the 1960s, when consciousness of social change and, more particularly, of creativity at the popular level made themselves felt. After about 1970, the trend towards concentration on more compact social units resulted in a deepening ethnographic depiction of the contexts, uses and purposes of traditional music. Concurrently one may note here the field activity of Central and Northern European scholars in the music of the Balkans and the Mediterranean: Samuel Baud-Bovy, Brandl (Greece), A. F. W. Bentzon, Bernard Lortat-Jacob (Sardinia), F. Hoerburger, B. Traerup (Yugoslavia), Lloyd, D. and E. Stockmann (Albania), though little or no field research, in Europe East or West, has been undertaken by ethnomusicologists who are not from a European background (however, see Dunn, 1980; Holst, 1975).

Gradually the term folk music in English-language usage began to be replaced by traditional music in order to highlight the broader spatial and temporal dimensions of the material rather than the social level at which it was vaguely thought to operate (communal) or the means by which it was exclusively transmitted (oral). 'Folk' frequently was, moreover, an irrelevant term when one referred to societies outside Europe. Traditional music, while equally difficult to define satisfactorily, was at least free of the condescension suggested by the older term, and indeed found its way into the new title of the IFMC in 1980. The designation 'folk music' or its equivalent still appears, however, in the title of some scholarly societies and the journals they issue (e.g. *Folk Music Journal, Jahrbuch für Volksliedforschung*).

New concepts of traditional music

By 1960 scholars in Europe had begun to move away from the concept of traditional music as exclusively of an older sort, or as produced only by peasants or rural artisans, and had come to look at factors of adaptation, change and creativity. As much was evident from a symposium on this topic published in the IFMC *Journal* (1960). More pointedly, the idea of 'folk music' underwent scrutiny in the European context, where reassessment was in response to external forces such as political ideology or tourism and their mounting effect on traditional life. At the same time in Eastern Europe, the 'new song', or 'modern song' became the focus of some scholarly work (e.g. Stoin and Kachulev, 1958, in Bulgaria; Popova, 1969, in the USSR deals only with the texts of songs).

In Western Europe scholars started to speak, rather, of a 'second existence' (*zweites Dasein*) of folk music (Wiora, 1959), or of 'folklore' singers who used traditional forms as a means for political expression (Bose, 1967). Terms such as these (Fr. *musique folklorique* as opposed to *traditionnelle*, Sp. *canción folklórico* vs *popular*) reflected notions of an authentic tradition self-consciously arranged for stage performance rather than as a spontaneous production within a natural context. Ernst Klusen characterized this distinction in terms of song function whereby, in the one case, a song arises naturally from a group as 'the serving object' (*das dienende Gegenstand*) while in the other, the group gathers in order to sing (the song as *triumphierendes Gegenstand*; Klusen, 1969). A similar distinction has been adapted by the Swiss scholar Max Peter Baumann in his treatment of Alpine music, where he contrasts a primary and a secondary group, the former being composed of traditional performers in face-to-face musical interaction, the latter made up of musicians who arrange traditional material for a public audience (Baumann, 1976). This last idea, of *folklorismus* or 'manipulated' folklore applied to music, is open to the criticism that it perpetrates the notion of an ideal folk culture against which latterday arrangements seem derivative or artificial, thereby suggesting false kinds of comparison. 'Folkloristic music' (*Musikfolklorismus*) is simply a set of musical behaviours adjusted to fit a changed context and need not be devalued when compared to more traditional kinds of performance (discussed in Bošković-Stulli, 1971; Gusev, 1977; Heimann, 1977).

Dissatisfied with current terminology, Klusen has argued further that the German word *Volkslied* carries with it objectionable overtones from the Nazi era, and proposed *Gruppenlied* ('group song') to replace it (1967). This led to a dispute between Klusen and Wiora that surfaced in the pages of the IFMC *Yearbook* (1972). To a large extent the argument, which ostensibly concerned Herder's introduction of the term *Volkslied* in the 18th century, was really about a demarcation of approach between historical and comparative research on the one hand and the sociological study of popular song and singing on the other. These differences not only of emphasis but of fundamental concept and approach had become increasingly apparent in symposia published in Germany, such as those of *Das Volkslied Heute* (1959), the *Deutsches Jahrbuch für Volkskunde* (1967) and *Heutige Probleme der Volksmusik* (1973).

The historical and comparative view of traditional music in Europe as espoused by Wiora in such works as *Europäische Volksgesang* (1952) was plainly being overtaken by a need for empirical field research to determine, as Klusen proposed, what music people were actually singing and not what music scholars ideally believed them to sing (1974–5). This need was stressed further by Wolfgang Suppan in his overview of strategies necessary to an 'ethnomusicology of Europe' (1970), although the deeper objectives and problems of such fieldwork remained unspecified.

The political dimensions of traditional song in Central Europe were meanwhile the object of investigation by Klusen's colleague at the Institut für musikalische Volkskunde at Neuss since 1968, Vladimir Karbusicky, whose book on song ideology (1973) involves semiotic analysis of political song in relation to traditional patterns of composition. A major thesis is the similarity of means used by political song writers, whatever their persuasion. Karbusicky had previously published a collection of Czech workers' songs (1958), and this no doubt lent him insights into the genesis of ideologically motivated song composition. His study stands, therefore, in contrast to that of Wolfgang Steinitz on the relationship between workers' songs and folk song (1965), or to the latter's two-volume survey of historical songs of oppression (1955–62). Another publication with political content preceded Karbusicky's although the English translation did not appear until 1974, namely that by János Maróthy (1966). This offers a picture of musical development in Western society from a Marxist viewpoint, but poses fundamental problems in linking the development to social structure and by comparing musical examples extrapolated from their performance contexts. Subsequent studies of popular song in Western Europe have sometimes drawn on Marxist models (e.g. Harker, 1980, especially in the light of Lloyd's 1967 book on traditional song in England).

In Eastern Europe the official policy of socialist governments formed on the Soviet model after World War II had recognized in traditional music (usually called 'national' or 'people's' music) the ideological expression of a newly emancipated peasant class and proceeded to build professional troupes of dancers and musicians based on village prototypes. The Soviet example of the Igor Moiseyev Ensemble was influential in this process, which 'revised' native conceptions of style. In some cases, for instance the Bulgarian State Ensemble for Folk Song and Folk Dances directed by Filip Kutev, village singers were invited to join an urban professional chorus and to adapt their singing to a smoother, more homogeneous texture. Regional idioms were thereby harnessed in creating a more 'collective' national style emphasizing musical unity. This idea was in turn fed back to the villages through the media and began to affect deeply rooted traditions of performance. Political ideology, therefore, has had a direct effect on the aesthetics of traditional music.

The very concept of 'folk music' (*narodnaya muzika*) in the Soviet Union, according to one view, has come to denote music performed by professional ensembles or academic 'folk choirs', or alternatively diminishing musical traditions in remote districts of interest only to scholars (Gronow, 1975). The official account, however, stresses that 'the distinctive character of folk art should not be understood as ethnic isolation, since folklore is an inseparable part of world musical culture' (USSR Union of Composers Bulletin, 1985, p.15). This is not to deny that concepts of an 'authentic folk music' exist in eastern Europe, for the situation in Yugoslavia, for example, is complicated by the use of *narodna muzika* to signify 'traditional music' in the sense of ethnic and regional identity (Bosnian, Croatian, Serbian, and so on), *izvorna muzika* (lit. 'source' music) to refer to an 'authentic' music practised in sparse rural areas or by revival groups who may otherwise reject the manifestations of popular culture found among peasants or the working classes, *folklorna muzika* to signify 'arranged folk music', and *komponovane narodne pesme* to mean popular commercial folk songs fashioned after traditional models. According to one commentator, these composed songs are a more dynamic response than the authentic to the rapid changes that have overtaken life in modern Yugoslavia (Simic, 1976). Such terms are now also encountered in the framework of 'folk festivals', which represent both a variety of and distillation of contexts since interaction between and among performers is not confined to the 'official', on-stage one.

Later directions in research

By the mid-1970s, the study groups of the IFMC had moved towards publishing the fruits of their colloquia, partly as a response to the different format of the Council's *Yearbook*, which no longer printed papers given orally at the plenary conferences as the *Journal* had done (1949–69). The Study Group on Musical Instruments in particular has now issued nine volumes of proceedings since 1969, while the Groups on Analysis and Systematization of Folk Music (1969, 1973, et seq.) and on Historical Sources of Folk Music (1978, 1979, 1981, 1985) have also published the collected papers of meetings. Other groups, such as the recently formed Study Group on Music Archaeology (1985), have developed their original newsletter into a mini-journal, *Archaeologia Musicalis* (1987–9). In addition, some national committees of the Council hold symposia and publish the results (e.g. the UK National Committee, 1980). The incentive to publish a series of handbooks of European folk instruments has come mainly from Ernst Emsheimer and Erich Stockmann, who edit the proceedings of the most senior study group (1969–). Four volumes in the *Handbook* series appeared, covering the instruments of Hungary (Sárosi, 1967), Czechoslovakia (Kunz, 1974; Elschek, 1983), and Switzerland (Geiser, 1981). Independent organological surveys by country include, for example, those by F. Anoyanakis for Greece (1979), E. Veiga de Oliveira for Portugal (1966), and K. Vertkov for the USSR (1963, Eng. trans., 1975).

Several monographs on single instruments in Europe have appeared: that on the Swedish keyed fiddle by Jan Ling (1967), the Sard triple clarinet or *launeddas* by A. F. Weis Bentzon (1969) and the hurdy-gurdy by M. Bröcker

(1973). These studies examine past scholarship, historical sources, social use, symbolism, repertory, tunings, and other features. They complement broader organological writings such as Werner Bachmann's on the origins of bowing (1966, Eng. trans., 1969) as well as the more general surveys, for instance Anthony Baines's on bagpipes (1960) or Frank Harrison and Joan Rimmer's overview of European folk instruments (1964). Mention may also be made of two modest symposia on the fiddle and the drone in Europe (Deutsch, 1975, 1981).

Occasional panels on traditional music in Europe emerged from proceedings of the International Musicological Society from the early 1960s, when ethnomusicologists brought growing influence into discussions. Of particular note for Europe have been panels on the contribution of ethnomusicology to historical musicology and criteria for acculturation (1961), oral and written traditions in the Mediterranean (1964), the problem of historicity in European folk song, traditional forms of epic singing, and sociology in music (1972) and multiple sessions at the 1977 IMS Conference in Berkeley, California.

The IFMC Conference at Regensburg, Germany (1975), included a panel on the current state of research in orally transmitted music. A point made by Bruno Nettl at that time was that scholars had become less interested in transcription, not only because of the arrival of automatic melody-writers such as that dubbed Mona at the University of Uppsala (Bengtsson, 1967) but because the insights of recent anthropology had redirected ethnomusicologists to central problems of meaning and value in traditional music (Nettl, 1975). Among Europeans, Doris Stockmann has continued to explore the problems of aural transcription in articles that link this process to other analytic modes such as, for example, musical semiotics (1966, 1970, 1976). Culturally specific questions of notational method, however, are still open to varied solutions (Bodley, 1973; Cooke, 1972).

In Western Europe, certainly, there has been a shift away from conventional methods of collecting and analysis as confidence in positivist conceptions waned and objectivity appeared an unobtainable ideal. Field research has turned instead to scrutiny of the scholar's role and how he or she affects the human subjects under study (e.g. Koning, 1980, in Ireland; Lortat-Jacob, 1982, in Sardinia). In contrast, the approach of Bartók and Brăiloiu has persisted in most parts of eastern Europe, where academies of science adhere in general to laboratory methods, the focus being firmly on the musical products rather than on context or performance (parts of Yugoslavia are something of an exception; see Petrović, 1983). Various ancillary systems of analysis were developed, however, during the 1960s and 1970s to supplement conventional methods: the computer scanning of melodies (the IFMC *Journal*, 1965), cybernetics and information theory (Goshovsky, 1965; Stockmann, 1972), semiotics (Giurghescu, 1974; Goshovsky, 1981), and the use of linguistic methods of analysis (e.g. Sundberg and Lindblom's generative grammar for eight-bar melodies resembling a set of Swedish nursery tunes, 1976).

While the traditional goals of research such as the history of a genre, formal or structural idioms and their evolution, or instrumental typology continued to be served in study group publications, these were challenged at the 1979

Oslo Conference of the IFMC by Kenneth Gourlay, who has since argued elsewhere for a 'humanizing ethnomusicology' that abandons the pretence of objectivity so prized by scholars such as Brăiloiu (Gourlay, 1982). This departure in method centres more upon intersubjectivity between the researcher and those whose music is studied, as well as upon the less elitist attitude of the former (1978).

A radical shift of this sort calls into question not only the preoccupation with musical products and their properties (what folklorists have called 'item-centred scholarship') but also the tradition of social ethnography as it had developed in Eastern Europe and, for example, France. While the approach of French ethnographers stood in marked contrast to the Central European tendency to theorize and systematize (sometimes without due regard for the observable musical facts), it tended to dwell on social function to the exclusion of the individual performer-creator and his or her concepts and values in making music. Younger scholars working at the Musée de l'Homme in Paris, such as Lortat-Jacob and Hugo Zemp, have begun to inject discussion of relations between scholar and performer into their work (e.g. Lortat-Jacob, 1982). As such, this novel direction in *ethnographie musicale* should be differentiated from its Polish counterpart, which retains a Central European comparative and systematic orientation (Bielawski, 1970; Czekanowska, 1972).

Topics of investigation since 1945

The study of traditional music in Europe since 1945 falls into several broad topic areas: (i) cross-cultural or intra-cultural comparative; (ii) historical or developmental; (iii) systematic (including organology and aesthetics); (iv) formal, structural, or stylistic; and (v) ethnographic, functional, or contextual. To some extent these research perspectives have co-existed with one another and should not be understood as following a linear development; rather, they have acted as points of reference which overlap from time to time. The last grouping in particular cannot easily be separated from some systematic work, yet its primary identifying feature is strong influence from other disciplines, particularly the social sciences since the mid-1960s.

The first of these areas preoccupied scholars between the wars and continued in the later work of Marius Schneider (e.g. 1940, 1946). Wiora notably carried on such work, in which identifying 'European' from 'non-European' traits, and 'folk' from 'primitive' musical layers was characteristic (1952). Tracing the distribution of a melodic formula cross-culturally, such as that which gave rise to both Smetana's 'Vltava' and the Israeli national anthem (List, 1979), or the syllabic rhythm of a European ballad (Baud-Bovy, 1977) represents, however, a more cautious approach. George Herzog (1950) and, more recently, Bruno Nettl have characterized European traditional music as a whole in terms of its basic traits: strophic form, diatonic intervals, isometric rhythms, 'wandering melodies', common song genres (ballad, carol, and so on), and shared dance and instrumental types, although considerable variation exists within individual regions (Nettl, 1965, 2/1973). Nettl also draws attention to the research of Alan Lomax on traditional singing styles in Europe, where the latter has isolated three distinct modes of singing based on social and economic factors: 'Old European', 'Modern European', 'Eurasian' (Lomax, 1968), later dubbed 'European peasant', 'Northwestern European', and 'Old High Culture' (1974).

This conception of three supranational styles which transcend the bounds of culture, politics and language, may identify major tendencies but it is based on small samples and cannot indicate the wide range of stylistic variance often present in one geographic region (e.g. the ornamental styles of Irish *sean-nós* or Hebridean psalm-singing, which appear to have more in common with Mediterranean styles than with the second of Lomax's style areas). 'Oriental' influence, at least in those areas formerly occupied by the Ottoman Turks, has been more closely studied by scholars such as Hoerburger (1967) and C. Rihtman (1966), though the precise extent of Islam's influence on such forms as *cante flamenco* in Spain has been much debated (Crivillé i Bargalló, 1983). Ostensible melodic ties exist, however, between the Spanish and Sephardic *romances* (Etzion and Weich-Shahak, 1988).

Intra-cultural contact and exchange, which has occurred in all areas of Europe to varying degrees, has been documented in specific cases: for Hungarian Gypsies (Šarosi, 1978) and for linguistically diverse cultures in Northwest Ireland (Shields, 1972), while K. Brambats has recently traced elements connecting the vocal drone in Baltic countries to their neighbouring Balkan analogues (1983). In several publications devoted to dance music, Joan Rimmer has demonstrated close connections among the Netherlands, Ireland and Britain (e.g. 1985). These researches are distinguished from earlier types by the freedom from simple diffusionist explanations, and as such are essential to understanding the supranational processes at which the complex of traditional music in Europe operates (cf. Ling, 1989).

Historical studies constitute a parallel, related direction in research from before 1939, and this link was maintained in works by Bence Szabolcsi (1950, 2/1957), in Paul Collaer's *Atlas Historique* (1960), and in that of Walter Salmen on the role of the itinerant musician in the Middle Ages (1960). 'History' was a focus for papers at the Budapest IFMC Conference in 1964 (see *Journal*, 1965). Bachmann's landmark study on the origins of bowing, however, includes ethnomusicological and iconographical evidence as well as historical source criticism (1964, Eng. trans., 1969). The question of origins was, of course, integral to earlier studies, but the nature of history and the process of historicization became a topic of renewed interest in the light of Wiora's work (1980; see Fukač, 1966, on periodization in European traditional music). This was evident in the symposium held at the IMS Conference in Ljubljana in 1967, when the question of historicity was addressed by a panel of Central and East European scholars (1970). Since then the focus has moved more towards matters of chronology and stratigraphy (Harrison, 1976; Schneider, 1978; Elschek, 1981), attempts to identify and explain different kinds of historical problem in ethnomusicology (Schneider, 1984; Bielawski, 1985), and musical archaeology (Lund, 1984; Hickmann and Hughes, 1988).

An essentially ahistoric approach has been followed by some scholars, for example Walter Graf, who investigated problems of musical perception, acoustics and psychology (1980). Aesthetics, as a traditional branch of this orientation, has been discussed by C. Vakarelski for peasant singers in Bulgaria (1957), by K. Kos for changing public taste for 'folk music' in

Yugoslavia (1966) and by Ginette Dunn for English rural singers (1980). Issues of local or native terminology, which more often than not house essential aesthetic concepts, began to be explored early in Scandinavia in relation to instruments (Väisänen, 1938), were taken up by Jan Ling (1967) and, with greater theoretical emphasis, by Radmila Petrović for Serbia (1971), Jan Stęszewski in Poland (1972) and Timothy Rice for Bulgaria (1980). Other approaches to analysis that may be included here are Erich Stockmann's application of information theory to the diffusion of instruments (1972), the subsequent trend towards semiotics (e.g. Blacking, 1981; Lange, 1982), the discussion of psychological features in improvisation (Suliţeanu, 1977) or vocal physiology (in the Swedish herding call, Johnson, 1984) and the advocacy of Asaf'yev's theory of 'intonation' as important to ethnomusicology (Zemtsovsky, 1977). The work of the ICTM Study Group on the Analysis and Systematization of Folk Tunes is a central thread in these developments (*JIFMC*, 1965; Study Group Proceedings, 1969, 1973; Elschek, 1977; see also the proceedings of the Soviet All-Union Seminar, Goshovsky, 1977).

Analysis of form, structure and style (in the technical sense of manner or execution) has likewise continued earlier work. Indeed of all analytical tools in use before 1960 this found the most favour, although with the arrival of alternative techniques such as those mentioned above formal analysis has become less of a conventional task. Attempts to outline a common architectonic process for traditional music in Europe as a whole have been few even though some geographical complexes (e.g. Northwest Europe and the Balkans) have comparable melodic and rhythmic features within them. The Report of the IFMC Study Group for Folk Dance Terminology (now the Group on Ethnochoreology), indeed, argued the necessity of treating the complex problems of dance beyond the limits of individual countries (1975). Marcel-Dubois has addressed the role of musical intervals (1960), ornamentation (1961) and tempo (1965) in European folk music, while a broad view of structural or tectonic principles has been undertaken by the Romanian scholars Emilia Comişel (1969) and Mariana Kahane (1984–6). The loosely unified area of Southeastern Europe, in which interpenetration of ethnic groups and musical styles is a marked feature, has become the focus for more intensive cross-cultural analysis, especially in a period of social change (Elschekova, 1981; cf. Kremenliev, 1975, Petrović, 1973).

As far as the basic structural elements of music are concerned (melody, rhythm, timbre, and so on), the thorough analyses of scholars such as Brăiloiu (on *aksak* rhythm, 1951, or on children's rhythms, 1954) are well-known. A recurring interest in metrical and rhythmic problems has been characteristic of East European work, which is often spurred by language idioms and other cultural factors: a typical example is the analysis of *tempo rubato* in Chopin and Polish folk music by Marian and Jadwiga Sobieski (1963); this was followed by Ludvik Bielawski's full treatment of the rhythms of Polish folk song (1970). Studies by Dzhudzhev (1954) and Dzhidzhev (1964) on the poetic and rhythmic structures of Bulgarian, and by Rudneva on those of Russian songs (1969), offer comparable examples. Although technically an outsider, Birthe Traerup (1971) has analysed rhythm and metre in Albanian historical songs and compared them with the epic songs of other Balkan peoples. In Western Europe, Diego Carpitella has scrutinized the metrical and rhythmic systems of

Italian folk song from the point of view of semiotics (1975), while Jan-Petter Blom relates the flexible rhythms of Hardanger fiddle music to body movement and dance figuration (1981). Dušan Holý has studied the sung units of folk songs from Czechoslovakia and Ukraine with some reference, in the final chapter, to the UNSAKAT computer program devised in Yerevan (Armenia), where precise but artificial syntactic categories have been worked out for comparing the division of the musical line with the structuring of the musical text (1988).

History, language and ethnic identity in Europe have tended to blur lines of tonal, rhythmic and textural demarcation, even in adjacent regions, although a simplified picture of tonality shows a preference for wide-ranging modal structures in Northwest Europe, merging into developed tonal and harmonic forms in Central Europe, and into typically narrow range concepts in Eastern Europe and some parts of the Mediterranean, especially in situations of custom and ritual. The modal structures of British-American balladry, for example, have been arranged by Bertrand Bronson on the basis of tune families rather than in terms of melodic classification (1959–72), the tune family concept having been developed by Samuel Bayard in particular for the ordering of British and British-American vocal and instrumental tunes (1950, 1954). Knudsen, Nielsen and Schiørring schematize Danish ballad melodies by model, type and variant (1976), while typological and classificatory studies have resulted in extensive studies in Poland (Czekanowska, 1972, 1977) and Hungary (Jardányi and Olsvai, 1973). Samuel Baud-Bovy has examined numerous aspects of Greek song structure (1956, 1968), and more recent analysis of melodic models in the music of the Mediterranean is by Giannattasio and Lortat-Jacob concerning improvised structures in Sardinian music (1982). Additional analyses of regional tonal structures can be found in, for instance, Peter Crossley-Holland (1968) for Wales and, with an organo-logical focus, Reidar Sevåg (1973) for Norway; Anna Czekanowska (1964–5) and Vinko Žganec (1963) for Slavic lands; Josep Crivillé i Bargalló (1983) for Spain and Wolfgang Laade (1981) for Corsica. The tentative survey of vocal polyphonic forms in Europe by Ernst Emsheimer (1964) has been supplemented by the research of the Stockmanns in Albania (1965), Knudsen in the Hebrides (1968), Petrović in Serbia (1972) and Brambats for the Baltic countries (1983); Gisela Suliţeanu has discussed antiphony in Romania (1979), and Christian Ahrens instrumental polyphony in the *touloum* playing of Pontic Greeks (1974).

Analysis of traditional music in Soviet Europe from 1945 to 1990 has been almost entirely confined to developmental or structural studies (e.g. Banin, 1973, 1978). V. M. Shchurov, for instance, can show how the modal structure of South Russian songs and instrumental tunes includes diatonic systems of seven tones as well as the more common anhemitonic structures within a 5th (1973). A. A. Banin himself (1978) writes on 'the syllabic-rhythmic method of analysis' that forms the familiar basis for much contemporary Russian work. The influence of folklorists such as Vladimir Propp has shaped much of the contemporary Russian concern with song genres, for instance calendrical and life cycle songs, their structure and development (see Zemtsovsky, 1975).

Studies of style, which stretch from Lajos Lajtha's analysis of Hungarian Gypsy instrumental music (1953) to Svend Nielsen's of the now moribund

Icelandic epic chanting called *kvedaskapur* (1982), normally focus on specific genres, although the ornamental style of *sean-nós* singing in Ireland treated by Bodley (1972–3) spans lyric and religious content (cf. Partridge, 1983). Holý's tracing of stylistic development in the traditional dance music from the Moravian side of the White Carpathians is notable (1969). Lawrence McCullough (1977) and Jos Koning (1979) have dealt with instrumental style in Irish music, the latter specifically with fiddle technique (see also Kotlyarov, 1973 on the interpretive style of Moldavian violin playing). More delimited focuses on technicalities of utterance are Hugh Shields's study of supplementary syllables in Irish singing (1974), J. L. Campbell and F. Collinson's interpretation of 'meaningless' syllables in waulking songs (1969), Bezić's description of Croatian *ojkanje*-singing (1967–8), and Stęszewski's view of the vocal apocope as a cross-cultural phenomenon (1967).

With the mounting influence of anthropology in the 1960s, later studies of traditional music, especially in Western Europe, have tended to become not only more ethnographic in tone but also more eclectic, often remaining faithful to historical viewpoints while exploring newer concepts. Empirical field research was well developed before 1939, for instance, in Eastern Europe with Klyment Kvitka (Goshovsky, 1971–3), Chybiński (Bielawski, 1961) and others (Vakarelski's study of music in his native village, 1952). The unit of the village was a central thrust to work by Romanian sociologists in the 1920s (Brăiloiu, 1960), and this was taken up by scholars in Hungary (Vargyas, 1957), with relatively more attention paid, after 1960, to the 'folk festival' (e.g., Bezić, 1979, on the classifying of Dalmatian *klapa* songs at the Omis festival. Humenjuk and Poricki on festivals in Ukraine, 1966, and Vorontsov and Dobrovol'sky on a festival in the Leningrad region, 1977).

In Western Europe scholars following an ethnographic approach were initially few, but Claudie Marcel-Dubois, prominently, has demonstrated her attachment to ethnography in a number of her studies (e.g. that on the whirling friction-drum of the Central Pyrenees, 1956). 'Regional ethnology' as an umbrella term in France, on the other hand, includes annotated collections of songs (Millien and others, 1977). Of special note are the ethnographic studies carried out in Italy (e.g. Leydi and Pianta, 1975); Carpitella's work on the ritual of tarantism is particularly notable (e.g. 1961). The function of traditional music in education found some response in the decade 1965–75: by Tiberiu Alexandru for teaching panpipes in Romania (1972), by Pál Jardányi for Hungarian folk songs (1975), and Helmut Segler for 'new' folk songs in Germany (1975). Some dichotomy is apparent in these studies, where a West European view of music education tends to stress social change and the creation of original songs, and the East European which, doubtless because of ideological and other factors, has maintained a more conservative concept of traditional music and its uses.

In the 1970s and 1980s the emphasis on context and performance, with special attention to factors relating to musical change, led to studies dwelling on individual creators and re-creators. The original notion of research into individual repertoires (Schiørring, 1956) was at the same time balanced by interest in the creative personalities of singers and instrumentalists (e.g. work by Bulgarian scholars in the early 1950s, also Henssen, 1953), but the effect of later anthropological work concentrated attention on the concepts of the performer: studies by Hopkins in Norway (1986), Lortat-Jacob in Sardinia (1981), Nielsen in Iceland (1982), Pekkilä and others in Finland (1983) and Porter in Scotland (1976, 1978, 1988) aimed at uncovering 'emic' explanations of communication, meaning, and value as well as concepts on composition and classification. These studies disclose a burgeoning interest in cognitive aspects of traditional music and its genesis, in stark contrast to the comparative and historical research in vogue before 1960.

It remains to note work on the relationship of traditional music to other factors in expressive culture; the interaction, as it were, of forms such as dance, verbal texts, or conventional categories ('art', 'church', 'folk'; the weak basis for these has been pointed out by Blacking, 1981, 'Making Artistic Popular Music', and Leisiö, 1983). The interface of music, dance and text was actually the topic of an early IFMC symposium (1960). With the growth of semiotics as a tool for analysing cultural forms other than language, some attempts have been made to explore the possibilities for music (Blacking, 1981, 'The Problem of "Ethnic" Perception') and dance (Giurghescu, 1974; Lange, 1982). But the basic assumption that musical metre, for instance, has no 'objective' existence, such as a typical semiotic analysis might demand, has led Blom and Kvifte (1986) to question further, in discussing the ambivalence of metre in Norwegian dance music, John Blacking's thesis of 'consensus of opinion about the principles on which music should be organized' in any society (1973) and to call for a general theory of rhythm and communication.

The use of traditional idioms by composers in the 19th century has been well documented, but studies of key transitional figures have been extended by Brăiloiu's study of Debussy (pentatonic structures, 1956), those of Geck (1975) and Vetterl (1968) on Janáček, Klusen's on Mahler (1963), as well as by continuing work on Bartók, Stravinsky and Vaughan Williams. Among younger 'art' music composers, Berio and Globokar stand out for their adaptations or arrangements of folk music, while Volkov (1981) has described the newer 'folkloristic' wave of Soviet composers. Church musical practice has likewise had close links with popular traditions over the continent (Anglès, 1964; Avenary, 1964; Dragoumis, 1971; D. Petrović, 1975; A. Petrović, 1982; Žganec, 1983), and the extent of mutual influence is only one of the many problems facing ethnomusicologists in Europe. Leydi and Rossi, for example, have made observations on non-liturgical religious songs (1965).

The most recent work on European musics has included the following concerns: the control and management of musical production in complex societies (in France, Romania, Sardinia: Lortat-Jacob, 1984; in Ireland: Henry, 1989), myth and ideology in northern Europe (Donner, 1985), class- and self-identity in relation to music (Krader, 1986; Manuel, 1989), dance behaviour (Garfias, 1984, on Romanian Gypsies; Giurghescu, 1986, on adolescent males and females in Transylvania; Stockmann, 1985, on the relationship with human evolution); acoustical analysis of herding calls in Sweden and Switzerland (Johnson, 1984; Bolle-Zemp, 1985), folk hymn singing (Suojanen, 1984); revival and innovation (Ledang, 1986; Ling, 1986); and music and trance (Rouget, 1980). The process of urbanization, or traditional forms in urban environments, is an overarching preoccupation, while the relation between gender and music, explored by Marcia Herndon and Norma McLeod for the Maltese form *bormliza* (1975), has come to the forefront with the formation of a new ICTM Study Group (1987; see also Auerbach, 1987; Sugarman, 1989; M. Herndon and S. Ziegler, 1990). Iconography, likewise, has become a recent focus for group research on the historical and social contexts of traditional music.

As Wachsmann proposed (1980), it may be that folk or traditional music has not yet been shown to have a stylistic identity of its own. Studies of the internal characteristics of such music, however, cannot provide the whole answer, since concepts of value, context, performance and use collectively override purely stylistic questions. Ethnomusicology in Europe, consequently, is as much a matter of shifting into novel research modes as it is of consolidating knowledge of the musical products or their stylistic character. We simply need to know more about the fundamental biological, cognitive and social factors involved in traditional music and its contexts throughout the subcontinent.

The most general problem in Europe, then, is to determine the essential features of music-making at basic levels, from the individual to the local region, thus suggesting that it is an ethnomusicology *in* or *throughout* Europe rather than one *of* Europe that is the current mandate. Particular problems, on the other hand, are the dichotomies that flourish in all complex societies: rural versus urban values, upper versus lower class tastes, indigenous ethnic minorities versus the nation state, local versus eclectic 'popular' musical idioms, consumerism versus musical activism, a historicized concept in performing traditional music versus the search for novel expression, often by technological means. Some of these issues have been explored in the past, but too often unimaginatively because of the researcher's preconceptions, poor research design or inadequate fieldwork.

The emphasis in the past forty years has been, as Wachsmann's remark suggests, almost entirely upon collection and analysis of musical products with a view to establishing, among other things, stylistic identity: the systematic aspects have tended to overwhelm the wider nature and humanistic purpose of research. Yet because of later questioning of past methods and objectives, many scholars are now aware that sensitive fieldwork forms the most vital part of any serious inquiry into Europe's regional music systems, and that such research must command scrupulous attention to ethics and personal interaction as much as to purely musical issues.

Bibliography

A. Galli: *Estetica della musica* (Turin, 1898)

J. Tiersot: 'Notes d'ethnographie musicale, i', *Le ménéstrel*, lxvi–lxviii (1900–02); pubd separately, 1905

C. J. Sharp: *English Folk-Song: Some Conclusions* (London, 1907)

P. Grainger: 'Collecting with the Phonograph', *JFSS*, iii (1908–09), 147–242

J. Kunst: *Terschellinger volksleven* (The Hague, 1915, 2/1937)

B. Bartók: 'Musikfolklore', *Musikblätter des Anbruch*, i (1919), 102

——: 'Mi a népzene? A parasztzene hatása az újabb műzenére: a népzene jelentőségérol' [What is Folk Music? The Influence of Peasant Music on Contemporary Composition], *Új idők*, xxxvii (1931), 626, 718, 818; Eng. trans. in *Béla Bartók Essays*, ed. B. Suchoff (London, 1976), 5

O. Seewald: *Beiträge zur Kenntnis der steinzeitlichen Musikinstrumente Europas* (Vienna, 1934)

C. Sachs: 'Prolégomènes à une préhistoire musicale de l'Europe', *RdM*, xx (1936), 22; Eng. trans., as 'Towards a Prehistory of Occidental Music', *PAMS 1937*, 91

A. O. Väisänen: 'Wirklichkeitsgrund der finnisch-estnischen Kantelerunen', *Acta Ethnologica*, i (Copenhagen, 1938), 31

W. Danckert: *Das europäische Volkslied* (Berlin, 1939/R1970)

A. M. Buchanan: 'Modal and Melodic Structure in Anglo-American Folk Music: a Neutral Mode', *PAMS 1939* (1940), 84

M. Schneider: 'Kaukasische Parallelen zur mittelalterlichen Mehrstimmigkeit', *AcM*, xii (1940), 52

——: 'A propósito del influjo árabe: ensayo de etnografia musical de la España medieval', *AnM*, i (1946), 31–141

——: *El origen musical de los animalos-simbolos en la mitología y la escultura antiguas* (Barcelona, 1946)

F. Bose: 'Vergleichende Musikwissenschaft heute', *Musica*, iii (1949), 255

W. Wiora: 'Concerning the Conception of Authentic Folk Music', *JIFMC*, i (1949), 14

S. Bayard: 'Prolegomena to a Study of the Principal Melodic Families of Folksong', *Journal of American Folklore*, lxiii (1950), 1–44

G. Herzog: 'Song: Folk Song and the Music of Folk Song', *Funk & Wagnalls Standard Dictionary of Folklore, Mythology and Legend*, ii, ed. M. Leach (New York, 1950), 1032

J. Kunst: *Musicologica: a Study of the Nature of Ethno-musicology, its Problems, Methods and Representative Personalities* (Amsterdam, 1950, enl. 2/1955 as *Ethnomusicology*, 3/1959; suppl., 1960)

B. Szabolcsi: *A melodia története* (Budapest, 1950, 2/1957; Eng. trans., 1965, as *A History of Melody*)

B. Bartók and A. B. Lord: *Serbo-Croatian Folk Songs* (New York, 1951)

C. Brăiloiu: 'Le rhythme *aksak*', *RdM*, xxx (1951), 71

G. Henssen: *Überlieferung und Persönlichkeit: Lieder und Erzählungen des Egbert Gerrits* (Münster, 1951)

C. Rihtman: 'Čičak Janja – narodni pjevac sa Kupresa' [Čičak Janja, Folksinger from Kupres], *Bilten Instituta za proučavanje folklore* (Sarajevo, 1951), 33

R. Kacarova: 'Tri pokolenija narodni pevici' [Three Generations of Folksingers], *IIM*, i (1952), 43

C. Vakarelski: 'Muzikata v zhivota na rodnoto mi selo: bitovi materiali ot s. Momina Klisura: Pazardzhishko' [Music in the Life of my Native Village of Momina Klisura: Pazardzhik District], *IIM*, i (1952), 167

W. Wiora: *Europäische Volksgesang: gemeinsame Formen in charakteristischen Abwandlungen* (Cologne, 1952; Eng. trans. 1967)

L. Lajtha: 'Egy "hamis" zenekar' [An 'out of tune' Band], *Emlékkönyv Kodály Zoltán 70-ik születésnapjára* [Memorial Book for Zoltán Kodály's 70th Birthday], ed. B. Szabolcsi and D. Bartha (Budapest, 1953), 169

C. Vranska: 'Djado Mano – avtor i izpalnitel na narodni pesni s. Maslovo, Sofisko' [Old Mano, Author and Singer of Folk Songs from the Village of Maslovo, District of Sofia], *Izvestija na Etnografskija institu i muzej – BAN*, i (Sofia, 1953), 143–92

S. Bayard: 'Two Representative Tune Families of British Tradition', *Midwest Folklore*, iv (1954), 13

C. Brăiloiu: 'Le rythme enfantin: notions liminaires', *Colloques du Wégimont*, i, ed. P. Collaer (Paris and Brussels, 1954), 64

S. Dzhudzhev: *Teoriia na bulgarskata narodna muzika* [Theory of Bulgarian Folk Music] i: *Ritmika i metrika* (Sofia, 1954)

G. Keremidchiev: *Narodnijat pevec djado Vico Bončev* [Folksinger Vicho Bonchev] (Sofia, 1954)

W. Steinitz: *Deutsche Volkslieder demokratischen Charakters aus sechs Jahrhunderten* (Berlin, 1954, 1962)

T. Alexandru: *Instrumentele musicale ale poporului Romĭn* [Folk Music Instruments of the Romanian People] (Bucharest, 1956)

S. Baud-Bovy: 'The Strophe of Rhymed Distichs in Greek Songs', *Studia memoriae Belae Bartók sacra* (Budapest, 1956, 3/1959), 359

C. Brăiloiu: 'Pentatonismes chez Debussy', *Studia memoriae Belae Bartók sacra* (Budapest, 1956, 3/1959), 385

C. Marcel-Dubois: 'Le Toulouhou des Pyrénées Centrales: usage rituel et parenté d'un tambour à friction tournoyant', *Colloques du Wégimont*, iii (1956), 55

N. Schiørring: *Selma Nielsens Viser* (Copenhagen, 1956)

C. Vakarelski: 'Belezki po musikalnata teorija i estetika na naroda' [Notes on Popular Music, Theory and Aesthetics], *IIM*, iv (1957), 123

L. Vargyas: 'Das Musikleben im ungarischen Dorf und die Methoden seiner Enforschung', *Deutsches Jb für Volkskunde*, iii (1957), 447

W. Wiora: *Europäische Volksmusik und abendländische Tonkunst* (Kassel, 1957)

V. Karbusicky: *Dělnicke pisně* [Workers' Songs] (Prague, 1958)

E. Stoin and I. Kachulev: *Balgarski savremenni narodni pesni* [Present-day Bulgarian Folk Song] (Sofia, 1958)

B. Bartók: *Slovenské ludové piesne* [Slovak Folk Songs] (Bratislava, 1959–)

B. H. Bronson: *The Traditional Tunes of the Child Ballads* (Princeton, NJ, 1959–72)

W. Wiora: 'Der Untergang des Volksliedes und sein zweites Dasein', *Musikalische Zeitfragen*, vii (1959), 9

A. Baines: *Bagpipes* (Oxford, 1960)

C. Brăiloiu: *Vie musicale d'un village: recherches sur le répertoire de Drăguş (Roumanie 1929–1932)* (Paris, 1960)

P. Collaer and others: *Atlas historique de la musique* (Brussels, 1960)

C. Marcel-Dubois: 'Présence ou absence de la constante de quarte, de quinte et d'octave: son rôle structurel dans l'ethnomusicologie européenne', *La résonance dans les échelles musicales* (Paris, 1960), 143

A. Häusler: 'Neue Funde steinzeitlichen Musikinstrumente in Osteuropa', *Wiss. Zeitschr. Martin Luther Univ. Halle-Wittenberg*, ix (1960), 321

W. Salmen: *Der fahrender Musiker im europäischen Mittelalter* (Kassel, 1960)

——: 'European Song (1300–1530)', *NOHM*, iii: *Ars Nova and Renaissance, 1300–1500* (London, 1960), 349–80

L. Bielawski, ed.: *A. Chybiński: O polskiej muzyce ludowej: wybór prac etnograficznych* [On Polish Folk Music: a Selection of his Ethnographic Works] (Kraków and Warsaw, 1961)

D. Carpitella: 'L'esorcismo coreutico musicale del tarantismo', in E. de Martino, *La terra del rimorsi* (Milan, 1961), appx. iii, 334

C. Marcel-Dubois: 'Remarques sur l'ornamentation dans l'ethnomusicologie européenne', *IMSCR*, viii (New York, 1961), i, 439

W. Wiora, *Die vier Weltalter der Musik* (Stuttgart, 1961; Eng. trans., 1965)

F. Rubtsov: *Intonacionnoye sjazi v pesennom tvoroestve slavjanskich narodov* [Relations in the Intonation of the Folk Songs of the Slavs] (Leningrad, 1962)

M. Sobieski and J. Sobieska: 'Das Tempo rubato bei Chopin und in der polnischen Volksmusik', *Chopin Congress, Warszawa 1960* (Warsaw, 1963), 247

E. Klusen: 'Gustav Mahler und das Volkslied seiner Heimat', *JIFMC*, xv (1963), 29

J. Kuckertz: *Gestaltvariationen in den Bartok gesammelten rumänischen Colinden* (Regensburg, 1963)

W. Laade: *Die Struktur der korsischen Lamento-Melodik* (Baden-Baden, 1963)

K. Vertkov and others: *Atlas of Musical Instruments of the Peoples Inhabiting the USSR* (Moscow, 1963; Eng. trans., 1975)

V. Žganec: 'La gamme istrienne dans la musique populaire yougoslave', *SM*, iv (1963), 101

H. Anglès: 'Relations of Spanish Folk Song to the Gregorian Chant', *JIFMC*, xvi (1964), 54

H. Avenary: 'The Hasidic Nigun – Ethos and Melos of a Folk Liturgy', *JIFMC*, xvi (1964), 60

W. Bachmann: *Die Anfänge des Streichinstrumentenspiels* (Leipzig, 1964, 2/1966; Eng. trans., 1969)

T. Dzhidzhev: 'Kam vaprosa za stikhovo-ritmichniya stroezh na balgarskite narodni pesni' [On the Question of the Poetic-rhythmic Structure of Bulgarian Folk Songs], *IIM*, x (1964), 217

E. Emsheimer: 'Some Remarks on European Folk Polyphony', *JIFMC*, xvi (1964), 43

F. Ll. Harrison and J. Rimmer: *European Musical Instruments* (London, 1964)

A. P. Merriam: *The Anthropology of Music* (Evanston, IL, 1964)

S. Chianis: *Folk Songs of Mantineia, Greece* (Berkeley and Los Angeles, CA, 1965)

V. Hadžimanov: 'Les melodies funèbres du séisme de Skopie', *SM*, vii (1965), 71

C. Marcel-Dubois: 'Le tempo dans le musique de tradition orale', *FAM*, xii (1965), 204

R. Leydi and A. Rossi: *Osservazioni sul canti religiosi non liturgici* (Milan, 1965)

B. Nettl: *Folk and Traditional Music of the Western Continents* (Englewood Cliffs, NJ, 1965, 2/1973)

W. Steinitz: *Arbeiterlied und Volkslied* (Berlin, 1965)

D. and E. Stockmann and W. Fiedler: *Albanische Volksmusik, i: Gesänge der Çamen* (Berlin, 1965)

W. Danckert: *Das Volkslied im Abendland* (Berne and Munich, 1966)

J. Fukač: 'K problému periodizace evropského hudebního folklóru' [On the Problem of Periodization in European Folk Music], *Strážnice* 1946–1966, ed. V. Frolec, D. Holý and J. Tomeš (Brno, 1966), 329

A. Humenjuk and A. Poricki: 'Lidové slavnosti na Ukrajine' [Folk Festivals in Ukraine], *Strážnice 1946–1966*, ed. V. Frolec, D. Holý and J. Tomeš (Brno, 1966)

J. Maróthy: *Zéne es polgar – zéne es proletar* [Music and the Bourgeois, Music and the Proletarian] (Budapest, 1966; Eng. trans., 1974)

C. Rihtman: 'Orientalische Elemente in der traditionellen Musik Bosniens und der Herzegovina',

Das orientalische Element am Balkan, ii: Balkanologen-Tagung (Graz, 1966), 97

D. Stockmann: 'Das Problem der Transkription in der musikethnologischen Forschung', *Deutsches Jb für Volkskunde*, xii (1966), 207

E. Veiga de Oliveira: *Instrumentos musicais populares portugueses* (Lisbon, 1966)

K. Vetterl and others: *A Select Bibliography of European Folk Music* (Prague, 1966)

B. Bartók: *Rumanian Folk Music*, ed. B. Suchoff (The Hague, 1967–75)

I. Bengtson: 'On Melody Registration and "Mona"', *Elektronische Datenverarbeitung in der Musikwissenschaft*, ed. H. Heckman (Regensburg, 1967), 136–74

J. Bezić: 'Muzički folklọr Sinjske krajine' [Folk Music of the Sinj District], *Narodna umjetnost*, v–v (1967–8), 175

F. Bose: 'Volkslied – Schlager – Folklore', *Zeitschrift für Volkskunde*, 63 (1967), 60

O. Elschek and others: *Annual Bibliography of European Ethnomusicology* (Bratislava, 1967–)

S. Erixon: 'European Ethnology in Our Time', *Ethnologia europaea*, i (1967), 3

F. Hoerburger: 'Oriental Elements in the Folk Dance and Folk Dance Music of Greek Macedonia', *JIFMC*, xix (1967), 71

E. Klusen: 'Das Gruppenlied als Gegenstand', *Jb für Volksliedforschung*, xii (1967), 21

J. Ling: *Nyckelharpan* (Stockholm, 1967)

A. L. Lloyd: *Folk Song in England* (London, 1967)

B. Sárosi: *Die Volksmusikinstrumente Ungarns* (Leipzig, 1967)

J. Stęszewski: 'Die Apokope, eine Eigentümlichkeit im Volksliedvortrag', *Festschrift für Walter Wiora* (Kassel, 1967), 641

S. Baud-Bovy: 'Equivalences métriques dans la musique vocale grecque antique et moderne', *RdM*, liv (1968), 3

P. Crossley-Holland: 'The Tonal Limits of Welsh Folk-Song', *Journal of the Welsh Folk-song Society*, v/2 (1968), 46

V. L. Goshovsky: *Ukrainskiye pesni Zakarpat'ya* (Moscow, 1968)

T. Knudsen: 'Ornamental Hymn/Psalm Singing in Denmark, the Faroe Islands, and the Hebrides', *DFS Information*, lxviii/2 (Copenhagen, 1968)

A. Lomax: *Folk Song Style and Culture* (Washington, DC, 1968)

J. V. S. Megaw: 'Problems and Non-Problems in Palaeo-organology: a Musical Miscellany', *Studies in Ancient Europe*, ed. J. J. Coles and D. D. A. Simpson (Leicester, 1968), 333

K. Vetterl: 'Janáček's Creative Relationship to Folk Music', *Leoš Janáček et musica europaea: Brno iii* (1968), 235

A. F. W. Bentzon: *The Launeddas: a Sardinian Folk Music Instrument* (Copenhagen, 1969)

B. H. Bronson: *The Ballad as Song* (Berkeley and Los Angeles, CA, 1969)

J. L. Campbell and F. Collinson: 'The Meaningless Refrain Syllables and Their Significance', *Hebridean Folksongs*, i (Oxford, 1969), 227

E. Comişel: 'La forme architectonique de la musique populaire', *IIM*, xiii (1969), 261

D. Holý: *Probleme der Entwicklung und des Stils der Volksmusik* (Brno, 1969)

E. Klusen: *Volkslied: Fund und Erfindung* (Cologne, 1969)

T. Popova: *O pesnyakh nashikh dney* [On the Songs of Today] (Moscow, 1969)

A. Rudneva: 'Ritmika stikha i napeva russkoy narodnoy pesne' [The Rhythm of Verse and Melody in Russian Folk Song], *IIM*, xiii (1969), 303–34 [with Fr. summary]

E. Stockmann, ed.: *Studia instrumentorum musicae popularis*, i (Stockholm, 1969)

L. Bielawski: 'Etnografia muzyczna w XXV-leciu PRL', *Muzyka*, ii/57 (1970), 3

——: *Rytmika polskich pieśni ludowych* [The Rhythm of Polish Folk Songs] (Warsaw, 1970)

J. Ling: *Musiksociologiska projekt i Göteborg* (Göteborg, 1970)

D. Stockmann: 'Musik als kommunikatives System: Informations- und zeichen-theoretische Aspekte insbesondere bei der Erforschung mündlich tradierter Musik', *DJbM* (1970), 76

W. Suppan: 'Zur Konzeption einer "europäischen" Musikethnologie', *Ethnologia europaea*, iv (1970), 132

M. Bošković-Stulli: 'O folklorizmu', *Zbornik za narodni život i običaje*, xlv (1971), 171

A. Czekanowska: *Etnografia muzyczna* [Musical Ethnography] (Warsaw, 1971)

M. Ph. Dragoumis: 'Some Remarks on the Traditional Music of the Greeks of Corsica', *Studies in Eastern Chant*, ii, ed. M. Velimirovic (London, 1971), 28

V. L. Goshovsky, ed.: *Kl. Kvitka: Izbranniye trudi* [Selected Works], 2 vols. (Moscow, 1971–3)

——: *U istokov narodnoy muziki slavyan* [The Sources of Slavic Folk Music] (Moscow, 1971)

B. Krader: 'Russian Folk Music Records: a Review Essay', *EM*, xv (1971), 432

R. Petrović: 'Some Aspects of Formal Expression in Serbian Folk Songs', *YIFMC*, ii (1971), 63

B. Traerup: 'Rhythm and Metre in Albanian Historical Folk Songs from Kosovo (Drenica)

Compared with the Epic Songs of Other Balkan Peoples', *Makedonski folklor*, vii–viii (1971), 247

T. Alexandru: 'An Account of the Teaching of Some Folk Instruments in Romania: the Panpipe', *YIFMC*, iii (1972), 143

S. Bodley: 'Technique and Structure in "Sean-Nós" Singing', *Éigse Cheol Tíre/Irish Folk Music Studies*, i (1972–3), 44

P. Cooke: 'Problems of Notating Pibroch: a Study of "Maol Donn"', *Scottish Studies*, xvi/1 (1972), 41

A. Czekanowska: *Ludowe melodie wąskiego zakresu w krajach słowiańskich* [Folk Melodies of Narrow Range in Slavic Countries] (Warsaw, 1972)

F. J. de Hen: 'Folk Instruments of Belgium', *GSJ*, xxv (1972), 87; xxvi (1973), 86

I. J. Katz: *Judeo-Spanish Traditional Ballads from Jerusalem: an Ethnomusicological Study* (New York, 1972–5)

K. Kos: 'New Dimensions in Folk Music: a Contribution to the Study of Musical Tastes in Contemporary Yugoslav Society', *IRASM*, iii/1 (1972), 61

R. Petrović: 'Dvoglas u muzičkoj tradiciji Srbije' [Two-Voiced Singing in Serbian Musical Tradition], *Rad XVII Congresa Saveza Udruzenja Folklorista Jugoslavije – Porec 1970* (Zagreb, 1972)

H. Shields: 'Singing Traditions of a Bilingual Parish in Northwest Ireland', *YIFMC*, iii (1972), 109

J. Stęszewski: 'Sachen, Bewusstsein und Benennungen in ethnomusikologischen Untersuchungen', *Jb für Volksliedforschung*, xvii (1972), 131

E. Stockmann: 'The Diffusion of Musical Instruments as an Inter-ethnic Process of Communication', *YIFMC*, iii (1972), 128

—— ed.: *Studia instrumentorum musicae popularis*, ii (Stockholm, 1972)

A. A. Banin, ed.: *Muzikal'naya fol'koristika*, 1 (Moscow, 1973)

J. Blacking: *How Musical Is Man?* (Seattle and London, 1973)

M. Bröcker: *Die Drehleier: Ihr Bau und ihre Geschichte* (Düsseldorf, 1973)

P. Jardányi and I. Olsvai, eds.: *Népdaltípusok* [Folksong Types], *Corpus musicae popularis hungaricae*, vi, ed. B. Bartók and Z. Kodály (Budapest, 1973)

V. Karbusicky: *Ideologie im Lied: Lied in der Ideologie* (Cologne, 1973)

B. Kotlyarov: 'O nekotorikh osobennostyakh ispolnitel'nogo stilya moldavskogo narodnogo skripichnogo iskusstva' [On Certain Characteristics of the Interpretive Style of Moldavian Fiddle Playing], *Problemi muzikal'nogo fol'klora narodov SSSR*, ed. I. I. Zemtsovsky (Moscow, 1973), 285

F. Rubtsov: *Stat'i po muzikal'nomu fol'kloru* (Leningrad and Moscow, 1973)

V. M. Shchurov: 'O ladovom stroyenii yuzhnorusskih pesen' [On the Modal Structure of South Russian Songs], Banin, ed. (1973), 107

R. Sevåg: 'Neutral Tones and the Problem of Mode in Norwegian Folk Music', *SIMP*, iii (1973), 207

I. I. Zemtsovsky, ed.: *Problemi muzikal'nogo fol'klora narodov SSSR* (Moscow, 1973)

C. Ahrens: 'Polyphony in *touloum* Playing by the Pontic Greeks', *YIFMC*, v (1974), 122

A. Giurghescu: 'La danse comme objet semiotique', *YIFMC*, v (1974), 175

G. Hillestrom, ed.: *Studia instrumentorum musicae popularis*, iii (Stockholm, 1974) [Festschrift for Ernst Emsheimer]

E. Klusen: *Zur Situation des Singens in der Bundesrepublik Deutschland*, i: *Der Umgang mit dem Lied*; ii: *Die Lieder* (Cologne, 1974–5)

L. Kunz: *Die Volksmusikinstrumente der Tschechoslowakei*, i (Leipzig, 1974)

A. Lomax: 'Singing', *Encyclopaedia Britannica*, xvi (1974), 789

R. Petrović: 'Folk Music of Eastern Yugoslavia: a Process of Acculturation, Some Relevant Elements', *IRASM*, v/1 (1974), 217

H. Shields: 'Supplementary Syllables in Anglo-Irish Singing', *YIFMC*, v (1974), 62

D. Carpitella: 'Sistema metrico e sistema ritmico nei canti popolari', *Actes du 1er congrès international de semiotique musicale, Beograd 17–21 Oct. 1973* (Pesaro, 1975), 40

W. Deutsch, ed.: *Die Geige in der europäischen Volksmusik* (Vienna, 1975)

A. Geck: *Das Volksliedmaterial Leoš Janáčeks* (Regensburg, 1975)

P. Gronow: 'Ethnic Music and the Soviet Record Industry', *EM*, xix (1975), 91

G. Holst: *Road to Rembetika* (Athens, 1975)

P. Jardányi: 'Folk Music and Musical Education', *Music Education in Hungary*, ed. S. Frigyes (Budapest, 1975), 13

V. Karbusicky: 'Soziologische Aspekte der Volksliedforschung', *Handbuch des Volksliedes*, ii, ed. R. W. Brednich, L. Röhrich and W. Suppan (Munich, 1975), 45

233

B. Kremenliev: 'Social and Cultural Changes in Balkan Music', *Western Folklore*, xxxiv (1975), 117

R. Leydi and B. Pianta, eds.: *Brescia e il suo territorio* (Milan, 1975)

N. McLeod and M. Herndon: 'The *Bormliza*: Maltese Folksong Style and Women', *Journal of American Folklore*, 88 (1975), 81

B. Nettl: 'The State of Research in Ethnomusicology and Recent Developments', *CMc*, xx (1975), 67

D. Petrović: 'Church Elements in Serbian Ritual Songs', *Beiträge zur Musikkultur des Balkans*, i: *Walter Wünsch zum 65. Geburtstag*, ed. R. Flotzinger (Graz, 1975), 109

H. Segler: 'Das "Volkslied" im Musikunterricht', *Handbuch des Volksliedes*, ii, ed. R. W. Brednich, L. Röhrich and W. Suppan (Munich, 1975), 681

W. Wiora: *Ergebnisse und Aufgaben vergleichender Musikforschung* (Darmstadt, 1975)

I. I. Zemtsovsky: *Melodika kalendarnikh pesen* [Melodies of Calendar Songs] (Leningrad, 1975)

M. P. Baumann: *Musikfolklore und Musikfolklorismus: eine ethnomusikologische Untersuchung zum Funktionswandel des Jodels* (Winterthur, 1976)

F. H. Harrison: 'Towards a Chronology of Celtic Folk Instruments', *SIMP*, iv (1976), 98

T. Knudsen, S. Nielsen and N. Schiørring, eds.: *Danmarks gamle folkeviser*, xi: *Melodier* (Copenhagen, 1976)

I. Markoff: 'Two-Part Singing from the Razlog District of Southwestern Bulgaria', *YIFMC*, vii (1976), 134

J. Porter: 'Jeannie Robertson's "My Son David": a Conceptual Performance Model', *Journal of American Folklore*, lxxxix (1976), 5

A. Schneider: *Musikwissenschaft und Kulturkreislehre: Zur Methodik und Geschichte der Vergleichenden Musikwissenschaft* (Bonn, 1976)

A. Simic: 'Country 'n' Western Yugoslav Style: Contemporary Folk Music as a Mirror of Social Sentiment', *Journal of Popular Culture*, x (1976), 156

D. Stockmann: 'Zur Analyse schriftlos überlieferter Musik', *BMw*, xviii (1976), 235

E. Stockmann, ed.: *Studia instrumentorum musicae popularis*, iv (Stockholm, 1976)

V. Atanasov: *Sistematika na balgarskite narodni instrumenti* (Sofia, 1977)

S. Baud-Bovy: 'Sur la ballade européenne', *SM*, xix (1977), 235

A. Czekanowska: 'On the Theory and Definition of Melodic Type', *YIFMC*, viii (1977), 108

O. Elschek: 'Zum gegenwärtigen Stand der Volksliedanalyse und Volksliedklassifikation: ein Forschungsbericht der Study Group for Analysis and Systematization of Folk Music der I.F.M.C.', *YIFMC*, viii (1977), 21

V. Goshovsky, ed.: *First All-Union Seminar on Machine Aspects of Algorithmic Formalized Analysis of Musical Texts (Yerevan-Dilijan, 27. Oct.–1. Nov. 1975): Materials* (Yerevan, 1977)

V. E. Gusev: 'Fol'klor i sotsialisticheskaia kul'tura' [Folklore and Socialist Culture], *Sovremennost'i fol'klor: stat'i i material'i*, ed. V. E. Gusev (Moscow, 1977), 7

W. Heimann: 'Zur Theorie des musikalischen Folklorismus: Idee, Funktion, und Dialektik', *Zeitschrift für Volkskunde*, lxvii/2 (1977), 181

L. E. McCullough: 'Style in Traditional Irish Music', *EM*, xxi (1977), 85

A. Millien and others: *Chansons du Nivernais populaires et du Morvan (documents d'ethnologie regionale*, v) (Grenoble, 1977)

J. Porter: 'Prolegomena to a Comparative Study of European Folk Music', *EM*, xxi (1977), 435

J. Shepherd and others: *Whose Music? A Sociology of Musical Languages* (London, 1977)

I. Semzowski: 'Die Bedeutung der Intonationstheorie Boris Asafiews für die Entwicklung der Methodologie der musikalischen Folkloristik', *Sozialistische Musikkultur: Traditionen, Probleme, Perspektiven*, ed. J. Elsner and G. Ordshonikidse (Berlin, 1977), 95

E. Stockmann, ed.: *Studia instrumentorum musicae popularis*, v (Stockholm, 1977)

G. Suliţeanu: 'Les implications psychologiques dans la structure du processus de l'improvisation: concernant le folklore musical roumain', *YIFMC*, viii (1977), 97

Y. Vorontsov and B. Dobrovol'sky: 'Festival fol'klora leningradskoye oblasti' [Folklore Festival in Leningrad], *Sovremennost' i folk'lor: stat'i i materiali*, ed. I. I. Zemtsovsky (Moscow, 1977), 312–19

T. Alexandru: *Folkloristica, Organologie, Muzicologie: Studii* (Bucharest, 1978)

E. Alekseyev and others: *Sotsiologicheskiye aspekti izucheniya muzikal'novo folk'lora* (Alma-Ata, 1978)

A. A. Banin, ed.: *Muzikal'naya fol'kloristika*, ii (Moscow, 1978)

B. Bartók and A. B. Lord: *Yugoslav Folk Music*, ed. B. Suchoff (Albany, NY, 1978)

O. Elschek: 'Stilbegriff und Stilschichten in der slovakisch Volksmusik', *Studia musicologica*, xx (1978), 263–303

K. A. Gourlay: 'Towards a Reassessment of the Ethnomusicologist's Role in Research', *EM*, xxv (1981), 185

M. Mazo: 'Nikol'skiye prichitaniya i ikh syazi s drugimi zhanrami mestnoy pesennoy traditsii' [The Nikolsky Laments and their Connections with other Genres of Local Traditional Songs], *Muzikal'naya fol'kloristika*, ed. A. A. Banin, ii (1978), 213–55

S. Oledzki: *Polske instrumenti ludowe* [Polish Folk Instruments] (Kraków, 1978)

J. Porter: 'Introduction: the Traditional Music of Europeans in America', *Selected Reports in Ethnomusicology*, iii/1 (1978), 1

——: 'The Turriff Family of Fetterangus: Society, Learning, Creation and Re-Creation of Traditional Song', *Folk Life*, xvi (1978), 7

B. Sárosi: *Gypsy Music* (Budapest, 1978)

A. Schneider: 'Stil, Schicht, Stratigraphie und Geschichte der Volksmusik: Zur historischen Erforschung oral tradierter Musik', *SM*, xx (1978), 341

A. Simon: 'Probleme, Methoden und Ziele der Ethnomusikologie', *Jb für musikalische Volks- und Völkerkunde*, ix (1978), 8

F. Anoyanakis: *Greek Folk Musical Instruments* (Athens, 1979)

J. Bezić and others, eds.: *Zbornik dalmatinskih klapskih pjesama izvedenih na festivalima u Omišu od 1967 do 1976* (Omiš, 1979)

S. Erdely: 'Ethnic Music in the United States: an Overview', *YIFMC*, xi (1979), 114

J. Koning: 'That Old Plaintive Touch': On the Relation between Tonality in Irish Traditional Dance-Music and the Left Hand Technique of Fiddlers in East Co. Clare', *SIMP*, vi (Stockholm, 1979), 80

G. List: 'The Distribution of a Melodic Formula: Diffusion or Polygenesis?' *YIFMC*, x (1979), 33

E. Stockmann, ed.: *Studia instrumentorum musicae popularis*, vi (Stockholm, 1979)

G. Suliţeanu: 'Antiphonal Performances in Roumanian Folk Music', *YIFMC*, xi (1979), 40

G. Dunn: *The Fellowship of Song: Popular Singing Traditions in East Suffolk* (London, 1980)

W. Graf: *Vergleichende Musikwissenschaft: Ausgewählte Aufsätze*, ed. F. Födermayr (Vienna, 1980)

D. Harker: *One for the Money: Politics and Popular Song* (London, 1980)

M. Karpeles: 'International Folk Music Council', *Grove 6*

J. Koning: 'The Fieldworker as Performer: Fieldwork Objectives and Social Roles in County Clare, Ireland', *EM*, xxiv (1980), 417

T. Rice: 'Aspects of Bulgarian Musical Thought', *YIFMC*, xii (1980), 43

J. Trojan: *Moravská lidová pisen: melodika, harmonika* [Moravian Folk Song: Melodies and Harmonies] (Prague, 1980)

K. Wachsmann: 'Folk Music', *Grove 6*, vi (1980), 693

W. Wiora: *Ideen zur Geschichte der Musik* (Darmstadt, 1980)

B. Bartók: *The Hungarian Folk Song*, ed. B. Suchoff (Albany, NY, 1981)

J. Blacking: 'Making Artistic Popular Music: the Goal of True Folk', *Popular Music*, i (1981), 9

——: 'The Problem of "Ethnic" Perception in the Semiotics of Music', *The Sign in Literature and Music*, ed. W. Steiner (Austin, TX, 1981), 184

J.-P. Blom: 'The Dancing Fiddle: On the Expression of Rhythm in Hardingfele Slåttar', *Norsk Folkemusikk*, i, ed. J.-P. Blom, R. Nyhus and R. Sevåg (Oslo, Bergen and Tromsø, 1981), 305

W. Deutsch, ed.: *Die Bordun in der europäischen Volksmusik* (Vienna, 1981)

O. Elschek: 'Die musikalische Individualität der slowakischen Primgeiger', *SIMP*, vii (1981), 70

A. Elschekova, ed.: *Stratigraphische Probleme der Volksmusik in den Karpaten und auf dem Balkan* (Bratislava, 1981)

B. Geiser: *Die Volksmusikinstrumente der Schweiz* (Leipzig, 1981)

V. Hoschowskyj: 'Ukrainische Wechselgesänge der Ostkarpaten als semiotisches System', *Stratigraphische Probleme der Volksmusik in den Karpaten und auf dem Balkan*, ed. A. Elschekova (Bratislava, 1981), 133

B. Krader: 'New Trends in Slavic Ethnomusicology', *Music of the Slavonic Nations*, ed. R. Pečman (Brno, 1981), 497

L. Kuter: 'Music and Identity in Britanny, France', *Discourse in Ethnomusicology*, ii: *a Tribute to Alan P. Merriam*, ed. C. Card and others (Bloomington, IN, 1981), 15

W. Laade: *Das korsische Volkslied: Ethnographie und Geschichte, Gattungen und Stil* (Wiesbaden, 1981)

B. Lortat-Jacob: 'Community Music and the Rise of Professionalism: a Sardinian Example', *EM*, xxv (1981), 185

S. Neilsen: *Flyv lille påfugl: tekster, melodier & kommentarer til traditionel sang blandt børn* (Copenhagen, 1981)

E. Stockmann, ed.: *Studia instrumentorum musicae popularis*, vii (Stockholm, 1981)

Ethnomusicology: Historical and Regional Studies

S. Volkov: 'The New "Folkloristic" Wave in Contemporary Soviet Music as a Sociological Phenomenon', *IMSCR, 1977*, ed. B. Wade and D. Heartz (Kassel, 1981), 49

L. Ballová: *Totožnost'a podonost' melódii* [Identity and Similarity of Melodies] (Bratislava, 1982)

F. Giannattasio and B. Lortat-Jacob: 'Modalità d'improvvisazione nella musica sarda: due modelli', *Culture musicali*, i (1982), 3

K. A. Gourlay: 'Towards a Humanizing Ethnomusicology', *EM*, xxvi (1982), 411

R. Lange: 'Semiotics and Dance', *Makedonski folklor*, xv (1982), 163

B. Lortat-Jacob: 'Theory and "Bricolage": Attilio Cannargiu's Temperament', *YTM*, xiv (1982), 45

S. Nielsen: *Stability in Musical Improvisation: a Repertoire of Icelandic Epic Songs*, trans. K. Mahaffy (*Acta Ethnomusicologica Danica*, iii) (Copenhagen, 1982)

A. Petrović: 'Sacred Sephardic Chants in Bosnia', *World of Music*, xxiv/3 (1982), 35

M. Slobin: *Old Jewish Folk Music: the Collections and Writings of Moshe Beregorski* (Philadelphia, PA, 1982)

P. Szöke: *A zene eredete es három világa* [The Origin of Music and its Three Worlds] (Budapest, 1982)

S. Band-Bory: *Essai sur la chanson populaire grecque* (Nauplion, 1983)

K. Brambats: 'The Vocal Drone in the Baltic Countries: Problems of Chronology and Provenance', *Journal of Baltic Studies*, xiv/1 (1983), 24

J. Crivillé i Bargalló: *El folklore musical* (Madrid, 1983)

O. Elschek: *Die Volksmusikinstrumente der Tschechoslowakei*, ii (Leipzig, 1983)

——: *Die slowakischen Volksmusikinstrumente* (Leipzig, 1983)

T. Leisiö: 'Surface and Deep Structure in Music – An Expedition into Finnish Music Culture', *Suomen Antropologi*, iv (1983), 198

A. Partridge: *Caoineadh na dTri Muire* (Dublin, 1983)

T. Pekkilä, ed.: *Suomen Antropologi* [Finnish Anthropology], iv (Helsinki, 1983)

A. Petrović: 'Muzička forma ganga – simbol tradicionalnog kulturnog zajedništva' [The Musical Form Ganga – Symbol of Traditional Cultural Co-operation], *Slovo Gorčina*, xi (1983), 50

C. Rahkonen: 'Twenty Five Years of Selected Films in Ethnomusicology: Europe (1955–1980)', *EM*, xxvii (1983), 111

A. Tokaji: *Mosgalom és Hivatal. Tömegdal Magyarorszàgon 1945–1956* (Budapest, 1983)

L. Vargyas: *Hungarian Ballads and the European Ballad Tradition* (Budapest, 1983)

V. Žganec: 'Der glagolitische Gesang als kostbares kulturhistorisches Erbgut der Kroaten', *Musikethnologisches Kolloquium zum 70. Geburtstag von Walther Wünsch (1978): Sudosteuropäische Volkskultur in der Gegenwart*, ed. A. Mauerhofer (Graz, 1983), 169

G. Adamo: 'Towards a Grammar of Musical Performance: a Study of a Vocal Style', *Musical Grammars and Computer Analysis: Atti di convegno*, ed. M. Baroni and L. Callegari (Florence, 1984), 245–54

P. V. Bohman: 'Central European Jews in Israel: the Reurbanization of Musical Life in an Immigrant Culture', *YTM*, xvi (1984), 67

P. Farwick: *Deutsche Volksliedlandschaften: Landschaftliches Register der Aufzeichnungen im Deutschen Volksliedarchiv: Teil II* (Freiburg im Breisgau, 1984)

R. Garfias: 'Dance Among the Urban Gypsies of Romania', *YTM*, xvi (1984), 84

A. Johnson: 'Voice Physiology and Ethnomusicology: Physiological and Acoustical Studies of the Swedish Herding Song', *YTM*, xvi (1984), 42

I. Lammel and others: *Lied und politische Bewegung: Materialen der Arbeitstagung zum 30 jährigen Bestehen des Arbeiterliedarchivs an der Akademie der Künste der DDR: 13–15 Februar 1984* (Leipzig, 1984)

B. Lortat-Jacob: 'Music and Complex Societies: Control and Management of Musical Production', *YTM*, xvi (1984), 19

C. Lund: *The Sounds of Prehistoric Scandinavia* (Stockholm, 1984)

M. MacLeod: 'The Folk Revival of Gaelic Song', *The Folk Revival in Scotland*, ed. A. Munro (London, 1984)

A. Munro, ed.: *The Folk Revival in Scotland* (London, 1984)

Y. Passeleau and others: *Musiques d'en France: Guide des musiques et danses traditionnelles 1984* (Paris, 1984)

A. Peresada: *Orkestry russkikh narodnykh instrumentov: Spravochnik* (Moscow, 1984)

A. Schneider: *Analogie und Rekonstruction: Studien zur Methodologie der Musikgeschichtsschreibung und zur Frühgeschichte der Musik*, i (Bonn, 1984)

H. Strobach: *Droben auf jenem Berge: Deutsche Volkslieder I: Balladen, Liebeslieder, Berufs- und Ständelieder* (Wilhelmshaven, 1984)

P. Suojanen: *Finnish Folk Hymn Singing: Study in Music Anthropology* (Tampere, 1984)

R. Wallis and K. Malm: *Big Sounds from Small Peoples: the Music Industry in Small Countries* (New York, 1984)

H. White: 'The Need for a Sociology of Irish Folk Music: a Review of Writings on Traditional Music in Ireland, with Some Responses and Proposals', *IRASM*, xv (1984), 3

I. Wilkinson: 'The Music of Hungary's Gypsies: an Annotated Bibliography', *Bulletin of the UK Chapter (ICTM)*, viii (1984), 7

J. Zhordania: 'Georgian Folk Singing: Its Sources, Emergence and Modern Development', *International Social Science Journal*, xxxvi/3 (1984), 537

G. Adamo and others: *Forme e comportamenti della musica folklorica italiana: Etnomusicologia e didattica* (Milan, 1985)

A. Arrebola: *Los cantes preflamencos y flamencos de Malaga* (Malaga, 1985)

J. Bezić: 'Etnomuzikološka djelatnost Božidara Širole', *Arti Musices*, xvi/1–2 (1985), 5–39

——: ed.: *Traditional Music of Ethnic Groups – Minorities: Proceedings of the Meeting of Ethnomusicologists on the Occasion of the European Year of Music 1985 and in Conjunction with the 20th International Folklore Festival, Zagreb, July 22–24, 1985* (Zagreb, 1985)

L. Bielawski: 'History in Ethnomusicology', *YTM*, xvii (1985), 8

S. Bolle-Zemp: 'Lyoba: Appel au bétails et identité en Haute-Gruyère (Suisse)', *YTM*, xvii (1985), 167

G. Boyes: 'Performance and Context: an Examination of the Effects of the English Folksong Revival on Song Repertoire and Style', *The Ballad Today*, ed. G. Boyes (Doncaster, 1985), 43

E. Brockpähler, ed.: *Lied, Tanz und Musik im Brauchtum: Protokoll der Arbeitstagung der Kommission für Lied-, Musik- und Tanzforschung in der Deutschen Gesellschaft für Volkskunde* (Münster, 1985)

E. Dahlig: 'Problem synkretyzmu w muzycznych i tanecznych zachowaniach wykonawcow ludowych w Polsce' [The Problem of Syncretism in Musical and Dance Performance of Folk Artists in Poland], *Muzyka*, xxx/3–4 (1985), 43

P. Donner, ed.: *Musiikin Suunta*, vii/1 [Idols and Myths in Music] (1985)

O. Elschek: 'Die ethnische Besonderheiten der slowakischen instrumentalen Volksmusik', *Ethnologica Slavica*, xiv (1985), 13–56

F. Hais: *Vzpominky pražškého pisničkare: 1818–1897* (Prague, 1985)

D. Harker: *Fakesong: the Manufacture of British 'Folksong' 1700 to the Present Day* (Milton Keynes, 1985)

B. Kjellström and others: *Folkemusikvågen: the Folk Music Vogue* (Stockholm, 1985)

D. Kristopaite: *Aš išdainavau visas daineles, i: Pasakojimai apie liaudies talentus – Dainininkus ir muzikantus* [I Have Sung All of the Songs, i: an Account of Folk Talent – Singers and Musicians] (Vilnius, 1985)

A. Lunačarskij: *Musik und Revolution: Schriften zur Musik* (Leipzig, 1985)

B. Ó Madagáin: 'Functions of Irish Song in the Nineteenth Century', *Bealoideas*, liii (1985), 130–216

L. Manush: 'K probleme muzykal'nogo fol'klora tsygan (Istoki tsyganskoi muzyki v Evrope)', *Sovetskaia Etnografiia*, v (1985), 46

G. Pemino: *Due repertori musicali tradizionali* (Palermo, 1985)

I. Polednak: 'Zur Problematik der nonartifiziellen Musik slawischer Volker', *BMw*, xxvii/3–4 (1985), 285

J. Rimmer: 'Some Irish-Netherlandish Musical Connections', *Éigse Cheol Tíre: Irish Folk Music Studies*, iv (1985), 30

W. Schepping: 'Europäische Volksmusikforschung', *Lehrbuch der Musikwissenschaft*, ed. E. Kreft (Düsseldorf, 1985), 621–92

D. Schuller and H. Thiel: 'Between Folk and Pop: the Stylistic Plurality in Music Activities in Several Austrian Regions', *Popular Music Perspectives*, ii (1985), 166

D. Stockmann, 'Music and Dance Behavior in Anthropogenesis', *YTM*, xvii (1985), 16

——: 'Tonalität in europäischer Volksmusik als historisches Problem', *Wegzeichen: Studien zur Musikwissenschaft*, ed. J. Mainka and P. Wicke (Berlin, 1985), 357–72

E. Stockmann, 'Zum Professionalismus instrumentaler Volksmusikanten', *Wegzeichen: Studien zur Musikwissenschaft*, ed. J. Mainka and P. Wicke (Berlin, 1985), 331

H. and E. Tampere: *Vana Kannel V: Mustjala regilaulud* (Tallinn, 1985)

J.-P. Blom and T. Kvifte: 'On the Problem of Inferential Ambivalence in Musical Meter', *EM*, xxx (1986), 491

B. Breathnach: *The Use of Notation in the Transmission of Irish Folk Music (O Riada Memorial Lecture)*, i (Cork, 1986)

P. Cooke: *The Fiddle Tradition of the Shetland Isles* (Cambridge, 1986)

A. Giurghescu: 'Power and Charm: Interaction of Adolescent Men and Women in Traditional Settings of Transylvania', *YTM*, xviii (1986), 37

P. Hopkins: *Aural Thinking in Norway: Performance and Communication with the* Hardingfele (New York, 1986)

M. Kahane: 'Du système sonore à la forme architectonique (sur l'indifférence fonctionnelle)', *Dialogue*, xii–xiii (1984–86), 119–66

O. K. Ledang: 'Revival and Innovation: the Case of the Norwegian Seljefløyte', *YTM*, xviii (1986), 145

J. Ling: 'Folk Music Revival in Sweden: the Lilla Edet Fiddle Club', *YTM*, xviii (1986), 1

J. Rimmer: 'Edward Jones's Musical and Poetic Relicks of the Welsh Bards, 1784: a Reassessment', *GSJ*, xxxix (1986), 77

G. Sandoval: *Flamenco et société andalouse* (Toulouse, 1986)

B. Sárosi: *Folk Music: Hungarian Musical Idiom* (Budapest, 1986)

N. Staiti: 'Iconografia e bibliografia della zampogna a Paro in Sicilia', *Lares*, lii/2 (1986), 197–240

H. Steinmetz and H. Schoffel: *Volksmusik im Landkreis Bayreuth: Dokumentation über die instrumentale Volksmusik* (Bayreuth, 1986)

G. Suliteanu: *Cîntecul de leagan* [The Lullaby] (Bucharest, 1986)

B. Krader: 'Slavic Folk Music: Forms of Singing and Self-Identity', *EM*, xxxi (1986), 9

C. Pegg: 'An Ethnomusicological Approach to Traditional Music in East Suffolk', *Singer, Song and Scholar*, ed. I. Russell (Sheffield, 1987), 55

S. Auerbach: 'From Singing to Lamenting: Women's Musical Role in a Greek Village', *Women and Music in Cross-Cultural Perspective*, ed. E. Koskoff (New York, 1987), 25

M. Beregovski: *Jevreskaja narodnaja instrumentalnaja muzyka* [Jewish Instrumental Folk Music] (Moscow, 1987)

V. Blankenhorn: 'The Connemara Sean-Nós since the Gramophone', *Bulletin of the UK Chapter (ICTM)*, xviii (1987), 6

E. V. Gippius and I. Macejevski: *Narodyne muzikalne instrumenti i instrumentanaya muzyka* [Folk Music Instruments and Instrumental Music] (Moscow, 1987)

O. K. Ledang: 'The Norwegian Seljefløyte: a Case of Melodic Pluralism', *Progress Reports in Ethnomusicology*, ii/2 (1987)

A. Michel: 'The Development of Ethnomusicology in the German Democratic Republic: an Overview', *YTM*, xix (1987), 171

M. Pickering and T. Green: *Everyday Culture: Popular Song and the Vernacular Milieu* (Milton Keynes, 1987)

P. K. Shehan: 'Balkan Women as Preservers of Traditional Music and Culture', *Women and Music in Cross-Cultural Perspective*, ed. E. Koskoff (New York, 1987), 45–53

T. Todorov: 'Old Forms of Professionalism in Bulgarian Folk Music', *International Folklore Review*, v (1987), 39

R. D. Cannon: *The Highland Bagpipe and its Music* (Edinburgh, 1988)

S. El-Shawan Castelo-Branco and M. M. Toscano: 'In Search of a Lost World: an Overview of Documentation and Research in the Traditional Music of Portugal', *YTM*, xx (1988), 158–92

O. Elschek, ed.: *Hudobnofolklórne druhy a ich systémové súvztažnosti* [Genres of Musical Folklore and their System Relations], *Muzicologica slovaca*, xiii (1988)

J. Etzion and S. Weich-Shahak: 'The Spanish and Sephardic Romances: Musical Links', *EM*, xxxii/2 (1988), 1–37

F. Ll. Harrison: *Irish Traditional Music: Fossil or Resource? (O Riada Memorial Lecture)*, iii (Cork, 1988)

E. Hickmann and D. W. Hughes, eds.: *The Archaeology of Early Music Cultures* (Bonn, 1988)

D. Holý: *Zpévni jednotky lidové pisné, jejich vztahy a význam* [The Sung Units of Folk Song, their Relations and Significance] (Brno, 1988)

E. Pekkilä: 'Tourism and Authenticity in the Kaustinen Music Festival', *Bulletin of the UK Chapter (ICTM)*, xxi (1988), 20

J. Porter: 'Context, Epistemics, and Value: a Conceptual Performance Model Reconsidered', *Selected Reports in Ethnomusicology*, vii (1988), 69

T. Rice: 'Understanding Three-Part Singing in Bulgaria', *Selected Reports in Ethnomusicology*, vii (1988), 43

E. Stockmann: 'The International Folk Music Council/International Council for Traditional Music – Forty Years', *YTM*, xx (1988), 1

J. Sugarman: 'Making Muabet: the Social Basis of Singing among Prespa Albanian Men', *Selected Reports in Ethnomusicology*, viii (1988), 1–42

E. O. Henry: 'Institutions for the Promotion of Indigenous Music: the Case for Ireland's Comhaltas Ceoltoiri', *EM*, xxxiii/1 (1989), 67

E. Kertesz-Wilkinson: 'Communal versus Individual Composition in Hungarian Folk Music Research', *Bulletin of the UK Chapter (ICTM)*, xxiv (1989), 4

J. Ling: *Folkmusiken 1730–1980 (Europas Musikhistoria)* (Göteborg, 1989)

S. Meier: 'Songs of the Hitler Youth', *Bulletin of the UK Chapter (ICTM)*, xxii (1989), 17

P. Manuel: 'Andalusian, Gypsy, and Class Identity in the Contemporary Flamenco Complex', *EM*, xxxiii/1 (1989), 47

J. Porter: *The Traditional Music of Britain and Ireland: a Research and Reference Guide* (New York and London, 1989)

J. Sugarman: 'The Nightingale and the Partridge: Singing and Gender among Prespa Albanians', *EM*, xxxiii/2 (1989), 191

M. Herndon and S. Ziegler, eds: *Music, Gender, and Culture* (Wilhelmshaven, 1990)

CHAPTER VII

Africa

CHRISTOPHER WATERMAN

The ethnomusicological literature on sub-Saharan Africa – a variegated land mass inhabited by more than 500 million people speaking over 800 languages – presents a fundamental dual image: on the one hand, a 'relatively compact musical area' (Nettl, 1986, p.17) characterized by a high degree of stylistic cohesion (Jones, 1959; Lomax, 1970); and, on the other, a 'vast area within which substantial [musical] diversity occurs' (Merriam, 1977, p.244). The notion that African music forms 'an indivisible whole' (Jones, 1959, p.200), despite evidence of variation within and between localized traditions, is historically grounded in European conceptions of sub-Saharan Africa as a unified geographic-ethnological entity. Senior Africanist scholars have, in the last two decades, become increasingly ambivalent about generalizing at the level of the entire subcontinent. Thus, Gerhard Kubik asserts that 'there is no African music, rather many types of African music' (1983, p.27, *trans. C.W.*), while Klaus Wachsmann suggests that variability in the orientation and rigour of field research makes it difficult to identify 'distinctly African features common to the whole continent' (1980, p.144). Kwabena Nketia's cautious characterization of African music as 'a network of distinct yet related traditions which overlap in certain aspects of style, practice or usage' probably indicates the current limits of reasonable generalization (1974, p.4).

Historical and geographical studies

Problems facing historical research in sub-Saharan Africa resemble those encountered in other areas without extensive written pre-colonial sources. Scholarly interest in African music prior to World War II was dominated by unilinear evolutionism and diffusionist approaches. While diffusionism (e.g. Hornbostel, 1933–4) has continued to exert some influence, the evolutionary hypotheses of scholars such as Henry Balfour (1907) and Percival Kirby (1934, pp.193–6) have largely been dismissed. Archaeology and the interpretation of prehistoric and early historic iconography have provided data on instruments and, to a lesser degree, performance techniques and symbolic associations (Hirschberg, 1969; Dark and Hill, 1971; Willett, 1977; Mugglestone, 1982). It is by now generally accepted that 'there is relatively little hope of reconstructing the aural shape of [prehistoric] African music with any accuracy' (Merriam, 1967 [1982, p.297]).

240

The historical interests of Africanists were encouraged anew in the 1960s, the decade that saw the initiation of *The Journal of African History* (1960) and publication of *The Historian in Tropical Africa* (Vansina, Mauny, and Thomas, eds., 1964). This efflorescence of interdisciplinary research encouraged the use of musical data as a source in the study of particular delimited problems of culture history, rather than the conjectural reconstruction of global or continental music history. Publications of the last two decades, including the pioneering collection *Essays on Music and History in Africa* (Wachsmann, ed., 1971), generally suggest that 'the best way of approaching the historiography of African music is . . . [to] combine the stylistic and the social dimensions of music history' (Nketia, 1982, p.98).

Historical topics investigated by ethnomusicologists include relationships between style and instrument distributions and population movements (Wachsmann, 1964; Lomax, 1970); the influence of territorial expansion, culture contact and political hegemony on musical style and song texts (e.g. articles by Blacking, Nketia and Rouget in Wachsmann, ed. 1971); the relationship of Black Africa to other areas, including the Americas (R. Waterman, 1952; Lomax, 1970; Roberts, 1972; Dauer, 1985), the Middle East (Anderson and Euba's articles in Wachsmann, ed. 1971), and Southeast Asia (see below); and histories of music in particular regions (Wachsmann, 1971; Kazadi and Mensah's articles in Gunther, ed. 1973; Fiagbedzi, 1977; Vidal, 1977; Kubik, 1982, 1989).

Two controversial hypotheses must be cited in any discussion of sub-Saharan African musical history. The first is a venerable diffusionist argument concerning Africa and insular Southeast Asia. Erich M. von Hornbostel (1911), Jaap Kunst (1936) and Curt Sachs (1938) based their arguments concerning links between Madagascar and Indonesia on instruments, tunings and linguistic relationships. A. M. Jones (1964, 1971) extended this line of argument, correlating musical features with a wide range of evidence (e.g. plastic arts, crop complexes, elephantiasis) and deducing prehistoric Indonesian colonization in western as well as southeastern Africa. Indonesian influence on Madagascar is generally accepted, but subsequent research has not confirmed Jones's extensions of the initial hypothesis (Jeffreys, 1961; Hood, 1966; Jeffreys, 1968; Rouget and Schwarz, 1969; McLeod, 1977; Blench, 1982).

The second argument (Lomax, 1970) concerns similarities between the song styles of central African Pygmy groups and the San ('Bushmen') of the Kalahari Desert. This historical hypothesis – that since the peopling of Africa by hunter-gatherers predates the Bantu expansion, the music of present day hunter-gatherers represents an 'ancient Pygmy-Bushman strain' – has been criticized by Alan Merriam who notes that it rests upon the assumption that:

> The African Hunter peoples have sustained a single music style for thousands of years. Yet during this time they have experienced dispersal across the continent, a sharp decline in number, and a mode of life which emphasizes tiny groups of people. While continuity of a single style is conceivable, nothing confirms it in such extraordinary detail (1977, p.245).

There is even disagreement about the degree of resemblance between the styles: where Charlotte Frisbie (1971, p.287) found 'overwhelming similarities' between San and Pygmy musics, Y. Grimaud wrote that such resemblances 'grew less clear as, through a greater knowledge of the two musics, the dissimilarities seemed more and more important' (Grimaud and Rouget, 1956, p.1). As Merriam concluded, 'the mystery remains, for San and Pygmy styles *are* highly similar, and the same style occurs sporadically in many parts of Africa among both Pygmy and non-Pygmy peoples' (1977, p.245). Some scholars have emphasized similarities between the musics of hunter-gatherers and neighbouring groups. Kubik, for example, suggests that the distinctive polyphonic singing and harmonic progressions of Bantu groups in Southern Africa are due to contact with San peoples around AD 300–400 (Kubik, 1988, p.71).

Areal studies of sub-Saharan African music have been closely linked with the development of historical hypotheses. A number of attempts have been made to demarcate musical areas for the entire subcontinent, including André Schaeffner (1946), Merriam (1959, 'African Music'), Gilbert Rouget (1960), Alan Lomax (1970), Merriam (1977), and Wachsmann (1980, pp.146–8). Merriam's influential seven-area scheme for music (1959, 'African Music', pp.76–80) largely parallels Melville Herskovits's nine culture areas (1930). Merriam later posited the existence of a central core area including most of tropical Africa, with several clusters of regional variation (1977, p.244). Lomax, on the basis of Cantometric analysis, proposed eight song style areas variously named after subsistence modes, geographical location and linguistic groupings (1970, p.195). His Gardener area, covering more than half of sub-Saharan Africa, coincides broadly with Merriam's core area. The difficulty of defining macro-regions is underlined by Kubik's classification of at least eight historically conditioned 'style regions' within Tanzania alone (1982).

Numerous scholars have attempted to map the geographical distribution of African musical instruments and style traits (e.g. Ankerman, 1901; Wieschoff, 1933, p.149ff; Schneider, 1937, p.87; Boone, 1936, 1951; Jones, 1959; Laurenty, 1960, 1962; Anderson, 1967, p.48; Zemp, 1971, pp.282–7; DjeDje, 1980, p.40; King, 1980, p.236; Wegner, 1984, p.66). These maps generally indicate the presence or absence of features, but not their frequency of occurrence. In general, patterns of musical conceptualization and social function have not been taken into account in distributional studies. The anthropological concept of culture clusters (Merriam, 1959, 'The Concept of Culture Clusters'), which relies in part upon indigenous accounts of cultural-historical relationships, has been applied by Lester Monts (1982) to the problem of musical linkages among ethnic-linguistic groups in Liberia and Sierra Leone. Ongoing processes of musical transmission between African societies have only rarely been studied; see, for example, Atta Mensah's study of Ndebele-Soli bimusicality (1970).

The study of African music history in the colonial period has been developed by scholars focussing on popular styles (e.g. Ranger, 1975; Collins, 1976; Low, 1982; Bemba, 1984; Coplan, 1985; Erlmann, 1988; C. Waterman, 1990). Colonial records, newspapers and the letters and memoirs of civil servants and literate Africans are important sources of information about urban musical events and values. In addition, the commercial mass-reproduction of music by European firms, beginning in South Africa by World War I and Anglophone West Africa by the 1920s, provides a potentially rich, though inevitably partial, source for the analysis of stylistic continuity and change.

Musical sound and performance practice

Ethnomusicological understanding of musical sound and practice in sub-Saharan Africa is extensive in some regards and undeveloped in others. Certain topics – most notably rhythm and polyphony – have attracted the interest of every major scholar since Hornbostel (1928). Matters of tuning, scale and melody have received attention, but tend to resist attempts at generalization. It might be argued that the relative amount of scholarly attention paid to these parameters is proportionate to their prominence in African musical thought and practice. The scarcity of detailed analyses of timbre (DeVale, 1984), a feature reported to be important in musical production and evaluation throughout Africa, belies this notion.

Theoretical advances in the study of musical sound and practice have often resulted from research overarching traditional musicological categories of description and analysis. Such research has in fact been demanded by musical systems in which timbre often plays a crucial role in foregrounding patterns within dense multi-part textures, and melodies are strongly conditioned by rhythmic and linguistic factors. Hyphenated terms such as 'melodic-rhythmic' and 'speech-song' may tell future scholars as much about the tenacity of Western analytical assumptions as about African musical thought and practice.

Much Africanist writing has dealt with four issues: (i) the establishment of temporal order in and through music; (ii) the generation of cumulative patterns from the interaction of multiple parts; (iii) the role of motor behaviour in performance; and (iv) the relationship of musical forms and processes to other patterns of cultural significance and social interaction. The approaches adopted by various scholars have been shaped by their training, the musics and societies they study, and the practical goals of their research. A survey of the literature suggests the existence of highly productive subtraditions. Scholars have sometimes converged on problems posed by particular musical traditions, the two most notable examples being Anlo Ewe drumming (e.g. Cudjoe, 1953; Jones, 1959; Koetting, 1970; Ladzekpo and Pantaleoni, 1970; Pantaleoni, 1972; Fiagbedzi, 1977; Chernoff, 1979; Locke, 1982; Pressing, 1983; Agawu, 1987) and Baganda royal music (e.g. Wachsmann, 1950, 1965; Kubik, 1960, 1969; Anderson, 1968, 1984; Cooke, 1970).

The rhythmic complexity of African music, cited by early Arabic and European observers, has been a focus of academic attention since the days of armchair comparative musicology. Three classic approaches have been particularly influential over the last 30 years: Hornbostel's emphasis upon motor behaviour and pattern perception, in which 'rhythmical shapes . . . present themselves to the ear as unities . . . without the smallest time units being counted out' (1928, p.54); Jones's notion of rhythmic tension or 'clash' created by the polymetric 'crossing of beats' against an 'inexorable mathematical background', often provided by clapping (1954, pp.28, 39–40); and Richard Waterman's psychocultural notion of the 'metronome sense' – a learned, unconsciously carried equal pulse framework 'assumed without

243

question or consideration to be part of the perceptual equipment of both musicians and listeners', and allowing performers and participants to orient themselves temporally 'whether or not the beats are expressed in actual melodic or percussion tones' (1952). The formulations of Hornbostel and Waterman both rest upon concepts derived from gestalt psychology. However, they differ in at least one crucial respect: whereas Hornbostel hypothesized that African rhythmic conception was fundamentally rooted in motion rather than hearing (1928, p.53), Waterman focussed upon the dynamic interaction of aural perception, music cognition, and motor behaviour.

Research in the Guinea Coast region of West Africa, the *locus classicus* of 'hot' drumming, has emphasized rhythmic organization, drawing upon the concepts of pattern perception and equal-pulse base. James Koetting, for example, grounds his analysis of Anlo Ewe drumming in the 'intimate interrelation of patterns on all component levels' (1970, p.120). The total configuration of patterns generates and is in turn maintained through a 'fastest pulse' or 'density referent' resulting from the interlocking of parts. His analysis thus relies implicitly upon the notion of gestalt patterning but downplays the importance of an internalized temporal framework of 'gross pulses', such as suggested by the 'metronome sense' concept (1970, p.122). In contrast, H. Pantaleoni, citing Anlo informants, asserts that all players orient themselves vis-à-vis a repeated asymmetric pattern, usually performed on an iron bell (1972). The temporal asymmetry of this 'time-line' is crucial, allowing it to 'put each pattern into its proper place, while a simple pulse can only regulate the speed with which the pattern is played' (1972, p.60).

Nketia's model of the organization of West African ensembles, a grand compromise among these various hypotheses, includes hierarchical layers of regular pulses – slow, moderate and rapid – and an asymmetric time-line (1974, pp.126–38). Divisive or additive rhythms may be played over this temporal infrastructure, creating complex cumulative patterns against a regularized background. The notion of graded levels of activity and foreground/background relations has also been applied by Lazarus Ekwueme (1975–6), who suggests that:

> ... the rhythm of African music is built on three distinguishable structural levels. The background material is a skeleton of the structure ... often reduceable to the antiphonal 'call and response' ... pattern; the middleground contains rhythmic motifs such as the standard patterns and other delimiters on which the music is based, while decorative motifs such as are employed by the master drummer are merely foreground material ... (pp.34–5).

John Chernoff emphasizes the role of silence in the interlocking of rhythms, suggesting that the Ewe or Dagomba drummer 'concerns himself as much with the notes he does not play as with the accents he delivers' (1979, p.60). Timbre and tone production have also been identified as important factors in co-ordinating component parts within a drum ensemble, and in the distribution of perceived accent patterns (Nketia, 1958, p.23; Cudjoe, 1958, pp.74–5).

The study of rhythm in sub-Saharan Africa has generally entailed the study of multi-part structures and techniques, a focus of scholarly symposia (see *JIFMC*, xix [1967], *Selected Reports in Ethnomusicology*, v [1984]) and dissertations (e.g. Kauffman, 1970; Schmidt, 1985). Scholars working in eastern, southern, and contiguous regions of central Africa – where the development of polyphonic choral/ensemble textures appears to be a primary aesthetic focus – have advanced our understanding of gestalt processes in the generation of composite patterns in multi-part music. David Rycroft's analysis of Zulu, Xhosa and Swazi vocal music stresses the generation of a cyclical, 'ever-changing balance' through multiple staggered entries and overlapping of individual phrases (1967). This approach to music-making is not only a pragmatic solution to the problem of co-ordination in group performance, but also a norm guiding solo performances:

> An isolated singer, if asked to demonstrate a song, will usually not complete one part and then the other, but will attempt to present the essentials of both parts, by jumping from one to the other whenever a new phrase-entry occurs (p.90).

Studies of Baganda music describe the close interlocking of parts, 'like the fingers of folded hands' (Wachsmann, 1980, p.147) and the emergence, in the perception of performers and listeners, of 'inherent rhythms' (Kubik, 1962) or 'resultant musical structures' (Anderson, 1984, p.136) within dense aural textures. Kubik (1962, p.33) posited that in some eastern and central African instrumental musics:

> The musicians playing together (or in the case of a soloist, his left and right hands or fingers) produce rhythmic patterns, which are not perceived by the listener as they are actually played by the musicians . . . *The image as it is heard and the image as it is played are often different from each other in African music.*

This formulation was an important advance in the analysis of dynamic relationships between motor and aural patterns in the flow of musical performance. The analytical importance of motor behaviour has also been discussed by John Blacking (1955, 1961), Rycroft (1971) and Alfons Dauer (1983). Nketia (1963, p.156) and Seth Cudjoe (1953, pp.280–1) cite the importance of movement in musical enculturation among the Akan and Ewe, while Blacking argues that Venda music:

> is not founded on melody or on metre, but on a rhythmical stirring of the whole body, of which singing and metre are extensions. When a rest is heard between two drumbeats, it must be understood that for the player it is not a rest; each drumbeat is part of a total movement in which the hand or a stick strikes the drumskin (1980, p.597).

The relationship of musical time to other systems of temporal organization is an under-researched topic on the border of technical and cultural analysis. As Merriam wrote in his last published statement on African rhythm:

> If the search is for how Africans conceptualize and organize their musical rhythms, and what it means to them, then we must . . . consider the organization, meaning, and application of time-reckoning in their cultural system (1981, p.141).

245

While ethnomusicological analyses have generally assumed some sort of equal-pulse framework, anthropological accounts of African time-reckoning systems describe them as non-linear and constituted of gross units based upon natural phenomena or social activity (Merriam, 1981, pp.133–7). The distinction between musical time and other systems of temporal organization has been explicitly discussed by only a few scholars, although hints abound in the literature. Roderic Knight (1984), for example, notes that Mandinka musicians do not conceptualize basic generative patterns in terms of 'beginnings' or 'endings', since they are fundamentally cyclic. According to Blacking (1980, p.597), the Venda view music as creating a continuous, 'special world of time'. Ruth Stone, drawing upon Schutz's distinction between inner and outer time, suggests that 'musical time cannot be reduced to a single dimension' and therefore involves 'the coordination of a number of simultaneously experienced flows' (1985, p.147).

The close integration of dance and music in African performance events also has implications for the analysis of rhythm and temporal experience. S. K. Ladzekpo and Pantaleoni explicitly incorporate dance into their analysis of Anlo Ewe drumming, suggesting that the basic temporal 'ground' is 'a rhythmic complex of high-voiced instruments and dance movements' (1970, p.13). Charles Keil, in an analysis of Tiv expressive culture, calls dance 'the ultimate time-space spanner' (1979, p.245), and suggests that drumming, in its use of movement and space, is 'midway between song and dance' (p.257).

The study of pitch organization in African music has yielded fewer broad generalizations than research into rhythm and multi-part techniques (e.g. Nketia, 1974, pp.116–21, 147–59). Beginning with global hypotheses concerning the development of musical scales and polyphony from natural harmonics (e.g. Kirby, 1926), analyses have become increasingly sophisticated. A variety of methods have been adopted: Wachsmann's pioneering work on tuning and pitch stability in East Africa, combining ethnographic methods and electronic measurement (1950, 1957, 1967); Merriam's statistical analysis of melodic movement within a repertory, influenced by Mieczyslaw Kolinski (1957); B. Aning's study of the tuning norms of a Mandinka musician (1982); and Kubik's comparative investigation of the cognitive representations guiding instrumental tuning, focussing upon 'the internal order of the tone material . . . in the minds of the musicians themselves' (1985, p.31).

There is a substantial literature on relationships between music and language in Africa, much of it concerned with the influence of linguistic tone upon melodic contour (e.g. Herzog, 1934; Jones, 1959, pp.230–51; Schneider, 1961; Blacking, 1967, pp.199–203; Agawu, 1984, 1988) and with surrogate languages and signalling systems (e.g. Herzog, 1945; Carrington, 1949; Nketia, 1971; Rouget, 1964; Locke and Agbeli, 1980; Mbabi-Katana, 1984). Such research has continued to focus attention upon the 'complex and subtle transitional forms between language and music' (Herzog, 1934, p.218). Numerous examples in the literature await careful examination and cross-cultural comparison: for example, Wachsmann's characterization of Baganda song as 'speech clothed in melody' (1954, p.45); Rycroft's explanation of portamento glides in Nguni song as the result of the pitch-lowering effects of voiced consonants (1957); Blacking's suggestion that, in Venda performance, 'the forces can be musical and the forms verbal, or vice-versa' (1982, p.21);

Akin Euba's hypothesis that Yoruba speech involves a high degree of 'sub-musical' activity (1975); Chernoff's description of the role of language in Dagomba drum education (1979, pp.75–82); and Kofi Agawu's analysis of speech rhythm as the most important factor shaping Akan and Ewe music (1987). In general, narrow analyses of the influence of linguistic tone on melody have given way to studies of the interaction of various systems of cultural communication. As Agawu phrases the matter:

> the way forward in our attempts to understand African rhythm does not lie in the production of more analyses of the mechanical aspects of its organization, but rather in a careful investigation of its basis in the various modes of signification that characterize West African life itself (1987, p.418).

Transcription has played a crucial role in the development of Africanist ethnomusicology, both as an analytical tool and as an emblem of professional competence. The visual representation of musical sound has, of course, been complicated by a fundamental dilemma: deciding what to notate, or, more fundamentally, what 'the music' is. One approach is represented by Blacking's transcriptions of Venda children's songs, based upon 'generalized norms of . . . songs' rather than 'the numerous ways in which Venda children sing the same songs' (1967, p.35). From this perspective a song is a normative structure, differentially embodied in any particular performance. The notion of musical structure as normative paradigm also appears in Blacking's analyses of Venda ocarina music (1959) and inter-genre transformations of the *tshikona* dance theme (1971, p.107), Lois Anderson's description of the derivation of Baganda instrumental performances from vocal models (1984) and Simha Arom's transcription of Banda-Linda trumpet ensemble music, a repertory composed of named pieces, each derived from a 'paradigmatic theme' realized in aleatoric variations (1984).

Most published transcriptions of sub-Saharan African music represent particular recorded performances. Jones, a pioneer in mechanical transcription and the visual presentation of entire performances, believed that the transcriber should be guided by the behaviourist question, 'When the African makes music, what exactly does he do?' (1959, p.7). A symposium on transcription (England and others, 1964), which took as its analytic object a recording of a *Hukwe* San song with musical bow accompaniment, suggests some of the philosophical and practical problems entailed in analysing sounds apart from the behaviour that produces them. The confrontation of text-centred musicological methods with African music has convinced some ethnomusicologists that, as Kubik puts it, 'it is impossible to understand the music by writing it down in its audible aspects only' (1972, p.29). Technology has played an important role in the development of transcription techniques; S. Arom, for example, has refined the use of multiple-track cumulative recording techniques in transcribing multi-part ensemble music (1985). Film and video recording have also, since the 1950s, become indispensable tools for the documentation and analysis of African musical performance (Rouget, 1965; Kubik, 1972; Thompson, 1974, pp.251–75; Stone and Stone, 1981).

Notation systems have been influenced by analytical and pedagogical considerations. The Time Unit Box System (TUBS), a graphic system developed for teaching purposes at UCLA during the late 1960s, adopts the density referent as a minimal unit of organization. Pantaleoni, working with Serwadda and Ladzekpo, developed a sophisticated tablature capable of indicating performance techniques, the linguistic content of drumstrokes, and dance patterns. Other innovative notational schemes include Rycroft's circular transcriptions of Nguni music (1967), Muyinda's cipher notation for Kiganda music (Kubik, 1969), and a variety of systems developed to represent techniques on specific instruments (Blacking, 1961; Knight, 1971; Ngumu, 1980).

African musical technology has been a major focus of ethnomusicological interest since the 19th century. The literature on musical instruments includes early diffusionist and evolutionary works, numerous studies based upon museum collections and focussed upon classification according to the Hornbostel-Sachs scheme (e.g. the *Annales of the Musée Royal de l'Afrique Centrale*, Tervuren, Belgium), and a small body of pioneering studies based upon more detailed ethnographic research (Kirby, 1934; Wachsmann, 1958). Ulrich Wegner synthesizes information on the construction, classification, functions and symbolism of African chordophones (1984). Additional information on the construction, social functions and cultural significance of instruments is scattered throughout the literature. Francis Bebey's introductory text includes a survey of the social roles of various African musical instruments (1975, pp.40–118), while Merriam (1969) and Paul Berliner (1980) provide detailed accounts of construction techniques.

The ethnography of music

The anthropological study of music is not strictly separable from the technical analysis of musical sound and performance practice. A distinction has nonetheless been posited between musicological approaches, in which 'the music itself' is analysed with minimal recourse to extra-musical factors and culture is reduced to 'context', and anthropological approaches which view musical patterns as cultural configurations and performance as social action, holding open the possibility that musical forms may result from non-musical causes, and vice versa. This epistemological distinction, however important in the ideological history of ethnomusicology, is not clearly defined in the practice of pioneering scholars, who include musicians with degrees in anthropology (e.g. Blacking, Kubik, Merriam, Waterman, Hugo Zemp) and anthropologically sophisticated musicologists (Hornbostel, Nketia, Wachsmann).

The influence of anthropology on the study of music in sub-Saharan Africa may be divided into several complexly intermingled streams. The impact of British structural-functionalism is represented by Blacking, who studied under Meyer Fortes at Cambridge. Blacking, like other British-trained anthropologists of his generation, continued to insist upon the analytical importance of social organization, while at the same time looking to symbolist, structuralist and linguistic theory for interpretive tools. American cultural anthropology is represented by Merriam, who studied at Northwestern University under Herskovits, a student of Franz Boas. The Boasian school's emphasis upon aesthetics, expressive behaviour, and psychocultural patterns encouraged the development of ethnomusicological theory and contributed during the 1960s to the emergence of ethnosemantic (Ames and King, 1971) and folkloristic (Stone, 1982) approaches. The impact of French anthropology is represented in part by the work of Zemp, a Swiss scholar trained by Claude Lévi-Strauss in Paris. Like other Francophone West Africanist scholars (e.g. M. Griaule, G. Rouget, Schaeffner, Zahan), Zemp has paid especially close attention to the role of music in indigenous philosophical and cosmological systems. Post-war German anthropology is exemplified by Kubik, whose work combines careful ethnographic description and comparativist goals with psychological interests. It must be emphasized that the schools of thought outlined here are not clearly bounded, and that the *oeuvre* of any creative scholar will bear the traces of many intellectual influences.

While a few scholars have attempted to provide a holistic overview of the musical life of an entire society or community (e.g. Blacking, 1965; Zemp, 1971; Ames and King, 1971), musical ethnography in Africa has more often focussed upon particular social categories or institutions. Thus we have ethnographic accounts of the music of children (Blacking, 1967), adults (Campbell and Eastman, 1984), women (Schmidt-Wrenger, 1979; Joseph, 1983; DjeDje, 1985), royalty (Brown, 1984), religious sects (Besmer, 1983), age-grades and initiation 'schools' (Blacking, 1969; Kubik, 1971), and musical specialists (e.g. Tracey, 1948; Schaeffner, 1960; Nketia, 1963; Zemp, 1967; Ames, Merriam, and Nketia's articles in d'Azevedo, ed. 1973; Erlmann and Magagi, 1981). Still other accounts have focussed primarily upon specific aspects of musical thought or behaviour in a given society, including the cultural role and symbolism of instruments (Schaeffner, 1951; Griaule, 1955; Ames and Gourlay, 1978; Berliner, 1978), interaction and interpretation in performance events (Stone, 1982), music and possession-trance (Rouget, 1980; Erlmann, 1982; Blacking, 1985), the social functions of praise singing (Smith, 1957), music and death (Hampton, 1982) and relationships between aesthetics, ethics and power (Chernoff, 1979; Keil, 1979). This concentration upon delimited problems has arguably resulted in richer ethnographic accounts at the local level. The drawbacks of holistic ethnography have been pointed out by social anthropologists working in Africa, including Jack Goody (1969, p.viii; cited in Nketia and DjeDje, 1984, p.xiv):

> To think that anyone can cover 'a culture', even a preliterate 'homogenous' one, in a year or two is a figment of the anthropologist's imagination and not one that he would be prepared to extend to his own personal situation.

Determination of analytical units – nation-states, societies, communities, conceptual systems, genres and instruments – entails the problem of comparison, an important issue in African studies from the days of grand ethnological theory to recent idiographic accounts. Rouget (1964), in an evaluation of the literature on 'funerary music', points out the complexities involved in establishing cross-cultural categories on the basis of social function, while Merriam (1982, p.46f) suggests that increasing concentration on micro-studies since the 1960s has inhibited comparison.

> We seem to have lost sight – at least temporarily – of the prime target of the anthropologist, which is not simply to understand better and better the finer and finer details of the workings of a particular society but, rather, to

understand how and why those details are like or unlike similar phenomena in other societies and, eventually, among mankind (p.47).

Nketia distinguishes several comparative strategies or levels and suggests that Africanist ethnomusicologists have too often been quick to generalize without engaging in systematic comparison (1984, pp.11–12).

The elicitation of indigenous musical terminology and cognitive categories has been an important focus of musical ethnography in Africa. Many languages do not include a term corresponding in semantic range to the Western word 'music'. When Keil investigated the problem:

> It became clear that a word corresponding to our term 'music' could not be found in one African language after another – Tiv, Yoruba, Igbo, Efik, Birom, Hausa, assorted Jarawa dialects, Idoma, Eggon, and a dozen other languages from the Nigeria–Cameroons area do not yield a word for 'music' gracefully. It is easy to talk about song and dance, singers and drummers, blowing a flute, beating a bell, but the general terms 'music' and 'musician' require long and awkward circumlocutions . . . So what seems to us a very basic, useful, and rather concrete term is apparently a useless abstraction from a Tiv, Yoruba, perhaps even a pan-African or non-Western point of view (1979, p.27).

Keil's list might be expanded to include Mandinka, Wolof, Serer, Bambara, Dogon, Dan, Kpelle, Twi, Ga, Ewe, Fulani, Bala-Basongye, Karimojong, Baganda, Shona, Venda, Zulu, Xhosa, various San languages and Chokwe. Systematic surveys of musical terminology within and between African culture areas and linguistic groupings have rarely been undertaken (Hause, 1948). The most thorough account of the musical terminology of an African people is D. W. Ames and A. V. King's *Glossary of Hausa Music and Its Social Contexts* (1971). Intended as a 'shorthand ethnography' (p.vii), it is widely cited though rarely emulated in terms of format.

The study of terminology is closely related to analysis of discourse about performance. Rich aesthetic vocabularies have been described among the Vai (Monts, 1987), Kpelle (Stone, 1982), Dan (Zemp, 1971), Dagomba (Chernoff, 1979), Yoruba (Thompson, 1974), Igbo (Nzewi, 1977), Tiv (Keil, 1979), Baganda (Kubik, 1969) and Basotho (Adams, 1975). There is, however, a great deal of variation among African peoples regarding the verbalization and systemicity of aesthetic norms. Merriam notes that societies with clear structural-cognitive parallels to Western notions of 'art' and 'aesthetics' have attracted disproportionate attention from scholars:

> What of societies like the Bala-Basongye . . . in which the basic categories simply do not fit, the outsider is forced to puzzle over the very nature of the phenomena he hopes to study, and transference of concepts will not work? These are potentially the most fruitful cases and the societies in which the problems of cross-cultural applicability must be solved. It would be foolish, even unthinkable, to suggest that the Yoruba of Nigeria do not have clear concepts of 'art' and 'aesthetics' which are structural parallels to our own, but it would be equally foolish to suggest that the Bala-Basongye do (1982, pp.322–3).

The study of categories and values leads to the consideration of whole ideational systems. As in the technical analysis of music, the most revealing ethnographies have overarched traditional categories of analysis – music, art, politics, economics, philosophy, religion and social organization – in responding to observed patterns of African life. Zemp's account of the Dan terms *wo* (voice) and *vi* (noise) exemplifies the relationship of musical concepts to a wider universe which grounds them and invests them with significance:

> The singer sings with his 'voice', *wo*. This term designates all sounds emitted by a being that possesses a 'mouth': humans, animals, supernatural beings and musical instruments that are . . . anthropomorphized and have a 'mouth' (the vent of a wooden slit-gong, the skin of a drum, the embouchure of a trumpet, etc) (1971, p.73).
> The term *vi* is fluently translated as 'noise' . . . In its verbal form it signifies 'to disturb'; for example, a hunter can say *wi ya vi*, 'the game was disturbed'. As a noun *vi* can be translated as 'a disturbance', with the associated idea of the noise that results . . . One can say of footsteps on the earth, of rain beating on the roofs, of the chops of an axe or machete, of a bunch of palm fronds being beaten on the earth, 'that is its noise' (*a vi*), but one cannot say 'that is its voice' (*a wo*). However, both terms are applicable to waterfalls, the creaking of a door, or the strokes of a blacksmith on a forge. These last things which may produce a 'noise', an audible 'disturbance', may also be assimilated with beings that possess a mouth. The water is like a living being (according to one of our informants, the voice of a waterfall may be the song of God), the closed door is the 'mouth' of a house, and the hammered fire of the blacksmith rings like a bell, which also possesses a mouth (pp.74–5; *trans. C.W.*).

Other scholars have focussed upon parallels between social and musical structures. Thus, Blacking (1971, p.104) suggests that Venda musical order is linked to social order at a number of levels – 'tone/companion tone, tonic/counter-tonic, call/response, individual/community, theme/variation, chief/subjects, etc' – while Robert Thompson (1966, p.91) characterizes the high-intensity interlocking patterns typical of Yoruba music, dance, and visual arts as 'a communal expression of percussive individuality'. Nicholas England suggests that the contrapuntal structures of !Kung music reflect 'the Bushman desire to remain independent . . . at the same time that he is contributing vitally to the community life' (1957, p.60). Musical style may symbolically contradict other aspects of ideology or interaction. These hypotheses are persuasive because they derive from careful ethnographic observation, rather than from the search for homologies between reified musical and social structures. Specific criteria for the evaluation of musical sound vary; for example, the Yoruba taste for high-affect contrast versus Baganda preferences for 'murmuring' ensemble textures (Wachsmann, 1965, p.3). Nonetheless, it appears that African peoples differing widely in social organization and language share a vital cultural imperative – the metaphoric enactment of values concerning individuality and communality through complex musical configurations built up from multiple repetitive patterns.

Wachsmann (1980, pp.148–9) has posited the principle of transaction as a normative tenet underlying musical expression throughout sub-Saharan Africa. The notion of transaction is related to yet another aspect of musical ethnography, the study of music-makers as social actors. The social status, role behaviour, and degree of specialization of musicians in Africa varies widely, ranging from hunter-gatherer bands, where any normal individual is expected to contribute to most musical events, to the professional praise musicians associated with centralized political authority. The role of music as a medium for rhetorical discourse is related to the position of musicians in many African societies as mediators between individuals, social-political units, and the human and supernatural realms. Veit Erlmann, for example, sees the ideological efficacy of Fulbe praise-singing as rooted in the role of performance as a mode of exchange and the 'quasi-magical' functions of speech and song (1980). In the realm of popular music, David Coplan has developed the notion of African urban musicians as cultural brokers, mobile individuals skilled at manipulating multiple cultural codes in heterogeneous environments (1981). In many parts of Africa the musician is conceptually linked with other deviant and potentially powerful social categories – blacksmiths (Michels-Gebler, 1984), prophets, herbalists, diviners and nomads. The study of music-makers as social actors remains an underdeveloped branch of Africanist ethnomusicology.

Reflexivity, an important philosophical and methodological issue in anthropology, history, and literary criticism, has not yet made a strong impact on Africanist ethnomusicology. Chernoff, in discussing the need for critical approaches to musical ethnography, has noted that:

> The most important gap for the participant-observer . . . is not between what he sees and what is there, but between his experience and how he is going to communicate it . . . Finding the proper level of abstraction to portray with fidelity both the relativity of his own viewpoint and the reality of the world he has witnessed necessarily involves an act of interpretation (1979, p.11).

This suggests that each ethnographer/interpreter of African music – the American anthropologist in Zaire, the Ghanaian musicologist in Tanzania, the Anlo Ewe drummer in his natal community – is involved in an interpretive project conditioned by his or her personal experience and socio-historical position. Although this notion renders the bipartite notion of emic and etic perspectives philosophically problematic, it also reaffirms the centrality of participant-observation and musical participation as research techniques, and grounds ethnography in the interaction of student and studied.

This intervention, the heart of ethnomusicological fieldwork in Africa as elsewhere, has been conditioned by colonialism, the penetration and transformation of indigenous economic and political structures, the emergence of socio-economic classes, and the development, within and outside Africa, of centres for the 'preservation' of culture. Although ethnomusicologists have generally lagged behind their colleagues in other branches of African studies in considering the impact of ideological factors upon their work, some notable exceptions appear in the literature. Thus, Wachsmann optimistically suggested in 1966 that the era when 'African performers and listeners alike were cast into a passive role' as objects of scholarly attention had come to an end (p.65), and Nketia and C. J. DjeDje have called for the 'decolonization' of fieldwork (1984, p.xiii). K. A. Gourlay discusses the effects of colonial languages on African scholarship, citing a study (Nwachukwu, 1981) in which *nkwa*, an Igbo term denoting singing, playing instruments and dancing, is uncomfortably glossed by an Igbo scholar as 'music':

By forcing the Igbo concept into the Procrustean bed of western conceptualization, she is in effect surrendering to the dominance of western ideas
– or at least to the dominance of the English language! How different things
would have been if the Igbo tongue had achieved the same 'universality' as
English! We should then have been seeking for universals in *nkwa* and
regarding the whole process of western 'serious' music as an aberration
because it excluded dance (1984, p.35).

Certain ubiquitous aspects of musical life in modern Africa are under-
represented in the ethnomusicological literature. There are still relatively few
accounts of women's and children's musics, the role of music in the formation
of class, ethnic and pan-African identity (e.g. Collins and Richards, 1982;
Hampton, 1983; Bemba, 1984; Coplan, 1985; C. Waterman, 1990), the
invention of musical tradition under colonialism (Ranger, 1983), and the part
played by music in black resistance to apartheid in South Africa (Erlmann,
1985). The application of ethnomusicological ideas, as well as materials, in
African music education is another underresearched topic (Laade, 1969,
pp.29–65; Nketia, 1978; Lo-Bamijoko, 1981). As elsewhere in the Third
World, the future of ethnomusicology in sub-Saharan Africa will depend not
only upon increasing sophistication of theory and method, but also upon the
ability of scholars to adapt to contemporary social and political realities.

Basic resources

The standard bibliographic sources are D. H. Varley (1936), Merriam (1951),
D. L. Thieme (1964) and L. J. P. Gaskin (1965). Sources of information on
sound recordings include Merriam (1970), H. Tracey (1973) and R. M. Stone
and F. J. Gillis (1976). Institutions producing and disseminating sub-Saharan
African field recordings include UNESCO; Office de Coopération Radiopho-
nique (OCORA), Centre Nationale de Recherche Scientifique (CNRS),
Office de la Recherche Scientifique et Technique Outre-Mer (ORSTOM) and
the Musée de l'Homme in France; the Musée Royal de l'Afrique Centrale in
Belgium; the Ethnomusicological Audio-Visual Archive of Cambridge University and the National Sound Archive (formerly the British Institute of
Recorded Sound) in England; the Museum für Volkerkunde in Germany; and
Ethnic Folkways, Nonesuch and Lyrichord record companies and the sound
archives of Indiana University and UCLA in the USA.

The scholar wishing to carry out long-term field research in an African
nation must generally obtain a research visa, contingent upon affiliation with a
scientific or educational institution. Such institutions include universities and
colleges, government cultural agencies, and co-operative organizations such
as CERDOTOLA in Yaounde, Cameroun, which administers the
Ethnomusicologie d'Afrique Centrale project, and the Association for Urgent
Anthropological Research, which supports research in Malawi, Kenya,
Angola and other countries. Tracey, Kubik and Tracey (1969) and Blacking
(1973) discuss field research in Africa. Wachsmann (1969) provides an
interesting overview of the role of ethnomusicology in African studies; students
interested in the development of other branches of African studies might begin
by consulting C. Fyfe, ed. (1976), and R. Oliver and M. Crowder, eds. (1981).

Bibliography

GENERAL

A. M. Jones: *Studies in African Music* (London, 1959/R1978)

A. Lomax: 'The Homogeneity of African-Afro-American Musical Style', *Afro-American Anthropology: Contemporary Perspectives*, ed. N. E. Whitten Jr and J. Szwed (New York, 1970), 181

J. H. K. Nketia: *The Music of Africa* (New York, 1974)

A. P. Merriam: 'Traditional Music of Black Africa', *Africa*, ed. P. M. Martin and P. O'Meara (Bloomington, IN, 1977), 243

K. P. Wachsmann and P. Cooke: 'Africa', *Grove 6*

A. P. Merriam: *African Music in Perspective* (New York and London, 1982)

G. Kubik: 'Musikgestaltung in Afrika', *Musik in Afrika*, ed. A. Simon (Berlin, 1983), 27

B. Nettl: 'Africa', *The New Harvard Dictionary of Music*, ed. D. M. Randel (Cambridge, MA, and London, 1986), 16

HISTORICAL AND GEOGRAPHICAL STUDIES

B. Ankerman: 'Die Afrikanischen Musikinstrumente', *Ethnologisches Notizblatt*, iii (1901), 1–134

H. Balfour: 'The Friction-Drum', *Journal of the Royal Anthropological Institute*, xxxvii (1907), 67

E. M. von Hornbostel: 'Über ein akustisches Kriterium für Kulturzusammenhänge', *Zeitschrift für Ethnologie*, xliii (1911), 601; repr. in *Beiträge zur Akustik und Musikwissenschaft*, vii (1913), 1

M. J. Herskovits: 'The Culture Areas of Africa', *Africa*, iii/1 (1930), 59

E. M. von Hornbostel: 'The Ethnology of African Sound Instruments. Comments on *Geist und Werden de Musikinstrumente* by C. Sachs', *Africa*, vi/2 (1933), 129; vi/3 (1934), 277–311

H. Wieschoff: *Die afrikanischen Trommeln und ihre ausserafrikanischen Beziehungen* (Stuttgart, 1933/R1968)

P. R. Kirby: *The Musical Instruments of the Native Races of South Africa* (London, 1934, 2/1965)

J. Kunst: 'A Musicological Argument for Cultural Relationship between Indonesia – probably the Isle of Java – and Central Africa', *PMA*, lxii (1935–36), 57

O. Boone: *Les xylophones du Congo Belge* (Tervuren, 1936)

M. Schneider: 'Über die Verbreitung afrikanischer Chorformen', *Zeitschrift für Ethnologie*, lxix/1–3 (1937), 78

C. Sachs: *Les Instruments de Musique de Madagascar* (Paris, 1938)

A. Schaeffner: 'La musique noire d'Afrique', *La Musique des origines à nos jours*, ed. N. Dufourq (Paris, 1946), 460

O. Boone: *Les tambours du Congo Belge et du Ruanda-Urundi* (Tervuren, 1951)

R. A. Waterman: 'African Influence on the Music of the Americas', *Acculturation in the Americas: Proceedings and Selected Papers of the 29th International Congress of Americanists*, ii, ed. S. Tax (Chicago, IL, 1952), 207

Y. Grimaud and G. Rouget: *Note on the Music of the Bushmen compared to that of the Babinga Pygmies*, LD 9, 1956 [disc notes]

A. M. Jones: *Studies in African Music* (London, 1959/R1978)

A. P. Merriam: 'African Music', *Continuity and Change in African Cultures*, ed. W. R. Bascom and M. J. Herskovits (Chicago, IL, 1959a), 49–86

——: 'The Concept of Culture Clusters Applied to the Belgian Congo', *Southwestern Journal of Anthropology*, xv (1959), 373

J. S. Laurenty: *Les cordophones du Congo Belge et du Ruanda-Urundi* (Tervuren, 1960)

G. Rouget: 'La musique d'Afrique noire', *Histoire de la Musique*, i, ed. M. Roland (Paris, 1960), 215

M. D. W. Jeffreys: 'Negro Influences on Indonesia', *African Music*, ii/4 (1961), 10

J. S. Laurenty: *Les sanza du Congo* (Tervuren, 1962)

A. M. Jones: *Africa and Indonesia: the Evidence of the Xylophone and Other Musical and Cultural Factors* (Leiden, 1964/R1971)

J. Vansina, R. Mauny and L. Thomas, eds.: *The Historian in Tropical Africa* (London, 1964)

K. P. Wachsmann: 'Human Migration and African Harps', *JIFMC*, xvi (1964), 84

M. Hood: 'Review of *Africa and Indonesia* by A. M. Jones', *EM*, x (1966), 214

L. A. Anderson: 'The African Xylophone', *African Arts*, i/1 (1967), 46

A. P. Merriam: 'The Use of Music as a Technique of Reconstructing Culture History in Africa', *Reconstructing African Culture History*, ed. C. G. Gabel and N. R. Bennett (Boston, MA, 1967), 83–114

M. D. W. Jeffreys: 'Response to G. T. Nurse', *African Music*, iv/2 (1968), 75

W. Hirschberg: 'Early Historical Illustrations of West and Central African Music', *African Music*, iv/3 (1969), 6

G. Rouget and J. Schwarz: 'Sur les xylophones équiheptaphoniques des Malinké', *RdM*, lv/1 (1969), 47–77

A. Lomax: 'The Homogeneity of African-Afro-American Musical Style', *Afro-American Anthropology: Contemporary Perspectives*, ed. N. E. Whitten Jr and J. Szwed (New York, 1970), 181

A. A. Mensah: 'Ndebele-Soli Bi-musicality in Zambia', *YIFMC*, ii (1970), 108

P. J. C. Dark and M. Hill: 'Musical Instruments on Benin Plaques', *Essays on Music and History in Africa*, ed. K P. Wachsmann (Evanston, IL, 1971), 65

C. J. Frisbie: 'Anthropological and Ethnomusicological Implications of a Comparative Analysis of Bushmen and African Pygmy Music', *Ethnology*, x/3 (1971), 265

A. M. Jones: 'Africa and Indonesia: An Ancient Colonial Era?', *Essays on Music and History in Africa*, ed. K. P. Wachsmann (Evanston, IL, 1971), 81

K. P. Wachsmann: 'Musical Instruments in Kiganda Tradition and Their Place in the East African Scene', *Essays on Music and History in Africa*, ed. K. P. Wachsmann (Evanston, IL, 1971), 93–134

——, ed.: *Essays on Music and History in Africa* (Evanston, IL, 1971)

H. Zemp: *Musique Dan: La musique dans la pensée et la vie sociale d'une société africaine* (Paris, 1971)

J. S. Roberts: *Black Music of Two Worlds* (New York, 1972)

R. Günther, ed.: *Musikkulturen Asiens, Afrikas und Ozeaniens im 19. Jahrhundert* (Regensburg, 1973)

T. O. Ranger: *Dance and Society in Eastern Africa, 1890–1970: the Beni 'Ngoma'* (London, 1975)

E. J. Collins: 'Ghanaian Highlife', *African Arts*, x/1 (1976), 62

N. Fiagbedzi: *The Music of the Anlo: Its Historical Background, Cultural Matrix, and Style* (diss., UCLA, 1977)

N. McLeod: 'Musical Instruments and History in Madagascar', *Essays for a Humanist: an Offering to Klaus Wachsmann*, ed. C. Seeger (New York, 1977), 189

A. P. Merriam: 'Traditional Music of Black Africa', *Africa*, ed. P. M. Martin and P. O. Meara (Bloomington, IN, 1977, 2/1986), 243

T. Vidal: 'Traditions and History in Yoruba Music', *Nigerian Music Review*, i (1977), 66

F. Willett: 'A Contribution to the History of Musical Instruments among the Yoruba', *Essays for a Humanist: an Offering to Klaus Wachsmann*, ed. C. Seeger (New York, 1977), 350–89

J. C. DjeDje: *Distribution of the One String Fiddle in West Africa* (Los Angeles, CA, 1980)

A. King: 'Nigeria', *Grove 6*

K. P. Wachsmann and P. Cooke: 'Africa', *Grove 6*

R. Blench: 'Evidence of the Indonesian Origins of Certain Elements of African Culture: a Review, With Special Reference to the Arguments of A. M. Jones', *African Music*, vi/2 (1982), 81

G. Kubik: *Musikgeschichte in Bildern: Ostafrika* (Leipzig, 1982)

J. Low: 'A History of Kenyan Guitar Music: 1945–1980', *African Music*, vi/2 (1982), 17

L. P. Monts: 'Music Clusteral Relationships in a Liberian-Sierra Leonean Region: a Preliminary Analysis', *Journal of African Studies*, ix/3 (1982), 101

E. M. H. Mugglestone: 'The Gora and the "Grand" Gom-gom: a Reappraisal of Kolb's Account of Khoikhoi Musical Bows', *African Music*, vi/2 (1982), 94

J. H. K. Nketia: 'On the Historicity of Music in African Cultures', *Journal of African Studies*, ix/3 (1982), 91

S. Bemba: *Cinquante ans de musique du Congo-Zaïre (1920–1970): De Paul Kamba a Tabu-Ley* (Dakar, 1984)

U. Wegner: *Afrikanische Saiteninstrumente* (Berlin, 1984)

D. B. Coplan: *In Township Tonight! South Africa's Black City Music and Theatre* (London and New York, 1985)

A. M. Dauer: *Tradition Afrikanischer Blasorchester und Entstehung des Jazz* (Graz, 1985)

V. Erlmann: 'A Feeling of Prejudice: Orpheus P. McAdoo and the Virginia Jubilee Singers in South Africa', *Journal of Southern African Studies*, xiv/3 (1988), 331

G. Kubik: 'Nsenga/Shona Harmonic Patterns and the San Heritage in Southern Africa', *EM*, xxxii/2 (1988), 39–76

——: *Musikgeschichte in Bildern: Westafrika* (Leipzig, 1989)

C. A. Waterman: *Jùjú: a Social History and Ethnography of an African Popular Music* (Chicago, IL, 1990)

MUSICAL SOUND AND PERFORMANCE PRACTICE

P. R. Kirby: 'Some Problems of Primitive Harmony and Polyphony with Special Reference to Bantu Practice', *South African Journal of Science*, xxiii (1926), 951

E. M. von Hornbostel: 'African Negro Music', *Africa*, i/1 (1928), 30–62

G. Herzog: 'Speech-Melody and Primitive Music', *MQ*, xx (1934), 452

P. R. Kirby: *The Musical Instruments of the Native Races of South Africa* (London, 1934, 2/1965)

G. Herzog: 'Drum-signalling in a West African Tribe', *Word*, i (1945), 217

J. F. Carrington: *Talking Drums of Africa* (London, 1949)

K. P. Wachsmann: 'An Equal-stepped Tuning in a Ganda Harp', *Nature*, clxv (1950), 40

R. Waterman: 'African Influence on the Music of the Americas', *Acculturation in the Americas: Proceedings and Selected Papers of the 29th International Congress of Americanists*, ed. S. Tax (Chicago, IL, 1952), 207

S. D. Cudjoe: 'The Techniques of Ewe Drumming and the Social Importance of Music in Africa', *Phylon*, xiv (1953), 280

K. P. Wachsmann: 'The Sound Instruments', *Tribal Crafts of Uganda*, ed. M. Trowell and K. P. Wachsmann (London, 1953), 311–422

A. M. Jones: 'African Rhythm', *Africa*, xxiv (1954), 26

K. P. Wachsmann: 'The Transplantation of Folk Music from One Social Environment to Another', *JIFMC*, vi (1954), 41

J. Blacking: 'Eight Flute Tunes from Butembo, East Belgian Congo – an Analysis in Two Parts, Musical and Physical', *African Music*, i/2 (1955), 24

A. P. Merriam: 'Yovu Songs from Ruanda', *Zaire*, xi (1957), 933–66

D. K. Rycroft: 'Linguistics and Melodic Interaction in Zulu Song', *Akten des xxiv Internationalen Orientalistenkongresses, München* (Wiesbaden, 1957), 726

S. D. Cudjoe: 'Problems of Notation, 3: the Notation of Drum Music', *Music in Ghana*, i/1 (1958), 70

J. H. K. Nketia: 'Traditional Music of the Ga People', *African Music*, ii/1 (1958), 21

J. Blacking: 'Problems of Pitch, Pattern and Harmony in the Ocarina Music of the Venda', *African Music*, ii/2 (1959), 15

A. M. Jones: *Studies in African Music* (London, 1959/R1978)

A. P. Merriam: 'African Music', *Continuity and Change in African Cultures*, ed. W. R. Bascom and M. J. Herskovits (Chicago, IL, 1959), 49–86

G. Kubik: 'The Structure of Kiganda Xylophone Music', *African Music*, ii/3 (1960), 6

J. Blacking: 'Patterns of Nsenga Kalimba Music', *African Music*, ii/4 (1961), 26

M. Schneider: 'Tone and Tune in West African Music', *EM*, v (1961), 204

G. Kubik: 'The Phenomenon of Inherent Rhythms in East and Central African Instrumental Music', *African Music*, iii/1 (1962), 33

J. H. K. Nketia: *Drumming in Akan Communities of Ghana* (Edinburgh, 1963)

N. M. England and others: 'Symposium on Transcription and Analysis: a Hukwe Song with Musical Bow', viii (1964), 223–77

G. Rouget: 'Tons de la langue en Gun (Dahomey) et tons du tambour', *RdM*, 1 (1964), 3

——: 'Un film experimental: Batteries Dogons, éléments pour une étude de rythmes', *L'Homme*, v/2 (1965), 126

K. P. Wachsmann: 'Some Speculations Concerning a Drum Chime in Buganda', *Man*, new ser., i (1965), 1

J. Blacking: *Venda Children's Songs: a Study in Ethnomusicological Analysis* (Johannesburg, 1967)

D. K. Rycroft: 'Nguni Vocal Polyphony', *JIFMC*, xix (1967), 88

K. P. Wachsmann: 'Pen-equidistance and Accurate Pitch: a Problem from the Source of the Nile', *Festschrift für Walter Wiora zum 30. December 1966*, ed. L. Finscher and C. -H. Mahling (Basel, 1967), 583

L. A. Anderson: *The Miko Modal System of Kiganda Xylophone Music* (diss., UCLA, 1968)

G. Kubik: 'Composition Techniques in Kiganda Xylophone Music: With an Introduction into Some Kiganda Musical Concepts', *African Music*, iv/3 (1969), 22–72

A. P. Merriam: 'The Ethnographic Experience: Drum-making Among the Bala (Basongye)', *EM*, xiii (1969), 74

P. Cooke: 'Ganda Xylophone Music: Another Approach', *African Music*, iv/4 (1970), 62

R. Kauffman: *Multi-part Relationships in the Shona Music of Rhodesia* (diss., UCLA, 1970)

J. Koetting: 'Analyses and Notation of West African Drum Ensemble Music', *Selected Reports in Ethnomusicology*, i/3 (1970), 116–46

S. K. Ladzekpo and H. Pantaleoni: 'Takada Drumming', *African Music*, iv/4 (1970), 6

J. Blacking: 'Deep and Surface Structures in Venda Music', *YIFMC*, iii (1971), 91

R. Knight: 'Towards a Notation and Tablature for the Kora and Its Application to Other Instruments', *African Music*, v/1 (1971), 23

J. H. K. Nketia: 'Surrogate Languages of Africa', *Current Trends in Linguistics*, vii (1971), 699–732

D. K. Rycroft: 'Stylistic Evidence in Nguni Song', *Essays on Music and History in Africa*, ed. K. P. Wachsmann (Evanston, IL, 1971), 213

G. Kubik: 'Transcription of African Music from Silent Film: Theory and Methods', *African Music*, v/2 (1972), 28

H. Pantaleoni: 'Three Principles of Timing in Anlo Dance Drumming', *African Music*, v/2 (1972), 50

J. H. K. Nketia: *The Music of Africa* (New York, 1974)

R. F. Thompson: *African Art in Motion* (Los Angeles, CA, 1974)

F. Bebey: *African Music: a People's Art* (Westport, CT, 1975)

L. E. N. Ekwueme: 'Structural Levels of Rhythm and Form in African Music with Particular Reference to the West Coast', *African Music*, v/4 (1975–76), 27

A. Euba: 'The Interrelationship of Poetry and Music in Yoruba Tradition', *Seminar on Yoruba Oral Tradition: Poetry in Music, Dance and Drama*, ed. W. Abimbola (Ile-Ife, 1975), 471

N. Fiagbedzi: *The Music of the Anlo: Its Historical Background, Cultural Matrix, and Style* (diss., UCLA, 1977)

J. M. Chernoff: *African Rhythm and African Sensibility: Aesthetics and Social Action in African Music* (Chicago, IL, 1979)

C. Keil: *Tiv Song: the Sociology of Art in a Classless Society* (Chicago, IL, 1979)

P. F. Berliner: 'John Kunaka: Mbira Maker', *African Arts*, xiv/1 (1980), 61

J. Blacking: 'Venda Music', *Grove 6*

R. Kauffman: 'African Rhythm: a Reassessment', *EM*, xxiv (1980), 393

D. Locke and G. K. Agbeli: 'A Study of the Drum Language in Adzogbo', *African Music*, vi/1 (1980), 32

P.-C. Ngumu: 'Modèle standard de rangées de carreaux pour transcrire les traditions africaines du Cameroun', *African Music*, vi/1 (1980), 52

K. P. Wachsmann and P. Cooke: 'Africa', *Grove 6*

A. P. Merriam: 'African Musical Rhythm and Concepts of Time-reckoning', *Music East and West: Essays in Honor of Walter Kaufmann*, ed. T. Noblitt (New York, 1981), 123

R. M. Stone and V. L. Stone: 'Event, Feedback and Analysis: Research Media in the Study of Music Events', *EM*, xxv (1981), 215

B. Aning: 'Tuning the Kora: a Case Study of the Norms of a Gambian Musician', *Journal of African Studies*, ix/3 (1982), 164

J. Blacking: 'The Structure of Musical Discourse: the Problem of the Song Text', *YTM*, xiv (1982), 15

D. Locke: 'Principles of Offbeat Timing and Cross-Rhythm in Southern Eve Dance Drumming', *EM*, xxvi (1982), 217

A. M. Dauer: 'Kinesis und Katharsis', *Musik in Afrika*, ed. A. Simon (Berlin, 1983), 166

J. Pressing: 'Rhythmic Design in the Support Drums of Agbadza', *African Music*, vi/3 (1983), 4

V. K. Agawu: 'The Impact of Language on Musical Composition in Ghana: an Introduction to the Musical Style of Ephraim Amu', *EM*, xxviii (1984), 37–74

L. A. Anderson: 'Multipart Relationships in Xylophone and Tuned Drum Traditions in Buganda', *Selected Reports in Ethnomusicology*, v (1984), 121

S. Arom: 'The Music of the Banda-Linda Horn Ensembles: Form and Structure', *Selected Reports in Ethnomusicology*, v (1984), 173

S. C. DeVale: 'Prolegomena to a Study of Harp and Voice Sounds in Uganda: a Graphic System for the Notation of Texture', *Selected Reports in Ethnomusicology*, v (1984), 285–315

R. Knight: 'The Style of Mandinka Music: a Study in Extracting Theory from Practice', *Selected Reports in Ethnomusicology*, v (1984), 3–66

S. Mbabi-Katana: 'The Use of Measured Rhythm to Communicate Messages among Banyoro and Baganda in Uganda', *Selected Reports in Ethnomusicology*, v (1984), 339

U. Wegner: *Afrikanische Saiteninstrumente* (Berlin, 1984)

S. Arom: *Polyphonies et Polyrythmies Instrumentales d'Afrique Centrale: Structure et Methodologie* (Paris, 1985)

G. Kubik: 'African Tone-Systems: a Reassessment', *YTM*, xvii (1985), 31–63

C. E. Schmidt: 'Multi-Part Vocal Music of the Kpelle of Liberia' (diss., UCLA, 1985)

R. M. Stone: 'In Search of Time in African Music', *Music Theory Spectrum*, vii (1985), 139

V. K. Agawu: 'The Rhythmic Structure of West African Music', *Journal of Musicology*, v/3 (1987), 400

——: 'Tone and Tune: the Evidence for Northern Ewe Music', *Africa*, lviii/2 (1988), 127–46

Ethnomusicology: Historical and Regional Studies

ETHNOGRAPHY OF MUSIC

H. E. Hause: 'Terms for Musical Instruments in Sudanic Languages: a Lexiographical Inquiry', *Journal of the American Oriental Society*, lxviii/1 (1948), 1–71

H. Tracey: *Chopi Musicians: Their Music, Poetry, and Instruments* (London, 1948)

A. Schaeffner: *Les Kissi: une société noire et ses instruments de musique* (Paris, 1951)

M. Griaule: 'Symbolisme des tambours Soudanais', *Mélanges d'histoire et d'esthetique musicales: offerts à Paul-Marie Masson* (Paris, 1955), 79

M. G. Smith: 'The Social Functions and Meaning of Hausa Praise-Singing', *Africa*, xxvii/1 (1957), 26

A. Schaeffner: 'Situation des musiciens dans trois sociétés Africaines', *Les Colloques de Wégimont, III, 1956: Ethnomusicologie*, ii (Paris, 1960), 33

J. H. K. Nketia: *Drumming in Akan Communities of Ghana* (Edinburgh, 1963)

G. Rouget: 'La musique funéraire en Afrique Noire: functions et formes', *Roundtable: Bericht über den Neunten Internationalen Musikwissenschaftlichen Kongress*, ii (Paris, 1964), 143

J. Blacking: 'The Role of Music in the Culture of the Venda of the Northern Transvaal', *Studies in Ethnomusicology*, ii (1965), 20–53

K. P. Wachsmann: 'Some Speculations Concerning a Drum Chime in Buganda', *Man*, new ser., i (1965), 1

R. F. Thompson: 'An Aesthetic of the Cool: West African Dance', *African Forum*, ii/2 (1966), 85

K. P. Wachsmann: 'The Trends of Musicology in Africa', *Selected Reports*, i/1 (1966), 61

J. Blacking: *Venda Children's Songs: a Study in Ethnomusicological Analysis* (Johannesburg, 1967)

N. M. England: 'Bushmen Counterpoint', *JIFMC*, xix (1967), 58

H. Zemp: 'Comment on deviant musicien', *La musique dans la vie*, ed. T. Nikiprowetsky (Paris, 1967), 77

J. Blacking: 'Songs, Dances, Mimes and Symbolism of Venda Girls' Initiation Schools', *African Studies*, xxviii (1969), 215–66

J. R. Goody: *Comparative Studies in Kinship* (Stanford, CA, 1969)

G. Kubik: 'Composition Techniques in Kiganda Xylophone Music: With an Introduction into some Kiganda Musical Concepts', *African Music*, iv/3 (1969), 22–72

W. Laade: *Die Situation von Musikleben und Musikforschung in den Ländern Afrikas und Asiens und die neuen Aufgaben der Musikethnologie* (Tutzing, 1969)

D. W. Ames and A. V. King: *Glossary of Hausa Music and Its Social Contexts* (Evanston, IL, 1971)

J. Blacking: 'Deep and Surface Structures in Venda Music', *YIFMC*, iii (1971), 91

G. Kubik: *Die Institution mukanda und assoziierte Einrichtungen bei den Vambwele–Vankangela und verwandten Ethnien in Sudostangola* (diss., U. of Vienna, 1971)

H. Zemp: *Musique Dan: La musique dans la pensée et la vie sociale d'une société africaine* (Paris, 1971)

W. L. d'Azevedo, ed.: *The Traditional Artist in African Societies* (Bloomington, IN, 1973)

C. R. Adams: *Ethnography of Basotho Evaluative Expression in the Cognitive Domain Lipapali (Games)* (diss., U. of Indiana, 1974)

R. F. Thompson: *African Art in Motion* (Los Angeles, CA, 1974)

P. F. Berliner: 'Music and Spirit Possession at a Shona Bira', *African Music*, v/4 (1975–76), 130

N. Nzewi: *Master Musicians and the Music of ese, ukori and mgba ensembles in Ngwa, Igbo* (diss., Queen's U., Belfast, 1977)

D. W. Ames and K. A. Gourlay: 'Kimkim: a Women's Musical Pot', *African Arts*, xi/1 (1978), 56

P. F. Berliner: *The Soul of Mbira: Music and Traditions of the Shona People of Zimbabwe* (Berkeley, CA, 1978)

J. H. K. Nketia: 'New Perspectives in Music Education', *ISME Yearbook*, v (1978), 104

J. M. Chernoff: *African Rhythms and African Sensibility: Aesthetics and Social Action in African Musical Idioms* (Chicago, IL, 1979)

C. Keil: *Tiv Song: the Sociology of Art in a Classless Society* (Chicago, IL, 1979)

B. Schmidt-Wrenger: *Rituelle Frauengesange der Tshokwe: Untersuchungen zu einem Sakularisierungsprozess in Angola und Zaire* (Tervuren, 1979)

V. Erlmann: *Die Macht des Wortes: Preisgesang und Berufsmusiker bei den Fulɓe des Diamaré (Nordkamerun)* (Hohenschaftlarn, 1980)

G. Rouget: *La musique et la transe: Esquisse d'une théorie générale des relations de la musique et de la possession* (Paris, 1980; Eng. trans., 1985)

K. P. Wachsmann and P. Cooke: 'Africa', *Grove 6*

V. Erlmann and H. Magagi: 'Data on the Sociology of Hausa Musicians in the Valley of Maradi (Niger)', *Paideuma*, xxvii (1981), 63–110

J. I. N. Lo-Bamijoko: *A Preliminary Study of the Classification, Tuning and Educational Implications of the*

Standardization of Musical Instruments in Africa: the Nigerian Case (diss., U. of Michigan, 1981)
C. Nwachukwu: *Taxonomy of Musical Instruments of Mbaise, Nigeria* (diss., Queen's U., Belfast, 1981)
J. Collins and P. Richards: 'Popular Music in West Africa: Suggestions for an Interpretative Framework', i, *Popular Music Perspectives: Papers from the First International Conference on Popular Music Research, Amsterdam, June 1981*, ed. D. Horn and P. Tagg (Goteborg and Exeter, 1982), 111–41
D. B. Coplan: 'The Urbanisation of African Music: Some Theoretical Observations', *Popular Music*, ii (1982), 113
V. Erlmann: 'Trance and Music in the Hausa *Bòorii* Spirit Possession Cult in Niger', *EM*, xxvi (1982), 49
B. L. Hampton: 'Music and Ritual Symbolism in the Ga Funeral', *YTM*, xiv (1982), 75–105
A. P. Merriam: *African Music in Perspective* (New York and London, 1982)
R. M. Stone: *Let the Inside be Sweet: the Interpretation of Music Events among the Kpelle of Liberia* (Bloomington, IN, 1982)
F. E. Besmer: *Horses, Musicians, and Gods: the Hausa Cult of Possession-Trance* (Zaria, Nigeria, 1983)
R. Joseph: 'Zulu Women's Music', *African Music*, vi/3 (1983), 53–89
T. Ranger: 'The Invention of Tradition in Colonial Africa', *The Invention of Tradition*, ed. E. J. Hobsbawm and T. Ranger (Cambridge, England, 1983/*R*1987), 211–62
S. Bemba: *Cinquante ans de musique du Congo-Zaïre (1920–1970): De Paul Kamba à Tabu-Ley* (Dakar, 1984)
E. D. Brown: *Drums of Life: Royal Music and Social Life in Western Zambia* (diss., U. of Washington, 1984)
C. A. Campbell and C. M. Eastman: '*Ngoma*: Swahili Adult Song Performance in Context', *EM* xxviii (1984), 467
K. A. Gourlay: 'The Non-Universality of Music and the Universality of Non-Music', *The World of Music*, xxvi/2 (1984), 25
R. Michels-Gebler: *Schmied und Musik: Über die traditionelle Verknupfung von Schmiedehandwerk und Musik in Afrika, Asien und Europa* (Bonn, 1984)
J. H. K. Nketia: 'Universal Perspectives in Ethnomusicology', *World of Music*, xxvi/1 (1984), 3
—— and J. C. DjeDje: 'Trends in African Musicology', *Selected Reports*, v (1984), ix
J. Blacking: 'The Context of Venda Possession Music: Reflections on the Effectiveness of Symbols', *YTM*, xvii (1985), 64
D. B. Coplan: *In Township Tonight! South Africa's Black City Music and Theatre* (London and New York, 1985)
J. C. DjeDje: 'Women and Music in Sudanic Africa', *More Than Drumming: Essays on African and Afro-Latin American Music and Musicians*, ed. I. V. Jackson (Westport, CT, 1985), 67
V. Erlmann: 'Black Political Song in South Africa – Some Research Perspectives', *Popular Music Perspectives*, ii (1985), 187
L. P. Monts: *An Annotated Glossary of Vai Musical Language* (Paris, 1987)
C. A. Waterman: *Jùjú: a Social History and Ethnography of an African Popular Music* (Chicago, IL, 1990)

BASIC RESOURCES

D. H. Varley, comp.: *African Native Music: an Annotated Bibliography* (London, 1936)
A. P. Merriam: 'An Annotated Bibliography of African and African-Derived Music since 1936', *Africa*, xxi/4 (1951), 319
D. L. Thieme, comp.: *African Music: a Briefly Annotated Bibliography* (Washington, DC, 1964)
L. J. P. Gaskin: *A Select Bibliography of Music in Africa* (London, 1965)
H. Tracey, G. Kubik and A. Tracey: *African Music: Codification and Textbook Project* (Roodepoort, 1969)
K. P. Wachsmann: 'Ethnomusicology in African Studies: the Next Twenty Years', *Expanding Horizons*, ed. G. Carter and A. Paden (Evanston, IL, 1969), 131
A. P. Merriam: *African Music on LP: an Annotated Discography* (Evanston, IL, 1970)
J. Blacking: 'Field Work in African Music', *Reflections on Afro-American Music*, ed. D. -R. de Lerma (Kent, OH, 1973), 207
H. Tracey: *Catalogue of the Sound of Africa Series* (Roodepoort, 1973)
F. Bebey: *African Music: a People's Art* (Westport, CT, 1975)
C. Fyfe: *African Studies Since 1945: a Tribute to Basil Davidson* (London, 1976)
R. M. Stone and F. J. Gillis: *African Music and Oral Data: a Catalog of Field Recordings 1902–1975* (Bloomington, IN, 1976)
R. Oliver and M. Crowder: *The Cambridge Encyclopedia of Africa* (Cambridge, England, 1981)

CHAPTER VIII

West Asia

AMNON SHILOAH

Historical survey

The study of musical traditions in West Asia (the Arab states of the Middle East, the Arabian Peninsula and the Gulf States, as well as the Magrib, and the nations of Israel, Turkey and Iran) has been largely determined by the co-existence and interaction of many different types of music. These include learned or 'art' music from the great tradition that developed after the advent of Islam; specific little traditions involving Beduin, folk and ethnic, linguistic and religious groups; and a variety of newer styles, including the mainstream practices as well as other combinations of old and innovative elements that reflect the ways different ethnic groups emerged and confronted the modern world. The combination of ethnic folk genres and styles is usually explained by their being mostly orally transmitted and interrelated by common attitudes towards music and towards its practice and place in life. The art music of West Asia, however, is distinguished by greater prestige and a wealth of written sources whose blossoming coincides with the establishment of the great tradition. Thus, unlike folk traditions, sources provide the scholar with evidence on art music, its concepts, nature, values and historical perspectives. These factors have had considerable effect on the scope and nature of research, resulting in continuous oscillation between the general and the particular, diatonic and synchronic approaches.

The first leading scholars were chiefly concerned with learned music and interpreting of sources. The studies of Jean-Benjamin La Borde (1780), Raphael Georg Kiesewetter (1842) and Johann Gottfried L. Kosegarten (1840) were based mainly on written sources but Guillaume-André Villoteau (1809, 'De l'état actuel'; 1809, 'Description historique'), Edward William Lane (1836), Francesco Salvador Daniel (1863) and Xavier Maurice Collangettes (1904–6) combined information from sources with analyses of their exposure to living music. These studies were later enriched by the contributions of Henry George Farmer (1925, 'Arabic Musical Manuscripts'; 1925, 'Clues for the Arabian Influence'; 1925–6; 1926; 1929/R1973; 1930, 'Greek Theorists'; 1930, 'Historical Facts'), Jules Rouanet (1922) and Julian Ribera y Tarrago (1922, 1927), and include broad historical surveys, translation and interpretation of sources, analysis of scales and modes, and rare treatment of folk music; the debt to Greece and the influence of Arabs on medieval Europe was explored and the vague distinction made between Arabian, Turkish, Persian and North African musical traditions emphasized their common antecedents and origin.

Indigenous scholarship

Indigenous scholarship continued in the spirit of the past, but by the end of the 19th century, new trends began to emerge. In Turkey, a circle of musical personalities committed itself to a new exploration of the development of Turkish music. They included M. N. Selcuk, Halil Bediî Yönetken, Sufi Ezgi (author of a five-volume treatise introducing the practice and theory of music 1935–53), Rauf Yekta Bey, author of the extensive French article in *EMDC*, Mahuut Ragip Gazimihal (1928, 1929) and Adnan Saygun (1960).

In Iran, Ali Naqi Vaziri, who adopted Western staff notation and wrote a textbook on the theory of classical music, was the most important early 20th-century writer. Ruholla Khaleqi's three-volume work, *Sargozasht-e-musigi-ye Iran*, dealt with the history and theory of Iranian classical music.

In Lebanon, Michail Mushaqa was an important theorist of the late 19th century.

In Egypt, musical theorists produced works covering a wide range of topics. Early scholars, such as Muhammad Dhakir, Mahmud Ahmad al-Hefni (collaborator of Robert Lachmann), Kamil al-Khulai, Mansur Awwad and Ahmad Taymur, produced musico-literary and biographical works in the old style; studies of scales, modes, forms and performance practice; and collections of song texts.

By the beginning of the 20th century, Cairo had become a major centre of recording activity. The phonograph era in Egypt has been described and documented by Jihad Racy (1976). Of special importance is the first scientific, documented collection of recordings made by the first International Congress of Arabic Music held in 1932 under the auspices of the Egyptian authorities. The commission responsible for these recordings comprised the eminent ethnomusicologists Lachmann, as president, and Erich M. von Hornbostel, who initiated the inclusion of Beduin and rural music, and the composer Béla Bartók, who later contributed two important studies on southern Turkish and Algerian folk music. The recordings provided samples of art music from Turkey, Iraq, Syria, Algeria, Tunisia, Morocco and Egypt, as well as various other Egyptian styles including dance and songs of exorcism, Muslim and Coptic religious music, and rural styles. Thus, despite concentrating on classical traditions, the Congress paved the way for thorough exploration of other genres, excluding however the alleged 'alterations' or 'imitations of inferior European productions'.

Many of the participants in the Congress were well-known. Others too had already made valuable contributions to the field, including two books by H. G. Farmer (1929, 1930, *Historical Facts*); comprehensive historical and theoretical surveys by M. Collangettes in *Journal asiatique* (1904); articles by Raul Yekta, Jules Rouanet and Clément Huart in *EMDC* (1922); and Rodolphe d'Erlanger's first volume of *La musique arabe* (1930). However, for those scholars as well as for the other eminent participants such as Lachmann, Curt Sachs,

Egon Wellesz, Hans Hickmann and Alexis Chottin, the opportunity to encounter local leading musicians and scholars, the direct exposure to living traditions, and the in-depth deliberations were of special inspiring impetus.

Indigenous scholarship after World War II

Indigenous scholarship was influenced by general developments in traditional cultures at this time. The increasing importance of the mass media, the ease of rapid communication, and much greater mobility, resulted in immediate contacts among people and greater exposure to Western and other musical cultures. Some of the resulting changes, which also involved conceptualization and behaviour, led to increasing patronage of musical activity by government agencies and international institutions. There also was a shift in emphasis on scientific exploration. Analysis of gradual trends became as essential to researchers as knowledge of historical events, and, parallel to generalizations about structures and the significance of past events, studies on special art and folk repertories, genres, and forms began to appear. Particularly important was the emergence of a young generation of local scholars, who either were familiar with Western scholarship and languages or had received their professional education in Western institutions. Their numerous contributions in Arabic, Turkish, Persian and European languages coincided with a general upsurge of publications in the 1960s and 1970s. Some of the published books in European languages by local authors were doctoral dissertations: four on the classical Persian systems, two of which are in English (P. Hahmud, 1957; H. Farhat, 1965) and two in German (Khatschi, 1962; Massoudieh, 1968); one on the Turkish classical system, in German (G. Oransay, 1964); and seven on different aspects of Arabian music, of which three are in English (Racy, 1977; El-Shawan, 1984, on musical change in Cairo; Sawa, 1983 on the musical life of the Abbassid era); three are in French (Hage, 1972, on Maronite church music; Guettat, 1980, on North African musical tradition; Scheherazade Q. Hassan, 1980, on instruments in Iraq and their social role); and one in German (Touma, 1968, on one *maqam*). Beyond these there has been an abundant outpouring from all the major regional centres, written in Arabic, Turkish, Persian and occasionally in European languages.

Problems concerning origins and the chain of past events have continued to concern many authors. The Arabic translation of Farmer's books, *History of Arabian Music* and *Sources*, provides a clue to this prevailing tendency. A related trend is the intensified publication of source materials (B. al-Athari, A. al-Azzawi, M. al-Hefni, G. al-Khashaba, Yusuf Shawqi and Yusuf Zakariya).

Another important development is the publication of textbooks and educational material, including methods for playing diverse instruments and introductions to the fundamentals of music for both Near Eastern and Western music.

An overview of the literature reveals several more general themes: (i) the analysis of musical systems in general (scales, modes, and rhythms) as in Michael Allawerdi's book, *The Philosophy of Oriental Music* (1949), and Yusul Shawqi's *The Measurement of the Arab Scales*; (ii) the presentation of part of or an entire repertory of a particular style using in most cases Western notation, such as the Ma'rufi entire Persian *radif* preceded by Barkecshli's historical and analytical survey (1963), Selim al-Helou's transcription of the important vocal form *muwashshahat* repertory accompanied by a historical survey (1965), el-Hitami's transcriptions of seven *faṣil*, modal groups of the classical instrumental music in Egypt (1983), and the books of Hashim M. al-Rajab (1961), Galab al-Hanafi (1964), Ibrahim Sha'ubi (1982), and Hammudi al-Wardi (1964) on the Iraqi *maqam*, a compound large musical form; (iii) studies on special aspects like Samha al-Kholy's work *The Tradition of Improvisation in Arab Music* (1978), or Medjid Rezvani (1962) on Iranian dance, and Metin Amd (1959) on Turkish dance – two rare studies on dance art.

In Iran, Turkey and Iraq, the exploration of the diverse musical traditions gradually increased. Good surveys analysing local scholarly activity were published in *Acta Musicologica* – xxxii (1960) and xliv (1972) on Turkey, xlviii (1976) and lii (1980) on Iran and liv (1982) on Iraq.

Western scholarship

Western scholarship after World War II was at first marked by the seal of former renowned scholars. The veteran Farmer continued his work, contributing 24 entries to the *New Grove Dictionary of Music and Musicians* (5th edn.), an extensive article for the *New Oxford History of Music*, and in the third volume of *Musikgeschichte in Bildern* a preface summarizing research in the field of Islamic music over the years, as well as articles dealing with problems of influence and musical heritage during the golden age of Islam. Hans Hickmann, in his authoritative works on ancient Egyptian civilization, has suggested links with present-day living music; he also contributed several studies on Egyptian folk music and instruments as well as a comprehensive work, *Die Musik des Arabish-Islamischen Bereichs* (1970), in which he deals with systematic, historical and social aspects. D'Erlanger pursued his enterprise, *La musique Arabe*, in which he provided French translations of important Arabic treatises and also two volumes codifying scales, modes, rhythms, and compositional forms of contemporary Arab music. Chottin who specialized in Moroccan musical styles, also provided general encyclopedic articles on Arabic and North African music. Three scholars, Eugène Borrel, Helmut Ritter and Fritz Meier, added further to their previous publications on the music and ceremonial dance of the mystical orders in Turkey.

The powerful resurgence of publication in the 1960s and 1970s resulted in hundreds of books and articles. This rich output has been characterized by versatility, multidirectionality, a growing interest in the different styles of living traditions and also a certain oscillation between the general and the particular accompanied by a marked decrease in studies based on the analysis of sources and by a decrease in the publication of source material.

Historical linguistic method

Only a few scholars have opted for the historical linguistic method. Owen Wright, in addition to publishing the ibn al-Munadjim treatise (1966) and articles in the *New Grove Dictionary of Music and Musicians* (1980), contributed a major work based on 13th-century sources, *The Modal System of Arab and Persian Music* (1978). Eikhard Neubauer dedicated much of his writing to the musical life of the Abbassid era (1965, 1969, 'Eine Musikalische Soirée', 1969 'Musik zur Mongolenzeit') and provided a German translation to al-Farabi's book on rhythm (1968–9) and articles in the *Encyclopedia of Islam, Grove 6,* and *Die Musik in Geschichte und Gegenwart.* Al-Farabi's *Grand Book on Music* was the object of two studies: Ellen Hickmann (1960) and George Sawa (1984), who also used al-Isfahani's *Book of Songs* in exploring aspects of medieval practice. Amnon Shiloah provided studies and annotated translations of treatises dealing with the theory of practice (*al-Hasan,* 1972), cosmology, the harmony of the universe (*The Ikhwan,* 1983), medicine and music (*ibn Hindu,* 1972), medieval dance (1962), theories of the origin of music (1979) and an extensive catalogue raisonné of Arabic sources (1979).

Some topics that had previously received great attention by scholars, such as the indebtedness of the Arabs to Greece, the influence on medieval Europe, and the ideological attitude of religious authorities towards music, have waned but not completely disappeared. One still finds works on the influence on medieval European dances (McGee, 1982), on music theory (Randel, 1976), on the Cantigas de Santa Maria (Bagby, 1973) and on the troubadours or the relation of their music to the *nuba* (Denoumy, 1953; Pacholczyk, 1983). Other studies have tended to focus on subjects related to living traditions and seeking to confirm or negate alleged influences on Muslim African music (Anderson, 1971; Simon, 1975), on South Europe and the Balkan states (Reinhard, ed., 1976; Rihtman, 1967) and on Spanish music (Schneider, 1946). Only a few studies have investigated problems over religious ideological attitudes (Choudhoury, 1957; During, 1982; Shiloah, 1984; al-Faruqi, 1985).

Two specific subjects were favoured by many scholars: (i) the cantillation of the Koran (Schneider, 1954; Talbi, 1958; Pacholczyk, 1974; al-Faruqi, 1978, Nelson, 1982); and (ii) the ceremonial music and dance of the Mystics – on the Turkish Mewlevi order (Reinhard, 1973; Seidel, 1972–3; Random, 1980), on the Persian music and dance of the mystics (Mokri, 1961–8; During, 1982), and on the North African brotherhoods' music and ceremony (Aisou, 1968; Dermengham and Barbes, 1951; Crapanzano's ethnopsychiatric study, 1973; Schuyler, 1985). A well-documented study has been done on ecstatic dance in Islam (Mole, 1963). Another subject held in great esteem by Arab writers is lexicography. The major related contribution in a European language is Lois al-Faruqi's annotated lexicon (1981).

Monographs and general surveys

The monographs and surveys tend to present a particular musical tradition either by stressing a common origin or by pointing out the special role played by a particular tradition in the elaboration of the great tradition. Thus, almost all monographical studies begin with a general historical survey, bringing up more or less the same facts: on Arab music (Jargy, 1971; Touma, 1977); on North Africa (al-Mahdi, 1972; Guettat, 1980); on Iran (Caton-Safvate, 1966; Zonis, 1973); and on Turkey (Reinhard, 1962/1967; Signell, 1973).

Modal analysis and repertory

The subject of musical structures and systems includes a few general studies:

on tonal and modal medieval systems (Liberty, 1969) and on the modal concept throughout the ages (Shiloah, 1981). Yet most of the studies refer essentially to living systems and repertories.

The *maqam* phenomenon has been well investigated, both in its broad sense and as a body of melody types, structures, compositional processes, and improvisation, with its derivational forms such as the instrumental *taqsim* (Elsner, 1970, 1975; Gerson-Kiwi, 1970; Nettl and Riddle, 1973; Neubauer, 1965; Okkay, 1976; Olsen, 1974; Oransay, 1957; and Touma, 1968, 1971, 1977, 'The Fidjri', 1977, *La musique arabe*). These studies range from generalities and principles to detailed structural analysis of several renditions of one *maqam*.

Similarly the Persian classical *dastgah* system, its principles, the *radif* repertory, individual *dastgah* and specific aspects have also received considerable attention by Margaret Caron and D. Safvate (1966); Hormoz Farhat (1973); Edith Gerson-Kiwi (1963); Khatchi Khatchi (1962); Mohammed Tashi Massoudieh (1968); Bruno Nettl (1969, 1972, 1979); and E. Zonis (1973). Undoubtedly this category of writings presents one of the area's highest achievements. In addition, several learned music compositional forms have been analysed (al-Faruqi's *muwashshahat*, 1975, and 'The Suite in Islamic History', 1985).

Instruments

The study of instruments and instrumental music has also been favoured, resulting in hundreds of books and articles encompassing learned and folk musics, historical aspects, diffusion and performance practice, morphology, terminology and social context. Some of the studies concentrate on separate instruments: the Egyptian frame drum *darbukkah*, and the single clarinet *uffāta* (Hickmann, 1951, 1952); the Egyptian double clarinet *arghūl* (Elsner, 1969); the Turkish double clarinet *cipte* (Reinhard, 1971); the Beduin lyre, *simsimiyya* (Shiloah, 1972); the Persian fiddle *rabāb* (Kuckertz, 1970); and the kemenche style of Ustad Faydullah in the province of Gilan (Caton, 1971). The typical instrument pair comprising drum and oboe-like *zurna ghaita*, which enhances open-air ceremonies in several countries, has also been examined (Snoussi, 1961 for Tunisia; Reiche, 1970 for Turkey; Simon, 1977 for Egypt). Some research has resulted in books dedicated to the instruments of a particular culture: on the folk instruments of Turkey (Picken, 1975), on Iraqi instruments in their social context (Hassan, 1980), and on Egyptian and Balkan folk instruments (Alexandru, 1968). The *New Grove Dictionary of Musical Instruments* (1984) provides many related entries.

Folk musical traditions

With studies on folk musical traditions the research attains its widest geo-cultural coverage, stretching from the Khorasan in northeast Iran and the Black Sea region in Turkey to South Yemen, the Sudan, the Sahara, the Atlas mountains and Mauritania. The research, which includes some hitherto unexplored groups and aspects, encompasses various styles of rural and nomadic musical traditions. Whether dealing with the repertory of a wide region involving a major ethnic group or with the repertory of a village, an individual informant or a specific genre, most of the studies give stylistic analyses based on transcribed examples and to some extent on inquiries about socio-cultural context. A number of exemplary studies have been based on extensive fieldwork including direct exposure to the culture under analysis: on Khorasan musical traditions (Blum, 1974, 1978; Nettl, 1970); on Busahr in southern Iran (Kuckertz-Massoudieh, 1975); on Egypt, Nubia and the Sudan (Simon, 1972, 1975); and on the nomads in Turkey and the Black Sea area (Reinhard, 1966, 1975). Many studies concentrate on particular genres: the *milhun*, a special style found throughout North Africa (Tahar, 1971; Schuyler, 1974); the Iraqi *abudiyya* and *mawwal* (Wegner, 1982); wedding songs and dances (Shiloah, 1974); the Persian Gulf *mahami* and *fidjri* (Olsen, 1961; Touma, 1977); Turkish and Egyptian epic songs (Reinhard, 1967; Alexandru, 1968); and funeral songs of the Druzes in Lebanon (Racy, 1971).

The relation between the musical and the social

A most important development during the second half of the 20th century is the growing emphasis upon the relationship between musical structure on the one hand and social structure and cultural value on the other, including questions about the urbanization of folk and tribal music and the fate of traditional musics after their contact with Western music. The resulting musical changes are usually examined in terms of sociologically significant variables, as in Nettl's study of Persian music – on attitude (1970) and on musical and social values (1978). Other socio-musicological studies are by Michel Guignard (1973) and Bernard Lortat-Jacob (1980) on Mauritania and the Highlands Atlas. Salwa el-Shawan (1980) discusses in detail a category of urban music in Cairo as it was practised from 1927 to 1977. Amnon Shiloah (1984) examines the phenomenon of cultural contact throughout the ages. Recent collections have been edited by William Kay Archer (1964), Robert Gunther (1973), Wolfgang Laade (1971), Nettl (1978) and Robert Falk and Timothy Rice (1982). A special number of *Asian Music* (vol. xiii) appeared in 1979.

The Eastern churches

The Eastern churches – that is to say the Coptic, Ethiopian, Syrian Orthodox (Jacobite), Assyrian (Nestorian), Maronite and Armenian congregations, including branches that have placed themselves under the authority of the Catholic church at Rome (uniate) – present the scholar with a variety of living musical traditions. They also offer possibilities for comparative studies of diverse old and more recent neighbouring musical traditions. One of the questions for instance that has occupied researchers is the relationship between the *oktoechos* and Syrian church modes, including the possible effects of Turkish, Persian and Arabic musical influences. Syrian church music is under study (Husmann, 1966, 1967, 1970, 1977). Work on Eastern chant has produced three volumes edited by Miloš Velimirović and Egon Wellesz (1969), and Hiroko Awakura (1977), provide comparison between the Iraqi *maqam* and the traditional melodies of the Syrian Orthodox church. Maronite church music has been analysed by Louis Hage (1972), and the liturgical music of the Christian Arabs in Israel by Dalia Cohen (1967, 1971). Coptic music has been surveyed by Margit Borsai (1970–71) and by René Menard (1969); Ethiopian liturgical music by Bernard Velat (1961, 1966) and M. Porone (1960); 29 recordings of diverse Eastern Churches musical selections are described in Laade (1969). Finally, information on the various Eastern rites is in the *Encyclopédie des musiques sacrées.*

Jewish music in Israel

Jerusalem at the beginning of the 20th century with its profusion of Jewish, Arab and Christian musical traditions, existing side by side and interacting with each other, has been a most propitious locale for ethnomusicological research. A. Z. Idelsohn, who arrived there in 1905, took full advantage of this variety of strains, capping his career with his 10-volume *Thesaurus* (1914–33), which has served a model for the discipline of ethnomusicology, as well as for generations of Israeli scholars. In 1935 another eminent ethnomusicologist arrived in Jerusalem – Robert Lachmann. He initiated a new style of research based on his achievements in the realm of 'comparative musicology' with an emphasis on the points of contact of Jewish music with neighbouring and parallel civilizations. His work, regarded as a major contribution to Jewish musicology, is an essay on Jewish cantilation and song on the Tunisian Isle of Djerba (1940). Edith Gerson-Kiwi, who re-edited Lachmann's essay in 1978, took over the recording projects of the archive that had been founded by Lachmann in 1935.

Musicological activities greatly increased during the last half of the 20th century. The National Sound Archive and laboratories were established, the Jewish Music Research Centre was founded and three departments of musicology have given impetus to research and to the publication of books, articles and records. After the mass immigration to Israel, the major goal was to investigate the musical heritage of Jewish communities from around the world. But a look at the subjects chosen reveals that scholars moved in all directions, often combining more than one field of interest and specialization. In this wide-ranging effort, both synchronic and diachronic viewpoints were included on many subjects: musical archaeology, Biblical and post-Biblical tradition (H. Avenary, 1979; B. Bayer, 1968, 1982; and E. Gerson-Kiwi, 1980), transmission of the Biblical and Synagogal tradition to the Christian church and related questions (H. Avenary and E. Werner, 1959, 1984); Jewish music throughout history and source material, with editing of sources (I. Adler, 1975; H. Avenary and A. Shiloah, 1985–7), living traditions of the surrounding Arab-Muslim and Christian musical heritage (A. Bahat, 1986; D. Cohen, 1967, 1971; E. Gerson-Kiwi, 1980; A. Hajdu, 1971; A. Herzog, 1963; S. Hofman, 1964, 1971; R. Katz, 1968, 1974; U. Sharvit, 1981; A. Shiloah and E. Schleifer, 1984). This multidirectional research activity is a fortuitous result of the rich material and diverse possibilities presented to those who were seeking both deeper and broader views on music.

Acta Musicologica (xxxviii, 1958 and liii, 1981) gives a detailed description of Israeli musicological scholarship from the 1950s to the 1980s.

Epilogue

The overall picture shows tremendous growth in the body of knowledge, a gradual move towards higher specialization, and incursion into unexplored areas. Yet there is still much to do. Little attention has been paid to some general topics such as music education, the process of learning and transmission in the oral tradition, psychological aspects of music-making, concepts and behaviour in historical perspective and to such specifics as the compound and sophisticated forms of the Iraqi *maqam* and the Nuba repertory, the various Kurdish musical and dance traditions, the dance as a form of art, and folk or religious expression. Moreover, researchers are now better equipped to attempt broad synthetical views combining systematic, historical sociological and anthropological approaches in order to place the picture obtained in a larger framework, to see the musical world studied in both its diversity and its unity.

Bibliography

J.-B. La Borde: *Essai sur la musique ancienne et moderne* (Paris, 1780)

G.-A. Villoteau: 'De l'état actuel de l'art musical en Egypte', *Description de l'Egypte: état moderne*, i, ed. E. F. Jomard (Paris, 1809), 607–845

——: 'Description historique, technique et littéraire des instrumens de musique des orientaux', *Description de l'Egypte: état moderne*, ed. E. F. Jomard, i (Paris, 1809), 846–1016

E. W. Lane: *An Account of the Manners and Customs of the Modern Egyptians* (London, 1836, 5/1860/ *R*1966)

J. G. L. Kosegarten: *Alii Ispahanensis liber cantilenarum magnus Arabice editus adjectaque translatione ad notationibus que illustratus* (Greifswald, 1840)

R. G. Kisewetter: *Die Musik der Araber* (Leipzig, 1842/*R*1968)

F. Salvador-Daniel: *La musique arabe* (Algiers, 1863)

M. Collangettes: 'Etude sur la musique arabe', *Journal asiatique*, iv (1904), 365–422; viii (1906), 149–90

A. Z. Idelsohn: *Hebräisch Orientalischer Melodienschatz* (Leipzig, Berlin, Jerusalem, 1914–32)

F. Salvador-Daniel: *The Music and the Musical Instruments of the Arabs*, trans. H. G. Farmer (London, 1915)

J. Ribera: *La música de las cantigas* (Madrid, 1922); Eng. trans. as *Music in Ancient Arabia and Spain* (1929/*R*1970)

J. Rouanet: 'La musique arabe', and 'La musique arabe dans le Maghreb', *EMDC* (1922), 2676–805, 2813–944

R. B. Yekta: 'La musique Turke', *EMDC*, v (1922), 2945–3064

H. G. Farmer: 'Arabic Musical Manuscripts in the Bodleian Library', *Journal of the Royal Asiatic Society* (1925), 639

——: 'Clues for the Arabian Influence on European Musical Theory', *Journal of the Royal Asiatic Society* (1925), 61 [pubd separately as *Influence on Musical Theory* (London, 1925)]

——: 'The Influence of Music: from Arabic Sources', *PMA*, lii (1925–6), 89–124

——: 'The Old Persian Musical Modes', *Journal of the Royal Asiatic Society* (1926), 93

J. Ribera: *Historia de la música arabe medieval y su influencia en la Española* (Madrid, 1927)

M. R. Gazimihal: *Andalou Türkuleri ve musiki Ikstikbalemiz* (Istanbul, 1928)

——: *Şarki Andalou Türkü ve Oyunlari* (Istanbul, 1929)

H. G. Farmer: *A History of Arabian Music to the Thirteenth Century* (London, 1929/*R*1973)

R. Lachmann: *Musik des Orients* (Breslau, 1929/*R*1965)

R. d'Erlanger: *La musique arabe* (Paris, 1930–59)

H. G. Farmer: 'Greek Theorists of Music on Arabic Translation', *Isis*, xiii (1930), 325

——: *Historical Facts for the Arabian Musical Influence* (London, 1930/*R*1970)

A. Chottin: *Corpus de musique marocaine* (Paris, 1931)

H. G. Farmer: *Studies in Oriental Musical Instruments*, i (London, 1931); ii (Glasgow, 1939)

S. Ezgi: *Nazari, ameli Türk musikisi* (Istanbul, 1933–53)

N. Vaziri: *Musiqi-ye Nazari* (Tehran, 1934)

A. Chottin: *Tableau de la musique marocaine* (Paris, 1939)

R. Lachmann: *Jewish Cantillation and Song in the Isle of Djerba* (Jerusalem, 1940); repr. *Posthumous Works*, ii, ed. E. Gerson-Kiwi (Jerusalem, 1978)

J. Ribera: *La musica arabe y su influencia en la musica Española* (Madrid, 1942)

M. Schneider: 'A proposáito del influjo arabe: ensayo de etnografia musical de la España Medieval', *AnM* (1946), 31–141

M. Allawerdi: *Philosophy of Oriental Music* (Damascus, 1948)

A. al-Azzawi: *Iraqian Music under the Mongols and the Turkmans, 1258–1534* (Baghdad, 1951)

E. Dermengham and L. Barbes: 'Essai sur la hadhra des Aissoua d'Algérie', *Revue Africaine* (1951) 289–314

H. Hickmann: 'The Egyptian Uffattah Flute', *Journal of the Royal Asiatic Society* (1952), 103

A. J. Denoumy: *Concerning the Accessibility of Arabian Influence in the Earliest Provencal Troubadours* (Toronto, 1953)

R. Khalqi: *Sargozasht-e musiqi-ye Iran* (Tehran, 1954–55)

H. Hickmann: 'Aegyptische Volkinstrumente', *Musica*, viii (1954), 49–97

F. Meier: 'Der Derwischtanz, Versuch eines Uberblicks', *Asiatische Studien* (1954), 107

M. Schneider: 'Le verset 94 de la sourate VI du Coran étudié en une version populaire et en trois nagamât de tradition hispano-Musulmane', *AnM* (1954), 80

H. Ritter: *Das Meer der Seele* (Leiden, 1955)

G. Oransay: 'Das Tonsystem der türkei-turkischen Kunstmusik', *Mf*, x (1957), 250

M. L. R. Choudhury: 'Music in Islam', *Journal of the Asiatic Society of Bengal*, xxiii/2 (1957), 43–102

P. Mahmud: *A Theory of Persian Music and its Relation to Western Practice* (diss., U. of Indiana, 1957)

E. Gerson-Kiwi: 'Musicology in Israel', *AcM*, xxx (1958), 17

M. Talbi: 'La qira'a bi-l-alhan', *Arabica*, v (1958), 183

M. Amd: *Dances of Anatolian Turkey*, *Dance Perspectives*, iii (New York, 1959)

E. Werner: *The Sacred Bridge*, i (London and New York, 1959)

E. Hickmann: *al-Fārābīs Músiklehre* (diss., U. of Hamburg, 1960)

P. R. Olsen: 'Enregistrements faits à Kuwait et à Bahrain', *Ethnomusicologie*, iii, 5 (1960), 137–70

M. Porone: *Ethiopian Music: a Survey of Ecclesiastical and Secular Ethiopian Music and Instruments* (London, 1960)

A. Saygun: 'Ethnomusicologie turque', *AcM*, xxxii (1960), 67

M. Snoussi: 'Folklore Tunisien, musique de plein air, l'orchestre de tabbal et zukkar', *Revue des Etudes Islamiques* (1961), 143

H. M. al-Ragab: *al-Maqām al'Irāqī* (Baghdad, 1961)

M. Mokri: 'Le Soufisme et la musique', *Encyclopédie de la musique, Fasquelle*, iii (1961), 1014

K. Khatchi: *Der Dastgah: Studien zur neuen persischen Musik* (Regensburg, 1962)

M. Rezvani: *Le théâtre et la danse en Iran* (Paris, 1962)

A. Shiloah: 'Réflexions sur la danse artistique musulmane', *Cahiers des civilisation mediévale*, vi (1962), 463

Y. Zakariya: *Six écrits sur la musique de Kindī* (Baghdad, 1962)

M. Barkechli: *Les systèmes de la musique traditionelle de l'Iran avec transcription en notation musicale par Moussa Ma'roufi* (Teheran, 1963)

E. Gerson-Kiwi: *The Persian Doctrine of Dastgah-Composition* (Tel Aviv, 1963)

A. Herzog: *The Intonation of the Pentateuch in the Herder of Tunis* (Tel Aviv, 1963)

M. Mole: 'La danse extatique en Islam', *Sources Orientales*, iv (1963), 145–280

A. Taymur: *al-mūsīqā wal-ghinā''ind al-'Arab* (Cairo, 1963)

G. al-Hanafi: *al-mughannūn al-baghdadiyyün wal-magam al-'iraqi* (Baghdad, 1964)

H. al-Wardi: *al-ghinā' al-'rāqī* (Baghdad, 1964)

W. K. Archer ed.: *The Preservation of Traditional Form of the Learned and Popular Music of the Orient and the Occident* (Urbana, IL, 1964)

G. Oransay: *Die traditionelle Türkische Kunstmusik* (Ankara, 1964)

S. A. Hofman: 'La musique Arabe in Israel', *JIFMC*, xvi (1964)

Y. Zakariya: *Risālat Nāṣir al-dīn al-ṭūsī fī 'ilm al-mūsīqā* (Cairo, 1964)

S. al-Helou: *Al-muwashshahāt al-andalusia* (Beirut, 1965)

H. Farhat: *The Dastgah Concept in Persian Music* (diss., UCLA, 1965)

E. Neubauer: *Musiker am Hof der Frühen 'Abbasiden* (Frankfurt, 1965)

Y. Zakariya: *Mu'allafat al-Kindī al-musīqīyya* (Baghdad, 1965)

M. Caton and D. Safvate: *Iran: les traditions musicales* (Paris, 1966)

H. G. A. Farmer: 'Music of Islam', *New Oxford History of Music*, i (1966), 421–77

——: *Musikgeschichte im Bildern-Islam*, iii (Leipzig, 1966)

H. Husmann: 'The Practice of Organum in the Liturgical Singing of the Syrian Churches of the Near and Middle East', *Gustave Reese B-day* (1966), 435

K. Reinhard: 'Musik am Schwarzen Meer', *Jb für Musikalische Volks und Völkerkunde*, ii (1966), 9–58

M. Velimirovic, ed.: *Studies in Eastern Chant* (London and Oxford, i, 1966, 2/1971)

O. Wright: 'Ibn al-munajjim and the Early Arabian Modes', *GSJ*, xix (1966), 26

D. Cohen: *The Liturgical Music of the Christian Arabs in Israel* (diss., Hebrew University, Jerusalem, 1967) [in Hebrew]

A. M. Khashabah Ghattas: *al-Fārābī: Kitāb al-musīqī al-kabīr* (Cairo, 1967)

H. Husmann, ed.: 'Die Melodien des Chaldaischen Breviers . . .', *Orientalia Christiana Analecta*, clxxxiii (1967)

C. Rihtman: 'Orientalische Elemente in der traditionellen Musik Bosniens und der Herzegovina', *Grazer und Munchener Balkananalogische Studien*, ii (1967), 97

T. Alexandru: 'Les instruments musicaux du folklore Egyptien et ceux des pays des Balkans', *Ib.*, (1968), 327

——: 'Les chansons épiques d'Egypte', *XV Kongress Saveza Udruzenya folklorista Yugoslavie* (1968), 243

B. Bayer: 'The Biblical Novel', *Yurvnal*, i (Jerusalem, 1968), 89–131

R. Katz: 'The Singing of Baggashot by Aleppo Jews', *AcM*, xl (1968), 65

M. T. Massoudieh: *Avaz-e-shur: Zur Melodiebildung in der Persischen Kunstmusik* (Regensburg, 1968)

E. Neubauer: 'Die Theorie vom Iqa'–Übersetzung des Kitab al-Iqa'at von Abu Nasr al-Farabi', *Oriens*, xii/xxi (1968/69), 196–232

J. Porte, ed.: *Encyclopedie des musiques sacrées* (Paris, 1968)

M. Powne: *Ethiopian Music, an Introduction, a Survey of Ecclesiastical and Secular Ethiopian Music and Instruments* (London, 1968)

H. H. Touma: *Der Maqam Bayati im Arabischen taqsim* (Berlin, 1968)

V. Arseven: *Bibliography of Books and Essays on Turkish Folk Music* (Istanbul, 1969)

J. Elsner: 'Remarks on the Big Arghul', *YIFMC*, i (1969), 234

H. Husmann: *Die Melodien der Jakobitischen Kirche* (Vienna, 1969)

J. Kuckertz: 'Die Melodietypen der Westsyrischen Liturgischen Gesange', *KJb*, liii (1969)

W. Laade: 'History of the Liturgical Music of the Eastern Churches on Records', *Schallplatte und Kirche*, xxxix/5 (1969), 109; xl/3 (1970), 225

L. Manik: *Das Arabische Tonsystem in Mittelalter* (Leiden, 1969)

R. Ménard: 'Tradition Coptique', *Encyclopédie des musiques sacrées*, ii (Paris, 1969), 317

E. Neubauer: 'Eine Musikalische Soirée am Hof von Harun al-Rashid', *Bustan* (1969), 27

——: 'Musik zur Mongolenzeit in Iran und den angrenzenden Ländern', *Der Islam*, xiv (1969), 233

K. Reinhard: *Türkische Musik* (Berlin, 1962). [French edn, *La musique Turque, les Traditions musicales* (Paris, 1969)]

B. Velat: 'Liturgical Music of Ethiopia', *Encyclopédie des musiques sacrées*, ii (Paris, 1969), 322

M. al-Hefni: 'Folk Music in Nubia: its Relation with Ancient Egyptian Music', *al-Funūn al-sha'bīyya*, xiii (1970), 9 [in Arabic with Eng. summary]

M. Borsai: 'Caractéristiques générales du chant de la messe Copte', *Studia Orientalia Christiana Aegyptica* (1970–71), 412–42

J. Elsner: *Der Begriff des Maqam in Aegypten in Neuerer Zeit Habschr. Musicology* (Berlin, 1970)

E. Gerson-Kiwi: 'On the Technique of Arab Taqsim Composition', *Musik als Gestalt und Erlebnis: Festschrift W.Graf* (1970), 66

H. Hickmann: 'Die Musik des arabisch-islamischen Bereichs', *Orientalische Musik*, ed. H. Hickmann and W. Stauder (Leiden and Cologne, 1970), 1–134

H. Husmann: 'Arabische Maqamen in Ostsyricher Kirchenmusik', *Musik als Gestalt und Erlebnis: Festschrift W.Graf* (Vienna, 1970), 102

J. Kuckertz: 'Origin and Development of the Rabab', *Sangeet-Natak*, xv (1970), 16

B. Nettl: 'Attitudes Towards Persian Music in Tehran 1969', *MQ*, lvi (1970), 183

——: 'Examples of Popular Music from Khorasan', *Musik als Gestalt und Erlebnis: Festschrift W.Graf* (Vienna, 1970), 138

J. P. Reiche: 'Stilelemente Sudtürkischer, Davul-Zurna Stücke', *Jb für musikalische Volks- und Völkerkunde*, v (Berlin, 1970), 9–54

L. A. Anderson: 'The Interrelation of African and Arab Music', *Essays on Music and History in Africa*, ed. K. P. Wachsmann (Evanston, IL, 1971), 143

E. A. Bowles: 'Eastern Influences on the Use of Trumpets and Drums in the Middle Ages', *AnM* (1971), 3

M. Caton: *The Kamanche Style of Ustad Faydullah of the Province of Gilan* (diss., U. of California, 1971)

D. Cohen: 'The Meaning of the Modal Framework in the Singing of Religious Hymns by Christian Arabs in Israel', *Yuval*, ii (Jerusalem, 1971), 23–57

A. Hajdu: 'Le Niggun Meron', *Yuval*, ii (Jerusalem, 1971), 73–114

S. Hofman: 'Karaites', 'Samaritans', *Encyclopedia Judaica* (Jerusalem, 1971)

S. Jargy: *La musique arabe* (Paris, 1971)

A. Kebede: *The Music of Ethiopia* (diss., Wesleyan U., 1971)

W. Laade: *Gegenwartzfragen der Musik in Africa und Asien: Eine Grundlegende Bibliographie* (Heidelberg, 1971)

M. Tahar: *Recherches sur le rythme, les mètres et les formes du melhun algérien* (Paris, 1971)

H. H. Touma: 'The Maqam Phenomenon: an Improvisation Technique in the Music of the Middle East', *EM*, xv (1971), 38

S. al-Mahdi: *La musique arabe* (Paris, 1972)

L. Hage: *Le chant de l'Eglise Maronite* (Beirut, 1972)

H. Husmann: *The Music of the Armenian Liturgy* (1972)

B. Nettl and B. Foltin Jr: *Daramad of Chahargah: a Study in the Performance Practice of Persian Music* (Detroit, MI, 1972)

———: 'Persian Popular Music in 1969', *EM*, xvi (1972), 218

K. Reinhard: 'Grundlagen und Ergebnisse der Erforschung türkischer Musik', *AcM*, xliv (1972), 266

H. P. Seidel: 'Studien zum Usul "Devri kebir" in den Peşrev der Mevlevi', *Mitteilungen der Deutschen Gesellschaft für Musik des Orients*, xi (Berlin, 1972–3), 7–70

A. Shiloah: 'Ibn Hindu, le medecin et la musique', *Israel Oriental Studies*, ii (1972), 447

———: *La perfection des connaissances musicales* (Paris, 1972)

———: 'The Simsimiyya: a stringed Instrument of the Red Sea Area', *Asian Music*, iv/1 (1972), 15

A. Simon: *Studien zur Aegyptischen Volkmusik* (Hamburg, 1972)

V. Crapanzano: *The Hamadsha: a Study in Moroccan Psychiatry* (Berkeley, CA, 1973)

H. Farhat: *The Traditional Music of Iran* (Tehran, 1973)

M. Guignard: *Musique, honneur et plaisir au Sahara: étude psychologique et musicologique de la société Maure* (Paris, 1973)

K. Gunther, ed.: *Musikkulturen Asiens, Afrikas und Ozeaniens im 19 Jahrundert* (Augsenburg, 1973)

B. Nettl and R. Riddle: 'Taqsim Nahawand: a Study of Sixteen Performances by Jihad Racy', *YIFMC*, v (1973), 11–50

K. Reinhard: *Musikalische Gestaltungsprinzipien der Ayin, dargestellt an der anonymen Komposition im Makam Pencgah* (Ankara, 1973)

M. Veilmirovic and E. Wellesz, eds.: *Studies in Eastern Chant*, iii (London and Oxford, 1973)

E. Zonis: *Classical Persian Music: an Introduction* (Cambridge, MA, 1973)

S. Blum: 'Persian Folksong in Meshhed', *YIFMC*, vi (1974), 86

I. Borsai: 'Die musikhistorische Bedeutung der Orientalichen christlichen Riten', *SM*, xvi (1974), 3

R. Katz: 'The Reliability of Oral Transmission: the Case of Samaritan Music', *Yuval*, iii (Jerusalem, 1974), 109

P. R. Olsen: 'Six versions de taqsim en maqam rast', *Studia Instrumentorum musicae popularis*, iii (1974), 197

J. Pacholczyk: 'Vibrato as a Function of Modal Practice in the Qur'an Chant of Shaikh 'Abdu'l-Basit 'Abdu'ṣ Ṣamad', *Selected Reports in Ethnomusicology*, ii/1 (1974), 33

P. Schuyler: *al-Milhun: the Fusion of Folk and Art Traditions in a Moroccan Song Poem* (Washington, DC, 1974)

A. Shiloah: 'A Group of Arabic Wedding Songs from the Village of Deyr al-Asad', *Studies of the Folklore Research Center*, iv (1974), 267

———: 'Traité sur le 'ūd d'abū Yūsuf al-Kindi', *Israel Oriental Studies*, iv (1974), 177

I. Adler: *Hebrew Writings Concerning Music*, RISM, B/ix/2 (Munich, 1975)

L. al-Faruqi: 'Muwashshah: a Vocal Form in Islamic Culture', *EM*, xix (1975), 1

J. Elsner: 'Zum Problem des Maqam', *AcM*, xlvii (1975), 208

M. Khashambah Ghattas: *al-Kātib: Kāmāl adab al-ghinā* (Cairo, 1975)

J. Kuckertz and M. T. Massoudieh: *Musik in Busehr, Sud-Iran* (Linz, 1975)

271

——: 'Volkgesange aus Iran', *Beiträge zur Musik des Vorderen Orients und seinen Einflussbereichen, K. Reinhard zum 60 Geburstag* (Berlin, 1975), 217

L. Picken: *Folk Musical Instruments of Turkey* (London, 1975)

K. Reinhard: 'Die Musik pflege Türkischer Nomadèn', *Zeitschrift für Ethnologei* (1975), 115

A. Simon: 'Islamische und Afrikanische Elemente in der musik des Nordsudan am Beispiel des Dikr', *Hamburger JB zur MW* (1975), 249

——: 'Feld forschungen in Aegypten in dem Sudan 1972–74', *Mitteilungen der Deutschen Gesellschaft für Musik des Orients*, xiii (1975)

H. Husmann: 'Madrase and Seblata Repertory: Studies of the Hymns of Ephraem the Syrian', *AcM*, xlviii/2 (1976)

D. M. Randel: 'al-Farabi and the Role of the Arabic Music Theory in the Latin Middle Ages', *JAMS*, xxix (1976), 173

M. T. Massoudieh: 'Die Musikforschung in Iran', *AcM*, xliii (1976), 12; lii (1980), 79

E. Okyay: *Melodische Gestaltelemente in den Türkischen Kirik Hava* (Ankara, 1976)

J. Racy: 'Record Industry and Egyptian Traditional Music, 1904–1932', *EM*, xx (1976), 23

K. Reinhard: 'Über Einige Beziehungen Zwischen Türkischer und Griechischer Volksmusik', *Studien zur Musik Sudost-Europas Beiträge zur Ethnomusikologie*, iv (1976)

Y. Shawqi: *Ibn al-Munajjim's Essay on Music and the Melodic Ciphers of Kitab al-Aghani* (Cairo, 1976)

K. Signell: *Maqam-Modal Practice in Turkish Art Music* (Seattle, WA, 1977)

A. Simon: 'Zur Oboen-Trommel-Musik in Aegypten', *Festschrift Felix Hoerberger* (1977), 153

H. H. Touma: *La musique arabe* (Paris, 1977)

——: 'The Fidjri: a Major Vocal Form of the Bahrein Pearl-Divers', *Wm* (1977), 121

L. I. al-Faruqi: 'Accentuation in Quranic Chant, a Study in Musical Tawazun', *YIFMC*, x (1978), 53

S. Blum: 'Changing Roles of Performers in Meshhed and Bojurn, Iran', *Eight Urban Musical Cultures*, ed. B. Nettl (1978), 19–95

S. A. al-Kholy: *The Tradition of Improvisation in Arab Music* (Giza, Egypt, 1978)

M. T. Massoudieh: *Radif vocal de la musique traditionnelle de l'Iran* (Teheran, 1978)

B. Nettl, ed.: *Eight Urban Musical Cultures: Tradition and Change* (Urbana, IL, 1978)

P. Schuyler: 'Moroccan Andalusian Music', *Wm*, i (1978), 33

A. Shiloah: *The Ikhwān al-Ṣafā's Epistle on Music* (Tel Aviv, 1978)

O. Wright: *The Modal System of Arab and Persian Music, A.D. 1250–1300* (London, 1978)

H. Avenary: *Encounters of East and West in Music: Selected Writings* (Tel Aviv, 1979)

B. Nettl: 'Musical Values and Social Values: Symbols in Iran', *Asian Music*, xii/1 (1979), 129

H. Powers, ed.: 'Symposium on Art Musics in Muslim Nations', *Asian Music*, xii/1 (1979)

A. Shiloah: *The Theory of Music in Arabic Writings* (Munich, 1979)

S. el-Shawan: *al-Mūsīqa al-ʿArabīyyaʿ: a Category of Urban Music in Cairo-Egypt 1927–1977* (diss., Columbia U., 1980)

M. Guettat: *La musique classique du Maghrib* (Paris, 1980)

E. Gerson-Kiwi: *Migrations and Mutations of the Music in East and West: Selected Writings* (Tel Aviv, 1980)

S. Q. Hassan: *Les instruments de musique en Iraq et leur rôle dans la société traditionnelle* (Paris, 1980)

B. Lortat-Jacob: *Musique et fêtes au Haut Atlas* (Paris, 1980)

M. Random: *Mawlana Djalal al-dīn al-Rūmī, le soufisme et la dance* (Tunis, 1980)

A. Shiloah: 'Arab Folk Music', *Grove 6*

L. I. al-Faruqi: *An Annotated Glossary of Arabic Musical Terms* (Westport, CT 1981)

S. Q. Hassan: *Masādir al-mūsīqā al-ʿiraqīyya, 1900–1978* (Baghdad, 1981)

U. Sharvit and Y. Adaqi: *A Treasury of Jewish Yemenite Chants* (Jerusalem, 1981)

A. Shiloah: 'Arabic Modal Concept', *JAMS*, xxxiv/1 (1981), 19

—— and E. Gerson-Kiwi: 'Musicology in Israel, 1960–1980', *AcM*, liii/2 (1981), 200

I. Kh. al-Sha'ūbī: *Dalīl al-anghām li tullab al-maqām* (Baghdad, 1982)

J. During: 'Revelation and Spiritual Audition in Islam', *Wm*, iii (1982), 68

R. Falck and T. Rice, eds.: *Cross Cultural Perspectives on Music, in Honor of M. Kolinski* (Toronto, 1982)

Sh. Q. Hassan: 'Die Entwicklung und Gegenwartige Stand der Musikforschung im Iraq', *AcM*, liv (1982), 148

T. J. McGee: 'Eastern Influence in Medieval European Dance', *Cross Cultural Perspectives in Music, in Honor of M. Kolinski*, ed. R. Falck and T. Rice (Toronto, 1982), 79

K. Nelson: 'Reciter and Listener: some Factors Shaping the *Mujawwad* Style of Qur'anic Reciting', *EM*, xxxvi (1982), 41

J. Racy: 'Musical Aesthetics in Present-Day Cairo', *EM*, xxvi (1982), 391

B. Bayer: 'The Titles of the Psalms: a Renewed Investigation of an Old Problem', *Yuval*, iv (Jerusalem, 1982), 29–123

U. Wegner: ''Abuḍiya und mawwal', *Beiträge zur Ethnomusikologie*, xii (1982)

M. Caton: *The Classical Tasnif: a Genre of Persian Vocal Music* (Los Angeles, CA, 1983)

P. Collaer and J. Elsner: *Musikgeschichte in Bildern* (Leipzig, 1983)

J. During: 'La musique traditionnelle Iranienne en 1983', *Asian Music*, xiv/2 (1983–84), 11

W. J. Krüger-Wust: *Arabische Musik in Europäischen Sprachen: Eine Bibliographie* (Wiesbaden, 1983)

J. Pacholczyk: 'The Relationship between the Nawba of Morocco and the Music of the Troubadours and Trouvères', *World Music*, xxv/2 (1983)

G. D. Sawa: 'Music Performance Practice in the Early Abbasid Era (730–932 AD)' (diss., U. of Toronto, 1983)

La musique Iranienne: tradition et évolution (Paris, 1984)

S. el-Shawan: 'Traditional Arab Music Ensembles in Egypt since 1967', *EM*, xxviii (1984)

——: 'Traditional Arab Music Ensembles in Egypt since 1967: the Continuity of Tradition within a Contemporary Framework?', *EM*, xxvii (1984), 271

J. Elsner: 'Zum Problem von Komposition und Improvisation', *BMw*, iii/4 (1984), 174

E. Schleifer, ed.: An Anthology of Hasidic Music (Jerusalem, 1984)

A. Shiloah: 'Transformation et phenomènes d'influence dans les musiques du Proche et Moyen-Orient hier et aujourdh'ui', *Douze cas d'interaction culturelle*, UNESCO (1984), 259

E. Werner: *The Sacred Bridge*, ii (New York, 1984)

L. I. al-Faruqi: 'The Suite in Islamic History and Culture', *World Music*, xxvii/3 (1985), 46

G. D. Sawa: 'The Status and Roles of the Secular Musicians in the Kitāb al-Aghānī (Book of Songs) of Abu al-Faraj al-Iṣfahānī', *Asian Music*, xvii/1 (1985)

P. H. Schuyler: 'The Rwais and the Zawia Professional Musicians and the Rural Religious Elite in SW Morocco', *Asian Music*, xvii (1985), 185

A. Shiloah and others: *The Musical Heritage of Jewish Communities* (Tel Aviv, 1985–7) [in Hebrew]

A. Bahat: 'The Hallelot in the Yemenite Diwan', *Yuval*, v (Jerusalem, 1986) [in Hebrew]

L. Hage: *Les strophes-types Syriaques et leur mètres poétiques du patriarch maronite Etienne Douayhi* (Kaslik, 1986)

H. Hickmann: 'Aegyptische Musik', *MGG*, i, 99

——: 'Die Aussereuropäischen und Antiken Klarinetteninstrumente', *MGG*, vii, 933–1005

CHAPTER IX

South Asia

NAZIR ALI JAIRAZBHOY, CYRIL DE SILVA KULATILLAKE

1: INDIA

NAZIR ALI JAIRAZBHOY

The field of ethnomusicology is constantly in the process of self-examination, and numerous definitions have been put forward by scholars since the term was first used by Jaap Kunst in the early 1950s. Some ethnomusicologists as well as musicologists have pointed out, however, that, in fact, the term is unnecessary and that musicology should not only embrace the music of the whole world but also involve the kinds of investigations of music as expressions of culture currently emphasized by ethnomusicologists. While this may be a future goal, historical factors necessitated the coining of this new term, since the word music in Western academia is still generally interpreted as referring to Western art music, and its study as being predominantly of the history and theory of this tradition.

In India one finds a parallel attitude: music (i.e. *saṅgīt*) refers to the classical art traditions of the Indian subcontinent, and emphasizes the history and theory of the two major traditions of the North and the South. Because of this parallel historical background, the term ethnomusicology is useful here to draw attention to the fact that other forms of music – not only those from other parts of the world, but also the myriad folk, tribal, devotional and popular forms which exist in the region – deserve study in their own terms, and as expressions of the many cultures that co-exist in the subcontinent.

It must be pointed out, however, that the term 'ethnomusicology' has a negative connotation to some scholars in India who tend to associate ethno-with ethnic, and interpret ethnomusicology as being limited to the study of the music of tribal and 'low caste' ethnic groups, and thus, like the pejorative word, primitive (implying 'simple' or 'rude'), is demeaning to those cultural traditions. It is not the purpose here to show that ethnomusicology is much more than this, but to emphasize that here no real distinction is made between musicology and ethnomusicology; music history and theory of the art traditions are considered as legitimate elements of study in both musicology and ethnomusicology. The primary purpose here is to trace the evolution of attitudes about music on the subcontinent from a primarily elitist art music 'history/theory' approach to the broader cultural view emphasized by ethnomusicologists.

The pre-war period

India has a long history of writings on music, beginning with the chapters on music in the *Nātyaśāstra*, which has been dated variously from the 2nd century BC to the 5th century AD. While most of these treatises have been concerned with music theory of what we might call 'art' music, descriptions of different regional and tribal forms are given in other works, such as the *Brihaddeśī* written by Matanga, around the 9th century AD, the title of which can perhaps best be translated as 'The Great Folk Traditions'. Treatises that follow, especially those from the 16th century, however, revert to an emphasis on the history and theory of art music. In order to comprehend this approach to music, certain historical, social, cultural and religious factors need to be examined.

The Indian subcontinent commonly includes present-day India, Pakistan, Bangladesh, Sri Lanka, and the Maldives; Nepal, Sikkim, Ladakh, and Bhutan and adjacent Himalayan regions are discussed in Chapter XI, 'Eastern Central Asia'. Music, both at the village and urban level, has traditionally been the province of the professional specialist musicians. In the social structure of Hinduism, they have tended to belong to the lower (and sometimes the lowest) of the occupational castes in society. In many areas of the subcontinent where the *jajmānī* (a kind of feudal) system has prevailed, the specialist musician has been the client (*yācak*) with a status not far removed from that of other service providers (such as barber, washerman or sweeper) often in virtual servitude to his patron, the *jajmān*. His duties have consisted of performing music at ritual occasions (and at the will of his patron) in exchange for which he received a portion of the patron's harvest and other gifts, as deemed fit by the patron or his guests. It should be made clear that there is no stigma attached to music itself: indeed it is widely recognized as a social grace and is perfectly acceptable as an amateur pursuit in the highest ranking families. The low caste ranking is derived primarily from the 'professional' nature of their musical activities in which the performance of their art is treated like a trade for which the tradesman must receive economic compensation. One other factor may have added to the low caste ranking of the musician in Hindu society. The making of music, and particularly the playing of certain essential instruments, necessitates the breaking of upper caste taboos (e.g. the handling of animal skins on drums, or making lip contact with flutes and reeds, which might have been touched by others). Even though Muslims do not recognize caste taboos, the specialist musician, whether Hindu or Muslim, in the role of professional client (*yācak*) to a Muslim overlord is treated in much the same way as by a Hindu *jajmān*.

This is not to deny that individual musicians have, by dint of musical excellence, enjoyed status and recognition from early times in the subcontinent; yet in substantive matters, such as those involving lineage (i.e. marriage relations and day to day contact with the upper castes), even the best of them have tended to be excluded until very recent times.

Existing side by side with these specialist musicians, there have always been gifted amateurs, both Hindu and Muslim, from all walks of life, ranging from weavers (e.g. the 15th-century saint-singer, Kabir Das) and tailors (e.g. the 15th-century Maharsashtrian saint-singer, Namadeva) to money lenders (Purandaradasa, 1480–1564), Brahmins (Tyagaraja, 1767–1847) and royalty (one of the early illustrations being the depiction on a coin of the 4th-century Emperor Samudra Gupta playing a bow harp). Hindu upper castes maintained their rankings by emphasizing vocal music and unexceptionable instruments, particularly chordophones. It is primarily these upper-caste amateurs, often belonging to royalty (the 15th-century Raja Man Singh Tomar and in more recent times, the late-19th-century Raja S. M. Tagore) or their governing ministers (the 13th-century writer Sarngadeva and the 16th-century Ramamatya), who tended to be the scholars and writers of music treatises. Their emphasis was naturally on the art music traditions of the courts, an activity patronized and enjoyed then only by the leisured classes, rather than on the myriad music-associated folk traditions.

Interacting with this courtly patron tradition were the devotional *bhakti* and *Sufi* traditions, the former leading to the song types, such as *bhajan, kīrtan, abhaṅg*, the latter to the vocal forms, *qawwālī* and, to some extent, *ghazal*. Many of these traditions were associated with temples or shrines of saints, and the composers of songs in these genres are themselves frequently referred to as poet- or singer-saints. Some of them travelled through the countryside, absorbing folk songs and themes which they incorporated into their sophisticated songs. The compositions of the South Indian singer-saint Tyagaraja (1767–1847), along with his contemporaries, Muttuswami Dikshitar and Syama Sastri, still form a significant part of the basic repertory of South Indian classical music, while some of their North Indian counterparts have left their marks in North Indian classical rāga names, for example *Sūrdāsī Malhār* (the Malhār of the blind 16th-century saint, Surdas) and *Mīrābāī kī Malhār* (the Malhār of Mirabai, a 15th-century queen who became a singer-devotee).

In their early contacts with India, the reactions of Europeans to Indian music were generally negative, yet scholars such as Sir William Jones, Sir W. Ousley, Captain Charles Russell Day and Capt. N. Augustus Willard recognized some measure of its importance and wrote on various aspects of the subject. These articles often contain valuable historical information on instruments and performance practices of the 19th century, when 'art' music was still a professional activity in court life (*see* Chapter III, Great Britain: 'Northern and Western Europe: The Empire and other territories').

Art music in India began to outgrow its association with professional performers and the leisured classes, and began to reach the middle classes largely as a result of the Nationalist movement in the second half of the 19th century. The indigenous performing arts, especially music and theatre, began to be recognized as cultural symbols of the movement. Bengal and Maharashtra were the two primary centres of this new vision. In Bengal, Sir Sourindro Mohun Tagore [Ṣaurīndramohana Ṭhākura] published music manuscripts, including *Hindu Music from Various Authors* (1875), which included some writings of European scholars, had others translated into

English, and sent them to scholarly organizations, especially museums in India and abroad, along with large numbers of musical instruments. This extraordinary gesture perhaps had more impact in Europe than India and there is good reason to believe that his gifts of instruments and manuscripts to the Brussels Museum in 1876 inspired Victor-Charles Mahillon (1841–1924) to develop the quadripartite classification of musical instruments which still prevails in Western organology. Other Indian scholars began to reassess traditional theoretical premises, notably, Kshetra Mohun Banerjee, who incorporated techniques of critical inquiry in his *Gītasūtrasāra*.

Not long after, the poet laureate, Rabindranath Tagore, began to compose his own music, drawing his inspiration not only from classical music, but also from the folk traditions around him, the songs of the Baul singer-mendicants, the Santal tribals and even the village boatmen. In seeking respectability for the arts, he began his arts college, Vishwa Bharati, in Santiniketan, which has had much influence on the emancipation of both music and dance in the subcontinent.

In Maharastra, two individuals, Vishnu Digambar Paluskar and Vishnu Narayan Bhatkhande, in the early years of the 20th century, had an immense influence on the course which Indian music studies were to take. Neither belonged to a community of professional musicians, yet both were able to tap these resources. Vishnu Digambar was primarily a vocalist and *kīrtankār* (performer of *kīrtan*, a form of religious discourse accompanied by song in Maharashtra). His goal was to make North Indian classical music available to the developing middle-class audience and thus developed teaching methods suited to group instruction, perhaps inspired by a modest music school for children initiated by the Poona Gayan Samaj in 1877. He established his music school, called Gandharv Mahavidyalay, in Lahore in 1901. This institution was later moved to Bombay, and although this parent school was closed in 1924 for lack of funds, many branches of the school have since been established and, as an examining body, its influence is felt throughout North India.

Bhatkhande, on the other hand, was a lawyer by trade and a musicologist by inclination. He was interested in music history and theory and studied a number of Sanskrit treatises, resulting in his Sanskrit work *Lakṣyasaṅgītam* on music theory, which was later followed by a monumental four-volume work, *Saṅgītśāstra*, on music history and theory written in Marathi, translated into Hindi in the 1950s. He also wrote two important historical surveys of Indian music in English. Bhatkhande, however, was also interested in performance practice and transcribed compositions by a number of musicians in many North Indian rāgas, which he published in seven volumes as *Kramik Pustak Mālikā*. This work has also been translated into Hindi. Bhatkhande's work culminated in the formation of the Marris College of Hindusthani Music (whose name was later changed to Bhatkhande University) in Lucknow in 1921. Bhatkhande Colleges and Universities of music have since sprung up in many cities, including some outside the country (e.g. San Jose, California).

In the many works on Indian music written in the pre-World War II period, three major trends can be detected. First were works on the history and theory of Indian classical music, exemplified by Bhatkhande's writings. Second were practical music instruction textbooks by Indian scholars usually in vernacular languages, which involved only a minimum of music theory such as Bhatkhande's *Kramik Pustak Mālikā*. Of the many others Phiroz Phramjee (Firoz Framjee), a Parsi music scholar (1893–1938), wrote more than 30 books on North Indian music in Hindi and Gujarati, including a music encyclopedia of rāgas in numerous volumes. The main feature of these works is that they included approximate transcriptions of songs, instrumental compositions, and phrases characteristic of individual rāgas. Since subtleties of intonation and melodic ornamentation were not included, it was scarcely possible for a student to learn new rāgas or composed pieces without guidance from a teacher, and thus the main purpose of the transcriptions was to serve as reference books and as reminders of materials learned aurally (and visually) from a teacher.

A third major trend involved a number of scholars, both European and Indian, who were attempting to interpret Indian musical theory in more precise scientific terms, particularly with regard to the exact intonation of the intervals used in the various North Indian rāgas. Although elements of this approach can be found in some of the Sanskrit treatises (more in connection with systems of classification than intonation), detailed discussions of intonation were initiated in the second half of the 19th century by writers such as J. D. Paterson ('On the Grāmas or Musical Scales of the Hindus') and R. H. M. Bosanquet ('On the Hindu Division of the Octave, with some additions to the Theory of Systems of the Higher Orders'), and were then continued by B. A. Pingle (1894), K. B. Deval (1910), E. Clements (1913), A. H. Fox Strangways (1914) and many others, including Alain Daniélou, Nilmadhab Bose, Antsher Lobo, Nazir Jairazbhoy and Mark Levy, to the present. In fact, it has been suggested that more words in English have been written on the subject of intonation in Indian classical music than perhaps any other Indian musical topic.

A major impact of the growing scholarship in Indian music was the institution of periodic so-called 'All-India' Music Conferences, inaugurated in 1916 in Baroda, at which scholars and performers from different parts of the country, mainly North India, were brought together, with the primary intent of reconciling regional differences and standardizing performance practices of North Indian classical music.

Music conferences were also organized in South India and became an annual occurrence sponsored by the Madras Music Academy founded in 1928. In 1930 this institution established one of the first Indian journals devoted solely to music, *The Journal of the Madras Music Academy*. In the same year Bhatkhande's Marris College in Lucknow also began publishing a quarterly journal, *Saṅgīta*. The former, which continues to this day, with only a brief interruption in its history, quite naturally focusses on the South Indian classical tradition, while the latter concentrated on the classical music of the North.

The many music schools that have arisen since the 1920s in virtually every major North and South Indian city have always emphasized the teaching of classical music performance over history and theory. At the university level, the University of Madras, through the affiliated Queen Mary's College and Stella Maris College, was the first to adopt academic instruction, which later led to the establishment of a music department at the University in 1937. A number of other universities have developed music departments since, including Benares Hindu University, University of Baroda, Bombay University, SNDT Women's University (Bombay), Khairagarh University (Khairagarh, MP) and Delhi University. They all tend to have strong performance components, with the academic thrust focussed on historical musicology and music theory as expressed in the Sanskrit musical literature of the past.

Recording and documentation

Ethnomusicologists recognize the advent of audio recording as an essential factor in the development of the field in the West. In India, however, the early period of recording had little influence on the development of ethnomusicology. The audio recording industry in India began in the early years of the 20th century with recordings of classical musicians presenting abbreviated (and studied) versions of their performances, reducing one hour plus materials into the three- or five-minute time frames of 78 rpm discs. These early discs were of urban classical or semi-classical music recorded in studios – the notion of recording in the live context was neither feasible in those early days, nor regarded as being particularly desirable.

Ethnographic studies of rural castes and groups, however, were being carried out before this century by British administrators, often with the collaboration of Indians, and in 1901 a scheme for a systematic and detailed ethnographic survey of the whole of India was sanctioned by the Government of India. Although these works – generally entitled, 'Tribes and Castes of . . .' or 'District Gazetteers . . .' of various regions – mention some regional music performance practices, they did not include detailed music studies. The one exception was that of Edgar Thurston, who produced the monumental 20-volume work, *Castes and Tribes of Southern India* (vol. i, 1909), with the assistance of K. Rangachari and others. Thurston states that he carried out musical research among some tribes in Ootacamund (Toda, Kota and Badaga) and elsewhere in South India (e.g. Chenchu and Khond) and actually made cylinder recordings of some of their songs as well as of classical music beginning as early as 1894. These recordings were initially housed in the Madras Government Museum, where Thurston was Superintendent, and the wax cylinders are now located in the National Sound Archive in London.

About 1910, A. H. Fox Strangways visited India expressly to carry out research on Indian music and made a great variety of cylinder recordings, which included such diverse items as tribal and folk songs, snake charmer's music, 'outdoor' *shannai* band music, Vedic chant, *ghazal* and *tappa*, as well as North and South Indian classical music. These cylinders, some of which have recently been transferred to magnetic tape, are also held by the National Sound Archive. Fox Strangways' major publication, *The Music of Hindostan* (1914), includes two chapters under the title of 'Musical Diary' which describe some of the non-classical music he encountered on his field trips and include a number of musical transcriptions.

While indigenous recordings made by commercial companies, such as HMV, Hindustan, Odeon and Columbia, focussed on urban 'greater tradition' music, transforming them to the studio context (sometimes with a select invited audience), visiting Western scholars (and some British administrators) had field recording equipment available to them which they used to record music outside the studio in both urban and rural contexts.

A major figure after Fox Strangways, for the documentation of non-classical music traditions of South Asia, was Arnold A. Bake. Although he began his research in the 1920s in Shantiniketan as a Sanskrit scholar of music (his dissertation being a translation of the 18th-century musical treatise, *Saṅgīta Darpana*), he was trained as a vocalist in the Netherlands, and during his stay in India learned to sing Rabindranath Tagore's songs, Bengali *kīrtana*, as well as folk and classical music. Subsequently he returned to South Asia on several occasions, his last trip being in the 1950s. In all, he spent more than 15 years in the area making many recordings on cylinders, film and tape, in a number of regions of the subcontinent, including Eastern India, South India, Sind (now in Pakistan), North India (i.e. Ladakh and the Punjab), Ceylon (now Sri Lanka) and Nepal. Most of these audio recordings, housed either in the School of Oriental and African Studies, London, or in the National Sound Archive, have now been transferred to magnetic tape and constitute an invaluable record of music in the subcontinent. Bake was an avid still photographer and also shot a number of 16mm (silent) films of the performing traditions he encountered. With the ethnographic notes and the song texts and translations he gathered, his work can be regarded as the most important ethnomusicological endeavour of this period in the area. It is exceedingly unfortunate that the major publication on the subject which Oxford University Press commissioned him to produce (in collaboration with J. R. Marr and N. A. Jairazbhoy) on the music of the subcontinent based on a holistic approach, could not be completed, owing to his death in 1963.

Mention must also be made of the Western anthropologists Verrier Elwin and Christoph von Fürer-Haimendorf, who carried out extensive research among the tribal populations, and although they were not ethnomusicologists, their works included important ethnographic data relevant to music and often included texts of songs.

Indigenous scholars were hampered by the lack of field recording equipment and of influence and the financial wherewithal to conduct ethnographical field recordings without the backing of (British) government officialdom. Local scholars often appear only as informants mentioned in forewords of publications by Westerners, or just in their field notes. For instance, Shamrao Hivale often assisted Verrier Elwin on his researches and Dr Shivram Karanth, a well-known author and dramatist, now in his eighties, helped to organize two of Arnold Bake's expeditions in Andhra Pradesh and Karnataka in 1938 and provided him with texts and translations of some of the songs. The contributions of these collaborator-informants were vital to the studies, although they received only minor credit for their work, an unfortunate circumstance which often continues to this day.

The post-war period

The first year after the conclusion of the war with Japan in 1946 was dramatic and turbulent, for India was in the process of negotiating the terms of independence with the British. When independence was finally achieved in 1947, it was only through a division of the subcontinent into two nations, India and Pakistan, determined on the basis of regional religious majority. The Muslim nation Pakistan was itself split into two parts, East and West, separated by more than a thousand miles of India in between and eventually, in 1971, resulting in the eastern part constituting the new nation Bangladesh.

In India, when the immediate trauma of mass migration was finally over, the government initiated a number of programmes which had a significant impact on the arts and the development of ethnomusicology in India. The most significant of these was the establishment of a national institution called Sangeet Natak Akademi, whose primary purpose was the preservation and development of the arts of music, dance, drama and film. Included in these purposes were the fostering of research and, where appropriate, the revival of ailing traditions. To serve these ends, state branches of the academy were established in many parts of the country, in addition to the central organization in New Delhi. Underlying the Akademi's purposes was a deeper motive, that the arts could and should serve to enhance the cultural unity of the country. The principal theme was unity through diversity. Thus the enormous variety of regional performing traditions was overtly lauded and paraded periodically through the streets of Delhi and other cities on occasions such as Republic Day. But in some government circles, at least, there was the fond hope that the exchange of ideas and techniques among performers of diverse backgrounds would result in a reconciliation of the differences and lead to the emergence of pan-Indian forms of expression to support the government's urgent need for unity in the country. In order to facilitate the exchange of ideas, the Sangeet Natak Akademi established its *Bulletin* and also organized conferences and exhibitions involving music, dance, drama and film. These have succeeded in stimulating research and publications on music, one clear example being that of the folk music instrument exhibition in 1968, which initially led to the publication of an important catalogue by Keshav S. Kothari (later Secretary of the SNA), assisted by Komal Kothari, and also provided data for two major publications on Indian musical instruments by the late B. C. Deva, musicologist on the staff of the Akademi.

One of the major continuing projects of the Akademi is the documentation, primarily through sound recordings and photographs (now also video tape), of regional performing traditions as well as the leading artists of the classical traditions. Most of the recordings were initially made in their studios, but, as portable recording equipment became available, a number of field trips were also conducted under the guidance of their field officer, Govind Vidyarthi, and others. The regional branches of the SNA also conducted field research independently, primarily with a view to locating the best regional performers for representation at national and regional functions. But limited resources prevented a systematic documentation of the nation's performing arts. In this connection, the heavy tariffs and penalties on electronic items such as tape recorders served to slow the collecting process. Even so, over the years, the central body and the regional branches have collected much recorded and visual material. Unfortunately, these have not always been satisfactorily catalogued and the accompanying written documentation is generally sparse.

Further, insufficient attention has been given to methods of preserving the aural and visual documents.

The government also established in many regional centres, Divisions of Song and Drama, with the purpose not only of preserving and stimulating folk traditions, but also of the 'upliftment of the masses' in the rural areas. This involved presentation of social (and sometimes political) themes in music drama format that would be comprehensible to rural audiences. The Song and Drama Division troupes toured extensively in both cities and villages. On the one hand, they provided employment to a number of genuine folk musicians, actors and dancers, but on the other, the folk performers were supported by city musicians and were placed under the direction of sophisticated urban artists, with the inevitable syncretic results of blurring distinctions.

The government has also established other institutions: the Indian Council for Cultural Relations, the Indira Gandhi Centre for the Arts, Bharat Bhavan, Lalit Kala Akademi, Kathak Kendra, Sahitya Kala Parishad, to mention a few, all of which play a part in supporting the arts, although overlapping of activities is inevitable.

Rajeev Sethi, originally an independent artist and designer, produced a number of exhibitions (e.g. *Aditi*, 'A Celebration of Life') both nationally and internationally, featuring a broad view of the visual and performing arts of India, with emphasis on the performers of Shadipur, a suburb of Delhi, to which many folk musicians, acrobats, magicians, puppeteers and story-tellers have migrated in recent times. Subsequently, he was appointed Director General of the Indian National Culture Festival which produced its first two-week 'extravaganza', called *Apnā Utsav* ('Our festival') in Delhi in 1986, involving 4000 artists and performers from all parts of the country. To facilitate the logistics of this enterprise, which was planned to be an annual one, India has been divided into seven culture zones, even though India has as many as 22 languages and innumerable linguistic (not to mention musical) dialects. Festivals of this nature undoubtedly involve considerable research and generally include educational 'lec-dems' (lecture-demonstrations), as they are called; yet the research and educational values are incidental to the government's political policy of exposing the diversity of culture in India as a means to achieving national unity. Needless to say, an ethnomusicologist would feel concern on at least two grounds: that these presentations are extracted from the natural contexts and thus convey little of their traditional meaning, and that the impact of exposing village musicians to the city world and to other forms of music could lead to the disintegration of their life styles and the artificial syncretization of their forms of expression.

The Indian government's influence has also extended in another area; that of broadcasting; first, radio and later, television. All India Radio is a government monopoly, and thus basically subject to the government's goals in connection with the issues of unity/diversity and notions of 'upliftment' of the population. In connection with the latter goal and to develop a growing sense of unity, urban classical music was featured every day on radio, in spite of the fact that very few listeners initially cared for it. Even in this area there were attempts to raise standards. One instance of this was in connection with the harmonium, which had been used by classical singers as an accompaniment from the early years of this century. The instrument was banned from radio for a number of years in the 1950s and 1960s on the grounds that it had an adverse influence on both the singer's and audience's perception of musical subtlety. This censorship was eventually relaxed after a major conference on the impact of the harmonium revealed very divergent views among scholars and musicians. Nevertheless, the policy of maintaining regular broadcasts of classical music appears to have had a significant impact on the urban population, at least, as interest in this form of music has increased greatly since the 1950s.

Similarly, songs from the films which contained syncretic elements derived largely from Western popular music, were, for a long period, banned from radio on moral grounds. This policy, too, was eventually reversed, after it became obvious that the so-regarded 'pirate' Radio Ceylon, a commercial short-wave station easily received in India, which featured film music and other modern forms, was drawing away a large segment of the audience.

To satisfy the diversity component of the government's policies, the All India Radio broadcasts frequently included folk music of individual communities. These were, for the most part, of limited ethnographic value, since they were generally recorded in their studios with the accompaniment of studio musicians, in 'arrangements' of the traditional songs.

Indian record companies also produced some records of folk music, but these, too, were generally 'studio-ized', by the use of individual microphones and orchestration provided by studio musicians. Their principal endeavours were, however, focussed on classical music and film music, since these were both urban, where their primary markets lay.

Important recorded documentation of Indian ethnographic materials relevant to music was, until the 1980s, still being collected by Western scholars or Indians living abroad. Among them were Alain Daniélou, John Levy, Deben Bhattacharya, Nazir Ali Jairazbhoy, Felix van Lamsweerde, Robert Brown, Louise Lightfoot, Caspar Cronk, David Lewiston, Edward Henry, Geneviève Dournon, Mireille Helffer, Bonnie Wade, Laxmi Tewari and Daniel Neuman. Some were concerned primarily with producing records in the West and thus their materials were selected on the basis of marketability and appeal. Others were concerned primarily with the documentation of particular traditions to further their own researches, sometimes towards the completion of doctoral dissertations. Much of this research tended to involve relatively stable and flourishing traditions. Only a few scholars were motivated by the urgent need to document performing traditions that were in the process of drastic change or under the threat of extinction, although at least one foreign proposal for the systematic documentation of all the performance traditions in India was rejected by a Western funding agency in the 1970s.

While academic institutions in India had neither the facilities nor the interest in ethnomusicological documentation, other indigenous institutions were beginning to carry out fieldwork in the 1960s and 1970s. The National Centre for the Performing Arts in Bombay, established by the Sir Dorab Tata Trust in 1966, acquired, through a substantial grant from the Ford Foundation, up-to-date studio and field-recording equipment. Although their primary focus was on the presentation of the performing arts, both Indian and foreign, they began the documentation of both city (i.e. classical and some semi-classical, not film songs) and village traditions. Not much progress was made with the latter until the 1980s (even though the Centre had a remarkable vehicle especially designed as a field studio) principally because no one on the staff had field experience or knowledge of rural traditions. On occasion they were able to recruit independent scholars, such as Komal Kothari, to lead expeditions, but these were infrequent. Under the direction of Dr Narayana Menon (later Chairman of the Sangeet Natak Akademi) their documentation of classical musicians stands as their most significant contribution to music studies, characterized by high-quality recordings with a concern for techniques of preservation and with a laboratory for research. Dr. Ashok Ranade has recently been appointed to supervise research.

In contrast, Komal Kothari with Vijaydan Detha in 1960 established a Folklore Institute, Rupayan Sansthan, in a remote village in Rajasthan, devoid of most physical amenities (including electricity for part of the time) and with the simplest recording equipment, but with great energy and knowledge of Rajasthani folk traditions. Although initially focussing on folk tales, proverbs and riddles, they soon expanded their range to include folk songs, being among the first of the Indian folklorists to recognize the importance of music as a vehicle for text. Since those early days, the Rupayan Sansthan has built up a remarkable archive of Rajasthani recordings with thorough documentation not only of the songs, but the background of the musicians as well. Kothari has contributed his expertise in many collaborative ventures with the Sangeet Natak Akademi, the National Centre for Performing Arts and many film makers as well as individual scholars from India and abroad.

A further contrast is provided by the organization, Indian National Theatre in Bombay, initially organized to promote the performing arts, particularly drama, and to raise funds for its own and other theatrical productions. It then established a Research Centre for the Performing Arts. Under the supervision of Damubhai Javeri, however, the organization has far exceeded its initial goals and has developed an active research team led by Mansukh Joshi, and Ashok Paranjape to document folk and religious music and the regional dramatic traditions of Gujarat and Maharashtra. Their approach, now quite characteristic of Indian organizations and institutions during the past 15 years or so, involves organizing folk festivals in villages or small towns featuring particular performance traditions (the dramatic form *Bhavai* and the music of the *Māldhāri*-'carriers' being two of their festivals). These festivals, which last several days, are publicized nationally and generally include evening performances with daytime presentations of scholarly papers, seminars and demonstrations. They are often attended by important scholars and administrators from diverse parts of the country as well as from abroad. In the preparations for these festivals, field researchers carry out detailed investigations in many villages and collect the audiovisual and written documentation needed for the selection of the 'best' groups to perform at the festivals.

Indian National Theatre is only one such sponsoring group, but there are many others located all over India: the Regional Resources Centre for Folk Performing Arts of the MGM College in Udupi (Karnataka), Bharat Bhavan in Bhopal (Madhya Pradesh), the Bharatiya Lok Kala Mandal in Udaipur (Rajasthan), and the School of Drama at the University of Calicut (Kerala), to mention just a few. There are also privately funded organizations, such as the

Karnataka Janapada Trust in Bangalore, which is concerned with the documentation of folk traditions of the state, and the Sangeet Research Academy in Calcutta, funded by the Indian Tobacco Company, whose emphasis is largely on classical music training and research. There are also many independent societies for the promulgation and presentation of music; one that has recently come to the fore is the Society for the Promotion of Indian Classical Music and Culture Amongst Youth (SPIC–MACAY), funded by many sources, which arranges 'lec-dems' and performances of classical music and other cultural events in schools and colleges.

Ethnographic documentation

Ethnographic documentation took a sharp upswing in the early 1980s as a result of grants for the purchase of recording equipment given to a number of organizations in India by the Ford Foundation. Among them were the Indian National Theatre and the Archives and Research Centre for Ethnomusicology (ARCE), a branch of the American Institute of Indian Studies funded by the Smithsonian Institution's Foreign Currency Program. The primary aims of ARCE are not to carry out fieldwork in India, but to return to India copies of recordings made by scholars from abroad and also to provide a professionally maintained archive where copies can be deposited by visiting scholars before they leave the country after their field trips. Copies of some early recordings (e.g. Bake and Jairazbhoy collections) have been returned to ARCE from abroad with funding from the Asian Cultural Council, and most foreign scholars are now depositing copies of their field materials before they leave the country. ARCE has also received generous support from the Ford Foundation for organizing conferences on technical equipment, fieldwork, archiving, documentation, retrieval, preservation, and also on ethnomusicological research (e.g. the 1986 conference 'Text, Tone and Tune'), drawing attention to the many aspects of ethnomusicology.

Scholarship and publications

In the post-war period there was a significant increase in the number of journals either devoted entirely to music, or with articles involving music (i.e. on the performing arts, folklore and anthropology). Some were in English, often with a section devoted to regional languages (or the reverse), while others were entirely in regional languages. *The Journal of the Music Academy, Madras*, published annually, has continued in strength. The Sangeet Natak Akademi began the publication of its semiannual *Bulletin* in 1965, and the National Centre for the Performing Arts began its quarterly journal in 1972. Both cover a wide range of the performing arts. But a number of other independent music journals were also introduced: *Saṅgīt* (Hathras, *c*1951, in Hindi, possibly a continuation of the Marris College quarterly), *Lakshya Sangeet* (Bombay, 1954), *Music Mirror* (Hathras, 1957?), *Kala Vikash Kendra* (Cuttack, 1960), *Indian Music Journal* (Delhi, 1963?), *Sangeet Kala Vihar, English Supplement* (Baroda, 1970) which was incorporated into the *Journal of the Indian Musicological Society* (1971), and *Shanmukha* (Bombay, 1976). Most of these journals operated on shoe-string budgets and some had a brief existence.

Many were obliged to solicit advertisers and memberships, in addition to occasional small private grants, in an attempt to cover their basic costs. Some included articles in both English and Indian languages and occasionally solicited articles from foreign authors or Indians domiciled abroad. Articles on music were also published in special commemoration issues and 'souvenir' volumes particularly for 'music conferences', which were generally more like music festivals, held in different cities lasting several days and featuring the leading classical musicians of the country.

While most of the articles in these journals and special issues show the usual predilection for the history and theory of classical music and dance, an occasional one recognizes the importance of an ethnomusicological perspective, for example the two articles published in *Lakshya Sangeet* in 1954–5, 'The Cultural Aspect of Indian Music' by S. N. Ratanjankar and 'The Interrelation that Exists Between Music and Society' by Sumati Mutatkar. In the following year, Alain Daniélou published an extensive article, entitled 'Ethno-Musicology', in *The Journal of the Music Academy, Madras* discussing several aspects of the field (but emphasizing the importance of laboratory methods of interval measurements). On the whole, however, the prevailing attitude seems to favour that expressed by V. Raghavan, in his review of Jaap Kunst's *Ethnomusicology* in 1960, 'ethno-musicology will have much to take from Indian music', rather than to emphasize the contribution that an ethnomusicological perspective might add to Indian music studies.

Among the many Indian writers on Indian music, the late P. Sambamoorthy was one of the most prolific. Although much of his writing was concerned with the classical idiom of South India, his experiences in Europe during 1931–2 (which evidently included study with Curt Sachs) and other travels around the world influenced him to adopt a broader view than most of his contemporaries. His major work, *South Indian Music* (1963–), in six volumes (some volumes of which have been through 7 editions), includes topics such as, 'Comparative Musicology', 'Folk Music', and 'Music in Europe and other Countries'. He published works on various musical instruments and tackled a monumental *Dictionary of South Indian Music and Musicians*, unfortunately completing only three volumes (extending to the letter N) before his death in the early 1970s. Although this, too, is based largely on classical music, a number of entries on non-classical forms indicate the vast scope of his researches.

The closest parallel to Sambamoorthy in the north, as to versatility and prolific production, was the late B. C. Deva (interestingly enough a South Indian by birth). Again, most of his research dealt with classical music, but having a scientific bent, he attempted to apply scientific method to analysing contemporary music practice, exemplified by his *Psychoacoustics of Music and Speech* (1967). His work *Musical Instruments of India* (1978) reveals his vast knowledge of both classical and folk traditions across a large part of the country.

The subject of musical instruments has received considerable attention, including publications by S. Krishnaswamy, Lalmani Mishra (in Hindi), H. S. Tarlekar and Komal Kothari, and the catalogue by K. S. Kothari. The most recent is the detailed study of the *sāraṅgī* by Joep Bor in *National Centre for the Performing Arts Quarterly Journal* (1987).

In 1968 two major publications on ethnomusicology, Sudibhusan Bhattacharya's *Ethno-musicology in India*, and Sankar Sen Gupta's article 'On Ethnomusicology and India', appeared in *Folklore*. In 1975 his *Folklore and Folklife in India* championed the cause and called for a comprehensive ethnomusicological survey of India by a collaborative team of anthropologists, linguists, and musicologists. Neither work had a significant impact on music studies in India. Bhattacharya, an anthropologist, reveals a good grasp of ethnomusicological principles and expresses useful notions applicable to the spectrum of Indian music. Yet his work may have had a negative impact on ethnomusicology in India because it seems to imply that the field is focussed on the study of folk and tribal (or 'uncultivated', to use his term) music, which is to be seen primarily as a generative or degenerative form of the classical musics of India.

Daniel Neuman's book, *The Life of Music in North India* (1980), on the other hand, profitably applies anthropological and ethnomusicological methods to classical music. The impression in India that ethnomusicology deals only with folk and tribal music was reinforced by publications that followed in Bhattacharya's footsteps; the short book entitled, *Ethnomusicology–Tribal Music*, with the subtitle in parentheses, *A Directory of Tribal Musicians of Kinnaur*, was published under the auspices of the Census of India, 1971, and obviously continued the association of ethnomusicology with tribal music. Notwithstanding the impression these writings created in the scholarly world, they reveal a far better comprehension of ethnomusicology than the many books and articles on the folk songs of particular areas, which began to be published as early as 1871 (*The Folk-Songs of Southern India* by Charles Gover), both in English and the regional languages. These focussed solely on the texts of songs as though the musical and cultural setting were irrelevant. Of the more than 4000 titles listed in Handoo's comprehensive *A Bibliography of Indian Folk Literature* (1977), nearly half deal with folk songs and ballads, but very few of these books and articles give any consideration to the musical properties of the songs, their social context, or their ramifications in the cultural environment.

There have, however, been notable exceptions. Komal Kothari, a folklorist in the first instance, as early as 1960 recognized the importance of the ethnomusicological approach in his *Monograph on Langas*, not only providing the texts and translations of the songs, but also describing elements of the life style of the Langa community, and including a set of records of their performances with the publication. Other scholars like Madhubhai Patel (*Folksongs of South Gujarat*, 1974) and Vinjamuri Seetha Devi (*Folk Music of Andhra Pradesh*, 1985) have attempted to provide basic transcriptions of melody and rhythm (in either Western or Indian notation systems). But these lack the kind of ethnographic data and musical instrument descriptions found in the articles of L. S. Rajagopalan, which examine the music of specific tribes and castes in South India. However, no work on Indian folk music compares in range, scope and ethnographic information to K. Vatsyayan's *Traditions of Indian Folk Dance* (1976), although *The Concise Encyclopaedia of Music, Dance and Drama in India*, when completed, will undoubtedly be an important work in this direction. This major cooperative endeavour initiated by Nikhil Ghosh through his institution, Saṅgīt Mahābhāratī in Bombay, has already been in progress for more than 20 years and is projected to encompass 20 volumes.

Since ethnomusicology has evolved to its present state in the West, it has naturally developed a Western bias and a primary concern with Westerners studying non-Western music. Many of the ideas that have grown out of this approach are applicable to music in India as well as other countries in which music not only serves functional purposes, but is also treated as a form of art. Nevertheless, the concepts of ethnomusicology, as they stand, cannot be transferred without modification to these non-Western countries, if for no other reason than that the field presently presumes knowledge of the Western notation system based on the prescriptive practices of Western music. 'Ethnomusicology in the Indian Context' by the present author begins to examine some of these problems and suggests academic course work that might eventually lead to a less-biased approach to the field. At present, no academic institution in India offers regular courses in ethnomusicology or 'world music', although experimental courses on the latter have recently been introduced at S.N.D.T. Women's University in Bombay. The return of Indian scholars from studies abroad, among them Ranganayaki Iyengar (formerly at Benares Hindu University), Prabha Atre (S.N.D.T. Women's University) and S. A. K. Durga in Madras, will no doubt have a further impact on the academic scene. Other scholar/musicians of Indian descent, such as Laxmi Tewari, T. Viswanathan and the present writer, though living abroad carry out research in India and prepare western students for field research, along with the many non-Indian scholars who have specialized in Indian music over the past thirty years and more. The following list, by no means complete, will give some idea of their numbers: Takahashi Akihiro, Joep Bor, Robert Brown, Charles Capwell, Amy Catlin, Alain Danielou, Alastair Dick, Kobinata Hidetoshi, Walter Kaufmann, Josef Kuckertz, Peter Manuel, Scott Marcus, Helen Myers, Harold Powers, Regula Qureshi, Peter Row, Neil Sorrell, Tanaka Takako, Emmie te Nijenhuis, Gordon Thompson, Fujii Tomoaki, Wim van der Meer, Bonnie Wade, and Richard Widdess. A special mention should be made of the late Jon Higgins, scholar and singer of South Indian classical music, whose career was ended in its prime by an accident of fate.

India has, as yet, no equivalent of the Society for Ethnomusicology, nor a regional branch of the International Council of Traditional Music. There are signs, however, that the term ethnomusicology and its implications are beginning to receive acceptance in the country with the founding of the Centre for Ethnomusicology in Madras (S. A. K. Durga, Director) and the Rajasthani Society for Ethnomusicology in Jaipur (U. B. Mathur, Hon. Secretary). These activities may well coalesce into a national organization.

India has clearly recognized its multi-cultural heritage since independence, and is beginning to recognize the importance of research in music and the performing arts in general. Sometimes political strategies dominate the present scene, taking precedence over scholarly endeavours, while traditional modes of expression struggle for survival in the face of festivalization and modernization.

Bibliography

C. Gover: *The Folk-Songs of Southern India* (Madras, 1871/*R*1959)
S. M. Tagore: *Hindu Music from Various Authors* (Calcutta, 1875, 2/1882 in 2 pts., 3/1965)

B. T. Sahasrabudhe: *Hindu Music and the Gayan Samaj* (Bombay, 1887)

C. R. Day: *The Music and Musical Instruments of Southern India and the Deccan* (London and New York, 1891/*R*1974)

A. H. Fox Strangways: *The Music of Hindostan* (Oxford, 1914/*R*1965)

C. Sachs: *Die Musikinstrumente Indiens und Indonesiens* (Berlin, 1914)

J. Grosset: 'L'Inde: Histoire de la musique', *EMDC*, I/i (1921), 257–376

V. Elwin: *Folk-Songs of the Maikal Hills* (Bombay, 1924)

V. N. Bhātkhaṇḍe: *A Short Historical Survey of the Music of Upper India* (Bombay, 1934)

V. Elwin: *Folk Songs of the Forest* (London, 1935)

C. Marcel-Dubois: *Les instruments de musique de l'Inde ancienne* (Paris, 1941)

P. Banerji: *Folk Dance of India* (Allahabad, 1944)

H. L. Spreen: *Folk-Dances of South India* (Bombay, 1945)

Asian Folklore Studies (Nagoya, 1946–)

S. C. Dube: *Folk Songs of Chhatishgarh* (Lucknow, 1947)

A. Bake: 'Indian Folk Dances', *JIFMC*, i (1949), 47

P. Bandyopadhyaya: *The Evolution of Songs and Lives of Great Musicians* (Delhi, 1949)

S. Bandyopadhyaya: *Indian Music Through the Ages: 2400 B.C. to the Present Era* (Delhi, 1949)

A. A. Bake: 'Some Hobby Horses in South India', *JIFMC*, ii (1950), 43

P. Sambamoorthy: *A Dictionary of South Indian Music and Musicians*, i–iii (Madras, 1952)

K. Das: *A Study of Orissan Folklore* (Santiniketa, 1953)

M. C. Achutha: *Ballads of North Malabar* (Madras, 1954)

V. Elwin: *Folk-Tales of the Mahakoshala* (Oxford, 1954)

College of Indian Music, Dance and Dramatics of Maharaja Sayajirao University (Baroda, 1956) [70th anniversary issue; several articles in English and Gujarati]

A. Daniélou: 'Ethno-Musicology', *Journal of the Music Academy, Madras*, xxvii (1956), 47

Folklore (Calcutta, 1956)

A. A. Bake: 'Indische Musik', *MGG* (1957), 1150–85

———: 'The Music of India', *NOHM*, i (1957), 195–227, 488

O. Guswami: *The Story of Indian Music* (Bombay, 1957)

Naushad: 'Film Music', *Music Mirror*, i/1 (1957), 29

M. L. Roychoudhury: 'Music in Islam', *Journal of the Royal Asiatic Society*, xxiii/2 (1957), 101

S. Devi: 'The Musico-Religious Traditions of Assam', *Journal of the Music Academy, Madras*, xxxix (1958), 63

V. Elwin: *Leaves from the Jungle* (London, 1958)

K. S. Karanth: 'Yakshagana: a Musical Dance Drama', *Sangeet Natak Akademi Bulletin*, x (1958), 26

R. Rao: 'Renaissance of Music in Andhra', *Music Mirror*, ii/1 (1958), 19

B. Behari: *Minstrels of God* (Bombay, 1959)

V. Elwin and V. Coverley-Price: *The Hill People of North-East India* (London, 1959)

P. Sambamoorthy: *Great Musicians* (Madras, 1959)

K. Kothari: *Monograph on Langas* (Borunda, 1960)

V. Raghavan: '*Ethno-Musicology* by Jaap Kunst', *Journal of the Music Academy, Madras*, xxxi (1960), 78 [review]

B. Shaw: *Folk Dance and Music of Orissa – Phulbani District* (Cuttack, 1961)

Tribal Research Bureau, ed.: *Adibasi* (Orissa, 1961–)

N. Bose: *Folk Dance and Music of Orissa – Bolangir* (Cuttack, 1962)

A. Halim: *Essays on History of Indo-Pak Music* (Dacca, 1962)

B. A. Pingle: *History of Indian Music* (Calcutta, 1962)

T. V. Subba Rao: *Studies in Indian Music* (Bombay, 1962)

C. H. Ranade: 'The Tamāshā', *Journal of the Music Academy, Madras*, xxxiii (1962), 140

T. V. Subba Rao: *Studies in Indian Music* (Bombay, 1962)

N. Shyamala: 'Collection and Publication of Folk Music', *Journal of the Music Academy, Madras*, xxxiii (1962), 28

K. Sing: *Shadow and Sunlight: an Anthology of Dogri-Pahari Songs* (1962)

H. Barua: *Folksongs of India* (New Delhi, 1963)

S. Krishnaswami: 'Research on Musical Instruments of India', *Journal of the Music Academy, Madras*, xxxiii (1963), 100

S. Prajnananda: *A History of Indian Music* (Calcutta, 1963)

P. Sambamoorthy: *South Indian Music* (Madras, 1963–)

B. Shaw: *Folk Dance and Music of Orissa – Kalahundi* (Cuttack, 1963)

N. Shyamala: 'Folk Music of Tamilnad', *Journal of the Music Academy, Madras*, xxxiv (1963), 70

W. Bryce: *Women's Folk Songs of Rajasthan* (Delhi, 1964)

Indian Music Journal (New Delhi, 1964–)

J. C. Mathur: *Drama in Rural India* (New Delhi and Bombay, 1964)

R. C. Mehta: 'Value of Folk Music', *Studies in Indian Folk Culture*, ed. S. Sen Gupta and K. D. Upadhyaya (Calcutta, 1964), 50

B. R. Raju: 'Telegu Folk Songs', *Studies in Indian Folk Culture*, ed. S. Sen Gupta and K. D. Upadhyaya (Calcutta, 1964), 54

N. A. Baloch: *Musical Instruments of the Lower Indus Valley of Sind* (Hyderabad, 1965)

S. Krishanaswami: *Musical Instruments of India* (New Delhi, 1965)

H. S. Powers: 'Indian Music and the English Language: a Review Essay', *EM*, ix (1965), 1

V. K. Agarwala: *Traditions and Trends in Indian Music* (Meerut, 1966)

B. Gargi: *Folk Theater of India* (Seattle, WA, 1966)

H. A. Popley: *The Music of India* (New Delhi, 3/1966)

V. Raghavan: *The Great Integrators: the Saint-Singers of India* (Delhi, 1966)

M. Singer, ed.: *Krishna: Myths, Rites and Attitudes* (Honolulu, HI, 1966)

V. R. Athavale: *Pandit Vishnu Digambar* (New Delhi, 1967)

B. C. Deva: *Psychoacoustics of Music and Speech* (Madras, 1967)

E. C. Dimock: *In Praise of Krishna: Songs from the Bengali* (London, 1967)

B. V. Keshkar: *Indian Music: Problems and Prospects* (Bombay, 1967)

S. Krishanaswami: 'Drums of India Through the Ages', *Journal of the Music Academy, Madras*, xxxviii (1967), 72

L. S. Rajagopalan: 'Music in Kootiyattam', *Journal of the Sangeet Natak Akademi*, x/12 (1967), 12

G. H. Ranade: *Music in Maharashtra* (New Delhi, 1967)

J. Spector: 'Samaritan Chant', *Journal of the Music Academy, Madras*, xxxviii (1967), 103

H. S. Upadhyaya: 'Some Annotated Indian Folksongs', *Asian Folklore Studies*, xxvi (1967), 63–98

S. Awasthi: *Who's Who of Indian Musicians* (New Delhi, 1968)

S. K. Babar: *The Folk Literature of Maharashtra* (New Delhi, 1968)

A. Baloch and N. A. Baloch: *Spanish Cante Jondo and Its Origin in Sindhi Music* (Hyderabad, 1968)

S. Bhattacharya: *Ethno-Musicology and India* (Calcutta, 1968)

N. A. Jairazbhoy: 'L'Islam en Inde et au Pakistan', *Encyclopédie des musiques sacrées* (Paris, 1968), 454

K. S. Kothari: *Indian Folk Musical Instruments* (New Delhi, 1968)

S. Seetha: *Tanjore as a Seat of Music during the 17th, 18th and 19th Centuries* (diss., U. of Madras, 1968)

S. Sen Gupta: 'On Ethnomusicology and India', *Folklore*, ix/7 (1968), 7

——: *Bibliography of Indian Folklore and Related Subjects* (Calcutta, 1968)

D. Bhattacharya: *Songs of the Bauls from Bengal* (New York and London, 1969)

P. Gopwami: *Ballads and Tales of Assam* (Gauhati, 1969)

W. Kaufmann: 'The Songs of the Hill Muria, Jhoria Muria and Bastar Muria Gond Tribes', *EM* (1969), 115

F. van Lamsweerde: 'Musicians in Indian Society: an Attempt at a Classification', *Tropical Man*, ii (1969), 7

L. Omchery: 'The Music of Kerala', *Journal of the Sangeet Natak Akademi*, xiv (1969), 12

R. Qureshi: 'Tarannum: the Chanting of Urdu Poetry', *EM*, xiii (1969), 425

J. Spector: 'Shingli Tunes of the Cochin Jews', *Journal of the Music Academy, Madras*, xl (1969), 80

A. A. Bake: 'Stick Dances', *YIFMC*, ii (1970), 56

N. A. Jairazbhoy: 'A Preliminary Survey of the Oboe in India', *EM* (1970), 63

S. Bhattacharya: 'Folk-Base of the Rhythmic Structures of Raga-Music', *Journal of the Music Academy, Madras*, xliii (1971), 149

I. E. N. Chauhan: *Ethnomusicology – Tribal Music* (Delhi, 1971)

V. H. Deshpande: 'Harmonium as Accompaniment for Hindustani Classical Music', *Journal of the Sangeet Natak Akademi*, xx (1971), 15

L. S. Rajagopalan: 'Thimila', *Journal of the Music Academy, Madras*, lxii (1971), 165

B. L. Sharma: 'Contribution of Rajasthan to Indian Music', *Journal of the Indian Musicological Society*, ii/2 (1971), 32

R. Ayyangar: *History of South Indian (Carnatic) Music* (Madras, 1972)

V. N. Bhatkhande: 'A Comparative Study of Some of the Leading Music Systems of the 15th, 16th, 17th and 18th Centuries', *Journal of the Musicological Society, Baroda* [Eng. suppl.], iii (1972), 2

V. H. Deshpande: *Maharashtra's Contribution to Music* (New Delhi, 1972)

R. Qureshi: 'Indo-Muslim Religious Music, an Overview', *Asian Music*, iii/2 (1972), 15

L. S. Rajagopalan: 'The Suddha Maddala of Kerala', *Journal of the Music Academy, Madras*, xliii (1972), 119

M. Singer: 'The Radha-Krishna *Bhajanas* of Madras City', *When a Great Tradition Modernizes*, ed. M. Singer (New York, 1972), 199

B. C. Wade: 'By Invitation Only: Field Work in Village India', *Asian Music*, iii/2 (1972), 3

——: 'Songs of Traditional Wedding Ceremonies in North India', *YIFMC*, iv (1972), 57

N. A. Baloch: *Development of Music in Sind* (Hyderabad, 1973)

V. H. Deshpande: *Indian Musical Traditions: an Aesthetic Study of the Gharanas in Hindustani Music* (Bombay, 1973)

B. C. Deva: *An Introduction to Indian Music* (New Delhi, 1973)

——: 'The Ethnic and Cultural History of Musical Instruments in India', *Journal of the Music Academy, Madras*, xliv (1973), 234

R. O. Dhan: 'Poetry in Oraon Songs of Bihar', *Essays in Indian Folklore*, ed. L. P. Vidyarthi (Calcutta, 1973)

E. O. Henry: *The Meanings of Music in a North Indian Village* (diss., Michigan State U., 1973)

S. Prajnananda: *Historical Development of Indian Music: a Critical Study* (Calcutta, 1973)

——: *Music of the Nations* (New Delhi, 1973)

S. Ray: *Music of Eastern India* (Calcutta, 1973)

L. P. Vidyarthy: *Folklore Researches in India* (Calcutta, 1973)

——, ed.: *Essays in Indian Folklore* (Calcutta, 1973)

L. S. Rajagopalan: 'Folk Musical Instruments of Kerala', *Journal of the Sangeet Natak Akademi*, xxxiii (1974), 40

——: 'The Mizhavu', *Journal of the Music Academy, Madras*, lxv (1974), 109

E. te Nijenhuis: *Indian Music: History and Structure* (Leiden and Cologne, 1974)

L. G. Tewari: 'Folk Music of India' (diss., Wesleyan U., 1974)

N. A. Jairazbhoy: '"Music", "South Asian Peoples, Arts"', *Encyclopedia Britannica* (1974), 150

M. Patel: *Folksongs of South Gujarat* (Bombay, 1974)

A. Brahaspati: 'Mussualmans and Indian Music', *Journal of the Indian Musicological Society*, vi/2 (1975), 27

J. Kuckertz: 'Origin and Construction of the Melodies in Baul Songs of Bengal', *YIFMC*, vii (1975), 85

N. A. Jairazbhoy: 'Indian Music', *A Cultural History of India*, ed. A. L. Basham (Oxford, 1975), 217–48, 485–6

L. S. Rajagopalan: 'The Kurum Khuzhal of Kerala', *Journal of the Music Academy, Madras*, xlvi (1975), 144

S. Sen Gupta: *Folklore and Folklife in India* (Calcutta, 1975)

R. L. Simon: *Bhakti Ritual Music in South India* (diss., U. of California, 1975)

E. O. Henry: 'The Variety of Music in a North Indian Village: Reassessing Cantometrics', *EM*, xx (1976), 49

H. S. Powers: 'The Structure of Musical Meaning: a View from Banaras', *PNM*, xiv/2–xv/1 (1976), 308

S. Sen Gupta: *Folklore of Bengal – a Projected Study* (Calcutta, 1976)

A. Siddiqui: *Folkloric Bangladesh* (Dacca, 1976)

B. Silver: 'On Becoming an Ustad: Six Life Sketches in the Evolution of a Gharana', *Asian Music*, vii/2 (1976), 27–58

K. Vatsyayan: *Traditions of Indian Folk Dance* (New Delhi, 1976)

A. R. Catlin: 'Whither the Manganihars? – an Investigation Into Change Among Professional Musicians in Western Rajasthan', *Bulletin of the Institute of Traditional Cultures, Madras* (1977), 165

R. Das: *Kala Vikash Kendra* (Cuttack, 1977)

J. Handoo: *A Bibliography of Indian Folk Literature* (Mysore, 1977)

E. O. Henry: 'The Ethnographic Analysis of Four Types of Performance in Bhojpuri-Speaking India', *Journal of the Indian Musicological Society*, viii/4 (1977), 5

N. A. Jairazbhoy: 'Music in Western Rajasthan: Stability and Change', *YIFMC*, ix (1977), 50

A. K. Maswani: 'Folk Songs and Dances of Pakistan', *Folk Heritage of Pakistan* (Islamabad, 1977), 41

B. Deva: *Musical Instruments of India: Their History and Evolution* (New Delhi, 1978)

K. L'Armand and A. L'Armand: 'Music in Madras: the Urbanization of a Cultural Tradition', *Eight Urban Musical Cultures: Tradition and Change*, ed. B. Nettl (Urbana, IL, 1978), 115–45

D. M. Neuman: '*Gharanas*: the Rise of Musical "Houses" in Delhi and Neighboring Cities',

Eight Urban Musical Cultures: Tradition and Change, ed. B. Nettl (Urbana, IL, 1978), 186–222

M. Z. Abbasi, ed.: *Folkloric Bangladesh* (Dacca, 1979)

P. Manuel: 'The Evolution of Modern *Thumri*', *EM*, xxx (1979), 470

——: 'The Light-Classical Urdu Ghazal-Song' (diss., U. of California, 1979)

D. M. Neuman: 'Country Musicians and Their City Cousins: the Kinship of Folk and Classical Music Culture in North India', *Proceedings of the XIIth Congress of the International Musicological Society* (Kassel, 1979)

O. Siddiqui: 'Our Ballad Songs', *Folkloric Bangladesh*, ed. M. Z. Abbasi (Dacca, 1979)

M. A. Talib: 'The Palanquin Bearers' Songs', *Folkloric Bangladesh*, ed. M. Z. Abbasi (Dacca, 1979)

A. R. Catlin: *Variability and Change in Three Karnataka Kriti-S: a Study of South Indian Classical Music* (diss., Brown U., 1980)

India Magazine (1980–)

N. A. Jairazbhoy: 'Embryo of a Classical Music Tradition in Western Rajasthan', *Communication of Ideas*, x/3 (1980), 99

——: 'The South Asian Double-Reed Aerophone Reconsidered', *EM*, xxiv (1980), 147

G. Kuppuswamy and M. Hariharan: *Indian Music: a Perspective* (Delhi, 1980)

D. Neuman: *The Life of Music in North India* (Detroit, MI, 1980)

H. S. Powers: 'India', *Grove 6*

L. S. Rajagopalan: 'The Pulluvans and their Music', *Journal of the Music Academy, Madras*, li (1980), 72

A. H. Saaduddin: 'Bangladesh', *Grove 6*

B. C. Deva and J. Kuckertz: 'Bharud, Vaghya-Murali, and Daff-Gan of the Deccan', *Studies in the Regional Folk Music of South India: a Research Report* (Munich, 1981)

R. R. Goswami: 'Some Aspects of the Performing Arts of the Dangs', *Mahostava of Tribal Arts-Dang* (New Delhi, 1981) [exhibition programme notes]

H. Myers: '"Normal" Ethnomusicology and "Extraordinary" Ethnomusicology', *Journal of the Indian Musicological Society*, xii 3–4 (1981), 3

G. A. Allana: *Folk Music of Sind* (Jamshoro, 1982)

Indian Music Newsletter (Amsterdam, 1982–)

J. Kuckertz: 'Folk Songs of Central India', *Journal of the Music Academy, Madras*, liii (1982), 141

M. Levy: *Intonation in Indian Music* (New Delhi, 1982)

B. Nettl: 'A Tale of Two Cities', *Journal of the Music Academy, Madras*, lxiii (1982), 105

C. R. Das: *Folk Culture* (New Delhi, 1983)

F. Hoff: '"Dojiji": a Woman and a Bell', *Dance as Cultural Heritage*, ed. T. Jones, i (New York, 1983), 32

J. Handoo, ed.: *Folklore of Rajasthan* (Mysore, 1983)

N. A. Jairazbhoy and A. Catlin: 'A Microcomputer Retrieval System for Indian Music', *Phonographic Bulletin: Journal of the International Association of Sound Archives*, xxxvi (1983), 49

M. Lath: 'Ancient Indian Music and the Concept of Man', *National Centre for the Performing Arts Quarterly Journal*, xxii/2–3 (1983), 1

A. Maitra: 'Tanbura (Tumbura or Tambura)', *Sangeet Research Academy Journal*, iv/1 (1983), 48

P. Manuel: *Thumri in Historical and Stylistic Perspective* (diss., U. of California, 1983)

B. R. Raju: 'South Indian Folksongs', *Journal of Intercultural Studies* (1983), 1–58

A. Ram: *Musical Instruments of India: History and Development* (New Delhi, 1983)

A. Ranganathan: 'The Relevance of Professor C. V. Raman to the Physical Theory of Musical Instruments (Some Aesthetic Considerations)', *National Centre for the Performing Arts Quarterly Journal*, xii/2–3 (1983), 11

R. Sathyanarayana: 'Indian Musicology: Research Methodology and Theory Construction', *Journal of the Sangeet Natak Akademi*, lxvii (1983), 45

D. M. Wulff: 'On Practicing Religiously: Music as Sacred in India', *Sacred Sound*, ed. J. Irwin (Chico, CA, 1983), 149

N. P. Ahmad: *Hindustani Music: a Study of its Development in the 17th and 18th Centuries* (New Delhi, 1984)

S. Bharati: 'Reviving Temple Music', *Indian Music Journal*, xiii (1984), 49

J. Bor: 'Baijis: Female Performers of the Past', *Indian Music Newsletter*, x (1984), 1

A. B. K. Choudhuary: *'Tribal Songs of North-East India' with Special Reference to Arunachal Pradesh* (Calcutta, 1984)

N. Jairazbhoy: 'Ethnomusicology in the Indian Context', *National Centre for the Performing Arts Journal*, xiii/3 (1984), 31

———: *Folk Music of Rajasthan* (Los Angeles, CA, 1984) [videotape with accompanying monograph]

K. Kothari: 'Epics of Rajasthan', *National Centre for the Performing Arts Journal*, xiii/3 (1984), 1

G. Kuppuswamy and M. Hariharan: *Royal Patronage to Indian Music* (Delhi, 1984)

B. Leela: 'Classical Music in the Mysore Court', *Quarterly Journal of the Mythic Society*, lxxv/4 (1984), 443

A. Le Normand: 'A propos de musiques-de-célébration', *Centre d'Etudes de Musique Orientale*, xxx (1984), 2

P. Moutal: 'Le sitar (Origines, developpement, techniques et maitres) – étude summaire', *Centre d'Etudes de Musique Orientale*, xxx (1984), 16

D. M. Neuman: 'The Ecology of Indian Music in North America', *Bansuri*, i (1984), 9

J. Pani: 'The Tradition of Orissi music', *National Centre for the Performing Arts Quarterly Journal*, xiii/1 (1984), 31

J. Pereira and M. Martins: 'Goa and its Music', *Boletim do Instituto Menezes Braganca*, cxxxxiv (1984), 75

A. D. Ranade: *On Music and Musicians of Hindoostan* (New Delhi, 1984)

S. Reys: 'Wandering Balladeers of Rajasthan: the Bhopa and His Phad', *India Magazine*, iv/4 (1984), 68

A. Catlin: '*Pallavi* and *Kriti* of Karnatak Music: Evolutionary Processes and Survival Strategies', *National Centre for the Performing Arts Journal*, xiv/1 (1985), 26

V. S. Devi: *Folk Music of Andhra Pradesh* (Madras, 1985)

N. Jairazbhoy: 'Performance, Music and the Child', *Aditi: the Living Arts of India* (Washington, DC, 1985), 219

R. Knight: 'The Harp in India Today', *EM*, xxix (1985), 9

K. Krishnamurthy: *Archaeology of Indian Musical Instruments* (Delhi, 1985)

O. Prasad: *Santal Music: a Study in Pattern and Process of Cultural Persistence* (New Delhi, 1985)

K. Rao: *Lavni of Maharashtra: a Regional Genre of Popular Music* (diss., U. of California, 1985)

Subbudu: 'Musings on Hari Katha – a Dyeing and Dying Art', *Shanmukha*, i/4 (1985), 25

B. C. Wade: *Khyāl: Creativity Within North India's Classical Music Tradition* (Cambridge and New York, 1985)

A. Chandola: *Music as Speech: an Ethnomusicological Study of India* (New Delhi, 1986)

C. Capwell: *Bauls: Music of the Bauls of Bengal* (Kent, OH, 1986)

P. Manuel: 'The Evolution of Modern *Thumri*', *EM*, xxx (1986), 470

R. Qureshi: *Sufi Music of India and Pakistan: Sound, Context and Meaning in Qawwali* (Cambridge and New York, 1986)

T. Skillman: 'The Bombay Hindi Film Song Genre', *YTM*, xviii (1986), 133

J. Bor: 'The Voice of the Sarangi', *National Centre for the Performing Arts Quarterly Journal*, xv–xvi (1987)

J. A. Greig: *Tarikh-i Sangita: the Foundations of North Indian Music in the Sixteenth Century* (diss., U. of California, 1987)

G. R. Thompson: *Music and Values in Gujarati-Speaking Western India* (diss., U. of California, 1987)

A. Arnold: 'Popular Film Song in India: a Case of Mass-Market Musical Eclecticism', *Popular Music*, vii/2 (1988)

J. Baily: 'Amin-e Diwaneh: the Musician as Madman', *Popular Music*, vii/2 (1988)

C. Capwell: 'The Popular Expression of Religious Syncretism: the Bauls of Bengal as Apostles of Brotherhood', *Popular Music*, vii/2 (1988)

G. N. Joshi: 'Concise History of the Phonograph Industry in India', *Popular Music*, vii/2 (1988)

E. O. Henry: *Chant the Names of God: Music and Culture in Bhojpuri-speaking India* (San Diego, CA, 1988)

P. Manuel: 'Social Structure and Music: Correlating Musical Genres and Social Categories in Bhojpuri-speaking India', *International Review of Aesthetics and Sociology of Music* (Zagreb, 1988), 217

———: 'Popular Music in India, 1901–1986', *Popular Music*, vii/2 (1988), 157

———: *Popular Musics of the Non-Western World: an Introductory Survey* (New York, 1988)

F. Nizami: *History and Development of Music* (Lahore, 1988)

P. Manuel: 'The Popularization and Transformation of the Light-Classical Urdu Ghazal-Song', *Folklore in South Asia* (Philadelphia, PA, 1989)

———: *Thumri in Historical and Stylistic Perspectives* (Varanasi, 1989)

S. Marcus: 'The Rise of Folk Music Genre, Birahā', *Culture and Power in Benares: Performance Community and Environment 1800–1980*, ed. S. Freitag (Berkeley, CA, 1989), 93

2: PAKISTAN

Nazir Ali Jairazbhoy

Pakistan was formed in 1947 from regions that had Muslim majority populations in the geographical area previously called British India. Thus much of its prior musical background is to be found under Indian music. The city, Lahore, for instance, which is now in Pakistan, was the original seat of Vishnu Digambar's music school, Gandharv Mahavidyalay. The western region of 'British India', however, which now constitutes Pakistan, had its own history, stretching back to the Indus Valley civilization in the 3rd millennium BC, and has been exposed to a much greater degree of influence from the West, and especially to Muslim influence, which began as early as the 8th century AD with the conquest of Sind by the Arab invader, Muhammad b. al-Qassim. It is not possible now to assess the precise impact of this early contact with the Muslim Arabic world and with Iran, but it is important to note that Pakistan has many cultural traditions not found in India, and many others which have developed in unique ways compared with their counterparts in India.

In discussing any aspect of music in an Islamic nation, mention must be made of the religion's ambivalent attitude towards music, which is generally proscribed by the legists but practised in folk and art traditions and wholeheartedly endorsed by many of the Sufi sects of Islam. The legists (*'ulema*), represented by the clergy, do not accept as legitimate any musical sounds that are not directly associated with Koranic texts; they do, however, generally condone the quasi-musical chanting of the Koran and the call to prayer (*āḍān*). In spite of this limitation, important music traditions are found at the shrines of Sufi saints, both in Pakistan and India, based, not on the text of the Koran, but on Sufi religious/devotional poetry (e.g. that by Jalaluddin Rumi and a great many others). Principally from oral tradition we are informed that the shrines of these Sufi 'saints', such as that of Shah Abdul Latif in Bhitshah, Sind, not only accepted music as a legitimate means of reaching the godhead, but also served as the equivalent of music colleges and provided musical training for Sufi initiates and musicians to the extent that a position comparable to that of a professor of music had been established at Bhitshah.

In the 1950s, there was indication that Pakistan, like India, was going to accord full recognition to classical music by regular broadcasts, since there were a number of excellent classical musicians in the country such as the vocalists Roshanara Begum, Barkat Ali Khan and the brothers Nazakat and Salamat Ali Khan, as well as instrumentalists such as the *sārangī* players Ustad Bundu Khan and his son Umrao Bundu Khan, to mention just a few. But Pakistani religious fundamentalist opposition to music as artistic expression prevented the kind of full-fledged support offered to classical music and other arts in India. The fact that the traditional texts of many of the classical songs were connected either with Hindu deities or with the separation of lovers probably reinforced opposition to this form of music. The government thus adopted a laissez-faire attitude, with the result that the market for classical music gradually diminished while popular film music became utterly dominant, especially in the cities.

After the chaotic partitioning of 'British India', Pakistan, like India, was also faced with the need to unify its diverse population, especially as eastern Pakistan was more than a thousand miles removed from its western section and shared very little with it apart from its religious persuasion. But Pakistan, in spite of its many problems of disparity, which led to its eastern section breaking away to form Bangladesh in 1971, eventually recognized the importance of the folk arts of the numerous minority cultural traditions within its bounds, and created the Institute of Folk Heritage (IFH, also known as Lok Virsa) in 1974 (although the process of collecting and documenting had begun much earlier) at Islamabad under the direction of Uxi Mufti, the son of a highly respected Pakistani poet. The Institute issued its first volume of *Folk Heritage* in 1977, in which its goals are expressed as follows: 'The IFH is endeavouring to create a science of the Folklore of Pakistan. In other words it is concerned primarily with scientific research, systematic collection, documentation, preservation and dissemination of oral traditions, folklore, folk wisdom and other aspects of indigenous heritage.' Receiving a substantial grant from the Ford Foundation for the purchase of field recording and studio equipment (including Nagra tape recorders), the IFH brought together an excellent staff and set about documenting the performing traditions. Realizing that a single central location was inadequate for their purposes, the staff established several regional offices in places such as Peshawar in the north and Hyderabad, Sind, in the south and placed them under the direction of local folklorists. Even by 1975 they had succeeded in documenting on tape and still photographs, with detailed written notes, a great deal of the folk and traditional music of the country and were able to pinpoint some of the best performers of the various regional genres, some of whom were brought to the USA by the Smithsonian Institution for its Bi-centennial Festival of American Folklife in 1976.

The IFH has also done much to disseminate materials from its collections and to make the broader Pakistani public aware of the regional performing traditions and other folk and classical arts. It has organized numerous exhibitions and performances, has increased publication of books and released many audio recordings of folk and classical music on cassettes. The folklorists have also put together slide-tape presentations for distribution to schools and programmes for radio and television. They have also begun to reissue out-of-print books (including the present writer's *The Rāgs of North Indian Music: their Structure and Evolution*) for sale in Pakistan. The income from these sales, as stated in the first publication, is 'utilized to further the objectives of the Institute and to preserve the folk heritage of Pakistan'.

Unquestionably the Institute has served an important purpose and has had a major impact particularly on the folk music traditions and the folk musicians of Pakistan. In field expeditions, the IFH has located excellent regional musicians many of whom they have brought to Islamabad to be recorded in a studio and have introduced them to the public through releasing recordings, as well as through arranging concerts and broadcasts. Some of these musicians who have become household names, such as the traditional singer Reshma, are in great demand as performers and have left their villages for residence in the cities. In the process, they have naturally acquired musical sophistication and have become accustomed to studio and concert musical practices (involving microphone techniques and new instrumentation) which have begun to feed back into the village styles. Thus among their many activities, a fundamental motivating factor has been to serve as talent scouts and impresarios with a view to dissemination of regional performing traditions to a larger public. Research has not been entirely neglected, however, and the appointment of Adam Nayyar as Research Director of the Institute (now Director, after Uxi Mufti's retirement) promises to expand this direction in the future.

The focus on research has been more evident in Hyderabad, Sind, both in the writings of N. A. Baloch, Professor of the University of Sind, and the direction of Ghulam Ali Allana, Professor in Charge of the Institute of Sindhology, in Jamshoro (near Hyderabad). Baloch's numerous publications deal with the history of music in Sind, the spread of gypsies from Sind to Andalusia (with Aziz Baloch), as well as ancient and contemporary musical instruments (1965).

The Institute of Sindhology established a sound and film archive as early as 1973, and has sent teams into many villages of Sind to record and document folk traditions. This institute has also helped to preserve and study Sufi music and dance, particularly the modes (called *sur* or *rāg*) and the compositions (called *kāfī*) of Shah Abdul Latif.

Unlike India, classical music has been receiving little attention in Pakistan. The Classical Music Research Cell in Lahore, sponsored by Radio Pakistan, under the advisorship of M. A. Sheikh, is the only visible organization of its kind, but even its activities are in a low key. Other support for classical music is also periodically provided by Arts Councils, for instance those of Punjab and Sind, which sponsor music performances. The former has recently funded publication of two books by the late Feroze Nizami in English, composed of his articles on classical music written for the *Pakistan Times*. The individual musician/connoisseur/scholar, such as Nizami, is still to be found in the country, many of them pursuing their own directions without much support. For instance, Luthfullah Khan has a vast collection of recordings in Karachi (made largely from radio broadcasts over the last 30 or 40 years), and G. Hyder Alidina has attempted to standardize the singing of the Khoja religious/devotional vocal genre known as *ginnan*. In addition, one continues to find performance instruction manuals in Urdu for various instruments, but all these, apart from the work of the IFH and the Institute of Sindhology, constitute together, a bare minimum of activity in the field.

Bibliography

See Bibliography *under* 1: India.

3: SRI LANKA

CYRIL DE SILVA KULATILLAKE

Music research is a recent field of study in Sri Lanka. Since the beginning of the 20th century the music of the country has been strongly dominated by the North Indian school of music, but in the 1950s there was agitation for a national musical identity. Scholars who responded to this enthusiasm, both musicians and academics, started their researches on the data given in ancient manuscripts belonging mostly to the Kandyan period (1587–1812). Some of these manuscripts were in the possession of traditional dancers, who had treasured them amid the introgression of modern trends. The local artists from the dance tradition who had been patronizing the folk-song belt of the National Radio had published some of this material in the manuscripts, but with no musical context (Sēdaraman, 1944).

As to theoretical data pertaining to the music of the Kandyan period, these artists quote from *Vādānkusa*, an ola-leaf manuscript written by a Buddhist monk of the Malwatta Chapter. Mahawelatenna Baṇḍāra, a connoisseur of music, also discussed this data in a lecture delivered under the auspices of the Royal Asiatic Society (1909, pp.129–64). Yet no sufficient attempt has been made to analyse the material in relation to the music as practised by the traditional artists. For instance the 5 *tāla*, 32 *tālam*, 4 *waṭṭam*, 7 *tit* and especially 32 *rāgams* have not received adequate analysis, for the interpretations given by the traditionalists to most of this material are disputed among themselves. The 32 *rāgams* bear no relevance to the rāgas of Indian music; these are played on the drum.

During this period of asymmetry W. B. Makulloluwe, a music graduate of Visva-Bhārati and one-time Chief Education Officer of Music, launched a dynamic programme of expounding new classifications of musical data. He was closely guided by Vincent Sōmapāla, a self-tutored musician, in analysing the 32 rhythmic measures based on the *tit* system (1959), which hitherto had not been researched. With his added knowledge of traditional dancing, Makulloluwe had a good approach to, and clear insight of the subject. He further expounded a new classification of popular folk songs on a system of Sinhala metrics (1962, pp.6–18, 26–66). Makulloluwe codified this material into syllabi and in his capacity as Chief Education Officer of Music introduced them to schools in the early 1960s. He conducted courses to brief teachers on the new syllabuses. Nevertheless Makulloluwe was strongly challenged by the performing musicians of the North Indian school, who were monopolizing the National Radio to propagate their view of music. The enthusiasm created by Makulloluwe resulted in a number of traditional music pageants.

The first government-sponsored Unit for Music Research was installed in 1970 in the National Broadcasting station, with C. de S. Kulatillake (the present writer) as its head. Kulatillake was a close associate of Makulloluwe.

With the recording equipment then available the unit launched an island-wide programme of field recordings including the Tamil regions of the North and the Christian areas along the Western coast, both of which had hitherto not received special attention. That the research unit was embodied within the only broadcasting centre created difficulties at the start, for the unit had to contribute programme productions on music. A series of discussion programmes was inaugurated where scholars and theorists who were engaged in music research and allied fields were invited to participate. Participants brought their own demonstrators to illustrate the examples. This scheme worked well for some time, and the unit gathered many different aspects of musical data from the past. The material thus collected has been published in a series of bulletins, where relevant examples from field collections too have been included (1980, 1982).

In 1974 the head of the unit was afforded an opportunity to study ethnomusicology under Josef Kuckertz, Professor at the Institute of Ethnomusicology, Cologne University.

Thus the first music research unit in the country has been able to create an interest in research among folklorists. New researchers have made promising contributions on past music cultures. Although the work initiated at the present University Aesthetic Institute is not wholly encouraging due to lack of equipment and personnel, professors from other universities with no sections for music or dancing have come out with private publications: *Baila-Kapiriñña* and *Passion Hymns* of the Catholic population are two recent works worth mentioning (Aniyarotne, 1985, 1987).

Many more strides are yet to be made in the development of music research in Sri Lanka. The absence of a research laboratory is a major drawback. The domination of North Indian music has discouraged the study of other music cultures in East and Southeast Asia (Ellingson, 1987), among countries that have had political and social contacts in the past. Scale dissimilarities evident in the stream of *nelum* singing found in the west-central and northwest regions of the island reveal non-Indian intervals. The local oboe, *ñoranē*, too has a scale quite different from the modern Indian or Western scales. Experiments carried out on the system of cents and the monochord have not been able to give distinct levels, as musicological sound experiments are hardly possible in the country owing to lack of sensitive scientific equipment. The music of the famous Kandyan ritual, Kohombā-Kankāriya, is another area for the study of scale dissimilarities (Walcott, 1980). Folk rituals, both Kandyan and low-country, have been areas where traditionalists can exhibit their skill and knowledge in the musical arts which during the times of Kandyan kings were performed in the courts.

Bibliography

OLA-LEAF MANUSCRIPTS

Rev. Badra: *Elu sañdäs Lakuna* (13th century; pubd in 1945) [94 leaves; treatise on Sinhalese metrics]

D. Adikaram: *Sringāraya hevat Daskon adikāramge Srī-nāmaya* (1707–29; pubd Colombo, 1958) [40 leaves; collection of court panegyrics]

Anon: *Vādānkusa* (Kandy, mid-18th century) [28 leaves]

P. J. Silva: *Detis talaya* (1833) [20 leaves; contains 32 drum rhythms in the form of *vrittas*]

OTHER STUDIES

J. Davy: 'Music in Ceylon', *An Account of the Interior of Ceylon and its Inhabitants* (London, 1821/ *R*1969)

M. Baṇḍāra: 'Kandyan Music', *JRAS, CB*, xli (1909), 129–64

J. E. Sēdaraman: *Sinhala nāṭya kalā* (Kandy, 1944) [in Sinhalese; dance ballads with notation and musical instruments]

——: *Sringāraya* (Colombo, 1955) [in Sinhalese; collection of court panegyrics with notation]

V. Sōmapala: *Tālagñanaya* (Colombo, 1959) [in Sinhalese; classification of calculated drum rhythms in Sinhalese music based on the Tit system]

W. B. Makulloluwe: *Hela gee maga* (Colombo, 1962) [in Sinhalese; codification of drum rhythms and melodies]

C. de S. Kulatillake: *Lankāwe sangeetha sambhavaya* (Colombo, 1974) [in Sinhalese; study of musical sources and culture]

A. Seneviratne: 'Music Rituals of the Daladā Māligāwa', *Sangeeth Natak* (New Delhi, 1974) [rituals and instruments of the Temple of the Tooth, Kandy]

C. de S. Kulatillake: '*Samudraghōsna* Metre and *Seepada* Styles of Singing in Lanka', *Mittelungen der deutschen Gesellschaft für Musik des Orients*, xiii (1974–5), 39

—— and J. Kuckertz: 'Darsteller und Music in Kōlam Maskenspiel Sri Lankas', *Studien zur Musikgeschichte des Rheinlandes*, iv (1975), 131

C. de S. Kulatillake: 'Gī Metre in Sinhala Music', *Proceedings of the National Symposium on Traditional Rural Culture of Sri Lanka* (Colombo, 1977), 132

——: *Metre, Melody and Rhythm in Sinhala Music* (Colombo, 1980)

R. Walcott: 'Kohoṁbā-Kankāriya' (diss., Sri Jayawardanapura U., 1980)

C. de S. Kulatillake: 'Buddhist Chant in Sri Lanka and its Musical Elements', *Jb für Musikalische Volks- und Völkerkunde*, x (1982), 20

——: *Daha-aṭa Vannama* (Colombo, 1982) [in Sinhalese; history, literature and styles of *vannams* in Sinhalese music]

S. Ariyaratne: *Baila Kapiriñña vimarshanayak* (Nugēgoḍa, 1985) [in Sinhalese; survey on *baila* and *kaffriñña*, with music exx.]

C. de S. Kulatillake: 'Vannama ia a Phono-metre', *Nava samskrite*, i/2 (Colombo, 1986), 36

S. Ariyaratne: *Carol, pasam, kantāru* (Colombo, 1987) [in Sinhalese; survey of evolution and styles of Christian music in Sri Lanka]

T. Ellingson: 'Kolam', *EM*, xxxi (1987), 187 [disc review]

CHAPTER X

Western Central Asia and the Caucasus

Theodore Levin

Western Central Asia as discussed here includes Afghanistan, the five (former Soviet) republics of Kazakhstan, Kyrgyzstan, Tajikistan, Turkmenistan, Uzbekistan, and the Transcaucasian massif that lies between the Caspian Sea and the Black Sea, comprising Azerbaijan, Georgia and Armenia. The diversity of peoples and cultures within the region so-defined is vast, and research by ethnomusicologists and folklorists has tended to focus on the distinct musical practice of particular ethnic or national groups rather than on common musical and cultural elements in the region as a whole. The Transcaucasus, lying to the west of the Caspian Sea, is commonly treated as a culture area distinct from Central Asia, which in most definitions extends eastward from the Caspian to Chinese Xinjiang.

Research on the music of Western Central Asia has been the product of three scholarly traditions. The first of these comprises the historical study of Christian liturgical chant and with regard to Western Central Asia, has focussed on the music of the Armenian and Georgian rites. The second tradition is exemplified by the 'armchair' historical and theoretical studies of Baron Rodolphe d'Erlanger, Henry George Farmer and Owen Wright, whose translations and analyses of medieval Persian and Arabic treatises have illuminated aspects of music theory and practice in urban centres of Islamic high culture, including such Central Asian cities as Bukhara, Samarkand and Herat. The third scholarly tradition embraces the disciplines of folklore, ethnography and musicology and has been centred on the collection, transcription and analysis of traditional music. Soviet scholarship on the music of Central Asia and the Transcaucasus arose largely from this third tradition.

Early research

Systematic collection of traditional music from Central Asia and the Transcaucasus came on the heels of Russian military and political advances in the region in the last third of the 19th century. These collecting activities were motivated by cultural and commercial interests that derived, in the first case, from an enthusiasm for Orientalism in Imperial Russia, and in the second, from the business acumen of a British recording company. In 1901, the Gramophone Company of the UK established a Russian subsidiary, A.O.

Grammofon, which soon after opened a branch office in Tiflis (now Tbilisi), Georgia, to promote the sale of gramophones and records to local ethnic markets. From this office, recording engineers were sent on expeditions throughout the Transcaucasus and Central Asia (then called Turkestan). Between 1901 and 1914, hundreds of titles were recorded, and these have been preserved in the EMI Archive and the National Sound Archive of the British Library, London.

Music recording activities ceased with the onset of World War I, but in the first two decades of Soviet rule following the Revolution of 1917, a succession of Soviet scholars published collections of Caucasian and Central Asian music notated during field expeditions (Uspensky and Belyayev, 1929, 2/1979; Romanovskaya, 1939; Zataevich, 1934, 2/1971) as well as social histories of music (Fitrat, 1927) and studies of musical instruments (Belyayev, 1933). The scope and emphasis of these early works to a large extent indicate the direction of subsequent work on the region.

Current research

Until the very last years of Soviet rule, fieldwork opportunities in the Central Asian and Transcaucasian republics were extremely limited for non-Soviet scholars. However, Soviet society's increasing openness in the Gorbachev era created the basis for new research initiatives in the humanities and social sciences. Most ethnographic research by foreign scholars has been collaborative, with a local scholar, and usually, a local institute or organization, providing a logistical and bureaucratic base within the Republics. Even if a great deal more territory is now officially accessible to foreigners, arranging research visits remains a cumbersome and bureaucratically complex procedure.

Since 1979, when Afghanistan was invaded by the USSR, access to that country has also been severely restricted for Western and Soviet scholars alike. In the late 1960s and 1970s, several Western ethnomusicologists did conduct fieldwork in Afghanistan, and the results of this work have been disseminated in articles, books and recordings (Slobin, 1976; Baily, 1977, 1988; Sakata, 1983). Afghani musicians living as refugees in Peshawar, Pakistan, have been the focus of a film by the British anthropologist and filmmaker, John Baily. With the exception of these studies of music from Afghanistan, scholarly publications on the music of West Central Asia have come largely from the USSR and its successor states. Even though Russian was the undisputed *lingua franca* of Soviet scholarship, several important musicological works from the Soviet period are in Central Asian or Caucasian languages. Some dual-language editions also exist in which Russian is accompanied by the major official language of one of the republics (Rajabi, 1978; Tbilisi State Conservatory, 1983).

The centre for research on the traditional music of Central Asia is the city of Tashkent, capital of the Republic of Uzbekistan. The Music Section of the Hamza Institute of Art Research (Khamsa Nomidagi San'atshunoslikInstituti), directed by F. M. Karomatov, conducts yearly expeditions to different regions of Central Asia to gather material for its extensive sound archive and maintains an ambitious publication programme that includes annotated collections of musical transcriptions as well as scholarly articles. Commercial recordings of Central Asian traditional music are released by the Tashkent branch of Melodiya, formerly the Soviet State record company. Recordings are plentiful and often of high quality, but beyond the rudiments of song titles and performers' names, record albums consistently lack documentary information about the music being performed. The Tashkent State Conservatory contains a department of Eastern music that trains young performers and music theorists, and the Tashkent radio station maintains several ensembles of traditional musicians. In a somewhat more popular vein, the Uzbek-language monthly *Sovet uzbekistani san'ati* prints many articles about music, musicians and musical lore.

Armenia, Azerbaijan, Georgia and Kazakhstan all have had similar institutions for the study and promulgation of indigenous traditional music, located in Erevan, Baku, Tbilisi and Alma-Ata. Dushanbe, Tajikistan, has an Institute of Arts. Kyrgyzstan and Turkmenistan are presently developing their own research centres.

In Western Central Asia, research by local scholars has focussed on the collection, transcription and publication of music from traditional sources, on the analysis of scales, melodic mode, metre and rhythm, and on the classification and characterization of musical genres with particular attention to the relation of musical form and prosodic structure. Rare are the sort of studies that have become increasingly central to American and European ethnomusicology, wherein music, musicians and music-making are examined as integral elements of a larger cultural Gestalt. This may in part reflect a tendency by local scholars to take for granted the social function of music in their own culture while outsiders are more likely to view 'social function' as an area of inquiry in itself.

Although indigenous musical terminology and musical concepts are studied by local scholars, analytical language and theoretical apparatus are chiefly drawn from Western music theory. For example, to designate 'modal' configurations and their melodic elements, Soviet folklorists and musicologists adopted the pseudo-Greek modal names which since the late 19th century have become increasingly identified – as others abandon them – with the Anglo-American folklore revival movement. This tendency was apparently part of an effort to synthesize for purposes both heuristic and comparative, a simplified and homogeneous morphology analytically applicable to the entire range of non-Western musics under scrutiny of Soviet investigators. Formulaic, motific or layered (e.g. Schenkerian) melodic analyses were regarded as overly abstract – lacking concreteness and reality in the actual music – and were eschewed in favour of an algebra representing large-scale formal divisions of pieces (e.g. $A\ B\ A\ +$).

Extant repertories that have received the most attention from scholars are those that represent the legacy of the musical great tradition of West Central Asia – the *maqam*. These include the Azeri *mugam* and the Uzbek and Tajik *shashmaqam*. In Georgia, polyphonic vocal music, both religious and secular, fills the role of a musical great tradition.

The *shashmaqam* and the *mugam* both assumed their present large-scale formal structure in the 19th century and underwent a process of systematization in the middle decades of the 20th century. In both cases, a single

302

individual – Uzeir Hajibeyov (1895–1948) in Azerbaijan and Yunus Rajabi (1897–1976) in Uzbekistan – was responsible for forging and reconstituting an authoritative musical system and repertory from disparate sources. Present-day performance practice as well as analyses of *mugam* and *shashmaqam* by local scholars rely heavily on the redactions of these men. Historical study of performance practice is restricted by the virtual absence of notation prior to the early 20th century (in the 19th century, some *shashmaqam* compositions were transcribed in a tablature system known as Khwarezm notation). However, theoretical treatises in the systematist tradition stemming from the mid-13th century *Kitāb al-adwār* of Safī al-Dīn al-Urmāwī, have been translated into European languages and analysed, most recently and most thoroughly by Owen Wright (1978). Many treatises that contain information about music survive in the archives of libraries and research institutes, particularly the Oriental Institute (Institut Vostokovedeniya) in Tashkent. Several young Uzbek musicologists have been trained in classical Arabic and Persian and are presently working on critical editions of treatises.

During the Soviet period, the hardening of political boundaries in Central Asia encouraged scholars to focus their research on the music of particular national or political units. However, as has become increasingly clear, these units often do not reflect the boundaries of ethno-linguistic entities or the congeries of cultural factors – ethnic, linguistic, religious and economic – that would more accurately delineate musical styles, repertories, and traditions. Ethnicity can itself be a grudging guide to both musical past and musical present. Centuries of commingling and consolidation of ethnic groups in Central Asia have made it difficult to correlate aspects of musical form, style and tradition to the histories of particular peoples. Conversely, a number of isolated ethnic groups still remain in the Caucasus and in the Pamir Mountains of Tajikistan whose languages are virtually mutually incomprehensible with those of nearby neighbours, and whose music has been little studied.

The investigation of what scholars trained in the Soviet tradition term 'professional oral tradition music' (e.g. *mugam, shashmaqam*), as well as that of folk music in Central Asia, awaits detailed comparative-analytic studies that are 'cross-cultural' within the region. The domination of research on Central Asian music by local scholars, whose primary focus is the music of their own region, creates additional obstacles to the establishment of such large-scale comparative studies that cross both international and intra-national lines. For example little work has been done on pan-Turkic elements in Central Asian music. Jean During has written about the similarities and common origin of the Iranian *dastgah* and the Azeri *mugam* (1985) and an Uzbek dissertation has reported on the relationship of the Azeri *mugam* to the Uzbek *shashmaqam*. Such comparative works are the exception rather than the rule.

Musicians' lives and social relations within the community in which they live have been the subject of three fine studies conducted in Afghanistan (Slobin, 1976; Sakata, 1983; Doubleday, 1988). In Uzbekistan and Azer-baijan, the canonized 20th century doyens of these republics' national musical traditions have been the subject of recent biographical accounts (Yunus Rajabi, Uzeir Hajibeyov). But local scholars have not produced anthropological studies of musicians, either individually, or as a social group, and this area of research remains untouched within Central Asia and Transcaucasia.

American and European conceptions of the study of ethnomusicology still contrast with those prevalent in the Central Asian and Caucasian republics. If ethnomusicology in the West is unequivocally interdisciplinary, the study of music in the Soviet Union and its successor states has remained divided between scholars trained in folklore, in musicology, and in 'Oriental Studies'. The strength of local scholars' work on Central Asia reflects the strength of these individual disciplines. Yet, they still await full integration into a discipline that could be called 'ethnomusicology'.

Bibliography

Afghanistan

M. Slobin: *Music in the Culture of Northern Afghanistan* (Tucson, AZ, 1976)

J. Baily: 'Movement patterns in playing the Herati *Dutar*', *The Anthropology of the Body*, ed. J. Blacking (London, 1977)

L. Sakata: *Music in the Mind: the Concepts of Music and Musician in Afghanistan* (Kent, OH, 1983)

J. Baily: *Music of Afghanistan: Professional Musicians in the City of Herat* (Cambridge, 1988)

V. Doubleday: *Three Women of Herat* (London and Austin, TX, 1988)

Soviet Central Asia

A. Fitrat: *Uzbek klassik muzikasi tarikhi* [The History of Uzbek Classical Music] (Tashkent, 1927)

V. Uspensky and V. M. Belyayev: *Turkmenskaya Muzika* (Ashkhabad, 1929, 2/1979)

V. M. Belyayev: *Muzikal'niye instrumenti uzbekistana* [Musical Instruments of Uzbekistan] (Moscow, 1933)

A. V. Zataevich: *250 kirgizskikh instrumental'nikh p'yes i napevov* [250 Kirghiz Instrumental Pieces and Melodies] (Moscow, 1934, 2/1971)

E. Romanovskaya: *Uzbek khalq kushiklari* (Tashkent, 1939)

V. M. Belyayev, ed.: *Shashmaqam* (Moscow, 1950)

I. Akbarov and others: *Uzbek khalq muzikasi/Uzbekskaya narodnaya muzika* (Tashkent, 1954–62)

V. S. Vinogradov: *Kirgizkaya narodnaya muzika* [Kirghiz Folk Music] (Frunze, 1958)

G. S. Golos: 'Kirghiz Instruments and Instrumental Music', *EM*, v (1961), 42

F. Karomatov: *O lokal'nikh stilyakh uzbeksoy narodnoy muziki* [On the Regional Styles of Uzbek Music] (Moscow, 1964) [Eng. trans. in *Asian Music*, iv (1972), 48]

Z. Zhanuzakov: *Kazakhskaya narodnaya instrumental'naya muzika* [Kazak Instrumental Folk Music] (Alma-Ata, 1964)

F. Karomatov and Yu. Rajabi: *Shashmaqam* (Tashkent, 1965–75)

J. Spector: 'Musical Tradition and Innovation', *Central Asia: a Century of Russian Rule*, ed. E. Allworth (New York, 1967), 434–84

M. Slobin: *Kirgiz Instrumental Music* (New York, 1969)

F. Karomatov: *Uzbekskaya instrumental'naya muzika* [Uzbek Instrumental Music] (Tashkent, 1972) [excerpts trans. in *Asian Music*, xv (1983), 11]

V. M. Belyayev: *Central Asian Music*, ed. and trans. M. and G. Slobin (Middletown, CT, 1975)

F. Karomatov and N. Nurjanov: *Muzikal'noe iskusstvo pamira* (Moscow, 1978–86)

F. Karomatov: *Uzbek Xalqi Muzika Merosi/Muzikaln'noe nasledie uzbekskovo naroda [v dvadtsatom veke]* [The Musical Legacy of the Uzbek People in the 20th Century] (Tashkent, 1978–)

Yu. Rajabi: *Muzika merosimizga bir nazar* [A View of Our Musical Heritage] (Tashkent, 1978)

D. A. Rashidova: *Makomi, mugami, i sovremennoe kompozitorskoe tvorchestvo* [Maqam-s, Mugam-s, and Contemporary Compositional Practice] (Tashkent, 1978)

O. Wright: *The Modal System of Arab and Persian Music, A.D. 1250–1300* (London, 1978)

M. Akhmedov: *Yunus Rajabi* (Tashkent, 1980)

N. Abubakirova and A. Kuliyev, eds.: *Turkmenskie narodni pisni* [Turkmenik Folk Songs] (Kiev, 1981)

Yu. Keldysh and F. Karomatov, eds.: *Professional'naya muzika ustnoi traditsii narodov blizhnevo, srednevo vostoka i sovremennost'* [Professional Oral Tradition Music of the Middle East and Central Asia and Modernity] (Tashkent, 1981)

F. Karomatov: '*Shashmaqam*', trans. T. Levin, *Asian Music*, xiii (1981), 97

A. Czekanowska: 'Aspects of the Classical Music of Uighur People: Legend vs. Reality', *Asian Music*, xiv (1983), 94

S. Zeranska-Kominek and others: 'Universal Symbols in the Bukharan *Shashmaqam*', *Asian Music*, xiv (1983), 74

T. Gafurbekov: *Fol'klornie istoki uzbekskovo professional'novo muzikal'novo tvorchestva* [Folklore Sources of Uzbek Professional Musical Creativity] (Tashkent, 1984)

T. Levin: 'The Music and Tradition of the Bukharan *Shashmaqam* in Soviet Uzbekistan' (diss., Princeton U., 1984)

J. Elsner, ed.: *Maqam, Raga, Zeilenmelodik: Konzeptionen und Prinzipien der Musikproduktion* (Berlin, 1989)

A. Jung: 'Quellen der traditionellen Kunstmusik der Usbeken und Tadshiken Mittelasiens', *Beiträge zur Ethnomusikologie*, xxiii (Hamburg, 1989)

Transcaucasia

U. Hajibeyov: *Osnovy azerbaydzhanskoy narodnoy muziki* [Principles of Azeri Folk Music] (Baku, 1945)

M. Ismailov: *Azerbayjan khalq musichisinin zhonrlary/zhanri azerbaydzhanskoy narodnoy muziki* [Genres of Azeri Folk Music] (Baku, 1960, 2/1984)

G. Chkhikvadze: *Osnovnie tipi gruzinskogo narodnogo mnogogolosiia* [Basic Types of Georgian Folk Polyphony] (Moscow, 1964)

D. Hajiyev, D. Danilov and others, eds.: *Azerbaydzhanskaya muzika* [Azeri Music] (Moscow, 1961)

F. Shushinskiy: *Narodnie pevtsi i muzikanti Azerbaydzhana* [Folk Singers and Instrumentalists of Azerbaijan] (Moscow, 1979)

S. Rustamov and others, eds.: *Azerbaydzhanskie narodnyie pesni* [Azeri Folk Songs] (Baku, 1982)

Tbilisi State Conservatory: *Lad, melodika i ritm gruzinskoy narodnoy muziki: sbornik nauchnikh trudov* [Mode, Melody and Rhythm in Georgian Folk Music: a Collection of Scholarly Articles] (Tbilisi, 1983)

E. Mansurov: *Azerbaydzhanskie daramedy i rengi* (Baku, 1984)

J. During: 'Azerbaijan: Musique', *Encyclopedia Iranica* (New York, 1985)

Z. Safarova: *Uzeir Hajibeyov* (Baku, 1985)

J. During: *La Musique Traditionnelle de l'Azerbayjan et la Science des Muqams* (Baden Baden, 1988)

CHAPTER XI

Eastern Central Asia

MIREILLE HELFFER

The second half of the 20th century has seen a considerable increase in our knowledge of the music of the Himalayan world (Nepal and areas of Tibetan culture), Central Asia and Mongolia. Musical instruments and sound recordings have been collected and lodged in the archives of many museums and educational institutions: discs, films and cassettes have appeared, constituting a basic body of material essential to any serious study. Before the 1950s, however, and sometimes even before the beginning of the 20th century, missionaries, travellers and Orientalists had described, noted down or recorded this music, which, unlike its Indian and Chinese neighbours, existed only in oral tradition and could not be approached by way of theoretical texts in the vernacular. Despite the progress that has been made, the standard of research remains uneven, varying from one to another of the countries, due to the difficulties of the subject as much as political conditions.

Areas of Tibetan culture

The establishment of a Moravian Brethren mission in Ladakh in 1885 enabled the Rev. A. H. Francke to do pioneering research into the oral literature and music of western Tibet over many years from 1898 to 1930; his findings were published often accompanied by musical notation in many periodicals in German and English. Another missionary, the Rev. Marion H. Duncan, who lived in the Batang area from 1921 to 1936, made valuable observations on the musical activities of the eastern Tibetans. However, despite the existence of several 78 rpm discs, brought out at the instigation of Sir Basil Gould between 1943 and 1945, not until the mass arrival of Tibetan refugees in the bordering countries in 1959 did work directed towards the knowledge of Tibetan music resume, just as tape-recording techniques were becoming common.

At the beginning of the 1960s, in the course of a mission undertaken for UNESCO, Peter Crossley-Holland, the musician and composer, collected the music for several discs that are now classics. Although he concentrated mainly on material relating to the ritual music of Tibetan Buddhism, he also turned his attention to folk songs (unfortunately he does not include the Tibetan texts). Later Ivan Vandor, also a musician by training, made an extensive study of aspects of Tibetan ritual music, with emphasis on the performance of instrumental music; he was the first foreigner to discover Tibetan musical notation for wind instruments.

As the Tibetan community in exile became organized (with centres developing around recognized religious personalities, and the creation of the Tibetan Institute for Performing Arts at Dharamsala), a new generation of researchers realized that a knowledge of Tibetan language and culture was essential for study of the music. Since the 1970s this approach has shaped my own work on the singing of the Tibetan epic and on Tibetan musical notation and also the studies of Ricardo Canzio and Ter Ellingson on the structure of ritual music in the Sa-skya-pa, Bka'-'gyur-pa and Bön-po schools.

During the same period, Tibetan exiles and the people of Ladakh and Bhutan have become aware of the necessity of preserving their musical traditions and began to collect song texts. Collections of Tibetan songs were also published in China.

With a better knowledge of Tibetan culture, it has become possible to understand the system of Tibetan musical notation for Buddhist chant, the drums, cymbals and trumpets and ritual dances. Examination of this wealth of material, concurrently with analysis of sound recordings, is now in progress; it ought to enable us to trace the broad outlines of a history of Tibetan music, in particular of the music of Tibetan Buddhism. Unfortunately studies of the different regional styles of Tibetan folk music have been comparatively neglected.

For Tibetan refugees, as for Tibetans living in the Autonomous Region of Tibet and in China, and for the people of Bhutan and Ladakh, contact with foreign music, whether Indian, Chinese or European, has varying consequences, but for the moment ritual music is still preserved in its traditional forms.

Nepal

We owe the first scanty observations on music of the kingdom of Nepal to British army officers in contact with Gurkha soldiers. The first recordings known in the West were made by the Dutch scholar Arnold Adrian Bake who combined the skills of a musician and Indologist; he collected primarily, first on cylinders (1931–2) then on tapes (1955–6), the music of the Newar people of the Kathmandu valley.

When Nepal opened its frontiers to Western research in the 1960s, ethnologists and linguists, followed by ethnomusicologists, began to make systematic sound recordings on tape. At the same time Nepalese scholars and writers, the best known being Dharma Raj Thapa, began collecting much information on the music of Nepal, musical instruments, the religious repertory, songs connected with the feasts of the Hindu and Buddhist calendar, repertories of musician castes such as the beggar-singers, *gâine*s. From 1961 onwards, a large corpus of the songs performed by the *gâine*s of the Kathmandu valley had been collected by Alexander-William Macdonald; this rich material has been subsequently studied by myself with a view for a joint publication (see Helffer and Macdonald, 1969). Between 1966 and 1969 my own field of research has extended to the *gâine*s of central Nepal and, with the collaboration of some ethnologists colleagues, to the tailor-musicians *damâi* and *hudkiya* (see Helffer, 1969 and 1977). It was only during the late 1980s that a young English ethnomusicologist was able to complete a fruitful fieldwork among the *damâi* in the Gorkha area and to justify the role of their auspicious music in the culture of Nepal (see Tingey, 1990).

For their part, German musicologists and scholars have concentrated on the music of the Newar of the Kathmandu valley, dealing mainly with musical instruments (see Hoerburger, 1975, and Wiehler-Schneider and Wiehler, 1980) and the repertory of various instrumental groups (see Wegner, 1986, 1988). Till now very few recordings of Newari music have been published in the West, and Laurent Aubert must be congratulated for the first compact disc of Newari music he has produced (Aubert, 1988). The music of the other ethnic groups of Nepal – Tharu, Gurung, Magar, Tamang, Limbu, Sherpa and so on – has so far been neglected. One must hope that these gaps will soon be filled since, with the development of the radio programmes and the spread of the official Nepali language through the whole country, there is the risk of a relative standardization of the specific musical repertories on a model which is itself influenced by Indian film songs and Western jazz or disco music.

Mongolia

The characteristic features of Mongolian music have attracted the attention of Russian travellers and scholars for years; it is significant that in 1909 A. D. Rudnev, while pursuing his own research, thought he should draw up a list of Mongolian tunes published by that date and reached a total of over a hundred. A Belgian missionary, Father J. van Oost, took a keen interest in the music of the Kuku-khoto area, which resulted in a series of publications in the journal *Anthropos* during the first two decades of the 20th century.

A major stage in the knowledge of the music of Inner Mongolia was reached with the work of Sven Hedin's Sino-Tibetan expedition, which enabled Henning Haslund-Christensen to make cylinder recordings in 1928; the same scholar pursued his musical quest as part of the Royal Danish Geographical Society expedition in 1936–7 and produced a series of discs which the Swedish musicologist Ernst Emsheimer analysed (1943).

The Stalinist era brought a halt to musical research in the People's Republic of Mongolia. Research was taken up with vigour towards the beginning of the 1960s, at a time when the Mongolian music previously collected had already undergone a partial process of 'folklorization' on the Soviet model. Monographs in Russian and publications in Mongolian proliferated, often accompanied by musical transcriptions – just preceding the first discs of Mongolian music published in the West. Thanks to recordings made in the field and to the tours of the official troupe of the People's Republic of Mongolia, researchers, whether students or musicians, whether Hungarian, French, English or Japanese, have embarked on detailed studies, mainly of the *urtyn duu* 'long song', the use of the *xöömij* (biphonic vocal technique) and the playing of the *morinkhuur* (fiddle). Few have followed the example of Gyorgi Kara, who combined a linguistic study with collection of the repertory of a single singer. Recent recordings reveal the progressive modification of vocal techniques, influenced as they now are by training in music colleges.

While we witness at present the development of compositions for orchestral groups – something foreign to the old tradition – it is to be hoped that ethnomusicologists will be given the opportunity to collect and analyse new material in both Inner Mongolia and the People's Republic of Mongolia, to document the originality of a musical tradition whose melodic richness risks impoverishment from contact with its Chinese and Russian neighbours.

Bibliography

Tibet
A. H. Francke: 'La musique au Tibet', *EMDC*, I/v (Paris, 1922), 3084

A. H. Francke and A. Paalzow: 'Tibetischer-lieder aus dem Gebiet des ehemaligen west-tibetischen Königreichs', *Mitteilungen des Seminars für Orientalischen Sprachen*, xxxiv (1931), 93–136

P. Crossley-Holland: *The Music of Tibetan Buddhism*, Unesco Collection – A Musical Anthology of the Orient, vol. 9–11, Bärenreiter Musicaphon 30L 2009–11 (1964?) [disc notes]

——: 'Form and Style in Tibetan Folksong Melody', *Jb für musikalische Volks- und Völkerkunde*, iii (1967), 9–69, 109

——: 'The State of Research in Tibetan Folk Music', *EM*, xi (1967), 170

——: 'rGya-gLing Hymns of the Karma-Kagyu: the Rhythmitonal Architecture of Some Tibetan Instrumental Airs', *Selected Reports in Ethnomusicology*, i/3 (1970), 80–114

W. Kaufmann: *Tibetan Buddhist Chant* (Bloomington, IN, 1975)

M. Helffer: 'Traditions musicales des Sa-skya-pa relatives au culte de Mgon-po', *Journal Asiatique*, cclxiv (1976), 357–404

G. Samuel: 'Songs of Lhassa', *EM*, xx (1976), 407–49

I. Vandor: *La musique du Bouddhisme Tibétain* (Paris, 1976)

M. Helffer: *Les chants dans l'épopée tibétaine de Ge-sar, d'après le livre de la course de cheval: version chantée de Blo-bzaṅ bstan-'jin* (Geneva and Paris, 1977)

R. Canzio: *Sakya Pandita's Treatise on Music: Rol-mo'i bstan-bcos and its Relevance to Present Day Tibetan Liturgy* (diss., U. of London, 1978)

M. Helffer: *Ladakh: musique de monastère et de village*, Chant du Monde LDX 74662 (1978) and LDX 274662–CM 251 (1989) [disc notes]

T. Ellingson: *"Don rta dbyangs gsum*: Tibetan Chant and Melodic Categories', *Asian Music*, x/2 (1979), 112–56

——: *The Mandala of Sound: Concepts and Sound Structures in Tibetan Ritual Music* (diss., U. of Wisconsin, 1979)

——: 'The Mathematics of Tibetan *Rol Mo*', *EM*, xxiii (1979), 225

J. Snyder: 'A Preliminary Study of the Lha Mo', *Asian Music*, x/2 (1979), 23–62

R. Canzio: *Les traditions rituelles des Bonpo tibétains*, OCR 558622 (1983) [disc notes]

M. Helffer: 'Le gandi: un simandre tibétain d'origine indienne', *YTM*, xv (1983), 112

A. Tsukamoto: 'The Music of Tibetan Buddhism in Ladakh: the Musical Structure of Tibetan Buddhist Chant in the Ritual *Bskaṅ-gso* of the *Dge-Lugs-pa* Sect', *YTM*, xv (1983), 126

M. Helffer: 'Essai pour une typologie de la cloche tibétaine *dril-bu*', *Arts Asiatiques*, xl (1985), 53

J. Norbu, ed.: *Zlos-gar* (Dharamsala, 1986)

D. A. Scheidegger: *Tibetan Ritual Music: a General Survey with Special Reference to the Mindroling Tradition* (Rikon/ZH, 1988)

M. Helffer: 'Organologie et symbolisme dans la tradition tibétaine: le cas de la clochette *dril-bu* et du tambour *damaru*', *Cahiers de musiques traditionnelles*, ii (1989), 33

——: 'Recherches récentes concernant l'emploi des notations musicales dans la tradition tibétaine', *Tibet: civilisation et société*, ed. Fondation Singer-Polignac (Paris, 1990), 59

Nepal
A. D. Percival: 'The Music of Nepal', *Unknown Nepal: an Anthology*, ed. R. N. W. Bishop (London, 1952), 115

Dharma Raj Thapa: *Mero Nepāl brahmana* (Kathmandu, 1959)

T. O. Ballinger and P. H. Bajracharya: 'Nepalese Musical Instruments', *Southwestern Journal of Anthropology*, xvi/4 (1960), 398

M. Helffer and A. W. Macdonald: 'Remarques sur le vers népâli chanté', *L'homme*, viii/3 (1968), 37–95; viii/4 (1968), 58–91

M. Helffer: *Castes de musiciens au Népal*, LD 20, 1969 [disc and notes]

——: 'Fanfares villageoises au Népal', *Objets et mondes*, ix/1 (1969), 51

F. Hoerburger: *Studien zur Musik in Nepal* (Regensburg, 1975)

M. Helffer: 'Une caste de chanteurs-musiciens: les *gâine* du Népal', *L'ethnographie*, lxxiii (1977), 45–75

A. H. Ross: *Catalog of the Terence R. Bech Nepal Music Research Collection* (Bloomington, IN, 1978)

S. Wiehler-Schneider and H. Wiehler: 'A Classification of the Traditional Musical Instruments of the Nevars', *Journal of the Nepal Research Centre*, iv (1980), 67–132

I. Shrestacharya and G.-M. Wegner: *Newar Music: an Illustrated Dictionary* (1984) [typescript]

C. Tingey: 'An Annotated Bibliography and Discography of Nepalese Musics', *ICTM UK Bulletin*, xi (1985), 4; xii (1986), 35

G.-M. Wegner: *The Dhimaybaja of Bhaktapur: Studies in Newar Drumming*, i (Wiesbaden, 1986)

L. Aubert: 'Les musiciens dans la société Newar', *Bulletin d'ethnographie du Musée de Genève*, xxx (1988), 31–67

G.-M. Wegner: *The Nâykhîbâjâ of the Newar Butchers* (Wiesbaden, 1988)

L. Aubert: *Musique de fête chez les Newar*, AIMP XIII, VDE Gallo CD–553 (1989) [disc and notes]

——: *NEPAL, Musique de fête chez les Newar*, Genève AIMP XII–CD553 (1989) [disc notes]

I. Grandin: *Music and Media in Local Life: Music Practice in a Newar Neighbourhood in Nepal* (Linköping, 1989)

C. Tingey: *Nepalese pancai baja Music: an Auspicious Ensemble in a Changing Society* (diss., U. of London, 1990)

Mongolia

J. van Oost: 'La musique chez les Mongols des Urdus', *Anthropos*, x–xi (1915–16), 358–96

N. de Torhout: *Dix-huit chants et poèmes mongols* (Paris, 1937)

E. Emsheimer: 'Preliminary Remarks on Mongolian Music and Instruments' and 'Music of Eastern Mongolia Collected by H. Haslund-Christensen, Noted Down by E. Emsheimer', *The Music of the Mongols*, i: *Eastern Mongolia* (Stockholm, 1943), 69–100, 101–197

H. Haslund-Christensen: 'On the Trail of Ancient Mongol Tunes', *The Music of the Mongols*, i: *Eastern Mongolia* (Stockholm, 1943), 13

B. Rintchen: *Folklore mongol* (Wiesbaden, 1960–72)

A. N. Aksenov: *Tuvinskaia narodnaia muzyka* [Tuvin Folk Music] (Moscow, 1964)

L. Vargyas: 'Performing Styles in Mongolian Chant', *JIFMC*, xx (1968), 70

G. Kara: *Chants d'un barde mongol* (Budapest, 1970)

S. A. Kondrat'ev: *Muzyka mongol'skogo éposa i pesen* [Music of Mongolian Epic and Song] (Moscow, 1970)

Urtïn duu [The Long Song], ed. Ulsïn Khevleliyn Gazar (Ulan Bator, 1970)

B. F. Smirnov: *Mongol'skaya narodnaya muzïka* [Mongolian Folk Music] (Moscow, 1971)

A. N. Aksenov: 'Tuvin Folk Music', *Asian Music*, iv/2 (1973), 7

R. Hamayon: *Chants mongols et bouriates*, Collection Musée de l'Homme, Vogue LDM 30138 (1973) [disc notes]

R. Hamayon and M. Helffer: 'A propos de "Musique Populaire Mongole", Enregistrements de Lajos Vargyas: coffret de deux disques Hungaroton Unesco co-opération, LPX 18013–14', *Etudes Mongoles*, iv (1973), 145–80

R. Hamayon: 'Quelques chants bouriates', *Etudes Mongoles*, vi (1975), 191

J. R. Krueger: '"Dix-huit chants et poèmes mongols" Revisited', *Etudes Mongoles*, vi (1975), 215

D. D. Dugarov: *Buryatskie narodnije pecne* [Buryat Folk Songs], i (Ulan Ude, 1980)

S. Gunji: 'An Acoustical Consideration of *xöömij*', *Musical Voices of Asia*, ed. R. Emmert and Y. Minegishi (Tokyo, 1980), 135

H. Hasumi: 'Understanding Mongolian Music', *Musical Voices of Asia*, ed. R. Emmert and Y. Minegishi (Tokyo, 1980), 142

S. Nakagawa: 'A Study of *Urtiin duu* – Its Melismatic Elements and Musical Form', *Musical Voices of Asia*, ed. R. Emmert and Y. Minegishi (Tokyo, 1980), 149

Trân Quang Hai and D. Guillou: 'Original Research and Acoustical Analysis in Connection with the *xöömij* Style of Biphonic Singing', *Musical Voices of Asia*, ed. R. Emmert and Y. Minegishi (Tokyo, 1980), 162

H. Zemp: *Le chant des harmoniques*, 16mm. film, CNRS Audiovisuel (1989)

CHAPTER XII

East Asia

ALAN R. THRASHER, DAVID W. HUGHES, ROBERT PROVINE

1: CHINA

ALAN R. THRASHER

Pre-imperial and imperial periods to early 20th century

The primary motivation for the growth of Chinese music scholarship over a 2500-year period rests in the traditional close association assigned to music in government theory. With the writing of the Confucian texts, beginning in the 5th century BC and during the next few centuries, comprehensive theories of music philosophy and pitch systems evolved. In function, these theories served to establish the principles of a refined music (believed to reinforce state-sanctioned norms of behaviour) and, through regulation of pitch systems, reconcile the state with the cosmological order. So important was the effort to bring all things into harmony that, in both the Zhou and early Han dynasties (before 1st century BC), offices of music were attached to the governments to oversee and coordinate this activity. Thus, in the early scholarship, the Confucian orientation was a powerful motivational force. Every important imperial compilation from the period of the Classics down to the 18th century has an extended section on music, including the large dynastic histories and imperial encyclopedias such as the 6th-century *Beitang Shuchao*, 14th-century *Wenxian Tongkao*, and 18th-century *Gujin Tushu Jicheng*. In this last-named important encyclopedia, for example, the music section is not included in the category of 'Arts and Sciences', but rather under 'Political Economy' (together with sections on the examination system, court ceremonies and military administration).

There are yet other motivations and orientations for scholarship in the imperial period. In the essays of the 3rd-century musician and philosopher Xi Kang, a well-developed music aesthetic reflecting Taoist philosophies is discussed for the *qin* zither. Literary writings and memoirs, such as those by Liu Xie (*c*500 AD) and Shen Gua (*c*1086), discuss musical matters from ethics and aesthetics to style and diction. The encyclopedias and dynastic histories include extensive documentation on the construction and use of musical instruments and biographies of important musicians and scholars. Practical treatises, mostly from the 13th century onward, document aspects of performance practice for the *ci* and *qu* songs and the *qin* zither. And of enormous importance to traditional scholarship is the collection of music in notation, with large collections from the 12th century onward. A good English-language survey of the types and orientations of traditional music scholarship in the Song dynasty alone (960–1279) is found in Rulan Chao Pian's *Sonq Dynasty Musical Sources and their Interpretation* (1967).

The large corpus of music scholarship and collecting from the 7th century BC to 1949 is indexed in the comprehensive bibliography *Zhongguo Yinyue Shupu Zhi* (Zhongguo, 1984, *ZGYYSPZ*). For the pre-imperial and imperial periods, ending with the fall of the Qing dynasty (1911), are 1859 entries, including classic texts, dynastic histories, encyclopedias, treatises and collections (the majority of which exist in unpublished manuscript). Owing to the topical listing, there is some duplication, and some important sources (such as the *Shijing* and the many *fu* poems) are omitted. For the post-imperial period of 1912 to 1949, there are 3198 entries, including historic studies, genre studies and collections, archival materials, and discographies, together with the numerous publications on Western music, music education reforms after the 1920s and revolutionary music.

The highly selective bibliography at the end of the present survey lists sources of the following types: Confucian classics and books of the philosophers with particular relevance to music, early poetic essays (*fu*) on music, treatises on music, collections of music in notation, literary works of importance and a few of the numerous dictionaries and encyclopedias (*leishu*) with large sections on music (but not the dynastic histories). Early 20th-century studies on specific topics are also listed, but discussed under contemporary developments. The entire listing is necessarily representative and publication histories are omitted.

The historic documentation touches upon many aspects of the old concepts and traditions, but focusses primarily on six areas, as follows.

ETHICS AND PHILOSOPHY (YUELUN) The ethics and philosophy of music, an area which is close to the centre of Confucian orthodoxy, is the dominant theme of the earliest writers. Most important are the classic texts attributed to Confucius and his disciples, especially the *Lunyu* of c5th century BC and the later *Yueji* (c1st century BC). In both books, music is treated largely as a medium to promote important values of the Confucian state. This philosophy is repeated and interpreted in works throughout the imperial period, including Liu Xie's literary masterpiece *Wenxin Diaolong* of c500 AD; Chen Yang's treatise *Yueshu* of 1104 (nearly half of its 200 chapters with commentary on the Confucian classics); Chen Yuanjing's *Shilin Guangji*, an encyclopedic compilation of c1270; and many later works. For the pre-imperial and imperial periods, 47 *yuelun* entries are listed in *ZGYYSPZ*, not including the music sections of the large compilations and dynastic histories.

PITCH SYSTEMS AND MODES (LÜLÜ) This area involves governmental attempts to establish the root pitch (*huangzhong*) of the cosmos and bring the theoretical pitch system (the 12 *lülü* chromatic pitches in particular) into correspondence with the cyclic aspects of the calendar. The earliest textual accounts to detail these theoretical developments are the *Guanzi* (4th century BC) and Lü Buwei's *Lüshi Chunqiu* (*c* 239 BC). In addition, it became known early in China that the circle of pure 5ths taken 12 times produces an interval sharper than the octave taken seven times. Initial attempts to shrink the size of the 5th and thus correct the discrepancy were made as early as the 2nd century BC and documented in the *Huai Nanzi* (Liu, *c*120 BC). With the publication of Zhu Zaiyu's treatises *Lüxue Xinshuo* (1584) and *Lülü Jingyi* (1596), this attempt was finally given a sophisticated formulation resulting in a type of equal temperament. The concept of mode (*diao*), which in the Chinese theoretical system exists in 5-note and 7-note forms, is well-documented in the 3rd-century BC dictionary *Erya* and other sources of the period. Summaries and interpretations of these theories of pitch and mode are found in most later treatises, including the 12th-century *Lülü Xinshu* (Cai, 1187) and 18th-century *Lülü Zhengyi* (Mei, 1713), among many other sources. For the imperial period, 149 *lülü* entries are given in *ZGYYSPZ*, without the large compilations.

RITUAL MUSIC OF THE COURT (DIANLI YINYUE) The musical ideals of Confucian philosophy and the historic pitch system are both strongly reflected in the style of the court ritual music, a tradition which forms a third area of scholarly interest. Between the 11th and mid-20th centuries, more than 80 treatises specifically on the ritual tradition (some including hymn notations) are listed in *ZGYYSPZ*, with the majority dating from the 17th century onward (Zhu, 1200; Liu, 1630; Qiu, 1840). The most widely available coverage of the theory, instruments, dance, costumes, and practice is found in the large general treatises on music. In addition, since court rituals were regular state-sanctioned activities, every important multi-volume encyclopedia and dynastic history routinely includes some discussion of the tradition. For other religious practices, *ZGYYSPZ* lists 30 sources dealing with Buddhist music and 26 sources on Taoist music.

MUSICAL INSTRUMENTS (YUEQI) Musical instruments are treated particularly well in the historic sources, though *ZGYYSPZ* lists only six books dealing entirely with instruments. The very early instruments are mentioned in the bone inscriptions (post-15th century BC) and *Shijing* (*c*7th century BC). Greater descriptive detail appears in later classic texts, such as *Zhouli* (which lists the known instruments according to the *bayin* '8-tone' classification system), and the dictionaries *Erya* (*c*3rd century BC) and *Shuowen Jiezi* (Xu, *c*121). Four centuries later, the 6th-century encyclopedia *Beitang Shuchao* (Yu, 6th century) provides important and well-documented information on pre-Tang instruments; and in the early 9th century, instruments are again systematically recorded in the Tang encyclopedia *Tongdian* (Du, 801), and later in the general music treatise *Yuefu Zalu* (Duan, 9th century). The most interesting, if not always accurate, record is Chen Yang's large 12th-century music treatise *Yueshu* (Chen, 1104). In 40 of the 200 chapters, the author discusses late Tang and early Song instruments in three categories, the 'refined', the 'barbarian', and the 'popular'. Of particular importance are the line drawings of most instruments, though these are the works of more than one artist and some are highly imaginative. Most of the later treatises and encyclopedias (such as Ma, 13th century, and Wang, 1619) also include ample coverage, with the monumental 18th-century encyclopedia *Gujin Tushu Jicheng* (Chen, 1725) providing a comprehensive review of earlier knowledge (e.g. over 700 pages on bells alone).

INSTRUMENTAL MUSIC (QIYUE) The one instrumental tradition which is documented more thoroughly than any other is that of the *qin* (7-stringed zither). In addition to lengthy coverage in the sources mentioned above, entire treatises are devoted to this instrument and its music. These include Cai Yong's 2nd-century treatise *Qin Cao*, Zhu Changwen's 11th-century *Qin Shi* (which contains a reprint of Xi Kang's 3rd-century essay 'Qin Fu') and Zhu Quan's large 15th-century treatise *Taigu Yiyin*. The *Taigu Yiyin* details aspects such as construction, stringing, tuning, performance techniques and ideology of the modes. The *qin* repertory is also the most comprehensively notated of all traditions, with more than 200 handbooks dating from the 6th to mid-20th centuries. The most prolific period of collection begins in the early 15th century with the printing of 63 notated pieces in the important *Shenqi Mipu* (Zhi, 1425). Among the many collections that follow, the 19th-century *Qinxue Rumen* (Zhang, 1864) and early 20th-century *Meian Qinpu* (Wang, 1931) are representative.

For the *pipa* (lute) repertory, 23 collections are listed in *ZGYYSPZ*, though the *Dunhuang Pipa Pu* (*c*9th century, a manuscript now held in Paris) is not included. Most *pipa* collections date to after the mid-18th century (such as Ju, 1790; Li, 1895; He, 1934). Collections of music for the *se* (large zither) date between the early 14th and 18th centuries and include the *Sepu* (Xiong, 1300). There are over 150 collections of repertory for the other more popular instruments, such as *zheng* (zither), *sanxian* (lute) and *di* (flute) in *ZGYYSPZ*. These mostly date to the 19th and early 20th centuries. The solo *erhu* (fiddle) repertory appears later, with several collections published in the 1930s and 1940s, including the compositions of Liu Tianhua (Liu, 1933).

The early 19th-century *Xiansuo Beikao* (Ming, 1814) is of particular importance for ensemble music. This source notates 13 pieces of music for string ensemble, showing full heterophonic detail of interpretation. With few other exceptions, the ensemble repertory is not well documented until the appearance of skeletal, single-line notations (in *gongche* and cipher systems) of regional repertories in the early 20th century (included within the 150 items mentioned above). The earliest of these include *Xiange Bidu* (Qiu, 1917) for the Cantonese repertory, *Xiaodi Xinpu* (Zheng, 1924) for the Jiangnan repertory, and others (Zhang, 1920; Yang, 1923).

VOCAL MUSIC (GEQU, QUYI, XIQU) The dominant Chinese vocal genres are of three broad types: *gequ* (songs), *quyi* (narrative), and *xiqu* (opera music). The first type, short songs often strophic in structure, is of numerous varieties dating between the 12th and mid-20th centuries. *ZGYYSPZ* lists over 1300 *gequ* entries, of which more than 90 per cent are war and revolutionary songs (1940s), school and children's songs (after 1920s) and composed songs (1940s). The remainder, about 100 entries, are historic songs and folk songs. The *ci* song, which became popular during the late Tang dynasty (618–907), is the subject of Zhang Yan's 13th-century treatise, *Ciyuan*. There are, in addition, *ci* of this period in notation, chiefly those composed by Jiang Kui (1195). Also, an important 14th-century treatise on singing is Zhi An's *Chang Lun*. In the late 18th century, scholars showed increased interest in the ancient classic *Shijing* ('Book of Songs', *c*10th–6th century BC), particularly in reconstruction of the lost melodies. The *Shijing Yuepu* (1788) is one of several such attempts. The collection and documentation of folk song and narrative for the most part began in the 1920s.

The vocal genre best represented in both theory and notation is *kunqu* (classical opera). Its principles are introduced in Wei Liangfu's famous treatise *Qulü* (1540). In 1610 another larger treatise of the same title was published by Wang Jide, followed by Li Yu's important 16-chapter treatise on vocal theory, *Xianqing Ouji* (1671). For *kunqu* collections between the 18th and mid-20th centuries, more than 1000 entries are listed in *ZGYYSPZ*, though most of these are unpublished manuscripts of separate acts. The important large collections include the 81-volume *Jiugong Dacheng Nanbei Ci Gongpu* (Yun, 1746), and the 24-volume *Liuye Qupu* (Zhang, 1911). Among the earliest studies of opera history and theory, those of Wang Guowei (1909) and Wang Guangqi (1934) are the most reliable.

The Peking Opera (*jingxi*) is not well documented until the early 20th century. Important collections date from the 1930s, and include Li Baishui's series *Pingju Huikan* (over 30 plays published separately) and Liu Tianhua's often reprinted collection of the interpretations of Mei Lanfang (1930).

Post-World War II developments

Contemporary Chinese music scholarship emerged in the years following the language and literature reform movement of 1919. Of the several important musical figures of this period, Wang Guangqi (PhD, Bonn, Germany, 1934) was probably most influential on the musicologists of the next generation (1926, 1931, 1934). During the years of war and internal conflict that followed, some scholars were active (Yang, 1937; Yin, 1945) but they had little opportunity to publish until several years after the new political order became established in 1949.

With the 'hundred flowers' pronouncement of 1956 (which eased earlier restrictions and encouraged scholars to become more active) came a flood of scholarly work on Chinese music. Much of this was carried out by the newly formed Chinese Music Research Institute (Beijing) and published in music journals, as collected articles, or in monograph form. The most honoured scholar of the 20th century, Yang Yinliu, was the director of this institute, and his many publications dominate the period. Among other scholars active during the mid-1950s, the names Yin Falu, Li Chunyi, and Cao Anhe stand out. Topics of publication include subjects of historic interest (history, pitch theory, old notation systems and instruments), development of the opera traditions, and repertory collection projects.

In the summer of 1957, the 'anti-rightist movement' sought to reverse the trend of liberal scholarship, and instead promote a scholarship that would better reinforce the prevailing ideology. Though some publication projects continued to be issued through the mid-1960s, for most of two decades music scholars were directed to turn out articles promoting the class struggle, praising Mao Zedong and the heroic efforts of the People's Army, and validating the new culture which served the needs of the workers and peasants. All scholars wrote articles on these themes. During the radical heights of the 'cultural revolution' (1966), countless numbers of old books and traditional instruments were burned, and scholars were sent out to the villages for 're-education'. Today, Chinese scholars make few references to publications of this period.

During these same two decades, music scholars in Taiwan, Hong Kong, Japan and the Western world became more active. In Taiwan, Liang Tsai-p'ing, Chuang Pen-li and Kao Tzu-ming (all from the Chinese mainland) promoted the mainstream Han traditions through their writings. In Japan, Hayashi Kenzō and Kishibe Shigeo wrote extensively on ancient Chinese music and its relationship with Japanese music; these are among the best writings of the period (with many translated into Chinese). In the West, Rulan (Chao) Pian, Laurence Picken and Fritz Kuttner continued the prevailing historical orientation in their documentation of the old traditions.

With the return of a more moderate government in the late 1970s, a second 'hundred flowers' movement emerged. Since 1979 the flow of scholarship has been staggering. Dozens of journals and occasional publications have been initiated by the conservatories and provincial presses. Regional research institutes have been greatly expanded and given more autonomy. Studies concerning every aspect of music, theatre and dance are being published and huge collection and recording projects instigated. Among the most active senior scholars have been Yang Yinliu (*d* 1984), Cao Anhe, Yin Falu, Wu Zhao, Li Chunyi, Huang Xiangpeng and Yuan Jingfang (all in Beijing), Chen Yingshi, Ye Dong and Li Minxiong (in Shanghai), Gao Houyong and Gan Tao (in Nanjing) and Huang Jinpei (Guangzhou). Many younger scholars are presently being trained.

ORIENTATIONS The primary focus of Chinese music scholarship up to the 1960s was upon historical developments. This discipline, known as *yinyue xue* ('musicology'), sought to document historic traditions based upon information in texts and old notations, together with the few surviving genres of the Han literati. The regional 'folk' traditions were largely neglected (with the exception of folk-song collection during the 1940s and documentation of major opera traditions) until the recent emergence of a second discipline, *minzu yinyue xue* (literally, 'nationalities' music study', a phrase which sometimes includes the term, *minjian*, 'folk'). This discipline, which today exists side by side with the older historic tradition (but is not entirely separate from it), seeks to document the many ongoing traditions in all their regional variants and to encourage their preservation. Both terms, 'folk' and 'nationalities', are misleading because many diverse types are represented. Indeed, some 'folk' genres preserve ancient traditions which the people themselves consider to be 'classical'. The recent tendency of translating *minzu yinyue xue* as 'ethnomusicology' is questionable, and is presently under review for possible modification (scholars have recently suggested 'sino-musicology' as a possibility). Ethnomusicology, as it is practised in the Western world, is a different discipline in many respects.

RESEARCH INSTITUTES Music scholars in the People's Republic of China (PRC) are typically members of research institutes, which in turn are often attached to

316

music conservatories. All are government sanctioned and funded. The most prestigious is the Beijing-based Zhongguo Yinyue Yanjiu Suo (Chinese Music Research Institute), established in 1954 under the Ministry of Culture and in association with the Central Conservatory of Music. The Institute, which attracts the most capable scholars and receives large government stipends, has a library of nearly 100,000 books, issues a regular journal and publishes numerous collections of reference materials. Research institutes associated with the other conservatories, especially those in Shanghai, Guangzhou, Shenyang, Xian and Chengdu, are less well-endowed but quite active. Because of China's huge labour force and prevailing socialist policies guaranteeing employment to all (under revision in the late 1980s), the institutes are usually quite large. At the major conservatories, as many as ten researchers have regular positions, though few teach classes. A full staff typically includes one or two senior members and a much larger number of younger scholars. Salaries are among the lowest of all Chinese jobs, though researchers often receive small subsidies for fieldwork and are always paid for articles published. This practice has had a stimulating effect on the recent cultural renaissance.

In regions where conservatories are absent, research is often conducted at the local universities, arts academies or local city-sponsored research institutes. In Xiamen (Fujian province), for example, several researchers are active at Xiamen University documenting Minnan music. In the smaller nearby city of Quanzhou (the oldest centre of Minnan culture), music research is conducted under the auspices of the Quanzhou Lishi Wenhua Zhongxin (Quanzhou Historical and Cultural Centre). In the city of Kunming (Yunnan province), research is being done on local minority musics by scholars attached to both the Yunnan Sheng Minzu Yishu Yanjiu Suo (Yunnan Nationalities' Arts Research Institute) and the Kunming Yishu Xueyuan (Kunming Arts Academy). Research projects are being carried out in many other cities with similar governmental support.

Music scholarship in Taiwan and Hong Kong follows the North American and British models. Scholars are typically faculty members at universities, with teaching obligations. Very often authors are paid for publication.

SOCIETIES Chinese music societies in the People's Republic of China assume a similar function to the institutes in sponsoring research and promoting traditional music, but differ in that their organization is defined almost entirely by interest. All have government funding. The largest is the Zhongguo Xiqu Yanjiu Yuan (Academy for Chinese Opera Research), which, under the direction of Zhang Geng, is engaged in publishing a large series of monographs on the regional opera traditions. Similarly, the Guqin Yanjiu Hui (Society for *Qin* Research), under the direction of Wu Jinglüe, is assembling a 20-volume series of historic materials (essays, handbooks, notations) for the *qin* (zither). The Guzheng Yanjiu Hui (Society for Zheng Research), directed by Cao Zheng, is also active, as are smaller societies for *pipa* and *erhu* research. There are other music societies with broader mandates. The oldest and most influential is the government-sponsored Zhongguo Yinyuejia Xiehui (Chinese Musicians' Association). Founded in 1949, with a branch in each province, the Association has many member musicians with diverse interests. They undertake some publishing, especially collections of traditional music in notation. The more recent Zhongguo Minzu Yinyuexue Xuehui (Ethnomusicology Society of China) was founded in 1980 for study and promotion of regional 'folk' traditions. Two conferences are held during even-numbered years, one for Han Chinese traditions, the other for minority traditions. In 1986, the Dongfang Yinyue Xuehui (Oriental Music Society) was founded in Shanghai; it holds occasional conferences and sponsors publications.

JOURNALS Journals may be classified in five general categories.

1. General circulation journals in the People's Republic. Approximately 20 Chinese-language journals dealing with music and theatre have wide circulation, including journals for folk song, children's song, popular music, composition, narrative and regional theatre traditions. For traditional music, the most significant are *Renmin Yinyue* (People's Music), a popular monthly, dating from 1950; *Yinyue Yanjiu* (Music Study), a scholarly quarterly, from 1958 (neither published during the years of the 'cultural revolution'); *Minzu Minjian Yinyue* (National Folk Music), a quarterly, from 1980; *Yueqi* (Musical Instruments), a bimonthly, from 1981; *Quyi* (Narrative Arts), monthly; *Wudao* (Dancing), bimonthly; and *Renmin Xiju* (People's Theatre), monthly, now renamed *Xiju Bao* (Journal of Dramatic Art). Though dealing only occasionally with music, but of importance to the study of archaeological finds of musical instruments and material culture, are the monthly journals *Kao Gu* (Archaeology) and *Wen Wu* (Cultural Relics). These journals are all printed in large numbers and available outside China by subscription.

2. *Xuebao*, journals of the music conservatories. Most of the nine music conservatories of China issue quarterly journals, most dating from the early 1980s. Best established are the *Zhongyang Yinyue Xueyuan Xuebao* (Journal of the Central Conservatory of Music), Beijing; *Zhongguo Yinyue* (Chinese Music), journal of the Chinese Conservatory of Music, Beijing; *Xinghai Yinyue Xueyuan Xuebao* (Journal of the Xinghai Conservatory of Music), Guangzhou; and *Yinyue Yishu* (The Art of Music), journal of the Shanghai Conservatory of Music. These are published in limited numbers and are intended primarily for internal circulation, though the *xuebao* from the largest conservatories are now listed for export. Regional traditions are well-represented in these publications.

3. Occasional publications by offices of culture and research institutes. Several local music periodicals are of high scholarly merit, including the *Quanzhou Lishi Wenhua Zhongxin Gongzuo Tongxun* (Newsletter of the Quanzhou Historical and Cultural Centre, published in Quanzhou), and *Minzu Yinyue* (National Music, published in Kunming). Other publications have emerged since the mid-1980s. Like the *xuebao*, these are printed in limited numbers primarily for internal circulation. Their contents are dominated by essays on local musics and instruments. The Beijing periodicals include the annual *Yinyue Luncong* (Collected Essays on Music), published by Renmin Yinyue; the annual *Yinyue Xue Congkan* (Musicology Series), and the more recent quarterly *Zhongguo Yinyue Xue* (Chinese Musicology), both published by the Chinese Music Research Institute; and the Beijing newsletter *Minzu Yinyue Gongzuo* (Work on National Music), a progress report on the general status of music research in China.

318

4. Journals in Taiwan. In Taiwan, *The Bulletin of the Institute of Ethnology, Academia Sinica* (Taipei) has published excellent studies during the 1960s and early 1970s on ancient Chinese musical instruments and Taiwan minority instruments (with summaries in English). The *Tunghai Ethnomusicology Journal* has published a single volume on Taiwan minority music (1974). For opera and narrative song, the journals *Guoju Yuekan* (Chinese Opera Monthly) and *Minsu Quyi* (Popular Narrative) are important. Articles on music are included in *Yishu Xuebao* (Arts Journal), published by the National Taiwan Academy of the Arts, *Minzu Yinyue* (National Music), and *Zhonghua Minsu Yishu Niankan* (Chinese Folk Arts Annual). With the exception of *Yishu Xuebao* (1966–), these journals date from the late 1970s and 1980s.

5. Western journals. *The Journal of the North China Branch of the Royal Asiatic Society* (Shanghai) has published some of the earliest studies on historic traditions, some undertaken in the late 19th century. *Asian Music* and *Musica Asiatica* contain many good articles on historic genres and regional traditions (together with studies on other Asian musics). *Chinese Music* contains a wide range of material primarily including short articles and translations, updates on contemporary developments, and orchestrations. *Chinoperl* is devoted to the vocal arts of opera, narrative, and folk song.

Post-World War II materials

BIBLIOGRAPHIC MATERIALS

1. *Historic sources* The standard Chinese-language bibliography of early books on music is the *Zhongguo Yinyue Shupu Zhi* (*ZGYYSPZ*), edited by the Chinese Music Research Institute (Zhongguo, 1984). This bibliography (which replaces Zhongguo (1962) and others in comprehensiveness) lists a wide variety of historic Chinese-language sources and notations from *c*7th-century BC to 1949. Entries are arranged according to topics, with a useful alphabetized index of abbreviated Romanized titles. Editions are differentiated and holding libraries in the People's Republic listed. A good selective bibliography of historic sources (including some 20th-century works) is found in Yang Yinliu's survey *Zhongguo Gudai Yinyue Shigao* (Yang, 1981, pp.1026–37). A standard English-language reference is Joseph Needham's *Science and Civilization in China*, iv/1 (1962), which selectively lists many pre-1800 sources in 'Bibliography A', and post-1800 sources (until 1960) in 'Bibliography B'. Another important index to a more limited holding of materials in the USA is the annotated 'Books on East Asiatic Music in the Library of Congress (Printed Before 1800)' (Wu, 1944). For archaeological studies and related texts, the most comprehensive listings are Feng Guang-sheng's catalogue of archaeological documents for music in the journal, *Yueqi* (1982–1984), and Kenneth DeWoskin's 'Sources for the Study of Early Chinese Music' (1989).

2. *Contemporary sources* The important Chinese-language music books of the 1950s and 1960s (including books by Japanese scholars on Chinese music) are listed in Cheung Sai-bung's *Zhongguo Yinyue Shilun Shugao*, ii (1975, pp.491–5). A selected number of these publications are reviewed in English in *Revue bibliographique de Sinologie*. A comprehensive bibliography of the works of three

predominant scholars of the 20th century is Han Kuo-huang's 'Three Chinese Musicologists: Yang Yinliu, Yin Falu, Li Chunyi', published in *Ethnomusicology* (Han, 1980, pp.483–529). For the large number of publications since the late 1970s, Chinese-language annual trade lists such as *Quanguo Zong Shumu* are the best sources.

3. *Chinese opera sources* Because of the special status of Chinese traditional opera, entire bibliographies are devoted solely to its sources. A good selective listing of historic sources is found in William Dolby's book *A History of Chinese Drama* (1976). For the Peking opera, extensive listings of materials are found in the bibliographies of D. Shih-p'eng Yang (1967) and Colin Mackerras (1972). In addition, many specialized listings are given in the *Chinoperl Papers*, such as I. Wong's of *kunqu* collections (1978) and C. K. Wang's of recent publications in Taiwan (1984).

4. *Western-language sources* For books and articles written in Western languages, the principal listing is Fredric Lieberman's *Chinese Music: an Annotated Bibliography* (1979). The second edition lists more than 2400 books and articles, with annotations. Up-to-date listings (without annotations) are found in 'Current Bibliography: Asia and Oceania' of each issue of the journal *Ethnomusicology*.

REFERENCE MATERIALS AND ANTHOLOGIES

1. *Publications by the Chinese Music Research Institute* The following reference tools are among the more important to have appeared since the mid-1950s: *Zhongguo Yinyue Shi Cankao Tupian* (Zhongguo, 1954–64), nine packets of unbound black-and-white photo reproductions (with descriptive notes) of musical instruments, historic notations, reliefs and stone rubbings on the subject of music making; *Zhongguo Gudai Yinyue Shiliao Jiyao* (Zhongguo, 1962), a large one-volume compilation in reproduction of 26 important music sections excerpted from the imperial encyclopedias dating between the 6th and 19th centuries; *Zhongguo Gudai Yuelun Xuanji* (Zhongguo, 1981), a one-volume compilation of historic passages relating to musical ethics and philosophy, excerpted from about 130 sources of the imperial period and reprinted in punctuated classical Chinese; *Zhongguo Yinyue Cidian* (Zhongguo, 1984), a one-volume music dictionary, containing 3560 entries on both traditional and modern subjects, together with biographical sketches of composers, performers and scholars and a useful 30-page topical index; *Yinyue Yanjiu Wenxuan* (Zhongguo, 1985), a two-volume collection of 81 articles selected from various Chinese-language music journals of the past 30 years; and *Zhongguo Yinyue Shi Tujian* (Zhongguo, 1988), a one-volume history of Chinese music in pictures. Publications of other reference materials are in preparation.

2. *Zhongguo Yinyue Shiliao* Another reproduction compilation of historic materials on music is the six-volume Taiwan publication *Zhongguo Yinyue Shiliao* (Yang, 1975). This series is more comprehensive than the Beijing collection (Zhongguo, 1962) in that it also includes sections from classic texts, dynastic histories, and the huge 18th-century encyclopedia *Gujin Tushu Jicheng*.

3. *Other reference materials* Reference materials on specific topics include: two multi-volume series of the most ancient texts and treatises, well annotated and translated into modern Chinese – the first a seven-volume series including

texts such as *Lüshi Chunqiu* and *Guoyu* (Ji, 1978), the second a five-volume series including the *Yueji* and other treatises (Ji, 1980); large one-volume dictionaries and encyclopedias of traditional opera and narrative (Wang, 1969; Shanghai, 1981; Zhang, 1983) and music and dance (Lü, 1989); collections of research materials and treatises on traditional opera (Ouyang, 1956; Zhongguo, 1959; Liu, 1965); a dictionary of famous historic personages in music, dance and opera (Cao, 1956); and an excellent dictionary on the musical instruments of minority cultures (Yuan, 1986).

4. *Comprehensive music anthologies* The most ambitious of all documentation projects ever attempted by Chinese scholars is the *Zhongguo Minzu Yinyue Jicheng* (Zhongguo Yinyuejia Xiehui, 1988), a huge anthology organized and edited by the Chinese Musicians' Association. This collection project documents in notation the surviving Chinese musical traditions, together with commentary and pictures. It is organized according to province, for which one or more large volumes each are given to the five categories of folk song, narrative song, opera music, instrumental music and *qin* music. The first volume to appear is on the folk songs of Hubei province (1988). When completed, this anthology will total approximately one hundred large volumes. Another anthology of smaller proportions is the *Zhongguo Minzu Yinyue Daxi* (Dongfang, 1989), edited by scholars of the Shanghai-based Oriental Music Society. One volume is given to each of eight categories: ancient music, opera music, instrumental music, narrative music, minority nationalities' music, folk song, dance-song music and religious music.

HISTORIC STUDIES

1. *Surveys* Several surveys of Chinese music history were written during the early 20th century, the most influential being Wang Guangqi's *Zhongguo Yinyue Shi* (1934). Following World War II, the celebrated music historian Yang Yinliu (whose publications number over 100) emerged as the pre-eminent scholar. His often reprinted book, *Zhongguo Yinyue Shigang* (1952), became the standard survey until his later two-volume revision *Zhongguo Gudai Yinyue Shigao* appeared in 1964 (most widely available in the 1981 edition). In this revision, the author documented the folk, art and court musics, musical instruments, theories and prevailing musical ideologies for each imperial period. At present, this work is the most comprehensive of all general surveys. Others of importance include the single-volume *Zhongguo Yinyue Shilue* by the Beijing scholars Wu Zhao and Liu Dongsheng (1983), which also attempts to put surviving traditions into historical perspective; the two-volume *Zhongguo Yinyue Shilun Shugao* by the Hong Kong scholar Cheung Sai-bung (1974); and the attractive four-volume Taiwan publication *Zhonghua Yuexue Tonglun* by Huang Tipei (1983), with one volume each given to music history, theory, instruments and notations. At the time of writing, no general Western-language survey (comparable to those of the Beijing scholars) has yet appeared, though introductions are available in the writings of Rulan Chao Pian (1980) and Liang Mingyue (1985).

2. *Shang-Zhou-Han periods* A major focus of Chinese musicology has been on period studies, with special emphasis on early developments. For Shang and Zhou dynasties (*c*16th–3rd centuries BC), the most active of the senior scholars is Li Chunyi. His major work, *Zhongguo Gudai Yinyue Shigao* (1958), is an

examination of Shang music based upon early inscriptions, archaeological finds, and later texts. Other of his many publications are listed under the section 'Musical Instruments'. Shorter studies include Yin Falu's investigation of early Han pitches (1944), Huang Xiangpeng's study of the ancient method of modulation based upon monthly cycles (1981), and many others. An excellent English-language study of musical concepts from the early Confucian period (following c5th century BC) is K. DeWoskin's *A Song for One or Two* (1982). The large studies of Tong Kin-woon (1983) and Fritz Kuttner (1990) are described under 'Musical Instruments'.

3. *Sui-Tang periods* The Tang period (618–907 AD) has attracted more scholarly attention than any other, a dynasty of extended cultural contact with other Asian peoples. Two Japanese scholars, Hayashi Kenzō and Kishibe Shigeo, have been particularly active in this field. Kishibe's work on Tang music history appears in the two-volume *Tangdai Yinyue Shi de Yanjiu* (1973, Chinese translation) and in an abridged English translation of an earlier book (1960). Hayashi's study *Sui Tang Yanyue Diao Yanjiu* (1936, Chinese translation) is an examination of the early modes of court entertainment music. His other Tang studies include examinations of the notation in the Dunhuang *pipa* manuscript from about the 9th century (1955, 1957), and major studies on musical instruments (below). The most active Chinese scholar in Tang music studies is Yin Falu. Among his early works is a detailed study of Tang-Song *daqu* form (1945; see also Wang, 1909). His later studies include examinations of musical developments along the 'silk road' (1951, 1980) and of early instruments. Western-language studies are represented by the recent four-volume project, *Music from the Tang Court*, edited by L. Picken (1981–87), the important German-language translation and analysis of the 9th-century treatise *Yuefu Zalu* by M. Gimm (1966), and E. Schafer's stimulating book on Tang culture, *The Golden Peaches of Samarkand* (1963).

4. *Song-Yuan-Ming periods* Fewer studies of post-Tang music have been made. The music of the 12th-century composer, Jiang Kui, has been thoroughly examined (Yang, 1957; Picken, 1957; Pian, 1967; Liang, 1980). Rulan Chao Pian's English-language *Sonq Dynasty Musical Sources and Their Interpretation* (1967) is an authoritative review of music literature between the 10th and late 13th centuries, with examination of modes and notations of the period. No period studies of the 14th century onward have yet appeared. However, the work of Zhu Zaiyu and 16th-century temperament theory has been studied (Kuttner, 1975; Yang, 1982; Huang, 1984). And the development of Yuan opera has been well-documented in English-language monographs (Shih, 1976; Crump, 1980; Johnson, 1980).

5. *Theory* The ethics and philosophy of music (*yuelun*) and the calculation of pitches (*lülü*) are treated as essential developments of the music systems of each period. Among the general studies, Wu Nanxun's Chinese-language book *Lüxue Huitong* (1964) is a thorough scientific study of the historic systems of pitch, temperament and mode. The standard English-language works are K. Robinson's study of theory and acoustics (Needham, 1962), and Nakaseko's study on symbolism in ancient theory (1957). Much is presently being published on theories of the 'folk' traditions, among which Gao Houyong's book *Minzu Qiyue Gailun* (1981) and a collection of articles on the structure of music (Zhongyang, 1986) stand out for their approach to several

genres of instrumental ensemble music. Another theoretical study is by He Luting (Ho, 1983) on scales and modes, translated into English by Han Kuo-huang. An important collection of essays on a variety of theoretical systems in common-practice music is the issue of *Asian Music*, 'Chinese Music Theory' (1989). Most studies on 'folk' theory, however, are journal articles on specific genres (cited below under 'Instrumental Music' or 'Vocal Music'). Historical notation systems are introduced in most general surveys and reference collections. Two volumes of Zhongguo (1954) are devoted to notations (shown in photo reproduction) and their transcriptions. For *gongche* notation, Yang Yinliu's introduction (1962) is good. In English-language studies, several systems are introduced in J. H. Levis (1936) and more thoroughly in W. Kaufmann (1967).

MUSICAL INSTRUMENTS

1. *Surveys* The documentation and study of musical instruments, already an important subject during the imperial period, became a particularly fertile field in the 20th century with entire monographs devoted to their development. The principal Han Chinese instruments are introduced in several short books (Zhongyang, 1957; Liang, 1982; Zhongguo, 1985), the latter two including minority and 20th-century reformed instruments. A larger general study is Cheng Deh-yuan's *Zhongguo Yueqi Xue* (1984), which examines backgrounds, construction and acoustics. The historic surveys of Yang Yinliu (1981) and Cheung Sai-bung (1974) include excellent chronological coverage. Introductory accounts in Western-language publications include a very good survey of the instruments known to A. C. Moule at the turn of the last century (Moule, 1908), an introduction by Liang Tsai-p'ing (1970), and the many entries in *The New Grove Dictionary of Musical Instruments* (1984).

2. *Shang-Zhou-Han periods* An extraordinary amount of research is currently being conducted by Chinese scholars on recent archaeological finds from tombs dating to about the 5th century BC and later, most results appearing in scholarly journals such as *Wenwu* (see *Wenwu* Index, 1986, and DeWoskin, 1989). Instruments found in the tombs of Mawangdui (Li, 1973; Li, 1974; Mok, 1978) and Zeng Houyi (Huang, 1979; Li, 1981; Hubei, 1980; Shen, 1986) have been well-examined. Studies on individual historic instruments have appeared by scholars on both sides of the Taiwan strait (Li, 1957; Yang, 1959; Chuang, 1963, 1965, 1966, 1972). Tong Kin-woon's English-language dissertation *Shang Musical Instruments* (1983) is a particularly thorough examination of the most ancient instruments, drawn from archaeological finds as well as literary documents. Another ambitious work which focusses on early instruments and temperaments is Fritz Kuttner's *The Archaeology of Music in Ancient China* (1990).

3. *Sui-Tang periods* For instrument studies of the Tang period (618–907), the Japanese scholar Hayashi Kenzō has been among the most active. His book *Dongya Yueqi Kao* (1962), a Chinese translation of the Japanese original, examines prototypes of the Japanese instrumentarium, and his jointly edited *Shōsōin no Gakki* (1967, with English summary) documents the physical characteristics of the instruments in that important 8th-century collection. A major recent study is Niu Longfei's book *Guyue Fayin* (1985), which examines at length the pre-Tang instruments represented in the Jiayuguan tomb paintings.

4. *Studies on individual instruments* The best-documented among the surviving Han Chinese solo instruments are the *qin* (zither) and *pipa* (lute). For the development of the *qin*, Xu Jian's *Qinshi Chubian* (1982) is a good historical introduction. (The monumental collection projects edited by the Society for *Qin* Research and others are cited below.) Standard English-language surveys include R. H. van Gulik's classic *The Lore of the Chinese Lute* (1940) and Liang's *The Chinese Ch'in* (1972). For the development of the *pipa*, the best account is Han Shude's *Zhongguo Pipa Shigao* (1985). English-language accounts include the articles by S. Kishibe (1940) and Picken (1955). Until recently, there has been only superficial examination of two other important instruments, the *zheng* (zither) and *sheng* (mouth organ). For development of the *zheng*, Cao Zheng (director of the Society for Zheng Research) has done recent important work on different phases of its evolution (1981); one of his articles is available in English translation (1983). Other studies include Cheng Deh-yuan's monograph (1977), Jin Jianmin's series in *Yueqi* on the ancient instrument (1982), and van Gulik's English-language introduction (1951). Gao Pei has been the most active scholar for documentation of the *sheng* (1986). Good introductions to other instruments are also found in the notes accompanying collections of music (below).

INSTRUMENTAL MUSIC

1. *Qin repertory* The collection of *qin* music in notation, another of the great achievements of the imperial period, has been continued through the mid-20th century. The most important collection work is presently being carried out by the Beijing-based Society for Qin Research, which is compiling the 20-volume *Qinqu Jicheng* (Guqin, 1963–), a comprehensive anthology of historic *qin* music begun in the early 1960s and now nearing completion. Another collection of importance is the three-volume *Ch'in-fu* (*Qin Fu*), compiled by the Hong Kong scholar Tong Kin-woon (T'ang, 1973). This includes a good cross-section of *qin* notations and handbooks, together with reprinted materials such as the *Guqin Qu Huibian* (Yang, 1956, with transcriptions in staff notation), and articles (such as Wang, 1957). Other studies on *qin* repertory include those by Yang Yinliu (1956) and Zha Fuxi (1956). English-language studies include Lui Tsun-yuen's introduction to *qin* technique and notation (1968), and F. Lieberman's translation and analysis of the handbook *Meian Qinpu* (1983).

2. *Zheng and pipa repertories* The *zheng* and *pipa* repertories have been slightly less well-preserved than the *qin*. In Taiwan active promotion of the *zheng* by Liang Tsai-p'ing has led to many publications; his two-volume *Guzheng Duzou Qu* (1978) is a good collection of *zheng* melodies from North China. In the People's Republic, the several regional *zheng* repertories have been reasonably well-collected in notation (Lin, 1980; Luo, 1985; Cao, 1986). Chen Anhua's brief comparison of Chaozhou and Hakka *zheng* musics (1982) introduces some important differences. Unfortunately, the historic *pipa* repertory has not been as well preserved in notation, though with the recent reprinting of 18th- and 19th-century collections (Lin, 1983; Li, 1982), some of this repertory is now more accessible.

3. *Ensemble traditions* Documentation of instrumental ensembles and their repertories was mostly neglected until the 1980s. Several short articles written in the 1950s and 1960s (Qin, 1958; Huang, 1960) identify the broad

outlines of ensemble musics, but the first good general study is Gao Houyong's book *Minzu Qiyue Gailun* (1981), an overview of ensemble organization, melodic sources and structures for various ensemble types. Other scholars dealing with ensemble repertories include Ye Dong (1983) and Li Minxiong (1983), the latter giving analyses for a large number of traditional ensemble and solo pieces. A good English-language introduction to ensemble development is Han Kuo-huang's discussion of the modern Chinese orchestra (1979).

4. *Regional ensemble repertories* The numerous regional repertories are reasonably well-collected in notation, but still not adequately studied. The following publications, organized according to region (from south to north) include both collections (in cipher notation) and studies.

For Hakka and Chaozhou traditions (eastern Guangdong province), the collections of Zhang Hanzai (1958), Luo Xu (1982), Luo Dezai (1982) and Chen Tianguo (1987) are standard. Historical backgrounds of Chaozhou music are examined by Chen Leishi (1978) and Chen Tianguo (1985), among others, and structural relationships between the Hakka and Chaozhou traditions by Alan Thrasher (1988).

For Guangdong (Cantonese) music (southern Guangdong province), the collections of Li Ling (1956), Taiping Shuju (1975) and Ning Yi (1983) are among the best sources. Backgrounds are well-documented in the writings of Huang Jinpei (1982, 1983, 1984).

For Minnan music (southern Fujian province and Taiwan), the early collection (in *gongche* notation) by the Philippine musician Lao Hong-kio (1953) is among the most important, a selection of which has been transcribed into staff notation and arranged in score form (Lao, 1973). Good scholarly works on Minnan music have been issued by Taiwan scholars, Lü Chuikuan's books (1982, 1986) and Nora Yeh's dissertation (1985) being the most thorough. In the People's Republic, the collection series *Zhipu Daguan* (Quanzhou, 1979) is important, and excellent articles are found in the *Journal of the Quanzhou Historical and Cultural Centre* (such as He, 1984 and Huang, 1984).

For Jiangnan music (central-eastern China), there are several collections of *sizhu* ('silk-bamboo'), the largest by Gan Tao (1985). Sizhu studies include Gao Houyong's book (1981), a good short introduction by Jin Zuli (1980), Thrasher's English-language examination of form (1985) and J. L. Witzleben's dissertation (1987). Jiangnan *luogu* ('gong-drum') music and other related types are found in collections by Cheng Wujia (1957) and Yang Yinliu (1982).

For ensemble music of the Northeast, collections of music from Shandong province dominate (Shandong, 1982; Zhongguo, 1984), though new publications are being issued at regular intervals.

VOCAL MUSIC

1. *Opera surveys* Opera is unquestionably the most popular genre of entertainment music in traditional culture. Its development is well-documented, though better in social and literary aspects than in structure. The opera scholar Zhou Yibai, active in the 1930s, published a good three-volume survey of Chinese opera (1953). However, the recent large survey by Zhang Geng and Guo Hancheng, *Zhongguo Xiqu Tongshi* (1980, also in three volumes),

is now considered to be the best of its kind. For Western-language surveys, W. Dolby's *A History of Chinese Drama* (1976) gives an excellent overview of the entire development, with a good general bibliography. Other bibliographies (Yang, 1967; Mackerras, 1972; Wong, 1978; Wang, 1984), opera dictionaries (Wang, 1969; Shanghai, 1981) and reference materials (Ouyang, 1956; Liu, 1965; Zhongguo, 1959; Zhang, 1983) are also available (listed above under 'Reference Materials').

2. *Kunqu* The 'classical' opera, *kunqu*, established in central-eastern China during the 16th century, is well documented in historic sources and collections (cited above) and in contemporary studies. The best general history is Lu Eting's *Kunqu Yanchu Shigao* (1980). More specialized in scope are studies on the principles of singing (Han, 1948; Chen, 1977; Wang, 1982) and a good collection in cipher notation of interpretations by the famous singer, Yu Zhenfei (1982). For Western-language surveys, Wang Guangqi's German dissertation (1934) and J. Hung's *Ming Drama* (1966) are useful. In addition, good specialized studies are found in the journal *Chinoperl Papers* (for example, Frankel, 1976; Strassberg, 1976; and Mark, 1983).

3. *Jingxi* The Peking opera, *jingxi*, which emerged in North China during the 18th century, is the best-known of the many regional opera variants. Collecting activity, well under way in the 1930s with publication of interpretations by Mei Lanfang (Liu, 1930) and others (Li, 1936; Yan, 1937), has continued, the recent series *Jingju Qupu* (He, 1983) being especially useful. For Chinese-language surveys, Liu Jidian's *Jingju Yinyue Gailun* (1981) is one of the largest. Specialized studies focus on the lives of famous performers and musicians (Xu, 1958; Scott, 1959; Wu, 1981) and the distinctive melody-types (Zhang, 1984; An, 1985; Liu, 1986). Two excellent surveys in English are A. C. Scott's *The Classical Theatre of China* (1957) and C. Mackerras's *The Rise of the Peking Opera 1770–1870* (1972).

4. *Other regional opera traditions* The study and collection of the several hundred regional opera traditions began in the 1940s and 1950s, but in-depth documentation projects were initiated only very recently. Among the important early books to be published are study-collections of southern Jiangsu opera (Jiangsu, 1955), Shanxi *jinju* (Zhang, 1955), Fujian *chensan wuniang* (Li, 1956), Guangdong *yueju* (Chen, 1956; Lin, 1958), and the northern *yangge ju* (Zhang, 1962). There are good studies by Taiwan scholars on the popular *gezaixi* of southern Fujian and Taiwan (for example, Lü, 1961; Zhang, 1982). Many books are being published in the large 'Opera Music Research Series' (Beijing), including thorough studies of Henan *yuju* (Wang, 1980), Hunan *xiangju* (Zhang, 1981), and Guangdong *yueju* (Huang, 1984). English-language studies have focussed mostly on Guangdong opera (Yung, 1983, 1989) and its preservation in North America (Leung, 1977; Riddle, 1983).

5. *Narrative* One of the oldest and richest genres of Chinese entertainment, *quyi* narrative exists in over 260 regional variants and is of several broad types (defined by length, conventions of presentation, region and use of instruments). Among the Chinese-language studies are an excellent history of *shuoshu* story-telling (Chen, 1958) and studies of Shandong *dagu* (Yu, 1957), *tanci* of central-eastern China (Lian, 1979), *kuaishu* of northern China (Chen, 1982), *nanyin* and other Guangdong narrative types (Cai, 1978). The major variants of these and other types are briefly introduced in the opera-narrative

dictionary *Zhongguo Xiqu Quyi Cidian* (Shanghai, 1981) and early essays collected in *Quyi Luncong* (Fu, 1954). For English-language studies, the genre as a whole is well introduced by C. Stevens (1980), and *Chinoperl Papers* contain many articles on individual types, including Tsao Pen-yeh's introduction to *pingtan* (1976), J. Walls's study of *kuaibanshu* (1977) and Rulan Chao Pian's translation of a *dagu* singer's autobiography (1984–5). C. Stevens's dissertation *Peking Drumsinging* (1972) and Tsao Pen-yeh's book *Su-chou T'an-tz'u* (1987) are major studies of these types.

6. *Nanguan qu* The important historic genre *nanguan qu* of Minnan song (Fujian province), also known as *nanyue* and *nanyin*, is best documented by Taiwan scholars such as Lü Chuikuan (1982) and Hsü Tsang-houei (1982). In the People's Republic, research is now being carried out in Xiamen and Quanzhou, with many articles in the Quanzhou journal (see 'Instrumental Music'). A collection series of songs (in cipher notation) is also in progress (Quanzhou, 1980).

7. *Folk song* Chinese folk song (*minge*), like narrative, exists in many regional styles. At present, collecting has far outweighed research. Two good recent collections are the four-volume *Zhongguo Minge* (Zhongguo, 1980), which includes a large selection of traditional, modern, and revolutionary songs for each province; and the two-volume collection *Zhongguo Minzu Geyao Xuanji*, published in Taiwan (Song, 1982), also arranged by province and including English summaries. A good general study of folk song is Jiang Mingdun's *Hanzu Minge Gailun* (1982). Of the separate regional traditions, Hakka folk song has been the best collected (Yang, 1974) and studied (Char, 1969; Yang, 1982; Lai, 1983), though numerous other studies and collections are being published.

MINORITY CULTURES The musical traditions of the numerous non-Han minority cultures have not received great attention until recently and are virtually unknown in the Western world. Among the earliest studies are those on Miao music (southwestern China) by the Chinese Music Research Institute (Zhongguo, 1958, 1959). For the music and instruments of minorities in Taiwan, studies include several good articles with English summaries (Ling, 1961; Li, 1967; Lü, 1974), and Hsü Tsang-houei's two-volume collection *Taiwan Shandi Minyao* (1978). Another good Taiwan publication is Hakan Chulun's collection of Mongolian songs (1972). On the Chinese mainland, minority studies have expanded rapidly since the early 1980s. Among the many collections and introductory articles (most of which appear in the journals *Yueqi* and *Minzu Yinyue*), the following are representative (identified by culture): Dong (Zhou, 1981), Dai (Yuan, 1981), Yi (Yuan, 1982; Liangshan, 1982; Zhang, 1985), Korean (Yun, 1983), Naxi (Yuan, 1984; Kou, 1984), Yao (He, 1986), Bai (Dali, 1986), Zhuang (Feng, 1985) and Lisu (Xiao, 1985). An overview of many of these traditions is found in Yang (1984), and instruments examined in Yuan (1986). Western-language studies include the Sino-Swedish expedition's early study of Mongolian music (Emsheimer, 1943), Mackerras's study of Uygur music (1985), and Thrasher's monograph on Yi dance-songs (1990).

20TH CENTURY: TRENDS, *GUOYUE* AND REVOLUTIONARY MUSIC Beginning in the

1930s, there were many changes in Chinese music, including new musical ideals, the development of a modern Chinese orchestra and its associated repertory, and the emergence of a new music education system. Some of these trends and institutions are introduced in Gao Ziming's book *Xiandai Guoyue* (1959). Good English-language summaries of these developments have been contributed by A. C. Scott (1963, 1980) and Han Kuo-huang (1979, 1980). The *guoyue* ('national music') repertory, a pan-Chinese genre of composed music for concert-hall presentation, is well preserved in notation. Among the important early collections are the *erhu* and *pipa* compositions by Liu Tianhua (Liu, 1933), others for the same instruments by the blind folk musician A Bing (Yang, 1952), and *dizi* (flute) compositions by Liu Guanyue (Liu, 1956) and Feng Zicun (Zhongyang, 1958). *Guoyue* ensemble repertory of the 1940s to 1960s is found in several People's Republic collections (Wenxue, 1955; Guangdong, 1973, 1977), and more recent trends are well summarized by Hu Dengtiao (1982). In Taiwan, the collections of Sun Peizhang (c1970), Huang Tipei (1960, including traditional music as well), and Xia Yan (1979) are representative.

The revolutionary doctrine of using music in the service of Communist ideals is particularly well documented. The thoughts of Mao Zedong and Jiang Qing are available in English translation (Mao, 1942/1967; Jiang, 1968). Many Chinese-language articles on these themes are published in music journals dating from the late 1950s (such as *Renmin Yinyue*), with earlier articles collected in the three-volume series *Yinyue Jianshe Wenji* (Zhongguo, 1959). Some of these issues are introduced in the English-language writings of Kagan (1963), Mackerras (1973), Wong (1984), and Perris (1983). The revolutionary songs of the 1960s (now out of favour) are notated in numerous collections, among them *Zhandi Xinge* (Guowu, 1972). Scholars on the Chinese mainland are showing a renewed interest in the early 20th century, with studies on a wide range of topics, from early school songs (Da, 1982) to biographies of famous national composers such as Xian Xinghai (Ma, 1980) and Nie Er (Nie, 1981).

Perspectives

SPECIAL CHALLENGES FOR THE FIELDWORKER Aside from questions of language, fieldwork techniques, ethics, and equipment (basic to work in any area), the following challenges are of particular importance in conducting fieldwork on Chinese music.

1. *Taiwan and Hong Kong as laboratories* Taiwan and Hong Kong (and most overseas Chinese communities) are dominated by regional populations from South and Southeast China. In Taiwan, the Minnan and Hakka musical traditions are well represented and well preserved (though they now differ in detail from those on the mainland); the tribal musics are related to those of the Philippines and other Pacific islands; the musics of North and central-eastern China (mostly introduced in the 1940s) are marginally represented in the city of Taipei, with fair representation of *qin*, *kunqu*, and *jingxi* (Peking opera). The *guoyue* ('national music'), however, is now very different from that played on the mainland. In Hong Kong, Guangdong and Chaozhou traditions domin-

ate, though other musics of South China are also occasionally found; traditions of more northern areas are for the most part absent, with the exception of *qin* and *jingxi* (which are preserved in southern variants); the *guoyue* is also largely different from that on the mainland. The numerous regional variants of opera, narrative, folk song, and instrumental music from northern areas of China are rarely performed in Taiwan or Hong Kong, and then to essentially foreign, or isolated, audiences.

2. *Local differences* In the preservation of 'folk' traditions, differences show up typically in form, style, and performance environment from city to city and ensemble to ensemble within the same subculture (e.g., Minnan music preserved in Xiamen, Quanzhou and Taipei). While there is generally a core of stylistic similarity within a regional tradition, many elements of its performance are not standardized for the entire region. These differences should be remembered before using the music of one city alone to characterize the subculture as a whole.

3. *Official and private research environments in the People's Republic* Chinese government policy toward foreign scholars changes regularly, and at any given time it is interpreted differently from one city to another. In general, it is proper for the foreign scholar to establish an official relationship with an organizational 'unit' (possibly a research institute, conservatory or ensemble) and work from that base. This official relationship makes rural or isolated traditions more accessible, though its implementation is often burdensome and very expensive when research fees are extracted. Scholars working in 'open cities' may, in fact, establish their own contacts and work privately with informants. However, some informants will fear government criticism of this practice because policies change and enforcement is selective. Some cities (especially those in the south, such as Guangzhou, Shantou and Xiamen) reflect the recent liberalization of policies and relaxation of government restrictions. The music is fairly accessible and private contacts can be established without great difficulty. Northern urban areas (such as Beijing and Shanghai) are more tightly controlled by the central government and display greater resistance toward the liberalization movement. Informants tend to be more cautious. At the gates of state-supported musical instrument factories and professional ensemble rehearsal buildings, guards carefully screen visitors, admitting those with recognized introductions to special reception rooms (where the flow of information is controlled and/or concerts pre-arranged). In the cities between these extremes (such as Kunming and Quanzhou), policies may be implemented arbitrarily, the result being that admission requests denied by a local Office of Culture may never even be questioned at the entrance gate. The amateur musical world, on the other hand, is larger than the professional world – and is, of course, more representative of the older milieu than is the highly polished ensemble. Since the late 1970s, amateur musical activity in all geographic areas is again flourishing. Afternoon or evening 'musical meetings', whether held in the teahouse, club-room or park, are now unregulated and easily accessible.

4. *Access to materials* In the People's Republic, policies of censorship and distribution restrict the availability of some publications (though these policies are reviewed yearly). At present only a select number of the many journals published in China are marked for external circulation (though these

can be obtained in China and personally taken out). Books, their publication better controlled by the central government, are routinely cleared for export. However, owing to the nature of the distribution system, they are usually more widely available in Hong Kong and on Western export lists (where they command higher prices) than in the bookstores of China itself. Access to library materials must not be assumed. The scholar may need special permission to gain entrance to libraries, and usage of material is restricted.

5. *Tradition and change* In the Chinese system, the dichotomies of 'old–new' and 'traditional–modern' are quite commonly employed by music scholars. These terms, however, must be used with care because each contains elements of the other. The term 'traditional', for instance, carries different meanings from one subculture to another. In South China it is used to identify both the centuries-old genres of the very conservative Hakka subculture, and the inherited repertory and 1930s compositions of the highly adaptable, innovative Cantonese subculture. As another aspect of this issue, scholars of the conservative traditions are in the habit of discussing the 'preservation' of ancient practices (e.g. Song dynasty music for the Hakka), implying there has been no change over a nearly one-thousand-year period. The mechanisms of this process need careful analysis before such assertions can be sustained, since most of these traditions have been passed on through oral transmission – a process in which change in some form is usually an integral part. Finally, the new professional ideal of the 20th century, involving fixed renditions and carefully rehearsed performances, has become an important force of change over both the old and new layers of music. These concepts need to be approached and described with great sensitivity.

RESEARCH AREAS IN NEED OF ATTENTION Because of the strength of China's long literary tradition, the study of music by Chinese and Western scholars alike has usually meant the study of historic or literati traditions. This orientation is solidly established, with research methods drawn from Sinology and historical musicology. For an ethnomusicology of Chinese music to take root (and I would suggest that it is at the margins of scholarship at present), a better balance needs to be sought between the historic and ethnographic perspectives on one hand, and literati and 'folk' traditions on the other. The application of ethnomusicological perspectives to the following areas and processes will assist in achieving this balance:

1. *Concept of 'music culture'* In China the cultural pluralism is great, not merely between the Han Chinese and minority (tribal) traditions, but also among Han traditions themselves. Therefore, the concept of 'music culture' must not be taken for granted. While the regional Han subcultures (e.g. Shandong, Jiangnan, Minnan, Hakka and many more) exhibit some shared musical characteristics, their specific differences are also quite pronounced. Is there a model of 'Chinese music' among these regional variants? Which characteristics are shared and which unique? Similar regional diversity has also existed in China's past, the most frequently cited example of this being the international Tang dynasty (618–907 AD). But, it is becoming clear from recent archaeological finds that more ancient periods were also quite pluralistic. What can be known about these historic regions and their music systems? Are there relationships between the surviving Han Chinese music cultures of

today and the historic music cultures about which we have some written information? And what has been the nature of interaction between Han Chinese music cultures and those of the old tribal cultures? It must be admitted that music scholars are at a great disadvantage in attempting to conduct culturally responsible work in these areas because neither the ethnohistory nor ethnography of China has yet been written.

2. *Music within culture* Chinese music at all times is related to cultural functions, from chamber and tea room entertainment to the accompaniment of lion dances, Confucian shrine rituals or the promotion of Communist ideologies. While each functional type represents one part of the whole, there are important aesthetic differences among them, which in effect demonstrate the various functional influences on music. For instance, in the entertainment genres, many old social ideals and literary stories are reflected in musical styles (especially in modes and tempos) and texts (or titles). Significantly, Chinese performers and listeners alike assign high importance to these associations. With a view towards understanding the deep cultural implications underlying Chinese music, ethnomusicological scholarship must seek to identify the specific symbolic values associated with both individual pieces (or operas) and entire repertories.

3. *Theory and the 'folk' traditions* The historic system of court music theory, primarily involving modes and temperaments, has been reasonably well analysed (though better in Chinese than Western sources). But the relationship between this body of theory and the numerous 'folk' genres (those in common practice) is not clear. In fact some striking differences between them in both modal organization and temperament suggest the possibility of a separate, centuries-old system of common theory having existed alongside the court theory. With the application of more sophisticated methods of analysis, the concepts of common-practice music – including the use of melodic models, fixed-beat forms, modal shift and modulation, simultaneous improvisation, and compositional practice – will become better understood.

4. *Chinese music within the Asian context* What are the relationships between Chinese musical traditions and those of non-Chinese peoples of Asia? Among the many relationships deserving better scrutiny are the following: the influences from Central and South Asia upon Chinese music throughout history (e.g. ancient horn and drum types, Buddhist songs and texts, the historic tribute orchestras during the Tang and Mongol influence during the Yuan); Chinese musical influence upon other East Asian traditions (e.g. court musics in Korea, Japan and Vietnam, the instrumental musics of the Chaozhou and Thai peoples, the *zheng* and related East Asian zither traditions); and the possibility of ancient East Asian musical influence on the New World (especially in tangible objects such as musical instruments). Of course, the retracing of history and the old cultural influences from incomplete documentation often causes insurmountable problems for the scholar (to say nothing of the problems caused by some nationalistic assumptions). But even when cultural contact cannot be shown with great precision, good comparative studies can be made of such aspects as melodic structures, temperaments and instrument forms. This work must be undertaken by scholars trained in musical analysis and the problems associated with comparative studies as well as in both geographic areas of comparison.

331

Bibliography

Bibliography is selective and representative of diverse areas of scholarship. General music anthologies are listed under REFERENCE MATERIALS. Studies on theoretical subjects are listed under HISTORIC STUDIES or under INSTRUMENTAL MUSIC or VOCAL MUSIC, depending upon orientation. Collections of music in notation are listed under INSTRUMENTAL MUSIC, VOCAL MUSIC or 20TH CENTURY, and are usually distinguished from related studies by their titles. Methods and teaching materials are omitted.

Pre-imperial and imperial periods to AD 1000

Confucius, ed. (attrib.): *Shijing* [Book of Songs] (*c*10th–6th cent. BC; trans. by A. Waley, 1937, and B. Karlgren, 1950)
—— (attrib.): *Lunyu* [Confucian Analects] (*c*5th cent. BC; trans. by J. Legge, 1861/*R*1872, and A. Waley, 1938)
Guan Zhong (attrib.): *Guanzi* [(the book of) Master Guan] (4th cent. BC)
Comp. unknown: *Erya* (*c*3rd cent. BC)
Comp. unknown: *Zhouli* [Rites of Zhou (dynasty)] (*c*3rd–2nd cent. BC)
Qu Yuan and others: *Chuci* [Elegies of (the state of) Chu] (*c*300 BC; trans. by D. Hawkes, 1959)
Han Fei: *Han Feizi* [(the book of) Han Fei] (*c*250 BC)
Xun Qing: *Xunzi* [(the book of) Master Xun] (*c*240 BC)
Lü Buwei, ed. (attrib.): *Lüshi Chunqiu* [Spring and Autumn Annals of Master Lü] (*c*239 BC)
Liu An and others, eds.: *Huai Nanzi* [(the book of the prince of) Huai Nan] (*c*120 BC)
Gongsun Nizi (attrib.): *Yueji* [Record of Music] (*c*1st cent. BC; trans. by W. Kaufmann, 1976)
Dai Sheng, ed. (attrib.): *Liji* [Record of Rites] (1st cent. BC–1st cent. AD; trans. by J. Legge, 1885)
Xu Shen: *Shuowen Jiezi* [Explanation of Graphs and Analysis of Characters] (*c*121 AD)
Cai Yong: *Qin Cao* [Qin Music] (*c*170 AD)
Ying Shao: *Fengsu Tongyi* [Meaning of Popular Customs] (*c*175 AD)
Fu Xuan: 'Pipa Fu' [Poetic Essay on the *Pipa*] (*c*265 AD)
Xi Kang: 'Qin Fu' [Poetic Essay on the *Qin*] (3rd cent.)
Pan Anren: 'Sheng Fu' [Poetic Essay on the *Sheng*] (4th cent.)
Liu Xie: *Wenxin Diaolong* [The Literary Mind and the Carving of Dragons] (*c*500; Eng. trans. by Shih Yu-chung, 1975)
Yu Shinan: *Beitang Shuchao* [Excerpts from Books in the Northern Hall], 2 vols. (6th cent.)
Wu Zetian, ed.: *Yueshu Yaolu* [Essentials from Treatises on Music] (*c*700)
Cui Lingqin, ed.: *Jiaofang Ji* [Record of the Teaching Ward] (801)
Du You: *Tongdian* [Encyclopedic History of Institutions] (801)
Nan Zhuo: *Jiegu Lu* [Record of the *Jiegu* (drum)] (*c*850)
Anon: 'Dunhuang Pipa Pu' [Dunhuang *Pipa* Music] (MS, *c*9th cent.)
Duan Anjie: *Yuefu Zalu* [Miscellaneous Notes on Music Scholarship] (late 9th cent.; trans. by M. Gimm, 1966)

Imperial period from 1000 to 1900

Zhu Changwen: *Qin Shi* [History of the *Qin*] (*c*1084)
Shen Gua: *Mengxi Bitan* [Memoirs from Mengxi] (*c*1086)
Chen Yang: *Yueshu* [Treatise on Music] (1104)
Wang Zhuo: *Biji Manzhi* [Random Notes from Biji] (1149)
Cai Yuanding: *Lülü Xinshu* [New Treatise on the System of Pitches] (1187)
Zhu Xi: *Qinlü Shuo* [Discourse on *Qin* Pitches] (*c*1190)
Jiang Kui: *Baishi Daoren Gequ* [Songs of Baishi the Taoist] (*c*1195)
Zhu Xi: *Yili Jingzhuan Tongjie* [Comprehensive Explanation of the *Yili* and Commentary] (*c*1200)
Chen Yuanjing: *Shilin Guangji* [Comprehensive Record of the Forest of Affairs] (*c*1270)
Wang Yinglin, ed.: *Yuhai* [Ocean of Jade] (*c*1270)
Zhang Yan: *Ciyuan* [Sources of Ci] (*c*1280)
Xiong Penglai: *Sepu* [Music for *Se*] (*c*1300)
Ma Duanlin, ed.: *Wenxian Tongkao* [A Comprehensive Investigation of Documents and Traditions] (13th cent.)

Zhou Deqing, ed.: *Zhongyuan Yinyun* [(Dictionary of) Rhymes of the Central Plain (North China)] (1324)
Zhi An, ed.: *Chang Lun* [Discourse on Singing] (*c*1350)
Zhu Quan: *Taigu Yiyin* [Ancient Traditional Sounds] (1413)
——: *Shenqi Mipu* [Mystical (*Qin*) Notations] (1425)
Wei Liangfu: *Qulü* [Principles of *Kunqu*] (*c*1540)
Zhu Zaiyu: *Lüxue Xinshuo* [New Account of the Study of Pitches] (1584)
——: *Lülü Jingyi* [Essential Meaning of the Pitches] (1596)
Wang Jide: *Qulü* [Principles of *Kunqu*] (*c*1610)
Wang Qi, ed.: *Sancai Tuhui* [Universal Encyclopedia] (1619)
Liu Minyue: *Wenmiao Liyu Quanshu* [Complete Book of Ritual Music for the Confucian Shrine] (*c*1630)
Shen Chongsui: *Duqu Xuzhi* [Essentials of *Kunqu* Writing and Singing] (1639)
Li Yu: *Xianqing Ouji* [Jottings During Moments of Leisure] (1671)
Mei Gucheng and others, eds.: *Lülü Zhengyi* [Basic Principles of the System of Pitches] (1713)
Chen Menglei and others, eds.: *Gujin Tushu Jicheng* [Synthesis of Books and Illustrations Past and Present] (1725)
Yun Lu and others, eds.: *Jiugong Dacheng Nanbei Ci Gongpu* [Jiugong Great Anthology of Southern and Northern Verse (of *Kunqu*) in Notation] (1746)
Xu Dachun: *Yuefu Chuansheng* [Transmitting the Sounds of the *Yuefu*] (1748)
Comp. unknown: *Shijing Yuepu* [Musical Notations for the *Book of Songs*] (1788)
Ju Shilin: *Ju Shilin Pipa Pu* [*Pipa* Music of Ju Shilin] (*c*1790)
Ming Yi [Rong Zai]: *Xiansuo Beikao* [String Music in Reference] (1814)
Qiu Zhilu: *Dingji Liyue Beikao* [Reference Notes on the Spring and Autumn Sacrificial Music] (*c*1840)
He Yuzhai: *Dapu He Yuzhai Xiansheng Zheng Pu* [Zheng Music of He Yuzhai of Dapu] (19th cent.)
Zhao Ziyong, ed.: *Yue Ou* [Cantonese Verse] (*c*1850)
Zhang He: *Qinxue Rumen* [Rudimentary *Qin* Study] (1864)
Wang Xichun, ed.: *Eyunge Qupu* [Eyunge *Kunqu* Music] (1870)
Li Zufen, ed.: *Nanbei Pai Daqu Pipa Xinpu* [New Notations of the Great Pieces of the Northern and Southern Schools of *Pipa*] (1895)

20th century to World War II
Wang Guowei: *Tang Song Daqu Kao* [Examination of Tang and Song Period *Daqu*] (1909)
——: *Song Yuan Xiqu Kao* [Examination of Song and Yuan Opera] (1909)
Zhang Yian, ed.: *Liuye Qupu* [Liuye *Kunqu* in Notation], 24 vols. (Shanghai, 1911)
Yang Zongji: *Qin Pu* [*Qin* Music], 3 vols. (1914)
Qiu Hechou: *Xiange Bidu* [Essential String and Vocal Music] (Guangzhou, 1917)
Zhang Hejing, ed.: *Qudiao Gongche Daguan* [Anthology of Melodies in *Gongche* Notation], 4 vols. (Beijing, 1920)
Qiu Hechou: *Qinxue Xinbian* [New Tutor for (*Yang*)*qin*], 2 vols. (Hong Kong, 1921)
Tan Rongguang: *Yuedong Luogu Yuepu* [Guangdong *Luogu* Music in Notation] (Guangzhou, 1921)
Yang Yinliu and Chen Dingjun: *Yayin Ji* [Collection of Refined Music], 2 vols. (Wuxi, 1923)
Zheng Jinwen, ed.: *Xiaodi Xinpu* [New Music for *Xiao* and *Di*] (Shanghai, 1924)
Wang Guangqi [Wang Kuang-ch'i]: *Dongxi Yuezhi Zhi Yanjiu* [Study of Eastern and Western Musical Systems] (Shanghai, 1926)
Tong Fei, ed.: *Zhongyue Xunyuan* [In Search for the Origin of Chinese Music] (Shanghai, 1926)
Zheng Jinwen: *Zhongguo Yinyue Shi* [History of Chinese Music], 4 vols. (Shanghai, 1929)
Chen Xiaohu, ed.: *Guoyue Diaopu* [(Hakka) Music in Notation] (Singapore, 1930)
Liu Tianhua, ed.: *Mei Lanfang Gequ Pu* [Opera Songs of Mei Lanfang in Notation] (Beijing, 1930)
Wang Jilie, ed.: *Jicheng Qupu* [Collection of *Kunqu* in Notation], 32 vols. (Shanghai, 1931)
Wang Guangqi: *Fanyi Qinpu zhi Yanjiu* [Study of the Transcription of *Qin* Music] (Shanghai, 1931)
Wang Binlu, ed.: *Meian Qinpu* [Meian *Qin* Handbook], 2 vols. (1931)
Liu Fu: 'Shier Deng Lüde Faming zhe Zhu Zaiyu' [Zhu Zaiyu, Inventor of the Equal-tempered Scale], in *Cai Yuanpei Xiansheng Liushiwu Sui Qingzhu Lunwen Ji* (Beijing, 1932)
——, ed. : *Liu Tianhua Xiansheng Jinian Ce* [Liu Tianhua Memorial Album] (Beijing, 1933)
Xiaxi Diaosou, ed.: *Qingyun* [Graceful Music], 2 vols. (Guangzhou, *c*1933)
Wang Guangqi: *Zhongguo Yinyue Shi* [History of Chinese Music] (Shanghai, 1934)
Xia Chengtao: 'Baishi Daoren Gequ Jiaolü' [Editing the Songs of Baishi Daoren], *Yenching Journal of Chinese Studies*, xvi (1934), 83–117

He Liutang and He Yunian: *Pipa Yuepu* [*Pipa* Music in Notation] (Shanghai, 1934)
Hayashi Kenzō: *Sui Tang Yanyue Diao Yanjiu* [Study of the Modes of Sui-Tang Court Entertainment Music] (Chinese trans. by Guo Moruo, Shanghai, 1936)
Li Baishui, ed.: *Pingju Huikan* [Collection of Peking Opera (Notations)], ser. (Shanghai, 1936–43)
Yang Yinliu: 'Pingjunlü Suanjie' [On the Calculation of (Chinese) Equal Temperament], *Yanjing Xuebao*, 21 (1937), 1–60 [Eng. abstract]
Yan Xianting, ed.: *Pingju Gepu* [Peking Opera Song Notations] (Shanghai, 1937)
Chen Yongyan, ed.: *Xiandai Qinxian Qupu* [Contemporary Instrumental Music in Notation], 2 vols. (Guangzhou, 1937)
Zhao Jingshen: *Tanci Kaozheng* [Textual Research on *Tanci*] (Shanghai, 1937)

Early Western-language studies and translations of historic works

J.-J. Amiot: 'De la musique des Chinois, tant anciens que modernes', in *Mémoires concernant l'histoire, les sciences, les arts, les moeurs, les usages, etc. des Chinois, par les missionnaires de Pe-kin*, vi (Paris, 1780), 1–254
J. Legge, trans.: *The Four Books* (London, 1861/*R*1872)
——: 'Li Ki' [Liji], *Sacred Books of China* (Oxford, 1885/*R*1926)
G. E. Moule: 'Notes on the Ting-chi, or Half-yearly Sacrifice to Confucius', *Journal of the North China Branch of the Royal Asiatic Society*, xxxiii (1900–01), 121–57
A. C. Moule: 'A List of the Musical and Other Sound Producing Instruments of the Chinese', *Journal of the Royal Asiatic Society, North China Branch*, xxxix (1908), 1–160
M. Courant: 'Essai historique sur la musique classique des Chinois', in A. Lavignac: *EMDC*, I/v (Paris, 1922), 77–241
Wang Guangqi [Wang Kuang-ch'i]: *Über die Chinesische Klassische Oper (1530–1860 n. Chr.)* (diss., U. of Bonn, 1934)
J. H. Levis: *The Foundations of Chinese Musical Art* (Beijing, 1936)
Chao Mei-pa: 'The Trend of Modern Chinese Music', *T'ien-Hsia Monthly*, iv/3 (1937), 269
A. Waley, trans.: *The Book of Songs* (London, 1937)
——: *The Analects of Confucius* (London, 1938)
Kishibe Shigeo: 'On the Origin of the P'i-p'a', *Transactions of the Asiatic Society of Japan*, xix (1940), 259–304
R. H. van Gulik: *The Lore of the Chinese Lute: an Essay in Ch'in Ideology* (Tokyo, 1940)
——: *Hsi K'ang and his Poetical Essay on the Lute* (Tokyo, 1941)
B. Karlgren, trans.: *The Book of Odes: Chinese Text, Transcription and Translation* (Stockholm, 1950)
D. Hawkes, trans.: *Ch'u Tz'u: the Songs of the South* (Oxford, 1959)
M. Gimm: *Das 'Yüeh-fu Tsa-lu' des Tuan An-chieh: Studien zur Geschichte von Musik Schauspiel und Tanz in der T'ang-Dynastie* (Wiesbaden, 1966)
Shih Yu-chung, trans.: *The Literary Mind and the Carving of Dragons* (Taipei, 1975; trans. of *Wenxin Diaolong*)
W. Kaufmann: *Musical References in the Chinese Classics* (Detroit, MI, 1976; trans. of *Yueji*)

Post-World War II sources: BIBLIOGRAPHIC AND REFERENCE MATERIALS

K. T. Wu and H. Bartlett: 'Books on East Asiatic Music in the Library of Congress (Printed Before 1800). 1. Works in Chinese', *The Library of Congress Catalogue of Early Books on Music . . . Supplement* (Washington, DC, 1944), 121
Zhongguo Yinyue Yanjiu Suo, ed.: *Zhongguo Yinyue Shi Cankao Tupian* [Chinese Music History in Reference Pictures], 9 vols. (Shanghai and Beijing, 1954–64)
Revue Bibliographique de Sinologie (Paris, 1955–)
Cao Chousheng, ed.: *Zhongguo Yinyue Wudao Xiqu Renming Cidian* [Dictionary of Famous Personages in Chinese Music, Dance, and Opera] (Hong Kong, n.d., orig. 1956)
Liang Tsai-p'ing, ed.: *Bibliography on Chinese Music* (Taipei, 1956)
Ouyang Yuqian, ed.: *Zhongguo Xiqu Yanjiu Ziliao Chuji* [Initial Collection of Research Materials on Chinese Drama] (Beijing, 1956)
Zhongguo Yinyue Yanjiu Suo, ed.: *Minzu Yinyue Yanjiu Lunwen Ji* [Collection of Essays on National Music Research], 3 vols. (Beijing, 1956–58)
Zhongguo Xiqu Yanjiu Yuan, ed.: *Zhongguo Gudian Xiqu Lunzhu Jicheng* [Collection of Classical Treatises on Chinese Opera], 10 vols. (Beijing, 1959)
J. Needham, K. G. Robinson and Wang Ling, eds.: 'Bibliographies', *Science and Civilization in China*, iv/1 (Cambridge, 1962), 335–97

Zhongguo Yinyue Yanjiu Suo, ed.: *Zhongguo Gudai Yinyue Shumu* [Bibliography of Ancient Chinese Music Books] (Beijing, 1962/*R*1965)

Zhongguo Yinyue Yanjiu Suo, ed.: *Zhongguo Gudai Yinyue Shiliao Jiyao* [Summary (Collection) of Historical Materials on Ancient Chinese Music] (Beijing, 1962/*R*1971)

Liu Shaotang and others, eds.: *Pingju Shiliao Congkan* [Historical Materials Series on Peking Opera], 12 vols. (Taipei, 1965)

D. Shih-p'eng Yang: *An Annotated Bibliography of Materials for the Study of the Peking Theatre* (Madison, WI, 1967)

Wang Peilun: *Xiqu Cidian* [Dictionary of Chinese Opera] (Taipei, 1969)

C. P. Mackerras: *The Rise of the Peking Opera 1770–1870: Social Aspects of the Theatre in Manchu China* (Oxford, 1972)

Cheung Sai-bung: *Zhongguo Yinyue Shilun Shugao* [Historical Studies of Chinese Music], 2 vols. (Hong Kong, 1974–5)

Yang Jialuo, ed.: *Zhongguo Yinyue Shiliao* [Historical Materials of Chinese Music], 6 vols. (Taipei, 1975)

W. Dolby: *A History of Chinese Drama* (London, 1976)

C. Dalhaus, ed.: *Brockhaus–Riemann Musiklexikon*, 2 vols. (Wiesbaden, 1978)

Ji Liankang, trans.: *Yinyue Shiliao* [Historical Materials on Music], 7 vols. (Shanghai, 1978–86)

I. Wong: 'The Printed Collections of K'un-ch'ü (kunqu) Arias and their Sources', *Chinoperl Papers*, viii (1978), 100

F. Lieberman: *Chinese Music: an Annotated Bibliography* (New York, 2/1979)

Han Kuo-huang: 'Three Chinese Musicologists: Yang Yinliu, Yin Falu, Li Chunyi', *EM*, xxiv (1980), 483–529

Ji Liankang, trans.: *Gudai Yinyue Lunzhu Yizhu Xiao Congshu* [Translation and Annotation Series on the Ancient Music Treatises], 5 vols. (Beijing, 1980)

Shanghai Yishu Yanjiu Suo, ed.: *Zhongguo Xiqu Quyi Cidian* [Chinese Opera and Narrative Dictionary] (Shanghai, 1981)

Yang Yinliu: *Zhongguo Gudai Yinyue Shigao* [Draft History of Ancient Chinese Music], 2 vols. (Beijing, 1981)

Zhongguo Yinyue Yanjiu Suo, ed.: *Zhongguo Gudai Yuelun Xuanji* [Collection (of Reference Materials) on Ancient Chinese Music Philosophy] (Beijing, 1981/*R*1983)

Feng Guangsheng, ed.: 'Zhongguo Yinyue Kaogu Ziliao Wenxian Mulu' [Catalogue of Archaeological Documents for Chinese Music], *Yueqi*, v (1982), 29 [cont. in later issues]

Zhang Geng and others, eds.: *Zhongguo Dabaike Quanshu: Xiqu Quyi* [Great Encyclopedia of China: Opera and Narrative] (Beijing, 1983)

S. Sadie, ed.: *The New Grove Dictionary of Musical Instruments* (London, 1984)

C. K. Wang: 'Research Activities in the Performing Arts in the Republic of China: a Bibliographic Report', *Chinoperl Papers*, xiii (1984–5), 139

Zhongguo Yinyue Yanjiu Suo, ed.: *Zhongguo Yinyue Cidian* [Dictionary of Chinese Music] (Beijing, 1984)

——: *Zhongguo Yinyue Shupu Zhi* [Record of Chinese Music Books and Notations] (Beijing, 1984)

——: *Yinyue Yanjiu Wenxuan* [Selection of Articles on (Chinese) Music Research], 2 vols. (Beijing, 1985)

Wenwu Sanwuling Qi Zongmu Suoyin (1950.1–1985.7) [Index to 350 issues of *Wenwu* (Jan. 1950–July 1985)] (Beijing, 1986)

Zhongguo Yinyuejia Xiehui, ed.: *Zhongguo Minzu Yinyue Jicheng* [Anthology of Chinese National Music], 5 ser. (Beijing, 1988–)

Zhongguo Yinyue Yanjiu Suo, ed.: *Zhongguo Yinyue Shi Tujian* [Pictorial Illustrations of Chinese Music History] (Beijing, 1988)

K. DeWoskin: 'Sources for the Study of Early Chinese Music', *Archaeologia Musicalis* (1989)

Dongfang Yinyue Xuehui, ed.: *Zhongguo Minzu Yinyue Daxi* [Anthology of Chinese National Music], 8 vols. (Shanghai, 1989–)

Lü Ji, He Luting and others, eds.: *Zhongguo Dabaike Quanshu: Yinyue Wudao* [Great Encyclopedia of China: Music and Dance] (Beijing, 1989)

'Current Bibliography: Asia and Oceania', in *EM*

Quanguo Zong Shumu [Nationwide Collected Booklist] (Beijing, annual)

HISTORIC STUDIES

Yin Falu: 'Xian Han Yuelu Chutan' [Preliminary Investigation of Pre-Han Pitches], *Huazhong Daxue Guoxue Yanjiu Lunwen Zhuankan* (Dali, 1944)

——: 'Tang Song Daqu Zhi Laiyuan Ji Qi Zuzhi' [Origin and Structure of the Tang-Song Daqu], *Huazhong Daxue Guoxue Yanjiu Lunwen Zhuankan* (Dali, 1945/*R*1948)

——: 'Cong Dunhuang Bihua Lun Tangdai de Yinyue he Wudao' [Tang Dynasty Music and Dance based upon Wall Paintings in the Dunhuang Caves], *Wenwu Cankao Ziliao*, ii/4 (1951), 107–139

Yang Yinliu: *Zhongguo Yinyue Shigang* [Draft History of Chinese Music] (Shanghai, 1952/*R*1953; Beijing, 1955; Taipei, 1977)

Hayashi Kenzō: 'Study on Explication of Ancient Musical Score of P'i-p'a Discovered at Tunhuang, China', *Bulletin of Nara Gakugei University*, v/1 (1955), 1

F. Kornfeld: *Die Tonale Struktur Chinesischer Musik* (Mödling bei Wien, 1955)

L. Picken: 'Twelve Ritual Melodies of the T'ang Dynasty', *Studia Memoriae Bela Bartok Sacra* (Budapest, 1956), 147

K. Reinhart: *Chinesische Musik* (Eisenach, 1956)

Yin Falu: 'Cong Yinyue Shi Shang Kan Zhongguo he Yindu de Wenhua Guanxi' [Cultural Relationship of the Music Histories of China and India], *Minzu Yinyue Yanjiu Lunwen Ji*, i (1956), 53

Hayashi Kenzō: *'Dunhuang Pipa Pu' de Jiedu Yanjiu* [Explanatory Study of the Dunhuang *Pipa* Notation], trans. by Pan Huaisu (Shanghai, 1957)

Li Chunyi: 'Shilun "Yuefu Chuansheng"' [Preliminary Discussion of (the Vocal Treatise) *Yuefu Chuansheng*], *Minzu Yinyue Yanjiu Lunwen Ji*, ii (1957), 67

Nakaseko Kazu: 'Symbolism in Ancient Chinese Music Theory', *JMT*, i/2 (1957), 147–180

L. Picken: 'Chiang K'uei's Nine Songs for Yüeh', *MQ*, xliii (1957), 201

Yang Yinliu and Yin Falu: *Song Jiang Baishi Chuangzuo Gequ Yanjiu* [Study of the Songs Composed by Jiang Baishi of the Song Dynasty] (Beijing, 1957/*R*1979)

Li Chunyi: *Zhongguo Gudai Yinyue Shigao* [Historical Sketch of Ancient Chinese Music] (Beijing, 1958; rev., 1964)

Yang Yinliu: 'Kongmiao Dingji Yinyue de Chubu Yanjiu' [Preliminary Study of the Music Used in the Spring and Autumn Sacrifices in the Confucian Temple], *Yinyue Yanjiu*, i (1958), 54

Kishibe Shigeo: *Tōdai Ongaku no Rekishi-teki Kenkyū* [Historic Study of the Music in the Tang Dynasty], ii (Tokyo, 1960–61) [Eng. summary, pp.1–46]

Dai Shengyu: 'The Confucian Philosophy of Music: a Theory in Jurisprudence', *Chinese Culture*, iv/1 (1962), 9

J. Needham and K. G. Robinson: 'Sound (Acoustics)', *Science and Civilization in China*, iv/1 (Cambridge, 1962), 126–228

Yang Yinliu: *Gongche Pu Qianshuo* [Brief Introduction to *Gongche* Notation] (Beijing, 1962)

E. Schafer: *The Golden Peaches of Samarkand* (Berkeley, CA, 1963)

Wu Nanxun: *Lüxue Huitong* [Comprehensive Study of (Chinese) Temperament] (Beijing, 1964)

M. Gimm: *Das 'Yüeh-fu Tsa-lu' des Tuan An-chieh. Studien zur Geschichte von Musik, Schauspiel und Tanz in der T'ang-dynastie* (Wiesbaden, 1966)

W. Kaufmann: *Musical Notations of the Orient: Notational Systems of East, South, and Central Asia* (Bloomington, IN, 1967)

R. C. Pian: *Sonq Dynasty Musical Sources and Their Interpretation* (Cambridge, MA, 1967)

L. Picken: 'T'ang Music and Musical Instruments', *Toung Pao*, lv (1969), 74–122

Kishibe Shigeo: *Tangdai Yinyue Shide Yanjiu* [Study of Tang Dynasty Music History], 2 vols. (Chin. trans. by Huang Zhijiong, Taipei, 1973)

Cheung Sai-bung: *Zhongguo Yinyue Shilun Shugao* [Historical Studies of Chinese Music], 2 vols. (Hong Kong, 1974–5)

Shi Weiliang: *Yinyue Xiang Lishi Qiuzheng* [History in Proof of Music] (Taipei, 1974)

J. Crump: 'Giants in the Earth: Yüan Drama as Seen by Ming Critics', *Chinese and Japanese Music-Dramas* (Ann Arbor, MI, 1975), 1–63

F. Kuttner: 'Prince Chu Tsai-yü's Life and Work: a Re-evaluation of his Contribution to Equal Temperament Theory', *EM*, xix (1975), 163–206

Shih Chung-wen: *The Golden Age of Chinese Drama: Yüan Tsa-chü* (Princeton, NJ, 1976)

L. Picken: 'The Shapes of the *Shi Jing* Song-texts and their Musical Implications', *Musica Asiatica*, i (1977), 85

J. Crump: *Chinese Theater in the Days of Kublai Khan* (Tucson, AZ, 1980)

D. Johnson: *Yuarn Music Dramas* (Ann Arbor, MI, 1980)

Kishibe Shigeo: 'China: II. Court Traditions', *Grove 6*

Liang Ming-yüeh: 'The Tz'u Music of Chiang K'uei: its Style and Compositional Strategy', *Song Without Music: Chinese Tz'u Poetry*, ed. S. Soong (Hong Kong, 1980), 211–46

336

R. C. Pian: 'China: I. General', *Grove 6*

Yin Falu: 'Sichou zhi Lushang de Yinyue Wenhua Jiaoliu' [Interaction of Music Cultures on the Silk Road], *Renmin Yinyue*, ii (1980), 25

Gao Houyong: *Minzu Qiyue Gailun* [Outline of National Instrumental Music] (Nanjing, 1981)

He Luting: *He Luting Yinyue Lunwen Xuanji* [Collected Essays on Music by He Luting] (Shanghai, 1981)

Huang Xiangpeng: 'Xuangong Gufa Zhong de Sui Yue Yong Lü Wenti he Zuoxuan Youxuan' [Questions about the Old Method of Modulation, Both Left and Right, Following the Monthly Cycles], *Yinyue Xue Congkan*, i (1981), 45

L. Picken: 'The Musical Implications of Chinese Song-texts with Unequal Lines, and the Significance of Nonsense-syllables, with Special Reference to Art-songs of the Song Dynasty', *Musica Asiatica*, iii (1981), 53

——, ed.: *Music from the Tang Court*, 4 vols. (London, 1981–7)

Xue Zongming: *Zhongguo Yinyue Shi* [History of Chinese Music] (Taipei, 1981)

Yang Yinliu: *Zhongguo Gudai Yinyue Shigao* [Draft History of Ancient Chinese Music], 2 vols. (Beijing, 1981)

K. DeWoskin: *A Song for One or Two: Music and the Concept of Art in Early China* (Ann Arbor, MI, 1982)

Sun Xingqun: 'Xixia Yinyue Shitan' [Exploration of Western Xia Period Music], *Yinyue Yanjiu*, ii (1982), 40

Yang Yinliu: 'San Lü Kao' [Study of Three Systems of Temperament], *Yinyue Yanjiu*, i (1982), 30

J. Crump: *Songs from Xanadu: Studies in Mongol-Dynasty Song-Poetry* (Ann Arbor, MI, 1983)

K. DeWoskin: 'Early Chinese Music and the Origins of Aesthetic Terminology', *Theories of the Arts in China*, ed. S. Bush and C. Murck (Princeton, NJ, 1983), 187

Ho Lu-ting [He Luting]: 'On Chinese Scales and National Modes', trans. by Han Kuo-huang, *Asian Music*, xiv/1 (1983), 132

Huang Tipei: *Zhonghua Yuexue Tonglun* [General Survey of Chinese Musicology], 4 vols. (Taipei, 1983)

Wu Zhao and Liu Dongsheng: *Zhongguo Yinyue Shilue* [Historical Sketch of Chinese Music] (Beijing, 1983)

Huang Xiangpeng: 'Lüxue Shi Shangde Weida Chengjiu ji Qi Sixiang Qishi' [Great Achievement in the History of Temperament Theory and its Ideological Inspiration], *Yinyue Yanjiu*, iv (1984), 2

Liang Mingyue: *Music of the Billion: an Introduction to Chinese Musical Culture* (New York, 1985)

Wan Yi and Huang Haitao: *Qingdai Gongting Yinyue* [Court Music of the Qing Dynasty] (Beijing, 1985)

Yang Yinliu: *Yang Yinliu Yinyue Lunwen Xuanji* [Selected Articles of Yang Yinliu] (Shanghai, 1986)

Zhongyang Yinyue Xueyuan Xuebao editorial board: *Minzu Yinyue Jiegou Yanjiu Lunwen Ji* [Collection of Articles on the Structure of National Music] (Beijing, 1986)

G. J. Cho: *Lu-lu: a Study of its Historical, Acoustical and Symbolic Signification* (Taipei, 1989)

'Chinese Music Theory', *Asian Music*, xx/2 (1989), ed. A. Thrasher

MUSICAL INSTRUMENTS

R. H. van Gulik: 'Brief Note on the Cheng, the Chinese Small Zither', *Journal of the Society for Research in Asiatic Music*, ix (1951), 10

L. Picken: 'The Origin of the Short Lute', *GSJ*, viii (1955), 32

Li Chunyi: 'Guanyu Yin Zhong de Yanjiu' [Concerning Research on Bells from the Yin Period], *Kaogu Xuebao*, iii (1957), 41

Zhongyang Renmin Guangbo Diantai, ed.: *Minzu Qiyue Jiangzuo* [Lectures on National Instrumental Music] (Beijing, 1957)

Yang Yinliu: 'Xinyang Chutu Chunqiu Bianzhong de Yinlü' [Tuning of the Chunqiu *Bianzhong* (bells) Excavated at Xinyang], *Yinyue Yanjiu*, i (1959), 77

Cha Fu-hsi [Zha Fuxi]: 'The Chinese Lute', *Chinese Literature*, iii (1960), 128

Hayashi Kenzō: *Dongya Yueqi Kao* [Examination of East Asian Instruments] (Beijing, 1962/R1978)

Chuang Pen-li: *Zhongguo Gudai zhi Paixiao* [Panpipes of Ancient China] (Taipei, 1963) [with Eng. summary]

Hayashi Kenzō: *Shōsōin Gakki no Kenkyu* [Study of the Musical Instruments in the Shōsōin] (Tokyo, 1964) [in Jap.]

Yang Yinliu: 'Chinese Drums', *Chinese Literature*, iv (1964), 107

Chuang Pen-li: 'Chi zhi Yanjiu' [Study of the *Chi* (flute)], *Bulletin of the Institute of Ethnology, Academia Sinica*, xix (1965), 139–203 [with Eng. summary]

L. Picken: 'Early Chinese Friction-chordophones', *GSJ*, xviii (1965), 82

Chuang Pen-li: 'Guqing Yanjiu Zhiyi' [Study of the Ancient *Qing* (chime-stone), Part I], *Bulletin of the Institute of Ethnology, Academia Sinica*, xxii (1966), 97–137 [with Eng. summary]

Hayashi Kenzō and others: *Shōsōin no Gakki* [Musical Instruments in the Shōsōin] (Tokyo, 1967)

Liang Tsai-p'ing: *Chinese Musical Instruments and Pictures* (Taipei, 1970) [in Chin. and Eng.]

Chuang Pen-li: 'Xun de Lishi yu Bijiao zhi Yanjiu' [Historical and Comparative Study of the *Xun* (flute)], *Bulletin of the Institute of Ethnology, Academia Sinica*, xxxiii (1972), 177–253 [with Eng. summary]

D. Ming-yüeh Liang: *The Chinese Ch'in: its History and Music* (Taipei, 1972)

Li Chunyi: 'Yueqi' [Musical Instruments], *Changsha Mawangdui Yihao Han Mu*, ed. Hunan Sheng Bowuguan (Beijing, 1973), 102 [Eng. trans. in Mok, 1978]

——: 'Han Se he Chu Se Tiaoxian de Tansuo' [Investigation of the Tunings of the Han *Se* (zither) and Chu *Se*], *Kaogu*, i (1974), 56

Cheng Deh-yuan: *Zhengyue Lilun Ji Yanzou* [*Zheng* Music in Theory and Performance] (Hong Kong, 1977)

R. Mok: 'Ancient Musical Instruments Unearthed in 1972 from the Number One Han Tomb at Ma Wang Tui, Changsha: Translation and Commentary of Chinese Reports', *Asian Music*, x/1 (1978), 39–91

Huang Xiangpeng: 'Xian Qin Yinyue Wenhua de Guanghui Chuangzao – Zeng Houyi Mude Gu Yueqi' [Brilliant Creation of Early Qin (dynasty) Music Culture – Ancient Instruments from the Tomb of Zeng Houyi], *Wenwu*, vii (1979), 32

Wu Zhao: 'Rare Find of Ancient Instruments', *China Reconstructs*, xxviii/5 (1979), 28

Hubei Sheng Bowuguan, ed.: *Suixian Zeng Houyi Mu* [Grave of the Marquis Yi of Zeng, Sui County] (Beijing, 1980)

Li Kunsheng and Qin Xu: 'Hulu Sheng' [Gourd *Sheng*], *Wenwu*, viii (1980), 85

Cao Zheng: 'Guzheng Yange Luetan' [Brief Discussion on the Evolution of the *Zheng* (zither)], *Yueqi*, iii (1981), 1

——: 'Lidai Wenyi Zuopin Zhongde Zheng' [*Zheng* in Old Literary Works], *Zhongguo Yinyue*, iv (1981), 35

Li Chunyi: 'Shuo Huang' [About the *Huang* (mouth-harp)], *Yueqi*, iv (1981), 1

——, Wu Zhao and others: 'Suixian Chutu Yinyue Wenwu Zhuanji' [Special Issue on the Musical Relics Excavated in Suixian County], *Yinyue Yanjiu*, i (1981)

R. Wolpert: 'The Five-stringed Lute in East Asia', *Musica Asiatica*, iii (1981), 97

Jin Jianmin: 'Gudai de Zheng' [Ancient *Zheng* (zither)], *Yueqi*, iv-vi (1982–)

Liang Guangcheng and Pan Yongzhang, eds.: *Yueqi Fa Shouce* [Handbook on the Principles of Musical Instruments] (Beijing, 1982)

Xu Jian: *Qinshi Chubian* [Initial Draft on the History of the *Qin* (zither)] (Beijing, 1982)

Cao Zheng: 'A Discussion of the History of the Gu Zheng', *Asian Music*, xiv/2 (1983), 1

Chen Shengtian: *Zhongguo Di zhi Yanjin yu Jiqiao Yanjiu* [Study of the Evolution and Techniques of the Chinese *Di* (flute)] (Taipei, 1983)

Li Chengyu: 'Zeng Houyi Bianqing de Chubu Yanjiu' [Preliminary Study of the *Bianqing* (stone chimes) of Zeng Houyi], *Yinyue Yanjiu*, i (1983), 86

Tong Kin-woon: *Shang Musical Instruments* (diss., Wesleyan U., 1983); repr. in *Asian Music*, xiv/2 (1983), xv/1 (1983) and xv/2 (1984)

Cheng Deh-yuan: *Zhongguo Yueqi Xue* [Study of Chinese Musical Instruments] (Taipei, 1984)

Fang Ronglin and Zhang Pinsheng: 'Suzhou Zhensi Xianxian de Lishi Yange' [Historical Development of Suzhou Silk Strings], *Yueqi*, vi (1984), 29

S. Sadie, ed.: *The New Grove Dictionary of Musical Instruments* (London, 1984)

Han Shude and Zhang Zhinian: *Zhongguo Pipa Shigao* [Historical Sketch of the Chinese *Pipa* (lute)] (Chengdu, 1985)

Jiang Yonghe: 'Dunhuang Bihua Zhongde Sui Tang Yueqi ji Qi Zuhe Xingshi' [Sui and Tang (dynasty) Instruments Depicted in the Dunhuang Wall Murals and Their Organizational Forms], *Quanzhou Lishi Wenhua Zhongxin Gongzuo Tongxun*, i (1985), 19

Lu Songling: 'Chiba Chutan' [Preliminary Investigation of the *Chiba* (flute)], *Quanzhou Lishi Wenhua Zhongxin Gongzuo Tongxun*, i (1985), 9

Niu Longfei: *Guyue Fayin* [Ancient Music Newly Discovered] (Lanzhou, 1985)

Zhongguo Yinyue Yanjiu Suo, ed.: *Zhongguo Yueqi Jieshao* [Introduction to Chinese Musical Instruments] (Beijing, 1985)

Gao Pei: 'Sheng de Yange he Fazhan' [Evolution and Development of the *Sheng* (mouth-organ)], *Yueqi*, i–ii (1986), 1 [cont. in later issues]

Liu Yu: 'Mantan Muyu' [Casual Discussion on the *Muyu* (woodblock)], *Yueqi*, ii (1986), 25

Shen Sin-yan: 'The Acoustics of the Bian-Zhong Bell Chimes of China', *Chinese Music*, ix/3 (1986), 53 [cont. in later issues]

F. Kuttner: *The Archaeology of Music in Ancient China: 2000 Years of Acoustical Experimentation (c 1400 BC–AD 750)* (New York, 1990)

INSTRUMENTAL MUSIC

Lao Hong-kio [Liu Honggou], ed.: *Minnan Yinyue Zhipu Quanji* [Complete Collection of Minnan *Zhi* and *Pu* Repertory] (Manila, 1953)

Cao Anhe and Jian Qihua, eds.: *Xiansuo Shisan Tao* [String Music in Thirteen Sets], 3 vols. (Beijing, 1955)

Shandong Sheng Yinyue Gongzuo Zu, ed.: *Shandong Minjian Yuequ Ji* [Collection of Shandong Folk (instrumental) Music] (Jinan, 1955)

Li Ling, ed.: *Guangdong Yinyue* [Cantonese Music], 2 vols. (Beijing, 1956–8)

Yang Yinliu: 'Dui Guqin Qu Yangguan Sandie de Chubu Yanjiu' [Preliminary Study of the *Qin* Melody *Yangguan Sandie*], *Minzu Yinyue Yanjiu Lunwen Ji*, i (1956), 41 [Eng. trans. by I. Wong in *Asian Music*, v/1 (1973), 10]

Yang Yinliu and others, eds.: *Guqin Qu Huibian* [Compilation of *Qin* Music] (Beijing, 1956)

Zha Fuxi: '"Youlan" Zhifa Jijie' [Explication of the Fingering of (the qin piece) *Youlan*], *Minzu Yinyue Yanjiu Lunwen Ji*, i (1956), 59

Zhang Zhengzhi, ed.: *Suona Qudi* [Collection of *Suona* Music] (Beijing, 1956)

Cheng Wujia, ed.: *Zhongguo Luogu Qu* [Chinese *Luogu* Music] (Shanghai, 1957)

Wang Shixiang: 'Guqin Qu "Guanglingsan" Shuoming' [Explanation of the Qin Melody *Guanglingsan*], in *Minzu Yinyue Yanjiu Lunwen Ji*, ii (1957), 13

Qin Pengzhang: 'Minzu Guanxian Yuedui' [(Chinese) National Orchestra], *Renmin Yinyue*, iv (1958)

Zhang Hanzai, ed.: *Chaozhou Minjian Yinyue Xuan* [Selection of Chaozhou Folk Music] (Guangzhou, 1958/R1973)

Huang Jinpei: 'Guanyu "Lao Liuban" de Bianti' [Concerning the Variants of *Lao Liuban*], *Renmin Yinyue*, x (1960), 38, [Eng. trans. by A. Thrasher in *Asian Music*, xiii/2 (1982), 19]

Zhongguo Yinyue Yanjiu Suo, ed.: *Minzu Yueqi Duzou Quxuan* [Selection of National Instrumental Solos] (Beijing, 1962/R1980)

Guqin Yanjiu Hui, ed.: *Qinqu Jicheng* [Anthology of *Qin* Music], 20 vols. (Beijing, 1963–)

Lui Tsun-yuen: 'A Short Guide to Ch'in', *Selected Report in Ethnomusicology*, i/2 (1968), 179

Lao Hong-kio, ed.: *Minnan Yinyue Zhipu Chuangzuo Quanji* [Complete Collection of Minnan Instrumental Music (*nanguan*)] (Taipei, 1973)

T'ang Chien-yüan [Tong Kin-woon], ed.: *Ch'in-fu: Collection of Materials on the Chinese Seven-stringed Zither*, 3 vols. (Taipei, 1973)

Li Zhiwei and Lu Dehua, eds.: *Zhongguo Minjian Qiyue Quji, Erbai Shou* [Collection of Chinese Folk Instrumental Melodies: 200 Pieces] (Hong Kong, 1975)

Taiping Shuju, ed.: *Guangdong Yinyue* [Cantonese (instrumental) Music] (Hong Kong, 1975)

Chen Leishi: *Chaoyue Juepu Ersi Pu Yuanliu Kao* [Examination of the Origin and Development of the Lost Chaozhou Notation *Ersi Pu*] (Hong Kong, 1978)

Liang Tsai-p'ing: *Guzheng Duzou Qu* [Solo Music for the *Zheng*], 2 vols. (Taipei, 1978)

Zhongyang Yinyue Xueyuan, Minzu Qiyue Xi, ed.: *Minzu Yueqi Chuantong Duzou Qu Xuanji* [Selection of Traditional National Instrumental Solos] (Beijing series: *suona*, 1978; *yangqin*, 1978; *pipa*, 1980; *sanxian*, 1981; *erhu*, 1982; *guan*, 1985)

Han Kuo-huang: 'The Modern Chinese Orchestra', *Asian Music*, xi/1 (1979), 1–40

Quanzhou Shi Nanyin Yanjiu She, ed.: *Zhipu Daguan* [Complete Collection of *Zhi* and *Pu*] (Quanzhou, 1979)

Jin Zuli and Xu Ziren: 'Jiangnan Sizhu Gaishu' [General Account of Jiangnan Sizhu], *Renmin Yinyue*, v (1980), 38

Lin Maogen and Chen Anhua, eds.: *Jinshang Tianhua* [Adding Flowers to the Embroidery] (Shantou, 1980)

Gao Houyong: *Minzu Qiyue Gailun* [Outline of National Instrumental Music] (Nanjing, 1981)

Yang Yong: 'Dui Xiansuo Qu "Shiliu Ban" de Chubu Fenxi' [Preliminary Analysis of the String Melody *Shiliu Ban*], *Yinyue Luncong*, iv (1981), 138

Chen Anhua: 'Zatan Chaoyue yu Hanyue' [Miscellaneous Discussion of Chaozhou and Hakka

Musics], *Guangzhou Yinyue Xueyuan Xuebao*, iv (1982), 57

Huang Jinpei: 'Lun Guangdong Yinyue de Xingti' [Discussion of the Waxing and Waning of Cantonese Music], *Guangzhou Yinyue Xueyuan Xuebao*, i (1982), 8

Li Guangzu, ed.: *Li Tingsong Yanzou Pu* [(*Pipa*) Performance Notations of Li Tingsong] (Beijing, 1982)

Lü Chuikuan: *Quanzhou Xianguan Yanjiou* [Study of *Xianguan* (*nanguan*) Music from Quanzhou] (Taipei, 1982)

Luo Dezai, Luo Qingtian and others, eds.: *Guangdong Hanyue Sanbai Shou* [300 Pieces of Guangdong Hakka Music] (Dapu, 1982)

Luo Xu and others, eds.: *Chaozhou Yinyue Quji* [Collection of Chaozhou Music] (Shantou, 1982)

Shandong Sheng Qunzhong Yishu Guan, ed.: *Lu Xinan Guchuiyue Xuanji* [Selection of *Guchui* Music of Southwestern Shandong] (Beijing, 1982)

Shen Fengquan, ed.: *Jiangnan Sizhu Yuequ Xuan* [Selection of Jiangnan *Sizhu* Music] (Hangzhou, 1982)

Yang Yinliu and Cao Anhe, ed.: *Sunan Shifan Guqu* [Shifan Percussion Music of Southern Jiangsu Province] (Beijing, 1982)

Huang Jinpei: 'Lun Yueyue Yifanxian Biaoxian de Yinyue Xingxiang' [Concerning *ti-fa* Tuning in the Expression of Musical Imagery in Cantonese Music], *Guangzhou Yinyue Xueyuan Xuebao*, ii (1983), 8

F. Lieberman: *A Chinese Zither Tutor: the Mei-an Ch'in-p'u* (Seattle, WA, 1983)

Li Minxiong, ed.: *Chuangtong Minzu Qiyue Qu Xinshang* [Appreciation of Traditional National Instrumental Music] (Beijing, 1983)

Lin Shicheng, ed.: *Ju Shilin Pipa Pu* [Pipa Notations of Ju Shilin] (Beijing, 1983)

Li Yan: '"Xian" Lun' [Discussion of 'String' (temperament)], *Guangzhou Yinyue Xueyuan Xuebao*, iii (1983), 12

Ning Yi, ed.: *Guangdong Yinyue 101 Shou* [101 Pieces of Cantonese Music] (Nan-ning, 1983)

Ye Dong, ed.: *Minzu Qiyue de Ticai yu Xingshi* [Types and Forms of National Instrumental Music] (Shanghai, 1983)

Zheng Shimin and Cai Yuwen: 'Chaozhou Yinyue Diaoshi Chutan' [Preliminary Look at Mode in Chaozhou Music], *Yinyue Yanjiu*, iii (1983), 105

Zhongguo Yinyue Yanjiu Suo, ed.: *Qin Ge* [Qin Songs] (Beijing, 1983)

He Changlin: 'Fujian Nanyin Yuanliu Shitan' [Preliminary Exploration into the Source of Fujian *Nanyin*], *Quanzhou Lishi Wenhua Zhongxin Gongzuo Tongxun*, ii (1984), 1–34

Huang Jinpei: *Guangdong Yinyue Xinshang* [Appreciation of Cantonese Music] (Guangzhou, 1984)

Huang Xiangpeng: '"Xianguan" Tiwai Tan' [Digression on the Topic of *Xianguan*], *Quanzhou Lishi Wenhua Zhongxin Gongzuo Tongxun*, i (1984), 9

Su Xia: 'Jianlun Lü Wencheng de Bufen Yinyue Chuangzuo' [Brief Discussion on Some of the Compositions of Lü Wencheng], *Yinyue Yanjiu*, i (1984), 6

Zhongguo Yinyuejia Xiehui, Shandong Fenhui, ed.: *Shandong Minjian Qiyue Quxuan* [Selection of Shandong Folk Instrumental Music] (Jinan, 1984)

Chen Bingji, ed.: *Fujian Nanyin ji Qi Zhipu* [*Zhi* and *Pu* (repertory) of Fujian *Nanyin*] (Beijing, 1985)

Chen Tianguo: 'Chaozhou Yinyue de Lishi Yuanyuan' [Historical Background of Chaozhou Music], *Guangzhou Yinyue Xueyuan Xuebao*, ii–iii (1985), 32

Gan Tao, ed.: *Jiangnan Sizhu Yinyue* [Jiangnan *Sizhu* Music] (Nanjing, 1985)

Luo Jiuxiang and Shi Zhaoyuan, eds.: *Hanyue Zhengqu Sishi Shou* [40 Pieces of Hakka *Zheng* Music] (Beijing, 1985)

Qi Ming: 'Zaitan Jiangnan Sizhu de Qushi Jiegou' [Further Opinions on the Formal Structure of Jiangnan *Sizhu*], *Yinyue Yanjiu*, iii (1985), 88

A. Thrasher: 'The Melodic Structure of Jiangnan Sizhu', *EM*, xxix (1985), 237

Wu Shizhong: 'Manhua Nanyin Gongche Pu' [Informal Discussion on the *Gongche* Notation of *Nanyin*], *Quanzhou Lishi Wenhua Zhongxin Gongzuo Tongxun*, ii (1985), 1

Xu Jian: 'Xianghege yu Qinqu' [*Xianghege* and *Qin* Music], *Yinyue Yanjiu*, iii (1985), 34

N. Yeh: *Nanguan Music in Taiwan: a Little Known Classical Tradition* (diss., U. of California, 1985)

Cao Zheng, ed.: *Zhengqu Xuanji* [Collection of *Zheng* Music] (Beijing, 1986)

Fujian Sheng Qunzhong Yishu Guan, ed.: *Fujian Minjian Yinyue Yanjiu* [Study of Fujian Folk Music], 4 vols. (Fuzhou, 1986)

Lü Chuikuan: *Taiwan de Nanguan* [*Nanguan* of Taiwan] (Taipei, 1986)

Zhou Hui and others, eds.: *Jiangnan Sizhu Chuantong Badaqu* [Traditional Eight Great Pieces of Jiangnan *Sizhu*] (Shanghai, 1986)

Chen Tianguo, ed.: *Chaozhou Da Luogu* [*Luogu* (notations) of the Chaozhou People] (Beijing, 1987)

J. L. Witzleben: *Silk and Bamboo: Jiangnan Sizhu Instrumental Ensemble Music in Shanghai* (diss., U. of Pittsburgh, 1987)

——: 'Jiangnan Sizhu Music Clubs in Shanghai: Context, Concept and Identity', *EM*, xxxi (1987), 240

Renmin Yinyue editorial board: *Minzu Yinyue Lunwen Ji* [Collection of Articles on National Music] (Beijing, 1988)

A. Thrasher: 'Hakka-Chaozhou Instrumental Repertoire: an Analytic Perspective on Traditional Creativity', *Asian Music*, xix/2 (1988), 1–30

VOCAL MUSIC

Han Feimu, ed.: *Quxue Rumen* [Rudiments for the Study of *Kunqu*] (Shanghai, 1948/*R*1976)

Zhou Yibai: *Zhongguo Xiqu Shi* [History of Chinese Opera], 3 vols. (Shanghai, 1953)

Fu Xihua: *Quyi Luncong* [Collected Essays on Popular Narratives] (Shanghai, 1954)

Lü Zhong and Shang Ke, eds.: *Jingju Jiban Changshi* [General Knowledge on the Foundation of Peking Opera] (Beijing, 1954)

Jiangsu Sheng Yinyue Gongzuo Zu, ed.: *Jiangsu Nanbu Minjian Xiqu Shuochang Yinyue Ji* [Collection of Opera and Narrative Music of Southern Jiangsu Province] (Beijing, 1955)

Zhang Pei and Guo Shaoxian, eds.: *Jinju Yinyue* [Music of Shanxi Opera] (Taiyuan, 1955/*R*1981)

Chen Zhuoying, ed.: *Yuequ Xiezuo Yu Changfa Yanjiu* [Study of the Composition and Singing Methods of Cantonese Song] (Guangzhou, 1956/*R*n.d.)

Li Qiuwu, ed.: *Chensan Wuniang* (Hong Kong, 1956)

A. C. Scott: *The Classical Theatre of China* (London, 1957)

Tao Junqi, ed.: *Jingju Jumu Chutan* [Preliminary Investigation of the Peking Opera Repertory] (Shanghai, 1957/*R*1963)

Yu Huiyong: *Shandong Dagu* [*Dagu* of Shandong Province] (Beijing, 1957)

Chen Ruheng, ed.: *Shuoshu Shihua* [History of Story Telling] (Beijing, 1958)

Lin Yun and others, eds.: *Yueju Yinyue* [Music of the Cantonese Opera], 2 vols. (Guangzhou, 1958)

Xu Lanyuan and Tang Ji: *Xu Lanyuan Caoqin Shenghuo* [Musical Life of (the *jinghu* performer) Xu Lanyuan], 3 vols. (Beijing, 1958/*R*1980)

A. C. Scott: *Mei Lan-fang: the Life and Times of a Peking Actor* (Hong Kong, 1959/*R*1971)

Xia Ye: *Xiqu Yinyue Yanjiu* [Study of (traditional) Opera Music] (Shanghai, 1959)

Zhongguo Xiqu Yanjiu Yuan, ed.: *Jingju Changqiang* [Peking Opera Arias] (Beijing, 1959)

Zhou Yibai: *Zhongguo Xiqu Lunji* [Collected Articles on Chinese Opera] (Beijing, 1960)

Lü Sushang: *Taiwan Dianying Xiju Shi* [History of Cinema and Drama in Taiwan] (Taipei, 1961)

Zhang Geng, ed.: *Yangge Ju Xuan* [Selection of *Yangge* Opera] (Beijing, 1962)

Zhou Zhifu: *Jin Bainian de Jingju* [Peking Opera over the Recent 100 Years] (Hong Kong, 1962/*R*1965)

Qi Rushan: *Qi Rushan Quanji* [Complete Works of Qi Rushan], 8 vols. (Taipei, 1964)

J. H. Hung: *Ming Drama* (Taipei, 1966)

D. Kalvodová: 'The Origin of Character of the Szechwan Theatre', *Archiv Orientální*, xxxiv (Prague, 1966), 505

Char Tin-yuke: *The Hakka Chinese: their Origin and Folk Songs* (San Francisco, CA, 1969) [Eng. trans. C. H. Kwock]

Li Chunren: *Zhongguo Fojiao Yinyue zhi Yanjiu* [Study of Chinese Buddhist Music] (diss., College of Chinese Culture, Taipei, 1971)

Shi Weiliang, ed.: *Chen Da he Tade Ge* [Chen Da and His Songs] (Taipei, 1971)

C. Mackerras: *The Rise of the Peking Opera 1770–1870: Social Aspects of the Theatre in Manchu China* (Oxford, 1972)

C. Stevens: *Peking Drumsinging* (diss., Harvard U., 1972)

Yang Zhaozhen: *Kejia Minyao* [Hakka Folk Song] (Taipei, 1974)

C. Mackerras: *The Chinese Theatre in Modern Times from 1840 to the Present* (London, 1975)

W. Dolby: *A History of Chinese Drama* (London, 1976)

C. Frankel [Chang Ch'ung-ho]: 'The Practice of K'un-ch'ü Singing from the 1920's to the 1960's', *Chinoperl Papers*, vi (1976), 82

R. Strassberg: 'The Singing Techniques of K'un-ch'ü and Their Musical Notation', *Chinoperl Papers*, vi (1976), 45

Tsao Pen-yeh: 'P'ing-t'an Music – A Preliminary Study', *Chinoperl Papers*, vi (1976), 95

Chen Fu-yen: 'Principles of K'un-ch'ü Singing', *Asian Music*, viii/2 (1977), 4

Leung Chun-kin: 'Notes on Cantonese Opera in North America', *Chinoperl Papers*, vii (1977), 9

J. Walls: 'Kuaibanshu: Elements of the Fast Clapper Tale', *Chinoperl Papers*, vii (1977), 60–91

341

Cai Yanfen: *Nanyin Longzhou he Muyu de Bianxie* [Composition of (the narratives) *Nanyin*, *Longzhou*, and *Muyu*] (Guangzhou, 1978)

T. Gee: *Stories of Chinese Opera* (Taipei, 1978)

Leung Chun-kin: 'The Cantonese Opera in Guangzhou in 1979', *Chinoperl Papers*, ix (1979–80), 92

Lian Bo, ed.: *Tanci Yinyue Chutan* [Preliminary Investigation of *Tanci* Music] (Shanghai, 1979)

Lu Eting: *Kunju Yanchu Shigao* [Draft History of *Kun* Opera Performance] (Shanghai, 1980) [revised by Zhao Jingshen]

C. Mackerras: 'China§III, 1 and 2. Musical Drama', *Grove 6*

Quanzhou Shi Nanyin Yanjiu She, ed.: *Nanqu Xuanji* [Selection of (Minnan) *Nanqu*] (Quanzhou, c1980)

C. Stevens: 'China§III, 3. Popular Narratives', *Grove 6*

Wang Jixiao: *Yuju Changqiang Yinyue Gailun* [Introduction of *Yuju* (Henan Opera) Arias] (Beijing, 1980)

Wu Guoqin: *Zhongguo Xiqu Shi Manhua* [Open Discussion on the History of Chinese Opera] (Shanghai, 1980)

Zhang Geng and Guo Hancheng: *Zhongguo Xiqu Tongshi* [General History of Chinese Opera], 3 vols. (Beijing, 1980)

Zhongguo Yinyue Yanjiu Suo, ed.: *Zhongguo Minge* [Chinese Folk Songs], 4 vols. (Shanghai, 1980–85)

Liu Guojie: 'Lun Jingju Pihuang Qiang de Gongdiao ji Qi Bianhua' [Concerning the Tonic Mode of Peking Opera *Pihuang* (melody-type) and its Variation], *Yinyue Luncong*, iv (1981), 77–114

Liu Jidian, ed.: *Jingju Yinyue Gailun* [Introduction to the Music of Peking Opera] (Beijing, 1981)

Liu Xuezhi and Liu Hongbin: *Shulaibao de Yishu Jiqiao* [Artistic Technique of *Shulaibao* (narrative)] (Beijing, 1981)

Shanghai Yishu Yanjiu Suo, ed.: *Zhongguo Xiqu Quyi Cidian* [Chinese Opera and Narrative Dictionary] (Shanghai, 1981)

Wu Zuguang and others: *Peking Opera and Mei Lanfang* (Beijing, 1981)

Zhang Jiu and Shi Shengchao: *Xiangju Gaoqiang Yinyue Yanjiu* [Study of *Gaoqiang* (melodic style) of Hunan Opera] (Beijing, 1981)

Chen Jinzhao: *Kuaishu Yanjiu* [Study of *Kuaishu* (narrative)] (Taipei, 1982)

Hsü Tsang-houei [Xu Changhui] and others: *Lugang Nanguan Yinyue de Diaocha yu Yanjiu* [Investigation and Study of *Nanguan* Music in (the city of) Lugang] (Taipei, 1982)

Hsü Tsang-houei: *Taiwan Fulao Xi Minge* [Fulao (Fujian) Folk Songs of Taiwan] (Taipei, 1982)

Jiang Mingdun: *Hanzu Minge Gailun* [Outline of Han Chinese Folk Song] (Shanghai, 1982)

Lü Chuikuan: *Quanzhou Xianguan Yanjiu* [Study of *Xianguan* (*nanguan*) Music from Quanzhou] (Taipei, 1982)

Song Chuyu [James Soong]: *Zhonghua Minzu Geyao Xuanji* [Collection of Chinese Folk Songs], 2 vols. (Taipei, 1982) [with Eng. summary]

Tan Fengyuan and others: *Danxian Yishu Jingyan Tan* [Discussion of the Artistic Experience of *Danxian* (narrative)] (Beijing, 1982)

Wang Shoutai: *Kunqu Gelü* [Rules and Forms of *Kunqu*] (Yangzhou, 1982)

Wang Zhenyi: *Taiwan de Beiguan* [Beiguan (music) of Taiwan] (Taipei, 1982)

Yang Zhaozhen: *Taiwan Kejia Xi Minge* [Hakka Folk Songs of Taiwan] (Taipei, 1982)

B. Yung: 'Popular Narrative in the Pleasure Houses of the South', *Chinoperl Papers*, xi (1982), 126

Yu Zhenfei: *Zhenfei Qupu* [*Kunqu* Notations of Yu Zhenfei] (Shanghai, 1982; rev. of 1953 collection)

Zhang Xuanwen: *Taiwan Gezaixi Yinyue* [Gezaixi (opera) Music of Taiwan] (Taipei, 1982)

He Shixi and others, eds.: *Jingju Qupu* [Peking Opera Notations], ser. (Shanghai, 1983)

Jiang Mingdun: 'Shilun Jiangnan Minge de Difang Secai' [Initial Discussion on the Local Colour of Jiangnan (district) Folk Songs], *Yinyue Yanjiu*, i (1983), 75

Lai Bixia: *Taiwan Kejia Shange* [Hakka Mountain Songs of Taiwan] (Taipei, 1983)

L. Li Mark: 'Tone and Tune in Kunqu', *Chinoperl Papers*, xii (1983), 9–60

Lu Wenqin and Wu Ying, eds.: *Mei Lanfang Changqiang Ji* [Collection of (Peking opera) Arias of Mei Lanfang] (Shanghai, 1983)

R. Riddle: *Flying Dragons, Flowing Streams: Music in the Life of San Francisco's Chinese* (Westport, CT, 1983)

Wen Ping: 'Kejia Shange Gaishu' [General Discussion of Hakka Mountain Songs], *Guangzhou Yinyue Xueyuan Xuebao*, iii (1983), 56 [cont. in later issues]

B. Yung: 'Creative Process in Cantonese Opera', *EM*, xxvii (1983), 29; xxvii/2, 297; xxvii/3, 439

He Ming: 'Dianju Sixian Qiang de Banshi ji Qi Jiegou' [Form of *Sixian* Arias of *Dianju* (Yunnan opera) and Their Construction], *Minzu Yinyue*, iv (1984), 66 [cont. in later issues]

Huang Jingming and others: *Yueju Changqiang Yinyue Gailun* [Introduction to *Yueju* (Cantonese Opera) Arias] (Beijing, 1984)

Zhang Bojie: 'Chaoju Shengqiang de Qiyuan ji Liubian' [Origin and Change in the Melody of Chaozhou Opera], *Yinyue Yanjiu*, iv (1984), 52

R. C. Pian, trans.: 'My Life as a Drum Singer: the Autobiography of Jang Tsueyfeng (As Told to Liou Fang)', *Chinoperl Papers*, xiii (1984–5), 6–106

Zhang Zelun: 'Shitan Woguo Xiqu Yinyue Tizhi' [Initial Discussion of the Musical System of (Chinese) Opera], *Yinyue Yanjiu*, i (1984), 12

An Luxing: 'Lun Woguo Xiqu Yinyue Liangda Tizhi' [Concerning Two Major Systems in Chinese Opera Music], *Yinyue Yanjiu*, ii (1985), 108

Liu Zhengwei: 'Erhuang Qiang Lunyuan' [Origin of *Erhuang* (melody-type)], *Yinyue Yanjiu*, i (1986), 73

Tsao Pen-yeh: *Su-chou T'an-tz'u: a study of the Structural Elements of the Chinese Southern Singing-Narrative* (Hong Kong, 1987)

N. Yeh: 'Nanguan Music Repertoire: Categories, Notation, and Performance Practice', *Asian Music*, xix/2 (1988), 31–70

B. Yung: *Cantonese Opera: Performance as Creative Process* (Cambridge, 1989)

MINORITY CULTURES

E. Emsheimer: 'Preliminary Remarks on Mongolian Music and Instruments' and 'Music of Eastern Mongolia Collected by H. Haslund-Christensen, Noted Down by E. Emsheimer', *The Music of the Mongols: Eastern Mongolia* (Stockholm, 1943), 69–100, 101–97

Zhongguo Yinyue Yanjiu Suo: *Miaozu Minge* [Folk Songs of the Miao Nationality] (Beijing, 1958)

——: *Miaozu Lusheng* [Lusheng (mouth organ) of the Miao Nationality] (Beijing, 1959)

Ling Manli: 'Taiwan Amei Zu de Yueqi' [Musical Instruments of the Taiwan Ami Minority], *Bulletin of the Institute of Ethnology, Academia Sinica*, xi (1961), 185–220 [with Eng. summary]

Li Hwei: 'A Comparative Study of the Jew's Harp Among the Aborigines of Formosa and East Asia', *Bulletin of the Institute of Ethnology, Academia Sinica*, i (1967), 85–140

Hakan Chulun and Wu Ronggui, eds.: *Menggu Minyao* [Mongolian Folk Songs] (Taipei, 1972)

Lü Bingchuan: 'Taiwan Tuzhuzu zhi Yueqi' [Instruments of the Taiwan Tribes], *Tunghai Ethnomusicological Journal*, i (1974), 85 [with Eng. summary]

Hsü Tsang-houei, ed.: *Taiwan Shandi Minyao* [Taiwan Mountain-tribe Folk Songs], 2 vols. (Taipei, 1978)

Yuan Bingchang and others: 'Daizu de Yueqi' [Musical Instruments of the Dai (Thai) Minority], *Yueqi*, i (1981), 14

Zhou Zonghan: 'Dongzu Yueqi' [Musical Instruments of the Dong Minority], *Yueqi*, iii (1981), 18; iv (1981), 11

Liangshan Yizu Zizhizhou Wenhua Ju, ed.: *Yizu Minjian Qiyue Quxuan* [Selection of Yi folk Instrumental Music] (Chengdu, 1982)

Yuan Bingchang: 'Yizu Yueqi' [Musical Instruments of the Yi Minority], *Yueqi*, iii (1982), 10; iv (1982), 15

Xiangxi Tujiazu Miaozu Zizhizhou Dangwei Xuanchuan Bu, ed.: *Xiangxi Tujiazu Miaoxu Minjian Gequ Yuequ Xuan* [Selection of Folk Songs and Music of the Xiangxi, Tujia, and Miao Minorities] (Shanghai, 1983)

Yun Hai: 'Chaoxian Zu Yueqi' [Musical Instruments of the Korean Minority], *Yueqi*, ii (1983), 15

Kou Bangping: 'Naxi Zu Yinyue Gaishu' [General Account of Naxi (minority) Music], *Minzu Yinyue*, iv (1984), 16

Yang Fang: 'Yunnan Minzu Minjian Yinyue Jianshu' [Overview of the (minority) Musics of Yunnan Province], *Yunnan Yishu Xueyuan Ershiwu Zhounian Yuanqing Zhuanji* (Kunming, 1984), 3

Yuan Bingchang and He Qing: 'Lijiang Naxi Guyue Yueqi' [Ancient Musical Instruments of the Lijiang Naxi Minority], *Yueqi*, iii (1984), 19; iv (1984), 25

Feng Mingyang: 'Zhuangzu "Shuangsheng" de Qiangdiao Lei Lun' [On the Classification of Zhuang (minority) Two-voice Melodies], *Yinyue Yanjiu*, iv (1985), 15

C. Mackerras: 'Traditional Uygur Performing Arts', *Asian Music*, xvi/1 (1985), 29

Xiao Li and Fu Xiao: 'Lisu Zu Sanxian Gewu Chutan' [Preliminary Investigation into *Sanxian* Song-dances of the Lisu Minority], *Minzu Yinyue*, ii (1985), 16

Zhang Nan: 'Honghe Yizu Minjian Yinyue de Diaoshi yu Xuanfa Chuxi' [Preliminary Analysis of Mode and Melodic Construction in Yi Tribal Music of Honghe (district)], *Minzu Yinyue*, iii (1985), 2

Zhu Zhuojian: 'Koqin Tanyuan' [Exploration into the Source of the *Koqin* (Jew's harp)], *Minzu Yinyue*, iv (1985), 23

Dali Shi Wenlian Wenhua Ju, ed.: *Baizu Dabenqu Yinyue* [*Dabenqu* Music of the Bai Minority] (Kunming, 1986)

Du Yaxiong, ed.: *Zhongguo Shaoshu Minzu Yinyue*, i [Chinese Tribal Minority Music, vol. i] (Beijing, 1986)

He Hong and others: 'Yaozu Minjian Yueqi' [Folk Musical Instruments of the Yao Minority], *Yueqi*, ii (1986), 24 [cont. in later issues]

Yuan Bingchang and Mao Jizeng, ed.: *Zhongguo Shaoshu Minzu Yueqi Zhi* [Dictionary of Musical Instruments of the Chinese Tribal Minorities] (Beijing, 1986)

A. Thrasher: *La-Li-Luo Dance-songs of the Chuxiong Yi, Yunnan Province, China* (Danbury, 1990)

Zhang Xingrong, ed.: *Yunnan Minzu Qiyue Huicui* [Cream of Yunnan Nationalities Instrumental Music] (Kunming, 1990)

20TH CENTURY

Yang Yinliu, Cao Anhe and others: *A Bing Quji* [Collected Music of A Bing] (Shanghai, 1952/*R*1979)

Wenxue Yishu Jielian Hehui, ed.: *Minzu Qiyue Quxuan* [Selection of National Instrumental Music], 3 vols. (Shanghai, 1955–6)

Liu Guanyue: *Dizi Duzou Quxuan* [Selection of Solos for *Dizi* (flute)] (Beijing, 1956)

Zhongyang Gewu Tuan, ed.: *Feng Zicun Dizi Quxuan* [Selection of *Dizi* (flute) Compositions by Feng Zicun] (Beijing, 1958/*R*1981)

Gao Ziming: *Xiandai Guoyue* [Present-day *Guoyue*] (Taipei, 1959)

Zhongguo Yinyuejia Xiehui, ed.: *Yinyue Jianshe Wenji* [Collected Essays on the Construction of (a new) Music], 3 vols. (Beijing, 1959)

Huang Tipei: *Guoyue Yuepu* [National Music in Notation], 7 vols. (Taipei, 1960)

Zhongguo Yinyuejia Xiehui, ed.: *Wei Gongnongbing Fuwu de Yinyue Yishu* [Musical Arts Serving the Workers, Peasants and Soldiers] (Beijing, 1961)

A. Kagan: 'Music and the Hundred Flowers Movement', *MQ*, xlix (1963), 417

A. C. Scott: *Literature and the Arts in Twentieth Century China* (London, 1963)

Mao Jizeng: 'Reform of Traditional Musical Instruments', *Chinese Literature*, viii (1965), 110

Mao Zedong [Mao Tse-tung]: *On Literature and Art (May 1942)* (Beijing, 1967)

Jiang Qing [Chiang Ch'ing]: *On the Revolution of Peking Opera* (Beijing, 1968)

Sun Peizhang and others: *Guoyue Mingqu Ji* [Collection of Famous Pieces of National Music] (Taipei, *c*1970)

Guowu Yuan Wenhua Zu, ed.: *Zhandi Xinge* [New Songs of the Battlefield] (Beijing, 1972)

Guangdong Renmin, ed.: *Qiyue Qu* [Instrumental Music] (Guangzhou, 1973)

C. Mackerras: 'Chinese Opera After the Cultural Revolution (1970–72)', *China Quarterly*, lv (1973), 478–510

Hu Yongguang, ed.: *Dizi Duzou Quxuan* [Selection of Solos for *Dizi* (flute)] (Hong Kong, 1974)

Guangdong Sheng Wenyi Chuangzuo She, ed.: *Guangdong Yinyue Quxuan* [Selection of (contemporary) Cantonese Music] (Beijing, 1977)

Han Kuo-huang: 'The Modern Chinese Orchestra', *Asian Music*, xi/1 (1979), 1–40

Xia Yan: *Guoyue Chuangzuo Zongpu* [Collection of *Guoyue* Compositions], ser. (Taipei, 1979)

Han Kuo-huang and Lindy Li Mark: 'Evolution and Revolution in Chinese Music', *Musics of Many Cultures*, ed. E. May (Berkeley, CA, 1980), 10

Ma Ke: *Xian Xinghai Zhuan* [Biography of Xian Xinghai] (Beijing, 1980)

A. C. Scott: 'China§VI. Since 1949', *Grove 6*

Nie Xulun: *Shaonian Shidai de Nie Er* [Nie Er in His Youth] (Tianjin, 1981)

Da Wei: 'Xinhai Geming Shiqi de Xuetang Gequ' [School Songs during the Period of the 1911 Revolution], *Yinyue Yanjiu*, iv (1982), 106

Hu Dengtiao: *Minzu Guanxian Yuefa* [National Wind-String Music] (Shanghai, 1982)

Lu Chunling: *Lu Chunling Dizi Quji* [Collection of *Dizi* (flute) Music by Lu Chunling] (Beijing, 1982)

A. Perris: 'Music as Propaganda: Art at the Command of Doctrine in the People's Republic of China', *EM*, xxvii (1983), 1

I. Wong: 'Geming Gequ: Songs for the Education of the Masses', *Popular Chinese Literature and Performing Arts in the People's Republic of China, 1949–1979*, ed. B. MacDougall (Berkeley, CA, 1984), 112–143

2: JAPAN

David W. Hughes

Much has been published in the field of Japanese traditional music. The present chapter characterizes rather than summarizes, aiming to catch the flavour of research done, including the approaches and attitudes of native scholars. More detailed introductory surveys by genre in Japanese can be found in Hirano and others (1987, pp.445–91) and at the end of the appropriate generic entry in *Ongaku daijiten* (1981–3) and *Nihon ongaku daijiten* (*NOD*, 1989). G. Tsuge's annotated bibliography (1986), indexed by topic, allows readers to explore Western-language sources (see also H.-D. Reese's 1987 supplement to Tsuge). Many shorter annotated bibliographies in Western languages are cited in Tsuge, several of which cover Japanese-language sources.

Early sources and studies

Sources from the 8th to the 19th centuries are numerous and varied. Aside from the wealth of musical notations mentioned below we have numerous musical encyclopedias, theoretical treatises, and other works, often containing illustrations. Most of the early works pertain to court or Buddhist music; E. Harich-Schneider (1973) provides a detailed, easily accessible English-language introduction to some of the more important of these. To suggest the wealth of materials, here is a partial list of the major early works mentioned in the summary of research on court music in *NOD* (pp.412f): music encyclopedias, for example *Kyōkunshō* (1233), *Taigenshō* (1512), *Gakkaroku* (1690); treatises on scales and modes, as *Gakusho yōroku* (before 735), *Kangen ongi* (1185), *Jinchi yōroku* (c1192), and many later works. The information contained in the encyclopedias is rich; for example, the *Taigenshō* lists programmes of concerts of the court vocal genre *saibara* covering some four centuries.

Sources pertaining to popular musical genres are abundant. A hint of what is available is given by D. Tanaka (1980, pp.239f), who cites various Edo period descriptions of the functions of particular off-stage mood-music patterns in the Kabuki theatre.

Finally, the treatises of Zeami (1363?–1443), the greatest noh theorist, are still cited and revered by performers and scholars. Numerous translations of his more important treatises are available (e.g. Rimer and Yamazaki, 1984), although his often cryptic references to musical practice are elusive in any language.

Several valuable scholarly studies date from around the turn of the century. R. Uehara (1895) made the first significant attempt at a general scale theory for Japanese music. A huge study of the Heike *biwa* tradition was made by Z. Tateyama (1910), an heir to one of its branches; it includes a wealth of data (if little analysis) on history, notation, and other aspects. The encyclopedia *Koji ruien* (1909–10) comprises two volumes on music and dance; although much of the information is repeated uncritically without attribution from earlier sources, it is a fine example of a transitional work linking traditional and modern Japanese scholarship. Finally, Tanabe Hisao (1883–1984) was a pioneer from whose efforts in a sense all modern work by native scholars on Japanese music and musical instruments, as well as the current interest in other East Asian musics, can be said to descend. Although no single work of his commands attention today, the serious researcher will read his books, and his influence can be detected in later writers.

Several early sources in Western languages deal with Japanese scale structure and are mentioned below in the discussion of Koizumi's tetrachordal theory. We also find C. Knott (1893) denying the relevance of the concept of 'tonic' to Japanese music – a view far ahead of its time in the West. Otto Abraham and Erich M. von Hornbostel (1903), working from recordings, concerned themselves with the detailed measurement of Japanese intervallic structure. Of these early researchers, only F. Piggott (1893) spent a significant period of time in Japan in close contact with music and musicians. His book depicts many aspects of musical life in Japan. In some cases he came upon instruments or genres scarcely noted by other researchers and little-known today. Serious fieldwork on Japanese music by non-Japanese, however, became common only from the 1950s.

Recent research

The recent rapid expansion of ethnomusicology in Japan can be considered to stem from the influence of Koizumi Fumio. Through his lectures at Tokyo University of the Arts and on radio and television, and through numerous popular writings, he almost singlehandedly raised Japanese consciousness of 'ethnic' musics. As a teacher, he encouraged fieldwork, comparative analysis and familiarization with Western ethnomusicological writings. His influence affected research on both Japanese music and other ethnic musics. Koizumi's effect can be gauged from the contents of the memorial volume of papers by his former students (Henshū-iinkai, 1986); these cover a wide range of topics, approaches and geographical areas (see also Ohtani and Tokumaru, 1983).

Most Koizumi pupils emphasized synchronic questions. However, historical (ethno-)musicology in Japan also has many skilled adherents, tempted by the abundance of early musical notations, theoretical treatises, and other documents pertaining to early music life. Hayashi Kenzō was a pioneer in this field; his most productive pupil is Hirano Kenji.

Sources and resources: availability and access

In Japan, as in neighbouring China and Korea, the tradition of written scholarship on indigenous music is of impressive antiquity. The present-day output of research on Japanese traditional music and performing arts is no less impressive. Although most of this is being produced by the Japanese themselves, the contribution of foreign scholars is also steadily increasing.

The Japanese-language output in particular can be gauged from the Japanese edition of *RILM*. Recent annual issues have averaged some 170 entries on traditional music. The 1987 compilation of 177 entries included 56 substantial books and 13 dissertations. Three other valuable bibliographical sources have recently appeared: G. Tsuge (1986) annotates 881 Western-language books and articles (with plans for periodic updates); *NOD* summarizes the research history of each major genre, citing significant works; K. Hirano and others (1987) annotate virtually all important native-language sources, including scholarly recordings, for Japanese 'art' music, and give sources for rare originals; the book is well-indexed by genre although works on folk and regional traditions, including Ryūkyū and Ainu music, are omitted. *NOD*, a dictionary-cum-encyclopedia, is the most compact and up-to-date source for the reader of Japanese to find introductions to different genres as well as specific information on technical terms and people; the work of E. Kikkawa (1984, *Hōgaku hyakka*), far less ambitious, is useful but idiosyncratic.

The visitor to Tokyo wishing to examine the range of books and recordings available can start at Toyoda Shobō in the Kanda bookshop district: the entire shop is devoted to new and used books on Japanese performing arts and a few recordings. Many of these are studies of theatre and dance without specific musicological content (as are many of the music works cited in Japanese *RILM*), and such works are generally ignored here. One of the best-stocked record stores is Tōyōdō in Asakusa, Tokyo where one can also obtain up-to-date information on the availability of recordings. These shops are willing to mail goods abroad once personal contact and trust has been established.

Given that books and scholarly recordings relating to Japanese music go out of print rapidly, and that the bulk of the extant premodern musical scores have never been issued in modern printed editions, the would-be researcher must often depend on libraries and archives. (Modern reprints generally lack the original music notation, and reprinting of facsimiles is still rare.) Outside Japan, extensive collections are found, for example, at such longstanding centres of Japanese music research as the universities of Cologne (over 1300 recordings) and Michigan; smaller collections exist at many other universities and libraries.

As for Japan itself, those seeking original manuscripts and notations dating back as far as 747 AD should contact the Research Archives for Japanese Music at Ueno Gakuen College, Tokyo. A representative sample of facsimiles of 68 notations from their astonishing collection is given by K. Hirano and K. Fukushima (1978). An idea of the wealth of other institutions harbouring such original manuscripts can be had from reading the acknowledgements by Harich-Schneider (1973). The most extensive research collections of books and recordings readily available to visiting scholars are in the libraries of Tokyo's Kunitachi College of Music and Tokyo National University of the Fine Arts and Music (also known as the Tokyo University of the Arts, or Geidai). More specialized collections are to be found at various institutions; for example, there are centres for research on noh music at Hōsei University and Musashino Women's University in Tokyo, and there is also an institute for research on Okinawan culture (including music) at Hōsei. Further information (slightly outdated) on archives can be found in the reports of the Music Librarians Association of Japan (1979–). Access to any such collections, however, requires a proper introduction such as a letter from your institution's librarian or from a mutual friend. A graduate student wishing to obtain regular access to materials at Geidai should apply at least six months in advance for the status of *kenkyūsei* (research student).

Finally, there are myriad journals dealing with Japanese music. The most important is *Tōyō ongaku kenkyū* (Journal of the Society for Research in Asiatic Music) (1936–), which publishes scholarly papers on Japanese and other Asian musics; it now includes English summaries of all major articles. *Kikan hōgaku* focusses on Japanese music and seemingly is intended for both academics and 'civilians'. Aside from scholarly articles, content ranges from interviews with leading performers regarding stage fright, to the questions from the entrance exam for the Japanese music division of Tokyo University of the Arts. *Geinō no kagaku*, the house organ of the Tokyo National Cultural Properties Research Institute, contains many excellent studies on a wide range of traditional performing arts; copies are available only to relevant libraries on special request. A recently issued monthly periodical, *Hōgaku Journal*, carries a detailed schedule of concerts throughout Japan as well as an English-language preview of selected events. Articles concerning aspects of traditional music may appear in a wide range of journals, including *Geinōshi kenkyū*, *Minzoku geinō kenkyū*, and *Ongakugaku*. Many more journals and newsletters relate to particular genres or performing arts organizations: *Gagaku-kai*, for example, deals only with the court music tradition; in English there is *Hōgaku*, published at the Graduate Center of the City University of New York, which has carried some useful analyses of pieces in the *sōkyoku-jiuta* repertory in particular.

Characteristics of Japanese publications

Given the enormous number of books and recordings produced in Japan, one might assume that many research topics have already been exhausted by the Japanese themselves, but the abundance of publications is somewhat misleading. The same material tends to reappear in slightly different guises. For example, M. Yokomichi's seminal work on the structure of noh music (1963; Yokomichi and Omote, 1960), originally issued as a booklet accompanying a disc set and as an introduction to a text collection, has recently been reprinted (in a useful collection of his articles) as well as reworked in various publications (1983–4, 1986). Impressionistic or romantic excursions by poets, painters, journalists, and others include several books dealing with the blind female folk singers (*goze*) of northern Japan; these contain significant amounts of descriptive data concerning the activities of the *goze* (Saitō, 1975). The problem for the reader is to sort out fact from interpretation, since sources are seldom cited. Further, there are countless books dealing with Japanese musical dramas and narrative forms (noh, kabuki, bunraku, heike epic recitation) which, while excellent in their treatment of historical and social context, texts etc, contain little that bears directly on music. For example, the volume on *jōruri* in the series *Nihon no koten geinō* (Geinōshi Kenkyūkai, 1970) has a single valuable chapter on *shamisen* melodic patterns by K. Inoue.

The most striking feature of Japanese scholarly output is the abundance of well-annotated thematic record sets of indigenous music. Many of these are devoted to in-depth coverage of one genre, as is a set of 60 discs surveying the repertory of koto and *jiuta-shamisen* vocal and instrumental pieces (Hirano, 1987, *Sōkyoku*) and cutting across the different schools of performers. The 220 compositions spanning four centuries are presented in near-chronological order. The discs are accompanied by an explanatory booklet (*kaisetsusho*) comprised of a mere 334 pages of A4 size. All song texts are included and given detailed textual explication, and the history of each composition is discussed. There are indexes of titles, performers, and first lines of lyrics. However, although the musical characteristics of each piece are described briefly, there is no attempt at analysis as such, nor are there any transcriptions. The book and discs thus constitute an excellent starting point for musical analysis.

Other record sets encompass only a sub-genre of a larger genre. The compound genre of *sōkyoku* and *jiuta* treated in the set mentioned above has also been covered in subdivided form in several other sets. Consider only the sub-genre of koto-accompanied song suites (*kumiuta*): Hirano in 1973 offered 50 compositions on 14 discs, with an 80-page booklet. Six years later the same editor issued another set (Kikkawa and Hirano, 1979) with 101 selections on 20 discs including virtually all the compositions in the earlier set. Justification for this second compilation was twofold: (i) wider coverage, including both ancestral forms and later imitations of the standard *kumiuta*; and (ii) more careful attention to differences between schools, so that up to four versions of some pieces are included. This comparative aspect makes the latter set much more useful, even though the annotations are far less complete than in the 1973 set and contain no analytical transcriptions.

Other sets are devoted to single performers. Referring again to *sōkyoku* and *jiuta*, there is a 22-record set by Kikuhara Hatsuko (Hirano, 1976). Another 12 discs of her performances form the bulk of a collection of shamisen-accompanied *kumiuta*, which includes detailed Western transcriptions of all selections (Hirano, 1974).

Other sets are devoted to a particular research problem or to a theme cutting across genres. Among the most valuable such sets are S. Kawatake and others (1965), including some analysis of the structure of classical dance pieces: M. Yokomichi and S. Gamō (1978), discussed further below; K. Machida (1965), which traces the musical genealogy of several families of folk song; Hirano (1978) and Hirano and others (1983), whose recordings demonstrate the results of the attempts at reading early notation described in the accompanying notes; and Hirano (1980), which charts the adoption of a particular ancient melody in various genres.

Nearly all such scholarly record sets give us the lyrics as well as the names of performers and are thus invaluable as research materials. However, they have two drawbacks: first, they are rarely commercially viable and therefore go out of print rapidly and second, the impressively bulky booklets, which contribute to the often prohibitive prices, tend primarily to have only two objectives – to provide basic (if extensive) information about the individual recorded selections and to give general historical background for the genre(s) treated.

Descriptively excellent, they contain little analysis except in those devoted to particular research problems.

Two ambitious sets attempted to survey nearly the entire range of Japanese music: S. Kishibe and others (1970–72) and E. Kikkawa and others (1980–82). The former includes folk music and some works by Western-style Japanese composers of the 20th century. The latter, despite its much greater size, does not include these although it does contain several research records (e.g. demonstrating various instrumental techniques or narrating the melodic patterns in a particular piece). Both sets would be invaluable – if they were still available.

It is obviously unfair to expect the *kaisetsusho* to do everything; certainly they far excel the skimpy annotations accompanying most non-Japanese re-cordings of 'ethnic' musics. The lack of analytical content is felt more acutely when these *kaisetsusho* are reprinted as parts of independent books, without recordings. Hirano's *Shamisen* (1987), for example, is cobbled together from the booklets of several of the above-mentioned recordings; it contains 84 pages of 'history and characteristics', 148 of lyrics and explanations of them, but virtually nothing about the music per se, and no transcriptions. The notes to K. Machida (1965) carry over nicely into book form (in Tōyō Ongaku Gakkai, 1967) because they contain extensive transcriptions.

Another characteristic of Japanese-language ethnomusicological studies is that much of the hard analytical work appears in the form of MA and even BA dissertations. Some of these are cited below; many more are abstracted in the Japanese edition of *RILM*. (As yet there have been few relevant doctoral dissertations; one of the best was published as Gamō, 1983.)

In sum, published monographs constitute a less important component of the work on Japanese music than do scholarly record sets, dissertations, and collections of shorter papers. For this reason the ratio of articles to books in the bibliography of Japanese research is high.

Cross-genre research topics

Japanese music comprises a number of distinct genres differing in such fundamental musical features as scale and mode, metric structure, and timbral 'sound ideal'. Just as Gregorian chant and the compositions of Machaut, Beethoven, and Webern are rarely analysed collectively as com-ponents of a single entity called 'Western classical music', so most research on Japanese music focusses on a single genre; there are, however, a number of topics that cut across generic or sub-generic boundaries.

SCALES AND MODES Despite generic diversity, a frequent concern has been to establish a modal theory that could encompass many or all types of Japanese traditional music. The best short surveys of such efforts are by Hirano and Kojima (1981) and Koizumi (1979, pp.149–88); longer examples of various approaches are in Tōyō Ongaku Gakkai (1982). Prior to the late 19th century, the only thoroughly elaborated modal theory was for *gagaku* (court music). Even for *gagaku*, early theorizing consisted chiefly of classifying pieces according to mode and did not extend to detailed analysis of tonal function or melodic patterns; the focus was mainly on scales (tonal material) and tunings.

It was recognized, however, that court music modes fell into two modal groups, *ritsu* and *ryo*: each had an anhemitonic pentatonic core with two 'exchange tones' (*hennon*) which could replace two of the core degrees (in ascending melodic passages in the case of *ritsu*, in descent for *ryo*). The modal terminology of *gagaku* was often applied to *shōmyō* (Buddhist chant), but the first true studies of distinctive *shōmyō* modal structure date only from the late 20th century.

The first significant Japanese attempt at an overview, which formed the basis for all subsequent work, was Uehara Rokushirō's *Zokugaku senritsu kō* (1895). Focussing on the non-court folk and popular musics, he distinguished two basic Japanese pentatonic 'modes': *senpō*, as opposed to *onkai* or 'scale' (a terminological distinction often ignored). These he called *in* and *yō* (in Chinese *yin* and *yang*), or *miyako-bushi* ('urban melody') and *inaka-bushi* ('rural melody'). If we start from C as 'tonic' (*kyū*; a court-music concept of Chinese origin), then Uehara's 'urban melody' *in* mode is C–Db –F–G–Ab –C but with Ab replaced by Bb (and sometimes Db by Eb) in ascending passages. The *yō* mode (identical in his thinking with the *ritsu* category of court modes) differed from this only in using Db and Ab instead of Db and Ab .

It was Koizumi Fumio who, in his 1959 book, created the model now followed by the majority of Japanese researchers. His theory differs from Uehara's in two crucial respects. First, he increased to four the ideal-typical modes he felt accounted for the majority of Japanese musics. Second, he abandoned Uehara's octave-based theory and focussed on the tetrachord as the basic unit of modal structure. In this he acknowledged R. Lachmann (1929) as his direct inspiration. However, other Western researchers had also proposed such an approach (Knott, 1891; Abraham and Hornbostel, 1903; Péri, 1934). Knott spoke of tetrachords but, since they contained only three notes, preferred to call them trichords; Péri followed this, while the Germans remained with tetrachord. The successful application of this ancient Greek approach to Japanese music is doubtless the major contribution of early Western researchers to Japanese music studies. Koizumi's tetrachord consists of two stable 'nuclear tones' (German *Kernton*, Japanese *kakuon*) a fourth apart plus a single infix whose position determines the species of tetrachord. He calls his four types the *in* or *miyako-bushi* (C–Db –F), *ritsu* (C–D–F), *yō* (C–Eb –F), and *ryūkyū* (C–E–F). These combine to form various octave species characteristic of particular types of music. An important difference from Uehara's theory is that Koizumi abandons the Chinese-derived tendency to think in terms of a single 'tonic' and recognizes that the various nuclear tones may compete as tonal centres, leading to various types of modulation. (For an English summary of his model, see Koizumi, 1977.)

Shibata Minao (1978) has proposed another general model, owing something to Koizumi's yet differing significantly. Whereas Koizumi focussed on the frame created by the fourths, Shibata shifts attention to the relations of the individual nuclear tones to their upper and lower neighbours. Among the few adherents to this main rival to Koizumi's model, Y. Tokumaru has applied it to *shamisen* music (1981) and J. Sawada to Buddhist chant (in Tōyo Ongaku Gakkai, 1982). The one other model to gain some currency is that of Kakinoki (in Tōyo Ongaku Gakkai, 1982; see also Kakinoki, 1975, in English), which, however, is more of a notational convention than a model of modal structures. T. Matsumoto (1965) seems to have had no influence.

ORAL MNEMONICS   It was only in the 1970s that researchers began to recognize the importance of the various systems of oral mnemonics for Japanese musical instruments. The accepted cover term for these systems is now *kuchi-shōga*. The transmission of many instrumental traditions has involved memorizing mnemonics rather than use of written notation; indeed, some written notations are directly derived from oral mnemonics (e.g. for the noh flute, or the flute and shawm of the court orchestra). This promises to be a growth field in Japanese music research.

The primary resource for the study of oral mnemonics is the record set *Kuchishōga taikei* (Yokomichi and Gamō, 1978), now unavailable, that contains recordings of most of the extant systems and comparisons with the actual instrumental performances. The extensive notes contain no serious attempt to analyse these systems; for that one must turn to several papers (by Tokumaru, Kawada, Gunji, Fujii, Fujita, and Kamisangō) in Tokumaru and Yamaguti, eds. (1986) and to Hughes (1989). The last-named work reveals that most Japanese systems show some degree of linkage between vowel colour (more precisely, the second-formant frequency) and musical pitch; in the case of the *ryūteki* flute of court music, the direction of melodic movement can be correlated with the vowel hierarchy of the mnemonics 98 percent of the time, with many exceptions explicable by reference to other features of vowel acoustics. Aside from this factor, other features of the consonants and vowels of these systems correlate with musical features such as timbre and onset. This sheds much light on the importance of these systems to musics that are primarily orally transmitted. Future research possibilities include a comparison of modern systems with the earliest extant printed collections of oral mnemonics (e.g. for noh flute, vol. xx of the 1687 work *Bugaku taizen*; see Hirano and others, 1987, p.359).

THE PAN-ASIAN CONTEXT   Another cross-genre, cross-cultural theme has generated increasing scholarly activity since the 1970s: the search for connections between Japanese and other Asian musics. This is often framed in terms of a search for the foreign antecedents or sources (*genryū, genten*) of Japanese music. Recent efforts in this direction include four collections of papers (Koizumi and others, 1977; Emmert and Minegishi, 1980; Fujii, 1985; Gamō and others, 1988). The bulk of the articles in these volumes, though, are not comparative but simply descriptive studies (often at an introductory level) of a single aspect of a single culture; it is left to the reader, and to future scholars, to try to find the connections among the various musics treated. Still, the impetus behind these efforts is laudable and healthy: Japan's rapidly increasing number of ethnomusicologists, with their broader perspective, are seeking to overcome the tendency among earlier Japanese scholars (in all fields of the humanities) to treat their country as a unique cultural isolate. The fact that it can now be admitted, tacitly or otherwise, that Japanese culture springs partly from foreign origins bodes well for the future of Japanese historical ethnomusicology in particular.

MELODIC PATTERNS OR FORMULAS   Given the prevalence of named vocal and/or instrumental melodic formulas (*senritsukei*) in many genres (e.g. Buddhist chant, Heike *biwa*, *gidayū*), it is not surprising that modern researchers have striven to find recurring melodic patterns even where they are not named (and occasionally where they do not seem to exist). The most interesting studies are by E. Kineya and G. Asakawa (1968), A. Tamba (1974), K. Machida (1981), M. Gamō (1983), L. Wakabayashi (1983), C. Yamada (1984), and A. Tokita (1988). The challenge is not only to discover such patterns but to elucidate the syntax of occurrence.

INSTITUTIONS: IEMOTO AND HOZONKAI   The *iemoto* ('househead') system has had a profound effect on the transmission of the arts in Japan. Most genres of traditional art music and dance, and recently even folk song, are organized into hierarchically structured 'schools' or 'lineages' with an autocratic *iemoto* at the head, who makes decisions about performance style, licensing of teachers etc. The leading researcher of this phenomenon and its effects has been Nishiyama Matsunosuke (1959, 1971), whose early work was summarized by B. Ortolani (1969) (see also Read and Locke, 1983; Shimazaki, 1953–4, which deals with the Kanze school of noh; and the special April 1978 issue of *Rekishi kōron*). Comparisons of stylistic differences between various schools of *nagauta* have been made by G. Kakinoki (1978) and W. Malm (1986).

Another institution deserving objective examination is the Preservation Society (*hozonkai*). An idea born near the turn of the century, preservation has swept the folk performing arts world, partly due to government encouragement. In simplest terms, this organization under local control is devoted to 'preserving' (but also usually developing and propagating) a local song or dance – often a single item, sometimes a suite. While 'preservation' may seem an inappropriate ideology to force on folk arts which are presumed by scholars to have continuous evolution as part of their nature, there is no denying that many folk forms would have disappeared without the growth of this concept. Thus scholars remain ambivalent about its value, as with the *iemoto* system. Little has yet been written about this phenomenon (for a general introduction, see Hughes, 1985, pp.224–41; see also Sasamori, 1981).

MUSICAL INSTRUMENTS   Introductory information on Japanese instruments, with some citation of sources, is available under individual entries in *The New Grove Dictionary of Musical Instruments* (1984). In addition, H. Tanabe (1964) goes into detail on most instruments, while K. Hayashi (1973) puts Japanese instruments into a pan-Asian context. Both writers explore various lines of evidence – textual, iconographic, ethnographic. S. Kishibe and L. Traynor puzzle out in English the evidence for substitute pipes on the mouth organ of the court ensemble (1952). A general survey of instrument manufacturing techniques (primarily in photographs) is provided by M. Shibata and others (1977).

Music archaeology is a growing field in Japan due primarily to the wealth of material turning up in the ever-increasing excavations since the 1960s. Collection has so far outstripped interpretation, which means there is fertile ground here for future researchers. Many fascinating questions arise, including the exact process of transmission and modification of vessel flutes, bronze bells, and various types of zithers from the continent during the last centuries BC; the use and social status of early instruments; and the apparent disinclination to standardize manufacture. A survey of these and other questions, as well as an introduction to data and sources, can be found in D. Hughes (1988), which takes us up to the 8th century. From that point on the most important resource for early East Asian instruments is the collection housed in the Shōsōin repository in Nara, containing numerous instruments primarily of Chinese origin given to a Japanese emperor of the mid-8th century. This collection comprises the early forms of several Japanese instruments and has been extensively researched and well reported by the Shōsōin Office (1967).

Several publications from Kunitachi College of Music have catalogued the iconographic occurrences of East Asian instruments (Kunitachi, 1980– and 1984–, the latter series covering the whole world). These are well-indexed and useful. Be warned, however, that the redrawings of the instruments in the former series are not intended to show fine detail, for which one must go to the original pictorial source.

Studies of instrumental acoustics are sparse. Most Japanese researchers, led now by Y. Andō, publish in Western languages. Some 15 Western-language entries are found under the heading 'acoustics' in Tsuge's bibliography; these deal with both instrumental and vocal intervals and timbre.

OTHERS There could be any number of other cross-genre research topics. To cite only one, there are still few good overviews of Japanese traditional musical aesthetics as a whole; the best are perhaps E. Kikkawa (1948 and 1984), *Nihon ongaku*.

Genres

Since the Japanese themselves tend to treat individual genres of music in isolation, it seems natural enough to include a brief survey by genre, citing only the most interesting works or research trends. The selection here is arbitrary and idiosyncratic, and for the most part lists works of particular interest without offering detailed annotation. Monographs, where they exist, are listed in preference to articles. Works mentioned above are generally not repeated here. In some genres more Western-language than Japanese-language sources are cited, where the former provide good guides to the latter. For further bibliography on most of the genres mentioned below, see the entry on Japan in *The New Grove Dictionary of Music and Musicians* (1980).

COURT MUSIC This section begins with a cautionary tale of relevance to any non-Japanese planning to do research on Japanese music. If a foreigner fails to demonstrate mastery of all possibly relevant sources, and/or reveals an occasional linguistic failing, then his/her work risks being largely ignored regardless of its value – even more so if it is complex. In that context, the initial Japanese reactions to the work of Laurence Picken and his pupils constitute a warning to beginning researchers.

Picken and his co-workers (primarily Wolpert, Marett, Condit, and Markham, but also the Japanese Mitani) have, in an impressive number of publications, sought to demonstrate their claim that performance practice in the *tōgaku* repertory of *gagaku* has changed markedly over the past 1200 years. They claim that a manyfold slowing of tempo and a concomitant increase in certain types of ornamentation in all five melodic instruments has rendered the original melodies all but unrecognizable (as when a Gregorian chant becomes the *cantus firmus* for a motet). The claims of the Picken school are beyond dispute for the most part, so carefully have these scholars marshalled different lines of evidence (see Marett, 1985, for a summary of the evidence; for details, see Picken and others, 1981, and Wolpert, 1981). Although their theories seem to be gaining grudging acceptance in Japan, several scholars in Japan initially waxed vitriolic in their reviews of the work of Picken and his followers. Their work is still ignored by many: the *NOD* review of research on reconstruction of early court music (1989) fails to mention any foreign researchers. It is worth considering the reasons for this.

It is clear that many Japanese cannot follow the tortuous English prose style of the Picken school, difficult even for native speakers: they were able to read only enough to detect several shortcomings but not enough to understand the details of the evidence assembled by the writers. Also, many Japanese working with early manuscripts emphasize the collation and examination of every possible relevant scrap, and refuse to accept the validity of work that fails to do so. At least two non-Japanese scholars, long resident in Japan and fluent in Japanese, seem to agree with their Japanese colleagues: they lit into the Pickenites first for errors in transliterating the pronunciation of (not necessarily in understanding) numerous Sino-Japanese ideograms, and second for failing to consult every possibly relevant primary and secondary source. Some manuscriptologists in Japan spend their time gathering rather than analysing. Third, the Japanese have long been proud of the continuity of their court music – 'the world's oldest continuous orchestral tradition', some boast inaccurately. To suggest that major changes have occurred does not sit well with some traditionalists. Fourth, many Japanese researchers seem to be unduly influenced by their familiarity with modern *tōgaku* performance practice. Even the admirable K. Hayashi, in overseeing the recording of several of his own reconstructions (1965), added lute and zither arpeggios and mouth organ chords of a modern type, for which there is no evidence in the scores or treatises of the 8th to 12th centuries.

A basic resource for the more important court music studies by Japanese scholars is provided by S. Shiba (1968–72, now out of print). This court musician transnotated much of the court repertory into Western notation. (Note that details of ornamentation and of codas and introductions may differ from actual performances.) K. Masumoto (1968) gives a good general introduction to the court traditions, with useful information on the structure of compositions, although there are virtually no modern full-length Japanese studies of court instrumental music. For court vocal music, useful attempts at transnotating early notations have been made by M. Yamanoi (1961 and 1966; the latter to be read in conjunction with Markham, 1983). Gamō (1983) gives a highly sophisticated musical analysis and reconstruction of the medieval court vocal genre *sōga*; among other things, she compares melodic movement in this genre and in related types of Buddhist and noh singing.

Aside from research on the music per se, another interesting line of investigation is the reconstruction of early court music life and practice from written sources such as novels, diaries, and official documents (Yamada, 1934; Sakamoto, 1983; Nishiyama, 1959, 1971).

In English, the principal works aside from those of the Picken school are by Harich-Schneider (1973) for the early sources in particular; R. Garfias (1975) for *tōgaku* and for an imaginative attempt to explain the chords played on the *shō* mouth organ; and Reid (1977) for *komagaku*. All of these guide the reader to relevant Japanese-language sources.

BUDDHIST MUSIC Resources pertaining to Buddhist chant (*shōmyō*) and instrumental music are extremely rich. The annual *shūnie* ceremony at Tōdaiji temple in Nara has been especially thoroughly and skilfully documented: Satō Michiko's huge 2500-page study of movement and text (1975–82) complements the recordings and music-analytical notes of Yokomichi and Satō (1971). The large record set *Shōmyō taikei* (Yokomichi and others, 1983–4) is another precious resource. H. Kindaichi (1964) analyses a genre of chant which has had profound influence on noh and other narrative musics. W. Giesen's commentary on several Tendai school treatises (1977) is one of the few major Western-language sources on Buddhist chant. E. Garner (1976) analyses modal structure in Shingon chant. Harich-Schneider (1973) gives much valuable information as well.

BIWA NARRATION A good English-language review of general *biwa* history is given by G. Gish (1967). Three particular record sets recommend themselves by their diversity of coverage of different genres of *biwa* music and/or by their annotations, those by Nihon Biwagaku (1963), Tanabe (1975) and Guignard (1988). The Heike *biwa* epic tradition barely survives; Fujii (1966) gives transcriptions of several of these pieces along with some melodic patterns. Ferranti (1991) sheds first light on Satsuma-school improvisation.

NOH MUSIC The 15th-century treatises of Zeami give early theories about noh music. Modern studies start with M. Yokomichi's seminal work (e.g. 1963; collections of his articles, 1984, 1986; Yokomichi and Omote, 1960). An English-language summary of Yokomichi's ideas is presented by F. Hoff and W. Flindt (1973). H. Kojima (1985) falls short of giving the characteristics promised in the title, but is worth a read. S. Yamaguchi (1987) gives a useful introduction to an important topic, the regional forms of noh. More than musical analyses, Japanese scholars have produced many excellent works tracing the history of noh (not its music) or analysing Zeami's theories.

Turning to Western-language works that relate more specifically to music, A. Tamba (1974) offers a useful analysis of song types as well as a general introduction to rhythm and instrumentation, drawing on and extending several Japanese analyses which he (mostly) cites. Y. Matsuyama (1980) takes a similar approach but focusses on one play, *Hagoromo*. M. Bethe and K. Brazell (1978, 1982, with videotapes) give invaluable source material and analyses. R. Emmert (1983) begins the task of showing how the different instrumentalists adjust to each other and to the dancer.

SHAKUHACHI The best recent interpretive historical overview of the *shakuhachi* and its music is by K. Ueno (1983). T. Tsukitani (1986) gives a brief but insightful study of the historical development of the classical repertory. She is the only Japanese scholar to have consistently published on the actual music of *shakuhachi*, in numerous articles in journals, festschrifts, and record booklets (for a partial listing, see *NOD*, 1989, p.505).

In English, Y. Kamisangō's half of C. Blasdel and Kamisangō (1988) is the best critical overview of *shakuhachi* history and also summarizes the ideas of Nakatsuka Chikuzen published in the 1930s. J. Sanford (1977) digs out the story of how the Tokugawa government, for reasons of its own, accepted what were clearly forged documents in granting a certain Zen sect a monopoly on playing *shakuhachi* for profit. A. Gutzwiller (1983, 1974) and I. Fritsch (1979) provide analyses of the Kinko and Tozan school repertories.

KOTO MUSIC, JIUTA, SANKYOKU S. Kubota's 1983 bibliography (in English) covers most sources of *koto* music and many valuable recordings and books have spun off from these sets, which constitute the principal Japanese sources. Major Western-language studies are those of P. Ackermann (1986, dealing with the Yamada school), B. Wade (1976, Ikuta and Yamada schools), C. Read (1975, Yamada school), and numerous works by W. Adriaansz (1973, 1978, and articles listed in Tsuge, 1987); all of these contain extensive transcriptions and analysis. Tsuge (1981) gives an excellent introduction to the symbolic value of particular *koto* melodic patterns.

OTHER SHAMISEN MUSICS Genres of *shamisen* music are numerous. Three recent excellent sources on *gidayū* are I. Tsunoda and others (1986), K. Inobe and others (1986), and D. Gerstle and others (1990). They cover almost every aspect of this genre; Tsunoda and others includes a taped research interview with a performer. Research on *nagauta* has consistently benefited from the attention of Malm (1963, 1986). A. Tokita's dissertation (1988) sheds first English-language light on *kiyomoto*. Much remains to be done in this area.

FOLK MUSIC A general English-language introduction to traditional folk song and its research resources is given by D. Hughes (1985). The single best source for transcriptions and comparative scores, annotations and analyses of folk song is NHK (1944–80). For the wider category of folk performing arts (*minzoku geinō*), the same collection is helpful, but the huge record set by Y. Honda (1975–6) is a wonderful resource. R. Uchida's study of rice-planting ritual music (1978) is excellent and can be read in conjunction with that of F. Hoff (1971). Malm and Fujie (1986) have published on Tokyo-area festival music, (1975, 'Shoden'). For studies of variants via comparative scores, see A. Higuchi and others (1986) or G. Kakinoki (1970).

M. Yamanoi (1961) and M. Gamō (1983) suggest respectively that the court vocal genres *fuzoku* and *sōga*, both long extinct, employed versions of the so-called *yō* or 'folk-song' scale/mode, unlike other court music genres. If correct, this suggests that this scale was associated with folk song in ancient times as well, since *fuzoku* at least may have been derived from folk songs.

Several monthly magazines are aimed at folk-song fans, but the first research journal treating folk music, *Minzoku ongaku* ('Japanese Folk Music'), dates only from 1986. Quality varies, but there are such gems as that by

M. Shijō (1988), which traces the spread of an 18th-century popular folk song and includes a comparative score of 12 versions.

THE RYUKYUS, AMAMI ŌSHIMA, THE AINU   Japanese researchers see the Ryūkyū Islands (Okinawa Prefecture) and Amami Ōshima, the islands just south of the main part of Japan, as a sort of museum preserving earlier folk music lifeways, as reflected in the spontaneity and communality of music-making in Amami and the liberated music-and-dance gatherings of young Okinawans even in the recent past. Studies of the Okinawan court vocal tradition, however, have been more numerous than of folk music; analytic studies include those of S. Yamanouchi (1959), J. La Rue (1952), and E. Higa (1976). K. Ohtani (1981) analyses the music and dance of a court musical-drama genre. The six-volume encyclopedia *Art of Okinawa* (1989) is a valuable general resource. The song tradition of the southernmost islands is treated by H. Iwata (1972).

Tōkyō Geijutsu (1981) provides transcriptions of Okinawan folk songs, including many variant versions, scale diagrams, and brief annotations. For Amami Ōshima, R. Uchida (1983) is the most thorough musical study to date. Much research is being done in both regions, and many publications are forthcoming.

Exploration of the Chinese roots of Okinawan music and musical theatre is still in its infancy, but two studies point the way. M. Kina (1980) has located the Chinese source for an Okinawan song text which is performed in pidgin Chinese; and R. Thompson (1984) presents persuasive evidence of musical continuity between the three-string lute music of China and Okinawa.

The principal work on Ainu music is from NHK (1965), which includes several phonodiscs. Studies of Ainu music since then are conspicuously rare.

Numerous other genres or types of music exist in Japan. Not mentioned above, for example, are Shintō music (see the Japan entry in *The New Grove Dictionary of Music and Musicians*, 1980) or *minshingaku* (music borrowed from China during recent centuries, Malm, 1975, 'Chinese music'). There are also studies of song texts, which constitute a major and discrete genre of research in Japan.

Topics for future research

Given the wealth of musics and music-related materials in Japan, the possibilities for future research are limitless, providing a wide range of subjects for scholars:

(1) further detailed comparative studies of musical differences between schools (as by Kakinoki, 1978, and Malm, 1986);

(2) further use of the melograph, especially in the study of vocal ornamentation (as in Kakinoki, 1979, and Gamō, 1986);

(3) systematic study of the interchange between folk and learned traditions;

(4) study of *kaede* (the countermelodies added to many *koto* and *shamisen* compositions) in terms of both their history and their musical relationships to the original melodies (Takeshita, 1987, is a beginning);

(5) the development of percussion patterns in noh and Kabuki dance music (using resources such as the early drum score described in Yokomichi, 1978);

(6) more systematic studies of oral mnemonic systems;

(7) study of the precise make-up of the audience for various Japanese musics;

(8) further studies of the musics of Japan's 'new religions' (see Shumway, 1974);

(9) detailed examination of the effects on performance and transmission exerted by three institutions: the *iemoto* system, the government's Important Cultural Property system, and Preservation Societies;

(10) critical Western-language translations of pre-modern treatises and other sources;

(11) serious analysis of connections between traditional and modern popular song styles (see Gamō, 1986; Koizumi, 1984;

(12) further study of the Japanese sense of rhythm and silence, as expressed in the concept of *ma*, felt by many native researchers to be a uniquely Japanese phenomenon.

For the future, more joint research between Japanese and foreign scholars, aside from its ideological soundness, would guarantee a broader, more universalistic perspective in the actual research as well as a more broadly accessible published presentation.

Bibliography

C. Knott: 'Remarks on Japanese Musical Scales', *Trans. As. Soc. Japan*, xix/2 (1891), 373

F. Piggott: *The Music and Musical Instruments of Japan* (London, 1893, 2/1909/R1971)

R. Uehara: *Zokugaku senritsu kō* [The Melodies of Popular Music] (Tokyo, 1895)

O. Abraham and E. M. von Hornbostel: 'Studien über das Tonsystem und die Musik der Japaner', *SIMG*, iv (1903), 302–60; [Eng. trans. in K. Wachsmann and others, eds., *Hornbostel opera omnia* (The Hague, 1975)]

Z. Tateyama: *Heike ongaku-shi* [History of Heike *Biwa* Music] (Tokyo, 1910)

R. Lachmann: *Die Musik des Orients* (Breslau, 1929)

N. Péri: *Essai sur les gammes japonaises* (Paris, 1934)

Y. Yamada: *Genji monogatari no ongaku* [Music in the *Tale of Genji*] (Tokyo, 1934)

NHK, ed.: *Nihon min'yō taikan* [Japanese Folk Song Anthology] (Tokyo, 1944–80)

E. Kikkawa: *Nihon ongaku no seikaku* [The Character of Japanese Music] (Tokyo, 1948/R1979; German trans., Kassel, 1984)

S. Kishibe and L. Traynor: 'On the Four Unknown Pipes of the Sho', *Tōyō Gakuhō*, xxxv (1952)

J. LaRue: *The Okinawan Classical Songs: an Analytical and Comparative Study* (diss., Harvard U., 1952)

M. Shimazaki: 'Geinō shakai to iemoto seido' [The Performing Arts World and the *iemoto* System], *Shakaigaku hyōron*, iii, 131; iv, 101–34 (1953–4)

W. Malm: *Japanese Music and Musical Instruments* (Tokyo, 1959)

M. Nishiyama: *Iemoto no kenkyū* [Research on *iemoto*] (Tokyo, 1959)

S. Yamanouchi: *Ryūkyū no ongaku geinō shi* [History of Musical Performing Arts in the Ryūkyūs] (Tokyo, 1959)

M. Yokomichi and A. Omote: *Yōkyoku shū* [Collection of Noh Plays] (Tokyo, 1960–63)

M. Yamanoi: *Fuzoku yakufu* [Transnotation of *fuzoku*] (Tokyo, 1961)

Nihon Biwagaku Kyōkai, ed.: *Nihon biwagaku taikei* [Compendium of Japanese Lute Music], Nihon Gramophone SLJM1031–37 (1963) [7 discs, disc notes]

W. Malm: *Nagauta: the Heart of Kabuki Music* (Tokyo, 1963/R1976)

M. Yokomichi, ed.: *Nō* [Noh], Japan Victor SJ3005–3006 (1963) [6 discs, disc notes]

H. Kindaichi: *Shiza kōshiki no kenkyū* [Research on *kōshiki* Chant] (Tokyo, 1964)

H. Tanabe: *Nihon no gakki* [Japanese Musical Instruments] (Tokyo, 1964)

K. Hayashi, ed.: *Tempyō, Heian jidai no ongaku* [Music of the Tempyo and Heian Periods], Japan Columbia CLS–5023 (1965) [disc and notes]

S. Kawatake and others, eds.: *Nihon buyō ongaku* [Japanese dance music], Japan Victor SJ3013–3015 (1965) [discs and notes]

K. Machida: *Min'yo genryū kō* [Tracing Folk-Song Roots], Japan Columbia AL5047–5050 (1965) [discs and notes], rev. text repr. in Tōyō Ongaku Gakkai (1967)

NHK, ed.: *Ainu dentō ongaku* [Ainu Traditional Music] (Tokyo, 1965)

T. Matsumoto: *Nihon senpō* [Japanese Modes] (Tokyo, 1965)

S. Fujii: *Saifubon: Heikyoku* [Heike *Biwa* Music in Transcription] (Nagoya, 1966)

M. Yamanoi: *Saibara yakufu* [Transnotation of *saibara*] (Tokyo, 1966)

G. Gish: *The Biwa in History* (diss., U. of Michigan, 1967)

Shōsōin Office, ed.: *Shōsōin no gakki* [Musical Instruments in the Shōsōin] (Tokyo, 1967)

Tōyō Ongaku Gakkai, ed.: *Nihon no min'yō to minzoku geinō* [Japanese Folk Song and Folk Performing Arts] (Tokyo, 1967)

E. Kineya and G. Asakawa: *Ōzatsuma-bushi*, Japan Victor SJ3018–19 (1968) [discs and notes]

K. Masumoto: *Gagaku: dentō ongaku e no atarashii appurōchi* [*Gagaku*: a New Approach to Traditional Music] (Tokyo, 1968)

S. Shiba: *Gosenfu ni yoru gagaku sōfu* [Gagaku Scores in Western Notation] (Tokyo, 1968–72)

B. Ortolani: 'Iemoto', *Japan Quarterly* (1969), 297

Gidayū Kenkyūkai, ed.: *Jōruri* (Tokyo, 1970)

G. Kakinoki: 'Kariboshi-kiri Uta no hikaku bunseki' [Comparative Analysis of the Song 'Kariboshi-kiri Uta'], *Ongakugaku*, xvi/1–2 (1970)

S. Kishibe and others, eds.: *Hōgaku taikei* [Collection of Japanese Music] (Tokyo, 1970–72) [26 discs, disc notes]

F. Hoff: *The Genial Seed: a Japanese Song Cycle* (New York, 1971)

M. Nishiyama: *Iemoto monogatari* [Tales of *iemoto*] (Tokyo, 1971)

M. Yokomichi and M. Satō, eds.: *Tōdaiji shunie kannon keka*, Japan Victor SJ3031–32 (1971) [6 discs, disc notes]

H. Iwata: *Yaeyama no dentō ongaku* [Traditional Music of Yaeyama] (diss., Nihon U., 1972)

W. Adriaansz: *The Kumiuta and Danmono Traditions of Japanese Koto Music* (Berkeley, CA, 1973)

——: 'Midare: a Study of its Historical Development', *Nihon ongaku to sono shūhen*, ed. F. Koizumi (Tokyo, 1973), 9–54

E. Harich-Schneider: *A History of Japanese Music* (London, 1973)

K. Hayashi: *Higashi Ajia gakki kō* [East Asian Instruments] (Tokyo, 1973)

K. Hirano, ed.: *Koto kumiuta zenshū* [Complete Collection of Koto Song Suites], CBS–Sony SOJZ17–30 (1973) [14 discs, disc notes]

F. Hoff and W. Flindt: 'The Life Structure of Noh: an English Version of Yokomichi Mario's Analysis of the Structure of Noh', *Concerned Theatre Japan*, ii/3–4 (1973), 209–56

A. Gutzwiller: *Shakuhachi: Aspects of History, Practice and Teaching* (diss., Wesleyan U., 1974)

K. Hirano, ed.: *Shamisen kumiuta zenshū* [Complete Collection of Shamisen Song Suites], CBS–Sony SOJZ59–72 (1974–82) [14 discs, disc notes]

L. Shumway: *Kibigaku: an Analysis of a Modern Japanese Ritual Music* (diss., U. of Washington, 1974)

A. Tamba: *La structure musicale du nō* (Paris, 1974; Eng. trans., Tokyo, 1981)

R. Garfias: *Music of a Thousand Autumns* (Berkeley, CA, 1975)

Y. Honda, ed.: *Nihon no minzoku ongaku* [Japanese Folkloric Music], Japan Victor SJL2166–2204 (1975–6) [39 discs, disc notes]

G. Kakinoki: 'A Method for the Comparative Analysis of Japanese Folk Melody by Structural Formulae', *Asian Music*, vi (1975), 60

W. Malm: 'Chinese Music in the Edo and Meiji Periods in Japan', *Asian Music*, vi (1975), 147

——: 'Shoden: a Study in Tokyo Festival Music', *YIFMC*, vii (1975), 44

C. Read: *A Study of Yamada-ryū Sōkyoku and its Repertoire* (diss., Wesleyan U., 1975)

S. Saitō: *Echigo goze nikki* [Diary of an Echigo *Goze*] (Tokyo, 1975)

M. Satō: *Tōdaiji shunie no kōsei to shosa* [Structure and Movements of the Tōdaiji *shunie* Ceremony] [= *Geinō Kagaku*, vols. vi, vii, xii, xiii] (Tokyo, 1975–82)

H. Tanabe, comp.: *Biwa: sono ongaku no keifu* [Genealogy of *biwa* Music], Japan Columbia CLS–5205–10 (1975) [6 discs, disc notes]

E. Garner: *Mode: Three Modes of Shingi Shingon Shōmyō as Analysed by ECG* (diss., Wesleyan U., 1976)

E. Higa: *Okinawan Classical Music: Analysis of Vocal Performance* (diss., U. of Hawaii, 1976)

K. Hirano, ed.: *Kikuhara Hatsuko zenshū* [Recording Collection by Kikuhara Hatsuko], CBS–Sony 00AG5–26 (1976) [22 discs, disc notes]

B. Wade: *Tegotomono: Music for the Japanese Koto* (Westport, CT, 1976)

W. Giesen: *Zur Geschichte des buddhistischen Ritualgesangs in Japan* (Kassel, 1977)

F. Koizumi: 'Musical Scales in Japanese Music', in Koizumi and others, eds. (1977), 73
—— and others, eds.: *Asian Musics in an Asian Perspective* (Tokyo, 1977)
J. Reid: *The Komagaku Repertory of Japanese Gagaku: a Study of Contemporary Performance Practice* (diss., U. of California, Los Angeles, 1977)
J. Sanford: 'Shakuhachi zen: the *fukeshū* and *komusō*', *Monumentica Nipponica*, xxxii (1977), 411
M. Shibata and others: *Nihon no oto o tsukuru* [Making the Sounds of Japan] (Tokyo, 1977)
W. Adriaansz: *Introduction to Shamisen Kumiuta* (Buren, 1978)
M. Bethe and K. Brazell: *Nō as Performance* (Ithaca, NY, 1978)
K. Hirano: *Rokudan*, Toshiba–EMI TH60054–60055 (1978) [2 discs, disc notes]
K. Hirano and K. Fukushima: *Sources of Early Japanese Music* (Tokyo, 1978) [Eng. summary and captions]
F. Hoff: *Song, Dance, Storytelling: Aspects of the Performing Arts in Japan* (Ithaca, NY, 1978)
G. Kakinoki: 'Nagauta *Kokaji* ni mieru ryūhasei' [Sectarian Differences as Seen in the Kabuki Dance *Kokaji*], *Geinō no Kagaku*, ix (1978), 153–204
M. Shibata: *Ongaku no gaikotsu no hanashi* [The Skeletal Structure of Music] (Tokyo, 1978)
R. Uchida: *Taue-bayashi no kenkyū* [Research on Rice-planting Music] (Tokyo, 1978)
M. Yokomichi: 'Nagauta narimono no kokei' [Old Percussion Patterns for Kabuki Dance], *Geinō no Kagaku*, ix (1978)
M. Yokomichi and S. Gamō, eds.: *Kuchishōga taikei* [Anthology of Oral Mnemonics], CBS–Sony OOAG457–461 (1978) [5 discs, disc notes]
I. Fritsch: *Die Solo-Honkyoku der Tozan-Schule* (Kassel, 1979) [Eng. summary]
G. Kakinoki: 'Nihonjin no kashō kōdō: merogurafu ni yoru bunseki' [Japanese Singing Activity, Analysed with Melograph], *Ongakugaku*, xxiv/2 (1979), 131
E. Kikkawa and K. Hirano, eds.: *Koto kumiuta taikan* [Anthology of Koto Song Suites], Toshiba–EMI TH60091–60110 (1979) [20 discs, disc notes]
F. Koizumi: *Minzoku ongaku kenkyū nōto* [Ethnic Music Research Notes] (Tokyo, 1979)
Music Librarians Association of Japan, ed.: *Ongaku shiryō tanbō* [Report on Music Resources] (Tokyo, 1979)
R. Emmert and Y. Minegishi, eds.: *Musical Voices of Asia* (Tokyo, 1980)
K. Hirano: *Etenraku to sono kayō* [Etenraku and its Vocal Versions], Toshiba–EMI 60130–60131 (1980) [2 discs, disc notes]
E. Kikkawa and others, eds.: *Nihon koten ongaku taikei* [1000 Years of Japanese Classical Music] (Tokyo, 1980–82) [74 discs, disc notes]
M. Kina: 'A Comparative Study on Okinawan Da-hua-gu Dance and Chinese Da-hua-gu Play', *Tōyō ongaku kenkyū*, xiv (1980), 73–126 [Eng. summary]
Kunitachi Ongaku Daigaku Gakki Shiryōkan, ed.: *Gakki shiryōshū* [Musical Instrument Resource Collection] (Tokyo, 1980–)
Y. Matsuyama: *Studien zur Nō-musik: Eine Untersuchung des Stückes 'Hagoromo'* (Hamburg, 1980)
D. Tanaka: 'Kabuki hayashi yōroku' [Catalogue of Kabuki Percussion and Flute Music], *Kabuki ongaku*, ed. Tōyō Ongaku Gakkai (Tokyo, 1980), 199–359
K. Hirano and T. Kojima: 'Nihon no onkai' [Japanese Scales], *Ongaku daijiten* (1981); updated in *Nihon ongaku daijiten* (1989), 139
K. Machida: 'Shamisen seikyoku ni okeru senritsukei no kenkyū' [Melodic Patterns in Shamisen Vocal Music], *Tōyō ongaku kenkyū*, xlvii/2 (1981)
Ongaku daijiten [Encyclopaedia of Music] (Tokyo, 1981–83)
K. Ohtani: *The Okinawan kumiodori: an Analysis of Relationships of Text, Music and Movement in Selections from Nidō Tekiuchi* (diss., U. of Hawaii, 1981)
L. Picken and others: *Music from the Tang Court* (London and Cambridge, 1981–)
T. Sasamori: 'The Preservation and Development of the Performing Art of Tsugaru', *Proceedings of the 4th International Symposium on the Conservation and Restoration of Cultural Property* (Tokyo, 1981), 55
Y. Tokumaru: *L'aspect mélodique de la musique de syamisen* (diss., Laval U., 1981)
Tokyo Geijutsu Daigaku Minzoku Ongaku Zeminaru: *Okinawa min'yō saifushū* [Okinawa Folk Song Transcription Collection] (Tokyo, 1981)
G. Tsuge: 'Symbolic Techniques in Japanese Koto Kumiuta', *Asian Music*, xii/2 (1981), 109
R. Wolpert: 'Tang–Music (Tōgaku) Manuscripts for Lute and their Interrelationships', *Music and Tradition*, ed. D. Widdess and R. Wolpert (Cambridge, 1981), 69–121
M. Bethe and K. Brazell: *Dance in the Nō Theater* (Ithaca, NY, 1982)
Tōyō Ongaku Gakkai, ed.: *Nihon no onkai* [Japanese Scales] (Tokyo, 1982)
R. Emmert: 'The Maigoto of No: a Musical Analysis of the Chū no mai', *YTM*, xv (1983), 5

M. Gamō: *Sōga no ongakuteki kenkyū* [Musical Research on *Sōga*] (Tokyo, 1983)

A. Gutzwiller: *Die Shakuhachi der Kinko-Schule* (Kassel, 1983) [Eng. summary]

K. Hirano and others, eds.: *Shamisen kofu no kenkyū* [An Investigation into the Old Shamisen Notations], Toshiba–EMI THX90212–90217 (1983) [6 discs, disc notes]

K. Komparu: *The Noh Theater: Principles and Perspectives* (1983)

S. Kubota: 'A Guide to the Basic Literature and Records for Research in *Jiuta* and *Sokyoku*', *Hogaku* i/1 (1983), 93

E. Markham: *Saibara* (Cambridge, 1983)

K. Ohtani and Y. Tokumaru: 'Ethnomusicology in Japan since 1970', *YTM*, xv (1983), 155

C. Read and D. Locke: 'An Analysis of the Yamada-ryu Sokyoku Iemoto System', *Hogaku*, i/1 (1983), 20–52

M. Sakamoto: *Chūsei gagakukai no kenkyū* [A Study of the 15th-century Gagaku Society] (diss., Ochanomizu U., 1983)

R. Uchida: *Amami min'yō to sono shūhen* (Tokyo, 1983)

K. Ueno: *Shakuhachi no rekishi* [The History of the Shakuhachi] (Tokyo, 1983)

L. Wakabayashi: *Yamada-ryū sōkyoku ni mirareru senritsukei* [Melodic Formulas in Yamada-school Koto Music] (diss., Tokyo U. of Arts, 1983)

M. Yokomichi and others, eds.: *Shōmyō taikei* [Compendium of Buddhist Chant], Nippon Columbia (1983–4) [32 discs, disc notes]

E. Kikkawa: *Nihon ongaku no biteki kenkyū* [Research on Japanese Musical Aesthetics] (Tokyo, 1984)

——, ed.: *Hōgaku hyakka jiten* [Japanese Traditional Music Encyclopedia] (Tokyo, 1984)

F. Koizumi: *Kayōkyoku no kōzō* [The Structure of Popular Song] (Tokyo, 1984)

Kunitachi Ongaku Daigaku Ongaku Kenkyūjo, ed.: *Nihon bijutsu ni hyōgen sareta ongaku bamen* [Music Scenes Depicted in Japanese Art] (Tokyo, 1984)

T. Rimer and M. Yamazaki, trans.: *On the Art of the Nō Drama: the Major Treatises of Zeami* (Princeton, NJ, 1984)

R. Thompson: 'Okinawa ni okeru Chūgoku ongaku no juyō ni tsuite' [On the Reception of Chinese Music in Okinawa], *Bungaku*, lii (1984), 163

C. Yamada: 'Gidayū-bushi ni okeru makura no ongaku gohō' [On the Melodic Pattern *Makura* in Gidayū-bushi], *Geinō no kagaku*, xv (1984)

M. Yokomichi: *Nōgeki shōyō* [A Noh Drama Ramble] (Tokyo, 1984)

T. Fujii, ed.: *Nihon ongaku to geinō no genryū* [The Sources of Japanese Music and Performing Arts] (Tokyo, 1985)

D. Hughes: *The Heart's Home Town: Traditional Folk Song in Modern Japan* (diss., U. of Michigan, 1985)

H. Kojima: *Yōkyoku no ongakuteki tokusei* [Musical Characteristics of Noh Music] (Tokyo, 1985)

A. Marett: 'Tōgaku: Where Have the Tang Melodies Gone, and Where Have the New Melodies Come From?', *EM*, xxix (1985), 409

P. Ackermann: *Studien zur Koto-Musik von Edo* (Kassel, 1986)

L. Fujie: *Matsuri-bayashi of Tokyo* (diss., Columbia U., 1986)

S. Gamō: 'Several Aspects of *enka* Singing Style: Comparison using Melograph . . .', in Henshū-iinkai (1986), 385 [in Jap. with Eng. summary]

Henshū-iinkai, ed.: *Shominzoku no oto* [The Sounds of Various Peoples] (Tokyo, 1986)

A. Higuchi and others: 'Kyōto no min'yō' [Folk Songs of Kyoto], in Henshū-iinkai, ed. (1986), 191–236

K. Inobe and others: *Gidayū-bushi no yōshiki tenkai* [Stylistic Development of Gidayu-bushi] (Tokyo, 1986)

W. Malm: *Six Hidden Views of Japanese Music* (Berkeley, CA, 1986)

Y. Tokumaru and O. Yamaguti, eds.: *The Oral and the Literate in Music* (Tokyo, 1986)

G. Tsuge: *Japanese Music: an Annotated Bibliography* (New York, 1986)

T. Tsukitani: 'A Study of the Classical *shakuhachi honkyoku* Tradition: the Formation and Change of its Repertory', in Henshū-iinkai (1986), 279 [in Jap. with Eng. summary]

I. Tsunoda and others: *Bunraku no ongaku* [Music of Bunraku] (Tokyo, 1986)

M. Yokomichi: *Nōgeki no kenkyū* [Research on Noh Drama] (Tokyo, 1986)

K. Hirano, ed.: *Sōkyoku jiuta taikei* [Anthology of *Sōkyoku* and *Jiuta*], Japan Victor SJ1051–1110 (1987) [60 discs, disc notes]

K. Hirano: *Shamisen to koto no kumiuta* [Shamisen and Koto Song Suites] (Tokyo, 1987)

—— and others, eds.: *Nihon koten ongaku bunken kaidai* [Annotated Bibliography of Sources for Japanese Traditional Classical Music] (Tokyo, 1987)

H.-D. Reese: Review of G. Tsuge, *Japanese Music: an Annotated Bibliography*, *World of Music*, iv (1987), 75

H. Takeshita: *A Study of Kaede in Nagauta* (diss., Tokyo U. of Arts, 1987) [in Jap.]

S. Yamaguchi: *Nō-ongaku no kenkyū: chihō to chūō* [Research on Noh Music: Centre and Periphery] (Tokyo, 1987)

C. Blasdel and Y. Kamisangō: *The Shakuhachi: a Manual for Learning* (Tokyo, 1988)

S. Gamo and others, eds.: *Nihon no ongaku, Ajia no ongaku* [Japanese Music, Asian Music] (Tokyo, 1988–)

S. Guignard, ed.: *Yoshitsune densetsu: Satsuma-biwa, Chikuzen-biwa* [The Yoshitsune Legend: Satsuma-biwa and Chikuzen-biwa], OAG CR10080–10081 (1988) [2 discs, disc notes]

D. Hughes: 'Music Archaeology of Japan: Data and Interpretation', *The Archaeology of Early Music Cultures*, ed. E. Hickmann and D. Hughes (Bonn, 1988), 55

M. Shijō: '*Kochae-bushi* and Ballads', *Minzoku ongaku* iii/1–2 (1988), 10 [in Jap.]

A. Tokita: *Kiyomoto-bushi: Narrative Music in Kabuki Dance* (diss., Monash U., 1988)

Art of Okinawa (Naha, 1989)

K. Hirano, Y. Kamisangō and S. Gamō, eds.: *Nihon ongaku daijiten* [Encyclopedia of Japanese Music] (Tokyo, 1989)

D. Hughes: 'The Historical Uses of Nonsense: Vowel-pitch Solfège from Scotland to Japan', *Ethnomusicology and the Historical Dimension*, ed. M. Philipp (Ludwigsburg, 1989)

D. Gerstle, K. Inobe and W. Malm: *Theatre as Music: the Bunraku Play 'Mt. Imo and Mt. Se'* (Ann Arbor, MI, 1990)

H. de Ferranti: 'Composition and Improvisation in Satsuma biwa', *Musica Asiatica*, vi (1991), 102

3: KOREA

ROBERT PROVINE

Korea, like its East Asian neighbours China and Japan, has a long history of native scholarship in music and the other arts. The literary tradition extends for more than a millennium, and as early as the 8th century AD, texts (at that time mostly Buddhist scriptures) were already being printed with woodblock technology. Korean scholarship exists in three languages: until the invention of a viable alphabetic script for the native Korean language in the 15th century, virtually the only language used in written works was literary Chinese, and indeed the vernacular was not widely employed in native scholarship until the 20th century. From 1910 to 1945, Korea was a colony of Japan, and a significant, if not large, amount of work on Korean music was carried out by Japanese scholars or under their influence; the language of writing was often Japanese. Since liberation in 1945, there has been an outpouring of writings in Korean of relevance to ethnomusicological investigation of Korean music.

In contrast to the sizable native contribution, Western studies of Korean music are still quite limited in quantity and scope, and are mostly confined to the second half of the 20th century. It is necessary therefore to consider seriously native scholarship, even though much of it may not be readily classifiable as 'ethnomusicological' in a Western disciplinary sense.

Early sources

The longevity and stature of Korea's scholarship might imply that a long survey of musical scholarship corresponding to that for China (*see* above) is required.

Unfortunately, however, several destructive invasions of Korea have eradicated large portions of the literary inheritance – Korea's geographical position and historical factors have long rendered her vulnerable to attack both from the north (Chinese, Mongols, Manchus) and the south (Japanese). Most notable of these invasions, from the standpoint of destruction of the written record, were those by the Mongols in 1231 and 1254, the Japanese in 1592–8 and the Manchus in 1627 and 1636. A number of the important handful of pre-17th-century materials that survive are official compilations originally printed in several copies and distributed for safekeeping to government book storage locations around the peninsula.

The earliest surviving Korean literary material with more than fragmentary information on music dates from the 12th century and is largely modelled on traditional Chinese Confucian scholarly methods: respect for and interest in past achievements, expressed by frequent and extended quotations from earlier writings considered to be authoritative, combined with newer interpretive insights in the form of commentaries. The chief early example is the 1145 *Samguk sagi* ('History of the Three Kingdoms') by Kim Pusik (1075–1151), which contains an essay on the music of three ancient Korean states: Silla (traditional dates BC 57–935 AD), Koguryŏ (BC 37–668 AD) and Paekche (18 BC–663 AD). Now the central source of information on music of the Korean peninsula to the 9th century, the essay quotes passages from a number of earlier Korean writings, none of which now survives. It tells the names and types of instruments used in each of the three kingdoms, names of pieces of music, musical contexts (ceremonies, rites etc), a few song texts, a very few names of musicians and substantial information on the background of the two most important Korean long zithers, *kŏmun'go* and *kayagŭm*. A standard translation of the whole work into modern Korean is by Kim Chonggwŏn (1960); the music essay has been studied and translated by Song Pangsong (1982).

Just as Kim Pusik's work looked back from the 12th century to past dynasties, the chief musical source for the Koryŏ dynasty (918–1392), the *Koryŏsa* ('History of the Koryŏ Dynasty'), was prepared in the succeeding Chosŏn dynasty (1392–1910). Written by Chŏng Inji (1396–1478) and officially promulgated in 1451, this work contains an extended essay (156 pages) that treats music history, instrumentation of performing ensembles, the use of music in court rituals and ceremonies, hymn and song texts, descriptions of dances and more. Music at the Korean court is divided here into three types: *aak* (ritual music of Chinese origin considered to be performed in authentic Chinese style), *tangak* (less ritualistic music of Chinese origin, played in a Koreanized style) and *sogak* (music of Korean origin). Music of the lower classes, or 'folk' music, is ignored in this and other compilations in the Confucian mould. This essay has been translated into modern Korean by Ch'a Chuhwan (1972). An important contemporary description of musical life in the Koryŏ court is provided by a travel diary of the Chinese envoy Xu Jing, 1124.

The 15th century

The 15th century is considered by many Koreans to be one of their cultural golden ages, a renaissance. It was a time of massive reconsideration and reformulation of the Korean court music tradition. During the reign of King Sejong (1418–50), the musicologist Pak Yŏn (1378–1458) and others carried out a thoroughgoing reform of court music, with the intention of imbuing it with the lofty traits described in ancient Chinese sources. Based on study of Chinese musical sources and imported instruments, they redesigned and reconstructed musical instruments, reorganized the performing ensembles, restructured the musical bureaucracy within the government, trained musicians, created a consistent scheme for incorporation of music into various rituals and court ceremonies, re-arranged or composed music for use in the various contexts and prepared written memorials and treatises. Under later kings, notably Sejo (1455–68) and Sŏngjong (1469–94), the scheme was further refined until a sort of codified standard was reached at the end of the century, described in the 1493 treatise *Akhak kwebŏm* ('Guide to the Study of Music') compiled chiefly by Sŏng Hyŏn (1439–1504). As a fascinating example of detailed theoretical research combined with practical fulfilment, this period has been much studied by scholars of succeeding centuries, though the scholarship has yet to find its way adequately into Western languages.

Most of the sources relating to the 15th-century reforms survive today. Memorials submitted to the throne and accounts of court discussions are preserved in official *Annals* (*sillok*; see *Chosŏn*, 1955–8) particularly the *Sejong sillok* ('Annals of King Sejong') of 1454. Some of Pak Yŏn's writings are also preserved in his collected writings, compiled in 1822. Descriptions of ceremonies and rituals, with precise specification of musical content and detailed illustrated rubrics on musical instruments and ensembles, are preserved in draft form in the *Annals* and in codified form in the 1474 *Kukcho oryeŭi* ('Five Rites of State') with its accompanying *Kukcho orye sŏrye* ('Rubrics for the Five Rites of State'). Materials on the musical bureaucracy and the training of musicians may be found in a volume of legal statutes, *Kyŏngguk taejŏn* ('National code') of 1471. A remarkably large quantity of music, mostly notated in precise mensural and pitch notations, is found in the *Annals* of King Sejong (about 760 pages of often densely packed score) and King Sejo (about 180 pages); these, the earliest preserved notations of music in Korea, have been carefully described by Condit (1979 and 1984, 'Korean Scores in the Modified Fifteenth-Century Mensural Notation'). Many of the sources are available in facsimile and have been translated into modern Korean (see the Bibliography); a selection of this music has been transcribed into Western notation with commentary (Condit, 1984, *Music of the Korean Renaissance*).

Sources to 1910

In succeeding centuries, the official compilations of the 15th century were taken as standard, and official publications for the most part were supplements, updates (e.g. ritual sections and hymn texts were added to sacrificial rites for recently deceased kings), or simple reprints of the standard text (e.g. the *Akhak kwebŏm* was twice reprinted intact in the 17th century). Following periods of decline and governmental economic straits, a resurgence of Confucian scholarship in the 18th century produced a number of these derivative works: official supplements to the *Kukcho oryeŭi* and *Kukcho orye sŏrye* were promulgated in 1744 and 1751, and the *Akhak kwebŏm*, describing what had become an unattainable ideal, was reprinted again in 1743. A new general treatise on music, the *Siak hwasŏng* ('Harmonious Sound of Poetry and Music') of 1780, examines history, theory, instruments, ensembles, song, dance and measurements (traditionally correlated with musical pitch); in the Confucian style, it consists mostly of quotations from earlier standard works, with commentary and updating to take account of diminished musical resources available in the 18th century.

A late and important example of the official publications is the *Chŭngbo Munhŏn pigo* (expanded edition of the *Korean Encyclopedia of Documents and Institutions*) of 1908, compiled by Pak Yongdae and others. The final version of an encyclopedia initially compiled in 1770, its music section (1160 pages) and ritual section (1550 pages) contain a useful, well-organized distillation of the earlier sources, occasionally quoting also from works now lost.

At the same time as these pieces of officially promulgated scholarship were being compiled, a great many less formal instruction manuals and notation books (most of them in a form of tablature for the six-string long zither *kŏmun'go*) were being written. While these manuals are not scholarly, their scores and explanations document much about the evolution of performance styles, and hence are essential source materials. In some cases, it is possible to trace the history of a given piece of music for several centuries; Condit (1977) has traced one important example from its tuneful 15th-century original down to its monumentally expanded present form. Lists and descriptions of the notated sources may be found in Yi Tongbok (1979), Song Pangsong (1981) and Chang Sahun (1984, *Kugak taesajŏn*); many have been recently published in facsimile (Kugnip Kuggawŏn, 1979–).

Early 20th century

During the Japanese occupation of Korea (1910–45), a number of Japanese scholars investigated Korean history, archaeology, folklore, and literature. A few turned their attention to music, often with the intention of describing the musical interconnections between China, Korea and Japan. While these scholars were genuinely interested in Korean music and were cordially respected by the few contemporaneous native Korean musicologists, it must be recognized that the essentially antagonistic relationship between Koreans and Japanese was not conducive to effective field research or thorough co-operation. Tanabe Hisao published a survey of Korean music as early as 1921, and late in life (1970) a diary and field notes on his 1921 research trip. Korean musical instruments, in the context of Chinese and Japanese relatives, were examined in detail in numerous articles by Hayashi Kenzō (1899–1976) (1962). Kishibe Shigeo contributed a study of the editions of *Akhak kwebŏm* (1943). Other significant writings include Aoyagi Tsunataro's early history of Korean music (1924), Iwaya Takechi's history of Korean court music (1928–9) and Tanaka Hatsuo's study of scale and pitch (1930). A bibliography of colonial-period Japanese studies of Korea, including many of ethnomusicological relevance, has been compiled by Suematsu Yasukazu (1980).

During the occupation, the Japanese authorities permitted a limited continuation of the earlier royal music institute (*Yiwangjik aakpu*), and much court and ritual music was taught, preserved, and performed (albeit not in original contexts). A very few Korean scholars published a number of studies, often in Japanese; chief among them were An Hwak, who wrote many short survey articles (e.g. 1930, 1931–2); Ham Hwajin (1889–1948), Director of the institute for many years, who contributed numerous articles and several significant books (1929, 1938, 1948); and Song Sŏkha, who attempted the first comprehensive list of historical notated sources (1943). While these native writings helped sustain Korean music scholarship during a difficult period, they are mostly simple surveys, lists, or compilations of earlier materials, now much outdated and primarily of historical interest. Important work on ancient Korean songs, still much consulted today, was done by Yang Chudong (1942).

The first half of the century also saw the first signs of Western interest in Korean music. Maurice Courant (1865–1925), an interpreter at the French legation (fluent also in Chinese and Japanese), wrote inter alia a respectable study of Korean music (1912) that was unsurpassed in Western languages until recent times; Courant is best known for a large bibliography of Korean sources (1894–6), a work that shows a commendable interest in and sympathy for musical materials. A German, Andreas Eckardt, wrote a survey of Korean music (1930) and one of Korean art, though he was an amateur in both areas; much later he revised the music work (1968). Keh Chung-sik (Kye Chŏngsik), a Korean violinist who went to Germany to study Western music in the 1930s, submitted the first Western doctoral thesis on Korean music (1934). Sara May Anderson wrote a short MA dissertation on Korean folk songs at the Eastman School of Music (1940), and J. L. Boots contributed a survey of Korean musical instruments (1940). Until the 1970s, these five works, despite their age and inadequacies, remained the main ones available to Western readers.

After 1945

At the end of World War II, Korea was released from Japanese control and placed under what was intended to be two temporary protectorates (the USSR in the north and the USA in the south). Relationships between the two parts became increasingly strained, eventually resulting in the Korean War of 1950–53 and subsequent decades of uneasy armistice between two disparate regimes (the Republic of Korea in the south and the Democratic People's Republic of Korea in the north).

THE NORTH Little is presently known of musical scholarship in the north; only tentative description is possible. Until the early 1960s, some useful research was carried out, especially of an archaeological nature – the Koguryŏ tombs in the north seem to have much more to offer musical studies than do the Silla tombs in the south. A landmark study of musical paintings in Koguryŏ tombs was done by Chŏn Chunong in 1957, but seemingly little comparable research since that time. Other northern writings are a translation of *Akhak kwebŏm* into modern Korean (Yŏm Chŏnggwŏn, 1956), a Chinese-language survey (Mun Hayŏn, 1962), and a study of music in the post-liberation period (Ri Hirim, 1956).

In the north, music has become increasingly a Marxist, utilitarian enterprise, expressing itself in a banal, heavily Westernized and 'modernized' style in which traditional instruments and performance practices are either replaced wholesale by Western instruments and norms, or at least 'improved' (by modification of instruments to suit Western scales and intonation etc). Publications of instrument manuals and of music collections reveal little that is traditionally Korean or old, and much that is derivative of the styles and theories of Stalinist Russia and Cultural Revolution China. In the absence of real scholarship on music in north Korea, a temporary guide to current instruments and practices is provided by entries in the encyclopedia *Paekkwa chŏnsŏ* (1982–4).

By the end of the 1980s, a hopeful easing of tensions in the peninsula was increasingly evident. Scholars from the north were travelling abroad, and publications gave first indications of a useful new scholarly productivity. Although still politically biased, a promising history of Korean music with emphasis on archaeological materials has been published (Mun Sŏngnyŏp, 1988).

THE SOUTH While musical scholarship is more substantial in the Republic of Korea than in the north, one must still recognize that the dominant musical culture in this rapidly developing and increasingly international country is Western music, both art and folk; traditional Korean music is a minority interest even on home soil, and at times (e.g. the 1960s) parts of it have come perilously close to extinction. Many of the traditional contexts of music, both court and country, have disappeared, and the survival of traditional music is increasingly dependent upon its adaptability to new packaging: court banquet music on a concert stage, sacrificial rites performed largely as tourist attractions, farmers' music at national festivals and on stage in the West, narrative forms with interpolated contemporary jokes, and so forth. Historical evidence suggests that Korean traditional music has always had to adapt to meet changing circumstances, and flexibility is itself part of the tradition; nevertheless, until the 20th century it had not faced the threat of complete replacement by imported music (a threat which has apparently been carried out in the north). In the 1980s, scholarship on and performance of traditional music survived and expanded, thanks to the perseverance and dedication of a remarkable minority in the Korean musical community.

The present descendant of the royal music institute, the Korean Traditional Performing Arts Centre (*Kungnip kugagwŏn*; until 1989, its English name was the National Classical Music Institute), is the focal institution for preservation, performance and propagation of court music and professionalized folk forms. Supported by government grants, the Institute has published many scores in both Western notation (1969–) and native notations (1974–), as well as a large series of facsimile reprints of traditional sources (1979–) and sound recordings (1972–). A new departure is a series of choreographic notations of court dances (1986–). These publications and recordings form a basic collection essential to any serious investigations of Korean music.

Another important institution with government sponsorship is the Cultural Properties Preservation Bureau (*Munhwajae kwalliguk*), which not only has provided subsidies to assist selected performing artists in continuing their art and training disciples, but also has commissioned several dozen studies of traditional musical forms (*Muhyŏng munhwajae chosa pogosŏ*) since 1964.

The most influential scholars of traditional Korean music in modern times are Lee Hye-Ku (Yi Hyegu, *b*1909) and his younger contemporary Chang Sahun (*b*1916). Between them they have written hundreds of articles, books, and pamphlets, given countless lectures and radio broadcasts, taught nearly the entire body of younger scholars, and generally shepherded the cause of traditional music through all vicissitudes to its present state of comparative vitality. Lee's initial training was in literature and broadcasting, Chang's in musical performance; while neither was trained in musicology as such, their breadth of experience, knowledge and insight, combined with phenomenal productivity, make their writings the core of modern scholarship (together they command 175 entries in Song Pangsong's 1981 bibliography).

Lee Hye-Ku's major work is mostly in the form of articles, of which several collections have been published (1957, 1967, 1970, 1976, 1985, *Mandang sok munch'aerok*; 1985, *Han'guk ŭmak nonjip*), but there are also a volume on musical instruments (1959), an annotated translation into modern Korean of *Akhak kwebŏm* (1979–80), and a study of Korean rhythmic notation (1987). A volume of his writings has also appeared in English translation (1981).

Important writings of Chang Sahun include his history of Korean music (1976), a study of musical instruments (1969), two books on dance (1977, 1984, *Han'guk muyong kaeron*), analyses of musical performances of the Korean poetic forms called *sijo* (1973) and *kasa* (1980), a history of music in the period of King Sejong (1982), a dictionary of Korean music (1984, *Kugak taesajŏn*), and several essay collections (1966, 1974, 1975, 1983). Virtually none of Chang's writings are available in Western languages.

Both Lee Hye-Ku and Chang Sahun taught at Seoul National University, until recently the only university with a department of traditional music. Under their guidance, a Korean Musicological Society (*Han'guk kugak hakhoe*) was founded, and two journals, *Han'guk ŭmak yŏn'gu* ('Studies in Korean Music', 1971–) and *Minjok ŭmakhak* ('Journal of the Asian Music Research Institute', 1977–).

The richness of untapped source materials and personal preferences have led Lee and Chang to focus primarily on court music, music history, and source studies. Their students have tended to move in different directions: Han Man-Young (Manyŏng), for example, has produced a volume on Buddhist chant (1981) and transcriptions of folk music in Western notation (1967, *Han'guk minyo chip*; 1967, *Sibi kasa*), and Lee Chae-suk (Yi Chaesuk), a leading performer on the 12-string long zither *kayagŭm*, has published transcriptions of all the major styles in the *sanjo* form (1971; 1983, *Chŏngak changdan*; 1983, *Kayagŭm sanjo*; 1987).

A very few scholars have steered their own direction, separate from this main tide. Two important figures are Yi Pohyŏng, a tireless collector and knowledgeable writer about folk music, who has published scattered articles, and Hwang Byungki (Pyŏnggi), a composer and performer on *kayagŭm* with highly original ideas on the core characteristics of traditional Korean music (1975–8). Other scholars among many have contributed to musical studies from other disciplines: Pak Hŭngsu, a physicist, has studied the measurement and history of pitch (1980); Im Tonggwŏn, in oral literature, has contributed six volumes of folk-song texts (1961–81); Kim Tonguk, in written literature, has published much on song texts in literary sources (1961, 1965, 1975, 1982); and Yi Tuhyŏn, a folklorist, has studied folk mask plays (1969).

New faces (including Western ones), ideas, and institutions started appearing in the mid-1960s. Departments of traditional music have materialized at Ewha Women's University (Seoul) (e.g. Chu Yŏngja, 1985), Hanyang University (Seoul), Yŏngnam University (Kyŏngsan), and the Academy of Korean Studies (Sŏngnam), among others. Two students of Lee Hye-Ku and Chang Sahun at Seoul National, Song Bang-song (Pangsong) and Lee Byongwon (Yi Pyŏngwŏn), went to North America for ethnomusicological training, Song at Toronto and Wesleyan (PhD, 1975), Lee at Seattle (PhD, 1974); in their works the catchwords of ethnomusicology begin to appear. Lee, who remained in the West, has produced a volume on Buddhist music (1987) and recently turned his attention to Korean communities outside of the Korean peninsula (e.g. in China). Song returned to Korea and appears about to out-produce his former teachers Lee Hye-Ku and Chang Sahun: in addition to reference works, he has published in Korean a source study dealing with the royal music institute of the Chosŏn period (1980, *Akchang tŭngnok yŏn'gu*), a general history of Korean music (1984), a set of studies of ancient music (1985), a volume on music of the Koryŏ dynasty (1988), and a volume of collected essays (1982); in English there is a volume of source readings (1980, *Source Readings in Korean Music*), a study of Korean folk song in Canada (1974), and a revision of his PhD thesis on music of the long zither *kŏmun'go* (1986). Significantly for the future of ethnomusicology in Korea, Song has drawn upon his American training and produced style sheets and research methodology for studies in Korean music (included in Song, 1982). These are supplemented by a volume of translations of major western ethnomusicological writings (1982), edited by Yi Kangsuk, who trained in music education at Michigan.

At the same time that Song and Lee were going to the West to learn ethnomusicology, a few Westerners without specifically ethnomusicological training were turning to Korea and delighted in the sounds and materials they found. An American, Jonathan Condit, arrived in 1966 with the Peace Corps, and studied performance and language, later writing an original and challenging interpretation of early Korean rhythmic notation for his PhD at Cambridge in 1976 (published in part in Condit, 1979 and 1984, 'Korean Scores'); he has since published a set of transcriptions for modern use of much of the early notated music (1984, *Music of the Korean Renaissance*). Lee Hye-Ku's volume on rhythmic notation (1987) is largely a reaction to Condit's publications. Condit translated a set of essays on Korean music for one of the few available English-language surveys of the subject (National Academy of Arts, 1973). Robert Provine, an American who went to Korea involuntarily in 1967 with the US Army, has mostly confined his work to the early history of Korean court music; he has published a bibliographic study of early written sources (1988), a study of music in state sacrificial rites (1989) and numerous articles. Apart from the focus on Korea, little in Condit or Provine's work distinguishes them from Western historical musicologists.

When Condit and Provine were first setting out, Walter Kaufmann published a study of Oriental music notation systems, including chapters on Korean notations (1967). Prepared from secondary sources with the collaboration of a Korean in the USA, this study broke new ground, but its mistakes and misunderstandings reveal the perils of attempting a foreign armchair study of Korean music.

An Englishman, Keith Pratt, came to Korean studies in the 1970s from Chinese history and initially investigated historically the role of music in diplomatic relations between Korea and China (1976, 1977, 1981), raising intriguing questions about the motives behind China's gifts of musical instruments to Korea. More recently, he has contributed a splendidly illustrated general survey of Korean music (1987), an excellent starting point for Western students.

Other foreign investigators include Alan Heyman, who has resided in Korea since 1960 and gained respect from Korean musicians as one who has both knowledge of and performing ability in traditional music. An Australian, Coralie Rockwell, submitted an MA dissertation at UCLA on the refined vocal genre *kagok* (published 1972). B. C. A. Walraven, from the Netherlands, has written a PhD thesis (1985) on Korean shaman song texts, giving many insights of use to ethnomusicology. Work of a high standard on Korean dance is being carried out by a few westerners, notably Judy Van Zile (e.g. 1987) and Christine Loken-Kim (1989).

A few Japanese scholars have continued to study Korean music in recent times. Leading figures have been the late Mitani Yoko, whose study of East Asian long zithers (1980) includes a close examination of Korean instruments, and Kusano Kaeko, who has published a number of articles.

A recent arrival is Keith Howard, an Englishman with training in Western music and ethnomusicology (anthropological hue). Unlike his predecessors, Howard has conducted extended field research in the remote countryside, and his PhD thesis at Belfast (1985) reports much hitherto unknown material and presents challengingly fresh ideas on the social role of musicians, musical preservation and change, and rhythmic modelling. Some of his research results are presented in a study of folk music bands (1989), and there is also a usefully detailed examination of seven musical instruments (1988).

Native scholarship is increasingly active, particularly in the publication of source material: an enormous country-wide collection of oral literature (Academy of Korean Studies, 1980); four volumes of shaman song texts (Kim T'aegon 1971–80); and a 24-disc recording of dramatic narrative singing (*p'ansori*), 11-disc set of folk song, and 12-disc set of instrumental music (*sanjo*) and songs of sorrow (Korea Britannica, 1982, 1984 and 1989).

Essential reference works

For the Western student, reference materials on Korean music in English are limited to bibliographies in the Western works already listed plus the useful bibliographies (1971, 1974–75, 1978) and discographies (1976–7, 1977) of Song Bang-song (Pangsong). Those who can read Korean are better served by Song's much improved later annotated bibliography (1981), which is the core reference work for the field. Other essential works are two dictionaries of Korean music, one by Chang Sahun (1984, *Kugak taesajŏn*) and one by multiple writers (National Academy of Arts, 1985). It is necessary to consult reference works in related fields in order to get access to context. Particularly useful are

In Kwŏnhwan's bibliography of folklore for 1900–77 (1978), supplemented by two more recent bibliographies (Ewha, 1983, 1984) and the dictionary of literature compiled at Seoul National University (1979).

Prospects and problems

The past survival and present expansion of native scholarship in Korean traditional music commands respect and admiration: but for the amazing perseverance and hard efforts of just a few Korean scholars and performers, little or nothing might remain of traditional Korean music for future generations of Koreans or for foreign investigators. Many useful projects are currently under way, including ever larger collections of oral material, recordings of performers both central and peripheral, and studies of written sources.

For Western students, investigating Korean musicology is arduous. The Korean language is appallingly difficult and requires years of study even to be able to locate a reference in a Korean bibliography, much less to read the item. Few Korean scholars have been properly trained in scholarly writing; the gems in their writings are roughly hewn and difficult to extract. The Westerner trained in a discipline such as musicology or ethnomusicology must learn to cope with native scholarship deficient in those disciplines.

A prime need for the future is translation into Western languages of key works of native scholarship. The problem is that Western perceptions of what needs to be revealed to a Western reader are usually radically different from what a Korean scholar thinks should be told a Korean reader. Translations must be heavily edited and sympathetically amplified in order to bridge the perception gap. Translations of historical primary sources would also be useful.

Some problems in the native scholarship arise from aspects of the native society. Traditional concepts of respect and loyalty make it awkward for a young scholar within the mainstream of musical scholarship spearheaded by Lee Hye-Ku, Chang Sahun, and their students to deviate from established results and procedures, and those few outside the mainstream have little access to the scholarly and monetary resources controlled by the insiders. Another problem is that scholars in related fields (literature, folklore, anthropology) continue to ignore music in their investigations, and the musicologists tend to respond in kind; each field has its own tight loyalties of descent, so that several independent strands of investigation of one topic may proceed simultaneously without the interchange that would benefit all involved. There is also a class problem: the farmer in the country usually regards the scholarly investigator from the city with considerable suspicion, and whole-hearted co-operation of informants is rare.

The Western scholar has the advantage of standing outside most of the internal cultural constraints; he enjoys, for example, a good chance of collecting better field materials than the native Korean scholar distrusted by the musician in the field. On the other hand, while Western interest in Korean music is welcomed by native scholars, understandably they are reluctant to take seriously persons foreign to the culture and language, who have not assimilated the extensive research already carried out by the Koreans. New methods of enquiry, such as ethnomusicology, are viewed with suspicion since they grow out of foreign models without knowledge of Korean music and culture. Lee Hye-Ku's serious consideration of the work of Jonathan Condit is a promising exception to the rule.

The written sources that concerned Korean musicology in its earlier stages still need comprehensive research. More historical notation books may yet be found and published, and much historical, theoretical, and textual work remains to be done. Korean government policy in recent years, however, has been to de-emphasize the study of Chinese characters and literary language, so that most of the younger generation are less well equipped to deal with Chinese-language sources than is a Westerner with adequate training in Chinese and Sinology.

Topics requiring further investigation include the music of Korean communities outside Korea (Central Asia, China and the USA), the music of north Korea, native perceptions of musical continuity, musical change (for which good sound resources are increasingly available), and the music of the remote countryside. A prime goal must be to change the incorrect (if geographically plausible) perception of many Westerners that Korea is essentially a cultural appendage of China or merely a cultural bridge to Japan.

Bibliography

Xu Jing: *Xuanhe fengshi Gaoli tujing* [Account of the Embassy to Korea in the *Xuanhe* Period] (1124/*R*1977)

Kim Pusik: *Samguk sagi* [History of the Three Kingdoms] (1145) [cf. Kim Chonggwŏn (1960)]

Chŏng Inji: *Koryŏsa* [History of the Koryŏ Dynasty] (1451/*R*1972) [cf. Ch'a Chuhwan (1972)]

Sejong sillok [Annals of King Sejong] (1454/*R*1955–8) [cf. *Chosŏn* (1955–8) and Sejong Memorial Society (1968–76)]

Ch'oe Hang: *Kyŏngguk taejŏn* [National Code] (1471/*R*1978) [cf. Office of Legislation (1978)]

Sin Sukchu: *Kukcho orye sŏrye* [Rubrics for the *Five Rites of State*] and *Kukcho oryeŭi* [Five Rites of State] (1474/*R*1979) [cf. Office of Legislation (1981–2)]

Sŏng Hyŏn: *Akhak kwebŏm* [Guide to the Study of Music] (1493/*R*1975) [cf. Yi Hyegu (1979–80)]

Siak hwasŏng [Harmonious Sound of Poetry and Music] (1780–*R*1983)

Pak Yŏn: *Nan'gye yugo* [Collected Writings of Pak Yŏn] (1822)

M. Courant: *Bibliographie Coréene* (Paris, 1894/*R*1968)

Pak Yongdae: *Chŭngbo Munhŏn pigo* [Expanded Edition of the *Korean Encyclopedia of Documents and Institutions*] (1908/*R*1957) [cf. Academy (1983) and Sejong (1978–)]

M. Courant: 'La musique coréene', appendix to his *Essai historique sur la musique classique des Chinois* (Paris, 1912), 211

Tanabe Hisao: 'Chōsen ongaku-kō' [A Study of Korean Music], *Tōyō gakugei zasshi*, xxxviii (1921), 277–84, 327–36, 378–87

Aoyagi Tsunataro: 'Chōsen ongaku-shi' [History of Korean Music], in his *Chōsen bunka-shi taizen* [Survey of Korean Cultural History] (Seoul, 1924), 643–91

Iwaya Takechi: 'Chōsen gakusei no hensen' [Evolution of the Korean Musical System], *Chōsen*, 4 instalments in nos. 163–167 (1928–9)

Ham Hwajin: *Chŭngbo Kagok wŏllyu* [Expanded Edition of the *Source and History of Kagok*] (Seoul, 1929/*R*1943)

A. Eckardt: *Koreanische Musik* (Tokyo, 1930)

An Hwak: 'Chosŏn ŭmak ŭi yŏn'gu' [Studies on Korean Music], *Chosŏn*, 7 instalments in xiv/3–xiv/12 (1930/*R*1980)

Tanaka Hatsuo: 'Chōsen gagaku no gakuritsu ni kansuru kaisetsu' [Explanation of the Pitches of Koreak *aak*], *Chōsen shi kenkyū* [Studies on Korea] (Seoul, 1930), 358

An Hwak: 'Chosŏn ŭmaksa' [History of Korean Music], *Chosŏn*, xv/12–xvi/1 (1931–2/*R*1980)

Ch. S. Keh [Kye Chŏngsik], *Die koreanische Musik* (Strasbourg, 1935/*R*1972)

Ham Hwajin: *Yijo akche wŏllyu* [Source and History of the Musical System of the Chosŏn Dynasty] (Seoul, 1938/*R*1954)

S. M. Anderson: *Korean Folk Songs* (diss., Eastman School of Music, 1940)

J. L. Boots: 'Korean Musical Instruments and an Introduction to Korean Music', *Transactions of the Korea Branch of the Royal Asiatic Society*, xxx (1940), 1–31

Yang Chudong: *Koga yŏn'gu* [Studies on Ancient Songs] (Seoul, 1942/*R*1957)

Kishibe Shigeo: 'Akhak kwebŏm no kaihan ni tsuite' [Editions of the *Guide to the Study of Music*], in *Tanabe sensei kanreki kinen tōa ongaku ronso* [Festschrift for Tanabe Hisao] (Tokyo, 1943), 213–44

Song Sŏkha: 'Genzon Chōsen gakufu' [Extant Korean Notated Sources], ibid., 387–432

Ham Hwajin: *Chosŏn ŭmak t'ongnon* [Introduction to Korean Music] (Seoul, 1948)

Chosŏn wangjo sillok [Annals of the Chosŏn Dynasty] (Seoul, 1955–8), 48 vols.

Ri Hirim: *Haebanghu Chosŏn ŭmak* [Korean Music after Liberation] (P'yŏngyang, 1956)

Yŏm Chŏnggwŏn: *Akhak kwebŏm* [Modern Korean translation of the *Guide to the Study of Music*] (P'yŏngyang, 1956)

Chŏn Chunong: 'Koguryŏ kobun pyŏkhwa e nat'anan akki e taehan yŏn'gu' [A Study of Depictions of Musical Instruments in Wall Paintings of Koguryŏ Tombs], *Nunhwa yusan*, i (1957), 41–71; ii (1957), 26

Yi Hyegu: *Han'guk ŭmak yŏn'gu* [Studies in Korean Music] (Seoul, 1957)

——: *Han'guk kojŏn akki haesŏl* [Explanation of Korean Traditional Musical Instruments] (Seoul, 1959)

Kim Chonggwŏn, trans.: *Wanju Samguk sagi* [Modern Korean translation of the *History of the Three Kingdoms*] (Seoul, 1960)

Im Tonggwŏn: *Han'guk minyo chip* [Collection of Korean Folksongs) (Seoul, 1961–81)

Kim Tonguk: *Han'guk kayo ŭi yŏn'gu* [Studies on Ancient Songs of Korea] (Seoul, 1961)

Hayashi Kenzō: *Dongya yueqi kao* [Studies on East Asian Musical Instruments] (Beijing, 1962)

Mun Hayŏn and Mun Chongsang: *Chaoxian yinyue* [Korean Music] (Beijing, 1962)

Kim Tonguk: *Ch'unhyangjŏn yŏn'gu* [Studies on the *Story of Ch'unhyang*] (Seoul, 1965)

Chang Sahun: *Kugak non'go* [Studies of Korean Music] (Seoul, 1966)

Han Manyŏng: *Han'guk minyo chip* [Collection of Korean Folk Songs] (Seoul, 1967)

——: *Sibi kasa* [12 *kasa*] (Seoul, 1967)

W. Kaufmann: *Musical Notations of the Orient* (Bloomington, IN, 1967)

Yi Hyegu: *Han'guk ŭmak sŏsŏl* [Topics in Korean Music] (Seoul, 1967)

A. Eckardt: *Musik, Lied, Tanz in Korea* (Bonn, 1968)

Sejong Memorial Society [Sejong taewang kinyŏm saŏphoe]: *Sejong changhŏn taewang sillok* [Modern Korean translation of the Annals of King Sejong] (Seoul, 1968–76)

Chang Sahun: *Han'guk akki taegwan* [Korean Musical Instruments] (Seoul, 1969)

Kungnip Kugagwŏn: *Han'guk ŭmak* [Korean Music] (Seoul, 1969–), in Western notation

Yi Tuhyŏn: *Han'guk kamyŏn'gŭk* [Korean Mask-Dance Drama] (Seoul, 1969)

Tanabe Hisao: *Chūgoku Chōsen ongaku chōsa kikō* [Musical Research Trips to China and Korea] (Tokyo, 1970)

Yi Hyegu: *Mandang munch'aerok* [Miscellaneous writings of Yi Hyegu] (Seoul, 1970)

Han'guk ŭmak yŏn'gu [Journal of the Korean Musicological Society] (Seoul, 1971–)

Kim T'aegon: *Han'guk mugajip* [Collection of Shaman Songs] (Seoul, 1971–80)

B. Song [Song Pangsong]: *An Annotated Bibliography of Korean Music* (Providence, RI, 1971)

Yi Chaesuk: *Kayagŭm sanjo* [Sanjo for the *kayagŭm* Zither] (Seoul, 1971)

Ch'a Chuhwan: *Koryŏsa akchi* [The Essay on Music in the *History of the Koryŏ Dynasty*] (Seoul, 1972)

Kungnip Kugagwŏn: *Han'guk ŭmak sŏnjip* [Selection of Korean Classical Music] (Seoul, 1972–), sound recordings

C. Rockwell: *Kagok: a Traditional Korean Vocal Form* (Providence, RI, 1972)

Chang Sahun: *Sijo ŭmangnon* [Studies on the Music of *sijo*] (Seoul, 1973)

National Academy of Arts (Yesurwŏn): *Survey of Korean Arts: Traditional Music* (Seoul, 1973)

Chang Sahun: *Yŏmyŏng ŭi tongsŏ ŭmak* [Eastern and Western Music in the Early 20th Century] (Seoul, 1974)

Kungnip Kugagwŏn: *Kugak chŏnjip* [Complete Collection of Korean Music] (Seoul, 1974–), [in Korean notation]

B. Song [Song Pangsong]: 'Supplement to an Annotated Bibliography of Korean Music', *Korea Journal*, 5 instalments in xiv/12–xv/4 (1974–5)

——: *The Korean-Canadian Folk Song: an Ethnomusicological Study* (Ottawa, 1974)

374

Chang Sahun: *Han'guk chŏnt'ong ŭmak ŭi yŏn'gu* [Studies in Korean Traditional Music] (Seoul, 1975)

Hwang Pyŏnggi: 'Han'guk chŏnt'ong ŭmakŭi mijŏk t'ŭksaek' [Aesthetic Character of Korean Traditional Music], series of 16 essays in *Konggan*, xcviii–cxxxv (1975–8)

Kim Tonguk: *Han'guk kayo ŭi yŏn'gu sok* [Additional Studies on Ancient Songs of Korea] (Seoul, 1975)

Chang Sahun: *Han'guk ŭmaksa* [History of Korean Music] (Seoul, 1976, 2/1986)

K. L. Pratt: 'Music as a Factor in Sung-Koryŏ Diplomatic Relations, 1069–1126', *T'oung Pao*, lxii/4–5 (1976), 199

B. Song [Song Pangsong]: 'A Discography of Korean Music', *Korea Journal*, xvi/12 (1976), 53; 'Subject Index of Discography', xvii/6 (1977), 57

Yi Hyegu: *Han'guk ŭmak nonch'ong* [Essays on Korean Music] (Seoul, 1976)

Chang Sahun: *Han'guk chŏnt'ong muyong yŏn'gu* [Studies on Korean Traditional Dance] (Seoul, 1977)

J. Condit: 'The Evolution of *Yŏmillak* from the Fifteenth Century to the Present Day', in *Chang Sahun paksa hoegap kinyŏm tongyang ŭmakhak nonch'ong* [Articles on Asian Music: Festschrift for Dr Chang Sahun] (Seoul, 1977), 231–62

Minjok ŭmakhak [Journal of the Asian Music Research Institute] (Seoul, 1977–)

K. L. Pratt: 'Some Aspects of Diplomatic and Cultural Exchange Between Korea and Northern Sung China', in *Chang Sahun paksa hoegap kinyŏm tongyang ŭmakhak nonch'ong* [Articles on Asian Music: Festschrift for Dr Chang Sahun] (Seoul, 1977), 313

B. Song [Song Pangsong]: 'A Discography of Korean Music', *Asian Music*, viii/2 (1977), 82–121

In Kwŏnhwan: 'Han'guk minsokhak nonjŏ ch'ongmongnok (1900–1977)' [Bibliography of Korean Folklore, 1900–1977], in his *Han'guk minsokhak sa* [History of Korean Folklore] (Seoul, 1978), 167–286

Office of Legislation [Pŏpchech'ŏ]: *Kyŏngguk taejŏn* [Modern Korean translation of the *National Code*] (Seoul, 1978)

Sejong Memorial Society [Sejong taewang kinyŏm saŏphoe]: *Kugyŏk Chŭngbo Munhŏn pigo* [Modern Korean trans. of the *Expanded Edition of the Korean Encyclopedia of Documents and Institutions*] (Seoul, 1978–)

B. Song [Song Pangsong]: 'Korean Music: an Annotated Bibliography, Second Supplement', *Asian Music*, ix/2 (1978), 65–112

J. Condit: 'A Fifteenth-century Korean Score in Mensural Notation', *Musica Asiatica*, ii (1979), 1–87

Kungnip Kugagwŏn: *Han'guk ŭmakhak charyo ch'ongsŏ* [Collection of Source Materials for the Study of Korean Music] (Seoul, 1979–)

Seoul National U.: *Kugŏ kungmunhak sajŏn* [Dictionary of Korean Literature] (Seoul, 1979)

Yi Hyegu: *Kugyŏk Akhak kwebŏm* [Modern Korean translation of the *Guide to the Study of Music*] (Seoul, 1979–80)

Yi Tongbok: 'Ko akpo haeje poyu (I)' [Supplementary Annotations on Old Music Scores], *Han'guk ŭmak yŏn'gu*, viii–ix (1979), 205–70

Academy of Korean Studies [Han'guk chŏngsin munhwa yŏn'guwŏn]: *Han'guk kubi munhak taegye* [Survey of Korean Oral Literature] (Sŏngnam, 1980–)

Chang Sahun: *Ha Kyuil Im Kijun chŏnch'ang sibi kasa* [12 *kasa* in the Vocal Tradition of Ha Kyuil and Im Kijun] (Seoul, 1980)

Mitani Yōko: *Higashi ajia koto no kenkyū* [A Study of Long Zithers and their Music in East Asia] (Tokyo, 1980)

Pak Hŭngsu: *Toryanghyŏng kwa kugak nonch'ong* [Essays on Measurements and Korean Music] (Seoul, 1980)

Song Pangsong: *Akchang tŭngnok yŏn'gu* [Studies on the *Record of the Royal Music Office*] (Kyŏngsan, 1980)

B. Song [Song Pangsong]: *Source Readings in Korean Music* (Seoul, 1980)

Suematsu Yasukazu: *Chōsen kenkyū bunken mokuroku* [Bibliography of Korean Studies] (Tokyo, 1980)

Han Manyŏng: *Pulgyo ŭmak yŏn'gu* [Studies on Buddhist Music] (Seoul, 1981)

Lee Hye-Ku [Yi Hyegu]: *Essays on Traditional Korean Music*, trans. R. C. Provine (Seoul, 1981)

Office of Legislation [Pŏpchech'ŏ]: *Kukcho oryeŭi* [Modern Korean translation of the *Five Rites of State* (and related works)] (Seoul, 1981–2)

K. L. Pratt: 'Sung Hui Tsung's Musical Diplomacy and the Korean Response', *Bulletin of the School of Oriental and African Studies*, xlvii/3 (1981), 509

Song Pangsong: *Han'guk ŭmakhak nonjŏ haeje* [Annotated Bibliography of Studies on Korean Music] (Sŏngnam, 1981)

Chang Sahun: *Sejongjo ŭmak yŏn'gu* [Studies on Music of the Sejong Period] (Seoul, 1982)

Kim Tonguk: *Kajip akpu aakpu kajip* [Collections of Song Texts] (Seoul, 1982)

Korea Britannica Corporation: *Ppuri kip'ŭn namu p'ansori* [The Deep-rooted Tree P'ansori Collection] (Seoul, 1982)

Paekkwa chŏnsŏ [Complete Encyclopedia] (P'yŏngyang, 1982–4)

Song Pangsong: *Han'guk ŭmaksa yŏn'gu* [Studies in Korean Music History] (Kyŏngsan, 1982)

Yi Kangsuk: *Chong jok ŭmak kwa munhwa* [Ethnic Music and Culture] (Seoul, 1982)

Academy of Korean Studies [Han'guk chŏngsin munhwa yŏn'guwŏn]: *Chŭngbo Munhŏn pigo saegin* [Index to the *Expanded Edition of the Korean Encyclopedia of Documents and Institutions*] (Sŏngnam, 1983)

Chang Sahun: *Kugak saron* [Essays on Korean Music History] (Seoul, 1983)

Ewha Univ., Korean Cultural Research Institute [Han'guk munhwa yŏn'guwŏn]: *Han'guk minsok kwan'gye charyo mongnok* [Bibliography of Korean Folk Culture] (Seoul, 1983)

Yi Chaesuk: *Chŏngak changdan kwa minsogak changdanbŏp e kwanhan yŏn'gu* [Studies on the Rhythmic Structure of Court and Folk Music] (Seoul, 1983) [includes Western transcription of *kayagŭm sanjo* in Ch'oe Oksan school]

——: *Kayagŭm sanjo: Kim Chukp'a yu* (Kayagŭm Sanjo of the Kim Chukp'a School) (Seoul, 1983) [Western notation]

Chang Sahun: *Han'guk muyong kaeron* [Survey of Korean Dance] (Seoul, 1984)

——: *Kugak taesajŏn* [Dictionary of Korean Music] (Seoul, 1984)

J. Condit: *Music of the Korean Renaissance: Songs and Dances of the Fifteenth Century* (Cambridge, 1984)

——: 'Korean Scores in the Modified Fifteenth-century Mensural Notation', *Musica Asiatica*, iv (1984), 1–116

Ewha Univ., Korean Cultural Research Institute [Han'guk munhwa yŏn'guwŏn]: *Han'guk minsok kwan'gye nonmun mongnok* [Article Index of Korean Folk Culture] (Seoul, 1984)

Korea Britannica Corporation: *Ppuri kip'ŭn namu p'alto sori* [The Deep-rooted Tree Collection of Korean Folk Songs] (Seoul, 1984)

Song Pangsong: *Han'guk ŭmak t'ongsa* [Complete History of Korean Music] (Seoul, 1984)

Chu Yŏngja: *Minsogak rhythm yŏn'gu* [Study of Rhythm in Korean Folk Music] (Seoul, 1985)

K. D. Howard: *Bands, Songs, and Shamanistic Rituals: Traditional Music on a Korean Island* (diss., Queen's U. of Belfast, 1985)

National Academy of Arts [Yesurwŏn]: *Han'guk ŭmak sajŏn* [Dictionary of Korean Music] (Seoul, 1985)

Song Pangsong: *Han'guk kodae ŭmaksa yŏn'gu* [Studies in the Ancient Music History of Korea] (Seoul, 1985)

B. C. A. Walraven: *Muga: the Songs of Korean Shamanism* (Leiden, 1985)

Yi Hyegu: *Mandang sok munch'aerok* [More Miscellaneous Writings of Yi Hyegu] (Seoul, 1985)

——: *Han'guk ŭmak nonjip* [Collection of Essays on Korean Music] (Seoul, 1985)

W. Burde, ed.: *Korea: Einführung in die Musiktradition Koreas* (Mainz, 1985)

Kungnip Kugagwŏn: *Kungjung muyong mubo* [Choreography of Court Dances] (Seoul, 1986–)

B. Song [Song Pangsong]: *The Sanjo Tradition of Korean Kŏmun'go Music* (Seoul, 1986)

B. W. Lee: *Buddhist Music of Korea* (Seoul, 1987)

Yi Chaesuk: *Kayagŭm sanjo: Sŏng Kŭmyŏn yu* [Kayagŭm Sanjo of the Sŏng Kŭmyŏn School] (Seoul, 1987) [Western notation]

K. L. Pratt: *Korean Music: its History and Its Performance* (Seoul and London, 1987)

J. Van Zile: 'Ch'ŏyongmu: an Ancient Dance Survives', *Korean Culture*, viii/2 (1987), 5

Yi Hyegu: *Chŏngganbo ŭi chŏnggan taegang mit changdan* [Studies on Korean Rhythmic Notation] (Seoul, 1987)

K. Howard: *Korean Musical Instruments: a practical Guide* (Seoul, 1988)

Mun Sŏngnyŏp: *Chosŏn ŭmaksa* [History of Korean Music] (P'yŏngyang, 1988)

R. C. Provine: *Essays on Sino-Korean Musicology: Early Sources for Korean Ritual Music* (Seoul, 1988)

Song Pangsong: *Koryŏ ŭmaksa yŏn'gu* [Studies on the History of Music in the Koryŏ Dynasty] (Seoul, 1988)

K. Howard: *Bands, Songs, and Shamanistic Rituals: Folk Music in Korean Society* (Seoul, 1989)

Korea Britannica Corporation: *Ppuri kip'ŭn namu Sanjo chŏnjip* [The Deep-rooted Tree Sanjo Collection] and *Ppuri kip'ŭn namu Han pando ŭi sŭlp'ŭn sori* [The Deep-rooted Tree Collection of Korean Songs of Sorrow], 12 discs (Seoul, 1989)

C. J. Loken-Kim: *Release from Bitterness: Korean Dancer as Korean Woman* (diss., U. of North Carolina, 1989)

R. C. Provine: 'State Sacrificial Rites and Ritual Music in Early Chosŏn', *Kugagwŏn nonmunjip* [Journal of the Korean Traditional Performing Arts Centre], i (1989), 239–307

CHAPTER XIII

Southeast Asia

JUDITH BECKER

Musical scholarship by Western scholars on the traditions of mainland Southeast Asia has been constrained by the political situations in Burma, Laos, Cambodia, Vietnam and most recently, Malaysia. Of the mainland countries, only Thailand and Malaysia (to some extent) have remained open and receptive to foreign musical researchers. The result has been that foreign researchers in the area are few, publications available in the West, even fewer. Related to this problem is the absence of a body of closely interacting scholars.

Burma

Musical research on Burma provides a good example of this problem. Before 1962, when Burma closed its borders to foreign researchers, the only notable essay on Burmese music was by U Khin Zaw from a pre-independence issue of the *Journal of the Burma Research Society* dating from 1941. Research in the late 1950s and early 1960s by Muriel Williamson (1975, 1981) and Judith Becker (1969) resulted in a few more articles. Then in the 1970s, Robert Garfias (1975, 1985) was able to obtain a research visa and added three essays. In 1978, a conference organized in Tokyo by Fumio Koizumi, Yoshihiko Tokumaru and Osamu Yamaguchi, at which Burmese musicians participated, resulted in a book that adds several articles to the outside world's knowledge of Burmese music (U Mya Oo, Ôtake, Tokumaru, 1980). These scholars are serious researchers, but are too few, too scattered in place, and too separated in time. To date, studies on the music of Burma are largely concerned with the description of instruments, repertories, scales and modal systems.

Laos

If the situation in Burma has been bleak, musical research in Laos and Cambodia has been worse. In Southeast Asia, Laos is the least represented by scholarly works on music. Laotian court traditions are considered to derive from those of Thailand and Cambodia, and Laotian rural traditions have been largely ignored. Although rural and popular musics are gaining the scholarly attention they deserve, researchers are not active in Laos. The works of Amy Catlin (1982, 1985) on Hmong refugee communities in the USA are thus particularly welcome, as is the linguistic study of Carol Compton (1979) on the sung poetry tradition *mawlam*. Compton's linguistic study and Terry Miller's musical study of the same genre from northeast Thailand comprise a fairly comprehensive set of resources for the genre *mawlam*.

Cambodia

Musical research in Cambodia has, since the early work by Alain Daniélou (1957), been centred on traditions of the royal court, thus following a pattern typical of most Southeast Asian research. The recent political upheavals of Cambodia have tended to solidify this focus, since new research from Cambodia has not reached the West. The presence of large refugee populations in the Western world has fostered a new kind of research for Southeast Asia, the study of refugee musical traditions. While adaptation may be the primary goal of the refugee communities, there are yet strong impulses to sustain and preserve the artistic traditions of the homeland. As in other Southeast Asian kingdoms, in Cambodia the ruler and his court embodied the forces which sustained prosperity, fertility and spirituality. Since immigrant populations in an alien environment need to invoke traditional sources of strength as well as to understand new ones, court music and dance are undergoing a popularization in the USA, where large groups of immigrant children are taught the court traditions of their ancestors. A few articles document this activity (Catlin, 1987; Sam Sam-Ang and Chan Moly Sam, 1987).

Vietnam

From the evidence presented by Trân Van Khê (1977) and Pham Duy (1975), musicological research is a vital part of the new Vietnam, encouraged and supported by the government. Apparently many manuscripts are available locally, written in Vietnamese. Though not presently available to outsiders, one could hazard a guess as to the style of this research based on the examples we have. Vietnamese scholarship has tended to follow the mode of Chinese research, which, as part of the larger entity of Chinese scholarship in general is predominantly historical and descriptive. This was also the predominant mode of historical musicology and has remained a strong element in ethnomusicology. Vietnamese scholarship, even as written by Westerners (Addiss, 1971, 'Music of the Cham Peoples'; 1971, 'Theatre Music'), follows this style (Trân Van Khê, 1962; Thai Van Kiem, 1964; Pham Duy, 1975). Anthropological, contextual issues are not discussed, but the reader is presented with ample information on the history of genres, musical instruments, scales and modes. However, the book by Pham Duy (1975) also includes many song texts, which although uninterpreted, add cultural information.

Malaysia

Researchers in Malaysia, both Malay and Western, have focussed attention on the rural genres with long histories, predating Islam. This emphasis, hardly

378

unique to Malaysia, has tended to exclude from scholarly discourse the most widespread kinds of music – the urban genres that have developed recently and have accommodated, more or less, to an Islamic society. This situation is changing (al Fārūqī, 1987; Chopyak, 1986, 1987), in part because of the general acceptance of popular musics as worthy of serious study, and in part because of repressive attitudes toward genres with ties to pre-Islamic religious beliefs and practices. One strong advantage for Malaysian research is the easy interchange of information and ideas between foreign and indigenous scholars. As a former British colony, English is widely understood, especially among the educated.

For a while it seemed possible that Malaysia would be the site of an institute for the study of performing arts of all Southeast Asia (Universiti Sains Malaysia, Penang). Given the geographically central location of Malaysia, its political non-alignment, its multi-racial make-up and the familiarity of Malaysian scholars with Western modes of scholarship, Malaysia seemed the ideal country both to build bridges between Western and Southeast Asian scholarship and also to facilitate greater communication between Southeast Asian performers and scholars. However, an ascendant fundamentalist Islamic movement (*Dakwah*) in Malaysia has taken a strongly negative stand against all pre-Islamic performance traditions in Malaysia, which includes many traditions unique to Malaysia (*main puteri, may ong*) and also many genres linking Malaysia to its neighbours (*wayang Siam, wayang kulit, gamelan Trengganu*). Malaysia remains, however, the focus of research of a number of outstanding scholars from several disciplines and covering several generations.

Thailand

Thailand stands as the most felicitous country of mainland Southeast Asia for musicological research. Thai music scholars have been active as long as foreign scholars, and have created a sizable bibliography of studies in Thai, few of which have been translated. In Southeast Asia, this Thai-language musical bibliography is rivalled only by the substantial Indonesian-language musical bibliography. (A complete listing has been compiled by Manop Wisuttipat of the Department of Music, Srinakharinwirot University in Bangkok.)

Research in Thailand, as in all countries of Southeast Asia except the Philippines, has focussed primarily on the urban court traditions of the 19th and early 20th centuries (Morton, 1976, 1980; Dhanit Yupho, 1957; Phra Chen Duriyanga, 1948). However, the Thai government has established over 70 cultural centres in the provinces to preserve, support and document regional traditions. Also, in keeping with Western research trends of the past two decades, studies of Thai regional music have been represented in Western publications as well (Miller, 1985; Miller and Chonpairot, 1979, 'The Musical Traditions'; Dyck, 1975, 'They Also Serve'; 1975, 'The Vanishing *Phia*').

The sequence of co-authored articles by Terry E. Miller and Jarernchai Chonpairot (1979, 'The Musical Traditions', 1979, 'Review Essay', 1981) is almost unique in Southeast Asian scholarship. Collaboration across cultural traditions and across languages is so difficult that most Western scholars prefer to learn from informants, not to write articles with them. Miller and Jarernchai Chonpairot have been able to alternate and reciprocate the teacher/student role and provide the field with models of Western/Southeast Asian collaborative articles.

Since many of the languages of mainland Southeast Asia are tonal, a number of scholars have studied the relationship between linguistic tone and musical pitch. For the Thai language, these include George List (1961), David Morton (1974) and S. T. Mendenhall (1975); for Burmese, Muriel Williamson (1981); for Hmong, Catlin (1981, 1985). These studies indicate that generalizations concerning the relationship between linguistic tone and melody are not easily constructed, and that the situation differs with each language, with each genre.

Philippine Islands

Musical research in the Philippines has been strongly focussed on the Islamic areas of Mindanao and the Sulu archipelago. One of the pioneers in ethnomusicology, José Maceda, wrote his dissertation on the drum and gong ensembles of the Magindanao, Muslims from the island of Mindanao (Maceda, 1963). This trend has continued with the work of Ricardo Trimillos, Usopay Cadar, and Steven Otto (Trimillos, 1972, 1974; Cadar, 1975, 1985; Otto, 1985). In part, this focus reflects an earlier attitude in ethnomusicology which held that assimilated genres, or genres including Western borrowings, were not worthy of serious study. Since most music of the Christian majority of the Philippine people is heavily influenced by Spanish music, and more recently by American music, scholars have tended to move away from the heavily populated central areas into the outlying islands in order to find 'indigenous' Philippine music.

Also, the ubiquitous drum-and-gong ensembles of Southeast Asia have stimulated scholars to pursue comparative studies, in which the Philippine scholars have taken an important role. Since gong-and-drum ensembles are found primarily in the Muslim areas of the Philippines, research has focussed on the southern regions. As the prejudice against musical forms of mixed heritage disappears, we can expect to see more studies of the music of the Christian majority peoples.

A notable aspect of Philippine musical research is that it has been largely pursued by Philippine nationals or Philippine-Americans. The closeness of the political ties between the Philippines and the Western world has made English the second language of educated Filipinos, and facilitated familiarity with Western modes of scholarship. Most scholarship in the Philippines is written in English. Thus, unlike Thailand, Vietnam and Indonesia, where the work of many scholars remains unknown in the West, the research of Philippine scholars is usually immediately accessible.

Indonesia

After decades of Indonesian musical research focussed primarily on the court gamelan traditions of Central Java and the gamelan traditions of Bali, the 1970s and the 1980s have been notable for a surge of interest in the regional musical traditions of urban and popular music. A number of scholars have turned from the romantic court traditions and have begun to pursue research in the villages of East Java (Sutton, 1985, 'Musical Pluralism'), the cassette shops of Jakarta (Frederick, 1982), and the ceremonies of the Mandailing peoples of Sumatra (Kartomi, 1981, 'Dualism in Unity', 1981, 'Lovely When Heard'). This broadening of musical research in Indonesia cannot be attributed to a single cause, or to a single scholar. It is too easy to attribute this change simply to a satiation of interest in the large gamelan ensembles of Central Java and Bali. These venerable traditions continue to provide an inexhaustible wellspring of pleasure and intellectual stimulation for a number of scholars (Vetter, 1981; Becker, 1980, Lindsay, 1985; Sumarsam, 1984; Sutton, 1984). But a perceptible shift has occurred, and works that were once at the centre of the discipline are no longer so.

New topics for study generate new questions, new approaches, new perspectives. Time-honoured aspects, such as modal studies, tuning comparisons, relationships of performance arts to kingship or historical reconstructions, are giving way to more contemporary approaches such as in-depth studies of the lives of musicians, the politics of music-making, interactions between village or regional and court styles, the impact of the cassette industry on music-making, or the analogies between music forms and other forms of cultural expression.

A factor that has contributed to this change of attitude is a degree of democratization of Indonesian musical studies in Indonesia itself. The gamelan traditions of Central Java are, for some Indonesian scholars, too closely identified with Javanese imperialism, a 'Greater Mataram' mentality. Central Javanese gamelan ensembles are sent to fine arts academies throughout the Republic, where they may remain unused and dusty, a silent reminder of Central Javanese cultural chauvinism. Sumatran or East Javanese researchers are beginning to find interest in and support for localized research, where the justification for the topic need not be ties, past or present, to court centres (Adam, 1970; Matsyachir, 1977; Manik, 1977).

What can be called the democratization of Indonesian musical studies is also influenced by Western trends in ethnomusicology. American and Australian scholars, along with their social science colleagues, are becoming more sensitive to the political aspects of all research, more receptive to the notion that the choice of an area of study cannot be based purely on scholarly or artistic grounds, but inevitably resonates into areas of social and political responsibility. Australian scholars, closer to Indonesia and more informed about day-to-day events in the archipelago than North Americans or Europeans, are continually reminded of the abuses of a Java-dominated political system. American scholars, on the other hand, are increasingly aware of the social, political or economic difficulties of their own underclasses, whose numbers and proportions have increased dramatically in the last decade. Thus, while it is still possible and still fascinating to study the artistic expressions of Java's cultural elite, scholars around the globe have become more circumspect about attributing these expressive forms exclusively to 'the Javanese'. The increased self-reflexivity of the scholar of the 1990s, the emphasis on the contextuality of the research situation, is producing a more politically sensitive type of research than that of earlier decades.

Before World War II, Indonesian musical scholarship was dominated by Dutch scholars and was framed within a European scholarly perspective. Those traditions considered to be 'high art', such as the Central Javanese shadow puppet theatre, court dance traditions, or gamelan traditions of Bali and Central Java, were the kinds of musical expression considered most worthy of scholarly interest. The emphasis of this scholarship was on the description of and the historical reconstruction of different genres (Groneman, 1890; Brandts Buys, 1934; Kunst, 1927, 1934).

Dutch scholarly interest in Indonesia, particularly Central Java, had an abiding impact on the ways in which Javanese scholars thought about and wrote about musical events. One of the Dutch concerns was the preservation of court gamelan repertories in some kind of notation. This European idea was embraced by Javanese musicians and led to the development, around 1900, of the now-standard *kepatihan* notation. The idea of writing a book or an article focussed exclusively on artistic forms introduced a new literary genre into Indonesia, a genre now firmly rooted. Previous to this late colonial period, there were no documents exclusively about music in Indonesia. In older texts, music, if mentioned at all, is integrated into a discussion of some larger issue such as kingly entertainment, ceremonial processions, or armies marching into battle. Today, the essays and books written by students and faculty members at the various arts academies are, like their Dutch predecessors, largely descriptive and, in Java, from an elite point of view (Warsadiningrat, 1987; Sindoesawarno, 1987; Martopangrawit, 1984). While the Dutch inspiration for these works is clear, musical treatises from Central Java are also influenced by the literary devices, stylistic conventions and assumptions about authorship that are indigenous to the millennium-old literary tradition in Java (see 'Preface', Becker and Feinstein, 1984).

The vast resource of Indonesian manuscripts in Dutch libraries, plus the legacy of colonial research and publication in many fields, continue to stimulate and inspire scholars of Indonesian music. Although The Netherlands is no longer the vital centre of Indonesian studies it once was, scholars of Indonesia from whatever field or country are likely, at some point in their careers, to make a trip to The Netherlands to study manuscripts (*see* Chapter III, 'Northern and Western Europe', 'The Netherlands').

Beginning in the 1950s, and increasingly each decade since, the centre for Western studies of Indonesian music has shifted from The Netherlands to the USA. At first, the models for American scholars were the earlier Dutch scholars; American scholarship did not differ in tone or in approach from its Dutch predecessors (Hood, 1954; McPhee, 1966). In the 1960s, however, American scholars began to feel the impact of the burgeoning social science disciplines, particularly since one of the giants of the field, Clifford Geertz, studied and wrote about Indonesia. Ever since, American scholars of Indonesian music have felt it necessary to keep abreast of current anthropological, linguistic, and historical studies on Indonesia. In fact, they often find themselves in more intellectual sympathy with Indonesianists in other fields than with Western historical musicologists, whose attitudes and approaches are often similar to the earlier research of Dutch musicologists.

While the writings of certain social scientists and historians are influential and often quoted in musical studies (Geertz, 1960, 1973, 1980; Ricklefs, 1974;

Anderson, 1972; Day, 1981), one aspect of contemporary anthropological and linguistic research that has not been adopted by scholars of Indonesian music is the tendency toward theory building. The social science approach in which one begins with theory and finds illustrations of the theory in one's field research has held little interest for scholars of Indonesian music. European, Australian and American researchers have quite consistently concentrated on particularity, on description, analysis and interpretation. They write about the cultural locus of a particular genre tied to a particular time and place, and avoid sweeping generalizations or global theories. One could see this phenomenon as a Geertzian legacy or as a reaction against the comparative, structuralist theories of 19th-century European ethnography, exemplified for Indonesianists in the works of the Dutch scholar W. H. Rassers (1959). Another aspect of the preference for particularity is the legacy of one of the earliest American scholars of Indonesian music, Mantle Hood, who insisted on the importance of learning to perform in the tradition studied. This injunction has been taken seriously and with several concomitant results; learning to perform tends to keep one's focus on the richness and complexity of performance traditions, on what can be called the phenomenological surface, rather than on theoretical abstractions.

While to social scientists, American scholars of Indonesian music may seem unnecessarily involved with performing, to another group they seem dryly academic and given to excessive intellectualizing. This group is the growing constituency of American gamelan musicians, whether performing traditional music on traditional ensembles, non-traditional music on traditional ensembles, or non-traditional music on non-traditional ensembles. It is estimated that there are, in the early 1990s, some 200 groups in the USA performing either on traditional Javanese or Balinese gamelan, or on American-made simulations of traditional instruments. American gamelan musicians even have their own journal; the well-produced periodical *Balungan* (1984–), that regularly includes gamelan scores by American composers. For the most part, these musicians and composers have little interest in scholarship. The American scholar of Indonesian music thus stands somewhat uneasily between social science colleagues with their theoretical models and subtle interpretive skills on the one hand, and the gamelan musicians whose interest is purely artistic and expressive on the other.

Another important centre for Indonesian music research is Australia. A burgeoning Australian scholarly interest in Indonesia is evident in the appearance of many fine studies from a number of academic disciplines such as anthropology, language and literature, and history. The proximity of Indonesia to Australia, plus the ample support given by Australian universities for research and for field trips have contributed to the development of Australia as a major centre for Indonesian studies. Musical researchers are in close contact with other Indonesianists and also with traditional musicologists. As ethnomusicology and historical musicology grew up together in Australia, ethnomusicology is not considered separate from musicology and was never in the parent–child relationship to musicology as in North America and in Europe. Thus, in Australia there was never any need to assert the autonomy of ethnomusicology. The slow rapprochement between the two disciplines, which progresses with a good deal of hesitation on both sides in North America and Europe, is, from an Australian perspective, the undoing of an unfortunate schism with which they never had to contend.

The centre of Indonesian musical research in Australia is at Monash University in Melbourne. Margaret Kartomi has written one book and several articles about Javanese music, but the bulk of her recent publications have been about musical traditions in Sumatra. Her numerous students tend to follow her lead and avoid research on the court traditions of Central Java, concentrating upon rural Javanese traditions and Sumatran traditions (Falk, 1978; Goldsworthy, 1978; Moore, 1984).

Australian musical research is not, however, the exclusive province of one university. Recently, a richly interpretive dissertation on the historicity of the Javanese concept of 'classical' music has come from the University of Sydney (Lindsay, 1985). Given the location of Australia and the number of Australian scholars of Indonesian music, it appears that Australian research will hold an increasingly important place in Indonesian musical studies.

Until around 1960, the number of scholars involved worldwide and the range of possible topics about Indonesian music were much more restricted than today. Early research on Indonesian music was constrained in two directions. Since very little had been written about Indonesian music, there was no body of scholarship to build upon or to butt against, and the kinds of questions one might ask were circumscribed by the prevailing intellectual context of musicology and history. Because of these limitations, it was possible for one person to think of writing a definitive work – a comprehensive book that covered all relevant topics of research pertaining to one kind of music. From research carried out in the 1930s, came two books which, at the time, were closer to this kind of definitive study than any work since. These were *De toonkunst van Java* by Jaap Kunst and *Music in Bali* by Colin McPhee. (Although McPhee's book was not published until 1966, the research was carried out in the 1930s.)

Kunst, after a brief introduction discussing pre-history, early historical references to Indonesian music and contemporary scholarship, plunges into Chapter 2, 'Tone and Scale-Systems'. Interest in tonal systems peaked in the late 19th century, when musicologists, restricted in travel, often had little more to study than a few instruments and some faulty transcriptions. Given the limitations of their data, the emphasis on scales and tunings is not surprising. Kunst was a participant in this European interest, which for many scholars had evolutionary implications. Only well into the 20th century were the evolutionary doctrines dropped, although the interest in scales and tunings persists into the 20th century (Hatch, 1980; Martopangrawit, 1984; Harrell, 1975; Hood, 1966). The remaining chapters of *De toonkunst van Java* are devoted to a description of ensembles and repertories that is intended to be exhaustive.

Music in Bali by Colin McPhee includes much more of the social context of music-making than the Kunst work, and less of the reconstructed historical background. Otherwise, it follows the predominant *modus operandi* of *De toonkunst van Java* with descriptions of ensembles and repertories. McPhee's daily interaction with many Balinese permitted him to write extensively about particular musicians, musical situations, and musical training in his other books, *A House in Bali* (1946) and *A Club of Small Men* (1948). These works read like novels and are different in tone as well as topic from *Music in Bali*.

One of the oldest concerns of musicologists and ethnomusicologists is musical modality. The Javanese equivalent, *paṭet* studies, was an interest of Kunst, and his contemporary M. A. Koesoemadinata (1969), and is the topic of the PhD dissertation of his student Mantle Hood (1954). The problem of *paṭet* has been addressed many times since by J. Becker (1980), M. F. Hatch (1980), Sumarsam (1984), R. L. Martopangrawit (1984), Sri Hastanto (1985), P. D. Poerbatjaraka (1987), Ki Sindoesawarno (1987), B. E. Brinner (1985) and S. P. Walton (1987) among others. All these studies are exclusively concerned with the music of Central Java, traditions either court derived or influenced by court traditions. Modal studies continue to interest scholars because of the complexity of the issues involved. The term '*paṭet*' is multivocalic, multi-meaningful. It covers a range of semantic fields, such as the sections of the shadow puppet theatre, tonality, modality (scale and melodic patterns), times of day, register, and mood. *Paṭet* is never defined in exactly the same way by any two musicians. The range of meanings of *paṭet* are never fixed, but continue to evolve as Central Javanese music adjusts to an ever-changing group of performers and listeners. Although scholarly interest in *paṭet* has been sustained up till the present, the turn away from Central Javanese studies and the increased importance of more thickly contextual, interpretive scholarship has made some of these works appear slightly old-fashioned. As it is no longer sufficient to describe ensembles and repertories without a context, it is no longer acceptable to abstract *paṭet* from the practice of particular musicians who are constantly redefining it.

The publication of the three-volume set of translations *Karawitan: Source Readings in Javanese Gamelan and Vocal Music* (Becker and Feinstein, 1984, 1987, 1988) continues the focus on Central Javanese court music of earlier decades. In another respect, however, it is a modern work. More than a dozen contemporary American and Javanese scholars have been involved as authors, translators, editors and consultants attesting to the high degree of cooperation and exchange among scholars of Indonesian music. This work also represents the first large-scale translation project of works by Southeast Asian scholars.

After decades of condescension and dismissal by traditional musicologists, popular music, which is often mass-produced urban music, has become a legitimate field of study for academics. Regionalism is still a strong element in all Indonesian music so that no clear line can be drawn between regional music and popular music. While some recording artists have pan-Indonesian appeal, each region, each locality also has its own favourites. The popular music of an older generation, *kroncong*, also has a number of stylistic variants determined by region. Some of the regional variants of *kroncong* received modest scholarly attention in the 1970s (Heins, 1975; Becker, 1975; Kornhauser, 1978). Studies of popular music are likely to become more important in the coming decades.

The rapid development of the cassette industry in Indonesia, producing quantities of cheap and easily available music, has provided a new and unforeseen stimulus to researchers. Not only do large Indonesian cassette companies produce the expected top hits from Jakarta, but also many small, regionally based companies record regional styles for regional consumption. Without an enormous output of time and energy, a researcher can have access to a variety of regional rural musical examples. Recently, articles have appeared with data including not only traditional fieldwork, but study of regional cassettes as well (Sutton, 1985). An annotated catalogue of cassette recordings made in Indonesia from 1957 to 1985 and totalling more than 3000 items has recently been published (Yampolsky, 1987). Collecting musical data by means of a tape recorder, the primary research activity of former times, is of less concern now. The musical record in many places is readily accessible. But the questions asked concerning that record continue to pose the greatest challenge.

Compared to the limited number of Western or Eastern scholars writing about the music of Burma, Thailand, Cambodia, Laos, or even the Philippines, Indonesian musical scholars seem numerous and highly interactive. There is often a feeling among ethnomusicologists that it may be more rewarding to study a musical tradition not yet written about, or one with only limited coverage. This privilege, so different from the research constraints of most traditional musicologists, is highly valued in the discipline. But the obverse side of the coin is that a little-studied area or topic lacks a framework for research, lacks previous scholarship and lacks contemporary scholarship with which to interact. Solitary scholarship was a 19th-century ideal, and commands few adherents in ethnomusicology, fewer yet among scholars of Indonesian music.

This overview of the state of Southeast Asian musical scholarship is of course one person's perspective and may not agree with the views of an observer from some other vantage point, with some other history. There are no 'hard facts' to be discovered, only a flow of events, selected, shaped and interpreted by each observer. As there is no privileged perspective, there is also no privileged observer. One of the conventions of traditional Indonesian literature was for the author to give a formal apology for his shortcomings at the beginning of his manuscript. This quotation illustrates the genre and can aptly express the sentiments of this ethnomusicologist: 'Informed readers will freely add and subtract, alter and contest, or completely throw out these theories and replace them with new ones' (Sindoesawarno, 1987, 'Ilmu Karawitan').

Bibliography

Burma
U Khin Zaw: 'Burmese Music (A Preliminary Enquiry)', *Bulletin of the School of Oriental and African Studies*, x (1941), 717–54
J. Becker: 'The Anatomy of a Mode', *EM*, xiii (1969), 267
D. A. Craig: 'The Music of Oboe and Drums', *Arts of Asia*, i/3 (1971), 13
J. Okell: 'The Burmese Double-Reed "Nhai"', *Asian Music*, ii/1 (1971), 25
R. Garfias: 'A Musical Visit to Burma', *World of Music*, xvii/1 (1975), 3
——: 'Preliminary Thoughts on Burmese Modes', *Asian Music*, vii/1 (1975), 39
M. Williamson: 'Aspects of Traditional Style Maintained in Burma's First 13 *Kyò* Songs', *Selected Reports in Ethnomusicology*, ii/2 (1975), 117–63
——: 'A Supplement to the Construction and Decoration of One Burmese Harp', *Selected Reports in Ethnomusicology*, ii/2 (1975), 111
R. M. Cooler: *The Karen Bronze Drums of Burma: the Magic Pond* (diss., Cornell U., 1979)

U Mya Oo: 'The Music of Burma', *Musical Voices of Asia*, ed. R. Emmert and Y. Minegishi (Tokyo, 1980), 7

T. Ôtake: 'Aspects of Burmese Musical Structure', *Musical Voices of Asia*, ed. R. Emmert and Y. Minegishi (Tokyo, 1980), 56

Y. Tokumaru: 'Burmese Music – A Brief Discussion of Its Present Situation', *Musical Voices of Asia*, ed. R. Emmert and Y. Minegishi (Tokyo, 1980), 68

M. C. Williamson: 'The Correlation between Speech-Tones of Text-Syllables and Their Musical Setting in a Burmese Classical Song', *Musica Asiatica*, iii (1981), 11

L. E. R. Picken: 'Instruments in an Orchestra from Pyū (Upper Burma) in 802', *Musica Asiatica*, iv (1984), 245

R. Garfias: 'The Development of the Modern Burmese Hsaing Ensemble', *Asian Music*, xvi/1 (1985), 1

Laos

A. Daniélou: *La musique du Cambodie et du Laos* (Pondicherry, 1957)

C. Archaimbault: 'Temple Drums', *Kingdom of Laos: the Land of the Million Elephants and of the White Parasol*, ed. R. de Berval (Saigon, 1959), 185

Prince Souvanna-Phouma: 'Music', *Kingdom of Laos: the Land of the Million Elephants and of the White Parasol*, ed. R. de Berval (Saigon, 1959), 87

E. Mareschal: *La Musique des Hmong* (Paris, 1976)

C. Compton: *Courting Poetry in Laos: a Textual and Linguistic Analysis* (DeKalb, IL, 1979)

A. R. Catlin: 'Speech Surrogate Systems of the Hmong: From Singing Voices to Talking Reeds', *The Hmong in the West: Observations and Reports*, ed. B. T. Downey and D. P. Olney (Minneapolis, MN, 1982), 170–200

——: 'Harmonizing the Generations in Hmong Musical Performance', *Selected Reports in Ethnomusicology*, vi (1985), 83

T. E. Miller: 'The Survival of Lao Traditional Music in America', *Selected Reports in Ethnomusicology*, vi (1985), 99

Cambodia

A. Daniélou: *La musique du Cambodie et du Laos* (Pondicherry, 1957)

J. Brunet: 'Music and Rituals in Traditional Cambodia', *Traditional Drama and Music of Southeast Asia*, ed. M. T. Osman (Kuala Lumpur, 1974), 219

The Royal University of Fine Arts, Cambodia: 'Pinpeat and Mohori Music', *Traditional Drama and Music of Southeast Asia*, ed. M. T. Osman (Kuala Lumpur, 1974), 196

——: 'Characteristic Aspects in the Interpretation of Cambodian Classical Music', *Traditional Drama and Music of Southeast Asia*, ed. M. T. Osman (Kuala Lumpur, 1974), 225

P. R. Cravath: *Earth in Flower: an Historical and Descriptive Study of the Classical Dance Drama of Cambodia* (diss., U. of Hawaii, 1985)

——: 'The Ritual Origins of the Classical Dance Drama of Cambodia', *Asian Theatre Journal*, iii (1986), 179

A. Catlin, ed.: *Apsara: the Feminine in Cambodian Art* (Los Angeles, CA, 1987)

S.-A. Sam and C. M. Sam: *Khmer Folk Dance* (Newington, CT, 1987)

Vietnam

P. Huard: 'Les instruments de musique chez les Muong', *Institut Indochinois pour l'étude de l'homme. Bulletin et Travaux*, ii/11 (1939), 135

Trân Van Khê: *La musique vietnamienne traditionelle* (Paris, 1962)

Thai Van Kiem: *Panorama de la musique classique vietnamienne: des origines à nos jours* (Saigon, 1964) [Extract from *Bulletin de la Société des Etudes Indochinoises*, xxxix/1]

S. Addiss: 'Music of the Cham Peoples', *Asian Music*, ii/1 (1971), 32

——: 'Theatre Music of Vietnam', *Southeast Asia: an International Quarterly*, i/1–2 (1971), 129

Pham Duy: *Musics of Vietnam* (Carbondale, IL, 1975)

Trân Van Khê: 'Situation de la Musique en République Socialiste du Viet-Nam', *AcM*, 1/1 (1977), 121

Malaysia

Tunku Nong Jiwa, Raja Badri Shah and Haji Mubin Sheppard: 'The Kedah and Perak Nobat', *Malaya in History*, vii/2 (1962), 6

Haji Mubin Sheppard: 'Joget Gamelan Trengganu', *Journal of the Malaysian Branch of the Royal Asiatic Society*, xl/1 (1967), 149

W. P. Malm: 'The Music of the Malaysian Ma'yong', *Traditional Drama and Music of Southeast Asia*, ed. M. T. Osman (Kuala Lumpur, 1974), 336

J. P. Ongkili: 'The Traditional Musical Instruments of Sabah', *Traditional Drama and Music of Southeast Asia*, ed. M. T. Osman (Kuala Lumpur, 1974), 327

M. T. Osman: 'Some Observations on the Socio-Cultural Context of Traditional Malay Music', *Traditional Drama and Music of Southeast Asia*, ed. M. T. Osman (Kuala Lumpur, 1974), 309

W. P. Malm: 'Music in Malaysia', *The World of Music*, xxi/3 (1979), 6

M. G. Nasaruddin: *Dance and Music of the Desa Performing Arts of Malaysia* (diss., U. of Indiana, 1979)

H. Mat Piah and others: *Tradisi gamelan di Malaysia* (Kuala Lumpur, 1980)

P. Matusky: *Music in the Malay Shadow Puppet Theatre* (diss., U. of Michigan, 1980)

J. D. Chopyak: 'Music in Modern Malaysia: a survey of the Musics Affecting the Development of Malaysian Popular Music', *Asian Music*, xviii/1 (1986), 111

L. I. al Fārūqī: 'Qūr'an Reciters in Competition in Kuala Lumpur', *EM*, xxxi (1987), 221

J. D. Chopyak: 'The Role of Music in Mass Media, Public Education and the Formation of a Malaysian National Culture', *EM*, xxxi (1987), 431

S.-B. Tan: 'From Popular to "Traditional" Theater: the Dynamics of Change in *Bangsawan* of Malaysia', *EM*, xxxiii (1989), 229

Thailand

Phra Chen Duriyanga: *Thai Music* (Bangkok, 1948); repr. as 'Siamese Music' in *Asian Music*, xiii/2 (1982), 55–91

D. Yupho: *Khrŷang dontri Thai* [Thai Musical Instruments] (Bangkok, 1957, 2/1967; Eng. trans., 1960, 2/1971)

Anon.: *Thai Classical Music: Book 1* (Bangkok, 1961)

G. List: 'Speech Melody and Song Melody in Central Thailand', *EM*, v (1961), 16

S. Moore: 'Thai Songs in 7/4 Meter', *EM*, xiii (1969), 309

———: *Traditional Thai Music for Voice, Wind, and Stringed Instruments* (diss., Columbia U., 1972)

D. Morton: 'Vocal Tones in Traditional Thai Music', *Selected Reports in Ethnomusicology*, ii/1 (1974), 88

Thai Delegation: 'Thai Traditional Music', *Traditional Drama and Music in Southeast Asia*, ed. M. T. Osman (Kuala Lumpur, 1974), 234

G. P. Dyck: 'They Also Serve' [Blind Musicians of North Thailand], *Selected Reports in Ethnomusicology*, ii/2 (1975), 205

———: 'The Vanishing *Phia*: an Ethnomusicological Photo-Story', *Selected Reports in Ethnomusicology*, ii/2 (1975), 217

S. T. Mendenhall: 'Interaction of Linguistic and Musical Tone in Thai Song', *Selected Reports in Ethnomusicology*, ii/2 (1975), 17

Prasidh Silapabanleng: 'Thai Music at the Court of Cambodia', *Selected Reports in Ethnomusicology*, ii/2 (1975), 3

D. Morton: *The Traditional Music of Thailand* (Berkeley, CA, 1976)

T. E. Miller and J. Chonpairot: 'The Musical Traditions of Northeast Thailand', *Journal of the Siam Society*, lxvii/1 (1979), 1

———: 'Review Essay: The Problems of Lao Discography', *Asian Music*, xi/1 (1979), 124

J. Becker: 'A Southeast Asian Musical Process: Thai *Thǎw* and Javanese *Irama*', *EM*, xxiv (1980), 453

D. Morton: 'The Music of Thailand', *Musics of Many Cultures: an Introduction*, ed. E. May (Berkeley, CA, 1980), 63

T. E. Miller and J. Chonpairot: 'The Ranat and Boon-Lang: the Question of the Origin of Thai Xylophones', *Journal of the Siam Society*, lvix (1981), 145

P. Fuller: 'Thai Music, 1968–1981', *YTM*, xv (1983), 152

T. E. Miller: 'Reconstructing Siamese Musical History from Historical Sources: 1548–1932', *Asian Music*, xv/2 (1984), 32

J. Marre: 'Two Faces of Thailand: a musical Portrait', *Beats of the Heart: Popular Music of the World*, ed. J. Marre and H. Charlton (New York, 1985), 198

T. E. Miller: *Traditional Music of the Lao: Kaen Playing and Mawlum Singing in Northeast Thailand* (Westport, CT, 1985)

P. A. Myers-Moro: 'Songs for Life: Leftist Thai Popular Music in the 1970's', *Journal of Popular Culture*, xx/3 (1986), 93

Philippines

J. M. Maceda: *The Music of the Magindanao in the Philippines* (diss., U. of California, 1963)

M. C. Conklin and J. Maceda: 'Hanunóo Music from the Philippines', *Readings in Ethnomusicology*, ed. D. P. McAllester (New York, 1971), 186

R. D. Trimillos: *Tradition and Repertoire in the Cultivated Music of the Tausuq of Sulu, Philippines* (diss., U. of California, 1972)

U. Cadar and R. Garfias: 'Some Principles of Formal Variation in the Kolintang Music of the Maranao', *EM*, xviii (1974), 43

J. Maceda: 'Drone and Melody in Philippine Musical Instruments', *Traditional Drama and Music of Southeast Asia*, ed. M. T. Osman (Kuala Lumpur, 1974), 246

R. D. Trimillos: 'Vocal Music of the Tausuq of Sulu, Phillipines', *Traditional Drama and Music of Southeast Asia*, ed. M. T. Osman (Kuala Lumpur, 1974), 274

U. H. Cadar: 'The role of *Kulintang* in Maranao Society', *Selected Reports in Ethnomusicology*, ii/2 (1975), 49

W. R. Pfeiffer: *Filipino Music* (Dumaguete City, 1976)

H. Rubio: 'The Roving Rondalla', *Filipino Heritage*, ix (1978), 2256

F. A. Prudente: *Musical Process in the Gasumbi Epic of the Buwaya Kalingga People of Northern Philippines* (diss., U. of Michigan, 1984)

U. H. Cadar: *Context and Style in the Vocal Music of the Muranao in Mindanao, Philippines* (Iligan City and Marawi City, 1985)

S. W. Otto: *The Muranao Kakolintang: an Approach to the Repertoire* (Iligan City and Marawi City, 1985)

A. M. Butocan: *Palabunibunyan: a Repertoire of Musical Pieces for the Maguindanaon Kulintangan* (Manila, 1987)

Indonesia

J. Groneman: *De gamelan te Jogjakarta* (Amsterdam, 1890)

J. Kunst: *Hindoe-Javaansche muziekinstrumenten, speciaal die van Oost Java* (Weltevreden, 1927; Eng. trans., 1963, rev. and enl. 2/1968)

J. S. Brandts Buys and A. Brandts Buys-van Zijp: 'De toonkunst bij de Madoereezen', *Djåwå*, viii (1928), 1–290

J. S. Brandts Buys: 'De muziek van de sekatèn-gamelans', *Djåwå*, xiv (1934), 243

J. Kunst: *De toonkunst van Java* (The Hague, 1934; Eng. trans., rev. 2/1949, enl. 3/1973)

C. McPhee: *A House in Bali* (New York, 1946/R1980)

——: *A Club of Small Men* (New York, 1948)

M. Hood: *The Nuclear Theme as a Determinant of Paṭet in Javanese Music* (Jakarta and Groningen, 1954/R1977)

W. H. Rassers: *Panji, the Culture Hero: a Structural Study of Religion in Java* (The Hague, 1959)

C. Geertz: *The Religion of Java* (Glencoe, IL, 1960/R1976)

M. Hood: 'Sléndro and Pélog Redefined', *Selected Reports in Ethnomusicology*, i/1 (1966), 28

C. McPhee: *Music in Bali: a Study in Form and Instrumental Organization in Balinese Orchestral Music* (New Haven, CT, 1966/R1976)

E. L. Heins: 'The Music of the Serimpi "Anglir Menḍung": Some Musicological Observations on Central Javanese Ceremonial Court Dances', *Indonesia*, iii (1967), 135

M. A. Koesoemadinata: *Ilmu Seni-Raras: Ilmu musik Indonesia asli* (Jakarta, 1969)

B. A. Adam: 'Seni Musik Klasik Minangkabau', *Himpunan Presaran den Kertas Kerdja Seminar Sedjarah den Kebudajaan Minangkabau* (Batusangkar, 1970)

E. L. Heins: 'Cueing the Gamelan in Javanese Wayang Performance', *Indonesia*, ix (1970), 101

R. Ornstein: 'The Five-Tone *Gamelan-Angklung* of North Bali', *EM*, xv (1971), 71

B. R. O'G. Anderson: 'The Idea of Power in Javanese Culture', *Culture and Politics in Indonesia*, ed. C. Holt (Ithaca, NY, 1972), 1–69

C. Geertz: *The Interpretation of Cultures* (New York, 1973)

M. J. Kartomi: *Matjapat Songs in Central and West Java* (Canberra, 1973)

——: 'Music and Trance in Central Java', *EM*, xvii (1973), 163–208

M. C. Ricklefs: *Jogjakarta under Sultan Mangkubumi 1749–1792: a history of the Division of Java* (London, 1974)

J. Becker: 'Kroncong, Indonesian Popular Music', *Asian Music*, vii/1 (1975), 14

M. Harrell: 'Some Aspects of Sundanese Music', *Selected Reports in Ethnomusicology*, ii/2 (1975), 81

E. Heins: 'Kroncong and Tanjidor: Two Cases of Urban Folk Music in Jakarta', *Asian Music*, vii/1 (1975), 20

A. F. Toth: 'The *Gamelan Luang* of Tangkas, Bali', *Selected Reports in Ethnomusicology*, ii/2 (1975), 65

M. F. Hatch: 'The Song is Ended: Changes on the Use of Macapat in Central Java', *Asian Music*, vii/2 (1976), 59

M. J. Kartomi: 'Performance, Music and Meaning of Reyog Ponorogo', *Indonesia*, xxii (1976), 85–130

T. Seebass and others: *The Music of Lombok: a First Survey* (Bern, 1976)

E. Heins: *Goong Renteng: Aspects of Orchestral Music in a Sundanese Village* (diss., U. of Amsterdam, 1977)

L. Manik: 'Suku Batak dengan "Gondang Batak'nya"', *Peninjau*, iv/1 (1977), 66

D. Matsyachir: *Jawa Timur Menuju Kesatuan Gaya Seni* (Surabaya, 1977) [typescript]

C. Falk: 'The Tarawangsa – A Bowed Stringed Instrument from West Java', *Studies in Indonesian Music*, ed. M. J. Kartomi (Clayton, Victoria, 1978), 45–103

D. Goldsworthy: 'Honey-Collecting Ceremonies on the East Coast of North Sumatra', *Studies in Indonesian Music*, ed. M. J. Kartomi (Clayton, Victoria, 1978), 1–44

B. Kornhauser: 'In Defence of Kroncong', *Studies in Indonesian Music*, ed. M. J. Kartomi (Clayton, Victoria, 1978), 104–83

J. Becker: 'Time and Tune in Java', *The Imagination of Reality: Essays in Southeast Asian Coherence Systems*, ed. A. L. Becker and A. A. Yengoyan (Norwood, NJ, 1979), 197

J. Lindsay: *Javanese Gamelan* (Kuala Lumpur, 1979)

J. Maceda and N. MacDonald: *Music of the Kenyah and Modang in East Kalimantan* (U. of the Philippines, 1979) [disc and notes]

J. Becker: *Traditional Music in Modern Java: Gamelan in a Changing Society* (Honolulu, HI, 1980)

M. Crawford: 'Indonesia', §V, *Grove 6*

C. Geertz: *Negara: the Theatre State in Nineteenth-Century Bali* (Princeton, NJ, 1980)

M. F. Hatch: *Lagu, Laras, Layang: Rethinking Melody in Javanese Music* (diss., Cornell U., 1980)

A. D. Jansen: *Gonrang Music: Its Structure and Functions in Simalungun Batak Society in Sumatra* (diss., U. of Washington, 1980)

M. J. Kartomi: 'Musical Strata in Sumatra, Java, and Bali', *Musics of Many Cultures: an Introduction*, ed. E. May (Berkeley, CA, 1980), 111

R. Schumacher: *Die Suluk-Gesänge des Dalang im Schattenspiel Zentraljavas* (Munich, 1980)

A. Toth: *Recordings of the Traditional Music of Bali and Lombok* (Ann Arbor, MI, 1980)

J. Becker and A. L. Becker: 'A Musical Icon: Power and Meaning in Javanese Gamelan Music', *The Sign in Music and Literature*, ed. W. Steiner (Austin, TX, 1981), 203

J. A. Day: *Meanings of Change in the Poetry of Nineteenth-Century Java* (diss., Cornell U., 1981)

M. J. Kartomi: 'Dualism in Unity: the Ceremonial Music of the Mandailing Raja Tradition', *Asian Music*, xii/2 (1981), 74–108

——: '"His Skyward Path the Rainbow Is": Funeral Music of the Sa'dan Toraja', *Hemisphere*, xxv/5 (1981), 303

——: '"Lovely When Heard from Afar": Mandailing Ideas of Musical Beauty', *Five Essays on the Indonesian Arts – Music, Theatre, Textiles, Painting and Literature*, ed. M. J. Kartomi (Melbourne, 1981), 1

Sumarsam: 'The Musical Practice of the Gamelan Sekaten', *Asian Music*, xii/2 (1981), 54

R. Vetter: 'Flexibility in the Performance Practice of Central Javanese Music', *EM*, xxv (1981), 199

W. H. Frederick: 'Rhoma Irama and the Dangdut Style: Aspects of Contemporary Indonesian Popular Culture', *Indonesia*, xxxiv (1982), 102

J. Diamond, ed.: *Balungan: a Publication of the American Gamelan Institute* (Oakland, CA, 1984–)

J. Becker and A. Feinstein: *Karawitan: Source Readings in Javanese Gamelan and Vocal Music* (Ann Arbor, MI, 1984, 1987, 1988)

R. L. Martopangrawit: 'Catatan-Catatan Pengetahuan Karawitan [Notes on Knowledge of Gamelan Music]', *Karawitan: Source Readings in Javanese Gamelan and Vocal Music*, i, ed. J. Becker and A. Feinstein (Ann Arbor, MI, 1984), 1–244

L. Moore: 'Ketuk', 'Kucapi', 'Lobat', 'Pongpong', 'Sarunai', and 'Taratoa', *Grove 6*

A. Simon: 'Functional Changes in Batak Traditional Music and Its Role in Modern Indonesian Society', *Asian Music*, xv/2 (1984), 58

Sumarsam: 'Inner Melody in Javanese Gamelan', *Karawitan: Source Readings in Javanese Gamelan and Vocal Music*, i, ed. J. Becker and A. Feinstein (Ann Arbor, MI, 1984), 245–304

390

H. Susilo: 'Wayang Wong Panggung: Its Social Context, Technique and Music', *Aesthetic Tradition and Cultural Transition in Java and Bali*, ed. S. Morgan and L. J. Sears (Madison, WI, 1984), 117–61

R. A. Sutton: '"Who is the *Pesindhèn*?" Notes on the Female Singing Tradition in Java', *Indonesia*, xxxvii (1984), 119

B. E. Brinner: *Competence and Interaction in the Performance of* Pathetan *in Central Java* (diss., U. of California, Berkeley, 1985)

Sri Hastanto: *The Concept of Pathet in Central Javanese Gamelan Music* (diss., U. of Durham, 1985)

J. Lindsay: *Klasik Kitsch or Contemporary: a study of the Javanese Performing Arts* (diss., U. of Sydney, 1985)

R. Supanggah: *Introduction aux styles d'interpretation dans la musique Javanaise* (diss., U. of Paris VII, 1985)

R. A. Sutton: 'Commercial Cassette Recordings of Traditional Music in Java: Implications for Performers and Scholars', *World of Music*, xxvii (1985), 23

——: 'Musical Pluralism in Java: Three Local Traditions', *EM*, xxix (1985), 56

P. Manuel and R. Baier: 'Jaipongan: Indigenous Popular Music of West Java', *Asian Music*, xviii/1 (1986), 91

M. A. Mohammed Nor: *Randai Dance of Minangkabau Sumatra with Labanotation Scores* (Kuala Lumpur, 1986)

R. A. Sutton: 'The Crystallization of a Marginal Tradition: Music in Banyumas, West Central Java', *YTM*, xviii (1986), 115

P. D. Poerbatjaraka: 'Radèn Inu Main Gamelan: Bahan Untuk Menerangkan Kata Pathet [Radèn Inu Plays Gamelan: Sources for the Explanation of the Word *Pathet*]', *Karawitan: Source Readings in Javanese Gamelan and Vocal Music*, ii, ed. J. Becker and A. Feinstein (Ann Arbor, MI, 1987), 261

Ki Sindoesawarno: 'Ilmu Karawitan' [Knowledge about Gamelan Music], *Karawitan: Source Readings in Javanese Gamelan and Vocal Music*, ii, ed. J. Becker and A. Feinstein (Ann Arbor, MI, 1987), 311–87

——: 'Menerangkan Kata Pathet' [Explaining the Word *Pathet*], *Karawitan: Source Readings in Javanese Gamelan and Vocal Music*, ii, ed. J. Becker and A. Feinstein (Ann Arbor, MI, 1987), 284

Sumarsam: 'Introduction to Ciblon Drumming in Javanese Gamelan', *Karawitan: Source Readings in Javanese Gamelan and Vocal Music*, ii, ed. J. Becker and A. Feinstein (Ann Arbor, MI, 1987), 171–203

S. P. Walton: *Mode in Javanese Music* (Athens, 1987)

R. T. Warsadiningrat: 'Wédha Pradangga' [The History, or Story, of Gamelan], *Karawitan: Source Readings in Javanese Gamelan and Vocal Music*, ii, ed. J. Becker and A. Feinstein (Ann Arbor, MI, 1987), 1–149

P. B. Yampolsky: *Lokananta: a Discography of the National Recording Company of Indonesia, 1957–1985* (Madison, WI, 1987)

M. Hatch: 'Popular Music in Indonesia', *World Music, Politics and Social Change*, ed. S. Frith (Manchester, 1989), 47–68

H. Susilo: 'The Logogenesis of Gendhing Lampah', *Progress Reports in Ethnomusicology*, ii/5 (1989), 1

R. Vetter: 'Animism, Hinduism, Islam, and the West: Fusion in Musical and Visual Symbolism in a Javanese Ceremony', *Progress Reports in Ethnomusicology*, ii/4 (1989), 1

——: 'A Retrospect on a Century of Gamelan Tone Measurements', *EM*, xxxiii (1989), 217

P. A. Wolbers: 'Transvestism, Eroticism, and Religion: in Search of a Contextual Background for the Gandrung and Seblang Traditions of Banyuwangi, East Java', *Progress Reports in Ethnomusicology*, ii/6 (1989), 1

General

J. Becker: 'Percussive Patterns in the Music of Mainland Southeast Asia', *EM*, xii (1968), 173

J. Maceda: 'A Concept of Time in a Music of Southeast Asia (a Preliminary Account)', *EM*, xxx (1986), 11–53

CHAPTER XIV
Oceania

MERVYN McLEAN

Oceania can conveniently be taken to encompass Australia, New Guinea (Papua New Guinea mainland and Irian Jaya), Island Melanesia (including the Bismarck Archipelago), Polynesia and Micronesia.

An Annotated Bibliography of Oceanic Music and Dance with *Supplement* (McLean, 1977, 1981) contains about 2700 references to books, journal articles, reviews, record notes, manuscripts on file in public institutions and theses in the most commonly read European languages, indexed by area. Further titles are accumulating for a second supplement or for possible merging into a second edition. Other bibliographies are those of K. Gourlay (1974) for Papua New Guinea and E. Tatar (1979) and A. K. Stillman (1982) for Hawaii. There are no general discographies for Oceania, although the McLean bibliographies take account of recent discs. W. Laade (1971, pp.47–50) includes a short discography, mostly of acculturated Maori and Polynesian items. D. Niles (1979) includes selected recordings from Oceania. G. S. Kanahele (1979, pp.419–502) contains a selected discography of popular Hawaiian music. Niles (1984, 1985, 1987, 1988) lists commercial recordings of Papua New Guinea.

Before and during World War II

The traditional music of Oceania, compared with other areas of the world, has been painfully under-researched. Much of the material comes from sources which are not always reliable (such as the reports of travellers, missionaries, explorers and other casual observers), and ethnographic reports written by persons who were generally not musicians. Before World War II, professional studies were few indeed. Erich M. von Hornbostel and his followers of the so-called Berlin School of the 1920s and 1930s provided some of the earliest. Their studies were based on recordings brought to the Berlin Phonogramm-archiv by ethnographers active in German New Guinea, Island Melanesia, and Micronesia. Hornbostel himself transcribed and analysed recordings from the Solomon Islands and from New Ireland (1912, 1914, 1922). Mieczyslaw Kolinski (1930) attempted a comparison of recorded Malayan and Samoan songs, the latter including items from a Samoan troupe that visited Berlin in 1910. George Herzog, in two classic studies (1932, 1936), transcribed and analysed the music of Truk and the Caroline Islands as recorded by a German South Seas expedition of 1908–10. Herbert Hübner (1938) did likewise for 88 early recordings of music from the Bismarck Archipelago, basing his conclusions on *Kulturkreis* ('culture circle') principles.

The work of the Berlin School, entirely dependent on fieldwork by others, gave little contextual information. Other work of the period also tends to be in this 'armchair' tradition (for example, Kunst's studies on Irian Jaya, first published from 1931 onwards and reissued in 1967). Even Charles S. Myers (1912), who very early had visited the Torres Straits Islands and recorded songs there with a Cambridge anthropological expedition, concentrated his efforts upon a meticulous musical analysis, leaving other aspects of music to the ethnographers of the expedition.

With the notable exception of Helen Heffron Roberts's *Ancient Hawaiian Music* (1926), the same pattern applied to the earliest work on Polynesian music sponsored by the Bernice P. Bishop Museum in Hawaii. In a long series of ethnographies, published as bulletins by the Museum, Peter Buck (Te Rangi Hiroa) provided systematic information, but no musical analysis, on song, dance, and musical instruments of Samoa (1930), Penrhyn (1932, *Ethnology of Tongareva*), Manihiki and Rakahanga (1932, *Ethnology of Manihiki and Rakahanga*), Mangaia (1934), Mangareva (1938), and the Cook Islands (1944). E. S. C. Handy and J. L. Winne's *Music in the Marquesas Islands* (1925) and the published version of Edwin G. Burrows's MA thesis *Native Music of the Tuamotus* (1933) appeared in the same series. Burrows's contributions continued with sections on music and dance in his ethnographies of Futuna (1936) and Uvea (1937) followed by a monograph specifically on *Songs of Uvea and Futuna* (1945).

After World War II

A good measure of scholarly activity in Pacific music is provided by the number of theses presented for higher degrees. In the immediate postwar period there was none. Excluding Australia, four theses were submitted from 1955–64; for 1965–74, seven; and for 1975–84, twenty-five. The earliest (Dieter Christensen, 1957; Norma McLeod, 1957; Raymond Clausen, 1958) continued the 'armchair' tradition, offering laboratory analyses of materials collected by others. The remainder, from about the time the present writer began work in New Zealand (McLean, 1958, 1965), have mostly been based on extended periods of fieldwork by the person undertaking the research. The best of this work (e.g. Richard Moyle, 1979; Vida Chenoweth, 1979; Kevin Salisbury, 1983) has involved working in the vernacular – sometimes exclusively so – and for long periods.

Most of the theses presented originate from the University of Hawaii, the University of Auckland, and Australian universities. Polynesia accounts for 16 theses, New Guinea for 10, Island Melanesia for 6 and Micronesia for 3.

Most Aboriginal research in Australia is now sponsored by the Australian Institute of Aboriginal Studies which was established as a corporate body by a Commonwealth Act of 1964. Besides promoting research and assisting co-operation among universities and other institutions, it serves as a repository for field recordings, holding close to 4500 hours of Aboriginal and Torres Straits music. Increasing numbers of graduate students in Australia are working on Aboriginal music topics with the assistance of the Institute. Monographs on Australian Aborigine music have been published by Trevor Jones (Elkin and Jones, 1957), Catherine Ellis (1964), Alice Moyle (1966) and Richard Moyle (1979, 1985).

There are local sound archives attached to museums and cultural centres throughout Oceania and three major sound archives that operate on a regional basis. The oldest is that of the Bernice P. Bishop Museum in Honolulu, which has recently begun to issue LP discs of holdings from its early cylinder recordings (Tatar, 1981). The Institute of Papua New Guinea Studies at Boroko, Port Moresby, is now the focal point for all officially approved music research in Papua New Guinea. In common with the Australian Institute of Aboriginal Studies it has an extensive sound archive with resident ethnomusicologists and has issued and sponsored both commercial discs and films of music. Finally, the Archive of Maori and Pacific Music is located at the University of Auckland, New Zealand. It is actively sponsoring collection and research by means of the UNESCO funded Territorial Survey of Oceanic Music (TSOM).

Recent research trends

Many publications have dealt with musical instruments, mostly at a descriptive level. Of the few that attempt comparative discussion the most notable is Hans Fischer's *Sound-Producing Instruments in Oceania* (1986, a reissue in English of a German monograph from 1958). Also worthy of mention are Don Niles (1983) on the distribution of the slit-drum in New Guinea and Hugo Zemp (1981), which compares 'Are'Are panpipes with non-graduated or 'irregular' instruments from elsewhere in Oceania. Mervyn McLean (1979, 'Towards the Differentiation') uses both musical instruments and elements of music structure to differentiate music areas for the whole of Oceania. The sole attempt at a diachronic study (limited to New Zealand Maori) is that of McLean (1982, 'A Chronological and Geographical Sequence').

Problems of 'Insider-versus-outsider' research are discussed by Barbara Smith (1981), Gordon Spearritt (1980, 1983), Peter Crowe (1981) and McLean (1983). Smith identifies differences of research emphases; Spearritt and Crowe see a need for both kinds of research; McLean advocates increased commitment to collaborative research.

Indigenous systems of classification is a topic taken up by Zemp (1978, 1979) in two papers that have emerged from his 1970s fieldwork with the 'Are'Are of Malaita. In 1978 he presented a three-dimensional paradigm encapsulating 'Are'Are use of the lexeme *'au* (meaning bamboo). Using qualifying terms, 'Are'Are distinguish instruments according to whether they are blown or beaten, solo or ensemble, as well as by scale. Further distinctions classify panpipes by shape, number of tubes, size of mouthpiece, regular or irregular arrangement of the tubes, and the like. Related terminologies apply to slit-drums and songs. Zemp concludes that besides meaning 'bamboo', the term *'au*, by extension, designates all music with melodic elements and in this sense comes close to an 'Are'Are equivalent of the Western concept of 'music'. In Zemp's 1979 paper the lexeme *'au* appears again, this time as a component of interval names that relate to differences in length of the bamboo tubes required to produce the intervals. Malaitan terms also exist for other elements of music structure.

Similar findings are described by Steven Feld (1981) for the Kaluli of Papua New Guinea, who use waterfall terms to designate both melodic contours and significant musical intervals within the contours. A common denominator of 'Are'Are and Kaluli appears to be that the two groups, using bamboo terminology in the one case and waterfall terms in the other, name and conceptualize those aspects of the system which are culturally meaningful or essential. Another is that most of the specialist vocabulary is drawn from the general vocabulary of the language (and on this account described as metaphor by Feld).

It is hoped that the work of Zemp and Feld will stimulate scholars to find similar terminologies elsewhere, for they are certainly more common than has been supposed. Both authors make the point that only by participant observation over a period of time was it possible to discover the vocabulary, by listening to singers' spontaneous comments and verbal corrections of their own and the authors' mistakes. Similar methods were used successfully by Richard Moyle (1979) in penetrating word groups that govern isometric units in Pintupi Aborigine music.

Linguistic approaches to ethnomusicology are exemplified in recent publications by several authors. For Papua New Guinea, Jacqueline Pugh-Kitingan (1982) discusses articulation of words in Huli and neighbouring peoples' performances on jew's harps and, in the case of the Huli, on musical bows and panpipes. In a later paper (1984), she examines the relationship between melody and speech-tone in the music of the Huli, who speak a tonal language, finding in a careful analysis that speech-tone is preserved in terms of musical contour. Rising melodic figures represent low-rising speech tone while falling patterns usually indicate high-falling speech tone and level progressions signify mid-level speech tone.

A paper by McLean (1982, 'The "Rule of Eight"') emerges from a discovery made by Bruce Biggs (1980). Biggs observed that in a significant proportion of Maori *waiata*, as notated in McLean and M. Orbell (1975), each half line of text (corresponding to a musical phrase) contained exactly eight vowels (or *morae*) counting short vowels as one and long vowels as two. In Maori the distinction between long and short vowels has phonemic significance, just as speech-tone has phonemic significance in the Huli language. McLean's concern was similar to Pugh-Kitingan's, in his case to find out the degree to which long and short vowels in the Maori texts were preserved in the music. In 'rule of eight' *waiata* an almost unexceptional correspondence was found between long vowels (the linguistically marked feature) and musical long notes, though not between short vowels and short notes. This was shown to result from the use of a rhythmic model such that any 'rule of eight' melody can accommodate any 'rule of eight' text. A linguistic 'spin off' is that a short *mora* count in a 'rule of eight' line indicates that a long vowel has mistakenly been treated as short. In such cases the close correspondence between music and text provides a means of determining the correct pronunciation of obsolete names.

Using similar methods Kevin Salisbury (1983) has discovered even closer associations between song texts and music structure in the northern Cooks island of Pukapuka. Like Maori, Pukapuka is a *mora*-timed language. In chant performance the short vowel (or single *mora*) is the basic rhythmic unit and the long vowel (two *morae*) is set to a note of twice the length. However, whereas the Maori half line contains eight *morae*, the Pukapukan contains six (Salisbury, 1983, pp.146–8). Even more remarkably, the most common Pukapukan chant style, the *mako*, is found by Salisbury to exhibit linguistic conditioning of pitch. *Mako* style is essentially monotonic with occasional descents to the minor third below the tonic. Salisbury discovered that this pitch is predictable according to the simple rule: 'The auxiliary pitch occurs on any mora containing a high vowel provided that the following mora does not also contain a high vowel' (p.156). Apparent exceptions are explained by a process of 'vowel assimilation', by means of which certain vowels of the song texts are systematically changed in performance. Salisbury's study is extremely valuable and his findings are certain to have application to other Polynesian styles when these have been fully studied.

Although some of the work already done is by established scholars, the remainder is the product of graduate students. The amount of work yet to be accomplished in Oceania provides an opportunity for many such students.

Research opportunities in Oceania

Before allowing research in their territories, most Pacific Island administrations require formal application for a research permit. Generally the application will be approved if the research can be shown to benefit the local community. Application should be made several months in advance of the proposed research to the appropriate embassy or consulate, or in Australia to the Australian Institute of Aboriginal Studies.

Compared with the rest of Oceania, Australia has fared relatively well. Increasing numbers of graduate students are turning to the study of Aboriginal music for higher degrees. (A register of work in progress is published in each issue of the Perth journal *Studies in Music*.) In the rest of Oceania the most pressing research need is documentation of music cultures that have received no scholarly attention. Others have been studied at survey level only or have been recorded but not studied. For these follow-up activity in the form of in-depth studies is urgent.

A list of islands and island groups requiring research was reported by McLean (1979, 'UNESCO'). Since then a number of gaps have been filled.

Information is now available on most areas in Eastern Polynesia. A thorough study of Pukapuka has been completed by Salisbury (1983) and Cook Islands drumming has been studied by Wayne Laird (1982). Tahitian dance is well described by Jane Moulin (1979) and Tahitian hymnody is the subject of doctoral work by Amy Stillman (Harvard University). Under the auspices of the writer's Territorial Survey of Oceanic Music (TSOM) studies at survey level have been carried out of Tubuai and Mangareva (by Amy Stillman), of Manihiki and Penrhyn (by Richard Moyle), of Atiu, Mauke and Mitiaro in the southern Cook Islands (by Jenny Little) and of the Marquesas Islands (by Jane Moulin). The original field recordings and documentation are housed in the Archive of Maori and Pacific Music (Auckland) and copies are available locally and elsewhere.

In Western Polynesia 14 of the 19 Polynesian Outliers are still almost completely unknown musically. (The exceptions are Tikopia, Ontong Java, Rennell and Bellona, and West Futuna.) Richard Moyle has completed monographs on the music of Tonga and Samoa (1987 and 1988) and has surveyed the music of Niue for TSOM. Alan Thomas (Victoria University of Wellington) has finished a thesis on Tokelau music (1986) and has conducted TSOM surveys there and on the Polynesian Outlier, West Futuna. Finally, recently Jane Rossen (1987) has published a two-volume monograph on songs of Bellona and McLean has collaborated with Raymond Firth on a study of Tikopia music (Firth and McLean, 1990).

In Island Melanesia the southern Massim has the benefit of a single preliminary study (Watson, 1979). The rest of the D'Entrecasteaux group – the Louisades, the Trobriands and nearby islands and almost the whole of the Bismarck Archipelago except the Admiralty Islands (Niles, 1980) – requires detailed study as do most of the Solomons except for the 'Are'Are of Malaita. Extensive recordings have been made in Vanuatu but analysis is still awaited. A beginning has been made in New Caledonia where Jean-Michel Beaudet (1984) was several years staff ethnomusicologist at the Office Culturel, Scientifique et Technique in Noumea. In Fiji, field recordings have been made by Chris Saumaiwai for the South Pacific Commission and more recently by David Goldsworthy for TSOM. But detailed study has been undertaken only for the *meke* dance (Good, 1978).

Over most of Micronesia there is a musical question mark. Lisa Lawson has recently completed a PhD thesis (1989) on Kiribati music and has also conducted a TSOM survey of the Marshall Islands. Except for Ponape (Bailey, 1978) nothing has been done in the Caroline Islands since Herzog's work in the 1930s. Finally all of the islands of Western Micronesia except Palau (Yamaguchi, 1967) remain to be studied.

In New Guinea the need for research is greatest where, despite an immense diversity of languages and cultures, only a handful of professional studies have been carried out. Although survey recordings have been made in a number of areas by the Institute of Papua New Guinea Studies, Irian Jaya, comprising the entire western half of New Guinea, is beyond the jurisdiction of the Institute and remains musically almost unknown.

The possibilities for music research in Oceania are almost inexhaustible. Field restudies could be undertaken of areas such as the Tuamotus, which were first studied more than 50 years ago. It is time for restudy of musics such as New Zealand Maori, first described 25 years ago. At similar remove, useful work can be done using archival resources, and these will become increasingly important in the future. Examples of this approach are D. Christensen and G. Koch (1964), G. Haase (1977), Niles (1980), Tatar (1982) and G. Van Waardenberg (1983). As time goes on, the study of acculturated forms will become more important, as these forms are dominant in most areas. Even Maori action song has not been studied musically, and Pacific hymnody has received little attention except for A. K. Stillman's recent work in Tahiti. Finally, comparative studies are sure to re-emerge once base studies have been completed in a sufficient number of the areas now lacking them.

Bibliography

E. M. von Hornbostel: 'Die musik auf den nordwestlichen Salomo-Inseln', *Forschungen auf den Salomo-Inseln und dem Bismarck-Archipel*, ed. R. Thurnwald, i (Berlin, 1912), 461–504

C. S. Myers: 'Music', *Report of the Cambridge Anthropological Expedition to Torres Straits*, iv, ed. A. C. Haddon (Cambridge, 1912), 238–69

E. M. von Hornbostel: 'Bemerkunge über eineger Lieder aus Bougainville', *Baessler Archiv*, vi (1914), 53

——: 'Notiz über die Musik der Bewohner von Süd-Neu-Mecklenburg', *Sammelbande für vergleichender Musikwissenschaft*, i (1922), 350

E. S. C. Handy and J. L. Winne: *Music in the Marquesas Islands* (Honolulu, HI, 1925)

H. H. Roberts: *Ancient Hawaiian Music* (Honolulu, HI, 1926/R1967)

P. Buck: *Samoan Material Culture* (Honolulu, HI, 1930)

M. Kolinski: 'Die Musik der Primitivstämme auf Malaka und ihre Beziehungen zur samoanischen Musik (Aus dem staatlichen Phonogramm-Archiv Berlin)', *Anthropos*, xxv (1930), 585–648

G. Herzog: 'Die Musik auf Truk', *Truk, Ergebnisse der Südsee-Expedition, 1908–1910*, iib/5, ed. A. Krämer (Hamburg, 1932), 384

P. Buck: *Ethnology of Tongareva* (Honolulu, HI, 1932)

——: *Ethnology of Manihiki and Rakahanga* (Honolulu, HI, 1932)

E. G. Burrows: *Native Music of the Tuamotus* (Honolulu, HI, 1933)

P. Buck: *Mangaian Society* (Honolulu, HI, 1934)

E. G. Burrows: *Ethnology of Futuna* (Honolulu, HI, 1936)

G. Herzog: 'Die Musik der Karolinen-Inseln', *Westkarolinen, Ergebnisse der Südsee-Expedition, 1908–1910*, iib/9, ed. A. Eilers (Hamburg, 1936), 263–351

E. G. Burrows: *Ethnology of Uvea* (Honolulu, HI, 1937)

P. Buck: *Ethnology of Mangareva* (Honolulu, HI, 1938)

H. Hübner: *Die Musik im Bismarck-Archipel: Musikethnologische Studien zur Kulturkreislehre und Rassenforschung* (Berlin, 1938)

P. Buck: *The Arts and Crafts of the Cook Islands* (Honolulu, HI, 1944)

E. G. Burrows: *Songs of Uvea and Futuna* (Honolulu, HI, 1945)

D. Christensen: *Die Musik der Kate und Sialum: Beiträge zur Ethnographie Neuguineas* (Berlin, 1957)

A. P. Elkin and T. Jones: *Arnhem Land Music (North Australia)* (Sydney, c1957)

N. McLeod: *The Social Context of Music in a Polynesian Community* (diss., London School of Economics, 1957)

R. Clausen: *A Musicological Study of the Layard Collection of Recorded Malekulan Music* (diss., U. of Oxford, 1958)

M. McLean: *Field Work in Maori Music* (diss., Otago U., 1958)

D. Christensen and G. Koch: *Die Musik der Ellice-inselis* (Berlin, 1964)

C. J. Ellis: *Aboriginal Music Making: a Study of Central Australian Music* (Adelaide, 1964)

M. McLean: *Maori Chant* (diss., Otago U., 1965)

A. M. Moyle: *A Handlist of Field Collections of Recorded Music in Australia and the Torres Strait* (Canberra, 1966)

J. Kunst: *Music in New Guinea: Three Studies* (The Hague, 1967)

O. Yamaguchi: *The Music of Palau: an Ethnomusicological Study of the Classical Tradition* (diss., U. of Hawaii, 1967)

W. Laade: *Neue Musik in Afrika, Asien und Ozeanien: Diskographie und historische-stilistischer Überblick* (Heidelberg, 1971)

K. Gourlay: *A Bibliography of Traditional Music in Papua New Guinea* (Port Moresby, 1974)

M. McLean and M. Orbell: *Traditional Songs of the Maori* (Wellington and Auckland, 1975)

G. Haase: *Studien zur Musik im Santa Cruz-Archipel: Ein monographischer Beitrag zur Musik Ozeaniens* (Berlin, 1976)

M. McLean: *an Annotated Bibliography of Oceanic Music and Dance* (Wellington, 1977)

C. R. K. Bailey: *Traditional Ponapean Music: Classification and Description* (diss., U. of Hawaii, 1978)

L. Good: *Fijian Meke: an Analysis of Style and Content* (diss., U. of Hawaii, 1978)

H. Zemp: ''Are'Are Classification of Musical Types and Instruments', *EM*, xxii (1978), 37–67

V. Chenoweth: *The Usarufas and Their Music* (Dallas, TX, 1979)

G. S. Kanahele, ed.: *Hawaiian Music and Musicians: an Illustrated History* (Honolulu, HI, 1979)

M. McLean: 'Unesco "World History of Music" Proposal: the Case for Field Research in Oceania', *Bulletin of the International Committee on Urgent Anthropological and Ethnological Research*, xxi (1979), 99

——: 'Towards the Differentiation of Music Areas in Oceania', *Anthropos*, lxxiv/5–6 (1979), 717

J. F. Moulin: *The Dance of Tahiti* (Papeete, 1979)

R. M. Moyle: *Songs of the Pintupi: Musical Life in a Central Australian Society* (Canberra, 1979)

D. Niles: *Musics of the World: a selective Discography, Part II: China, Indonesia, Korea, Oceania, Taiwan, Thailand* (Los Angeles, CA, 1979)

E. Tatar: 'Annotated Bibliography [of Hawaiian Music]', *Hawaiian Music and Musicians: an Illustrated History*, ed. G. S. Kanahele (Honolulu, HI, 1979), 503

M. V. Watson: *Southern Massim Music: a Preliminary Survey* (diss., Queensland Conservatorium of Music, Annerly, 1979)

H. Zemp: 'Aspects of 'Are'Are Musical Theory', *EM*, xxiii (1979), 6–48

B. Biggs: 'Traditional Maori Song Texts and the "Rule of Eight"', *Paanui*, iii (1980), 48

D. Niles: *The Traditional and Contemporary Music of the Admiralty Islands* (diss., U. of California, 1980)

G. D. Spearritt: 'Music Research in Papua New Guinea: the Past and the Future', *Studies in Music*, xiv (1980), 1

P. Crowe: 'After the Ethnomusicological Salvage Operation – What?', *Journal of the Polynesian Society*, xc/2 (1981), 171

S. Feld: '"Flow Like a Waterfall": the Metaphors of Kaluli Musical Theory', *YTM*, xiii (1981), 22

M. McLean: *Supplement: an Annotated Bibliography of Oceanic Music and Dance* (Auckland, 1981)

B. B. Smith: 'Indigenous and Non-Indigenous Researchers: Implications for Content and Method in the Study of Music in Oceania', *International Musicological Society: Report of the Twelfth Congress, Berkeley 1977*, ed. D. Heartz and B. Wade (Kassel, 1981), 132

E. Tatar: *Nā Leo Hawai'i Kahiko: Voices of Old Hawai'i*, ARCS–1 [2 discs and notes]

H. Zemp: 'Melanesian Solo Polyphonic Panpipe Music', *EM*, xxv (1981), 383–418

W. Laird: *Drums and Drumming in the Cook Islands* (diss., U. of Auckland, 1982)

M. McLean: 'A Chronological and Geographical Sequence of Maori Flute Scales', *Man*, new ser., xvii (1982), 123–57

——: 'The "Rule of Eight" and Text/Music Relationships in Traditional Maori *Waiata*', *Anthropological Linguistics*, xxiv/3 (1982), 280

J. Pugh-Kitingan: 'Language Communication and Instrumental Music in Papua New Guinea: Comments on the Huli and Samberigi Cases', *Musicology*, vii (1982), 104

A. K. Stillman: 'Annotated Bibliography of Hula', *The Hula*, ed. J. Hopkins (Hong Kong, 1982), 180

E. Tatar: *Nineteenth-Century Hawaiian Chant* (Honolulu, HI, 1982)

H. Fischer: *Sound-Producing Instruments in Oceania: Construction and Playing Technique – Distribution and Function* (Boroko, 1983, rev. 1986; Eng. trans. of *Schallgeräte in Ozeanien: Bau und Spieltechnik – Verbreitung und Funktion*, Strasbourg and Baden-Baden, 1958)

M. McLean: 'Approaches to Problems of Field Ethics in Oceania', *Pacific Studies*, vi/2 (1983), 51

D. Niles: 'Why Are There No Garamuts in Papua?', *Bikmaus* (Boroko), iv/3 (1983), 90

K. Salisbury: *Pukapukan People and Their Music* (diss., U. of Auckland, 1983)

G. D. Spearritt: 'Traditional Music of Petspets Villages (Hahon, N.W. Bougainville): an Exercise in Outsider/Insider Research', *Bikmaus* (Boroko), iv/3 (1983), 67

G. Van Waardenberg: *Songs of Tai Tokerau: an Analysis of 135 Northland Songs* (diss., U. of Auckland, 1983)

J.-M. Beaudet: 'Les instruments de musique kanaks: Kanak Musical Instruments', *Pacific 2000* (Noumea), vi (1984), 25

D. Niles, comp.: *Commercial Recordings of Papua New Guinea Music 1949–1983* (Boroko, 1984)

J. Pugh-Kitingan: 'Speech-Tone Realisation in Huli Music', *Problems and Solutions: Occasional Essays in Musicology Presented to Alice M. Moyle*, ed. J. C. Kassler and J. Stubbinton (Sydney, 1984)

D. Niles, comp.: *Commercial Recordings of Papua New Guinea Music 1984 Supplement* (Boroko, 1985)

R. M. Moyle: *Alyawarra Music: Songs in a Central Australian Community* (Canberra, 1986)

A. Thomas: *The Fatele of Tokelau: Approaches to the Study of a Dance in Its Social Context* (diss., Victoria U. of Wellington, 1986)

R. M. Moyle: *Tongan Music* (Auckland, 1987)

D. Niles, comp.: *Commercial Recordings of Papua New Guinea Music 1985 Supplement* (Boroko, 1986)

——: *1986 Supplement* (Boroko, 1987)

J. M. Rossen: *Songs of Bellona Island (Na Taungua a Mungiki)* (Copenhagen, 1987)

R. M. Moyle: *Traditional Samoan Music* (Auckland, 1988)

D. Niles, comp.: *Commercial Recordings of Papua New Guinea Music 1987 Supplement* (Boroko, 1988)

M. E. Lawson: *Tradition, Change and Meaning in Kiribati Performance* (diss. Brown U., 1989)

R. Firth and M. McLean: *Tikopia Songs* (Cambridge, 1990)

CHAPTER XV

North America

HELEN MYERS

Formation of the modern discipline

World War II ended the isolation of the North American continent, and with it parochial approaches to folk music research. American and Canadian service personnel returned from Europe and the Pacific with renewed respect for the complexity of their New World heritage, a heritage that included immigrants from many European countries as well as Africa, India, China, Japan, Southeast Asia and Latin America. From the 1950s, change swept through American universities. New emphasis was given to interdisciplinary topics, and folklore programmes including music were inaugurated. The fledgling field of 'comparative musicology', the study of 'primitive' and 'exotic' music, found a home, the North American university, and a name, 'ethno-musicology'.

Previous attempts to institutionalize the study of comparative musicology had collapsed in the 1930s. The two newly formed scholarly societies had been disbanded: in Berlin, the Gesellschaft für vergleichende Musikwissenschaft, and in the USA its affiliated organization, the short-lived American Society for Comparative Musicology (1934–7; founded by George Herzog, Helen Heffron Roberts, Charles Seeger, Henry Cowell and Dorothy Lawton). The classes in world music that Seeger and Cowell had initiated at the New School for Social Research in New York City (1932–5) were discontinued. The eminent musicologist Erich M. von Hornbostel fled Germany in 1933 and died in 1935. The Berlin Phonogrammarchiv was partly destroyed, partly dispersed during the war, completing a picture of an academic discipline whose institutional base had crumbled (Merriam, 1956).

After World War II attempts were made to reunite the rapidly growing community of music scholars. The first *Ethno-musicology Newsletter* was issued in 1953 under the editorship of Alan Merriam (1923–80), and in 1955 the Society for Ethnomusicology was founded in Philadelphia by Merriam, David McAllester (*b* 1916), Charles Seeger (1886–1979), and Willard Rhodes (*b* 1901). The society began to hold annual meetings in 1956; at the first of these, the hyphen was ceremoniously removed from the name, indicating unification of the field as well as the indivisibility of music from its cultural setting. The *Newsletter* was superseded in 1958 by the journal, *Ethnomusicology*, published three times a year. The Society held three meetings in Canada

(Toronto, 1972, Montreal, 1979, and Vancouver, 1985) and published a Canadian issue of the journal (xvi, September, 1972). The society also publishes the *SEM Newsletter* (begun in 1966) and a monograph series. In 1966, SEM was admitted to the American Council of Learned Societies.

In 1964, the first textbooks in ethnomusicology were published in the USA: *Theory and Method in Ethnomusicology* by Bruno Nettl (*b* 1930) and *The Anthropology of Music* by Merriam. Nettl's essentially musicological approach, firmly rooted in American and European traditions, stressed fieldwork, transcription and analysis, but included the study of music in its cultural context. Merriam's text drew a sharp distinction between ethnomusicologists with a musicological bent, such as Nettl and Mantle Hood (*b* 1918), and those like himself with anthropological orientation. Merriam criticized the deductive theories of the Berlin school, and defined ethnomusicology as a subdivision of anthropology.

The solitary American figure to oppose these trends in the 1960s was the anthropologist and folk-song scholar Alan Lomax (*b* 1915). In *Folk Song Style and Culture* (1968) he outlined the Cantometrics project, an international study of folk song and its relation to the cultural matrix. Cantometrics was not well received by the majority of American ethnomusicologists, some of whom demonstrated how its conclusions did not hold up for the area in which they had conducted fieldwork (Henry, 1976). This controversy proved a further setback for broadly based comparative studies.

Members of the Society for Ethnomusicology, mostly Americans and Canadians, study musical traditions of all continents, music past and music present. North American traditional music represents only a small percentage of the group's enterprise, though insights and interpretations gained abroad have stimulated Americans to re-examine their native culture. Many American and Canadian scholars, still comparative musicologists at heart, have first studied distant traditions and later turned to investigate music closer to home.

Ethnic diversity of the continent

Research on the traditional music of North America mirrors the history of human migration to the continent, a history that dawned during the last glacial period, 20,000 to 30,000 years ago, when the Mongoloid peoples, ancestors of the modern American Indians, moved across the Bering Strait and southwards across Canada, the USA, and into Central and South America, arriving at land's end, Tierra del Fuego, sometime around 6000 BC. A few scholars have speculated about vestigial links between Siberian tribal music and the music of Native Americans, for example, Nettl, who noted that both groups share a predominance of monophonic forms, large intervals, tense vocal style, and use of the single-headed frame drum (1956, pp.117–19). Lack of written records and sparse archaeological remains have limited speculation on Indian music during the pre-contact period. Research before World War II was largely devoted to the period of contact with European Americans and the reservation period; many modern studies deal with the pan-Indian era.

The African-American experience, rich, complex, challenging, begins with the forced transplantation of some 15 millions from West Africa to the New

World, to the age of slavery, the age of emancipation, the civil rights era and the modern post-civil rights movement – each period beset with its own brand of social and economic deprivation, each represented by a distinctive musical repertory.

Of Europeans, Hispanic-Americans have the longest history in the New World, dating from the mid-16th century in the southwestern USA, with the explorations of Spanish conquistadores in Texas, New Mexico, Arizona and southern California. In modern times, Mexican immigrants flood across the southwestern US border, while immigrants from Puerto Rico and other islands of the Hispanic Caribbean inundate the eastern ports, Miami and New York, where they add their music to the kaleidoscope of urban life.

The musical heritage of British and French settlers in the New World has received the earliest and most thorough research, beginning with the Colonial era predominated by the Protestant ethic, to the westward movement and expanding frontier, warfare with American Indians, contact with African-Americans, and with 19th- and 20th-century European and Asian immigrant groups.

During the years following World War II, scholars have turned to the immigrant music of the some 50 million people, largely European, who reached American shores between 1820 and 1960. New immigrants often settled in ethnic communities, postponing assimilation into Anglo-Saxon culture. Recent studies show how music has been a powerful force for conservation in some groups, for change in others.

The traditional music of North America – Native American, African-American, British-American, Hispanic-American and of recent immigrant groups – has developed, interacted and modernized, fostering new musicological research. Anglo-American ballad research, for generations the province of literature students, was claimed by musicologists, with the monumental work of Bertrand H. Bronson on the tunes of the Child ballads (1959–72). Scholars gave attention to modern folk forms influenced by popular music, especially from the southern USA – country-western, rhythm & blues, rock 'n' roll and bluegrass. The contribution of recent immigrants to the music of North America's great cities was examined, drawing on the methods of urban anthropology. The study of American Indian music was approached in a new light as, on the one hand, a full century of sound recording gave historical depth to research, and, on the other, American Indians readapted their music to post-war society.

Increasingly, scholars study music of the group to which they belong: Polish-Americans study Polish-American music, Native Americans, Native American music, African-Americans, African-American music. Inside researchers bring the special understanding of a member of the culture. The new generation of 'ethnic' researchers, trained in North American universities, can claim as much scholarly objectivity as can any other graduate, although in the 1990s the notion of objectivity in musicology and anthropology has itself come under question.

Bibliography

G. Herzog: *Research in Primitive and Folk Music in the United States* (Washington, DC, 1936)

C. Haywood: *Bibliography of North American Folklore and Folksong* (New York, 1951)

G. Chase: *America's Music: From the Pilgrims to the Present* (New York, 1955, rev. 2/1966, 3/1987)

A. Merriam: 'Notes and News', *Ethno-Musicology Newsletter*, vi (1956), 1

B. Nettl: *Music in Primitive Culture* (Cambridge, MA, 1956)

B. H. Bronson: *The Traditional Tunes of the Child Ballads; With their Texts, According to the Extant Records of Great Britain and America* (Princeton, NJ, 1959–72)

A. P. Merriam: *The Anthropology of Music* (Evanston, IL, 1964)

B. Nettl: *Theory and Method in Ethnomusicology* (New York and London, 1964)

T. P. Coffin, ed.: *Our Living Traditions: an Introduction to American Folklore* (New York, 1968)

A. Lomax: *Folk Song Style and Culture* (Washington, DC, 1968)

H. Wiley Hitchcock: *Music in the United States: a Historical Introduction* (Englewood Cliffs, NJ, 1969, 3/1988)

W. Lichtenwanger, D. Higbee, C. A. Hoover and P. T. Young, eds.: *A Survey of Musical Instrument Collections in the United States and Canada* (Chapel Hill, NC, 1974)

J. Hickerson: *American Folklore: a Bibliography of Major Works* (Washington, DC, 1975)

E. O. Henry: 'The Variety of Music in a North Indian Village: Reassessing Cantometrics', *EM*, xx (1976), 49

B. Nettl and H. Myers: *Folk Music in the United States: an Introduction* (Detroit, MI, 1976), orig. pubd as *An Introduction to Folk Music in the United States* (1960)

C. C. Flanagan and J.T. Flanagan: *American Folklore: a Bibliography, 1950–1974* (Metuchen, NJ, and London, 1977)

D. Horn: *The Literature of American Music in Books and Folk Music Collections: a Fully Annotated Bibliography* (Metuchen, NJ, 1977; suppl. 1, 1988)

C. Seeger: *Studies in Musicology, 1935–1975* (Berkeley, CA, 1977)

H. Kallmann, G. Potvin and K. Winters: *Encyclopedia of Music in Canada* (Toronto, Canada, 1981)

D. W. Krummel, J. Geil, D. J. Dyen and D. L. Root: *Resources of American Music History: a Directory of Source Materials from Colonial Times to World War II* (Urbana, IL, 1981)

Ethnic Recordings in America: a Neglected Heritage (Washington, DC, 1982)

J. W. Hickerson and K. Condon: *Folklife and Ethnomusicology Serial Publications in North America* (Washington, DC, 1982)

C. Hamm: *Music in the New World* (New York, 1983)

R. Benton: *Directory of Music Research Libraries in the United States and Canada*, i (Kassel, rev. 2/1983)

J. R. Heintze: *American Music Studies: a Classified Bibliography of Master's Theses* (Detroit, MI, 1984)

S. Field: 'Sound Structure as Social Structure', *EM*, xxviii (1984), 383

T. E. Miller: *Folk Music in America: a Reference Guide* (New York, 1986)

S. Sadie and H. Wiley Hitchcock, eds.: *The New Grove Dictionary of American Music* (London, 1986)

D. W. Krummel: *Bibliographical Handbook of American Music* (Urbana, IL, 1987)

B. Nettl: 'The IFMC/ICTM and the Development of Ethnomusicology in the United States', *YTM*, xx (1988), 19

1: NATIVE AMERICAN MUSIC

HELEN MYERS

Native American music, despite its stylistic simplicity and lack of written tradition, has contributed more than any other repertory to the development of American ethnomusicology. Scholarship following World War II built on the early studies of Jesse Walter Fewkes (1850–1930), Benjamin Ives Gilman (1852–1933), Alice Cunningham Fletcher (1838–1923), Francis La Flesche (1857–1932), John Comfort Fillmore (1843–98) and Frances Densmore (1867–1957), who with pioneering spirit, fired by musical nationalism, were fascinated that so rich and varied a musical culture had persisted in North America despite the domination of Euro-American society. The post-war generation inherited an extensive literature on the music of many tribes, supported by large collections of wax cylinders, dating from Fewkes's first recordings of 1890. With these data they also inherited a theoretical orientation, the 'musical area' (based on the anthropological theory of culture areas), proposed by George Herzog (1901–84) and Helen Heffron Roberts (1888–1985), as a rationalization for the diverse styles described in early studies.

1945–1966

The promising career of George Herzog, whose research synthesized the approaches of his mentors Erich M. von Hornbostel at the Berlin Phonogrammarchiv and Franz Boas at Columbia University, was cut short by illness in the early 1950s; his post-war publications include a brief statement on spoken versus sung language amongst the Pima (1946) and a study of Coast Salish music (1949; bibliography in Krader, 1956). The late monographs of Frances Densmore, *Seminole Music* (1956; based on fieldwork in 1931–3) and *Music of Acoma, Isleta, Cochiti, and Zuñi Pueblos* (1957; based on fieldwork in 1928, 1930–31, and 1939–40), came under the critical scrutiny of a new generation, who denounced her use of Western key signatures, classification of songs into major and minor keys, regularizing of rhythms to accommodate Western time signatures, and disregard for repetition, variation, and beginning and ending formulas (Rhodes, 1958, pp.83–4; Nettl, 1959, pp.34–5). Densmore remained untouched by developments in ethnomusicology; her last monographs are surprisingly similar in approach to those written half a century earlier, but lack the freshness and empathy of her seminal work (bibliography in Rhodes, 1956). For Canada, the major figure of this period was Marius Barbeau (1883–1969), who worked amongst Huron and Algonquin at Forette, Quebec, the Iroquois (Mohawk, Seneca), and the Tsimshian of British Columbia. His many hundreds of cylinder recordings and transcriptions are housed at the National Museum of Man, Ottawa (Barbeau, 1951, 1954, 1957; bibliographies in Cardin, 1947, and Katz, 1970).

The year 1954 was a watershed with the publication of *North American Indian Musical Styles* by Bruno Nettl (*b* 1930) and *Enemy Way Music* by David McAllester (*b* 1916), Nettl's work marking the end of an era, McAllester's a beginning. Nettl, a student of Herzog, took up the culture-area approach of his teacher, surveying available recordings and transcriptions to identify musical 'traits' – melodic contour and range, interval size, rhythm, tempo, form, antiphony and vocal production. He delineated six musical areas for the North American continent, coinciding more or less with culture areas (less so with language areas): Eskimo-Northwest Coast, Great Basin, California-Yuman, Athabascan, Plains-Pueblo and Eastern – a more sophisticated map than that

405

proposed by Helen Heffron Roberts based primarily on the distribution of instruments and vocal style (1936). Nettl's scheme was greeted with caution since of the approximately 1000 Indian groups, some had not been studied thoroughly, some had not been studied recently, and some not studied at all. In 1953, Gertrude Prokosch Kurath (*b* 1903) proposed a similar map for Indian dance styles, based on the distribution of such traits as dance steps, body movements and ground plans. In a reappraisal of musical areas (1969), Nettl redrew his map, contrasting 'good' areas, with homogeneous style and unique traits (Plains, California-Yuman, Great Basin), with 'bad' (Athabascan, East). He defended musical areas as the best compromise between the view of Indian music as a stylistic unit and the study of tribal styles in isolation from their continental context, but acknowledged the distortion caused on such maps by the forced migration of Indians to reservations during the 18th and 19th centuries. Like Newton's laws, culture areas and musical areas were found imprecise but useful; in the first college text on Indian music, Marcia Herndon denounces them as fossils, then devotes 26 pages to the trait lists and the maps (1980, pp.91–112, 186–202; also Kurath's review of musical areas, 1969, 'A Comparison').

By contrast, McAllester's *Enemy Way Music* was the first cross-cultural investigation, based on native perceptions, of musical values as a cultural manifestation. He conducted fieldwork with the Rimrock Navajo and used a questionnaire/interview to elicit aesthetic concepts. The first part of the study describes the public portion of the Enemy Way ceremony and gives analyses and musical and textual transcriptions of the secular songs, in the style of Hornbostel and Herzog; the second identifies Navajo musical concepts in a manner theretofore untried in ethnomusicology (relationship of the good to the beautiful, musical knowledge and prestige, music as power or danger), and relates musical style to such social attributes as shyness, reticence, hostility, competitiveness, provincialism, formalism and individualism. The integration of music and culture in McAllester's study had immeasurable influence on ethnomusicology, leading to research focussed on native ('emic') concepts, and honouring the distinction between normative and existential values ('what music should be' and 'what music is conceived to be', pp.4–6, 86–8). Following McAllester's lead, subsequent studies were based on personal fieldwork with individual tribes (Nettl, 1955; List, 1962; Black, 1964; Johnson, 1964; Frisbie, 1967; Nettl, 1967–68; Powers, 1968; Ware, 1970; Hauser, 1977); surveys and distributional studies were generally abandoned (exceptions are Collaer, 1967; Erickson, 1969; and Haefer, 1975).

The invasion of the Americas by Europeans resulted in loss of many Indian musical cultures; those that survived were transformed through modernization, Westernization and conversion to Christianity. Studies of acculturation during the 1940s and 1950s focussed on the Peyote Cult (Native American Church), a native movement with Christian overtones and a new musical repertory, synthesizing styles of several tribes: the long tunes with short phrases typical of Navajo and Apache music; the incomplete repetition form and undulating or descending terraced melodies of Plains style; the relaxed vocal production unique to Peyote songs. McAllester's impressive doctoral study of Peyote music (1949) based primarily on Plains material, includes comparative data and well-crafted transcriptions and analyses. Peyote studies by Nettl (1953) and Rhodes (1958) supplement McAllester's study.

Other research on acculturation and Western influence includes Nettl's study of texts and musical style in pan-Indianism (1966), Kurath's investigation of Hispanic elements in southwestern dance and ritual, including the *matachina* dance of Tewa Pueblo (Kurath and Garcia, 1970), and E. Z. Vogt's paper (1955) on the interaction among seven southwestern groups, describing Indian attitudes towards Indians and non-Indians (Frisbie, 1977, p.29). Willard Rhodes (*b* 1901) examined Indian songs with English words as an index to acculturation in different groups (1963; Rhodes bibliography in Korson and Hickerson, 1969). An unusual illustration of early acculturation is the Apache fiddle (*kízh kízh díhí*, 'buzz buzz sound'), possibly of aboriginal design, possibly a hybrid between the musical bow and a Western chordophone, mentioned by Roberts (1936, pp.15–16), by Frances Densmore (1927, p.98) and described by McAllester (1956).

Following 1946, research on American Indian dance was dominated by the solitary figure of Gertrude Prokosch Kurath, dancer, choreographer, art historian, linguist and ethnomusicologist, whose prolific output on the American and Canadian Iroquois and Southwest Pueblos are early examples in the fledgling field of dance ethnology (Kurath, 1964, 1981; survey of dance ethnology in Kurath, 1960; bibliography in Kealiinohomoku and Gillis, 1970). Other research during the 1930s and 1940s on dance, ritual, and ceremonial life includes Father Bernard Haile's work on Navajo War and Fire-Corral dances (1946, 'The Navaho Fire Dance'; 1946, 'The Navaho Snake Dance'); studies of Navajo and Apache ceremonial by Moskowitz and J. Collier (1949); research on Papago ritual by J. Hayden and C. R. Steen (1937) and A. W. Jones (1937); and studies of the Hopi Snake Dance (primarily on the lack of snake bites during the ritual) by C. M. Bogert (1941), R. F. Heizer (1944), N. W. Sterling (1941), and T. B. Hall (1953; based on photos taken in 1913–14, a year before the ban on photography). Later research on ceremonial life includes E. R. Forrest's Hopi Snake Dance study (1961; with photos taken 1906–8) and the comparison of Hopi and Polynesian dance by J. Kealiinohomoku (1967).

1967–1990

In 1964, Merriam offered in *The Anthropology of Music* his exegesis on ethnomusicology as the holistic study of music in culture, and in 1967 published a demonstration of this approach, *Ethnomusicology of the Flathead Indians*. Though a masterful ethnography of Flathead music, Merriam defeated his aim by divorcing culture (Part I) from music (Part II; reviews by Kolinski, 1970, and Powers, 1970).

Research in the 1970s and 1980s considered acculturation, revival, revitalization, and preservation of American Indian music. Indian music was transformed by the forced migrations of the early 19th century, when the American government moved Eastern groups west of the Mississippi, and in the mid-20th century, with the relocation of Native Americans to cities. V. L. Levine illustrates different patterns of acculturation and the transformation of musical concepts, using examples of the social dance repertory of three bands of Choctaw – those in their original homeland, Mississippi, and dislocated groups in Louisiana and Oklahoma (1985, 1990). Nettl describes Arapaho William Shakespear, informant for the summer institute in linguistics at Indiana University, 1951; Shakespear read the works of A. L. Kroeber and James Mooney (requesting interlibrary loans), and returned to his Wyoming reservation prepared to teach lost traditions as preserved in Western anthropological texts (1984, pp.174–7; 1985, pp.108–9). Native American song revival is discussed by C. Chiao (1971), who offers guidelines for training Indian singers. S. Dyal's 'toolkit' for cultural preservation and documentation includes the location of resources, funding applications, as well as technical information for native fieldworkers (1985).

Since World War II, modernization, Westernization and the pan-Indian movement resulted in the homogenization of musical styles, as different groups met and mixed at inter-tribal powwows. This movement affected each group differently. Nettl describes the incompatibility of European and Indian musical styles, the impoverishment of Indian music after the European invasion of North America, the transformation of music into a symbol of cultural identity and the acceptance of the Plains idiom as a pan-Indian style (descending terraced melodic contours; stanza structure; high, harsh, pulsating vocal production; and vocables). He interprets the intertribal powwow of the 1960s as the descendant of the 19th-century Plains Indian Sun Dance and the Montana 'North American Indian Days' of the 1940s – all musically eclectic midsummer public ceremonies, emblematic of tribal identity (1975, pp.113–21; 1985, pp.33–6). Acculturated popular music such as chicken scratch (*waila*), a form of the Arizona Pima and Papago that blends Anglo, Hispanic, and Indian forms has been studied by J. Griffith (1979, 1981) and J. Richard Haefer (1986).

From the 1960s, tribal identity has been nurtured at the expense of pan-Indianism. Kurath documented the Indianization of the Hispanic *matachina* dance dating from 16th-century fiestas (1970), and the blend of aboriginal and Hispanic Catholic elements in the Yaqui Easter fiesta (1980). William Powers noted during the 1960s that the 'northern' style of Sioux groups at the Standing Rock and Cheyenne River reservations became popular at Pine Ridge and other reservations in South Dakota, and that acculturation within the pan-Teton complex became more influential with the Sioux than pan-Indianism (1968). Thus the Sioux preserve the distinctiveness of their music by emphasizing regional diversity over conformity with national norms and cultural homogeneity, the inevitable consequences of pan-Indianism.

Disdain for early research transformed to sympathy and respect as scholars reissued cylinder collections on LP discs (List, 1963; Fewkes, 1964; Densmore, 1965, 1972; Lee and La Vigna, 1985), reprinted the pioneering studies (Baker, 1882/R1976; Fletcher and La Flesche, 1893/R1967; Curtis, 1907/R1968; Burlin, 1907, rev. 2/1923/R1968; Burton, 1909/R1969; Densmore, 1910–13/R1972, 1918/R1972, 1929/R1972, 1956/R1972, 1957/R1972) and prepared catalogues and bibliographies of these materials (Cardin, 1947; Haywood, 1951, pp.749–1159; Rhodes, 1952–3; Hickerson, 1961, 1974; 'Special Bibliography', 1967; Katz, 1970; Briegleb, 1971; Cavanagh, 1972; Guedon, 1972; Heth, 1973; Lee, 1979; Nattiez, 1981; Hirschfelder, Byler, and Dorris, 1983 ['Music and Dance', p.243]; Maguire, 1983; Brady and others, 1984;

Gray and Lee, 1985). They analysed early sources in the light of cultural biases that guided their collection and documentation (Crawford, 1967; Hofmann, 1968; Stevenson, 1973, 'English Sources', and 1973, 'Written Sources'; Frisbie, 1977), and wrote biographical studies of early scholars (Katz, 1970; Archabal, 1977; Moses, 1984). Archaeological work, especially in the Southwest, provided information about aboriginal practices (Bakkegard, 1960; Bakkegard and Morris, 1961; Brown, 1967, 1971, 1974).

During the 1980s scholars developed new methods of historical research, for example, combining research on archival materials with contemporary fieldwork (Levine, 1990, 1991; Vennum, 1982) or working with informants of different age groups (Vander, 1988). Guided by analysis of early works, scholars conducted historical studies comparing Indian music recorded in the late 19th and early 20th centuries with that of contemporary times: J. Cazeneuve's restudy of the Zuni Shalako (1955) as first described by M. C. Stevenson (1904); George List's comparative study of recordings of the Black Beetle Hopi lullaby dating from 1903 to 1960 (1987); H. Pantaleoni's re-examination of Densmore's analysis of Dakota rhythm (1987); McAllester's comparative textual analysis of nine translations of the Navajo 'The War God's Horse Song', 1930–80 (1980); and Thomas Vennum Jr's historical research on Ojibwa song form, comparing Densmore's cylinders, 1907–11, with a commercial disc by Canyon Records, 1971, and his own field tapes, 1968–71 (1980). Studies of recent change in Indian music, particularly the pan-Indian movement, led to rejection of older anthropological theories, such as evolutionary theory and the culture area, whereby music was seen as a bundle of 'traits', in favour of dynamic processual models, recognizing music as everchanging and inextricably enjoined with its cultural context (as in Ware, 1970).

Nonlexical vocables (formerly referred to as 'nonsense' or 'meaningless' syllables), a conspicuous feature of most tribal styles, was neglected by early scholars in transcription (and even appear to have been deleted upon request of the recordist from some cylinder recordings). Recent writings on vocables have investigated their significance and categorized them into types, to suit melodic flow and desired vocal style. Different genres have different proportions of vocables; by contrast with lexical text, vocables may promote solidarity amongst groups with mutually unintelligible languages, an especially important function at modern pan-tribal powwows (Densmore, 1943; Nettl, 1953; Bursill-Hall, 1964; Halpern, 1976; Frisbie, 1980; McAllester, 1980; Hinton, 1980).

In recent decades the Southwest and the Plains have continued as the most thoroughly studied areas. For the Southwest (surveyed in Frisbie, 1977), substantial research has been conducted on the Hopi (Black, 1964, 1967, 'Hopi Grievance Chants', 1967, 'Hopi Rabbit-hunt Chants'; Kealiino-homoku, 1967; List, 1962, 1968, 1985, 1987; Rhodes, 1973, 1977) and Navajo (McAllester, 1961; McAllester with S. W. McAllester, 1980; C. Johnson, 1964; C. Johnson Frisbie, 1967, 1968, 1980, 'An Approach to the Ethnography of Navajo Ceremonial'). Recent research on the Great Plains includes Nettl's studies of the Blackfoot (1967–8, 1989), R. Witmer's of the Canadian Blood Indians (1973, 1982), and Powers's of the Oglala (1968, 1971, 1980). Surprisingly little work has furthered that of Franz Boas (1858–1942; bibliography by

Andrews and others, 1943) and his students on Northwest Coast tribes (other than the idiosyncratic work of Ida Halpern, 1976, there is Stuart, 1968; Goodman, 1977; Kolstee, 1982; and Myers, 1986), or that of Herzog, A. L. Kroeber, and Leslie Spier on California-Yuman groups (but see Keeling, 1982; Hinton, 1980, 1984; Hinton and Watahomigie, 1984). A curious exception is Nettl's study of Ishi (the 'last wild Indian'), a Yahi native discovered in the northern California wilderness in 1911, whereupon he became an informant for Kroeber and T. T. Waterman at the University of California; Ishi's repertory of some 60 songs illustrates the 'simple style' of American Indian singing, with similar paired phrases (Nettl, 1965). Other studies devoted to biography and the repertory of a single informant include Nettl's biography of an unnamed Blackfoot singer (1968), Frisbie and McAllester's edition of Mitchell's autobiography (1978), and Judith Vander's studies of Shoshone women (1986, 1988). For Canada, the Iroquois have been studied by Jack Frisch (1968, 1970) and Michael Foster. Native music of Western Canada has been investigated by Michael Asch (1975), C. W. Mischler (1981) and Robin Ridington (1971). The Maritimes (Micmac and Malecite) await serious research.

The 1970s and 1980s brought the systematic discussion of Native American music to standard reference works and college texts including the *Encyclopedia of Music in Canada* (1981; music of four culture areas discussed by Ida Halpern [Pacific Northwest Coast], Thomas Johnston [Athabaskan], Kenneth Peacock [Plains] and Mieczyslaw Kolinski [Eastern Woodlands]); *The New Grove Dictionary of Musical Instruments* (1984; advisor for ethnomusicology, Helen Myers; some 40 instruments discussed by David McAllester and Mary Riemer-Weller); *The New Grove Dictionary of American Music* (1986, advisor, Myers; articles on some 50 individual tribes by various contributors, and overview of music and dance by Nettl and Kurath); and college texts by Marcia Herndon (1980), David McAllester in E. May (1980), and McAllester in J. T. Titon (1984, 2/1992). Major collections of Native American music are held at the Archive of Folk Culture, Library of Congress, Washington, DC; the Archives of Traditional Music, Indiana University, Bloomington, Indiana; the National Museum of Canada, Ottawa; the Lowie Museum of Anthropology, University of California, Berkeley; the Southwest Museum, Los Angeles; the Arizona State Museum, Tucson; the Archive of World Music, Wesleyan University, Middletown, CT; and the Library of the American Philosophical Society, Philadelphia. Commercial recordings of Indian music are available from Canyon Records, Indian House, Folkways, Tom Tom Records, Archive of American Folk Song and Thunderbird, Soundchief.

By the 1970s, generations of research had sensitized Native Americans to the invasiveness of anthropological inquiry, nurtured mistrust of scholarship, and awakened Indian awareness to minority rights and the intrinsic value of their cultural property. Ethics and field method are discussed by Kealiinohomoku (1974, 'Field guides'; 1974, 'Dance Culture'), Merriam (1974) and J. Valenzuela (1974). A new generation of American Indianists including Charlotte Frisbie, J. Richard Haefer, Charlotte Heth, Marcia Herndon, Dorothy Sara Lee, William Powers, Thomas Vennum, Jr., Maria La Vigna, Mary Riemer-Weller and Robert Witmer, were concerned to respect these sensitivities, and broke new ground in the ethics of research on human subjects, including such issues as the suitability of reproducing or publishing music divorced from its cultural context, the training of Native American ethnomusicologists, assisting Native Americans to preserve their traditions, and multidisciplinary teamwork in Indian studies. They published full acknowledgement of Native American contributions to scholarly work, and disseminated cultural materials back to donor communities through the Federal Cylinder Project (Brady and others, 1984; Lee and La Vigna, 1985; Gray and Lee, 1985).

Research since the 1970s has reflected increasing sensitivity to the human subject of research, the perspective of the Native American, his perception of musical categories and musical change. In the tradition of Fletcher and La Flesche (1893), many works of this period were written by or in collaboration with a native expert (Garcia, Trujillo and Trujillo, 1966; Garcia and Garcia, 1968; Kurath and Garcia, 1970; Herndon, 1971; Fogelson, 1971; Hinton and Hanna, 1971; Bahr, Gregorio, Lopez and Alvarez, 1974; Ben Black Bear and Theisz, 1976; A. White Hat, ed., 1983; Hinton and Watahomigie, 1984; Heth, 1975; Shapiro and Talamantez, 1986; Evers and Molina, 1987; and an early description of the Hotevilla Flute Ceremony written by the Hopi, Netquatewa, 1946). A landmark in scholarly collaboration was *Navajo Blessingway Singer: the Autobiography of Frank Mitchell, 1881-1967*, a co-operative enterprise spanning some 18 years, during which Frisbie and McAllester helped Mitchell to tell his own life story (1978). Scholarly opinion is divided between those who feel the ethnicity of the scholar is not an issue (as in Nettl, 1982) and those who regard it as a potential resource (Frisbie, 1980, 'An Approach').

Inuit

The Inuit ('Eskimo') are a Palaeo-asiatic Mongolid people, distinct from other Native American groups by virtue of physical characteristics (especially blood type) and language. Their many groups (population some 90,000) are sparsely distributed around the Arctic Ocean – in Alaska, northern Canada, the coast of Greenland and on the eastern Chukchi peninsula of Siberia. Inuit groups are distinct although linked by key traits such as use of the frame drum, especially for dancing, and ceremonial music relating to survival in an Arctic habitat. Acculturation varies depending on the degree of contact with outsiders (Olsen, 1972); the populations in Labrador (Moravian influence) and western Greenland (various European settlers) are the most acculturated groups.

Seminal anthropological studies of Inuit culture were made by Franz Boas of Columbia University (1888). After World War II, studies of Inuit music appeared with increasing frequency. Zygmunt Estreicher (*b* 1917), Swiss musicologist of Polish origin, wrote his doctoral dissertation on Canadian Caribou Eskimo dance-songs (1946), and in 1954, Laura Boulton (1899–1980) issued her Folkways recording and booklet summarizing the Hudson Bay and Alaskan traditions.

Canadian Inuit came to Greenland in waves between *c* 2000 BC and the mid-19th century. Eastern and northern groups, isolated by ice barriers, still preserve old traditional songs. Greenland song contests, shaman rituals, magic songs and musical instruments (*gilain* frame drum, bullroarer and

411

rattles) have been documented by the Danish scholars Poul Rovsing Olsen (1963, 1968) and Christian Leden (1952, 1954).

Palaeo-asiatic Inuit groups of eastern Siberia include the Koryak, Kamchadal, Nivkhi, Yukagir, Chukchi and Ket. Chukchi Eskimos have been studied by Voblov (1934–6), who documents their ceremonial music and dance, including *atigak* (boat-launching), as well as other rituals associated with hunting sea mammals. The *sekuyak* frame drum is analogous to those used in other Inuit areas.

The music and dance of the Alaskan Inuit groups (Yupik of the Bering Sea and Inupik of Norton Sound) have much in common with those of the Siberian population. Genres include ceremonial music for the hunting of whales and polar bears, exchange of gifts, dedication of boats and honouring of seal spirits. These ritual forms, in addition to game songs, children's songs and juggling songs, have been studied by Thomas Johnston (1976 *Eskimo Music*, 1976 'The Eskimo Songs', and 1979) and Lorraine D. Koranda (1964, 1972, 1981).

The 1970s brought a flourish of research on Canadian groups. Systematic studies revealed distinct customs and styles in each of the many Iniut groups, and ethnographic work led to the delineation of cultural areas for Canadian Inuit: the Yukon and Mackenzie Delta in the west; the Copper, Netsilik, Caribou and Iglulik of the central Arctic; and the Baffinland, northern Quebec, and Labrador groups of the east (Cavanagh, 1981).

In particular the many studies of Inuit vocal games have a special place in ethnomusicological research, serving as a showpiece for sophisticated French semiotic methods (Nattiez, 1975). This repertory has been systematically studied since 1974 by the Groupe de Recherches en Sémiologie Musicale of the University of Montreal: Claude Charron in the Belcher Islands, Denise Harvey in the Caribou and Netsilik area and in Payne Bay, Nicole Beaudry in Cape Dorset and Ivujivik, and J.-J. Nattiez in Pond Inlet and Iglulik (Beaudry, 1978 'Toward Transcription', 1978 'Le katajjaq'; Charron, 1978, and Nattiez, 1982). A form unique to the Canadian Inuit, the 'throat' or vocal game (*katajjait, piqusiraqtut*), is sung by pairs of women sitting face to face, indeed nose to nose. These competitive and highly rhythmic games, which include the noise of inhaling and exhaling and voiced and unvoiced syllables, have challenged ethnomusicologists to readdress many fundamental questions: what is music (laughter and running out of breath are cadences for this vocal form); what is the relationship between performers and audience (clustered tightly together in these festive competitions); what is the meaning of nonlexical vocables woven into text fragments; and finally, how can the scholar record for transcription polyphonic music performed without physical separation between performers? The issues that these song-like forms have raised, together with the scintillating racing quality of the music, make Inuit vocal games an attractive avenue for future research.

In recent years a search for unified ethnic identity, expressed in activities such as the Pan-Arctic Games, have spawned a revival of interest in traditional Inuit songs, games and dances. Acculturated forms such as accordion music, box fiddles, *agiarut, tautirut*, the 'Eskimo dance' (drawing on jigs and reels of 19th-century whalers), country and western music in Inuktitut, and Inuit composers such as Charlie Panagoniaq are being discussed in newer studies (Cavanagh, 1981).

Bibliography

T. Baker: *Über die Musik der nordamerikanischen Wilden* (diss., U. of Leipzig, 1882; Leipzig, 1882/ *R*1976 with Eng. trans.)

A. C. Fletcher and F. La Flesche: *A Study of Omaha Indian Music* (Cambridge, MA, 1893/*R*1967)

M. C. Stevenson: *The Zuni Indians: Their Mythology, Esoteric Fraternities, and Ceremonies* (Washington, DC, 1904)

N. Curtis [Burlin]: *The Indians' Book* (New York, 1907, rev. 2/1923/*R*1968)

F. R. Burton: *American Primitive Music with Especial Attention to the Songs of the Ojibways* (New York, 1909/*R*1969)

F. Densmore: *Chippewa Music* (Washington, DC, 1910–13/*R*1972)

——: *Teton Sioux Music* (Washington, DC, 1918/*R*1972)

——: *Handbook of the Collection of Musical Instruments in the United States National Museum* (Washington, DC, 1927)

——: *Papago Music* (Washington, DC, 1929/*R*1972)

H. H. Roberts: *Musical Areas in Aboriginal North America* (New Haven, CT, 1936/*R*1970)

J. Hayden and C. R. Steen: 'The Vikita Ceremony of the Papago', *Southwestern Monuments Monthly Reports* (April 1937), 263

A. W. Jones: 'Additional Information about the Vikita', *Southwestern Monuments Monthly Reports* (May 1937), 338

C. M. Bogert: 'The Hopi Snake Dance', *Natural History*, xlvii (1941), 276

N. W. Sterling: 'Snake Bites and the Hopi Snake Dance', *Annual Reports, Bureau of Regents, Smithsonian Institution* (Washington, DC, 1941), 551

J. A. Andrews and others: 'Franz Boas, 1858–1942', *American Anthropologist*, xlv/3 (1943) [incl. complete list of writings]

F. Densmore: 'The Use of Meaningless Syllables in Indian Songs', *American Anthropologist*, xlv (1943), 160

R. F. Heizer: 'The Hopi Snake Dance, Fact and Fancy', *Ciba Symposium*, v (1944), 1681

B. Haile: *The Navaho Fire Dance or Corral Dance: a Brief Account of its Practice and Meaning* (Saint Michaels, AZ, 1946)

——: *The Navaho War Dance: a Brief Narrative of its Meaning and Practice* (Saint Michaels, AZ, 1946)

G. Herzog: 'Some Linguistic Aspects of American Indian Poetry', *Word*, ii (1946), 82

E. Nequatewa: 'A Flute Ceremony at Hotevilla', *Plateau*, xix (1946), 35

C. Cardin: 'Bio-bibliographie de Marius Barbeau', *Les Archives de Folklore*, ii (1947), 17–96

G. Herzog: 'Salish Music', *Indians of the Urban Northwest*, ed. M. W. Smith (New York, 1949), 93

D. P. McAllester: *Peyote Music* (New York, 1949/*R*1971)

I. Moskowitz and J. Collier: *Patterns and Ceremonials of the Indians of the Southwest* (New York, 1949)

Z. Estreicher: 'Die Musik der Eskimos', *Anthropos*, xlv (1950), 659–720

M. Barbeau: 'Tsimshian Songs', *The Tsimshian: Their Arts and Music* (New York, 1951)

C. Haywood: *A Bibliography of North American Folklore and Folksong*, ii: *The American Indians North of Mexico, Including the Eskimos* (New York, 1951, rev. 2/1961)

W. Rhodes: 'North American Indian Music: a Bibliographical Survey of Anthropological Theory', *Music Library Association Notes*, x (1952), 33

W. N. Fenton and G. P. Kurath: *The Iroquois Eagle Dance: an Offshoot of the Calumet Dance* (Washington, DC, 1953)

T. B. Hall: 'Dancing the Snakes', *Arizona Highways*, xxix/7 (1953), 4

G. P. Kurath: 'Native Choreographic Areas of North America', *American Anthropologist*, lv (1953), 60

B. Nettl: 'Observations on Meaningless Peyote Song Texts', *Journal of American Folklore*, lxvi (1953), 161

M. Barbeau: 'Folk Music: Canadian', *Grove 5*

D. P. McAllester: *Enemy Way Music: a Study of Social and Esthetic Values as Seen in Navaho Music* (Cambridge, MA, 1954)

B. Nettl: *North American Indian Musical Styles* (Philadelphia, PA, 1954)

——: 'Text-Music Relations in Arapaho Songs', *Southwestern Journal of Anthropology*, x (1954), 192

J. Cazeneuve: 'Some Observations on Zuñi Shalako', *El Palacio*, lxii (1955), 347

B. Nettl: 'Musical Culture of the Arapaho', *MQ*, xli (1955), 325

E. Z. Vogt: 'A Study of the Southwestern Fiesta System as Exemplified by the Laguna Fiesta', *American Anthropologist*, lvii (1955), 820

F. Densmore: *Seminole Music* (Washington, DC, 1956/*R*1972)

B. Krader: 'Bibliography: George Herzog', *EM*, i/6 (1956), 11

D. P. McAllester: 'An Apache Fiddle', *EM*, i/8 (1956), 1

W. Rhodes: 'Bibliography: Frances Densmore', *EM*, i/7 (1956), 13

M. Barbeau: 'Indian Songs of the Northwest', *Canadian Music Journal*, ii, No. 1 (1957), 16

F. Densmore: *Music of Acoma, Isleta, Cochiti and Zuñi Pueblos* (Washington, DC, 1957/*R*1972)

W. Rhodes: 'A Study of Musical Diffusion Based on the Wandering of the Opening Peyote Song', *JIFMC*, x (1958), 42

———: 'Review, *Seminole Music*, F. Densmore', *EM*, ii (1958), 83

B. Nettl: 'Review, *Music of Acoma, Isleta, Cochiti and Zuñi Pueblos*, F. Densmore', *EM*, iii (1959), 34

B. M. Bakkegard: 'Music in Arizona Before 1912', *Journal of Research in Music Education*, viii (1960), 67

G. P. Kurath: 'Panorama of Dance Ethnology', *Current Anthropology*, i (1960), 233

B. M. Bakkegard and E. A. Morris: 'Seventh-Century Flutes from Arizona', *EM*, v (1961), 184

E. R. Forrest: *Snake Dance of the Hopi Indians* (Los Angeles, CA, 1961)

J. Hickerson: *Annotated Bibliography of North American Indian Music North of Mexico* (diss., Indiana U., 1961)

D. P. McAllester: *Indian Music in the Southwest* (Colorado Springs, CO, 1961)

B. Nettl: 'Polyphony in North American Indian Music', *MQ*, xlvii (1961), 354

G. List: 'Song in Hopi Culture, Past and Present', *JIFMC*, xiv (1962), 30

———, ed.: *The Demonstration Collection of E. M. von Hornbostel and the Berlin Phonogramm-Archiv*, FE 4175 (New York, 1963) [disc notes with commentary by K. Reinhard and G. List; includes Greenland Eskimo, Canadian Cree, American Pawnee, American Hopi]

W. Rhodes: 'North American Indian Music in Transition: a Study of Songs with English Words as an Index of Acculturation', *JIFMC*, xv (1963), 9

R. A. Black: *A Content-Analysis of Eighty-one Hopi Indian Chants* (diss., Indiana U., 1964)

G. L. Bursill-Hall: 'The Linguistic Analysis of North American Indian Songs', *Canadian Linguistic Journal*, x (1964), 15

J. W. Fewkes: *Hopi Katcina Songs: and Six Other Songs by Hopi Chanters*, FE 4394 (New York, 1964) [disc notes by C. Hofmann]

C. J. Johnson [Frisbie]: 'Navaho Corn Grinding Songs', *EM*, viii (1964), 101

G. P. Kurath: *Iroquois Music and Dance: Ceremonial Arts of Two Seneca Longhouses* (Washington, DC, 1964)

A. P. Merriam: *The Anthropology of Music* (Evanston, IL, 1964)

F. Densmore: *Healing Songs of the American Indians*, FE 4251 (New York, 1965) [disc notes by C. Hofmann]

B. Nettl: 'The Songs of Ishi: Musical Style of the Yahi Indians', *MQ*, li (1965), 460

A. Garcia, J. Trujillo and G. Trujillo: 'Tanoan Gestures of Invocation', *EM*, x (1966), 206

B. Nettl: 'Some Influences of Western Civilization on North American Indian Music', *New Voices in American Studies*, ed. R. B. Brown, D. M. Winkelman and A. Hayman (Lafayette, IN, 1966), 129

R. A. Black: 'Hopi Rabbit-hunt Chants: a Revitalized Language', *American Ethnological Society, Essays on the Verbal and Visual Arts*, ed. J. Helm (Seattle, WA, 1967), 7

———: 'Hopi Grievance Chants: a Mechanism of Social Control', *Studies in Southwestern Ethnolinguistics: Meaning and History in the Languages of the American Southwest*, ed. D. H. Hymes and W. E. Bittle (The Hague, 1967), 54

D. N. Brown: 'The Distribution of Sound Instruments in the Prehistoric Southwestern United States', *EM*, xi (1967), 71

P. Collaer: *Amerika: Eskimo und indianische Bevölkerung, Musikgeschichte in Bildern*, i (Leipzig, 1967; Eng. trans., 1971)

D. E. Crawford: 'The Jesuit Relations and Allied Documents, Early Sources for an Ethnography of Music Among American Indians', *EM*, xi (1967), 199

C. J. Frisbie: *Kinaaldá: a Study of the Navaho Girl's Puberty Ceremony* (Middletown, CT, 1967)

J. Kealiinohomoku: 'Hopi and Polynesian Dance: a Study in Cross-Cultural Comparisons', *EM*, xi (1967), 343

A. P. Merriam: *Ethnomusicology of the Flathead Indians* (Chicago, IL, 1967)

414

B. Nettl: 'Studies in Blackfoot Indian Musical Culture', *EM*, xi (1967), 141, 293; xii (1968), 11–48, 192

'Special Bibliography: Helen Heffron Roberts', *EM*, xi (1967), 228

C. J. Frisbie: 'The Navajo House Blessing Ceremony', *El Palacio*, lxxv/3 (1968), 26

A. Garcia and C. Garcia: 'Ritual Preludes to Tewa Indian Dances', *EM*, xii (1968), 239

C. Hofmann, ed.: *Frances Densmore and American Indian Music: a Memorial Volume* (New York, 1968)

G. List: 'The Hopi as Composer and Poet', *Proceedings of the Centennial Workshop on Ethnomusicology Held at the University of British Columbia, Vancouver, June 19 to 23, 1967*, ed. P. Crossley-Holland (Vancouver, Canada, 1968, 3/1975), 43

B. Nettl: 'Biography of a Blackfoot Indian Singer', *MQ*, liv (1968), 199

W. K. Powers: 'Contemporary Oglala Music and Dance: Pan-Indianism versus Pan-Tetonism', *EM*, xii (1968), 352

E. E. Erickson: *The Song Trace Song Styles and the Ethnohistory of Aboriginal America* (diss., Columbia U., 1969)

R. Korson and J. Hickerson: 'The Willard Rhodes Collection of American Indian Music in the Archive of Folk Song', *EM*, xiii (1969), 296

G. P. Kurath: 'A Comparison of Plains and Pueblo Songs', *EM*, xiii (1969), 512

B. Nettl: 'Musical Areas Reconsidered: a Critique of North American Indian Research', *Essays in Musicology in Honor of Dragan Plamenac on his 70th Birthday*, ed. G. Reese and R. J. Snow (Pittsburgh, PA, 1969), 181

'A Special Bibliography: Willard Rhodes', *EM*, xiii (1969), 305

I. J. Katz: 'Marius Barbeau 1883–1969', *EM*, xiv (1970), 129

J. W. Kealiinohomoku and F. J. Gillis: 'Special Bibliography: Gertrude Prokosch Kurath', *EM*, xiv (1970), 114

G. P. Kurath and A. Garcia: *Music and Dance of the Tewa Pueblos* (Santa Fe, NM, 1970)

W. K. Powers: 'Review Essay, *Ethnomusicology of the Flathead Indians*, A. P. Merriam', *EM*, xiv (1970), 67

M. Kolinski: 'Review Essay, *Ethnomusicology of the Flathead Indians*, A. P. Merriam', *EM*, xiv (1970), 77

N. Ware: 'Survival and Change in Pima Indian Music', *EM*, xiv (1970), 100

A. Briegleb, comp.: *Directory of Ethnomusicological Sound Recording Collections in the United States and Canada* (Middletown, CT, 1971)

D. N. Brown: 'Ethnomusicology and the Prehistoric Southwest', *EM*, xv (1971), 363

C. Chiao: *Continuation of Tradition in Navajo Society* (Taipei, 1971)

R. Fogelson: 'The Cherokee Ballgame Cycle: an Ethnographer's View', *EM*, xv (1971), 327

D. Hanna and L. Hinton: 'Havasupai Medicine Song', *Alcheringa*, iii (1971), 68

M. Herndon: 'The Cherokee Ballgame Cycle: an Ethnomusicologist's View', *EM*, xv (1971), 339

N. McLeod: 'The Semantic Parameter in Music: the Blanket Rite of the Lower Kutenai', *Yearbook for Inter-American Musical Research*, vii (1971), 83

W. K. Powers: *Yuwipi Music in Cultural Context* (diss., Wesleyan U., 1971)

R. Ridington: 'Beaver Dreaming and Singing', *Anthropologica*, xiii, No. 12 (1971), 115

B. Cavanagh: 'Annotated Bibliography: Eskimo Music', *EM*, xvi (1972), 479

F. Densmore: *Songs of the Seminole Indians of Florida*, FE 4383 (New York, 1972) [disc notes by C. Hofmann]

M.-F. Guédon: 'Canadian Indian Ethnomusicology: Selected Bibliography and Discography', *EM*, xvi (1972), 465

M. Kolinski: 'An Apache Rabbit Dance Song Cycle as Sung by the Iroquois', *EM*, xvi (1972), 415–64

W. B. Stuart: *Gambling Music of the Coast Salish Indians* (Ottawa, Canada, 1972)

C. Heth: 'Select Bibliography on American Indian Music', *Music Library Association Newsletter*, xiv (1973), 2

R. W. Rhodes: *Selected Hopi Secular Music: Analysis and Transcription* (diss., Arizona State U., 1973)

R. Stevenson: 'English Sources for Indian Music until 1882', *EM*, xvii (1973), 399–442

——: 'Written Sources for Indian Music until 1882', *EM*, xvii (1973), 1–40

R. Witmer: 'Recent Change in the Musical Culture of the Blood Indians of Alberta, Canada', *Yearbook for Inter-American Musical Research*, ix (1973), 64–94

D. Bahr, J. Gregorio, D. I. Lopez and A. Alvarez: *Piman Shamanism and Staying Sickness (Káicim Múmkidag)* (Tucson, AZ, 1974)

415

D. N. Brown: 'Evidence for Dance from the Prehistoric Southwest', *CORD Research Annual*, vi (1974), 263

J. C. Hickerson: 'History of Field Recording of North American Indian Music', *Phonographic Bulletin* (Utrecht), ix, No. 6 (1974)

J. Kealiinohomoku: 'Dance Culture as a Microcosm of Holistic Culture', *CORD Research Annual*, vi (1974), 99

——: 'Field Guides', *CORD Research Annual*, vi (1974), 245

A. P. Merriam: 'Anthropology and the Dance', *CORD Research Annual*, vi (1974), 9

J. Valenzuela: 'Roots, Branches, and Blossoms', *CORD Research Annual*, vi (1974), 299

M. Asch: 'Social Context and the Musical Analysis of Slavey Drum Dance Songs', *EM*, xix (1975), 245

J. R. Haefer: 'North American Indian Musical Instruments: Some Organological Distribution Problems', *JAMIS*, i (1975), 56

C. A. Heth: *The Stomp Dance Music of the Oklahoma Cherokee: a Study of Contemporary Practice with Special Reference to the Illinois District Ceremonial Ground* (diss., UCLA, 1975)

B. Nettl: 'The Western Impact on World Music: Africa and the American Indians', *Contemporary Music and Music Cultures*, ed. C. Hamm, B. Nettl and R. Byrnside (Englewood Cliffs, NJ, 1975), 101

W. K. Powers: 'The Study of Native American Music', *Keystone Folklore*, xx/1–2 (1975), 39

Ben Black Bear Sr and R. D. Theisz: *Songs and Dances of the Lakota* (Rosebud, SD, 1976)

I. Halpern: 'On the Interpretation of "Meaningless-Nonsensical Syllables" in the Music of the Pacific Northwest Indians', *EM*, xx (1976), 253

N. M. Archabal: 'Frances Densmore: Pioneer in the Study of American Indian Music', *Women of Minnesota: Selected Biographical Essays*, ed. B. Stuhler and G. Kreuter (St Paul, MN, 1977)

C. J. Frisbie: *Music and Dance Research of Southwestern United States Indians: Past Trends, Present Activities, and Suggestions for Future Research* (Detroit, MI, 1977)

L. J. Goodman: *Music and Dance in Northwest Coast Indian Life* (Tsaile, AZ, 1977)

M. Hauser: 'Formal Structure in Polar Eskimo Drumsongs', *EM*, xxi (1977), 33

R. W. Rhodes: *Hopi Music and Dance* (Tsaile, AZ, 1977)

C. J. Frisbie and D. P. McAllester, eds.: *Navajo Blessingway Singer: the Autobiography of Frank Mitchell, 1881–1967* (Tucson, AZ, 1978)

D. Bahr, J. Giff and M. Havier: 'Piman Songs on Hunting', *EM*, xxiii (1979), 245–96

J. Griffith: '*Waila* – the Social Dance Music of the Indians of Southern Arizona: an Introduction and Discography', *JEMF Quarterly*, xv (1979), 193

D. S. Lee: *Native North American Music and Oral Data: a Catalogue of Sound Recordings, 1893–1976* (Bloomington, IN, 1979)

C. J. Frisbie: 'An Approach to the Ethnography of Navajo Ceremonial Performance', *The Ethnography of Musical Performance*, ed. N. McLeod and M. Herndon (Norwood, PA, 1980), 75

——: 'Vocables in Navajo Ceremonial Music', *EM*, xxiv (1980), 347–92

M. Herndon: *Native American Music* (Norwood, PA, 1980)

L. Hinton: 'Vocables in Havasupai Song', *Southwestern Indian Ritual Drama*, ed. C. J. Frisbie (Albuquerque, NM, 1980), 275–306

G. P. Kurath: 'North America, §II, 2: Indian Dance', *Grove 6*

D. P. McAllester: 'North American Native Music', *Musics of Many Cultures: an Introduction*, ed. E. May (Berkeley, CA, 1980), 307

——: '"The War God's Horse Song": an Exegesis in Native American Humanities', *Selected Reports in Ethnomusicology*, iii/2 (1980), 1

—— with S. W. McAllester: *Hogans: Navajo Houses and House Songs* (Middletown, CT, 1980)

W. K. Powers: 'Oglala Song Terminology', *Selected Reports in Ethnomusicology*, iii/2 (1980), 23

T. Vennum Jr: 'A History of Ojibwa Song Form', *Selected Reports in Ethnomusicology*, iii/2 (1980), 42–75

J. Griffith: '*Waila* Music since 1979', *Southwest Folklore*, v (1981), 57

H. Kallmann, G. Potvin and K. Winters, eds.: *Encyclopedia of Music in Canada* (Toronto, 1981), 'Indians', p.448

G. P. Kurath: *Tutelo Rituals on Six Nations Reserve, Ontario* (Ann Arbor, MI, 1981)

C. W. Mishler: *Gwich'in Athapaskan Music and Dance: an Ethnography and Ethnohistory* (U. of Texas, 1981)

J.-J. Nattiez: 'La musique indienne sur disque: cent ans d'ethnomusicologie', *Recherches Amérindiennes au Québec*, xi, No. 3 (1981), 251

R. H. Keeling: *Songs of the Brush Dance and Their Basis in Oral-Expressive Magic: Music and Culture of the Yurok, Karok, and Hupa Indians of Northwestern California* (diss., UCLA, 1982)

A. Kolstee: *Bella Coola Indian Music: a Study of the Interaction between Northwest Coast Indian Structures and their Functional Context* (Ottawa, Canada, 1982)

B. Nettl: 'Review, *Native American Music*, M. Herndon', *EM*, xxvi (1982), 161

T. Vennum Jr: *The Ojibwa Drum Dance: its History and Construction* (Washington, DC, 1982)

R. Witmer: *The Musical Life of the Blood Indians* (Ottawa, Canada, 1982)

A. B. Hirschfelder, M. G. Byler and M. A. Dorris: *Guide to Research on North American Indians* (Chicago, IL, 1983)

J. H. Howard: 'Pan-Indianism in Native American Music and Dance', *EM*, xxvii (1983), 71

M. Maguire: *American Indian and Eskimo Music: a Selected Bibliography Through 1981* (Washington, DC, 1983)

A. White Hat Sr, ed.: *Lakota Ceremonial Songs* (Rosebud, SD, 1983)

E. Brady and others: *The Federal Cylinder Project: a Guide to Field Cylinder Collections in Federal Agencies*, i: *Introduction and Inventory* (Washington, DC, 1984)

C. Heth, ed.: *Sharing a Heritage: American Indian Arts* (Los Angeles, CA, 1984)

L. Hinton: *Havasupai Songs: a Linguistic Perspective* (Tübingen, 1984)

—— and L. J. Watahomigie, eds.: *Spirit Mountain: an Anthology of Yuman Story and Song* (Tucson, AZ, 1984)

D. P. McAllester: 'North America/Native America', *Worlds of Music: an Introduction to the Music of the World's Peoples*, ed. J. T. Titon and others (New York, 1984, 2/1992), 12–63

L. G. Moses: *The Indian Man: a Biography of James Mooney* (Urbana, IL, 1984)

B. Nettl: 'In Honor of Our Principal Teachers', *EM*, xxviii (1984), 173

S. Sadie, ed.: *The New Grove Dictionary of Musical Instruments* (London, 1984)

S. Dyal: *Preserving Traditional Arts: a Toolkit for Native American Communities* (Los Angeles, CA, 1985)

J. A. Gray and D. S. Lee: *The Federal Cylinder Project: a Guide to Field Cylinder Collections in Federal Agencies*, ii: *Northeastern Indian Catalog, Southeastern Indian Catalog* (Washington, DC, 1985)

D. S. Lee and M. La Vigna, eds.: *Omaha Indian Music: Historic Recordings from the Fletcher/La Flesche Collection*, AFC L71 (Washington, DC, 1985) [disc notes]

V. L. Levine: 'Duck Dance', in B. Nettl: *The Western Impact on World Music: Change, Adaptation, and Survival* (New York, 1985), 139

G. List: 'Hopi Melodic Concepts', *JAMS*, xxxviii (1985), 143

B. Nettl: *The Western Impact on World Music: Change, Adaptation, and Survival* (New York, 1985), 'Powwow', p.33; 'Old-Time Religion', p.93; 'Americans', p.108

E. Keillor: 'The Role of Youth in the Continuation of Dogrib Musical Traditions', *YTM*, xviii (1986), 61

J. R. Haefer: 'Chicken Scratch', *The New Grove Dictionary of American Music* (London, 1986)

G. P. Kurath: *Half a Century of Dance Research: Essays by Gertrude Prokosch Kurath* (Flagstaff, AZ, 1986)

A. D. Shapiro and I. Talamantez: 'The Mescalero Apache Girls' Puberty Ceremony: the Role of Music in Structuring Ritual Time', *YTM*, xviii (1986), 77

H. Wiley Hitchcock and S. Sadie, eds.: *The New Grove Dictionary of American Music* (London, 1986)

H. Myers: 'Salish', *The New Grove Dictionary of American Music*, ed. H. Wiley Hitchcock and S. Sadie (London, 1986)

J. Vander: *Ghost Dance Songs and Religion of a Wind River Shoshone Woman* (Los Angeles, CA, 1986)

L. Evers and F. S. Molina: *Yaqui Deer Songs, Maso Bwikam: a Native American Poetry* (Tucson, AZ, 1987)

D. W. Krummel: *Bibliographical Handbook of American Music* (Urbana, IL, 1987)

G. List: 'Stability and Variation in a Hopi Lullaby', *EM*, xxxi (1987), 18

H. Pantaleoni: 'One of Densmore's Dakota Rhythms Reconsidered', *EM*, xxxi (1987), 35

J. Vander: *Songprints: the Musical Experience of Five Shoshone Women* (Urbana, IL, 1988)

R. Keeling, ed.: *Women in North American Indian Music: Six Essays* (Bloomington, IN, 1989)

B. Nettl: *Blackfoot Musical Thought: Comparative Perspectives* (Kent, OH, 1989)

V. L. Levine: *Choctaw Indian Musical Cultures in the Twentieth Century* (diss., U. of Illinois, 1990)

——: 'Arzelie Langley and a Lost Pantribal Tradition', *Ethnomusicology and Modern Music History*, ed. S. Blum, P. Bohlman and D. Neuman (Urbana, IL, 1991)

F. Boas: 'The Central Eskimo', *Sixth Annual Report of the Bureau of Ethnology*, ed. J. W. Powell (Washington, DC, 1888/R1964), 299–669

Z. Estreicher: *La musique des esquimaux-caribous* (diss., U. of Fribourg, 1946)

——: 'Die Musik der Eskimos: eine vergleichende Studie', *Anthropos*, xlv (1950), 659–720

C. Leden: *Über die Musik der Smith Sund Eskimos* (Copenhagen, 1952)

417

C. Leden; *Über die Musik der Ostgrönländer* (Copenhagen, 1954)

L. Boulton: *The Eskimos of Hudson Bay and Alaska* (FE 4444, 1955) [disc notes]

E. Groven: *Eskimo melodies fra Alaska* (Oslo, 1956)

I. K. Voblov: 'Eskimo Ceremonies', *Anthropological Papers of the University of Alaska*, vii/2 (1958), 71

L. D. Koranda: 'Some Traditional Songs of the Alaskan Eskimos', *Anthropological Papers* (University of Alaska), xii (1964), 17

P. R. Olsen: 'Intervals and Rhythm in the Music of the Eskimos of East Greenland', *Proceedings of the Centennial Workshop in Ethnomusicology* (Vancouver, 1968), 54

B. Cavanagh: 'Annotated Bibliography: Eskimo Music', *EM*, xvi (1972), 479

L. D. Koranda: *Alaskan Eskimo Songs and Stories* (Seattle, 1972)

P. R. Olsen: 'Acculturation in the Eskimo Songs of the Greenlanders', *YIFMC*, iv (1972), 32

J.-J. Nattiez: *Fondements d'une sémiologie de la musique* (Paris, 1975)

T. F. Johnston: *Eskimo Music by Region: a Comparative Circumpolar Study* (Ottawa, 1976)

T. Johnston: 'The Eskimo Songs of Northwestern Alaska', *Arctic*, xxix (1976), 7

C. Charron: *Quelques mythes et récits de tradition orale Inuit: essai d'analyse sémio-culturelle* (Diss., U. of Montreal, 1977)

N. Beaudry: 'Le katajjaq, un jeu Inuit traditionnel', *Etudes Inuit Studies*, ii (1978), 35

——: 'Toward Transcription and Analysis of Inuit Throat-Games: Macro-structure', *EM*, xxii (1978), 261

M. M. Lutz: *The Effects of Acculturation on Eskimo Music of Cumberland Peninsula* (Ottawa, 1978) [includes disc]

C. Charron: 'Toward Transcription and Analysis of Inuit Throat-Games: Micro-structure', *EM* xxii (1978), 245

T. F. Johnston: *Inupiat Dance Songs* (Anchorage, 1979)

L. D. Koranda: 'Music of the Alaskan Eskimos', in E. May, ed.: *Musics of Many Cultures: an Introduction* (Berkeley, ca, 1980), 332–62

B. Cavanagh: 'Inuit', ed. H. Kallmann, G. Potvin, and K. Winters, *Encyclopedia of Music in Canada* (Toronto, 1981), 458

R. Pelinski: *La musique des Inuit du Caribou: cinq perspectives méthodologiques* (Montreal, 1981)

B. Cavanagh: *Music of the Netsilik Eskimo: a Study of Stability and Change* (Ottawa, 1982)

M. M. Lutz: *Musical Traditions of the Labrador Coast Inuit* (Ottawa, 1982)

J.-J. Nattiez: 'Comparison within a Culture: the Katajjaq of the Inuit', R. Falck and T. Rice, eds., *Cross-Cultural Perspectives on Music* (Toronto, 1982), 134

M. Asch: *Kinship and the Drum Dance in a Northern Dene Community* (Edmonton, Alberta, 1988)

J.-J. Nattiez: *Canada: Jeux Vocaux des Inuit* (Harmonia Mundi, 1989) [disc notes]

L. A. Wallen: *The Face of Dance: Yup'ik Eskimo Masks from Alaska* (Calgary, 1990)

2: AFRICAN-AMERICAN MUSIC

HELEN MYERS

The heritage of the American black – his African ancestry, slavery and emancipation, life in the rural South, lynching and Jim Crow, rednecks and the Klan, the migration to northern cities, poverty and ghetto life, Montgomery, Watts, Harlem, two hundred years of racism and ever-present discrimination – has shaped that distinctive body of music called African-American. Since the coming of the first African slaves to Virginia in 1619, the American black's history has been one of struggle: for survival, for equality, for dignity, for ethnic pride, for civil rights and full participation in a predominantly white culture. The distinctiveness of the black experience (so different from that of the white European immigrant groups of the 19th century) gives the African-

American a unique perspective. His music, from spirituals, blues, ragtime to jazz, gospel and soul, reflects his special point of view and his complex heritage.

American blacks are the descendants of Africans who were brought as slaves from regions of West and West-Central Africa. In 1727, there were 75,000 blacks in the 13 colonies; by 1800, the number had increased to one million. Many of these slaves first worked on the British, French, Dutch or Spanish sugar-growing islands of the Caribbean before being brought to the USA. This forced migration of an estimated 15 million African blacks to all parts of the New World – from Brazil to the northeastern USA – was one of the largest movements of peoples in modern history. It resulted in the contact of two distinct musical styles: the African traditions of the slaves and the various European traditions in the Americas; after contact, neither remained unchanged.

Early studies of black music tried to pinpoint the origins of African-American style. Scholars focussed their efforts on identifying African 'survivals' and explaining their presence in the music of the New World Negro. Melville J. Herskovits (*The Myth of the Negro Past*, 1941) and his student, Richard Waterman ('African Influence in American Negro Music', 1952), used the theory of culture change, syncretism, to demonstrate how European and African forms had blended to produce new genres – the black music of the Americas – bearing features of both parent musics. European and African music, they argued, have many features in common – among them diatonic scales and polyphony – and thus are compatible. When these two musics met, during the slave era, therefore, it was natural for them to mesh, to blend, to syncretize. A lack of shared features, on the other hand, explains why European and American Indian musics failed to combine and remained two separate, distinct systems.

Herskovits and Waterman maintained that musical survivals, 'Africanisms', were stronger in areas of the New World where blacks predominated numerically. In the West Indies, particularly in Haiti, Jamaica and Trinidad, for example, Shango and Voodoo cult songs which derive directly from Africa are still sung today (*see* Chapter XVI, 'The West Indies'). Ironically, African songs that persist in the Caribbean may have changed or even died out in their original African setting. In the USA, the cotton plantation system placed blacks and whites and their two musical styles in close association, and fewer pure Africanisms can be identified in black folk songs of the American South (Waterman, 1948, 1951, 1952).

Reference materials and general studies

The novice student of African-American music inherits a rich and diverse body of research written since World War II, by black and white scholars alike. But unlike the music of most American minorities, investigated first and foremost by members from the community, African-American music was studied by whites decades before black Americans turned their attention to this task. Richard Crawford finds that 'Black scholars' relationship to their subject may be said to invite a particular quality of empathy in their work, but the quantity of that work is not large' (1986, p.1). Crawford divides African-American research into two broad categories, one of them musicological and the other literary. The two streams can be represented by two well-known books: the musicological by Eileen Southern's *The Music of Black Americans* (1971; 1983) and the literary by LeRoi Jones's *Blues People* (1963) . . . Southern tells the story of Afro-American musicians in generous detail. *The Music of Black Americans* is a chronicle. It celebrates the ingenuity, adaptability, and artistry of people whose artistic achievements have often been misunderstood and undervalued by the culture in which they have been forced to live. But Southern's emphasis is on what those people have accomplished, not on what they have had to overcome. In contrast, *Blues People* is not a chronicle at all. It is a pointed search for an explanation of black music and its essence. According to Jones, that essence is to be found in a relationship – the relationship of American blacks to American whites, the evolving recognition by blacks of themselves as a particular kind of American and the ways in which the tension brought about by each change in their position in American society has created new sensibilities and hence new musical styles (1986, pp.2–4).

Bibliographies of African-American music include Dominique-René de Lerma's monumental four-volume *Bibliography of Black Music* (1981–4), including one volume on reference materials (2800 entries), one on African-American idioms (minstrelsy, spirituals, ragtime, gospel, blues, jazz and others), a third on geographical studies including the Americas, the Caribbean and Africa, and a final volume on theory and education (relating mainly to composed music). Samuel Floyd Jr and Martha J. Reisser (1983) give some 400 entries on reference and research materials. Zelma Watson George lists over 12,000 titles, based on the collection at Howard University, including 'art music by Negro composers or based on Negro thematic material' (1953). John F. Szwed and Roger D. Abrahams supply brief annotations for some 3300 items relating to African-American folk music in North America (1978). Irene V. Jackson's *Afro-American Religious Music: a Bibliography and Catalogue of Gospel Music* (1979) is unannotated but does include material on folklore and dance; it covers North America as well as the Caribbean. Other unannotated bibliographies include Portia K. Maultsby (1975) and J. Skowronski (1981). The discographer beyond compare for African-American music is Michel Ruppli, whose five volumes cover the major record companies that, beginning in the 1940s, have specialized in black music (1979; 1980, *The Prestige Label*; 1980, *The Savoy Label*; 1983; 1985).

General introductions to African-American music include Tilford Brooks's *America's Black Musical Heritage* (1984), Harold Courlander's *Negro Folk Music U.S.A.* (1963), Dena J. Epstein's thoroughly documented *Sinful Tunes and Spirituals* (1977), Alain Locke's (the first black Rhodes scholar) *The Negro and His Music* (1936/R1968) and Eileen Southern's three indispensable works – *Biographical Dictionary of Afro-American and African Musicians* (1982), which offers some 1500 short biographies of personalities in the field of African-American music; *The Music of Black Americans: a History* (1971), the standard text for most college courses on the topic, intended to be used in conjunction with *Readings in Black American Music* (1971), an anthology of writings dating from the African heritage (including Mungo Park), early America (including 18th-century newspaper slave advertisements, journals, and letters), documentation of 19th-century religious music (Richard Allen, John F. Watson, Daniel Alexander Payne), the plantation era (excerpts from the popular slave autobiographies) and passages by 20th-century stars including W. C. Handy,

John Birks 'Dizzy' Gillespie, Mahalia Jackson, and Imamu Amiri Baraka (formerly LeRoi Jones).

Beginning in the 1960s many of the pioneering studies of African-American music were reprinted (Allen, Ware and Garrison, 1867, rev. 1965; G. D. Pike, 1874/*R*1971; Marsh, 1875/*R*1969; Barton, 1899, repr. 1969; Krehbiel, 1913/*R*1976; Johnson and Odum, 1925, repr. 1964; Scarborough, 1925/ *R*1963; Odum and Johnson, 1926, repr. 1969; Hurston, 1935, rev. 5/ 1978; Cuney-Hare, 1936/*R*1974; Locke, 1936/*R*1968; Work, 1940/*R*1976; and Handy, 1941/*R*1970).

Spirituals

Spirituals are the most characteristic product of 19th-century American black folklore. Probably originating in the late 1700s, the Negro spiritual first achieved renown among white audiences with the dramatically successful USA and European tour of the Fisk Jubilee Singers in 1870 (Marsh, 1875). In the 1990s, the label 'spiritual' covers a wide range of religious song-types, including call-and-response chants, Fundamentalist Protestant hymns, and the so-called 'shout' or 'ring-shout'. Spirituals were the first black musical genre to receive comprehensive scholarly attention. Early in the 20th century, a controversy arose which lingers in the 1990s: in *Afro-American Folksongs* (1913), Henry Edward Krehbiel asserted that black American music was purely African material, that it sprang, without any outside influences, from the unique historical position of the American Negro; in *White and Negro Spirituals* (1943), George Pullen Jackson (1874–1953) put forward the 'white origin theory', arguing that black music had been influenced by Anglo-American song and constituted an integral part of the British tradition. Jackson discovered many of these white spirituals published in shape-note hymn books of the early 19th century. For example, the black spiritual, 'Down by the Riverside', is derived from the white spiritual, 'We'll Wait Till Jesus Comes', published in an 1868 upstate New York hymnal, *The Revivalist*. The black spiritual 'I Want to Die A-Shouting' uses a variant of the tune from the white spiritual, 'New Harmony', but takes parts of its text from three other white spirituals: 'Amazing Grace', 'Jesus My All' and 'Am I a Soldier'. This 'white origin theory' was rejected by James Weldon and J. Rosamund Johnson (1925–6/*R*1940), John W. Work (1940), Mieczyslaw Kolinski (1969) and John Lovell Jr (1972). In his summary of this historical debate, blues scholar Paul Oliver maintains that 'considerable evidence has been brought by Newman I. White, Guy B. Johnson and George Pullen Jackson to support the contention that both the black spiritual and the white originated from a common source in the camp meetings and the white Southern rural churches. . . . It can thus be assumed that the exchange between black and white traditions was considerable' (1980). In her detailed exposition of the 'white origin' debate Dena J. Epstein rejects Oliver's compromise ('A White Origin for the Black Spiritual? An Invalid Theory and How it Grew', 1983).

Studies of spirituals and other black church music are diverse in approach and focus. Archie Green has documented early spirituals preserved on wax cylinder (1970). The major opus on the spiritual by John Lovell Jr (1972) discussed the origins and diffusion of the form, the degree of African influence,

421

the texts and their cultural importance. Many other studies are available, including Horace Clarence Boyer's research in Rochester, NY (1973); Jacqueline Cogdell DjeDje's monograph on spirituals from Southeast Georgia (1978); Doris Jane Dyen's study of shape-note singing in Southeast Alabama (1977); William R. Ferris Jr's study of an oral-tradition folk service in Warren County, Mississippi (1972, 'The Rose Hill Service'); Maultsby's historical surveys of the pre-Civil War spiritual (1974, 1976); Sara M. Stone's study of performing practice in the Church of God and Saints of Christ, founded in 1896 (1985); and Robert Williams's research on black hymnody in Georgia and Florida (1973). Researchers on black preaching and chanted prayer include Henry W. Mitchell (1970), Bruce A. Rosenberg (1970, *The Art of the American Folk Preacher*; 1970, 'The Formulaic Quality of Spontaneous Sermons') and Therese Smith (1985).

Gospel

A concise overview of gospel from a black perspective is in Lawrence Levine, *Black Culture and Black Consciousness* (1977), an attempt to 'present and understand the thought of the people who, though quite articulate in their own lifetimes, have been rendered historically inarticulate by scholars who have devoted their attention to other groups and problems' (p.ix). The early gospel career of Thomas Dorsey is documented in A. Duckett (1974) and Boyer (1974). Performances from the Dorsey era to the 1960s are discussed by Tony Heilbut in *The Gospel Sound* (1971), including a discography and index of song titles. Performer-scholars also have contributed insights: Pearl Williams-Jones (1970, 1975), who presents gospel as an expression of the black aesthetic; and Boyer (1973, 1979), whose focus is the early gospel style of Dorsey, Roberta Martin and Mahalia Jackson. Biographical and autobiographical accounts include *Just Mahalia, Baby* (Goreau, 1975) and *Movin' on Up* (Mahalia Jackson, 1966). The life and career of Martin has been treated by Irene Jackson (1974). The issue of African retentions and reinterpretations in black church music, north and south, is addressed by George Robinson Ricks, a student of Melville Herskovits (1960). Gospel song in two Chicago churches has been researched by June Delores Paul (1973), and music in 20 black churches in New York State by Boyer (1973). Mellonee Burnim conducted fieldwork in two Indiana churches for her doctoral dissertation, *The Black Gospel Music Tradition: Symbol of Ethnicity* (1980). (Other gospel studies include Burnim, 1985; DjeDje, 1986; Feintuch, 1980; Tallmadge, 1968; and Waterman, 1951.) Reference sources for gospel include Irene Jackson, *Afro-American Religious Music: a Bibliography and a Catalogue of Gospel Music* (1979). An overview of gospel music research has been given by Burnim (1980).

Ragtime

Ragtime, a popular music form based on 'ragged', that is syncopated, rhythm was brought to public attention during the World's Columbian Exposition in Chicago, 1893. Pioneer performers included Ben Harney, Scott Joplin, Johnny Seamore (or Seymour) and Jesse Pickett. During the 1940s and again in the 1960s ragtime underwent a revival, including the collection, research and performance of classic compositions, and focussing primarily on the works of Scott Joplin. Recordings by Joshua Rifkin (1970) and Gunther Schuller (1973), and the New York Public Library two-volume edition of Joplin's works (1971) brought ragtime to the fore among musicologists and conservatory performers. Collected editions of piano rags appeared, including Rudi Blesh's *Classic Piano Rags* (1973), Tichenor's *Ragtime Rarities* (1975) and *Ragtime Rediscoveries* (1979), and Jasen's *100 Authentic Rags* (1979). General studies of the subject have been made by E. A. Berlin (1980) and J. E. Hasse (1982, 1985).

Blues

At the turn of the century, as industry in the North flourished and the agricultural importance of the South waned, blacks migrated to northern cities. From 1910 to 1920, the black population of Harlem doubled and that of Chicago trebled. By the 1930s, blacks constituted a major work force in New York, Philadelphia, Detroit and Chicago. In the northern cities, blacks sought employment opportunities, higher wages, better education for their children and greater personal freedom and social mobility. At the same time, in the North they encountered racism, which prompted them to live in the segregated, ethnic folk-like communities of the inner city ghettos.

This period of the first massive migration of blacks to northern cities saw the rise of the blues as a major black folk expression. Urban blues derived from several rural southern forms: 'field blues' or 'field hollers', short unaccompanied calls originally sung by cotton pickers; 'rural blues' or 'country blues', a solo form often accompanied by guitar; and the spirituals, particularly those such as 'Lay this Body Down', which expressed personal emotion and sorrow. Charles Keil documents how the 'city blues' of the 1920s and 1930s and urban blues after the 1940s broke away from these rural forms and reflected the new social dilemma of the American black as he faced the upheaval of urbanization (*Urban Blues*, 1966).

Early studies saw the blues as the musical antecedent of jazz (e.g. E. Simms Campbell's chapter on blues in Ramsey and Smith, 1939; Blesh, 1946; and Winthrop Sargent, 1946). In the late 1960s, approaches diversified as scholars from folklore, anthropology, poetry and black studies encouraged musicologists to look beyond the mere notes. Charles K. Wolfe describes the 'blues Renaissance' of the 1970s, noting the many scholarly publications and the abundance of historic recordings (1972).

Blues scholarship has been inhibited by a lack of primary written and pictorial sources; the many early recordings that have survived compensate in some measure for the slender written accounts. More documentation is available for post-war modern blues than for the pre-war 'classical' and 'country' forms, although it is these early forms that have most fascinated researchers. *Recording the Blues* by Robert Dixon and John Godrich (1970) documents early field trips made by recording companies, beginning in the 1920s and 1930s with records made of Ma Rainey, Bessie Smith, and Alberta Hunter of 'city blues' and later recordings of 'country blues' by venturesome companies like Bluebird and Vocalion, made both on location in such centres as Kansas City, Hot Springs, Atlanta and Memphis as well as in the studios of New York and Chicago. An account of fieldwork by talent scout Frank Waller is in *The New Lost City Ramblers Song Book* (ed. Cohen and Seeger, 1964, pp.26–9). An essential reference tool for blues discography is John Godrich and Robert Dixon's *Blues and Gospel Records, 1902–1942* (1963).

On the African features of the blues, Paul Oliver's *Savannah Syncopators: African Retentions in the Blues* (1970) is a comparative study based on his research in the southern USA and in Ghana. Other studies by Oliver emphasize the historical and biographical aspects of the subject (*Blues Fell This Morning*, 1960, and *Conversation With the Blues*, 1965, both based on interviews; see also his popular history, *The Story of the Blues*, 1969). In *Screening the Blues*, Oliver explores the cultural themes of blues lyrics, including the image of the church, Christmas themes, the John Henry-Joe Louis mythologies and hidden sexual themes, mostly expressed in slang (1968). The interchange between black and white genres, particularly between blues and hillbilly music, is discussed in Tony Russell, *Blacks, Whites and Blues* (1970), from the racial roles of the 19th-century minstrel show to the different worlds of white country and black music of the 1960s. Scholars of blues lyrics include Ralph Ellison, who concluded that 'the blues speak to us simultaneously of the tragic and comic aspects of the human condition and they express a profound sense of life shared by many Negro Americans' (1964, p.256). Texts are discussed by folklorist Samuel Charters in a brief and somewhat limited study, *The Poetry of the Blues* (1963) and by Stanley Edgar Hyman in 'American Negro Literature and the Folk Tradition' (1958), in which he compares lyrics with motifs in black literature. In a series of short articles in *Down Beat*, Rod Gruver studied blues prosody, maintaining that the lyrics are 'anti-lyrics', and do not necessarily express personal experience (1967, 1969, 1971).

A valuable reference aid is Eric Sackheim and Jonathan Shahn's *The Blues Line*, a compilation of some 250 lyrics transcribed from old country records and including artists Robert Johnson and Blind Lemon Jefferson (1969). Another anthology of lyrics is *Living Country Blues* (1969) by Harry Oster, which contains 230 thematically grouped poems transcribed from Louisiana singers during the late 1950s. In *Blues Lyric Poetry: an Anthology* (1983), Michael Taft presents over 2000 texts (1920–42) by more than 350 singers. In his three-volume *Blues Lyric Poetry: a Concordance* (1983), Taft 'deconstructs' the texts into words and phrases to analyse their poetic structure. A comprehensive study of country blues, their musical and poetic texts as well as social and cultural context is Jeff Todd Titon's *Early Downhome Blues* (1977), particularly effective for classroom use when read together with Titon's *Downhome Blues Lyrics* (1981), with 125 texts (1946–64; see also Titon, 1971, *Ethnomusicology of Downhome Blues: Phonograph Records 1926–1930*; 1977, 'Thematic Pattern in Downhome Blues Lyrics'; 1978). Despite this rich literature, the cultural and literary dimension of blues awaits further research; Wolfe points out that 'someone needs to think about the blues as well as research them' (1972, p.165).

Rhythm & blues

The term rhythm & blues (R & B) was coined in June 1949 in the tradepaper *Billboard* to replace 'Race', a term used from 1920 onwards to identify black records by black artists. Rhythm & blues was the predominant black popular style during the 1940s and 1950s. The musical and social characteristics of this style have been thoroughly investigated by Arnold Shaw (1978), who describes rhythm & blues as a 'product of the black experience in a segregated world that excluded blacks from night clubs, showrooms, theatres and first-run movie houses, forcing them to find entertainment in ghetto clubs and mainly through recordings . . . a combination of several sounds: boogie woogie, jump blues, electric instruments, and especially black gospel music' (1978, pp.51–168; 1980, p.74). Greil Marcus describes in *Mystery Train* (1976) the indebtedness of rock'n'roll to the unique character of R & B, beginning in the mid-1950s and including much of early Elvis Presley, Jerry Lee Lewis, Eddie Cochran and Buddy Holly. Presley said, 'I dug the real low-down Mississippi singers, mostly Big Bill Broonzy and Big Boy Crudup, although they would scold me at home for listening to them. *Sinful music*, the townsfolk in Memphis said it was – which never bothered me' (Shaw, 1980, p.72). Charles Hamm (1979) cites the well-known example, 'Hound Dog', which was originally recorded in 1953 by Big Mama Thornton.

Research in rhythm & blues is fraught with the difficulties of any folk art: the paucity of oral history and the unreliability of written sources such as tradepaper charts or records of small independent record companies. Consequently, rhythm & blues awaits thorough study and has often suffered from denigration. The renowned black scholar LeRoi Jones presents R & B as 'more easily faked', 'a less personal music than the older blues forms, if only because the constant hammering of the overwhelming rhythm sections often subverts . . . the lyrics' (1963, pp.172–3). Blues scholars such as Paul Oliver and Sam Charters tend to pass over rhythm & blues; Phyl Garland tells how Ray Charles was dismissed 'by jazz-loving, middle class blacks . . . as merely another hoarsely-shouting R & B man' (Garland, 1969, p.95; Shaw, 1980). Rock scholars of the early 1970s also tended to neglect rhythm & blues (exceptions are Charlie Gillette, 1970, and Arnold Shaw, 1970), though by 1977 this relationship had been established (Ewen, 1977; Hamm, 1979).

The central role of small radio stations in rhythm & blues is a topic that awaits investigation as are individual histories of rhythm & blues labels; the careers of figures like Chuck Berry, B. B. King, Little Richard, Fats Domino, Ray Charles, Muddy Waters and Dinah Washington; the relationship between rhythm & blues and gospel, soul and jazz; record producers; songwriters including Lincoln Chase, Rose Marie McCoy, Jeff Barry, Jessie Mae Robinson and many others; and the rhythm & blues revival of the late 1960s (Shaw, 1980).

Soul

During the 1960s and 1970s, blues lost popularity in northern cities, representing to African-Americans the resignation and complacency of a past era. The new mood, the aspirations and expectations of blacks, was expressed in a new musical genre – 'soul'. It originated in the mid-1950s with the songs of Ray Charles and soon superseded all other African-American styles in popularity. Michael Haralambos reported that more than 90 per cent of the music played on Chicago's WVON, Detroit's WCHB, and New York's WWRL was soul (1970). Soul music and the total 'soul' concept – including grits and greens, hog maws and potato pie – celebrated blackness and was seen as a validation of black values, thus became a symbol of racial solidarity for the African-American community.

The soul ethos was a natural consequence of several political events that have touched the lives of American blacks: the civil rights movement of the 1950s and 1960s under the leadership of the late Reverend Dr Martin Luther King Jr, the momentous Supreme Court decisions on school integration, the ghetto riots of the early 1960s, the assassinations of Dr King and of Malcolm X. These events brought the persistent problems of American blacks to the full attention of the white community. During this period, blacks sought a cultural revitalization, expressed in labels ('black is beautiful'), political slogans ('black power'), and group affiliations (Black Muslims). Soul lyrics affirmed these upsurgent feelings of black confidence and strength. While the blues commonly expressed a note of hopelessness (such as Albert King's 'I've been down so long it don't bother me'), soul conveys optimism. James Brown ('Soul Brother Number One') sings 'Say it loud, I'm Black, I'm proud'. The theme of 'Together we shall overcome', was echoed throughout soul: 'I got it', 'We're a winner', 'We're rolling on', 'Free at last' (Nettl and Myers, 1976).

Scholarly work on soul music began to appear in the late 1960s, just as the genre was losing popularity in favour of disco. General studies of soul music include P. Garland, *The Sound of Soul* (1969), R. Larkin, *Soul Music* (1970), A. Shaw, *The World of Soul* (1970), M. Haralambos, *Right on: from Blues to Soul in Black America* (1974), and G. Hirshey, *Nowhere to Run: the Story of Soul Music* (1984).

Jazz

Jazz, the classical music of African-Americans, is one of the major contributions to the 20th-century American musical scene. Jazz, composed and performed by trained musicians, is largely an urban phenomenon. Early jazz music has some of the characteristics of African music. The emphasis on rhythm and rhythmic instruments, the theme-and-variations structure reminiscent of call-and-response patterns with variations, the improvisation of variants by individuals in the ensemble, all these tie jazz closely with Africa. Another manifestation of George Pullen Jackson's 'white origin theory' is presented by H. O. Brun, who maintains in his *The Story of the Original Dixieland Jazz Band* (1960) that jazz was invented by whites. This theory was dismissed by Gunther Schuller (*Early Jazz*, 1968).

A comprehensive work on all aspects of jazz is *The New Grove Dictionary of Jazz* (London, 1988). For a summary of the field, see James Lincoln Collier, 'Jazz', in *The New Grove Dictionary of American Music* (1986). General surveys and histories include R. Harris, *Jazz* (1952, 5/1957), L. Feather, *The Book of Jazz: a Guide to the Entire Field* (1957, rev. 2/1965), and F. Tirro, *Jazz: a History* (1977). Researchers of jazz in particular cities or areas include F. Ramsey Jr, *Chicago Documentary: Portrait of a Jazz Era* (1944), S. B. Charters, *Jazz New Orleans: 1885–1957* (1958, rev. 2/1963), S. B. Charters and L. Kunstadt, *Jazz: a History of the New York Scene* (1962), R. Russell, *Jazz Style in Kansas City and the Southwest* (1971, 2/1973), J. Schiffman, *Uptown: the Story of Harlem's Apollo Theatre* (1971), and W. J. Schafer and R. B. Allen, *Brass Bands and New Orleans Jazz* (1977). Scholars of the jazz technique and repertory of individual instruments include A. McCarthy, *The Trumpet in Jazz* (1945), T. D. Brown, *A History and Analysis of Jazz Drumming to 1942* (1976), M. J. Summerfield, *The Jazz Guitar* (1978), M. Glaser and S. Grapelli, *Jazz Violin* (1981), B. Taylor, *Jazz Piano* (1982), K. Grime, *Jazz Voices* (1983) and M. Unterbrink, *Jazz Women at the Keyboard* (1983).

Jazz has a rich inventory of reference works. Bibliographies include those of A. P. Merriam and R. J. Benford (1954/*R*1970), H. Panassie and M. Gautier (1954), T. G. Everett (1976, 1977, 1979), D. Allen (1981), B. Hefele (1981) and E. Meadows (1981). Iconographic works are by A. Heerkens, *Jazz Picture Encyclopaedia* (1954), O. Keepnews and B. Grauer, *A Pictorial History of Jazz* (1955, rev. 4/1968), B. Case and S. Britt, *The Illustrated Encyclopedia of Jazz* (1978) and F. Driggs, *Black Beauty, White Heat: a Pictorial History of Classic Jazz, 1920–1950* (1982).

Some 25 periodicals are devoted largely to jazz, including *Down Beat* (1934–); *Jazz Magazine* (1954–); *Jazz Forum* (1967–); *Journal of Jazz Studies*, from 1982 *Annual Review of Jazz Studies* (1973/4–); and *Cadence* (1976–). Periodicals of interest to the jazz specialist include *Guitar Player* (1967–); *National Association of Jazz Educators: Newsletter*, later *NAJE Educator*, from 1980/81 *Jazz Educators Journal* (1968–); *Modern Drummer* (1977–); and *Directory of Female Jazz Performers* (1980–). Discographies include *Matrix* (1954–75), *Jazz Catalogue* (1960–), and *Journal of Jazz Discography* (1976–). Collections of essays and interviews of leading figures in the jazz world have been made by N. Shapiro and N. Hentoff, eds., *Hear me Talkin' to ya* (1955/*R*1966); M. James, *Ten Modern Jazzmen* (1960); R. Blesh, *Combo, USA: Eight Lives in Jazz* (1971); L. Feather, *From Satchmo to Miles* (1972); R. Gleason, *Celebrating the Duke* (1975); and Z. Knauss, ed., *Conversations with Jazz Musicians* (1977).

A new direction in jazz research during the 1980s and 1990s is the contribution made by black women; for example, S. Placksin, *American Women in Jazz, 1900 to the Present: their Words, Lives, and Music* (1982); L. Dahl, *Stormy Weather: the Music and Lives of a Century of Jazz Women* (1984); and Antoinette Handy, *Black Women in American Bands and Orchestras* (1981), which documents the role of women in the development of early jazz.

Post-civil-rights-movement era

During the post-civil-rights-movement era of the 1980s and 1990s, research on African-American music reflects new concerns. Samuel A. Floyd Jr puts the question, is research on black music 'a subspeciality of American music, or is it a separate field of study?' (1983, p.47). Most of the research on black-American music has been conducted by whites, a situation that has perhaps biased our understanding, particularly concerning the origins of various genres. Floyd finds that between 1879 and 1984, only 70 of the many hundreds of books on black music were written by blacks (1983, p.48). He cites the 'white origin theory', a 'slanted account of history', as the mandate for a separate field of black-music studies, a necessary force to counteract the denial of black achievement, the 'artistic counterpart of social denial' (p.48). Black-music history has been twisted 'under the guise of objective scholarship' (Floyd, 1983, p.48), a bias evident in statements such as Frank Tirro's disclaimer, 'Contrary to popular belief, jazz does not owe its existence to any one culture or race' (1977, p.5), or the claim of Michael Bane that black music died in the 1960s at the hands of British rock groups (1982; also Floyd, 1983, p.48).

African-American music is a lively and growing field. J. H. Kwabena Nketia, the renowned scholar of African music, looks towards the integration of African and African-American music studies, 'a new trend which sees the relationship between African and Afro-American music as dynamic and unbroken at the conceptual level in spite of the differences in materials to which these concepts are applied' (1973, p.9). Contemporary black-music studies 'vacillate between ethnomusicology and musicology, between anthropology and history, between music, folklore and even linguistics' (Nketia, 1973, p.12). Those who wish to claim expertise in this new integrated field will need, like Charles Keil and others, to gain field experience in Africa and the Americas. Other scholars, such as Samuel A. Floyd Jr, advocate the 'splintering' of disciplines and the establishment of separate departments of black studies. Floyd outlines nine areas for future research: music iconography studies, including photographs, paintings and sculpture; sources for out-of-print books and sound recordings; oral history studies; bibliographical studies of black musicians; critical studies of music by black composers; the role of music in the Harlem renaissance; manuscript collections; lexicographical studies; and studies of the negative black image, including 'coon songs' and 'blackface performances' (Floyd, pp.49–54).

The 1970s and 1980s have seen the consolidation of black research. The Society of Black Composers was founded in 1968, the Black Artist Group in 1972, *The Black Perspective in Music* in 1973, the *Black Music Research Newsletter* in 1978, and the *Black Music Research Journal* in 1980.

Bibliography

W. F. Allen, C. P. Ware and L. M. Garrison: *Slave Songs of the United States* (New York, 1867, repr. 1951, rev. 1965)

G. D. Pike: *The Singing Campaign for Ten Thousand Pounds* (London, 1874, rev. 3/1892 with suppl./ R1971) [with music]

J. B. T. Marsh: *The Story of the Jubilee Singers, with Their Songs* (London, 1875/R1969)

W. E. Barton: *Old Plantation Hymns* (Boston, MA, 1899); repr. in *The Social Implications of Early Negro Music in the United States*, ed. B. Katz (New York, 1969), 75–118

H. E. Krehbiel: *Afro-American Folksongs: a Study in Racial and National Music* (New York, 1913/ R1976)

J. W. Johnson and J. R. Johnson: *The Books of American Negro Spirituals* (New York, 1925–6/R1940, 1969)

G. B. Johnson and H. W. Odum: *The Negro and His Songs: a Study of Typical Negro Songs in the South* (Chapel Hill, NC, 1925, repr. 1964, 1968, 1972)

D. Scarborough: *On the Trail of Negro Folk-Songs* (Cambridge, MA, 1925, repr. 1963)

H. W. Odum and G. B. Johnson: *Negro Workaday Songs* (Chapel Hill, NC, 1926, repr. 1969, 1977) *Down Beat* (1934–)

Z. N. Hurston: *Mules and Men* (Philadelphia, PA, 1935, rev. 5/1978)

M. Cuney-Hare: *Negro Musicians and their Music* (Washington, DC, 1936/R1974)

A. Locke: *The Negro and His Music* (Washington, DC, 1936/R1968)

F. Ramsey Jr and C. E. Smith, eds.: *Jazzmen* (New York, 1939)

J. W. Work, ed.: *American Negro Songs: a Comprehensive Collection of 230 Folksongs, Religious and Secular* (New York, 1940/R1976)

A. Bontemps, ed.: *W. C. Handy: Father of the Blues: an Autobiography* (New York, 1941/R1970)

M. Herskovits: *The Myth of the Negro Past* (New York, 1941)

R. Ames: 'Art in Negro Folksong', *Journal of American Folklore*, lvi (1943), 241

G. P. Jackson: *White and Negro Spirituals: their Life Span and Kinship* (Locust Valley, NY, 1943/R1975)

F. Ramsey Jr: *Chicago Documentary: Portrait of a Jazz Era* (London, 1944)

A. McCarthy: *The Trumpet in Jazz* (London, 1945)

R. Blesh: *Shining Trumpets: a History of Jazz* (New York, 1946)

W. Sargent: *Jazz: Hot and Hybrid* (New York, 1946)

R. A. Waterman: '"Hot" Rhythm in Negro Music', *JAMS*, i (1948), 24

J. W. Work: 'Changing Patterns in Negro Folk Songs', *Journal of American Folklore*, lxii (1949), 136

R. Blesh and H. Janis: *They All Played Ragtime* (New York, 1950, rev. 4/1971)

E. R. Clark: 'Negro Folk Music in America', *Journal of American Folklore*, lxiv (1951), 281

R. A. Waterman: 'Gospel Hymns of a Negro Church in Chicago', *JIFMC*, iii (1951), 87

R. Harris: *Jazz* (London, 1952, 5/1957)

R. A. Waterman: 'African Influence on the Music of the Americas', *Acculturation in the Americas, Proceedings and Selected Papers of the XXIXth International Congress of Americanists*, ed. S. Tax (Chicago, IL, 1952, repr. 1967), 207

Z. W. George: *A Guide to Negro Music: an Annotated Bibliography of Negro Folk Music and Art Music by Negro Composers or Based on Negro Thematic Material* (diss., New York U., 1953)

T. Fletcher: *100 Years of the Negro in Show Business* (New York, 1954)

A. Heerkens: *Jazz Picture Encyclopedia* (Alkmaar, The Netherlands, 1954)

Jazz Magazine (1954–)

Matrix (1954–75)

A. P. Merriam and R. J. Benford: *A Bibliography of Jazz* (Philadelphia, PA, 1954/R1970)

H. Panassie and M. Gautier: *Dictionnaire du jazz* (Paris, 1954, 3/1980; Eng. trans. as *Guide to Jazz*, 1956/R1973)

O. Keepnews and B. Grauer: *A Pictorial History of Jazz* (New York, 1955, rev. 4/1968)

N. Shapiro and N. Hentoff, eds.: *Hear Me Talkin' to Ya* (New York, 1955/R1966)

L. Feather: *The Book of Jazz: a Guide to the Entire Field* (New York, 1957, rev. 2/1965)

S. B. Charters: *Jazz New Orleans: 1885–1957* (New York, 1958, rev. 2/1963)

P. Oliver: *Bessie Smith* (London, 1959)

H. O. Brun: *The Story of the Original Dixieland Jazz Band* (Baton Rouge, LA, 1960)

M. James: *Ten Modern Jazzmen* (London, 1960)

Jazz Catalogue (1960–)

P. Oliver: *Blues Fell This Morning: the Meaning of the Blues* (London, 1960/R1961, repr. 1963 as *The Meaning of the Blues*)

G. R. Ricks: *Some Aspects of the Religious Music of the United States Negro: an Ethnomusicological Study with Special Emphasis on the Gospel Tradition* (diss., Northwestern U., 1960)

S. B. Charters and L. Kunstadt: *Jazz: a History of the New York Scene* (Garden City, NY, 1962)

H. A. Kmen: 'Old Corn Meal: a Forgotten Urban Negro Folksinger', *Journal of American Folklore*, lxxv (1962), 29

S. B. Charters: *The Poetry of the Blues* (New York, 1963/R1970)

H. Courlander: *Negro Folk Music USA* (New York, 1963)

D. J. Epstein: 'Slave Music in the United States Before 1860: a Survey of Sources', *Music Library Association Notes*, xx (1963), 195, 377

——: 'Lucy McKim Garrison, American Musician', *New York Public Library Bulletin*, lxvii (1963), 529

J. Cohen and M. Seeger, eds.: *The New Lost City Ramblers Song Book* (New York, 1964)

J. Godrich and R. M. W. Dixon: *Blues and Gospel Records, 1902–1942* (Hatch End, London, 1963, rev. and enl. 3/1982 as *Blues and Gospel Records, 1902–1943*)

S. E. Hyman: 'American Negro Literature and the Folk Tradition', *The Promised End* (Cleveland, OH, 1963), 295

L. Jones: *Blues People: the Negro Experience in White America and the Music that Developed from it* (New York, 1963/R1967, 1980)

R. Ellison: 'Blues People', *Shadow and Act* (New York, 1964), 256

P. Bradford: *Born with the Blues: the True Story of the Pioneering Blues Singers and Musicians in the Early Days of Jazz* (New York, 1965)

P. Oliver: *Conversation with the Blues* (London, 1965)

M. Jackson: *Movin' On Up* (New York, 1966)

C. Keil: *Urban Blues* (Chicago, IL, 1966)

I. A. Baraka [LeRoi Jones]: *Black Music* (New York, 1967, repr. 1980)

R. Gruver: 'A Closer Look at the Blues', *Down Beat Yearbook* (1967), 50

B. Jackson, ed.: *The Negro and his Folklore in Nineteenth-Century Periodicals* (Austin, TX, 1967)

Guitar Player (1967–)

Jazz Forum (1967–)

P. Oliver: *Screening the Blues, Aspects of the Blues Tradition* (London, 1968; repr. as *Aspects of the Blues Tradition*, New York, 1970)

G. Schuller: *Early Jazz: its Roots and Musical Development* (New York, 1968)

W. H. Tallmadge: 'The Responsorial and Antiphonal Practice in Gospel Song', *EM*, xii (1968), 219

W. R. Ferris Jr: 'Records and the Delta Blues Tradition', *Keystone Folklore Quarterly*, xiv (1969), 158

P. Garland: *The Sound of Soul* (Chicago, IL, 1969)

R. Gruver: 'Blues as Poetry', *Down Beat Yearbook* (1969), 38

B. Katz, ed.: *The Social Implications of Early Negro Music in the United States [With Over One Hundred Fifty of the Songs, Many of them with their Music]* (New York, 1969)

M. Kolinski: 'Return of the Native', *Bulletin d'information No. 3, Premier Festival Cultural Panafrican* (May, 1969)

P. Oliver: *The Story of the Blues* (London, 1969/R1982)

H. Oster: *Living Country Blues* (Detroit, MI, 1969)

E. Sackheim and J. Shahn: *The Blues Line: a Collection of Blues Lyrics* (New York, 1969)

D.-R. de Lerma, ed.: *Black Music in our Culture* (Kent, OH, 1970)

R. M. W. Dixon and J. Godrich: *Recording the Blues* (New York, 1970)

W. R. Ferris Jr: 'Racial Repertories Among Blues Performers', *EM*, ix (1970), 439

C. Gillette: *The World of Soul: the Sound of the City* (New York, 1970)

A. Green: 'Hear These Beautiful Sacred Selections', *YIFMC*, ii (1970), 28

M. Haralambos: 'Soul Music and Blues: Their Meaning and Relevance in Northern United States Black Ghettos', *Afro-American Anthropology: Contemporary Perspectives*, ed. N. E. Whitten Jr and J. F. Szwed (New York, 1970), 367

R. Larkin: *Soul Music* (New York, 1970)

A. Lomax: 'The Homogeneity of African-Afro-American Musical Style', *Afro-American Anthropology*, ed. N. E. Whitten Jr and J. F. Szwed (New York, 1970), 181

P. Oliver: *Savannah Syncopators: African Retentions in the Blues* (London, 1970)

H. W. Mitchell: *Black Preaching* (Philadelphia, PA, 1970/R1979)

B. A. Rosenberg: *The Art of the American Folk Preacher* (New York, 1970)

——: 'The Formulaic Quality of Spontaneous Sermons', *Journal of American Folklore*, lxxxiii (1970), 3

T. Russell: *Blacks, Whites and Blues* (London, 1970)

A. Shaw: *The World of Soul: Black America's Contribution to the Pop Music Scene* (New York, 1970)

D. Stewart-Baxter: *Ma Rainey and the Classic Blues Singers* (London, 1970)

J. F. Szwed: 'Afro-American Musical Adaptation', *Afro-American Anthropology: Contemporary Perspectives*, ed. N. E. Whitten Jr and J. F. Szwed (New York, 1970), 219

P. Williams-Jones: 'Afro-American Gospel Music: a Brief Historical and Analytical Survey (1930–1970)', *Development of Materials for a One-Year Course in African Music for the General Undergraduate Student*, ed. V. Butcher and others (Washington, DC, 1970), 201

R. Blesh: *Combo: USA; Eight Lives in Jazz* (Philadelphia, PA, 1971)

W. R. Ferris Jr: *Blues from the Delta* (London, 1971, rev. 1978/R1984)

R. Gruver: 'The Origin of the Blues', *Down Beat Yearbook* (1971), 16

T. Heilbut: *The Gospel Sound: Good News and Bad Times* (New York, 1971/R1975)

L. W. Levine: 'Slave Songs and Slave Consciousness: an Exploration in Neglected Sources', *Anonymous Americans: Explorations in Nineteenth-Century Social History*, ed. T. K. Hareven (Englewood Cliffs, NJ, 1971), 99–130

R. Russell: *Jazz Style in Kansas City and the Southwest* (Berkeley, CA, 1971, 2/1973)

J. Schiffman: *Uptown: the Story of Harlem's Apollo Theatre* (New York, 1971)

E. Southern: *The Music of Black Americans: a History* (New York, 1971, rev. 2/1983)

——, ed.: *Readings in Black American Music* (New York, 1971, rev. 2/1983)

J. T. Titon: *Ethnomusicology of Downhome Blues Phonograph Records, 1926–1930* (diss., U. of Minnesota, 1971)

C. Albertson: *Bessie* (New York, 1972/R1980)

J. H. Cone: *The Spirituals and the Blues: an Interpretation* (New York, 1972/R1980)

L. F. Emery: *Black Dance in the United States from 1619 to 1970* (Palo Alto, CA, 1972)

L. G. Feather: *A History of the Blues* (New York, 1972)
——: *From Satchmo to Miles* (New York, 1972)
W. R. Ferris Jr: *A History of the Blues* (London, 1972)
——: 'The Rose Hill Service', *Mississippi Folklore Register*, vi (1972), 37
B. Jackson: *Wake Up Dead Man: Afro-American Worksongs from Texas Prisons* (Cambridge, MA, 1972)
B. Jones and B. L. Hawes: *Step it Down: Games, Plays, Songs, and Stories from the Afro-American Heritage* (New York, 1972)
J. Lovell Jr: *Black Song: the Forge and the Flame* (New York, 1972)
J. S. Roberts: *Black Music of Two Worlds* (New York, 1972)
C. K. Wolfe: 'Where the Blues is At: a Survey of Recent Research', *Popular Music and Society*, i (1972), 152
D. N. Baker: 'A Periodization of Black Music History', *Reflections on Afro-American Music*, ed. D. R. de Lerma (Kent, OH, 1973), 143
H. C. Boyer: *An Analysis of Black Church Music with Examples Drawn from Services in Rochester, New York* (diss., U. of Rochester, 1973)
D.-R. de Lerma, ed.: *Reflections on Afro-American Music* (Kent, OH, 1973)
D. E. Draper: *The Mardi Gras Indians: the Ethnomusicology of Black Associations in New Orleans* (diss., Tulane U., 1973)
D. J. Epstein: 'African Music in British and French America', *MQ*, lix (1973), 61–91
Journal of Jazz Studies, from 1982 *Annual Review of Jazz Studies* (1973/4–)
J. H. K. Nketia: 'The Study of African and Afro-American Music', *Black Perspective in Music*, i (1973), 7
J. D. B. Paul: *Music in Culture: Black Sacred Song Style – Slidell, Louisiana, Chicago, Illinois* (diss., Northwestern U., 1973)
E. Southern: 'Afro-American Musical Materials', *Black Perspective in Music*, i (1973), 24
R. Williams: *Preservation of the Oral Tradition of Singing Hymns in Negro Religious Music* (diss., Florida State U., 1973)
H. C. Boyer: 'Thomas A. Dorsey: Father of Gospel Music', *Black World*, xxiii (1974), 20
A. Duckett: 'An Interview with Thomas A. Dorsey', *Black World*, xxiii (1974), 4
M. Haralambos: *Right On: From Blues to Soul in Black America* (London, 1974)
I. V. Jackson: *Afro-American Gospel Music and its Social Setting with Special Attention to Roberta Martin* (diss., Wesleyan U., 1974)
P. K. Maultsby: *Afro-American Religious Music: 1619–1861* (diss., U. of Wisconsin, 1974) [Pt.1, 'Historical Development'; Pt.2, 'Computer Analysis of One Hundred Spirituals']
R. Gleason: *Celebrating the Duke* (Boston, MA, 1975)
L. Goreau: *Just Mahalia, Baby* (Waco, TX, 1975)
P. K. Maultsby: 'Music of Northern Independent Black Churches During the Ante-Bellum Period', *EM*, xix (1975), 401
——: 'Selective Bibliography: United States Black Music', *EM*, xix (1975), 421
P. Williams-Jones: 'Afro-American Gospel Music: a Crystallization of the Black Aesthetic', *EM*, xix (1975), 373
T. D. Brown: *A History and Analysis of Jazz Drumming to 1942* (diss., U. of Michigan, 1976)
D. J. Epstein: 'Documenting the History of Black Folk Music in the United States: a Librarian's Odyssey', *FAM*, xxiii (1976), 151
T. G. Everett: 'An Annotated List of English-language Jazz Periodicals', *Journal of Jazz Studies*, iii/2 (1976), 47; iv/1 (1977), 110; iv/2 (1977), 94; v/2 (1979), 99
Cadence (1976–)
Journal of Jazz Discography (1976–)
G. Marcus: *Mystery Train: Images of American Rock'n'Roll Music* (New York, 1976)
P. K. Maultsby: 'Black Spirituals: an Analysis of Textual Forms and Structures', *Black Perspective in Music*, iv (1976), 54
B. Nettl and H. Myers: *Folk Music in the United States: an Introduction* (Detroit, MI, 1976) [orig. pubd as *An Introduction to Folk Music in the United States* (1960)]
J. Wright and E. Southern: 'On Folk Music', *Black Perspective in Music*, iv (1976), 132
B. Boggs: 'Some Aspects of Worship in a Holiness Church', *New York Folklore*, iii (1977), 29
D. J. Dyen: *The Role of Shape Note Singing in the Musical Culture of Black Communities in Southeast Alabama* (diss., U. of Illinois, 1977)
D. J. Epstein: *Sinful Tunes and Spirituals: Black Folk Music to the Civil War* (Urbana, IL, 1977)
D. Ewen: *All the Years of American Popular Music* (Englewood Cliffs, NJ, 1977)
Z. Knauss, ed.: *Conversations with Jazz Musicians* (Detroit, MI, 1977)

431

L. W. Levine: *Black Culture and Black Consciousness* (New York, 1977)

N. Ruecker: *Jazz Index: Bibliography of Jazz Literature in Periodicals* (Frankfurt am Main, 1977–)

W. J. Schafer and R. B. Allen: *Brass Bands and New Orleans Jazz* (Baton Rouge, LA, 1977)

F. Tirro: *Jazz: a History* (New York, 1977)

J. T. Titon: *Early Downhome Blues: a Musical and Cultural Analysis* (Urbana, IL, 1977)

——: 'Thematic Pattern in Downhome Blues Lyrics: the Evidence on Commercial Phonograph Records Since World War II', *Journal of American Folklore*, xc (1977), 316

Modern Drummer (1977–)

J. Barnie: 'Formulaic Lines and Stanzas in the Country Blues', *EM*, xxii (1978), 457

B. Case and S. Britt: *The Illustrated Encyclopedia of Jazz* (London, 1978)

J. C. DjeDje: *American Black Spiritual and Gospel Songs from Southeast Georgia: a Comparative Study* (Los Angeles, CA, 1978)

D. Jarrett: 'The Singer and the Bluesman: Formulations of Personality in the Lyrics of the Blues', *Southern Folklore Quarterly*, xlii (1978), 31

A. Shaw: *Honkers and Shouters: the Golden Age of Rhythm and Blues* (New York, 1978)

M. J. Summerfield: *The Jazz Guitar: its Evolution and its Players* (Gateshead, 1978)

J. F. Szwed and R. D. Abrahams: *Afro-American Folk Culture: an Annotated Bibliography of Materials from North, Central, and South America and the West Indies* (Philadelphia, PA, 1978)

J. T. Titon: 'Every Day I Have the Blues: Improvisation and Daily Life', *Southern Folklore Quarterly*, xlii (1978), 85

H. C. Boyer: 'Contemporary Gospel Music', *Black Perspective in Music*, vii (1979), 5, 22

C. Hamm: *Yesterdays: Popular Songs in America* (New York, 1979)

S. Harris: *Blues Who's Who: a Biographical Dictionary of Blues Singers* (New Rochelle, NY, 1979)

I. V. Jackson: *Afro-American Religious Music: a Bibliography and a Catalogue of Gospel Music* (Westport, CT, 1979)

P. K. Maultsby: 'Influences and Retentions of West African Musical Concepts in U.S. Black Music', *Western Journal of Black Studies*, iii (1979), 197

H. Ottenheimer: 'Catharsis, Communication, and Evocation: Alternative Views of Socio-psychological Functions of Blues Singing', *EM*, xxiii (1979), 75

M. Ruppli: *Atlantic Records* (Westport, CT, 1979)

E. A. Berlin: *Ragtime: a Musical and Cultural History* (Berkeley, CA, 1980/R1984 with addenda)

J. Beyer: *Baton Rouge Blues* (Baton Rouge, LA, 1980)

M. V. Burnim: *The Black Gospel Music Tradition: Symbol of Ethnicity* (diss., Indiana U., 1980)

——: 'Gospel Music Research', *Black Music Research Journal*, i (1980), 63

B. Feintuch: 'A Noncommercial Black Gospel Group in Context: We Live the Life We Sing About', *Black Music Research Journal*, i (1980), 37

P. Oliver: 'Spiritual', *Grove 6*

M. Ruppli: *The Prestige Label: a Discography* (Westport, CT, 1980)

——: *The Savoy Label: a Discography* (Westport, CT, 1980)

H. T. Sampson: *Blacks in Blackface: a Source Book on Early Black Musical Shows* (Metuchen, NJ, 1980)

A. Shaw: 'Researching Rhythm & Blues', *Black Music Research Journal*, i (1980), 71

Black Music Research Journal (Nashville, TN, 1980–)

Directory of Female Jazz Performers (Kansas City, MO, 1980–)

D. Allen: *Bibliography of Discographies*, ii: *Jazz: 1935–1980* (New York, 1981)

S. B. Charters: *The Roots of the Blues: an African Search* (Boston, MA, 1981)

D.-R. DeLerma: *Bibliography of Black Music* (Westport, CT, 1981–4)

S. A. Floyd Jr: 'Toward a Philosophy of Black Music Scholarship', *Black Music Research Journal* (1981–2), 72

M. Glazer and S. Grapelli: *Jazz Violin* (New York, 1981)

A. D. Handy: *Black Women in American Bands and Orchestras* (Metuchen, NJ, 1981)

B. Hefele: *Jazz Bibliography* (Munich, Germany, 1981)

S. Lieb: *Mother of the Blues: a Study of Ma Rainey* (Amherst, MA, 1981)

E. Meadows: *Jazz Reference and Research Materials: a Bibliography* (New York, 1981)

E. J. Nelson: *Black American Folk Song: an Analytical Study with Implications for Music Education* (diss., Stanford U., 1981)

J. Skowronski: *Black Music in America: a Bibliography* (Metuchen, NJ, 1981)

W. H. Tallmadge: 'The Black in Jackson's White Spirituals', *Black Perspective in Music*, ix (1981), 139

J. T. Titon: *Downhome Blues Lyrics: an Anthology from the Post-World War II Era* (Boston, MA, 1981)

M. Bane: *White Boy Singin' the Blues: the Black Roots of White Rock* (Middlesex, 1982)

E. Brooks: *The Bessie Smith Companion: a Critical and Detailed Appreciation of the Recordings* (New York, 1982)

F. Driggs: *Black Beauty, White Heat: a Pictorial History of Classic Jazz, 1920–1950* (New York, 1982)

D. Evans: *Big Road Blues: Tradition and Creativity in the Folk Blues* (Berkeley, CA, 1982)

J. E. Hasse: *The Creation and Dissemination of Indianapolis Ragtime, 1897–1930* (diss., Indiana U., 1982)

S. Placksin: *American Women in Jazz, 1900 to the Present: their Words, Lives, and Music* (New York, 1982)

E. Southern: *Biographical Dictionary of Afro-American and African Musicians* (Westport, CT, 1982)

B. Taylor: *Jazz Piano* (Dubuque, IA, 1982)

W. Balliett: *Jelly Roll, Jabbo and Fats* (New York, 1983)

D. J. Epstein: 'A White Origin for the Black Spiritual? An Invalid Theory and How it Grew', *American Music*, i (1983), 53

S. A. Floyd Jr: 'On Black Music Research', *Black Music Research Journal* (1983), 46

—— and M. J. Reisser: *Black Music in the United States: an Annotated Bibliography of Selected Reference and Research Material* (Millwood, NY, 1983)

K. Grime: *Jazz Voices* (London, 1983)

B. Jones and J. Stewart: *For the Ancestors: Autobiographical Memories* (Urbana, IL, 1983)

M. Ruppli: *The Chess Labels: a Discography* (Westport, CT, 1983)

M. Taft: *Blues Lyric Poetry: an Anthology* (New York, 1983)

——: *Blues Lyric Poetry: a Concordance* (New York, 1983)

M. Unterbrink: *Jazz Women at the Keyboard* (Jefferson, NC, 1983)

T. Brooks: *America's Black Musical Heritage* (Englewood Cliffs, NJ, 1984)

L. Dahl: *Stormy Weather: the Music and Lives of a Century of Jazz Women* (New York, 1984)

G. Hirshey: *Nowhere to Run: the Story of Soul Music* (New York, 1984)

P. Oliver: *Songsters and Saints: Vocal Traditions on Race Records* (New York, 1984)

D. Toop: *The Rap Attack: African Jive to New York Hip* (Boston, MA, 1984)

M. V. Burnim: 'Culture Bearer and Tradition Bearer: an Ethnomusicologist's Research on Gospel Music', *EM*, xxix (1985), 432

J. E. Hasse, ed.: *Ragtime: its History, Composers, and Music* (New York, 1985)

I. V. Jackson, ed.: *More than Dancing: Essays on Afro-American Music and Musicians* (Westport, CT, 1985)

M. Ruppli: *The King Labels: a Discography* (Westport, CT, 1985)

T. Smith: 'Chanted Prayer in Southern Black Churches', *Southern Quarterly*, xxiii (1985), 70

S. M. Stone: *Song Composition, Transmission, and Performance Practice in an Urban Black Denomination, the Church of God and Saints of Christ* (diss., Kent State U., 1985)

R. Crawford: 'On Two Traditions of Black Music Research', *Black Music Research Journal* (1986), 1

J. C. DjeDje: 'Change and Differentiation: the Adoption of Black American Gospel Music in the Catholic Church', *EM*, xxx (1986), 223

S. A. Floyd Jr and M. J. Reisser: 'On Researching Black Music in California: a Preliminary Report about Sources and Resources', *Black Music Research Journal*, ix (1989), 109

3: HISPANIC-AMERICAN MUSIC

HELEN MYERS

The USA has assimilated from Spain and Portugal, Mexico and the Caribbean, and Central and South America a variety of Hispanic musical traditions, from the Spanish Jesuit missions of the Southwest, dating back to the explorations in mid-16th century to the urban music of newly arrived Hispanic Caribbean immigrants to the eastern ports, Miami and New York City. Traditional Portuguese music is preserved in New England as are remnants in Idaho of Basque traditions from the Spanish Pyrenees. This interesting and complex field awaits extensive study. Broad summaries have been compiled by Bruno Nettl and myself, *Folk Music in the United States* (1976, Chapter 7, 'Hispanic-American Folk Music'), Gilbert Chase, *The Music of Spain* (1959, Chapter 17, 'Hispanic Music in the Americas) and Gerard Béhague, *The New Grove Dictionary of American Music* (1986, 'Hispanic-American Music'). Bibliographic and reference aids are in M. Simmons's *A Bibliography of the Romance and Related Forms in Spanish America* (1963).

The oldest Hispanic tradition, of the Southwest and California, dates back some 400 years to the explorations of Spanish conquistadores in Texas, New Mexico, Arizona, Southern (Alta) California and as far north as Colorado. By the early 19th century, 21 missions were established along the California coast, each with a thriving music life based on the liturgical services of the Catholic Church (Summers, 1980). During the 16th and 17th centuries the Spanish Jesuits built schools, libraries and missions, taught music to Native American peoples, and were first in the New World to print books with music. The musical heritage of the California missions, including plainsong, some 24 complete cycles of the Ordinary, individual mass movements, settings of the Proper, Psalms, canticles and hymns, has been investigated by O. da Silva (1941), M. Geiger (1959, 1965), N. Benson (1969–70), T. Göllner (1970), R. Stevenson (1970, 1982), W. Summers (1976, 1977, 1980, 1981, 'Santa Barbara Mission', 1981, 'Spanish Music in California') and G. A. Harshbarger (1985). A bibliographic reference guide to this Mission material has been edited by M. Crouch, W. Summers, and K. Lueck-Michaelson (1976).

Lota May Spell (1885–1972), librarian in the Latin American section, University of Texas, was a prolific writer on the colonial music of Texas and Mexico. Her doctoral dissertation, *Musical Education in North America During the Sixteenth and Seventeenth Centuries* (1923), deals primarily with Mexico but also treats musical education in the French and English colonies. Her work on the Hispanic cultures of the Southwest includes 'Music in the Early Southwest' (1930) and 'The Contribution of the Southwest to American Music' (1931) and a major historical work, *Music in Texas* (1936). According to Spell's archival research, the first music teacher in the USA was one Franciscan, Cristóbal de Quiñones, who probably worked in New Mexico between 1598 and 1609.

Much of the American Southwest remained under Spanish rule until the 18th century, and this region retains powerful cultural bonds with Mexico. Mexican immigrants who flood across the border each year continually renew and revitalize the Hispanic-American repertory. Mexican genres common in the Southwest include the *romance, corrido, décima, verso, cancione, indita, alabado* and *truvo* – mostly strophic forms based on the *copla*, a verse of four octasyllabic rhyming lines. *Décimas* and *corridos* flourished in 19th- and 20th-century Mexico, especially during the Revolution (1910–30), when they were sold as broadsides and transmitted information about current events.

The earliest sound recordings in the Southwest were made on wax cylinder by Charles Fletcher Lummis (1859–1928), founder of the Southwest Society of the American Institute of Archaeology and author of the pioneering study of Southwest Hispanic culture, *The Land of Poco Tiempo* (1906). By 1905 he had recorded some 400 *romances* and other Hispanic folk songs at fiestas and folk gatherings. He collaborated with the composer Arthur Farwell who transcribed and annotated this material; 200 of these cylinders survive and are held at the Southwest Museum, Los Angeles, which Lummis founded (Newmark, 1950; Fiske and Lummis, 1975; Fleming, 1981).

An early collection of popular Hispanic songs and lyrics from the Southwest is by Eleanor Hague (1917). Marginal survivals of Spanish folklore in New Mexico have been documented by Aurelio M. Espinosa, particularly some ten archaic *romances tradicionales* ('traditional ballads') in 27 versions (1926). Juan B. Rael (1940) presents seven versions of one New Mexican *entrega de novios*, a traditional wedding song, accompanied by violin and guitar, comprising up to 24 *coplas*. Studies of the *corrido* and the *romance* include Auturo L. Campa's collections from New Mexico (1933, 1946) and Terrence L. Hansen's anthology of 33 *corridos* from southern California (1959). The folk songs of the Lower Rio Grande Border ('Lower Border' or 'Border') have been collected by Américo Paredes, a Mexican scholar who began collecting around 1920 (1958, 1976; Paredes and Foss, 1966). A *Texas-Mexican Cancionero* contains a selection of 66 Hispanic songs that 'record an important aspect of the Mexican-American's long struggle to preserve his identity and affirm his rights as a human being' (1976, p.xviii). Paredes has also documented the *décima* tradition in Texas (1958, 1966, 'The *Décima* on the Texas-Mexican Border', 1966, 'The *Décima Cantada*'). Terrence L. Hansen gives 33 *corrido* texts with music and English translations in 'Corridos in Southern California' (1959).

Music of Mexican-American 'Chicanos' has been studied by Manuel Peña, who analysed the *orquesta* repertory as a 'rite of intensification . . . wherein . . . the dances . . . served to reinforce the ethnic identity and values of Chicanos who otherwise lived in an American society known to be hostile to Mexicans and their culture generally' (1987, p.230). He distinguishes 'quality music' (*música moderna, música de orquesta, música buena*) of middle-class Mexican-American orchestras from 'vulgar music' (*música ranchera, música de conjunto, música arrabalera*), preferred by working-class audiences (1980, 1985, 1987).

Since 1900, thousands of Hispanics from the Caribbean have flooded to urban areas of the eastern USA, where they have maintained many folk genres, and introduced over the decades new Afro-Cuban dance styles: the rumba in the 1930s, the samba in the 1940s, the mambo and cha-cha-cha in the 1950s, the bossa nova in the 1960s and salsa in the 1970s. The tango was introduced to the USA via Broadway in 1913 (Béhague, 1986, p.398). Early studies of Hispanic music in American cities include two interesting but limited studies, by Carlota Garfias, 'Mexican Folklore Collected in New York City' (1938), and Shulamith Rybak, 'Puerto Rican Children's Songs in New York' (1958). A more ambitious project was undertaken by Adelaida Reyes-Schramm (1975) on the role of music in the interaction of African-Americans and Puerto Rican Hispanos of East Harlem. In the analysis of very diverse data, from Pentacostal and Catholic services to informal conga drumming sessions, Reyes-Schramm was particularly concerned to develop appropriate strategies for research in the urban environment.

Music of the New England Portuguese has little documentation. A useful early article is 'Portuguese Folk-Songs from Provincetown, Cape Cod, Mass.' by Maud Cuney-Hare (1938), which includes some 15 *fados, carrasquinha*, and *chamarrita* with Portuguese texts, English translations, and cultural notes. For the modern traditions of this community, graduate students in New England universities have made preliminary research (Rehm, 1975).

Bibliography

C. F. Lummis: *The Land of Poco Tiempo* (New York, 1906)

A. M. Espinosa: 'Romancero nuevomejicano', *Revue hispanique*, xxxiii (1915), 446–560; xl (1917), 215; xli (1917), 678

E. Hague, ed.: *Spanish-American Folk-Songs* (New York, 1917)

C. F. Lummis and A. Farwell: *Spanish Songs of Old California* (Los Angeles, CA, 1923, repr. 1929)

L. M. Spell: *Musical Education in North America During the Sixteenth and Seventeenth Centuries* (diss., U. of Texas, 1923)

A. M. Espinosa: 'Los romances tradicionales en California', *Homenaje ofrecido a Menéndez Pidal*, i (Madrid, 1925), 299

L. M. Spell: 'Mexico is the Cradle of American Music', *The Texas Outlook*, ix/3 (1925), 1

A. M. Espinosa: 'Spanish Folk-Lore in New Mexico', *New Mexico Historical Review*, i (1926), 135

L. M. Spell: 'Music Teaching in New Mexico in the Seventeenth Century', *New Mexico Historical Review*, ii/1 (1927), 27

J. González: 'Tales and Songs of the Texas-Mexicans', *Man, Bird and Beast*, ed. J. F. Dobie (Austin, TX, 1930), 86–116

L. M. Spell: 'Music in the Early Southwest: Some Sidelights on the Beginnings of Music in a Colorful Region', *The Texas Monthly*, v (1930), 63

——: *The Contribution of the Southwest to American Music* (Austin, TX, 1931)

A. L. Campa: *The Spanish Folksong in the Southwest* (Albuquerque, NM, 1933)

P. S. Taylor: 'Songs of the Mexican Migration', *Puro Mexicano*, ed. J. F. Dobie (Austin, TX, 1935), 221

Sister Joan of Arc: *Catholic Music and Musicians in Texas* (San Antonio, TX, 1936)

L. M. Spell: *Music in Texas: a Survey of One Aspect of Cultural Progress* (Austin, TX, 1936/R1973)

C. Garfias: 'Mexican Folklore Collected in New York City', *Journal of American Folklore*, li (1938), 83

M. C. Hare: 'Portuguese Folk-songs from Provincetown, Cape Cod, Mass.', *MQ*, xxiv (1938), 35

A. B. McGill: 'Old Mission Music', *MQ*, xxiv (1938), 186

E. Grenet: *Popular Cuban Music* (Havana, Cuba, 1939)

J. B. Rael: 'New Mexican Wedding Songs', *Southern Folklore Quarterly*, iv (1940), 55

G. Chase: *The Music of Spain* (New York, 1941, rev. 2/1959)

O. F. Da Silva, ed.: *Mission Music of California* (Los Angeles, CA, 1941)

G. Durán: *14 Traditional Spanish Songs from Texas* (Washington, DC, 1942) [transcr. from recordings made by J. A. Lomax and others]

A. L. Campa: *Spanish Folk Poetry in New Mexico* (Albuquerque, NM, 1946)

M. Newmark: 'Charles Fletcher Lummis', *Historical Society of Southern California Quarterly*, xxxii/1 (1950), 44

J. B. Rael: *The New Mexican Alabado* (Stanford, CA, 1951)

M. W. Hiester: *Los Paisanos: Folklore of the Texas-Mexicans of the Lower Rio Grande Valley* (diss., U. of Texas, 1954)

V. T. Mendoza: *El corrido mexicano* (Mexico City, 1954)

J. D. Robb: *Hispanic Folk Songs of New Mexico* (Albuquerque, NM, 1954)

——: 'The Music of *Los Pastores*', *Western Folklore*, xvi (1957), 263

M. E. Simmons: *The Mexican Corrido as a Source for Interpretive Study of Modern Mexico (1870–1950)* (Bloomington, IN, 1957)

A. Paredes: *With His Pistol in His Hand, a Border Ballad and its Hero* (Austin, TX, 1958)

S. Rybak: 'Puerto Rican Children's Songs in New York', *Midwest Folklore*, viii (1958), 5

M. J. Geiger: *The Life and Times of Fray Junipero Serra OFM; or The Man Who Never Turned Back, 1713–1784, a Biography* (Washington, DC, 1959)

T. L. Hansen: 'Corridos in Southern California', *Western Folklore*, xviii/3–4 (1959), 203, 295

S. G. Armistead and J. H. Silverman: 'Hispanic Balladry Among Sephardic Jews of the West Coast', *Western Folklore*, xix (1960), 229

M. E. Simmons: *A Bibliography of the Romance and Related Forms in Spanish America* (Bloomington, IN, 1963)

L. B. Spiess: 'Benavides and Church Music in New Mexico in the Early 17th Century', *JAMS*, xvii (1964), 144

M. J. Geiger: *Mission Santa Barbara 1782–1965* (Santa Barbara, CA, 1965)

A. Paredes: 'The Décima on the Texas-Mexican Border: Folksong as an Adjunct to Legend', *Journal of the Folklore Institute*, iii (1966), 154

A. Paredes and G. Foss: 'The Décima Cantada on the Texas-Mexican Border: Four Examples', *Journal of the Folklore Institute*, iii (1966), 91

N. A. Benson: 'Music in the California Missions: 1602–1848', *Student Musicologists at Minnesota*, iii (1968–9), 128; iv (1970–71), 104

R. B. Stark, T. M. Pearce and R. Cobos: *Music of the Spanish Folk Plays in New Mexico* (Santa Fe, NM, 1969)

T. Göllner: 'Two Polyphonic Passions from California's Mission Period', *Yearbook for Inter-American Musical Research*, vi (1970), 67

R. M. Stevenson: *Renaissance and Baroque Musical Sources in the Americas* (Washington, DC, 1970)

D. D. Rogers: 'A Memorial Tribute to Lota May Spell (1885–1972)', *Yearbook for Inter-American Musical Research*, x (1974), 194

T. L. Fiske and K. Lummis: *Charles F. Lummis: the Man and his West* (Norman, OK, 1975)

M. Geiger: 'Harmonious Notes in Spanish California', *Southern California Quarterly*, lvii (1975), 243

B. Rehm: *A Study of the Cape Verdean Morna in New Bedford, Massachusetts* (diss., Brown U., 1975)

A. Reyes-Schramm: *The Role of Music in the Interaction of Black Americans and Hispanos in New York City's East Harlem* (diss., Columbia U., 1975)

M. Crouch, with W. Summers and K. Lueck-Michaelson, eds.: 'An Annotated Bibliography and Commentary Concerning Mission Music of Alta California from 1769 to 1834: in Honor of the American Bicentennial', *CMc*, xxii (1976), 88

B. Nettl and H. Myers: *Folk Music in the United States: an Introduction* (Detroit, MI, 1976) [orig. pubd as *An Introduction to Folk Music in the United States*, 1960]

A. Paredes: *A Texas-Mexican Cancionero: Folksongs of the Lower Border* (Urbana, IL, 1976)

P. Sonnischen: 'Chicano Music', *The Folk Music Source Book* (New York, 1976)

W. Summers: 'The Organs of Hispanic California', *Music (AGO-RCCO) Magazine*, x (1976), 50

——: 'Music of the California Missions: an Inventory and Discussion of Selected Printed Music Books Used in Hispanic California, 1769–1836', *Soundings, University of California Libraries, Santa Barbara*, ix (1977), 13

D. W. Dickey: *The Kennedy Corridos: a Study of the Ballads of a Mexican/American Hero* (Austin, TX, 1978)

R. B. Stark, ed.: *Music of the Bailes in New Mexico* (Santa Fe, NM, 1978)

J. S. Roberts: *The Latin Tinge: the Impact of Latin American Music on the United States* (New York, 1979)

M. H. Peña: 'Ritual Structure in a Chicano Dance', *Latin American Music Review*, i (1980), 47

J. D. Robb: *Hispanic Folk Music of New Mexico and the Southwest: a Self-Portrait of a People* (Norman, OK, 1980)

W. Summers: 'Orígenes hispanos de la música misional de California', *Revista musical chilena*, cxlix–cl (1980), 34

R. E. Fleming: *Charles F. Lummis* (Boise, ID, 1981)

W. Summers: 'Santa Barbara Mission Archive Library', *Resources of American Music History*, ed. D. W. Krummel (Urbana, IL, 1981), 41

——: 'Spanish Music in California, 1769–1840: a Reassessment', *IMSCR*, xii (Kassel, 1981), 360

L. Warkentin: 'The Rise and Fall of Indian Music in the California Missions', *Latin American Music Review*, ii (1981), 45

R. Stevenson: 'California Music, 1806–24: Russian Reportage', *Inter-American Music Review*, iv/2 (1982), 59

G. A. Harshbarger: *The Mass in G by Ignacio Jerusalem and its Place in the California Mission Music Repertory* (diss., U. of Washington, 1985)

M. H. Peña: 'From *Ranchero* to *Jaitón*: Ethnicity and Class in Texas-Mexican Music (Two Styles in the Form of a Pair)', *EM*, xxix (1985), 29

——: *The Texas-American Conjunto: History of a Working-Class Music* (Austin, TX, 1985)

G. Béhague: 'Hispanic-American Music', *The New Grove Dictionary of American Music* (London, 1986)

M. Peña: 'Music for a Changing Community: Three Generations of a Chicano Family *Orquesta*', *Latin American Music Review*, viii (1987), 230

4: BRITISH-AMERICAN FOLK MUSIC

HELEN MYERS

World War II did not bring to American scholarship the interruption it forced on Europe. Distanced from the theatres of war, American and Canadian research continued, but at a diminished pace. By mid-century, Anglo-American folk-song scholarship had achieved if not maturity, at least adolescence, with regional collections – some systematic and scholarly, some amateur and eclectic – filling the shelves of municipal libraries, archives, and state folklore societies. The state of folk music research during the war years is reflected in *Funk and Wagnalls Standard Dictionary of Folklore, Mythology, and Legend* (1949–50), including MacEdward Leach's entry on the ballad, and George Herzog's on song. A useful review of the scholarship of this generation is in D. K. Wilgus's *Anglo-American Folksong Scholarship since 1898* (1959).

The years after World War II brought 'Americanization', the homogenization of American culture, particularly through radio and television. Recording technology served on the one hand to preserve traditions and on the other to accelerate their change. Through magnetic tape and LP records, folk songs were transformed and restyled into a household commodity. Popular arrangements of plantation songs and pseudo-cowboy songs were disseminated through the commercial disc. Some scholars derided the commercial folk records as corrupt debased renditions, others welcomed them as indigenous musical documents.

The Archive of American Folk Song at the Library of Congress, established in 1928, was renamed the Archive of Folk Song in 1956 and then the Archive of Folk Culture in 1981, throughout remaining a centre for study, collection, and dissemination. From 1963, the Recorded Sound Section has held commercial recordings. In the bicentennial year, 1976, the Library issued 15 LP recordings under the title *Folk Music in America* (ed. Richard K. Spottswood) drawing on field and commercial recordings.

Reference materials, checklists, catalogues

From the 1930s to the 1950s, priority in folk-song research was given to the preparation of checklists, bibliographies, discographies and guides to this material: the bibliographical appendix of G. H. Gerould's *The Ballad of Tradition* (1932); Alan Lomax and Sidney Robertson Cowell's brief guide to studies and collections, *American Folk Song and Folk Lore: a Regional Bibliography* (n.d.) [1942], now dated and somewhat rare; Mellinger E. Henry's *A Bibliography for the Study of American Folk-Songs* (n.d.) [1937], marred by lack of a subject index; and Charles Haywood's *A Bibliography of North American Folklore and Folksong* (1951), with more than 40,000 entries (mostly unannotated) on topics including the ballad, dance and song games, African-American and European-American folk music, work songs, spirituals and American Indian music (organized in ten cultural areas).

During the 1940s, numerous regional bibliographies of state folklore collections were prepared including such titles as Helen H. Flanders's 'Index of Ballads and Folk-Songs in the Archive of Vermont Folk-Songs at Smiley House, Springfield, Vt.' (1940); E. C. Kirkland's 'A Check List of the Titles of Tennessee Folksongs' (1946); Austin E. Fife's *A Bibliography of the Archives of the Utah Humanities Research Foundation* (1947); and A. K. Davis's *Folk-Songs of Virginia: a Descriptive Index and Classification* (1949). Later bibliographies, and checklists include Bruce A. Rosenberg's checklist of WPA holdings in West Virginia (1969), Vance Randolph's Ozark bibliography (1972), and Jennifer Post Quinn's index of the Flanders Ballad Collection at Middlebury College, Vermont (1983).

Regional studies

The regional collecting of British-American song had its heyday during the 1930s and 1940s, when a veritable army of folklorists set out to the rural areas to document American folklife (*see* Chapter II, 'North America'). The shelves of state folklore societies were soon filled with hundreds of collections – recorded on cylinder, wire or early disc, or simply notated with pad and pencil – from amateurs and professionals alike.

Regional collecting has continued, at a slower pace, into the 1990s. Recent collections from Appalachia include Thomas G. Burton and Ambrose N. Manning's transcriptions of Tennessee ballads (1967); Jean Ritchie's autobiography with texts and tunes of 42 songs (1955); Anne Warner's collection of some 1000 North Carolina songs recorded during the 1930s (1984); Newman Ivey White's seven-volume edition of the Frank C. Brown Collection from North Carolina (1952–64), including 49 Child ballads, and other types of courting, drinking and gambling, play-party, dance, occupational and children's songs; and Charles K. Wolfe's Kentucky collection (1982), including hillbilly music, string band, swing, gospel, bluegrass, honky-tonk and contemporary Nashville.

Collections from the Middle Atlantic States include Walter E. Boyer, Albert F. Buffington, and Don Yoder's anthology from Mahantongo Valley, Pennsylvania (1951); Norman Cazden, Herbert Haufrecht, and Norman Studer's Catskill collection (1982, *Folk Songs of the Catskills*; 1982, *Notes and Sources for Folk Songs of the Catskills*); Charles H. Kaufman's study of the 'Jackson Whites' of the Ramapo Mountains (1967); and Harold W. Thompson's anthology of texts from the Stevens-Douglass Manuscript of Western New York, 1841–56 (1958). Among New England collections are Helen Hartness Flanders's four volumes of New England ballads (1960–65, compiled in the 1930s); and Edward D. Ives's Maine collection (1966).

Midwestern studies include Ben Gray Lumpkin's collection from the Cummings family of Beatrice, Nebraska (1972); Harry B. Peters's Wisconsin anthology with material from a 1919 journal (1977); and Roger L. Welsch's pioneer songs from Nebraska (1967). Song collections from the southern and southwestern states include Ray B. Browne's study of the dissemination of

Alabama folk lyrics (1979); Ethel Moore and Chauncey O. Moore's Oklahoma songs of British, Scots, and American origin (1964); William A. Owens's collection from northeastern Texas (1950, 1983); Vance Randolph's Ozark work (1972, 1982); and Art Rosenbaum's collection from North Georgia (1983). Collections from the western states include Thomas E. Cheney's study of Rocky Mountain Mormon songs (1968); Lester Hubbard's 250 ballads from Utah, many from Mormons (1961); and Ben Gray Lumpkin's examples of Colorado folk songs (1960).

Ballad research

Ballad studies have overshadowed research on such other genres of Anglo-American song as work songs, folk lyrics, the play-party song, and religious songs including the spiritual. Reference aids for ballad scholarship from the post-World War II era include Tristram P. Coffin's *The British Traditional Ballad in North America* (1950), focussing on plot and poetic structure, and George Malcolm Laws's critical and bibliographical study, *Native American Balladry* (1950; also Laws's *American Balladry from British Broadsides*, 1957). Indices and reference aids for individual genres are in Helen Cushing's *Children's Song Index* (1936) and the comparative notes and bibliography in Annabel Morris Buchanan's *Folk Hymns of America* (1938). At mid-century, the emphasis in scholarly work was still very much on collection, hence, guides and lists of 'finders' for collectors were published, including Althea Lea McLenden's 'A Finding List of Play-Party Games' (1944); and Fletcher Collins's 'An Aid in the Discovery of Folksongs: a List of Finders for Traditional Ballads, Songs, and Play-Parties in the Southeast' (1941). Indices of place names, subject matter and other formulae were also designed to aid the collector, such as those of Bartlett Jere Whiting, 'Proverbial Material in the Popular Ballad' (1934); W. E. Richmond, *Place Names in the English and Scottish Popular Ballads and their American Variants* (1948); Stith Thompson, in his six-volume *Motif Index* (1932–36); and Coffin, 'An Index to Borrowing in the Child Ballads of America' (1949).

Scholars also devoted their attention to the history, classification and analysis of folk song. Textual variations prompted different analyses that were used to support opposing theories of ballad origin and evolution. The overriding concern for the purists among folk-song scholars was tallying the number of Child ballads recovered in the various collections (ballads included in the collection by F. J. Child, *The English and Scottish Popular Ballads*, 1882–98/R1956, 1962, 1965). Altogether nearly half of the 305 in Child have been reported in the USA, but some are merely 'traces', others cases of mistaken identity. The mere existence of the Child canon forced on scholarship an artificial classification between Child and non-Child material, reflected in many publications. Several early collections were devoted to songs of the Child canon: Reed Smith, *South Carolina Ballads* (1928); Arthur Kyle Davis Jr, *Traditional Ballads of Virginia* (1929) and *More Traditional Ballads of Virginia* (1960); Phillips Barry, Fannie Hardy Eckstorm and Mary Winslow Smyth, eds., *British Ballads from Maine* (1929); and Dorothy Scarborough, *A Song Catcher in the Southern Mountains* (1937). Scholars have compared the texts of British and American ballads and broadsides, for example, David Mason

Greene's study 'The Bold Soldier' and Norman Cazden's 'The Bold Soldier of Yarrow'. The rhythmic aspects of the Child ballads have been investigated by Donald M. Winkelman (1966). In *The British Traditional Ballads in North America* (1950), Coffin includes a bibliography of American scholarship on Child ballads.

Occupational songs

Collections, anthologies and surveys of occupational genres include studies of cowboy songs such as Austin E. and Alta S. Fife's anthology (1969); Katie Lee's history of the American cowboy including texts and tunes (1976); cowboy-singer Glenn Ohrlin's collection of some 100 songs (1973); Jim Bob Tinsley's anthology with contextual notes, tunes, and guitar chords (1981); and cowboy-singer John I. White's personal account of life in the West (1975). Lumberjack studies include E. C. Beck's *Lore of the Lumber Camps* (1948), Edith Fowke's anthology from Ontario and Quebec (1970) and Edward D. Ives's biography of Maine lumberjack, Joe Scott (1867–1918) (1978). Collections of miners' songs include those of J. T. Adams, *Death in the Dark: a Collection of Factual Ballads of American Mine Disasters* (1941); Duncan Emrich, 'Songs of the Western Miners' (1942); Wayland D. Hand, Charles Cutts, Robert C. and Betty Wylder, 'Songs of the Butte Miner' (1950); and Archie Green, *Only a Miner*, a highly regarded study with a portrait through song texts of mining life 1925–70 (1972; also see Green, 1969). George G. Korson compiled anthologies of Pennsylvania Dutch mining songs (1960), of the repertory of the anthracite industry (1938/*R*1964), and of the repertory of the bituminous industry (1943/*R*1965). Studies of railroad songs include Sterling Sherwin and H. K. McClintock's *Railroad Songs of Yesterday* (1943); Norm Cohen's historical account based on commercial recordings, 1920–50; and Katie Letcher Lyle's collection of songs and stories of railroad disasters (1983). Collections of sea songs and shanties include Mary Wheeler's *Steamboatin' Days: Folksongs of the River Packetboat Era* (1944); Joanna Colcord's *Roll and Go: Songs of American Sailormen* (1924, 2/1938/*R*1964); George G. Carey's 'songbag' (1976); Stan Hugill's edition of 117 songs relating to sailing ships, 1818–1920 (1977); and John Holstead Mead's collection of shanty (on duty) and fo'c'sle (off duty) songs (1973) (see Taylor, 1953, p.104).

British-American children's songs, rhymes, sung riddles and teasing and counting games have been a popular subject of investigation since the 1930s. There are collections by Carl Withers, *A Rocket in My Pocket* (1948); Ruth Seeger, *American Folk Songs for Children* (1948), a popularized anthology; B. A. Botkin, *The American Play-Party Song* (1937); Eugenia Millard, 'Sticks and Stones: Children's Teasing Rhymes' (1945); and Dorothy Mills Howard, 'The Rhythms of Ball-Bouncing and Ball-Bouncing Rhymes' (1949); also by Barbara Castagna, a collection of jump rope, jeering and counting songs from New Rochelle (1969); Joseph S. Hall, a study of the play-party song in the Great Smoky Mountains (1941); E. Henry Mellinger, a collection of 24 nursery rhymes (1934); Myra E. Hull, play-party songs from Kansas (1938); and Florence Warnick, a study of the play-party in Western Maryland (1941).

Musical analysis

The post-war years brought deeper analysis of the music of the ballads. Systems for the classification of tunes according to numerical, alphabetical and various other arrangements were devised by researchers: S. B. Hustvedt, *A Melodic Index of Child's Ballad Tunes* (1936); W. J. Entwistle, 'Notation for Ballad Melodies' (1940); S. P. Bayard, 'Ballad Tunes and the Hustvedt Indexing Method' (1942); B. H. Bronson, 'Folksong and the Modes' (1946); and Bronson, 'Mechanical Help in the Study of Folk Song' (1949) (see Taylor, 1953, p.110). George List suggests a method for indexing ballad tunes, omitting the first stanza, which is generally the least stable (1963).

The dean of ballad-tune study is Bertrand Harris Bronson, whose *The Traditional Tunes of the Child Ballads with their Texts, According to the Extant Records of Great Britain and America*, in four volumes (1959–72), treats 246 of the Child ballads and is the musical complement to Child's anthology of texts (1882). Bronson arranges the songs according to their order in the Child canon and accompanies each with an introductory headnote, comments on sources, the tunes and texts, extensive documentation and cross referencing; an extensive bibliography is in Volume 4. Although Bronson's analytic scheme, in which the ballad tunes are assumed to be based on 'gapped' modal scales, is now under question, the value of his monumental work is undeniable. The abridged version, with 167 ballads is a compact, convenient and relatively inexpensive aid to study (Bronson, 1976). In a series of articles, Bronson discusses the important musical aspects of ballad scholarship: tune resemblance, tune families and recurring melodic *Gestalten*; scales and modality; and the influence of tune on text (1942, 1954, 1958, 1959, 1975).

Histories of particular melodies, including preliminary researches on tune families, are in Bronson (1942) and H. Nathan (1943). Studies of oral transmission include those by Bronson (1950), Sirvart Poladian (1942) and S. P. Bayard, 'Prolegomena to a Study of the Principal Melodic Families of British-American Folk Songs' (1950), a study of extended tune families and the process of variation through communal re-creation. More recent studies of the tune-family concept are by Anne Dhu Shapiro (1975) and James R. Cowdery (1984). Examining 153 variants of a single Anglo-American lyric song, Judith McCulloh develops a method of defining a 'folk song cluster' (1970). The melodies and rhythms of the Appalachian repertory that were published by Cecil Sharp and O. A. Campbell (1917) have been re-examined by Eugene Armour (1961). The tunes for Child 1 and 2 have been reviewed by Bayard (1951).

Two lengthy and important studies of 'Barbara Allen' (Child 86) are Mieczyslaw Kolinski's theoretical study of tonal and melodic structure based on his idiosyncratic analytic system (1968), and Charles Seeger's examination of versions and variants based on the collection in the Archive of American Folk Song, Library of Congress (1966). The metrical aspect of 859 Tennessee songs has been analysed by George W. Boswell (1972); Boswell also has examined the influence of melody on textual accents (1951), and looked at melodic ornamentation and its relationship to text (1969). Bronson recommends the study of ballad tune as well as text, and highlights their interdependence (1944). Winkelman supports the view that tune study has been neglected (1960–61). Coffin argues that ballad tunes are in fact dominated by their text, and dismisses the notion of melodic dominance (1965).

Hymnody and singing schools

British-American sacred music includes genres from many sources – folk songs and ballads, hymns, composed songs, minstrel songs and dance and march tunes. During the 19th century, hymns were sung at church services and also at 'camp meeting', an open-air service lasting several days. Camp-meeting spirituals are characterized by repetition, simplicity, refrains, and tags. Often the tunes are derived from folk sources, many dating from the Great Revival, beginning around 1800.

British-American religious music has been well documented since World War II. The seminal work of George Pullen Jackson records hundreds of black and white spirituals (1933, 1937, 1941, 1943, 1952). Leonard Ellinwood has made a general survey of American religious music (1961). Essential reference tools are in Ellinwood and Elizabeth Lockwood's *Bibliography of American Hymnals* (1983; published on microfiche, including 7500 hymnals from 1640 to 1978) and in *The Dictionary of American Hymnology: First Line Index* by the same authors (1984). Bruce Jackson has summarized research on spirituals (1968) and Daniel W. Patterson scholarship on the white spiritual (1970–71; with discography). Issues of fieldwork among Baptists and Pentecostals are raised by Jeff Todd Titon (1985).

The transition from psalmody to hymnody in early America has been examined by musicologists and scholars of American culture. Hamilton C. MacDougall provides a historical discussion of early New England psalmody, 1620–1820 (1940). Brethren hymnals from 1720 to 1884 are discussed by Donald R. Hinks (1986), revival music of the late 18th century by James C. Downey (1968) and the camp meeting, 1800–45, and its hymnody by Charles Albert Johnson (1955), Dickson Davies Bruce Jr (1974) and Ellen Jane Lorenz (1980).

The religious songs of modern rural groups await thorough investigation. But the oral-tradition Baptist hymnody of Southern Appalachia has been researched by William H. Tallmadge (1975); the influence of modern Pentecostalism on popular southern culture by Stephen R. Tucker (1982); and styles of singing and preaching at Otter Creek Predestinarian Baptist Church, Putnam County, Indiana, by Terry E. Miller, who finds that the heterophonic texture similar to that of lining out survives (1975; also Miller, 1986, p. 240).

Singing schools and shape-note hymnody have been studied by Beula Blanche Eisenstadt Blum (1968), Jack S. Bottoms (1972), Joe Dan Boyd (1971), Richard Crawford (1976, 1984), Charles Linwood Ellington (1969), Harry B. Eskew (1966), John R. Graham (1971), George Pullen Jackson (1933, 1944), Earl Oliver Loessel (1959), Charles Seeger (1940), Brett Sutton (1982) and Paula Tadlock (1978).

Instrumental studies

Studies on British-American instrumental traditions have been thin in comparison with research on the vocal genres. 'How to play' books and popular guides to guitar technique or banjo fingerings abound. Scholarly writings for the banjo repertory include Hans Nathan's anthology of banjo tunes from 19th-century manuscript sources (1956); Jay Bailey's historical source study of the five-string banjo (1972); Cecilia Conway's study of the Afro-American banjo tradition (1980); Michael Theodore Coolen's comparative investigation of Senegambian archetypes for the American banjo (1984); Dena J. Epstein's painstaking documentation of US banjo history (1975); Robert B. Winans's research on African-American banjo traditions in Virginia and West Virginia (1979; see also his study of the 19th-century repertory, 1976).

Studies of the guitar and its repertory include Stefan Grossman's research on Delta blues guitar style (1969); Julius Lester and Pete Seeger's instructional manual for 12-string guitar as played by Leadbelly (1965); and Mike Longworth's chronicle of the Martins guitar company (1975).

Fiddle studies include Bayard's collections of more than 700 fiddle tunes and variants from Pennsylvania (1944, 1982; also 1956 for western Pennsylvania) and the thorough and well-documented writings of Linda C. Burman-Hall on traditional fiddling, particularly in the southern states (1968, a detailed study of one 1926 performance; 1974, an overview; 1975, identifies four dialects, Blue Ridge, Southern Appalachian, Ozark, Western; 1978, a Schenkerian analysis of one fiddle tune; and 1984, performing practice study with extensive bibliography and discography).

Research on plucked and hammered dulcimers include Gerald R. Alvey's account of instrument maker Homer Ledford's techniques (1984); Charles W. Joyner's study of dulcimer making in the mountains of North Carolina (1975); folk artist Jean Ritchie's *The Dulcimer Book* (1963); L. Allen Smith's illustrated catalogue of pre-folk revival Appalachian dulcimers (1983); and Charles Seeger's study of the history, tunings, and performing practice of the Appalachian dulcimer (1958). A useful source for autoharp history and style is to be found in Becky Blackley's research (1983). The history of US mandolin performance since 1880 has been documented by Scott Hambly (1977). A helpful source for harmonica style is by Michael S. Licht (1980). The social importance of the American 19th-century reed organ tradition is examined by Russell Eugene Schulz (1974).

Country music

Country music (from the southeast) and country-western (from the southeast and southwest), first known as hillbilly music, originated in the southern USA as Anglo styles mixed with African, Cajun, Latin American and other ethnic musics, and urban commercial music. Studies in the 1960s and 1970s describe its development from a domestic form to an industry after the 1920s through radio broadcasts, its survival during the Depression, and its growing popularity during and after World War II, when southern servicemen spread their musical tastes around the continent (A. Green, 1965; Malone, 1968; Malone and McCulloh, 1975; Malone, 1979). Country music reflected the homogenization of American life; formerly an exclusive white male Protestant domain, by the 1960s performers included blacks (Charley Pride), Chicanos (Johnny Rodriguez) and females (Loretta Lynn, Dolly Parton).

Bluegrass

Bluegrass, a style of country music, took its name in the 1940s from Bill Monroe and his 'Blue Grass Boys'. The style borrows from social, dance and religious folk styles. Ensembles usually have from four to seven string players (guitars, banjo, mandolin, double bass). The repertory includes traditional material as well as newly composed items. Bluegrass music was disseminated in the 1940s through radio and the phonograph. L. M. Smith has provided an introduction to bluegrass, its cultural context and musical features (1965). The most complete and scholarly work on the topic is Neil V. Rosenberg's *Bluegrass: a History* (1985), a chronological study from the hillbilly origins to the folk revival to 'newgrass'. The role of the traditional ballad in bluegrass is examined by Thomas Adler (1974) and the blend of African and European styles in bluegrass by Robert Cantwell (1984). An innovative study of the 'musical geography' of bluegrasses has been made by George O. Carney (1974), who traces the migration of the style throughout the USA and its popularity at music festivals. An anthology of 130 bluegrass songs, from old-time to newgrass is in Peter Wernick's songbook (1976).

Folk-song revival, political song

The Anglo-American folk-song revival of the 1950s and 1960s highlighted the relationship of folk song with democracy and with political protest. A succinct historical introduction to the revival has been done by Bruce Jackson (1985). Samuel P. Bayard describes the 'decline and revival' of Anglo-American folk music from a historical perspective (1962). Raymond R. Allen supplies a brief history of the instrumental music revival, especially fiddle and banjo styles (1981). Benjamin A. Botkin's transcription of the 1962 symposium on the folk-song revival includes statements by Mike Seeger, Alan Lomax, Frank Warner, Ellen J. Stekert, and other figures of the movement (1963). David A. Deturk and A. Poulin's collection (1967) includes articles on the revival by folk-song scholar-performers such as Pete Seeger (topics include protest songs) and Woody Guthrie (commercialism). The urban folk-song movement, 1930–66, is documented by Ellen J. Stekert (1966).

In a series of publications Serge R. Denisoff explores the interrelationship of revival folk song and the American left (1971; 1972; bibliography and discography of protest songs, 1973). A study by Denisoff and Richard A. Peterson (1972) includes 25 articles on various aspects of social change and popular folk song. Richard A. Reuss examines the tension between the political right and left as expressed in songs, 1935–56 (1975). Bert Spector (1982) takes the Weavers, formed in 1948, as a case history in blacklisting during the anti-communist hysteria of the 1950s. John Greenway's research on industrial songs (miners, migrant labourers, textile workers, farmers) broadens the concept of 'folk', a development that ultimately led to the rejection of the term in academic circles (*American Folksongs of Protest*, 1960). Historical studies of soldiers' songs are included in E. A. Dolph's *'Sound Off': Soldier Songs from Yankee Doodle to Parley Voo* (1929) and in Francis

D. Allan's collection of southern Confederate patriotic songs (1970). Bernice Johnson Reagon has examined the cultural history of the Civil Rights movement through freedom and protest songs, 1955–65 (1975).

The personalities of the folk-song revival are described in Edwin Cohen's biography of Woody Guthrie (1971), Guthrie's autobiography (1943), biographical studies of Bob Dylan by John Herdman (1981) and Anthony Scaduto (1971), David King Dunaway's study of Pete Seeger (1981) and Richard A. Reuss's summary biography of Charles Seeger (1979).

Bibliography

F. J. Child, ed.: *The English and Scottish Popular Ballads* (Boston, MA, 1883–98/*R*1956, 1962, 1965)

C. J. Sharp and O. A. Campbell, comps.: *English Folk Songs from the Southern Appalachians, Comprising 273 Songs and Ballads with 968 Tunes, Including 39 Tunes Contributed by Olive Arnold Dame Campbell, Edited by Maud Karpeles* (London, 1917) [without acc.; 2/1932, ed. M. Karpeles; 3/1960]

R. Smith: *South Carolina Ballads* (Cambridge, MA, 1928/*R*1972)

J. C. Colcord: *Roll and Go: Songs of American Sailormen* (Indianapolis, IN, 1924, rev. and enl. 2/1938 /*R*1964]

P. Barry, F. H. Eckstorm and M. W. Smith: *British Ballads from Maine: the Development of Popular Songs with Texts and Airs* (New Haven, CT, 1929)

A. K. Davis Jr, ed.: *Traditional Ballads of Virginia* (Cambridge, MA, 1929/*R*1969)

E. A. Dolph: *'Sound Off': Soldier Songs from Yankee Doodle to Parley Voo* (New York, 1929; repr. as *'Sound Off': Soldier Songs from the Revolution to World War II*, 1942)

M. E. Henry: *A Bibliography for the Study of American Folk-Songs with Many Titles of Folk-Songs (and Titles that Have to Do with Folk-Songs)* (New York, 1931)

G. H. Gerould: *The Ballad of Tradition* (Oxford, 1932)

S. Thompson: *Motif-Index of Folk Literature* (Bloomington, IN, 1932–6)

G. P. Jackson: *White Spirituals in the Southern Uplands* (Chapel Hill, NC, 1933/*R*1964, 1965)

M. E. Henry: 'Nursery Rhymes and Game-Songs from Georgia', *Journal of American Folklore*, xlvii (1934), 334

B. J. Whiting: 'Proverbial Material in the Popular Ballad', *Journal of American Folklore*, xlvii (1934), 22

H. G. Cushing: *Children's Song Index: an Index to more than 22,000 Songs in 189 Collections Comprising 222 Volumes* (New York, 1936)

S. B. Hustvedt: *A Melodic Index of Child's Ballad Tunes* (Berkeley, CA, 1936)

B. A. Botkin: *The American Play-Party-Song: a Collection of Oklahoma Texts and Tunes* (diss., U. of Nebraska, 1937/*R*1963)

G. P. Jackson, ed.: *Spiritual Folk-Songs of Early America* (New York, 1937/*R*1964)

D. Scarborough: *A Song Catcher in Southern Mountains: American Folk Songs of British Ancestry* (New York, 1937/*R*1966)

A. M. Buchanan, ed.: *Folk Hymns of America* (New York, 1938)

M. E. Hull: 'Kansas Play-Party Songs', *Kansas Historical Quarterly*, vii (1938), 258

G. G. Korson: *Minstrels of the Mine Patch: Songs and Stories of the Anthracite Industry* (Philadelphia, PA, 1938/*R*1954)

H. H. Flanders, E. F. Ballard, G. Brown and P. Barry, eds.: *The New Green Mountain Songster: Traditional Folk Songs of Vermont* (New Haven, CT, 1939/*R*1966)

P. D. Jordan: 'A Further Note on "Springfield Mountain"', *Journal of American Folklore*, lii (1939), 118

E. D. Andrews: *The Gift to Be Simple: Songs, Dances, and Rituals of the American Shakers* (New York, 1940/*R*1967)

W. J. Entwistle: 'Notation for Ballad Melodies' (1940)

H. H. Flanders: 'Index of Ballads and Folk-Songs in the Archive of Vermont Folk-Songs at Smiley Manse, Springfield, Vt', *Proceedings of the Vermont Historical Society* (1940), 214

H. C. MacDougall: *Early New England Psalmody: an Historical Appreciation, 1620–1820* (Brattleboro, VT, 1940/*R*1969)

C. Seeger: 'Contrapuntal Style in the Three-Voice Shape-Note Hymns', *MQ*, xxvi (1940), 483; repr. in *Studies in Musicology, 1935–1975* (Berkeley, CA, 1977)

J. T. Adams: *Death in the Dark: a Collection of Factual Ballads of American Mine Disasters* (Big Laurel, VA, 1941/*R*1974, 1977)

F. C. Collins Jr: 'An Aid in the Discovery of Folksongs: a List of Finders for Traditional Ballads, Songs, and Play-Parties in the Southeast', *Southern Folklore Quarterly*, v (1941), 235

J. S. Hall: 'Some Play-Party Games of the Great Smoky Mountains', *Journal of American Folklore*, liv (1941), 68

I. T. Ireland: '"Springfield Mountain"', *Oldtime New England*, xxxii (1941), 1

G. P. Jackson: *Down-East Spirituals and Others* (New York, 1941, 2/1953/*R*1975)

S. M. Shiver: 'Finger Rhymes', *Southern Folklore Quarterly*, v (1941), 221

F. Warnick: 'Play-Party Songs in Western Maryland', *Journal of American Folklore*, liv (1941), 162

S. P. Bayard: 'Ballad Tunes and the Hustvedt Indexing Method', *Journal of American Folklore*, lv (1942), 248

B. H. Bronson: 'Professor Child's Ballad Tunes', *California Folklore Quarterly*, i (1942), 185

——: 'Samuel Hall's Family Tree', *California Folklore Quarterly*, i (1942), 47

D. Emrich: 'Songs of the Western Miners', *California Folklore Quarterly*, i (1942), 213

A. Lomax and S. R. Cowell: *American Folk Song and Folk Lore: a Regional Bibliography* (New York, 1942)

S. Poladian: 'The Problem of Melodic Variation in Folk Song', *Journal of American Folklore*, lv (1942), 204

W. Guthrie: *Bound for Glory* (Garden City, NY, 1943/*R*1968, 1976)

G. P. Jackson: *White and Negro Spirituals: their Life Span and Kinship, Tracing 200 Years of Untrammeled Song Making and Singing Among Our Country Folk, with 116 Songs as Sung by Both Races* (New York, 1943/*R*1975)

G. G. Korson: *Coal Dust on the Fiddle: Songs and Stories of the Bituminous Industry* (Philadelphia, PA, 1943/*R*1965)

H. Nathan: 'The Career of a Revival Hymn', *Southern Folklore Quarterly*, vii (1943), 89

S. Sherwin and H. K. McClintock: *Railroad Songs of Yesterday* (New York, 1943)

S. P. Bayard, ed.: *Hill Country Tunes: Instrumental Folk Music of Southwestern Pennsylvania* (Philadelphia, PA, 1944/*R*1970)

B. H. Bronson: 'The Interdependence of Ballad Tunes and Texts', *California Folklore Quarterly*, iii (1944), 185

L. J. Davidson: '"Home on the Range" Again', *California Folklore Quarterly*, iii (1944), 208

G. P. Jackson: *The Story of the Sacred Harp, 1844–1944* (Nashville, IN, 1944; repr. in *The Sacred Harp*, ed. B. White and E. J. King, 3/1860/*R*1968)

A. L. McLenden: 'A Finding List of Play-Party Games', *Southern Folklore Quarterly*, viii (1944), 201–234

M. Wheeler: *Steamboatin' Days: Folksongs of the River Packet Era* (Baton Rouge, LA, 1944)

W. L. Alderson: 'The Comical History of Baldy Green', *Southern Folklore Quarterly*, ix (1945), 1

L. J. Davidson: 'Mormon Songs', *Journal of American Folklore*, lviii (1945), 273

W. H. Jansen: 'Changes Suffered by "The Wife Wrapped in Wether's Skin"', *Hoosier Folklore Bulletin*, iv (1945), 41

J. A. Lomax: 'Half-Million Dollar Song: Origin of "Home on the Range"', *Southwest Review*, xxxi (1945–6), 1

E. L. Millard: 'Sticks and Stones: Children's Teasing Rhymes', *New York Folklore Quarterly*, i (1945), 21

P. G. Brewster: '"The Hanging of Sam Archer": an Indiana Ballad', *Hoosier Folklore*, v (1946), 125

B. H. Bronson: 'Folksong and the Modes', *MQ*, xxxii (1946), 37

E. C. Kirkland: 'A Check List of the Titles of Tennessee Folksongs', *Journal of American Folklore*, lix (1946), 423

A. E. Fife: 'A Bibliography of the Archives of the Utah Humanities Research Foundation', *Bulletin of the University of Utah*, xxxviii (1947)

—— and A. S. Fife: 'Folk Songs of Mormon Inspiration', *Western Folklore*, vi (1947), 42

J. A. Lomax: *Adventures of a Ballad Hunter* (New York, 1947)

W. E. Richmond: *Place Names in the English and Scottish Popular Ballads and their American Variants* (diss., Ohio State U., 1947)

E. C. Beck: *Lore of the Lumber Camps* (Ann Arbor, MI, 1948)

R. C. Seeger: *American Folk Songs for Children in Home, School, and Nursery School* (Garden City, NY, 1948)

447

C. Withers, comp.: *A Rocket in My Pocket: the Rhymes and Chants of Young Americans* (New York, 1948)

B. H. Bronson: 'Mechanical Help in the Study of Folk Song', *Journal of American Folklore*, lxii (1949), 81

T. P. Coffin: 'An Index to Borrowing in the Child Ballads of America', *Journal of American Folklore*, lxii (1949), 156

——: 'Traditional Texts of "Geordie" in America', *Southern Folklore Quarterly*, xiii (1949), 161

A. K. Davis: *Folk-Songs of Virginia: a Descriptive Index and Classification of Material Collected under the Auspices of the Virginia Folklore Society* (Durham, NC, 1949/R1965)

D. M. Howard: 'The Rhythms of Ball-Bouncing and Ball-Bouncing Rhymes', *Journal of American Folklore*, lxii (1949), 166

G. G. Korson: *Pennsylvania Songs and Legends* (Philadelphia, PA, 1949/R1960)

M. Leach, ed.: *Funk and Wagnalls Standard Dictionary of Folklore, Mythology and Legend* (New York, 1949–50)

C. Seeger: 'Professionalism and Amateurism in the Study of Folk Music', *Journal of American Folklore*, lxii (1949), 107

S. P. Bayard: 'Prolegomena to a Study of the Principal Melodic Families of British-American Folk Songs', *Journal of American Folklore*, lxiii (1950), 1–44

B. H. Bronson: 'Some Observations about Melodic Variation in British-American Folk Tunes', *JAMS*, iii (1950), 120

T. P. Coffin: *The British Traditional Ballad in North America* (Philadelphia, PA, 1950, rev. 2/1963/R1977 with suppl.)

——: 'The Problem of Ballad-Story Variation and Eugene Haun's "The Drowsy Sleeper"', *Southern Folklore Quarterly*, xiv (1950), 87

W. D. Hand, C. Cutts, R. C. Wylder and B. Wylder: 'Songs of the Butte Miners', *Western Folklore*, ix (1950), 1–49

G. M. Laws Jr: *Native American Balladry: a Descriptive Study and a Bibliographical Syllabus* (Philadelphia, PA, 1950, rev. 2/1964)

B. G. Lumpkin: *Folksongs on Records* (Boulder, CO, 1950)

W. A. Owens: *Texas Folk Songs* (Austin, TX, 1950)

S. P. Bayard: 'Principal Versions of an International Folk Tune', *JIFMC*, iii (1951), 44

G. W. Boswell: 'Shaping Controls of Ballad Tunes over their Texts', *Tennessee Folklore Society Bulletin*, xvii (1951), 9

W. E. Boyer, A. F. Buffington and D. Yoder: *Songs Along the Mahantongo Valley* (Lancaster, PA, 1951)

C. Haywood: *A Bibliography of North American Folklore and Folksong* (New York, 1951, rev. 2/1961)

G. M. Laws Jr: 'The Spirit of Native American Balladry', *Journal of American Folklore*, lxiv (1951), 163

G. P. Jackson: *Another Sheaf of White Spirituals* (Gainesville, FL, 1952)

N. I. White, ed.: *The Frank C. Brown Collection of North Carolina Folklore* (Durham, NC, 1952–64)

J. Greenway: *American Folksongs of Protest* (Philadelphia, PA, 1953/R1970)

A. Taylor: 'Trends in the Study of Folksong, 1937–1950', *Southern Folklore Quarterly*, xvii (1953), 97

B. H. Bronson: 'The Morphology of the Ballad-Tunes', *Journal of American Folklore*, lxvii (1954), 1

J. W. Hendren: 'The Scholar and the Ballad Singer', *Southern Folklore Quarterly*, xviii (1954), 139

C. A. Johnson: *The Frontier Camp Meeting: Religion's Harvest Time* (Dallas, TX, 1955)

J. Ritchie: *Singing Family of the Cumberlands* (New York, 1955/R1963)

S. P. Bayard: 'Some Folk Fiddlers' Habits and Styles in Western Pennsylvania', *JIFMC*, viii (1956), 15

H. Nathan: 'Early Banjo Tunes and American Syncopation', *MQ*, xlii (1956), 455

H. Gower: *Traditional Scottish Ballads in the United States* (diss., Vanderbilt U., 1957)

S. E. Hyman: 'The Child Ballad in America: Some Aesthetic Considerations', *Journal of American Folklore*, lxx (1957), 235

G. M. Laws Jr: *American Balladry from British Broadsides: a Guide for Students and Collectors of Traditional Song* (Philadelphia, PA, 1957)

B. H. Bronson: 'The Music of the Ballads', *Virginia Quarterly Review*, xxxiv (1958), 474

C. Seeger: 'The Appalachian Dulcimer', *Journal of American Folklore*, lxxi (1958), 40; repr. in *Studies in Musicology, 1935–1975* (Berkeley, CA, 1977)

H. W. Thompson: *A Pioneer Songster: Texts from the Stevens-Douglass Manuscript of Western New York, 1841–1856* (Ithaca, NY, 1958)

B. H. Bronson: *The Traditional Tunes of the Child Ballads* (Princeton, NJ, 1959–72)

448

——: 'Towards the Comparative Analysis of British-American Folk Tunes', *Journal of American Folklore*, lxxii (1959), 165

T. P. Coffin: 'The Folk Ballad and the Literary Ballad: an Essay in Classification', *Midwest Folklore*, ix, ed. H. P. Beck (1959), 5; repr. in *Folklore in Action: Essays for Discussion in Honor of MacEdward Leach* (Philadelphia, PA, 1962/R1972)

E. O. Loessel: *The Use of Character Notes and Other Unorthodox Notations in Teaching the Reading of Music in Northern United States during the Nineteenth Century* (diss., U. of Michigan, 1959)

D. K. Wilgus: *Anglo-American Folksong Scholarship since 1898* (New Brunswick, NJ, 1959/R1982)

A. K. Davis Jr: *More Traditional Ballads of Virginia: Collected with the Cooperation of Members of the Virginia Folklore Society* (Chapel Hill, NC, 1960)

H. H. Flanders: *Ancient Ballads Traditionally Sung in New England* (Philadelphia, PA, 1960–65)

G. G. Korson: *Black Rock: Mining Folklore of the Pennsylvania Dutch* (Baltimore, MD, 1960)

R. M. Lawless: *Folksingers and Folksongs in America: a Handbook of Biography, Bibliography, and Discography* (New York, 1960, rev. 2/1965/R1968)

B. G. Lumpkin: 'Colorado Folk Songs', *Western Folklore*, xix (1960), 77

D. M. Winkelman: 'Musicological Techniques of Ballad Analysis', *Midwest Folklore*, x (1960–61), 197

E. Armour: *The Melodic and Rhythmic Characteristics of the Music of the Traditional Ballad Variants Found in the Southern Appalachians* (diss., New York U., 1961)

L. Ellinwood: 'Religious Music in America', *Religious Perspectives in American Culture*, ed. W. Herbert (Princeton, NJ, 1961), 289–359

L. Hubbard: *Ballads and Songs from Utah* (Salt Lake City, UT, 1961)

M. Leach and T. P. Coffin, eds.: *The Critics and the Ballad* (Carbondale, IL, 1961)

S. P. Bayard: 'Decline and "Revival" of Anglo-American Folk Music', *Folklore in Action and Essays for Discussion in Honor of MacEdward Leach*, ed. H. P. Beck (Philadelphia, PA, 1962/R1970), 21

P. Seeger and J. Silverman: *The Folksinger's Guitar Guide* (New York, 1962)

B. A. Botkin: 'The Folksong Revival: a Symposium', *New York Folklore Quarterly*, xix (1963), 83–142

G. List: 'An Approach to the Indexing of Ballad Tunes', *Folklore and Folk Music Archivist*, vi (1963), 7

J. Ritchie: *The Dulcimer Book* (New York, 1963, 2/1974)

M. C. Boatright, W. M. Hudson and A. Maxwell, eds.: *A Good Tale and a Bonnie Tune* (Dallas, TX, 1964)

E. Moore and C. O. Moore: *Ballads and Folk Songs of the Southwest* (Norman, OK, 1964)

T. P. Coffin: 'Remarks Preliminary to a Study of Ballad Meter and Ballad Singing', *Journal of American Folklore*, lxxviii (1965), 149

J. Lester and P. Seeger: *The 12-String Guitar as Played by Leadbelly: an Instruction Manual* (New York, 1965)

L. M. Smith: 'An Introduction to Bluegrass', *Journal of American Folklore*, lxxviii (1965), 245

H. B. Eskew: *Shape-Note Hymnody in the Shenandoah Valley 1816–1860* (diss., Tulane U., 1966)

E. D. Ives: *Folksongs from Maine* (Orono, ME, 1966)

C. Seeger: 'Versions and Variants of "Barbara Allen" in the Archive of American Folk Song in the Library of Congress', *Selected Reports in Ethnomusicology*, i/1 (1966), 120–67; repr. in *Studies in Musicology, 1935–75* (Berkeley, CA, 1977), 273–320

E. J. Steckert: 'Cents and Nonsense in the Urban Folksong Movement: 1930–1966', *Folklore and Society: Essays in Honor of Ben A. Botkin*, ed. B. Jackson, (Hatboro, PA, 1966), 153

D. M. Winkelman: 'Some Rhythmic Aspects of the Child Ballad', *New Voices in American Studies*, ed. R. B. Browne, D. M. Winkelman, and A. Hayman (Lafayette, IN, 1966), 151

T. G. Burton and A. N. Manning: *The East Tennessee State University Collection of Folklore: Folk Songs* (Johnson City, TN, 1967)

D. A. Deturk and A. Poulin Jr, eds.: *The American Folk Scene: Dimensions of the Folksong Revival* (New York, 1967)

G. Foss: 'A Methodology for the Description and Classification of Anglo-American Traditional Tunes', *Journal of the Folklore Institute*, iv (1967), 102

C. H. Kaufman: 'An Ethnomusicological Survey Among the People of the Ramapo Mountains', *New York Folklore Quarterly*, xxiii (1967), 3–42, 109–31

R. L. Welsch: *A Treasury of Nebraska Pioneer Folklore* (Lincoln, NE, 1967)

R. Abrahams and G. Foss: *Anglo-American Folksong Style* (Englewood Cliffs, NJ, 1968)

B. B. E. Blum: *Solmization in Nineteenth-Century American Sight Singing Instruction* (diss., U. of Michigan, 1968)

L. C. Burman: 'The Technique of Variation in an American Fiddle Tune: a Study of "Sail Away Lady" as performed in 1926 by Uncle Bunt Stephens', *EM*, xii (1968), 49

T. E. Cheney: *Mormon Songs from the Rocky Mountains: a Compilation of Mormon Folksongs* (Austin, TX, 1968)

J. C. Downey: *The Music of American Revivalism* (diss., Tulane U., 1968)

B. Jackson: 'Glory Songs of the Lord', *Our Living Traditions: an Introduction to American Folklore*, ed. T. P. Coffin (New York, 1968), 103

C. L. Ellington: *The Sacred Harp Tradition of the South: its Origin and Evolution* (diss., Florida State U., 1969)

M. Kolinski: 'Barbara Allen: Tonal Versus Melodic Structure', *EM*, xii (1968), 208; xiii (1969), 1–73

G. W. Boswell: 'Text-Occasioned Ornamentation in Folksinging', *Southern Folklore Quarterly*, xxxiii (1969), 333

B. H. Bronson: *The Ballad as Song* (Berkeley, CA, and Los Angeles, CA, 1969)

B. Castagna: 'Some Rhymes, Games, and Songs from Children in the New Rochelle Area', *New York Folklore Quarterly*, xxv (1969), 221

A. E. Fife and A. S. Fife: *Cowboy and Western Songs: a Comprehensive Anthology* (New York, 1969)

A. Green: *Recorded American Coal Mining Songs* (diss., U. of Pennsylvania, 1969)

S. Grossman: *Delta Blues Guitar* (New York, 1969, 2/1972)

W. R. Murphy: *Melodic Contour in White Anglo-American Traditional Narrative Song in North America* (diss., U. of Pennsylvania, 1969)

F. D. Allan: *Allan's Lone Star Ballads: a Collection of Southern Patriotic Songs Made During Confederate Times* (New York, 1970) [1874]

E. Fowke: *Lumbering Songs from the Northern Woods* (Austin, TX, 1970)

J. Greenway: *American Folksongs of Protest* (New York, 1970)

J. M. McCulloh: *In the Pines: the Melodic-Textual Identity of an American Lyric Folksong Cluster* (diss., U. of Indiana, 1970)

J. D. Boyd: 'Negro Sacred Harp Songsters in Mississippi', *Mississippi Folklore Register*, v (1971), 60

E. Cohen: *Woody Guthrie and the American Folk Song* (diss., U. of Southern California, 1971)

R. S. Denisoff: *Great Day Coming: Folk Music and the American Left* (Urbana, IL, 1971)

J. R. Graham: 'Early Twentieth-Century Singing Schools in Kentucky Appalachia', *Journal of Research in Music Education*, xix (1971), 77

A. Jabbour: *American Fiddle Tunes* (Washington, DC, 1971)

A. Scaduto: *Bob Dylan: an Intimate Biography* (New York, 1971)

J. Bailey: 'Historical Origin and Stylistic Developments of the Five-String Banjo', *Journal of American Folklore*, lxxxv (1972), 58

J. S. Bottoms: *The Singing School in Texas: 1971* (diss., U. of Colorado, 1972)

R. S. Denisoff: *Sing a Song of Social Significance* (Bowling Green, OH, 1972, rev. 2/1983)

R. S. Denisoff and R. A. Peterson, eds.: *The Sounds of Social Change: Studies in Popular Culture* (Chicago, IL, 1972)

H. Glassie, E. D. Ives, and J. F. Szwed: *Folksongs and their Makers* (Bowling Green, OH, 1972)

A. Green: *Only a Miner: Studies in Recorded Coal-Mining Songs* (Urbana, IL, 1972)

B. G. Lumpkin: 'Folksongs from a Nebraska Family', *Southern Folklore Quarterly*, xxxvi (1972), 14

V. Randolph: *Ozark Folklore: a Bibliography* (Bloomington, IN, 1972)

E. V. Spielman: 'Fiddling Traditions of Cape Breton and Texas: a Study in Parallels and Contrasts', *Yearbook for Inter-American Music Research*, viii (1972), 39

R. G. Alvey: 'Phillips Barry and Anglo-American Folksong Scholarship', *Journal of the Folklore Institute*, x (1973), 67

R. S. Denisoff: *Songs of Protest, War & Peace: a Bibliography & Discography* (Santa Barbara, CA, 1973)

J. H. Mead: *Sea Shanties and Fo'c'sle Songs, 1768–1906, in the G. W. Blunt Library, Mystic Seaport, Mystic, Connecticut* (diss., U. of Kentucky, 1973)

W. R. Ferris Jr: 'Folk Song and Culture: Charles Seeger and Alan Lomax', *New York Folklore Quarterly*, xix (1973), 206

G. Ohrlin: *The Hell-Bound Train: a Cowboy Songbook* (Urbana, IL, 1973)

D. K. Wilgus: 'The Future of American Folksong Scholarship', *Southern Folklore Quarterly*, xxxvii (1973), 315

T. Adler: 'The Ballad in Bluegrass Music', *Folklore Forum*, vii (1974), 3–47

D. D. Bruce Jr: *And They All Sang Hallelujah* (Knoxville, TN, 1974)

L. C. Burman-Hall: *Southern American Folk Fiddling: Context and Style* (diss., Princeton U., 1974)

G. O. Carney: 'Bluegrass Grows All Around: the Spatial Dimensions of a Country Music Style', *Journal of Geography*, lxxiii (1974), 34

J. C. Hickerson: 'A Bibliography of American Folksong', *American Folk Poetry: an Anthology*, ed. Duncan Dmrich (Boston, MA, and Toronto, 1974), 775–816

R. E. Schulz: *The Reed Organ in Nineteenth-Century America* (diss., U. of Texas, Austin, 1974)

B. H. Bronson: 'Traditional Ballads Musically Considered', *Critical Inquiry*, ii (1975), 29

L. C. Burman-Hall: 'Southern American Folk Fiddle Styles', *EM*, xix (1975), 47

D. J. Epstein: 'The Folk Banjo: a Documentary History', *EM*, xix (1975), 347

P. S. Foner: *American Labor Songs of the Nineteenth Century* (Urbana, IL, 1975)

C. W. Joyner: 'Dulcimer Making in Western North Carolina: Creativity in a Traditional Mountain Craft', *Southern Folklore Quarterly*, xxxix (1975), 341

M. Longworth: *Martin Guitars: a History* (Cedar Knolls, NJ, 1975, 2/1980)

T. E. Miller: 'Voices from the Past: the Singing and Preaching at Otter Creek Church', *Journal of American Folklore*, lxxxviii (1975), 266

B. J. Reagon: *Songs of the Civil Rights Movement, 1955–65: a Study in Culture History* (diss., Howard U., 1975)

R. A. Reuss: 'American Folksongs and Left-Wing Politics', *Journal of the Folklore Institute*, xii (1975), 89

A. D. Shapiro: *The Tune-Family Concept in British-American Folk-Song Scholarship* (diss., Harvard U., 1975)

E. V. Spielman: *Traditional North American Fiddling: a Methodology for the Historical and Comparative Analytical Style Study of Instrumental Musical Traditions* (diss., U. of Wisconsin, 1975)

W. H. Tallmadge: 'Baptist Monophonic and Heterophonic Hymnody in Southern Appalachia', *Yearbook of Inter-American Musical Research*, xi (1975), 106–36

J. I. White: *Git Along, Little Dogies: Songs and Songmakers of the American West* (Urbana, IL, 1975)

B. H. Bronson: *The Singing Tradition of Child's Popular Ballads* (Princeton, NJ, 1976)

G. G. Carey: *A Sailor's Songbag: an American Rebel in an English Prison, 1777–1779* (Amherst, MA, 1976)

R. Crawford: 'Watts for Singing: Metrical Poetry in American Sacred Tunebooks, 1761–1785', *Early American Literature*, xi (1976), 139

D. Emblidge: 'Down Home with the Band: Country-Western Music and Rock', *EM*, xx (1976), 541

K. Lee: *Ten Thousand Goddam Cattle: a History of the American Cowboy in Song, Story, and Verse* (Flagstaff, AZ, 1976)

I. Lowens: *A Bibliography of Songsters Printed in America Before 1821* (Worcester, MA, 1976)

B. Nettl and H. Myers: *Folk Music in the United States: an Introduction* (Detroit, MI, 1976) [orig. pubd as *An Introduction to Folk Music in the United States*, 1960]

P. Wernick: *Bluegrass Songbook* (New York, 1976)

R. B. Winans: 'The Folk, the State, and the Five-String Banjo in the Nineteenth Century', *Journal of American Folklore*, lxxxix (1976), 407

D. K. Dunaway: 'A Selected Bibliography: Protest Song in the United States', *Folklore Forum*, x (1977), 8

S. Hambly: *Mandolins in the United States Since 1880: an Industrial and Sociocultural History of Form* (diss., U. of Pennsylvania, 1977)

S. Hugill: *Songs of the Sea: the Tales and Tunes of Sailors and Sailing Ships* (New York, 1977)

H. B. Peters: *Folk Songs Out of Wisconsin* (Madison, WI, 1977)

L. C. Burman-Hall: 'Tune Identity and Performance Style: the Case of "Bonaparte's Retreat"', *Selected Reports in Ethnomusicology*, iii/1, ed. J. Porter (Los Angeles, CA, 1978), 77

J. W. Eldridge: *A Preface to the Study of Anglo-American Ballad Variation* (diss., U. of Oregon, 1978)

E. D. Ives: *Joe Scott: the Woodsman-Songmaker* (Urbana, IL, 1978)

P. Tadlock: 'Shape-Note Singing in Mississippi', *Discourse in Ethnomusicology: Essays in Honor of George List*, ed. C. Card and others (Bloomington, IN, 1978)

R. B. Browne: *The Alabama Folk Lyric: a Study in Origins and Media of Dissemination* (Bowling Green, OH, 1979)

D. K. Dunaway: 'Unsung Songs of Protest: the Composers Collective of New York', *New York Folklore*, v (1979), 1

N. Porterfield: *Jimmie Rodgers: the Life and Times of America's Blue Yodeler* (Urbana, IL, 1979)

R. A. Reuss: 'Folk Music and Social Conscience: the Musical Odyssey of Charles Seeger', *Western Folklore*, xxxviii (1979), 221

R. B. Winans: 'The Black Banjo-Playing Tradition in Virginia and West Virginia', *Journal of the Virginia Folklore Society*, i (1979), 7

C. Conway: *The Afro-American Traditions of the Folk Banjo* (diss., U. of North Carolina, 1980)

M. S. Licht: 'Harmonica Magic: Virtuoso Display in American Folk Music', *EM*, xiv (1980), 211

E. J. Lorenz: *Glory Hallelujah! The Story of the Campmeeting Spiritual* (Nashville, IN, 1980)

R. R. Allen: 'Old-Time Music and the Urban Folk Revival', *New York Folklore*, vii (1981), 65

N. Cohen: *Long Steel Rail: the Railroad in American Folksong* (Urbana, IL, 1981)

D. K. Dunaway: *How Can I Keep from Singing: Peter Seeger* (New York, 1981)

J. L. Goldenberg: 'Folk Song is Alive and Well and Living in the City', *Journal of American Culture*, iv (1981), 167

J. Herdman: *Voice Without Restraint: a Study of Bob Dylan's Lyrics and their Background* (New York, 1981)

J. B. Tinsley: *He was Singin' This Song: a Collection of Forty-eight Traditional Songs of the American Cowboy with Words, Music, Pictures, and Stories* (Orlando, FL, 1981)

S. P. Bayard: *Dance to the Fiddle, March to the Fifes: Instrumental Folk Tunes in Pennsylvania* (University Park, PA, 1982)

C. A. Bean: *An Index to Folksongs Contained in Theses and Dissertations in the Library of Congress* (Loughborough, 1982)

N. Cazden, H. Haufrecht and N. Studer: *Folk Songs of the Catskills* (Albany, NY, 1982)

——: *Notes and Sources for Folk Songs of the Catskills* (Albany, NY, 1982)

P. K. Eberly: *Music in the Air: America's Changing Tastes in Popular Music, 1920–1959* (New York, 1982)

B. Spector: 'The Weavers: a Case History in Show Blacklisting', *Journal of American Culture*, v (1982), 113

B. Sutton: 'Shape-Note Tune Books and Primitive Hymns', *EM*, xxvi (1982), 11

S. R. Tucker: 'Pentecostalism and Popular Culture in the South: a Study of Four Musicians', *Journal of Popular Culture*, xvi (1982), 68

C. K. Wolfe: *Kentucky Country: Folk and Country Music of Kentucky* (Lexington, KY, 1982)

B. Blackley: *The Autoharp Book* (Brisbane, CA, 1983)

L. Ellinwood and E. Lockwood: *Bibliography of American Hymnals* (New York, 1983)

K. L. Lyle: *Scalded to Death: Authentic Stories of Railroad Disasters and the Ballads that were Written About Them* (Chapel Hill, NC, 1983)

W. A. Owens: *Tell Me a Story, Sing Me a Song: a Texas Chronicle* (Austin, TX, 1983)

D. W. Patterson: 'Hunting for the American White Spiritual: a Survey of Scholarship, with Discography', *The Bible in American Arts and Letters*, ed. G. Gunn (Philadelphia, PA, 1983), 187–217

J. P. Quinn: *An Index to the Field Recordings in the Flanders Ballad Collection at Middlebury College, Middlebury, Vermont* (Middlebury, VT, 1983)

A. and M. Rosenbaum: *Folk Visions and Voices: Traditional Music and Song in North Georgia* (Athens, GA, 1983)

L. A. Smith: *A Catalogue of Pre-Revival Appalachian Dulcimers* (Columbia, MO, 1983)

G. R. Alvey: *Dulcimer Maker: the Craft of Homer Ledford* (Lexington, KY, 1984)

B. B. Boggs and D. W. Patterson: *An Index of Selected Folk Recordings* (Chapel Hill, NC, 1984)

L. C. Burman-Hall: 'American Traditional Fiddling Performance Contexts and Techniques', *Performance Practice: Ethnomusicological Perspectives*, ed. G. Béhague (Westport, CT, 1984), 149–211

R. Cantwell: *Bluegrass Breakdown: the Making of the Old Southern Sound* (Urbana, IL, 1984)

M. T. Coolen: 'Senegambia Archetypes for the American Folk Banjo', *Western Folklore*, xliii (1984), 117

J. R. Cowdery: 'A Fresh Look at the Concept of Tune Family', *EM*, xxviii (1984), 495

R. Crawford, ed.: *The Core Repertory of Early American Psalmody* (Madison, WI, 1984)

L. Ellinwood and E. Lockwood: *The Dictionary of American Hymnology: First Line Index* (New York, 1984)

J. Warner and J. S. Epstein, eds.: *Traditional American Folk Songs from the Anne & Frank Warner Collection* (Syracuse, NY, 1984)

C. Goertzen: 'American Fiddle Tunes and the Historic-Geographic Method', *EM*, xxix (1985), 448

B. Jackson: 'The Folksong Revival', *New York Folklore*, xi (1985), 195

N. V. Rosenberg: *Bluegrass: a History* (Urbana, IL, 1985)

J. T. Titon: 'Stance, Role, and Identity in Fieldwork among Folk Baptists and Pentecostals', *American Music*, iii (1985), 16

D. R. Hinks: *Brethren Hymn Books and Hymnals, 1720–1884* (Gettysburg, PA, 1986)

T. E. Miller: *Folk Music in America: a Reference Guide* (New York, 1986)

5: EUROPEAN-AMERICAN and ASIAN-AMERICAN MUSIC

HELEN MYERS

Beginning around 1880, the new wave of immigration brought millions of European and Asian immigrants to American shores. In the USA they added their musical styles to the already diverse American tradition. Most of the arrivals settled in cities, but some groups, particularly those from western and northern Europe – the Germans, French, Scandinavians and Irish – settled in the rural countryside, where they lived in ethnic enclaves, preserving their culture in isolation from their motherland. Some of the more conservative groups still maintain practices in oral tradition that, under the intense pressure of modernization, were abandoned during the early part of the 20th century in Europe. Other European groups have adopted various strategies, such as acculturation and revitalization, to modify their musical cultures for an American setting.

Research on the music of European and Asian minorities has been late and scattered, following in the wake of the studies of cultural anthropologists and historians of immigration. More attention has been paid to texts than tunes. Ethnomusicological research on American 'ethnic' music typically is undertaken as a summer project, to serve as a second area of concentration, as a topic for a master's thesis or as a seminar project for graduate students. As a consequence, many of the writings in this area lack intellectual distinction. The music of these minority groups, urban and rural, often has been studied in the hope that the data will shed light on the larger question of ethnicity.

In his overview of ethnic music in the USA, Stephen Erdely identifies topics of research including liturgical music, folk singing, singing societies (such as German song fests, urban amateur glee clubs) and instrumental groups (including Scottish bagpipers, Croatian and Serbian tamburitzans, Gypsy ensembles, old-time fiddling and Balkan-American instrumental groups) (1979, pp.117–28). James Porter focusses on 'the paradoxical elements in respect of which change [in European-American music] is encouraged or counterbalanced: tradition and innovation, stability and variability, continuity and atrophy' (1978, p.2). Non-English-speaking groups are generally more conscious of their folk music heritage than native-born Americans. For these immigrants, music provides a way of retaining the cohesion of their group and gaining the respect of mainstream society. Oral tradition is often abandoned in favour of more concrete means of transmission, such as books and cassettes. European and Asian enclaves often organize societies, clubs (bands and choirs) and religious groups; they sponsor entertainers and promote musical specialists. In cities, musical organizations are one means of adapting to a tough unfamiliar environment. Membership is typically heterogeneous, drawing together persons who share a common ethnic identity but are from different socio-economic groups, individuals who would not normally have met in their homeland. I found such examples in my own research with some 50,000 recent immigrants from India to New York City (Nettl and Myers, 1976, pp.127–39). Alison Arnold worked with Indians in Chicago (1985) and Gordon Thompson and Medha Yodh with Gujaratis in Los Angeles (1985). Most immigrants arrived in the USA after World War II, and are well-educated professionals. Regional and caste differences tend to break down in the USA. Indians have founded over a dozen temples that hold regular services, drawing together Hindus from all parts of the subcontinent. These groups have combined their musical repertories, with the finest singers leading the services.

The oldest European music preserved in the USA is mostly religious. The Old Order Amish, a German-speaking sect related to the Mennonites, came in the early 18th century, settling in Pennsylvania, Ohio, Indiana, Illinois, Iowa and Maryland. In the 1990s, they live in virtual musical isolation, practising a monophonic style that no longer survives in Germany or Switzerland – a marginal survival that apparently has vanished in its original home. Bruno Nettl found that American Amish tunes are slowed down and highly ornamented versions of old German hymn tunes (1957; also see Umble, 1939; Jackson, 1945, 1946; Frey, 1949; Burkhart, 1953; and Hohmann, 1959). Music of the Mennonite community, founded in the USA in 1860, has been studied by Walter Jost (1966) and Charles Burkhart (1953). Hymn singing of the German Amana Society, established in Iowa in 1859, has been analysed by Lloyd Winfield Farlee (1966); 16th-century Canadian Hutterite songs by Helen Martens (1969); Canadian Doukhobors by Kenneth Peacock (1970). General analyses of Pennsylvania-German hymnody, a combination of South German and Anglo traditions, have been made by George Pullen Jackson (1952), Philip Bohlman in Wisconsin (1980, 1984), Edward C. Wolf (1960, 1985) and Don Yoder (1961). Secular songs of the Pennsylvania Germans ('Dutch') have been recorded by Walter E. Boyer, Albert F. Buffington and Don Yoder (1951), Buffington (1974) and Theodore J. Albrecht in Texas (1975).

Jewish liturgical music has a long history in the USA. Samuel Armistead and Joseph H. Silverman (1981) and Raymond MacCurdy and Daniel Stanley (1951) treat the traditions of the Spanish Sephardic community. Ellen Koskoff has published on the music of the Lubavitcher Hasidic community, particularly the tradition of *nigun* singing (1976, 1978). Yiddish folk song is documented by Ruth Rubin (1946, 1961, 1963). Mark Slobin has written on *klezmer*, a secular instrumental genre (1984) in addition to his well-documented *Tenement Songs: the Popular Music of the Jewish Immigrants* (1982). A survey of Jewish-American music is under that title in *The New Grove Dictionary of American Music* (Slobin, Schiff and Katz, 1986).

The French have lived in North America for more than 300 years. The most tenacious tradition has been maintained in French-speaking northeastern Canada, where before 1680 some 7000 French settled. The more than 20,000 songs that have been recorded from their descendants testify to the richness and conservatism of this tradition. The foremost collector of these materials was anthropologist and ethnologist Charles Marius Barbeau (1883–1969), whose publishing career on French-Canadian material extended from 1915 to

1965. In 1946, in collaboration with his leading disciple, Luc Lacourcière, he founded the Archives de Folklore at Laval University, the first of several folklore programmes at Canadian Universities and the repository (together with the National Museums of Canada, Quebec City) for field recordings of the French tradition. The publication of *Les archives de folclore*, organ of the Archives, began in the same year. Barbeau's writings include *Alouette: nouveau recueil de chansons populaires* (1946), 'La guignolée au Canada' (1946) and *Le rossignol y chante* (1962). (For Barbeau's life and works, see Katz, 1970.)

The Anglo-Canadian tradition has been documented by Helen Creighton (1950, 1960, 1962, 1971), Edith Fowke (1963, 1965, 1970) and Edward D. Ives (1962, 1964, 1971). Folk songs of Newfoundland have been collected and documented by Kenneth Peacock (1954, 1960, 1965) and the eminent English folk-song scholar, Maud Karpeles (1930, 1971). An ethnomusicological survey of the Maritime Provinces is available in Creighton (1972).

The Lithuanian tradition has been studied by Peacock (1971), and that of Ukraine by Robert B. Klymasz (1970; also Klymasz and James Porter, 1974). Armenian musical culture in Toronto has been studied by Margaret Sarkissian (1987). The music of Canada's Arab and East Indian populations has been summarily analysed by Regula Qureshi (1972). Canadians of Korean origin have been treated by Song Pangsong [Song Bang-song] (1974). A résumé of research on Canadian ethnomusicology, including bibliographies, now somewhat dated, is in the 'Canadian Issue' of *Ethnomusicology* (xvi/3, 1972). Summaries of Canadian folk and ethnic traditions, including Inuit and Native Americans as well as biographies of researchers, are in the *Encyclopedia of Music in Canada* (1981).

The French Cajun-American musical tradition of southern Louisiana dates from the mid-18th century, when Acadians were forcibly deported from Nova Scotia to the English Colonies. Cajun songs have been influenced by French, African-American, and Creole styles. An early study is Irène Thérèse Whitfield's *Louisiana French Folk Songs* (1939/R1969); later research includes that of Pierre V. Diagle (1972), Claudie Marcel-Dubois (1978), B. J. Ancelet (1982), John Broven (1983) and Ancelet and E. Morgan (1984).

Research on Italian-American music has moved forward with the studies of Regina and Roy D'Adriano on ballads (1976), A. Virgilio Savona and Michele Straniero on immigrant songs (1976), Joseph Sciona on music and ethnicity (1989) and Anthony T. Rauche on the Italian-American community of Hartford, Connecticut (1992).

Such studies show that Italian-Americans have maintained the songs, dances and marches which accompany saints' feasts and other religious celebrations. This repertory has endured to the present day and usually reflects the regional and village traditions maintained in the USA. The 'festa' bands and community choral groups have been two types of musical organizations important in community life. Other traditional music includes worksongs, lullabies (*ninne nanne*), funeral laments, narrative songs (*ballata* and *storie*) and the lyric forms (*stornelli* and *strombotti*).

The music of the immigration experience was also an important part of life in the USA, and one of the most popular musical genres has been that of the Neapolitan art song, which reflected the love of the homeland as well as nostalgia for the romance of peasant life. These themes also appeared in the music associated with immigrant theatre.

In the 1930s and throughout the 1940s recordings targeted for the Italian community were produced (Gualerzi, 1977–8), though most of these were imported, and very little was actually recorded in the USA. Italian language and music on radio stations were popular, and Italians trained in classical music joined the ranks of major orchestras, opera companies and music conservatories as conductors, performers, teachers and composers.

After World War II Italian singers and entertainers helped to generate a more modern and assimilated Italian-American musical identity, which very often used comic and stereotypical images. Prominent among these were Nicola Paone, Lou Monte (the 'Godfather of Italian-American song'), and Louis Prima (the 'Italo-Satchmo').

In the 1990s, Italian contemporary music recordings, along with radio and television programmes, help maintain contact with the current trends of popular culture in Italy. At the other end of the spectrum organizations like the Italian Folk Arts Federation of America help to preserve the older traditional music and customs (Rauche, 1992).

During the 17th and 18th centuries, Irish immigrants brought folk ballads and dance tunes to the USA, including the reel, hornpipe, jig and set dance played by fiddle, flute, tin whistle and bagpipes. Scots-Irish pioneers blended their repertory with Anglo and to some extent Afro traditions. During the 19th century the hybrid idiom of Irish-American music won popularity in vaudeville, on Tin Pan Alley and in Hollywood. Irish-American music has been studied by G. Malcolm Laws Jr (1962/*R*1972), Lawrence E. McCullough (1974, 1975, 1978), Robert L. Wright (1975) and D. K. Wilgus (1979).

Although Scandinavians first immigrated to the USA in the 17th century, the heaviest period of immigration was from 1850 to World War I, when they settled mainly in Michigan, Minnesota and Wisconsin. Instrumental dance music such as the Norwegian *springar* and *springeleik* and the Swedish *polska* have survived, as well as numerous religious and secular vocal types. Studies of Scandinavian-American music have been published by Marjorie Edgar, 'Finnish Folk Songs in America' (1935; also 'Ballads of the Knife-Men', 1949); K. A. Swanson, 'Music of Two Finnish-Apostolic Lutheran Groups in Minnesota' (1970–71); Theodore C. Blegen and Martin B. Ruud, 'Norwegian Emigrant Songs and Ballads' (1936/*R*1979); Robert L. Wright, 'Swedish Emigrant Ballads' (1965); Leroy Wilbur Larson, *Scandinavian-American Folk Dance Music of the Norwegians in Minnesota* (1975); and R. and R. L. Wright, *Danish Emigrant Ballads and Songs* (1983). The outstanding discographer for Scandinavian-American music is Pekka Gronow (1977).

Research on Slavic music in the USA includes that by C. Merton Babcock, 'Czech Songs in Nebraska' (1949); Robert Joseph Ficca, *A Study of Slavic-American Instrumental Music in Lyndora, Pennsylvania* (1980); Bruno Nettl and Ivo Moravcik, 'Czech and Slovak Songs Collected in Detroit' (1955); and Brownlee Waschek, *Czech and Slovak Folk Music in Masaryktown and Slovenska-Zahrada, Florida* (1969). Research on Polish-American music has focussed on the polka, for example, Charles Keil, 'The Dyna-Tones: a Buffalo Polka Band in Performance' (1984) and Janice Ellen Kleeman, *The Origins and Stylistic*

Development of Polish-American Polka Music (1982). Baltic studies include Jonas Balys's research on Lithuanian folk songs (1958, 1978) and Christina Niles's study of the Latvian *kokle* zither (1978).

The 3.5 million American Asians include Chinese, Japanese, and Koreans (about half the total), Indians and Pakistanis, Filipinos and recent arrivals from Vietnam, Cambodia and Laos. Like all immigrant peoples, Asian-Americans try to preserve their native customs while assimilating into the mainstream of American society. A general survey of Asian-American music is under that title in *The New Grove Dictionary of American Music* (1986).

The Chinese arrived in the USA in the 1850s to build the western railroads. Cantonese operas that date from this period flourished between 1870 and 1890. Cantonese opera in North America has been investigated by Ronald Riddle (1976, 1977, 1978, 1983) and Chun-kin Leung (1977). The music of Korean-Americans has been documented by Riddle (1985); classical Indian music in North America by Bonnie Wade (1978); the Gujarati community of Los Angeles by Gordon Thompson and Medha Yodh (1985); Southeast Asian music in the USA by Amy Catlin (1981, 1982).

As the field of urban studies has grown, the music of non-English-speaking groups in American cities has been collected and documented by several scholars including Harriet Pawlowska, *Polish Folksongs Gathered in Detroit* (1940) and *Merrily We Sing: 105 Polish Folksongs* (1961); George Korson, *Pennsylvania Songs and Legends* (1949); D. Borcherdt, 'Armenian Folk Songs and Dances in the Fresno and Los Angeles Areas' (1959); Stephen Erdely, 'Research on Traditional Music of Nationality Groups in Cleveland and Vicinity' (1968) and 'Folksinging of the American Hungarians in Cleveland' (1964); Ronald Riddle, 'Music Clubs and Ensembles in San Francisco's Chinese Community' (1978); Mark Forry, 'Bećar Music in the Serbian Community of Los Angeles' (1978); and R. K. Spottswood, 'The Sajewski Story: Eighty Years of Polish Music in Chicago' (1982).

Bibliography

M. Karpeles: 'British Folk Songs from Canada', *JFSS*, xxxiv (1930), 218

M. Edgar: 'Finnish Folk Songs in America', *Minnesota History*, xvi (1935), 319

T. C. Blegen and M. B. Ruud, eds.: *Norwegian Emigrant Songs and Ballads* (London, 1936/R1979)

J. Umble: 'The Old Order Amish, Their Hymns and Hymn Tunes', *Journal of American Folklore*, lii (1939), 82

I. T. Whitfield: *Louisiana French Folk Songs* (Los Angeles, CA, 1939/R1969)

H. M. Pawlowska: *Polish Folksongs Gathered in Detroit, with an Analysis of the Music by Grace L. Engel* (diss., Wayne State U., 1940)

M. D. Ramirez: 'Italian Folklore from Tampa, Florida', *Southern Folklore Quarterly*, v (1941), 101

G. P. Jackson: 'The Strange Music of the Old Order Amish', *MQ*, xxxi (1945), 275

C. M. Barbeau: *Alouette: nouveau recueil de chansons populaires* (Montreal, Canada, 1946)

——: 'La guignolée au Canada', *French Folklore Bulletin* (1946), 115

G. P. Jackson: 'The American Amish Sing Medieval Songs Today', *Southern Folklore Quarterly*, x (1946), 151

R. Rubin: 'Yiddish Folksongs in New York City', *New York Folklore Quarterly*, ii (1946), 15

C. M. Babcock: 'Czech Songs in Nebraska', *Western Folklore*, viii (1949), 320

M. Edgar: 'Ballads of the Knife-Men', *Western Folklore*, viii (1949), 53

J. W. Frey: 'Amish Hymns as Folk Music', *Pennsylvania Songs and Legends*, ed. G. Korson (Philadelphia, PA, 1949/R1960), 129

G. Korson, ed.: *Pennsylvania Songs and Legends* (Philadelphia, PA, 1949/R1960)

H. Creighton: *Folklore of Luneburg County, Nova Scotia* (Ottawa, Canada, 1950)

W. E. Boyer, A. F. Buffington and D. Yoder, eds.: *Songs Along the Mahantongo Valley* (Lancaster, PA, 1951)

R. R. MacCurdy and D. D. Stanley: 'Judeo-Spanish Ballads from Atlanta, Georgia', *Southern Folklore Quarterly*, xv (1951), 221

G. P. Jackson: 'Pennsylvania Dutch Spirituals', *MQ*, xxxviii (1952), 80

C. Burkhart: 'The Church Music of the Old Order Amish and Old Colony Mennonites', *Mennonite Quarterly Review*, xxvii (1953), 34

K. Peacock: 'Nine Songs from Newfoundland', *Journal of American Folklore*, lxvii (1954), 123

B. Nettl and I. Moravcik: 'Czech and Slovak Songs Collected in Detroit', *Midwest Folklore*, v (1955), 37

B. Nettl: 'The Hymns of the Amish: an Example of Marginal Survival', *Journal of American Folklore*, lxx (1957), 323

J. Balys: *Lithuanian Folksongs in America: Narrative Songs and Ballads* (Boston, MA, 1958)

D. Borcherdt: 'Armenian Folk Songs and Dances in the Fresno and Los Angeles Areas', *Western Folklore*, xviii (1959), 1

R. K. Hohmann: *The Church Music of the Old Order Amish of the United States* (diss., Northwestern U., 1959)

H. Creighton: 'Songs from Nova Scotia', *JIFMC*, xii (1960), 84

K. Peacock: *The Native Songs of Newfoundland* (Ottawa, Canada, 1960)

E. C. Wolf: *Lutheran Church Music in America during the Eighteenth and Early Nineteenth Centuries* (diss., Northwestern U., 1960)

H. Pawlowska: *Merrily We Sing: 105 Polish Folksongs* (Detroit, MI, 1961)

R. Rubin: 'Yiddish Folksongs of Immigration and the Melting Pot', *New York Folklore Quarterly*, xvii (1961), 173

D. Yoder: *Pennsylvania Spirituals* (Lancaster, PA, 1961)

C. M. Barbeau: *Le rossignol y chante* (Ottawa, Canada, 1962)

H. Creighton: *Maritime Folk Songs* (Toronto, Canada, 1962)

E. D. Ives: 'Satirical Songs in Maine and the Maritime Provinces of Canada', *JIFMC*, xiv (1962), 65

G. M. Laws Jr: 'Anglo-Irish Balladry in North America', *Folklore in Action: Essays for Discussion in Honor of MacEdward Leach*, ed. H. P. Beck (Philadelphia, PA, 1962/R1972), 172

E. Fowke: 'British Ballads in Ontario', *Midwest Folklore*, xiii (1963), 133

R. Rubin: *Voices of a People: the Story of Yiddish Folksong* (New York, 1963, 2/1973)

S. Erdely: 'Folksinging of the American Hungarians in Cleveland', *EM*, viii (1964), 14

E. D. Ives: *Larry Gorman: the Man Who Made the Songs* (Bloomington, IN, 1964)

E. Fowke: *Traditional Singers and Songs from Ontario* (Hatboro, PA, 1965)

K. Peacock: *Songs of the Newfoundland Outports* (Ottawa, Canada, 1965)

R. L. Wright: *Swedish Emigrant Ballads* (Lincoln, NE, 1965)

L. W. Farlee: *A History of the Church Music of the Amana Society, the Community of True Inspiration* (diss., U. of Iowa, 1966)

W. J. Jost: *The Hymn Tune Tradition of the General Conference Mennonite Church* (diss., U. of Southern California, 1966)

S. Erdely: 'Research on Traditional Music of Nationality Groups in Cleveland and Vicinity', *EM*, xii (1968), 245

H. Martens: *Hutterite Songs: the Origins and Aural Transmission of their Melodies from the Sixteenth Century* (diss., Columbia U., 1969)

B. Waschek: *Czech and Slovak Folk Music in Masaryktown and Slovenska-Zahrada, Florida* (diss., Florida State U., 1969)

E. Fowke: *Lumbering Songs from the Northern Woods* (Austin, TX, 1970)

I. J. Katz: 'Marius Barbeau, 1883–1969', *EM*, xiv (1970), 129

R. B. Klymasz: *An Introduction to the Ukrainian-Canadian Immigrant Folksong Cycle* (Ottawa, Canada, 1970)

K. Peacock: *Songs of the Doukhobors: an Introductory Outline* (Ottawa, Canada, 1970)

K. A. Swanson: 'Music of Two Finnish-Apostolic Lutheran Groups in Minnesota: the Heidemanians and the Pollarites', *Student Musicologists at Minnesota*, iv (1970–71), 1–36

H. Creighton: *Folksongs from Southern New Brunswick* (Ottawa, Canada, 1971)

E. D. Ives: *Lawrence Doyle: the Farmer Poet of Prince Edward Island* (Orono, ME, 1971)

M. Karpeles: *Folk Songs from Newfoundland* (London, 1971)

K. Peacock: *A Garland of Rue* (Ottawa, Canada, 1971)

H. Creighton: 'Canada's Maritime Provinces – an Ethnomusicological Survey', *EM*, xvi (1972), 411, 414

P. V. Diagle: *Tears, Love and Laughter: the Story of the Acadians* (Church Point, LA, 1972)

R. Qureshi: 'Ethnomusicological Research among Canadian Communities of Arab and East Indian Origin', *EM*, xvi (1972), 381

W. W. Kolar: *A History of the Tambura* (Pittsburgh, PA, 1973–5)

A. F. Buffington: *Pennsylvania German Secular Folksongs* (Breinigsville, PA, 1974)

R. B. Klymasz and J. Porter: 'Traditional Ukrainian Balladry in Canada', *Western Folklore*, xxxiii (1974), 89–132

L. E. McCullough: 'An Historical Sketch of Traditional Irish Music in the United States', *Folklore Forum*, vii (1974), 177

Song Pangsong: *The Korean Canadian Folksong: an Ethnomusicological Study* (Ottawa, Canada, 1974)

——: *German Singing Societies in Texas* (diss., North Texas State U., 1975)

T. J. Albrecht: 'The Music Libraries of the German Singing Societies in Texas, 1850–1855', *Music Library Association Notes*, xxxi (1975), 517

L. W. Larson: *Scandinavian-American Folk Dance Music of the Norwegians in Minnesota* (diss., U. of Minnesota, 1975)

L. E. McCullough: 'An American Maker of Uillean Pipes: Patrick Hennelly', *Eire-Ireland*, x (1975), 109

R. L. Wright: *Irish Emigrant Ballads and Songs* (Bowling Green, OH, 1975)

R. Ariano and R. D'Ariano: *Italo-American Ballads, Poems, Lyrics, and Melodies* (Parsons, WV, 1976)

T. C. Grame: *America's Ethnic Music* (Tarpon Springs, FL, 1976)

P. Hopkins: 'Individual Choice and the Control of Musical Change', *Journal of American Folklore*, lxxxix (1976), 449

J. K. Kardas: *Acculturation in the Folk Music of a Polish-American Community in Lackawanna, New York* (diss., Brown U., 1976)

E. oskoff: *The Effect of Mysticism on the Nigunim of the Lubavitcher Hasidim* (diss., U. of Pittsburgh, 1976)

B. Nettl and H. Myers: *Folk Music in the United States: an Introduction* (Detroit, MI, 1976) [originally published as *An Introduction to Folk Music in the United States*, 1960]

R. Riddle: 'The Cantonese Opera: a Chapter in Chinese-American History', *The Life, Influence, and Role of the Chinese in the United States, 1776–1960*, ed. T. Chinn (San Francisco, CA, 1976), 40

——: *Chinatown's Music: a History and Ethnography of Music and Music-drama in San Francisco's Chinese Community* (diss., U. of Illinois, 1976)

A. Virgilio Savona and M. Straniero: *Canti dell'emigrazione* (Milan, 1976)

Chun-kin Leung: 'Notes on Cantonese Opera in North America', *Chinoperl Papers*, vii (1977), 9

P. Gronow: *Studies in Scandinavian-American Discography* (Helsinki, 1977)

R. Riddle: 'Music in America's Chinatowns in the Nineteenth Century', *Chinese Historical Society of American Bulletin*, xii/5 (1977), 1

M. Gualerzi: *La musica popolare italiana in dischi commerciali 78 rpm 1900–1959 in Italia e negli State Uniti* (Bologna, 1977–8)

J. Balys: *Lithuanian Folksongs in America*, ii (Silver Springs, MD, 1978)

S. G. Davis: 'Utica's Polka Music Tradition', *New York Folklore*, iv (1978), 103

S. Erdely: 'Traditional and Individual Traits in the Songs of Three Hungarian-Americans', *Selected Reports in Ethnomusicology*, ed. J. Porter, iii 1 (Los Angeles, CA, 1978), 99–151

M. Forry: 'Becar Music in the Serbian Community of Los Angeles: Evolution and Transformation', *Selected Reports in Ethnomusicology*, ed. J. Porter, iii 1 (Los Angeles, CA, 1978), 175–210

E. Koskoff: 'Contemporary Nigun Composition in an American Hasidic Community', *Selected Reports in Ethnomusicology*, ed. J. Porter, iii/1 (Los Angeles, CA, 1978), 153

C. Marcel-Dubois: 'Réflexions sur l'heritage musical français en Louisiane', *Selected Reports in Ethnomusicology*, ed. J. Porter, iii/1 (Los Angeles, CA, 1978), 25–76

L. E. McCullough: *Irish Music in Chicago: an Ethnomusicological Study* (diss., U. of Pittsburgh, 1978)

C. Niles: 'The Revival of the Latvian Kokle in America', *Selected Reports in Ethnomusicology*, ed. J. Porter, iii/1 (Los Angeles, CA, 1978), 211

J. Porter, ed.: *Selected Reports in Ethnomusicology*, iii/1 (Los Angeles, CA, 1978)

R. Riddle: 'Music Clubs and Ensembles in San Francisco's Chinese Community', *Eight Urban Musical Cultures: Tradition and Change*, ed. B. Nettl (Urbana, IL, 1978), 223–59

B. C. Wade: 'Indian Classical Music in North America: Cultural Give and Take', *Contributions to Asian Studies*, xii (1978), 29

459

S. Erdely: 'Ethnic Music in the United States: an Overview', *YIFMC*, xi (1979), 114

D. K. Wilgus: '"Rose Connoley": an Irish Ballad', *Journal of American Folklore*, xcii (1979), 172

P. V. Bohlman: 'The Folk Songs of Charles Bannen: the Interaction of Music and History in Southwestern Wisconsin', *Transactions of the Wisconsin Academy of Sciences, Arts and Letters*, lxviii (1980), 167

——: *Music in the Culture of German-Americans in North-Central Wisconsin* (diss., U. of Illinois, 1980)

R. J. Ficca: *A Study of Slavic-American Instrumental Music in Lyndora, Pennsylvania* (diss., U. of Pittsburgh, 1980)

S. Armistead and J. H. Silverman, eds.: *Judeo-Spanish Ballads from New York: Collected by Mair José Benardete* (Berkeley, CA, 1981)

A. Catlin: *Music of the Hmong: Singing Voices and Talking Reeds* (Providence, RI, 1981)

H. Kallmann, G. Potvin and K. Winters, eds.: *Encyclopedia of Music in Canada* (Toronto, Canada, 1981)

B. J. Ancelet: *The Makers of Cajun Music* (Austin, TX, 1982)

A. Catlin: 'Speech Surrogate Systems of the Hmong: From Singing Voices to Talking Reeds', *The Hmong in the West: Observations and Reports*, ed. B. T. Dowling and D. P. Olney (Minneapolis, MN, 1982), 170

J. E. Kleeman: *The Origins and Stylistic Development of Polish-American Polka Music* (diss., U. of California, Berkeley, 1982)

H. W. Marshall, ed.: *Ethnic Recordings in America: a Neglected Heritage* (Washington, DC, 1982)

M. Slobin: *Tenement Songs: the Popular Music of the Jewish Immigrants* (Urbana, IL, 1982)

R. K. Spottswood: 'The Sajewski Story: Eighty Years of Polish Music in Chicago', *Ethnic Recordings in America: a Neglected Heritage* (Washington, DC, 1982), 133–73

J. Broven: *South to Louisiana: the Music of the Cajun Bayous* (Gretna, LA, 1983)

M. K. Hom: 'Some Cantonese Folksongs on the American Experience', *Western Folklore*, xlii (1983), 126

R. Riddle: *Flying Dragons, Flowing Streams: Music in the Life of San Francisco's Chinese* (Westport, CT, 1983)

R. Wright and R. L. Wright: *Danish Emigrant Ballads and Songs* (Carbondale, IL, 1983)

B. J. Ancelet and E. Morgan Jr: *The Makers of Cajun Music/Musiciens cadiens et creoles* (Austin, TX, 1984)

P. V. Bohlman: 'Hymnody in the Rural German-American Community of the Upper Midwest', *Hymn*, xxxv (1984), 158

C. Keil: 'The Dyna-Tones: a Buffalo Polka Band in Performance, in Rehearsal, and on Record', *New York Folklore*, x (1984), 117

M. Slobin: *Klezmer* Music: an American Ethnic Genre', *YTM*, xvi (1984), 34

A. Arnold: 'Aspects of Asian Indian Musical Life in Chicago', *Selected Reports in Ethnomusicology*, vi: *Asian Music in North America*, ed. N. A. Jairazbhoy and S. C. DeVale (Los Angeles, CA, 1985), 25

N. A. Jairazbhoy and S. C. DeVale, eds.: *Selected Reports in Ethnomusicology*, vi: *Asian Music in North America* (Los Angeles, CA, 1985)

R. Riddle: 'Korean Musical Culture in Los Angeles', *Selected Reports in Ethnomusicology*, vi: *Asian Music in North America*, ed. N. A. Jairazbhoy and S. C. DeVale (Los Angeles, CA, 1985), 189

G. Thompson and M. Yodh: 'Garba and the Gujaratis of Southern California', *Selected Reports in Ethnomusicology*, vi: *Asian Music in North America*, ed. N. A. Jairazbhoy and S. C. DeVale (Los Angeles, CA, 1985), 59

E. C. Wolf: 'Two Divergent Traditions of German-American Hymnody in Maryland circa 1800', *American Music*, iii (1985), 299

M. Slobin, D. Schiff, and I. J. Katz: 'Jewish-American Music', *The New Grove Dictionary of American Music* (London, 1986)

M. Sorce Keller: 'European American Music, §II, 5 'Italian', *The New Grove Dictionary of American Music* (London, 1986)

'Asian-American Music', *The New Grove Dictionary of American Music* (London, 1986)

'European-American Music', *The New Grove Dictionary of American Music* (London, 1986)

M. Sarkissian: *Armenian Musical Culture in Toronto: Political and Social Divisions in an Immigrant Community* (diss., U. of Illinois, 1987)

J. Sciorra: '"O' Giglio e Paradiso": Celebration and Identity in an Urban Ethnic Community', *Urban Resources*, v./3 (1989)

A. T. Rauche: 'The Tarantella: Musical and Ethnic Identity for Italian-Americans', J. Scelsa, S. LaGumina and L. Tomasi, eds., *Italian Americans in Transition* (New York, 1990)

E. S. Rocco: *Italian Wind Bands: a Surviving Tradition in the Milltowns of Pennsylvania* (New York, 1990)

460

CHAPTER XVI

The West Indies

HELEN MYERS

The Creole cultures of the West Indies (from the Portuguese *crioulo*, 'locally raised') have been the object of intensive study since World War II by anthropologists, political scientists, and linguists, who have regarded these highly stratified small-scale societies as virtual laboratories for social science research (Weatherly, 1923; Lowenthal, 1960, 1972; Wagley, 1960; bibliography, Comitas, 1968). Ethnomusicologists have been slow to explore the diverse music of these island cultures, a situation difficult to explain in view of the lively carnival arts practised there, the relatively tame fieldwork conditions and the proximity to the USA. The West Indies have lacked the lure of the East Indies, Africa and the Orient; the miniature scale of the some 50 societies and the virtual absence of authentic aboriginal traditions put off scholars of earlier generations. Ethnomusicological interest developed in the wake of anthropological studies of the New World Negro, particularly the seminal work of Melville J. Herskovits (1938, 1941, 1949, 1958; M. J. and F. S. Herskovits, 1947). His conclusions about cultural change, marginal survival, acculturation, reinterpretation and syncretism were tested in the world of music by his students, including Richard Waterman (retention of African patterns in Trinidad, 1943) and Alan Merriam (Afro-Bahian cult groups, 1951).

The West Indies is a crescent-shaped archipelago more than 2400 sq km in length, stretching from near Florida to the Venezuelan coast, separating the Atlantic Ocean on the east from the Gulf of Mexico and the Caribbean Sea on the west. The islands (total area 236,000 sq km) can be divided by cultural orientation into those with British, French and Dutch affiliation – the West Indies proper – and those with an Iberian background – Cuba, Puerto Rico and the Dominican Republic (*see* Chapter XVII, 'Latin America'). Culturally and musically the three Guianas – French Guiana, Guyana (formerly British) and Surinam (Netherlands) – belong to the West Indies as does Belize (former British Honduras) in Central America. The islands are known collectively as the Antilles – the Greater Antilles (an ancient Central American mountain chain), including the large islands of Cuba, Jamaica, Hispaniola (Haiti and the Dominican Republic) and Puerto Rico, and the Lesser Antilles (small volcanic and limestone islands), including the Windward and Leeward Islands as well as the Bahamas, Trinidad and Tobago and numerous islands on the continental fringe. Eleven million people inhabit the more than 50

distinct geographical and political West Indian units, including the independent states of Barbados, Dominica, Grenada, Jamaica, St Lucia, and Trinidad
and Tobago; states in free association with the UK comprising Anguilla,
Antigua, St Kitts and St Nevis (Leeward Islands), and St Vincent (Windward
Islands); dependent territories of the UK comprising the Cayman Islands,
Turks and Caicos Islands and Montserrat; overseas departments of Metropolitan France comprising Guadeloupe and Martinique; internally self-
governing states within the Kingdom of the Netherlands comprising the
Netherlands Antilles, St Eustatius, Saba and St Martin; and islands
associated with the USA comprising Puerto Rico (commonwealth), the Virgin
Islands (unincorporated territory) and Navassa Island (possession).

Caribbean culture is diverse, reflecting the many racial and linguistic
groups that have settled there – African, Asian and European. Spanish,
English, Dutch, and French are spoken in various regions in addition to Creole
dialects such as Papiamento (Spanish Creole) in Aruba and Curaçao, Srana
(Taki-Taki or English Creole) in Surinam, and Bhojpuri, a Hindi dialect, in
Trinidad and Guyana. Aboriginal American Indian culture is largely extinct
except in Belize amongst the so-called Black Caribs and on the mainland
amongst Mayan- and Tupi-Guarani-speaking peoples. Diverse though the
islands are in culture, language and political organization, they share a
common history of monocrop plantation economies, manned by Asian and
African labourers and governed by European metropolitan powers (Wagley,
1960).

Musicologists have concentrated on the large British islands, Jamaica and
Trinidad (Jamaica: Beckwith and Roberts, 1923; Roberts, 1924, *Jamaican
Anansi Stories*, 1924, 'Some Drums and Drum Rhythms', 1925, 1926, 1928,
1989; also see Miller, 1989; Lewin, 1968, 1971, 1973, 1980; Hopkins, 1984.
Trinidad: Waterman, 1943; Espinet and Pitts, 1944; Carr, 1954; Adams, 1955;
Cameron, 1955; Crowley, 1956, 1959; Merriam, Whinery, and Fred, 1956;
Pearse, 1956; Attaway, 1957; Seeger, 1958; Elder, 1961, 1964, 1965, 1966,
'Evolution of the Traditional Calypso', 1966, 'Kalinda', 1968; Hill, 1972;
Malm, 1978; Myers, 1978, 1980, 1984, 1990). Music of the smaller British
islands of the Lesser Antilles has been studied by D. J. Crowley (1958), R.
Abrahams (1967, 1972, 1974, 1983), and J. S. Handler and C. J. Frisbie
(1972); music of the former British territory of Guyana by V. P. Vatuk (1964,
1965).

Studies of the French Creole traditions of Haiti have been made by
Courlander (1939, 1941, 1944, 1955, 1960), Kolinski (1980) and Welch
(1977). Little musicological research has been conducted on the Dutch and
French territories (but see for Surinam, M. J. and F. S. Herskovits, 1936, and
L. C. van Panhuys, 1936; for Curaçao, de Goeje, 1948, 1950, and Boskaljon,
1958; for Martinique, Horowitz and Klass, 1961, Horowitz, 1963, and
Desroches, 1980). The Hispanic influences in Trinidadian music, which
derive more from recent contact with Venezuela than from the period of
Spanish rule, have been investigated by K. Malm (1978).

Much of the information about the aboriginal population comes from the
chronicles of early Spanish settlers but research on music is rare (but see T. E.
and A. P. Penard, 1925). Archaeological excavations indicate that the first
inhabitants were of the New Stone Age, their culture dating back 2000 years.

Arawaks and Caribs apparently engaged in agriculture, ceramics and weaving, but no musical instruments have been unearthed, possibly indicating that their music was primarily vocal. The 19th-century historical sources from Trinidad mention an Arawak dance, the *arectoe*, performed at sporting events with music by choral groups and accompanied by drums and conch shells. Some authorities have argued that calypso has its roots in the topical humorous songs *carieto* or (*arieto*) also attributed to the Arawaks, but there is little evidence to support this view. It is unlikely that much music of the rapidly dwindling aboriginal populations survived after the influx of Europeans, Africans and East Indians throughout the 18th and 19th centuries.

Afro-Caribbean music

The most widespread music of the Caribbean islands is of the African-derived black and Creole populations. From the 16th to the 19th century black slaves were brought to the West Indies from the Guinea Coast (groups such as the Fon, Ewe and Yoruba), the Western Sudan (Nupe, Hausa and Mandinka), and the Congo area (Kongo). Following emancipation in the British Empire in 1838, former slaves continued to migrate to the British West Indies from the French West Indies, from the Hispanic Caribbean and from West Africa. In the 1940s, M. J. Herskovits posited the then novel theory that these various populations brought to the New World African cultural practices (including musical forms) which persisted into the 20th century. In *Trinidad Village* (1947) Herskovits used the newly developed anthropological theory of acculturation to explain aspects of a number of African musical retentions among the Spiritual Baptists ('Shouters') and the Shango cult.

The musical traditions of African-American syncretic cults, for instance Vodun in Haiti, Santeria in Cuba and Shango (or Xangô) in Trinidad and Brazil have been a focus of research (Waterman, 1943; Merriam, 1951; Herskovits, 1941; M. J. Herskovits and F. S. Herskovits, 1947; Merriam, Whinery and Fred, 1956; Courlander, 1939, 1941, 1944, 1955, 1960; Simpson, 1970; Welch, 1977). All these hybrid or syncretized cults feature spirit possession, animal sacrifice, drumming and dancing, and a combination of African and Christian deities. Each deity has an individual personality with distinctive powers and is identified by one or several special songs and drum patterns.

The Shango music that Herskovits recorded in Toco was transcribed and analysed by R. A. Waterman (1943), who concluded that drumming, an important feature of Shango ritual, derives from West African drumming. Some Shango songs are accompanied by a single box-drum, but generally, three double-headed drums resembling the Yoruba *bata* drums are used. It is believed that the two larger drums speak to the gods, one to St Michael, the other to St John the Baptist – Catholic identifications of the Yoruba deities Ogun and Shango. The use of rattles and also of hand-clapping (with cupped, rather than flattened, palms) is common to both Nigerian and Trinidadian Shango.

Herskovits stressed African retentions in Shango song style, including body swaying and other movements during singing, antiphony between leader and chorus, and polyrhythm. He assumed that such 'survivals' dated from the pre-emancipation period. Subsequent research indicates, however, that many Africanisms of contemporary West Indian cult music were introduced by free blacks who came to the islands in the second half of the 19th century. Merriam, for instance, found retention of African musical traits in the music of the Rada cult, a community from Benin (formerly Dahomey) founded in Trinidad in 1855 by a free black immigrant who had been a *bokono* (diviner) in Africa. Waterman (1963) also examined African musical survivals in Trinidad, drawing on Herskovits's concepts of reinterpretation (assigning new values to borrowed cultural forms) and syncretism (similarities between distinct cultural forms providing a basis for their fusion). He pointed out that 'since there was little reason, in terms of pressure from the rest of the [New World] culture, to change many diagnostic elements of the West African musical style, it changed only through the incorporation of new musical elements that could be reinterpreted to fit it'.

Other syncretized folk forms of the West Indies include the *bongo*, the *bele*, and the reel; dance-songs in either English or French Creole have been documented by Helen Heffron Roberts, during her pioneering fieldwork in Jamaica, 1920–21 (Beckwith and Roberts, 1923; Roberts, 1924, *Jamaican Anansi Stories*, 1924, 'Some Drums and Drum Rhythms', 1925, 1926, 1928, 1989; also see Miller, 1989). Crowley, D. K. Midgett and J. Guilbaut have studied the English and African traditions of song and story telling of St Lucia, a Windward island of the Lesser Antilles (Crowley, 1955, 1957, 1958; Guilbaut, 1984, 1987, 'Fitness and Flexibility', 1987, 'The La Rose and La Marguerite'; Midgett, 1977).

Calypso and Carnival

West Indian topical songs, including calypso, developed in the 19th and 20th centuries. Although calypso retains African elements, it is a highly eclectic form: Hispanic, British, French and African influences blend in a uniquely Creole expression that has spread from its original source in Trinidad to the entire circum-Caribbean area (studies include Espinet and Pitts, 1944; Carr, 1954; Adams, 1955; Attaway, 1957; Crowley, 1959). J. D. Elder has documented the history of calypso, primarily an urban phenomenon, intimately linked with the celebration of Carnival in Port of Spain (1966, *Evolution of the Traditional Calypso*; 1968). During the 18th century, Trinidadian Carnival was principally for the European ruling classes. Following emancipation it was rapidly taken over by newly freed blacks, by Creoles and by Spanish peasants, who transformed the formerly sedate religious holiday into a lively and sometimes disorderly festival, introducing the *canboulay* (*cannes brûlées*: 'cane burning'), a night-time torchlight procession often including rowdy stick fights between *batoniers*, and the singing of *kalindas*, the antecedent of calypso (Elder, 1966, *Kalinda*). The *kalindas* in these processions celebrated black liberation; the principal singers, *chantuelles* (*shantrelle, shantwell*) were accompanied by horns, conch shells, rattles and African hourglass drums (*doun doun*).

The history and significance of the Carnival arts, including masquerade, music, dance, drama and spectacle have been studied by A. C. Pearse (1956), Crowley (1956), Abrahams (1972) and E. Hill (1972). In the 1850s and 1860s the white ruling classes made repeated attempts to suppress masquerades and revelries on the grounds that they often resulted in violence and street riots. They protested, too, against the obscenity of the *kalindas*, with their lewd dancing and noisy instruments. In 1881 conflict between blacks and whites resulted in two days of rioting in Port of Spain ('the Cannes Brulles Riots') and subsequently led to the prohibition of such torchlight processions. The Peace Preservation Act of 1884 banned the use of African drums, but such political opposition did not prevent the growth of Carnival into a national celebration.

During World War II, Trinidad Carnival gave birth to a uniquely Caribbean instrument, the steel drum or 'pan', 55-gallon oil drums tempered and beaten to produce specific pitches, played in orchestras (Cameron, 1955; Seeger, 1958; Hill, 1972; Myers, 1980; Rimmer, 1984). Instruments are not standardized, as the fierce competition between rival bands has fostered innovation and experimentation in pan design and tuning. Steel bands first became popular in the poorer sections of Port of Spain, where barrack yards attracted gangs of youths. In the 1990s they are an integral part of Carnival celebrations in the West Indies as well as in overseas West Indian communities, particularly in New York City and London.

East Indian cultures

A distinctive musical culture in the Caribbean is preserved by the Hindu and Muslim populations of Trinidad, Grenada, St Lucia, St Vincent, St Kitts, St Croix, Guyana, Jamaica and Martinique. Known originally as the 'Gladstone Coolies', these people were shipped out from India, beginning in 1838, as indentured labourers from India to work the sugar plantations of the Caribbean. They refer to themselves as East Indians to distinguish themselves from other West Indians (all peoples of the West Indies) and from the American Indians (the indigenous Arawaks and Caribs). This export of East Indian labour was suspended during World War I and legally abolished by Act of Parliament in 1921. Study of East Indian music and culture has led to refinement of the theories of acculturation, and syncretism, originally based only on the African-American experience.

Intensive anthropological studies of East Indian communities in the Caribbean were undertaken beginning in the 1950s (Crowley, 1954, 1957; Freilich, 1960; Horowitz, 1963; Horowitz and Klass, 1961; Jha, 1974; Klass, 1959, 1960, 1961; Nevadomsky, 1977; Schwartz, 1963, 1964, 1965, 1967; R. J. Smith, 1963; Smith and Jayawardena, 1958, 1959; Stewart, 1973).

Morton Klass, the first anthropologist to study in Felicity, Trinidad, was particularly interested in the questions of acculturation and cultural persistence. During his stay (1957–8), he examined these opposing forces in relation to five areas of Indian culture: caste, extended family, religion, economics and politics. He concluded that cultural persistence had predominated; the Trinidad Indians had managed to reconstruct a South Asian culture in the Caribbean.

Musical studies of the East Indian community have drawn on anthropological findings (Vatuk, 1964, 1965; Myers, 1978, 1980, 1984, 1990; Desroches, 1980). The primary sources for music research also include fragments from the logs and diaries of the voyages of the indentured labourers from Calcutta and Madras to the West Indies: 'the Madrasee is a lively, singing fellow'; 'coolies and crew were very subdued, there was no music'; 'should be permitted to play their drums till 8 bells'; 'getting music up to amuse the Coolies'; 'Coolies having some native games and war dances'; 'the Coolies are very musical'; 'Coolies performing' (Carlyle, 1859, pp.8–11; Tinker, 1974, pp.160, 164). Nothing about the steps of the dances, the verses of the songs, the types of drums, the groups of singers; here only the sparsest evidence of cultural persistence and the wonderful image of songs and dances at the very moment that they were transported from one world to another as the passengers on these ships; rural folk, leaving home for the first time, members of different castes, different language families, learned to sing together. The amalgam that has become Caribbean East Indian music originated on shipboard as new songs were passed from one voyager to the next and strangers learned to dance hand in hand.

In addition to cultural revitalization, I have found marginal survival in the East Indian community of Felicity, Trinidad, where cultural practices no longer maintained in India are preserved (1980, 1984, 1990). 'How can I explain my feelings of outrage', writes the renowned Trinidad East Indian writer V. S. Naipaul, 'when I heard that in Bombay they used candles and electric bulbs for the Diwali festival, and not the rustic clay lamps of immemorial design, which in Trinidad we still used?' (1968, p.36).

'What is striking', writes John La Guerre, Professor of Government at the University of the West Indies, is 'the virtual demise of some of the more crucial features of East Indian culture – of *panchayat* [village council of five] and of caste – and the retention of those with more symbolic value' (Jha, 1974, p.xiii). These contradictions are the very heart of East Indian life in the Caribbean, and it is this cultural and social complexity that has drawn so many scholars to the West Indies.

Since Herskovits's generation, two opposing views of the cultural diversity in the West Indies have been put forward. Both views, 'pluralism' and 'consensualism', are useful to the musicologist, highlighting the divisions in the multi-ethnic societies of the West Indies. Anthropologists M. G. Smith and L. Despres describe West Indian social organization as 'plural', characterized by 'formal diversity in the basic system of compulsory institutions . . . kinship, education, religion, property and economy, recreation. . . . It does not normally include government' (Smith, 1960, p.769). The pluralists maintain that in Trinidad, Guyana and Surinam, Indians and blacks each have individual systems of agriculture, buying and selling, worship, schools, the arts and music, dance and so on (Benedict, 1962; Crowley, 1957, 1960; Skinner, 1955; and Smith, 1955, 1960, 1965). These separate institutional structures were unified before independence by the European metropolitan powers – England, Holland, France – and now by newly formed local governments. In the pluralist view, Creoles and other minority ethnic groups are antagonistic forces; Indians have no assigned place in the colour-class hierarchy of Trinidad, as it is perceived by Creoles, a hierarchy in which white colour has high status and black low.

Opponents of the pluralist viewpoint, especially Lloyd Braithwaite and R. T. Smith, maintain that the functional, consensual model of society developed by Talcott Parsons best describes these Caribbean societies

(Braithwaite, 1953, 1960, 'The Present Status, 1960, 'Social Stratification'). Pointing out that Indians and blacks share many concepts, they claim that the Indian community is not a separate enclave, but rather one class in a highly stratified but unified society. 'Values are not co-terminous with norms, nor norms with behaviour,' D. Lowenthal points out. 'West Indian social groups often maintain separate institutions and exhibit divergent behaviour while they share underlying values' (1972, p.90).

Competition, Daniel J. Crowley claims, is the motivation behind the Indian's renewed search for his Asian heritage. '"This latter day 'revival' of Indian culture is not Indian at all". In the typical competitive Creole way, East Indians are using Indian culture and often mythical caste for "making style" and as a club with which to beat contemptuous Creoles' (1960, p.853).

The authenticity of Indian cultural survivals has been questioned by C. Jayawardena:

> What is meant by 'persistence' of Indian culture? Since the period of emigration to various countries ranges from three or four decades to more than a century, and since, presumably, society and culture in India were also changing during that time, a question arises as to which point in this flux should be used as the base time to measure change. Is 'persistence' to mean that the customs and organizational principles of peasant communities of Oudh before the mutiny persist in, say, Trinidad, whereas in all likelihood they have changed in India? If the Kenyan grandsons of a Patidar farmer from Gujarat lead the life of the Bombay urban upper class, learned from the *Indian Illustrated Weekly*, does this represent persistence or change? (1968, pp.438–9).

Since World War II the music of Caribbean East Indians and West Indians alike has undergone rapid change, change that follows patterns observed in many other cultures in which the impact of Western culture seems to be endangering the very survival of indigenous expression. Electronic instruments and urban popular genres are replacing hand-crafted instruments and traditional folk song. During the 1980s, research on West Indian music documented these substitutions, spurred by the quickened pace of urban life, the impact of technology, the introduction of mass media and the development of global communications. It is not unusual for ethnomusicologists to return to West Indian communities they studied a decade earlier, to find the musical scene transformed through modernization and Westernization. Scholars of these up-beat islands, lands of competition and Carnival, are able, perhaps, to accept these innovations more gracefully than those working in more rigid societies; students of West Indian music quickly learn to celebrate change and to applaud revitalization as they mourn the passing of traditional folkways.

Bibliography

J. Carlyle, ed.: *Journal of a Voyage with Coolie Emigrants from Calcutta to Trinidad. By Captain and Mrs. Swinton, Late of the Ship, 'Salsette'* (London, 1859)

467

M. W. Beckwith and H. H. Roberts: *Christmas Mummings in Jamaica* (Poughkeepsie, NY, 1923)

U. G. Weatherly: 'The West Indies as a Sociological Laboratory', *American Journal of Sociology*, xxix (1923), 290

M. W. Beckwith: 'English Ballad in Jamaica: a Note Upon the Origin of the Ballad Form, With Music and Texts', *Publications of the Modern Language Association of America*, xxxix (1924), 455

H. H. Roberts: *Jamaican Anansi Stories: Collected by Martha Warren Beckwith, with Music Recorded in the Field by Helen H. Roberts* (New York, 1924)

——: 'Some Drums and Drum Rhythms of Jamaica', *Natural History*, xxiv (1924), 241

T. E. Penard and A. P. Penard: 'Four Arawak Indian Songs', *West-Indische Gids*, vii (1925), 497

H. H. Roberts: 'A Study of Folk Song Variants Based on Field Work in Jamaica', *Journal of American Folk-Lore*, xxxviii (1925), 149–216

——: 'Possible Survivals of African Song in Jamaica', *MQ*, xxii (1926), 340

——: *Jamaican Folk-lore: Collected by Martha Warren Beckwith, with Music Recorded in the Field by Helen H. Roberts* (New York, 1928)

M. J. Herskovits and F. S. Herskovits: *Suriname Folk-Lore* (New York, 1936)

L. C. van Panhuys: 'Aard en Karaketer van Surinaamische Liederen' [Nature and Character of Surinam Songs], *West-Indische Gids*, xviii (1936), 1

M. J. Herskovits: *Life in a Haitian Valley* (New York, 1937)

——: *Acculturation: the Study of Culture Contact* (New York, 1938)

H. Courlander: *Haiti Singing* (Chapel Hill, NC, 1939)

——: 'Musical Instruments of Haiti', *MQ* (1941)

M. J. Herskovits: 'Patterns of Negro Music', *Transactions of the Illinois State Academy of Science*, xxxiv/1 (1941), 19

R. A. Waterman: *African Patterns in Trinidad Negro Music* (diss., Northwestern U., 1943)

H. Courlander: 'Abakwa Meeting in Guanabacoa', *Journal of Negro History* (1944)

C. S. Espinet and H. Pitts: *Land of Calypso: the Origin and Development of Trinidad's Folk-Song* (Port of Spain, 1944)

M. J. Herskovits and F. S. Herskovits: *Trinidad Village* (New York, 1947)

C. H. de Goeje: 'De Wiri-Wiri, een Muziek-Instrument van Curaçao' [The Wiri-Wiri, a Musical Instrument of Curaçao], *West-Indische Gids*, xxix (1948), 225

M. J. Herskovits: *Man and His Works* (New York, 1949)

C. H. de Goeje: 'Verwanten van de Curacaose Wiri' [Relatives of the Curaçao Wiri], *West-Indische Gids*, xxxi (1950), 180

A. P. Merriam: *Songs of the Afro-Bahian Cults: an Ethnomusicological Analysis* (diss., Northwestern U., 1951)

L. Braithwaite: 'Social Stratification in Trinidad: a Preliminary Analysis', *Social and Economic Studies*, ii (1953), 5–175

A. T. Carr: 'Trinidad Calypso in Unique Folk Culture', *Caribbean Commission: Monthly Information Bulletin*, vii (1954), 162

D. J. Crowley: 'East Indian Festivals in Trinidad Life', *Caribbean Commission: Monthly Information Bulletin*, vii (1954), 202, 208

T. Van Dam: 'The Influence of the West African Songs of Derision in the New World', *African Music Society Journal*, i (1954), 53

A. A. Adams: 'Whence Came the Calypsos? *Caribbean*, viii (1955), 218, 230, 235

N. E. Cameron: 'Harmony in Steel Bands', *New Commonwealth, British Caribbean Supplement*, xxx/11 (1955), xviii

H. Courlander: 'The Loa of Haiti: New World African Deities', *Miscelanea de estudios dedicandos a Fernando Ortiz por sus discipulos, colegas y amigos* (Havana, 1955)

D. J. Crowley: 'Festivals of the Calendar in St Lucia', *Caribbean Quarterly*, iv (1955), 99

A. Merriam: 'The Use of Music in the Study of a Problem of Acculturation', *American Anthropologist*, lvii (1955), 28

A. C. Pearse: 'Aspects of Change in Caribbean Folk Music', *JIFMC*, vii (1955), 29

E. P. Skinner: *Ethnic Interaction in a British Guiana Rural Community: a Study in Secondary Acculturation and Group Dynamics* (diss., Columbia U., 1955)

M. G. Smith: *A Framework for Caribbean Studies* (Mona, Jamaica, 1955)

D. J. Crowley: 'The Traditional Masques of Carnival', *Caribbean Quarterly*, iv (1956), 194

A. P. Merriam, S. Whinery and B. G. Fred: 'Songs of a Rada Community in Trinidad', *Anthropos*, li (1956), 157

A. C. Pearse: 'Carnival in Nineteenth Century Trinidad', *Caribbean Quarterly*, iv (1956), 175

W. Attaway: *Calypso Song Book* (New York, 1957)

D. J. Crowley: 'Plural and Differential Acculturation in Trinidad', *American Anthropologist*, lix (1957), 817

——: 'Song and Dance in St Lucia', *EM*, ix (1957), 4

R. Boskaljon: *Honderd Jaar Muziekleven Op Curaçao* [Hundred Years of Music on Curaçao] (Assen, The Netherlands, 1958)

D. J. Crowley: 'La Rose and La Marguerite Societies in St Lucia', *Journal of American Folklore*, lxxi (1958), 541

——: 'The Shak-Shak in the Lesser Antilles', *EM*, iii (1958), 112

M. J. Herskovits: *The Myth of the Negro Past* (Boston, MA, 1958)

P. Seeger: 'The Steel Drum: a New Folk Instrument', *Journal of American Folklore*, lxxi (1958), 52

R. T. Smith and C. Jayawardena: 'Hindu Marriage Customs in British Guiana', *Social and Economic Studies*, vii (1958), 178

D. J. Crowley: 'Toward a Definition of "Calypso"', *EM*, iii (1959), 57, 117

M. Klass: *Cultural Persistence in a Trinidad East Indian Community* (diss., Columbia U., 1959)

R. T. Smith and C. Jayawardena: 'Marriage and the Family Amongst East Indians in British Guiana', *Social and Economic Studies*, viii (1959), 321–76

L. Braithwaite: 'The Present Status of Social Sciences in the British Caribbean', *Caribbean Studies: a Symposium*, ed. V. Rubin (Seattle, WA, 1960)

——: 'Social Stratification and Cultural Pluralism', *Annals of the New York Academy of Sciences*, lxxxiii, Art. 5: *Social and Cultural Pluralism in the Caribbean* (20 Jan 1960), 816

H. Courlander: *The Drum and the Hoe: Life and Lore of the Haitian People* (Berkeley, CA, 1960) [with 186 transcr. by M. Kolinski]

D. Crowley: 'Cultural Assimilation in a Multiracial Society', *Annals of the New York Academy of Sciences*, lxxxiii, Art. 5: *Social and Cultural Pluralism in the Caribbean* (20 Jan 1960), 850

M. Freilich: *Cultural Diversity Among Trinidadian Peasants* (diss., Columbia U., 1960)

M. Klass: 'East and West Indians: Cultural Complexity in Trinidad', *Annals of the New York Academy of Sciences*, lxxxiii, Art. 5: *Social and Cultural Pluralism in the Caribbean* (20 Jan 1960), 855

D. Lowenthal: 'The Range and Variation of Caribbean Societies', *Annals of the New York Academy of Sciences*, lxxxiii, Art. 5: *Social and Cultural Pluralism in the Caribbean* (20 Jan 1960), 786

M. G. Smith: 'Social and Cultural Pluralism', *Annals of the New York Academy of Sciences*, lxxxiii, Art. 5: *Social and Cultural Pluralism in the Caribbean* (20 Jan 1960), 763

C. Wagley: 'Plantation America: a Cultural Sphere', *Caribbean Studies: a Symposium*, ed. V. Rubin (Seattle, WA, 1960)

J. D. Elder: *Song Games from Trinidad and Tobago* (Delaware, OH, 1961)

M. M. Horowitz and M. Klass: 'The Martiniquan East Indian Cult of Maldevidan', *Social and Economic Studies*, x (1961), 93

M. Klass: *East Indians in Trinidad: a Study in Cultural Persistence* (New York, 1961)

B. Benedict: 'Stratification in Plural Societies', *American Anthropologist*, lxiv (1962), 1235

E. Hill: *The Artist in West Indian Society: a Symposium* (Mona, Jamaica, 1963)

M. M. Horowitz: 'The Worship of South Indian Deities in Martinique', *Ethnology*, ii (1963), 339

B. M. Schwartz: *The Dissolution of Caste in Trinidad* (diss., UCLA, 1963)

R. J. Smith: *Muslim East Indians in Trinidad: Retention of Ethnic Identity under Acculturative Conditions* (diss., U. of Pennsylvania, 1963)

R. A. Waterman: 'On Flogging a Dead Horse: Lessons Learned from the Africanisms Controversy', *EM*, vii (1963), 83

J. D. Elder: 'Color, Music and Conflict: a Study of Aggression in Trinidad with Reference to the Role of Traditional Music', *EM*, viii (1964), 128

B. M. Schwartz: 'Caste and Endogamy in Trinidad', *Southwestern Journal of Anthropology*, xx (1964), 58

V. P. Vatuk: 'Protest Songs of East Indians in British Guiana', *Journal of American Folklore*, lxxvii (1964), 220

J. D. Elder: *Song Games from Trinidad and Tobago* (Philadelphia, PA, 1965, rev. 2/1974)

B. M. Schwartz: 'Patterns of East Indian Family Organization in Trinidad', *Caribbean Studies*, v (1965), 23

M. G. Smith: *The Plural Society in the British West Indies* (Berkeley, CA, 1965)

V. P. Vatuk: 'Craving for a Child in the Folksongs of East Indians in British Guiana', *Journal of the Folklore Institute*, ii (1965), 55

J. D. Elder: *Evolution of the Traditional Calypso of Trinidad and Tobago: a Socio-historical Analysis of Song-change* (diss., U. of Pennsylvania, 1966)

——: '*Kalinda*: Song of the Battling Troubadours of Trinidad', *Journal of the Folklore Institute*, iii (Bloomington, IN, 1966), 192

R. Abrahams: 'The Shaping of the Folklore Traditions in the British West Indies', *Journal of Inter-American Studies*, ix (1967), 456

B. M. Schwartz: *Caste in Overseas Indian Communities* (San Francisco, CA, 1967)

L. Comitas: *Caribbeana 1900–1965: a Topical Bibliography* (Seattle, WA, 1968)

C. Dumerve: *Histoire de la musique en Haïti* (Port-au-Prince, 1968)

J. D. Elder: 'The Male-Female Conflict in Calypso', *Caribbean Quarterly*, xiv (1968), 23

C. Jayawardena: 'Migration and Social Change: a Survey of Indian Communities Overseas', *Geographical Review*, lviii (1968), 437

O. Lewin: 'Jamaican Folk Music', *Caribbean Quarterly*, xiv (1968), 49

V. S. Naipaul: *An Area of Darkness* (London, 1968)

R. Stevenson: 'The Afro-American Musical Legacy to 1800', *MQ*, liv (1968), 475

G. E. Simpson: *Religious Cults of the Caribbean: Trinidad, Jamaica, and Haiti* (Rio Piedras, Puerto Rico, 1970)

M. M. Horowitz, ed.: *Peoples and Cultures of the Caribbean* (New York, 1971)

O. Lewin: 'Jamaica's Folk Music', *YIFMC*, iii (1971), 15

R. D. Abrahams: 'Christmas and Carnival on Saint Vincent', *Western Folklore*, xxxi (1972), 275

J. S. Handler and C. J. Frisbie: 'Aspects of Slave Life in Barbados: Music and its Cultural Context', *Caribbean Studies*, xi (1972), 5–46

E. Hill: *The Trinidad Carnival: Mandate for a National Theatre* (Austin, TX, 1972)

D. Lowenthal: *West Indian Societies* (London, 1972)

O. Lewin: *Forty Folk Songs of Jamaica* (Washington, DC, 1973)

J. O. Stewart: *Coolie and Creole: Differential Adaptation in a Neo-Plantation Village – Trinidad West Indies* (diss., UCLA, 1973)

R. D. Abrahams: *Deep the Water, Shallow the Shore: Three Essays on Shantying in the West Indies* (Austin, TX, 1974)

J. C. Jha: 'The Indian Heritage in Trinidad', *Calcutta to Caroni: the East Indians of Trinidad*, ed. J. La Guerre (Port of Spain, 1974)

J. S. Roberts: *Black Music of Two Worlds* (New York, 1974)

H. Tinker: *A New System of Slavery: the Export of Indian Labour Overseas 1830–1920* (London, 1974)

D. K. Midgett: 'Performance Roles and Musical Change in a Caribbean Society', *EM*, xxi (1977), 55

J. J. Nevadomsky: *The Changing Family Structure of the East Indians in Rural Trinidad* (diss., U. of California, Berkeley, 1977)

D. Welch: 'West African Cult Music Retentions in Haitian Urban Vaudou: a Preliminary Report', *Essays for a Humanist: an Offering to Klaus Wachsmann* (New York, 1977), 337

K. Malm: 'The Parang of Trinidad: a Case of Transformation through Exploitation', *Anthropologiska Studier*, xxv–xxvi (1978), 42

H. Myers: 'The Process of Change in Trinidad East Indian Music', *Journal of the Indian Musicological Society*, ix (1978), 11

M. Desroches: 'Validation empirique de la méthode sémiologique en musique: les cas des indicatifs de tambour dans les cérémonies Indiennes en Martinique', *YIFMC*, xii (1980), 67

M. Kolinski: 'Haiti', *Grove 6*

O. Lewin: 'Jamaica', *Grove 6*

H. Myers: 'Trinidad and Tobago', *Grove 6*

R. D. Abrahams: *The Man-of-Words in the West Indies: Performance and the Emergence of Creole Culture* (Baltimore, MO, 1983)

J. Guilbaut: *Musical Events in the Lives of the People of a Caribbean Island, St Lucia* (diss., U. of Michigan, 1984)

J. B. Hopkins: 'Jamaican Children's Songs', *EM*, xxviii (1984), 1–36

H. Myers: *Felicity, Trinidad: the Musical Portrait of a Hindu Village* (diss., U. of Edinburgh, 1984)

J. Rimmer: 'Steel band', *The New Grove Dictionary of Musical Instruments*, ed. S. Sadie (London, 1984)

I. V. Jackson, ed.: *More Than Drumming: Essays on African and Afro-Latin Music and Musicians* (Westport, CT, 1985)

J. Guilbaut: 'Fitness and Flexibility: Funeral Wakes in St Lucia, West Indies', *EM*, xxxi (1987), 273

——: 'The La Rose and La Marguerite Organizations in St Lucia: Oral and Literate Strategies in Performance', *YTM*, xix (1987), 97

T. E. Miller: 'Introductory Essay on H. Roberts's "Spirituals or Revival Hymns. . . ."', *EM*, xxxiii (1989), 405

H. H. Roberts: 'Spirituals or Revival Hymns of the Jamaica Negro', *EM*, xxxiii (1989), 409–474

H. Myers: 'Indian, East Indian, and West Indian Music in Felicity, Trinidad', *Ethnomusicology and Modern Music History*, ed. S. Blum, D. Neuman and P. Bohlman (Urbana, IL, 1990)

CHAPTER XVII

Latin America

The early history of ethnomusicology in Latin American countries dates back to the late 19th century when historians began to recognize the importance of local oral cultural phenomena. This recognition resulted as a reaction against the domination of European and European-related music in Latin America under the control of elite social classes, music that tended to obliterate the nationalizing qualities of local musical expression. At the same time, Latin America, like other Third World regions, provided a similar interest in folk and traditional music by comparative musicologists such as Erich M. von Hornbostel and Curt Sachs, or ethnologists as Theodor Koch-Grünberg, all related to the Berlin School. Not until the 1920s and 1930s, however, were the first music histories of Latin American countries written with specific attention to traditional, folk and urban popular music. Up to that time both European and native scholars of Latin American music paid little attention to actual fieldwork. With a few exceptions, only since about the end of World War II has field research been undertaken, and since about the early 1960s has study *in situ* become systematized. Indeed, a most innovative factor in ethnomusicological research over the last 30 years has been that researchers became aware of the need for first-hand knowledge and experience in the musical traditions they sought to describe and interpret. Such awareness made possible a better, more representative account of folk and traditional music, but an essentially descriptive approach has continued in most places, no doubt resulting from the lack of specific factual data on oral musics in general. Whether in organological studies, in the relationships of music, dance and ritual or in music and traditional poetry used in various contexts, the majority of ethnomusicologists and folklorists have focussed on descriptions.

Particularly important for Latin American ethnomusicologists has been the study of origins along the continuum of the tri-ethnic cultural make-up of Latin American music (Iberian, American, Indian and African). Naive, simplistic generalizations over this question of origins have resulted from the search for 'pure' retention of a given musical trait believed to be attributable to a specific primal cultural root. The essentially mestizo or creole nature of folk and popular culture in Latin America was recognized by ethnomusicologists in the 1940s, with specific attention to the levels of syncretism that account for unique musical features, repertories, instruments, practices, functions and values. But only in the 1960s did scholars begin to recognize the diversity of Latin American musics. Yet insufficient knowledge of the vast music corpora continues, disallowing the possibility of meaningful, cross-cultural comparisons among music cultures that share a similar ethnohistory, as, for example, the Afro-Caribbean communities of Cuba and Haiti or those of western Colombia and northeastern Brazil. In addition, little attention has been given to the significance of the prominent social stratification that typifies Latin America and elucidates the musical expressions that function as class identity symbols. This stratification will provide the keystone to account for the various practices found in rural and urban areas (Béhague, 1982).

Mexico and Central America

Pre-Columbian musical practices have received much attention since the 1930s, concentrating on the acoustical properties and functions of archaeological instruments and early missionary descriptions. Robert Stevenson (1952, 1968) provided detailed descriptions of musical instruments used by the Aztecs, the Mayas and other tribes, as well as the predominantly ritual contexts in which they were played. He also reported on the symbolic carvings and drawings attesting to specific ritual functions that sacred instruments were supposed to fulfil. Stevenson paid close attention to 16th-century Spanish chronicles, iconographic references (including the Mexican codices) and dictionaries of Indian languages compiled by Spaniards, all this allowing the reconstruction of musical practices in pre-Conquest Mesoamerica and the ascription of a pre-Columbian origin to some contemporary Indian musical practices – thereby establishing the continuity of Indian musical cultures. Thomas Stanford (1966, 'A Linguistic Analysis') studied the linguistic evidence that points to the constant union of music and dance and to the ideal sound qualities of loudness, clarity and high pitch, elements still much favoured in contemporary Indian music performance. In his early Mexican music history, Miguel Galindo (1933) dedicated one section to pre-Cortesian music. Gabriel Saldívar's study (1934) deals with the pre-Cortesian and colonial periods of music history, devoting part of his work to music in the pre-Columbian era, then several chapters on music and dance of Mexican Indians since the conquest, and a part to folk music in contemporary Mexico.

The major publications of Vicente T. Mendoza, Mexico's foremost folk music scholar of his generation, appeared from the 1930s to the 1950s. Particularly important in the area of pre-Cortesian music are his studies of pre-Columbian musical instruments (especially 1933 with Castañeda). Charles Boilès also gave detailed information and insights on multiple flutes (1965) and the overall Mesoamerican tradition of pipe and tabor (1966). Samuel Martí (1955, 1968) summarized the various findings on pre-Columbian organology (with liberal illustrations) and provided in his overview of pre-Cortesian music, dance and poetry (1961, *Canto, danza . . .*) a vivid, if sometimes highly subjective and speculative, image of the ancient Mexicans' practices.

The most extensive annotated bibliography on Indian instruments in Mexico and Central America was compiled by John Schechter (1977). Martí joined efforts with Gertrude Kurath (1964) in a study of ancient music and dance, primarily derived from iconographic and archaeological sources. Another useful survey on pre-Hispanic music is by Pablo Castellanos (1971). Although some attention has been given to native conception of sound (through study of lexicographic sources), much remains to be done towards better appreciation of the sophisticated musical systems of the pre-Columbian Mesoamericans.

Contemporary Indian music has been studied sporadically since the 1940s and reported in short articles. No major general overview on the numerous Indian musical traditions of 20th-century Mexico and Central America is available. The 1930 field expeditions in various Mexican states, sponsored by the National Institute of Fine Arts, and reported in *Investigación folklórica en México* (1962, 1964), did not have continuity in later decades as government-sponsored research.

Individual efforts have been the rule since the 1950s. Henrietta Yurchenco worked assiduously among the Purépecha (or Tarascan), Cora, Huichol, Seri, Tarahumara, Yaqui and Tzotzil Indian groups in the 1940s and 1950s, and reported on her field experience (1943, 1946, 'Grabación de música', 1946, 'La recopilación', 1963). Vicente Mendoza studied Otomi musical traditions in general (1951–4), while Boilès (1969, 1971) dealt with the Otomi Carnival and Tepehua ritual music (1967). Frank and Joan Harrison (1968) provided detailed analyses of music and musical instruments of two Mayan groups in Chiapas with the aim of identifying Spanish elements. Thomas Stanford, who studied Indian Carnival songs (1966, 'Three Mexican Indian Carnival Songs') and courtship music in Oaxaca (1969), has been concerned with the acculturation of Indian groups as seen through musical expression. A major comprehensive document dealing with a Mazatec shamanistic performance is provided by Gordon Wasson and others (1974) with 'musicological notes' on the ceremony by Willard Rhodes. *The Proceedings of the First Round Table on Folklore and Ethnomusicology* (Zamora, Michoacán, 1982), published by J. Arturo Chamorro (ed., 1983) included several papers relevant to Mexican Indian music by Stanford, Abraham Cáceres, Felipe Ramírez Gil, Yurchenco, Maria de P. Rosario Pérez and Max Jardow Pedersen (ch.3), and to the state of ethnomusicology in Mexico by Ramírez Gil and Jaime González Quiñones (ch.2). Chamorro contributed an historical study on Tarascan musical instruments (ch.5); his study of percussion instruments (1984) is fairly comprehensive. Stanford provided a general overview on present-day Indian music (1984, pp.46–77).

The mestizo folk music traditions of Mexico and Central America have been regularly studied since about 1945. In Mexico, in addition to a few surveys on folk music (e.g. Mendoza, 1956, *Panorama*), the main focus has been on specific song and dance genres or folk instrumental ensembles. The ballad genre known as *corrido* has received wide attention, including its history, text, and repertory. Mendoza's earlier study on the *corrido*'s relationship to the Spanish *romance* (1939) was followed by studies on specific *corrido* repertories (1956, *El corrido*) and by substantial anthologies (1954, 1964). Merle Simmons's volume *The Mexican Corrido as a Source of an Interpretive Study of Modern Mexico (1870–1950)* (1957) is important for the history of the genre in the period 1870–1950. A special repertory of *corridos* (on the death of President John F. Kennedy) among Mexican American communities was the subject of Dan Dickey's study (1978). Stanford (1974) also dealt with the history of the *villancico* and *corrido* in

Mexico, with detailed descriptions of their musical and literary features. Mendoza's study of *glosas* and *décimas* (1957) stressed the historical development of both genres, primarily from the literary perspective. On the *canción mexicana*, Mendoza (1961) proposed the most comprehensive attempt at classification together with an anthology of music and texts of 311 pieces. He also studied the origins and musical characteristics of the *canción chilena* in Mexico (1948). Unfortunately, the *canción* (in its generic sense) has been classified almost strictly according to function and text-based criteria. Musical analyses are lacking for the *canción* perhaps because of its heterogeneous nature. The specific type of popular song known as *canción ranchera* or simply *ranchera* is more frequently associated with urban popular music and has been mentioned in very general terms (e.g. Reuter, 1981; Stanford, 1984).

The complex of the *son* has occupied students of Mexican folk and popular music, partly because the *son* represents concurrently a song with its poetic contents and a dance, and partly because there are numerous regional variants, such as the *son jarocho, huasteco, jaliscience, abajeño* and *son marimba* associated with specific folk instrumental ensembles. Most studies are concerned with description of the *son* music and song-text repertories, of their musical and choreographic characteristics, and of the specific instrumental make-up of the ensembles. By far the most popular of these ensembles is the *mariachi*, which cuts across regional boundaries and has thus become an identity symbol of Mexico. A general survey of the *son* is provided by Stanford (1972); the *huasteco* and *jarocho* genres have been studied in detail by Lawrence Saunders (1974) and Daniel Sheehy (1979).

The Indian and mestizo musical traditions of the Central American countries have received scant attention since the mid-1940s. Guatemala and Panama have had better treatment than their neighbours but the general paucity of critical studies remains for the entire Central American area. David Vela (1972) has provided a short but informative overview on Central American music.

Indian music of Maya stock in Guatemala has been subject to most consideration: Jesus Castillo (1941), Paul Collaer (1956), Lise Paret-Limardo de Vela (1962) and Norman Hammond (1972). Linda O'Brien's doctoral dissertation (1975) provides an in-depth study of Indian song repertory in truly ethnomusicological terms. The marimba's origins and development are most important for Guatemalans since it is considered the national instrument. In addition to Vela's study (1962), Vida Chenoweth's substantial volume (1964), Mariano López Mayorical's debate (1978) and Carlos Monsanto's article (1982) raise the issue of African or Indian origin of the Guatemalan marimba. 'Ladino' or mestizo music in Guatemala is described in general terms by Paret-Limardo de Vela (1962).

The general description of Panamanian folk music provided by Narciso Garay (1930) was followed by more specialized studies from the 1950s. The Spanish-related folk-song genres, the *décima* and *copla*, were studied by the Zárates (1953). Manuel Zárate (1958) attempted a classification of folk materials and studied the Afro-Panamanian tradition (1968). Ronald Smith (1976) dealt specifically with Afro-Panamanian music and dance. Songs of the Cuna Indians were researched by Sandra McCosker (1974) and the relationships of Cuna language and music by Joel Sherzer and Sammie Ann Wicks

(1982). A descriptive overview of Panama's folk music and dances was published by the Chevilles (1977).

Musical research in Costa Rica, Honduras, El Salvador and Nicaragua has been severely limited. The history of traditional music in El Salvador was undertaken by Maria de Baratta (1951–2) but had no follow-up. In Honduras, Rafael Manzanares (1963, 1967) gave a general view on the main sources of traditional music and described musical instruments, and Terry Agerkop (1976) studied the Miskito Indian musical bow. Some aspects of Costa Rican popular music are mentioned in Bernal Flores's historical survey (1978) and Jorge Luis Acevedo V. surveys the music in Costa Rican Indian reservations (1986) and the music and dances in the province of Guanacaste (1986). There are only a few, very general articles on the music of Nicaragua. Ritual music of the Black Caribs of Nicaragua is the subject of Idalberto Suco Campos's study (1987). Virtually, Central America is one of the most depressed areas of the continent in ethnomusicological research (see Smith, 1982, for further assessment and sound archive data).

Spanish Caribbean

Cuba and Puerto Rico are the two most important areas of the Spanish Caribbean for ethnomusicological research since the 1950s. In Cuba, Alejo Carpentier, Fernando Ortiz and Argeliers León stand out. Carpentier's music history (1946) covers several aspects of Cuban folk and popular music, particularly the dance and music genres known as *contradanza, son* and *danzón*, and the Afro-Cubanism revival of the 1920s a source essential for understanding Cuba's musical formation. The seven-volume study by Ortiz (1950, 1951, 1952–5) on Afro-Cuban music antecedents, songs, dances, theatre and musical instruments, remains a substantial contribution to Cuban ethnomusicology; no subsequent study shows such depth and comprehensiveness. The composer-ethnomusicologist Argeliers León has provided an overview on Cuban folk music (1964), updated 1984, and including the 'guajiro' folk music genres frequently ignored in favour of the Afro-Cuban tradition. Maria Teresa Linares (1958) has considered the Spanish heritage in Cuban music and aspects of Cuban popular music (1970). Carlos Borbolla (1975) has studied the musical nature of the Cuban *son*, Larry Crook (1982) the rhythmic complexities of the *guaguancó* type of rumba, and Peter Manuel (1987) popular music in socialist Cuba.

The musics of Puerto Rico have been investiged systematically since the late 1960s. Anna Figueroa de Thompson (1974) has provided a professional *catalogue raisonné*, Héctor Campos Parsi (1976) a historical overview of the musical traditions, Maria Luisa Muñoz (1966) historical and analytic sketches, and Francisco López Cruz (1967) a study of folk music. Martha Ellen Davis (1972) has analysed the Fiesta de Cruz in San Juan. Afro-Puerto Rican song and dance genres have been studied only sporadically. Edwin Figueroa Berríos (1963) discovered an important music repertory associated with the *bomba*, whose probable African origins are examined in H. Vega-Drouet's dissertation (1979), but the other main genre, the *plena*, still awaits adequate treatment. The *danza puertorriqueña*, on the other hand, has been thoroughly studied by Angel Quintero Rivera (1986).

Folk and popular music in the Dominican Republic was first studied rather thoroughly by J. Arzeno (1927) and updated by J. A. Hernández (1964, 1969). The *merengue*, the national dance and music, received special attention from Emilio Rodríguez Demorizi (1971), Luis Alberti Mieses (1975) and Bernarda Jorge (1982), folk dance music by Lizardo (1975), children's song by Emilio Garrido (1947) and Edna Boggs (1955). Ritual music of predominantly black Dominicans has been analysed by Martha Ellen Davis, who worked at the 'Museo del Hombre Dominicano' for several years; her work on the music of Afro-Dominican religious brotherhoods (1976) and on the *salve* (1981) results from thorough field experience.

Venezuela and the Andean area

The presence in Venezuela of Isabel Aretz and her husband, Luis Felipe Ramón y Rivera, has had beneficial results not only for ethnomusicology in Venezuela but for all Latin America. The Instituto Interamericano de Etnomusicología y Folklore (INDEF), established in Caracas in 1970 under the auspices of the Venezuelan Council of Culture and the Organization of American States and under the directorship of Isabel Aretz, provided the much-needed basic training for numerous young scholars from Mexico, Central and South America and the Caribbean. The Institute also promoted a multinational plan in Latin America for field research and collection, published monographs (including Aretz's own overview of Latin American oral musics, 1980) and the journal *Revista INIDEF* (six issues to 1983), issued audio-visual materials and films, and organized the First Inter-American Congress of Ethnomusicology and Folklore (October 1983). The Institute was reorganized in 1985 and ceased to exist in its previous format and directorship.

Both Aretz and Ramón y Rivera have been prolific on all aspects of Venezuela's oral musical traditions. Besides his in-depth study of the *joropo* (1953), Ramón y Rivera wrote on work songs (1955) and Afro-Venezuelan folk music (1962, 1971), and has published broad surveys on the folk music of his country (1967, 1969), folk song (1972) and popular music (1976). His study of the phenomenology of Latin American traditional music (1980) appeared in the INIDEF series. Aretz's work on Venezuelan music has focussed on folk music and folklore of the Department of Táchira (with Ramón y Rivera, 1961–3), Christmas songs (1962), musical instruments (1967) and the *tamunangue*, a traditional fiesta for San Antonio (1976). Venezuelan Warao Indian music was the subject of Dale Olsen's dissertation (1973), several portions of which appeared in articles (1974, 1975, 1980, 1981). Istvan Halmos (1974) and Terry Agerkop (1976) dealt with Piaroa Indian music and instruments. Jonathan Hill (1985) has presented an engaging study of the linguistic and musical structuring of a special genre of sacred vocal music among the Wakuénai Indians. Afro-Venezuelan music of the Barlovento area interested Juan Liscano (1960), and Max Brandt (1979) wrote his doctoral thesis on Barlovento drum ensembles. A general bibliography on Venezuelan music with 412 entries was compiled by Alberto Calzavara (1986) and an Afro-Venezuelan bibliography by A. Pollak-Eltz (1976).

In Colombia, ethnomusicology has had only a few well-trained, experienced scholars. The folk music traditions of the mountain area, the eastern

477

plains and the Atlantic and Pacific coastal areas have received the main attention. Indian music of the Amazon basin has been neglected, and urban popular music still awaits treatment. Carmen Ortega Ricaurte's extensive bibliography on Colombian music (1973) includes a section on Colombian folk music and dances (121–32). The most prolific writers have been Guillermo Abadía, Manuel Zapata Olivella, and Andrés Pardo Tovar (1970, 1973) providing data on folk and popular musical genres, Zapata Olivella (1962) dealing with the popular *cumbia* (see also Delia Zapata Olivella, 1962, and 1963 describing carnival parades). Pardo Tovar's major introduction to Colombian music (1966) is one of the most comprehensive, and his studies of the traditional songs of Baudó (1960), of the rhythmic and melodic traits of Chocó folk music (with Jesus Pinzón Urrea, 1961), and of the popular guitar making in Chiquinquirá (with Jesús Bermúdez Silva, 1963) are models of serious, detailed work. Specific organological works include those by L. C. Espinosa (1968), G. Abadía Morales (1981) and Egberto Bermúdez (1985), this last providing an interesting discussion of the application in Colombia of the Hornbostel–Sachs classification. Numerous writers have paid attention to the *bambuco*, Colombia's national dance, among them Daniel Zamudio (1961) and Lubia Mazuera (1972). A thoroughly documented study on Colombian musical instruments, folk and popular music and dances is Harry Davidson's Colombian folk dictionary (1970). Octavio Marulanda's general survey (1973) is also useful. The American ethnomusicologist George List carried on extensive field research in the Atlantic coastal area in the 1960s, and his work resulted in several important articles (particularly 1968 and 1973) and a detailed monograph (1983) on the music and poetry in the village of Evitar. List (1966, 'Ethnomusicology in Colombia') and previously S. Marti (1961) wrote about ethnomusicology in Colombia. The American anthropologist Norman Whitten Jr studied the music and social context of the marimba dance, *currulao*, of the Pacific area of Colombia and Ecuador (1967, 1970, 1974). Ronald Smith (1982) describes the sound archival materials on Colombian music available at the Indiana University Archives of Traditional Music. Karl Izikowitz's classical study of Indian musical instruments (1935) is still the major source for Colombian Indian cultures. In 1985 the Instituto de Investigaciones Estéticas of the Universidad Nacional issued the first volume of the *Revista Colombiana de investigación musical*, under the editorship of Egberto Bermúdez.

Although quite old and inaccurate, R. and M. d'Harcourt's volume (1925) provides a basic foundation for study of the folk and traditional music of Ecuador, Peru and Bolivia. The main Ecuadorian scholar has been Segundo Luis Moreno, whose first major work (1930) was followed by a bilingual survey (1949), a study of origins and survivals (1957), and then a collection of his numerous writings (1972); his approach was either descriptive with a frequent diffusionist bias or speculative. Charles Sigmund's doctoral thesis (1971) assesses Moreno's contributions to Ecuadorian musicology. Paulo de Carvalho Neto's dictionary of Ecuadorian folklore (1964) relies almost exclusively on Moreno's writings for its music entries. List gave an assessment of ethnomusicology in Ecuador (1966) and wrote on Jíbaro Indian music (1965). Inés Muriel (1976) also supplied a general view of Jíbaro music. B. Seitz (1981) provided insight into the meaning of the Quichua songs of Indian women of the eastern lowlands of Ecuador. William Belzner (1981) has worked among the Shuar. The Instituto Ecuatoriano de Folklore was active in the late 1960s, under the leadership of Paulo de Carvalho Neto, Napoleón Cisneros, Osvaldo Viteri and the artist Oswaldo Guayasamin. No trained ethnomusicologist, however, was recruited into the Instituto's ranks. Since then, another organization, the Instituto Otavaleño de Antropología, has opened a department of ethnomusicology, under the directorship of Carlos Alberto Coba Andrade, trained at INIDEF. That institute publishes the journal *Sarance*. Coba Andrade's own work includes studies of black folk genres (1980, *Literatura popular afroecuatoriana*) and of musical instruments (1980, *Instrumentos musicales*, 1984). Coba Andrade (1985) contributed a survey of Ecuadorian folk dances. In the 1970s, a number of non-Ecuadorian scholars examined the country's musical expressions. The American ethnomusicologist John Schechter wrote a doctoral dissertation (1982) on Quechua harp and vocal music in the highland (outside Cotacachi) in the context of a child's wake, part of which appeared as an article (1983).

Since the 1930s, pioneers in the study of Peru's traditional musics have been Carlos Vega, Andrés Sas, Rodolfo Holzmann, Josafat Roel Pineda, and later, the composers César Bolaños and Fernando García. Vega provided insights into scales used by pre-Columbian Peruvians (1934) and also brought perspective to the origin and development of such dances as the *zamacueca* in Peru, Argentina, Chile and Ecuador (1952). Vega was also among the first 20th-century scholars to study pre-Columbian organology in the Andean area (1946). Sas, in his 1930s studies of Inca and Nazca music and musical instruments, disclaimed the exclusive use of pentatonicism by the ancient Peruvians and denied the likelihood of polyphony in their musical practices (1935, 1936, 1938). Arturo Jiménez Borja (1951) relied on iconographic evidence to explain possible characteristic methods of playing instruments. Robert Stevenson (1960, 1968), in studies during the 1950s and 1960s, discovered much information about pre-Columbian musical instruments and has provided insights into the pre-Inca and Inca musical cultures by considering linguistic and literary evidence relevant to determining the development of music functions and values over the centuries.

In the 1960s, the composer-musicologist Rodolfo Holzmann published anthologies of contemporary Peruvian folk music (1966, 1967, 1988) and dealt with analytical questions of traditional Indian and mestizo music. His analytical focus rested essentially on scale formations, rhythmic organization and formal structures, and particularly on the characteristic traits of what he called 'primitive melody' (1968, 1980). Roel Pineda, an experienced student of contemporary highland music in Peru, has accumulated much data on facets of Indian and mestizo musical traditions. His article on the *wayno* in Cuzco (1959) follows Carlos Vega 'phraseology' method and generally ignores contextual considerations. Ever since the Casa de la Cultura in Lima was transformed into the Instituto Nacional de Cultura (in the early 1970s), there have been renewed efforts to promote Peruvian music research and publication, primarily through the Oficina de Música y Danza. In the mid-1970s, a large research project concerned with the study, classification and mapping of folk and popular musical instruments in Peru was undertaken and results published (1978) under the supervision of Bolaños, with Fernando García,

Alida Salazar and Roel Pineda as collaborators. The Instituto has also contemplated the more ambitious project of a general atlas of music in Peru (see Olsen, 1979, a preliminary to the project). John Schechter (1979, 1980) has shed light on the ancient Inca 'historical chant'. Thomas Turino (1983, 1984) has dealt with the Peruvian *charango* and its symbolic meanings and identity keying. Turino's dissertation (1987) addressed the rural–urban dichotomy of Aymara Indian music and its adaptive mechanism in Lima as a result of shifting power relations and the need for identity markers. Highland Peruvian panpipe tradition comprises the work of Americo Valencia Chacón (1983 and 1989). Theodore Lucas (1971) has analysed the songs of Shipibo Indians of the Upper Amazon, and Amuesha Indian music of the Peruvian *montaña* has been studied in its ritual performance context by Richard Chase Smith (1977, 1984). Elisabeth den Otter (1985) has presented a comprehensive study of the contexts of music and dance making in Callejón de Huaylas, in North-Central Peru Raúl Romero has provided an overview of Peruvian traditional and popular music (1985).

Urban popular music in Peru has been neglected as a scholarly subject. Besides the descriptive historical account of the *vals criollo* by Santa Cruz (1977) and studies of song texts (e.g. Sergio Zapata Agurto, 1968, and Steve Stein, 1982) a general study of popular music in Lima by José Antonio Lloréns Amico (1983) is short but well-conceived in terms of socio-cultural analysis. Afro-Peruvian music still awaits adequate treatment despite the rediscovery of that tradition since the 1960s (William Tompkins's dissertation, 1981). In 1984 the Lima Catholic University's Instituto Riva Agüero established a new Archival Centre for Traditional Peruvian music under the direction of Raúl Romero, with the aim of centralizing all sorts of recorded materials and of promoting new field recordings. Indeed, one of the major difficulties for developing a Peruvian ethnomusicology comprising all facets of Peru's music heritage still lies in the lack of such centralized primary sources, both oral and written, as an archival centre, with the proper support and continuity of efforts, could provide.

Bolivia does not yet have the necessary institutional foundation to develop ethnomusicological studies of its rich musical traditions. Aspects of pre-Columbian Indian music have received attention, particularly in the general history of José Diaz Gainza (1962). Organological studies of contemporary Indian groups by Bolivian and foreign scholars began in the 1930s with Izikowitz (1932), Manuel Paredes (1936) and Antonio González Bravo (1937, 1949), and continued with Max Peter Baumann (1979, 1981, 'Julajulas'), who also wrote a survey of Andean highland Indian music in Bolivia (1982) and a more focussed study of Chipaya musical culture (1981, 'Music, Dance, and Song'). The d'Harcourts (1959) studied field recordings of Aymara Indian music made in the 1950s and reassessed in the process their earlier pentatonic and retention thesis. Folk festivities and dances have attracted a number of scholars. Olsen (1976) attempted to isolate some pre-Conquest musical elements among the Mojo Indians of Bolivia. Julia Elena Fortún (1957, 1961) studied the Christmas cycles of music and dance in several Bolivian provinces and the famous Devils' Dance (*diablada*). Antonio Paredes Candia (1966) gave an overview of Indian and mestizo dances with commentaries on corresponding music and musical instruments. In the 1960s, the journal *Archivos del folklore boliviano* published useful articles on Bolivian folk music, especially by Angel Olmos Agreda (1966) and Hugo Ruíz Ruíz (1966). On Bolivian urban popular music, in addition to a few studies of the *cueca* (see Porfirio Díaz Machicao, 1968), Gilka Céspedes (1984) stressed the relationship of music in La Paz since the 1950s to indigenous music, and Ernesto Cavour (1974), although providing primarily an instruction manual on playing the panpipe, included some cautious remarks about international cultural colonialism.

Ethnomusicology in Chile has had the good fortune since the 1940s not only of being able to rely on dynamic scholars (e.g. Eugenio Pereira Salas, Carlos Lavin, Carlos Isamitt, Manuel Dannemann, Raquel Barros, Mana Ester Grebe, to name but a few) but also of counting on continuous institutional support through the University of Chile, specifically its Instituto de Investigaciones Folklóricas, created in 1943 and renamed Instituto de Investigaciones Musicales in 1947. The Institute from 1947 to 1970 has promoted activities of all sorts, from exchange programmes, publications of monographs and sound recordings of Chilean traditional music, to university instruction, organization of symposia and festivals and fundamental support of research projects on Chilean music (for a brief summary of these activities see Claro, 1970). An early bibliographic guide on Chilean folklore (Pereira Salas, 1952) included a chapter on music which attested to an incipient tradition of folk music studies. Over the years, the Instituto published a substantial number of essays (in its 'Colección de ensayos') that provided important data on folk music of both Hispanic and Indian derivation. In addition, Chilean scholars have had the most regular scholarly music journal in Latin America, the *Revista musical chilena* (began publication in 1945).

Although the Indian population of Chile represents a minute percentage of the total population, its musical traditions have attracted the attention of several generations of scholars. Studies of Indian musical instruments were first undertaken by Isamitt in the 1930s, followed by C. Vega (1946, a study which, in spite of its title extends to several South American Countries), Juan Orrego-Salas (1966), Jorge Iribarren (1971), Luis Merino (1974) and M. E. Grebe (1973, 1974, 'Instrumentos musicales', 1980). Alejandro Henríquez's volume (1973) deals with Chilean musical instruments in general. Prior to the 1950s, the culture of the Mapuche (Araucanians) received treatment to the neglect of the northern (Aymara, Atacameño, Diaguita) and southernmost (Alacaluf, Ona, Yahgan) Indian groups. Mapuche ritual and social music was studied by Mischa Titiev (1949) and by Grebe (1974, 'Presencia del dualismo'), who provided insight into Mapuche symbolic dualism and its presence in musical forms, ritual dances, and the internal structures of song, and music performance. Grebe (1974, 'La música alacalufe') also studied the dramatic changes in Alacalufe music and with Cristina Alvarez (1974) considered the tritonic melodic structure of Atacameña peasant music. Jorge Urrutia Blondel (1967) described the ritual dances and their music associated with the festivities of San Pedro de Atacama. An interesting festival, Our Lady of Las Peñas in the northern region of Livílcar, in which various ethnic groups participate, was described with some choreographic and musical detail by Lavín (1948–9). Aymara music in Chile was neglected for many years until the major investigation carried out by Grebe (1980) was completed. Knowledge of Fuegian music (of those groups of Tierra del Fuego) continues to be

481

based on Erich von Hornbostel's articles (1936, 1948), supplemented by Grebe (1974, 'La música alacalufe').

Chilean folk mestizo music has been surveyed in the general music history of S. Claro Valdés and Urrutia Blondel (1973) and in Claro Valdés's general introduction (1979). R. Barros and M. Dannemann (1970) studied quite thoroughly the Chilean *romancero* or balladry. In an attempt to draw a comprehensive picture of the problems facing Chilean folk music studies, Dannemann (1972) convincingly discussed the general methodology necessary to establish the atlas of Chilean folklore. He also analysed the situation of Chilean folk music (1975), deploring the 'pseudo' folk styles that emerged in the early 1970s. The retention of old Spanish modes in Chile prompted Grebe (1967, 'Modality'; 1971–2) to search for correspondence between Spanish Renaissance music and Chilean folk music. Her study of the *verso* (1967, *The Chilean Verso*) considered all factors of this genre of song poetry. Among dance genres, the Chilean *cueca* has been treated by Vega (1947) and more recently by Claro Valdés (1984) and Pablo Garrido (1979). Of all phases of urban popular music in Chile the 'nueva canción' movement has received the most attention; Eduard Carrasco (1982) has given an overview, and Bernardo Subercaseaux (1980) and Shu Cohen (n.d.) have examined the repertories of the 1960s and 1970s, particularly the songs of Violeta Parra and Victor Jara.

In Paraguay, there are no strictly ethnomusicological studies. The only major survey that has appeared since 1945 is by Boettner (n.d., mid-1950s), who gave some attention to indigenous music and musical instruments.

The Río de la Plata area and Brazil

Even before the turn of the 20th century, Argentine scholars, notably the literary historian Ricardo Rojas, paid close attention to the folk music of their country. From the late 1920s until his death in 1966, Carlos Vega was the major force in Argentine folk music research, not only through his own work as an assiduous researcher but also as a successful promoter of institutionalized folklore studies in general. His major contributions include his controversial theoretical classification of Latin American music corpora ('cancioneros') according to origin, melodic structure and geographical-cultural distribution (1944), and his proposed method of transcription and analysis of melodic units, which he called 'phraseology' (1941). Vega's basic views of the discipline were strongly influenced by the Hornbostel–Curt Sachs school of thought, based on unidirectional evolutionist and comparative theories. Thus Vega firmly believed in a historically definable folklorization process, from high to low social class. Several of his studies of origin (1952, 1956) reveal this interest in looking for European precedents in some aspects of South American folk music. Gilbert Chase (1967) has sketched Vega's theories. Vega's most illustrious disciple, Isabel Aretz, was an active field researcher in the 1940s and 1950s. Her survey of Argentine folk music (1952) and her studies of traditional music in Tucumán (1946) and La Rioja (completed in 1967, published in 1978) are typical of the conceptualization of ethnomusicology at that time – descriptive approach with little attention to context, a static view of culture and general neglect of musical change. Indian music in Argentina has received only sporadic attention. Of special importance are the studies of

Carol Robertson (1975, 1979) on Mapuche music in Argentina, as she provides sophisticated analyses of the interface of music and ritual. The Instituto Nacional de Musicología 'Carlos Vega' published a series of short articles by Vega (1981), of rather difficult access, which shed some light on the history of folklore and folk music research in Argentina in conjunction with the nationalist movement in the arts. The Institute also provided a useful descriptive booklet (1980) on traditional Argentine musical instruments and two important essays (1984) by Jorge Novati on the songs of the Mataco in the Chaco region and by Irma Ruiz on the Ñemongarai ceremony of the Mbiá of the Misiones province.

Historical study of the origin and development of certain folk song and dance genres was carried out by Josué Teófilo Wilkes and Ismael Guerrero Cárpena (1946), especially the *cifra*, *estilo* and *milonga*, and by Vega (1936, 1956). Sociological analyses of certain aspects of popular music of the Río de la Plata and southern Brazil were pursued by Daniel Mendoza de Arce (1981), while Pablo Vila (1987) at the other end of the spectrum interpreted the Argentine *rock nacional* of the late 1970s and early 1980s as strongly reflective of political counteraction to the established military regime. Among Argentine popular music genres, the *tango* has been paramount. Gerard Béhague (1985) gives a detailed discussion of *tango* scholarship.

In Uruguay the work of Lauro Ayestarán (1913–66) on traditional and popular music dominated the 1950s and early 1960s. Although Indian cultures have long disappeared in Uruguay, Ayestarán (1949) has studied thoroughly 16th- to 19th-century sources for information about Indian musical instruments and dances (especially the Chaná-Charrúa and the Tupí-Guaraní groups). This study emphasizes the indigenous musical bow and its distribution throughout the Americas; it was reproduced in the author's major work on Uruguayan music (1953) as the first chapter of the first part 'Primitive music'. He also surveyed 'black music' from the *comparsas* of 1760, the *tangos* of 1807 and 1808, to the *candombe* complex of the 19th century. The project was to include a third part on folk music in Uruguay which was never completed, but his study of musical folklore was published posthumously (1967, *El folklore musical*). On the *candombe* Paulo de Carvalho Neto (1962) stressed its dramatic features, its integration into Carnival and its overall change. Nestor Ortiz Oderigo (1969) dealt with the history of the *candombe* on both sides of the River Plate. Ayestarán also studied the Afro-Uruguayan drum ensembles (1967, 'La "conversación"').

In Brazil Mário de Andrade was the true pioneer in the conceptualization of ethnomusicology. His essay on Brazilian music (1928) was the first perceptive attempt to delineate and analyse the various sound-structural elements of Brazilian folk music. His concept of music was dynamic, as opposed to the prevailing views of his time. In his studies of Luso-Brazilian, Afro-Brazilian and, to a lesser degree, Brazilian Indian music, he conceived of musical dynamics as multidirectional. His studies of the dramatic dances, which he labelled *bailados* (1959), and of 'witchcraft music' (1963) remain the most stimulating of Brazil's ethnomusicological literature because, with his unique prose style, he was able to combine sociocultural and musical matters. Andrade considered the ethnographic basis and justification of musical-performance contexts, which made him a true ethnomusicologist in concept, if

483

not in actual method. His only student was Oneyda Alvarenga, who adhered, nevertheless, to the prevailing descriptive approach to folklore studies in her survey (1950) and her analyses of black influence on the music of Brazil (1946).

Luso-Brazilian folk music has been studied by Rossini Tavares de Lima (1954, 1964, 1971, *Romanceiro folclórico do Brasil*, 1971, *Folclore das festas círclicas*, 1978) and by Andrade himself in the south-central folk cultural area (1941). Father José Geraldo de Souza (1963) revealed analytically the influences of Gregorian chant, through the work of missionaries, on Brazilian folk songs. Luiz Heitor Corrêa de Azevedo (1944) was among the first to turn his attention to the *cantoria* tradition (the narrative, ballad-like tradition of improvising singing) of the northeastern provinces, and José Jorge de Carvalho (1975) provided specific musical analyses of songs of the same repertory. Dances and music associated with popular religious rituals, such as the Festa do Divino, the Folias de Reis, or the Bailes Pastoris, have been studied by Corrêa de Azevedo (see Universidade do Brasil, 1953, 1956, 1959), and by folklorists like Alceu Maynard de Araújo (1964). The Portuguese tradition of the festivities of the Dança de São Gonçalo and the Dança de Santa Cruz, together with the whole complex of *romanceiro* (balladry), has been thoroughly documented in Brazil by folklorists and musicologists (Câmara Cascudo, 1954; Souza, 1966; Corrêa Giffoni, 1973). For the most part, however, their approach has been geared towards historical questions, attempting to clarify various kinds of syncretism. Regarding organology, in spite of the supremacy of the *viola* (folk guitar of Portuguese origin) in Brazilian folk music, instruments of African derivation have received more attention, particularly percussion instruments. Organological studies, such as those of Araújo (1953) and Tavares de Lima (1964, 1965), are physical descriptions of the instruments and do not explain their functions and potential symbolic meanings. Northeastern instrumental ensembles and festivals have been described by César Guerra Peixe (1956, 1970) and Beatriz Gois Dantas (1972).

Little has been achieved in the area of Afro-Brazilian musical traditions, despite the substantial folkloric, anthropological and sociological literature on black culture. Andrade's study on the *samba* of São Paulo (1937) has no counterpart for the numerous regional varieties of the *samba*. Luciano Gallet (1934) provided the best general coverage of black music in Brazil for its time, but his analyses are conceived in Eurocentric terms and the information provided did not result from extensive field experience. Since then, some good but sporadic studies have emerged, such as Edison Carneiro's posthumous work (1974), which includes a study on *batuque* and *samba*, and Ralph Waddey's study of the *samba de viola* from Bahia (1980–81). The Bahian group of anthropologists who were the first to study the sociocultural significance of Afro-Brazilian popular religions (especially Nina Rodrigues, Artur Ramos and Carneiro) generally neglected the musical aspect of religion. The American anthropologist Melville Herskovits (1944) recognized the importance of music and dance as integral to the ritual structures. His essay with Richard Waterman (1949) is informative but does not provide ethnographic and musical integration. In-depth study of *candomblé*, *Xangô* cult, *macumba* and *umbanda* music repertories is still not available. Alan Merriam's dissertation (1951) gives pertinent analysis of Herskovits's material. Gisèle Binon-Cossard

(1967) treated *candomblé* music competently in general terms. Béhague (1975, 1984) has dealt with Bahian *candomblé* music in relation to other national trends of popular religious music and in the context of performance. J. J. de Carvalho's doctoral thesis in anthropology (1984) represents the type of study needed in this area. But questions dealing with codification of repertories, music's relationship to belief systems and practices, music as part of religious behaviour and as performance understood in ethnographic terms, all are open for investigation in the numerous regional versions of cult music from the state of Pará to Rio Grande do Sul. Secular music of predominantly black Brazilians has received more attention. Waldeloir Rego (1968) treated *capoeira* songs and dances, amplified by Tiago de Oliveira Pinto (1986). E. Carneiro (1961) dealt with the *samba de umbigada* and Valdemar de Oliveira (1971) with the *frevo* and the *passo* of Recife. The Austrian Africanist Gerhard Kubik (1979) searched for Angolan origins in Afro-Brazilian music and dances, while the Zairan scholar Kazadi wa Mukuna (1979) stressed the Bantu contribution. The Bahian carnival *afoxê* (carnival associations of cultsmen) still awaits a proper ethnomusicological treatment. Carnival in Recife was studied by Katarina Real (1967).

The most neglected area of Brazilian musical studies has been traditional Indian music. Indian music has remained foreign to most Brazilian researchers despite a substantial social scientific literature on Brazilian Indian cultures. Helsa Cameu's Indian music survey (1977) is a useful compendium by a dedicated musician who describes musical features and instruments competently, but with no attention to ethnomusicological methods. I. Halmos's analysis (1964) of the music of the Nambicuara is strictly musicological. A general introduction to Indian music of Brazil is provided by R. J. de M. Bastos (1974), who also studied in great detail Kamayurá music and culture (1978, 1986, 1989). The American anthropologist and ethnomusicologist Anthony Seeger, who taught at the Museu Nacional for a number of years and exerted beneficial influence on young Brazilian scholars, worked among the Suyá Indians of the Upper Xingu and has published ethnomusicological studies on the subject (1979, 1980, 1987). One of his students, Elizabeth Travassos, has researched music and shamanism among the Kayabi (1985, 1986).

Conclusions

Latin American and Caribbean ethnomusicology has suffered from lack of attention in local institutions of higher learning. Schools of music, conservatories or music departments in universities recognize the need to provide instruction in local musical traditions, but conceive of the courses as 'musical folklore', an exotic subject separate from the main music disciplines traditionally associated with music education. Whenever it is acknowledged as a discipline, ethnomusicology has tended to receive more attention from social scientists than musicians, although this attitude is changing with the younger generation of scholars, trained abroad or in anthropology.

Another major problem confronting current ethnomusicology in Latin America and the Caribbean comes from the scarcity of reliable field-recordings collections. Recent efforts of government-sponsored cultural agencies (FUNARTE, [i.e. Fundação Nacional de Arte in Brazil], the Instituto Nacional de Cultura in Peru, the Documentation Centre of the Instituto Colombiano de Cultura, the CENIDIM of Mexico City, the Cuban Music Department of the Casa de las Américas) to issue field recordings have not been entirely successful either because the selections are not fully representative of a particular tradition or genre and the recordings lack ethnographic documentation.

Ethnomusicological research in Latin America and the Spanish Caribbean faces a problematic future, with the following specific needs.

1. Systematic gathering of musical and ethnographic data of folk and traditional music.

2. Authentic field recordings with thorough documentation to enable students to assess the diversity of musical expressions in a particular cultural area.

3. On the part of Latin American ethnomusicologists development of relevant theoretical approaches (anthropological focus, relevant analytic models, ethnographic descriptions and interpretations).

4. Better communication between researchers in the area through specialized publications, now lacking.

5. Development of serious and continuous academic programmes for training Latin American ethnomusicologists.

6. A realistic reassessment by Latin American researchers of the relationships between their cultural focus and the actual cultural values of the social group under study.

An examination of the current state of bibliographic research in Latin American ethnomusicology was made by John Schechter in 1985 and published in 1987 by the SALALM (Seminar on the Acquisition of Latin American Library Materials) Secretariat. Schechter emphasized Latin American urban popular-music scholarship. Béhague (1985) assessed that scholarship and has provided also an historic outline of popular music trends, a survey of reference works, an annotation of historical and critical works, a brief listing of centres and research collections, and some suggestions for future research.

Bibliography

R. and M. d'Harcourt: *La musique des Incas et ses survivances* (Paris, 1925)

J. Arzeno: *Del folk-lore musical dominicano* (Santo Domingo, 1927)

M. de Andrade: *Ensaio sobre a música brasileira* (São Paulo, 1928)

N. Garay: *Tradiciones y cantares de Panamá* (Brussels, 1930)

S. L. Moreno: 'La música en el Ecuador', *El Ecuador en cien años de independencia, 1830–1930*, ii, ed. J. Gonzálo Orellana (Quito, 1930), 187–276

M. Galindo: *Nociones de historia de la música mejicana*, i (Colima, 1933)

V. T. Mendoza and D. Castañeda: *Instrumental precortesiano*, i: *Instrumentos de percusión* (Mexico City, 1933)

L. Gallet: *Estudos de folclore* (Rio de Janeiro, 1934)

G. Saldívar: *Historia de la música en México (épocas precortesiana y colonial)* (Mexico City, 1934)

C. Vega: 'Escala com semitonos en la música de los antiguos peruanos', *Actas y Trabajos Científicos del XXV Congreso Internacional de Americanistas (La Plata, 1932)*, i (Buenos Aires, 1934), 349

K. G. Izikowitz: *Musical and Other Sound Instruments of the South American Indians* (Göteborg, 1935)

A. Sas: 'Ensayo sobre la música Inca', *Boletín latinoamericano de música*, i (1935), 71

E. M. von Hornbostel: 'Fuegian Songs', *American Anthropologist*, new ser., xxxviii (1936), 357

M. R. Paredes: 'Instrumentos musicales de los Kollas', *Boletín latinoamericano de música*, ii (1936), 77

A. Sas: 'La formación del folklore peruano', *Boletín latinoamericano de música*, ii (1936), 97

C. Vega: *Danzas y canciones argentinas* (Buenos Aires, 1936)

M. de Andrade: 'O samba rural paulista', *Revista do Arquivo Municipal*, xli/4 (1937), 37–116

A. González Bravo: 'Kenas, pincollos y tarkas', *Boletín latinoamericano de música*, iii (1937), 25

A. Sas: 'Ensayo sobre la música nazca', *Boletín latinoamericano de música*, iv (1938), 221

V. T. Mendoza: *El romance español y el corrido mexicano: estudio comparativo* (Mexico City, 1939)

M. de Andrade: *Música do Brasil* (Curitiba, 1941)

J. Castillo: *La música Maya-Quiché (región guatemalteca)* (Quetzaltenango, 1941)

C. Vega: *La música popular argentina. Canciones y danzas criollas*, ii: *Fraseología* (Buenos Aires, 1941)

H. Yurchenco: 'La música indígena en Chiapas, México', *América indígena*, iii/4 (1943), 305

L. H. Corrêa de Azevedo: 'A arte da cantoria', *Cultura política*, xlii (1944), 183

M. J. Herskovits: 'Drums and Drummers in Afrobrazilian Cult Life', *MQ*, xxx (1944), 477

C. Vega: *Panorama de la música popular argentina, con un ensayo sobre la cienca del folklore* (Buenos Aires, 1944)

O. Alvarenga: 'A influência negra na música brasileira', *Boletín latinoamericano de música*, vi (1946), 357–407

I. Aretz: *Música tradicional argentina: Tucumán, historia y folklore* (Buenos Aires, 1946)

A. Carpentier: *La música en Cuba* (Mexico City, 1946)

C. Vega: *Los instrumentos musicales aborígenes y criollos de la Argentina* (Buenos Aires, 1946)

J. T. Wilkes and I. Guerrero Cárpena: *Formas musicales rioplatenses. Su génesis hispánica* (Buenos Aires, 1946)

H. Yurchenco: 'Grabación de música indígena', *Nuestra música*, i/2 (1946), 65

——: 'La recopilación de música indígena', *América indígena*, vi/4 (1946), 121

E. Garrido: 'El folklore del niño dominicano. Juegos infantiles', *Boletín del folklore dominicano*, ii/2 (1947), 54

C. Vega: 'La forma de la cueca chilena', *Revista musical chilena*, iii/20–21 (1947), 7; iii/22–3 (1947), 15

E. M. von Hornbostel: 'The Music of the Fuegians', *Ethnos*, xiii (1948), 61–102

C. Lavín: 'Nuestra señora de las Peñas. Fiesta ritual del norte de Chile', *Revista musical chilena*, iv/31 (1948), 9; iv/32 (1949), 27

V. T. Mendoza: *La canción chilena en México* (Santiago, 1948)

L. Ayestarán: *La música indígena en el Uruguay* (Montevideo, 1949)

A. González Bravo: 'Clasificación de los sicus aimaras', *Revista de estudios musicales*, i (1949), 93

M. J. Herskovits and R. A. Waterman: 'Música de culto afrobahiana', *Revista de estudios musicales*, i/2 (1949), 65–127

S. L. Moreno: *Música y danzas autóctonas del Ecuador* (Quito, 1949)

M. Titiev: *Social Singing among the Mapuche* (Ann Arbor, MI, 1949)

O. Alvarenga: *Música popular brasileira* (Porto Alegre, 1950)

F. Ortiz: *La africanía de la música folklórica de Cuba* (Havana, 1950)

M. de Baratta: *Cuzcatlán típico. Ensayo sobre etnofonía de El Salvador* (San Salvador, 1951–2)

A. Jiménez Borja: 'Instrumentos musicales del Perú', *Revista del Museo Nacional* (Lima), xix–xx (1951), 37–190

V. T. Mendoza: 'La música otomí. Una investigación en el valle del Mezquital (1936)', *Revista de estudios musicales*, ii/5–7 (1951–4), 351–530, 221–46

A. P. Merriam: *Songs of the Afro-Bahian Cults: an Ethnomusicological Analysis* (diss., Northwestern U., 1951)

F. Ortiz: *Los bailes y el teatro de los negros en el folklore de Cuba* (Havana, 1951)

I. Aretz: *El folklore musical argentino* (Buenos Aires, 1952)

F. Ortiz: *Los instrumentos de la música afrocubana* (Havana, 1952–55)

E. Pereira Salas: *Guia bibliográfica para el estudio del folklore chileno* (Santiago, 1952)

R. Stevenson: *Music in Mexico: a Historical Survey* (New York, 1952)

C. Vega: *Las danzas populares argentinas* (Buenos Aires, 1952)

L. Ayestarán: *La música en el Uruguay*, i (Montevideo, 1953)

A. Maynard Araújo: 'Instrumentos musicais e implementos: achegas ao folclore paulista', *Revista do Arquivo Municipal*, clvii (1953), 147–217

487

L. F. Ramón y Rivera: *El joropo, baile nacional de Venezuela* (Caracas, 1953)

Universidade do Brasil: *Relação dos discos gravados no Estado do Ceará* (Rio de Janeiro, 1953)

M. F. Zárate and D. Pérez de Zárate: *La décima y la copla en Panamá* (Panama City, 1953)

L. da Câmara Cascudo: *Dicionário do folclore brasileiro* (Rio de Janeiro, 1954)

V. T. Mendoza: *El corrido mexicano* (Mexico City, 1954)

R. Tavares de Lima: *Melodia e ritmo no folclore de São Paulo* (São Paulo, 1954)

E. G. Boggs: *Folklore infantil de Santo Domingo* (Madrid, 1955)

S. Marti: *Instrumentos musicales precortesianos* (Mexico City, 1955, 2/1968)

L. F. Ramón y Rivera: *Cantos de trabajo del pueblo venezolano* (Caracas, 1955)

P. Collaer: 'Cariban and Mayan Music', *Studia memoriae Belae Bartók sacra*, ed. B. Suchoff (Budapest, 1956), 123

C. Guerra-Peixe: *Maracatus do Recife* (São Paulo, 1956)

V. T. Mendoza: *Panorama de la música tradicional de México* (Mexico City, 1956)

——: *El corrido de la revolución mexicana* (Mexico City, 1956)

Universidade do Brasil: *Relação dos discos gravados no Estado de Minas Gerais* (Rio de Janeiro, 1956)

C. Vega: *El origen de las danzas folklóricas* (Buenos Aires, 1956)

J. M. Boettner: *Música y músicos del Paraguay* (Asunción, 1956)

J. E. Fortún (de Ponce): *La navidad en Bolivia* (La Paz, 1957)

V. T. Mendoza: *Glosas y décimas de México* (Mexico City, 1957)

S. L. Moreno: *La música de los Incas* (Quito, 1957)

M. E. Simmons: *The Mexican Corrido as a Source of an Interpretive Study of Modern Mexico (1870–1950)* (Bloomington, IN, 1957)

M. T. Linares: 'Ensayo sobre la influencia española en la música cubana', *Separata Revista Pro-Arte Musical* (Havana, 1958)

M. F. Zarate: *Breviario de folklore* (Panama City, 1958)

M. de Andrade: *Danças dramáticas do Brasil* (São Paulo, 1959)

R. and M. d'Harcourt: *La Musique des Aymara sur les Hauts Plateaux Boliviens* (Paris, 1959)

J. Roel Pineda: 'El wayno del Cuzco', *Folklore americano*, vi–vii (1959), 129–246

Universidade do Brasil: *Relação dos discos gravados no Estado do Rio Grande do Sul* (Rio de Janeiro, 1959)

J. Liscano: 'Lugar de origen de los tambores redondos barloventeños', *Revista Shell*, viii/35 (1960), 22

A. Pardo Tovar: *Los cantos tradicionales del Baudó* (Bogotá, 1960)

R. Stevenson: *The Music of Peru* (Washington, DC, 1960)

I. Aretz and L. F. Ramón y Rivera: *Folklore tachirense* (Caracas, 1961–3)

E. Carneiro: *Samba de umbigada* (Rio de Janeiro, 1961)

J. E. Fortún (de Ponce): *La danza de los diablos* (La Paz, 1961)

S. Marti: *Canto, danza y música precortesianos* (Mexico City, 1961)

——: 'Ethnomusicología en Colombia', *Revista colombiano de folklore*, ii/6 (1961), 133

V. T. Mendoza: *La canción mexicana: Ensayo de clasificación y antología* (Mexico City, 1961)

A. Pardo Tovar and J. Pinzón Urrea: *Rítmica e melódica del folklore chocoano* (Bogotá, 1961)

D. Zamudio: 'El bambuco', *Boletín de programas* (Radiotelevisora Nacional de Colombia), ccii (1961), 4 (repr. in *Textos sobre música y folklore*, 1 [1978], 409)

I. Aretz: *Cantos navideños en el folklore venezolano* (Caracas, 1962)

P. de Carvalho Neto: 'The Candombe: a Dramatic Dance from Afro-Uruguayan Folklore', *EM*, vi/3 (1962), 164

J. Diaz Gainza: *Historia musical de Bolivia: época pre-colonial* (Potosí, 1962)

Instituto Nacional de Bellas Artes: *Investigación folklórica en México* (Mexico City, 1962–4)

L. Paret-Limardo de Vela: *Folklore musical de Guatemala* (Buenos Aires, 1962)

L. F. Ramón y Rivera: 'Rhythmic and Melodic Elements in Negro Music of Venezuela', *JIFMC*, xiv (1962), 56

D. Vela: *La Marimba* (Guatemala City, 1962)

D. Zapata Olivella: 'La cumbia, síntesis musical de la nación colombiana', *Revista del Folklore*, iii/7 (1962), 187–204

——: 'Los pasos del folklore colombiano: la cumbia', *Vínculo Shell* (Bogotá, 1962), 4

M. de Andrade: *Música de feitiçaria no Brasil* (São Paulo, 1963)

E. Figueroa Berríos: 'Los sones de la bomba en la tradición popular de la costa sur de Puerto Rico', *Revista del Instituto Puertorriqueño de Cultura*, v (1963), 46

R. Manzanares: 'La etnomusicología hondureña', *Folklore americano* (Lima), xi–xii (1963), 68

A. Pardo Tovar and J. Bermúdez Silva: *La guitarrería popular de Chiquinquirá* (Bogotá, 1963)

J. G. de Souza: 'Contribuição rítmica modal do canto gregoriano para a música brasileira', *Revista Conservatório Brasileiro de Música*, xxi–xxii (1963), 17

H. Yurchenco: 'Survivals of Pre-Hispanic Music in New Mexico', *JIFMC*, xv (1963), 15

M. Zapata Olivella: 'Comparsas y teatro callejero en los carnavales colombianos', *Boletín cultural y Biblográfico*, vi/11 (1963), 1763

P. de Carvalho Neto: *Diccionario del folklore ecuatoriano* (Quito, 1964)

V. Chenoweth: *The Marimbas of Guatemala* (Lexington, 1964)

I. Halmos: 'Melody and Form in the Music of the Nambicuara Indians (Mato Grosso, Brazil)', *Studia Musicologica*, vi/3–4 (1964), 329

J. A. Hernández: *Música folklórica y popular de la República Dominicana* (Santo Domingo, 1964)

A. León: *Música folklórica de Cuba* (Havana, 1964)

R. Tavares de Lima: 'Estudo sobre a viola', *Revista Brasileira de Folclore*, iv/8–10 (1964), 29

S. Marti and G. P. Kurath: *Dances of Anáhuac: the Choreography and Music of Precortesian Dances* (Chicago, IL, 1964)

A. Maynard Araújo: *Folclore nacional* (São Paulo, 1964)

V. T. Mendoza: *Lírica narrativa de México; el corrido* (Mexico City, 1964)

C. Boilès: 'La flauta triple de Tenenexpan', *La palabra y el hombre*, xxxiv (1965), 213

G. List: 'Music in the Culture of the Jibaro Indians of the Ecuadorian *montaña*', *Primera Conferencia Interamericana de Etnomusicología* (Washington, DC, 1965), 131

R. Tavares de Lima: 'Música folclórica e instrumentos do Brasil', *Boletín interamericano de música*, xlix (1965), 3

C. Boilès: 'The Pipe and Tabor in Mesoamerica', *Inter-American Institute for Musical Research Yearbook*, ii (1966), 43–74

R. Holzmann: *Panorama de la música tradicional del Perú* (Lima, 1966)

G. List: 'Ethnomusicology in Colombia', *EM*, x (1966), 70

——: 'Ethnomusicology in Ecuador', *EM*, x (1966), 83

M. L. Miñoz: *La música en Puerto Rico* (Sharon, CT, 1966)

A. Olmos Agreda: 'Cancionero popular en Cochabamba', *Archivos del Folklore Boliviano*, ii (1966), 102–46

J. Orrego-Salas: 'Araucanian Indian Instruments', *EM*, x (1966), 48

A. Pardo Tovar: 'La cultura musical en Colombia', *Historia extensa de Colombia*, vi (Bogotá, 1966)

A. Paredes Candia: *La danza folklórica en Bolivia* (La Paz, 1966)

H. Ruíz Ruíz: 'Fiesta patronal de San Pedro en Achacachi', *Archivos del Folklore Boliviano*, ii (1966), 164

J. G. de Souza: *Folcmúsica e liturgia* (Petrópolis, 1966)

E. T. Stanford: 'A Linguistic Analysis of Music and Dance Terms from Three Sixteenth-Century Dictionaries of Mexican Indian Langauges', *Inter-American Institute for Musical Research Yearbook*, ii (1966), 101–59

——: 'Three Mexican Indian Carnival Songs', *EM*, x (1966), 58

I. Aretz: *Instrumentos musicales de Venezuela* (Cumaná, 1967)

L. Ayestarán: *El folklore musical uruguayo* (Montevideo, 1967)

——: 'La "conversación" de tamboriles', *Revista Musical Chilena*, xxi/101 (1967), 32

G. Binon: 'Musique dans le Candomblé', *La musique dans la vie*, i, ed. T. Nikiprowetsky (Paris, 1967), 159–207

C. Boilès: 'Tepehua Thought-Song: a Case of Semantic Signaling', *EM*, xi (1967), 267

G. Chase: 'Recordando a Carlos Vega', *Revista Musical Chilena*, xxi/101 (1967), 36

M. E. Grebe: 'Modality in Spanish Renaissance Vihuela Music and Archaic Chilean Folksongs: a Comparative Study', *EM*, xi (1967), 326

——: *The Chilean Verso: a Study in Musical Archaism* (Los Angeles, CA, 1967)

R. Holzmann: *Perú-cánticos, 15 piezas de música tradicional del Perú* (Lima, 1967)

F. López Cruz: *La música folklórica en Puerto Rico* (Sharon, CT, 1967)

R. Manzanares: 'Instrumentos musicales tradicionales de Honduras', *Music in the Americas*, ed. G. List and J. Orrego-Salas (Bloomington, IN, 1967), 123

L. P. Ramón y Rivera: *Música indígena, folklórica y popular de Venezuela* (Buenos Aires, 1967)

K. Real: *O folclore no carnaval de Recife* (Rio de Janeiro, 1967)

J. Urrutia Blondel: 'Danzas rituales en las festividades de San Pedro de Atacama', *Revista musical chilena*, xxi/100 (1967), 44–80

N. E. Whitten Jr: 'Música y relaciones sociales en las tierras bajas colombianas y ecuatorianas del Pacífico', *América indígena*, xxvii/4 (1967), 635–66

P. Díaz Machicao: *Testificación de la cueca* (La Paz, 1968)

L. C. Espinosa: 'Organología y organografía folklóricas', *Boletín del Instituto de Antropología de la Universidad del Cauca*, xi/5 (1968), 15

F. and J. Harrison: 'Spanish Elements in the Music of Two Maya Groups in Chiapas', *Selected Reports in Ethnomusicology*, i/2 (1968), 2–44

R. Holzmann: 'De la trifonía a la heptafonía en la música tradicional peruana', *Seperata revista San Marcos* (1968), 5–51

G. List: 'The Mbira in Cartagena', *JIFMC*, xx (1968), 54

W. Rego: *Capoeira Angola* (Salvador, Bahia, 1968)

R. Stevenson: *Music in Aztec and Inca Territory* (Berkeley, CA, 1968)

S. Zapata Agurto: 'Psicoanálisis del vals peruano' (Contribución al estudio de la personalidad básica del hombre peruano), *Revista de ciencias psicológicas y neurológicas*, v/1–2 (1968), 5–61

M. F. Zarate: *Tambor y socavón* (Panama City, 1968)

C. Boilès: *Cognitive Process in Otomi Cult Music* (diss., Tulane U., 1969)

J. A. Hernández: *Música tradicional dominicana* (Santo Domingo, 1969)

N. Ortiz Oderigo: *Calunga, croquis del candombe* (Buenos Aires, 1969)

L. F. Ramón y Rivera: *La música folklórica de Venezuela* (Caracas, 1969)

E. T. Stanford: 'Courtship Music in Present-Day Mexico', *Inter-American Institute for Musical Research Yearbook*, v (1969), 90

G. Abadia Morales: 'Panorama de las músicas folklórica y popular', *Revista Espiral*, cxvi–cxvii (1970), 22

R. Barros and M. Dannemann: *El romancero chileno* (Santiago, 1970)

S. Claro Valdés: *Memoria. Instituto de Investigaciones Musicales* (Santiago, 1970)

H. C. Davidson: *Diccionario folklórico de Colombia (Música, instrumentos y danzas)* (Bogotá, 1970)

C. Guerra-Peixe: 'Zabumba, orquestra nordestina', *Revista brasileira de folclore*, x (1970), 15

M. T. Linares: *La música popular* (Havana, 1970)

N. E. Whitten Jr: 'Personal Networks and Musical Contexts in the Pacific Lowlands of Colombia and Ecuador', *Afro-American Anthropology: Contemporary Perspectives*, ed. N. E. Whitten Jr and J. F. Szwed (New York and London, 1970), 203

C. Boilès: 'Síntesis y sincretismo en el carnaval otomí', *América Indígena*, xxxi/3 (1971), 555

P. Castellanos: *Horizontes de la música precortesiana* (Mexico City, 1971)

M. E. Grebe: 'Modality in the Spanish Vihuela Music of the Sixteenth Century and Its Incidence in Latin American Music', *Anuario musical*, xxvi (1971), 29; xxvii (1972), 109

J. Iribarren: 'Instrumentos musicales del norte chico chileno', *Boletín* (Publicaciones del Museo Arqueológico de La Serena), xiv (1971), 12

R. T. de Lima: *Romanceiro folclórico do Brasil* (São Paulo, 1971)

——: *Folclore das festas cíclicas* (São Paulo, 1971)

T. D. Lucas: 'Songs of the Shipibo of the Upper Amazon', *Yearbook for Inter-American Musical Research*, vii (1971), 59

V. de Oliveira: *Frevo, capoeira e 'passo'* (Recife, 1971)

L. F. Ramón y Rivera: *La música afrovenezolana* (Caracas, 1971)

E. Rodríguez Demorizi: *Música y baile en Santo Domingo* (Santo Domingo, 1971)

C. E. Sigmund: *Segundo Luis Moreno: His Contributions to Ecuadorian Musicology* (diss., U. of Minnesota, 1971)

M. Dannemann: 'Atlas del folklore chileno, metodología general', *Revista musical chilena*, xxvi/118 (1972), 3

B. Gois Dantas: *A taieira de Sergipe, una danca folclórica* (Petrópolis, 1972)

M. E. Davis: 'The Social Organization of a Musical Event: the *Fiesta de Cruz* in San Juan, Puerto Rico', *EM*, xvi (1972), 38

M. E. Grebe: 'Cosmovisión mapuche', *Cuadernos de la realidad nacional*, xiv (1972), 46

N. Hammond: 'Classic Maya Music: Part 1, Maya Drums', *Archaeology*, xxv/2 (1972), 124

L. E. Mazuera M.: *Orígenes históricos del bambuco, teoría musical y cronología de autores y compositores colombianos* (Cali, Colombia, 2/1972)

S. L. Moreno: *Historia de la música en el Ecuador, i: Prehistoria* (Quito, 1972)

L. P. Ramón y Rivera: *La canción venezolana* (Maracaibo, 1972)

E. T. Stanford: 'The Mexican "Son"', *YIFMC*, iv (1972), 66

D. Vela: 'Música tradicional y folklórica en América Central', *Guatemala Indígena*, vii (1972), 227

G. Abadia Morales: *La música folklórica colombiana* (Bogotá, 1973)

S. Claro Valdés and J. Urrutia Blondel: *Historia de la música en Chile* (Santiago, 1973)

M. A. C. Giffoni: *Danças folclóricas e suas aplicações educativas* (São Paulo, 3/1973)

M. E. Grebe: 'El kultrún mapuche: un microcosmo simbólico', *Revista musical chilena*, xxvii/123–4 (1973), 3–42

A. Henríquez: *Organologia del folklore chileno* (Valparaiso, 1973)

G. List: 'El conjunto de gaitas de Colombia: la herencia de tres culturas', *Revista musical chilena*, xxvii/123–4 (1973), 43

O. Marulanda: *Folklore y cultura general* (Cali, Colombia, 1973)

D. A. Olsen: *Music and Shamanism of the Winikina-Warao Indians: Songs for Curing and Other Theurgy* (diss., U. of California, 1973)

C. Ortega Ricaurte: 'Contribución a la bibliografía de la música en Colombia', *Revista de la Dirección de Divulgación Cultural* (Universidad Nacional de Colombia), xii (1973)

C. Alvarez and M. E. Grebe: 'La trifonía atacameña y sus perspectivas interculturales', *Revista musical chilena*, xxviii/126–7 (1974), 21

R. J. de Menezes Bastos: 'Las músicas tradicionales de Brasil', *Revista musical chilena*, xxviii/125 (1974), 21–77

E. Carneiro: *Folguedos tradicionais* (Rio de Janeiro, 1974)

E. Cavour: *La zampoña, aerófono boliviano* (La Paz, 1974)

M. E. Grebe: 'Instrumentos musicales precolombinos de Chile', *Revista musical chilena*, xxviii/128 (1974), 5–55

——: 'Presencia del dualismo en la cultura y música mapuche', *Revista musical chilena*, xxviii/126–7 (1974), 47–79

——: 'La música alacalufe: aculturación y cambio estilístico', *Revista musical chilena*, xxviii/126–7 (1974), 80–111

I. Halmos: 'Preliminary Report on a Field Work among Piaroa Indians', *Revista venezolana de folklore*, v (1974), 58

S. S. McCosker: 'The Lullabies of the San Blas Cuna Indians of Panama', *Etnologiska studier*, xxxiii (1974), 1–190

L. Merino: 'Instrumentos musicales, cultura mapuche, y el *Cautiverio feliz* del maestre de campo Francisco Nuñez de Pineda y Bascuñán', *Revista musical chilena*, xxviii/128 (1974), 56–95

D. A. Olsen: 'The Function of Naming in the Curing Songs of the Warao Indians of Venezuela', *Yearbook for Inter-American Musical Research*, x (1974), 88–122

L. Saunders: 'The Son Huasteco', *Changing Perspectives in Latin America*, iii (1974), 141

E. T. Stanford: *El villancio y el corrido mexicano* (Mexico City, 1974)

A. F. de Thompson: *An Annotated Bibliography of Writings about Music in Puerto Rico* (Ann Arbor, MI, 1974)

G. Wasson and others: *María Sabina and her Mazatec Mushroom Velada* (New York and London, 1974)

N. E. Whitten Jr: *Black Frontiersmen: a South American Case* (Cambridge, MA, 1974)

L. Alberti Mieses: *De música y orquestas bailables dominicanas, 1910–1959* (Santo Domingo, 1975)

G. Béhague: 'Notes on Regional and National Trends in Afro-Brazilian Cult Music', *Tradition and Renewal: Essays on Twentieth-Century Latin American Literature and Culture*, ed. M. H. Forster (Urbana, IL, 1975), 68

C. Borbolla: 'El son, exclusividad de Cuba', *Yearbook for Inter-American Musical Research*, xi (1975), 152

J. J. de Carvalho: 'Formas musicais narrativas do nordeste brasileiro', *Revista INIDEF*, i (1975), 33–68

M. Dannemann: 'Situación actual de la música folklórica chilena. Según el "Atlas del folklore de Chile"', *Revista musical chilena*, xxix/131 (1975), 38–86

F. Lizardo: *Danzas y bailes folklóricos dominicanos* (Santo Domingo, 1975)

L. O'Brien: *Songs of the Face of the Earth: Ancestor Songs of the Tzutuhil-Maya of Santiago Atitlan, Guatemala* (diss., U. of California, 1975)

D. A. Olsen: 'Music-Induced Altered States of Consciousness among Warao Shamans', *Journal of Latin American Lore*, i/1 (1975), 19

C. E. Robertson: Tayil: *Musical Communication among the Mapuche of Argentina* (diss., Indiana U., 1975)

T. Agerkop: 'Lunku, el arco musical de los Miskitos', *Revista INIDEF*, ii (1976), 28

I. Aretz: *El tamunangue* (Barquisimeto, 1976)

H. Campos Parsi: *La música. La gran enciclopedia de Puerto Rico*, vii (San Juan, 1976)

M. E. Davis: *Afro-Dominican Religious Brotherhoods: Structure, Ritual and Music* (diss., U. of Illinois, 1976)

491

I. Muriel: 'Contribución a la cultura musical de los jíbaros del Ecuador', *Folklore americano*, (1976), 141

D. A. Olsen: 'Música vesperal Mojo de San Miguel de Isidoro, Bolivia', *Revista musical chilena*, xxx/133 (1976), 28

A. Pollak-Eltz: *Bibliografía afrovenezolana* (Caracas, 1976)

L. F. Ramón y Rivera: *La música popular de Venezuela* (Caracas, 1976)

R. R. Smith: *The Society of Los Congos of Panama: an Ethnomusicological Study of the Music and Dance-Theater of an Afro-Panamanian Group* (diss., Indiana U., 1976)

H. Camêu: *Introdução ao estudo da música indígena brasileira* (Rio de Janeiro, 1977)

L. R. Cheville and R. A. Cheville: *Festivals and Dances of Panama* (Panama, 1977)

C. Santa Cruz G.: *El waltz y el valse criollo* (Lima, 1977)

J. M. Schechter: 'Non-Hispanic Instruments in Mexico and Central America: an Annotated Bibliography', *CMC*, xxiv (1977), 80

R. C. Smith: *Deliverance from Chaos for a Song: a Social and Religious Interpretation of the Ritual Performance of Amuesha Music* (diss., Indiana U., 1977)

I. Aretz: *Música tradicional de La Rioja* (Caracas, 1978)

C. Bolaños and others: *Mapa de los instrumentos musicales de uso popular en el Perú* (Lima, 1978)

D. W. Dickey: *The Kennedy Corridos: a Study of the Ballads of a Mexican American Hero* (Austin, TX, 1978)

B. Flores: *La música en Costa Rica* (San José, 1978)

M. López Mayorical: *La polémica de 'La marimba'* (Guatemala City, 1978)

R. J. de Menezes Bastos: *A musicológica Kamayurá: para uma antropologia da comunicação no Alto-Xingu* (Brasilia, 1978)

R. Tavares de Lima: *A ciência do folclore* (São Paulo, 1978)

M. P. Baumann: *Música Andina de Bolivia: Comentario* (Cochabamba, 1979) [disc LPLI/S–062 and notes]

M. H. Brandt: *An Ethnomusicological Study of Three Afro-Venezuelan Drum Ensembles of Barlovento* (diss., Queen's U. of Belfast, 1979)

S. Claro Valdés: *Oyendo a Chile* (Santiago, 1979)

P. Garrido: *Historia de la cueca* (Valparaiso, 1979)

G. Kubik: *Angolan Traits in Black Music, Games and Dances of Brazil* (Lisbon, 1979)

K. wa Mukuna: *A contribuição bantu na música popular brasileira* (São Paulo, 1979)

D. A. Olsen: *Doce conferencias en etnomusicología para iniciar el estudio de un atlas musical del Perú* (Lima, 1979)

C. E. Robertson: '"Pulling the Ancestors": Performance Practice and Praxis in Mapuche Ordering', *EM*, xxiii (1979), 395

J. M. Schechter: 'The Inca *Cantar Histórico*: a Lexico-Historical Elaboration on Two Cultural Themes', *EM*, xxiii (1979), 191

A. Seeger: 'What Can We Learn When They Sing? Vocal Genres of the Suyá Indians of Central Brazil', *EM*, xxiii (1979), 373

D. E. Sheehy: *The 'Son Jarocho': the History, Style, and Repertory of a Changing Mexican Musical Tradition* (diss., U. of California, 1979)

H. Vega-Drouet: *Historical and Ethnological Survey on Probable African Origins of the Puerto Rico Bomba, Including a Description of Santiago Apostol Festivities at Loiza Aldea* (diss., Wesleyan U., 1979)

C. A. Coba Andrade: *Literatura popular afroecuatoriana* (Otavalo, Ecuador, 1980)

——: *Instrumentos musicales populares registrados en el Ecuador*, i (Otavalo, Ecuador, 1980)

M. E. Grebe: *Generative Models, Symbolic Structures, and Acculturation in the Panpipe Music of the Aymara of Tarapaca, Chile* (diss., Queen's U. of Belfast, 1980)

R. Holzmann: 'Cuatro ejemplos de música Q'ero (Cusco, Perú)', *Latin American Music Review*, i/1 (1980), 74

Instituto Nacional de Musicología 'Carlos Vega': *Instrumentos musicales etnográficos y folklóricos de la Argentina* (Buenos Aires, 1980)

D. A. Olsen: 'Magical Protection Songs of the Warao Indians, Part I: Animals', *Latin American Music Review*, i/2 (1980), 131–61

L. F. Ramón y Rivera: *Fenomenología de la etnomúsica en el área latinoamericana* (Caracas, 1980)

J. M. Schechter: 'El cantar histórico incaico', *Revista musical chilena*, xxxiv/151 (1980), 38

A. Seeger: 'Sing for Your Sister: the Structure and Performance of Suyá *Akia*', *The Ethnography of Musical Performance*, ed. N. McLeod and M. Herndon (Norwood, PA, 1980), 7–42

B. Subercaseaux: 'El canto nuevo en Chile (1973–1980)', *Cuadernos Americanos*, xxxix/4 (1980), 88

R. C. Waddey: '*Viola de Samba* and *Samba de Viola* in the Recôncavo of Bahia (Brazil)', *Latin American Music Review*, i/2 (1980), 196; ii/2 (1981), 252

492

G. Abadía Morales: *Instrumentos de la música folklórica de Colombia* (Bogotá, 1981)

M. P. Baumann: 'Julajulas – ein bolivianisches Panflötenspiel und seine Musiker', *Studia instrumentorum musicae popularis*, vii (1981), 158

——: 'Music, Dance, and Song of the Chipayas (Bolivia)', *Latin American Music Review*, ii/2 (1981), 171–222

W. Belzner: 'Music, Modernization and Westernization among the Macuma Shuar', *Cultural Transformations and Ethnicity in Modern Ecuador*, ed. N. Whitten Jr (Urbana, IL, 1981)

M. E. Davis: *Voces del purgatorio. Estudio de la salve dominicana* (Santo Domingo, 1981)

D. Mendoza de Arce: 'A Structural Approach to the Rural Society and Music of the Río de la Plata and Southern Brazil', *Latin American Music Review*, ii/1 (1981), 66

D. A. Olsen: 'Magical Protection Songs of the Warao Indians, Part II: Spirits', *Latin American Music Review*, ii/2 (1981), 1

J. Reuter: *La música popular de México. Origen e historia de la música que canta y toca el pueblo mexicano* (Mexico City, 2/1981)

B. Seitz: 'Quichua Songs to Sadden the Heart: Music in a Communication Event', *Latin American Music Review*, ii/2 (1981), 223

W. D. Tompkins: *The Musical Traditions of the Blacks of Coastal Peru* (diss., U. of California, 1981)

C. Vega: *Apuntes para la historia del movimiento tradicionalista argentina* (Buenos Aires, 1981)

M. P. Baumann: 'Music of the Indios in Bolivia's Andean Highlands (Survey)', *World of Music*, xxv/2 (1982), 80

G. Béhague: 'Folk and Traditional Music of Latin America: General Prospect and Research Problems', *World of Music*, xxv/2 (1982), 3

E. Carrasco: *La nueva canción en América Latina* (Santiago, 1982)

L. Crook: 'A Musical Analysis of the Cuban Rumba', *Latin American Music Review*, iii/1 (1982), 92–123

B. Jorge: *La música dominicana: siglos XIX–XX* (Santo Domingo, 1982)

C. Monsanto: 'Guatemala a través de su Marimba', *Latin American Music Review*, iii/1 (1982), 60

J. M. Schechter: *Music in a North Ecuadorian Highland Locus: Diatonic Harp, Genres, Harpists, and Their Ritual Junction in the Quechua Child's Wake* (diss., U. of Texas, 1982)

J. Sherzer and S. A. Wicks: 'The Intersection of Music and Language in Kuna Discourse', *Latin American Music Review*, iii/2 (1982), 147

R. R. Smith: 'Latin American Ethnomusicology: a Discussion of Central America and Northern South America', *Latin American Music Review*, iii/1 (1982), 1

S. Stein: 'El vals criollo y los valores de la clase trabajadora en la Lima de comienzos del siglo XX', *Socialismo y participación*, xvii (1982), 43

A. Chamorro, ed.: *Sabiduría Popular* (Zamora, Michoacán, 1983)

S. Claro Valdés: 'La cueca chilena, un nuevo enfoque', *Anuario musical*, xxxvii (1983), 82

G. List: *Music and Poetry in a Colombian Village* (Bloomington, IN, 1983)

J. A. Lloréns Amico: *Música popular en Lima: Criollos y andinos* (Lima, 1983)

J. M. Schechter: *Corona y Baile: Music in the Child's Wake of Ecuador and Hispanic South America, Past and Present*, *Latin American Music Review*, iv/1 (1983), 1–80

T. Turino: 'The Charango and the *Sirena*: Music, Magic, and the Power of Love', *Latin American Music Review*, iv/1 (1983), 81–119

A. Valencia Chacón: *El siku bipolar altiplánico* (Lima, 1983)

I. Aretz: *Síntesis de la etnomúsica en América Latina* (Caracas, 1984)

G. Béhague: 'Patterns of Candomblé Music Performance: an Afro-Brazilian Religious Setting', *Performance Practice: Ethnomusicological Perspectives*, ed. G. Béhague (Westport, CT, and London, 1984), 222–54

J. J. de Carvalho: *Ritual and Music of the Sango Cults of Recife* (diss., Queen's U. of Belfast, 1984)

G. W. Céspedes: 'New Currents in *Música Folklórica* in La Paz, Bolivia', *Latin American Music Review*, v/2 (1984), 217

A. Chamorro, ed.: *Los instrumentos de percusión en México* (Zamora, Michoacán, 1984)

C. A. Coba Andrade: *Instrumentos musicales populares registrados en el Ecuador*, ii (Otavalo, Ecuador, 1984)

Instituto Nacional de Musicología, 'Carlos Vega': *Temas de etnomusicología* (Buenos Aires, 1984)

A. León: *Del canto y el tiempo* (Havana, 1984)

R. C. Smith: 'The Language of Power: Music, Order, and Redemption', *Latin American Music Review*, v/2 (1984), 129–60

E. T. Stanford: 'La música popular de México', *La música de México*, ed. J. Estrada (Mexico City, 1984), 46–77

T. Turino: 'The Urban-Mestizo Charango Tradition in Southern Peru: a Statement of Shifting Identity', *EM*, xxviii (1984), 253

G. Béhague: 'Popular Music', *Handbook of Latin American Popular Culture*, ed. H. E. Hinds Jr and C. M. Tatum (Westport, CT, and London, 1985), 3–38

E. Bermúdez: 'Las clasificaciones de instrumentos musicales y su uso en Colombia: un ensayo explicativo', *Revista colombiana de investigación musical*, i/1 (1985), 3–78

J. Hill: 'Myth, Spirit-Naming, and the Art of Microtonal Rising: Childbirth Rituals of the Arawakan Wakuénai', *Latin American Music Review*, vi/1 (1985), 1–30

E. den Otter: *Music and Dance of Indians and Mestizos in an Andean Valley of Peru* (Leiden, 1985)

R. Romero: 'La música tradicional y popular', *La musica en el Perú* (Lima, 1985), 217–83

E. Travassos: 'Xamanismo, rituais terapêuticos e modalidades vocais de comunicação com o sobrenatural entre os Kayabi', *Revista pesquisa e música* (Rio de Janeiro), i/1 (1985),

J. L. Acevedo V.: *La música en las reservas indígenas de Costa Rica* (San José, 1986)

——: *La música en Guanacaste* (San José, 1986)

R. J. de Menezes Bastos: 'Música, cultura e sociedade no Alto-Xingu: a teoria musical dos indios Kamayurá', *Latin American Music Review*, vii/1 (1986), 50

A. Calzavara: *Prospecto para una bibliografía de la música en Venezuela* (Caracas, 1986)

T. de Oliveira Pinto: 'Capoeira, das Kampfspiel aus Bahia', *Brasilien Einführung in Musiktraditionen Brasiliens*, ed. T. de Oliveira Pinto (Mainz, 1986), 146

A. G. Quintero Rivera: 'Ponce, the Danza, and the National Question: Notes Toward a Sociology of Puerto Rican Music', *Cimarrón*, i/2 (1986), 49

E. Travassos: 'Die Musik der Kayaabi: Schamanen- und Kriegslieder', *Brasilien Einführung in Musiktraditionen Brasiliens*, ed. T. de Oliveira Pinto (Mainz, 1986), 14–47

P. Manuel: 'Marxism, Nationalism and Popular Music in Revolutionary Cuba', *Popular Music*, vi/2 (1987), 161

J. M. Schechter: 'The Current State of Bibliographic Research in Latin American Ethnomusicology', *Latin American Masses and Minorities: Their Images and Realities*, i (Madison, WI, 1987), 334

A. Seeger: *Why Suyá Sing: a Musical Anthropology of an Amazonian People* (Cambridge, 1987)

I. Suco Campos: *La música en el complejo cultural del Walagallo en Nicaragua* (Havana, 1987)

T. Turino: *Power Relations, Identity and Musical Choice: Music in a Peruvian Altiplano Village and among Its Migrants in the Metropolis* (diss., U. of Texas, 1987)

P. Vila: '*Rock nacional* and Dictatorship in Argentina', *Popular Music*, vi/2 (1987), 129

S. Cohen: *La nueva canción chilena. Notes to Chile Vencerá: an Anthology of Chilean New Song* (Somerville, MA, n.d.), Rounder Records, 4009–4010

R. J. de Menezes Bastos: *A Festa da Jaguatirica: uma partitura critico-interpretativa* (diss., University of São Paulo, 1989)

A. Valencia Chacón: *El Siku o Zampoña* (Lima, 1989)

Index

of Densmore, 409
Archaeologia Musicalis, 221
archaeology
Africa, 240; European studies, 224; Japan, 353–54; Korea, 367, 368; Mexico and Central America, 473; southwestern USA, Indians, 409; West Indies, 462
Archer, William G., research on Indian music, 142
Archer, William Kay, research on West Asian music, 266
Aretz, Isabel: research on Argentine folk music, 482; research on Venezuelan music, 477
Argentina, research activities, 482–83
'armchair anthropology', defended, 90
Armenia, research activities, 200, 202, 300–03
Armistead, Samuel, research on American Sephardic music, 454
Armour, Eugene, Anglo-American ballad analysis, 442
Arnberg, Matts, radio broadcasts, 217
Arnim, Ludwig Achim von, influence on Swiss folk-music research, 97
Arnold, Alison, research on Indian-American immigrants, 454
Arom, Simha: field recording techniques, 9; transcription of African music, 247
Arzeno, J., research on Dominican Republic music, 477
Asaf'yev, Boris, intonation theory, 225
Asakawa, G., analysis of Japanese music, 353
Asch, Michael, research on North American Indian music, 410
Asch, Moses, founding of Asch Records, 42
Ash, Alan, instrumental music manuscript book, 68
Asia. *See also* specific countries
Central, research activities, 202, 300–04
Eastern Central, research activities, 306–09

Southeast, musical connections with Africa, 241
West
methodology: folk music traditions, 265–66; historical linguistic, 263–64; instruments, 265; Israeli scholarship, 267; modal analysis and repertory, 264–65; religious music, 266–67; research topics, 268; social-musical relationships, 266; surveys, 264
research: to World War II, 260–62; World War II to present, 262–63
Asian-American music, research, 453–54, 456–57
Atre, Prabha, research on Indian music, 288
Attaway, W., research on Trinidad music, 462, 464
Aubert, Laurent, recordings of Newari music, 308
Auerbach, Susan, research on gender and music, 229
Australia: Aboriginal music, research, 393–94; research activities, 396; research on Indonesian music, 383–84
Austria: comparative musicology, beginnings, 77–79; 19th-early 20th c., 79–83; Vienna school, 83–85; to World War II, 85–91
Avenary, Hanoch, research on Jewish music, 267
Awakura, Hiroko, research on Eastern chant, 266
Awwad, Mansur, research on Egyptian music, 261
Ayestarán, Lauro, research on Uruguayan music, 483
Ayyar, C. S., influenced by British research, 141
Azerbaijan, research activities, 202, 300–03
Azevedo, A. Rodríguez de, Portuguese folk-text collections, 120
Azevedo, Luiz Heitor Corrêa de, research on Brazilian music, 484
d'Azevedo, Warren L., research on African music, 249
Azoulay, L., recordings of

ethnic groups, 113

Babcock, C. Merton, research on Czech-American music, 456
Bachmann, Werner, organological research, 222, 224
Back, George, collection of French-Canadian songs, 66
Bahat, Avner, research on West Asian music, 267
Bahr, Donald, research on North American Indian music, 411
Bailey, C. R. Kim, research on Ponapean music, 397
Bailey, Jay, study of five-string banjo, 444
Baily, John, research on Afghan music, 301
Baines, Anthony, bagpipes research, 222
Bake, Arnold A.: research on Indian music, 280, 285; research on Nepalese music, 307
Baker, Theodore: research on North American Indian music, 408; *Über die Musik der nordamerikanischen Wilden*, 20, 71
Baker, Thomas, arrangement of *Go Down Moses*, 49
Bakkegard, B. M., research on North American Indian music, 409
Bal y Gay, J., field recording of Spanish music, 121
Balakirev, Mily, Russian folk-song collection 198
Balfour, Henry: evolutionary hypotheses, 240; organological research, 139
Balinese music. *See* Indonesia
ballad study, communalist vs. individualist theories, 36–37
Ballanta, N. G. J., Sea Islands research, 54
Ballantyne, R. M., on decline of voyageur songs, 65
Baloch, Aziz, research on Gypsies, 296
Baloch, N. A., research on Pakistani music, 296
Balys, Jonas, research on Lithuanian-American music, 457
Bandara, Mahawelatenna, research on Kandyan music, 297

497

501

510

Morris, Alton C., ballad collecting, 39

Morton, David: research on Thai language and music, 380; research on Thai music, 379

Morris, E. A., research on North American Indian music, 409

Moses, L. G., biography of Mooney, 409

Moshkov, V., Volga-Ural research, 201

Moskowitz, I., research on Navajo and Apache ceremonies, 407

Moszyński, Kazimierz, research activities, 174

Motherwell, William, lowland ballad collection, 132

Moule, A. C., accounts of Japanese music, 139; research on Chinese instruments, 323

Moulin, Jane: research on Marquesas music, 396; research on Tahitian dance, 396

Moyle, Alice: research on Australian Aborigine music, 394

Moyle, Richard: research on Australian Aborigine music, 393, 394, 395; research on Oceanic music, 396, 397

Muddy Waters, career, 425

Mufti, Uxi, and Institute of Folk Heritage, 295, 296

Mukuna, Kazadi wa, research on Afro-Brazilian music, 485

Mun Hayŏn, research on Korean music, 367

Mun Sŏngnyop, research on Korean music, 368

Muñoz, Maria Luisa, research on Puerto Rican music, 476

Murie, James: collaboration with Roberts, 29; research activities, 25

Muriel, Inés, research on Ecuadorian music, 478

Murko, Matija, field recordings, 166–67; Slovenian folk-song collection, 163

Murphy, James, *Songs and Ballads of Newfoundland Ancient and Modern*, 68

Mushaqa, Michail, research on Lebanese music, 261

musicology: establishment of discipline, 80; relation to ethnomusicology, 6–7; systematic, Adler schemata, 4

'*Musikethnologie*', 216

'*Musikfolklorismus*', 97

Musorgsky, Modest, Russian folk-song collection, 198

Mutatkar, Sumati, research on Indian music, 286

Muyinda, notation of Kiganda music, 248

Myers, Charles S., analysis of Torres Straits music, 393

Myers, Helen: *Folk Music in the United States*, 434; research on Indian music, 288; research on Indian-American immigrants, 454; research on North American Indian music, 410; research on Trinidad music, 462, 465

Myklebust, Rolf, radio broadcasts, 217

Myrand, Ernest, *Noëls anciens de la Nouvelle-France*, 67

Nadel, Siegfried, research activities, 83

Naipaul, V. S., writings on East Indian music, 466

Nakaseko, Kazu, research on Chinese theory, 322

Nakatsuka, Chikuzen, research on *shakuhachi* music, 357

Namadeva, musical activities, 276

Nataletti, Giorgio: radio broadcasts, 217; research on Italian folk music, 126

Nathan, Hans: anthology of banjo tunes, 444; research on Anglo-American ballads, 442

National Conservatory of Music (New York), Dvořák students, 24

nationalism: influence on development of ethnomusicology, 5–6; USA, 55. *See also* cultural policies; ideology

Nattiez, Jean-Jacques, bibliography of North American Indian music, 408; research on Inuit music, 412

Naumann, Hans, debased

culture theory, 36

Nayyar, Adam, and Institute of Folk Heritage, 296

Neal, J., Irish music anthology, 148

Neal, W., Irish music anthology, 148

Neal, Will, *43*

Needham, Joseph, *Science and Civilization in China*, 319

Neely, Charles, ballad collecting, 39

Nelles, Walter R., ballad studies, 40

Nelson, Kristina, on Koran cantillation, 264

Nepal: research activities, 307–08; sound recordings made by Bake, 280

Nerval, Gérard de, literary works, influence on interest in French folk music, 112

Netherlands, the: colonial research, 101–06; Kunst research, 106–10, 382

Netquatewa, E., research on North American Indian music, 411

Nettl, Bruno: cross-cultural research, 223; *Folk Music in the United States*, 434; methodology, viewed by Hood, 402; *North American Indian Musical Styles*, 405; on anthropological research directions, 222; research on Arapaho music, 408; research on Czech- and Slovak-American music, 456; research on modal systems, 265; research on North American Indian music, 405–06, 407, 408, 409, 410, 411; research on Persian music, 266; research on Siberian-Native American style connections, 402; *Theory and Method in Ethnomusicology*, 402

Neubauer, Eikhard: research on Arabic music, 263–64; research on modal systems, 265

Neuman, Daniel; *The Life of Music in North India*, 287; research on Indian music, 283

Nevadomsky, J. J., research on East Indian music, 465

Neves e Melo, A. A. das,

529

535